ARCHEOLOGY
of
EASTERN
UNITED STATES

FAY-COOPER COLE

ARCHEOLOGY

of

EASTERN

UNITED STATES

EDITED BY JAMES B. GRIFFIN

THE UNIVERSITY OF CHICAGO PRESS

CHICAGO & LONDON

THE UNIVERSITY OF CHICAGO PRESS, CHICAGO 60637
The University of Chicago Press, Ltd., London

Copyright 1952 by The University of Chicago. All rights
reserved. Published 1952. Fifth Impression 1971. Printed in
the United States of America

International Standard Book Number: 0-226-30861-8
Library of Congress Catalog Card Number: 52-14698

FAY-COOPER COLE *was born in Plainwell, Michigan, August 8, 1881. His undergraduate training was at Northwestern University, where he received a Bachelor of Science degree in 1903. His advanced studies were at the University of Chicago, the University of Berlin, and Columbia University, where he received the Ph.D. degree in 1914. He was on the staff of the Field Museum of Natural History from 1906 to 1923, where he specialized in Southeast Asia. In 1923 he became an Assistant Professor of Anthropology at the University of Chicago, and in 1929 he was named Professor of Anthropology and Chairman of the Department of Anthropology. He held these positions until his retirement in 1947. During his tenure at the University of Chicago, one of his major fields of interest was the development of a summer training program in archeology which was concentrated in Illinois. As a result of this development not only did the archeology of Illinois receive a considerable impetus, but a great many of the practicing archeologists in the United States received part of their training and experience under his direction. This volume was prepared in his honor and in appreciation for the part he has played in the study of Eastern United States archeology.*

PREFACE

THIS volume is a summary of eastern United States archeology prepared, except for one chapter, by various former students of Professor Fay-Cooper Cole, Chairman Emeritus of the Department of Anthropology at the University of Chicago. Between 1925 and 1950 there developed under his direction an outstanding training center for archeologists, particularly, in the field of the eastern United States. As the time neared for Professor Cole's retirement it was agreed among the members of the Department of Anthropology, and among many of the former students who had received advanced degrees, that a volume of contributions by his former students in the anthropological field in which he had performed such signal service would be both a testimonial to his lasting influence in American archeology and a volume which would also have meaning in terms of its unity around a central theme.

The outline for this volume was completed during the summer of 1946 by Dr. F. R. Eggan and Dr. J. B. Griffin. The Department of Anthropology at the University of Chicago agreed to sponsor the volume, and the University of Chicago Press agreed to consider it for publication. The first deadline for submission of chapters was September 1, 1947. A second deadline of December 1, 1947, also failed to provide the requisite coverage. In order to remove possible criticism of any of the individual authors for failure to include references to publications or ideas current in the last few years, the date of reception by the editor of the various chapters is placed in a footnote at the beginning of each chapter. There is also included in the footnote a brief statement of the author's association with the University of Chicago and his present position.

The majority of the chapters in the volume present an interpretation of the succession of prehistoric human cultures in various geographical regions east of the Rocky Mountains. Unfortunately, the chapter which would have discussed the geographical background of this broad area and its influence on the prehistoric cultural development was not submitted, nor was the section on the Central Plains completed. The initial chapter by Dr. Carl E. Guthe, "Twenty-five Years of Archeology in the Eastern United States," provides a broad understanding of the men, methods, and problems of this area. As a professional colleague of Dr. Cole's he participated in the support

and encouragement given to American archeology by its outstanding leaders. The second chapter by Georg K. Neumann, "Racial Differentiation in the American Indian," is a summary of his interpretation of significant physical divisions within what has been somewhat loosely called the "American Indian." The basis for his physical groups has been the inbreeding human populations associated with specific archeological cultures. A knowledge of population varieties in any cultural area in historical perspective is essential in any attempt to assess the role which diffusion, migration, and internal development has played in the gradually shifting cultural picture. The chapter by Dr. Fred R. Eggan, "The Ethnological Cultures and Their Archeological Background," presents a relatively new tool for the organization and interpretation of archeological units. By an intensive study of population density, the size of individual site units, and other factors bearing on economic and social life at any given archeological horizon, it should be possible to recognize and correlate the significant ethnological cultural orientations over wide areas. By this means the more basic varieties of cultural organization and their change through time can be understood without the presence of minutiae which are important only in identifying minor temporal and areal focal units.

Accompanying most of the areal chapters is a series of figures which present many of the more important cultural traits which serve to characterize the archeological units in the various time periods. These figures may be regarded as one of the most important parts of this publication. They provide in one volume a means of visual comparison of cultural content over a large geographical area, and extending over some five to ten thousand years of time. The volume should be viewed not as a definitive summary but as a representative of a particular stage in the continuing study of human cultural development which took place in the area east of the Rocky Mountains before this area came under the influence of Western civilization.

During the period of years when this volume was in preparation the several secretaries of the Museum of Anthropology at the University of Michigan have aided the editor in many ways. To Phyllis Worth, Ruby Griffin, Mary Hurt, Alma Anderson and Jeanne Scully the authors and the editor are obligated for their considerable assistance. In so far as is known to the editor the following artists have prepared the illustrations for certain chapters: C. W. Angell for Chapter 17, W. L. Brudon for Chapter 22, Eleanor Chapman for Chapters 11 and 19, A. R. Janson for Chapter 24, and H. K. Strauch for Chapter 15.

Publication of this volume has been made possible by a generous subvention from the Wenner-Gren Foundation for Anthropological Research, Incorporated, supplemented by additional funds from the Marian and Adolph Lichtstern Fund of the Department of Anthropology of the University of Chicago. The editor and contributors wish to express their gratitude for this financial support and to thank Dr. Paul Fejos, director of research of the Wenner-Gren Foundation, for his encouragement and aid.

TABLE OF CONTENTS

TWENTY-FIVE YEARS OF ARCHEOLOGY IN THE EASTERN UNITED STATES. By Carl E. Guthe*

THE origin and history of the Indians encountered by the Europeans settling on the eastern seaboard were a source of speculation as early as the latter part of the eighteenth century. The serious study of Indian archeology began with surveys in the eastern United States before the close of the first half of the nineteenth century, as recorded in the famous classic, *Ancient Monuments of the Mississippi Valley*, published by the Smithsonian Institution in 1848.[1] This report and many others of lesser significance by scientifically-minded men in a variety of often obscure publications issued by societies and institutions led inevitably to a tremendous growth of pioneer interest in our subject. The great American custom of collecting "Indian relics" was well launched.

During the last quarter of the nineteenth century organized surveys and careful excavations increased in number. By 1880 Cyrus Thomas started his extensive survey of the mound area of the eastern United States.[2] About the same time W. H. Holmes began his studies of pottery which were to have a profound influence upon the development of research in eastern United States archeology. In the 1870's Frederick W. Putnam became interested in the archeological sites of the Ohio Valley. Ernest Volk spent twenty years, between 1872 and 1892, with the support and endorsement of Frederick W. Putnam, in careful excavations at the Abbott Farm in New Jersey. In the last decade of the nineteenth century Clarence B. Moore began his explorations of archeological sites in the southern states.

During this period there were many men who brought their scientific abilities to bear upon the archeological problems of their immediate local regions. Nearly every state east of the Rockies recognizes local archeological pioneers, such as Lapham in Wisconsin, Winchell in Minnesota, and Beauchamp in New York, whose reports were published under the auspices of local or state organizations.

Cyrus Thomas, a leading scientist of his day, probably expressed the point of view of the serious students of eastern United States archeology at the turn of the century when he wrote, in 1898: "The work of archeology in its broad sense is to revivify the dead, to put life into the past, and, so far as possible, to bring before the mind the ancient people with their activities, characteristics and customs. In other words, the chief object in view in the study of archeology is the man of bygone ages."[3]

We who are familar with modern archeological techniques must give proper credit to these early pioneers of the nineteenth century. They were explorers in a new subject field of science. Their first concern was to assemble evidence. Today we know that they failed to recognize the need for recording various kinds of evidence which we consider important. Nevertheless, their objective statements concerning the archeological conditions and objects which they found are still an integral part of the modern archeologists' fund of knowledge. Great credit is due these serious students of eastern United States archeology who laid the foundations upon which our modern studies are built.

By the turn of the century the period of pioneer explorations was approaching an end. A great number of archeological sites had been discovered and studied, a tremendous quantity of archeological specimens had been collected, and the opportunity had emerged to develop classifications of evidence and to make certain deductions.

One of the earliest of such classifications was the famous monograph, *Aboriginal Pottery of the Eastern United States*, by W. H. Holmes, published in 1903.[4] He divided the eastern United States into eleven pottery provinces, yet cautiously made the following prophetic qualifications. "Within the limits, however, of their areas are numerous subgroups which do not possess such strong individuality and such clear geographic definition as the larger ones, but which may well be studied separately and may in time be found to have an ethnic importance quite equal to that of the better-defined groups of ware."[5] A few years later,

* University of Michigan, B.S., 1914; Harvard University, A.M. 1915, Ph.D., 1917; Director, New York State Museum, 1944. Chapter received December, 1948.

1. Squier and Davis, 1848. 2. Thomas, C., 1894.

3. Thomas, C., 1898, pp. 1–2. 5. *Ibid.*, p. 21.
4. Holmes, 1903.

in 1910, a similar classification of stone implements appeared in W. K. Moorehead's classic two-volume work, *The Stone Age in North America*.[6]

In 1914 W. H. Holmes published an article in the *American Anthropologist*[7] which later became one chapter in Part I of the *Handbook of American Aboriginal Antiquities*.[8] Herein he assigned five archeological culture areas to the eastern United States: (1) the North Atlantic area; (2) the Georgia-Florida area; (3) the Middle and Lower Mississippi Valley area; (4) the Upper Mississippi and Great Lakes area; and (5) the Great Plains and Rocky Mountain area.[9] In this evident compromise between his earlier pottery provinces and the recognized ethnological areas of the eastern United States he established a pattern which influenced archeological thinking in the eastern United States for many years.

In the meantime, at the very beginning of the twentieth century, another kind of classification of archeological records makes its appearance. This is the publication of the first of a long series of volumes devoted to the archeological materials and problems within individual states, a series of publications which has not yet run its full course.

At the turn of the century W. M. Beauchamp published an extensive list of archeological sites in New York State arranged alphabetically by counties.[10] These data were later expanded and interpreted by A. C. Parker in the two-volume work, *The Archeological History of New York*.[11] The most comprehensive of these early state archeological histories was the *Archeological History of Ohio* by Gerard Fowke.[12] In 1912 Moorehead began a survey of the archeology of Maine, and Pearce started studying the archeological materials in Texas in 1918. Yet most of the state archeological surveys come at a later period.

Coincident with these earliest systematic efforts at both geographical and cultural classifications of archeological records, the explorations of general areas and the excavations of individual sites continued. Clarence B. Moore continued the surveys of the river valleys of the southern states. W. K. Moorehead undertook similar surveys of the Susquehanna, the Connecticut, the Arkansas, and the Canadian river valleys. M. R. Harrington made intensive studies of sites in Arkansas and Tennessee.[13] S. A. Barrett excavated the important site of ancient Aztalan.[14] And Moorehead began excavations at Cahokia, which led to the purchase of this great archeological landmark by the Illinois State Legislature in 1923.

The publications resulting from these and many other surveys and excavations demonstrate that more careful and exacting field records were being kept. Factors contributing to this improvement in field methods were the growing interest in the analysis and classification of archeological records in the eastern United States and the demonstration of the existence of true stratigraphy in the Southwest.

The advent of the third decade of the twentieth century marks the beginning of a period of co-ordination of archeological research in this area. It had its origin in the newly created Division of Anthropology and Psychology of the National Research Council, which, in 1920, formed the Committee on State Archeological Surveys "to encourage and assist the several states in the organization of state archeological surveys similar to the surveys conducted by the states of Ohio, New York, and Wisconsin."[15] Within four years such surveys had either been organized or given encouragement in Georgia, Illinois, Indiana, Iowa, Louisiana, Michigan, Mississippi, Missouri, Pennsylvania, South Carolina, South Dakota, and Tennessee. In 1922 the Committee published in the *American Anthropologist* the first of a long series of annual summaries of the archeological field work in North America. That for 1927 contains reports from nineteen state agencies and thirteen other institutions.[16] These summaries broadened the professional interests of archeological students working within the boundaries of single states. Another co-ordinating stimulus was the compilation in 1923 by Clark Wissler, then chairman of the Committee, of a mimeographed statement on the aims and methods most applicable to state archeological surveys, which was printed later the same year by the State Historical Society of Iowa.[17]

In these same fateful years the Central Section of the American Anthropological Association was organized in Chicago.[18] The annual spring meeting of this regional branch of the national organization afforded an opportunity for archeologists throughout the Middle West to meet, become acquainted, and discuss informally problems of mutual interest.

In 1924 Fay-Cooper Cole accepted a position on the faculty of the University of Chicago, and the influence of this institution on eastern United States archeology was inaugurated. At that time the status of eastern United States archeology was still uncertain.

Progress, during the previous ten years, in the study of southwestern archeology had made possible A. V. Kidder's *An Introduction to the Study of Southwestern Archeology*. The impact of this report upon the students of eastern United States archeology is epitomized in one sentence in the final paragraph: "If a single outstanding fact has become apparent in our survey, it is the great value of stratigraphy, first

6. Moorehead, 1910.
7. Holmes, 1914.
8. Holmes, 1919.
9. *Ibid.*, pp. 95 and 96.
10. Beauchamp, 1900.
11. Parker, 1922.
12. Fowke, 1902.
13. Harrington, M. R., 1920 and 1922.
14. Barrett, 1933.

15. National Research Council, 1921, p. 54.
16. Guthe, 1930, p. 56.
17. State Historical Society of Iowa, 1923.
18. *American Anthropologist*, Vol. 24, pp. 247–249.

for determining the sequence of local types and for solving local problems, secondly, for the possibilities that it holds out for providing crossfinds of contemporaneous non-local types and so for solving the broader and more important problems of inter-area chronology."[19]

The general existence of true physical superimposition of archeological strata in sites in eastern United States was still very much in doubt. Clark Wissler, in the 1922 edition of *The American Indian,* discussed the chronological records of Peru, Central America, and the Southwest, recognized a few sporadic cases of stratification in New York, Nebraska, and New Jersey, and added: "Hence, considering the small number of exceptions just cited, we can truthfully say that so far, archeological work outside of the regions of higher culture has given negative stratification."[20] Cyrus Thomas had recognized evidence that some mounds had been built by successive additions. Archeological conditions in New York and New Jersey, in Arkansas and Tennessee, could only be explained on the basis of sequences of cultures. Students in the eastern part of the country were confidently looking for evidences of true stratification.

The great variety of archeological materials accumulated by this time and the inability to establish clear-cut distribution limits of particular complexes either in space or in time led to a feeling of frustration, partly reflected in the tendency to use logical interpretations of existing evidence to establish working hypotheses. Shetrone, in 1920, offered as "a tentative working hypothesis" that the Algonquian group was the earliest, the most persistent, and the last of Ohio's prehistoric peoples; that the Fort Ancient, Hopewell, and Stone Grave groups were contemporaneous; that the time relations of the Adena group could not be defined; and that the Iroquoian group, of late prehistoric time, disappeared about the middle of the seventeenth century.[21] Parker postulated four major culture groups in New York.[22] Wissler, describing the Mississippi-Ohio area, wrote: "The center of the ceramic art may be roughly defined by a circle inscribed about Memphis, intersecting Nashville, Tennessee. We have already noted that other artifacts tended to center in this region, so that we have a true culture center here."[23] M. R. Harrington reasoned that the Ozark Bluff-dwellers may have originated in the Southwest but had cultural affiliations with the Muskhogean, Caddoan, Siouan, and Algonkian peoples.[24]

It is evident that the research work of the first

19. Kidder, 1924, p. 135.
20. Wissler, 1922, p. 293.
21. Shetrone, 1920, pp. 168–169.
22. Parker, 1922.
23. Wissler, *op. cit.,* p. 268.
24. Harrington, M. R., 1924a, pp. 14–15.

quarter of the twentieth century had served to emphasize the complexity of the archeological problems in the eastern United States. The urge to organize the accumulated data led to the formulation of various working hypotheses, practically all of which were based, of necessity, upon insufficient evidence, and have now become obsolete. The problem was further complicated by the continued use of ethnological terms which implied a direct link between historic tribes and archeological cultures, a relationship which in most cases could not be proved.

The outstanding characteristic of the last twenty-five years has been the tremendous progress made in the interpretation of the prehistory of the Indians of the eastern United States. A demonstration of the present status of these scientific achievements constitutes the subject matter of the other contributions to this volume. This paper seeks only to review the major historical developments which played significant roles in bringing about this scientific progress.

The two most noteworthy factors which influenced archeological work in the eastern United States were the rapid growth of organizational activities, on the one hand, and the tremendous stimulus given to research by federal agencies, on the other.

The increase in the organizational approach began to be felt in the twenties, through the work of universities, state agencies, and state societies. Closely correlated activities included the organization of regional conferences, the publication of state archeological histories, the establishment of co-operative research projects, and the development of training centers.

Prior to the 1920's a few universities had conducted archeological studies in the area, notably Harvard, Texas, and Wisconsin. By 1926 archeological work was also being sponsored by Beloit College, Columbia University, and the universities of Chicago, Kentucky, Michigan, Nebraska, Ohio, and South Dakota. Within the next ten years this list more than doubled with the addition of Yale and the universities of Alabama, Arkansas, Illinois, Louisiana, Missouri, North Carolina, Oklahoma, Pennsylvania, and Tennessee. By 1935 at least twenty-one institutions of higher learning were supporting research in eastern United States archeology.

During the latter half of the 1920's state historical societies and geological agencies also contributed to the expansion of archeological work. They sponsored studies in Alabama, Illinois, Indiana, Iowa, Kentucky, Minnesota, Mississippi, Nebraska, North Dakota, Oklahoma, and Texas. Some of these organizations later retired from the field as the work of the universities and the state archeological societies increased.

Another aspect of the organizational growth was the rapid development of state societies. A number of state societies had been in existence for some time: the Ohio State Archeological and Historical Society (founded 1885), the Wisconsin Archeological Society (1903), the Alabama Anthropological Society (1909), The New York State Archeological Association (1916), and the St. Louis Anthropological Society. Between 1922 and 1925 state societies were organized in Michigan, Mississippi, Louisiana, Tennessee, and South Carolina. During the next ten years similar societies were created in Connecticut, Delaware, Georgia, New Jersey, North Carolina, and Pennsylvania. In 1939 the Massachusetts Archeological Society was established. By 1940 there were societies in at least seventeen states dedicated to the study of eastern United States archeology.

Not all of these societies were of equal strength, nor did they all develop with equal rapidity. Yet the majority of them have issued journals or newsletters which have recorded contributions to archeological knowledge on the part of lay students as well as professionals. It is obvious they have also been a strong factor in developing a better understanding of archeological problems on the part of their respective memberships.

A direct result of the rapid increase in state archeological societies was the formation of the Eastern States Archeological Federation in 1934[25] and of the more recent Mississippi Valley Archeological Federation.[26]

In one sense, the culmination of the growth of archeological societies was the creation of the national Society for American Archeology, in December, 1934.[27] Its quarterly journal, *American Antiquity*, was first issued in July, 1935. Two years later the Committee on State Archeological Surveys of the National Research Council was disbanded because its functions had been taken over by the national society. Today, the Society for American Archeology is recognized as the official professional organization of American archeologists in this country. It has maintained throughout its existence a policy of seeking to serve all serious students of American Archeology regardless of whether they be professional scientists or interested laymen.

Another stimulus for the integration of archeological research was the development of regional conferences. The meetings of the Central States Branch of the American Anthropological Association had given students of the subject an opportunity to discuss mutual problems and exchange informal progress reports with their colleagues in other states. The success of these meetings led to the holding of more formal conferences. The Committee on State Archeological Surveys sponsored three of these conferences; one on midwestern archeology in St. Louis in 1929,[28] another on southern prehistory in Birmingham in 1932,[29] and the third in Indianapolis in 1935.[30]

Two regional conferences which met a number of times were organized in the 1930's. The first Plains Archeological Conference was held in Vermillion, South Dakota, in 1931. After the interruption caused by World War II, the fifth Plains Conference was held at the University of Nebraska in 1947. In 1938 the first Southeastern Archeological Conference was held at the University of Michigan. The fifth Southeastern Conference took place at Louisiana State University in 1940. Through its sponsorship of ten issues of a mimeographed newsletter, this Conference had a significant influence upon the development of southeastern archeology.

The organizational expansion in eastern United States archeology was soon reflected in increased publications, as articles in the professional journals and as long and short reports in publication series of state government agencies, various societies, museums, and other research centers. Among the latter is the series of books on the archeology of individual states. The first of these, on New York and Ohio, have been mentioned. In the late 1920's three more appeared on Michigan, Mississippi, and Kentucky. Between 1932 and 1937 six more were published on Delaware, Illinois, Indiana, Kentucky, and Nebraska. In more recent years, since 1940, three additional volumes have been added, on New Jersey, New York, and North Carolina.

These books differ considerably in content and scientific importance, ranging all the way from a descriptive catalogue of archeological sites and specimens to a thoughtful analysis of archeological evidence in terms of existing scientific problems. The one thing they have in common is that they deal with the archeological data from individual states, yet each of them has contributed in its own way to the combined knowledge of the archeology of the eastern United States which has made possible the great scientific progress in this field during the past quarter-century.

Another derivative of this organizational growth stemmed from the personal associations established among colleagues at the meetings of the societies and at the conferences. It became obvious that collections of similar materials assembled in one laboratory from many organizations would greatly facilitate comparative research upon regional topics. The concept of co-operative projects which began with the creation of central laboratories later expanded to include field

25. Osgood, 1940.
26. *American Antiquity*, Vol. 12, pp. 65–67.
27. *American Antiquity*, Vol. 1, pp. 141–151.
28. National Research Council, 1929.
29. National Research Council, n.d.*a*.
30. National Research Council, n.d.*b*.

expeditions sponsored by several organizations and comparative studies by a single archeologist from one organization working for extended periods in a series of museums or laboratories as the guest of co-operating organizations.

The first of the central laboratories was the Ceramic Repository for the Eastern United States founded at the University of Michigan under the auspices of the National Research Council in 1927. A similar Ethnobotanical Laboratory was also established at the University of Michigan in 1930. Under the leadership of Fay-Cooper Cole, an extensive pictorial survey of the archeological materials of eastern United States was begun in 1931. The University of Chicago also undertook a survey on the dendrochronology of the eastern United States, stimulated by the preliminary studies in this field undertaken during the 1934 surveys of the Tennessee Valley Authority. Slightly later, a Lithic Laboratory was begun at the Ohio State Museum. About this time, ethnohistorical studies were begun almost simultaneously at the University of Chicago and the University of Michigan.

The growing interest in eastern United States archeology on the part of a variety of organizations obviously increased professional opportunities for trained American archeologists. Training schools were badly needed. The first and most important of these in the Middle West was started at the University of Chicago shortly after Dr. Cole joined the faculty in 1924. During his twenty years of service at that institution a large number of students received a rigorous training in the subject. The volume of which this essay is a part is a partial measure of the tremendous contribution to the study of eastern United States archeology which has been made by the men and women who received training at the University of Chicago.

Twenty-five years ago the University of Texas had been giving courses in archeology and anthropology for some years. During the late 1920's and early 1930's departments of anthropology and archeology, offering courses in eastern United States archeology, were established at the universities of Illinois, Kentucky, Michigan, Minnesota, Nebraska, and Tennessee. At the same time, some of the eastern universities added courses on eastern United States archeology to their older established departments of anthropology. Twenty years ago the University of Chicago was just beginning its training school as a pioneer in the field. Today, quite a number of colleges and universities are teaching courses in anthropology and American archeology, and several of them offer well-rounded training programs for professional students of eastern United States archeology.

The second most noteworthy factor which influenced archeological work in the eastern United States during the past twenty-five years was the tremendous stimulus given to research by federal agencies, which started in a rather mild form in the late 1920's.

In May, 1928, Congress appropriated $20,000 to the Smithsonian Institution, which had been conducting archeological work as a part of its research program since the days of Squier and Davis, to enable it to co-operate with any state, educational institution, or scientific organization in the United States for continuing ethnological researches among the American Indians and the excavation and preservation of archeological remains, provided the monies appropriated be matched by the institution to whom the grant was made and not more than $2,000 be allocated to any one state. In the four years which followed, out of a total of forty allotments, fifteen were made in support of archeological projects in the Upper Great Plains, Illinois, Indiana, Kentucky, Michigan, Mississippi, Nebraska, Oklahoma, Tennessee, and New England.[31]

In 1929 the Rockefeller Foundation made a grant to the National Research Council, which was renewed several times, for the creation of the Research Aid Fund. During the next seven years, out of a total of more than one hundred grants-in-aid to research projects, two gave assistance in the classification of data in eastern United States archeology, and thirteen were in support of archeological field work in Alabama, Kentucky, Louisiana, Mississippi, Oklahoma, Pennsylvania, and Tennessee.[32]

This financial aid was especially timely for, in some instances, it made possible the continuation of projects which would otherwise have been forced to close because of the economic conditions resulting from the depression of the early thirties, which did cause the curtailment or abandonment, in some cases, of field research by a number of institutions.

The creation in 1933 of the Civil Works Administration, a federal relief program for reducing unemployment, brought about a virtually explosive expansion of field work in eastern United States archeology. On very short notice, in January, 1934, the Smithsonian Institution inaugurated eleven archeological CWA projects employing about 1,500 people. Seven of these were in Florida and one each in Georgia, North Carolina, Tennessee, and California.[33]

In the fall of 1933 the National Research Council, acting on advices from the chairman of the Tennessee Valley Authority and in co-operation with the Science Advisory Board and the Smithsonian Institution, created a subcommittee on the archeology of

31. Smithsonian Institution, *Annual Reports,* 1928–1932, inclusive.
32. National Research Council, n.d.*c.*
33. Setzler and Strong, 1936, p. 301.

the Tennessee Valley. A grant of $2,000 was secured from the Carnegie Corporation.[34] Professor William S. Webb of the University of Kentucky was appointed archeologist in charge by the Tennessee Valley Authority. By the end of the first week in January, 1934, field work had been started by a staff consisting of twenty-two field supervisers and over 1,000 laborers, in the Norris and Wheeler basins. As in the case of the Smithsonian Institution projects, the work was done by CWA and FERA labor, until the projects closed on July 1, 1934.[35]

The spring months of 1934 will stand in history as a period of greatest field activity in eastern United States archeology. In spite of almost insurmountable physical and administrative difficulties, these projects contributed immensely to our knowledge of the subject, as is evidenced by the publications resulting from the work. The leaders of the several projects, and particularly William S. Webb, as co-ordinator of the Tennessee Valley Authority projects, are entitled to great credit for their accomplishments.

The comments made by Setzler and Strong with reference to the Smithsonian Institution projects are equally applicable to the work done in the Tennessee Valley Authority project.

Considering the speed with which they were put in motion the above mentioned archeological projects under the CWA were surprisingly successful. From the standpoint of relief they provided immediate work for numerous people. Over 90 per cent of the funds expended went for labor, since the tools for manual work, both skilled and unskilled, as well as the materials for the preservation of the archeological remains, cost very little; and because the values produced were entirely scientific and educational, there was no resultant overproduction. The main difficulties encountered were due to the failure of the original plans to provide for the supervision of the various aspects of each project by staffs adequately manned by technically trained archeological assistants, and to the fact that the exact amount of time and expenditure allotted to each project was constantly uncertain. This last factor prevented the accurate planning essential for the completion of a thoroughly productive piece of scientific excavation.[36]

In the spring of 1936 with the creation of the Public Works Administration, the integration of relief projects with archeological work underwent another period of expansion. The Tennessee Valley Authority undertook archeological field surveys in three new dam basins, again under the general direction of Professor Webb. The number of organizations throughout the country that used WPA labor in connection with archeological projects increased at an alarming rate. The variety of procedures used and the diversity of sponsoring organizations were causing some concern.

In the spring of 1939 the National Research Council Committee on Basic Needs in American Archeology,[37] appointed at the request of WPA officials, issued confidential mimeographed recommendations concerning the policies, methods and techniques, and publication plans which should be considered in connection with archeological projects, which were subsequently published in synoptic form in *Science*.[38] The Works Progress Administration established a national office in charge of the archeological projects and deposited the quarterly progress reports of the several projects in the Department of Anthropology of the United States National Museum.

In the spring of 1942, after this country had entered World War II, the archeological projects of the Works Progress Administration were terminated. Thus ended a fourteen-year period of direct federal aid to archeological studies. An overwhelming quantity of archeological material and records had been assembled under varying degrees of expert sponsorship. Reports on some of the projects had appeared in published form, but the herculean task of preparing technically sound reports on the great majority of the WPA projects seemed almost insurmountable.

Another equally important result of the federal aid programs was the experience it brought to archeologists in the handling of large projects and the education they received in the complex problems of administration, especially in connection with government organizations. A critical review of the programs is contained in a committee report of the Society for American Archeology.[39] One result of this experience was the establishment of a permanent planning committee of the Society for American Archeology in July of 1944. In January, 1945, it became evident that the plans before Congress to establish various authorities to carry on work in a number of river valleys analogous to that which had been done in the Tennessee Valley and to create conservation authorities made it necessary for archeologists to formulate some policy on these subjects. The combined efforts of the Planning Committee of the Society for American Archeology and the Committee on Basic Needs in American Archeology resulted in the creation in the late spring of 1945 of a Joint Committee for the Recovery of Archeological Remains, composed of one representative from the Society for American Archeology and another from the American Anthropological Association, with two representatives from the American Council of Learned Societies. A representative of the Smithsonian Institution and of the National Research Council acted in a liaison capacity to this committee.[40] This Joint Committee has been

34. National Research Council, 1935, p. 41.
35. Webb, W. S., 1938, pp. 1–7; 1939, pp. 1–7.
36. Setzler and Strong, 1936, pp. 306–307.

37. National Research Council, 1941, p. 49.
38. Guthe, 1939.
39. *American Antiquity*, Vol. 11, pp. 142–144 (1945).
40. National Research Council, 1946, p. 50; *American Antiquity*, Vol. 11, p. 143.

instrumental in making possible the archeological surveys in a number of river valleys which are now being carried forward under the general supervision of the Smithsonian Institution.

By the mid-1940's the period of rapid expansion of facilities for research in eastern United States archeology was drawing to a close. Local and state archeological societies had been organized throughout the area. Research centers had been established in state agencies, universities, colleges, and museums. The integration of activities had been strengthened through conferences, annual meetings of specialists, and the creation of comparative laboratories. Instructional facilities in eastern United States archeology had grown tremendously. Closer relations were being developed between the professional and the lay students of archeology. The national Society for American Archeology had been founded. An almost overwhelming amount of field investigations had been carried out with federal support. In short, the organizational tools for the study of eastern United States archeology had been greatly diversified and improved and the available research data had increased enormously.

The impact upon the study of eastern United States archeology of this relatively rapid expansion of facilities has resulted in an increased public interest in the subject, a vast quantity of work accomplished, and a definite progress in the analysis and interpretation of the archeological record of the eastern United States.

The desirable increase of public interest in archeology, amply demonstrated by the newspaper and magazine articles of recent years, is the result of the expansion of field work. The record shows that by the mid-1930's archeological research was being conducted in thirty-one of the thirty-seven states east of the Rocky Mountains. Yet this growing public appreciation of the subject also made more acute the "amateur" problem, inherited from the pioneers of the nineteenth century, which runs like a sinister thread through the archeological story of the twentieth century.

At first, stimulated by the Federal Antiquities Act of 1906, a number of individual states passed legislation to restrict or prohibit the collection or sale of archeological specimens by unauthorized persons. As the years have passed it has become increasingly evident that the problem of the "amateur" archeologist cannot be solved by legislative enactment.

The feeling of many professional archeologists in the 1920's was expressed by one spokesman as follows:

We who are engaged with these problems of prehistory will not actually solve them, however much we contribute to their ultimate solution. Meanwhile, the very evidence from which conclusions are finally to be drawn is left a prey to vandals and curio seekers. That is the tragedy of it all! Every mound pillaged, every cliff dwelling despoiled, means just so much less with which the student has to work—just so many more pages torn from the record he seeks to interpret. With existing laws inoperative and rather lacking in public support, I fail to perceive any practical means of checking this destruction. It will continue so long as pot hunters find a market for their plunder; so long as cliff dwellings and mounds remain to tempt the curious. It would seem that only by greater industry, concentration of effort, and closer cooperation between research organizations and their trained personnel can sufficiently reliable data be assembled from the major culture areas to answer every need of that historian who some day will write the prehistory of the United States.[41]

Early in the 1920's the Committee on State Archeological Surveys began to use the educational process in combating the destruction of archeological records by laymen. Many individual archeologists sought to educate laymen by direct contacts. Laymen were encouraged to attend the meetings of the Central States Branch of the American Anthropological Association. The 1929 St. Louis Conference on Midwestern Archeology was oriented toward the problems encountered by the laymen. In the early 1930's the growth in the number of state societies created more opportunities for laymen to discuss mutual problems and made possible informal and closer relations between these laymen and the professional archeologists working in the same state. The rapid expansion of field work brought more professional archeologists into direct contact with laymen in a larger number of communities.

In 1930 when Fay-Cooper Cole was chairman of the Division of Anthropology and Psychology, the National Research Council issued the famous "Guide Leaflet for Amateur Archeologists." Its wide distribution certainly had an influence upon the activities of archeological laymen, an objective stated in the introductory paragraphs: "In presenting this booklet, the Committee hopes to enlist the active cooperation of all intelligent laymen in the preservation of archeological sites. It seeks to give information which will enable the local investigator to carry on work according to the most approved methods, so that he may assist in unraveling the story of human development on the American continent."[42]

Dr. Strong writing in 1932 of his work in Nebraska archeology recognized the assistance given by archeological laymen but at the same time sounded a note of warning:

It must be obvious that the present paper is actually a cooperative piece of work wherein the writer has been directly and materially aided by a large number of persons. Of this latter group only a small proportion have been professional archeologists, the majority being persons in other walks of life who have been drawn to archeology as an avocation. Owing to the increasing interest in prehistoric research in this country, the number of amateur archeologists is growing rapidly.

41. Judd, 1929, p. 417.   42. National Research Council, 1930.

Encouraging as this rising interest in archeology undoubtedly is, it must frankly be admitted that inasmuch as it is often unaccompanied by technical knowledge, it is both a potential and an actual danger. This is demonstrated by the rapidly increasing destruction of important archeological sites, either by enthusiastic but untrained amateurs or by persons who are frankly mere collectors or relic hunters. . . . Persons of the first type may be scientific archeologists in the making; those of the second type uselessly destroy the very stuff of human history.[43]

In December, 1934, one of the three major reasons for creating the Society for American Archeology was that a large number of nonprofessional students could not be reached through existing channels and that some permanent national group preferably with a journal should be able to reach these students. An editorial in the first issue of *American Antiquity* contains the following statement: "We feel that American Indian archeology has many friends, and we are anxious to become acquainted with them. At the suggestion of one of them, the idea of a national Society for American Archeology came into being. Its purpose is to make it possible for everyone, professional and non-professional alike, to become acquainted with the story in which all are interested."[44]

The case for the serious minded lay student of archeology was well stated by McKern in 1935:

Unfortunately, there is a classification that divides those who rise to the name archeologist into two distinct and separate groups: students and collectors. I believe that such a classification is fundamentally wrong. All archeological students, if not themselves collectors, study the collections of others, since collections that are properly made and catalogued are storehouses of facts pertinent to scientific problems. And all collectors are potential students, since fact-revealing materials that pass through their hands may at any time engage their interest in some related problem. . . . Unquestionably, the activities of amateurs, when motivated by the purpose to find the truth at any price, and when conducted with studious care and according to methods which insure accurate and complete data, can be of inestimable value to the professional student. In fact, it is difficult to see how the work of the specialist can progress satisfactorily, if indeed it can survive, without the support of a constantly growing element of amateur student.[45]

The extreme opposite viewpoint held by many archeologists, was recorded in 1936:

The present actual status of archeological conservation in the United States, however, is deplorable. . . . From motives of mere curiosity or greed, dealers and relic hunters in practically every state are steadily destroying an irreplaceable heritage. The Antiquities Act of 1906 forbids unauthorized archeological excavation on public lands, but the law is difficult to enforce and, so long as archeological specimens can be sold on the open market, can have at best a very limited effect. This annihilation of our readable past which, due to the great popularity of relic hunting, is steadily growing worse, indicates the need for a carefully planned archeological pro-

gram before it is too late. At present a race between the scientist and the curio seeker is on. Scientists are relatively few in number and must work slowly and carefully, whereas relic hunters are extremely numerous, and loot sites with great rapidity. The probable outcome, unless definite action is taken very soon, is only too obvious. . . . It is a sad paradox that at this time, when trained men are becoming available and new techniques for determining archeological history are reaching a high pitch of development, the materials themselves should be vanishing like snow before the sun. It is even more tragic since an enlightened national policy in this regard could save them for all time.[46]

The expansion of facilities and activities in the study of eastern United States archeology has resulted in a more widespread public interest in the subject. Yet this interest in turn has increased the danger of destruction of irreplaceable records. The situation has received constructive study during the past quarter century. The achievements are measurable but seem relatively insignificant in terms of the immensity of the problem. The educational process is a slow one, yet it should be pursued unremittingly, since it seems to be the only practical means of ultimately establishing a strong public opinion in support of the proper conservation of archeological resources.

Another broad measure of achievement resulting from increased facilities is the gross quantity of work accomplished in field and laboratory investigations. In terms of publication alone the tremendous increase in the annual productivity of students of eastern United States archeology is made apparent by a comparison of the lists of recent publications in the issues of the *American Anthropologist* of the early 1920's with those in the current issues of *American Antiquity*.

It would be a herculean and dangerous task to attempt to review the progress in eastern United States archeology in terms of an analysis of these publications. The increase in the amount of research they record presented a wealth of new data and raised new scientific problems which required solution. In the aggregate they reflect the recognition of the need for improved research techniques and procedures, and the progress made in their development and use.

In the 1920's the existing conception of eastern United States archeology was still confused. Judd, as retiring president of the Anthropological Society of Washington, expressed in 1928 the attitude of many archeologists:

We who seek to construct the groundwork for future knowledge of Indian peoples, past and present, within the United States have assumed an obligation to make our studies as thorough as is humanly possible. We have not been thorough heretofore simply because no one perceived the present requirements of our science. We are not being thorough today since the current tendency toward specialization leads natu-

43. Strong, 1935, p. 4.
44. *American Antiquity*, Vol. 1, p. 4.
45. McKern, 1935, pp. 81–82.

46. Setzler and Strong, 1936, pp. 308–309.

rally to omission of significant data—data which may prove highly desirable a few years hence.[47]

Early in the 1930's A. V. Kidder wrote:

Archeologists, noting that modern biology has mounted above the plane of pure taxonomy, have attempted to follow that science into the more alluring fields of philosophic interpretation, forgetting that the conclusions of the biologist are based on the sound foundation of scientifically marshalled facts gathered during the past century by an army of painstaking observers. This groundwork we utterly fail to possess. Nor will it be easy for us to lay, because the products of human hands, being unregulated by the more rigid genetic laws which control the development of animals and plants, are infinitely variable. But that is no reason for evading the attempt. It has got eventually to be done, and the sooner we roll up our sleeves and begin comparative studies of axes and arrowheads and bone tools, make classifications, prepare accurate descriptions, draw distribution maps and, in general, persuade ourselves to do a vast deal of painstaking, unspectacular work, the sooner shall we be in position to approach the problems of cultural evolution, the solving of which is, I take it, our ultimate goal.[48]

One expression of this feeling of inadequacy took the form of efforts to create practical classifications of archeological objects. The results of many of these studies appear in the published records. Two of the papers at the St. Louis conference in 1929 dealt with the subject. The problem is well stated in a significant article in the first volume of American Antiquity:

It is a very bold individual indeed who will suggest ideas concerning descriptive methods pointing toward a system for the simplification of classifications for archeological artifacts. The chief difficulty in the way of arriving at simplified classifications lies in the great diversity of irregular forms. Consequently, the problem becomes so intricate, so full of pitfalls, that one is apt to become lost in a maze of detail out of which there is but slight possibility of gathering together and properly grouping the essentials.[49]

Pottery requires a specialized terminology. The archeologists of the eastern United States tended to follow the methods first used in southwestern archeology. Types of pottery were established on the basis of objective attributes of the vessels. A binomial name was invented by combining a geographical site name with the type name. This method has been widely adopted throughout the eastern United States in technical reports. Its use tends, however, to make a technical report on ceramic materials unintelligible to anyone except a specialist.

The present status of descriptive classifications of objects is succinctly phrased by Whiteford in a recent article:

American archeology is far removed from general agreement on terminology. . . . Each individual seems to know what he is talking about but no one else can be quite sure. With such a situation, it is certain that there is no broadly established, generally accepted series of terms which can be used in descriptive analysis.[50]

While these efforts were being made to establish more satisfactory methods of describing and classifying archeological objects, it was becoming apparent that the archeological culture areas formulated by Holmes and Wissler were obsolete. Even the word "culture" was losing its significance archeologically, because of the variety of contexts in which it was used. There was a need for a re-evaluation of archeological culture complexes. At the Birmingham Conference in December, 1932, Stirling outlined tentatively for the Southeast thirteen archeological culture areas, characterized by recognizable traits.[51]

In the same month, a group of archeologists met in Chicago, stimulated by a suggestion made by McKern in the spring of 1932, to discuss the same subject from a slightly different standpoint. This conference resulted in the formulation of "The Midwestern Taxonomic Method" of culture classification. The taxonomic frame of this method, to quote McKern "consists of five major divisions: focus, aspect, phase, pattern, and base, progressing from localized detailed to large general classes. The manifestation of a focus at any site is called a component of that focus. The method is comparable to a filing cabinet equipped with labeled drawers to facilitate the orderly arrangement of culture-indicative data."[52]

The discussions caused by this proposed method of culture classification led to the calling of the Indianapolis Conference in 1935, a symposium upon the archeological culture complexes of the north central United States. The mimeographed report of this conference contains as an appendix McKern's discussion of this taxonomic method, presented at the annual meeting of the Central Section of the American Anthropological Association in May, 1934.[53] The most extended analysis of this method has been published by Griffin.[54]

The formulation of the Midwestern Taxonomic Method of Culture Classification came at a moment when it was most needed. It was the single most constructive achievement in the eastern United States during the past twenty-five years in attacking the problem of the description and classification of archeological evidence. Its value is demonstrated many times over in the publications in which it has been used that have appeared in the past fifteen years. It has led to a more objective recognition of cultural relationships and has forced into the discard practically all of the earlier working hypotheses which were based upon inadequate evidence.

47. Judd, 1929, p. 410. 49. Black and Weer, 1936, p. 280.
48. Kidder, 1932, p. 8.
50. Whiteford, 1947, p. 228.
51. National Research Council, n.d.a, pp. 20–31.
52. McKern, 1939a, p. 310.
53. National Research Council, n.d.b, pp. 70–82.
54. Griffin, J. B., 1943a, pp. 327–341.

However, these changes in techniques of analysis were not accepted without discussion. The other viewpoint is best illustrated by quoting from the record. In 1938 Steward and Setzler wrote:

We believe that it is unfortunate for several reasons that attempts to state broad objectives which are basic to all cultural anthropology and to interpret data in terms of them should be relegated to a future time of greater leisure and fullness of data. First, although technological advancement is of the utmost importance, techniques alone neither state nor solve problems. Techniques are tools. . . . Techniques, therefore, may be perfected only with reference to their purpose, which involves the question of research objectives. Second, no one will in the future be able to interpret data one tenth as well as the persons now immersed in them. . . . It is only to the extent that archeological findings are interpreted in terms of broad problems that they are useful to the general student of culture.[55]

In 1940 Stirling commented:

At the present time there is a school of archeological thought represented for the most part by earnest scholars who, revolting against careless looting of sites primarily for specimens, have installed meticulous methodologies for the excavating and recording of material and equally elaborate and systematic nomenclatures to be applied to various kinds of ceramics and combinations of artifacts, to be used for comparative purposes. The wisdom of this application of American high-pressure business methods and systems to the scientific pursuit of archeology might be open to some question. It perhaps goes without saying that over-carefulness is much more desirable than lack of care, but the question might be asked as to whether or not there is a danger in permitting techniques to become an objective in themselves.[56]

While this testing of the midwestern taxonomic method was under way, progress was also being made in improving the techniques of using the other, long-recognized temporal approach to the comparative study of archeological complexes. The Birmingham Conference in 1932, gave special attention to the relation between the historic tribes and the archeology of the southeast.[57] About the same time Strong wrote:

It is the firm belief of the author that the possibilities of historic archeology in North America are not fully realized by the majority of anthropologists at the present time. Wherever the approach has been from the known historic into the unknown prehistoric, the results have more than justified the method, as the present superior status of archeology in the Iroquoian and Pueblo areas amply demonstrates. It seems surprising, therefore, that even today there are archeologists more interested in segregating obscure early cultures of unknown periods and affiliations than they are in determining the historic cultures and sequences represented in the regions to be worked. Obviously, in such work the historic cultures need not be an end in themselves, but they do seem to represent the threads that give most promise of untangling the complex skein of prehistory. The prehistoric past comes remarkably close to the historic present in the New World, and it is this fact that especially favors the ethnological and historical approach to archeology on both continents.[58]

In past decades this temporal approach had given rise to hypotheses of relationships between historic Indian groups and archeological manifestations and to the uncritical use of ethnological terms for archeological complexes, which the more exact archeological techniques of analysis had shown to be more apparent than real. Therefore many archeologists, in order to avoid implied ethnological associations which could not be demonstrated by archeological evidence, deliberately eliminated the use of such terms in their reports. What was needed were new ways of using this temporal approach to the comparative study of archeological complexes.

The point of view expressed at the Conference on Southern Prehistory was used in interpreting the field work conducted in the Tennessee Valley two years later. The project on dendrochronology of the Mississippi Valley undertaken by the University of Chicago was an effort to apply a new tool to this approach. Another experiment, started at the universities of Michigan and of Chicago, attempted through ethnohistorical studies to bridge the apparent gap between ethnology and archeology.

The most comprehensive exposition of the temporal approach to archeological problems is found in the large volume *Essays in Historical Anthropology of North America,* published in honor of John R. Swanton. This volume contains, among others, six articles dealing with various aspects of eastern United States archeology. Herein Strong records the more constructive attitude which had developed by 1940 with regard to the integration of ethnological and archeological records.

With the protohistoric period the need for a general methodology to supplement and extend the direct historic approach becomes acute. Once beyond the historic period specific tribal organization merges into the complex streams of culture history. The known tribal terminations of these streams are essential to link history and prehistory. They convert archeological sequence into historic reality and anchor archeology to social science. Yet, from the protohistoric to the earlier periods, all tribal and linguistic appelations become increasingly fallacious. The anthropologist can legitimately trace the history of a specific tribe or even linguistic stock down into the successive prehistoric archeological constellations of which it becomes a part, but the archeologist as a technician must eschew ethnic terminology for prehistoric horizons.[59]

During recent years archeological publications have shown over and over again that the more critical use of documented Indian historical records can furnish valuable data for use in interpreting the results obtained with the greatly refined tools and methods of modern archeological research. Among the first of such publications is *An Introduction to Nebraska Archeology.*[60] More recent examples are *The Fort*

55. Steward and Setzler, 1938, p. 5.
56. Stirling, 1940, p. 118.
57. National Research Council, n.d.*a*
58. Strong, 1935, p. 296.

59. Strong, 1940, p. 377.
60. Strong, 1935, pp. 7–30.

Ancient Aspect,[61] *The Pre-Iroquoian Occupations of New York State,*[62] and *Hiwassee Island.*[63]

The taxonomic method and the temporal method of determining relationships between two or more archeological communities are coming to be recognized as complementary to one another, although based upon quite different approaches to the subject. Each has its limitations as well as its advantages. The taxonomic method concentrates upon the physical factor of similarity of evidence and almost disregards the time and space factors. The temporal method, on the other hand, emphasizes the time and space factors, giving only secondary consideration to the physical factor of similarity of evidence. The exclusive use of either method cannot fully explain archeological relationships. The interdependence of these two methods is analogous to that of horizontal and vertical stratigraphy. The resultant construct is a three-dimensional pattern of relationships in which data are furnished by the taxonomic method for the horizontal associations and by the temporal method for the vertical ones. Both methods need to be improved and refined through further experimentation. In the end the potential results of their combined use will approach more closely the axiomatic objectives of archeological research. An illustration of the use of both methods is Griffin's "Cultural Change and Continuity in Eastern United States Archeology," in which he "attempts to place cultural aggregates recognized by various students, in their areal, cultural, and chronological context."[64]

The progress made in establishing more critical means of identifying and classifying archeological complexes in the eastern United States has increased attention upon the interpretations of this classified body of data. It has taken two forms. One is the synthesis, within larger frames of reference, of the archeological evidence. The other is the demand that archeological data be related more closely to the cultures of bygone peoples.

There are at least three varieties of synthesis. One is the co-ordination of the temporal and taxonomic relationships of currently identifiable complexes within a particular state, as in *An Introduction to Nebraska Archeology,*[65] *Rediscovering Illinois,*[66] and *The Pre-Iroquoian Occupations of New York State.*[67] A second is the analysis of a large but discrete archeological unit, such as *The Fort Ancient Aspect*[68] and *The Adena People.*[69] A third is the integration of the results of recent archeological studies throughout large areas. An outstanding example of this approach is *An Interpretation of the Prehistory of the Eastern United States.*[70] A similar objective is implicit in the group of archeological articles which appeared in *Essays in Historical Anthropology of North America*[71] and *Man in Northeastern North America.*[72] Finally, the volume of which this article is a part is another illustration of this third variety of synthesis.

Another form of review of recent research is the compilation of existing knowledge in the recently published *Indians before Columbus.*[73] A comparison of this book with a similar review of fifty years ago[74] reveals vividly the progress which has been made during this half-century in securing a clearer understanding of the archaeological records of the eastern United States.

The other product of the progress made in the study of eastern United States archeology is the growing insistence that present methods and procedures be critically evaluated in terms of the contributions which they make to culture history. Strong was among the first to record a plea for a closer integration of the three techniques of anthropology (ethnology, archeology, and physical anthropology).[75]

Two years later Steward and Setzler published a critical evaluation of current archeological activities, which contains the following statement:

We criticize not commissions but omissions of modern archeology. Though modern field techniques, intensive ceramic studies, listing of elements, and taxonomic methodologies serve important purposes, it is unfortunate that emphasis on them alone should be at the expense of clarifying the general problems. Though the conception of ultimate objectives will develop as the science of archeology matures, we believe that a deliberate effort should be made at present to ascertain whether or not our daily research is likely to fit into a general scheme of cultural research. Otherwise, the fruits of archeology will continue to have little apparent bearing on other fields of cultural research and to hold little interest for persons other than antiquarians.[76]

Evidence that this revised approach to the interpretation of archeological data has been receiving attention is found in John Bennett's summary of "Recent Developments in the Functional Interpretation of Archeological Data." He concludes: "A new set of premises must be accepted if the archeologist is to adapt a functional outlook. Perhaps the most fundamental of these is the one concerned with the nature of his data. Archeological data must be considered as essentially similar to that gathered by any social sci-

61. Griffin, J. B., 1943a, pp. 11–35.
62. Ritchie, 1944, pp. 11–25.
63. Lewis and Kneberg, 1946, pp. 10–20.
64. Griffin, J. B., 1946, p. 39.
65. Strong, 1935.
66. Cole and Deuel, 1937.
67. Ritchie, 1944.
68. Griffin, J. B., 1943a.
69. Webb and Snow, 1945.

70. Ford and Willey, 1941.
71. Smithsonian Institution, 1940.
72. Johnson, (ed.), 1946.
73. Martin, Quimby, and Collier, 1947.
74. Thomas, C., 1898.
75. Strong, 1936.
76. Steward and Setzler, 1938, p. 10.

entist. The difference is one of degree, not kind."[77]

The most comprehensive statement calling for a critical evaluation of current archeological procedures and a reorientation of archeological research has just been published, after the major portion of this manuscript was completed.[78] In it Walter Taylor contends that current archeological research, called the comparative or taxonomic approach,

is primarily an attempt to determine the significance of specific cultural items with regard to relationships *outside* the cultural unit being investigated. . . . The conjunctive approach, on the other hand, has as its primary goal the elucidation of cultural conjunctives, the associations and relationships, the 'affinities,' *within* the manifestation under investigation. It aims at drawing the completest possible picture of past human life in terms of its human and geographic environment. It is chiefly interested in the relation of item to item, trait to trait, complex to complex (to use Linton's concepts) *within* the culture-unit represented and only subsequently in the taxonomic relation of these phenomena to similar ones outside of it.[79]

These two recent developments constitute the final episode in the story of the achievements of the past twenty-five years in the analytical study of the archeological records of the eastern United States. One marks the beginning of the close of a trend in research procedures. The other, at present a challenge, may indicate the start of a new trend.

The progress made during the past quarter-century in advancing the cause of eastern United States archeology stems from the rapid expansion of facilities brought about by the growth in the number of archeological organizations and by the increased governmental support of field studies. The achievements of this period may be grouped into three great categories. First, a greater public appreciation of local archeological work has established a more enlightened public opinion and a closer association between professional and lay students. Second, the amount of field work accomplished has greatly increased the published record of much additional archeological data and of a correspondingly significant improvement in technical field methods. Third, the necessity of incorporating the additional raw data and the newly encountered problems into the body of archeological knowledge has required a searching study of research tools and procedures, resulting in the improvement and revision of the techniques of nomenclature and classification of archeological objects and associations and of the methods of comparative analysis and interpretation of archeological complexes.

A large number of factors contributed to these accomplishments. Yet in last analysis they are the result of the devoted efforts of many students working cooperatively to perfect the tools and improve the methods of their chosen research field. Recent achievements are in large measure the contributions of those who had not yet joined the archeological ranks twenty-five years ago, a fact amply demonstrated by the remainder of this volume. They received their training in the field, the laboratory, and the classroom from many teachers, of whom Fay-Cooper Cole is an outstanding example. It is now their turn to stimulate and guide those who will contribute to the progress to be achieved in the next quarter-century.

The study of eastern United States archeology stands, at the mid-century point, on the threshold of maturity as a discipline.

77. Bennett, 1943, p. 219.   79. *Ibid.*, pp. 95, 96.
78. Taylor, 1948.

ARCHEOLOGY AND RACE IN THE AMERICAN INDIAN.

By Georg K. Neumann*

THIS paper provides a framework for the recon-struction of the racial history of the American Indian north of Mexico. It is a study based on archeologically documented skeletal material from the earliest times to the period of first contacts with Europeans. Each of the series has been previously described but are now for the first time clearly de-limited as varieties and placed into a chronological and cultural framework.

Some of the earlier attempts at syntheses showed certain shortcomings. Thus one of Hooton's papers is in a sense too broad in that he examined the skele-tal remains of a pueblo to find to what extent it re-tained morphological features that are now more or less diagnostic of Australoids, Negroids, Caucasoids, or southeastern Asiatic Mongoloids—all end prod-ucts of human evolution—and applied the results of this study to the American Indian as a whole.[1] In other syntheses the crania were pooled on a broad geographical basis irrespective of the time element involved,[2] or, in a sense, were considered too local to obtain a proper perspective,[3] or the groupings were based on as few as three indices.[4] Most studies, finally, largely omitted morphological characteristics, which are much more likely to reflect genetic relationships than absolute dimensions or indices, and gave too few measurements to obtain an adequate description of the group. The main shortcoming, however, was that too often the crania were examined without due re-gard to their archeological affiliations.

Because of space limitations only a small portion of the research can be presented in this paper; and it is to be regarded as a condensation of a more exten-sive monograph: *Racial Differentiation in the Ameri-can Indian*. With the exception of a brief summary table in the last section, all tables of morphological observations, measurements, and indices have been omitted here. Although the study is based on the ex-amination of more than 10,000 skulls, the eight type series total only 471 crania of adult undeformed males.

The ultimate Asiatic origin of the natives of the Western Hemisphere is a generally accepted fact,[5] just as that the peopling of the New World was not the result of a single wave of people, but rather a continuing series of migrations lasting from perhaps immediately post-glacial times to around the begin-ning of the Christian Era.[6] The immediate ancestors of the immigrants were in all probability inhabitants of the boreal coniferous forest lands of northern Asia and the grassland belt to the south.[7] These mid-lati-tude grasslands and adjoining boreal forests were not especially favorable to primitive food gatherers and hunting groups. In the competition for hunting grounds in the past, groups must have been pushed off toward the west and northeast again and again. To the west migration routes were open and, as the racial history of man shows, often followed; but at other times, while deserts and mountains formed barriers to the south, human groups repeatedly may have constituted a barrier against further expansion to the west. In that case small groups, perhaps at first closely related to the Upper Cave people of Choukoutien,[8] followed the path of least resistance and were channeled off to the northeast.

The boreal forests of Siberia were barriers in themselves limiting migration in that they were pene-trated only by small groups. The Sea of Okotsk to the east and the tundra to the north served as stronger barriers, but the north-flowing rivers and mountain ranges of northeastern Siberia determined migration routes to a great extent and made it inevitable that group after group was directed to Bering Strait. Simi-lar factors were at work in Alaska: the arctic coast would beckon only to members of a culture that had become adapted to sea-mammal hunting in Asia, the tundra acted as an effective barrier, nor can the deeply dissected mountainous coast of southern Alaska be considered a natural highroad for migration. Most immigrants from across the strait therefore probably pushed up the Yukon and the Porcupine rivers, over a low divide to the Mackenzie and then south, or fol-lowed the Yukon and the Pelly further upstream, keeping south of the Mackenzie Mountains, eventu-ally to arrive in the Peace River area and the open

* University of Chicago, Ph.B., 1930; A. M., 1936; Ph.D., 1950; Associate Professor, Indiana University, 1950. Chapter received August, 1949.

1. Hooton, 1933, pp. 154–162.   3. Wissler, 1926, pp. 118–121.
2. Hrdlička, 1927, p. 48.   4. Dixon, 1923, pp. 3–23.
5. Hrdlička, 1925, p. 493.   7. Chapple and Coon, 1942, p. 90.
6. Jenness, 1941, pp. 383–396.   8. Weidenreich, 1939, p. 172.

plains.[9] Minor movements may have been along the coast, but most of them probably were by way of the western plains and thence to the more peripheral parts of the continent in quest of better hunting grounds or yielding to pressure of newly arrived groups. With the exception of the chief migration routes to the south into Middle and South America, the earlier immigrants were thus pushed into refuge areas and the less accessible margins of the continent, while those that arrived later settled more centrally located areas.[10] With certain limitations, and especially a careful consideration of physiographic conditions, distributions may give us important leads to sequences of migrational movements. In itself this may not mean too much, but often the appearance of new varieties in an area can be checked by stratigraphic and typological evidence from archeology.

Since this work has certain taxonomic aspects, it may not be amiss to mention here that no super-groupings of varieties have been attempted. I feel that as yet we do not have enough information of the total range of variability of the American Indian, especially of the natives of South America, nor have we enough data on early Asiatic races, to attempt to solve the interrelationship of all Mongoloids at this time. All groups dealt with in this paper are regarded on the level of zoölogical varieties of the subspecies *asiaticus* of *Homo sapiens*. In other words, at present we sidestep the issue as to whether there are any morphological traits that set off all American Indians from any of the Mongoloid races of Asia. In my estimation it will be very difficult to find such characteristics. This would make the appellation "American Indian" a purely geographical term.

Just as in any other form of animal life there is, of course, no set limit to the number of varieties that may have differentiated in the American Indians over a period of, say, twenty thousand years. It is therefore quite likely that additional varieties will be described, and even possible that it will be necessary to combine several of them with the gaining of additional knowledge as some of the gaps are filled in the archeological story of the Americas and northeastern Asia. It would be erroneous to force the people of any area into a preconceived system.

As the concept is used in this study we may define a variety as a zoölogical group of a certain order of differentiation characterized by the possession of a combination of a selected number of inherited morphological attributes. The criteria by which race classifications are established are admittedly physical. Generally they are morphological, although they might find metrical expression. To attain varietal rank the group must be more than a family line or a very local physical type. The formation of new

varieties takes place constantly in nature. This differentiation under conditions of isolation allow full play for various selective processes. On the other hand, mixture, with a recombination of traits, may give rise to secondary varieties. In any case, the rate of change varies. One variety may remain relatively undifferentiated, while another may change rapidly. In thus regarding lower taxonomic categories as dynamic entities in various stages of differentiation we can only say that a variety is a grouping of an order somewhere between a subspecies and a local strain. Following Keith,[11] in general 30–80 per cent of its members should be identifiable as such. Of course, it would be much more desirable to be able to express this variability in terms of differences in gene frequencies, but as yet our information on the inheritance of normal morphological traits is much too scanty to do this.

The traits by which a variety can be identified are necessarily multiple. No single bodily character exhibits a sufficient range of variation to enable us to assign even to each of the three or four recognized subspecies a distinct and exclusive development of that feature. In other words, there are more distinct kinds of men than distinct categories of hair form, head shape, eye color, etc. This makes most of these traits quantitative in nature, and makes it necessary to assign a certain range of the feature to the subspecies, variety, or local physical type under consideration. Many of the morphological attributes can be expressed metrically, but this should serve as a tool for the reduction of a mass of data on variables to constants rather than for purposes of the establishment of varieties. Some overlapping of characteristics is to be expected, but this does not mean that differences do not exist or that they are not significant. The uniqueness of a variety lies in possessing a certain combination of traits. Similar to taxonomic problems in other animals the diagnostic traits need not be used for the entire group but may differ from variety to variety. Man exhibits some traits by virtue of being a vertebrate, mammal, primate, one of the Hominidae, a member of the genus *Homo*, the species *sapiens,* and even smaller divisions such as subspecies. It is the work of the taxonomist to determine in the light of the evolutionary history of the group the diagnostic value of the different traits. Thus, if a morphological trait is so old that it is a general primate characteristic, it would be too much to expect it to shed much light on human differentiation on a varietal level. In this sense the traits are "selected" in the above definition.

Finally, in order to have a large number of inherited morphological traits in common, the group must have formed an inbreeding community, a premise which requires that when we deal with archeological material at the outset we have to work within a given archeological horizon and usually a fairly circumscribed area. It is only after the older varieties are described that we can go farther afield and interpret what has happened in case of the more recent ones.

In this paper eight varieties have been established —varieties which to a large extent satisfy the conditions that have just been discussed. It must be emphasized that these groups do not represent types in the sense of selecting from various populations individuals representing certain metrical or indicial combinations, but consist of relatively homogeneous units, each a stabilized related community, from a number of archeological horizons, from marginal or refuge areas, or from continuous continental areas of distribution as yet undisturbed by the shattering effect of the arrival of a new group. These nuclear groups are scattered widely over the continent in their distribution and may range on a conservative estimate over a period from 2000 B.C. to the end of the nineteenth century. The older varieties, such as the Otamids, Iswanids, and Ashiwids, almost certainly can be traced back far beyond that date, although the series described here may be relatively recent.

A Texas Coast series (Otamid), a Kentucky shell heap series (Iswanid), an Arizona Basket-Maker series (Ashiwid), a Middle Mississippi series (Walcolid), a Central Algonkin series (Lenapid), an Eskimo series (Inuid), a series from the interior of the Canadian Northwest (Deneid), and a series from the northern Plains (Lakotid) should represent an adequate sample to give the anthropologist a fair idea of the variability of the North American Indian from both a distributional and a temporal point of view (see distribution map, Fig. 4 C). Numerically the Otamid series is represented by 18, the Iswanid series by 33, the Ashiwid series by 15, the Walcolid series by 45, the Lenapid series by 24, the Inuid series by 241, the Deneid series by 32, and the Lakotid series by 63 undeformed adult male crania. The populations of the centers of culture areas, in contrast to these series, generally represent considerable degrees of mixture.

The determining of the varieties was done in four steps. The first consisted of gathering observations and measurements from as many as possible series of crania that were associated with archeological material, both stratigraphic and typological, the relative homogeneity of which indicated that one is dealing with a physically closely related group rather than a population representing a mechanical mixture of diverse strains. The second step, after reduction of the morphological observations and measurements —tabulating modal distributions of the former and

computing the means and standard deviations and their probable errors of the latter—was to examine the variability of the physical data of each group and determine which of the traits were more or less diagnostic of the group. The third step consisted of eliminating groups that were too small to be certain that they might represent groups of a varietal order, or those groups that were intermediate in too many traits—groups that could be explained on the basis of mixture between others. The fourth step, finally, consisted of making comparisons and determining what kind of correlations there existed between the physical data and cultural and linguistic groupings in order to reconstruct the history of the Indians of various areas.

The only secondary variety that has been included is the Lakotid variety of the northern Plains. Although it probably has not had time to stabilize itself in its entire extent it may be relatively homogeneous locally, a condition which seems to hold for our type series.

THE OTAMID VARIETY

The evidence of physical anthropology is perhaps the most striking in tracing the Asiatic relationships of the American Indian. But here too, just as in cultural and linguistic connections, time relationships have to be kept in mind when comparisons are made. First of all, it must be considered as established that the peopling of the New World was not the result of a single wave of people, but rather that the process consisted of a series of migrations lasting from perhaps immediately postglacial times to around the beginning of the Christian Era. If we accept this time factor as basic, this Asiatic stock had perhaps 25,000 years at its disposal–enough time for physical differentiation to take place in northeastern Asia, and some of the later groups to differentiate after their arrival in North and South America.

The earliest finds of man in the New World for this reason should be compared with archeological material from northeastern Asia of approximately the same age, and the same applies to the comparison of peripheral surviving groups. The latter is more difficult as it would presuppose that changes in each have been of a parallel nature, rather than showing evolution in different directions. When Matthew[12] formulated his principles of dispersal of mammals from an Asiatic center, and the distribution of the most conservative forms to the peripheries, he naturally did not assume that the latter would remain entirely static. Dixon, on the other hand, who applied Matthew's principles of dispersal to man, assumed that at least those traits were stable that he used for classification.[13] This still has to be demon-

12. Matthew, 1915, p. 181.   13. Dixon, 1923, pp. 393–406.

strated. It is much more likely that, although various racial groups exhibit different rates of change, all are to be regarded as dynamic rather than static.

Upper Palaeolithic material from northeastern Asia is as yet too scanty for wide comparisons with the few finds of skeletal material of possibly Mesolithic or earliest Neolithic data in the New World. The three Late Palaeolithic crania from the Upper Cave at Choukoutien are suggestive, and may well be regarded as ancestral to the Otamid, the Inuid, and possibly some South American varieties. Closely related to the questions of origins is whether all such groups as the Lagoa Santa people, the Pericue from Lower California, and the Early Sacramento Valley people can be considered as representing a single variety. A considerable number of skeletal finds that suggest some antiquity have been reported. Most of them lack cultural associations, and those that can be shown to be relatively old are still isolated cases which cannot indicate the variabilities of their respective groups.

On the basis of a considerable amount of skeletal material, which is either early archeologically or extreme marginal in distribution, I believe that a varietal group can be established. This is a widely dispersed group that is represented by the Early Woodland Black Sand Focus people in Illinois, the Coastal Focus people on the Atlantic Coast, and the Karankawa on the Texas Coast. In this study the latter, consisting of a series of 18 adult undeformed male crania, shall serve as a type series. Since there is some evidence that such tribes as the Mohave, Pima, and Papago may, in part at least, be descended from this variety (Fig. 5), I have used the name members of the latter tribe use for themselves as the basis for the varietal name Otamid (Papago: *O'otam*, "people"). There can be very little doubt that the people of the Oso site formed a closely inbred group for both culturally and physically the material is quite homogeneous. Woodbury published a brief metrical description of part of this series and made some comparisons with two other series.[14] For purposes of standardization, especially from a morphological point of view, the series was remeasured and is briefly described here.

The Otamid male skull, if we take the Texas Coast series as representative for the present, is relatively large in size, judging by its cranial module of 155.0, a glabello-occipital length of 189.3 mm., a maximum breadth of 133.5 mm., and a basion-bregma height of 140.4 mm. Of course, the absolute diameters may be somewhat misleading in this respect as they do not take the degree of recession of the forehead, the temporal fullness, the development of sagittal cresting, nor the amount of lambdoidal flattening

14. Woodbury, 1937, pp. 5–16.

into account. If all of these factors were considered, as in cranial capacity, more moderate size may be indicated. The braincase is dolichocephalic with a cranial index of 70.66, orthocranial or moderately high with a length-height index of 73.77, and acrocranial or high according to a breadth-height index of 104.71. From above, the vault tends to be ellipsoid or ovoid with medium to pronounced muscular relief, generally with large rather than medium brow ridges, large to medium glabellar prominence, pronounced to medium frontal slope, a medium amount of sagittal elevation, small to medium parietal eminences, a medium amount of lambdoid flattening, a medium to low-placed bun-shaped occiput, and large-sized mastoid processes. The combination of morphological traits gives the skull an appearance that is generally described as Australoid, but an actual comparison of contour drawings of Otamid skulls with those of one hundred Australian skulls did not reveal a single one that was identical.

The face is morphologically less diagnostic, although the Texas Coast series stands out more sharply than would a Long Island or Early Woodland Otamid series from Illinois (Fig. 4, D). In the Karankawa series the face is elongated: total facial height 128.3 mm., upper facial height 78.0 mm., and a bizygomatic breadth of only 134.2 mm. These measurements yield a mean total facial index of 97.39, hyperleptoprosopic; and an upper facial index of 58.99, leptene. Cheek bones are only moderately prominent; orbits are quite square with little inclination of the horizontal axis, and mesoconch; and the nose is leptorrhine with a mean nasal index of 44.26. Nasal breadth tends to be moderate, 25.2 mm., but the height is considerable, 56.7 mm. In profile the nose was probably straight. Face size can be described as moderate, and prognathism is generally absent. The mandible, in contrast to that of the Ashiwids to be described later, is medium to large, rather massive, with a wide bilateral type of chin, and only a small amount of gonial eversion.

In order to demonstrate that the Karankawa series represents more than a local type, Clauser made a detailed comparison between this series and a marginal one from Long Island and Manhattan Island.[15] The resemblance is rather striking, considering the great distance that separated these groups geographically. Both evidently represented survivors which persisted marginally until historical times. A comparison of the New York coast series with the Early Woodland series of the Black Sand Focus from central Illinois indicates that the Karankawa were somewhat specialized in that they differed in exhibiting greater facial length, narrower noses, and slightly higher orbits. Both morphologically and metrically the oldest series

15. Clauser, 1948, pp. 18–23.

from Illinois and the most marginal one on the Atlantic Coast can be considered identical in almost every respect, a circumstance that validates the establishment of the Otamid variety as an archeologically early population stratum.

Two detailed metrical comparisons have been made in order to demonstrate the nature of the difference between the Otamid and a Lenapid series, on the one hand, and between the Otamid and an Ashiwid series, on the other. Although series like that were never pooled by Hrdlička, he considered the crania that have been separated into Otamid and Lenapid varieties to form one group,[16] and states that the Basket-Makers approach the Algonkin very significantly.[17]

The Otamid series is shown to be more longheaded, slightly lower in vault height, narrower and longer faced, and narrower nosed. Facial and nasal proportions, however, vary considerably from local group to group. Greater weight therefore has to be given to morphological traits, the Otamids differing considerably from the Lenapids in having heavier supra-orbital ridges, a more prominent glabellar region, a forehead that is generally more retreating, more sagittal cresting, less developed parietal eminences, more lambdoid flattening, and an occipital region that tends to be low-placed and bun-shaped.

In a metrical comparison between our Otamid and Ashiwid series, that is, between the Karankawa and Arizona Basket-Maker crania, fully half of the measurements and indices differ significantly. Morphological characteristics fully substantiate the existence of the differences, and Hrdlička's conclusion has to be interpreted as based only on more general morphological resemblances. In other words, the Basket-Makers can be regarded as more like the marginal dolichocephals than the Apache, for example.

Many finds of reputed antiquity, such as Brown's Valley Man,[18] the Clark's Fork skeleton from Idaho, the Wyoming crania,[19] Nebraska Loess Man, and others, undoubtedly fit well into the range of this variety. It is therefore quite evident that originally the Otamid variety enjoyed a very wide distribution and was subsequently pressed off into refuge areas. One of these, as Dixon pointed out long ago, was the northeastern part of North America.

During the time the Early Woodland culture flourished from Nebraska east to the Atlantic seaboard this variety is practically the only one that is encountered archeologically; skeletal remains are relatively plentiful from Wisconsin, Illinois, Indiana, and Ohio, but usually lack documentation. In New York there are some indications that this variety may be represented in the Archaic, and certainly in the

Coastal Focus. Howells in his excellent summary on the physical anthropology of the northeastern area reports essentially the same variety from the Maine shell heaps and crania associated with the Red Paint manifestation of New England.[20] In Illinois and the Ohio Valley the variety persisted well into Hopewellian times and was after that replaced by Lenapid groups. Earlier, even as far back as during the Late Archaic of New York a brachycranial element is found intrusively in the vicinity of the eastern end of Lake Ontario. Since this element is found with a different culture, it is safe to suppose that this was the first group that exerted population pressure on the Otamids, beginning thereby to crowd them to the eastern seaboard, where they persisted in places until historic times.

THE ISWANID VARIETY

The Iswanid variety owes its establishment as a separate taxonomic entity to an archeological grouping. In this case it is the time element separating the Archaic of the eastern United States as a pre-pottery horizon that gave the lead to pool cranial material from this early archeological manifestation and compare it to later less closely related series from the same area. When the measurements of the first series of Archaic skeletons, which were excavated by Clarence B. Moore at Indian Knoll, Kentucky, were listed in the "Catalogue of Human Crania" by Hrdlička the crania were grouped on a more or less general morphological basis with other supposedly Algonkin crania from Kentucky.[21] Hrdlička assumed the Indian Knoll people to be historically recent, and in all probability to represent the inhabitants of a village of an Algonquian-speaking tribe. This view was expressed by him in a brief report in which he stated that "none of the skulls is deformed and their type is that of the Algonquin. . . . The location is in the region still generally ascribed to the Shawnee, but the remains evidently represent another tribe. This may have been the Miami, or one of the tribes from Illinois, or one of the Lenape."[22]

The antiquity of the pre-ceramic Indian Knoll people, who were responsible for the shell middens along the larger water courses of eastern United States, was not fully realized until Webb's excavations of such sites in Kentucky, Tennessee, and Alabama from 1934 on. Even as late as 1939 in their first report on a shell-mound site, the Chiggerville site, Webb and Haag refer to the antiquity of this complex only in an indirect way by making comparisons with Basket-Maker II sites in Arizona, and cautiously state that the shell-mound group preceded, at this

16. Hrdlička, 1927, pp. 46–48. 18. Jenks, 1937, pp. 18–29.
17. Hrdlička, 1931b, p. 94. 19. Howells, 1938.

20. Howells, 1946, pp. 168–177.
21. Hrdlička, 1927, pp. 26–29.
22. Moore, C. B., 1916a, p. 448.

locality, the Middle Mississippi people. Subsequently dates roughly equivalent to those for Basket-Maker and Modified Basket-Maker have found general acceptance. This would date the Archaic series provisionally between A.D. 100 and A.D. 700, although some archeologists feel that the complex with which the skeletal material is associated should be dated as early as 3000 B.C.

It is very likely that after more early skeletal material has been collected in the northwestern part of the continent the distribution of the Iswanids will prove to be a very wide one. Nor is it very improbable that a variety ancestral to it can be traced to northeastern Siberia. In the collections of the American Museum of Natural History there are some crania from the lower Yukon Valley which resemble those from the Indian Knoll site both morphologically and metrically, and other scattered series for the northern Plains. But as yet these series cannot be used to demonstrate the presence of this variety over this large area because of the smallness of the sample.

On the other hand, along the Ohio, Cumberland, and Tennessee rivers and their tributaries, and to a lesser extent along the Atlantic seaboard, the Iswanid variety is well represented. As the putative bison hunters migrated east into the woodlands, dependence on the deer and small mammals became greater, and seasonally, at least, their economy must have shifted to a large extent to one of gathering fresh water mussels in the shallows of the larger streams. As a result we find extensive shell middens, which besides being utilized as camp sites, served as places of interment. These sites with a concentration of skeletal material were not tapped until Moore's work along the Green River and Webb's excavations in connection with the flood-control projects in the Tennessee Valley. Since then some of the most extensive series of American Indian skeletal material have been recovered from these middens (Fig. 1, C–D). The largest series of crania comes from a re-excavation of the Indian Knoll site, smaller series from sites in the Pickwick Basin in northern Alabama,[23] the round graves in eastern Tennessee, the Chiggerville site in northern Kentucky,[24] and a number of sites in southern Indiana. In Maryland, New Jersey, and southern New England a fair number of crania that could be classed as Iswanid occur, but as yet there is no evidence that they formed an early inbreeding group. In eastern Oklahoma the Iswanid variety is represented in the Fourche-Maline complex and may have survived in the Bryan Focus population. Farther to the south an early cultural manifestation related to the Archaic has been recognized in the Tchefuncte complex. Some of these sites are coastal shell heaps; others are earth mounds in the interior. The fact that, unlike the Kentucky sites, they all yield pottery may indicate a temporal difference in occupation. The skeletal material from the Copell place, a Tchefuncte site on Pecan Island, Vermillion Parish, southern Louisiana, was described by Collins, who considers this group to represent a variant of the Indian Knoll people.[25] That the Iswanid variety extended also along the Atlantic Coast is demonstrated by the small crania from the Savannah River shell heaps and the Melbourne skull from Florida.

The largest available series for comparative purposes is that from Indian Knoll. Clarence B. Moore's excavation yielded 33 and that of the University of Kentucky 219 measurable adult male crania, which gives us a statistically adequate sample of 252 adult underformed male skulls of this ancient group. Moore's original series, now part of the collections of the United States National Museum, may serve here as a type sample for wider comparisons. It was measured again—omitting those Kentucky crania that could not be assigned to the Archaic horizon—detailed morphological observations were made, and both checked against the larger sample that has been described by Dr. C. E. Snow.[26] The smaller sample was found representative of the group as a whole in every respect, and, since the variability of the series is less than that of other Archaic series, it is evident that it represents one of the most homogeneous varieties among the early inhabitants of the eastern part of the continent.

When von Bonin and Morant came to the conclusion that the Indian Knoll people obviously defines a separate type, it became evident that neither Hrdlička's "Algonkin type" nor von Eickstedt's "Sylvid race" is applicable to it. It then becomes necessary to supply a new term for this variety. In this paper it is designated as the Iswanid variety (Catawba: *iswa*, "river," and *nie*, "people"). This name was selected on the basis of identification of some skeletal material from historic Catawba and Tutelo villages as closely related to the Indian Knoll series (Fig. 6, C). Since, according to this, it is very probable that the eastern Siouan tribes represent an eastern extension of the Archaic people of the Ohio Valley, a Catawba name was thought to be preferable for this group.

The Iswanid variety can be briefly described as follows: the skull is relatively small with an average capacity of 1366.9 cc., a glabello-occipital length of 177.0 mm., a maximum breadth of 134.9 mm., and a basion-bregma height of 138.8 mm. These dimensions yield a cranial index of 76.25, and a length-height index of 78.27. The cranial vault is therefore on the lower border of mesocrany and high in relation to its length. It is ovoid in form, with medium

23. Newman and Snow, 1942, pp. 393–507.
24. Skarland, 1939.
25. Collins, 1941.   26. Snow, 1948.

muscular relief, small to medium brow ridges, medium frontal slope, small frontal breadth, a slight amount of sagittal cresting, medium parietal eminences, only a slight amount of lambdoidal flattening, and an occiput that has a medium high position.

The face as a whole is of gracile rather than rugged build and not large in relationship to the braincase. All facial dimensions tend to be moderate (total facial height 118.0 mm., upper facial height 70.9 mm., and bizygomatic breadth 135.9), and the same applies to the proportions (total facial index 87.09, mesoprosopic, and upper facial index 52.14, mesene). The size of the zygomatic bones and their anterior projection are only moderate, but the lateral projection of the zygomatic arch is generally pronounced. The orbits are most frequently somewhat oblong, often square with a small amount of inclination; and the left orbital index is mesoconch (77.92, if the breadth is taken from maxillofrontale, 83.33 from dacryon). The nasal index is leptorrhine, 46.60, on the border of mesorrhiny. Absolute diameters of the nasal structures are small with a breadth of 23.8 mm., and a height of 51.2 mm.; both root and bridge dimensions are moderate. Prognathism is medium to submedium. The size of the mandible is medium, the most common chin form is bilateral, and gonial eversion small to medium.

The presence of an hunting and gathering culture group that gradually changed to a pottery-using agricultural one has been recognized for a long time in both the northeastern portion of the United States as well as in the Southwest. Despite the approximate contemporaneity of the two populations, it has not been until recently, however, that both have begun to be considered manifestations of one underlying cultural base.[27] This does not mean that such relatively primitive cultural units as the Basket-Makers and Archaic shell-heap people can be grouped together in a classificatory sense, but in each manifestation a number of traits, some of which have since been linked to an earlier Folsom-Yuma culture in the Southwest, continue into these cultures. Following the time the first hunters with a Folsom-Yuma culture penetrated to the Southwest there must have been a fairly long period during which a large division of this group gradually spread from the northern plains toward the east. In the Ohio Valley and the Tennessee Valley there are few sites that exhibit a culture complex which can be equated typologically with a Folsom-Yuma culture, yet Folsom-Yuma influences are strong throughout this area. In at least two instances Folsomoid points have been discovered in the earliest pre-ceramic strata of Archaic sites, and it is more than a coincidence that in southern Indiana, for example, most Folsomoid and Yuma points

are coterminous in their distribution with the known Archaic sites.

Now the question arises whether this group of people that carried the Folsom-Yuma tradition at a somewhat later period as far east as the Atlantic seaboard represents an entirely separate group from the one that penetrated to the Southwest. On a cultural basis a considerable period must be allowed for the differentiation to have taken place. The morphological and metrical data fully substantiate this contention.

When von Bonin and Morant made a statistical comparison of the Indian Knoll series with a number of others, they found that it obviously represented a type that differed widely from all other series that were considered.[28] In my own detailed comparison of forty-six morphological observations, twenty-two measurements, and eight indices, the Iswanid Indian Knoll series shows closer relationships to the Ashiwid Basket-Maker series than to any other. Morphologically there is a striking similarity between the modes of the observations: identity in fourteen, overlapping of one of the two modes in thirty, and significantly differing modes only in two of the traits, namely, lateral projection of the zygomatic bones and eversion of the gonial angles. In the position of the occipital bone, orbit shape, nasal bridge height, and nasal sill form there is considerable difference. In the Iswanid variety the occipital position tends to be medium or high, in the Ashiwid variety medium or low; the orbits oblong or square, and rhomboid or square, respectively; nasal bridge height medium or high in the former, and medium or low in the latter; while the nasal sills tend to be duller in Ashiwids.

Metrically the two type series are especially similar in their small size, a feature that was noted by von Bonin and Morant, but something that is not expressed sufficiently by the cranial module alone as this average takes little cognizance of the fullness of the curved surfaces which make up the cranial vault. Except for basion-bregma height and the indices derived from it, there are no statistically significant differences in vault dimensions. The total facial breadth and biangular breadth is significantly greater in the Iswanid series, on the other hand, the Ashiwid nasal opening exceeds the Iswanid one in breadth. As a whole, then, this physical comparison would substantiate the assumption that the Basket-Makers and Indian Knoll people had an immediate common ancestry, that a split must therefore have occured somewhere in the plains area, and that subsequently differentiation must have taken place. Later each group was probably further modified through contacts with other varieties.

27. Griffin, J. B., 1946, p. 40.

28. Von Bonin and Morant, 1938, p. 106.

A second comparison of racial as well as of archeological interest is between the Iswanid and Lenapid varieties. As was pointed out above, Hrdlička grouped the Indian Knoll series with others of supposedly Algonkin type of the northeastern United States. Here the great difference is quite obvious, for the number of statistically significant differences in mean measurements and indices is quite large, a circumstance which justifies the establishing of separate groups of varietal order.

THE ASHIWID VARIETY

The racial history of the Southwest is a long and complex one. The area, well watered in postglacial times, is situated so that most migration routes to Mexico and South America must have traversed it, and each of the groups that wandered south probably left traces of its presence either as archeological remains or as survivors in a refuge area as the country became progressively more dessicated. The physical diversity of the tribes, too, if the area is not too sharply delimited, has been recognized for a long time. More marginal groups, such as the Pericue from Lower California, the people from the Texas Coast, the Pima, Papago, Mohave, as well as a number of Shoshonean-speaking tribes have been regarded as remnants of earlier populations. The latter have also been considered comparatively late immigrants, either preceding or even being linked with the more recent Athapascan migration.

Whether the earlier peripheral groups are pooled in the sense of von Eickstedt's "Margide Rasse"[29] or Gladwin's "Southern Longheads"[30] or eventually will be found to represent a number of isolates, there remains a core of people on the Southwestern Plateau who form the subject of this section. Hrdlička did not consider the Pueblo Indians a homogeneous group.[31] He described a substantial dolichoid as well as a fairly strong brachycranic element. The former were identified essentially with the Basket-Makers and were recognized as having persisted as the predominant element in the later Pueblo population. In the Puyé Pueblo population and in the Hopi, on the other hand, he recognized a naturally brachycranial element strongly represented.

More recently Seltzer confirmed the persistence of the Basket-Maker type in the Pueblo population and showed that even the Puyé Pueblo group falls within the range of what he calls the Southwestern Plateau type.[32] On that basis Seltzer would argue that the intrusion of the naturally brachycranial element is a relatively late one and that it had only a very limited effect in changing the Pueblo peoples.

29. Von Eickstedt, 1934, pp. 704–711.
30. Gladwin, 1937, p. 54.
31. Hrdlička, 1931b, pp. 91–95.
32. Seltzer, 1944.

In this connection Brew takes a strong stand in denying a mass invasion or even a peaceful mass penetration of a large alien population with a strikingly different culture between Basket-Maker III and Pueblo I times.[33] Yet a brachycranial element is certainly in the area by early Pueblo IV times and there is too small a time span for this type to have developed out of the earlier one. If it were merely a matter of an increase in brachycephaly, which in part at least could be explained by the coming into fashion of artificial cranial deformation, it would be rather simple, but the later brachycephals exhibit a complex of other morphological traits that leaves us no explanation except that they must have been introduced from the outside. This would suggest an intermittent immigration of relatively small groups that became acculturated rather quickly. But just how early this began and whether this immigration can be linked with the arrival of certain Shoshonean-speaking groups, such as the Hopi, is still an unanswered question.

Here we shall sidestep the question of an influx of a new group, and for the present deal only with the Basket-Makers and Early Pueblo people as a relatively inbred stabilized group in order to explore more distant relationships which might shed light on their origin (Fig. 1, A–B). Then, too, it cannot be reiterated enough that in order to determine what elements may have been involved in a mixture to form a new physical variety, the older possible strains which may have gone into it must be known.

Hooton's series of fifteen undeformed adult male Arizona Basket-Makers has been used here as a type series for comparative purposes.[34] Because of the physical identity of the Old Zuni people with various Basket-Maker series, the Zuni term for themselves has been used as a name to designate the variety: Ashiwid, from A'shiwi, "the flesh" (Fig. 6, A–B).

As with the Iswanid variety, the Ashiwid skull is relatively small, the cranial module of 148.1 mm. being 2.3 mm. smaller in the latter. In fact, all cranial dimensions are relatively small. The mean glabello-occipital length is 179.9 mm., the maximum breadth 134.5 mm., and the basion-bregma height 129.9 mm. —dimensions yielding a mean cranial index of 74.9 (on the upper border of dolichocrany), and mean length height index of 72.6 (orthocranial). From above the cranial vault is ovoid in form with only small to medium muscular relief, generally small brow ridges, medium frontal slope, medium to narrow frontal breadth, sagittal elevation absent to slight, medium developed parietal eminences, a slight amount of lambdoid flattening, and an occiput with a medium to low position.

The face, in general, is of gracile rather than

33. Brew, 1946, pp. 67–73. 34. Hooton, 1930, p. 234.

rugged build and in absolute dimensions fairly small. Thus, the total facial height is only 116.3 mm., the upper facial height 73.1 mm., and the bizygomatic breadth only 132.4 mm. The indices derived from these dimensions tend to be moderate: a total facial index of 86.8, mesoprosopic, and an upper facial index of 54.8, mesene. Morphologically the face is characterized by a nasion depression either absent or slightly depressed, zygomatic bones which are small in overall size and especially small in their superior-inferior extent, with only slight to medium anterior, and medium to slight lateral projection. Orbits tend to be rhomboid or square with a medium amount of inclination in their modal distribution. The orbital dimensions are moderate with a height of 34.3 mm., a dacryal breadth of 39.1 mm., and mesoconch with a mean index of 87.5. Characteristically the nasal root is medium in height and breadth, the bridge medium in breadth, but only medium or low in height. In absolute breadth the piriform aperture is not wide, averaging 25.4 mm., with a rather short nasal height of 50.8 mm. we get a mesorrhine nasal index of 50.1. Prognathism is medium, the mandible tends to be small in size, it lacks robusticity, tends to exhibit either a median or medio-bilateral type of chin, usually negative in projection, and lacks eversion of the gonial angles.

A comparison between an Iswanid and an Ashiwid series was made in the preceeding section and a common ancestor was postulated for the two. A satisfactory late prehistoric or protohistoric Walcolid type series from the Southwest is not available for comparison, but such a comparison would probably be of about the same order as that between an Ashiwid and a Walcolid series from the South.

THE WALCOLID VARIETY

When Dixon presented his ideas of the racial history of the natives of the central part of the continent of North America he was forced by the limitations of his method into pooling a large number of tribes under the grouping "Central Brachychephals."[35] Since he took the nasal index as his next criterion for further subdivision, lacked adequate material, did not recognize platybasia as the reason for the lowness of certain series of crania, and did not know of the diagnostic value of this trait in combination with certain other ones, this grouping included too much and obscured the unraveling of the sequence of at least two separate varieties moving from the northwest over the continent.

In this section we shall separate these two groups and deal exclusively with the earlier high-vaulted one, a variety whose existence as an inbreeding group is demonstrated by its occurring as a relatively un-

mixed form in certain archeological horizons and by its distribution in areas to which the later low-vaulted Deneid variety did not have time to penetrate.

For convenience we shall refer to this racial group as the Walcolid variety (Muskogee: *wahali*, "south;" *cola*, "people"). As a whole it corresponds to von Eickstedt's Centralid race and Hrdlička's Gulf type, but since these two groupings do not have the same coverage, nor correspond quite to the findings outlined in this section, a new varietal name is necessary. This is especially true, since a number of series have been included in the older designation because of the assumption that they were hypsi- and brachycranial in their artificially undeformed states. As in many other parts of the New World, earlier groups in the Southeast have been absorbed by later ones, and both natural brachycephalization and the introduction of various forms of artificial cranial deformation have helped to obscure the picture.

The Walcolids present a typical shatter pattern in their distribution. Small groups are found as islands among the people of the North Pacific Coast, as a relatively solid block in central California and the Great Basin—in a refuge area, and as archeological entities in the Southeast.

Craniologically a Middle Mississippi archeological series may serve for a type description. This is the Spoon River Focus series from central Illinois, a series of forty-five adult undeformed male skulls, a group that occupied the Illinois River Valley during late prehistoric times. It is relatively homogeneous and closely related to the people responsible for the Tennessee-Cumberland stone graves farther to the south (Fig. 2, *C–D*).

The Walcolid variety can be briefly described as follows: the skull is relatively large, with a cranial module of 154.3, a glabello-occipital length of 180.8 mm., a maximum breadth of 138.9 mm., and a basion-bregma height of 143.9 mm. These dimensions yield a cranial index of 76.84, and a length-height index of 80.02. The braincase is therefore mesocephalic and high in relation to its length. However, the factor of artificial cranial deformation may not have been eliminated entirely. The forty-five crania comprise a group of skulls that seemed entirely undeformed in a series of about 300 skulls in which simple occipital deformation is very common. It is likely that the selection may have been too rigorous, and that some undeformed brachycranial skulls may have been excluded from the series on the basis of seeming to show a slight amount of artificial deformation. An inclusion of borderline cases would raise the basion-bregma height to 145.6 mm., the cranial index to 77.79, and the length-height index to 81.17.[36] From above, the vault tends to be short ovoid in form, with

35. Dixon, 1923, pp. 420–442.

36. Neumann, 1941b.

pronounced to medium muscular relief, medium brow ridges, medium to slight frontal slope, medium frontal breadth, the sagittal elevation generally absent or slight, medium parietal eminences, lambdoidal flattening more frequently absent than slight, and an occiput that has a medium high position.

The face is large to medium in size and rugged in build. Absolute dimensions tend toward being large (total facial height 125.5 mm., upper facial height 75.6 mm., and bizygomatic breadth 139.0), but are not extreme, and indicial relationships tend to be moderate (total facial index 90.29, leptoprosopic, and upper facial index 54.37, mesene). The leptoprosopy is not extreme, as an index of 90 forms the lower limit of the index class. The size of the zygomatic bones is about equally distributed between the large and medium categories, and the same holds for anterior and lateral projection of the cheek bones. The orbits tend to be rhomboid to square, conditions accompanied by medium to small inclination of the horizontal axis; indicially the orbits are mesoconch (the left index is 79.44, if the breadth is taken from maxillofrontale, almost hypsiconch, 84.59, if the dacryal breadth is used). The nasal index is mesorrhine, 48.96, with absolute diameters of 26.3 mm. (breadth) and 53.8 mm. (height); both root and bridge dimensions are moderate. Prognathism is medium to submedium. The size of the mandible is as often large as medium, the most common chin forms are medio-bilateral and bilateral, and gonial eversion is either absent or small.

It is of interest to make a metrical comparison of the Walcolid series with a Lenapid one to get an idea of the nature and magnitude of the differences between a group that may have been Chickasaw with another that probably can be identified with a central Algonkin group. The second set of comparisons have been made with the Deneid means to indicate the differences between two groups that were formerly lumped under the term Central Brachycephals. In the former comparison the differences are perhaps not as marked as could be desired—a circumstance that might be due to mixture between these two late prehistoric groups—but in the writer's opinion they are nevertheless great enough to warrant the establishment of separate varieties. About a third of the measurements and approximately an equal number of indices differ significantly. The skulls of the Walcolid series are significantly higher-vaulted, broader and flatter-faced, exhibit a lower nasal root, and a broader palate. A trait by trait comparison of morphological attributes substantiates the statistical results fully. If the comparison had been made between a Lenape and a Seminole series, for example, the differences would have been greatly accentuated.

The comparison of a Walcolid and Deneid series indicates that in this case the differences are much more marked, fully validating the subdivision of the group that was once considered homogeneous. Fully two-thirds of the metric and three-fourths of the indicial constants differ significantly. The Deneid skull is smaller and lower vaulted, the base is flattened, broader and rounder, with a broader and flatter face, higher orbits, more salient nasal bones, and a much greater biangular mandibular breadth. In fact the metrical and morphological differences are of such magnitude that it is usually fairly simple to diagnose over 80 per cent of the individuals from a pooled series.

Both from a metrical and an indicial standpoint, as well as morphologically, an early Tchefuncte series from southern Louisiana, does not differ too greatly from our Walcolid series, and it is quite likely that we may deal in this case with the earliest Walcolids in the far Southeast. Whether the differentiation actually occurred in North America or represents a migration from Asia, at about the time the first granular and fiber-tempered pottery appears, has been a much debated question. If the Walcolid variety differentiated from earlier elements this process must have taken place over a wide area, for we find such replacements all the way from the North Pacific Coast as far north as among the Haida, southward into the Intermountain area where the Southern Utes and part of the Hopi (Fig. 8, C) may represent this variety, into the southeastern states, where it forms a later overwash,[37] and then far into southern Mexico and South America, where it almost certainly formed the basis for further local differentiation. A separate migration of the more "Mongoloid" group from Asia seems the better explanation. Except for a few imperfectly documented instances, the Walcolid variety is usually associated with material from late archeological horizons. A parallel local differentiation from earlier varieties such as the Otamid, Ashiwid, Iswanid, and later Lenapid varieties, with which we find the Walcolid variety associated in various areas is very unlikely and would run counter to all archeological evidence. Nor is a backwash of Walcolids from either the Southeast, the Southwest, or even Mexico to the Northwest Pacific Coast likely.

As a whole, the distribution of the Walcolids suggests a variety whose former continuous distribution was shattered by later immigrants. In the Northwest and West the Deneids made inroads on them, so that a number of tribes preceded them into the Intermountain refuge area, from where they descended on some of the predominantly Ashiwid Pueblo people. On the Southwestern Plateau they played a minor role (Fig. 8, A), for the variety is not well represented among the Pueblo groups of the Rio Grande. Part of

37. Hrdlička, 1940, pp. 315–464.

the Shoshonean-speaking Hopi form the latest link to the north. Physically, as well as culturally there exists a gap between the Walcolids of the Mexican Mesa Central and the Huaxteca, and those of the Southeast. Here the westernmost Walcolids are the Atakapa of Louisiana and the northern portion of the Texas Gulf Coast. In all probability the Walcolids entered the southeastern states from the northwest (Fig. 8, B), while farther to the west another component wandered to Mexico. A major migrational backwash from Mexico to the Southeast has not been substantiated. However, this does not mean that no such movements took place. There were late contacts in this direction, but they came about at the time of a widely recognized secondary expansion in association with Middle Mississippi cultural manifestations.

Along the northeastern seaboard evidence points to two possible movements of Walcolids to New York State during the late Archaic period. The new element intruded itself into this area either by way of the Ohio Valley or Ontario. This was a relatively large-skulled, rugged, brachycranial group that falls typologically into the Walcolid classification. Throughout the Northeast and Middle West it is associated with cultural manifestations of the Laurentian and Early Woodland Horizon. In Illinois the brachycranial people of the Red Ochre Phase[38] and in upper New York State the people of the Point Peninsula Focus belonged to this group.[39] On Frontenac Island in Cayuga Lake mixture took place between the Archaic and Point Peninsula Focus populations.[40] Whether the Beothuk, who have been described as moderately brachycranial and the later more roundheaded element in such tribes as the Mohawk, Huron, Ojibwa, Naskapi, and Montagnais, and Connestoga can be linked with this Early Woodland people is still open to question.

The rugged brachycepals that appear in the Adena and Copena cultures of the Ohio and Tennessee valleys may provide the geographical link with the southern Walcolids if the movement should have been from the south. However, it is just as likely that there was an early spread of Walcolids from the west, a movement which may have encompassed the whole of the northeastern part of the continent, and may have brought this element both north as well as south of the Great Lakes. For the Ohio Valley the most important Walcolid series are from the Tennessee stone graves and the Madisonville Focus of the Fort Ancient Aspect. Like the Middle Mississippi people in Illinois, the Upper Mississippi occupation in southern Ohio and northern Kentucky was late, in fact, probably protohistoric.

THE LENAPID VARIETY

Although the tribes that were predominantly of the Lenapid variety played a very important role in the history of the Northeastern Woodland area, it was not until relatively late that they entered the archeological scene of this region. The chief affiliations of this group are certainly with the hunters to the northwest of the Great Lakes. As we have seen in an earlier section, the Lenapid variety was preceded by an Otamid dolichocranial population in the northern Plains, in Minnesota, in central Illinois, in the Ohio Valley, in the state of New York, and in New England. People of the Iswanid variety occupied especially the Ohio and Tennessee drainages, but the northeastern limits of their distribution are as yet only vaguely defined, due mainly to the fact that no Archaic series from a pure Lamoka Focus site has so far been discovered. Whether such a population formed an isolate that could be grouped with others of either the Otamid or Iswanid variety is still an unanswered question.

A satisfactory type series of Lenapids was described as early as 1916 by Hrdlička.[41] In his later work, however, all of the more recent series, which in general are to be attributed to historic Algonquian and Iroquoian tribes, were pooled with the earlier Otamid and Iswanid series under the term Algonkin type.[42] Von Eickstedt largely followed Hrdlička and even broadened the grouping to include the group that is described under the term "Lakotid variety" below.[43] In this study we shall deal with this entity in a narrow sense again, as an inbreeding strain during a fairly well defined archeological and historic period.

Since the crania of the Lenape are representative of this entity, which is physically homogenous within the protohistoric Castle Creek Focus, the name Lenapid variety (Delaware: *Lenape*, "real men") has been adopted here. This group which has recently been identified as having belonged to the Munsee division, in turn is closely linked to protohistoric Seneca and a number of Central Algonkin series (Fig. 7, A–B). As the Munsee type series is still in the process of being described, an almost identical series—the Maples Mills Focus series of 24 undeformed adult male crania—has been used here for comparative purposes. Recent field work since the publication of the data of this series[44] has increased this number to 54, an increment that has not changed the modal observations or means of measurements appreciably.

The Lenapid variety can be briefly described as follows: the skull is relatively large, with a cranial

38. Neumann, 1937, pp. 232–234.
39. Ritchie, 1944, p. 186. [Ritchie now considers this broadheaded group to be the dominant Laurentian type.—ED.]
40. Ritchie, 1945, pp. 19–20.

41. Hrdlička, 1916.
42. Hrdlička, 1927, pp. 4–48.
43. Von Eickstedt, 1934, pp. 696–704.
44. Neumann, 1941b, pp. 79–82.

module of 153.5, a glabello-occipital length of 182.5 mm., a maximum breadth of 137.4 mm., and a basion-bregma height of 141.7 mm. These dimensions yield a mean cranial index of 75.39, and a length-height index of 77.76. The cranial proportions are therefore on the lower border of mesocrany and high in relation to cranial length. From above the vault is ovoid to ellipsoid in form, yet the temporal region is never as full as in European crania. Muscularity is above medium, as are the size of brow ridges, frontal slope, breadth of frontal, development of parietal eminences, and position of the occiput. Sagittal cresting on the other hand, tends to be either slight or absent, and lambdoid flattening is about evenly divided between medium and slight.

The face, on the whole, is only moderate in ruggedness and size in relation to the braincase. All facial dimensions tend to be on the plus side of moderate, with a total facial height of 123.1 mm., an upper facial height of 75.1 mm., and a bizygomatic breadth of 136.5 mm., and the same applies to the indices, which run as follows: total facial index, 89.65, or mesoprosopic, and upper facial index, 54.88, or mesene. But both indices are on the border of leptoprosopy and meseny. Although the size of the zygomatic bones and their anterior projection is greater than in Europeans, they are only moderate for American Indians. Lateral projection of the zygomatic arches is medium to pronounced. The orbits are most frequently rhomboid with medium to submedium inclination of the transverse axis; the mean index for the left orbit is 81.82 or mesoconch if the orbital width is taken from maxillofrontale, and 86.39 or hypsiconch if the width measurement is taken from dacryon. The nasal index is mesorrhine, 48.52, derived from the mean nasal breadth of 26.1 mm., and the mean nasal height of 54.0 mm. The proportions of the nasal root and nasal bridge breadth tend to be moderate, nasal bridge height high to medium, at least in this series. Prognathism is submedium to medium, while the size of the mandible is medium to large, generally accompanied with a bilateral chin and only a small amount of eversion of the gonial angles.

A number of metrical comparisons have been made to demonstrate the uniqueness of the Lenapid variety and to indicate the possible degree of relationship to several other varieties. Although the Lenapids differ enough to be considered a variety, it is interesting to see just how close their relationship is to a number of groups with which this variety has been formerly pooled or with which it has had extensive contacts.

The first comparison was made with the Otamids. It was demonstrated in the foregoing section dealing with this variety that, although the two groups had basically a good deal in common morphologically, there has been considerable metrical differentiation.

Thus about 40 per cent of the measurements and indices can be said to differ significantly. Yet if any group can be considered as ancestral to the Lenapid variety it would have to be the Otamid or a closely related one.

Two other comparisons were made with the Iswanid and Ashiwid varieties, respectively. In the former instance the comparison was made because of Hrdlička's pooling of crania of these two varieties, in the latter, because of his insistence that the Basket-Makers were closely related to the pooled Algonkin series. There is really a profound metrical difference between the former two series. It has been seen previously that the Iswanid-Ashiwid relationship is by far the closer one. The Lenapids differ from the Ashiwids in absolute skull size, ruggedness, muscularity, vault height, in at least half of the absolute measurements, the Ashiwid series exhibiting smaller dimensions in nearly every instance. Size of zygomatic bones, differences in vault form, structural features of the nasal skeleton, size of zygomatics, and eversion of the gonial angles are almost diagnostic.

A fourth comparison was made with the Walcolid series. Here the differences are clearer morphologically than metrically, and possible mixture between the two varieties in central Illinois, a region peripheral to the Southeast, make the groups stand out less than one could wish. Both series, too, are of late prehistoric date, the Spoon River Focus series almost certainly has a mean date of A.D. 1400. It is well known that this was a period of extensive contacts between sedentary southern groups, such as Chickasaw and Central Algonkin hunting tribes expanding to the south.

The fifth and final comparison was made with the Inuid series in the section that deals with the Eskimo, mainly because of attempts to derive the Eskimo variety from a Lenapid group, such as a Huron series.

The earliest appearance of the Lenapids in the northwestern part of the continent is as yet unknown, mainly due to the lack of archeological work in this area. Cord-marked and granular tempered pottery has been traced to Montana and is encountered to the north of the Great Lakes. In all probability a number of migrations took the Lenapids east. In the Middle West the earliest appearance of the variety, if the Otamids and Iswanids are considered separate biological entities, is in the Glacial Kame and the Hopewellian cultures of the Early to Middle Woodland periods. In this last period extensive mixture took place between the earlier Otamid people, such as those of the Black Sand Focus of central Illinois, and the less long-headed Lenapids. Even the burials of the developed Hopewell manifestation still include an appreciable percentage of Otamids. The same conditions obtained in southern Ohio, and some Hopewellian crania from western New York are clearly Lenapid.

A later movement, associated with a Late Woodland culture and largely associated with the Algonkin movement to the eastern seaboard, may not have taken place until three hundred years later. I am thinking here primarily of the Lenape and closely related groups. Sometime between 1400 and 1600 they came under strong Iroquois culture pressure in western Pennsylvania. However, this could not have affected them in a physical sense, since these groups to the north with which they had their contacts, such as the Seneca, undoubtedly represent the same variety as early as 1350. Of course, this poses the problem of Iroquoian origins—a question that involves extensive integrated archeological, physical, and linguistic research before it can be answered.

All in all, the Lenapid variety is most closely linked on the cultural side with the Central Algonkin tribes. Tribes such as the Menominee, Miami, Illinois, Shawnee, and Delaware exhibit a predominant percentage of individuals of this variety. It is here too where the Indians of the northern foci of the Fort Ancient Aspect belong (Fig. 2, *A–B*).

THE INUID VARIETY

The question as to which was the last variety of man to enter the New World via Bering Strait has not been entirely settled. The consensus is that the Eskimo migration represents the last one, a claim that is based (1) on the continuity of distribution of the Eskimo; (2) on the fact that there is no sharp break between the earliest known archeological remains and those of the nineteenth century; and (3) on the observation that even the oldest Bering Sea cultures, dating back to about the beginnings of the Christian Era, require a fairly long developmental period. From the latter, one might argue that, since the maritime Chukchee and Bering Strait Eskimo had no place to go in order to allow the Deneid migration to cross their territory, the latter must have crossed it before the development of the whole sea-mammal hunting complex. Then too, the break in the continuity of the distribution of certain physical traits from central Siberia to the American Southwest, which shall be brought up again in connection with the description of the Deneids in the following section, indicates that the Eskimo were the latest intruders.

On the other hand, there is some evidence for a late migration of the Deneid variety across Bering Strait. The break in the continuity in the distribution of certain physical traits could be explained by the fact that the Chukchee, who are closely related to the Eskimo, were by-passed to the north at a time when they occupied the maritime area south of the Anadyr River, and Deneid pressure may have dis-

placed the Bering Strait Eskimo and pushed them toward the Coronation Gulf area around A.D. 500. The above-mentioned distributional discontinuity could then be explained by the late reoccupation of the Chukotsk Peninsula by the Yuit and the well-authenticated late southward expansion of the Kenai Peninsula and Kuskokwim Eskimo. The South Alaskan Eskimo then cut off that part of the Deneid migration that became the Aleut. If the crossing of Bering Strait by the Deneids was a rapid one instead of a prolonged occupation, little would be left in the way of archeological remains in such places as the Diomedes. On the return of the Eskimo later, the identical sites that had been lived on before could have been reoccupied and have given the deposits a semblance of continuous occupation. A late migration of the Deneids would also explain the presence of a considerable number of Late Asiatic cultural traits in the northwestern part of North America; many of them could have been introduced in the migration instead of being borrowed from Kamchatka by the Aleuts and then diffused to the Mackenzie area and southward along the coast. The isolation necessary to give the Athabaskan languages their stationary, stagnant, or resistant character may have been found on the Lena Platform in Siberia as well as in the Canadian Northwest.

Not only is the uniformity of language, of physical type, and of culture in the Eskimo area a matter of common knowledge, but it is a correlation that is used as a classical example in every textbook on the subject. Nevertheless, this correlation is by no means a perfect one. It may be true that the Eskimo speak a single mutually intelligible language, but they share a language of the same stock with the Aleuts, who represent a different variety. Culturally the Eskimo share quite a number of traits with the Chukchee and Aleut, and physically, too, there is a transition into other varieties (Fig. 6, *D*).

Ever since the first description of the Eskimo, because of a number of specializations, he has been regarded as forming a distinct racial group; thus he is generally considered to differ more from other American Indian groups than any of these groups differ from each other. There is some justification for this view, both on morphological and on metrical grounds, but as a whole the uniqueness of the Eskimo may have been overstressed.

The magnitude of intraracial variability recently has been examined by Morant,[45] and the degree of metrical differentiation from other related Old and New World groups has been demonstrated in a paper by von Bonin and Morant.[46] Metrically it may be shown that the Western Eskimo is more closely related to the Asiatic Chukchee than the Central Es-

45. Morant, 1937.   46. Von Bonin and Morant, 1938.

kimo to the Greenland Eskimo. Furthermore, we find among the Central Eskimo a so-called "blond Eskimo" element representing either Palaeolithic survivors with a tendency toward depigmentation, greater hairiness, and finer cut features, or an early historic Norse admixture. And, finally, the Alaskan Eskimo exhibit a number of characteristics that are transitional in their resemblance to traits of Athabaskan-speaking Indians of the Yukon Valley and farther to the east.

This resemblance has been utilized by Shapiro in an attempt to derive the Eskimo from a dolichocephalic eastern Indian stock.[47] He found metrical resemblances between a Seward Peninsula–Point Barrow Eskimo and Huron series, as well as a resemblance between the Seward Peninsula series and a Chipewyan Indian one. At the most this indicates a relationship to a northern longheaded American Indian group, because the comparison was made between evolutionary end products, and with pooled series from a number of archeological horizons. Shapiro's method is open to criticism in that, with the exception of the Old Igloo series, he did not deal with ancestral Eskimo groups. In other words, his method was somewhat like Hooton's in his attempt to analyze a number of contemporaneous groups in order to reconstruct their genetic relationships. The result may be correct, but they can only be proved by a comparison of archeological material.

The chronological framework that is so necessary for the reconstruction of the racial origins and relationships of man in the Arctic area still presents many serious gaps in the chain of evidence. Many areas are as yet unexplored archeologically, most collections of crania consists of surface material without definite stratigraphic and other archeological documentation, many series of skulls are too small to be reliable for comparative purposes, and the number of measurements and observations that have been published are only too often too few or not comparable. Nevertheless, much valuable work has been done, especially in the North American sector, so that prehistory has been carried back to the beginning of the Christian Era with a fair degree of completeness.

The archeological aspect of the historical reconstruction has been admirably summarized by Collins.[48] The essential points pertinent to the racial history of the Eskimo are the following. An old Eskimo-like culture preceding that of the present Samoyed has been discovered at the mouth of the Ob River and a generalized maritime Proto-Eskimo culture between the Kolyma Delta and Bering Strait. This helps to extend the earlier Eskimo cultures back toward an Asiatic Mesolithic boreal culture, which must have existed after the Upper Palaeolithic cultural manifestation at Choukoutien, among the population of which Eskimoid tendencies are already manifested. Unfortunately no skeletal material from this Asiatic Proto-Eskimo culture has been described as yet. On the other hand, the Neolithic Angara River culture, dated back to approximately 2700 B.C., which might have been utilized to fill in the gap in the development, cannot be regarded as directly ancestral to the earliest Eskimo cultures. An older stage of Eskimo culture that has been fully described is the Old Bering Sea. On St. Lawrence Island this developed into the Punuk under Siberian influences, and along Point Barrow and the Arctic coast of Alaska first into the Birnirk around A.D. 400, and in turn into the Thule culture in the central area around A.D. 1000. From the central regions the Thule culture spread to Greenland, where it had been preceded by the Dorset culture, another derivative of the Proto-Eskimo culture. Unfortunately, an exact description of this Proto-Eskimo culture awaits further work in Siberia. So far it has not been clearly delimited, nor is its exact distribution known, and though we know of older generalized Eskimo remains from the Alaska Peninsula, Kodiak Island, and Cook Inlet, exact relationship to northern stages of related cultures are not yet clear. As matters stand, therefore, there is considerable evidence for a generalized Proto-Eskimo culture, which gave rise to (1) Old Bering Sea, (2) Dorset, and (3) the Kachemak Bay I Culture. In addition, a pre-Eskimo culture has recently been discovered at Point Hope, Alaska. This Ipiutak culture differs widely from the Old Bering Sea, but, because of its relationships in its art forms, it may be roughly contemporaneous with Old Bering Sea.

The earliest Eskimo cranial material that I have been able to examine consists of a few skulls which were found associated with the Old Bering Sea complex. As far as the crushed condition and the paucity of the material permit any conclusions to be drawn, they can be characterized by an attenuation of the specialized traits that distinguish later Eskimo skulls. In this they approximate the cranial form of Lenapids. They are not extremely dolichocranial, somewhat lower in vault height, the orbits are somewhat lower, the zygomatic bones are less prominent, the sagittal cresting is less, etc. In some respects too they seem to be more like the Pre-Aleut crania, although it is unlikely that the latter can be regarded as ancestral to the Eskimo. The Ipiutak material has not been described as yet, but it should vary in the same direction.

Later cranial series should reflect the rate of specialization and admixtures of other varieties. The Old Igloo series[49] from near Point Barrow finally has

47. Shapiro, 1934.   48. Collins, 1940; 1943.   49. Hrdlička, 1930, pp. 318–329.

been identified as Birnirk[50] and thus may give us an idea of the Eskimo that spread east from Point Barrow to Greenland around A.D. 500. The vault especially is characteristic—narrow, long, high, more or less keel-shaped. The cranial index for twenty-seven males is 69.1, lowest among Eskimo. A comparison of the Old Igloo and a southern Greenland series shows striking similarities. In all probability these southern Greenland Eskimo arrived with a Thule culture but represent members of the older stratum of people. As an alternative, there are possible Dorset influences in Greenland, but these have not been fully examined as yet. With the exception of a single skull, there is no Dorset skeletal material available, and this individual specimen is, of course, not enough to go on in tracing closer relationships. The physical type associated with the Thule culture was identified by Fischer-Møller.[51] As a whole, the Central Eskimo take a more intermediate position between the Alaskan and Greenland Eskimo, although the relation to the latter may be a somewhat closer one. According to Stewart, the Labrador Eskimo, similarly, may be somewhat more closely related to the Greenland than to the Central Eskimo.[52] The Alaskan Eskimo, finally, represents the group that has been modified most by Asiatic influences, first, possibly by Lenapid and Deneid elements, and later by Tungid ones, as is attested by a higher frequency of the Mongoloid fold and other specialized traits (Fig. 4, A–B).

The name Inuid (Eskimoan: *Inuit,* "men") used here has been selected to keep the nomenclature for varieties parallel. In this paper the constants of Morant's Greenland series of 241 adult males are compared with those of the Lenapid series. This shows that the differences between the measurements and indices of the two series are statistically significant ones in nearly every instance. Since only Lenapid elements have been considered as possible ancestral ones to the Eskimo, this may help in shifting the explanation for any resemblances to admixture.

The Deneid Variety

If the Northwest Pacific Coast region is considered from the point of view of an area it is obvious, when the time factor and its whole geographical extent is included, that we deal racially with a number of varieties of man. This is almost necessarily the case for a number of reasons: (1) this region is located along or near the migration route from Siberia, along which all the original immigrants must have wandered; (2) the topography is such that, with its islands, fjords, and steep valleys extending inland from the deeply dissected coast, many marginal refuge areas

are provided, which are likely to shelter remnants of the earlier migrants; and (3) coastal connections by boat provide contacts for the development of a culture center, which, if not in the first place greatly influenced by the contacts of diverse groups, acts as a stimulus to trade, immigration, and mixture.

While the Northwest Pacific Coast area is one of the most intensively studied regions of North America, interest has not primarily been historical. For that reason the delimitation and examination of cultural subareas has only been tentative, archeological work has only been sporadic, comparative linguistic data has not as yet been correlated to any extent with other historical information, and from a racial standpoint, the bulk of the cranial material has been considered only by tribal groups and as a whole without a consideration of the time factor.[53] Another factor that makes a racial analysis of the area difficult is the widespread practice of artificial cranial deformation, especially in the southern half of the coastal area.

Since this immediate study does not primarily deal with analyses of various populations into their racial elements, but deals with the description and comparison of relatively homogeneous imbreeding groups in various archeological horizons, it was thought advisable to consider the almost continuous block of inland people and test it for its homogeneity. The discussion in this section therefore deals rather with the hinterland of the area, which Wissler placed into his Mackenzie and Plateau areas.[54] A number of tribal groups had to be eliminated because of the inclusion of a predominant number of individuals of widely differing elements. One was a small series of putative Athabaskan crania from the Yukon Valley which were found to be similar to the Iswanid variety described earlier. A second series of crania from an area occupied by Salishan-speakers, as well as a Haida series were eliminated on the basis of including an archeologically earlier high-vaulted, dolichoid element that is most closely related to the Lenapid variety. This left a series of thirty-two undeformed adult male crania, from tribes that were either Athabaskan-speaking, Salish from the interior, and historic Haida. Practically every measurable skull from these groups was included.

The pooled series is morphologically quite homogeneous and both statistically and morphologically very closely related to Aleut, Koniag, and Apache series (Fig. 3, A–B).[55] The establishing of a distinct variety in this case is based on the occurrence of an almost continuous block of tribes, which represent a relatively homogeneous physical appearance. With the exception of the Aleut and some groups that migrated to the coast, it is, according to present knowl-

50. Stewart, 1939a, p. 22.   52. Stewart, 1939a, pp. 31–42.
51. Fischer-Møller, 1937.

53. Oetteking, 1930.   55. Richards, n.d.
54. Wissler, 1926.

edge, chiefly a group that for the most part traveled in the interior, and represents the people of one of the two last migrations from Siberia to the New World.

Historically it was Boas who first recognized this variety as a physical entity, but this recognition was not immediate.[56] When he began his researches in this area, he designated the population of the coast of British Columbia as "almost homogeneous."[57] As von Eickstedt points out, he contrasts the natives of the whole area with tribes of the eastern United States. Then he analyzes his data and detects Siberian, and an early dolichoid admixture, and an extremely small brachycephalic local type in the Lillooet of the Harrison Lake area, and groups in the Western Plateau area that form the basic element considered here.[58] Thus he states later in his concluding survey of the identical population of British Columbia that it is not homogeneous at all.[59]

All the above makes it clear that we need a new designation for the variety described here. The term "Northwest Coast type" used by Haddon is too inclusive,[60] and von Eickstedt's "Pacifid race" does not have the same coverage. We shall therefore refer to this group as the Deneid variety (Athabaskan: *Tiṅne*, "people"). The term was selected on the basis that the bulk of this group is associated with the expansion of speakers of languages of the Athabaskan stock. It is hardly necessary to point out that a linguistic and physical correlation will not prove to be too high. There are also Skittagetan, Wakashan, Penutian, and other groups that are Deneid.

The Deneid skull is medium in size, with a cranial module of 152.4, a glabello-occipital length of 179.9 mm., a maximum breadth of 145.0 mm., and a basion-bregma height of 132.2 mm. The lowness of the latter dimension is almost entirely due to a flattened base, a characteristic of diagnostic value. The braincase is brachycranial and orthocranial with indices of 80.74 and 73.55 (length-height), respectively. From above, the vault tends to be sphenoid or ovoid in form, generally the former, with medium muscular relief, most commonly small brow-ridges, medium frontal slope, small frontal breadth, a small amount of sagittal cresting, medium but often low-placed parietal eminences, with lambdoidal flattening generally absent or slight, and a broad low-placed occiput. The more specialized Aleut diverge from the rest by showing lower foreheads, more sagittal cresting, and a flatter base.

The face as a whole gives the impression of ruggedness and large size, mostly due to the large, high, and flat zygomatic bones. The facial height is moderate (total facial height, 122.4 mm., upper facial height

73.3 mm.), the breadth is great (141.9 mm.). These dimensions yield a total facial index of 85.03 on the eury-mesoprosopic border, and an upper facial index of 52.05, which falls into the mesene class. In contrast to pronounced anterior and lateral projection of the cheek bones resulting in a very broad face (that even exceeds our Greenland Eskimo sample), the interorbital diameter is small. The orbits are round with little declination of the horizontal axis; the orbital index is mesoconch—high in some subgroups—with an orbital index of 81.28. The nasal index is mesorrhine, 48.97; absolute diameters of the nasal structure are narrow in breadth (25.7 mm.) and moderate in height (52.4 mm.). A considerable bridge height, a rather straight profile of the nasal bones, and their general parallel-sidedness are diagnostic traits. They are exceeded in saliency only by those of the Lakotid variety. Prognathism is medium, gonial eversion medium to marked, and the chin form more often medio-bilateral than bilateral.

As to comparisons, the marked divergence of the Deneid from the Walcolid series has already been discussed in the section of the Walcolid variety. The divergence of the Deneids from the Lakotids, to whom they are more closely related, will be taken up in the next section.

From a racio-historical point of view the Deneid variety is of considerable importance. It represents one of the last of the major migrations to the New World, it is the group that exhibits the most marked Asiatic connections, it exercised profound influences on both North Pacific Coast and Southwestern cultures, and it contributed from perhaps A.D. 1200 onward to the differentiation of the Lakotid variety in the northern Plains (Fig. 9).

The Aleuts may perhaps best serve as a point of departure in a reconstruction of the racial history of the Deneids. Undoubtedly they form a specialized form of the larger group. There is strong physical anthropological evidence that they made up the tail end of the wave of Siberian hunting people which can be identified now to a large extent with the Athabaskan-speaking tribes of northwestern Canada. This makes it necessary to explain their Esquimauan linguistic affiliations by assuming that they took over their language from the Eskimo, probably at the same time they borrowed the trait complex involved in the hunting of sea mammals.

Like the Eskimo, the Aleut should be regarded as the end-product of specialization; like the Tungid of eastern Siberia they developed from a less-round-headed, higher-vaulted, and more delicate-featured element. Indeed, in both eastern Siberia[61] and in the Aleutian Islands an earlier group showing these attributes has been described. Hrdlička and later Rich-

56. Von Eickstedt, 1934, p. 693.
57. Boas, 1892, p. 447.
58. Boas and Farrand, 1899.
59. Boas, 1905.
60. Haddon, 1925, p. 36.
61. Coon, 1939, pp. 226–236.

ards pointed out wider relationships of these Pre-Aleuts, and in the light of the discovery of a likely ancestral and somewhat different early Deneid population a reconstruction of the movements of this variety is now possible.

The earliest Deneids, being much closer to a common ancestor of the later Deneids and the Eskimo, were in all probability very much like the Pre-Aleut, or better Proto-Aleut. In the maritime regions both east and west of Kamchatka, this element must have adapted itself to sea-mammal hunting and may have taken over its language through contact with the Proto-Eskimo. Southern Alaskan Eskimo contacts were probably much later. Yielding to the pressure of other somewhat more specialized Deneid groups, the Pre-Aleut crossed Bering Strait, wandered south, and, in order to be able to retain its sea-mammal hunting practices, took over the coastal area of the Alaska Peninsula and gradually expanded westward over the Aleutian chain of islands. They were closely followed by Deneid inland tribes with a boreal hunting culture, which continued in its eastward movement into Alaska and southward into British Columbia. It is fairly safe to assume that these tribes were Athabaskan speakers.

In their migrations southward, probably after 1300, some of the Deneids wandered to California, for example, the Hupa; others reached the Southwest as the Apache; others again became mixed with high-vaulted brachycephals west of the lower reaches of the Mississippi where they contributed to such tribes as the Osage, and with low-mesocephalic elements along the river courses of the northern Mississippi Valley and the northern plains. Here the newcomers were not able to impose their language but took over the Siouan that was spoken by such tribes as the Mandan and Dakota. Smaller groups made their presence felt north of the Great Lakes as far east as Labrador, where they introduced a new physical type and some late Asiatic boreal culture traits, but adopted the Algonquian dialects of the people among whom they settled.

Meanwhile, other groups of the interior penetrated to the North Pacific Coast, becoming mixed with Salishan-speakers and others, contributing to the mixed coastal elements responsible for the high Northwest Coast culture. Farther to the north the Tsimshian and to a lesser extent the Haida evolved from a mixture of earlier more dolichocranial and later Deneid elements. The later Aleut, on the other hand, at the most represent an addition of a more recent group of Deneids to an older element of the same variety. Whether this was a part of the main Deneid group that occupied the area of Alaska south of the Yukon or late emigrants from Kamchatka and the west shore of Bering Sea regions, with which the

Aleuts maintained trade relationships, still remains to be determined. It is quite certain that a considerable part of the wave of people that became the Deneids in North America must have remained in the Transbaikal area to become subsequently the specialized Tungids. This would explain the existence of a complex of morphological traits common to many groups extending from Lake Baikal to the Aleutians, and from there south to the Apache of Arizona and New Mexico. Among these characteristics are platybasia associated with brachycephaly, low foreheads narrow in comparison to the bizygomatic breadth, massive zygomatic bones with marked anterior and lateral projection, a relatively narrow nasal root, somewhat parallel-sided relatively salient nasal bones, relatively high orbits, and considerable gonial eversion.

THE LAKOTID VARIETY

Unlike the varieties which have been considered up to now, the Lakotid variety is a secondary one in the sense that it probably represents the results of hybridization of two or three other varieties.[62] This is quite evident from the fact that, despite the mobility of the tribes within the Plains area, the people grade off into the surrounding varieties in every direction and that according to all archeological evidence the first appearance of this variety is in the main of proto-historic date. Yet just this mobility, if a different set of morphological traits is used, may have given the groups of the Plains a similarity which allows us to recognize a type characteristic of the area.

Almost three decades ago Sullivan, analyzing Boas' material, noted this homogeneity of descriptive and anthropometric characters in the Sioux of the northern Plains.[63] Wissler[64] and Hrdlička[65] also take cognizance of this specialization but, like Sullivan, deal only with northern Plains groups of limited distribution. Hrdlička ignores the grading off into other varieties by simply calling the Iowa, Osage, and Winnebago unrelated to the Sioux, and attempts to substantiate this also on the basis of cranial material.[66] If this cutting-down process were applied to all varieties so that only a core of typical tribes were left, the bulk of anthropometric data would have to be discarded, or a large number of varieties established. In case of the prehistoric Winnebago we evidently deal with a Lenapid group closely related to the Algonquian-speaking Menominee. The historic Winnebago, on the other hand, are obviously Lakotid, and it is only through pooling of the two series that they become atypical of the Sioux of the northern Plains. The Osage, like other tribes of the Dhegiha subdivision,

62. Neumann, 1942.
63. Sullivan, 1920, p. 170.
64. Wissler, 1926, pp. 117–179.
65. Hrdlička, 1931a, p. 124.
66. Hrdlička, 1927, p. 78.

exhibit a number of facial characteristics which link them obviously with northern Lakotids, yet show morphological and metrical traits of the cranial vault that are reminiscent of those of a number of southeastern tribes.

Before we can consider the question of origin of the specialized Plains type, attention must be called again to the groups that we find peripheral to the area. It is first of all obvious that we deal with a highly specialized type that evolved somewhere in the North American continent. It is thus very unlikely that we shall ever find a very closely related group in the archeological deposits of eastern Siberia that could serve as an immediate ancestral group. There are certainly no archeological indications that would indicate that a Plains type of Indian like the Lakotid variety with its flat-based, low-vaulted skull, its heavy features and aquiline nose developed in the Southeast and then migrated west. Nor does the Canadian Northwest, from the west of the Great Lakes into the Mackenzie area, seem a likely region to have served as an evolutionary center for such a populous group. This predominantly wooded territory probably never supported a fairly large and concentrated population from which this comparatively inbred variety could have evolved.

The fact that the tribes grade off into other major varieties gives us also a number of leads as to possible origins. It is thus known that certain tribes, which became typical northern Plains tribes, did not get to their historic locations until very late. Thus the common ancestors of the Hidatsa and Crow probably came from the vicinity of Devil's Lake in northeastern Dakota sometime before 1845; the Teton Dakota moved from west-central Minnesota into the open plains sometime prior to 1742; the Santee Dakota were beginning to move south and west from the Mille Lacs region of east-central Minnesota in 1860; the Assiniboine were still around Lake Winnipeg in 1670; and the Cheyenne abanded their semisedentary life in the valley of the Minnesota ca. 1750.[67] Now it is just these tribes that show the greatest number of morphological and metric features in common with the predominantly Lenapid Central Algonkin tribes to the east. Most of the remainder of the traits are shared with the Athabascan-speaking Deneids who are their neighbors just to the north.

The Plains tribes that lived along the Missouri and other river courses that flowed toward the southeast, on the other hand, shared some of the same Deneid traits with the northern Plains groups, but also shared a considerable number of characteristics with the predominantly Walcolid Muskogean-speaking tribes of the Southeast. This applies especially to the Siouan-speaking tribes of the Dhegiha division, possibly with the exception of the Quapaw. A trihybrid origin—Lenapid-Deneid-Walcolid—of the Lakotid variety as a whole, seems therefore to fit the facts of distribution best.

In order to keep the varietal designations parallel we shall use the term "Lakotid variety" (Teton Dakota: *lakota,* "allies"), instead of the geographical term *Prairid* that was used earlier (Fig. 7, C–D; 3, C–D). The term is synonymous with Hrdlička's "Siouan type" but covers a somewhat wider range of tribal groups and does not imply that it is coterminous with tribal groups of the Siouan linguistic stock.

The series on which the type description is based consists of the measurements of sixty-three undeformed adult male crania of various bands of Dakota of the northern Plains, which Hrdlička described in the 1927 section of his "Catalogue of Human Crania in the United States National Museum Collections."

The Lakotid skull is medium in size, with a cranial capacity of 1486 cc. and a cranial module of 152.7; a glabello-occipital length of 184.8 mm., a maximum breadth of 143.8 mm., and a basion-bregma height of 129.8 mm. As in the Deneid skull, the lowness of the latter dimension is almost entirely due to a flattened base. The braincase is high-mesocranial and orthocranial, with indices of 77.89 and 70.27 (length-height), respectively. From above, the vault tends to be sphenoid in form, with medium to large muscular relief, commonly small brow-ridges, pronounced to medium frontal slope, small frontal breadth, sagittal elevation generally absent, medium but often low-placed parietal eminences, lambdoidal flattening usually absent, and a broad, low-to medium-placed occiput.

The face as a whole is large and rugged, an impression mainly due to the large, high, and flat zygomatic bones. The facial height is moderate (total facial height, 123.6 mm., upper facial height 75.6 mm.), and the bizygomatic breadth is great (142.8 mm.). These dimensions yield a total facial index of 87.08, mesoprosopic, and an upper facial index of 53.13, which falls into the mesene class. The orbits tend to be rhomboid in shape, a condition accompanied by pronounced declination of the horizontal axis; the mean orbital index is hypsiconch, 90.15, if the dacryal breadth is used. The nasal index is mesorrhine, 48.90, with absolute diameters of 26.9 mm. (breadth) and 55.0 mm. (height); the nasion depression is slight, the nasal root height high to very high, combined with medium breadth; the nasal bridge, likewise, is high, and narrow to medium in breadth. The very large nasal bones tend to be straight or slightly concavo-convex in profile. The whole nasal skeleton is salient, a trait of diagnostic value. Total prognathism is small, gonial eversion small to me-

67. Strong, 1940, pp. 358–359.

dium, the chin is usually wide bilateral in form and rather massive.

Since there is very little resemblance between those Lenapid series that probably represent Central Algonkin groups and the Lakotid type series from the northern Plains, detailed morphological and statistical comparisons of such groups have not been attempted in this study. Transitional forms, which might be directly ancestral to the Lakotid series, are to be sought in mound crania from Minnesota. The dolichocranial Mandan crania show affiliations to earlier eastern varieties but have little in common with Deneid series.

The closest relationships of the Lakotid type series are unquestionably with the Deneid one. This is especially true of the morphological traits. In such a comparison, despite the fact that they have so much in common morphologically, more than half of the measurements and indices exhibit significant statistical differences. As indicated by the similarity in the cranial module, there is probably little difference in actual skull size. The 76 cc. discrepancy in cranial capacity may be explained by differences in techniques of the two investigators.

Statistically significant differences indicate that the Lakotid skull is somewhat longer, yielding a cranial index approximately three units lower; that it is very slightly less in basion-bragma height; that the base is not quite as flat; that the face is slightly higher; that the nasal height is somewhat more; and that the orbital breadth is less than in the Deneid skull. On the whole, the figures show that the values are on the plus side in favor of the Lakotid skull: values, which in the case of the module, glabello-occipital length, total facial height, upper facial height, nasal breadth, and nasal height, vary toward the Lenapid means. In case of maximum breadth of the braincase and orbital breadth the tendency is in the same direction although the values vary on the negative side. On the other hand, such characters as basion-bragma height and total facial breadth invite Deneid comparison.

Let us turn briefly to the archeological picture again. We have seen that gradually evidence is accumulating that the earliest finds in the Plains represent the remains of a group that eventually will prove to be of the Otamid or another closely related variety. These migratory hunters dominated the area over a long span of time. Later, judging by less marginal distributions, to both the east and the southwest, of peoples of the Ashiwid and Iswanid varieties who probably had a common ancestor in the intermediary area, a second group can be assumed to have occupied the plains. A people with a Folsom-Yuma culture has been suggested, and the similarity of crania of eastern Siouan groups to those of the Archaic of Kentucky

lend support to such an early connection. The dolichocranial Mandans may possibly represent the westernmost remnant of a proto-Siouan people. Next in chronological order we find a widespread Early Woodland people filtering into the Plains. This relatively thin but widespread occupancy probably came from the northwest and extended into the Ohio Valley. This settlement in turn was followed by a stronger movement, extending mainly along the great river valleys, of a semi-sedentary horticultural group that can be linked with the Hopewellian expansion from the east into the Plains. The crania from the stone vault graves that are found along the Mississippi, the Missouri, and up the Kansas River represent the same varieties as those which are encountered in the Hopewell mounds of the Illinois Valley. There can therefore be little doubt that we have a backwash of Otamid plus Lenapid people re-entering the Plains area as a mixed agricultural group. As has been pointed out in an earlier section, the early Lenapids may have entered the East in post-Archaic times both from around the south as well as the north of the Great Lakes. The practices of artificial cranial deformation of the bifronto-occipital type, found along the Missouri, the Mississippi, and southern Ohio provides another link and temporal marker as well.

The Upper Republican and Nebraska aspects, which follow the Hopewellian thrust into the Plains, are protohistoric. According to Wedel, there is at present no indication of direct contacts between Hopewellian and the two later arrivals,[68] which eventually may be placed in a Plains Phase of the Mississippi Pattern. Although these manifestations may be derived from a Middle Mississippi base, it is likely that they may be the earliest ones to yield crania which show Lakotid traits. At any rate, protohistoric Pawnee and Arikara crania exhibit a strong Deneid influence. These and other groups, which lived in large fortified villages, were clearly on the defensive against the more typical Plains tribes to the north and west. The Oneota Aspect people of Upper Mississippi affiliations, which may be identified with the Siouan-speaking Iowa of the Chiwere division, were comparatively late arrivals on the middle Missouri. Like the Arikara they should represent a rather mixed group, which, though primarily Lakotid, also clearly show Lenapid and Walcolid characteristics. As the Lakotids of the northern Plains became more stabilized in historic times, they became the undisputed masters of the area.

CONCLUSIONS

The purpose of this paper is to provide a framework for the reconstruction of the racial history of the American Indian, a task that called for a close

68. Wedel, 1940, p. 344.

integration of archeological and physical anthropological data. It is hoped that it will serve as a basis for further efforts in identifying additional series, aid in tracing migrations, and elucidate the nature of the relationships of various groups to one another. Such a clear-cut taxonomic framework is necessary in order to be able to analyze the obviously more mixed populations of various centers of cultural development. Because of the nature of the problem constant revision will be necessary. This is due to the fact that we are dealing with dynamic or continually changing groups and that we are constantly securing new archeological data that necessitate revision in our concepts of relationships. The problems are continental and even intercontinental in scope. Attack of the problems of the racial history of northeastern Asia and South America may contribute a great deal to the answers to problems of this continent.

The conclusions that may be drawn from this study at the present time are the following:

Varieties can best be established through an examination of relatively homogeneous units from a number of archeological horizons, from marginal or refuge areas, from continuous continental areas of distribution as yet undisturbed by the shattering effect of new immigrants, or from a historically known tribal unit. Some sort of evidence for the actual physical relatedness of the group is necessary. In this respect the method employed in this reconstruction differs widely from that in which individuals exhibiting a preconceived combination of traits are selected

out of a number of populations.

At present eight varieties appear to be sufficient to explain subsequent mixtures encountered in various archeological manifestations that exhibit concomitant mixtures of cultural elements. These eight varieties consist of a Texas Coast series (Otamid), a Kentucky shell-heap series (Iswanid), an Arizona Basket-Maker series (Ashiwid), a Middle Mississippi series (Walcolid), a Central Algonkin series (Lenapid), a series of Greenland Eskimos (Inuid), a series of Athabaskan and other related groups of the Canadian Northwest (Deneid), and a series from the northern Plains (Lakotid). In the preceding sections it was pointed out that Woodbury described the Otamids as a separate entity; that the Iswanids were regarded as unrelated to a large number of other series by von Bonin and Morant; that the Ashiwids have been considered separately by Hooton; that the Walcolids were pooled as a Gulf type by Hrdlička; that the Lenapids have been recognized in a very broad Algonkin type, which also included the Iswanids and possibly the Ashiwids, by the same author; that the Inuids have generally enjoyed an independent status; that Boas at one time recognized a Deneid Northwest Coast type; and that the Lakotids were treated as a distinct type by Sullivan. The contribution of this study lies in delimiting these varieties more clearly and placing them into a more concise archeological framework.

The anthropometric data are briefly summarized in Table 1.

TABLE I

SUMMARY OF COMPARATIVE MEASUREMENTS AND INDICES

	Otamid (18)	Iswanid (33)	Ashiwid (15)	Walcolid (45)	Lenapid (24)	Inuid (241)	Deneid (32)	Lakotid (63)
Glabello-occipital length	189	177	180	181	183	189	180	185
Maximum breadth	133	135	135	139	137	135	145	144
Basion-bregma height	140	139	130	144	142	139	132	130
Cranial index	71	76	75	77	75	71	81	78
Length-height index	74	78	73	80	78	73	74	70
Total facial height	128	118	116	125	123	—	122	124
Upper facial height	78	71	73	76	75	75	73	76
Total facial breadth	134	136	132	139	136	140	142	143
Total facial index	97	87	87	90	90	—	85	87
Upper facial index	59	52	55	54	55	54*	52	53
Nasal breadth	25	24	25	26	26	23	26	27
Nasal height	57	51	51	54	54	54	52	55
Nasal index	44	47	50	49	49	44	49	49
Orbital height	34	33	34	35	35	36	36	36
Orbital breadth (mf)	41	42	42†	44	43	40	44	43†
Orbital index	82	78	81*	79	82	91	81	84*

*Calculated from means.
†Corrected from dacryal breadth.

This table gives the number of crania that made up each of the groups and a summary of the most frequently published measurements and indices. Here the values have been rounded off to the nearest millimeter. Alone, these means of a few conventional measurements and indices do not tend to be diagnostic. In order to characterize each variety, it therefore becomes necessary to combine them with brief morphological descriptions.

In the measurements and indices of the braincase the Otamids strikingly resemble the Inuids. The face of the Otamid is narrower and higher, the nose higher, and orbit lower, but these differences may decrease in magnitude with a larger sample of Otamid crania. Yet when two such series of marginal dolichocephals and Eskimos are placed side by side, diagnosis is relatively easy. The Otamid variety stands out in that there is a high incidence of large brow ridges, large glabellar prominence, pronounced frontal slope, a medium amount of sagittal elevation, a medium amount of lambdoid flattening, a somewhat low-placed bun-shaped occiput, and large-sized mastoid processes.

Similarly, the Iswanids and Ashiwids do not differ too greatly in a metrical sense. Both varieties exhibit small absolute dimensions, resemble each other in the total facial index, nasal and orbital proportions. They do differ in cranial vault height, but that feature may be partly due to the smallness of the Basket-Maker sample. Morphologically, the Iswanid skull is moderate in its development, and can be distinguished from the Ashiwid or Basket-Maker skull by showing larger zygomatic bones, greater nasal root height, more oblong orbits, greater vault elevation, more rounded piriform aperture, and larger size of the mandible.

The Walcolid Middle Mississippi people and the Lenapid Late Woodland group, again, show considerable similarity from a metrical point of view. Morphologically, however, there are considerable differences in vault shape, with a tendency toward roundheadedness in the Walcolids. A flatter face, a less pronounced nasal skeleton, a smaller incidence of sagittal cresting, a more posteriorly placed greater vault elevation, a more highly placed occiput, and greater muscular relief is much more frequent in the Walcolid variety.

Due to an extensive contribution of a Deneid element to the Lakotid variety of the Plains, our summary of measurements exhibits a considerable number of similarities, not only in vault height and cranial breadth, but also in nasal proportions and orbital dimensions. Yet few investigators confronted with the tall, heavy-faced aquiline-nosed Plains Indian would mistake him for his Athapaskan relative of the interior of the Canadian Northwest. The Lakotid skull is larger and longer, the nose is more salient and higher, and the orbits narrower. The Deneid nasal bones are more often parallel-sided, the interorbital distance tends to be smaller, the mandible lighter in build, and the gonial eversion more marked.

Considerable supporting evidence has been brought out that peripheral groups tend to be the older. This is illustrated by the linkage of Early Woodland Otamids from Illinois with the people of the Coastal Focus along the Atlantic seaboard and the dolichocephals of the Texas coast. Further, there is sufficient evidence that groups in refuge areas also tend to represent survivals of older population strata. The shell-heap people of the Ohio and Tennessee valleys and the Basket-Makers of the Southwest are examples, who also turned out to be related. It may be pointed out here that if Keresan is related to Siouan, as has been suggested by an Hokan-Siouan grouping, it may reflect the old Iswanid-Ashiwid physical relationship. The data for the postulation of migrations to the New World are as yet too scanty to furnish positive evidence for more than four; an Otamid, Iswanid-Ashiwid, Inuid, and Deneid migration appear well established. The Walcolid and Lenapid varieties could have developed from strains on the continent, although personally I would favor a theory of immigration for them; and the Lakotid variety almost certainly differentiated in North America. The sequence of migrations or appearance of these varieties, on the basis of archeological and distributional data was probably in the sequence in which they have been described in this paper: Otamid, Iswanid, Ashiwid, Walcolid, Lenapid, Inuid, Deneid, and Lakotid.

Archeologically, the Otamids practiced cultures that have been classified as of the Rockport Focus, without wider known affiliations; the "Early" Focus of the Coastal Aspect, and of the Black Sand Focus—both of the Woodland Pattern. The Iswanid series described here has been identified as of the Archaic Pattern and the Ashiwids represent the Basket-Makers of the Southwest. The Walcolid variety has been most frequently linked with various subgroupings of the Middle Phase of the Mississippi Pattern, and the Lenapid variety most frequently with Late Woodland and a few Upper Mississippi manifestations. As yet very little has been done with the archeology of the Athabaskans, and the sites in which skeletons of the Lakotid variety have been discovered up to now have been designated as remains of Siouan Plains and Algonquian Woodland tribes.

As to the last three varieties to appear on the continent, the best data available at the present suggests an Otamid origin for the Inuid variety; the oldest Eskimo remains resemble those of the northern Otamids most closely. The more Mongoloid features may indicate late Asiatic contacts. The Deneids, similarly, show many late Mongoloid relationships. These are of importance in indicating the distinctness of the Deneid variety from the earlier Walcolid variety. The Lakotid variety almost certainly represents a very late product of mixture. In the northern Plains a predominantly Deneid element probably took over the Siouan languages from an Iswanid or Otamid-Iswanid population. This is the only explanation for the fact that the Lakotid variety does not occur among the older peripheral Siouan-speakers of the East.

Finally, a few speculations concerning possible linguistic affiliations may not be amiss here. From this standpoint the Otamids have been linked with Karankawan-, Coastal Algonquian-, Piman-, and Yuman-speaking groups. It is obvious that not all of these linguistic stocks were represented by this early group; most likely they represent languages which were taken over by various groups of this variety. Karankawan, or perhaps Coahuiltecan, seems to furnish the best contender for the position, but this is merely a suggestion until it is checked by more archeological and linguistic research. With the next oldest varieties a possible Iswanid-Siouan and a possible Ashiwid-Keresan linkage have been mentioned. These super-groupings have been suggested by Sapir's somewhat vague Hokan-Siouan relationship, a linguistic type grouping with very little historical support. The Walcolid variety is most frequently linked with Muskogean and Uto-Aztecan-speaking tribes; the Lenapid variety to a very large extent with Algonquian- and Wakashan-speaking ones; and the Deneids with Athabaskan-, Penutian-, and to a lesser extent with Salishan-speaking ones. The Inuid-Esquimauan correlation hardly needs more than brief mention. The Lakotid variety, finally, because of its close physical relationship to the Deneids, in all probability took over Siouan, Algonquian, and Caddoan after contacts with groups speaking those languages in the Plains area. All of these associations are merely to be taken as suggestions for whatever they may be worth.

THE ETHNOLOGICAL CULTURES AND THEIR ARCHEOLOGICAL BACKGROUNDS.

By Fred R. Eggan*

IN ALMOST all areas of the New World the traditional relationships between the historic cultures and their archeological backgrounds are in process of radical revision as the archeologists begin to reveal the full complexity of the past.[1] In this process of revision the roles of the ethnologist and the archeologist have been shifting; the integrating and synthesizing functions are more frequently assumed by the archeologist as his contributions to culture history grow in significance. The ethnologist, in turn, has frequently shifted from the problems of culture history and its reconstruction to the direct study of culture dynamics and the processes of cultural continuity and change or to the comparative study of social structures and ritual. In the reconstruction and re-creation of the cultural past it is essential that the new insights and new knowledge so gained be fully utilized; the present paper offers some suggestions along these lines.

In the eastern United States the relative uniformity of the historic cultures long obscured their archeological diversity, and the reconstructions of culture history for the area were correspondingly inadequate. Up to about 1930 the major anthropological activities in the region east of the Rockies were in connection with the collection of ethnographical data and its ordering for specialized ethnological interpretation. In this area there were, at the time of first contact, some one hundred and fifty tribes divided into eleven linguistic stocks (see map, Fig. 10).[2] The events concerned with the conquest and settlement of the New World resulted in the rapid extinction, coalition, acculturation, or removal of many of these tribes, particularly along the eastern seaboard and the Gulf Coast, so that our knowledge of their historic cultures will forever be incomplete, despite the efforts of Speck and Swanton. In addition,

the once heavily populated Ohio Valley was temporarily deserted, or inhabited by shifting groups, in the early historic period. The Plains tribes, on the other hand, retained their cultural integrity almost up to the present century.

Concentration of ethnological investigation in the Plains area was therefore natural. Under the auspices of the American Museum of Natural History and other institutions a considerable number of Plains tribes were studied. On the basis of a series of distributional and comparative studies by our foremost ethnologists, Wissler formulated the Plains culture type and its variations, outlined the chronological development of Plains culture, and developed a theory of the relation of culture to environment which was designed to explain the general form of the culture area.[3] There seemed little left to do in this area except to fill in the spaces.

No such organized effort took place in the Great Lakes–Gulf regions in the period before 1930. Less than one-third of the still extant groups had been studied systematically, and there were preliminary surveys only for the Southeast and the extreme Northeast.[4] Many of the older monographs were incomplete or not oriented in terms of modern problems. The degree of cultural diversity or unity east of the Mississippi was not easily determined therefore, and the relationships with neighboring areas were correspondingly vague.

This situation was reflected in the classifications of the eastern United States in terms of culture areas. Thus Wissler, without reference to historical relationships, classified the cultures east of the Rockies into three culture areas: the Plains, Eastern Woodlands, and Southeast, thereby allocating to this region one-third of the areas he recognized north of Mexico.[5] In a notable revision made a decade later, Kroeber reduced the number of major areas to six, each of

---

* University of Chicago, Ph.B., 1927; M.A., 1928; Ph.D., 1933. On the staff since 1935, now Professor of Anthropology. Chapter received December, 1947.

1. See, e.g., Strong, 1943, and Martin, Quimby, and Collier, 1947.
2. Our limited knowledge of many groups makes it impossible to indicate the exact number of tribes or dialect groups. Wissler, 1922, Appendix, gives a convenient list. Cf. also the tribal maps in Kroeber, 1939, and Murdock, 1941.

3. Wissler, 1920; 1926. See also Lowie, 1916, and Spier, 1921, and the papers on which they are based.
4. Speck, 1907a; 1926; and Swanton, 1928c. Some of the more important monographs for this period are those of Skinner (1913; 1915; 1921b; 1925; 1927), Radin (1923), Speck (1907b; 1909), and Swanton (1928a; 1928b; 1928d).
5. Wissler, 1914; 1922.

which was "believed to represent a substantial unit of historical development, or of a prevailing characteristic current of culture."[6] Only one of these major areas was allotted to the region here under consideration:

East of the Rockies there is not a single native culture of as high a degree of characterization as occurs west; nor, except in some regions near the minimum of subsistence potentiality, any as culturally uncharacterized as some of the western transitional cultures. In other words the Atlantic side of North America is relatively uniform in its native culture. Its bent or direction is fundamentally similar everywhere. Once local subsistence adaptations and local culture imports are allowed for, there remains little in the way of local development; and, concomitantly, no great degree of difference in culture intensification.[7]

Within his Eastern area (in itself a subdivision of his major Eastern and Northern area) Kroeber recognized some thirteen subdivisions or specialized types of culture (see map, Fig. 11). The division between his Eastern and Northern areas is placed at the line of the northern Great Lakes, in contrast to Wissler's trifold distinction centering on the mouth of the Missouri River; within the Eastern area pre-eminence is accorded the Southeast, but Kroeber found it difficult to organize his subdivisions in terms of their historical relations or cultural dependences.

During the same period (before 1930) archeology was making rather slow progress in the eastern United States. A considerable amount of work had been carried out in the mound area by Thomas,[8] Moore,[9] and others. The mound areas had been partly surveyed and mapped, and excavations had been carried out in the Southeast and Ohio areas. Holmes[10] had made a comprehensive study of the pottery of the eastern United States which gave some hint of the complexities of cultural development which lay beneath the surface. But the objectives of research were limited by museum needs and state boundaries, and the problems formulated were frequently narrow and inadequate. To dispel the mystery of the "Mound Builders" and to equate their finds with historic tribes were the dominant objectives.

In the Southeast and in portions of the Great Lakes region there appeared to be a close tie-up between the prehistoric and the historic cultures; only in Ohio and neighboring areas did there appear to be a sharp discontinuity. Archeological classifications on the pattern of culture areas were proposed by Holmes[11] and Wissler[12] which varied only slightly from one another and from the ethnological groupings. But Holmes warned archeologists that

it is by no means assumed that the culture phenomena of any considerable area are uniform throughout. There may be much diversity, possibly great complexity of conditions. There may be a number of somewhat independent centers of development of nearly equal importance, or a single center may have spread its influence over a wide area. The mapping of the cultures will, in the end, take forms that cannot now be foreseen.[13]

The elaboration and documentation of this point of view was to take a long time, and the first steps were taken by the ethnologists. But with the decade of the thirties the center of gravity shifted to archeological research. The large-scale excavations of the depression period crowded a half-century of archeological research into a decade[14] and furnished a mass of material that is not yet completely digested. The prehistoric period was divided into some five cultural horizons, with complex interrelationships extending over an unknown but considerable time. Griffin, writing in 1941, summarized the results of the decade:

Within the last ten years there has been an unusually large amount of activity in the region east of the Rockies and this has completely altered the general picture presented by Holmes, Wissler, and Shetrone. More material has been made available for study than in all the previous years of excavation, and it is natural that the interpretation of the history of the area has changed. We have experienced a shift in our conception of aboriginal culture in the Mississippi Valley. Formerly it was considered a province where there was no stratigraphy, where the archeological scheme was a static one, divided into culture areas. Now definite stratigraphic sequences are recognized throughout the area. If a culture area exists it includes almost the whole territory.[15]

The documentation of this revolution has already begun to appear. Preliminary syntheses have been published covering most of the region under consideration, and the studies to follow in this volume will add considerably to our over-all knowledge. But it is in a notable series of monographs by Griffin,[16] Lewis and Kneberg,[17] Ritchie,[18] Strong,[19] Wedel,[20] Webb and Snow,[21] and others, that there is found the best evidence for a new approach to the study of archeological cultures and their development. Here one finds an awareness that prehistoric communities did not exist in a vacuum but were selectively adapted to certain features of the geographical and ecological environment and that the material remains may be interpreted in terms of major cultural activities as well as classified and tabulated in terms of form. A classification of culture types, conditioned on the comparison of detailed lists of traits, is well under

6. Kroeber, 1939, p. 20. It is one of the tragedies resulting from the depression that this study, completed in 1931, was delayed so long in publication. It represents a landmark in North American ethnology.

7. *Ibid.*, p. 60.
8. Thomas, C., 1894.
9. Moore, C. B., 1894–1918.
10. Holmes, 1903.
11. Holmes, 1914.
12. Wissler, 1922.

13. Holmes, 1914, p. 416.
14. Setzler, 1943, p. 207.
15. Griffin, J. B., 1946, pp. 39–40.
16. Griffin, J. B., 1943a.
17. Lewis and Kneberg, 1946.
18. Ritchie, 1944.
19. Strong, 1935.
20. Wedel, 1936.
21. Webb and Snow, 1945.

way and will, I believe, contribute to more precise historical inferences. Documentary materials and historical methods are utilized in competent fashion. In short, the archeologists show evidence that they are aware of their new responsibilities for making as complete an interpretation of the archeological record as is possible.

The major source of assistance to the archeologists in carrying out their task of interpreting the past comes from the study of living cultures. Here ethnology and linguistics are the traditional disciplines, but we shall see that their newer sister, social anthropology, has much to offer as well.[22] The most obvious way of integrating archeological and historic cultures would be to work from the historic period back into the past. Steward notes that "the direct historical approach is not only crucially important in ascertaining cultural sequences, but integrated with recent endeavors in ethnology, it has a tremendous potential value to the more basic problems of anthropology."[23] For various reasons this approach was late in application to the eastern United States, but it has already achieved important results in specific areas. One problem has been the difficulties and pitfalls of documentary research, even when documents are available. Furthermore, the direct historical approach frequently does not lead to deeper sequences; beyond the protohistoric or late prehistoric periods the trail is lost or becomes uncertain. At the historic end of the sequence the adding of a tribal name is without much significance unless there is information available as to the tribal culture which once prevailed. Despite these difficulties the potential values of ethno-historical research, combined with the direct historical approach to archeology, offer so much in the way of rewards that they should be strongly encouraged. But ethno-historical research is so specialized and time-consuming that its activities need to be coordinated and centralized.

Even where a direct tieup of archeological cultures and historic tribes is not possible, inferences from ethnology and linguistics can be extremely valuable. In Ohio the complex archeological situation resisted clarification for almost three decades. The initial confusion of Fort Ancient and Hopewell was replaced by a conception of their separate but contemporaneous existence. Kroeber,[24] in a review of Shetrone's[25] conclusions, criticized this view on *ethnological* grounds. He found it difficult to conceive of two such sharply differentiated cultures retaining their individuality under conditions of close contact over a considerable period of time, and suggested that the situation would make more sense, in terms of our knowledge of cultural behavior, if the two were separated in time. He further suggested that Fort Ancient might well be considered the later culture, despite its wider distribution. The influence of these ethnologically oriented hypotheses was limited through delay in publication, but their general accuracy can be attested by comparing the conclusions reached by Griffin[26] on the basis of archeological data.

The various methods and techniques of achieving time perspective have been known for some time, but they have seldom been applied in any co-ordinated way in the area here under discussion. Sapir's[27] brilliant essay contains many insights and techniques, particularly in the field of culture and language, which will be extremely useful, particularly in connection with the archeological record. For the general validity of the broad reconstructions of culture history in various areas will depend in considerable measure on the coincidence of inferences arrived at independently from the data of ethnology, linguistics, and archeology.

It is in connection with these comparisons that the nature of classification in each field becomes of vital importance. The ethnologist, linguist, and archeologist each has a variety of classifications adapted to his immediate needs, but the broader problems require some co-ordination. The ethnologist uses the tribe as a convenient unit for cultural study; for larger groupings the trend is away from the "culture area" to the concept of "culture type,"[28] which emphasizes similarities in culture content rather than geographical grouping, and offers a basis for the determination of genetic relationships. For analytical studies of culture Linton[29] has pointed out the need for more objective classification of culture elements and has proposed a grouping in terms of item, trait, trait complex, and activity, which makes it possible to consider both form and function.

The classification of languages in terms of dialect, language, stock, and "superstock" represents a grouping based directly on genetic principles which is exceedingly useful in linguistics but which students of culture have made little use of because the language classifications frequently cut across cultural groupings. The less differentiated dialect groupings, however, frequently coincide with cultural divisions; the larger groupings, once more is learned about the rates of change in various language stocks, will offer a powerful tool for investigating the past.[30]

---

22. I have omitted discussion of physical anthropology in this connection since Neumann is making a basic contribution to this problem in the preceding paper.

23. Steward, J. H., 1942, p. 339.

24. Kroeber, 1939, pp. 106–107.

25. Shetrone, 1920; 1930.

26. Griffin, J. B., 1943a.   27. Sapir, 1916.

28. Cf. Linton, 1936, Chap. xxii, and Kroeber, 1939, p. 2.

29. Linton, 1936, pp. 397–398.

30. The limited number of linguists working in the eastern United States makes it imperative that anthropologists working in the area do something with the linguistic materials available. Such

The nature of archeological knowledge in the eastern United States made it impossible to utilize immediately either the conventional ethnological and linguistic classifications, or the chronological classifications developed in the Southwestern archeological field. Early in the thirties the problem of archeological classification became acute, and a group of midwestern archeologists under the leadership of McKern developed the Midwestern Taxonomic Method to clarify the confusions resulting from the labeling of every assemblage as a "culture."[31] The basic concept is the "culture type," divorced from all temporal and geographical connotations. Through the comparisons of culture content five divisions are recognized, ranging from the *focus* made up of sites with a degree of correspondence suggestive of cultural identity, to the *base* which is characterized by fundamental traits relating to subsistence and organization. The task of linking these arbitrary culture types with ethnological and linguistic groupings is a difficult one but can be done in time. The broader problems of the relevance of the Midwestern Taxonomic Method for the problems of historical reconstruction have been raised[32] but will not be further considered here.

So far archeologists have not gone much beyond the reconstruction of the material aspects of prehistoric life. But recent developments in social anthropology hold out the possibility of reconstructing the social institutions of many prehistoric communities, without recourse to evolutionary or other formulas. For certain recent archeological cultures the direct historical method, once valid connections are established, offers an avenue by which late manifestations may be enlarged through inferences from ethnological horizons. For earlier cultures insights from the comparative study of social institutions will make it possible to determine with reasonable certainty the type of social organization prevailing and even to infer changes where the archeological data are adequate.

Social structures are mechanisms to organize the members of a society to carry out various objectives in a relatively efficient manner. Comparative studies are beginning to show that there are a limited number of forms and that these are shaped by a combination of social and ecological factors. Steward's[33] pioneer study of the economic and social basis of primitive bands offers an excellent start in this direction. After noting the social and economic factors which make the "autonomous, land-owning socio-political group" greater than the elementary family in all known societies, he analyzes the functional and necessary relationships involved in the adjustment of various types of band organization. He shows that "the patrilineal band is most common because it is produced by recurring ecological and social factors which may be formulated into something akin to cultural law, and that the composite band occurs where there are special factors, which may readily be ascertained in each instance."[34] By a comparative study of existing band types Steward has determined the essential social and ecological factors in rather specific terms.[35] In a related paper he has applied his conclusions to the study of the development of Southwestern society.[36] His summary of the conditions of development is important enough to be quoted practically in its entirety:

First, a low culture and/or unfavorable environment prevents dense population and precludes large population aggregates. It produces groups which, barring special contrary factors, are unilateral, localized, exogamous, and land owning. Descent is male or female largely according to the economic importance of man or woman in that culture.

Second, increased food supply or other factors making for a denser population will produce either larger bands, occupying the same territory, more bands each occupying less territory, or multi-band villages.

Third, large multi-band villages will be produced if tribal movements, war, or some other factor dislocates the unilateral band, causing concentration, or if, in an increasing population, newly founded lineages fail to move away.

Fourth, it is not inevitable that these unilateral groups become clans, but they will do so if possession of a group name, common ceremonies, or other factors create solidarity and prevent the loss of recognition of kindred in succeeding generations. . . .

Fifth, in the course of these transformations political autonomy passes from the localized lineage to a wider group. . . .[37]

Here are conclusions which may be applied to the reconstruction of the *earliest* cultures in the eastern United States, as well as to later forms. Careful archeological research in favorable areas can reveal the level of population density at different periods, the size of the local groups and their concentration or dispersion, the arrangement of houses in the village and the outlines of household activity and division of labor, the subsistence patterns and ecological adjustment, the continuity or replacement of populations, and the outlines of ceremonial organization and practice.[38] From such data it should be possible

activities will result in more useful linguistic classifications. See, e.g., Voegelin, 1941; Voegelin, C. F. and E. W., 1946.

31. See McKern, 1939a, and Griffin, J. B., 1943a, Appendix, for a discussion of the system.

32. See Brew, 1946, pp. 44–66, and Jennings, 1947, for critical comments and appraisals.

33. Steward, J. H., 1936.

34. *Ibid.*, p. 331.   35. *Ibid.*, pp. 343–345.

36. Steward, J. H., 1937a. See also his important study of Great Basin sociopolitical groups (Steward, J. H., 1938).

37. Steward, J. H., 1937a, pp. 101–102.

38. Recent excavations at Kincaid, the Angel site, in Kentucky, Tennessee, Alabama, Georgia, and other regions furnish evidence that such data are obtainable. For examples see Bennett, 1944b; Lewis and Kneberg, 1946; and others.

to say a good deal about the social organizations of the Archaic and Early Woodland horizons of the eastern United States, as well as to trace the development of more complex institutions with the introduction of large scale agriculture and town life. Such reconstructions need not remain mere guesses. By a more adequate analysis of historical social structures and their projections into the past through the direct historical approach it should be possible to check the conclusions reached through the application of social anthropology. Furthermore, if the the hypothesis for the Asiatic origins of Woodland culture proposed by McKern[39] is verified, comparison with northern ethnological cultures may be relevant on the basis of Cooper's concept of marginal cultures.[40]

We have reviewed in the last few pages some of the ways in which the various disciplines of anthropology may contribute to the reconstruction and interpretation of cultural development. It will be useful now to turn to an examination of the present state of our knowledge in two or three areas of the eastern United States in order to see in what ways this knowledge may be applied.

We have noted above the differing perspectives on Plains culture and its classification developed by Wissler and Kroeber. From the vantage point of Late Plains institutions, and in the relative absence of archeological data, Wissler came to view Plains culture as static and essentially timeless. The introduction of the horse intensified these patterns; this intensification, reaching its peak in the eighteenth and nineteenth centuries, was responsible for reversing cultural values in the marginal areas and inhibiting the further development of sedentary life.[41] Kroeber, in a notable paper on "Native Culture in the Southwest,"[42] dissented from this interpretation on ethnological grounds. He viewed the High Plains as only sparsely inhabited for a long period. The basic culture was an Eastern Woodlands one along the margins of the Plains; as these people gradually moved out into the Plains, they divided their time between farming and bison-hunting. The introduction of the horse led to a florescense of the hunting life, and the focus of Plains culture shifted to the northern High Plains.

This historical hypothesis was confirmed in a striking manner by the archeological researches of Strong[43] and Wedel[44] in Nebraska, Kansas, and the Dakotas.

In these regions they found that early hunting cultures were succeeded by semi-sedentary village-dwelling peoples who practiced both horticulture and bison-hunting; these in turn were succeeded by the protohistoric and historic tribes. The evidence further suggested several semi-sedentary prehistoric occupations, some of which had affiliations with protohistoric sites. By utilizing the direct historical approach, the historic Pawnee were linked with protohistoric sites on the Lower Loup River (Lower Loup Focus),[45] and the movement of the Cheyenne out onto the High Plains was confirmed.[46] In this view tribes such as the Pawnee were typical of the area in late prehistoric times, and the historic High Plains culture represented merely "a thin overlay associated with the acquisition of the horse."[47] Both Strong and Kroeber lean to the view that the uniformity of Plains culture is largely the result of historic factors rather than the result of environmental control.

But the High Plains area was not a cultural vacuum before the introduction of the horse. The early Spanish explorers of the southern Plains found two well-defined modes of life, a nomadic, buffalo-hunting, dog-transporting, and tipi-using one in the western portions, and a sedentary, village-dwelling, agricultural one in the east. In Coronado's time[48] the basic techniques for continuous life on the High Plains were well established, and the Folsom finds suggests a long occupancy of the region by bison-hunters. Granted that the groups were small before the introduction of the horse, and without the elaborations of ceremonial and societal life which came with greater wealth and leisure, the patterns of material life were still distinctive and formed the basic substratum for the historic cultures.

When first described most of the tribes of the northern High Plains had centered their culture around the horse, but this culture seems a logical development of the type of life described by Coronado.[49] If we examine the typical tribes of this area, however, there is good evidence that practically every group entered the High Plains in historic or protohistoric times,[50] the majority of them from the east and north. Whether the northern High Plains culture of historic times is primarily a development of earlier Plains patterns or an amalgam of modified northeastern and eastern traits is not yet clear; there is evidence that both processes were involved.[51] It is

39. McKern, 1937.
40. Cooper, J. M., 1941.
41. Kroeber, 1939, pp. 76 ff., presents a summary of interpretations of Plains culture. The following discussion is largely drawn from an independent analysis of "The Plains Area" which I presented at the annual meeting of the American Anthropological Association in December, 1939, in connection with a symposium on the present state of our knowledge of various fields.
42. Kroeber, 1928.
43. Strong, 1935; 1940.
44. Wedel, 1938; 1940; 1947.

45. Wedel, 1938.
46. Strong, 1940.
47. Strong, 1936, p. 362.
48. See Winship, 1896.
49. Winship (ed.), 1904, pp. 111–112 and 230, as quoted in Wissler, 1927, pp. 155–156.
50. The Kiowa, who may be an exception, unfortunately moved into the southern Plains before they were studied.
51. Archeological evidence will ultimately give us an outline of the sequence of events in this area.

important to note for our purposes, however, that these diverse tribal cultures came to have a similar form, under the influence of environmental and historical factors.

Wissler attempted to work out the mechanisms involved in terms of a tendency for specialization to take place in the center of the ecological area and to diffuse to the margins.[52] The Plains area shows this central clustering of traits, and there is evidence that diffusion is an important process; but the historical evidence does not support the assumption of central origin and dissemination. The Cheyenne and Arapaho, generally considered the most typical High Plains tribes, entered the central plains in relatively late times. Strong has shown that the Cheyenne, in particular, shifted from a sedentary, agricultural, village-dwelling group to a typical nomadic plains tribe in the short period between 1750 and 1800.[53] They therefore borrowed or adapted practically their entire historic culture complex in very short order.

It is clear that Wissler's search for a dynamic factor in the ecological pattern led him to underestimate the importance of contact and migration in the Plains. If contact be given its proper weighting, the margins of culture areas, rather than their centers, may become the places where new developments take place. The increased mobility provided by the horse would make it possible for a marginal tribe moving to the center to assimilate and integrate a large number of new cultural ideas from all sides, thus building up a complex culture in a relatively short time. The application of such a hypothesis may give us a more adequate explanation for the development of at least some of the Plains culture patterns.

Such hypotheses are, however, inadequate to account for the uniformities observed in social structure. We have noted that there is a limited number of forms of social organization and that these are adjusted to social and ecological factors; furthermore, the patterns of kinship organization, like those of language, are not readily observable, and therefore difficult to borrow, even if consonant with the existing institutions. I have suggested elsewhere[54] that the basic features of Plains local organization and kinship represented adjustments to the conditions of Plains life. These conditions are both social and ecological, involving not only the need for protection against hostile raids but also the necessity for adjusting to the annual cycle of the buffalo. The uncertainties of Plains existence were great, compared with those of the village dwellers, and a flexible type of social structure was required.

Collier[55] has noted that the social organization of the Plains tribes took a series of forms: the camp circle, two types of large bands, the camp based on extended kinship, and the temporary hunting camp, each of which was adapted to the annual cycle of subsistence as well as to the social environment. It is important to note that tribes coming into the Plains with more complex formal social structures were in the process of giving them up in favor of the more flexible band and camp organization, and, conversely, the more simply organized Great Basin groups developed a more complex organization. To explain such uniformities in terms of borrowing is an oversimplification; the Crow, for example, in modifying their clan organization and kinship system in the direction of Plains patterns,[56] were adapting their own more complex organization to new requirements. They had not borrowed Plains social institutions outright in these cases but had modified their own in the direction of a more efficient adjustment to the exigencies of Plains life.

The events of the historic periods throw some light on the past; archeological evidence suggests a series of incursions by horticultural peoples from the east out into the Plains. In historic times very rapid readjustments were made by groups moving into the High Plains, and older patterns were obliterated or modified in a short period of time. In this process ecological factors are important, as well as historical factors; where these ecological factors are of long standing they can be utilized, as Steward suggests, in the analysis of social organization.

Our understanding of the High Plains will be greatly enhanced when more is known about the Prairie Areas along the eastern border. The recognition of this region as a distinct culture type, rather than as marginal to the High Plains, has the advantage of not subordinating culture type to geographical area to the extent that Wissler's formulation did. Within this area the great majority of the tribal groups speak Siouan languages, so that the ethnologist turns first to the classifications worked out by the linguists. Voegelin[57] has summarized our present knowledge of Siouan groupings in terms of four groups, two of which are relevant to the areas under discussion. In his Missouri River grouping he places Hidatsa and Crow, pointing out that they have differentiated more from each other than is generally recognized. Evidence that Chiwere and Dhegiha belong together has resulted in a new Mississippi Valley grouping, to which Mandan and Dakota are tentatively added. These conclusions are of considerable

52. Wissler, 1926.
53. Strong, 1940, p. 359.
54. Eggan, 1937b, pp. 85, 88, 89 ff., especially. This analysis was made independently of Steward's studies noted above, and adds another series of cases.

55. Collier, n.d. His forthcoming study of local groupings in the northern plains will discuss these organizations in detail.
56. Eggan, 1937b, p. 94; Collier, n.d.
57. Voegelin, 1941, p. 249.

importance in view of the growing archeological evidence in this important region.

Kroeber's divisions of his Prairie Areas correspond rather closely with this new alignment: his Southern Prairie is composed entirely of Chiwere- and Dhegiha-speaking tribes, his Central Prairie is occupied by tribes speaking Dakota dialects, and his Northern Prairie area is occupied by the related Assiniboin- and intrusive Algonkian-speaking groups such as the Plains Cree and Plains Ojibwa. But while the Siouan-speaking tribes of this area have many cultural features in common, their basic social structures are quite different. Recent evidence on the Eastern Dakota[58] suggests a form of social organization and mode of life much closer to that of the Ojibwa than to that of the Southern Siouans; the Mandan and Hidatsa, on the other hand, shared common patterns.

Archeological research is beginning to document these similarities and differences and, indeed, in some cases has called them to attention. The Oneota Aspect comprises a series of foci, belonging in the Mississippi horizon, which have been tentatively identified with Chiwere-speaking tribes;[59] a further extension to Dhegiha-speaking groups is highly probable in terms of the close linguistic connections noted above and basic similarities in social organization and other aspects of culture. The archeological sites identified with Eastern Dakota groups, on the other hand, appear to belong in the Woodland horizon, along with the Menominee and other Algonkian-speaking groups.[60]

The linguistic distribution and the evidence of migration legends points to the possibility of an earlier homeland in the Ohio Valley. Thus Kroeber, in speaking of the decline in this area, suggests: "The legendary southwestward movement of the Dhegiha-Chiwere Siouans may have been part of one of the last phases of this period of evacuation and decay. It is tempting to think of the Mandan, Hidatsa, and Winnebago as similar emigrants; but it would be speculative to follow this idea out until a clearer picture of Mound Builder culture is available."[61] This hypothesis has received reinforcement by Voegelin's conclusion that Biloxi, Ofo, and Tutelo form an Ohio Valley Siouan group, with the implication that they dispersed from this region,[62] but the degree of linguistic and cultural differentiation among the Missouri River and Mississippi Valley groups sug-

gests that such a series of movements, if ultimately demonstrated, took place over a fairly long period. The possible role of these Siouan-speaking groups in the development of Mississippi cultures will be briefly considered below.

A complex problem, the solution to which will throw considerable light on the development of culture types in the Prairie-Plains areas, is that of the earth lodge complex. In the historic period circular earth lodges were used by the Dhegiha-speaking Omaha, Osage, Kansa, and possibly Ponca, the Chiwere-speaking Iowa and Oto, the Mandan, Hidatsa, and Arikara of the Village Area, and the Pawnee of the Middle Platte. This grouping not only cuts across Siouan linguistic divisions but includes Caddoan-speaking tribes as well.[63] In the archeological horizons, while little or no trace of dwellings has been found in connection with the earlier Woodland occupations of the Plains, the rectangular semisubterranean earth lodge is an integral feature of the Upper Republican and Nebraska aspects of the Mississippi horizon. The distribution of the earth lodge during this period was much wider than in historic times;[64] the comparable distributions in the northern Plains are now in the process of being worked out in connection with the Missouri Valley Survey.[65]

The situation in the central Plains suggests that the protohistoric and historic Pawnee structures developed out of Upper Republican forms. As Wedel notes:

It is reasonable to believe that the historic circular Plains lodge evolved in the region out of the closely similar and clearly earlier rectangular structure. Architecturally, the earlier is if anything the more complicated of the two types, and it must have had a fairly long developmental background. Nothing so far found in the Plains suggests an incipient or formative stage, from which fact it might be inferred that the developed type was an importation.[66]

The historical relations between the earth-lodge complex of the central Plains and that of the Upper Missouri need to be clarified before the source of the complex can be adequately investigated. Wedel has examined parallels from the Southeast and Southwest without arriving at any definite conclusions; in view of the extensions of earth-lodge sites along the tributaries of the Upper Missouri and the historic occurrences of earth lodges in the Plateau, the Northwest must also be thoroughly investigated.[67]

Despite the complexities of historical development

58. Landes, n.d.; see also Wallis, 1947.

59. See Griffin, J. B., 1937a, and Wedel, 1940.

60. Strong, 1940, pp. 358 ff., presents a summary of their historic movements.

61. Kroeber, 1939, p. 91.

62. Voegelin, 1941, p. 247. This is still a highly controversial question, since there is no good historical documentation for the Siouan groups in the Ohio Valley according to Griffin, and the area is marked as "Uninhabited in Early Historical Period" on the "Map of North American Indian Languages" by C. F. and E. W. Voegelin.

63. Strong's (1940) evidence makes it possible to add the Algonkian-speaking Cheyenne to this list.

64. Wedel, 1940, p. 328.

65. Strong, 1940, gives a preliminary summary of the data and suggests that there may be differences between the central and northern plains.

66. Wedel, 1940, p. 321.

67. The possible relation of the semisubterranean houses at the Fisher site to the Plains types should also be investigated in view of the affiliations of Fisher with Oneota.

all the tribes of the Prairie Areas using earth lodges had a complex social organization centering around the village, with a formal clan organization and kinship systems of a "lineage" type. The Dhegiha- and Chiwere-speaking tribes of the Southern Prairie were organized in terms of patrilineal clans grouped into exogamous moieties, with kinship systems of the Omaha subtype; the Mandan and Hidatsa of the Village Area were organized in terms of matrilineal clans and moieties, with kinship systems of the Crow subtype.[68] The Pawnee and Arikara show certain specializations in village organizations, but accord with the village tribes in their emphasis on matrilineal descent.

The objective differences between these areas preclude direct borrowing of social institutions, but the parallel organization suggests the influence of some common factors. The increased density of population requisite for village life was made possible by the increased food supply resulting from combining maize agriculture with hunting and gathering. The utilization of fertile bottomlands along the Missouri and its tributaries made it possible for these villages to be both large and relatively permanent; the problems of integrating the population around common activities in connection with agriculture and hunting, with regard both to subsistence and to rituals, made the development of a segmentary clan organization highly probable.[69] Wherever it is essential to hold property in trust or to maintain rituals from generation to generation, unilateral organizations or "corporations" are far more efficient than bilateral ones.[70] The clan gives a greater degree of stability and permanence but has in turn a limited flexibility and adaptability to new situations.

The difference in descent pattern, from this point of view, is of less significance. Steward has suggested that descent is male or female, largely according to the economic importance of the sexes in the culture. In the village tribes the earth lodges were occupied by extended families based on matrilocal residence so that the women of a lodge represented a lineage group. These women co-operated in the activities connected with cultivating their fields and in various household tasks. Hunting and ceremonial activities were in the hands of the men and were organized largely on a clan or village basis. It is conceivable that the relatively greater importance of agriculture in the subsistence pattern and the greater efficiency of household co-operation were important factors in emphasizing the matrilineal line in residence, inheritance, and descent.

The patrilineally organized Southern Prairie groups offer a crucial case, but the details of local organization are not available. For the Omaha, however, Fortune[71] offers an important clue in a footnote. He notes that the earth lodge, which was inhabited during the agricultural periods, was organized in terms of matrilocal residence, whereas the tipis used during the hunting periods were organized on the basis of patrilocal residence. The women of the earth lodge co-operated in agricultural and household activities, despite the patrilineal organization of the society; for hunting activities tipi-mates and clansmen co-operated, with their wives taking care of the meat and skins. With the reversal in values brought about by the horse it is possible that hunting activities came to dominate to a greater extent and brought about a greater emphasis on the patrilineal line.[72] In this connection it is important to note that the moiety organization was expressed in the camp circle, where each clan had a specific place, and not in the village, where matrilocal residence precluded any spatial arrangement of the earth lodges in terms of moiety and clan patterns. Matrilineally organized groups such as the Pawnee and Crow apparently responded to such changes by shifting from a clan toward a band type of organization and becoming more "bilateral" in their kinship practices.

The above discussions may have some relevance to the Iroquois problem so ably discussed in its various aspects by Fenton,[73] Griffin,[74] and others. Fenton has pointed out that "the major problem in Iroquois culture history is that of explaining their intrusive linguistic and cultural position."[75] Griffin has briefly characterized their cultural position as follows:

The semisedentary villages of the Iroquois based on a maize economy certainly present a subsistence picture different from that of their Algonquian neighbors on the west, the north, and the northeast. The Iroquois agricultural-hunting economy included relatively permanent large villages, with a social structure highlighted by the matrilineal household unit within the clan and by the possession of two moieties. The Iroquois tribal organization was of a high order, and the conceptual framework of the "League" was a still further advance. Much of this sociopolitical organization is at marked variance with the Algonquian tribes to the north and west and, to a somewhat less degree, with the bordering Algonquian groups to the east and south.[76]

---

68. See Eggan, 1937b, p. 93, for a preliminary classification of these kinship systems.

69. Cf. Steward's, J. H., (1937a, pp. 101–102), conclusions quoted above.

70. See Radcliffe-Brown, 1935, for an exposition of this point of view.

71. Fortune, 1932, p. 24, note to chap. ii.

72. The testing of this generalization obviously requires a much wider comparative survey than can be carried out here, but I hope to bring together the relevant evidence in the near future. The Ponca and Kansa emphasized hunting to a greater extent than the Omaha; the Osage and Quapaw apparently were more agricultural. An analysis of this series, if the data were available, would be of great importance.

73. Fenton, 1940.

74. Griffin, J. B., 1944b.

75. Fenton, 1940, p. 164.

76. Griffin, J. B., 1944b, p. 360.

Fenton notes the assumption that the Iroquois brought some basic patterns of their culture, such as village life based on maize agriculture and matrilineal clans, from a place where they were in contact with an area of higher cultures, but states that the Iroquois did not necessarily ever reside in the Southeast.[77]

There is a growing belief among students of the Iroquois that they may have developed much of their distinctive mode of life in the lower Great Lakes area. Flannery[78] has presented data which indicate that the Iroquois have much in common with their neighbors and that they have mutually influenced one another as well as having been affected by influences from the south; Griffin[79] believes that part of their culture is derived from the Hopewell horizon through the Owasco and that the ancestors of the Iroquois may have been Hopewellian, or, as part of Point Peninsula, been in the Lower Great Lakes region in Hopewellian times.

The distinctive and advanced character of Iroquois social and political structure has been one of the major features, along with maize agriculture and the associated ceremonial cycle, by which they were linked to the Southeast. But it is quite possible for the basic features of their social and political organization to have developed in the north. Given maize agriculture, which they may have brought with them or received by diffusion, a greater concentration of population would result. Greater emphasis on agriculture in a favorable environment might well lead to the further organization of women for agricultural co-operation and, ultimately, to the utilization of matrilineal principles for residence, inheritance, descent, and succession. The tribal and intertribal organizations represent devices designed to integrate larger groups for the purpose of protection, and were further elaborated under conditions of contact; there is no adequate source from which they could have been borrowed. In this connection it might be noted that the kinship systems are "bilateral" and resemble those of neighboring areas to a much greater extent than they do the "lineage" systems of the Southeast. If they turn out to be originally based on cross-cousin marriage, their tie with adjoining groups will be much more definite. There is no necessity, therefore, to postulate a southern origin for the Iroquois on the basis of their social organization. While the linguistic and cultural situation may point in that direction as their original homeland, there is no need to assume that they arrived with their full cultural equipment.

Griffin[80] has suggested that the ancestors of the Iroquois were probably in the north by A.D. 1200, which would give them plenty of time to develop their complex institutions.

Turning now to the Southeast, we find an area where the potential values of ethno-historical research and the direct historical approach are beginning to be realized on a large scale. Here the archeologists can draw on Swanton's great researches;[81] the archeologists in turn can illuminate the course of cultural development underlying the historic tribes.[82]

Even where direct tieups of archeological cultures and historic tribes are not possible, influences from ethnology and linguistics may be extremely valuable. There is a general feeling that Mississippi cultures were brought into the Southeast by the ancestors of the historic Muskogean-speaking tribes in late prehistoric times.[83] Such an inference is based in part on the linguistic and cultural situation at the time of first contact. While the linguistic differentiation between the major branches of Natchez-Muskogean is fairly deep, the dialectic differentiation of the Muskogean group is much less marked, and Haas's[84] revision of Swanton's classification indicates a center of gravity for the latter in the west-central portion of the Southeast, with dialectic differentiation at the margins. More distantly related languages such as Natchez and Timucuan are found on the peripheries. The ethnological picture presents a similar pattern. The cultural distinctions between the Creek, Hitchiti, and Alabama were slight in comparison with their uniformities; Choctaw and Chickasaw varied somewhat from the Creek patterns but obviously belonged with them. The linguistic and cultural differentiations, therefore, are on approximately the same level and suggest either a recent expansion of these groups or the effects of the Creek Confederacy in the historic period.

The possibility of a relationship between Mississippi cultures and the later Creek-Choctaw-Chickasaw groups is made more probable by the identification of Mississippi archeological complexes in Tennessee,[85] Georgia,[86] and Mississippi,[87] with historic Muskogean-speaking tribes, with evidence of cultural discontinuity and replacement in most instances.

77. Fenton, 1940, p. 165.

78. Flannery, 1939.

79. Griffin, J. B., 1944b, p. 372, and personal communication. See also the chapter by MacNeish in this volume.

80. *Ibid.*, pp. 372–373. [This date would now be extended backward some 500 to 600 years.—Ed.]

81. See Swanton, 1946, for a summary and bibliography.

82. See Ford and Willey, 1941, and Griffin, J. B., 1946.

83. I am indebted to Moreau Maxwell for many suggestions incorporated in the following discussion.

84. Haas, 1941. Kroeber (1939, pp. 65–67) had criticized Swanton's (1922) groupings on the basis of dialect distribution.

85. Lewis and Kneberg, 1946, chap. ii, equate the Hiwassee Island Focus with Muskogean peoples and the Dallas and Mouse Creek foci with the Creek and Yuchi, respectively.

86. See Jennings, 1939; Kelly, 1938; and Willey, 1939, for the probable relations of Lamar and Ocmulgee Fields cultures to the protohistoric and historic Creeks.

87. Jennings, 1941; 1944, discusses the relationships between Mississippi cultures and the historic Choctaw and Chickasaw.

The marginal areas, on the other hand, show cultural continuity at several points. In the Lower Mississippi region there is apparently an unbroken development from early Tchefuncte to historic Natchez; a similar continuity is apparent in the cultural developments in northwestern Florida and the Georgia coast. All of these marginal areas appear to derive from or share in a widespread Southeastern Woodland cultural horizon, and each was affected in varying degrees by Mississippi influences in its later stages.

The evidence from linguistics and archeology thus reinforces and makes more precise a hypothesis with regard to the dynamics of southeastern cultural development originally formulated by Swanton[88] on the basis of ethnological evidence alone. The conception of an indigenous Woodland culture into which Mississippi intrusions took place, with the forcing of the earlier populations to the margins, and the fusing of the two traditions and populations in varying degrees, offers a situation in which problems of culture process and culture change can be attacked on an archeological level and checked with ethnological data. A comparison of the marginal cultures holds out the possibility for reconstructing the earlier cultures in the area, as well as explaining the cultural similarities noted by Swanton[89] and Speck[90] between the Natchez, on the one hand, and the Eastern Siouans, Algonkians, and Cherokee, on the other.

The probability that languages more distantly related to Muskogean proper, such as Natchez and Timucuan, were early in the Southeast is strongly reinforced by the cultural continuity displayed by the marginal areas. In historic times tribes speaking Siouan, Yuchi, Iroquois, Caddoan, Tunican, and Algonkian were also marginal to the Southeast proper. Sapir[91] has suggested that Siouan-Yuchi may form an enlarged group comparable to Natchez-Muskogean and that Iroquois-Caddoan makes up a similar group; these with Tunican, form the eastern portion of his proposed Hokan-Siouan "superstock." The genetic relations of such a stock, if ultimately demonstrated, would take us far into the past, but detailed studies of the proposed substocks such as Siouan-Yuchi and Iroquois-Caddoan will be extremely useful in working out the relative chronology of the archeological horizons in relationship to linguistic differentiation. The possibility that all the languages of an enlarged Southeast may be genetically related[92] further suggests that their differentiation may have taken place largely within the area and that a considerable period of time may be involved.

That Muskogean-speaking peoples were bearers of

Mississippi cultures in the Southeast does not solve the problem of the origins of Mississippi cultures but does give some useful hints. The Yuchi, as noted above, have also been identified with this horizon in Tennessee; the Cherokee remains, on the other hand, appear to derive from a different tradition. The general direction of the Mississippi intrusion into the Southeast seems to have been from the northwest. Griffin is inclined not to look for a single center but postulates, instead, a gradual growth throughout the Mississippi Valley, in which "various ideas and complexes developed in several centers the whole to be welded into classic Middle Mississippi."[93] Within the area so labeled on his maps,[94] there were, in early historic times, only Siouan- and Algonkian-speaking tribes in addition to the groups already mentioned. The Algonkians of the Wisconsin and Illinois areas, while ultimately derived from northern centers, had developed fairly complex cultures comparable to those of their Siouan-speaking neighbors and show evidence of having been in the region for a considerable time. Only the Illinois and Shawnee were far enough south to participate in the development of Mississippi cultures, however, and the probability that Menominee ancestral culture belongs in the Woodland horizon suggests that the former have played a minor role. This leaves the Mississippi Valley Siouan-speaking tribes, particularly the Osage, Quapaw, Omaha, Ponca, and Kansa, as the most likely series of tribes, in addition to the Muskogean groups, to be involved in the development of Mississippi cultures. The place of the Caddoan area in the development of Mississippi cultures depends on the evaluation of the newly discovered role of Spiro as an intermediary for Middle American influences and, of course, on its chronological relationships with Mississippi sites.[95]

In view of the evidence so far available I would look for the center of development for Mississippi cultures in the general Lower Missouri–Lower Ohio region, where we find some of the largest Mississippi sites: Cahokia, Kincaid, Angel and others. The establishment of tree-ring dates for one level at Kincaid[96] gives a basis for establishing correlations with other sites through trade materials and intrusive sherds and for estimating the period of development required. The assumed primacy of the lower Mississippi in earlier archeological periods and the reputed position of the historic Natchez have led us to look gulfward too long. Kroeber[97] assigns to the Natchez a pre-eminent position in the Southeast, mainly on

88. See Swanton, 1928c; 1946.   90. Speck, 1920.
89. Swanton, 1928c; 1935.   91. Sapir, 1929.
92. Except, of course, the Algonkian-speaking Shawnee who entered the area in historic times.

93. Griffin, J. B., 1946, p. 75.   94. Ibid., Fig. 7, p. 76.
95. If Krieger's (1947a, p. 148) views as to the age of the Spiro materials hold up, it may be an important factor.
96. See Bell's paper in this volume and the forthcoming Kincaid report.
97. Kroeber, 1939, pp. 62 ff.

the basis of their class system and sun symbolism. But while the Natchez social structure was unique in its combination of class and exogamy, both class systems and exogamy were widespread in the Southeast.[98] Only among the Chitimacha is a true caste system reported, and here apparently only for the nobility.[99] The archeological evidence likewise does not support the assumption of a climax culture—in fact, the archeology of the contact period shows a relative decline.[100]

The central Mississippi region has been an important meeting place for diverse cultures, situated as it is on the borders of the Prairie, Ohio Valley, and Southeast areas, and at the confluence of the Missouri, Upper Mississippi, and Ohio rivers. We have pointed out above the importance of contacts in the development of culture,[101] and in this respect the region deserves important consideration. The direct historical approach and ethno-historical research may be able to verify, or disprove, the legendary history of the Mississippi Valley Siouan-speaking groups which brings them to their later homes from the lower Ohio. The close relationship of the Dhegiha-speaking groups to the Chiwere, who have been identified with the Oneota Aspect, further suggests a relationship of these Siouan tribes with Mississippi cultures; their division into "Upstream" and "Downstream" peoples is suggestive of a former home on the Mississippi. Their possible connection with the Late Mississippi sites waits on further research but is, in my opinion, a useful working hypothesis.

The combination and coincidence of inferences from ethnology, linguistics, and archeology, then, promises to be very useful in unraveling the complex prehistory of the Southeast. Until the archeologists had progressed sufficiently to relate their materials to the ethnological horizons, such multidisciplinal approaches to cultural development were not possible. Griffin has noted that "this growing ability to assign definitely, or even tentatively, cultural blocks to known tribes is one of the most fortunate results of the recent archeological activity in the Southeast."[102] With the tentative identification of such sites as Moundville and Etowah as Creek, it will be possible to expand greatly our knowledge of the protohistoric and contact cultures by putting together the archeological and the ethnological complexes.

But the problem of reconstructing cultures and cultural development in the periods preceding the Mississippi horizons is more difficult. There is no continuity with historic cultures, except in modified form at the margins, and our limited knowledge of Natchez, Chitimacha, Timucua, and Cusabo will be a handicap in reconstruction. But it may well be possible that we can utilize our greater knowledge of Cherokee, Yuchi, and Caddo cultures in this connection, once their role in Southeastern cultural development is better known.

In connection with such problems recent studies of social organization in the Southeast should prove useful.[103] The basic patterns of social structure in the historic Muskogean-speaking groups are similar to those we have noted for the Iroquois and the village tribes, and have developed, in my opinion, in response to similar social and ecological factors. Studies with reference to the factors bringing about social change in Southeastern tribes in historic times[104] support this view and will be of great assistance in evaluating the possibilities of earlier changes. For the Mississippi horizons we should be able ultimately to project back the historic social patterns, at least in general terms. For earlier horizons there is the possibility, mentioned above, of interpreting the archeological record along the lines suggested by Steward. Some of the cave and shell-mound occupations, as well as the various occupations described for Hiwassee Island,[105] suggest that sharp differences from later forms will be found.

The great advances in archeological techniques and materials in the eastern United States during the last fifteen years offer both a challenge and a promise. The challenge involves nothing less than the necessity of bringing the entire resources of our accumulated knowledge of man and his environment and culture to bear upon the interpretation of the archeological record. The promise is that through the cooperation of all the disciplines of anthropology this task can be carried out. The increasing specialization within the field of anthropology, as each discipline grows in complexity, makes this task of co-operation more difficult, but it can be met in at least two ways: by collaboration of groups of specialists on related or common problems and by broader training for students in universities and museums. Dr. Cole saw this challenge and met it with a program of training and research adequate to its needs; part of the promise is in this volume and in the work of his students and associates who are already realizing a good portion of his goal of "making the past live again."

98. Several writers have pointed out that the system, as described by the French, is unstable; Kroeber, himself, finds "something of the quality of a remnant" about it.

99. Swanton, 1946, p. 661.

100. Personal communication from George I. Quimby, Jr. This conclusion is based largely on ceramics, and he recognizes that it is not conclusive.

101. See Dixon, 1928, for an exposition of this point.

102. Griffin, J. B., 1946, p. 80. J. Joe Bauxar has made a detailed study of the Yuchi which illustrates the value of a multidimensional approach.

103. See, e.g., Eggan, 1937a; Gilbert, 1937; 1943; Haas, 1939; 1940; and Spoehr, 1941; 1942; 1944; 1947.

104. See, especially, Spoehr, 1947.

105. Lewis and Kneberg, 1946.

THE ARCHEOLOGY OF THE NORTHEASTERN
UNITED STATES. *By Richard S. MacNeish* [*]

INTRODUCTION

THIS article is an attempt at a synthesis of the aboriginal history of the Northeast from earliest prehistoric times until the contact period (or the period of the arrival of European articles). The area here called the Northeast consists of New York State, northern New Jersey, and the New England States. This region has been divided into a number of subareas which are:

1. Central and northern New York.
2. The Hudson River Valley of New York, northern New Jersey, and coastal New York and Connecticut.
3. Rhode Island and eastern Massachusetts.
4. Coastal New Hampshire and Maine.

Justification for subdividing the Northeast in this manner is due in part to the distribution of cultures at historic time and to the natural areas. It will, of course, be apparent that "culture areas" have changed frequently during prehistoric times. When it is pertinent to the particular subject, reference will be made to data from the unexplored areas of the Northeast, as well as to such surrounding regions as the Susquehanna and Delaware drainages, northern Ohio, northeastern Pennsylvania, Ontario, and the St. Lawrence River Valley.

The prehistoric and early historic periods of each subarea have been divided into a number of temporal horizons. These periods are (from early to late) Archaic, Early Woodland, Middle Woodland, Late Woodland, and Final Woodland.[1] In many of the subareas the material warrants subdividing these major periods. The subdivisions will be marked by Arabic numerals. A problem concerning the temporal periods of the Northeast arises from the fact that some of the subareas show definite cultural lag. Occurrences of this lag will be noted.

In studying the materials of the Northeast, I have attempted to employ the "Direct Historic Method." One's archeological or analytical approach is governed by the problem or the available facts. In New York the ethno-historical field has been lucrative, and archeological sites of numerous tribal groups can be readily identified. Therefore, the first step in my study was to link a certain material culture with a tribal group. With this as a starting point I endeavored to trace the histories of each tribe back into the prehistoric. Such tracing was done by comparison of the traits of historic and prehistoric sites as well as the establishment of trends in ceramics, pipes, combs, and projectile points from historic to prehistoric times. Since these articles present summaries of the prehistories of various areas, I shall present only the conclusions of my study and shall leave the proof of these conclusions to a future publication. Also, I shall present the sequence of culture from the earliest to historic times for each area and, wherever possible, point out the development of culture of the various tribal groups. This sequence of presentation of data is done so that my paper shall conform to the other articles even though it de-emphasizes the developmental differentiation and identification of the material culture of tribal groups in the Northeast.[2]

[*] University of Chicago, 1940, B.A.; 1944, M.A.; 1948, Ph.D.; National Museum of Canada, 1949——. Chapter received October, 1949; reduced by one-third, January, 1951.

1. These time-markers agree with the general periods presented in the other articles of this volume, except the last one, which I have called Final Woodland (not Late Mississippi). I believe this change is justified in that there are none of the basic Mississippi pattern traits in this area in the final period (such as truncated pyramids, plaza arrangement of villages, villages in river bottoms, wall trench houses, extended burials, burials with large amounts of burial furniture, "buzzard cult" materials, shell-tempered pottery, pottery with handles, pottery vessel forms such as bowls, bottles, plates, and ollas, native copper ornaments, shell ornaments, and cradleboard occipital deformation).

2. I should like to explain that this article is based upon my observations of materials in numerous collections and museums, gleanings from the literature concerning sites of this area, and information obtained from individuals familiar with the sites and material culture of the Indians of the region. The factual data pertaining to the artifacts under consideration in this study are almost entirely the contribution of individuals other than myself; the interpretations for the most part are my own, and no one else can be held directly accountable for them. In every case of the mention of a site or an object from a site, I shall attempt to mention the individual who so generously allowed me the privilege of examining his materials. Since I have examined over three hundred site collections, belonging to more than a hundred individuals or institutions, it is impossible to mention the collections from the various sites along with the individual owners in this brief introduction. I wish to express my gratitude to them collectively and individually. Special thanks are due to Dr. William A. Ritchie, who so generously gave his time and energy in helping me carry on this work and allowed me to examine and analyze the materials in the Rochester Museum. He also directed me to other individuals who had pertinent materials. The bulk of the material presented in this paper is in agreement with his earlier paper, and most of the major

CENTRAL AND NORTHERN NEW YORK SUB-AREA
ARCHAIC PERIOD

Perhaps the earliest evidence of man in this area are those mentioned by Parker in the Ripley Site report.[3] He indicates that in the swamps along Lake Erie near the Ripley Site, fire hearths and fire-cracked rocks have been found supposedly in the same deposits as mammoth bones. Folsom-like points and large weathered argillite points found in western New York have also been thought of as having considerable antiquity.[4] However, proof of the presence of early man in this area (and of the entire northeast) is still lacking. So far, the earliest evidences of human culture are to be found in the pre-ceramic foci—Lamoka, Frontenac, and Brewerton. These cultures are not only nonagricultural and nonceramic, but all have been found stratigraphically below early ceramic types. Fortunately, stratigraphic data are such that the Lamoka, Frontenac, and Brewerton foci can be arranged in chronological order and something can be said concerning the genetic relationships of the three. At the Lamoka Lake Site, Brewerton Focus artifacts appear near the top of the midden and above most of the Lamoka Focus materials (as well as under Vinette 1 pottery).[5] Since the Frontenac Culture has traits of both Brewerton and Lamoka Lake, it is thought of by Ritchie as being chronologically between the Brewerton Focus and the Lamoka Focus.[6]

Thus, the earliest peoples in western New York of whom there is good evidence are represented in the Lamoka Focus (Fig. 12).[7] The main components of this focus are in western New York at Geneva, Scottsville, and Lamoka Lake,[8] though some Lamoka artifacts were found in the lower levels of the Vinette site. Distinctive traits of this focus are narrow stemmed points, beveled adzes, plano-convex adzes, heavy grinding implements, and a wide variety of bone implements including awls made from many kinds of animal bones, double-pointed pins, gorges, scapula scrapers, pierced bone weaving tools, bone whistles, pierced bone awls, deer ulna knives, notched antler pendant-like artifacts, and bone daggers. Various authors have pointed out the relationship of this

focus with those of the shell-mound people in the central part of the United States,[9] and a fairly large number of specific resemblance occur with the McCain site in Dubois County, Indiana,[10] as well as in the lower levels of the Annis Mound in Butler County, Kentucky.[11]

As has been stated previously, the Frontenac Focus has been designated, on typological grounds, as chronologically between the stratified Brewerton and Lamoka foci (Fig. 13).[12] The Frontenac shares with the Lamoka Focus the narrow-bladed stemmed and side-notched points, the beveled adze, the chopper, antler pendants, and the notched pendant-like objects, as well as sixty-two other more general traits. It is linked with the Brewerton Focus by such traits as broad-bladed stemmed and side-notched points, plummets, bannerstones, unilaterial single barb harpoons with a line hole, gouges, copper awls, and ground slate artifacts, as well as other more general traits. The physical type also reveals a mixture of dolichocephals (of the Lamoka type) with brachycephals (of the Brewerton Focus). In spite of the great mixture of Lamoka and Brewerton foci traits in Frontenac, it does have some differentiating elements, such as round and elongated pendants of shell, receptacles of shell, bird effigy combs, bone whistles of new types, ground wolf mandibles, perforated elk and bear teeth, and unilateral multi-barbed, bilateral multi-barbed, and unilateral single-barbed harpoons. Interpretation of the Frontenac as an early Brewerton Focus which has moved into western New York, amalgamating with and replacing the Lamoka people both physically and culturally, appears possible. However, the occurrence of its many distinctive traits such as the harpoons that somewhat resemble Point Peninsula and the comb that resembles Iroquois do not strengthen the above hypothesis. Certainly study of more components of this culture are necessary before much can be said as to where it came from or to where it went.

One of the final Archaic cultures, the Brewerton Focus (Fig. 14), is represented by the Smoky Hollow components in western New York[13] and in central New York at Brewerton at the Oberlander, Robinson, and Vinette sites.[14] At the Oberlander and Robinson sites pre-pottery remains were found under a thin top layer of Vinette I and II and exterior cord-marked sherds. The artifact complexes of the two nonceramic manifestations were sufficiently similar to warrant placing them in the Brewerton Focus.[15]

points have been discussed with him. Thanks are also due to Dr. James B. Griffin, of the Museum of Anthropology of the University of Michigan, who instigated this survey, and to the Indiana Historical Society which financially assisted it. I also should like to express my gratitude to three individuals who unknowingly contributed to the methodology employed in this survey: Dr. Waldo Wedel, Dr. James Ford, and Dr. Fay-Cooper Cole.

3. Parker, 1907.
4. Ritchie, 1944, pp. 310–313.
5. This statement is based upon observations of the material from Lamoka in the Rochester Museum.
6. Ritchie, 1945.
7. Ritchie, 1944, pp. 292–310.
8. Ritchie, 1932, 1936.

9. Ritchie, 1944; Webb and Haag, 1940.
10. Miller, 1941.
11. Webb, W. S., 1950.
12. Ritchie, 1944, p. 229; 1945.
13. Ritchie, 1944.
14. Ritchie, 1940; 1944.
15. The upper levels of Robinson and Oberlander I sites have Vinette I exterior cord-marked and Vinette II pottery along with a

The Brewerton Focus is characterized by winged bannerstones; plummets; copper awls, gorges and adzes; thick, broad-bladed, notched, and stemmed projectile points; eared notched points and eared triangular points; choppers; gouges; plano-convex adzes; celts; curved-eyed needles; perforated weaving tools; crescentic chert end scrapers; conical antler points; bone spear points; and beaver incisor cutting tools.[16]

Of perhaps wider implication are the ulos and ground slate points that point to affiliations with the north.[17] In fact, many items of this culture show similarities to other cultures in the Northeast, such as the so-called Vergennes Focus, the Vosburg Focus, the Blue Hill Focus, and early materials in New Jersey and Pennsylvania.[18] Spaulding has interpreted the occurrence of some of the artifacts of this culture as indicating linkage with earlier circumpolar cultures of the Old World.[19] A series of sites without pottery and similar in their projectile point complex as well as in many other items of their culture to that of the Brewerton and Vosburg foci extending westward across Ontario toward Manitoba tend to confirm such a hypothesis.

In northern New York the Vosburg Focus appears to be about contemporaneous and related to the Brewerton Focus.[20] The components of the Vosburg Focus are the Fitch Site, near Glenn Falls, New York; the Round Lake and the Manning sites near Saratoga Lake, New York; the Vosburg and Covered Bridge sites near Guilderland, New York; the Dunsback Ferry Site near Dunsback Ferry, New York; and the Clapper Site near Glenville, New York. Characteristic of this focus are steatite; short broad gouges; plano-convex adzes; celt-like scrapers; pitted stones; ground arrow-shaft rubbers; single grooved sinew-stones; plummets; anvilstones; choppers; banner-stones; triangular, oval and oval notched scrapers; drills; stemmed, side- and corner-notched, semilozenge, triangular with straight or concaved-based projectile points; and ulos of ground slate.[21]

Generally speaking, this area has as its first occupancy semi-sedentary food-gathering peoples (Lamoka Focus) related in physical type and culture to the early Kentucky shell-mound groups (and very possibly derived from them) who are later superseded by brachycephalic semi-sedentary food-gathering groups (Brewerton and Vosburg foci) who appear to have invaded the area from Canada. No pre-pottery manifestation in the area can be shown to be definitely related to the Early Woodland period. This remains one of the major problems.

EARLY WOODLAND PERIOD

Two foci—Middlesex and Point Peninsula I–appear to be of the Early Woodland Period. The Middlesex Focus is placed in this time period because of its similarities with Adena (Fig. 15). Some of the more important similarities are: flexed, cremated, and bundle burials, powdered hematite over the burials, willowleaf-shaped knives with a notched or truncated base, blocked-end tubes, cache blades, discoidal shell beads, rolled tubular copper beads, copper awls square in cross-section, and the heavy grit-tempered pottery cord-marked on the interior and exterior (called Vinette I in New York and Fayette Thick in Ohio and Kentucky). Distinctive elements of Middlesex are to be found in the bolas stones, willowleaf knife, bone gouge, boatstones, and the pentagonal gorget.[22] Unfortunately, much of our knowledge of Middlesex is drawn from a few burial sites, most of which have not been professionally excavated. Therefore, any conclusions as to the history of this culture must await further data. Nevertheless, the similarities with Adena certainly hint a possible derivation from that direction (or vice versa).

Evidently at the same time or just slightly later than Middlesex, the earliest Point Peninsula people were moving into New York (Fig. 16). At present only two stations of this stage are known, the lower levels of the Vinette Site[23] and the burial site at Cuylerville, New York.[24] Though our data are sparse, certain tentative conclusions can be drawn. Typical of Point Peninsula I is Vinette I pottery. Stratigraphically Vinette I pottery (as well as diagnostic Point Peninsula I traits) are found under Vinette I and II of Point Peninsula II at the Vinette site.[25] As stated

---

Brewerton Focus artifact complex. At the Vinette site, the Vinette I pottery types precede the Vinette II and exterior cord-marked types, though some Vinette I is still present for a time. Therefore, two interpretations are possible concerning the pottery found in the Brewerton Focus—either this pottery was that of a short Point Peninsula occupation that injected (via indistinguishable pits, etc.) a small scattering of sherds into the upper level pre-pottery deposits of Oberlander and Robinson sites; or there is a continuous development of the Brewerton Focus from pre-pottery, through a dominantly Vinette I stage to a Vinette II stage that is not apparent in the other materials. Dr. Ritchie and I now prefer the former interpretation until more data are available (see Ritchie, 1940, p. 85).

16. Ritchie, 1944.
17. Spaulding, 1946; de Laguna, 1946.
18. Ritchie, 1944.
19. Spaulding, 1946.
20. A Vergennes Focus has been established in the Champlain area. The materials from the type site, however, reveal considerable heterogeneity, since there are Owasco and Point Peninsula artifacts and pottery types as well as Brewerton-like artifacts. Therefore, I consider this to be a mixed site some of which may have belonged to a separate focus that might be called Vergennes. However, one must await clear evidence and definition for such a complex.

21. Ritchie, 1940; 1944.
22. Ritchie, 1940.
23. Ritchie, 1944, p. 187.
24. I should like to thank Mr. Robert Hill of Rochester, New York, for the privilege of examining the material he carefully excavated from this key site.
25. Ritchie, 1944; Ritchie and MacNeish, 1949.

before, this interior-exterior cord-marked pottery is like that in the Adena of Early Woodland. Therefore Point Peninsula I is probably of Early Woodland time and certainly earlier than Point Peninsula II of Middle Woodland time. Traits of this latter culture include contracting stemmed, thin, semilozenge, broad side-notched and corner-notched points; thin cache blades; barrel shaped copper beads with punched holes; elongated round-ended gorgets; extended burials in pits covered with red ocher; and Vinette I pottery. This Point Peninsula culture in its earlier stages shows more resemblance to Adena than to Hopewell, but in its later stages Point Peninsula certainly becomes very Hopewell-like. Similarity of traits and ceramics as well as stratigraphy indicate Point Peninsula I as ancestral to Point Peninsula II and ultimately Point Peninsula III. As I shall point out, there are indications that Point Peninsula III is ancestral to Owasco and that some Owasco is ancestral to some Iroquois groups. In other words there is some evidence for culture continuity from Early Woodland through Point Peninsula I to historic Iroquois. Thus the proto-Iroquois may have entered New York bearing a Point Peninsula I culture in Early Woodland time. The origins of Point Peninsula I are at present unknown. What evidence we do have is negative, namely, that few resemblances to Point Peninsula I are found in the east and south, so Point Peninsula may have come from some unknown culture to the north (or west?).

MIDDLE WOODLAND

The New York Focus of Hopewell is found mainly in the Western New York subarea. Seven components of this focus have been discovered and are: Kane, Liddydyke, Murray Hill, Squawkie Hill, Geneseo, Bamber, and Kipp Island mounds.[26] The pottery from these sites is of Vinette I and Geneseo Cord Marked types (except for one pot of Vinette II type found in the Geneseo mound) and certainly suggests a Middle Woodland I temporal position, as do the semilozenge points, effigy platform pipes, broad-stemmed round-based points, pearl beads, flat copper celts, cremations, broad side-notched points, and long ellipsoidal gorgets. Rude thick cache blades, straight- and concave-based triangular points, and platform pipes suggest a contemporaneity with the Point Peninsula III horizon but certainly do not outweigh the traits supporting the early Middle Woodland dating. The majority of the traits of this focus are also in the Point Peninsula Focus except for the eight diagnostic New York Hopewell traits: effigy platform pipes, pearl beads, burial mounds, copper ear plugs, copper breast ornaments, large conch containers, thin lanceolate and triangular

knives. Recent evidence from western Pennsylvania points to that area as a likely source of these mounds that are certainly intrusive in the New York area.[27]

Point Peninsula I of Early Woodland time is ancestral to Point Peninsula II. Sites of this latter stage are West Rush, Sea Breeze, Wickham, Oberlander 2, Pickins, the middle and upper levels of the Vinette Site, and the Muskalonge Lake Component.[28] Certain traits diagnostic of this time period are as follows: Vinette I, Vinette II and exterior cord-marked pottery; thin semilozenge, turkey-tailed, broad-stemmed, broad side-notched with expanded bases or round ends, and double side-notched projectile points; clay tubular pipes; trapezoidal convex-topped rectangular broad gorgets, birdstones of two types (bar and broad base with transversal ridges), narrow rectangular round-ended gorgets, thin elongated objects of slate, flat copper celts, cylindrical beads of rolled sheet copper, polished perforated-base splinter awls, sinew-stones of the ovoid flat pebble type, expanded-base drills with scraper edge, cremations (both single and multiple), and bundle burials. There is a great predominance of thin triangular cache blades over the thick, crude type.

Many of the traits of the Point Peninsula II complex are in Adena (as well as in Hopewell), and I have therefore placed this complex in the early part of the Middle Woodland period. Certainly it includes all the traits in the poorly defined Point Peninsula I, as well as the notable addition of Vinette II pottery. This type of pottery seems to have been added to an already existing Point Peninsula I complex. Dr. J. B. Griffin has pointed out the affinities of this pottery to Illinois Hopewell.[29] These suggested affinities appear to me to be of a very general nature.

The components in the Western New York subarea that appear to belong to Point Peninsula III time are Kipp Island, Jack's Reef burial and middens 1 and 2, the Avon (Durkee) Site, and perhaps the Fall Brook Site (and in other areas the Point Peninsula Site, the Northrop Site, Port Maitland Site, and perhaps the Rene Menard Bridge No. 1, and Bay of Quinte sites).[30] Characteristic traits of this stage are the presence of isosceles points with V-shaped bases, equilateral triangular points with straight bases, pentagon-shaped points, corner-notched points with angular edges, and a greater frequency of equilateral triangular points with concave bases; stone platform pipes of the curved-based and straight-based varieties, stone and clay pipes with the bowl and stem at obtuse (rarely right) angles, and cigar-shaped pipes of polished slate; numerous large rough cache blades (as against a minority of thin triangular ones), seed-

26. Ritchie, 1944; 1938a.

27. Carpenter, n.d.
28. Ritchie, 1944.
29. Ritchie, 1944, p. 166; Ritchie, 1946, p. 17.
30. Ritchie, 1944.

shaped gaming stones, large elaborate combs, shell columella beads of numerous varieties, fishhooks with knobbed shanks and barbs, antler wedges, bar amulets, harpoons of the unilateral and multi-barbed types, bone gorgets, antler flakers large and cylindrical, deer scapula scrapers, large ovate knives, serrated-end bone tubes, shark teeth pendants, straight drills, graves lined with mica, fire pits associated with burials containing grave goods and Vinette II pottery along with pottery decorated with a corded paddle edge similar to Canandaigua pottery.

It is interesting to note that this stage of Point Peninsula bears resemblance to the Hopewell of Ohio and to the post-Hopewellian Intrusive Mound Culture found at Mound City.[31] Tentatively, it may be temporally equated with Middle and Late Ohio Hopewell and the just post-Hopewellian horizon of that region.[32] In other words, Point Peninsula III occupies the middle and late parts of the Middle Woodland period. Many of the diagnostic traits of Hopewell which are present in New York only in Point Peninsula III (such as platform pipes, mica-lined graves, bar amulets, shell beads, etc.)[33] appear to have been grafted onto an already existing Point Peninsula II complex. Whether these increments came from Ohio or from New York Hopewell or from some poorly defined Hopewell center in Ontario, Canada, is yet to be established.

However, perhaps even more important than what influences affected Point Peninsula III is the question of what happened to this manifestation. Ceramic linkage between the Canandaigua Focus and Point Peninsula are numerous[34] and, furthermore, Dr. Ritchie has often pointed out the many link traits between the two manifestations in question.[35] Thus it would appear that there is much cultural continuity from Point Peninsula III to the Canandaigua Focus, except in the elaborate mortuary complex which is absent in the latter. This loss of an elaborate ceremonial complex (often Hopewell or Hopewell-like) by a group has many parallels in other parts of the eastern United States.[36] However, in New York it may have had special significance. For in the period following this loss of a mortuary ceremonialism (religious institution?) of Middle Woodland, there is considerably more cultural variation (in Owasco foci and components) than in the ancestral Point Peninsula III, though there were already many marked variations from site to site. I have interpreted this as meaning that earlier or proto-Iroquois (Point

Peninsula), with the loss of the cohesive, conservative force of a ceremonial or religious nature, began to change during Late Woodland time into what became the tribal units (or historic foci). Considerably more work is necessary to test the above hypothesis.

LATE WOODLAND

For this time period we have a more complete picture of the way of life of the people.

Villages are larger in size and placed in defensible positions. Often they were surrounded by palisades and moats. Tribal warfare was evidently of some importance. The people appear to have been agriculturalists growing corn, beans, and possibly squash, supplementing their diet with hunting and fishing. Projectile points, generally speaking, are triangular with variations in proportions. A variety of bone tools were used. Pipes were widely used and were of various elbow forms. The dead were flexed and buried in refuse pits and graves in cemetery areas with few if any grave goods. This way of life appears to have continued until historic time.

At present the materials of this period are classified into two foci, the Castle Creek and Canandaigua of the Owasco Aspect (Fig. 18). The Canandaigua Focus is composed of the following components: Sackett Farm, Levanna, St. Helena, Fall Brook, Klink, Rapp, Waneta, Owasco Lake, Carpenter Brook, and Wickham. Characteristics of the focus are: broad, triangular, isosceles points with straight or concave bases; strike-a-lights; drills; rectanguloid celts; incised stones; split bone awls of numerous varieties; small cylindrical antler flakers; multiple-bilateral barbed harpoons; awls with incised designs; spoons made from animal skulls; tubular shell beads; obtuse-angle elbow pipes decorated by stamping; and a distinctive ceramic complex.[37]

Components of the Castle Creek Focus are spread over a wide area and were found at a site at Athens, Pennsylvania; the two Willow Point sites in Broome County, New York; the Castle Creek Site in Broome County, New York; the Damascus Site in Broome County, New York; the Bell-Philhower Site in New Jersey near Port Jervis, New York; the Bainbridge Site in Chenango County, New York; and the Headquarters Site on Lake Champlain.[38] Distinctive of this focus are thin sandstone disks with smooth or notched edges; wide and narrow-based isosceles triangular points; arrowpoints from the terminal phalanx of a deer; three-tooth combs; human skull pendants; pendants from deer epiphyses; utensils made from box-turtle shell; grooved, split, and pierced bear canines; bone pins decorated by notching, incising, or carved heads; bone spatulas; sinewstones; and a distinctive pottery complex.

31. Mills, 1922a, pp. 572–584.
32. Ritchie, 1944, pp. 117–118; cf. 1937.
33. Cole and Deuel, 1937.
34. Ritchie and MacNeish, 1949, pp. 120–121.
35. Ritchie, 1944, p. 52.
36. Marksville to Troyville in Louisiana and Ogden Fettie Focus to Weaver Focus in Illinois and Candy Creek to Hamilton Focus on the Tennessee River.

37. Ritchie, 1944.   38. Ritchie, 1944.

However, it is now becoming apparent that on this time level there are other cultural grouping (foci?) closely related to the Owasco foci and in the same general area. Overpeck II of northern New Jersey, the Snell Site from Montgomery County, New York, the Pillar Point and the Calkins farms from Jefferson County, New York, and the Goessins, Krieger, and other sites in southern Ontario appear to compose at least four other related groupings. All four are still too poorly defined to warrant description in this brief summary.

Perhaps even more important than the static classification of the various components of this time level has been the recognition of a series of developing sequences within this time period and within Owasco. The recognition is based upon a study of the ceramic seriation and trends of the various components.

One of these developments seems to be from Wickham to Castle Creek to Bainbridge. Ceramics indicate such to be possible, and artifact trends appear to confirm the ceramic trends. Furthermore, the final stage of these sequences, Bainbridge, is very similar to Iroquoian remains and specifically to early Mohawk. Carpenter Brook to Levanna to Sackett Farm to the Hummel Site seem to represent another development. The final site of this sequence previously undescribed needs further comment.

The site is located on a hill on the Hummel farm just north of Bristol Center, Ontario County, New York.[39] The pipes from this site are mainly Iroquoian-looking like those from Richmond Mills though having a few Owasco features. Decoration of pottery is the Owascoid cord-wrapped stick but it is on vessel shapes specifically Iroquoian like those of Richmond Mills. Projectile points are both Owasco and Iroquois in type.

Thus in the Late Woodland period of upper New York it would appear that there are at least three regional developing series, all getting gradually more and more Iroquoian.

FINAL WOODLAND

The Final Woodland period of most of New York is characterized by the presence of the remains of the Iroquois. The general way of life and many of the actual artifacts are closely similar to those of the former period (Figs. 19 and 20). However, the elbow pipe in a wide variety of forms, ornate bone combs, the narrow-based isosceles projectile point, single unilateral harpoon with a square base, small pottery celts and ceramics characterized by globular bodies, incised decoration on collar, castellations and smooth surface finish make it distinguishable from other remains. Different types of the above diagnostic arti-

facts as well as differences in occurrences or absences of the more general traits make it possible to delineate various artifacts assemblages. In many cases it is possible to connect these assemblages with artifact complexes found on sites which can be identified as historic tribal villages.

In central and northeastern New York are to be found components of the Chance Focus which are: the Weaver Lake Site near Cooperstown, New York, the Chance Site in Schoharie County, New York,[40] the upper levels of the site just above Fort Plain (Oak Hill),[41] the second Woods Site near by,[42] the upper levels of the Chipman's Point Rock Shelter near Fort Ticonderoga,[43] the Goodyear Lake site near Oneonta, New York,[44] and a site near Baldwinsville in Onondaga County, New York.[45] None of these have produced a large cultural inventory but on each early Mohawk pottery types are in association with Owascoid or Owasco pottery types, as well as Iroquois and Owasco projectile points. Some of the pipes found have both Iroquois and Owasco features, and some of the artifacts are like those of the Castle Creek Focus. Though the evidence is far from conclusive it rather appears that the Chance Focus may have evolved from a Bainbridge-like culture of the Wickham–Castle Creek–Bainbridge Owasco development in the general area between Binghamton and Corning, New York. Ceramic trends and pottery seriation indicate that the Fonda Focus (Mohawk) developed from the Chance Focus.

On the basis of ceramic trends the Fonda Focus follows the Chance Focus. At present the former focus is composed of six components: the prehistoric Garoga,[46] Cayadutta,[47] and Otstungo sites[48] and the historic Mohawk sites, Martin,[49] Wagoner's Hollow,[50] and Rice Woods.[51] Sixty-one per cent of the traits (ex-

39. I am indebted to Mr. Harry Schoff and Mr. J. Hummel for their assistance in working at this site.

40. Ritchie, personal communication and from the Van Epps–Hartley Chapter.

41. I would like to thank members of the Van Epps–Hartley Chapter for allowing me to study these materials.

42. Ritchie, personal communication.

43. Bailey, 1940.

44. Materials from this site are in the Yaegar Collection of Oneonta, New York, and in the Ceramic Repository of the University of Michigan.

45. I would like to thank Mr. Stanley Gifford of Syracuse, New York, for allowing me to see his materials from this site.

46. In the collections of the Peabody Museum of Harvard and excavated by Harrington in 1905.

47. I should like to thank the Rochester Museum, the Van Epps–Hartley Chapter and Mr. Naylon of the Chapter, for the use of their materials.

48. I am grateful to the Van Epps–Hartley Chapter, Mr. Naylon, and the New York State Historical Society of Cooperstown for data from this site.

49. These materials are in the collections of the Van Epps–Hartley Chapter.

50. I am indebted to Mr. Lenig, of the Van Epps–Hartley Chapter, and the New York State Historical Society, for their cooperation in studying the artifacts from this site.

51. Mr. Naylon and the New York State Historical Society generously allowed me to analyze their materials from this site.

cluding pottery and pipes) of the Fonda Focus are held in common with Castle Creek.[52] Significantly distinctive traits of the Fonda Focus are: decorated phalanx tinklers; incised, notched, or carved headed bone awls; tubular bone pottery markers; wolf tooth beads; stone and pottery disks; squared netsinkers; grooved bear teeth; turtle shell scoops and dishes; long bone pins; effigy combs; a few pipe types; and the ceramic complex. Mohawk pottery is characterized by two kinds of ware: a series of types having well-pronounced high collars decorated with incised opposed triangulars often separated by a series of parallel lines and a type with thickened lips decorated with incising on surfaces and notched at the edges. Most Mohawk pottery is grit-tempered and smooth surfaced, and vessels have globular bodies.

In the general area of Broome and Delaware counties, New York, northern New Jersey, and northeastern-most Pennsylvania, the ethnohistorians have placed the Munsee. The largest documented village of the Munsee appears to be on and adjacent to Minisink Island.[53] In 1914, Heye and Pepper excavated a large portion of this site and uncovered early historic goods, presumably in association with aboriginal Munsee material.[54] From their collections it is not possible to determine exactly which native remains occurred with European trade objects. Therefore, in 1947 Dr. Ritchie conducted further excavation at this site.[55] During these last excavations on the Bell-Philhower farms, a large number of pits were uncovered which belong to three components. Typologically it is possible to arrange these pits in chronological order. The "earliest" pits contained Castle Creek pottery; the intermediary pits contained pottery called Castle Creek Epigonous, which is similar to that of the Chance Focus and Clasons Point I (of the New York City area); while the "latest" pits contained most of the Fonda Focus ceramic types. (The Mohawk thickened-lip type was absent.) Thus it seems probable that the Munsee had developed a Mohawk-like culture from a Castle Creek or a Clasons Point base, probably the latter.

While on the subject of the Munsee, it seems appropriate to touch upon their linguistic, political, and spatial relatives, the Unami. In 1947, John Witthoft and the author excavated two sites south of Easton, Pennsylvania, on the Delaware River.[56] The Diehl Site had a material culture similar to the Fonda Focus and contained European objects in rather poor association with the aboriginal materials. This site also agrees in a general way with the location of the historic Unami village near Durham, Pennsylvania. This site at Diehl's belongs to Final Woodland. At the Overpeck Site the top materials were closely similar to the Diehl Site in displaying a Fonda Focus–like trait complex but lacked historic goods and therefore are in the early part of the Final Woodland period. Underlying these materials was Overpeck II, which is provisionally considered to be of Late Woodland times. The complex included Owasco and isosceles triangular points and pottery of the Overpeck Complicated Incised type. Mr. Witthoft believes it ties with the Abbott Farm sequence and is in no way genetically related to the Castle Creek–Fonda Focus sequence farther north. Final publication should illustrate this more graphically than I can. Overpeck I was a single pit containing Vinette I sherds and a fish-tailed point.

In north central New York and the adjacent area of Canada are to be found Iroquois sites having pottery that appears to connect with the Pillar Point–Calkins–Ivey Owascoid sites. The largest of these sites is near Lanorie, Quebec and may in the future be the basis of a Lanorie Focus. Characteristic of this site are sherds with Onondaga-Oneida designs done by dentate stamping or the edge of a cord-wrapped paddle (or stick?). Projectile points are both Iroquoian and Owasco, while pipes exhibit features of both.

Following, and possibly developing from, this earlier culture type are the components of the Madison Focus. The components of this focus are: the prehistoric Roebuck Site in Ontario,[57] the prehistoric Hochelaga Site in Montreal,[58] the prehistoric Durfee Site near Watertown,[59] the prehistoric Atwell Fort Site south of Syracuse,[60] the prehistoric Nichols Pond Site in Madison County, New York,[61] the historic Onondaga sites of Indian Hill and Pompey Center near Manlius, New York,[62] and the historic Oneida sites of Thurston and Quarry (Munnsville) in Madison County.[63] Characteristic traits of this focus are unilateral single- and multiple-barbed harpoons, and bilateral multiple-barbed harpoons with a single hole in the shaft, conical antler points some of which are pierced, skull gorgets, tinklers made from a split phalanx, bone projectile points, flat bone dolls, and num-

52. A comprehensive list will be presented in MacNeish's forthcoming article on the Iroquois.

53. Heye and Pepper, 1915.

54. *Ibid.*

55. Ritchie, 1949a.

56. See John Witthoft's unpublished report in the files of the University of Michigan.

57. Wintemberg, 1936.

58. I should like to thank Dr. Douglas Leechman of the National Museum of Canada for allowing me to read Mr. Wintemberg's manuscript on Hochelaga.

59. Materials are in Peabody Museum of Harvard.

60. Materials are in the Rochester Museum and the Warder Collection of Geneva.

61. Materials are in the Lothrop Museum of Colgate University, Hamilton, New York.

62. I should like to thank Mr. Haberle, of Syracuse, New York, for allowing me to see his collection from those sites.

63. I should like to thank Mr. H. Bigford, of Earlville, New York, and Mr. Thurston, of Oneida, New York, for permission to study their materials.

erous distinctive comb, pipe, and pottery types (see illustration for some of these types).[64] On the basis of the present evidence it has been impossible to distinguish materials from historic Oneida and Onondaga sites.

It has been previously indicated that the Richmond Mills Focus might have developed out of the Hummel Site (or focus). The Richmond Mills Focus has seven components: Richmond Mills,[65] Dansville Fort,[66] California Ranch,[67] the Belcher Site,[68] the Le Roy Site,[69] and the Locke Site.[70] Characteristic of this focus are: unilateral barbed harpoons, bilateral multi-barbed harpoons, bone pottery markers, basically pierced bone awls, bone projectile points, three-toothed antler combs, conical antler points with or without a single tang, short-collared flaking tools, cut bear teeth pendants, shell artifacts, square-topped trumpet pipes, cone-shaped pipes, helmet-faced trumpet pipes, potsherd discs pierced or unpierced, and distinctive pottery types.

The Richmond Mills Focus appears to have been directly ancestral to the Genoa Fort Focus composed of Genoa Fort and Myer's Station components.[71] Almost all of the Richmond Mills diagnostic traits are to be found in this focus in addition to historic goods, antler combs, the pregnant effigy bone dolls, foot-shaped pendant made of a bear molar, effigy pipes, ring bowl pipes, and three new pottery types. Shell artifacts and potsherd discs are absent from this focus. A comparison of the few artifacts I was able to examine from the Great Gully Site with those of Genoa Fort Focus reveals the two complexes as being almost identical. The Great Gully Site is a Cayuga village of 1688.[72]

Just what is ancestral to the Seneca is unknown. Ceramic trends indicate the possibility that it, like the Cayuga, may have developed from the Owascoid-Carpenter-Brook-Levanna-Canandaigua-Hummel sequence; however, confirmation is lacking. The earliest Seneca materials so far discovered compose the West Sparta Focus.

The West Sparta Focus is composed of the Portageville, Fall Brook, and Dansville Flats components.[73] The presence of cut human jaws, human skull pendants, wide and narrow based isosceles points, large tubular beads, beads from phalanges which have notched sides, foot-shaped bear molar pendants, and short cylindrical antler flakers is considered to be diagnostic traits of the focus. Perhaps of equal distinction are the pipe and pottery complexes. Flaring bowl trumpet, ring bowl trumpet, reel-shaped bowl, and barrel-shaped bowl pipes are very common. The pottery is characterized by cord-marked, grooved paddle, check stamped, or smooth surface finish. Decoration consists of cord-wrapped paddle edge, incising and dentate parallel lines on an incipient short collar often with notching at the base and top of an applied collar. Vessel forms include globular-bodied jars with narrow applied or incipient collar or no collar.

The Factory Hollow Focus, composed of the prehistoric Long Point Site[74] and the Factory Hollow,[75] Dutch Hollow,[76] Cornish,[77] and Warren historic[78] components is derived from the West Sparta Focus. Though the human jaw and skull pendants are absent, the majority of the traits carry over from the early focus. However, the presence of historic goods, the dominance of the ring-bowl pipes, the occurrence of distinguishing effigy pipes and the occurrence of new pottery types show some significant differences. The majority of the pottery has smooth surfaces, and may either have short collars with large diagonal basal notches or no collars but notched thickened lips. Bodies are globular.

64. Further details to be found in MacNeish's forthcoming report.

65. I am indebted to Dr. Ritchie of the Rochester Museum and to Joseph Quinlan of Dansville, New York, for allowing me to examine their materials from Richmond Mills.

66. I should like to thank G. N. Gessner of Dansville, New York, for the privilege of his materials from this site.

67. Rochester Museum and J. Quinlan, of Dansville, New York, have material from this site.

68. Rochester Museum, J. Quinlan, and Mr. Clair Carpenter of Canandaigua, New York, are to be thanked for the use of their materials.

69. Materials from this site is in the Harry Schoff Collection.

70. I am indebted to the Museum of the American Indian, Heye Foundation of New York City, for the use of their materials on this site.

71. I am here acknowledging the kindness of Mr. M. Cramer and the Cayuga County Historical Society of Auburn, New York; Rochester Museum; Mr. J. Quinlan of Dansville, New York; St. Bernard's Seminary of Rochester, New York; Mr. Thurston of Oneida, New York; Mr. C. Warder, Mr. Farwell, and Mr. Phillips of Geneva, New York; Mr. J. Ward of Cayuga, New York; Mr. H. Bigford of Earlville, New York; Mr. Harry Schoff of West Bloomfield, New York; and the New York State Historical Society of Cooperstown, New York, who so generously allowed me to study their collections from these sites.

72. Thwaites, (ed.), Vol. 51, p. 293.

73. I am grateful to: Mr. J. Quinlan, of Dansville, New York, for allowing me to examine his artifacts from the Portageville and Dansville Flats sites; to Mr. G. Gessner, of Dansville, New York, for the privilege of seeing his material from the Dansville Flats Site; and to Dr. W. A. Ritchie, of the Rochester Museum, for making available to me the materials from the Fall Brook Site.

74. I should like to acknowledge the co-operation and assistance of Mr. G. Wright, of Pittsford, in studying his carefully excavated materials from this site.

75. Monseigneur Goggin, of St. Bernard's Seminary of Rochester, Mr. Farwell and Mr. Phillip, of Geneva, Mr. Schoff, of West Bloomfield, and Mrs. Yaeger, of Oneonta, made available to me materials from this site.

76. I am indebted for information about this site to the following: Mr. R. Hill, of Rochester, A. Hoffman, of East Bloomfield, C. Carpenter, of Canandaigua, J. Quinlan, of Dansville, H. Schoff, and K. Pierce, of West Bloomfield, and to Dr. Ritchie, of the Rochester Museum.

77. This material is derived from the collection of Carpenter, Hamlin, Pierce, and Hoffman.

78. Messrs. Pierce, Farwell, Wray, Schoff, and Hamlin, and the American Museum of Natural History are thanked for the use of their materials.

Various authors have noted that there appears to be a dual division of the Seneca.[79] Houghton has hypothesized that one of the divisions developed similar to the above described Seneca sequence while the other developed from Richmond Mills.[80] The historic Steele Site[81] situated in the center of the Seneca area does resemble Richmond Mills (while the other sites mentioned above do not) and may represent such a derivation. Unfortunately a large sample of materials is not available, and other similar sites are unknown.

At the Kienuka Site near Lewiston, New York, Mr. R. McCarthy, Mr. A. Muller, and Dr. L. Pechuman have rather carefully excavated an ossuary and a village.[82] Both the ossuary and the upper levels of the village have historic goods in association with aboriginal materials. Since ossuaries ethnologically are reported for only the Neutral and Huron, since the materials from the site are similar to material excavated by Wintemberg in Neutral territory (and dissimilar to Huron materials),[83] and since the site is in the area which Beauchamp (based on Sansan's map of 1661 and other ethno-historical data) indicates was Neutral-Wenro territory,[84] I believe this is a historic Neutral site. Ceramically, the lower levels of the site are somewhat similar to the Middleport[85] Southwald, and Lawson material from Ontario.[86] However, materials are sparse, and more are necessary for correct temporal correlations of these levels. The historic component has yielded an ossuary, trumpet pipes, shell disks and tubular beads, conch shell gorgets(?), bird bone beads, narrow isosceles triangular projectile points, net-sinkers and distinctive Neutral pottery. The pottery has smooth and grooved paddle surface, globular bodies with a narrow vertical collar, a single pointed castellation, and decorations consisting of oblique lines or opposed oblique lines on the collar. Since no materials like those from the Uren site of Ontario,[87] thought by Wintemberg to be developmental or proto-Neutral, are present in western New York, it would seem that the Neutral-Wenro moved into New York from the peninsula area of Ontario during very late prehistoric times. The earlier Neutral development thus lies outside the scope of this paper.

Ethnologically the Erie occupied the Lake Erie region of western New York. However, like the Neutral, they were decimated by the League of the Iroquois at an early date,[88] and no documented villages have been found. In 1906, Parker,[89] and in 1904, Harrington,[90] excavated the Ripley village site at Ripley, Chautauqua County, New York. Here they found a distinctive material culture associated with European trade goods. It has been postulated that this site represents an Erie village. The artifact complex of this supposedly Erie village has been described at some length in the literature and is quite similar to that of the Neutral except for the pipes and pottery. The shapes and decoration of the pottery are somewhat similar to those of the Neutral, but the undecorated jars with or without collars and having a smooth or cord-marked surface finish are different. A developmental stage of this culture has been found at the prehistoric Goodyear Site near Buffalo, New York, by Miss Cummings, Miss Dickinson, and Miss White. These materials, though showing close resemblance to the Ripley site, show more resemblance to the Southwald site than does Ripley. I interpret this as indicating that the Neutral and Erie had separated at a time just previous to that of the Lawson Site occupation.

NORTHERN NEW JERSEY, HUDSON RIVER VALLEY, COASTAL NEW YORK, AND COASTAL CONNECTICUT

ARCHAIC PERIOD

Underneath the Clasons Point materials at the Finch Site, and under the Clasons Point and Bowmans Brook components at the Grantville Site, pre-pottery levels have been uncovered.[91] Sufficient materials have been found, I believe, to warrant the establishment of a Finch Focus. Projectile point types do show some overlapping with North Beach Focus as well as relationships with other pre-pottery horizons in the Northeast and to the Old Stone Culture of Labrador.[92] The projectile points include many Lamoka Lake forms as well as Brewerton, Vosburg, and Koens-Crispin forms. The lithic assemblage includes, besides projectile points, winged bannerstones, netsinkers, roller pestles, plummets, full-grooved axes, plano-convex adzes, asymmetrical knives, thumbnail scrapers, humpbacked scrapers, choppers, and flake scrapers.

EARLY WOODLAND

Just what culture is ancestral to the North Beach Focus is at present not demonstrated. However, Carlyle Smith is of the opinion that the pre-pottery com-

79. Fenton, 1940.
80. Houghton, 1922.
81. I should like to express my appreciation to Mr. Lester Bill and Mr. C. Carpenter, of Canandaigua, Mr. A. Hoffman, of West Bloomfield, Mrs. J. Hamlin, of West Bloomfield, and Mr. H. Schoff, of East Bloomfield, for allowing me to analyze their materials.
82. I am very grateful to these gentlemen for assisting me in studying these materials.
83. Wintemberg, 1928; 1939.
84. Beauchamp, 1900.
85. Wintemberg, 1948.
86. Wintemberg, 1939.
87. Wintemberg, 1928.

88. Fenton, 1940.
89. Parker, 1907.
90. I am indebted to Dr. Phillip Phillips, and Dr. D. Scott, of the Peabody Museum of Anthropology at Harvard University, Cambridge, Massachusetts, for making possible the study of these materials.
91. Smith, C. S., 1950.
92. Strong, 1930.

plex from the Grantville Site is a very likely prospect for this position. The North Beach Focus has been relegated to the Early Woodland because of its Vinette I pottery and Vosburg artifact similarities.

Manifestations of this focus in New York at North Beach, Matinecock Point, and Pelham Boulder sites and in Connecticut at the Basto and Eagle Hill sites. C. S. Smith believes the Orient Focus to be merely the burial complex of the North Beach Focus. Four Orient Focus components have been found near Orient, eastern Long Island.[93] Pottery is mainly Vinette I though sherds with interior and exterior brushing appear. Vessels are elongate with pointed bottoms with slightly flaring contracting rims. Projectile points are narrow stemmed, broad stemmed, narrow side-notched, broad side-notched, lozenge, semilozenge, fish-tailed, and broad corner notched. Other artifacts include three-quarter grooved ax, steatite vessels with side lugs, gorgets (Orient) bannerstones (Orient), chipped celts (Orient) and plano-convex adzes (Orient). The burial complex include large pits filled with cremated human bones, red ocher, artifacts, and occasionally bundle burials. The focus including the burial complex is somewhat reminiscent of the Middlesex Focus.

MIDDLE WOODLAND

Found at Throgs Neck, Dyckman Street, Clearview, and Manhasset Rock sites in New York, and at Eagle Hill in Connecticut are materials that have been assigned to the Clearview Focus. It appears to be derived from the North Beach Focus, and there are many overlapping traits. It has been assigned to the Middle Woodland period, since the Clearview Focus ceramics are suggestive of the Vinette II of Central New York, Middle Woodland times. The pottery is characterized by heavy interior channeling (like Vinette II) and is shell-tempered as well as having interior and exterior dentate stamping. Surface finishes include net impressions, cord-wrapped paddle-edge impressions, heavy cord marking, and scouring. A few sherds with incising are present. Vessel forms show the bases to be pointed and the rims vertical. Projectile points include large equilateral triangular forms with straight bases, lozenge-shaped points, pointed-based types, corner-removed pointed-stemmed types, narrow-stemmed, and side-notched types. Steatite vessels are in evidence, as are a number of heavy grinding tools. Winged bannerstones (or atlatl weights) and boatstones are said to occur.[94]

LATE WOODLAND

In the eastern part of the area Clearview materials develop into those of the Sebonac Focus. Ultimately these materials develop into the Niantic Focus, which has been identified as belonging to the Niantic tribe of central coastal Connecticut.

Sebonac sites are known from eastern Long Island at the Old Field, Aquebogue, Sebonac, and Squaw Cove sites. In Connecticut, Sebonac remains have been found at Old Lynne, East Windsor, Woodstock, Laurel Beach, and Pine Orchard Swamp components. Projectile points of this complex are large, equilateral triangular points of quartz as well as elongated, poorly defined stemmed points of quartz and corner-notched points. Steatite sherds, ground axes, and celts also belong to this complex.[95]

The ceramic decorations include wares with combed rectangular designs on the neck, wares with rows of deep, widely spaced punctations, wares with dentate and scallop shell stamping, wares with incised lines encircling the neck, and wares with cord-wrapped paddle-edge designs. Surface finish is cord-wrapped paddling, exterior scouring, combing, and overlapping impressions of a cord-wrapped paddle edge. Occasionally the inner surfaces of sherds are scoured. Tempering is of shell. At Old Lynne in the Sebonac section of this site, Bowmans Brook Incised and Castle Creek Punctate types are found as trade wares.[96]

In the western part of the area there appears to be an invasion of new peoples. These new peoples appear to be ancestral to the Wappinger, western Metoac, and some Delaware in the Hudson River Delta area. The resemblance of the materials of the Bowmans Brook Focus, the earliest manifestations of these invaders to those from the Abbott Farm and Overpeck II of south central New Jersey would seem to indicate that the homeland of the Bowmans Brook Focus was somewhere in south central New Jersey and southeast Pennsylvania.

The Bowmans Brook Focus is composed of materials from three components: the Bowmans Brook site of Staten Island and the Wilkins and Grantville B sites of western Long Island. The trait complex includes split bone awls of numerous varieties, turtle cups, deer phalanx tinklers, stone ovoid gorgets, and elbow pipes decorated with fine dentate stamping. Projectile points are for the most part convex-sided equilateral triangular points. A few stemmed points occur, as well as thin side-notched points. The dominant pottery is a stamped ware, Bowmans Brook Incised occurs (which is related to the Overpeck Complicated Incised ware in New Jersey), while secondary wares include cord-wrapped paddle sherds with neck plats, and horizontal ring decorations made by a cord-wrapped paddle-edge. Many sherds with an all-over cord-wrapped paddle surface are also present. Generally speaking, the pottery is more like that of the

93. Smith, C. S., 1950.   94. Ibid.   95. Ibid.   96. Ibid.

Canandaigua Focus than the Castle Creek Focus of central New York.[97]

Developing from the Bowmans Brook Focus is the Clasons Point Focus. The twelve components of the focus are distributed over the western portion of Long Island, Manhattan Island, Staten Island, and up along the Hudson River at least as far as Peekskill. Evidently the focus covers a considerable span of time from Late Woodland to the historic period. Therefore it has been divided into early and late divisions. The early division is the Late Woodland period and is characterized by Bowmans Brook Incised wares, a series characterized by collars and decorations by a corded paddle-edge and scallop shell edges, in Mohawk designs and outflaring jars with horizontal corded paddle-edge decorations. The tempering is usually of grit, though shell occurs, and the surface of sherds show cord marking. Generally speaking, the pottery resembles that of the Castle Creek Focus of central New York and is extremely similar to that of the Castle Creek-Epigonous stage at Bell-Philhower Site in northwestern New Jersey.[98]

FINAL WOODLAND

In roughly the same area the Late Clasons Point manifestation develops from Early Clasons Point. It is characterized by Mohawk-like pottery, Mohawk pottery, Bowmans Brook Incised pottery, narrow-based isosceles triangular projectile points, small-stemmed projectile points, turtle cups, celts, split bone awls, and shell ornaments. In Westchester County this assemblage has been discovered in association with historic goods. Since Westchester County was Wappinger territory, it has been postulated that the Clasons Point II assemblage represents the material cultural remains of the Wappinger. Also, historic goods have been found in association with Clasons Point II remains on western Long Island. There Smith has tentatively correlated the Clasons Point II remains of that area with the western Metoac. One of the components of western Long Island has been identified as Fort Massapeag, a village of the Massapequa branch of the Metoac between 1640 and 1654. Owing to the occurrence of many traits of European origin, this has been called the Massapeag Focus.[99]

On the central Connecticut coast the Niantic Focus appears to develop from the Sebonac Focus. Historic goods have been found in association with Niantic remains at the Niantic Site and the Indian River Site in Connecticut.[100] The distribution of the Niantic Focus materials may be roughly equated with the tribal location of the Nehantic.[101]

The artifact complex of this focus is not well defined, but a great deal is known concerning the ceramics. The pottery is predominantly shell-tempered, surfaces are cord-marked, scored, and smooth, and vessel forms include globular bodies, constricted neck and collars. Decoration consists mainly of Iroquois-like designs impressed with shells on the collars or scoring on the collars.

Intrusive on the coast in Final Woodland times is the Fort Shantok Aspect. My personal opinion is that these people moved in from northwestern Connecticut and western Massachusetts. Each of the three foci of the aspect have been identified with historic tribes. The Pantigo Focus has been identified as a cemetery used by the Montauk between 1650 and 1750. The Fort Corchaug Focus has been identified as a stronghold of the Corchaug between 1650 and 1700, while the Fort Shantok Focus has been identified at a fort of the Mohegan after 1645. The trait complexes of the foci are extremely similar, so I will only describe the salient features of the aspect.

The pottery is shell-tempered but with many Iroquoian features. Particularly noticeable are collar with basal nodes, high castellations with vertical lugs at their apexes, and appliqued ridges around the rims. Decorations are in incising on the neck and collars; bodies are smooth. Other traits include long bird bone beads, pitted and unpitted hammerstones, isosceles and small equilateral triangular points, stemmed points, bone projectile points, and short tubular central hole (wampum) beads.[102]

RHODE ISLAND AND EASTERN MASSACHUSETTS SUBAREA

ARCHAIC

The earliest human remains so far found in this subarea were uncovered at Boyleston Street in Boston.[103] Here parts of a fishweir was found in a geological context indicating some antiquity, but unfortunately no artifacts were associated with it.

The earliest artifact complex, which I shall call the Maud Eaton complex, was found in lower levels of the Hofmann, Foster's Cove, Maud Eaton Test VI, Pringle sites of the Shawsheen River Valley and in the lower levels of the Peaked Hill and Rose sites of Cape Cod.[104] The complex is characterized by corner-removed arrowpoints, corner-removed spear points, pointed based points, large straight stemmed points, choppers and semilunar knives, expanded based drills, and battered ball hammerstones. Artifacts are mainly of felsite. A thumbnail scraper was found in the early levels at Foster's Cove, but this trait is usually absent from the complex. The Maud Eaton complexes appear to be definitely related to

97. Ibid.   100. Rouse, 1945, 1947.
98. Ibid.   101. Kroeber, 1939.
99. Ibid.

102. Smith, C. S., 1950, pp. 110–116.
103. Johnson et al, 1942; 1949.
104. Bullen, 1948; 1949.

the Koens Crispin Site of New Jersey, some of the materials from the pre-ceramic levels at Grantville in coastal New York, Stallings Island pre-ceramic in Georgia, nonceramic sites in Nova Scotia, and the "Big Blade" culture found near Hopedale, Labrador.[105] It is only tenuously related to the south-eastern shell mound complex and the pre-ceramic foci of central New York and may be a representative of an early basic coastal substratum roughly contemporaneous with the southeastern Archaic.

Evidently following and developing from the Maud Eaton complex is what I shall call the Grassy Island complex. This complex is widespread throughout this area, and there is probably some local variation of the complexes that, when more material is available, may be the basis for a series of foci. The middle levels of the Pringle, Maud Eaton Test VI, and Foster's Cove sites in the Shawsheen Valley,[106] and the Ford,[107] Grassy Island,[108] and Stewart's Island of southeastern Massachusetts and the lower levels of the Clark's Pond shell heap of northeastern Massachusetts[109] are components of the complex. Artifacts are often made of quartz or quartzite and typical of the complex are corner-removed, small stemmed and small triangular projectile points, gouges, choppers, pebble hammerstones, expanded based drills, and asymmetrical triangular knives. Semilunar knives, side-notched and corner-notched points, plummets, grooved axes, celts, bannerstones, and steatite occur at various of these sites but are hardly reoccurring diagnostic traits. Generally speaking, the Grassy Island complexes appear to be related to the Laurentian of central New York. Perhaps occasionally in this area this complex lasted up into and through the Early Woodland period.

EARLY WOODLAND

Early Woodland materials are found only in the middle levels of Pringle, Maud Eaton, and Foster's Cove sites of the Shawsheen River Valley. Small stemmed, and side-notched points, gouges, drills and Vinette I pottery characterize these assemblages which I shall call the Foster's Cove complex. It appears to be little more than the Grassy Island complex plus Vinette I pottery.[110]

MIDDLE WOODLAND

Middle Woodland sites are fairly numerous, and I suspect that some of them developed directly from pre-pottery manifestations, while others developed from the Foster's Cove complex. The upper levels of the Pringle and Maud Eaton, Test VI sites,[111] the Hornblower Site,[112] the middle levels of the Clark's Pond Site,[113] the Faulkner Springs Site,[114] the Rich Site,[115] the Holden Site,[116] and possibly the middle levels of the Seth Swamp sites[117] appear to belong to a single cultural manifestation that is called the Hornblower complex. Diagnostic of this horizon are mineral-tempered sherds decorated with punctations, dentate stamp, rocker dentate and scallop shell impressions (a few Vinette I sherds and shell-tempered sherds may occur); corner-removed, corner-notched, triangular, and small-stemmed projectile points predominate; drills; choppers; plummets, notched stones; graphite, and hammerstones occur rather often while bannerstones, pestles, grooved axes, gouges and gorgets occur rarely.[118]

LATE WOODLAND

Late Woodland manifestations which compose the Railroad complex have been discovered as follows: the Squam's Pond Site of Nantucket Island,[119] the Railroad Site,[120] and Rose Site of Cape Cod, and in the loam of the Hoffmann Site.[121] The pottery at this time is mainly shell-tempered, although mineral-tempered sherds do occur. The pottery is decorated by the use of the edge of a cord-wrapped paddle, dentate stamp, and the edge of a scallop shell, and much of the pottery at Railroad is incised over cord-paddled surface. Projectile points are mainly the large and small triangular types, while small-stemmed and corner-notched points do occur. Other artifacts include unilateral barbed harpoons, celts, grooved axes, netsinkers, and cylindrical pestles.

FINAL WOODLAND

Final Woodland archeological remains and historic goods in association with aboriginal materials have been found at a number of sites in the humus levels. Owing to the association of these materials in the humus levels, I do not believe that these can be the basis for defining the Final Woodland artifact complexes.

However, at Titicut, in southeastern Massachusetts, graves with triangular points, pipes, Fort Shantok–like pottery, and historic goods have been uncovered. These remains, though unpublished and unanalyzed, may be the basis for a Titicut Focus and may represent the material remains of the Narragansett.[122]

At Clark Pond, in northeastern Massachusetts, in the upper levels of the site, triangular points, clay pipes, celts, fine mineral-tempered pottery with punc-

105. Strong, 1930.
106. Bullen, 1948.
107. Robbins, 1946.
108. Johnson and Raup, 1947.
109. Bullen, 1949.
110. Bullen, 1949.
111. Bullen, 1949.
112. Byers and Johnson, 1940.
113. Bullen, 1949.
114. Robbins, 1944.
115. Moffett, 1946.
116. Ibid.
117. Bullen, 1949.
118. Bullen, personal communication.
119. Bullen and Brooks, 1947.
120. Moffet, 1946.
121. Bullen, 1949.
122. I would like to thank Fred Johnson of the Peabody Museum of Andover, Massachusetts, for showing me these materials and discussing them with me.

tated and incised rims were found with European pipe fragments and European metal artifacts. Bullen tentatively suggests these remains belong to the Aggawam tribe (Massachusetts).[123] However, further work seems necessary.

COASTAL MAINE AND COASTAL NEW HAMPSHIRE[124]

ARCHAIC AND EARLY WOODLAND

The earliest cultural remains have been found in the lower levels of the Taft's Point shell heap (and possibly in the shell heaps Moorehead excavated).[125] However, I do not consider all these remains to be Archaic in spite of their lack of pottery. Thus on the Maine coast pre-ceramic peoples existed into Early Woodland time, and pottery did not arrive in this area until Middle Woodland time.

Cultures of this period are characterized by no pottery, plummets, bannerstones, stone crescent gorgets, swordfish swords, burials covered by red paint, plummets, gouges, slate spears, harpoons, corner-removed points, and long-stemmed points.

Exactly where this complex is derived from is at present unknown, though it appears to be very tenuously related to the so-called Laurentian Phase of New York. It appears to be another example of a very early mortuary complex (equivalent in time to Adena) which continues into Middle Woodland time.

MIDDLE WOODLAND

The middle horizon of Taft's Point[126] and the Waterside shell heap[127] appear to be of this time period (as well as the Nevin's shell heap).[128] Some of the pottery is very similar to (if not identical with) the Vinette II pottery of central New York. The interior channeling, the plain rocker stamp decoration, the dentate rocker stamp decoration, the plain dentate decoration, and the vessel forms having pointed bottoms and outflaring rims, or very small collars at the rim, are ceramic resemblances to Vinette II, which certainly indicate a spatial and temporal connection (though not ancestral). Other wares include pointed bottom vessels decorated with marking from the edge of a cord-wrapped paddle and plain ware having punctates round the rim. Much of the earlier burial complex carries on into this period, with the addition of a few large triangular points.

LATE WOODLAND

The upper horizons of shells and fine dirt from the Taft's Point shell mound appear to be of this time period.[129] This conclusion is based on the presence of a few triangular points and the Owascoid pottery.[130] Present also in this time period are celts, harpoons, beaver teeth gouges, bone awls, needles, bodkins, flint drills, adzes, flake knives, and bannerstones. The many overlappings of traits between the upper and middle horizons of the Taft's Point shell heap certainly indicate continuity. However, the pottery of the middle level appears to be of Middle Woodland times.

FINAL WOODLAND

As yet I have seen no materials that appear to be of this time period, nor have associations of aboriginal materials with European trade goods been reported.

123. Bullen, 1949.
124. I would like to thank Mr. Douglas S. Byers for discussing these materials with me. He was most helpful and went to great lengths to show the materials he so carefully excavated at Nevins shell heap thereby illustrating our discussion of the Maine sequence.
125. Hadlock, 1939.   126. *Ibid.*

127. Rowe, 1940.
128. Byers, personal communication.
129. Hadlock, 1939, and Rowe, 1940.
130. Hadlock, 1939, and Byers, personal communication.

ARCHEOLOGICAL CHRONOLOGY OF THE MIDDLE ATLANTIC STATES.[1] *By Karl Schmitt**

INTRODUCTION

THE area to be considered comprises the territory of the present states of Virginia, Maryland, Pennsylvania, New Jersey, and Delaware. The data available for the analysis of the area consist of published reports, which vary widely as to time of publication and as to usefulness for the purpose at hand, plus unpublished information on sites in the states of Virginia and Maryland. The methodological procedure in establishing the chronology of the Middle Atlantic area consisted of two steps. The first of these was the comparison of complexes from historic sites with those from prehistoric sites. Such a procedure, when stratigraphy is lacking, as is almost the case in the area under discussion, is the best means for the establishing of a relative chronology. A second step was the comparison of Middle Atlantic complexes with those of chronological significance in neighboring areas. Both steps represent application of the typological method and serve to check one another. A further check was available in the small indications of stratigraphy present.

Beneath the time period headings to follow will be presented summaries of archeological manifestations considered to have resulted from occupations in those periods. Because of wide variance in reporting, it has not been possible to standardize the size or level of archeological classification; some of the manifestations to be considered are single sites or even single components of a given site; others are on the focal level; while one, the Monongahela Culture, consists of several foci. In conclusion, a summary of the archeological history of the area will be presented.

* George Washington University, B.S., 1938; University of Chicago, M.A., 1942; Ph.D., 1947; Assistant, 1946–1947; Assistant Professor of Anthropology, University of Oklahoma, 1947–1952. Chapter received December, 1947. While this volume was in page proof word was received of the death of Karl Schmitt in an automobile accident in New Mexico in August.

1. Without the co-operation of personnel of the United States National Museum, particularly of Messrs. Neil Judd, Frank Setzler, T. Dale Stewart, and Waldo R. Wedel, in furnishing material and aid, this work could not have been undertaken. Other individuals to whom thanks are due are Mr. Richard G. Slattery and Mrs. Alice L. L. Ferguson of Washington, D.C.; Dr. James B. Griffin of the University of Michigan; Dr. Dorothy Cross of the New Jersey Site Survey; Drs. Fay-Cooper Cole, Robert J. Braidwood, Fred Eggan, and Kenneth G. Orr of the University of Chicago; and Mr. Alfred Harris and Miss Grace Gredys, also of the University of Chicago.

ARCHAIC

KOENS-CRISPIN COMPONENT

On the Crispin property in Burlington County, New Jersey (Fig. 21), Hawkes and Linton[2] reported finding three artifact-bearing levels: an upper layer of leaf mold containing tools attributed to the Lenape; a middle layer of yellow sand containing a concentration of artifacts two feet below the leaf mold; and a third concentration of artifacts at the juncture of the yellow sand with a "white glacial sand" from five to seven feet below the surface. The lowest level contained caches of artifacts and had no pottery. The caches of the non- pottery level consisted of numerous well-finished artifacts (Fig. 21, *A–C, G–J, N, R, T*), which included winged bannerstones, large projectile points with straight-sided and straight-based stems, chipped argillite celts or adzes with ground blades, a tanged adze or knobbed celt, a rectangular polished celt, large flaked choppers, nodular hammerstones, pestle-like objects, a polished gouge, fossil brachiopods bearing traces of red paint, a polished crystal ball, white quartz pebbles, "fish-spears" or thick, relatively narrow projectile points with rounded stems, and diamond-shaped points, which were relatively long narrow points with slight stemming and narrowing near the base. Cross's later excavations on the adjoining Koens property[3] appear corroborative of the earlier finds.

RED VALLEY COMPONENT

Cross also made excavations at the Red Valley Site in Monmouth County, New Jersey.[4] The stratification here was similar to that of the Koens-Crispin Site. A basal nonpottery level and caches of well-made artifacts, not associated with pottery, were present. Contents included broad-winged bannerstones, a gouge, a full-grooved ax, a knobbed celt, and large projectile points (Fig. 21, *D, K*).

POPLAR ISLAND COMPONENT

This site in the Susquehanna River in Dauphin County, Pennsylvania,[5] revealed an artifact complex,

2. Hawkes and Linton, 1916; Cross, 1941, pp. 81–90.
3. Cross, 1941.
4. *Ibid.*, pp. 117–127.   5. Witthoft, 1947, pp. 123–124.

lacking in pottery, which was overlaid by over thirteen feet of deposits. Included were argillite "fish-spears," large triangular blades of argillite and ryolite, rectangular and oval choppers, a portion of a rectangular bannerstone, chipped and ground adzes, an argillite celt, a roller pestle, an almost circular celt or scraper, a broken, partially-ground projectile point of red slate, and numerous burned and broken stones.

MISCELLANEOUS COMPONENTS

The Abbot Farm Site near Trenton, New Jersey,[6] and the Chickis rock shelter in eastern Pennsylvania,[7] appear to have Archaic components; but, either because later information is rumored to disprove the presence of such a horizon or because the method of excavation appears to have obscured stratification, their chronological position is uncertain. Both sites, however, have produced artifacts similar to those from the three sites discussed above. The Abbot Farm Site in particular has yielded a tremendous number of artifacts which may be referable to an early time period. These last types are semilunar knives[8] and hammered and multiple-notched copper blades (Fig. 21, F, N).[9] The Zakiah Swamp area in Charles County, Maryland, which has produced literally thousands of large projectile points (Fig. 21, E), hundreds of bannerstones, and little, if any, pottery, almost certainly would reveal Archaic horizons on excavation.[10]

EARLY WOODLAND
KOENS-CRISPIN COMPONENT

At the Koens-Crispin Site in New Jersey, Hawkes and Linton[11] noted that the intermediate or middle level contained pottery and described it in the following manner:

The pottery of the intermediate culture was quite distinct from that of the Modern Lenape, many bits of which were found on the surface. . . . The fragments from the intermediate level were composed of red clay and pounded steatite, the latter composing more than half the bulk. The red clay could have been obtained from the small strips of the same running through the yellowish soil. Judging from its consistency it had been sun-dried and not baked. It could be easily scratched with the fingernail. Nevertheless the fragments showed a uniform thickness, and one piece showed the curve of a rim. It is possible that here we have the very beginnings of pottery among these people and the steatite, which is not used to temper the recent pottery, marks the transition from the bowls of that material used for similar purposes.

Cross's report[12] of her excavations does not separate the artifacts by levels, nor does she describe pottery by types, but her series included steatite-tempered and mat-impressed sherds. All three workers noted the continuity of artifact types from the lower pre-

pottery horizon to the middle level. A long chipped drill was noted as an additional middle type.

RED VALLEY COMPONENT

At the Red Valley Site the pre-pottery or Archaic level appears to shade into the Early Woodland level with only the appearance of pottery indicating the transition. Cross[13] reports a number of modes of surface finish, temper and decoration, but gives no correlation of such attributes. There is an absence of steatite-tempered pottery and it would appear that other pottery types may occur in Early Woodland manifestations of the area. All pottery from this site should not be interpreted as Early Woodland.

SALISBURY AND GOOSE ISLAND COMPONENTS

Cross[14] reports these two sites in Gloucester County, New Jersey. The interpretation of remains is complicated by the presence of an upper humus layer containing sherds of Late Woodland types and Colonial trade material. However, the presence of flat-based, mat-impressed, steatite-tempered pottery indicates a strong possibility of an early component on these sites. Other artifacts recovered included large stemmed points, chipped stone drills, an adze, fragments of steatite bowls (Fig. 21, M), a two-holed gorget, a bannerstone fragment, full and three-quarter grooved axes, and cord-wrapped stick impressed pottery. Much of this material belongs to the Early Woodland period.

SELDEN ISLAND SITE

Slattery[15] has reported a highly significant site near Washington, D.C. Pottery from this buried site was largely of steatite temper with net and mat-impressed flat bases and cord-marked exteriors (Fig. 21, P, Q). A minority ware had crystalline temper and a cord-marked surface. Other artifacts were several types of large points, including one with bifurcated expanding base, fragments of full grooved axes, and a piece of a steatite vessel. The Marcy Creek Site[16] also near Washington has artifacts which appear very closely related to those of Selden Island.

MIDDLE WOODLAND (FIG. 22)
MOUNTAIN FOCUS

The components considered to form this focus are mainly described by Fowke[17] and were a series of mounds in Allegheny, Bath, Page, Rockingham, and Shenandoah Counties, Virginia, and one mound in Hardy County, West Virginia. A complex of traits (Fig. 22, A, L, O), namely, mound structures involving subsoil or subfloor pits and inclusive large rock piles;

6. Spier, 1918.
7. Haldeman, 1881.
8. Cross, 1941, p. 3.
9. Putnam, 1882, pp. 123–125.
10. Personal observation.
11. Hawkes and Linton, 1916, p. 77.
12. Cross, 1941, pp. 81–90.
13. Ibid., pp. 117–127.
14. Ibid., pp. 52–66.
15. Slattery, 1946.
16. Manson, 1948.
17. Fowke, 1894.

cremation, bundle and articulated burials; platform pipes; quartz crystals; mica sheets; triangular cache blades; and single- or double-perforated stone gorgets, can be compiled by grouping the traits present in the mounds. Other traits of unique occurrence indicate a Middle Woodland horizon; such traits are obtuse angle pottery pipes, elaborately carved bone combs and pottery vessels from the Linville mound (Fig. 22, D, N, P, Q),[18] and a copper crescent from the Rileyville mound.[19] The two vessels from the Linville mound appear related to more southern types: one sand-tempered, cone-shaped vessel with surface treatment of cord-wrapped stick impressions resembles the ware found in Coe's second archeological horizon of the Carolina area;[20] and one sand-tempered vessel with a simple stamped or wrapped paddle-impressed surface finish most closely approaches the pottery type known as Wilmington Heavy Cord Marked found on the south Atlantic coast of the Carolinas and Georgia.[21] However, many of the other traits have affiliations west to Hopewellian or Hopewellian-like manifestations in the Ohio River drainage, or to the Point Peninsula complex[22] in New York and Canada. It is to be regretted that the Mountain Focus is represented solely by traits from burial practices and does not include village-site material.

CLOVER CREEK FOCUS

Two mound sites, one on Clover Creek in Highland County, Virginia,[23] and the other known as the Bell or Battle mound in Rockbridge County, Virginia,[24] are grouped together because of the absence of the trait complex of the Mountain Focus and because they share a pottery type not found in the latter focus. In this type (Fig. 22, S), the cord-marked surface finish, the thin added fillet below the rim, and the presence of fingernail incising, pinching, and punctating seen to foreshadow the greater development of the added rim strip and fingernail decoration technique found on the Gala type of pottery to be considered under the Late Woodland section of this chapter. The similarity—by no means to be construed as identity—of the Clover Creek type pottery to the Late Woodland types and its associations with a burial mound complex which appears to be an attenuated form of the Mountain Focus burial complex lead to the conclusion that the Clover Creek Focus belongs to a late Middle Woodland time period and that it may continue into Late Woodland times.

THOMAS FOCUS

A mound near the town of Irvinetown,[25] and a mound cluster near Kinzua,[26] in Warren County, Pennsylvania, comprise this focus. Both were earth burial mounds (Fig. 22, B), which included stone cists made by lining subfloor pits with rocks and by covering burials with slabs. The second mound unit near Kinzua exhibited a peripheral arrangement of stone slabs much like that at Squawkie Hill Mound 2 of Ritchie's New York Focus of the Hopewellian phase.[27] The rock-covered burials of the Geneseo mound, also of the New York Focus, resemble those of the Thomas Focus. The presence in the latter focus of copper-covered ornaments, curved-base platform pipes, mica, gorgets, and galena is very suggestive of Hopewellian manifestations and indicates a Middle Woodland time period for the Thomas Focus. This focus is particularly closely related to the New York Focus and perhaps the two should be combined.

JONES FOCUS

The two components of this focus are a mound on Clemson's Island in the Susquehanna River in Dauphin County, Pennsylvania, and a mound in Juniata County, Pennsylvania.[28] Single and multiple disarticulated burials were recovered at both sites. Pottery was plentiful in both excavations and was described as having crushed quartz temper, cord-marked surface finish, and nodes or bosses made by punctating the opposite surface of the vessel. The high incidence of punctates and corresponding raised nodes does not occur in Late Woodland pottery types in this area. The presence of mound burial indicates that the site is comparable to other more western Middle Woodland sites. The high incidence of triangular arrow points and the possible cord-wrapped stick impressed designs leads one to suspect that the date for this focus is a rather late one. Until fuller information on the sites is available, the mounds are tentatively placed in Middle Woodland and probably at a point near the arbitrary division between that period and Late Woodland.

MISCELLANEOUS COMPONENTS

The Crall mound[29] in Monongahela City, Pennsylvania, has been classed by Webb and Snow as an Adena structure.[30] Features included a subfloor pit, a prepared floor, a reel-shaped copper gorget (Fig. 22, H), a thin copper plate, and a clay tube or pipe. Possibly this manifestation should be considered Early

18. *Ibid.*, pp. 37–44. For recent discussion and pictures see Carpenter, 1950.
19. Fowke, 1894, p. 55.
20. Griffin, J. B., 1945c.
21. Haag, 1939c, p. 6.
22. Ritchie, 1944, pp. 184–185.
23. Fowke, 1894, pp. 31–32.
24. The Valentine Museum, 1898, p. 58.

25. Thomas, Cyrus, 1894, pp. 499–502.
26. Bliss, 1942.
27. Ritchie, 1944, Pl. 95.
28. Jones, R. W., 1931.
29. Thomas, Cyrus, 1894, pp. 494–495.
30. Webb and Snow, 1945, p. 101.

Woodland. Two other mound sites in western Pennsylvania, the Finleyville mound in Washington County[31] and the McKees Rocks mound near Pittsburgh,[32] are related to Hopewellian manifestations to the west: included in them were many burials, stone cists, a clay platform, perforated bear canines, a bear canine incased in a copper sheath, and a slate gorget.

In the eastern Pennsylvania–New Jersey–Delaware area no typical complex for a Middle Woodland period has been set forth. Typologically many of the cord-marked sherds from the Salisbury,[33] the Red Valley, and Goose Island sites could belong to this period. Other artifact types—such as the grooved ax, knobbed celt,[34] stemmed and side-notched points, bannerstones, chipped flint drills, scrapers, pestle-like forms, hammerstones, and net-sinkers—appear to continue into Middle Woodland from the earlier time periods. On the basis of gorget types the Larrison and Fairy Hole Rock Shelter sites[35] may have Middle Woodland components.

Two caches in the Wolves Den Rock Shelter[36] in eastern Pennsylvania yielded large leaf-shaped blades and a number of worked fossil shark's teeth. The latter in particular indicate a relationship to the Point Peninsula Focus of New York.[37] An unusual occurrence of artifacts from Cambridge, Maryland,[38] also has a relationship to the same focus. At this place a group burial, or possibly an ossuary, yielded many perforated stone gorgets, stone tubes, large stone points, cylindrical copper beads, a rectangular copper plate, an effigy pipe, a birdstone, a boatstone, and fossil shark's teeth. This site should not be included with other nearby ossuaries found by Mercer.[39]

Christopher Wren figures a number of sherds and restored vessels from eastern Pennsylvania which exhibit characteristics related to other specimens from Middle Woodland sites. One large vessel found near the junction of the Lackawanna and Susquehanna Rivers possesses a cord-marked surface; punctates producing raised nodes on the interior surface; patterned arrangements of cord-wrapped edge impressions, and possibly dentate stamping, over the upper half of the vessel; a conical bottom; and a slightly everted rim.[40] Scattered finds of related pottery in the Wyoming Valley and from Lock Haven in eastern Pennsylvania are also reported by Wren.[41]

LATE WOODLAND (FIG. 23)

GALA FOCUS

At present a single published site comprises this focus. It is situated on the James River in Botetourt County, Virginia. Here Fowke[42] excavated refuse pits and flexed burials in pits. Artifacts included beads, awls of many varieties, perforated needles, fishhooks, beamers, perforated animal scapulae, all of bone; mortars, mullers, polished celts, fragments of steatite pipes, many triangular arrowpoints, all of stone; disk beads, marginella beads, conch columella beads, and a perforated shell disk. Charred kernels of corn were also found.

Large numbers of pot sherds were recovered from the Gala Site. The vessels appear to have been predominantly round-based and relatively full-bodied and to have had a slightly constricted neck and an added rim strip which produced a collared effect. The temper was a mixture of limestone and grit, while the surface finish was largely cord- or net-malleated. Decoration was almost always confined to the rim strip and consisted of fingernail pinchings and gouges, with secondary techniques of incising and impressing with cord-wrapped sticks. A secondary ware with sandy temper and a surface finish made by impressing various fabrics, and with buff exteriors and dark grey core, was also present.

MONTGOMERY FOCUS

Detailed information for the Montgomery Focus is limited to a single component, the Shepard Site on the Potomac River in Montgomery County, Maryland.[43] At present there appears no major difference between the Gala and Montgomery foci except for that of pottery and the presence of obtuse angle pottery pipes in the latter (Fig. 23, H, N). The predominant pottery type, Shepard Cord Marked (Fig. 23, J), is characterized by cord-roughened surfaces with impressions arranged linearly and perpendicular to the lip; crushed dark igneous rock or crushed quartz for temper; the presence of an added rim strip and decoration of the strip by impressions of cord-wrapped sticks; bold gashes at the juncture of the strip and vessel body; and occasional incising and punctating. Two minority wares, Page Cord Marked[44] with limestone temper and Keyser Cord Marked[45] with shell temper, are present.

LURAY FOCUS

Two sites are known for this focus, the Keyser Farm component located on the South Fork of the Shenandoah River near Luray, Virginia,[46] and the

31. Cadzow, 1933.
32. Swauger, 1940.
33. Cross, 1941, Pl. 22a, Figs. 1–3.
34. See Ritchie, 1944, Pl. 15, Fig. 23, for a similar specimen from approximately the same time horizon.
35. Cross, 1941, Pls. 21a, 51b, 69a.
36. Clausen, 1932.
37. Ritchie, 1944, Pls. 69, Figs. 6–9; Pl. 76, Fig. 40.
38. Weslager, 1942, pp. 146–149.
39. Mercer, 1897, pp. 87–98.
40. Wren, 1914, Pl. 2.
41. Ibid., Pls. 16, 17, Fig. 1; Pl. 19, Figs. 3, 6; Pl. 22.

42. Fowke, 1894, pp. 17–23.
43. Schmitt and Slattery, n.d.
44. Manson, MacCord, and Griffin, 1944.
45. Ibid.   46. Ibid.

Hughes component very close in distance to the Shepard Site in Montgomery County, Maryland.[47] The burial (Fig. 23, M) and artifactual complexes (Fig. 23, O, P, T), except for pottery, are similar to those of the Gala and Montgomery foci. Additional traits not noted for the latter foci are a huge oval pattern of refuse pits at the Hughes Site and oval post mold outlines, indicating habitations, and cache or refuse pits surrounded by post molds at the Keyser Farm Site.

The major pottery type, Keyser Cord Marked (Fig. 23, K, L), is characterized by wide-mouthed jars with rounded bases, slightly constricted necks, and slightly flared rims; small solid lugs; cord-roughened surface finish; temper of crushed river mussel shells; predominant decoration technique of impressing rims and lugs with cord-wrapped stick; alternative decoration techniques of incision and circular punctating; and absence of added rim strips. A minority type, Page Cord Marked, was found at the Keyser Farm Site and differs from the previously mentioned Shepard Cord Marked by presence of limestone temper instead of granite temper. Trade sherds of Potomac Creek Cord Impressed and pottery pipes of tidewater Potomac types were found at the Keyser and Hughes sites and indicate a near historic horizon for this focus.

POTOMAC CREEK FOCUS

Two large village sites of the tidewater Potomac area comprise this focus. One site has been identified beyond doubt as the village of Patawomeke visited by Captain John Smith in 1608,[48] and the other has been identified as Moyaone, also a village visited by Smith.[49] Both sites were fortified by concentric palisades and encompassing ditch. The burial complex included large ossuaries and the majority of the bones had been buried in a fleshless condition (Fig. 23, A). Some pits had as many as five hundred individuals interred. Grave goods were relatively rare. The general artifactual material, except for pottery vessels, pipes, and shell gorgets, of the two sites does not differ greatly from that of the Gala, Montgomery, and Luray foci.

The predominant pottery type, Potomac Creek Cord Impressed (Fig. 23, B,C),[50] has crushed quartz gravel temper; a cord-roughened surface finish, which often was partially smoothed for application of decoration; predominant decoration technique of impressing with cord-wrapped sticks, edges, and strings; secondary decoration techniques of cord and fingernail impressing and circular punctating; design motifs of short parallel elements, continous bands, and pat-

terned areas of cord and cord-wrapped edge impressions, placed about the rim area; vessel form with sub-conoidal bases, cylindrical body, constricted neck, and straight or slightly flaring rim.

A minority ware, Rappahannock Fabric Impressed (Fig. 23, D), was decorated by incising and punctating and has relationships south, particularly along the Rappahannock River in Virginia and north through the coastal area to New Jersey.[51]

The pottery pipes of obtuse angle shape often have delicate dentate stamp impressed designs and are common in the Potomac area (Fig. 23, H). Shell gorgets with drilled dot designs of stars, circles and diamonds and shell masks with "lightning" designs beneath perforated eyes are associated with sites of this focus. (Fig. 23, E, F).

One complication concerning this focus should be stressed; the site of Moyaone produced artifacts of a wide range of time periods and evidently was inhabited over a considerable period of time; the last component is of the Potomac Creek Focus.

MONONGAHELA CULTURE (FIG. 24)

The appelation Monongahela Woodland Culture was originally applied by Butler to a series of sites found in western Pennsylvania.[52] Sites yielding similar material are common throughout that area.[53] All the completely excavated sites, except two, revealed circular or oval patterns of post molds, indicating stockade lines (Fig. 24, A). Of the exceptions, the Hanna Component possessed houses arranged in an oval pattern and the first Powell Component possessed a three-quarter circle of houses with the fourth quarter closed off by a stockade. House types were oval or circular in pattern at all the completely excavated sites except the Montague site. At the latter, although the oval or circular type was important, the rectangular form was predominant. Pits, often pearshaped and attached to house outlines, and surrounded by post molds, were common at excavated sites. Burials were predominantly individual and flexed in pits dug into the subsoil. Bone and antler artifacts seem to have been particularly plentiful at all sites, and tubular bone beads, perforated phalanges, awls of many types, antler cylinders, socketed antler points, turtle shell receptacles, bone chisels, and beaver incisors seem almost ubiquitous. Shell artifacts shared by most sites are marginella and small disc beads, small pendants basically triangular in shape, and serrated mussel shells. In general, the bone and shell artifacts are essentially the same from site to site (Fig. 24, R–V).

A consideration of the stone artifacts reveals both

47. Stearns, 1940.
48. Stewart, 1939b.
49. Ferguson, 1937a; 1937b.
50. Manson, MacCord, and Griffin, 1944, Pl. XIII.

51. Schmitt, n.d.
52. Butler, M., 1939.
53. Augustine, 1938a; 1938b; 1938c; 1938d; Engberg, 1930; 1931.

similarities and differences (Fig. 24, *L–Q*). Presence of celts, perforated discoidals—many with incised decorations, flint drills, and hammerstones seems characteristic of the Monongahela culture. Projectile point type varies from the Clouse component, where only one of twenty-nine was of triangular shape, to the Fullerton Farm component, where almost all points were triangular in shape.

Pottery type reveals the general similarity of rounded base, swelling body, slightly constricted neck, and slightly flaring rim. Cord marking is predominant (Fig. 24, *B–E*). The foregoing attributes appear to have been found with both grit- and shell-tempered wares. A grit-tempered type with added rim strips and decorated variously with incised bands, "roulette" or cord-wrapped stick impressions, and gashes at the lower edge of the strip was present at the Montague, Troutman, and two Powell sites. Another type, which was smoothed and presumably shell-tempered, bearing broad-line incised or trailed decorations, and wide flanged rims was found at the Montague, First Peck, Steele, and several river valley sites reported by Engberg. Some sherds, particularly at the Montague Site, bore a variety of lugs, knobs, and rim points (Fig. 24, *F–H*).

Because of the differences in pottery and types of projectile points, it seems that the sites of the Monongahela culture could be arranged in a time series of their own and into several foci; sites with stemmed projectile points and grit-tempered pottery with added rim strips represent the earlier occupation while those with triangular points and smoothed, shell-tempered pottery represent a later time period.

SUSQUEHANNA FOCUS

This focus (Fig. 25) is composed of three sites, the Strickler, Washington Borough, and Schultz Farm sites, along the banks of the Susquehanna River in eastern Pennsylvania.[54] These sites contained varying amounts of European or Colonial trade material (Fig. 25, *Q–V*) and have been attributed to the historic Susquehannock Indians. This identification appears valid.

The material culture of the three sites is closely related to that of known sites of Iroquoian-speaking peoples to the north. The collared vessels with elaborate incised paneled designs, raised rim points, and conventionalized human and animal effigies applied below the rims are known from many Iroquoian sites in New York (Fig. 25, *A–D*). The pipe complex—including the sharply flared bowl forms ("trumpet"), the collared and often incised type ("coronet"), the conventionalized dog or wolf type with the orifice of the bowl below an upraised upper jaw, the vase-shaped stone form, and the large simple terra cotta

types—is common on known Iroquoian sites to the north. Small stone masks, elaborately carved bone combs, and triangular arrowpoints are also part of the known Iroquoian complex (Fig. 25, *E–P*).

Specifically the pottery exhibits more detailed relationships to that from the more western Iroquoian sites. Skinner, in writing on Iroquoian archeology, divided Iroquoian groups into an Eastern or Mohawk-Onondaga group and a Western group, which was subdivided into Neutral-Seneca-Cayuga, Susquehanna, and Huron-Tobacco Nations divisions.[55] The double-neck jar, the vessel with narrow collar and mammiform projections or incising at the lower edge of the collar, modeled human faces and bodies below the vessel rim, and roughened surface finish are characteristic of Susquehanna Focus pottery and also occur in Seneca pottery as illustrated by Skinner.[56]

MINISINK FOCUS

This focus is at present limited to one cemetery site located on the Delaware River in Sussex County, New Jersey (Fig. 26). The location is at or near the site of the historic seventeenth century Munsee village of the Minisink, a subdivision of the Delaware.[57] No traces of fortifications or house types were noted. Many of the burials were accompanied by grave goods, including a variety of European or Colonial materials.

The ceramic material from the Minisink Focus can be differentiated into two types. Heye and Pepper did so and labeled the types "Algonkian" and "Iroquois". The first type includes vessels with rounded bases and bodies and more elongated forms, sometimes called "melon-shaped." Vessels of this type (Fig. 26, *A, D–F, K–L*) commonly have constricted necks and slightly everted rims or narrow collars. Decoration consists of herringbone, horizontal bands, columnar arrangements, and short oblique lines produced with cord-wrapped sticks or edges. Occasionally punctating, sharp or narrow line incising, and rim points occur. Surfaces are cord-marked and occasionally the cord-wrapped stick decoration continues a short distance into the interior. Temper is of grit. This type closely approximates that of Castle Creek pottery of New York.

The second pottery type of "Iroquoian" form is characterized by rounded bases and bodies and a constricted neck, above which flares a pronounced collar. The collar bears patterned decorations of vertical, horizontal, and slanting incised and punctated lines. The lower edge of the collar is usually gashed or nicked with the incising implement. Conventionalized faces were made by bounding a triangular

54. Cadzow, 1936.

55. Skinner, 1921*a*, pp. 24–36.
56. *Ibid.*
57. Heye and Pepper, 1915. Recent additional information on this archeological manifestation is in Ritchie, 1949*a*.

smoothed area with incised lines and punctating eyes and mouth in that area. Examples of vessels with one, three, or four rim points are illustrated (Fig. 26, *B, C*). Surface finish is smoothed and temper is of grit. This type is related to that of Skinner's Eastern Iroquois or Mohawk-Onondaga group. The narrower collar and the style of punctating the conventionalized human faces on pot rims in the "Iroquoian" pottery style is particularly close to some specimens from the Putnam Site, an Onondaga site in Jefferson County, New York.[58] In addition, some sherds at the Minisink Site appear to have the "Iroquoian" collar and design elements, but the latter have been executed with some type of stamp or by a series of punctates.[59]

Other artifacts from the Minisink cemetery included pottery pipes, turtle shell rattles and cups, antler arrowpoints, and large numbers of shell beads, runtees and pendants.

MISCELLANEOUS COMPONENTS

Information concerning a large number of sites throughout the Middle Atlantic area is not suitable for classification of the sites into foci, but is sufficient for assigning them to the Late Woodland period. A number of ossuaries have been located throughout the tidewater area; namely, along the Choptank River on the eastern shore of Maryland;[60] on the Potomac River near Anacostia, D.C.;[61] on Port Tobacco, Accotink, and Piscataway Creeks—all tributaries of the Potomac;[62] and on the York River near Poropotank Creek.[63] Some of these ossuaries contained European or Colonial material which is further proof for the late date of this particular burial complex.

Throughout eastern Pennsylvania and in New Jersey, a large number of rock shelters have been excavated. Stratigraphy seems to have been present in many of these shelters but this is not certain because of the nature of reporting. Much of the material is undoubtedly of the Late Woodland period. Extreme caution should be used in assigning the entire artifact complex of any shelter to a historic tribe. Pot sherds comprise the majority of artifacts from the shelters and most are of either Owasco or "Iroquoian" types.[64] Some of the pottery appears to be more closely related to types occurring in coastal New Jersey south to the tidewater Virginia area.[65] Other open sites have also produced material difficult to classify. At

the Rosenkrans Site in northern New Jersey, Cross recovered pottery of both Owaso and Eastern-Iroquoian types, as well as sherds which typologically lie between those extremes.[66] Also, Cross's Indian Head and Salisbury sites produced some sherds which bear extremely close resemblance to the pottery type of Potomac Creek Cord Impressed from Virginia.[67] Those from the Salisbury Site were apparently in association with the Colonial or European material present in the humus layer.

DISCUSSION OF SPATIAL AND CHRONOLOGICAL RELATIONSHIPS

In the preceding section a very condensed description of the known important archeological manifestations of the Middle Atlantic area has been presented and these manifestations have been classified into major time periods and, in so far as possible, focal groups. Only four sites were located which could with any certainty be assigned to the Archaic period, and the knowledge of their artifactual complex is far from complete.[68] The Koens-Crispin and Red Valley components in New Jersey furnish most of the known material from this horizon in the Middle Atlantic region. An artifact complex consisting of winged bannerstones, gouges, knobbed celts, full-grooved axes, adzes, pestle-like implements, flaked choppers, large flake scrapers, and a variety of large projectile points—mostly of the straight-stemmed and semilozenge shapes—is indicated. There is a possibility that handled steatite bowls occurred in this horizon. Also the Red Valley and Koens-Crispin sites indicate the presence of a ceremonial practice of caching well-made artifacts such as bannerstones, gouges, adzes, and projectile points.

Data on the components classified in this chapter as of the Archaic period indicate a numerically small, scattered occupation at that time. There is no evidence of agriculture, in spite of functional identification of some chopper-like implements as hoes. Subsistence was by hunting and gathering and probably did not vary greatly over a major part of the area. The coastal or tidewater area was probably inhabited at this period but is little known archeologically. Some of the large shell mounds of the coastal area are almost certain to possess Archaic levels and would indicate a variant (characterized by greater dependence on shell fish) of the hunting and gathering culture type.

The Early Woodland components were also limited in number. The New Jersey sites at which mani-

---

58. Skinner, 1921*a*, Pl. XXVIII.
59. Heye and Pepper, 1915, Pl. XXVII.
60. Mercer, 1897.
61. Stewart and Wedel, 1937.
62. Graham, 1935; Reynolds, 1880–1881*a*; 1880–1881*b*; Ferguson, 1940.
63. Stewart, 1940.
64. Schrabisch, 1926.
65. Schrabisch, 1915.

66. Cross, 1941, Pls. 66, 67
67. *Ibid.*, Pl. 10, Figs. 1, 2; Pl. 22*b*.
68. [In January, 1951, Mr. John Witthoft informed the editor of a fluted blade complex in Lebanon County, Pennsylvania, east of Harrisburg. This material from the Shoop Site is apparently older than the Archaic sites mentioned in this chapter.]

festations occurred appeared to indicate a gradual transformation from the Archaic. Perhaps the most abrupt feature was the introduction of pottery, which serves here as the only marker between the two periods. Since Cross found that artifact types at New Jersey sites varied slowly in time, the only conclusion to be drawn is that the introduction of pottery did not significantly change the mode of life or adjustment of the inhabitants to the environment. Steatite-tempered pottery with flat bases, lug handles, and smooth sides is found in New Jersey. A related pottery type which has been found in Virginia and Maryland has similar flat, fabric-impressed bases and lug handles but seems to be predominantly cord-marked. Pottery of this temper is the only variety which can certainly be assigned to the Early Woodland period. However, there is a strong possibility that some sites show a direct transition from an Archaic prepottery horizon to one with grit-tempered and cord-marked pottery. Information on the remainder of the artifact complex of the Early Woodland period indicates that the winged bannerstone, knobbed celt, gouge, and other artifacts of the Archaic continued to be used in this period. Additional artifact types are long chipped drills and stone gorgets.

With the advent of Middle Woodland times there is evidence of much "foreign" influence in the area. The western portion of the states of Virginia, Maryland, and Pennsylvania contain many mounds which include objects related to the more western manifestations of the Ohio Valley. The Thomas Focus and the Crall Site of western Pennsylvania have traits which are more specifically Hopewellian than those of the Mountain Focus of Virginia and West Virginia and the Jones Focus of western Pennsylvania.

The Irvineton and Sugan Run components making up the Thomas Focus possess ornaments covered with silver and copper foil, mica sheets, pottery platform pipes, and gorgets—all of which suggest, not a strong, but a definite Hopewellian affiliation. The actual mound structures here are closely related to those of the New York Focus of the Hopewellian Phase.

In the mountain area of western Virginia a large number of mounds were grouped into a Mountain Focus. The components as a group include mounds with subfloor pits, stone platform pipes, mica, quartz crystals, stone gorgets, a single copper crescent, individual burials, ossuary burials, and cremation. All these traits have some Hopewellian affinities. However, some of the pipe forms, the unusual bone combs, and shell bead types from the Linville Component definitely indicate a connection with the Point Peninsula Focus of New York. The pipe forms and comb type also indicate a relationship to the

Intrusive Mound Culture of the Ohio area. The two pottery vessels recovered from the Linville Component have their closest relationships east and south to the Carolina area in Coe's second archeological horizon and to the Middle Woodland Wilmington series in Georgia.

Two other mounds in the western Virginia area have been placed in a Clover Creek Focus. The burial complex, involving mound structures, rock covered burials, and apparently disarticulated burials, seems to be an attenuated form of the Mountain Focus burial complex. In this same area were many small mounds of rock and earth which Fowke investigated and reported to contain nothing. Though these mound components have not been classified, it is possible that they belong to the Clover Creek Focus. Pottery was found in both mounds classified in this focus and though it has a few resemblances to that from the Linville mound, it appears to bear a closer relationship to pottery from the Gala and Montgomery foci of the Late Woodland period.

The mounds included in the Jones Focus of western Pennsylvania are in some ways analogous to those of the Clover Creek Focus in that they may represent an attenuated form of the burial complex found at the Thomas Focus and the Crall mound and probably are later in time than these latter manifestations. The pottery from the Clover Creek Focus differs from that of the Jones Focus in that it does not possess grit temper, circular punctates, and raised nodes characteristic of the latter, but is limestone-tempered and bears narrow appliqued fillets decorated with fingernail incisions or punctates.

Considering the distribution and maximum density of Hopewellian and Adena remains to the west, the Virginia and Pennsylvania manifestations discussed above can be said to be peripheral to the Ohio area. To explain the occurrence of Hopewellian-like practices in the area, it is not necessary to postulate migrations though they may have occurred to a small degree. Since the manifestations of Middle Woodland in western Virginia and western Pennsylvania are limited to burial complexes, it is more probable that a diffusion of burial practices and some trade took place. These burial practices could have been a result of adaptation and integration by local people of ideas emanating from the west. There are, of course, other evidences of wide trade relations in this Middle Woodland period. So many large conch columellas and beads made from shells from the Gulf or Atlantic region were found in the Linville mound of Virginia and in Point Peninsula sites of New York that this portion of trade must have been of high importance. The fossil shark's teeth of Point Peninsula sites may have originated in the famous Miocene beds of Chesapeake Bay.

Turning to the Piedmont Plateau, the remainder of Pennsylvania, and the coastal area of all the Middle Atlantic states, we find there is little, if any, evidence of mounds and also little evidence from excavated sites for the presence of a Middle Woodland horizon. In all probability, the Middle Woodland period was one of increasing differentiation in local pottery types with perhaps some diffuse western influence in the way of use, or increased use, of gorgets and other specialized stone forms and possibly the adoption of group burial practices. The find reported by Weslager on the eastern shore of Maryland which contained a large number of skeletons and many unusual artifacts may represent such a last vestige of western influences reaching people on the Atlantic coast. The time for such manifestations may lag somewhat behind that of the Mountain and Thomas foci. The gorgets, birdstones, and other artifacts may indicate a connection with the Point Peninsula Focus of New York.

The general picture of the Middle Atlantic area in Middle Woodland times is that of cultural continuity from the Early Woodland period with more local diversification in pottery. In the mountain areas of Virginia the pottery types seem more closely related to the heavy cord-marked, simple stamped, and fabric-impressed or cord-wrapped stick impressed types to the south in what is now the southern Virginia–North Carolina area. In Pennsylvania the wares seem to be more closely related to the types with cord marking, punctates, nodes, and dentate stamping found in what is now New York State. The pottery types in the area which now includes New Jersey and Delaware are less surely known and probably are local continuations from the Early Woodland period, with perhaps a somewhat closer affiliation to the cord-wrapped stick impressed wares of more southern areas. These relationships imply some influences from the adjoining areas. However, at this time period, the major influence is that of the Hopewellian manifestation, through its burial and perhaps ornamental complexes to the west. Such an influence was strongest in the western part of the Middle Atlantic region and its strength fades out to the east.

The Late Woodland manifestations in the Middle Atlantic area are much better known and considerably more differentiated than the cultures in the preceding periods. Again local continuity appears to be an important characteristic. To the south in the mountain area of Virginia, the continuity from the Middle Woodland period to Late Woodland may be through the Clover Creek Focus. The pottery of this focus, with its limestone temper, cord-marked surface, and appliqued fillet with punctates and fingernail decorations, is an excellent typological forerunner to the limestone- grit-tempered and cord- and

net-impressed ware, with added rim strip and fingernail marks, belonging to the Gala Focus. Somewhat to the east and north, the pottery type, Shepard Cord Marked, of the Montgomery Focus and the minority type, Page Cord Marked, of the Luray Focus have relationships to the pottery of the Gala Focus. Page Cord Marked is granite-quartz-tempered while both share added rim strips with cord-wrapped edge impressed decorations. Descriptions of what must be a very similar ware to the last two are given for a minority type at some Monongahela Culture sites in western Pennsylvania and similar sherds are occasionally pictured for eastern Pennsylvania and New Jersey. At this time, the strong mortuary complex centering in mound burial that appears to have prevailed in the mountain area in Middle Woodland times has largely given way to single interments in pits in the village area. This type of burial also is found north into Monongahela country. A last holdover of mound burial, but now developed into a definite ossuary type of burial may occur in the Piedmont region of Virginia. As evidenced by the excavation of Thomas Jefferson.[68a]

The pottery types so far discussed might be considered as local variants of a widespread tradition common at this time period. It appears possible to arrange pottery from this horizon in a typological series ranging from types in the Baum Focus of the Fort Ancient Aspect,[69] through types present in the Gala-Montgomery Foci and some collared wares of the Monongahela Culture, to types present in the Owasco Aspect of New York. In general, the pottery in this distribution is characterized by cord-marked surface finish, rounded or semi-conoidal base, slightly constricted neck, and collar often produced by adding a rim strip; but the decoration changes from emphasis on incising and fingernail incising in Fort Ancient types to impressing with cord-wrapped stick and with various dentate stamps in Owasco types. Pottery of these types, wherever found in the area, may safely be assigned to the Late Woodland period and probably to the earlier portion of the period. Such types exhibit features which indicate a continuity from the earlier Middle Woodland types.

If the collared type with the added rim strip decorated by fingernail marks or cord-wrapped stick impressions is considered to be earlier Late Woodland, then other somewhat more differentiated types can be considered as influenced by the Fort Ancient Aspect, or possibly even by Middle Mississippi groups to the west. Holmes figures sherds which possess both loop and strap handles from the New River Valley of southwestern Virginia.[70] Since the New River is on the eastern margin of the distribution of handled

68a. Jefferson, 1794.
69. Griffin, J. B., 1943a, Pl. 7, Figs. 1, 2, 7.
70. Holmes, 1903, Pl. CXXXIII.

pottery, it appears logical to consider the presence of such pottery in the southwestern Virginia area as a result of influences of the Fort Ancient Aspect reaching the area via the Ohio, Kanawha, and New River valleys. Further to the north in the vicinity of Luray, Virginia, a shell-tempered ware associated with a variety of lugs and occasionally a small handle has been found. Similar sherds were found at the Hughes Site near Washington, D.C., and trade sherds of the same ware occurred at the historic site of Patawomeke on the tidewater Potomac. This type has its closest relationship north to the Monongahela Culture, specifically to the Montague Site, in western Pennsylvania. Again this type is on the periphery of a related series and it appears logical to consider its presence in northern Virginia and Maryland as a result of influences from the Fort Ancient area following the Ohio, Monongahela-Youghiogheny valleys across to the Potomac and Shenandoah valleys. Other items or traits which are referable to a Monongahela influence are the perforated discoidals and the pits surrounded by post molds found at the Keyser Site. Trade sherds and pipes similar to those of Patawomeke and Moyaone in the tidewater area indicate that the Hughes and Keyser sites are of proto-historic times.

From the vicinity of Washington, D.C., in more eastern Virginia and southern Maryland, considerable information is available. A number of sites of villages, including one which belonged to the Powhatan Confederacy, have been partially excavated in the Potomac tidewater area. The most complete information comes from the sites of Patawomeke and Moyaone, where large fortified villages existed. The majority pottery type, Potomac Creek Cord Impressed, is related to Shepard Cord Marked of the Montgomery Focus; but the added rim strip is of less importance, and the decoration by cord-wrapped edges and twisted cord has increased in importance so that highly patterned designs of triangles and rectangles occur. Pottery of the type, Potomac Creek Cord Impressed, was made by Algonkin-speaking people at the sites of Patawomeke and Moyaone. Bushnell figures many sherds which, on the basis of illustrations, are referable to this type,[71] and which he considered to come from Siouan sites. Since at least some of the sites visited by Bushnell were inhabited by Siouan speaking peoples, it is highly probable that in this local area these people also utilized pottery belonging to the Potomac Creek Cord Impressed type.

At the site of Patawomeke, another pottery type, Rappahannock Fabric Impressed, was found. This type has a surface finish produced by impressing a plain plaited fabric, or possibly a cord-wrapped stick, and bears incised decorations of hatchured triangles and rectangles and lines fringed by punctates. Unlike Potomac Creek Cord Impressed, which appears to be largely confined to the upper Potomac tidewater and the central Virginia Piedmont region, the Rappahannock type appears to become more important to the south and possibly east to the Chesapeake Bay area.

In this tidewater Virginia area and extending into the coastal areas of Maryland and Delaware, the practice of ossuary burial in pits is important in the Late Woodland period. Those burials apparently predating the contact period, which commences in 1607, except for a few shell beads and other artifacts, contain only cremated, bundled, and occasionally articulated remains. After the contact period the amount of grave goods becomes considerable and includes much Colonial and European material. Ossuaries of this late date have produced a number of shell masks, including some with the "weeping" or "lightning eye"[72] of the type often attributed to a southern death cult. These masks probably were brought into the Chesapeake tidewater area from southwestern Virginia. As is to be expected, in the latter area there are sites which produce artifacts similar to those from eastern Tennessee. A mound excavated in Lee County, Virginia, included, among other materials attributable to the Middle Mississippi Phase, a shell mask with zigzag engraved lines below the eyes.[73]

Another type of shell gorget was found in an ossuary of the contact period of Patawomeke. These gorgets were decorated with central four-pointed stars or circles and with peripheral triangles. The designs were produced by a drilled dot technique. One of these gorgets and a gorget from the Irene mound,[74] a site of the Lamar period in coastal Georgia, are so nearly identical that the possibility of independent invention seems impossible. The drilled dot technique extends to the New Jersey area where it is found on the shell birds and runtees from the Minisink burial ground. Similar runtees and decoration technique are found throughout the Iroquois country.

To return to the question of ossuary burial in the Virginia area, it does not appear necessary to rely wholly on a "Southeastern" influence for the burial practices of the Powhatan Confederacy and the groups of the Delmarva Peninsula. The practice of interring disarticulated bones was present in the mountain and Piedmont areas in Middle Woodland times and was apparently diffusing in the direction of the coast. The ossuary burial found in the coastal groups may well be a continuation of an initially

71. Bushnell, 1935, Pls. 3, 7, 8, 13, 17e. Not all the sherds in these plates are of the Potomac Creek Cord Impressed type.

72. Holmes, 1883, Pl. LXVII, Fig. 2.
73. *Ibid.*, Pl. LXVIII.
74. Caldwell and McCann, 1941, Pl. XIXc.

Hopewellian practice transmitted and reintegrated by several groups.

In western Pennsylvania, evidences of the Late Woodland period consist mainly of manifestations of the Monongahela culture. A very large number of sites belonging to this unit have been excavated, but only a few have more than incomplete notes published concerning them. The indication from two varying pottery styles and two major projectile point types is that the sites of the Monongahela culture could be arranged into a time series within the Late Woodland period. The earlier ware appears to have been grit-tempered and to have a cord-roughened surface finish and a moderately to sharply flared rim. A later ware, influenced by Fort Ancient Aspect types to the west, has shell temper, smoothed surfaces, and a variety of lugs and appendages. The increasing frequency of triangular projectile points within the Monongahela components also indicates that they make up such a time series.

Present at some Monongahela sites is a pottery type with added rim strip and cord-wrapped edge decoration which has close relationships south to the Page Cord Marked and Shepard Cord Marked types and which also has some relationship north to Owasco Aspect types. The pottery pipe form in Monongahela sites appears to occupy an intermediate position between the Montgomery, Luray, and Potomac Creek foci types and the Owasco Aspect type. As a general impression, many of the decorations resemble southern specimens in style and design while the over all proportion of the pipes tends more to the large, swollen bowl found in the Owasco Aspect and often includes the narrow rim band also found at sites of the latter.

Butler has pointed out the probability of Fort Ancient influences on the Monongahela culture and also has noted that Iroquoian "trade sherds" occur at some sites. Although the people responsible for the Monongahela manifestations probably approached historic times, no evidence of European or Colonial contact has been found in the sites. This leaves a gap between the historic Seneca inhabitants of the area and the known archeological manifestations. Further to the east in Clinton County, Pennsylvania,[75] two "long house" sites associated with "Andaste" pottery, but with no contact material, were excavated and indicate that archeological remains of the "Iroquoian" type at least partially overlap in time those of the Monongahela culture.

Moving further to the east in Pennsylvania and to adjoining portions of New Jersey, we find that the archeological picture of Late Woodland times is somewhat confused. From the collections and excavations of the Wyoming Historical and Geological

Society in central Pennsylvania, it is evident that an occupation related to, or part of, the Owasco Aspect was strongly present in the area. A similar manifestation was present at the Minisink cemetery in New Jersey. Excavations of Schrabisch in many rock shelters, of Heye and Pepper at the Minisink cemetery, and of Cross at the Rosenkrans Ferry Site revealed the presence of much "Iroquoian" pottery in association with Owasco-like material. In all probability the Owasco types are earlier, but overlap the "Iroquoian" in time. At the Minisink cemetery the "Iroquoian" pottery and other artifact types are associated with remains left by the Algonkin-speaking Munsee of the late seventeenth century. It is probable that other "Iroquoian" remains of the area are also to be associated with Algonkin-speaking groups.

Southeastern Pennsylvania in the early seventeenth century was the home of the Susquehannocks of possible Iroquoian linguistic affinity. As a result of Cadzow's work, a number of sites can be grouped into a Susquehanna Focus. The major affiliations of this grouping are up the Susquehanna River to the so called "Andaste" remains in the vicinity of Athens, Pennsylvania, and to Skinner's Western Iroquoian Group. Points of similarity are: the double-necked vessel, high collared vessel, other vessel forms with narrow collars and mammiform projections, and modeled faces on vessel collars. On the other hand, the presence of shell temper, some appendage forms, and cord marking in Susquehannock pottery is suggestive of Monongahela Culture pottery.

The presence of two types of "Iroquoian" manifestations in the eastern Pennsylvania and western New Jersey area, is of such a nature that they appear intrusive—that is, intrusive in that they do not represent local developments in situ. The more northeastern manifestations are largely limited to pottery, except at the Minisink cemetery. It is probable that here a large proportion of the "Iroquoian" material items were used by Algonkin speaking groups and that they replaced older forms by a combination of the processes of diffusion and trade. These "Iroquoian" remains of northeastern Pennsylvania and New Jersey resemble Skinner's Eastern or Mohawk-Onondaga remains.

The Susquehannock artifacts of the lower Susquehanna Valley more closely resemble those of the Western Iroquoian Group of Skinner. The Susquehannocks are generally thought to have been Iroquoian speaking, and since their material culture appear to have replaced an older form called "Algonkin" by Cadzow and which is also of the Late Woodland time period, the possibility of a migration down the Susquehanna by an Iroquoian-speaking group is strong. The cord-marked surface finish of the Susquehannock pottery and some narrow collars with the lower

75. Godcharles, 1934.

edges nicked or incised, however, suggest a continuation of older Woodland traditions into the Iroquoian material.

In the greater part of what is now the state of New Jersey, the indications of cultural continuity from the earliest period through to Late Woodland are strong. This continuity is so striking that it appears to have discouraged workers from any attempts to determine chronology. There are, however, pottery types in the New Jersey area which have close relationships south to historic types in Virginia and Maryland and probably north to types on Long Island. The Owasco-Iroquois influence does not seem to have affected the New Jersey material culture as strongly as it did that of coastal groups in the vicinity of Long Island Sound.

SUMMARY

A widely scattered prepottery, pre-agricultural population has been postulated for the Archaic period in this region. This early period, by the addition of pottery, was transformed into the Early Woodland period. During Early Woodland times the type of hunting and gathering existence was probably very similar to that of the Archaic. Agriculture may have been introduced into the area in the latter part of the Early Woodland period though this is at best inferential.

By Middle Woodland times, considerable local diversity existed and particularly the Mountain and Piedmont region was strongly influenced by burial practices emanating from Hopewellian developments in the Ohio area. Trade was highly developed in this period and particularly shells and stone gorgets appear to have traveled far. A secondary center of influence seems to have been that occupied by the Point Peninsula Focus of New York, and articles which may have come from that culture have been found in Virginia and Delaware. Agriculture may have been present in the area at this time.

The Late Woodland period is one of considerable diversity, though continuity with the preceding period is present. The population may have increased substantially over that of former times though it is possible that this only seems to be the case for the reason that late sites are more obvious than earlier ones. The prevalence of fortified sites during Late Woodland times may indicate an increase of unfriendly relations. Two strong influences from outside areas are discernible. One, from the Fort Ancient area, appears to have entered the Middle Atlantic region both to the south via the New River Valley of Virginia and to the north via the Youghiogheny and Monongahela Valleys in Pennsylvania. The second strong influence was from "Iroquoian" groups in the New York area. The "Iroquoian" influence may have been from two centers, an Eastern and a Western. At this time the more western people of the Middle Atlantic area had given up mound, ossuary, and group burial practices in favor of single interments. However, the practice of ossuary burial was prominent in the Chesapeake area.

SIXTY YEARS OF ONTARIO ARCHEOLOGY.
By Kenneth E. Kidd*

ARCHEOLOGICAL research in the Province of Ontario has had a long history attended with not unrewarding results. A great deal more was accomplished by the early students of the subject than is generally realized, and at present their work is being carried forward by various institutions. Intensive work, leading to the classification of cultures, has not proceeded as fast here as in other parts of the continent, it is true, but the prospects for increased activity are encouraging. Whatever is done in the future will be based to a large extent on what has already been done. Since the history and results of that work are so little known, it is hoped this paper will serve a useful purpose by outlining them. But before one can grasp the problems in their full reality, it is necessary to understand something of the geographical background in which they are set.

The Province of Ontario is a vast region of diverse climatic, geologic and ecologic conditions. It embraces within its borders a large segment of the ancient Laurentian Shield, part of which is sub-arctic in climate and contains country never yet trodden by white men. In its southern extremities it contains the fertile, often level country of the St. Lawrence Valley, temperate in climate and always a hospitable land. The Laurentian Shield portion, by contrast, is characterized by a somewhat severe climate. Innumerable lakes and streams run through a rocky country where the soil is scattered and shallow, yet sufficient to support an almost impenetrable forest of softwoods, mostly evergreen. That part of the Province known as Southern Ontario, really a triangle formed between Lake Huron on the west, Lakes Erie and Ontario on the southeast, and the Ottawa Valley on the north, is on the other hand temperate in climate, possessing deep, fertile lands, supporting for the most part deciduous hardwoods. Such in briefest outline are the main contrasts in the two great subdivisions of the vast Province stretching a thousand miles from east to west and nearly as much from north to south.

The same contrasts account not only for differences in aboriginal cultural adjustments, but are equally responsible for our present inadequate knowledge of them. The difficulties of travel in the deep forest, and the near-absence of agriculture, have contributed to leave archeological sites undisturbed; whereas in the south, systematic surveying, intensive agriculture and a certain amount of leisure have brought to light many hundred of sites and innumerable surface finds. What we know of archeology in the north, aside from Greenman's work at Killarney, has been learned primarily from chance finds made during the construction of highways, railroads, and occasionally from observations made along watercourses and in building.

In southern Ontario antiquarians began the work of exploration in pioneer times.[1] David Boyle, the first systematic archeologist in the Province, was able to devote to such work all of his time after about 1887 until his death in 1911. During that period, he trenched several mounds in various parts of Ontario and built up a large surface collection from all over the same region. The catalogue which he kept gives in most cases the provenience of individual specimens. His is the first archeological work in Ontario which may safely be called scientific. He did not, it is true, have altogether the same objectives as a modern archeologist, nor did he have the same appreciation of time depth and culture sequence, but his approach was nevertheless that of a careful empiricist who expected to learn by observing.

Around Boyle there developed a group of able men who undoubtedly laid the foundations of archeology in the Province. One of these, George Laidlaw by name, made important contributions to our knowledge of aboriginal occupation in the country east of Lake Simcoe, principally Victoria County, but his life was cut short some twenty years ago. W. G. Long will be remembered best for his careful work on certain mounds in the Trent Valley system. But the most outstanding followers of Boyle are undoubtedly William J. Wintemberg and Andrew F. Hunter, both of whom have died within the present decade. Hunter, to take the last named first, was perhaps more of an historian than an archeologist for he did

* University of Toronto in Arts, 1931; M.A., 1937; Department of Anthropology, University of Chicago, 1939–1940; Deputy Keeper, Ethnological Collections, Royal Ontario Museum of Archeology, Toronto. Chapter received March, 1948.

1. Pioneer times in Ontario are of recent date, reaching back not more than 150 years, compared with parts of the East which have a recorded history of more than 300 years.

71

little actual digging. We shall, however, be forever indebted to him for recording with all possible fidelity and completeness every Indian site of which he could find evidence. Most of his research was done in his native county of Simcoe which, as it happens, was also the historic homeland of the Hurons. His notebooks contain 637 site references, each carefully and fully described as to type (whether village, ossuary, or trail), location and whether or not it contained European goods. By far the largest portion of these refer to Simcoe County, and the remainder to counties adjacent to it, so that by a strange stroke of fortune, we have a remarkably full and critical record of the historic homeland of the Hurons, made at a time when the old pioneers still recalled the location of sites which are now obliterated by cultivation. No other portion of the Province has a record anywhere near so complete. This circumstance, taken in conjunction with the invaluable records of this extinct people preserved in the *Jesuit Relations,* opens the way for an ideal ethnohistorical approach to the archeology of this particular region.

Wintemberg, however, is Boyle's best known protégé. He was brought to the Provincial Museum of which Boyle was head, and worked there for a number of years before joining the staff of the National Museum at Ottawa. From there most of his field work was conducted. During his thirty years with that institution, Wintemberg carried out numerous excavations, about six or seven of which have been published. Until the entry of the Royal Ontario Museum into the field of active investigation, Wintemberg's work embodied almost our entire knowledge of systematic archeology in Ontario.

This résumé is based essentially on (1) recent work by the Royal Ontario Museum, (2) Wintemberg's reports,[2] (3) Boyle's activities and those of his associates as described in the Ontario Archeological Reports, and (4) the surface collections which have accumulated during the past 70 years and are now in the above Museum. To this end, Wintemberg's reports are summarized, except those which are readily available; certain other reports not generally accessible are cited; the essential features of Boyle's work are reviewed, and the work of the Royal Ontario Museum staff is indicated. Various other important contributions are also brought together in order to make the paper as comprehensive as possible.

It seems to have been entirely fortuitous that most of the sites so far excavated in Ontario have been Iroquoian or proto-Iroquoian. That they are the largest and most prolific in the Province may have had some influence upon their selection. A meager legacy of knowledge concerning the non-Iroquoian cultures

has come down to us, although some of Boyle's work had to do with others such as mound-building cultures. That such had existed in Ontario is beyond question, as hundreds or even thousands of artifacts bear witness. But as these latter are for the most part surface finds, not always clearly documented, little attempt is made in this paper to classify Ontario cultures except on the broadest terms. That we have Iroquoian we know, and we likewise are aware of the presence of Woodland, Hopewellian and some archaic cultures, but beyond such an elementary classification it would be unwarranted to proceed at this stage of our knowledge.

Because of the profound geographical and other differences existing between southern Ontario and the rest of the Province, the description of its archeology has been cast into two sections, one dealing with the southern portion, and the other with that great area which lies upon the Laurentian Shield. Southern Ontario may be treated first.

SOUTHERN ONTARIO

HISTORIC HURON

The historic Hurons are known from many sites in the north part of Simcoe County, south of Georgian Bay. They were found there by Champlain in 1615, and by the Recollets and Jesuits who dwelt among them until their destruction by the Five Nations in 1649. While no publication has appeared upon an excavated site of this people as yet,[3] large surface collections are in existence which seem to be fairly reliable. The situations which the Hurons chose are well known. They preferred a high headland surrounded on three, or at least two, sides by ravines; sandy or gravelly soil seem always to have been their choice. A small stream was generally within easy distance, but the site was located far from large rivers and lakes. Large refuse dumps are situated at the edges of ravines, often continuing down their slopes even to the bottom. Or they may occur on the surface of the headland, usually in original hollows. These consist mainly of ashes and camp refuse, as well as greater or lesser amounts of potsherds, broken and unbroken tools of stone, bone, and antler, and ornaments. Quantities of fish, mammal and bird bone, in that order, are commonly found in them. Projectile points are small, triangular, unnotched, made of grey chert, and relatively rare (Fig. 27, *A*). Scrapers of the same material are of the snub-nosed and thumbnail varieties, often delicately chipped along the working edges. Rectanguloid axes, adzes and chisels of diorite, diabase, granite, etc. are roughly shaped and usually unfinished. Mortars of large field stones have a con-

---

2. Since this paper was written, Wintemberg's last report, *The Middleport Prehistoric Village Site,* has appeared, 1948.

3. A report on a historic Huron site is in preparation by Professor T. F. McIlwraith, Mr. J. N. Emerson, and Miss M. Thomson.

cave hollow on one face and are frequently too large to be portable. Small disks of stone, sometimes centrally perforated, are not uncommon. Bone is used freely and worked rather well. Conical projectile points of bone, unsocketed except for the hollow end are fairly plentiful (Fig. 27, B). Harpoon points of bone, multi-barbed on one side with a perforation near the shaft end are found occasionally (Fig. 27, C). Bone awls and netting needles are abundant and of several forms. Tubular beads made of sections of bird bone (Fig. 27, E), and discoidal or cylindrical beads made from conch shells are common. Small carvings of human beings, often paired, are skilfully executed in bone (Fig. 27, D, F). Beads of a red slate resembling catlinite are long and square in cross-section. Other beads of the same material are zoomorphic, representing turtles and other animals (Fig. 27, K). A typical shell bead found on historic Huron sites is about one inch square, perforated lengthwise.

Pottery is abundant and well diversified within its pattern. It is grit-tempered, usually with crushed gneiss containing spicules of mica. The paste is fine and of a reddish, buff or grey hue. Exteriors of vessels are usually polished or smoothed. Forms of vessels are basically globular with constricted neck, flaring rim and one or more castellations (Fig. 27, M). Shoulders are often pronounced. A typical though not common form is keel-shaped (Fig. 27, N). Traces of red paint apparently occur on a few pieces, probably accidentally. Decoration is confined to the outside of the rim, the neck, and the shoulder, and consists of punctations, trailed and incised lines. The latter two are applied in the form of hatched triangles, the lines in adjacent triangles running in opposite directions. Size ranges from diminutive vessels to others with a diameter of one foot or slightly more. Very large vessels seem to be rare. Disks made from potsherds are very common (Fig. 27, I).

Pottery pipes are extremely abundant and of many forms. They are elbow-shaped, right-angled or obtuse-angled, and made of a fine, homogeneous paste, devoid of tempering so far as the eye can tell, which bakes to a bright buff, red or sometimes almost a white. Black pipes are also common, made no doubt by greasing and burning or by holding in smoke. Pipes of all forms are frequently carefully scraped and often highly polished. Stems are medium to long, and usually rather slender. They may be plain or decorated with three longitudinal rows of notches along raised ridges. Cross-sections have various shapes. There is great variety in shapes of bowls, most of them being basically cylindrical with square rims with or without castellations at the corners, or cylindrical with modeled effigies of birds, mammals or humans on the rim (Fig. 27, L). These, with the exception of the effigy forms, are often further elab-

orated with punctate or incised designs. Incised lines radiating outward on the rim of the trumpet-shaped pipe, for instance, convert it into the semblance of a blossom resembling the squash, the datura or the convolvulus. Effigy pipes made with the bowl in the form of a crouching human figure with hands beneath the chin are common to this horizon (Fig. 27, J). Such pipes are generally of a highly polished black.

Stone pipe bowls are commonly made from a greenstone like serpentine or steatite, as well as from slate, limestone and even harder materials. They were made for use with a detachable stem of reed or wood. These bowls are most frequently vasiform, though sometimes conoidal, rectanguloid and wedge-shaped (Fig. 27, G, H), and almost always have a small perforation at the bottom of the bowl for suspension when not in use.

The mortuary practices of the historic Hurons are well enough known from Jesuit accounts not to require repetition here.[4] Numerous ossuaries have been opened from time to time by relic hunters until few remain. Some of these have been estimated to contain the remains of as many as a thousand individuals, disarticulated and in bundles. A few bodies—those recently dead—were buried in the flesh in pits. Traces of beaver skin, quantities of discoidal wampum and trade goods, particularly copper kettles and fragments of copper, were deposited with the dead.

It remains to be added that these contact sites yield considerable quantities of trade goods, especially iron axes, iron knives and awls, some of which are set in bone handles of various types, conical brass points, and a few triangular, tanged points of iron, and glass beads of several types.

PREHISTORIC HURON

Certain sites in the territory of the Hurons which yield no European materials are thought to be those of prehistoric Huron villages. The material from them is so similar to that from historic Huron sites and to that from Wintemberg's Sidey-Mackay Site in the nearby Petun country[5] that one may be justified in accepting them as prehistoric Huron until such time as one of them is excavated. Such sites are frequently in less defensible locations than the later ones, as for instance, in an open plain, but yet a good distance from rivers. Refuse dumps are spotted irregularly over the plain. The bones of fish are abundant; those of birds and mammals seemingly less so. Pipes appear to be less common. Pottery decoration is probably less diversified.

4. Thwaites (ed.), 1897, Vol. 10, pp. 265–305. Sagard (in *Trois Voyages au Canada*), n.d., pp. 203–204; Kinietz, 1940, pp. 99–119.
5. Wintemberg, 1946.

PREHISTORIC NEUTRAL

The Neutral Indians, also of Iroquoian stock, are known to have inhabited that part of Ontario which lies west of the great escarpment running from Niagara to Collingwood, with most of their villages in the fertile country north of Lake Erie. No historic site, so far as the writer is aware, has been excavated or reported upon. The "Lawson Site," formerly known as the "Shaw-Wood" Site, in Middlesex County, was probably a late prehistoric Neutral station however.[6] Its excavator, the late William J. Wintemberg, was of this opinion, and at least a large segment of the pottery which he recovered from it conforms well to the Iroquoian pattern. He was evidently not satisfied that all the material pertained to one culture for he writes: "it was impossible to ascertain if there was a chronological sequence of types [of pottery], owing to the disturbed condition of the deposits"; and again, "A few fragments appear to be of non-Iroquoian origin." A study of Wintemberg's descriptions and illustrations indicates that a large percentage of the sherds show a slightly collared rim, incipient castellations, constricted necks, overhanging collars and rounded bodies. Decoration is confined practically to the rim, sometimes rim and shoulders, and consists of incising and punctating. The incised lines are arranged in plats and triangles on the rims, sometimes with the addition of horizontal lines; the punctating serves to outline triangles or to border a zone. Several of the pottery pipes found at the site fit well into the late prehistoric Iroquoian picture also, notably the elbow pipes with cylindrical bowls decorated with horizontal grooves and rows of punctate notches below. Those with incised triangles and chevron designs, the human effigy forms, and the stem fragments bear notches arranged in lengthwise series. The stone pipes carved with human face masks are likewise known from late Iroquoian sites, as well as the vasiform and conoidal forms. It would be unprofitable, in view of the confused nature of the deposits, to speculate in detail on the cultural attributions of the bone and stone industries represented at the site, other than to point out that the conical bone point and various awl forms have Iroquoian affinities.

The Lawson Village Site also bore a number of resemblances to the Younge Site of southern Michigan, which Dr. Emerson F. Greenman excavated. For the sake of brevity, it seems best to cite these comparisons rather than to give a detailed account of them. Both sites were situated on small plateaus near or on streams, the plateaus in both cases running in an east-west direction. Both showed a long, narrow arrangement of post molds, probably outlining the habitations, the Younge Site being much the larger in this regard. On the latter there were 61 pits,[7] on the Lawson, 120. At both locations these contained ashes and a few artifacts, although those on the Michigan site yielded in addition a good deal of bone and mussel shell which was not the case at Lawson. Projectile points at both sites were of chipped chert, triangular and unnotched or notched, and in a few cases were leaf-shaped and notched. What were probably net-sinkers were found at both sites, as were also whetstones or hones of sandstone. There is likewise a large degree of correspondence in ceramics. Grit tempering was employed at both; one case of shell tempering occurred at Lawson. Body sherds show fabric roughening,[8] paddle-marking;[9] rim sherds show cord-wrapped paddle impressions, punctate lines and stamped designs. Notable in many sherds from both sites are the rows of small punctate dots on the rims. Clay pipes of the right-angled or elbow variety are common to both; these usually possess short, stubby stems and cylindrical bowls decorated with numerous little punctate dots,[10] or simple incised designs. Wintemberg reported that he found only one grave, which contained parts of the skeleton of a child and of two adults. Another grave opened previously had contained four skeletons "buried in a pile," with the long bones below and the skulls on top, while still another discovered by early diggers was surrounded by clam shells. These can be matched respectively, albeit somewhat roughly, with Greenman's Burials No. 32 (three apparently disturbed bundle burials); Group 1, Burial 6; and as for the last-mentioned Lawson burial, no direct correspondence occurred at the Younge Site, except that Burial 16 included a few mussel shells. Wintemberg remarked particularly upon two human tibiae in the possession of a local collector who found them under unspecified circumstances on the Lawson Site, and one of which he illustrated in his Figure 6. "Both its tuberosities and the whole top of its head have been removed and flattened, and both sides of its lower extremities have also been flattened, the internal malleolus being entirely removed."[11] The practice at Lawson of the modification of the long bones is one of the strongest similarities between the two sites. Cranial disks cut from human skulls also occur at both though the Lawson village specimens were both perforated and incised, in contradistinction to the plain, unperforated ones at the Younge Site.

There is thus a considerable degree of similarity in the cultures at these two sites. The fact that burials

6. Wintemberg, 1939.

7. Greenman, 1937, p. 13.

8. Wintemberg, 1939, Pl. IV, Figs. 3, 4; Greenman, 1937, Pl. XX, Fig. 2.

9. Wintemberg, 1939, Pl. IV, Fig. 14; Greenman, 1937, Pl. XX, Fig. 1.

10. Greenman, 1937, Pl. XXI, Fig. 2a; Wintemberg, 1939, Pl. XV, Fig. 13.

11. Wintemberg, 1939, p. 43. Cf. Greenman, 1937, pp. 38–39.

were not found in greater numbers at the Ontario village makes it impossible to use this important trait to better advantage in assessing the linkage.

There are strong similarities also between the site presently being discussed and the second occupation at Clearville in Kent County, particularly in pottery pipes, and cranial disks; and between this site and Uren. Indeed, all three sites have a great deal in common. Stronger bonds, no doubt, exist between them than between any single one and any more distant culture, such as the Younge Site manifests, despite many apparent link-traits.

THE UREN VILLAGE SITE

Wintemberg excavated in 1920 another village site, in South Norwich township, Oxford County.[12] He called it the Uren Site, after the owner of the farm where it was located. The station is prehistoric, or at least no European artifacts were found on it. Wintemberg considered that probably "the people were Neutrals, among the earliest Neutrals, perhaps, to arrive in this region, their culture possibly modified by contact with Algonkian predecessors. . . . The inhabitants of Uren, therefore were probably proto-Neutrals."

The site was about 15 acres in extent, situated on a piece of undulating land of sandy loam, south of a small stream. Some ten other village sites, believed to be of the same culture, are scattered over an area of 20 square miles. These are close together, mostly on the banks of large streams, "in which," remarks Wintemberg, "they differ most from later Neutral sites." There were no hillside dumps, although the 20 or so ash beds were irregularly placed on the site itself, and not clearly defined. In some of these deposits there was a layer of burnt sand, or rather "the sand below the ash layer . . . had been hardened by fire." The middle layer comprised ashes from two to five inches thick, the upper consisted of black soil. Refuse pits three and one-half feet deep and four and one-half feet in diameter, some more, some less, were dug through the ash beds and contained in addition to discoloured soil, some charcoal and a few artifacts, such as sherds. The bottom of one pit was hardened by fire.

Corn, sunflower seeds, and butternuts were found, though not abundantly. Mammal bones made up 88 per cent of all bones found, with bird, fish, shell and amphibian remains next and in that order. Consequently, the people of Uren probably lived largely by hunting and fishing, ekeing out this livelihood with a little farming. The chert, quartz and quartzite points were leaf-shaped, triangular or pentagonal and either stemmed or notched. Triangular points with concave bases appear to have been the most numerous variety. Those which were notched were so made that the cross-section where the notches came was rhomboidal. Scrapers of chert were carefully finished. Hammerstones were pitted, oval to round. Adzes were trianguloid and rectanguloid. Axes were ungrooved, thick and wedge-shaped. Whetstones were made of shale or sandstone in irregular, thin slabs. Mortars were small and portable. Pendants were made of notched and perforated pebbles. An apparently unfinished gorget of slate is rectangular with two biconical perforations. One piece of hematite was the only paint material. From antler, the people of Uren had fashioned conical projectile points, unilaterally barbed harpoon points, little cylinders and flakers, and perhaps most of striking of all, combs with large trapezoidal heads bearing incised chevron designs. Circular gorgets with several perforations were made from human skull. Freshwater clam shells were used probably as spoons or knives, while beads were made from the shell of *Marginella apicina,* an oceanic form.

Pottery was fabricated either from clay alone or from clay mixed with crushed stone, coarse sand or limestone for tempering material. It baked to a light buff, dark brown, gray or black and was often mottled in these colors. A trace of red paint was found on one sherd. The vessels were symmetrically proportioned, being globular with round bottoms, slightly constricted necks, flaring mouths and more or less incurved or rolled rims. Another form possessed round bottoms, with walls rising nearly perpendicularly and either slightly incurved at the top, or with the rim slightly everted. Castellations occurred on three vessels. Decoration was applied to the outside and inside of rims, and to the exterior of the entire vessel. The bodies were scarified with wisps of dry grass, malleated with grooved and check stamped paddled or cord-wrapped tools, or impressed with textiles. Rims were incised, embossed from the inside, stamped and punched. Punctate marks were of various shapes, as round, oval, and angular. Short, vertical elements were present on the inside and outside of some rims; short, crescentic impressions mostly on the interior. Oblique and crescentic impressions in a double row with the elements slanting in opposite directions constituted another design. The same elements were sometimes arranged into a zigzag pattern. Horizontal lines singly or in bands of from two to seven lines, small circles, always part of a compound design; V- or U-shaped grooved lines, usually concentric, and a triangular grouping of circles, oval or round depressions are other characteristic features. The author remarks upon the following negative traits: the absence of chevrons, the undecorated shoulders and the paucity of rectilinear and curvilinear designs in comparison to Iroquois work. Clay

12. Wintemberg, 1928.

pipes are light to dark grey or reddish buff, and are of a type now called the elbow pipe, although Wintemberg describes one as a monitor type.[13] Stems are various in form and short. Bowls are conical and cylindrical. A noteworthy form is knobbed, at least on the stem.

THE ROEBUCK SITE

There remains to be considered the Roebuck Village Site excavated in 1912–1915 by Wintemberg.[14] Situated in Augusta Township, Grenville County, this site is about eight miles north of the St. Lawrence River, where it occupies the top of a long sandhill surrounded on three sides by an alder swamp. It covers approximately eight acres, and had 24 large refuse deposits, oval in outline, containing ashes and quantities of bones and artifacts. Some of the deposits were stratified into as many as five layers, the one separated from the other by ashes. They were as much as four feet deep by 95 feet long and 50 feet wide. Some were on level ground, others on the slopes of ravines. Burials within them were numerous. The site yielded large quantities of material in the form of pottery, bone, stone, antler, and some shell and wood artifacts.

A defensive outwork or palisade originally stood across the narrow part of the spit of land on which the site was located.

The 83 burials were found in all parts of the site, but 46 were in areas covered with refuse and 39 of these were found in the largest of the refuse deposits. Half of the total number were placed in deep holes evidently before refuse was present. In addition to single burials, there were three groups of double burials, two of which had the skeletons arranged in opposite directions, and three triple burials. Legs were all more or less flexed, some of them acutely. Positions varied, for some skeletons lay face down, some on the back, others on the right or left side. Only nine were adult male burials. Grave goods were sparse. One pot and possibly a few bone awls, charred corn and potsherds exhaust the list. Besides the burials, there were large numbers of scattered human bones found on the refuse heaps, mostly in broken condition, hacked and sawed, and sometimes boiled and scorched.

Chipped stone was not abundant. A few triangular notched or unnotched points, triangular and stemmed points, leaf-shaped knives and thumbnail scrapers practically exhaust the list.

Ground stone objects were more plentiful. Whetstones, hammerstones, portable mortars, discoidal soapstone beads, irregular imperforate disks, three fragmentary slate gorgets and three pipes come under this heading. One of the slate gorgets was hexagonal, four inches long, and had two perforations, another was rectanguloid and imperforate. The slate pipe was wedge-shaped; a soapstone pipe was probably obtuse-angled.

Beads were made of snail shells, and of the columellae of conchs. Conical points were fashioned from antler, one type of which had channelled bases. Harpoon points of antler were unilaterally barbed. Other tools made of this material included corn husking pins, probably chisels or wedges, handles for knives and combs.

Bone was used extensively for both utilitarian and ornamental purposes. Points of bone were wedge-shaped with pointed or notched bases, or with channeled bases. Harpoon points were both uni- and bilaterally barbed. There were four barbed fish hooks, and numerous small barbs and gorgets. Awls were extremely abundant, numbering 1,210. Beads were plain and cylindrical. Phalanges of deer were shaped, according to Wintemberg, for use in the cup-and-pin game, while other deer phalanges were flattened to varying degrees. Pipes were made of deer scapulae to the number of 29.

Teeth of dogs were made into beads. Beaver teeth served as chisels and knives.

Over 11,000 sherds were recovered from the site, but only very small pots were entire. For tempering, crushed gneiss was used. The color was buff, red, brown, pinkish, and gray to black, with the first three most common. There was no evidence of painting. Surfaces were mostly smooth, except for the decorated areas. In general, the vessels were smaller than those on Wintemberg's Neutral sites. The basic shape was globular, with a few cup-like forms. The rims might be vertical, but more often there was a constricted neck with an everted or an overhanging rim. Rims frequently had castellations. Handles were found on 29 vessels, extending from the base of the overhanging rim to the top of the shoulder. Sometimes they were decorated. Shoulder shapes varied. Some were plain, others ridged, flattened, or possessed a raised, encircling band.

The bodies of vessels were usually left smooth, though some showed the effect of scarifying with grass, or of malleating with a grooved paddle. Some also showed textile impressions and checker stamping, but these were few. Decoration was confined to rim, neck and shoulder, and very rarely on the body.

Decoration techniques included pinching, trailing, incising, punctating with, in 1,100 cases, stamping. The latter usually took the form of square markings, but rectangular marks are not uncommon. Pinching the wet clay into notches along the upper or lower

---

13. *Ibid.*, Pl. XXIII, Fig. 11. The illustration is not very satisfactory; the author describes this specimen on p. 39 as "nearly [approaching] the typical form in having a prow-like projection apparently at the front of the bowl."

14. Wintemberg, 1936.

margin of the rim is a common feature, and the notches may be of several shapes and sizes. Modeling the outer surface of rims into ridges which are then horizontally grooved or incised is also characteristic. When the treatment shows numerous small ridges of this sort, the excavator used the term "corn-ear" to describe the design. Most rims possess a narrow band along the top consisting of hatching, usually slanting. Below this is a main zone of decoration, occupying the greater portion of the rim. This zone shows considerable variety of treatment; a chevron design of some sort, usually with incised hatching running in opposite directions on either side of the central line is a common feature; so also are triangles of hatching, and at this site, such triangles show a tendency to be elongated, isosceles or right-angled. In some cases, the the rim is hatched in one direction only, with bands of grooved lines at intervals crossing the hatching at an angle to give the effect of a chevron, or there may be horizontal grooves crossing it and bordering it top and bottom. Another common feature is the arrangement of impressed circles, usually in threes in triangular arrangement, either set off by themselves or impressed upon the hatching. There may also be single or double vertical lines of circles, or hollow squares or rectangles. Occasionally small human masks are modeled on the rim, usually below a castellation.

Clay pipes were mostly of the elbow type, but two were almost tubular, one of them in the shape of a fish, the other resembling a corn-cob, with the incised "corn-ear" design. Wintemberg divides these pipes into five main types as follows: (a) nearly tubular; (b) cylindrical; (c) trumpet; (d) ovoid; and (e) conoid. The trumpet form was the most abundant. Modeling was important on pipes, with human faces and bird or animal effigies most frequent. Nearly half the stems were round in section. There was no apparent tempering in the clay used. The color was gray to terra cotta, none was black. The surface on most was polished, frequently very highly. Stem-holes were made by modeling around a small stick or piece of reed; twisted grass was never used, as it was at Huron and other Iroquoian sites.

The age of this site is not estimated, other than that it is prehistoric. The people subsisted on wild and cultivated plant foods, and on the flesh of animals, with evidence for the use of human flesh in the number of boiled and broken bones on the site. They were proficient in making pottery, which showed a high degree of elaboration of the rim and the possession of handles. A fragment of twined weaving testifies to the knowledge of that technique. The excavator felt that the Roebuck people "seem to have advanced to a higher degree of culture than the Neutrals; were as advanced as the early Tionontati and

Hurons, to whom they were certainly not inferior in their modeling of life forms on earthenware pipes; and they exceeded all three in the elaboration of pot forms."[15] He saw the closest similarity on the one hand in the culture of the Mohawk, and on the other to the Onondaga and suggested that "at the period when this and the nearby sites of the same culture were occupied, the Mohawk and Onondaga had not become separated into the present distinct tribes."[16]

THE CLEARVILLE SITE

Another location clearly of the Iroquois Aspect but in western Ontario, and which may likewise be late prehistoric, is the upper level of the Clearville Site in Orford Township, Kent County. This large palisaded village was situated on a small plain surrounded by bluffs from 10 to 35 feet high. Further afield on the north the land was level, while along the west ran a small stream. The soil is a sandy loam and quite fertile. The place was occupied three times, both of the upper occupation levels being separated from the one below by several inches of drift sand. Mr. Wilfrid Jury of the University of Western Ontario has begun the excavation of this important site, which he hopes to continue in the near future.[17] Enough evidence has already been obtained to justify a few conclusions regarding it. Mr. Jury considers that "the inhabitants of this site belonged to the Iroquoian stock and were probably Neutrals." A study of the pottery shown in the report indicates its close kinship with much of that from the Lawson site, which Wintemberg postulated as late prehistoric and probably Neutral. It shows incised decoration on the rim, in triangles with rows of punctate dots bordering it in some cases, and decoration of oblong and lenticular punctations arranged, like the incised lines, in triangles with the direction in adjacent triangles being opposed. Rims are overhanging and castellated. Clay pipes are conical, obtuse-angled or elbow form. Decoration seems to be confined to rows of horizontal grooves below the rim. Projectile points are made of flint, small, triangular with straight or concave bases, and unnotched.

During the second occupation at Clearville, subsistence included the use of corn, beans and squash, but with a seeming predominance of hunting, particularly of the deer, bear, squirrel, raccoon and woodchuck. Pits were dug through the deposits below into the sand. Chipped points were triangular, as well as notched and stemmed. Pottery comprised globular vessels with plain or decorated rims. The decoration was simple and seemingly often crudely done; the designs illustrated show a slanting hatching on the rim with or without a row of punctations to mark the shoulder. Gorgets were made of human skull, per-

15. *Ibid.*, p. 124.　　16. *Ibid.*, p. 124.　　17. Jury, 1941.

forated and decorated with incised rectilinear designs. Pipes were of the elbow type. In some of these respects a linkage with Lawson is evident; in others also with Uren.

The first occupation at Clearville shows pottery with shoulder and rim decoration consisting of roughly scratched line or incised lines, sketchily arranged into triangular plats. Still another type shows the use of a stamp below the rim, combined with short incised lines arranged in series on the shoulder. The first occupation yielded no human bones and no corn. Houses, however, are said to have been floored with rushes and corn-stalks.

THE ALWAY SITE

The Alway Site in Lobo Township, Middlesex County, also excavated by Jury, appears to be very closely related to the culture last described.[18]

THE PORT MAITLAND SITE

The work of Mr. Peter Pringle, as reported by Dr. William A. Ritchie, leaves us in no doubt of the existence of the Point Peninsula culture within the borders of Ontario.[19] The site referred to is situated at the mouth of the Grand River, near Dunnville, in Dunn Township, Haldimand County. As a matter of fact, two discoveries have been made at the same site at intervals of thirty years. The earlier find, called the "Chief's Grave," revealed a skeleton sitting upright, surrounded by red paint, and two deposits of mortuary objects. The later was a child's burial, flexed with head to the east. Accompanying artifacts included a platform pipe of stone, two large combs of antler incised with designs on the head, a trianguloid pendant of slate, the typical tool made of beaver incisors mounted in an antler handle and other material. Ritchie accepts also the presence of this focus at the Bay of Quinte, citing the account of Wallbridge in 1860. The Royal Ontario Museum of Archeology collections contain a certain number of specimens belonging to this culture, suggesting its presence in Huron, Peel, and York counties as well as Haldimand and Prince Edward (Fig. 28, *A, B*).

It is worthy of note here that a site almost certainly belonging to this culture is known to exist in Nottawasaga Township, Simcoe County, whence have come the antler-hafted beaver incisors so characteristic of Point Peninsula and several conical, socketed points of antler. No pottery was reported from it, nor any stone points, although the above material was associated with a burial.[20]

Moreover, as Ritchie has pointed out, there are parallels to Point Peninsula in the so-called Intrusive

Mound culture. In Ontario, intrusive burials in mounds are known to occur at Cameron's Point on Rice Lake, on Sugar Island, Rice Lake; possibly in Prince Edward County. They vary from one to two feet below the surface, surrounded by stones, but are devoid of grave goods.[21] Original descriptions do not allow of a much more detailed picture than this.

MIZANG'S POINT, RICE LAKE MOUNDS

On Mizang's Point, Rice Lake, is a complex of mounds, one of which is described by Boyle as being 189 feet long with two pronounced convolutions, giving it a resemblance to a serpent, with another oval mound opposite the head end, and three or four smaller mounds nearby.[22] The so-called Serpent Mound on sampling yielded besides intrusive burials, at least one original burial on the ground level, a few burnt human bones near the centre of the mound, and one human skull, also an original burial. Still nearer the centre, Boyle found a bed of black soil and ashes mixed with mussel shells, beneath which again was a circle of stones, some of which appeared to be fire-cracked. But there was no trace of ashes or charcoal inside the circle. The only artifacts were a few sherds and they were not directly associated with any of the burials, being below the bed of ashes. There are certain correspondences with the Effigy Mound culture of Wisconsin demonstrated here.

OTHER MOUND STRUCTURES IN ONTARIO

Boyle and some of his co-workers, especially W. G. Long and Phillips, excavated in whole or in part a number of mound structures in Ontario, and have left reasonably adequate reports on their work. Most of them may be found in the *Annual Archeological Report for Ontario, 1896–1897*. For that time, their methods were good. Notes were kept on the nature of the construction of the mounds, their shape, size and orientation; on the contents, the number, orientation, and condition of burials, whether they were original or intrusive; and on the quantity, nature and disposition of grave goods where present. However, it was seldom that a mound was completely excavated, and descriptions are often rather brief, so that we have to be satisfied with a reference to a "circle of stone" around a skeleton or are left to guess the nature of the intrusive burials. Reference has already been made to the connection existing between Point Peninsula and intrusive burials, so that no more need be said on that score. Enough is thus available to permit one to give a generalization of the culture, or cultures, which produced them. None of them seems to offer a complete correspondence with any known cul-

18. Jury, 1937.

19. Ritchie, 1944, p. 181.

20. From information accompanying specimens donated to the Royal Ontario Museum of Archeology.

21. *Annual Archeological Report for Ontario, 1896–1897*, pp. 32–34.

22. *Annual Archeological Report for Ontario, 1896–1897*, pp. 19–24 (article by Boyle, "Otonabee Serpent Mound").

ture outside of the Province, but nevertheless the similarities are great enough to indicate close ties with some. One group exhibits circular to oval mounds from 25 to 40 feet in diameter and heights from 3½ to 5 feet. Burials are on the original ground level, which has been prepared by burning in certain areas. In one case the skeletons radiate outwards from the centre, apparently in extended positions. In others they were possibly the same, but one of them contained a number of partial burials as well as an entire one. In this structure were found a few pieces of mica, a rough stone net-sinker, a few mussel shells, a large slate knife or chisel, a small rough stone axe, a trapezoidal slate gorget with one perforation, and roughly made chert points, both triangular and un-notched and triangular notched.[23] In other mounds a like amount of grave furniture was found. In the Leeds County structure there were about ten huge chert blades, some copper beads, two conical slate pendants, and a copper ax. Similar structures in Peterboro County showed the burned-area feature or else a pit-like affair in which there were evidences of fire, as much as eight feet below the crest of the mound. Two other mounds in the same country had floors made of extremely hard clay, which the excavators thought had been indurated by fire, although there was no other evidence of that agency. Associated specimens here included chert points, a stone pendant, and a fragment of pottery, two axes, a bone point, and two large conical antler tools. In mounds on Pelee Island, Essex County, and the Leeds County mounds, large flat stones were placed over the skeletons, especially over the heads. No artifacts were associated with the Pelee Island burial. There is almost certainly a connection between some of these manifestations and the Hopewellian Phase, but much more will have to be done before the details are clear.

Three oblong mounds at Cameron's Point, Rice Lake, excavated by Boyle and his associates, revealed flexed burials which were virtually devoid of grave accompaniments. A good deal of the mounds was taken up with stones, which had been carefully arranged in rows on edge (concentric circles?) ending "at the angle on the opposite side"[24] (vestibule-like?). The stones had damaged the skeletons considerably. The striking feature of these mounds is not so much their structure as the fact that wood, apparently from logs, was found near the burials, a similarity to the Adena culture of Ohio. Not far distant in the same county of Peterboro are other mounds indicative of a similar connection, namely at Mizang's Point. One of these was a small, nearly circular structure, within which was a half-sitting skeleton resting on a pre-

pared bed of stiff clay and sand, four feet below the surface. Accompanying it were a small stone adze, a broken slate gorget and a copper bracelet. Nearby was a second mound, containing a similar burial with abundant grave offerings. These included three strings of copper beads, two strings of *Marginella conoidalis* shells, a copper axe and a stone tablet. The latter was rectanguloid with long sides concave, and made from beautiful white marble or calcite.[25] The diagnostic feature is that the perforations are conically, and not biconically, bored, a trait found in Adena but seldom elsewhere.

THE ARCHAIC PATTERN

No site of the Archaic Pattern has yet been reported in southern Ontario. There is no doubt, either on concrete or hypothetical grounds, that stations do exist, for the very considerable number of surface finds obviate the first, and the existence of such cultures in northern Ontario and in all adjacent States, the second. This surface material will in fact indicate suitable sites to explore in order to expand our knowledge of this horizon.

We have attempted to isolate congeries of artifacts to illustrate the presence in southern Ontario of some of the more important cultures such as the Laurentian and the Lamoka. In this we have had some degree of success, although such congeries, instead of being derived from a single site or even from such an area as a township or a county have had to be assembled from various finds all over the Province. For this reason, they can be taken only as probably representative, for anyone who has had to proceed on the basis of typology knows how dangerous a tool that can be. It is, moreover, highly probable and indeed likely that cultures as yet not identified occur within Ontario's borders, but at the present time these must go unrecognized. Perhaps some of the traits which do occur here, for instance the chopper-like copper tools assumed to be diagnostic of the Laurel culture of Minnesota may in fact be shared by another culture, as yet unknown, in this Province. Only excavation can make such points clear.

Laurentian-like material is fairly abundant and widespread. Chipped and notched projectile points, knives and scrapers made of reworked points are common, for instance, in Brant County. Ground slate points of the types found in both early and late Laurentian also occur, though much less frequently in Lambton, Perth, and Peterboro counties (Fig. 28, *C*). Ulus of slate come from Prince Edward, Renfrew, Lanark, Northumberland, York, and Simcoe counties. Slate butterfly stones occur in Brant, Ontario, Kent, Middlesex counties and Western Ontario generally, and in a somewhat specialized form as far east

23. *Annual Archeological Report for Ontario, 1901*, pp. 25–29.
24. *Annual Archeological Report for Ontario, 1896–1897*, p. 32 (article by Boyle, "Cameron's Point").

25. *Ibid.*, p. 57.

as Grenville County. Half and fully grooved gouges are widespread as are also the axes. A few specimens resembling Lamoka Lake material, especially two or three bevelled adzes, have been found in the Niagara peninsula, but the existence of the focus here is still problematical.

Material resembling the so-called Old Copper culture of Wisconsin, Minnesota, and Upper Michigan has turned up in several parts of Southern Ontario. (Fig. 28, D, E). There are awls, particularly from the eastern half of the area, socket-tanged points, (Fig. 28, I), all from the same region and more especially the Trent Valley subarea; knives, bracelets, and a few beads from the east; a long copper pick from Renfrew County (Fig. 28, G), and one "spud" from York County (Fig. 28, H). All of these conform to the types occurring in Wisconsin. Other forms seemingly peculiar to Ontario may also belong to this category, as for instance a large copper knife with broad, convex blade with serrations along the back. The specimen came from the southern Georgian Bay region, and a similar one was found in Algoma District north of Sault Ste. Marie. A site apparently of this culture is said to exist in Leeds County on a high and sandy location overlooking a bay of Lake Ontario; here a "great many objects of stone and chert have been found" in addition to two copper spear points of the socket-tanged type.[26] Until a site of this culture has been carefully studied, little more can be said about it. It is, of course, a Woodland culture in any case.

MISCELLANEOUS NOTES

In addition to the cultures referred to above, specimens which would seem to indicate the presence of other cultural units, or at least trade relations with them, are to be found in the Royal Ontario Museum of Archeology collections. Reference has already been made to the chopper-like tools of copper considered diagnostic of the Laurel culture of Minnesota. Two specimens have been found in Ontario, one in the Lake Rideau region and the other in Victoria County. Sandal-shaped gorgets of shell with three perforations and circular gorgets suggest the Glacial Kame culture of northeastern Ohio and adjoining area (Fig. 28, J, K, M, N). The sandal-shaped specimens were found in Kent and Prince Edward counties, while four examples of the circular gorgets derived from Middlesex County and all apparently from the one site. Large circular gorgets of conch shell with two perforations, worked animal jaws, and guilloche-impressed pottery from widely separated points are indicative of the Fort Ancient culture. Indeed from Wentworth County a considerable amount of pottery probably akin to this culture exists in the Museum collections (Fig. 28, F). Much of it is

shell-tempered and shows a wide range in form and decoration. Unfortunately, it was a surface collection and not much in the way of documentation accompanies it, but it appears to have been found along with circular shell gorgets and worked animals jaws.

NORTHERN ONTARIO

Except for that done by Greenman, no systematic work has been carried out in northern Ontario. Occasional explorations have been made, it is true, for example, by Boyle who visited certain petroglyphs on Lake Nipigon in 1894–1895. But by and large, the north has remained an unknown land archeologically. It is particularly regrettable that this should be so, because there can be little doubt that great and important movements have passed through parts of the territory at least, probably with profound effects on the history of the Northeast. For all our ignorance of this vast region, the former existence of certain cultures may be postulated with some degree of assurance on the evidence of surface finds which have accumulated in the Royal Ontario Museum of Archeology over a long period of time. That there are not more is due to fairly obvious reasons. Northern Ontario is for the most part unsuited to agriculture and hence little land has been cleared with the result that the surface has hardly been scratched.

The most striking cultural manifestation, apart from those revealed by Greenman is the Old Copper. Excellent examples of something akin to this have been found all the way from Rainy River District in the west to Renfrew County in the east, and as nearly as we can judge, from Parry Sound District on the south to the Height of Land on the north. Specimens include "spuds," hair-parters, "gaffs,"[27] socketed knives, knives with tangs, long chisels, axes, socketed points, and a pike about 18 inches long. Indeed, most of the type specimens illustrated by Ritzenthaler[28] can be duplicated in them. Moreover, the meager data which came with them indicated that in many instances they were found under conditions suggesting considerable antiquity. Both the hair-parters, for instance, were found in gravel pits, one of them eight feet below the surface. So also were the socketed knife (at a depth of six to seven feet), and one of the gaffs. One of the copper axes was recovered from a grave at Mamainse, Algoma District. It retained about one-half of the beaver-skin sheath in which it had been encased. More needs to be known about the details of this Old Copper culture in northern Ontario but its presence seems demonstrated.

There are suggestions of the presence of other cultures. Some of these are possibly identifiable with cultures known elsewhere, some probably are en-

26. *Annual Archeological Report for Ontario, 1923*, pp. 112–113.

27. *Annual Archeological Report for Ontario*, 1928, p. 54.
28. Ritzenthaler, 1946.

tirely new. For example, two rectanguloid slate gouges and two slate ulus in the surface collections point to a Laurentian-like culture in the Nipissing-Renfrew region. A fragmentary butterfly stone from Manitoulin Island may also indicate it there. Slate gorgets, slate knives and bar amulets indicate Woodland cultures. Particularly interesting in this connection are three slate dual-purpose tools, rectanguloid in outline and large in size, one end of which is a gouge and the other an axe. Such tools are found in Ontario so far only in the Ottawa Valley. Again, much later cultures, some probably of historic occurrence, are attested by catlinite elbow pipes, small points of exotic materials such as obsidian and agate, found near Sault Ste. Marie, and pottery from Thessalon, the Michipicoten River and Manitoulin Island, all of late Iroquoian type. A chipped and polished hoe of chert from Manitoulin Island and two grooved mauls are also likely of late origin. Thus there is evidence to indicate that northern Ontario has been inhabited from very early times. But it obviously requires much attention.

THE ROCK LAKE EXCAVATIONS

In 1939, Mr. Emerson and the writer made a study of a small site at the southern edge of the Shield, on Rock Lake, for the Royal Ontario Museum.[29] The place had apparently been occupied for two brief periods and the amount of material was extremely limited. It deserves to be mentioned here only from the fact that it was apparently stratified, the upper level containing both cord-marked and incised pottery, and the lower only large, roughly flaked slate blades.

THE KILLARNEY STATIONS

Dr. Emerson F. Greenman of the University of Michigan has uncovered five ancient sites on the north shore of Lake Huron, as reported in preliminary papers. The oldest site yields only quartzite tools and flakes, many of them water-worn. Its discoverer places the time of occupation as "towards the close of the Pleistocene ice age, late in the Wisconsin glacial stage."[30] Another but lower site is estimated by Dr. Stanley to date between 1,960 and 2,632 years old, while a still lower one yielding both quartzite and flint tools and pottery he estimates at from 1,100 to 1,400 years. A site on Great Cloche Island, Georgian Bay, which Dr. Greenman excavated is thought by him to be the most recent, dating from about A.D. 500 to 800.

It is evident that the occupation of northern Ontario dates from the close of the Pleistocene Age, and occurred at certain intervals thereafter. Since the excavator of the early sites has not assigned the earliest phase to any culture pattern other than to indicate that it is microlithic and Levalloisian-like, it is not yet time to do so. The Laurentian-like ulu-using people of the Ottawa Valley seem to pertain to the Archaic horizon. The fabricators of the dual-purpose ax-gouges of slate may be either an Archaic or a Woodland folk. The first definite indicators of Woodland people however are possibly the Old Copper culture specimens, the culture having been estimated to be previous to A.D. 700 in Wisconsin.[31] The Great Cloche Island occupation explored by Greenman is dated as about co-eval. The mound-building cultures of the Rainy Lake District may overlap, but more probably postdate the Old Copper and may extend down to the beginning of the historic period. The carriers of the catlinite elbow pipes and the small points of exotic stone have a temporal connection with late Plains culture. Iroquoian influences are attested by the presence of pottery over much of the area south of the Divide, thus bringing down to historic times the list of cultures which have made their impact felt on this vast region. It remains only to make the obvious statement that the historic Algonquin tribes of the north participated at the time of the discovery in the Woodland Pattern.

SUMMARY

The work of Boyle and the able men whom he gathered around him gave a brilliant launching to archeological studies in Ontario over half a century ago. The evidence they gathered has made it possible for modern students to piece together something of the story of culture sequence particularly in southern Ontario. Boyle's work must always remain as a stepping stone from the unknown to the known in the history of archeology in this Province.

As for northern and southern Ontario, it is apparent that due essentially to profound physical and climatic differences they are two distinct archeological areas, and the fact is reflected in the history of the science in the two segments of the Province. Progress is likely to be much slower in the north due to the natural difficulties which the region presents.

The presence of the George Lake culture attests the great antiquity of occupation upon the Laurentian Shield, followed in later time by the Old Copper and presumably other cultures down to the historic Algonquin. The fact that apart from Dr. Greenman's work, no sites of even these later occupations has been studied indicates how very much awaits to be done, and how incomplete is the information regarding the area.

Compared with this situation, the archeology of southern Ontario is somewhat better understood. It

29. A more detailed report on this site will appear shortly.
30. Greenman and Stanley, 1943, p. 528.

31. Martin, Quimby, and Collier, 1947, p. 299.

is true that virtually all of the systematic excavations of recent years have been done upon Iroquoian, and usually prehistoric, sites. Huron sites in particular have been approached from the historic end. On the other hand, evidence is slowly accumulating upon the development of the Iroquoian complex. As for the earlier occupations, we have still to rely upon the work of Boyle and his associates. This, though excellent as far as it goes, does little more than hint at the presence and complexity of the early cultures. It is in this field perhaps that the major part of the work of the future will lie.

OUTLINE OF CULTURES IN THE OHIO REGION.

By Richard G. Morgan*

IN THIS paper the prehistoric Indian cultures of the Ohio region are summarized and placed in their apparent cultural and chronological position. This region is here defined as including all of Ohio, northern Kentucky, eastern Indiana, southeastern Michigan, and northwestern West Virginia. As Ohio occupies the central portion of the region, and since archeological work has been carried on for a greater length of time in that state, greater emphasis has been placed upon its cultural complexes. The cultures of the region are discussed in chronological order, beginning with those considered to be the oldest and ending with those which are transitional between the historic and prehistoric eras. In those cases where the time period is in doubt the culture is placed in an arbitrary position for convenience in discussion. Each well-defined cultural unit is illustrated by a figure depicting characteristic artifact traits.

ARCHAIC PERIOD

The presence in the Ohio region of archeological material that could not be assigned to the well-defined cultures has long been recognized. Attention was called to this fact when the "grooved-ax-bannerstone" complex was attributed to an Early Algonquian group which was thought might have been ancestral to the Adena and Hopewell peoples.[1] Later on, the same author reported upon the occurrence of Folsom-like points in Ohio and discussed their relationship to the Folsom culture of the High Plains area.[2] As the result of recent work in other parts of the eastern United States, it is now recognized that there were in the Ohio region representatives of the early hunting-fishing-gathering peoples who lived during the Archaic Period. Under this heading will be discussed the Folsom-like points and the Indian Knoll-like material that is present in Ohio.

FOLSOM-LIKE POINTS OR FLUTED BLADES (FIG. 29, P–R)

With the finding of flint points at Folsom, New Mexico, and later at other places in the West, associ-ated with the remains of extinct Pleistocene animals, workers in the Ohio region became interested in what seemed to be related types. It was noted that there were numerous specimens of fluted projectile points similar to the Folsom points of the Western states.[3] In the Ohio State Museum collections there are over one hundred and twenty fluted blades which are surprisingly similar to the western forms in their general shape, in their characteristic fluting, in having the ground edges at the base, and in their concave base. They average, however, about an inch longer than the western types.[4] The Ohio points are all surface finds with the exception of two specimens that were incidental inclusions in the earth fill of sites of later cultures. They cannot be assigned to any of the defined cultures, nor have they been found in association with extinct animal forms. Considered on typological grounds, it is now generally held that they probably belong to the same early time horizon as the western Folsom complex.[5]

Folsom-like points have been noted generally for the Ohio region, but none have been found along with extinct animal forms. It has been recorded that there are about one hundred in the collections of the Indiana Historical Society.[6] In Kentucky three fluted blades were found at the Parrish Site in the western part of the state.[7] At the same site occurred points without fluting, but otherwise like those that were fluted, Yuma-like points, and small snub-nosed scrapers similar to specimens from the Lindenmeier site in Colorado. Pottery was absent at this site.

Certain forms of points in Ohio seem to be related to the fluted blade type. There is the type that is similar in most respects, but without the fluting (Fig. 29, T). Then there are some other specimens like those depicted on Figure 29, S, U, which seem to be cognate forms (Yuma-like) in that they share certain of their features (such as ground edges) with fluted types. A likely place to look for Folsom-like artifacts in association with extinct animals would be in the cave district of Kentucky where the bones of the ground sloth and those of the mastodon have been recovered from collapsed cave entrances.[8]

* Ohio State University, B.A., 1926; M.A., 1929; Graduate work, Department of Anthropology, University of Chicago, 1929–1932; Curator of Archeology, Ohio State Museum, 1936–1948. Chapter received, February, 1948; reduced one-third, January, 1951.

1. Shetrone, 1920, pp. 160–170.
2. Shetrone, 1936.
3. Ibid.
4. Ibid., pp. 246–247.
5. Griffin, J. B., 1946, p. 42.
6. Lilly, 1937, p. 27.
7. Haag, 1942a, pp. 217–218
8. Webb and Funkhouser, 1934.

INDIAN KNOLL-LIKE COMPLEX (SHELL MOUND COMPLEX)
(FIG. 29, *A–O*)

In the area there is a great variety of artifact types which have not been specifically classified. Included in this category are grooved axes, stone pestles, bannerstones, cylindrical pestles, subrectangular bars and certain "problematical" specimens. Such objects rarely occur in or on sites of known cultural groupings, however, they are present in great numbers in private and museum collections. Since little excavating has been done on sites where such objects occur as the trait assemblage, workers have hesitated to place the material within the cultural sequence.

This vaguely defined complex was thought by earlier archeologists to represent an old Algonquian occupation,[9] while later writers have viewed it as pertaining to Early Woodland groups.[10] As the result of recent excavations in the eastern United States, cultural complexes of the Archaic Period have been recognized and defined. Several workers have called attention to local and regional expressions of this period and have pointed out likenesses and differences.[11] They have noted occurrences in New York, Kentucky, Alabama, Georgia, and in other states. Here it can only be indicated that certain of the traits in the Ohio region which have been considered Early Woodland occur as a definite recurring complex in Kentucky known as the Green River Focus of the Shell Mound Complex[12] or the Indian Knoll Focus.[13] The artifacts illustrated are in the Ohio State Museum collections and, with the exception of the atlatl, are types found commonly in the Ohio region. These traits are all found at the Indian Knoll Component in Ohio County, Kentucky.[14] Some of them also occurred at the Chiggerville Site and at the Cypress Creek and other sites in McLean County, Kentucky.[15] Several nonpottery sites in southern Indiana have also produced trait assemblages similar to Indian Knoll.[16]

A surface collection from a newly reported site in Preble County, Ohio, also makes it clear that an Indian group having Indian Knoll-like artifacts once existed in southwestern Ohio.[17] Both in Ohio and in Kentucky rock shelters were used in Archaic times. In Ohio an antler atlatl hook was found in a rock shelter in Hocking County.[18] In a nearby shelter occurred an ovate slate artifact with a central hole which may have been used as an atlatl weight.[19] In Kentucky a rock shelter in McLean County produced Archaic material.[20]

In pointing out the presence of Indian Knoll-like material in the Ohio region we do not mean to imply cultural identity, but merely wish to show that the region was occupied by related peoples during the general Archaic Period. It is not possible to clearly differentiate the traits belonging to the Early Woodland Period from those pertaining to the Archaic Period. In a recent report on Archaic sites in McLean County, Kentucky, it is noted that a number of Shell Mound traits are also present in Woodland.[21]

EARLY WOODLAND PERIOD

GENERAL

In discussing the Early Woodland Period it must be kept in mind that the archeological record in most cases is very fragmentary. The classification of such material, therefore, is in a very tentative stage. It is clear, too, that there is no discontinuity between the Archaic Period and the Early Woodland Period.

Material classified as Woodland[22] is common in the Ohio region at several different types of sites, including village sites, rock shelters, stone-slab mounds and earth mounds. In Ohio, Woodland artifacts have been found in a number of rock shelters, although in most cases under circumstances not conducive to accurate records.[23] Such material includes plain and cord-marked pottery, stemmed and notched points, and textile objects of various kinds. It should be noted that some of the rock shelters also contain material relating to the well-recognized Adena, Hopewell, and Fort Ancient cultures,[24] although their stratigraphic sequence was not established by the type of excavating done. The rock shelters of Kentucky present a similar picture, with Woodland material being present in some of them.[25] Woodland material occurs in stone-slab mounds of varied forms on ridges along the Ohio River. Some of these sites have produced crania classed with the long-headed Sylvid group of Woodland nature.[26] Since few artifacts have been found in these sites, the complex has been poorly defined. Stone-slab mounds explored in Brown County, Ohio, had traits evidently pertaining to the

9. Shetrone, 1920, pp. 165–168; Willoughby, 1935, p. 3.

10. Cole and Deuel, 1937, pp. 33–38; Byers (ed.), 1943; Morgan and Ellis, 1943, pp. 63–64.

11. Ford and Willey, 1941, pp. 332–334; Ritchie, 1944, pp. 321–323; Griffin, J. B., 1946, pp. 40–43.

12. Webb and Haag, 1939, p. 59.

13. Webb and Haag, 1947*a*, p. 44.

14. Webb, W. S., 1946; C. B. Moore, 1916*a*.

15. Webb and Haag, 1939; 1940; 1947*a*.

16. Lilly, 1937, p. 100; Miller, 1941, pp. 7-8.

17. Moffett, 1949, Raish-Smith Site; also recently excavated by the Ohio State Museum.

18. Goslin, 1944.

19. Department of Archaeology, Ohio State Museum.

20. Webb and Haag, 1947*a*, pp. 22–30.

21. *Ibid.*, p. 44.

22. Byers, (ed.), 1943.

23. Department of Archaeology, Ohio State Museum; Mills, 1912; Shetrone, 1928.

24. Mills, 1912, Figs. 5–7; Department of Archaeology, Ohio State Museum.

25. Haag, 1942*a*, pp. 214–216.

26. Neumann, 1942, p. 540.

Hopewellian Period.[27] In southeastern Indiana, stone-slab mounds with Woodland traits were excavated in Franklin and Dearborn counties.[28] In the latter county a village site was recorded with Woodland traits comprising grooved axes, slate objects, stemmed and notched points and grit-tempered cord-marked pottery.[29] Woodland traits have also been described for sites in Randolph County, Indiana.[30] A site in Henry County, Kentucky, contained material similar to that from stone-slab mounds in Indiana.[31] In Ohio, sites with Woodland trait complexes also have been noted for Franklin,[32] Fairfield,[33] and Hamilton counties.[34] Woodland sites have likewise been recorded for West Virginia.[35]

On typological grounds, some of these Woodland components may be classed as Early Woodland, or even Archaic, others with little question could be assigned to the Middle Woodland Period (Hopewellian). They have been discussed for convenience in this section, and to make it clear that the region was occupied extensively by groups which can be classified in the Woodland Pattern.[36] The basic Woodland character of most of the cultures of the Ohio region will become manifest as they are described in this article.

GLACIAL KAME CULTURE

The Glacial Kame Culture (Fig. 30) was named and partially characterized around forty years ago,[37] but it still remains poorly defined culturally and chronologically.[38] This is due to the fact that most of the sites have been accidentally discovered during gravel pit operations, farm cultivation or construction work with the result that there has been little accurate documentation and the artifacts have been widely scattered in collections.

The culture is known almost entirely from artifacts found with burials that occur in glacial kames or knolls composed of gravel and sand. It centers in the region of northwestern Ohio,[39] northeastern Indiana, and southern Michigan. The people, who were long-headed Sylvids,[40] buried their dead in pits which were dug into the kames. Some of these pits were very deep. At the Richardson Kame in Hardin County, Ohio, the burial pits ranged in depth from two to eighteen feet,[41] while one burial at the Zimmerman Kame in the same county was reported to have been twenty feet deep in a pit which could be traced to the surface.[42]

Burials were generally flexed, although extended, partially cremated and mass reburials(?) were reported for the Richardson Kame.[43] The custom of burying dogs along with human burials was practiced at the Richardson Site and at the Cedar Point Site in Indiana.[44] Where grave offerings occurred they were restricted to a relatively few recurring types. Red ocher was sometimes used in connection with the burial rites.

Artifacts placed with burials were mainly ornamental so little is known of their tools.[45] Ornaments made from conch-shell fragments predominate, indicating trade with the Gulf or Atlantic coastal region. Characteristic among these are the sandal-shaped shell gorgets with three holes for attachment. Commonly, these were plain, but some bear incised line decorations on their concave surface or rarely animals are depicted.[46] Shell gorgets include circular and rectanguloid forms. Large barrel-shaped beads cut from the columella of conch-shells and disk-shaped marine shell beads are common.

Gorgets, made of banded slate, are similar in type to the forms in shell. Birdstones of slate served for ornaments, or perhaps for atlatl weights. Stone pipes of the simple tubular type[47] apparently indicate the use of tobacco, although they may have been shaman tubes.

Crude spherical beads of copper occur, and a copper breastplate(?) with a row of bosses was reported for one site.[48] Ivory specimens include a gorget and a sphere. Tools and weapons include copper awls, stone celts, stemmed projectile points, antler flint chipping tools, harpoons and antler tines. No pottery has been definitely recorded for this group.

The Glacial Kame Culture is basically Woodland (probably early), but its exact relationships to other

27. Fowke, 1902, pp. 391-406.
28. Setzler, 1930; Black, 1934, p. 240.
29. Black, 1934, pp. 192–194.
30. Setzler, 1931, pp. 39–42.
31. Funkhouser and Webb, 1937.
32. Merion Village Site, Ohio State Museum Collection; Mc-Guerer Burial Site, Shetrone, 1924, pp. 353–358.
33. Swinehart Village Site, Ohio State Museum Collection.
34. Sites near mouth of the Great Miami River, Ohio State Museum Collection; Turpin Site, Cincinnati Museum of Natural History Collection; and Oehler, 1950.
35. Griffin, J. B., 1946, p. 55.
36. See references to paucity of data on Woodland sites in Ohio, Byers (ed.), 1943, p. 395.
37. Moorehead, 1909, pp. 138, 141–142.
38. A report on the culture by W. M. Cunningham has now appeared. Cunningham, 1948.
39. Ohio State Museum collections contain material from Hardin, Mercer, Fayette, Marion, Fulton, Auglaize, Williams, Allen, Erie and Crawford counties, Ohio, and Randolph County, Indiana.

40. Lilly, 1942; Neumann, 1942, p. 540.
41. Read and Whittlesey, 1877 (description of site by J. S. B. Matson) pp. 126–131.
42. Greenman, 1931.
43. Read and Whittlesey, 1877, pp. 126–131; Lilly, 1942, pp. 31–32.
44. Lilly, 1942.
45. This artifact summary is based mainly on material in Ohio State Museum Collections; and secondarily on sources indicated in the footnotes; recurring traits were selected as typical of the complex.
46. Snodgrass, 1894, pp. 114–115.
47. Platform pipes are reported to be associated with the complex, but they have not been documented, Lilly, 1942; Martin, Quimby, and Collier, 1947, p. 263.
48. Read and Whittlesey, 1877, pp. 126–131.

cultures of the region are poorly understood.[49] On typological grounds, the complex has been assigned to the general Adena-Hopewell time period.[50] Some writers, emphasizing apparent Hopewell-like traits reported for the complex, have placed it within the Hopewellian time period.[51] Others have thought these people were contemporaneous with late Adena groups and to have lived on into Hopewellian times.[52] It has been suggested that the Middlesex Focus of the Vine Valley Aspect of New York represents a people of the same approximate time interval.[53]

ADENA CULTURE

The Indians of the Adena culture (Fig. 31)[54] occupied a region consisting of the southern half of Ohio, northern Kentucky, southeastern Indiana, northwestern West Virginia and southwestern Pennsylvania.[55] Physically, they belong to the roundheaded Centralid type. Occipital deformation was almost universal among them and bifrontal flattening was common. Both types of deformation are attributed to the custom of binding infants in cradleboards. Diseased bones show that they suffered from apical abscesses, dental caries, rickets, arthritis, osteitis, osteoporosis symmetrica (from diet deficiency) and perhaps syphilis.

The Adena culture is known mainly from artifacts, burial traits and structural features found in or beneath burial mounds. Excavations of village sites beneath mounds in Kentucky in recent years, however, have added measurably to a more rounded knowledge of the complex. Several kinds of sites pertain to the culture, including mounds, earthen enclosures, and village sites. In addition, in some areas in Ohio and Kentucky, Adena material has been found in rock shelters. Mounds are the most common, occurring usually in groups, but sometimes singly. They are subconical in form and vary in height from a few feet up to almost seventy feet. The majority of subconical mounds in the region probably pertain to the Adena culture.

Enclosures include square, rectangular, and circular earthen embankments. The most common type is the circular earthwork which varies from about fifty to five hundred feet in diameter. These "sacred circles" have a gateway, and an interior ditch which was partially formed by the removal of earth to form the embankment.

Villages consisted of from two to five houses. The "greater" village being made up of a number of such house groups dispersed over a considerable area.

Post-mold house patterns beneath mounds show that Adena houses were circular in form, about thirty-seven feet in diameter and built of paired wooden posts set in line with the wall in individually dug holes. All of the posts slanted outward, allowing the eaves to protect the walls more readily from the weather. Four to six interior post-molds suggest supports for roofs. Central hearths were no doubt situated beneath smoke holes in the roof. A large post-mold pattern beneath one mound in Kentucky with a special dais seems to indicate a council house.

Very large post-mold patterns may represent structures which had living quarters arranged around their walls on the interior with an open area in the center. Circular fire basins in the village area were probably used for domestic purposes.

Their implements are known from specimens found buried with the dead, from caches in mounds and village sites, and from scattered material in the village refuse. Typical of the flint objects are the large straight-stemmed projectile points which may have been used for spears hurled by atlatls. Side-notched points were also made. Leaf-shaped blades are often found as ceremonial burial offerings in the mounds. Small ungrooved axes were chipped from flint and then ground and polished. Scrapers consisted of the stemmed, thumbnail and flake varieties. Gravers with sharp curved points were made from large flint flakes, and flint drills of several types were used.

Ungrooved axes, fashioned from igneous rock and hematite were commonly employed. Large hoes were chipped from slabs of stone and saws were made by notching the sharp edges of thin stone slabs. Cup-stones, hammerstones, rectangular abrading stones, and disks were used. Awls of several kinds were used, one type being made from deer and elk shoulder blades while others were cut from bone splinters and ulnas. Antler was used for making flint flaking tools, tine projectile points and implement handles. Large spatulas were cut from deer leg bones, and spoons from the carapace of the turtle.

Mussel-shells served for spoons and were perforated for hafting as hoes. Copper was used primarily for ornaments, but a few ungrooved axes were hammered from that metal. Stone gorgets of slate with holes drilled from one side only are of common occurrence. Among the types are expanded-center bar gorgets with two perforations, reel-shaped forms and flat rectanguloid, elliptical and diamond-shapes. It

49. Excavations in the Trent Waterway, Ontario, Canada, seem to indicate that the Glacial Kame culture is Early Woodland, (Ritchie, 1949*b*).

50. Morgan and Ellis, 1943, p. 63.

51. Lilly, 1942; Griffin, J. B., 1946, p. 56.

52. Martin, Quimby, and Collier, 1947, p. 263.

53. Ritchie, 1944, p. 325.

54. The culture takes its name from the Adena Mound, Ross County, Ohio, which was excavated by Mills in 1901 (Mills, 1902).

55. This summary is based upon *The Adena People* by Webb and Snow, 1945; "Excavation of the Coon Mound and an Analysis of the Adena Culture" by Greenman, 1932; Ohio State Museum Collections; Griffin, J. B., 1946; Ford and Willey, 1941; Black, 1936; and Ford and Quimby, 1945.

has been suggested that some of these may have been atlatl weights.

Beads were made of shell, bone, pearl and copper. Disk-shaped beads cut from shell were most common, although Marginella shells were used, as well as cylindrical beads cut from columella of conch shells. Copper bracelets were frequently buried with the dead, occurring in place on the forearm or thrown into the mound earth. Other copper objects were rings, pendants, pins, gorgets and crescents.

Designs cut from mica were used for ornamental purposes, with certain crescent forms probably representing parts of headdresses. Circular gorgets cut from human skulls, rarely engraved with a raptorial bird design, were also made. Bone combs made in two parts were used for the hair or perhaps as carding tools for preparing textile fibers. Small cones or hemispheres of stone had an unknown function. Circular earrings with a central perforation were worn in the pierced and extended ear lobe.

Engraved stone tablets, while not common, show a very close relationship to one another in form and design. Rectanguloid in shape, they usually bear on one surface a conventionalized incised design of a raptorial bird. A few tablets bear curvilinear geometrical designs. The reverse side of the tablets are usually plain, but may have grooves seemingly formed by sharpening bone awls or other tools.

Adena pipes are tubular in form with flattened and blocked-end mouth pieces or flaring mouthpieces. Tubular pipes in human effigy form occur, but are extremely rare. It has been assumed that tobacco was smoked in these stone tubes, but they may have been blowing or sucking tubes used by medicine men. Elbow pipes occur rarely, as do the platform types.

The Adena people made clothing of skin and fabric. The human effigy pipe from the original Adena Mound shows a male figure wearing a breachcloth (Fig. 92, C–D). Fragmentary fabrics, preserved by contact with copper objects, indicate several weaving techniques including plain plaiting, twilled plaiting, braiding, and plain and twilled twining.

Pottery was not buried with the dead but enough sherds have been found to give a general picture of the pottery complex. Vessels were generally small with rounded or flat bases, although four legged forms were also made. They commonly had slightly flaring rims with a thickened rim-strip and rim nodes. Most of the vessels had plain surfaces, although some were cord-marked and a few had incised diamond-shaped designs. In Ohio and Indiana the pottery was mainly grit-tempered, while in Kentucky limestone tempering was largely used. A rarer and probably earlier type was a thick, crude, plain surfaced, grit-tempered ware sometimes having large cylindrical handles on the body.

The Adena people had elaborate burial customs as is shown by their tombs, but apparently only people of importance in the community were given mound burial. Cremation, burial in the flesh and reburial were all employed. Burial in the flesh in log tombs was evidently reserved for the most important personages, while people of lesser importance generally were cremated. Burials were commonly made on the floors of houses and in subfloor tombs, while others were placed in a partly constructed mound and then covered with earth. Small mounds were built over burials on house floors after which the house was burned. Weathered layers and superimposed tombs indicate that some mounds were built over a period of time. Lenticular masses of earth in the mounds reveal that the earth was carried in baskets. Borrow pits from which earth was dug are present near some of the larger mounds.

Individuals buried in the flesh were placed in an extended position on the back in a simple grave on the floor, in earthwalled tombs, or in log tombs. These were often located centrally in the mound, and in some cases contained two or three extended burials. Red ocher was strewn on burials and in some cases applied directly to the bones, indicating apparently that graves stood open for a long enough time for the flesh to have decayed. Graphite was used to mark skulls. Bundle burials and flexed burials were rarely made. Separate skulls were sometimes placed in graves and sometimes buried alone.

Cremation took place in large circular fire-basins of puddled clay. The ashes were usually gathered up for special burial, but sometimes were left in place and covered with clay or a log tomb. Cremations were redeposited in mounds, in the village site, with extended burials in log tombs, or separately in log tombs. The remains of several individuals might also be put in one deposit. Artifacts, sometimes "killed," were burned along with the body or placed with the cremated remains afterwards. Red ocher was sprinkled on artifact offerings and sometimes on cremations.

The simple form of log tomb consisted of four logs placed to form a rectangle with poles laid across for a covering. Bark was laid on top of the poles and sometimes puddled clay was added. Tombs were two logs high in most cases, and three or more logs were frequently laid on the floor parallel to the logs forming the sides of the structure. Burial pits were sometimes shored up with logs, and smaller post-molds around tombs suggest temporary canopies or perhaps posts on which offerings were hung. This evidence along with the fact that some tombs had passageways, suggests that burials were left accessible for a certain period of time before final rites were performed. Bark was placed beneath and over burials. Log tombs were frequently burned, either accidently, or perhaps intentionally when the houses were destroyed by fire. Such burning resulted in the partial cremation of the burials within them.

The Adena people were probably sedentary in nature, raising corn and the plants associated with it, including tobacco. Hunting and collecting were probably of more importance than agriculture. "Sacred circles," council houses and the elaborate burial customs point to a people with well-developed social groups with standardized rituals. The large mounds and earthworks, likewise imply a social fabric in which communal undertakings were common. Marine shells, copper and mica indicate contact with other regions and peoples.

The culture is essentially Woodland, with burials, pottery and artifact traits all connecting it with similar cultures in the eastern United States in the same general period. The Middlesex Focus of New York, the Red Ocher, Baumer and Morton complexes of Illinois, and the Tchefuncte culture of Louisiana all represent related regional expressions of Early Woodland time.

On typological grounds, and on the basis of similar sequences in other regions, it is now generally held that the Adena culture preceded the Ohio Aspect of the Hopewellian Phase and is partly ancestral to it. The burial traits of the two cultures are basically alike, although in some respects there is a greater elaboration in Hopewell. Certain Adena mounds containing traits typical of Hopewell are regarded as Late Adena, while those lacking such traits are considered to be Early Adena. The Late Adena people, in this view, were contemporaneous with Early Hopewell peoples.

Adena and Hopewell pottery belong to the Woodland ceramic complex, and the plain and cord-marked utilitarian types of both cultures have certain general resemblances. Specific Adena pottery traits, however, are generally absent in Ohio Hopewell, and there are no decorative elements in Adena pottery that would have formed a basis for the development of decorative motifs present in Ohio Hopewell. Thick, coarse ware at some sites seems to indicate Early Adena, for such pottery in other regions seems to pertain to the Early Woodland Period. Tchefuncte pottery has certain of its traits in common with Adena pottery. In the Louisiana region, stratigraphy shows that Tchefuncte preceded the Marksville culture and on the basis of typology was probably ancestral to it. Since the Ohio Hopewell and Marksville cultures have considerable in common, this suggests that the Adena-Hopewell relationship in Ohio was similar.

The Adena and Hopewell peoples were of divergent types, the former being roundheads and the latter longheads. Biologically speaking, then, there is little genetic connection between the two peoples. The theory that the Adena People came from Mexico bringing with them their basic culture has little evidence to support it, for their culture is primarily Woodland, with many of its roots in the Archaic Period.

MIDDLE WOODLAND PERIOD

HOPEWELLIAN PHASE: OHIO ASPECT

The Hopewell[56] Indians (Figs. 32 and 33) in Ohio lived mainly along the major rivers forming a part of the Ohio River drainage system.[57] Many of their important sites are in the Ross County area in the valley of the Scioto or its tributaries. Other occupation centers were in the Great Miami, the Little Miami, and the Muskingum valleys. Evidences of related Hopewellian people are present in the adjacent states of Indiana, Kentucky, Pennsylvania, and Michigan and in other regions of the Eastern states. In physical type, the Hopewell peoples in Ohio were predominantly a longheaded group pertaining to the Sylvid classification of the Eastern Woodlands.[58] One-fourth of the skulls show bifrontal deformation, and a few occipital deformation. Diseased bones indicate that they were subject to dental caries, apical abscesses, arthritis, and perhaps syphilis.

The Hopewellian people in Ohio were the "Great Earthwork Builders," erecting enclosures of two general types, the geometrical earthworks and the hilltop enclosures or "forts." The former, located in the valleys, include circles, rectangles, octagons and combinations of these forms. At the larger sites, such geometrical enclosures are often connected by long parallel walls which evidently served as passageways. The walls of the earthworks, some with interior ditches, vary from several feet up to sixteen or more feet in height and often are broken by a number of openings or "gateways". Burial mounds are usually associated with the enclosures, often being located within them. They vary considerably in shape and size, ranging from small sub-conical or elongate mounds to large elongated mounds up to thirty feet in height and two hundred and forty feet long. Earthworks may enclose from ten to fifteen acres to over a hundred acres. Usually there are depressions near the earthworks from which the builders dug earth

56. The culture was named for the Hopewell Mound Group, Ross County, Ohio (Mills, 1906, p. 135).

57. This summary is based primarily on the following Ohio sites: Hopewell, Seip, Harness, Tremper, Mound City, and Turner; and collections in the Ohio State Museum and other museums: see particularly Shetrone, 1926; Moorehead, 1922; Mills, 1907; 1909; 1916; 1922a; Shetrone and Greenman, 1931; and Squier and Davis, 1848.

58. The physical type summary is based on Webb and Snow, 1945; Willoughby and Hooton, 1922; Martin, Quimby, and Collier, 1947, p. 267.

for their construction. Among some of the well-known sites of this kind are the Hopewell, Newark, Marietta, Seip, Mound City, Turner, Harness, and the Tremper earthworks.

These geometrical enclosures were used as centers by the Hopewell peoples for social, religious and burial purposes. Their sacred character is testified to by the achieving of privacy by walls and connecting passageways, their symbolical form, and their use for the burial of important personages in the group. This latter fact is supported by the evidence of extremely elaborate burial practices, the placing of great ceremonial offerings or "sacrifices" in the burial mounds, and the final erection of large mounds over certain of the sacred structures. It is likely that the chief-priests of the tribe lived at the earthworks and that the important burials and offerings pertained to them and their families.

The second kind of earthworks is typified by Fort Ancient, a hill-top enclosure, on the Little Miami River in Warren County,[59] Ohio. Sites of this type, located mainly in southwestern Ohio, are characterized by earthen or stone walls enclosing the relatively level tops of hills isolated from the surrounding country side by steep sided valleys or ravines. Burial mounds were built within and adjacent to the hill-top enclosures in a few cases, and they have features such as parallel walls, paved ways and burial mounds which seem to have had ceremonial functions. Although the hill-top enclosures have been termed "forts," it is evident that they were used as ceremonial centers as well as for defense.

Since the Hopewell Culture in Ohio has been mainly defined from artifacts and other traits associated with the burial cult, a well-rounded picture of the village and everyday life of these people cannot be given. However, village refuse in the mounds and earthworks, and beneath and around them, gives abundant evidence that at least some of the Hopewell people lived at the sites of the major enclosures. Sites showing thick deposits of village debris have not so far been found in Ohio.

Pottery vessels were made for both utilitarian and ceremonial usages, but as they were rarely buried with the dead, few whole ones are found. A number of forms were made, including jars, bowls, platters and plates. The bottoms of the pots were rounded or flattened, and a few of the smaller vessels were made with four conical-shaped legs. All were without handles. Tempering material was either grit or limestone, with 80 per cent of the sherds having grit and about 19 per cent limestone, the remainder being sand or clay-tempered. All are gray or buff in color. Ordinary containers had cord-wrapped paddle impressions on their exterior surfaces or were plain.

59. Morgan, 1946b.

Sixty-four per cent of all sherds are cord-marked and 23 per cent are plain.

The finer or ceremonial vessels were all decorated by various stamping, incising and cord-impressing techniques. The upper rim was usually thickened and decorated with cross-hatched incised lines bordered by a row of hemiconical punctate impressions. The body surface was covered with an over-all stamped design, or by curvilinear zones or bands with stamped impressions set off from plain smooth areas by incised lines. Some of the smaller vessels were made with four body-lobes with bird designs on them. Ceramic artifacts include platform pipes, button cores for covering with copper, beads, circular ear ornaments, and human figurines.

The Hopewell people, on the whole, produced the best made tools, weapons and ornaments of any group in the Eastern United States. A study of their artifacts indicates that they had specialized craftsmen, for some objects required skills which could only be acquired by long practice. They worked not only in stone, bone and shell but extensively in wood, hides, feathers and other perishable substances. When certain materials or natural objects were scarce, they would imitate them in other substances.

Their projectile points, knives, scrapers and drills were chipped largely from local flint. There is strong evidence that the atlatl or spear-thrower was in common use, although they may also have had the bow and arrow. The large size of most of the points, the occurrence of certain stone artifact types which seem to be atlatl weights, and the presence of what has been interpreted as an effigy atlatl in mica, all point to the use of the spear-thrower. Furthermore, several antler objects were found which are considered to be atlatl hooks. Projectile points are mainly corner-notched, side-notched and stemmed for hafting, although some blades were made in leaf-shaped or triangular forms. Very large blades of several forms, evidently ceremonial in nature, were chipped from obsidian, quartz, or flint. Some cone-shaped points were rolled from copper, while others were made of antler tines. Curved and straight bladed knives were made, and small flake knives with razor-sharp edges were struck from flint cores. Flint scrapers were made in ovoid, rectanguloid and notched forms, and flint drills were of the plain or notched-for-hafting types. A few chisels, some with bone handles, were pounded out of copper and meteoritic iron.

Axes of the ungrooved type (no doubt hafted in a wooden handle) were pecked from hard stones and polished. Axes and adzes were also hammered from copper nuggets and pieces of meteoritic iron. Hammerstones and abrading stones were used, but stone mortars and pestles were very rare. Bowls and cups were very rarely made out of stone, but charred fragments of wooden bowls and other objects hint at an extensive use of wood. Containers were also fashioned from conch shells (mainly Busycon perversum) and from the carapace of turtles. Bone objects include needles, awls, flint-chipping tools, skewers and pins, spatulas and digging implements. Spoons were cut from fresh-water mussel shells.

The Hopewell people made a great variety of ornamental objects, with beads being the most common form. Beads cut from fresh-water mussel shells and marine snail shells occur in great quantities with burials. A common form was disk-shaped, but barrel-shaped, globular and cylindrical beads were also used. Beads made from Marginella and Anculosa shells were common, and drilled fresh-water pearls were used abundantly as grave offerings. Beads of stone, copper, bone and seeds were also used. Animal canine teeth were drilled for pendants, as were bird and animal claws. Bear canines were sometimes elaborately carved, and occasionally set with pearls. A few perforated alligator and shark teeth were used, with the possibility that the latter may have formed the cutting edges of swords and clubs.

Ornaments worn directly on the person included earrings, bracelets, headdresses, combs, and finger rings. The common form of ear ornament was the spool-shaped one of copper, which was sometimes overlaid with silver or meteoritic iron. Finely made circular ear ornaments of stone and wood were also used, some of which were perforated possibly for the attachment of small pendents. Bracelets of copper were not common, while copper finger rings were very rare. Copper breastplates with two holes for attachment were common, some being decorated with scrolls or bosses, or cut in the form of birds (usually the hawk). Carved tortoise shell combs and copper rods were used in the hair. Copper plates served as foundations for headdresses. Some were plain, some had cut-out designs and others were set with copper antlers. Impressions of fabric and feathers on the copper and the presence of pearls and mica designs, indicate some of the headdresses were elaborate.

Pendants and plummets were made from stone, copper, bone and shell. Button-like objects of wood or stone covered with copper were fairly common. Designs cut from sheets of copper or mica were made in the forms of animals, humans, birds, fish, crescents, circles, triangles, scrolls, and swastikas. Usually they were perforated for attachment to clothing. Stone gorgets perforated with one or two holes for suspension, include rectanguloid, expanded-center, reel-shaped and diamond-shaped forms. The reel-shaped form was also made of copper, and the rectanguloid form sometimes of copper, bone, shell, or tortoise shell. Circular gorgets and disks were made from shell, wood, stone, bone, copper, and iron. Boat-stones, perhaps used as atlatl weights, were usually made of stone. Some represent birds and animals, including the hawk and the mythical horned serpent.

Animal and human jaws were cut and perforated for suspension, with some of the former having incised and painted designs. Hollow copper turtle effigies containing pebbles served as rattles on a leather belt. Human parietal bones were cut into circular gorgets and incised with conventional bird designs. Animal long bones were sometimes incised with expertly executed designs in the form of animals, birds, geometric figures and mythological beings. Other ornamental objects comprise incised spadefish bones, bones banded with copper, hawk skulls, a tablet with a rattlesnake design, and oval and rectanguloid stone tablets. It is likely that some of these were used by medicine men and formed the contents of medicine bags. Copper noses were used in connection with three burials. A few small sheets of gold indicate that this material was known, but was extremely rare. Musical instruments include rattles, and triple con-joined-tubes (of reed, wood, or bone covered with copper, silver, or meteoritic iron) which are apparently pan pipes.

Tobacco, judging from the great quantities of pipes in ceremonial offerings, played an important part in the ceremonial life of the Hopewell people. Their pipes, usually carved from a hard flint clay (Ohio pipestone) were of the platform type with either a curved or straight base. Some were plain, while others had their bowls expertly carved in the forms of various birds and animals native to the region. In all cases the animal faces the smoker. It is noteworthy that most of the effigy pipes were found in two great ceremonial offerings. Tubular and modified pipes were very rare.

The Hopewell people had a well-developed weaving art. Cloth preserved by copper objects shows they used the techniques of plain plaiting, twilled plaiting, looping, plain twining, and twilled twining. Thread was made from plant fibers as well as rabbit hair. Some of the weaving may have been done on a simple loom, although there is no tangible evidence of such implements. Twine served for a variety of uses, and mats, bags, and baskets were woven. Some fabrics were decorated in color with painted geometrical designs. (Fig. 94).

From pottery figurines and designs depicting the human figure, light is thrown upon their manner of dress and personal adornment. Women wore wrap-around skirts and footwear of woven grass. Their hair was parted in the center and gathered into a knot at the back of the head. Men wore breechcloths, belts, and moccasins of Algonquian type to which short leggings were fitted. Their hair was worn in several styles, in one of which, a knot was formed in the center of the forehead. In another, it was gathered into a hairnet, and in some cases they shaved the sides of the head leaving a ridge of hair from front to back in the center. Their ears were pierced and distended for the insertion of several types of ear ornaments. Facial painting or tattooing, or perhaps both, were practiced. Garments were made of skin, fur, and fabric, although little may be said of the form they took.

The Hopewell people had the most elaborate burial customs of any prehistoric group in the region, or perhaps in North America. Their ceremonies took place within their geometrical enclosures, and interment of the dead was made in structures within or adjacent to them. Post-mold patterns beneath the mounds indicate that circular, oval, and elongated rectanguloid structures were built in which burial rites were conducted and tombs placed. Large wooden posts were placed in separately dug holes to form the sides of the structures which varied in size from about fifteen or twenty feet across to over fifty. Some of the elongate forms were as much as two hundred feet in length. Some of the smaller structures were houses, judging from the arrangement of fireplaces and the presence of post-molds which may indicate roof supports. The great size of other structures would seem to show that they were not roofed; however, some were divided into smaller compartments which may have been covered. Characteristically, these "houses" had level sand-covered floors of clay, compacted by intentional puddling or by long continued use. Their burial practices may be summarized as follows. Upon the death of an individual who was to be buried in the flesh, the body was dressed in the finest garments and ornaments and placed in an extended position on the back in a charnel house upon a rectangular burial platform on the floor. This puddled clay platform was surrounded by a log tomb from one to three logs in height, and covered by logs or slabs, with layers of bark often placed beneath and over the logs. The logs were held in place with vertical stakes or stone slabs. Implements and ornaments, usually ceremonially "killed" or broken to release their "spirits," were then placed in the grave. Artifacts were often placed symmetrically around the rectangular tomb, while in other cases burials were encircled by ornaments or small stones. A copper ear ornament was commonly placed at each hand and a conch shell at each corner of the platform.

Burials were sometimes accompanied by thousands of pearl or shell beads, and dozens of other ornaments and implements. Red ocher was strewn over the body and artifacts, or applied directly to the bones, a fact showing that the bodies sometimes laid in state long enough for the flesh to have decayed. In some cases as many as six bodies were placed in one large tomb. Separate skulls placed in some graves are considered to have been those of revered ancestors, since they conform in physical type to those of the main burials. Extended burials in the flesh were also placed in stone-slab graves. Flexed burials occurred at one site and bundle burials at another, the later custom being indicative of some form of reburial.

Cremation was practiced more than burial in the flesh, with over three-fourths of all burials being of that type. Cremation took place in rectangular basins of puddled clay which had sloping sides and flat bottoms. They were from three to five inches deep and varied in length from three to over ten feet. Some show evidence of long and repeated use, and in rare cases they were used for depositories for the cremated remains and accompanying artifacts. A few bodies were cremated in the flesh, but most cremations were apparently of dismembered defleshed skeletons. This argues for a practice in which the bodies were exposed for a considerable period of time, perhaps on platforms or scaffolds, as among some historic tribes. After cremation the charred bones and ashes were deposited on prepared platforms surrounded by log tombs. Some tombs were used for the ashes of one person, while in others the remains of a number of cremated bodies were placed.

Artifacts were burned with the body or placed with the ashes at the time of deposition on the prepared platforms. Large offerings were also placed in special depositories separate from the tombs or upon wooden platforms. Certain "houses" or compartments were used for cremation, some for tombs and others for the storage of ceremonial objects. Well-made circular fire basins of puddled clay may represent the sites of ceremonial fires. After a lapse of time, individual tombs were covered with small mounds. In a few cases "canopies" of woven fabric were placed over these mounds and pinned down with bone skewers, while others were covered with layers of sand or gravel. Following this, the wooden structures forming the walls of the houses were burned. Earth was then piled over the small mounds forming a larger mound which took the outline of the pre-mound wooden structure. In some cases, the larger primary and secondary mounds were encircled by retaining walls and coverings of stone and gravel, with a gravel layer frequently extending over the entire mound. When the enclosures became filled with burial mounds they were apparently abandoned in favor of new sites.

The Hopewell people apparently lived in permanent villages. Their large earthworks, with all the sustained labor they imply, point to this conclusion. The fact that they practiced agriculture, raising corn and no doubt its associated plants,[60] likewise indicates a nonnomadic people. Hunting was probably important, while gathering of wild foods played only a secondary role. A people capable of building the

60. Charred corn was found at Turner and Harness.

great earthworks and who had such elaborate burial customs must have had a well-developed social organization. There may have been totemic clans, for certain animals and birds were used extensively for ceremonial motifs. Sites of the Hopewell culture by no means have complete cultural identity. Some differences may no doubt be attributed to local variations at a given time level, while others may indicate that some sites are older. The Tremper Site for example differs considerably from the other major sites and may be an early Hopewell expression.[61]

The Ohio Aspect of the Hopewellian Phase is essentially Woodland in its traits, as are the other regional developments of that culture throughout the Mississippi Valley and its peripheries.[62] Its roots were apparently in the simpler Adena Culture which is considered to have preceded it in the region. The closest ties of Ohio Hopewell seem to be with sites of the Ogden-Fettie Focus in Illinois.[63] Many burial customs and artifacts of that focus are the same as those of the Ohio Aspect, although the pottery is different. The presence of platform pipes of Ohio pipestone at that focus, identical in type with those of Ohio, and of chipped implements of Ohio flint, argues for a close relationship. Ohio Hopewell also has much in common with such Hopewellian cultures as the Goodall Focus of Michigan and Indiana,[64] the Trempeleau Focus of Wisconsin,[65] the Nickerson Focus of Illinois and Iowa,[66] and the Kansas City Focus.[67] In addition, there are Hopewellian sites, and Woodland sites showing Hopewellian influence, in practically every portion of the Upper Mississippi Valley. Some Hopewellian sites in Pennsylvania and New York are closely related to those in Ohio as they contain artifacts of identical types made of Ohio materials.[68]

In the southern United States there were also Hopewellian cultures which had ties with the Ohio centers, such as the Indians of the Copena Focus who lived along the Tennessee River.[69] Their pottery, largely limestone-tempered, is related to Adena pottery but apparently was made at a later period.[70] They made the large zoomorphic steatite pipes which were found in Seip Mound No. 1 in Ohio. This trade material shows the two cultures to have been partially contemporaneous.

The Marksville Focus people of Louisiana also had cultural ties with Ohio.[71] This is especially true of pottery vessels, some bearing bird designs like those from Ohio Hopewell sites. The Troyville Focus, classed with the Marksville Focus in the Delta Aspect, also has Ohio Hopewellian affinities.[72] The Ohio Aspect people likewise had connections with those of the Gulf Coast Aspect of Florida, including the Santa Rosa-Swift Creek Focus and the Crystal River Focus.[73] Artifacts made of exotic materials show the extent and direction of trade, travel, and general interregional contacts of the Ohio Hopewellians. From the northwest came copper and silver of the Lake Superior district, brown chalcedony from North Dakota, obsidian from the Rocky Mountains, grizzly bear teeth, and possibly meteoritic iron. From closer sources to the West came galena (Illinois and Missouri) and nodular flint from southern Indiana. From the southern Appalachian Mountains came mica, quartz, steatite, and graphite. From the Gulf Coast came alligator teeth, tortoise shell, shark teeth, spadefish bones, and barracuda jaws. From the same region came the marine gastropods *Busycon, Cassis,* and *Fasciolaria,* as well as *Marginella, Oliva,* and *Olivella.* The tropical conchs suggest that the Gulf Coast of Florida was the main source of materials coming from the Gulf, for they are scarce in the Delta region.[74] Complicated stamp and check stamp sherds, as well as the T-shaped lip in Ohio Hopewell were also apparently derived from the Florida area.[75] Out of Ohio, largely to northern Hopewell sites, went pipes made of Ohio pipestone and implements made of Flint Ridge flint.

It is not possible to point to one region or to one culture for the ultimate origin of Ohio Hopewell. Like Hopewellian in other regions it was a regional expression of a widespread cultural phase during a particular time interval which may have lasted over two or three hundred years. The influence the Ohio Hopewell culture had upon later cultures in the region seems to have been slight. One author has suggested that the early Woodland-like Fort Ancient Aspect sites in Ohio had a genetic connection with Hopewell and that the Iroquois Aspect developed out of a culture which was in the northeast in Hopewellian times.[76] The relationship of the "Intrusive Mound Culture" to Ohio Hopewell will be taken up later. Survival of general Hopewellian concepts, and their modification by later groups, has been noted for the Weeden Island Culture,[77] the Caddoan[78] and

61. See Webb and Snow, 1945, pp. 200–217; and Morgan, 1946a.

62. The interpretation in this section, in the main, is based on Griffin, J. B., 1946; limitations of space preclude detailed trait comparisons.

63. Griffin, J. B., 1946, p. 62; Cole and Deuel, 1937, p. 19; Griffin and Morgan (eds.), 1941, pp. 17–19.

64. Quimby, 1941b.

65. McKern, 1931.

66. Bennett, 1945, p. 121.

67. Wedel, 1940, p. 309; 1943, pp. 201–203.

68. Ritchie, 1937; 1938b; 1944, pp. 202–227.

69. Webb, W. S., 1939, pp. 188–201.

70. Griffin, J. B., 1945d, in *The Adena People,* pp. 228–234.

71. Setzler, 1933; Ford and Willey, 1940.

72. Griffin, J. B., 1946, pp. 63–67.

73. Griffin, J. B., 1946, pp. 62, 64; Martin, Quimby, and Collier, 1947, p. 392.

74. Griffin, J. B., 1946, p. 65.

75. *Ibid.*

76. *Ibid.,* p. 92.

77. *Ibid.,* p. 77.

78. Setzler, 1933, p. 21.

for certain elements in the "Southern Cult"[79] of Mississippian times.

INTRUSIVE MOUND CULTURE

The "Intrusive Mound" Culture (Fig. 34), although discovered and recognized as distinctive over one hundred years ago,[80] was not characterized until the report on the final explorations at the Mound City Group appeared.[81] At Mound City, Ross County, Ohio, burials of this culture occurred in intrusive pits dug into Hopewellian mounds. At Portsmouth in Scioto County, Ohio, the Heinisch Mound and the Hilltop Mound apparently pertained entirely to the "Intrusive Mound" Culture. Although many artifacts were salvaged from these mounds, no records were kept as the mounds were removed by construction work. At Mound City both extended and flexed burials were present but nothing was reported on the physical type of these people. Most of the burials were accompanied by numerous artifacts, as well as by unworked and partially worked bone and antler objects.

Although the culture has to be defined from grave goods, fortunately the bulk of the artifacts are implements. Characteristic of the culture are the angular bladed pentagonal flint points. Large trianguloid flint blades occur as do corner-notched projectile points. Projectile and spear points were also made from antler tines hollowed out at the base to receive a shaft. The large size of the points indicate the use of the atlatl. Ungrooved axes, chipped from flint and polished, are typical of the culture. Scrapers were made from large curved spalls of Indiana flint, from metapodial bones of the deer (beamers) and from mussel shells. Typical for this group are the cutting tools consisting of a beaver incisor tooth hafted crosswise in an antler handle. Characteristic, too, are the unilaterally barbed harpoons with from two to five barbs, and with either a perforated or enlarged base for attachment to a line. Various types of awls were cut from animal and bird bones. Clubs, flint chipping tools, and gouges were made from elk antler, and bone needles from elk shoulder blades.

Beads of Marginella and Anculosa shells were used, as well as cylindrical beads cut from the columella of conch shells. Hair combs were fashioned from elk antler and incised with parallel lines on the handle portion. Pendants, rectangular in form, were of slate with one hole for suspension.

Tobacco was smoked in platform pipes similar to those of the Hopewell Culture, but made of steatite with a ridge on the stem portion above the stem hole. The use of marine shells and steatite reveals contact with people to the southeast. They were no doubt hunters and gatherers and may have had some agriculture. They were of a later period than the Hopewell people who lived at Mound City, for their burials are intrusive into the mounds at that site. This fact, in conjunction with the typological differences in their artifacts, implies that they followed the entire Hopewellian occupation of the region. Platform pipes may indicate an attenuated Hopewellian influence, while bone beamers and perhaps chipped and polished axes may be a tie with the later Fort Ancient Culture.[82]

The "Intrusive Mound" Culture of Ohio is distinctly Woodland in its nature and closely related to the Point Peninsula Focus of the Vine Valley Aspect of New York which centers in the area south of Lake Ontario.[83] It should be noted that pottery of the Woodland type is present in New York and that there seems to be more Hopewellian influence on the Point Peninsula Focus than on the "Intrusive Mound" Culture. Chronologically, the Point Peninsula Focus has been classified in the Intermediate Period between the Archaic and Late Prehistoric periods.[84] Its exact relationship in time with the Hopewellian Phase in New York and with the Middlesex Focus of the Vine Valley Aspect is not clear, but it is considered to have overlapped, or to have been influenced by, both of these cultures. It is also thought to have influenced the Owasco Aspect. The "Intrusive Mound" material is also similar to a complex of traits found in a mound in Montmorency County, Michigan in a sub-floor burial pit with a flexed skeleton,[85] and it shares traits with the Arvilla Focus of the Red River Aspect of Minnesota and North Dakota.[86]

MISSISSIPPI PERIOD

FORT ANCIENT ASPECT

The Fort Ancient Indians (Fig. 35)[87] lived in southern Ohio, southeastern Indiana, northern Kentucky, and apparently in northwestern West Virginia.[88] Sites of the culture have been classified into four foci. The Madisonville Focus sites are located in the lower valleys of the Great and Little Miami rivers, along the

---

79. Krieger, 1945, pp. 503–507.

80. Squier and Davis, 1848, pp. 144–154.

81. Mills, 1922a, pp. 563–584. This summary is based on Mills, Squier and Davis, 1848, and on the artifacts in the Ohio State Museum. Intrusive burials of other cultures into mounds should not be confused with the "Intrusive Mound" culture.

82. Griffin, J. B., 1943a, p. 307.

83. Ritchie, 1937, pp. 188–194; 1938b, pp. 100–102; 1944, pp. 112–186, 324.

84. Ritchie, 1944, Pl. 2 and 4.

85. Hinsdale, 1930, pp. 127–128.

86. Wilford, 1941, pp. 243–246.

87. The culture was named for the Fort Ancient Earthworks, Warren County, Ohio, in the belief that the people who left their remains in the nearby valley also built the hill-top enclosure. Later it was established that the Hopewell people built the enclosure (Mills, 1906, p. 135; Morgan, 1946b, p. 9).

88. This summary is based primarily upon The Fort Ancient Aspect (Griffin, J. B., 1943a, and the collections of the Ohio State Museum).

Ohio, and along the Licking River drainage in Kentucky. Sites of the Anderson Focus are situated along the central valleys of the two Miamis, those of the Baum Focus mainly along the central Scioto Valley, while sites of the Feurt Focus are near the mouth of the Scioto and along the Ohio.

Physically, the people of this culture were not homogeneous in type. Some were longheaded Sylvids, some were roundheaded Centralids, and at certain sites both types occurred.[89] Among the diseases which have been noted for this group are dental caries, apical abscesses, arthritis, rickets, osteitis, auditory abscesses, and possibly syphilis.[90] Some of the skulls show occipital deformation or cradleboard flattening.

The people are known from their village sites, cemeteries, and burial mounds, hence a well-rounded description of their material culture is available. Their villages were usually in the valleys, often situated on terraces, but sometimes they were in the lowlands directly on the stream banks. Patterns of post-molds and ridges of earth indicate that their houses were circular in ground plan and around thirty or forty feet in diameter. Some of the houses had centrally situated circular fireplaces made of puddled clay. In other cases the fireplaces were located outside of the house, and were sometimes marked by a group of fire-cracked stones. Houses were sometimes arranged in rows, and there is evidence that entire villages may have been protected by wooden stockades.[91] Usually near the house were food storage pits three or four feet in diameter and from three to five feet deep. These were lined with bark, leaves or grass for the protection of their contents. When such storage pits were abandoned they served as refuse pits, becoming filled with ashes, animal bones, sherds, broken and lost tools and ornaments, and fire-cracked stones.

The Fort Ancient people used pottery vessels extensively for utilitarian purposes as shown by the great quantities of sherds in the village deposits. Complete vessels occur with burials and broken ones are occasionally found in storage pits. There is considerable variation in the pottery from focus to focus, although a number of the main types occur to a greater or lesser degree in most of the foci. Pottery was tempered with grit or shell, or a combination of the two materials, and is gray, brown, or buff in color. Exterior surfaces of the vessels were smoothed or impressed with a cord-wrapped paddle before firing, leaving cord marks over most of the area. Rim areas were often smoothed over the cord marking. Some vessels bore no decoration but many were deco-

rated around the rim and a few on the shoulder area by incising, notching and punctating. A common incised design was the curvilinear guilloche. Another common motif was a band of line-filled triangles filled with groups of punctate marks. Punctate marks were also sometimes placed at the base of the thickened rim band. Some vessels had handles or lugs, while others were without them. Handles were ordinarily either two or four in number, and occasionally decorated with punctate marks or notching. They were of the strap or loop variety, while lugs were of the semicircular or horizontal form, often notched and with two on each vessel. A few rims were decorated with animal or bird effigies. The open-mouth jar with straight or slightly flaring rim and a rounded bottom predominates. Bowls were made, as well as flat salt pans for evaporating brine in the manufacture of salt

Fort Ancient village sites contain an abundance of artifacts of stone, bone and shell. Tools and ornaments were also commonly placed in the graves as offerings. The bow and arrow was evidently the main weapon employed in hunting and fighting, for they made great numbers of small triangular flint arrowpoints. They also used a few side-notched, corner-notched and stemmed flint points. Other points, with a hollow base which is sometimes perforated, were made from antler. Wooden shafts were straightened by running them through a hole in a large piece of antler, and were smoothed by grooved abrading stones. Flint was chipped with small cylindrical tools of antler.

They employed the ungrooved stone axe hafted through a wooden handle. Ungrooved adzes of the narrow poll type were used in woodworking. Large oblong pebbles, completely grooved for hafting were employed as club-heads. The most common form of hoe was made from a mussel-shell perforated for hafting on a wooden handle. However, some were made of stone, some from deer and elk shoulder blades, and others from sections of elk antler. Corn and other seed foods were ground with small ovoid hand stones on mortars consisting of small sandstone slabs with a slightly curved grinding surface. Hand-sized water worn pebbles served as hammerstones. Trianguloid and ovoid flint knives were used, as well as flake knives and side and corner-notched types. Implements cut from deer and elk shoulder blades and mussel shells served as both knives and scrapers. Flint scrapers include the ovoid types and end scrapers. In addition, large scrapers or beamers were commonly cut from the metapodial bone of the deer.

Drills of flint consist of the expanded-base, single pointed and double pointed forms. Awls were cut from whole mammal bones, bone splinters, and bird bones. A common variety was made from the turkey meta-

89. Neumann, 1941a, p. 488; 1942, p. 541; Hooton and Willoughby, 1920, p. 88.

90. Hooton and Willoughby, 1920, pp. 114–115, 127, 130–133; Mills, 1906, pp. 126–135.

91. Field notes, 1941, Ohio State Museum.

tarsal bone which was sometimes decorated by notching. Flattened awls or spatulas were likewise utilized. Flat sections of deer rib with a hole in one end were probably used in weaving. Small irregular pieces of sandstone, bearing grooves, evidently were used as abrading stones for shaping and sharpening awls.

Bone fishhooks were made from a flat rectanguloid piece of bone by removing the center and cutting the resultant form into two pieces. These were then pointed on the curved end and grooved or eyed on the straight shaft for the line. Antler harpoons, with a single barb and a hole in the shaft for the line, were apparently used for catching large fish. Small double-pointed bone gorges may have also been tied to a line and used in fishing.

Mussel shells, some with well-formed and decorated handles, functioned as spoons; and slightly modified turtle carapaces served either as spoons or containers. Charred fragments indicate that wooden bowls, some with animal effigies on the rim, were carved by these people. Halves of the lower jaw of the deer, occurring in abundance, may have been used for removing green corn from the cob as among the Iroquois.

Ornaments were commonly made of shell or bone. Pendants of many forms, usually with one hole for suspension, were cut from marine (*Busycon*) shell or occasionally from mussel shell. They were also fashioned from stone, cannel coal, bird digits and bone and antler. The canine teeth and incisors of various mammals were perforated or grooved for suspension. Beads were cut from hollow bird and animal bones, and were occasionally decorated. Other forms cut from shell comprise the disk-shaped, globular and cylindrical varieties. Modified *Marginella* and *Oliva* shells were also used as beads. Circular gorgets of marine shell, some with a central hole and some with one or two marginal perforations were used. A few of these bear decoration such as crosses, circles and spiders. Other shell gorgets are of the mask type, with some having the "weeping eye" design below the two holes. Crescent-shaped forms, some with two holes, were also made. Hair ornaments include decorated antler combs perforated for attachment, bone holders for eagle feathers, bone hair pins decorated with grooves or animal effigy heads, and possibly shell pins.

Musical instruments consisted of turtle shell rattles, turkey skull rattles, notched ribs or rasps and bird-bone flutes.

Discoidal stones, some plain and others perforated and decorated, seem to pertain to the game of "chunkey" as played by some of the southern historic Indians. Perforated deer phalanges apparently represent the cup and pin game as played by various historic tribes. Tobacco must have been smoked as a common practice, as well as ceremonially, for pipes are found in relative abundance. They were usually made from stone, but a few are of pottery, and practically all are of types requiring stems. Two common forms are the conoidal and elbow types. Incised designs on tobacco pipes and other artifacts include the "weeping eye", thunderbird, horned serpent, mythical monster, rattlesnake, cross, circle, and human and animal figures.

Little is known of Fort Ancient textiles, although charred fragments found in pits show that they made bags of bast fiber in which they stored corn. They also braided fibers into rough cord.

The Fort Ancient people buried their dead in mounds built within the village, in cemeteries and in their village deposits. Mounds were gradually built up by placing burials on their surfaces and covering them with earth. Some burials were evidently made within houses, some were grouped around houses, while still others were placed in separate burial grounds. The most common type of burial was the extended form, although many flexed burials were made. Bundle burials, indicating reburial of some kind, were not too rare; and there is a little evidence that cremation was sometimes practiced. On an average, the burial pits were around three feet in depth. Where suitable stone occurred, graves were often partly or completely lined with stone slabs and covered with slabs. Many were covered with a layer of bark.

The Fort Ancient people were a sedentary group who relied heavily upon their food crops, supplementing them with fish and game. Their only domestic animal was the dog. Their agriculture centered around the raising of corn. Charred remains of corn, beans, and sunflower seeds have been found in their storage pits, as well as wild foods such as nuts and berries. Little evidence is at hand relating to the social structure of these people, but it is likely that they had a clan system of some form. Certain burial finds are suggestive of "medicine bundles" and point to the presence of medicine men or shamans.[92]

The Fort Ancient Aspect has been classified in the Upper Mississippi Phase of the Mississippi Pattern along with the Iroquois and Oneota Aspects. Stratigraphic evidence shows Fort Ancient material intrusive into Hopewell mounds in Ohio and hence later than that culture in time. Furthermore, the European trade material at the Madisonville Site definitely established that component as existing into historic times, perhaps until the last quarter of the seventeenth century. Efforts have failed to identify the Fort Ancient people with any specific historic tribe, although there is a possibility that they may have been Shawnee.

The Fort Ancient Aspect has a number of traits in common with the Iroquoian cultures of New York and with the Whittlesey Focus of the Iroquois Aspect

92. Morgan, 1946b, pp. 25-26.

of Ohio. The Fort Ancient and Iroquoian peoples of Ohio were evidently contemporaneous, and it is not unlikely that the latter may have been responsible for the disappearance of the former in early historic times. While there are definite connections between the Fort Ancient and Oneota materials, the similarities of the former with the Iroquoian are stronger. The Oneota people were contemporaneous with both groups.

There are traits in the Fort Ancient Aspect, especially the southern foci, connected with those of the Dallas Focus of the eastern Tennessee region.[93] In this connection should be mentioned a number of traits such as rattlesnake and mask gorgets of shell, shell "buttons", check-stamp pottery, handles, jars and bowls, large flint knives, discoidal stones, and the spider, cross and "weeping eye" designs. A number of these traits, as well as the thunderbird, horned-serpent, mythical monster, and circle and cross, have been attributed to the Southern Cult.[94] The Fort Ancient Aspect was contemporaneous with other Middle Mississippi manifestations to the west and south west, and shows definite influence from those regions which evidently came in along the Ohio River.

In conclusion, the Fort Ancient Aspect represents a people with a mixed Woodland-Mississippi background. There may have been an actual movement of Mississippi people into the southern part of the Ohio region who mixed with a Woodland group already modified by Mississippi influences.

WHITTLESEY FOCUS, IROQUOIS ASPECT

The Indians represented by the Whittlesey Focus (Fig. 36)[95] cultural material lived south of Lake Erie in Ohio from the Pennsylvania boundary to the western end of the lake, and on some of the islands. In addition, they or similar peoples lived in northern Indiana[96] and in southern Michigan.[97] The principal sites so far excavated are located in Lake and Cuyahoga counties, Ohio.

Little information is yet available concerning the physical type or types to which the Whittlesey people belonged, but it is probable that they were long-headed Sylvids like the Iroquois Indians of New York,[98] although a few of the crania seem to be of Centralid type.

They lived in fortified villages along streams draining into the lake. These villages, many of them three or four acres in extent, were usually located on high bluffs at stream bends, or on high or inaccesible points of land at stream junctions. These defensive positions were enclosed by wooden stockades or by earthen walls with exterior ditches. Some of the village sites or forts are marked by thick deposits of black soil resulting from long periods of occupancy. These deposits contain layers of ashes, fire-cracked stones, whole and broken artifacts, potsherds and many broken animal bones. Nothing is known of their houses, but certain localized concentrations of refuse seem to mark house sites. Circular pits, as much as six feet in depth, were used to store corn and other food materials, while some of the smaller ones seem to have been used for cooking purposes for they contained charcoal and fire-cracked stones. Most of them were filled with village debris, including potsherds and artifacts.

Pottery vessels were used extensively for cooking and storage purposes. Thousands of sherds are found in their village debris, and occasionally whole vessels were buried with the dead. Pottery was modeled from local clays tempered with grit, shell or a combination of the two materials. In color it varies from dark gray through various shades of brown. The outer surfaces were usually impressed with a cord-wrapped paddle held to leave more or less vertical cord-markings. Most of the vessels were open-mouthed jars with elongated globular bodies and rounded bottoms. A very few were made with loop handles or lugs. Many were decorated on the rim area with impressed or incised designs. The most common design consisted of notches around the outer edge of the lip or on an added rim-strip. Also made of baked clay were a few pipes of the modified elbow type, with tapering stems and incised lines around the bowl as on some Iroquois pipes of New York.

The principal weapon was the bow and arrow. Arrows were tipped mainly with small unnotched, triangular flint points chipped from local material. Small cylindrical flaking tools of antler were used in shaping the flint points. Axes were of the ungrooved variety, some being pecked and polished from igneous rocks, others being chipped from slate with their blades sharpened by grinding. A few adzes were used, as well as chisels of stone, elk antler, bone, and beaver incisor teeth. Several types of knives with their bases modified for hafting in wooden or antler handles were chipped from flint. Flint scrapers are of the end, round, elongate, ovoid and rectanguloid types. Mussel-shells, slightly modified, served as knives, scrapers and spoons. Deer jaws may have been used for removing green corn from the cob. Flint drills are of the straight and expanded-base types and two com-

93. Lewis and Kneberg, 1941, pp. 12–20; 1946; Krieger, 1945, pp. 486–487.

94. Krieger, 1945.

95. Named after Charles Whittlesey, who was the first to describe sites of this culture (Greenman, 1937b, p. 351); this summary is based on Whittlesey, 1871; Greenman, 1935a; 1935b; and 1937b; and Morgan and Ellis, 1943.

96. The Secrest-Reasoner Site in Blackford County, Indiana, produced artifacts similar to those of the Whittlesey Focus (Black, 1935).

97. Greenman, 1939b, p. 25.

98. Griffin, J. B., 1944b, p. 363.

mon awls are the splinter and metatarsal types. Pitted and faceted hand-sized pebbles were used as hammerstones. The ground was cultivated with hoes of mussel-shell perforated for hafting. Bone fish-hooks, some with knobbed shafts for attachment of the line, were used for catching lake and river fish. Flat stones, usually unmodified except for two notches on their opposite edges, were evidently used as net-sinkers.

Ornaments were few and crude. Long pins, perhaps for use in the hair, were cut from antler. Beads of cut and polished sections of bird and small mammal bones predominated. Crude one-holed slate gorgets were made, as were canine teeth pendants. Hair combs with five teeth and with animal effigy handles were carved from elk antler.

Musical instruments included bird-bone flutes, deer or elk rib rasps and turtle-shell rattles. Hollowed and perforated deer toe bones apparently represent the cup-and-pin game which had a wide distribution among historic tribes.

Tobacco was smoked in pipes of stone or clay, with those of stone predominating. Conoidal, rectanguloid, and vase-shaped forms were common, as well as both the plain and effigy keel-shaped type. In the latter type the effigy, usually a bird, faces away from the smoker. All of the pipes, except those of clay, had to be smoked with added stems. A few of the pipes were decorated with notches, incised lines or crude incised animal or human forms.

The Whittlesey Indians buried their dead in cemetery areas near or within their villages. Burial was in simple pits two or three feet in depth. The flexed position was the most common type, although their customs included the extended form of burial, bundle burial and interment in ossuaries. Burial offerings were not common, although they sometimes placed ornaments, implements or pottery in the grave.

The people lived in permanent villages subsisting upon wild game and plant food gathered from the forests. They raised corn and no doubt the plants associated with it in the maize complex. In addition, their diet was enlarged by shell-fish and fish taken from streams and lakes. No evidence is available concerning their dress, and nothing is known of their social organization, but both were probably similar to the historic Iroquois.

Some European trade goods was found at the Fairport Harbor Site, apparently in association with the Indian material. This suggests that the site may have been occupied up to the middle of the seventeenth century. It is possible that the Whittlesey material represents the Erie Indians who are reported to have been destroyed as a functioning group by the Iroquois around 1654.[99]

The Whittlesey Focus has been classified in the

Iroquois Aspect of the Upper Mississippi Phase of the Mississippi Pattern.[100] Its general relationship to the Fort Ancient Aspect of the same phase has already been indicated, and it is evident that the two peoples were generally contemporaneous.[101] The presence of a pottery vessel of an Oneota type at one of the Whittlesey sites, and a number of shared artifact traits, link the culture with the Oneota Aspect of Iowa. The two cultures were at least partially coexistent.

The basic similarities between the Whittlesey Focus and the Iroquoian cultures to the east have long been recognized.[102] General resemblances are also to be noted between the Whittlesey Focus and the Owasco Aspect of the Woodland Pattern of New York.[103]

The Whittlesey material has a notable Woodland character, especially in its pottery.[104] The Taylor Site[105] in Erie County, Ohio, and the Younge[106] and Wolf[107] sites in Michigan also reflect a strong Woodland influence. In conclusion, the suggestion has been made that in the northern Ohio region there was a development from a Woodland pottery tradition into the Iroquoian pottery complex which began toward the end of the Hopewellian period, for a number of basic similarities can be pointed out between Hopewellian and Iroquoian pottery.[108]

SUMMARY

The prehistoric Indian cultures of the Ohio region which have been characterized in this paper cannot be considered in isolation, but must be viewed in the light of the general cultural sequence in the eastern United States. When this is done, the individual cultures may be seen as regional expressions of broad cultural patterns at certain time periods. They have been placed in a general time sequence which at the present time seems to best fit the known facts.[109]

The earliest inhabitants of the region seem to be represented by the Folsom-like points. These people, living in the early Archaic period, were hunters, fishers and gatherers, using the atlatl or spear-thrower. They raised no plants and were without pottery.

Later on in the Archaic period, a people with an Indian Knoll-like culture lived in the area. They, too, were hunters and food gatherers, using the atlatl

99. Morgan and Ellis, 1943, pp. 59–60.

100. Greenman, 1937b, p. 351.
101. Griffin, J. B., 1943a, p. 237.
102. Greenman, 1937b, pp. 357–366; Griffin, J. B., 1943a, p. 237; Ritchie, 1944, pp. 26–29; Parker, 1907.
103. Ritchie, 1944, pp. 29–101.
104. Griffin, J. B., 1944b, p. 368.
105. Ibid.
106. Greenman, 1937a, p. 95.
107. Greenman, 1939b, pp. 25–26. Greenman places the Wolf component in the Whittlesey Focus.
108. Griffin, J. B., 1944b, pp. 368–370.
109. See particularly Griffin, J. B., 1946; Martin, Quimby, and Collier, 1947; and Ritchie, 1944.

which was tipped with an antler hook and weighted with artifacts of the bannerstone type. Pottery was either unknown or was just beginning to make its appearance toward the end of the period. The Indian Knoll-like assemblage of traits contains many elements of a Woodland nature, and it is evident that the people represented by it were transitional to the early stages of that period.

In the Early Woodland period the longheaded people of the Glacial Kame culture lived in the northwestern part of the region. It is likely that they were hunters and gatherers, and their numerous conch-shell ornaments indicate contact with the Gulf Coast region. Their pipes were of the simple tubular type. On typological grounds they have been assigned tentatively to the Early Woodland period, and they may have been coexistent with the people of the Adena culture.

Indians of the Adena culture, a roundheaded people, occupied the southern portion of the region in the Early Woodland period, burying their dead in log tombs in mounds. They were evidently a sedentary people with their economy based partly upon agriculture and partly upon hunting. The size of their flint points suggests that they used the atlatl rather than the bow and arrow. They worked copper mainly for ornamental purposes, and they possessed cloth. They had tubular pipes, and their pottery is of the Woodland type. Available facts point to a people with a formalized social organization permitting the planning and completion of communal undertakings such as the building of large mounds and enclosures. Their use of exotic materials reveals their contacts with other areas and cultures. Although stratigraphic evidence is lacking, it is thought that the culture preceded the Hopewell culture in Ohio, and that it may have been culturally ancestral to it.

The longheaded people of the Ohio Aspect of the Hopewellian Phase had their main centers in the southern part of Ohio. They lived in permanent villages, built great earthworks, raised corn, and buried their dead in log tombs with large ceremonial offerings. They used exotic materials indicating extensive trade relations. Their pottery was basically Woodland.

Strong evidence points to the use of the atlatl, although they may have also had the bow and arrow. Copper was used for implements and ornaments. Weaving was well developed. Tobacco must have played an important part in their ceremonies, for they made great offerings of plain and effigy platform pipes to the dead.

The Ohio Hopewell trait assemblage is funda-mentally Woodland, with strong ties with the Adena culture which evidently preceded it in the area. Likewise, it is related to other expressions of the Hopewellian Phase in various parts of the Mississippi Valley and peripheral areas. Attenuated Hopewellian influences manifest themselves in some of the later cultures of the region.

Following the Hopewell people in the area were the Woodland people of the "Intrusive Mound" culture who sometimes buried their dead in Hopewell mounds and sometimes built mounds of their own. Some of their artifacts, such as pentagonal flint points, large spall scrapers, beaver teeth hafted in antler, and multiple barbed harpoons, are not found in other cultures of the region. Their pipes are of the platform type, but differ from Hopewell pipes in having a keeled stem. Culturally, they were closely related to the people of the Point Peninsula Focus of the Vine Valley Aspect of New York.

Later occupants of the region were the people of the Fort Ancient Aspect. They were of mixed ancestry, some being longheaded and some roundheaded. They lived in circular houses in permanent villages that were surrounded by stockades, and they buried their dead in cemeteries or mounds. The bow and arrow was in general use by this time in place of the atlatl. Tobacco was in everyday use, and was smoked in conoidal or elbow pipes of stone. Their trait assemblage is indicative of a people with a mixed cultural background, both Woodland and Mississippi elements being involved. White trade goods at one site show that some of these people were probably still in existence as late as the last quarter of the seventeenth century.

Roughly contemporaneous with the Fort Ancient people were the longheaded people of the Whittlesey Focus of the Iroquois Aspect. They were a sedentary group subsisting upon game and wild plant foods, and upon corn and its associated plants. They lived in fortified villages and buried their dead in cemeteries. The bow and arrow was their principal weapon, and tobacco was in common use. Their culture has a definite Woodland cast and may have been ancestral to the historic Iroquois. European trade material suggests that these people may have lived on past the middle of the seventeenth century. It is possible that they may have been the Erie Indians.

In conclusion, it is apparent that the underlying and pervading cultural tradition throughout the Ohio region in prehistoric times was Woodland in character, with Mississippi influences modifying certain cultures toward the end of that period.

THE ARCHEOLOGY OF THE UPPER GREAT LAKES AREA.

By George I. Quimby*

THE upper Great Lakes area is an arbitrary archeological division and not a geographical or cultural area. It includes eastern Wisconsin, part of Minnesota, all of Michigan, some portions of Ontario, northern Indiana, and northern Ohio. The archeology of some parts of this area has been treated elsewhere in this volume, consequently my discussion shall be limited to Michigan, northern Indiana, and parts of Ontario bordering on Lake Superior and northern Lake Huron.

At the time of its discovery by Europeans all of the area was forested. The sandy plains and low rock hills of the north were covered with coniferous trees whereas the undulating clay belts and moraines of the south were covered by deciduous forest.

The northern part of the upper Great Lakes area had a continental forest climate with severe winters. The southern portions had a moderate marine forest climate with mild winters.[1]

About 70,000 years ago the upper Great Lakes area was covered by ice. At that time the great continental glaciers had pushed their way southward for the last time. Moving sheets of ice more than three miles thick scooped up soil; ground down mountains into sand, clay, and boulders; gouged out lake beds; displaced rivers; and compressed the land under an over burden of billions of tons of ice. All living things, plants and animals alike, were driven southward before the ice or else perished.

About 30,000 years ago the climate became milder and the glaciers began to retreat northward. As the glaciers diminished, soils, gravel, and boulders were deposited in front of the ice; lakes were formed; rivers began to cut their way to the sea; and the compressed land slowly began to rise. Plants and animals moved northward again following the retreating ice.

It was during this glacial retreat that the Indians came to America from Asia. And not long after their entry into the New World some groups of Indians found their way into the upper Great Lakes Area.

THE GEORGE LAKE COMPLEX

The earliest Indians so far known in the upper Great Lakes area lived in the Manitoulin District of Ontario, Canada. Remains indicative of these Indians were excavated by Dr. Emerson F. Greenman and dated geologically by Dr. George M. Stanley.[2]

Dr. Greenman's excavations revealed a complex of large tools made of flaked quartz (Fig. 37, R'–X'). This complex was named "George Lake" after the locale of the type site.

The George Lake complex consisted of semilunar knives; choppers; ovate blades; quadrangular blades; retouched flakes; perforators; and other tools and weapons, all of which were of flaked quartzite. The thousands of quartzite flakes found in the site indicate that the stone tools and weapons were manufactured on the spot.

The George Lake complex was associated with an old beach of glacial Lake Algonquin 300 feet above the present level of Lake Huron. Tools and weapons were found not only in the beach deposits but also some were waterworn, presumably by wave action. By its association with this old beach of glacial Lake Algonquin the George Lake complex must be dated at the close of the Pleistocene ice age, late in the Wisconsin glacial stage[3] or possibly 10,000 to 15,000 years ago.

At this time the front of the glacier stood fifty or a hundred miles north of present-day lake Huron and the Great Lakes were larger than now. The George Lake Indians then lived on a long narrow, windswept peninsula jutting out from a rugged coast of "Quartzite cliffs with ragged indentations and small rocky islands."

From the archeological and geological evidence it is possible to infer that these Indians lived by hunting, fishing, and food gathering. They probably had boats of some kind; and adequate shelter and clothing. They were among the earliest Indians known in North America.

* University of Michigan, B.A., 1936; M.A., 1937; Graduate Student, University of Chicago, 1937–1938; Curator of Exhibits, Department of Anthropology, Chicago Natural History Museum, 1943——; Lecturer in Anthropology, University of Chicago, 1949. Chapter received December, 1947.

1. Geographical and climatological data from *Goode's School Atlas* (1937).

2. Greenman, 1943; Greenman and Stanley, 1943.

3. Greenman and Stanley, 1943. [These time estimates will be revised downward if the radiocarbon dates for the pre-Lake Algonquin Two Creeks bog at 11,000 years ago is accurate. Ed.]

FLUTED POINTS

Perhaps indicative of considerable antiquity are the fluted or Folsom-like points of chipped flint that occur sporadically in the upper Great Lakes area. Fluted points are known to be very ancient in the west and the generalized Folsom or Ohio fluted type points in the east are suspected of possessing a respectable antiquity, because of their typological relationships with the western forms.

Among other places these fluted points have been found on a sandy outwash plain in Newaygo County, Michigan and on a morainic deposit of sand and gravel along an old terrace of the Thornapple River in Kent County, Michigan (Fig. 37, Q').

THE CHICKANISING CULTURE

Somewhat later than the George Lake complex previously described was the Chickanising culture found by Greenman in a raised beach six miles east of Killarney in the Manitoulin District of Ontario.[4] Excavation of the site has produced two components, one in the beach gravels, and the other in the top soil. This site has been a functional beach three times in the advance and recession of the waters since Lake Algonquin times, and the two components are apparently separated in time by several thousand years.

The cultural material in the gravels is comparable to that of the George Lake Site, and is taken to represent an occupation during the first recession from that level. That in the topsoil was deposited during the recession of the waters from the Nipissing Great Lakes. The surface of this beach is 56 feet above the level of Lake Huron, and Stanley, using the Antevs-Niagara Falls method of estimating ages of beaches, assigns to this component an antiquity of 2,632 years.

Thus in 685 B.C., and earlier, the Chickanising Indians lived on the shore of a post-glacial great lake. They likely made their living by hunting, fishing and food gathering and made their tools and weapons of chipped stone. Perhaps they were descendants of the George Lake Indians who lived in the same region at a much earlier date. But, what is most interesting about the archeological sequence in the Manitoulin District is the long time-span between George Lake and Chickanising without any apparent *basic* culture change observable from the archeological evidence. There were, of course, minor changes: differences in forms and techniques of making tools and weapons. However during 7,000 to 12,000 years (and even longer as will be shown presently) the paleo-Indian pattern of living persisted in this area.

EARLY WOODLAND CULTURES

THE KILLARNEY BAY FOCUS

In the Manitoulin District of Ontario the archeological record shows a span of 8,000 to 12,000 years before the appearance of the Early Woodland cultures in the upper Great Lakes area. For at least 8,000 years the Indians lived by hunting, fishing, and the gathering of wild foods. They did not have pottery or agriculture.

However, by A.D. 500 some of the Indians in the Manitoulin had pottery and exhibited other traits characteristic of Early Woodland. This Early Woodland culture is called the Killarney Bay Focus.[5]

The Killarney Bay Focus was the product of Indians who seem to have lived by hunting, fishing, and food gathering. They made grit-tempered pottery jars with semi-conoidal bottoms and notched lips. Vessel surfaces were predominantly plain although some were fabric impressed and others were cord-marked (Fig. 37, U). Decoration, when present, consisted of typical Woodland impressed elements including dentate stamping.

Other Killarney Bay cultural characteristics were stemmed (Fig. 37, V) and notched (Fig. 37, W) projectile points of chipped flint; flakes and end scrapers (Fig. 37, W) of flint; crude celt-like blades of flaked sedimentary rock; and leaf-shaped blades of chipped flint.

At two different sites this culture was associated with old strand lines 28 feet above the present level of Lake Huron. By means of the Antevs-Niagara Falls method of clocking postglacial time these beaches have an age of about 1,400 years[6] and the cultural remains associated with them probably can be dated at about A.D. 500.

THE OLD COPPER INDUSTRY

The Old Copper industry is the name given to a complex of heavy copper implements occuring for the most part as surface finds in Wisconsin and Michigan. The complex is largely without cultural affiliations, but occasional types have appeared in Early Woodland contexts. And to the best of my knowledge none of the Old Copper types has been associated with any post-Hopewellian remains or Middle Woodland groups with the possible exception of the Effigy Mound Aspect in Wisconsin. Thus the lack of association with cultures of later periods argues for an Early Woodland or Archaic context for the Old Copper industry.

Recent excavations by the Milwaukee Public Museum produced evidence of the Old Copper industry in what may be an Early Woodland or Late Archaic culture. A typical Old Copper type gouge has been found in an early Laurentian site in New York.

Some years ago W. C. McKern recognized the Old Copper industry as an assemblage of related types of heavy tools unassociated with later known cultures and often marked by deep acid erosions and dense patination. He hypothecated that the Old Copper

---

4. Greenman and Stanley, 1941.

5. *Ibid.*　　6. Greenman and Stanley, 1940; 1941.

industry was Archaic and largely antedated the Woodland cultures in the upper Great Lakes region.[7]

Although this hypothesis cannot yet be demonstrated I suspect that the Old Copper industry had its beginnings in the Archaic period and persisted strongly into Early Woodland times. I further believe that there is the possibility of an early Eskimo (Dorset perhaps) connection with the Old Copper assemblage.

COPPER MINING

Although some, if not much, of the copper used by Indians of the upper Great Lakes occurred as erratics in the glacial drift, certainly a great deal of copper was mined. There are literally hundreds, perhaps thousands, of aboriginal copper pit-mines in Ontonagon County, on Isle Royale, and on the Keweenaw Peninsula of upper Michigan. These pit-mines have contained grooved and ungrooved mauls and occasionally other artifacts most of which seem to have no diagnostic value culturally. The probable reason for this state of affairs is that copper mining is a specialized activity requiring specific tools and techniques not useful in other contexts. Such artifacts would not be found in the habitation sites and burials that archeologists usually deal with. And artifacts typical of habitation sites and cemeteries would not be found in the copper pits. Furthermore, there is a good chance that Indians of diverse cultures would use identical tools and techniques in mining operations. Thus the mining pits provide no answer to the question of who used them.

Despite the paucity of direct evidence there is some information available from camp sites, burials, and random finds in the area in which the mining pits occur. If one assumes that the main attraction of the copper mining area was the copper itself, then one may assume that most if not all of the cultural remains found in that area are indicative of Indian groups that were engaged in mining operations.

Tools and weapons of types belonging to the Old Copper assemblage have been found in the copper mining region. Some, in fact, have come from mining pits. Hinsdale[8] mentions socketed spear heads of copper found in an old mining pit and Moore[9] mentions a gad or pike of copper and a socketed copper chisel, presumably found in ancient mining pits. Thus it is probable that the copper pits were worked in Archaic and Early Woodland times.

The Middle Woodland period is represented by the finding of one obsidian projectile point on Isle Royale. The point presumably is connected with Hopewellian or some related Middle Woodland group; for this was the period of widespread trade when copper and obsidian were exchanged over great areas.

The only habitation sites found on Isle Royale are Late Woodland and Iroquoian.[10] Copper knives were a part of the cultural complex found in the camp sites so presumably copper fabricating and mining were carried on even in these protohistoric times.

Thus the available evidence, meager as it is, suggests that the numerous pit-mines in Ontonagon County, the Keweenaw Peninsula, and on Isle Royale were in operation from Early Woodland (perhaps Archaic) times up to and including the Late Woodland period.

THE GLACIAL KAME FOCUS OR ASPECT

A cultural complex that I intuitively feel is Early Woodland, but which Griffin[11] allocates to Middle Woodland is the Glacial Kame Focus or Aspect. However, this disagreement is not at all serious, as I would place Glacial Kame late in the Early Woodland period, and I believe that it persisted well into Middle Woodland times.

The Glacial Kame complex is found in southern Michigan, northwestern Ohio, and northeastern Indiana. The complex can be recognized in terms of varying associations of traits including such things as cremated bones or flexed skeletons buried in glacial kames; copper bar-gorgets, awls, celts, and beads that were spheroidal and thick; stemmed projectile points; birdstones; tubular and platform pipes of stone; and various ornaments of conch shell. Particularly characteristic of the complex were shell gorgets shaped like shoe-lasts some of which bore engraved designs.

Although much of the content of Glacial Kame complex seems Middle Woodland in character, there are other characteristics that suggest an earlier period for some of the sites. For instance, a copper bar-gorget and awls have been found in an Archaic site in McLean County, Kentucky.[12] Gorgets made of conch shell and similar to some of the types of the Glacial Kame complex have also been found in Archaic sites in Kentucky.[13]

The apparent lack of pottery leads me to suspect an Early Woodland context for this complex. Although Woodland pottery has been found in at least one site it seems to be very scarce or absent from most.

The sites that produce platform pipes are most likely coeval with Hopewell and other Middle Woodland groupings, but I believe some sites antedate Middle Woodland.

10. Quimby, 1939a.

11. Griffin, J. B., 1946. [See also Morgan's chapter. Excavations by W. A. Ritchie in Lower Ontario in 1948 rather clearly place this culture in Early Woodland. See Ritchie, 1949b.]

12. Webb and Haag, 1947a, p. 22.

13. Ibid., p. 26 and Fig. 8,B.

7. McKern, 1942.   8. Hinsdale, 1931.   9. Moore, C., 1897.

MIDDLE WOODLAND CULTURES

HOPEWELLIAN GROUPS

The Middle Woodland period in the upper Great Lakes area is best exemplified by the Hopewellian groups and particularly the Goodall Focus. The term "Goodall Focus," which is applied to one of many foci belonging to various aspects of the Hopewellian Phase, designates the archeological remains of a group of culturally related Indians who lived in southwestern Michigan and northwestern Indiana in Middle Woodland times.[14] These Indians probably were farmers who were also dependent upon hunting, fishing, and the gathering of wild foods. They had elaborate funeral rituals in which fine ornaments, tools, and clothing were placed in graves that were then covered by dome-shaped burial mounds of earth.

Tools and ornaments were made of copper, silver, stone, bone, wood, shell, and mica. Garments were manufactured from animal skins and woven cloth. Beautifully executed platform pipes were made of stone.

The types of pottery characteristic of the Goodall Focus are Hopewell Zone Stamped; Naples Dentate Stamped, which I formerly called Goodall Dentate Stamped; Sumnerville Incised (Fig. 37, O); Norton Crosshatched (Fig. 37, P); Brooks Plain; and cord-marked Woodland ware of perhaps several varieties (Fig. 37, N).[15]

Stratigraphic, typological, and distributional studies of various Hopewellian foci suggest convincingly that the Goodall Focus was the product of a cultural movement into southwestern Michigan and northwestern Indiana, probably from Illinois by way of the Kankakee River.

Within southwestern Michigan and northwestern Indiana the components of the Goodall Focus are distributed along westerly flowing drainage systems in such a way that it looks as if there had been a progressive movement northward from one river valley to another. In testing the temporal significance of the distribution of components by river valleys, I tentatively concluded that the life-span of the Goodall Focus could be divided into at least four periods.[16] Pottery types are the most obvious determinants of these four or more periods.

Naples Dentate Stamped (Goodall Dentate Stamped) is a type indicative of the earliest two periods—very popular in the earliest or Kankakee period and less popular in the following St. Joseph period. Sumnerville Incised is not represented in the earliest period; is most popular in the

St. Joseph period; less popular in the Grand River period; and waning rapidly in the Muskegon period. Norton Crosshatched is representative of only the last two periods and Brooks Plain is found only in the last or Muskegon period. Cord-marked Woodland pottery is present in all periods as is also a fine limestone-tempered type called Hopewell Zone-Stamped.

The Naples Dentate Stamped (Goodall Dentate Stamped) pottery previously mentioned as popular in the Kankakee period of the Goodall development was a common type in Illinois where it probably appeared at a slightly earlier date. The relative chronological position of the Goodall Focus and foci in Illinois may be obtained by assuming approximate contemporaneity of periods marked by the Naples and Goodall Dentate Stamped pottery.

The Goodall Focus is known primarily from the excavation of burial mounds. The village sites in the vicinity of these ceremonial centers never have been excavated. But there have been some investigations of Goodall Focus campsites.

These campsites are located in the sand-dune country of western Michigan. Such sites usually were situated in a hollow between two dunes and were adjacent to a river mouth or were between Lake Michigan and a small inland lake.

Cultural evidence found at these sites consisted of Woodland pottery with a scattering of crudely made Hopewellian types; chipped flint projectile points and scrapers; and bone tools. Food refuse included the bones of birds, mammals, particularly deer and beaver; a profusion of fish bones; and some mussel shells.

These dune sites presumably were summer camps occupied by Hopewellian peoples who must have lived elsewhere in the winter. Such sites would not have been suitable for winter occupancy. However, the inland burial-mound sites and adjacent village areas were better fitted for year-round occupancy. Here there were good agricultural lands; a better climate; and sheltering stands of forest.

The Goodall Focus Indians seem to have been fond of the deciduous or transitional deciduous forest zone. They never really settled in the coniferous forest zone of Michigan. This apparent correlation between Hopewellian choice of occupancy and vegetation cover may have been the result of their presumed agricultural activities, although the reason for this is far from clear.

SAGINAW VALLEY HOPEWELL

In the Saginaw Valley of eastern Michigan there are a number of village or campsites that produce Goodall Focus pottery types as a minority ware in a cord-marked, grit-tempered pottery assemblage.

14. Quimby, 1941b; 1944.
15. Quimby, 1941a; 1941b.
16. Quimby, 1943.

Probably both the obviously Hopewellian and the general Woodland pottery are part of the same complex at each of these sites. Moreover, it seems probable that these sites are Hopewellian villages or camps. None, however, has been excavated insofar as I know.

The most common of the Hopewellian pottery types found on the Saginaw Valley village sites is Naples (Goodall) Dentate Stamped. This is a marker type for the early periods of the Goodall Focus. Therefore, I suspect that this unknown Hopewellian complex in eastern Michigan is coeval with early Goodall Focus. Although the eastern Michigan complex might have lasted as long as the Goodall Focus in the west, I rather doubt it, because the late period Goodall types do not seem to have counterparts in eastern Michigan.

However, the late Hopewellian in eastern Michigan is well represented by the Gibraltar Focus which I shall discuss later, because this Focus seems to have been transitional between Middle Woodland and Late Woodland.

OTHER MIDDLE WOODLAND COMPLEXES

Although an examination of both public and private collections in the upper Great Lakes area indicates that Middle Woodland complexes were distributed throughout the region, very few sites indicative of these complexes have been excavated. Moreover, these Middle Woodland complexes are recognized by their typological relationships with Middle Woodland foci in other areas or in terms of their typological relationships with Hopewellian in the upper Great Lakes area.

THE GOGEBIC FOCUS

In Gogebic County in the upper peninsula of Michigan there was a small Middle Woodland site excavated some years ago by Dr. C. E. Guthe for the University of Michigan. The site consisted of a small, dome-shaped mound built over an oblong pit which contained a flexed skeleton. Accompanying the burial were elbow pipes of fired clay; lumps of red ocher; a copper awl; notched and stemmed projectile points of chipped flint; bone awls; antler flakers; and cord-marked pottery sherds indicative of semi-conoidal bottomed jars with rather straight rims and notched lips. Except for occasional impressed designs on the outer and inner surfaces of the upper rim this style of pottery was extremely simple. This general culture, as represented by the Gogebic Focus is distributed over all of Michigan.

MIDDLE WOODLAND IN WESTERN MICHIGAN

In the western half of the lower peninsula of Michigan there were numerous Middle Woodland

sites. These sites usually consisted of one or more dome-shaped burial mounds near a lake, river, or stream. Flexed burials or cremations, often in oblong pits beneath the mound, were often accompanied by awls of bone and antler, drills and scrapers of chipped flint; notched and stemmed projectile points of chipped flint; copper awls and axes; celts and grooved axes of ground stone; elbow pipes of fired clay; and cord-marked pottery either plain or very simply decorated with impressed designs. Occasional finds at such sites were copper beads; bannerstones; birdstones; conch shell dippers and elliptical or oblong gorgets of ground slate.

Associated with some of these sites were geometric earthworks or enclosures. These enclosures were walls of earth arranged to enclose a circular, elliptical, curvilinear or rectilinear space. Such enclosures were a prominent feature of some Ohio Hopewell sites. Two, perhaps three of the Goodall Focus components were probably associated with enclosures. But most of the enclosures of Michigan were of a non-Hopewellian brand of Middle Woodland.

Although some of these Middle Woodland enclosures were in association with burial mounds many of them stood alone. Most of the enclosures were circular in outline. They ranged in diameter from 50 to 180 feet and in height from six inches to seven feet.

A typical circular enclosure located near the edge of a high bluff above the Muskegon River in Muskegon County, Michigan, was one hundred feet in diameter with low walls of earth ten feet across and six to twelve inches high. Excavations in the wall of the enclosure produced six cord-marked sherds and one flint flake.

Two large circular enclosures in Missaukee County were excavated by Dr. Emerson F. Greenman.[17] One of these was 175 feet in diameter; the other 156 feet in diameter. Cord-marked sherds were abundant in each of these enclosures. Greenman concluded that the enclosures might be the remains of dwelling structures made of logs and bark arranged side by side in a circle and covered with earth. Entryways to the individual compartments faced the inside of the circle. The circular earth-covered village was entered through an opening or gateway that may have been fortified from time to time by upright posts.[18]

If Greenman's hypothesis is correct, then earthcovered, circular villages or community apartments were a rather common feature of Middle Woodland times.

MIDDLE WOODLAND IN EASTERN MICHIGAN

The Middle Woodland culture of eastern Michigan was much the same as that just described for the

17. Greenman, 1927. 18. Hinsdale, 1931, p. 30.

western part of the state. The major difference was in pottery decoration. Whereas in the western part of the state Middle Woodland pottery decoration was relatively simple, in eastern Michigan it ranged from simple to complex. In the fancy cord-marked wares the impressed decoration exhibited a broader range of impressing techniques and a greater wealth of geometric patterns. This difference in pottery between east and west persisted into Late Woodland times.

As one can readily see from this line of survey, there is very little known about Middle Woodland in the upper Great Lakes area with the exception of the Hopewellian remains. The identification and temporal assignment of Middle Woodland elements is based on typological relationships with Middle Woodland cultures in other areas.

GARDEN BEDS

So called "garden beds" were symmetrical, low earth ridges about 18 inches high, arranged precisely in geometric forms, and somewhat superficially resembling a formal garden. Some garden beds were shaped like a wagon wheel, but most of them were of rectilinear forms of varying complexity. The largest garden bed covered an area of 120 acres. Of more than 30 garden beds reported to be in the upper Great Lakes area, the majority were situated in southern and southwestern Michigan.

Although there is no direct evidence for assigning garden beds to any particular culture or period, I feel that they best fit Middle Woodland times. Garden beds seem to have been the product of the same kind of concepts that produced certain kinds of enclosures. I could tentatively assign garden beds and enclosures to the Middle Woodland period and perhaps to the period of transition from Middle Woodland to Late Woodland.

THE TRANSITION FROM MIDDLE WOODLAND TO LATE WOODLAND

Two cultural complexes or foci seem to represent a transition from Middle Woodland to Late Woodland. The Gibraltar Focus, a late Hopewellian complex in southeastern Michigan is the earliest of the two transitional complexes. Chronologically, it belongs in the latter part of the Middle Woodland period.

THE GIBRALTAR FOCUS

The Gibraltar Focus is known from one component found at a site fifty miles south of the mouth of the Detroit River.[19] Among the traits characteristic of this focus are the following: ovate projectile points with oblique corner notches; leaf-shaped blades;

copper beads; copper rods with bone handles; a copper gorget; slate pendants or gorgets; celts of polished stone; a stone platform pipe with a straight base and a median ridge above the stem-hole; a large elbow pipe in the effigy of a bird; and cord-marked pottery.

This decorated, cord-marked pottery seems to foreshadow some of the characteristics of Owasco pottery styles (Fig. 37, G–I). It also seems to have partaken of Hopewellian ceramic concepts.[20] Similarly the nonceramic traits of Gibraltar impress one as representing the beginning of a transition from Hopewellian–Middle Woodland to Owasco–Late Woodland perhaps to Iroquoian.[21]

Another cultural complex that is here interpreted as being transitional between Middle and Late Woodland is the West Twin Lake Focus of northern Michigan. Like the Gibraltar Focus, it is late in the Middle Woodland period. And although it may overlap Gibraltar in time, I suspect that on the whole West Twin Lake is slightly later than Gibraltar.

THE WEST TWIN LAKE FOCUS

The cultural assemblage called the West Twin Lake Focus was obtained from one of a group of mounds, on the north shore of West Twin Lake in Montmorency County, Michigan. This focus is characterized by flexed burial and grave offerings in an oblong pit beneath a dome-shaped mound; side-notched projectile points of chipped flint (Fig. 37, J); a socketed, antler-tip projectile point; an elbow pipe of fired clay (Fig. 37, K); slate gorgets; miscellaneous fragments of worked bone; unique implements made by the insertion of beaver incisors through transverse holes in antler tines (Fig. 37, L); bone harpoons (Fig. 37, M), unilaterally barbed; and a grit-tempered, cord-marked pottery jar with simple impressed decoration around the rim.

Much of this cultural assemblage is closely related to the Intrusive Mound culture of Ohio, a complex that stratigraphy shows to have been later than Hopewell. Many significant traits of the West Twin Lake Focus are identical to those of the Point Peninsula Focus which seems to overlap and follow the Hopewellian Focus in New York.[22] Because the West Twin Lake Focus is so closely allied to the Intrusive Mound Focus in Ohio and the Point Peninsula Focus of the Northeast, one may assume approximate contemporaneity for all three foci. And since two of these foci, Point Peninsula and Intrusive Mound, seem to have been post Hopewellian, it is likely that West Twin Lake also is post Hopewellian.

---

19. Greenman, 1945.

20. *Ibid.*
21. See Griffin's hypothesis for the role of Hopewellian and Woodland in the ancestry of the Iroquoian Aspect (Griffin, J. B., 1944b).
22. Ritchie, 1944.

THE LATE WOODLAND COMPLEXES

Evidence of Late Woodland occupancy is found over all of the upper Great Lakes area. Although most of this evidence never has been placed in any classificatory framework or otherwise synthesized, sufficient data are available to allow the presentation of some of the Late Woodland foci.

THE PORTER FOCUS

The various components of the Porter Focus are situated in the middle part of western Michigan. This focus is manifested by such traits as burial mounds; flexed skeletons; cremations; bundle burials; grave offerings; red ocher with burials; sub-floor, oblong burial pits; notched projectile points; unilaterally barbed harpoon heads of bone; awls of bone and antler; awls of ground stone; elbow pipes of fired clay; and cord-marked, grit-tempered pottery.

Were it not for a few significant traits, this complex could not be separated from Middle Woodland foci. These seemingly significant traits involve the pottery and the elbow pipes. The pottery, for instance, seems to show a greater incidence of flaring rims than straight rims, although this is hard to demonstrate. Moreover, both occasional jar fragments and pipes are decorated with a kind of pseudo cord-wrapped stick impressing technique that seems to have been a Late Woodland characteristic, when present. Also at least one effigy pipe found in a component of this focus exhibits qualities that suggest Late Woodland. The effigy pipe in question is of elbow form with a spotted lizard modeled on the under-side of the stem, and the outer side of the bowl. Lizards of very similar style have been noted on pipes and/or pottery of the Iroquois, Fort Ancient and Mississippi peoples.[23] All previous occurances of lizard effigies seem to belong to time levels that are the equivalent of Late Woodland. Therefore, I suspect, the lizard effigy from one component of the Porter Focus is likewise indicative of Late Woodland.

By and large it is difficult to separate Middle and Late Woodland components in western Michigan. Part of the difficulty arises from lack of data. Another stumbling block is the persistence of many Middle Woodland traits into Late Woodland. And, finally, and perhaps most important is the fact that at any given component there may not be a sufficient range of traits present to provide an opportunity for adequate classification.

THE YOUNGE FOCUS

In eastern Michigan the investigations of Dr. E. F. Greenman have revealed a comparatively rich and interesting cultural assemblage called the Younge Focus.[24] The Younge Focus is related to the Owasco Aspect[25] and may have some ancestral ties with Hopewellian as manifested by the Gibraltar Focus. Moreover, the Younge Focus may be an expression of the same kind of process that hypothetically produced Iroquois from a Middle Woodland–Hopewellian base.

The Younge Focus was the product of a farming, hunting, and fishing economy. Although there was no use of burial mounds, death rituals were nonetheless elaborate and manifested in part by the burial of rearticulated skeletons with holes drilled in the long bones and skulls; disks cut from the skulls; and portions cut from the heads of long bones. These and a number of other burial traits suggest the ethnologically known ceremony of the Huron called the Feast of the Dead.

IROQUOIAN COMPLEXES

Although Iroquoian pottery of the western type (Erie-Neutral) has been found near Sault Ste. Marie, Michigan and near Lake Nipigon, Ontario in small quantities, it appears in campsites on Isle Royale, Michigan as part of a mixed assemblage of Iroquoian and Late Woodland.[26] Included in this mixed Woodland-Iroquoian assemblage were copper knives of a specific type, scrapers, a notched projectile point, and hammerstones. There was no evidence of contact with Europeans, nevertheless, the presence of Iroquoian pottery suggests a rather late period for the occupancy of these particular sites. In all likelihood these archeological remains were left by a protohistoric Woodland group who had absorbed some Iroquois, probably women.

The Iroquoian materials reported from southwestern Michigan and northwestern Indiana by Parker[27] actually came from a well known Iroquoian site near Richmond Mills in New York. This fact was verified beyond any reasonable doubt by the writer and Glenn A. Black during their co-operative archeological survey of the St. Joseph Valley in 1937. Both Dr. Parker and the collector who brought these materials to his attention seem to have been the victims of a hoax or perhaps an unfortunate error.

With the elimination of the spurious Iroquoian sites in southwestern Michigan and northwestern Indiana, all of the undeniably Iroquoian materials are confined to the northern part of the upper Great Lakes region. The absence of European trade goods with these Iroquoian remains suggests a protohistoric rather than an historic period for the Iroquoian intrusion into the northern part of the upper Great Lakes area.

23. Griffin, J. B., 1943a, pp. 202–205.

24. Greenman, 1937a; 1939a; 1939b.
25. Greenman, 1939a; Ritchie, 1944.
26. Quimby, 1939a.
27. Parker, 1922, Pl. 55.

THE WHITTLESEY FOCUS

In southeastern Michigan and particularly in northern Ohio there are a series of components that comprise the Whittlesey Focus.[28] Although Woodland-like in many of its characteristics, the Whittlesey Focus has heretofore been classified in the Iroquoian Aspect of the Upper Mississippi Phase.[29] At least one component of this focus seems to represent members of the Erie tribe of the period *ca.* 1590–1650.[30] Other components may have been earlier.

The principal component of this focus in southeastern Michigan is found at the Wolf Site.[31] There is some question that this component should be included in the Whittlesey Focus.[32] The Wolf component in addition to showing relationship with Whittlesey materials shows stronger evidence of relationship with the cultural content of the Younge Focus.

A FISHER-ONEOTA, UPPER MISSISSIPPI COMPLEX

In northwestern Indiana and southwestern Michigan there are found occasionally the remains of an Upper Mississippi cultural assemblage. Sites near South Bend, Indiana, near Niles, Michigan, and in the vicinity of Grand Rapids, Michigan have produced shell-tempered pottery jars of globular form and decorated with broad, shallow, incised lines arranged in rather simple geometric patterns. In some instances small, narrow, triangular points of chipped flint accompany the pottery. This complex does not seem to have been associated with European trade materials although such materials were present at the Fisher site in northeastern Illinois. However, Oneota-Fisher cultural manifestations in adjoining areas are securely anchored in the historic horizon which varies slightly from area to area. And there is no reason to believe that the Fisher-like material in northwestern Indiana and southwestern Michigan is not similarly late. There is strong probability that this vaguely defined focus, termed Moccasin Bluff by Greenman[33] and McCartney by Griffin[34] can be assigned to either the Potawatomi or the Miami. Bands of both tribes were known to have been in the specific area in early historic times.

SHELL-TEMPERED POTTERY IN THE SAGINAW VALLEY

Surface collections from sites in the Saginaw Valley of eastern Michigan have revealed the presence of shell-tempered pottery decorated in several different ways. One style is best represented by a jar with a smooth surface and a rim decoration consisting of four encircling impressions of a twisted cord. Beneath and above the band of horizontal cord impressions are single rows of closely spaced punctate impressions. Another type is characterized by jars with smooth surfaces and applique bands or fillets some of which have a pinched decoration. Both types also occur with grit tempering, but shell temper is common. This seems to be the only occurrence of shell-tempered pottery in eastern Michigan.

I suspect that this pottery shows relationships with types found along the Mississippi and west of the Mississippi. There is a very remote possibility that this ceramic complex is related to the traditional occupancy of the Saginaw Valley by the Sauk and Fox.

THE HISTORIC TRIBES

The historic horizon in the upper Great Lakes area began about 1660, for it was not until then that European explorers began to come into contact with the native peoples of this region. The historic tribes resident in the upper Great Lakes area between 1660 and 1760 were the Huron, Ottawa, Potawatomi, Chippewa or Ojibwa, Miami, and Menominee. Visitors in the area during this period were the Sioux, Cree, Kickapoo, Fox, and Sauk.[35]

Thus far I do not know of any archeological cultural assemblage that has been definitely identified with any of these tribes. Nevertheless, I feel sure that most of the Woodland archeological complexes of the late period are related to Algonkin speaking tribes, particularly the Chippewa, Ottawa, and Potawatomi. I would further guess that the Potawatomi played the most important role in protohistoric Michigan for the following reasons. At the beginning of the historic period the Ottawa, Huron, and Chippewa were recent arrivals in the area. They were products of a westward drifting of peoples, although it is possible that they had moved eastward out of the area at a much earlier date. The Potawatomi had recently moved westward and later they reentered the state along with the Miami. But thinking primarily in terms of the westward drifting of tribes that can be inferred from all of the sources cited by Kinietz,[36] it looks as if the Potawatomi moved westward just prior to the beginning of the historic period. And they would be the best suspects as a native population. Some day archeological evidence and ethnohistorical identification will settle this problem.

But in the meantime I would suggest that the Potawatomi, Ottawa and Chippewa are descended from Woodland groups of the late period. The ancestral Potawatomi may have been a Woodland group

28. Greenman, 1937*b*; 1939*b*; Morgan and Ellis, 1943; also see Morgan, this volume, pp. 96-97.

29. Greenman, 1937*b*; 1939*b*; see also the chapter by MacNeish, pp. 46 and 51.

30. Morgan and Ellis, 1943.

31. Greenman, 1939*b*.

32. Greenman, 1939*a*; 1939*b*.

33. Greenman, 1939*a*.

34. Griffin, J. B., 1946. [McCartney should be dropped as a focal name.]

35. Kinietz, 1940.   36. *Ibid.*

or an Upper Mississippi group. If, for instance, the Moccasin Bluff-McCartney Focus in Southwestern Michigan and northwestern Indiana should turn out to be Miami, then I would suspect that the Potawatomi were a Woodland group. The Huron probably are represented by Late Woodland remains in eastern Michigan or possibly they are manifested by a Woodland-like Upper Mississippi group such as the one that occupied the Wolf Site (Whittlesey Focus).

All of these hypotheses about the identification of historic tribes could be tested by excavating sites of the early historic period, 1660–1760. Such sites exist, but never have received professional attention. These sites could be identified by the presence of European trade goods diagnostic of the early historic period.[37]

A number of late historic sites, 1760–1820, have been analyzed, but they are too late to reveal anything of significance for archeological-tribal identification.[38] These late sites represent Ottawa, Chippewa, and Potawatomi, but by 1760 these Indians were so acculturated that such items as pottery and manufactures in stone had disappeared; burial customs had changed; and in general the culture was specifically different from what it must have been a hundred years earlier. Thus, archeology of the late historic period is interesting in terms of acculturation, but it offers nothing of value in the identification of archeological groupings with tribal groups. Only the archeology of the early historic period can do this.

Methodological Note

In presenting this summary and interpretation of the archeology of the upper Great Lakes area I have placed chronologically a number of taxonomic units without making any clear statement about the evidence for so doing.

In most instances there is no internal evidence, such as stratigraphy, within the area. With the exception of the Manitoulin area where the archeological complexes are associated with a stepped succession of beaches that can be dated geologically, there is no published evidence of stratigraphy within the upper Great Lakes area. It is possible, however, to provide a relative chronology for some of the archeological units of the upper Great Lakes area by means of typology and a knowledge of the stratigraphy of adjoining areas.

The chronological position of the Goodall Focus can be established by means of its close typological relationship with some Hopewellian foci in Illinois and the known stratigraphic position for those foci in Illinois.

The West Twin Lake Focus is typologically similar to the Intrusive Mound culture which is stratigraph-

ically known to have been post-Hopewellian in Ohio. Presumably then, the West Twin Lake Focus follows Hopewellian in the upper Great Lakes area.

The West Twin Lake Focus is typologically close to the Point Peninsula Focus of New York where it is known stratigraphically to have preceded Owasco. The Younge Focus is typologically close to Owasco. Thus West Twin Lake Focus is believed to have been earlier than Younge.

The above cases are good examples of the method used in lieu of actual stratigraphy within the area. The basic assumption underlying this method is that archeological complexes that are basically similar had approximate contemporaneity. Cultural lags if present are negligible. And distribution from a "center" may apply to individual traits or limited trait complexes but is of little significance in the manipulation of large trait assemblages or taxonomic units. To put this last assumption another way: the same forces of culture change seem to be manifested over broad areas simultaneously. And all of these assumptions must be understood to be operative in a rather general frame of reference rather than in a specific limited context.

Summary

The archeology of the upper Great Lakes area reveals a history of the occupancy of the area by man from early post glacial times until the arrival of European explorers in the seventeenth century. The earliest Indians lived in the area while there were still glaciers within a hundred miles or less. These Indians were hunters and food collectors—a way of life that persisted until about A.D. 500.

Around A.D. 500 there were a number of cultural changes. These may not have taken place all at once; some may have been earlier, others later. The cultural changes involved such traits as the presence of pottery, tools of ground stone, tools of copper, burial mounds, and agriculture.

By Middle Woodland times agriculture and burial mounds were well established in parts of the upper Great Lakes area.

In Late Woodland times there seems superficially to have been a degeneration of culture, but I believe that this degeneration was merely the result of changes in technology and social organization that brought about an increase in the efficiency of food production. The old styles of tools, weapons, and ornaments eventually became obsolete and with the shift in cultural values the archeologist was left without anything much to work with except what he sees as a cultural degeneration. And what he sees as a cultural degeneration may actually represent a cultural climax in terms of efficiency of food production and social organization.

37. Quimby, 1939b.   38. Quimby, 1938.

THE PREHISTORY OF THE NORTHERN MISSISSIPPI VALLEY. *By John W. Bennett**

O F THE various regional provinces of eastern United States archeology, the northern Mississippi Valley perhaps is least deserving of the appellation, "glamorous". Up there are found no important and mysterious hints of Middle American influences; no cross-dating with Pueblo pottery; no vast towns with ceremonial plazas and elaborate temple mounds; no large and complex cultural remains of the classic stature of Ohio Hopewell or southern Middle Mississippi. The Aztalan Site, representing a Middle Mississippi push into southern Wisconsin, provides some exception to these generalizations, but it is an isolated case and its duration was short.

In most cultural epochs, the northern valley was a story of migratory or semi-sedentary Indians who, only in the later periods, possessed the art of pottery-making, who lived in small and medium-sized villages and simple campsites, who often built burial mounds, and who subsisted mainly on hunted and gathered foods.

Although lacking in glamor, the northern Mississippi Valley possesses a number of important historical problems. These may be listed briefly: (1) the emergence of western Woodland from an Early Woodland stage; (2) the emergence, blending, and disappearance of Hopewellian manifestations from and in the generalized Middle Woodland cultures; (3) the origins of the western Upper Mississippi cultures; and (4) the status of late glacial and early postglacial man in the north and east. Evidence has accumulated in sufficient quantity to hint at solutions, but much more work remains to be done. An equal amount needs to be published.

The definition of "northern Mississippi Valley" as used in this paper is as follows: All of the states of Minnesota and Wisconsin; the northwestern section of Illinois and northern Iowa; and border regions in the Dakotas and Canada. Wisconsin and Minnesota constitute the heartland.

* Beloit College, A.B., 1937; University of Chicago, M.A., 1940; Ph.D., 1946; Associate Professor of Anthropology and Sociology, Department of Sociology (Division of Anthropology), Ohio State University, 1945—; Chief, Public Opinion and Sociological Research Division, C.I.E., G.H.Q., S.C.A.P., 1949–1951. Chapter received January, 1948. Cut by the editor to one-third its original length, January, 1951.

Geologically, the northern portions of the area under consideration, northern Wisconsin and northeast Minnesota, are part of the Laurentian upland. This is a great rock shield with topographic, mineral, and soil conditions distinct from the Eastern Lake section of the Central Lowland regions to the south, and which constitute the remaining portions of the northern valley region. The Upland is a region of streams, glacial lakes, and swampland, and possesses rocky soils suitable for pine and specialized flora. Fauna characteristic of northern forests abounded. The Lowland area contains prairie areas and runs toward open mixed pine and hardwood forests, and less rocky soils. The climate, as we shall see later, is also more conducive to agriculture, and its fauna was smaller. The climate of the whole region was in general a Continental Forest type, running to moisture the year round and with severe-to-variable winters. Precipitation varies from 20 to 40 inches yearly.

The cumulative effect of the physiographic and climatic factors in the northern valley is to make the area a transitional one between typically northern forest regions and more southerly prairie-open forest country. This transition is seen in topography, drainage, plant cover, fauna, temperature, length of summer, length of growing season, and mineral deposits. There are differences in all of these factors as between the northern and southern sections of the northern Mississippi Valley. These differences also generally correlate with cultural differences.

The archeological record of the northern valley (leaving aside the remains of early postglacial man) contains two basic cultural divisions: First, the Woodland peoples, who inhabited the entire area for a very long time, and who developed simple though distinctive cultures in the Wisconsin-Minnesota areas.[1] That is, these states seem to represent the most characteristic Woodland areas, with the region to the south being marginal or modified considerably by more southerly cultures. Second, the region saw Mississippi peoples, both Middle and Upper, who in later times inhabited the southern parts of Wisconsin and Minnesota and all areas to the south, where agriculture was possible with limited technologies and knowledge.

1. Byers (ed.), 1943; McKern, 1937; McKern, 1945, pp. 174–175.

These two cultural horizons in the northern valley correspond well to the environmental division described earlier. Woodland cultures, with their hunting-collecting adjustment, were especially typical for the northern reaches of the region, but were also able to range throughout the north and south. Mississippi cultures stopped near the boundary of the 100–120 day frost-free growing season.

THE ARCHAIC

The term "Archaic" is to a certain extent a chronological grab-bag into which is thrown a variety of cultural developments and human remains which antedate the oldest horizon in the more recent cultural developments with continuity in the eastern United States, referred to in this book as Early Woodland. Thus within the Archaic in the northern valley we shall include artifact complexes and skeletal remains which potentially cover a chronological spread of at least 12,000 years ago, to the beginning of the Christian era.

There have been a number of claims for great antiquity of man in this area going as far back as 1870. The first of these was the discovery made at the Little Falls Site[2] on the upper flood terrace of the Mississippi River at Little Falls, Morrison County, central Minnesota (Fig. 38). The artifacts or stones were found embedded and scattered in the outwash deposit made by a small gully or cut in the bank for a road. This site received intensive investigation by a number of individuals in Minnesota and was subsequently examined by such individuals as Holmes and Chamberlain.[3] In general they tended to be unconvinced of the antiquity of this material. At present the deposits are recognized as probably postglacial, but perhaps fairly early within that period.[4] The status of the quartzite flakes as artifacts is still quite cloudy. This is one of the most interesting of the Early Man problems and should receive further study by present day archeologists.

The find of a skeleton of a young girl ("Minnesota Man") during the excavations for a modern road bed near the town of Pelican Rapids in the northern part of Otter Tail County, in western Minnesota, has received considerable study and been the object of more controversy. There are individuals who are skeptical that this particular skeleton actually was the result of an accidental death in the waters of glacial Lake Pelican, and it will probably never be certainly established as to whether the skeletal material was found under undisturbed deposits. Perhaps the majority of individuals connected with the problem of Minnesota Man have leaned to the opinion that it is

a genuine find. It has received extensive description from A. E. Jenks,[5] and has been studied by an unusual number of geologists.[6] There is also controversy as to the status of the skeletal material. Some individuals, notably Jenks, insist on its possession of a number of primitive features,[7] while other physical anthropologists do not seem to believe it varies significantly from some of the modern Indians of the northern Mississippi Valley.[8]

Somewhat more certain in its geological dating is Brown's Valley Man (Fig. 38). It was excavated in a large gravel bar, which had been formed during the third (Tintah) beach stage of glacial Lake Agassiz. The present topsoil was undisturbed and no humus was found in the burial gravel which Jenks interprets as an indication that no plant life was in existence when the burial was made. This, plus the artifact types and the physical type, suggested to Jenks that the find belonged to a period, roughly, of some eight to ten thousand years ago.[9] The skeletal material has been interpreted as belonging to an early dolichocephalic group. With the burial were found six projectile points, two asymmetrical blades which have been called knives, and two sandstone abrading implements. Dr. Jenks interpreted the projectile points as belonging to what was then called the Folsom-Yuma tradition. They are now referred to, because of their distinctive character, as the Brown's Valley points.

Sauk Valley Man was uncovered in a gravel pit in central Minnesota and was probably a natural deposition, as no artifacts were found with the body and there were no clear indications of its being a burial.[10] It was an accidental find and was called to the attention of the University of Minnesota archeologists. It has a physical resemblance both to Minnesota Man and to Brown's Valley Man, thus indicating that in the northern part of the area an early dolichocepahlic people were well established and probably existed over some period of time.

In various parts of the northern Mississippi Valley projectile points which resemble Folsom fluted and Yuma type flaking have been found.[11] Unfortunately, most of these are scattered finds, and as such, are not associated with a cultural complex, nor can they be tied in with geological events. The accumulating evidence, however, in the northern Mississippi Val-

2. Winchell, 1878; Babbitt, 1884; Brower, 1898–1903.
3. Holmes, 1893; 1919, pp. 85–86; Chamberlain, T. C., 1902.
4. Wilford, 1941, p. 233.

5. Jenks, 1936.
6. Bryan, 1935; Bryan and McClintock, 1938; Kay and Leighton, 1938; Antevs, 1935; 1937; 1938.
7. Jenks, 1938.
8. Hrdlička, 1937a; Howells, 1938.
9. Jenks, 1937.
10. Jenks and Wilford, 1938; Bryan, Retzek, and McCann, 1938.
11. Flaskerd, 1945; Jenks, 1937, pp. 30–47; Byers, 1942; Bennett, 1945, pp. 14–15. See also the several available summaries and directories of early man sites and culture in North America, e.g., Roberts, 1940; Sellards, 1940; Fischel, 1939; Cotter, 1937; Haag, 1942a.

ley, if considered with that in the rest of the east, begins to suggest the widespread existence of an early hunter horizon or Paleo-Indian in the eastern United States area.

THE OLD COPPER CULTURE

For many years specimens of copper implements of a rather unusual and distinctive character have been found principally in Wisconsin, Minnesota, and northern Michigan, with rare and often undocumented finds in northern Illinois, northeast Iowa, and southern Ontario (Fig. 39). These implements, often found in caches,[12] have attracted attention because of the resemblance of some of the types to Arctic artifacts of stone and bone. The geographical location, plus the distinctive forms and types, indicate a native copper industry dependent upon the Lake Superior mines and apparently detached from and earlier than any possibility of Middle American influences. The exact position of this so-called "Old Copper" culture and industry with respect to Woodland cultures of the north is not entirely clear, but it appears early.[13] In the area to the south and east of Wisconsin, copper objects which almost certainly have been derived from the Old Copper area[14] have been found in late Archaic and Early Woodland horizons.

In 1945, a burial site, apparently Old Copper, was excavated by the Milwaukee Public Museum following discovery of the location by local people.[15] The Osceola Site is located on the bank of the Mississippi River, south of the town of Potosi in Grant County, Wisconsin. There was a large burial pit or shallow depressed cemetery area. The cultural deposit consisted of a five-foot deep stratum of very black, humus-stained sand, resting on an old beach of sterile white sand. The lower two to two-and-one-half feet of the black sand contained burials and artifacts, and scattered stone chips and Woodland potsherds. The top zone was nearly sterile, containing only a few Woodland sherds and broken stone points and chips. Burials were concentrated in the center, and in one (at least) area to the side. As the burials and copper artifacts diminished, Woodland sherds and other village debris increased. All burials were of secondary bundle type, single and multiple. A few showed partial cremation. Three had a layer of small stones placed over the bones. Copper and stone artifacts appear to have been associated with the burials, but the report is not definite on this matter. At any rate, artifacts were most numerous where burials were

most common. The skeletal material was not salvagable, and this poor condition contrasted with the relatively excellent state of a flexed burial outside of the "Old Copper" burial area, and in a thick Woodland refuse deposit. This general assemblage of traits of a highly concentrated mass of secondary burials in a large shallow depression or pit is unique for Wisconsin, although the individual traits composing the assemblage are generalized Woodland in character.

The full range of copper types is not found at Osceola, although enough appear to make identification of this site with the complex certain. Probably most abundant and typical in the Old Copper complex in general, are awls and tanged knives, or spear points, of copper. Awls are predominantly square in cross section and are double pointed. Round awls occur rarely. Points show a considerable range in size, from large spear points with socket-tangs, plain tangs, rat-tailed, and forked-tailed tangs, to smaller spearheads or knives with less variety of tangs and sockets, although some of the smaller types may have serrated stems. The shapes of these points or knives are variable, from rather broad leaf-shaped to long ellipses. The tendency is toward elongated, graceful forms, like long pine trees and long ellipses. There are socketed spuds or adzes, which are square or rectangular bevelled-edged implements with the sides curled over to form a socket. These are probably next in abundance to the awls and knives. Plain chisels or small axe-blades, expanding toward the edge, are also found. Conical points made by rolling sheet copper into a cone are fairly common. Bilateral-barbed harpoons, with enlarged and triangular base are somewhat more rare. Equally rare, but consistent, are crescent-shaped knives with curled or sharply-angled-back prongs (for hafting?) at the ends of the crescent. Of the above tools, the crescent-shaped knives, ax-chisels, and the more elaborate socketed points or knives were not found at Osceola. The smallest utilitarian artifacts associated with Old Copper are "gorges", short double-pointed pins possibly used for fish hooks. The largest artifacts have been called "pikes" and range from 20 to 40 inches in length. These are square in the middle and pointed at the ends. Neither of these forms was found at Osceola. One of the large "pikes" was found in an Ohio Hopewell mound. Ornamental objects consist of flat bracelets, tubular copper beads, a small clasp or clip, and other problematical or fragmentary forms.

Chipped stone is known only from the Osceola specimens apparently associated with the burials and copper artifacts. The projectile points are quite distinctive and show excellent techniques of manufacture, with fine secondary retouching on the edges.

12. Brown, C. E., 1907.
13. McKern, 1945, p. 119.
14. Knoblock, 1939, pp. 201–210; Griffin, J. B., 1941a, pp. 196–206, refers to the Hemphill site. Pottery from this site seen by the editor in 1950 indicates an Early Woodland period.
15. Ritzenthaler, 1946.

The general appearance is reminiscent of the Early Woodland levels in Illinois to the south. The other artifacts at the Osceola site were smoothing stones, pecked hammerstones, small, unworked galena cubes, and small lumps of red ocher. The pottery is not regarded as part of the Osceola culture by the archeologists who excavated the site, and according to one authority it resembles Lake Michigan Phase ceramics rather than that of earlier Woodland levels.

Until additional excavations are made it is perhaps wisest to postpone judgment on the correct placement of this material with the clear understanding, however, that it is either somewhere in the late part of the Archaic or in Early Woodland.

Another feature of the northern Mississippi Valley area which cannot, unfortunately, accurately be associated with known local cultural groups is the large number of polished stone forms with the ubiquitous bannerstone holding the honors as the most abundant. The work of Byron Knoblock in studying bannerstone distribution has indicated that there is a considerable concentration in the northern Mississippi Valley.[16] In other areas to the south and east it is known that some of these problematical forms belong in cultures ranging from the Archaic to the Middle Woodland. Seen in long perspective, the bannerstone, boatstone, birdstone forms merge into a general Woodland polished stone tradition which includes, in addition to these interesting forms, more commonplace bar and rounded gorget forms, and also the pipe complex. Like the copper artifacts, the polished stone tradition tends to diminish as one approaches the later Woodland cultures.

EARLY WOODLAND

The precise circumstances of the emergence of pottery making Woodland cultures from Archaic horizons are unknown. Stray materials in collections furnish most of the evidence; sites are virtually unlocated. Typical of the pottery occasionally observed in collections in the northern valley which suggest Early Woodland cultures is that obtained by local excavators from the Cooper rock shelter in Sauk County, in southwestern Wisconsin (Fig. 40). The writer's information extends only to the pottery remains, which consist of a number of restored vessels. These appear in simple shapes, of two major types: One is a pot with a flattened conoidal base, outcurving walls, and a straight-to-slightly flaring rim—a kind of small based flowerpot shape rather typical for Early Woodland and some sections of Hopewellian. These vessels are thick, granular-tempered, and are imprinted with cord-wrapped-paddle with widely spaced cords, or what may appear as random impressions by long,

single cords. Lips may be notched. The appearance is reminiscent of Baumer in southern Illinois.

The second vessel type is a round-bottomed jar, with rounded shoulder and straight rim. The body is cord-marked, and the rim has two horizontal impressions of single cords running around the vessel below the lip. This type appears as a rather simple and crude form of the more elaborate (and later?) Wisconsin Woodland pottery. The "flowerpot" type is much more indicative, perhaps, of Early Woodland as it is defined for the Illinois-Missouri-Indiana area.

The Lamoille Rock Shelter, in the Mississippi bluffs in Winona County, southeastern Minnesota, has yielded a 15-foot deep refuse deposit with thick, cord-marked sherds in the upper layers.[17] The shelter had been sealed by talus and debris, suggesting a considerable antiquity for the site. Fish bones were predominant in the refuse. Additional evidence for an Early Woodland level in the northern Mississippi Valley, particularly in Wisconsin, is suggested in a recent publication where pottery comparable to Vinette I in New York and Fayette Thick in the Ohio Valley has been identified.[18] There are also in Wisconsin materials typologically similar to Black Sand Incised of Illinois, which also belongs in the Early Woodland period.

MIDDLE WOODLAND

The general time period and cultural stage known as Middle Woodland is, for the northern valley, the horizon which provides the largest number of sites and the widest dispersion of cultural remains. The abundance of sites, burial mound groups and ceramics suggests the presence of some form of agriculture and a fairly sedentary village life, but definite evidence of corn and other domesticated crops is lacking in this region. The great efflorescence of Woodland-Hopewellian cultures of this period has been conventionally explained in part by the addition of agriculture or horticulture to the simpler hunting-collecting cultures of Early Woodland. The steps in this transition are as yet unclear in the northern valley.

At the present time the question of distinguishing between Hopewellian and non-Hopewellian manifestations and traits has become confused, largely because of the persistence of the older mindset which viewed Hopewellian as *a specific, historical culture,* instead of a horizon or style within a certain general period of the development of Woodland culture. The most serious confusion pertains to pottery. For the purposes of this paper, we shall make three generalized ceramic groupings, recognizing that these grade into one another and that revisions are to be expected.

16. Knoblock, 1939.

17. Wilford, 1941, p. 247.   18. Hall, 1950.

(1) *Middle Woodland pottery* is a phrase referring to a complex of stamped-incised-punctated-cord-marked wares of medium crudity, and possessing definite antecedents in Early Woodland horizons. An example from the northern Mississippi Valley is the pottery found in the village site below the Schwert (Hopewellian) mounds in Wisconsin. (2) *Hopewellian pottery* refers mainly to the fine, limestone-tempered, zoned-decorated jars, usually with cross-hatched rims, distributed in burial mounds in Ohio, Illinois, Wisconsin, Iowa, and elsewhere. This pottery probably grades into "Middle Woodland pottery", but many sites simply have the Middle Woodland series but lack the "Hopewellian pottery". Both types of pottery are found in mounds assigned to "Hopewellian culture". (3) *Lake Michigan pottery* is a phrase referring to the later Woodland wares in the northern valley, distinguished by much cord-marking on bodies and rim decoration, but still possessing, in lesser degree, the older stamped-incised-punctate features. Raised corners and thickened upper rims are common. A good example is the pottery found associated with Middle Mississippi wares at the Aztalan site in Wisconsin. Naturally local expressions of these three "types" vary in their resemblance to the type definitions. The three "types" are listed here in their rough chronological order of development—at least, such is the hypothesis. (Incidentally, the term "Hopewell" is reserved here exclusively for the Ohio Hopewellian developments).

It also appears that certain basic shapes, like the narrow base flowerpot and the rounded jar, and such decorations as stamping and incising are inherited from Early Woodland horizons and are expanded in the Middle Woodland cultures. Some of the burial traits, like the use of red ocher, subfloor pits, bundle burials, and long blades probably have an origin in Early Woodland. The long blade-red ocher tradition may trace back to Brown's Valley. The Old Copper artifacts also continue into this period in several of the northern cultures. Laurel of northern Minnesota contains a large proportion of these implements, including the unique pronged cresent-shaped knives. The effigy mound group of Wisconsin contains awls, harpoons, chisels, and axes. Scattered finds of similar utilitarian forms have been made in other Middle Woodland components in the region.

In handling these various cultural manifestations of this stage we shall have two major groupings: Middle Woodland cultures without definitive Hopewellian traits, or, "generalized Middle Woodland", and Middle Woodland cultures possessing those traits. We do not separate these groups by the terms Hopewell and Woodland because we recognize that these terms are extreme ends of a stylistic continuum, with relatively few manifestations belonging at the extremes.

GENERALIZED MIDDLE WOODLAND

In the extreme northern counties of Minnesota, particularly along the course of the Rainy River, occur sites of the Laurel Focus (Fig. 41), usually consisting of large and small round domed burial mounds, a few to a group, constructed over village refuse. These mounds contain multiple burials, usually of bundle type, although a few are in a sitting position. Often the long bones have been cracked and opened at the ends, and the occiputs from some skulls have been removed. Clay plugs adorn the orbits of others. Total cremation, as deposits of bone ash, occur rarely. Burials are placed in distinct layers in the mounds, often as many as a hundred or more to a mound. The mounds are thus accumulative. "Long continued" fires burned on the dirt floors of the successive strata before the burials were laid down, and sometimes ash and charcoal layers cover burials. Artifacts with burials are rare, but about one-third had small pottery vessels, ocher, clam shells, and beaver teeth.

Pottery from the mounds and village areas indicated a variety of vessel forms. Mortuary vessels have flattened bottoms and are often bell-shaped, with maximum width at the mouth (the narrow base flowerpot). Other vessels were globular, with short necks while others had angular shoulders with higher necks. Deep and shallow bowls also occur. Flat-based, straight-sided, wide-mouth ("bucket") forms are present. A single vessel was in the form of a rocker-curved tube.

Surfaces are predominantly plain, although 5 per cent are cord-marked and another 6 per cent had net-fabric markings. Decorations occur on the rim running down to shoulder level. They consist of a Middle Woodland punctate-stamped-incised complex, featuring columns of dentate stamps, masses of a wavy-line or curved single stamp, small triangles, and semi-circular stamps. Several parallel rows of these stamped units at right angles to the lip is the commonest motif. Bosses produced by both interior and exterior punching are fairly common, as are lines of punctates and bands of short, vertical, incised lines. Single-cord impressions are rare.

Projectile points are all stemmed. Five triangular, unstemmed specimens were found at the McKinstry Mound, which also possessed much Blackduck Focus pottery, a later Transitional Woodland culture. Leaf-shaped and rectangular knives are common, and a few diamond-shaped knives were found. Side-scrapers appear as thin blades, some with parallel double edges. Snub nosed, flat, triangular end-scrapers are common. Ground stone includes schist and greenstone flattened cylinders, belled tubes of schist and steatite (pipes?), round and elliptical flat stones with rounded edges, one in the shape of a half-cone.

Bone and antler implements are all very common and quite characteristic of the focus. These are large, socketed antler points and angular-cut beaver teeth—these artifacts being virtually "diagnostic" of Laurel.[19] Also occurring are antler and bone harpoon heads, unilaterally barbed. Ulnae and split-bone awls, long-bone awls, and pointed bird bones are common. A bone pipe or receptacle with hollow interior was found, and tubes and whistles made of bone are present. Antler chisels and anvils, scapulae ladles or hoes, bone arm bands, spatulae, a carved bone dagger, a skin dresser with serrated ends, and perforated lynx and bear teeth are all found.

Ornaments consist of beads made from copper and clam shells, copper bracelets, clam shell pendants, and columnella pendants from *Busycon* shells. Red ocher is also common. Copper artifacts included gorges, longer awls, square in cross-section and double-pointed tubular beads, bracelets, thin knives, or stemless points, small chisels, crescent-shaped knives with prongs at the ends, and pieces of sheet and strap copper.

The affiliations of Laurel are predominantly to the generalized Middle Woodland manifestations of the north. Cross-finds and simple stratigraphy in Minnesota indicate that Laurel overlapped in time with later Blackduck and Howard Lake cultural units. There is a strong suggestion of Hopewellian in the Laurel Focus and the presence of the copper artifacts is an indication of a carry-over from Archaic or Early Woodland. The diamond-shaped knives are of interest in suggesting a Plains connection.

The Howard Lake and Kathio foci (Fig. 46) were grouped by Wilford into the Mille Lacs Aspect, and these two constitute the clearest case for a cultural sequence in the Minnesota Woodland manifestations.[20] Of the two, Howard Lake is the older and can be assigned typologically to Middle Woodland in its later phases. Kathio represents the later, or Transitional-to-Late Woodland culture. In discussing the two together we are violating the order of presentation by stage, but feel this is worthwhile since it clarifies the picture considerably.

The area occupied is the central area of Minnesota from the Minnesota River on the south to Mud Lake on the north. This region has a considerable number of mounds, running to at least 10,000. Quite a number of traits are held in common, although there are certain differences which appear to segregate the two chronologically. Mounds are circular, elliptical, and rarely linear in form and are used almost entirely for burials. Individuals are found as bundle burials, primary flexed. Sometimes in shallow subfloor pits and also in the mound fill. "Fairly common" is the practice of placing logs or poles over the burials, and cremations are evidenced by bone ash deposits. Small stone cairns are sometimes piled over the burial on the floor. Wilford believes that the log and cairn features may be associated with the Howard Lake Focus, the older of the two. Grave goods with the burials is rare. One of the outstanding features of the culture is the occasional placement of skeletons, or the skull of a food animal, particularly buffalo, on the mound floor. This is paralleled by the appearance of a horse skull in a mound of the Clam River culture in northwestern Wisconsin.

Projectile points include plain triangular and stemmed types, the former predominating, and this situation is particularly representative of the later Kathio Focus. Knives are leaf-shaped and triangular. End-scrapers are flat, of both the thumbnail and elongated types. Side-scrapers also occur, and a few drills. There are not many polished stone artifacts, a few small stone bowls, a platform pipe, some possible atlatl weights, and a flat, polished stone with the ends notched to make imprints similar to those of the dentate stamped pottery. There are very few bone artifacts. Copper awls occur in Howard Lake sites only.

Howard Lake pottery has a high proportion of plain surface vessels with quite a bit of incising on the rims and dentate stamping placed in zones. Bosses are common on the rims. Some of the upper rims are cross-hatched, resembling the Hopewellian rim.

The Kathio pottery is almost entirely cord-marked on the exterior surface, and while dentate stamping continues most of the decoration is made by the cord-wrapped stick. Punctates are arranged in single horizontal rows around the vessel, or as a border for the cord-wrapped stick or stamped units. Bosses are all produced by internal punches. The rim areas are smoothed before decorating and incising occurs very rarely.

The early period of the Mille Lacs Aspect is characterized by a typical Middle Woodland ceramic series. If the logs and cairns associated with burials are early, this fits in with the ceramic complex. The interpretation of these differences as resulting from a "Hopewell influence" on Howard Lake is probably too mechanical an explanation. It is perhaps more in accordance with known facts to interpret the Howard Lake manifestation as a Middle Woodland culture in Minnesota which had some of the characteristics associated with the Hopewellian end of the Middle Woodland continuum.

The identification of Kathio as Dakota Sioux is accurate at least for a few sites.[21] But the proportion and complexity of sites and certain traits suggests

19. Wilford, 1941, p. 242.   20. Wilford, 1941; 1944.

21. For an early identification see Winchell (ed.), 1911, and Brower, 1898–1903, Vol. 3, p. 125.

that the ethnic identification may turn out to be more complex than now thought.

There are effigy mounds in southeastern Minnesota, but these have not been extensively investigated. Another cultural unit belonging to this period has been identified by Wilford as the Judson-Hanel culture along the Minnesota River.[22]

THE EFFIGY MOUND ASPECT OF WISCONSIN

Some of the oldest literature in American archeology relates to the "emblematic mounds" of the Wisconsin area (Fig. 42)[23] and their overlap into the adjacent states of Illinois, Iowa, and Minnesota. This complex is generally of Middle Woodland status in mounds, burial practices, pottery, and implements, but it stands as a distinct manifestation. It appears as one of the Middle Woodland cultures in Wisconsin with suggestive Early Woodland antecedents, but persists throughout the period in which Hopewellian developments were present, and its echoes, in pottery at least, persisted into historic times with the Menominee and other late tribes.

Effigy Mound sites consist of groups of effigy, domed, double-domed, and linear mounds, often aligned along the axes of natural features, and frequently with the effigy forms aligned in definite directions. Campsites are found both with and away from mound groups. Mounds are generally for burial purposes, but it is not uncommon to find mounds with simple features minus burials. Humus layers are usually removed below the mounds. Burials are placed in the center of round, domed mounds, at focal points of effigy mounds (such as the heart area), and along with the long axes of linears. Burials are primary and bundled, the former flexed, with single individuals and compound interments. Cremations of bundle burials are fairly common. Rarer are mass cremations involving the whole mound. Stone cists and stone paving with burials is frequent. Animal bones are sometimes found in association with burials. Other burial furniture is pottery, stone and bone artifacts, shell beads, and copper objects. Burial artifacts are not abundant.

Pottery is thin-walled, grit-tempered, with a granular texture and the surfaces usually cord-wrapped-paddle-impressed, but often smoothed (plain). Two principal vessel forms exist: First, the conoidal-based, straight-to-slightly flaring wide-mouthed shape; and second, the round-bottom, rounded-shoulder, short-rim jar. The upper rim is sometimes treated by folding over or applying wedge-shaped strips to the outside to produce a thickened or slanting-collar-like effect. More frequent, however, are simple rims with square or rounded lips. Decoration has already been suggested: the cord-wrapped-stick and cord-impres-

sions are common, along with punctates, incising and fingernail-impressing, pinching, simple and dentate stamping, and exterior bosses. Decoration, as is typical for Middle Woodland pottery, is confined to the rim on the jar forms, but can extend down an indefinite extent on the conoidal shape. Interior rim decoration is fairly common. A typical, but not too common form consists of the jar form with very short rim, with a rounded-thickened upper rim impressed with single, horizontal cords, and below that, punctates or cord-wrapped-stick imprints. This type gives some evidence of being later than the varieties described above.

A classic Effigy Mound pipe form is present: The bowl is conoidal, often with two incised lines running around the top, and with a short, tapered stem at right angles to the bowl, and made of pottery or pipeclay. Curved-tube and "horn-of-plenty" pipes are also present.

Chipped stone appears as a Woodland complex of no particular distinctiveness. The ovate and triangular notched, and stemmed and notched points and blades are common. Ovate and ellipsoidal scrapers are found, and occasional drills. An unnotched blade-scraper-blank tradition, as found in Hopewellian, associated with burials, is rare, although a few of the specimens are reported. Ground stone artifacts include some highly characteristic types. Among the most unique are the famous fluted-blade axes, which are exclusive to Wisconsin. Plain types are also present, and most axes are three-quarter or full grooved. The fluted types commonly have the groove surrounded by a high ridge. There are small crude celts and oval-ended spuds. Problematic forms include serrated stone plates, smoothed stones, and some evidence of a gorget-bannerstone complex, although this is rare.

Bone artifacts are not common, but some typical forms are present. Harpoons with unilateral, multiple barbs (Point Peninsula type?) appear in one focus. More general are ulnae awls and perforators, cannon-bone beamers, and assorted awls and blunter tools made from animal bones. Shell is confined to anculosa beads, fairly common with burials. Copper artifacts consist of small celts, chisels, awls, and rare specimens of other forms.

McKern has called attention to three Effigy Mound foci.[24] The actual variety within the complex as suggested by surveys and collections is probably greater than this, but the evidence is sufficient only for these at this time. McKern has recognized a Buffalo Lake Focus, a Horicon Focus, and a Beetown Focus. No doubt these groupings will be modified as future excavations continue. Unfortunately, there is no clear evidence as yet as to the temporal succession of the

22. Wilford, 1941, pp. 246–247.   23. Lapham, 1855.   24. McKern, 1945, p. 118; McKern and Ritzenthaler, 1945.

various types of mounds or of the materials. This is one of the most desirable phases of future research in the northern Mississippi Valley.

Middle Woodland Cultures in Iowa

The Woodland cultures of Iowa (Fig. 43) are known only sketchily owing to the slender body of published material. Until recently Iowa Woodland was viewed largely as a single cultural unit with regional variations, and sharply distinguished from the Hopewellian cluster in the northeastern part of the state. More recently, it has become apparent that Woodland in this state can be separated into several different manifestations at different time periods.[25] One of these is an effigy mound area in the east and northeast. Some of these sites, at least, are apparently on a Hopewellian time level.

There are a number of different cultural units which probably belong in this general Middle Woodland period. One of these might be called the "Amana" culture. A brief description of the complex to which Bennett gave this name is as follows: (1) Large numbers of mounds, several thousand, generally small and containing secondary burials without artifacts; (2) a few cases of sherds apparently placed intentionally in mounds, sometimes a whole pottery vessel, points, a large number of stone axe types, generally surface finds which were frequently specialized and polished. There is a great variety of chipped flint projectile points, drills, and scrapers. Dr. Keyes also believes that many of the polished stone forms, such as bannerstones, gorgets, birdstones, and plummets so abundant in Iowa belong to this level. Dr. Keyes is, at present, working upon a cultural division which he proposes to call the Maquoketa Aspect, which is located in rock shelter and river terrace sites in eastern and northern Iowa. This material, on the basis of a brief description, seems to belong to the Lake Michigan (Transitional Woodland) culture.

Another Woodland division Keyes proposes to call the Boone River Aspect. It is located in northern, eastern, and central Iowa and seems to have some relationship to the Upper Mississippi Phase. This unit will probably belong in the Transitional to Late Woodland. Dr. Keyes has also identified a number of Woodland divisions which have connections with Hopewellian, to a greater or less extent. These are located in central and eastern Iowa.

Middle Woodland Cultures with Definitive Hopewellian Characteristics

The distinctive Hopewellian of the northern valley is limited to the more southerly portions of the re-

gion: northwestern Illinois, northeastern Iowa, southern Minnesota, and southern-central Wisconsin generally. Collections from several sites in southeastern Minnesota near the Iowa border indicate a continuity of Hopewellian burial and ceramic traits up the Mississippi Valley through eastern Iowa to southeastern Minnesota.

Mounds and burials excavated in the St. Paul area have yielded platform pipes, perforated bear canines, perforated copper plates, cremations, stone cists, and suggestions of clay funerary masks like those found in the Red Cedar River Focus of Wisconsin Hopewellian.[26]

The most intense area of Hopewellian culture in Wisconsin lies in the southwestern part of the state, where it has been identified as the Trempealeau Focus. Another center is in the southeastern area where it has tentatively been called by McKern the Waukesha Focus. In the latter center mounds have yielded characteristic Hopewellian burials and artifacts. Pottery from the mounds and from scattered camp or village sites in the area shows much closer resemblances to the Illinois Valley than to the Trempealeau Focus. "Black Sand" type sherds, with incising over cord-wrapped-paddle, and sherds with "ticked line" indentations, and incisions, ovate dentate stamps, herringbone incising, and reed-punctating strongly suggest the so-called 2A Middle Woodland pottery defined by Cole and Deuel.[27] This would accordingly appear to be a northern frontier of Hopewellian developments of the northern Illinois River Valley.

The mounds of the Trempealeau Focus (Fig. 44) occur in groups of round and elliptical domed types.[28] Linears and effigies interspersed are probably earlier or later additions by Effigy Mound peoples. Some mounds are aligned in rows along natural features. Humus is often removed from the mound floor before the burials were laid down, but artificial floors are absent. Mound fill is of earth, without stratification. Camp and village sites are within and around the mound groups, and isolated from mounds in numerous cases.

Burials were of bundle and primary extended and flexed types. They were placed on the floor of the mound, grouped in the center, or in fairly large, rectangular, shallow subfloor pits, with embankments around the edges created by throwing out the dirt from the pit. Some pits were lined with bark. Burials in the pits were multiple, from 2 to 45 individuals, and were extended with bundle burials placed in the corners or along the sides. One pit in the Nicholls Mound had poles placed over the embankments, and bark over the poles. Floor burials were from 2 to 31

25. Dr. Charles R. Keyes of Mt. Vernon, Iowa, kindly furnished Dr. Bennett with a summary of his interpretations. This was condensed by Bennett in his manuscript and has been reduced further in the editing of this chapter.

26. Lewis, T. H., 1896; and Bennett, John, 1944a.
27. Gerend, 1904, Pl. 1; West, 1905, pp. 122, 126; Wood, 1936.
28. McKern, 1931; Thomas, Cyrus, 1894, pp. 63–83.

individuals, of bundle and flexed types. A few intrusive burials also of Hopewellian type occurred in the mound fill. Burials have abundant artifact and pottery offerings.

Copper artifacts found with burials are simple in type and relatively abundant. Celts or gouges are fairly common, the former being flat, thin, angular, and slightly flaring to bit, the latter having a slightly curved blade. Awls are square and double-pointed. Ornaments are most frequent, consisting of tubular beads; biconcave rivetted earspools and ear disks, consisting of one-half of an earspool; copper rolled cones, some used as pendants; sheet copper plaques or breastplates, rectangular with straight or incurving sides and sometimes with rounded indentations on the edges and perforations for suspension. One copper plate is spearhead-shaped, with punctating on the ends. Also found are copper and silver-covered wooden buttons, one hemispherical copper-silver bead or button, and copper conjoined tubes or "pan pipes."

Chipped stone artifacts with burials are very abundant and constitute a kind of Trempealeau specialty. Various materials rare in the vicinity and doubtlessly traded in, are used: Quartzite, obsidian, jasper, and the brown chalcedony from the Dakotas which first appears in the Brown's Valley-Yuma points and is also found in the Nickerson Focus of Hopewellian and in some of the Ohio and Illinois Valley Hopewellian mounds. Types include large and small knives, of long, narrow side-notched forms, and leaf-shaped, broad-leaf or ovates, elliptical and asymmetrical types. Notched types are more frequent than unnotched. Obsidian forms include large, unnotched, pear-shaped ovates, and large, round-corner-notched types. Smaller notched and unnotched types are also present. Some of the very large obsidian unnotched "blanks" are also evident. A few asymmetrical scrapers have been found. Projectile points from village sites are the familiar stemmed Woodland types with a few of the broad leaf-shaped forms more characteristic of the Hopewellian. Polished stone artifacts are rare. Two platform pipes, with plain, concave bases have been found, and one "bar amulet," a slightly curved, bar-shaped object with slightly concave base and with grooves around the ends, like a few specimens found in Ohio Hopewell.

Also present are pearl beads, textiles of twined weave, and bear canines with lateral biconical drilled perforations, like Ohio types. Some are also split longitudinally.

Pottery is known from excavated specimens with burials and from village sites. It is grit-tempered, with at least one fine, polished Hopewellian mortuary vessel having limestone temper. Most of the pottery has smooth surfaces, but a fair proportion is cord-marked. A few cord-marked pots were found with burials, but the bulk is found in village debris. Two principal vessel forms are known: (1) Semiconoidal, with faint shoulder and slightly flaring rim and wide orifice—the "narrow-based flowerport" type. The cruder wares of generalized Woodland occur in this shape. (2) The finer specimens are pots with round bases, rectangular, lobed shape at the shoulder, with short, straight necks, constricted orifice, and thickened upper rim-lip. Decoration on rims is predominantly of a dentate-stamped character. Incising is present as border and as trailing for zoned-stamped motifs. Some cord-wrapped-stick is present. Rims are frequently cross-hatched. McKern distinguishes three types of rim decoration: (1) Parallel arrangements of dentate stamping in vertical and diagonal lines, or both. When "both," cross-hatched effects appear. These parallel units occur in bands around rim, sometimes with punctate borders, or with internal and external bosses. (2) Rocker-dentate-stamped, or thumbnail-incised motifs form bands below lip. (3) The fine, limestone tempered ware occurs in zone stamping of various types, with cambered and cross-hatched rims bordered with slanting punctates. This is indistinguishable from Illinois or Ohio specimens. Body decoration can be of an all-over type, like stamping, or it can occur in zones bordered by trailed lines. A few of the elaborate curvilinear zoned unit-designs on the body are present on the finer wares, but zoned stamping is found on utilitarian pottery also, in cruder execution, and in different designs.

The pottery as a whole presents the usual division found in Hopewellian sites between a cruder Middle Woodland type utilitarian ware and a finer, more ornate pottery. The difference between Trempealeau and some other reported Hopewellian cultures is that at Trempealeau the utilitarian pottery is also found regularly associated with burials. The pottery from the village site underlying the Schwert mounds is a generalized Middle Woodland stamped-incised-punched-cord-wrapped-stick impressed complex, perhaps leaning toward Hopewellian in the abundance of rocker-dentate stamp and curvilinear zone-stamped motifs.

In general, the Trempealeau Focus displays a rather simple mound and burial complex, analogous to some Middle Woodland developments in Minnesota and probably related also to Effigy Mound. Pottery is more Middle Woodland than Hopewellian of the finer variety, but stone artifacts are abundant and Hopewellian in type.

The Red Cedar River Focus is located in northwestern Wisconsin.[29] As an assemblage it does not seem to be any more typical of Hopewellian than

29. Cooper, L. R., 1933; Thomas, Cyrus, 1894, pp. 94-98.

Laurel of Minnesota. The clay masks may however bring it into the Hopewellian end of the Middle Woodland continuum: Pottery is the same Middle Woodland complex found at Trempealeau sites, and no limestone tempered Hopewellian ware is present. The emphasis on bundle burials, cremations, primary mounds, and the presence of whole mounds devoted to crematory practices is reminiscent of Minnesota Middle Woodland, the Buffalo Lake Focus of Effigy Mound, and the Nickerson Focus Hopewellian in the Iowa-Illinois area.

Nickerson Focus (Fig. 45) is a term tentatively applied to the Hopewellian manifestations of northwest Illinois and northeast Iowa.[30] Its cultural characteristics are only generally known, but in many respects the sites are intermediate between the Trempealeau Focus and the Ogden-Fettie Focus of central Illinois. Many instances of relationship to Ohio Hopewellian linking the Wisconsin and Illinois Valley manifestations are also present in Nickerson. Nickerson Focus shares with Wisconsin the interest in ceremonial chipped stone-work, including specimens of the brown chalcedony from the Dakotas, which is relatively abundant in Trempealeau, occurs in Ohio, and in Calhoun County, Illinois, at the Snyders site. Cremation appears to be heavily emphasized. Copper artifacts seem somewhat more common than in Trempealeau, especially awls, an Illinois Valley specialty. The copper ear-disc, or half of an earspool, a typical Trempealeau feature, is also frequent in Nickerson. Pottery seems most closely related to the Illinois River Valley traditions, though heterogeneous Middle Woodland elements are present. In general, this Nickerson Focus seems to be more closely connected with the Illinois Valley complex than is Trempealeau, and it is not unlikely that future research will show that the Nickerson belongs with the Illinois Valley Hopewellian groups.

The foregoing descriptions have merely scratched the surface of an overlapping and complex cultural development which deserves careful and extensive investigation. The manifestations described must be only a few of many, and they are defined almost entirely by burial traits alone. Complexity of the actual Middle Woodland situation can be grasped by reading the reports of the Bureau of American Ethnology investigations in the region, the scattered accounts in the Smithsonian Annual Reports and similar publications, and the papers in local academy publications, like the Davenport group. We have, then, an overlapping cultural record which will eventually be given historical depth and cultural continuity. The present simple breakdown into cultures and foci, with the possible exception of the more conservative

30. Bennett, John, 1945, pp. 113–122.

groupings like the Effigy Mounds, is sketchy and conceals the genuine complexity of the situation.

TRANSITIONAL WOODLAND

The Middle Woodland cultures of the northern valley appear to have made the transition into later Woodland toward the end of the Hopewellian dominance in the region. That is, the Hopewellian style of Middle Woodland is probably the final one in most areas except Minnesota and northern Wisconsin, where the more traditional Middle Woodland persisted. On the extreme margins, especially south-central Canada, Middle Woodland traditions probably continued into historic times. There occurred a gradual disappearance of the characteristics often defined as "typically Hopewellian" and the reversion to a Woodland tradition of more generalized scope but with some traits of its own. The ceramic complex known as "Lake Michigan pottery" is typical of the period.

The Blackduck Focus (Fig. 46) is located in the north-central lake area of Minnesota. Mounds are of round and elliptical domed types. Burials are found in village areas and mounds, and are rare in the latter. They are generally flexed, in a sitting posture, but a few bundle and cases of multiple bundle burials are known. Flexed burials are commonly found in shallow pits in village refuse, or in deeper subfloor pits in the mounds. A few have been found on the mound floors and in the mound fill. Grave goods are relatively scarce, consisting of red ocher, birch bark, tubular copper beads and two spear points or knives, and small pottery vessels.

Pottery is the most homogenous series of all the Minnesota Woodland manifestations. Utilitarian vessels are globular and round-bottomed, with wide mouths, short necks, flaring rims and thickened lips. The bodies are predominantly cord-wrapped-paddled, with varying proportions of net-impressed, and with only 5 per cent plain. Decoration occurs on the neck and rim area, and consists of the following motifs: most frequent are cord-wrapped-stick impression below the lip, in continuous lines around the vessel, or arranged in panels of horizontal impressions, or as oblique impressions. Also frequent are sherds with *interior* bosses, made by deep external punching. Lips are characteristically crenellated by cord-wrapped sticks. These three elements—cord-wrapped-stick impressions on the rim, interior bosses, and crenellated lips—constitute the entire decorative complex. Rim areas are usually combed and smoothed before applying designs.

Chipped stone artifacts include projectile points of triangular, side-notched triangular types predominating, with a few stemmed points. Knives are thick, generalized types, leaf-shaped and broad convex in shape. Some slate specimens are known, one being shaped like an Eskimo ulo. End scrapers are snub-nosed, with flat backs and rectangular in form. Long and short specimens are found. Drills are present. Ground and polished stone is rare. No axes have been found. One short tubular pipe of schist, and one oval, flat schist gorget, no perforations, have been found. Bone artifacts are fairly common. Harpoons, of uni-laterally-barbed, multiple-barbed types are frequent. Awls are made from ulnae, split bones, and long-bone shafts. Spatulae are present. Bone tubes and bird-bone "whistles" are rare. Antler-tip points are present in a few socketed types. Copper is known from tubular beads, and a spearhead or knife form, the latter wrapped in moose hair.

Blackduck shows its intermediate position by its conservative adherence to such older traits as copper artifacts, slate scrapers, and the basic designs of the pottery rims (individual impressions in panels). The simpler burial complex, prevalence of cord-marking and cord-impressing on the pottery, and triangular projectile points are traits of generally late prove-nience. Wilford has found Blackduck pottery strati-graphically later than the Howard Lake Focus (ear-lier Middle Woodland) of Mille Lacs, but strati-graphically earlier than Kathio Focus (later Wood-land and identified as Siouan). Typologically, the Blackduck pottery is closer to Kathio, with its preva-lence of cord-marking and rim designs, since it lacks the dentate stamping and external bosses of Howard Lake.

Wilford has suggested that Blackduck is early (six-teenth century) Assiniboin, since the distribution of sites correspond to the movements of this tribe in Minnesota, and since no other sites have been found which might be attributed to the Assiniboin. The similarities with Mille Lacs Kathio pottery are also to be expected because of Siouan-Assiniboin relation-ships. The difference between Siouan secondary-bundle and Blackduck primary-sitting burial types is also documented historically.[31] Definite assignments, however, must await further research.

The Arvilla Focus (Fig. 46) is located in northern Minnesota and along the Minnesota-Dakota state lines. The grouping defined as Arvilla Focus seems typical of the northern part of the distribution, the southern components should be segregated into at least one other focus. The name "Arvilla" is that of the type site at Arvilla, North Dakota.[32]

Mounds are round, domed, or long, low linears. The linear mounds are remarkably long, running from 100 to 200 feet, about 5 to 25 feet wide. Mounds

31. Wilford, 1945a, p. 329; and Bushnell, 1927, pp. 42–43.
32. See Jenks, 1932; 1935; and Wilford, 1941, for descriptions. Montgomery, 1906, describes sites of the southern branches of the general culture. Jenks' original chronological placement of Arvilla was far too early.

can be found as single units or in groups. Burials are single or multiple, almost always of primary flexed type, sitting position, in pits sunk into sterile sand below mounds. In addition, burials flexed on the side, and a few extended burials, on back, occur. A very few mounds have yielded multiple bundle bur-ials in large pits (ossuary). Artifacts with burials are very common. Clam shells, red ocher, pottery vessels, shell ornaments, bone and stone tools, and rare cop-per objects, are found.

Pottery is not well known as yet, but it appears to be another variant of the Minnesota-Wisconsin Mid-dle Woodland wares going toward cord-marking. Like Blackduck pottery, vessels are globular, with short necks and flaring rims. Rim decoration is mainly cord-wrapped-stick, but a large proportion of dentate stamping, lines of punctates, and exterior and interior bosses occur. These features are more suggestive of Howard Lake and Laurel. Pottery pipes have an elbow shape, with large bowls, short stems, and flat bases. This is a somewhat modified Effigy Mound type.

Chipped stone artifacts: Half the available speci-mens are made of the familiar brown chalcedony en-countered elsewhere, the rest of poor grade flint. Pro-jectile points are mainly stemmed, with stems ex-panding to base. A few notched triangular types oc-cur. Knives are plentiful, of leaf-shape with wavy edges. End-scrapers are snub-nosed, with rectangular shape, and of thick and flat type. Ground stone is ex-tremely rare. Flat stones with dressed edges; sand-stone shaft abraders; and full-grooved mauls are known.

Bone artifacts, including in this category antler, teeth, shell and bone, constitute the richest assem-blage known for any Minnesota culture. Awls and long pins are made from split long bones, and are frequently found in pairs with burials. Harpoons are unilateral and multiple barbed, with highly charac-teristic type of barbing consisting of notches cut in from edge, giving a toothed appearance. Scapulae were made into knives or scrapers. Spatulae and spatulate skin dressers or polishers are found. A ser-rated ulo form is present. Whistles are made from bone tubes with notches; arm bands are of open types, circular and rectangular; tubular beads; and epiphysis pendants are all typical. A pipe of belled-tube shape is known. Antler artifacts include dressed antler tips cut squarely off, as projectile points. Short, thick sections of antler with convex ends seem to have been used as pounders for hides and other uses. Small, curved tines are used as scrapers by inserting beaver incisors near the tip, on the sides. Elk antler hafts for stone tools are common. One pipe is made from a straight section of polished antler.

Beaver teeth are inserted in antler and are also

found alone, with evidence of use as chisels. They are cut on the lingual surface to sharpen the biting edge, indicating an entirely different use than that in the earlier Laurel, where the incisors are cut obliquely to form sharp points. Bear and wolf teeth are perforated and were probably ornamental. Large bear canines are found with burials suggesting their use as single pendants. They are perforated in various ways, including the "Hopewell" type of double holes, drilled from both sides of the tooth, and often with grooves for suspension.

The great use of shell Wilford feels to be the "outstanding trait" of the focus. Large *Busycon* columnella beads are common, clam shell pendants and gorgets of trapezoidal shape and three vertical grooves at the base for ornamentation, are found. One pendant was shaped like an equal-armed Latin cross. A variety of flat discs and snail-shell beads are also found. Clam shells are frequently associated with red ocher in burials. Copper is rare, and always found in burials. A large, flat-crescent-shaped breastplate, a pendant in the form of a hollow boss with serrated edge, and two grooved bear teeth made up a single compound chest ornament. Two copper spearheads or knives, one with socketed tang with basal perforation, the other with a straight base and no tang, have been found.

Arvilla shows conservatism and basic continuity with the older Minnesota Woodland cultures, in such details as the prevalence of dentate stamping on the pottery, linear mounds, pipes, and general burial type. Other features, however, serve to place Arvilla in a group of poorly-known cultures of the northern Plains, northwest Mississippi Valley, and Canada.[33] These Transitional Woodland cultures all tend to show Middle Woodland continuities, especially in pottery, and lie somewhere in the background of such historic tribal groups as the Blackfoot. The later features appear in the well-preserved bone and antler artifacts, the style of shell and copper gorgets and pendants, and bone arm bands.

Transitional to Late Woodland Cultures

In southern Minnesota, in addition to the Judson-Hanel culture, identified as Middle Woodland, there are other Woodland divisions (Fig. 47) which have been recognized in sites such as the Tudahl Rock Shelter in Fillmore County, and the Fox Lake site in Martin County.[34]

In the adjacent areas of Wisconsin, Illinois, Iowa, and Minnesota, along the Mississippi River, there can now be recognized a Stone Vault burial complex which is associated with pottery belonging to the Lake Michigan Phase, as defined by McKern, indicat-

ing its position in the Transitional-to-Late Woodland period. It is now suggested that the term Chapman Focus be given to this complex in northwestern Illinois.[35] It is characterized by groups of small, elliptical round-domed burial mounds, often with small subfloor pits, and linear mounds. Projectile points are of notched and unnotched triangular form with some stemmed types present. "Unio" shell caches have been found, and charred corn is known from one mound. The mortuary pottery is all cord-marked, with round jar forms, raised corners, panels of cord-impressing or several horizontal cord impressions running around the rim, bordered with cord impressions, or occasionally punctates. Rounded and wedge shaped thickened upper rim-lips decorated with cord impressions are also common. Interior rim decoration is usual.

A localized Transitional development in Wisconsin of considerable importance is the Woodland (Lake Michigan) pottery found at Aztalan, abundantly mixed and actually blended typologically with Middle Mississippi wares in the refuse deposits. The associations of the pottery, as well as many other features of the site, indicate contemporaneity with the Middle Mississippi people at Aztalan.

Early Mississippi Cultures

As the evidence now stands, the first Mississippi culture in the northern valley, Aztalan, came as a migration from the Cahokia center at St. Louis, with only a few sites in northwestern Illinois of similar culture between the two communities. The typological features of Aztalan belong to the older Cahokia manifestation now called Old Village Focus, to be regarded here as Early Mississippi. The evidence suggests, however, that Aztalan probably lasted into later times than the Old Village Component at St. Louis.

The beginnings of western Upper Mississippi (Oneota) are also to be found in this general period. These origins are still obscure, but the presence of sites (Cambria and Apple River Foci) showing Aztalan-Cahokia characteristics integrated with Upper Mississippi traits suggests that Aztalan-Cahokia culture had much to do with the origin of Upper Mississippi in this region. This interpretation is strengthened by the fact that the Late Mississippi culture of the Cahokia site, the Trappist Focus, is contemporaneous with developed Oneota and one Illinois site (Crable) shows a clear case of *mixture* of the two cultures—producing a result totally different from the *transitional* character of the Cambria-Apple River manifestations.[36]

The great palisaded village of Aztalan (Fig. 48) is located on the west bank of Crawfish River, a north-

33. See Mulloy, 1942a; Strong, 1940; Thomas, Cyrus, 1894, pp. 35–37, and the chapter on the northern Plains in this volume.
34. Wilford, 1941, pp. 246–247; 1942, p. 22.

35. Bennett, 1945, pp. vii–viii, 68–73, Pls. 6–8.
36. For discussion, see the appropriate chapter in this volume, also Bennett, 1945, pp. vii–ix, and Part II; Bennett, 1944b, pp. 18–21; Griffin, J. B., 1943a, p. 302; 1946, pp. 86–90.

ern tributary of Rock River, in Jefferson County, southern Wisconsin. This is a region of many streams and marshes, affording plenty of environmental advantages for an agriculture-hunting community of sedentary existence. Water communication with major rivers and lakes was also permitted.

Information on Aztalan is concentrated in two concise and available sources, and a lengthy survey is not required here.[37] The major feature of the site is a huge palisade, marked by an embankment with outcurving sections every 60 feet or so, for square bastion towers. This palisaded portion has its long axis along the river, extending for some 1600 feet, and in depth about 600 feet back from the river. The river shore had a smaller wall. The northwest corner entrance was defended by two extra segments of wall, making a corridor. A smaller wall enclosed the mound area within the great palisade. In the northwest and northeast corners of the area inside the palisade were two pyramidal mounds, the former with a terraced setback and a long ramp—a simpler and smaller version of the Monks Mound at Cahokia. A plaza lay in the center of the enclosure, with village debris elsewhere.

Village sites lay outside the palisade. A long row of large, round domed mounds lay several hundred feet to the northwest, on a higher terrace of the river. These mounds contained the remains of large posts which apparently once protruded above the mounds, making a long avenue of standards. One of the mounds contained an elaborate female burial, with thousands of shell beads. Considerable detailed information relating to the height of the plastered walls, construction of towers, runways along the walls, and house features has been found, due to the excellent preservation of all details, (even to the pottery vessels and stones placed on the tower platforms for quenching fires and discouraging wall-scalers).

No village plan has been found, and not many dwellings have been excavated. The village complex is identical to other large Middle Mississippi sites, with abundant evidence of pottery and tool manufacture, corn-bean-squash agriculture, and abundant remains of edible wild animals. Outdoor stone hearths are fairly common. Refuse deposits in an area along the riverbank are 6 feet deep, and were probably deeper elsewhere. Trash pits are abundant. Houses were probably mainly rectangular, with wattle-and-daub construction and bark, rather than thatch, covered roofs. Some circular houses are known. Fireplaces were of baked clay, and circular. The mounds had large rectangular public buildings. A burial area has not been found. One of the stimulating aspects of life in ancient Aztalan was the practice of cannibalism, evidenced by the presence of hands, arms, split human bones and cut skulls found in refuse pits and cooking areas. Aztalan arrowpoints have been found elsewhere in the region embedded in the bones of Woodland burials.

Aztalan pottery is virtually identical with the Old Village Focus material of Cahokia. It is shell-tempered, smoothed, and often polished. Colors are brownish-buff, through gray, to deep black on the finer polished, angular-shouldered jars. A rare series of limestone tempered, polished red bowls with incurving rims and incised and punctated designs on the body is also found (called Monks Mound Red at Cahokia). A general division between coarser utilitarian wares and finer decorative-ceremonial wares is present, but is not as sharply marked off as in the later Middle Mississippi cultures. Vessels occur in a wide variety of shapes. Cooking pots are of wide-mouthed globular form, with and without short rims and handles. Handles are of loop type, some of them grooved in the middle and with small projecting knobs at the top. Lip lugs occur, often notched and typically asymmetrical. Lips on all vessels tend to be slightly outcurving or flared outward. Another common vessel shape is globular, but with sharply-angled shoulders and a low, flat, or slightly convex rim. Bowls are of simple hemispherical form or of the converging-rim "seed bowl" type. The Monks Mound Red bowls are of this shape. But of rare occurrence are straight-sided beakers, some with projecting bar handles. Plates with straight, low sides are found, some with lug handles. Rectangular plates are rare. Very rare forms are the long-necked bottle, with shoulders, the gourd-shaped bowl or deep ladle, and bowls with conventionalized head-and-tail effigy attachments.

Decorated vessels consist of jars with angular shoulders and flat to concave rims. The rim area is decorated with an incised or trailed motif, consisting of simple spirals, continuous scrolls, concentric semicircles, nested squares, zig-zags, chevrons, and combinations of the curvilinear and rectilinear elements. Most of these vessels, in browns, grays, and black are polished and can have excessively thin walls. Pottery trowels, of squat mushroom shape, are found.

Chipped stone artifacts include the typical Aztalan-Cahokia small triangular point, with or without narrow side-notches. Some larger forms, with stems and basal notches, also occur. Knives are well-made, of long ovate, triangular and narrowed-stem "Folsom-like" shape. Plain drills, with slight bases, are found. Hoes are large oval implements, with no retouching and showing wear-polish. Ground stone artifacts seem rare, with some celts and full-grooved hammers known. One biconical block pipe is known, and a few biconcave discoidals. A small variety of earspools, of collar-button shape, decorated with incised lines

37. Barrett, 1933, and McKern, 1946; McKern and Ritzenthaler, 1946, the last two constituting one issue of the *Wisconsin Archeologist*.

and made of steatite is fairly common at both Aztalan and Cahokia. In the rougher categories are found flat, shallow mortars, mullers, and unshaped sandstone abraders.

Bone artifacts are abundant. Found are awls of various types, slender needles or skewers, splint needles, and a few rare triangular bone projectile points. Shell beads of several types and large columnella pendants are found. Shell hoes with large perforations are also common. Antler flaking tools, and projectile points of several types are common. The simple conical type is most frequent. Copper occurs as disc-shaped ornaments with concentric corrugations; as copper overlay on stone earspools; as rare triangular points, and in awl, fish-hook, and slender knife-blade forms. Examples of the long nosed god similar to the artifacts from Gahagan were also found at Aztalan.

Aztalan is typologically an Early Middle Mississippi culture, derived from the full-blown Old Village Focus of Cahokia. Associated with the Aztalan material at the site are large quantities of Lake Michigan pottery and Woodland stone artifacts of all kinds. These are present in abundance throughout refuse deposits, and it must be concluded that a contemporaneous occupation of the site by Woodland peoples was present. The two artifact inventories are too distinct to admit of one people, but there is plenty of evidence of transitional forms in the pottery. This evidence is in the form of body and rim form on vessels, tempering, the presence of the thickened, overhanging upper rim on Aztalan vessels, Aztalan-type handles on Woodland jars, and other features.

The Apple River Focus (Fig. 49) in northwestern Illinois is representative of a cultural complex which is most important in discussing the relationships between Middle Mississippi and Upper Mississippi.[38] This has been reviewed at some length in another publication. As a result of the study of this material plus other more recent finds in the northern Mississippi Valley area, it appears that the Apple River Focus is a manifestation basically Aztalan in character, but persisting into later times, and becoming involved in the transformation of Middle Mississippi of a Cahokia-Aztalan type into western Upper Mississippi. No stratigraphic separation of the middle and upper Mississippi features was present at any of the excavated sites. The later time period is attested to not only by the occurrence of Oneota characteristics, but also by the presence of Trappist Focus material, completely absent at Aztalan, and known to be contemporaneous in its final stages with Oneota in Illinois. Several phases of Trappist discussed elsewhere in this volume should be reviewed in connection with this tentative interpretation.

The Cambria Focus of southern Minnesota fits into the same general culture as Apple River and probably could be included in a broader cultural classification (see Fig. 49).[39] There is a fairly strong Plains element present in the Cambria material which is absent at Apple River.

LATE WOODLAND AND LATE MISSISSIPPI

In general we have considered as Late Woodland those cultures which can be linked ethno-historically to known tribal entities. It will be recalled that two of the Minnesota developments—Kathio and Arvilla—are so identified, but they were treated in earlier sections for editorial and typological reasons.

The Keshena culture is located in northeastern Wisconsin,[40] but surface collections indicate a much wider range for this material. Certainly the Menominee and possibly part of the Sac, Fox, and Chippewa-Ojibwa were involved. Sites are of campsite type, located on streams. Probably small round-domed burial mounds were constructed, but the majority of burials are found in shallow pits near the camp area, in cemetery groups. The sites indicate small populations and a more migratory life than that of the Middle Woodland occupations. Burials are of bundle, flexed, and cremation type, the latter consisting of small clusters of burned bones deposited in pits. Burial furniture is rare, consisting of pottery vessels and implements when found. Pottery is a Late Woodland variety, occurring in round-shoulder jar forms, with rounded or conoidal bases, necks, and wide orifices. The thickened rims and raised corners are not nearly as common as in some of the Transitional Woodland cultures discussed earlier. The flamboyant cord-marked styles appearing elsewhere in Late Woodland are not present.

Chipped stone included stemmed and notched points, and stemmed points, some leaf-shaped and some triangular. Small unnotched triangular points also occur. Drills and scrapers are present and knives are triangular and ovate. Ground stone artifacts attributed to this division are full- and three-quarter-grooved axes. There is a simple oval gorget with two perforations. Pipes have considerable variety including the Micmac form, catlinite elbow pipes with broad, disk bowls or rectilinear bowls, and small conoidal forms. This may indicate a heterogeneous tradition, or considerable trade.

The Clam River culture,[41] located in northwestern Wisconsin, has been tentatively connected to the

---

38. Bennett, 1945, pp. 131–158 and appropriate plates; Griffin, J. B., 1943a, p. 302; 1946, p. 80.

39. Wilford, 1945b. In this publication Cambria is called an "aspect," but this designation seems premature. Perhaps related to this complex is the Oneota vessel described in Griffin, J. B., 1945e.

40. McKern, 1942; Barrett and Skinner, 1932.

41. McKern, 1939b; 1942.

Santee (Dakota Sioux). The mounds are a round domed type which grew by accumulation. Floors were sometimes prepared with sand and red and yellow ocher before the first stratum of burials was laid down. Burials were all of a bundle type, and were deposited in successive layers, each layer adding to the height of the mound. Five mound layers were identified at the Clam Lake mound. A single burial stratum included from one to 15 individuals, most of these having been wrapped in bark or in sewn, circular birch-bark containers.

An interesting discovery was the skull of a horse placed with one of the burials, a trait reminiscent of the Kathio practice of including buffalo skeletons in the mounds. The presence of the skull, and the absence of white trade material, provides a date of approximately 250 years ago, which points to the Dakota as the inhabitants of this area.

Pottery is known from a few specimens only. It is grit-tempered, and occurs in the form of crude round-bottomed jars, with slightly constricted neck and slightly flaring rim. Bodies are cord-wrapped-paddle impressed, and are decorated on the rim by cord-wrapped-stick impressions, in simple rows and lines. Lips are sometimes crenellated with the same instruments. There are elbow pottery pipes with flaring bowls and right-angled stems, decorated with single cord impressions or cord-wrapped-sticks. Chipped stone includes triangular points of asymmetrical shape, with concave bases. There are a few triangular scrapers. Cannon-bone beamers and dressed rectangles of turtle plastrons ("net spacers") were made of bone.

THE ONEOTA ASPECT

The geographical distribution of this aspect now extends from central Wisconsin, through southern Minnesota, through Iowa, to Missouri, with close relatives in Kansas, Nebraska, Illinois, and South Dakota. It has been positively identified with the Ioway and Oto in Iowa, the Oto in Nebraska, the Missouris in Missouri, and the Winnebago in Wisconsin. An Oneota-like culture has been identified as late eighteenth century Osage in Missouri.[42]

All of the Oneota foci, with the possible exception of Grand River, are more like one another than different, and some of the focal distinctions, like the division between Orr and Blue Earth, are difficult to see on the basis of the slender published materials. Apparently the archeologist is dealing here with a late culture complex which differentiated rapidly from an original tribal nucleus. Despite its wide geographical diffusion, the culture is remarkably homogeneous (Fig. 50).

Oneota sites are usually medium to large villages, but many small campsites are also found. The Winnebago villages of the Green Bay area in Wisconsin are probably the largest, covering many acres. Associated with villages are cemeteries, in which the dead are almost always buried in rectangular graves, in an extended position. Flat stones are sometimes associated with these graves. The village materials indicate a semi-sedentary existence, with corn-bean-squash agriculture, much hunting, and extensive bone and stone tool industries. House data is not abundant, but the Nebraska branch used earth lodges, while the eastern groups may have used pole and bark houses. Many cache and refuse pits characterize the sites. Burial furniture is abundant.

Pottery is shell-tempered, smooth-surfaced, and lacks slips and polishing in nearly all manifestations. It ranges from buff to dark gray, depending on the amount of firing. A dull brownish-orange is most common. Vessel forms varied around one basic shape: A medium-sized globular jar, with round bottom, incurving sides, and sharply flaring rim, with paired loop and strap handles. Variations could take the form of size differences, absence of the flaring rim, presence of thickened, collar-like rims, and variation in decorative treatment. Decoration consisted almost entirely of slight variations on a basic theme: Combinations of narrow or broad incised and trailed lines on the rim-shoulder area, usually with punctates as borders or elements within the incised units. Designs were almost entirely rectilinear. Lips were frequently crenellated with fingers or sticks.

Pottery disks, often perforated, are common.

Chipped stone implements included the ubiquitous triangular projectile points, with flat base, and very well-chipped. Knives of long, oval shapes are fairly common. Stone drills with plain and expanding bases are found. The scraper complex is especially typical, including the snub-nosed type as most common, with other triangular, rectangular, and irregular shaped forms.

Sandstone shaft abraders, of definite shapes and often found in pairs in graves are also very typical. Sandstone whetstones of irregular and formed shape are also present. An assortment of plain and grooved hammerstones and mauls, and sandstone mortars and mullers are all common artifacts.

Polished stone artifacts consist of small stone celts and the highly characteristic "Siouan disk" pipe—a pipe with a broad, flat disk-shaped projection surrounding the bowl, and resting on a single or equal-arm stem. Material was stone or catlinite. Some variations on this form occur. Dressed catlinite tablets occur.

42. Orr, E., 1914. For general surveys of the culture see Mott, 1938; Griffin, J. B., 1937a; 1943a; Keyes, 1942; McKern, 1945, esp. pp. 153–157; Wedel, 1940, pp. 334–337; Berry, Chapman, and Mack, 1944.

Bone materials included an assortment of ulnae and split-bone awls. Spatulae are rare. Bone fishhooks were used in Wisconsin. Bone tubes, incised or plain, are also typical. Buffalo or elk scapulae hoes and "fiber shredders" were characteristic of the more westerly manifestations. Antler was used for socketed projectile points, "flakers," and other minor artifacts. Shell beads and spoons, and perforated hoes were not common. Copper was present in the form of long, tubular beads and pendants made of cut sheet copper. Trade materials, such as brass ear coils, glass beads, and iron objects are found in many sites.

Of the various subdivisions of Oneota, Grand River, located principally in Green Lake County, Wisconsin, is the most aberrant. It shows some traces of Middle Mississippi, and also some connections to Lake Winnebago. No historical materials have been found with this particular division of Oneota, and perhaps an earlier time period is indicated. No affiliations to Apple River can be perceived.

The Lake Winnebago Focus is found in sites around Green Bay and Lake Koshkonong, the historic home of the Winnebago tribe. It has a number of minor variations, such as the importance of shell work, both utilitarian and ornamental forms, and flexed burials are found as well as extended. The pottery has considerable variety in forms and decoration. It is perhaps the most impressive of the Oneota pottery.

The Orr Focus along the Mississippi has the largest number of sites, and was the first unit to be definitely identified in the literature. Some of its variations are the use of stone slab graves for burials and evidence of cannibalism.

Much of the interpretation of the cultural materials described in the preceding pages is tentative and is based on an admittedly hypothetical theory or viewpoint of the nature of eastern United States prehistory. The general sequences, however, whatever they are called and whatever their duration may be, are based on stratigraphic evidence. Some of this evidence is equivocal, but enough of it is securely established so that a reasonable picture can be drawn.

THE NORTHERN PLAINS.

By William Mulloy*

THE complex prehistory of the Great Plains is only beginning to be understood. The historic period is best known, but in many areas archeological antecedents are entirely unknown, and even in the best-studied regions great gaps in information still exist.

Since the beginning of the seventeenth century when the earlier European visitors first saw the northern Plains, the area has been traversed by a constant stream of soldiers, explorers, and pioneers who provided eyewitness descriptions of peoples in various stages of acculturation. Later in the nineteenth century, the Plains Indians became involved in resistance to western expansion of the United States. Accounts of spectacular conflicts in which they figured were widely read and did much to influence popular thinking about Indians. As the locale of one of the most striking of native American cultures, the region attracted unusual public attention which was to culminate in the concept of the Plains equestrian as the archetype of American Indian.

Because much of historic Indian culture persisted until recent times and because its appeal fired the imagination of the average man as well as the student, it received much attention. A body of literature resulted which made the historic culture one of the best documented in America. Men such as Robert Lowie and Clark Wissler made the region a proving ground for some of the ethnological theory of the early twentieth century and the concepts of "culture area" and "age-area hypothesis" will always be linked with this area.

Though historic cultures were well known before the last two decades, little attention was given to archeological antecedents of the spectacular florescence built upon the horse-bison economic foundation. The very existence of much of a culture history was doubted for a long time for what appeared to be good reasons. It was felt that the bison economy, which seemed to be the only possible adjustment in the greater part of the area, would have been impossible before the introduction of the horse. It was difficult to understand how a prehistoric Plains population could have maintained itself. It appeared that the Plains had been populated in relatively recent times by an influx of peoples from surrounding areas only when the horse-bison economy tapped a vast and easily available food supply. There was evidence for this. The reconstructed histories of such peoples as the Cheyenne,[1] Teton Dakota,[2] Assiniboine,[3] Crow,[4] and others, suggest that they entered their historic area late. Even in the prairies, the Mandan seems to be the only tribe of proven long residence, the Hidatsa, and the Arikara apparently having moved from the east and south respectively.[5] To the west, the Shoshoni must be regarded as basically a Plateau rather than a Plains people, until late.[6] There is little evidence for the time of entry of the Arapaho and Blackfoot, though the latter seem to have been moving gradually southward into Montana.

In 1907, Wissler felt that "the peopling of the Plains proper was a recent phenomenon due in part to the introduction of the horse and the displacement of tribes by white settlements."[7] As late as 1939, Kroeber maintained much the same view, regarding the Plains as having been "one of the well-developed and characterized cultures of North America only since the taking over of the horse from Europeans, and that previously there was no important Plains culture, the chief phases in the area being marginal to richer cultures outside."[8] These views are characteristic of past thinking about Plains prehistory. Principally, they predate archeological evidence. In view of the evidence of the late entry into the area of many tribes coupled with the facts that most of the Plains would not have been satisfactory for Indian agriculture, and that bison-hunting without horses appeared difficult, conclusions reached seem reasonable. They can only be modified by archeological facts which, though scanty, are becoming available. It is proposed here to examine some of these facts. It is impossible to present a complete survey. Much evidence will have to be ignored or barely mentioned, and a selection presented to illustrate the various culture types and sequences.

The prehistoric picture has been approached from two different points of view which are now beginning

* University of Utah, B.A., 1936; University of Chicago, M.A., 1948; Assistant Professor, Department of Economics and Sociology, University of Wyoming, 1948——. Chapter received December, 1947; revised January, 1951.

1. Grinnell, 1923, Vol. 1, pp. 1–46, Vol. 2, pp. 382–384.
2. Swanton, 1930, pp. 156–160.
3. Lowie, 1909b, pp. 7–10.
4. Mulloy, 1942a, pp. 99–103.
5. Strong, 1940, pp. 357–360.
6. Lowie, 1909a, pp. 171–173.
7. Wissler, 1907, pp. 39–52.
8. Kroeber, 1939, p. 76.

to become integrated. The historic period has been used as a springboard for archeological investigations into the antecedents of groups known ethnologically. In 1906, Will and Spinden produced *The Mandans,* a classic study coordinating material then available on the ethnology, history, archeology, linguistics, and physical anthropology of this group. This was the first effort to push back the historical record of a known tribe by archeological means. Later investigators, including Strong[9] and others, have used this method with the result that a picture of the archeological background of such peoples as the Mandan, Hidatsa, Crow, Cheyenne, and Arikara is appearing (Fig. 51).

The other approach focused attention upon a period far back in the cultural sequence. In 1926, the first Folsom finds were made near the town of Folsom, New Mexico.[10] Later additional discoveries provided a body of evidence of what appear to be nomadic hunters who lived in the area from perhaps ten to twenty thousand years ago in association with extinct mammals. In 1928, the first artifacts of types formerly called Yuma were noted. These are projectile points of several types and associated artifacts. Subsequent finds in this category suggested the presence of several other groups of hunting nomads. A picture of some of the Yuma complexes is beginning to emerge, together with a suggestion that several complexes are represented.[11]

An impressive gap lies between. Lately, scattered material has come partially to fill it. Most suggestive are Signal Butte in Scottsbluff County, Nebraska, on the extreme southern boundary of the area, excavated by Strong, in 1932,[12] and Pictograph Cave near Billings, Montana, excavated by the Montana Archeological Survey, 1937–1941. Each is a stratified site demonstrating a similar sequence of three cultural horizons underlying historic materials. These together with corroborative evidence from smaller and less clear sites provide the first glimmerings of at least one of the cultural sequences which fills part of this hiatus.

Archeological evidence now suggests a broad, tentative, classification into three temporal divisions: an *Early Period,* including Folsom, Yuma and similar materials; a *Late Period,* including historic materials and what appear to be their immediate prehistoric antecedents; and between these, a long and little known *Middle Period.* These wide, vague divisions are not expected to reflect detailed culture historical changes with accuracy, but are a useful framework in which to discuss the evidence. Frequently in the ceramic cultures of the *Late Period,* divisions ap-

proximating tribal lines are suggested. In the earlier potteryless horizons, classification must rest upon artifacts of stone and bone which have similarities over wide areas and which can indicate only general trends and broad differences in a small portion of the material culture. Broad and vague as they may seem, differences do exist. They cannot be regarded as of the order of those demonstrable in cultures with ceramic guideposts. They should be thought of as horizon styles including many cultural variations.

THE EARLY PERIOD

Only a segment of the Folsom problem is pertinent here.[13] Much evidence comes from outside the area. The Folsom people were nomadic hunters who lived in the High Plains between ten and twenty-five thousand years ago. The characteristic artifact is a projectile point. These are excellently pressure flaked, thin and more or less leaf shaped and average about two inches in length, frequently being broadest about two-thirds of the distance from the base and having a rather blunt point. Bases are concave and usually have ear-like projections. The main distinguishing characteristic is the removal of large longitudinal flakes from one or usually both faces. Associated with the points is a complex including snub-nosed, plano-convex scrapers; side scrapers; end scrapers; turtle back scrapers; gravers with minutely worked points; and a variety of bone tools and other artifacts.[14] Unfortunately, most of these occur widely in later times and it is difficult to identify them as Folsom artifacts unless they occur with the characteristic points.

Another type of projectile point similar to the Folsom is called fluted. These are usually larger and more generalized than the classic type and have more rudimentary longitudinal grooves. They are widely distributed in the United States, showing a strong concentration in the Missouri, Mississippi, and Ohio drainages.[15] Some may be a typical true Folsom and others, later evolutionary developments.

Evidence for the Folsom complex in the northern Plains is seen in the fact that the characteristic Folsom points are seen frequently in surface collections from Montana and Wyoming and less frequently farther to the east. Fluted points are more common and are reported from many parts of the area. At the Lewis site some twenty miles south of Glendive, Montana, which has not yet been investigated in detail, but seems to be an early camp site or series of camp sites, several fluted points were found which are very similar to Folsoms, although the bulk of the artifacts

9. Strong, 1940.
10. Wormington, 1949, pp. 19–32.
11. *Ibid.,* pp. 48–62.
12. Strong, 1935, pp. 224–239.

13. A good introduction to this problem is to be found in Martin, Quimby, and Collier, 1947, pp. 79–94, and Wormington, 1949, pp. 19–32.
14. Roberts, 1935; 1936.
15. Cotter, 1937. [These two types recognized by Mulloy correspond roughly to Folsom Fluted and Clovis Fluted. Ed.]

are "Yuma" (Fig. 52).[16] In the lowest horizon of Pictograph Cave near Billings, Montana, which will be described later, a fluted point also turned up. Fluted points are frequent in Minnesota, but are rare in North and South Dakota.[17] Others similar to the classical Folsom also occur to the north in Alberta and Saskatchewan.[18]

The distributions of the categories formerly called Yuma are not now known. Though similar material occurs widely, with a few exceptions, items for which there is some evidence of antiquity appear to be concentrated in the western Plains. Only the northern Plains facets of the problem are pertinent here.[19] Evidence suggests several groups of early, primitive, nomadic hunters probably somewhat later than Folsom.

Three types of points are diagnostic in the northern Plains. One is the Eden Valley point which is narrow and parallel sided, with a point at one end and a flat base at the other. The basilar portion is slightly narrowed to form a stem and a slight, though definite, shoulder. Edges of basilar portions are sometimes ground smooth. Flaking is excellent with large, transverse flake scars extending uniformly half way across the face of the blade to produce a lozenge shaped cross section. A variant, called the Scottsbluff point, is wider relative to its length, has more pronounced shoulders, and more lenticular cross section. A third type is the Browns Valley point which is a long, slender, usually concave based point, stemless, with long slender flake scars which run diagonally across the face of the blade, and a lenticular cross section. Sometimes, the edges of the base are ground smooth.[20]

Evidence in these categories from the northern Plains includes the Finley site in Sweetwater County, southwestern Wyoming. Here were found Eden Valley and Scottsbluff points. They occurred in surface blowouts and in a clay stratum resting on the Farson terrace, which being formed probably during the late Wisconsin ice advance, establishes post glacial age. Associated were many bison bones.[21] The dating is significant in terms of Folsom relationships, as the Lindenmeier Folsom site to the south tentatively suggests an earlier dating and precedence for Folsom, at least in this area.[22]

A site now being excavated near Cody, Wyoming, by Jepson appears to be a camp site and includes, in addition to Eden Valley points, many bison bones and a considerable material culture complex. A car-

bon 14 date of 6876 ± 250 years ago was determined here.

Eden Valley and Browns Valley points were found near Red Lodge, Montana mixed with artifacts of later horizons.[23] At Pictograph Cave, two Eden Valley points were found in the lowest horizon, associated with types presumably later.[24]

In the lowest horizon at Signal Butte were a number of blades which possibly should be classed with the Browns Valley points.[25]

More convincing are six blades associated with a skeleton found in Browns Valley, Traverse County, Minnesota, on the extreme eastern boundary of the area.[26] Two are Browns Valley points while others are difficult to classify.[27] The find was made in gravels of the Tintah beach stage of glacial Lake Agassiz and has been dated by Jenks at from eight to twelve thousand years ago.

Two other skeletons from western Minnesota may be mentioned here, but because they lack accompanying cultural material which can be related to anything else at present, they are of interest only in passing, though they may turn out to represent valid evidence of considerable antiquity of man in the area. One is "Minnesota Man," found near Pelican Rapids, Minnesota,[28] which may or may not be associated with silt beds antecedent to the formation of Lake Agassiz some eighteen thousand years ago.[29] The other is "Sauk Valley Man" found near Lake Guerney, West Union Township, Minnesota.[30] This find has not been proved to be contemporaneous with the gravels with which it was found nor have the gravels been accurately dated. Nevertheless, it may have considerable antiquity.

The finds mentioned are elements of the scanty evidence on which is based the idea of the earliest inhabitants we know in the northern Plains. Though Folsom people probably antedated users of Yuma artifacts, their time periods may well have overlapped. The bulk of evidence suggests that both groups ranged mostly in the western part of the area though this point is not at all clear. The picture is one of small groups of nomadic hunters. The few grinding tools and the excellence of the projectile points suggests an emphasis on hunting rather than gathering. *Bison taylori* and other extinct forms were important to the earlier Folsom people and were later replaced by *Bison bison* and other modern forms. It appears that bison were the important source of food supply

16. Mulloy and Lewis, 1943.
17. Strong, 1940, p. 389.
18. Howard, E. B., 1939; Bird, 1939.
19. A good introduction to this problem is to be found in Wormington, 1949, pp. 48–66.
20. *Ibid.*
21. Howard, E. B., 1943.
22. Bryan and Ray, 1940.

23. Mulloy, 1942*b*.
24. See p. 127.
25. Strong, 1935, p. 25.
26. Jenks, 1937.
27. Wormington, 1949, pp. 64, 142.
28. Jenks, 1936.
29. Bryan and MacClintock, 1938, and Antevs, 1937.
30. Bryan, Retzek, and McCann, 1938, and Jenks and Wilford, 1938.

throughout this period. Undoubtedly, items preserved are a small part of the total culture.

THE MIDDLE PERIOD

The long *Middle Period* is also known from scanty evidence in a few areas. At present it can only be said that it is intermediate without attempting to set its temporal boundaries. Like the previous period, it is pre-ceramic so far as is known.

The outline of one, probably only partially complete, sequence is known. It rests upon two similar series of stratigraphically superimposed horizons. One is at Signal Butte, Nebraska and the other at Pictograph Cave, Montana.

Signal Butte[31] is a high mesa in Scottsbluff County, Nebraska on the extreme southern boundary of the area. On it, in a stratum of windborn material, are three cultural levels (Signal Butte I to III from bottom to top) separated from each other by sterile windborne strata. The lowest level lies directly on silt and gravel thought to be of Pleistocene age. A correlation of the aeolian deposits with sand dunes suggested a minimum date for Signal Butte I of fifty-two hundred years though Strong points out that it may be greater. A correlation of soil zones with climatic fluctuations suggested a rough date of from eight thousand to ten thousand years for Signal Butte I and around five thousand for Signal Butte II. These dates are tentative and remain to be corroborated by future work.

Pictograph Cave[32] is a large erosional recess in a cliff side about seven miles above the mouth of Bitter Creek, a southern tributary which enters the Yellowstone near Billings, Montana. In it were about twenty-three feet of culture-bearing deposit. Stratigraphically superimposed were three prehistoric complexes and one historic. (Pictograph Cave I to IV from bottom to top.) Levels I and II were distinct but not separated by sterile material while above them a sterile stratum separated them from Levels III and IV.

In both Signal Butte and Pictograph Cave, levels I and II are of interest in this period. The two sites are not identical but similarities in both content and sequence are suggestive. There is no pottery and the most convincing similarities are seen in projectile points, though other items are corroborative.

Signal Butte I and Pictograph Cave I have in common lanceolate or leaf-shaped projectile points with concave bases which may be thinned by removal of flakes from each face, leaf shaped knives or projectile points with convex or flat bases, a range of variation of triangular stemmed points usually with large shallow notches and predominantly concave bases, plano-convex end scrapers with retouched and unretouched backs, choppers, ovoid side scrapers, retouched flakes, spoke shaves, gravers, pestles, shaft smoothers, awls, knapping tools, bone "game counters" with one or two transverse lines across one surface, and small bone tubes (Fig. 52, *K–H'*). Pictograph Cave I lacks triangular side notched points with basal notch or concave base, plano-convex scrapers with stems and concave bases, T-shaped drills, grooved axes or mauls, and certain other minor artifacts of Signal Butte I. The latter lacks flat metates and Eden Valley Yumas of Pictograph Cave I.

Signal Butte II and Pictograph Cave II have in common triangular, corner notched points with bases concave to convex, comparable ranges of variation of triangular stemmed points usually with large, shallow notches and predominantly concave bases similar to those from Level I; leaf shaped blades with convex or flat bases; plano-convex end scrapers with unretouched backs; side scrapers; retouched flakes; awls; knapping tools; and hammerstones (Fig. 52, *I'–S'*). Pictograph Cave II lacks lap stones, grinding stones, plano-convex end scrapers with retouched backs and drills and gravers of Signal Butte II.

These two sequences are not identical either in content or proportional occurrence of traits, but general similarity is indicated in type and stratigraphic relation. Levels III at both sites should probably be regarded as properly belonging to the *Late Period*. They are difficult to compare because Signal Butte III is ceramic and Pictograph Cave III is not (Fig. 53). There are similarities in stone and bone work, particularly projectile points, which are reflections of a common trend in these items.[33]

In the suburbs of Billings, Montana, are the remains of a prehistoric bison trap.[34] Bison were driven over a low cliff to fall on a rocky talus. Along the front of the cliff was a deposit several feet in thickness containing bison bones and divided by an old soil surface line into upper and lower strata, which suggested that some time elapsed between the deposition of the upper and lower layers. Included were many projectile points presumably shot into the animals as they were driven over the cliff. A few knives, retouched flakes, and other artifacts were also found. The projectile points in the lower stratum were like those described for Pictograph Cave II and those in the upper like Pictograph Cave III.[35] As the cave and the bison trap are within a few miles of each other, the groups who used the cave might well have been the ones who used this particular bison trap.

31. Strong, 1935, pp. 224–236.
32. Excavated in 1937–1941 by the Montana Archeological Survey but as yet unpublished.

33. See p. 136.
34. Excavated in 1941–1942 by the Montana Archeological Survey but as yet unpublished.
35. See p. 136.

Many small campsites in the Shoshoni Basin of the Big Horn River in north-central Wyoming show a complex similar to Pictograph Cave II, but here the number of metates and paucity of projectile points and animal bones suggest more food gathering and less hunting than at Pictograph Cave. Present indications are that this variant will turn up widely in the Wyoming Basin.

Both horizons I and II of Pictograph Cave, together with later material, are probably represented at the much mixed Red Lodge Site[36] near Red Lodge, Montana, but the material is too scanty and confused to add much to the picture. Some of the projectile point types characteristic of these horizons were found at the Lewis Site[37] south of Glendive, Montana. Similar projectile points and other artifacts, some of which are also characteristic of later horizons, are frequent surface finds in Montana and Wyoming and are also reported from North and South Dakota.

As in the *Early Period,* the picture here is one of small groups of people living in caves or impermanent shelters. Subsistence in the Plains variant was probably based primarily on game animals as suggested by the number and excellence of the projectile points and the many animal bones. Bison was probably of primary importance though other game animals were also used. Existing species have taken the place of the extinct forms of the early part of the previous period. Minor occurrence of metates and other grinding tools suggest some gathering of food plants. Plano-convex, snub nosed scrapers, side scrapers, and other artifacts indicate a possibility of hide working and perhaps skin clothing. Cache pits at Signal Butte suggest storage of food. The type of life deduced further indicates small groups and at least a restricted nomadism based upon the habits of game animals. In the Wyoming Basin, food gathering appears to have been more and hunting less important.

One fact of significance is the association of bison traps with the second horizon in this period, and possibly also the first. One of the reasons why earlier writers doubted prehistoric occupations of the Plains involved presumed difficulties in taking bison on foot. Bison traps partially answer this question. Many are in Montana. Some have bone deposits up to twenty feet or more in thickness, suggesting either long use or enormous catches or both. Articulated skeletons in them suggest that more meat was taken than could be used. Bison traps are also reported from eastern Wyoming and the western Dakotas.

Bison trapping usually involved driving a herd over a cliff, usually high enough to offer a chance of killing or injuring.[38] Occasionally an enclosure may have been built about its foot (Fig. 54). Usually, though apparently not always, at the top of the cliff were long converging lines of piles of stones varying from five or ten to several hundred feet apart and leading in a long, narrow, and frequently irregular V to a narrow opening at the cliff edge. In some cases, these piles extend for several miles and are arranged in several lines which seem to be parts of different systems and are occasionally complicated.

Such traps were used in the later periods also and in historic times. Descriptions of the technique indicate that a herd of buffalo was driven into the open mouth of the V and kept within the lines by men stationed behind the piles of stones who waved blankets or brush and shouted to stampede the animals toward the edge. When enclosures were used at the base of the cliff, men were stationed about to shoot the wounded with arrows and finish them off with stone mauls.[39]

This technique, probably supplemented by other forms of communal hunting, was important in the *Middle Period* as well as in later and possibly earlier times. If the people customarily lived in small groups, it would seem that this sort of hunting would necessitate their uniting into larger organized groups, at least for the period of the hunt.

The Late Period

This period includes the well-known historic cultures, their protohistoric and prehistoric predecessors and some other prehistoric manifestations which cannot be linked with any known tribe. Two related culture types appear. In Montana and Wyoming were prehistoric hunting peoples living a life similar to that of the *Middle Period.* In protohistoric and historic times, these were replaced by or, in some cases, possibly converted into High Plains historic cultures, characterized by use of the skin tipi, dog or horse travois, excellent skin working, simple band organization, the camp circle, Sun Dance, Scalp Dance, and other traits. They lacked agriculture, basketry, pottery, weaving, and did little work in stone and bone. They were highly mobile and had a strong war complex.[40]

To the east, centered about the Missouri in North and South Dakota in historic times and extending into the prehistoric period, were sedentary peoples who had many of the traits of the historic western groups, but who lived in villages of earth lodges, and had well developed agricultural and pottery complexes. Their communities were larger and relatively stable. One of the important trends in historic and

36. Mulloy, 1942b.
37. Mulloy and Lewis, 1943.
38. See Brown, B., 1932 for a description of a bison trap near Livingston, Montana.
39. Wissler, 1910, pp. 33–38.
40. Wissler, 1938, pp. 221–222.

protohistoric times was a movement of peoples from this locality to the west where they gradually discontinued their pottery making and agriculture and took over the historic horse culture. There is some evidence that this tendency was also present in prehistoric times, probably in a less pronounced form.

As the later phases of this period are better known, and cultural relationships are increasingly blurred as one moves backward through time, most sequences will be discussed from later to earlier and as far as possible by tribes.

Strong[41] provides an excellent summary of the eastern groups in much more detail than can be presented here and much of the information to follow comes from his work.

THE MANDAN

The Siouan speaking Mandan are the only eastern tribe which can be proved to have lived for a long time in its present location. Such early records as those of Verendrye, Lewis and Clark, Mackenzie, and Henry all mention from six to thirteen major villages in the vicinity of the Heart River in North Dakota. Though the locations of other villages are known,[42] the historic Mandan are best represented from two excavated and documented sites. The older Double Ditch (or Burgois) Site[43] is on the Missouri just north of the mouth of the Heart River. This may have been one of the sites visited by Verendrye in 1738. The latter, though in part contemporaneous, Old Fort Abraham Lincoln Site[44] is across the river from Bismark. Historical evidence suggests its abandonment *ca.* 1765. These two sites have similar culture and are the remains of large fortified towns.

The picture of Mandan culture of this early historic period, as seen at these sites, includes large, permanent villages, with surrounding moats, earthworks, and palisades (?). Lodges were large, circular, dome-shaped structures covered with earth and supported by rows of interior posts, with a central fire and lateral entrance. There were many cylindrical or bottle shaped cache pits either near or inside the houses. Within the village was an open ceremonial area. Burial customs seem to have differed from later times, both bundle burials and flexed bodies in pits having been found, in contrast to the scaffold deposition in conjunction with surface skull and subsurface bundle burials of later Mandan. Horticulture was important with the scapula hoe as the usual tool, though bones indicate that bison and other game animals were also used. Artifacts include completely grooved stone mauls, celts, discoidals, shallow dishes or palettes of stone, shallow mortars, and flat metates. The pre-

dominant projectile points are small and triangular with side notches and concave bases. Knives are bifacially flaked ovoid, piriform, subtriangular, and lunate blades some of which were hafted. Bone work is well developed and includes scapula hoes, notched and unnotched metapodial fleshers, shaft straighteners of bison rib, horn, and bison scapula, scrapers, awls, eyeless needles, fish hooks, tubular beads, narrow bracelets of bone or antler, small baton-like objects with a bird head carved on one end, and other minor objects. Pottery is important. Paddle and anvil technique is present. Color ranges from black through gray, to dull orange and red. Temper is pulverized granite. Shapes are jars with constricted necks, round to sub-piriform bottoms, and a characteristic S-shaped rim and shoulder. Less common are forms with flaring rim profiles. Ornamentation is usually in bands about shoulder area and rim. About the shoulder are incised, zigzag, diagonal, or herringbone patterns. Sometimes there is a band of vertical brush roughening about the shoulder area. About the rim are cord or infrequently, wrapped rod impressions in bands of horizontal or diagonal lines interspersed with characteristic elements made up of a series of concentric semicircles. Rims may be straight, scalloped, or wavy, with cord-marked or incised, transverse, diagonal, or concentric lines and may be thickened in various ways. Punctates of several kinds, depressed spouts, lugs, and ears also occur. Body treatment is frequently grooved paddle and rarely check paddle impressed or smooth (Fig. 55, *A–C*).

An earlier, undocumented village reported by Strong,[45] who regards it as Mandan, awaits full publication. It is the Rygh Site on the east side of the Missouri above the mouth of the Grand River in South Dakota. Traditions of up-river movements and an eastern origin for the Mandan make its downstream location significant. Strong regards it as the most southerly location yet demonstrated for this group. It is known from a stratification test in one of the middens, and other limited excavations. Practically all historic Mandan traits are found here as well as additional ones. In appearance, it is similar to the previously described Mandan sites. Cache pits are frequent though house floors are not proved. Several pieces of iron of European origin occurred in the upper half of the test, which was divided into seven levels which showed significant differences. Among these were: progressive decrease in stone work and increase in pottery; decrease in incising and increase in cord-marking, though at the top there are still twice as many incised as cord marked sherds; elaboration of types just below middle of deposits including sherds painted in black on lighter background, and wrapped rod impressions less rare than

41. Strong, 1940.
42. Will, 1924; Will and Hecker, 1944.
43. Will and Spinden, 1906, pp. 148–185.
44. Strong, 1940, pp. 360–365.

45. Strong, 1933, p. 76; 1940, pp. 378–380.

at later sites; cord impressions remain more or less static and incising becomes more intricate; collared and S-shaped rims appear in the second level and in the third and later levels the S-shaped type is much more numerous than the collared type, although the latter continues to increase gradually throughout; color is lighter than later Mandan pottery with more variety in rim forms and designs; thickness is frequently less with lugs and castellations lacking. Bone work differs in infrequent occurrence of fleshers of notched ribs and spinous processes rather than metapodials.

Other investigators, such as Will and Hecker, have regarded the Rygh Site as Arikara rather than Mandan.

Further into the past, Strong does not trace the Mandan, though he regards certain elements at the Rygh Site as suggestive of Upper Republican or protohistoric Pawnee influence.[46] He also speculates on Mandan similarities to the Mill Creek Aspect of northwestern Iowa and southeastern South Dakota.[47]

Pottery and other artifacts from Ludlow Cave[48] might also be regarded as prehistoric Mandan, but are more likely Hidatsa or Crow.[49]

Will and Hecker have established a Mandan archeological sequence on the basis of sherd collections and excavations in a large number of sites. They regard Mandan material culture as indistinguishable from Hidatsa in the present state of knowledge and indicate a sequence of four temporal periods: Archaic, Middle, Later Heart River, and Decadent. Their Archaic Period is characterized by unfortified villages of rectangular lodges and has a simple pottery complex with similarities to Mill Creek and Nebraska Aspects and to the wares at the Mitchell Site. The Middle Period has villages with progressively developing fortifications, rectangular and later circular lodges, and ceramic changes in which cord impressions become more frequent at the expense of incising, and bowl shapes at the expense of constricted neck types. In the Later Heart River Period, which is regarded as having ended shortly after 1750, villages are more populous though more compact, earthworks are better developed, and circular lodges and material culture are similar to that described for the Double Ditch Site. The Decadent Period includes the subsequent disintegration of Mandan culture under White influence.

The Hidatsa

According to native traditions the Siouan speaking Hidatsa once lived near a lake northeast of the Missouri, possibly Devil's Lake. There they lived in circular earth lodges similar to those of the Mandan, and also used skin tipis. Later they joined the Mandan on the Heart River. Some time before 1796, they moved northward to the Knife River where they established villages.[50]

Hidatsa culture is not well known archeologically. No detailed accounts of excavated, historic Hidatsa villages have yet been published. Seven villages are known near the mouth of the Knife River.[51] Of these, four are documented.[52] These are apparently the remains of large fortified villages with earth lodges similar to the Mandan. Strong made tests in some of these villages and found that the pottery and other artifacts were similar to the Mandan, but less well made and of more limited types. Pottery is thicker, of predominantly dark color, has cord decoration on outer and inner rim, concentric semicircle motif, S-shaped neck and shoulder form, and Mandan-like paddle marks. The material known all suggests Mandan influence. In comparison to this pottery, later sherds from the Fort Berthold Reservation show marked decadence in form, design and symmetry.[53]

An earlier, undocumented site with contact materials is regarded by Strong as Hidatsa and is located on the Missouri near Mobridge, South Dakota. Limited excavations were made. The village consists of haphazardly arranged, deep house pits and has no moat. Pottery suggests extremely simplified Mandan, is mostly plain, but includes a few sherds with fine cord and incised decoration. S-shaped and collared rims are rare, as are the elaborate decorations and rim forms of the Mandan.[54]

The Crow

According to traditional and other evidence, the Crow were once one with the Hidatsa. In late prehistoric times, they split off and moved westward to their later range on the Yellowstone in Montana.[55] This schism may have taken place while the Hidatsa were living on the Missouri. Hayden, following Crow tradition, placed the time of the break at about 1776,[56] though the writer feels that it may have been earlier. This movement is particularly interesting because the Crow apparently left the Missouri, a sedentary, horticultural people who made pottery and lived in earth lodges and were much like the Mandan and other Hidatsa, to turn up at the beginning of the 19th century on the Yellowstone as typical Plains nomads. Extremely rapid cultural reorientation under new environmental conditions is indicated.

46. Strong, 1940, pp. 379–383.
47. Strong, 1935, p. 286; 1940, pp. 384–385.
48. Over, 1936.
49. Will and Hecker, 1944.

50. Mooney, 1907a, p. 548.
51. Will, 1924, pp. 323–326.
52. Will, 1924; Bushnell, 1922.
53. Strong, 1940, pp. 365–366.
54. Ibid., p. 380.
55. See Will, 1924, pp. 305–310, and Hodge, 1907–1910, Pl. I, pp. 367–369, for summary of Crow movements.
56. Hodge, op. cit., p. 367; Hayden, 1862, pp. 391–392.

There is some archeological evidence of a westward movement of a group or groups of general Mandan-Hidatsa culture of a progressively more simplified form extending as far as the Continental Divide in Montana. At present, none of the material is positively identified with Crow, though the suggestion is that they were responsible for at least part of it.

Three sites reflect the first phase of this movement. They are Ludlow Cave,[57] in northwestern South Dakota; the Hagen site,[58] near Glendive, Montana; and the Ash Coulee site[59] near Terry, Montana.

Ludlow Cave is a small cavern which contained three feet of stratified deposit including two horizons, one prehistoric and one with contact material. In the earlier were found a small number of sherds with crushed granite temper, dark color, bands of diagonal incised or cord impressed lines, grooved paddle impressions, and everted and sometimes thickened lips. Strong regards them as of general Mandan-Hidatsa type.[60] Other items also present in Mandan-Hidatsa culture are thin, side notched projectile points with concave bases, a piriform blade with pitch on its base suggesting hafting, awls, knapping tools, tubular bone beads, perforated disks and piriform pendants of shell. Noteworthy is the presence of fragments of coiled basketry. Over feels that the cave may have been intermittently occupied and that the material in the lower level may not be culturally homogeneous. Nearby is a row of stone cairns and there are petroglyphs in and near the cave.

The Hagen Site is a prehistoric village on a low terrace above the banks of the Yellowstone. Only one house and no fortifications were noted. The house was circular with slightly excavated floor, central fireplace, east entrance, two central posts surrounded by a sixteen-foot circle of twelve posts. Had other houses been present, excavation should have disclosed them. The large artifact series and many cache pits of both bottle and cylindrical shapes suggest many more than one habitation. The remainder of the village may have been of hide tipis or other impermanent structures. Nearby was a truncated conical mound forty-five feet in diameter and two feet high. It contained scattered human bones, principally skull fragments.

Pottery is somewhat more simplified, though highly similar to that described for the historic Mandan with the following differences: rim band ornamentation is most frequently wrapped rod impressions and less frequently in cord (Fig. 55, D–E). In the Mandan material wrapped rod impressions are apparently

rare, though it is noteworthy that they are more frequent at the Rygh site than in later Mandan sites.[61] Incising is also more frequent here than at later Mandan sites, though this is also true at the Rygh site. Also in contrast to Mandan, more vessel bottoms are smooth than paddle impressed, and check paddle marks, though still infrequent, are more common at the Hagen site. Also present are a few dentate stamped designs on vessels otherwise typically Mandan. The majority of the large stone and bone work series can also be matched by the historic Mandan.

The Ash Coulee site is about nine miles above the mouth of Ash Coulee, a southern tributary of the Yellowstone, near Terry, Montana. Excavation in the culture-bearing surface stratum disclosed a small series of artifacts but no structures. Dwellings may have been hide tipis or other impermanent structures.

The pottery falls within the range of variation at the Hagen site, though it seems simpler and cruder, and perhaps partly because of the small sample, many of the former elements are not found here. Present are jars with constricted necks and flaring, frequently thickened rims, bands of incised lines much more frequent than cord impressions, little brush roughening, lines of various kinds of punctates on lips, and grooved paddle impressed and smooth body treatment. Stone artifacts are side notched, concave based projectile points and a few corner notched points with convex or concave bases, drills, ovoid, piriform, and subtriangular bifacially flaked knives. Bone work includes serrated and unserrated metapodial fleshers, knife handles for blades placed obliquely at one side or at the end, awls, knapping tools, and tubular beads.

Because of lack of published material, the desirable comparisons to Hidatsa material culture cannot be made, and Mandan similarities have been stressed. Detailed differences between Mandan and Hidatsa artifacts are not known to the writer, but it appears that the two complexes are rather similar. The three sites described suggest a westward movement of the generalized Mandan-Hidatsa material culture. This might be interpreted as westward movement of the Crow, but the case is not clear. The three sites are not identical, and particularly the Ash Coulee Site looks as though it might be something somewhat different from the other two. Ludlow Cave might be evidence of buffalo hunting trips by small groups of Mandan, Hidatsa, or both. The Hagen Site shows longer and more intensive occupation, and might be Crow, or some other group who moved westward and tried horticulture, only to give up and return.

Significant is the change which appears already to have taken place in the new environment. The great earthworks and fortified villages are not present. The earth lodge is smaller and simpler and seems largely

57. Over, 1936.
58. Mulloy, 1942a.
59. Excavated by the Montana Archeological Survey and as yet unpublished.
60. Strong, 1940, p. 384.
61. See p. 129.

to have been superseded by hide tipis or other perishable structures, though cache pits are still common. Horticulture is not proven here, though scapula hoes suggest it. Large numbers of animal bones, particularly bison, indicate increasing dependence on meat.

Further up the Yellowstone, the movement becomes more difficult to trace. Permanent villages of long occupation were not noted, though some may yet be found. The usual manifestations become small camp sites on mesa tops and in the bottoms along the Yellowstone and its tributaries. Typically, these show a few burned stones, occasionally the remains of a sudatory pit, a few small potsherds, and stone tools. The sites are widely distributed and frequent, but the material in them is so scanty that it is difficult to assess them culturally. Until the central Yellowstone is reached the pottery, in the sites observed, remains entirely an increasingly simplified form of the Hagen site wares. Cord and wrapped rod impressions as well as incising become rarer and tend to occur in simpler and smaller bands. A larger proportion of design seems to be confined to the region of the lip. Most body treatment is smooth, but check and grooved paddle impressions occur. The S-shaped rim is found occasionally though everted rims are more common.

This simplified ware is found as far west as the Continental Divide and in the central and upper Yellowstone country and sometimes occurs in sites which have contact material. The camp sites are too small to have merited identifiable mention in historic documents. A single large sherd with an S-shaped rim and the typical wrapped rod decoration was found in a grave reported as late historic Crow near Billings.

Log lodge villages as well as isolated lodges, some of which may be Crow, occur in several localities along the Yellowstone.[62] Both villages and lodges are small and usually occur in wooded areas, on and around mesas and escarpments, and in sheltered spots in broken country. Several lodge types sometimes occur in the same villages. One type is conical and made of vertically placed poles with a row of stone slabs outside. Frequently, support is provided by a standing tree. A variation is hemi-conical and built against a cliff wall. Another type is rectangular or pentagonal and built of horizontally laid logs, also with an outside row of slabs. This also frequently includes a standing tree and is varied by having one side formed by a cliff wall. There are few associated artifacts and intermittent occupation is possible.

In the village areas of two of these sites, though not in the lodges, sherds were found. One is the Thirty Mile Mesa site[63] about thirty miles north of Billings, Montana (Fig. 57). It consists of three pentagonal, one conical, and one hemiconical lodges, as well as one of irregular truncated conical construction and a small U-shaped structure of horizontally laid logs. The sherds are of the simplified Mandan-Hidatsa tradition, but lack any decoration. Some sherds show grooved paddle impressions. No rimsherds were found. In and near the lodges were small side notched concave based projectile points; ovoid and flat based, bifacially flaked knives; retouched flakes; and several small, lenticular, rose quartz beads. Contact material included home made and commercial gunflints and petroglyphs showing men in boats with flintlock weapons (Fig. 57, inset 2). With a semiflexed burial in the area were similar projectile points and knives, plano-convex snub nosed scrapers, mussel shell and a large, perforated, bituminous shale disk (Fig. 57, inset 1).

The other is the Pompey's Pillar Cuesta site[64] about fifteen miles north of Pompey's Pillar on the Yellowstone. Here are the foundations only of six lodges, no superstructures remaining. Here the lodges were made to fit rock crevices and floor plans are irregular in shape. Sherds similar to those at Thirty Mile Mesa were found and in addition a number of sherds from the flat bottomed vessels to be described. Projectile points are predominantly side notched with concave bases, though a few are large and corner notched. Present also are plano-convex snub nosed scrapers, retouched flakes, hammerstones, and flat, subrectangular, mano-like stones smoothed on one edge.

Other log lodge sites which have been investigated include the Little Cayuse Mountains site east of Melville, in Sweetgrass County, Montana; the Blue Mountain site some twenty miles south of Glendive, Montana; the Tipi Pole Spring site near the source of Lodge Grass Creek in Big Horn County, Montana; sites along Razor Creek in northern Yellowstone County, Montana;[65] and the Teepee Creek site in the Clarks Fork region of Wyoming.[66] Many others have been reported throughout the Yellowstone.

Lines of piles and individual piles of stones are of frequent occurrence in the Yellowstone country as well as further east in the Dakotas.[67] Two of these are of interest because of possible Crow connections. One lies along a probable trail through Pryor Gap in western Big Horn County, Montana. It is an irregular line of some sixty-four piles of stones. Most piles are only two or three feet in diameter, but near the south end three are larger. The largest of these is about thirty-six feet in diameter and about five and a half feet high. Among the stones of this larger cairn and a somewhat smaller one next to it were found charcoal, bison bones, and a number of artifacts. Some sherds are of the Mandan-Hidatsa tradition,

62. Mulloy, 1945.   63. Ibid., pp. 512 and 520.

64. Ibid.   66. Frost, 1941.
65. Ibid.   67. Will, 1924, pp. 295–298.

but lack most decorative features. S-shaped rims and grooved paddle impressions are present, but no decorations. There are also sherds from flat-bottomed vessels to be described. Other artifacts are side notched, concave based projectile points; plano-convex, snub nosed scrapers; knives with flat bases; discoidal game counters; awls; pierced coyote canines and elk incisors; small bone tubes; olivella and dentalia beads; and glass trade beads.

A similar though shorter line of piles lies near the Yellowstone River about five miles south of Livingston, Montana. This also may have extended along a trail. Present here also are sherds from the flat-bottomed vessels.[68]

Within the top one foot of deposit in Pictograph Cave[69] and in the area about its mouth was found a complex which included contact material and pottery (Pictograph Cave IV) and which could be distinguished from underlying Pictograph Cave III[70] material largely by the presence of these two items, though other differences might have appeared had the Level IV artifacts been more abundant. Most sherds are Mandan-Hidatsa tradition but lack most decorative features. The majority are smooth, but grooved paddle and check stamp impressions occur. A few rims have simple incised lines and there are occasional rows of punctates. Some lips are slightly thickened. A minority are from flat-bottomed vessels.[71] Other artifacts are frequently side notched, concave based projectile points and less frequent similar ones with a basal notch; plano-convex snub nosed scrapers; large, irregular percussion flaked choppers; ovoid knives, hammerstones; wooden skewers, gaming sticks of split peeled branches; and brass and iron projectile points, brass tubes, and glass beads. Near the mouth of the cave were the remains of a house site of fifteen elliptically arranged post molds surrounding two interior post molds near the south end. Southeast of center was a fireplace.

Historic material in these sites as well as in many of the smaller campsites indicates that pottery persisted in the Yellowstone country into the contact period. It cannot be unquestionably attributed to the Crow merely because the Yellowstone was Crow territory. Throughout the historic period, there was much movement in this area and during the eighteenth century, much of the central Yellowstone was held by the Shoshoni.[72] The Northern Shoshoni are known to have made pottery though the details of the ware are not clear.[73] Some of the flat-bottomed vessels described might be attributable to this group, but where elements of a simplified Mandan-Hidatsa tradition occur, Crow is more probable.

Log lodges frequently are described by explorers in the area, but descriptions do not distinguish tribal variations.[74] Crow informants stated[75] that in earlier times their forefathers constructed lodges of both the horizontal and vertical log types, though most frequently the latter. They also said that all the tribes they knew constructed both kinds, though the Blackfoot, Blood, and Piegan preferred the horizontal type while the Araphao, Arikara, Assiniboine, Cheyenne, Flathead, Gros Ventre, Hidatsa, Mandan, Nez Perce, Shoshoni (Wind River), and Sioux preferred the vertical pole, tipi-like structure. The lodges apparently were used both as winter camps and as war lodges.

A Crow informant said that his people were formerly accustomed to stop at the line of rock piles at Pryor Gap and add stones to the piles and make offerings, but there is no evidence that other groups may not also have done this. No statements were obtained regarding rock piles near Livingston. A similar custom is recorded in connection with a rock pile near Sanger, South Dakota.[76]

Crow informants are reported as having said that they avoided Pictograph Cave for superstitious reasons. The cave might well have been occupied intermittently by war parties of other tribes on expeditions into the Crow country.

These archeological manifestations of the central and upper Yellowstone, if they may be regarded in part at least as ancestral Crow, reflect a further stage of the cultural reorientation which had already begun on the lower Yellowstone. The remains suggest a nomadic people who moved about in small bands and were dependent on the buffalo and other game animals. No longer is there any suggestion of horticulture or earth lodges. Pottery remained into the contact period though in a simplified form and was probably less important than formerly. Essentially, the picture is similar to historic Crow culture.

THE ARIKARA

The Caddoan-speaking Arikara seem once to have been in close relationship with the ancestral Pawnee and their history is a constant northward movement up the Missouri. From the vicinity of the Nebraska–South Dakota line, they moved northward to the vicinity of Pierre, South Dakota, where they had large fortified villages about the middle of the eighteenth century. In 1795 they were on the Cheyenne River whence they moved northward and lived for a short time in close contact with the Mandan. Later they moved south to the mouth of the Grand River.

68. See p. 136.
69. See p. 127.
70. See p. 127.
71. See p. 136.
72. Teit, 1930, pp. 304–305.
73. Lowie, 1909a, p. 177.

74. E.g., Stuart, 1876, pp. 176–178; Coues (ed.), 1893, Vol. 1, pp. 295–296, Vol. 3, p. 1140; Thwaites (ed.), 1906, pp. 42–43, 351.
75. Information obtained by Mr. Fred Voget at Lodge Grass, Montana.
76. Will, 1924, p. 295.

Subsequently, they moved back to Nebraska with the Skidi Pawnee to return to Fort Clark in 1838. Thirty years later, they again moved north to live with the Mandan and Hidatsa on the Fort Berthold Reservation.[77]

Published archeological evidence of Arikara backgrounds is scarce. Strong[78] provides a summary of the Leavenworth site about five miles above the mouth of the Grand River on the Missouri. This well-documented site may have been occupied from around 1797 until its abandonment in 1823. The site is a large village of one hundred thirty-nine earth lodges on both sides of a small creek. On each side of the stream is an open plaza. Originally the whole village was surrounded by a stockade, but there was no ditch. Earth lodges are similar to Mandan, have a four post central support surrounded by a ring of posts, and both interior and exterior cache pits. Also present is a ceremonial lodge somewhat larger than the usual dwellings and a "grandfather" rock. Deep, flexed inhumations covered with boards and accompanied by abundant grave goods were made in a hill near the village. Unlike the Mandan, there were no cache pit burials encountered.

Arikara of this period was influenced by Mandan, and ceramics, though distinctive, reflect this. Color is tan to gray-brown, sometimes with hematite slip. Temper is crushed granite. Necks of vessels are grass rubbed, usually vertically, and bodies are indistinctly grooved paddled. Shapes are little known, but vessels were probably smaller and more rounded than those of the Mandan, while walls are somewhat thicker. Rims are usually thickened and everted with a small collar, which is decorated by diagonal or vertical cord impressions. Some simple, geometric, cord designs are found and the concentric semicircle design of the Mandan is rare. Both collared, narrow, and everted rims are found and these are often decorated by heavy punctates or finger corrugations. Some sherds have linear incisions on rim and body. Decoration is cruder and rarer than among the Mandan. Strap handles and lugs are rare. Other material culture items are common shaft polishers, elk scapula hoes, bone "squash knives," notched fleshers, perforated rib arrow wrenches, "snow snakes," and rare shallow mortars and mullers, grooved and ungrooved hammerstones, celts, end and side scrapers, triangular points, and catlinite pipes.

Three protohistoric and presumably older Arikara sites are also mentioned by Strong.[79] These are the Lower Cheyenne River site near the mouth of the Cheyenne River, and the Fort Sully and Buffalo Pasture sites, both somewhat farther down the Missouri. All are collections of earth lodges. The Cheyenne River and Buffalo Pasture sites have surrounding ditches which the Fort Sully site lacks. At Buffalo Pasture, there was a stockade inside the ditch, and an excavated earth lodge here was similar to the Leavenworth site. Artifacts and ceramics are similar to those at the Leavenworth site, but show less Mandan influence in having less cord marking on the rim and more incised and punctate decoration. The predominant rim form is thickened and everted, and suggests derivation from a collared type.

In the late prehistoric period there are suggestions that Arikara antecedents become confluent with those of the Pawnee to the south in a horizon which is basically Upper Republican. Strong[80] indicates that the Arzberger site about seven miles down the Missouri from Pierre, South Dakota, suggests this development. This fortified prehistoric village consists of forty or more shallow house pits surrounded by a ditch with bastions jutting out at intervals. A stockade had been present. Two excavated earth lodges were round with four post central support, and were similar to those previously described. Another was sub-rectangular and similar to Upper Republican houses. Ceramics show Upper Republican similarities and incline more toward the Pawnee line of development than to the Arikara in being more similar to Lower Loup material than to protohistoric Arikara. The pottery has marked collars, frequently with scalloped bases, and has both cord wrapped and grooved paddle impressions. Incising is important and punctates occasional. Combined incised and punctate shoulder decoration suggests Oneota influence. Other material culture includes practically all the stone and bone artifact types characteristic of Upper Republican, and in addition, catlinite pipes, grooved stone mauls, large scrapers, and a predominance of unnotched, triangular points.

As far as Arikara culture can be traced, the picture is one of a sedentary, earth-lodge-dwelling, agricultural people broadly similar to the Mandan and the other tribes of the eastern fringe of the Northern Plains, though with a culture which differed in detail. They appear to have come out of the Upper Republican substratum, which also gave rise to the Pawnee, to move up the Missouri later to become influenced by Mandan culture.

THE CHEYENNE

According to tradition, the Algonkian-speaking Cheyenne once lived in the valley of the Minnesota whence they moved gradually westward to their later historic habitat in the western Plains. At the beginning of this movement, they were settled horticulturalists, living in earth lodges and raising crops of corn, beans, and squash.[81]

77. Strong, 1940, pp. 357–360.   79. Ibid., pp. 380–381.
78. Ibid., pp. 366–370.

80. Ibid., pp. 382–383.   81. Bushnell, 1922, p. 21.

The most easterly location from which we have archeological evidence is the Sheyenne-Cheyenne site, a large village in the great bend of the Sheyenne River about twelve miles southeast of Lisbon, North Dakota (Fig. 58). This site is described by Strong,[82] who regards it as having been abandoned around 1770. The site contains contact material, and is documented. Lying on a terrace near the river are remains of about seventy earth lodges, surrounded by a ditch. The existence of a stockade was not established. Excavated lodges were circular with four central posts and either with or without a surrounding ring of additional posts. Only external cache pits were noted, and many may have been refuse rather than storage pits.

Pottery is predominantly light in color, ranging from buff and tan to mottled gray and black. A minority of sherds have a hematite inner slip. Grit temper is fine to coarse. Average thickness is about 8 mm. Vessels were probably globular and a few sherds have angular shoulders. Strap handles and triangular, horizontal lugs are found. The one basal fragment recovered is flat.[83] Vertical grass wiping is usual on necks as are partially smoothed horizontal grooved paddle impressions on bodies. Occasionally punch stamps or plaited matting impressions occur. Rims are usually thickened with protruding, flat topped lips directed outward and downward at an angle varying around 45°. There are both constricted and straight necks. Lip decoration is predominantly vertical, horizontal, and diagonal parallel lines of cord or wrapped rod impressions. In a few cases, the inner lip is decorated with wrapped rod or cord impressions, incisions or punctates. A few necks have horizontal, parallel lines of wrapped rod or cord impressions, and shoulder decorations of incised herringbone or opposed diagonal bands occur. Roulette technique is present though minor, as is a decoration of inset glass beads on the outer rim. This pottery suggests more Woodland influence than the wares hitherto described though it has many of the generalized traits of northeastern Plains ceramics. It differs more markedly from the Mandan than from the Arikara wares. Strong feels that possibly, in view of its resemblance to pottery of the Black Duck Focus of Minnesota, it may eventually be linked to one of the aspects of Minnesota's Lake Michigan Phase.

The rest of the material culture is similar to that of the other sedentary tribes along the Missouri. Present are grooved mauls, oval and discoidal hammer stones, rubbing stones, flat grinding stones and mullers, triangular arrowpoints with notched or expanding stems, subrectangular scrapers chipped on all four sides, triangular knife blades, scapula hoes, notched fleshers, rib knife handles, shaft wrenches, knapping tools, end scraper handles of rib, and crescentic, triangular, and rectangular mussel shell knives. Rare are elbow catlinite pipes, shaft polishers, bone beads and pendants, bone bracelets, and cancellous bone hide dressing tools. The three burials recovered consisted of one bundle burial and two skulls outside one of the lodges, though additional burials near the village are mentioned.

Animal bones suggest secondary dependence on game and the horse is attested to by frequent bones.

Farther west along the Missouri, near Fort Yates, North Dakota, are two additional, presumably earth lodge villages,[84] older than or contemporaneous with the Sheyenne-Cheyenne site. Tradition states that one of these was abandoned around 1784, for a point some twenty miles above the mouth of the Grand River. The new village, which existed until about 1840, appears to have been composed of skin tipis rather than earth lodges and suggests a change toward the historic nomadism of the Cheyenne.[85]

Strong points out that nineteenth century Cheyenne campsites, one of which he examined near Scottsbluff, Nebraska, in lacking pottery, earth lodges, fortifications, and other evidence of a sedentary life, indicate that a tremendous change from the culture of the Sheyenne-Cheyenne village toward Plains nomadism seems to have taken place in about two generations.[86] This is interesting in comparison with the similar cultural reorientation described for the Crow.

OTHER HISTORIC GROUPS

Archeological evidence is largely lacking for the Dakota, Assiniboine, Shoshoni, and Blackfoot.

The Teton Dakota moved or were forced into the Plains from the vicinity of west-central Minnesota, acquiring horses and developing rapidly into typical Plains nomads of considerable military strength.[87] Though a possible Dakota stratum is mentioned in Ludlow Cave, this is too late and too scanty to be useful.[88] The closely related Assiniboine were noted in the vicinity of Lake Winnepeg in 1670 whence they moved southward and westward about the beginning of the nineteenth century to their historic habitat.[89]

The northern Shoshoni or Snakes occupied a large area from western Montana and Wyoming, central and southern Idaho, northern Utah and Nevada, to eastern Oregon. In Wyoming their special territory was on the Green and Sweetwater Rivers and they are said to have extended as far east as the North Platte.[90] It has been suggested that they once lived

82. Strong, 1940, pp. 370–375.
83. See also Grinnell, 1923, Vol. 1, p. 238.
84. Grinnell, 1918, pp. 359–380.
85. Bushnell, 1922, p. 23.
86. Strong, 1940, p. 376.
87. Bushnell, 1922, pp. 59–71.
88. Over, 1936, p. 126.
89. Lowie, 1909b, pp. 7–10.
90. Lowie, 1909a, p. 171.

further east in the Plains,[91] but on linguistic,[92] mythological, and cultural evidence, Lowie thinks they have lived in the Basin-Plateau region for a long time.[93] Their basic culture was that of the mountains with a superficial Plains superstratum acquired late.[94] They are reported to have lived in part of the central Yellowstone country in the eighteenth century.[95]

The flat-bottomed pottery mentioned as associated with some possible Crow manifestations in the central Yellowstone may be Shoshoni. It is known from the central Yellowstone where it occurs separately in camp sites, and sometimes with Mandan-Hidatsa tradition ware to which it is foreign; from a camp site near Laramie, Wyoming, where it is associated with an Upper Republican–like ware; and from camp sites near the Great Salt Lake in Utah. Color is buff to brown and temper is sand or crushed rock. Surface is carelessly smoothed and slightly undulating with occasional peculiar dimpled appearance. It tends to be thick and is without decoration. A presumably typical vessel comes from a camp site near Billings (Fig. 56).

The Blackfoot, in recent historic times, held the immense territory stretching almost from the North Saskatchewan River in Canada to the southern headstreams of the Missouri in Montana, and from the mountains on the west almost to the North Dakota line on the east. About 1790, they were noted along the Saskatchewan in a process of gradual migration to the north and west.[96] Though archeological information about them is lacking, two points are important to previous discussions. They erected war lodges in enemy country of both horizontal and vertical log types, the latter with a covered entryway.[97] Some of the lodges described for the central Yellowstone may have been Blackfoot structures. They also formerly made flat bottomed pots. Descriptions suggest an appreciable difference from those just described,[98] but they may be related.

OTHER ARCHEOLOGICAL MANIFESTATIONS OF THE LATE PERIOD

Other prehistoric complexes in the area are probably late but have not been related to historic cultures. Pictograph Cave III[99] is a late prehistoric nonceramic material culture overlying Pictograph Cave II[100] and separated from it by a sterile stratum, and underlying Pictograph Cave IV.[101] It is abundantly represented both in Pictograph Cave and in Ghost Cave, a nearby cavern.

The remains, which include perishable items, have a number of generalized resemblances to the nonceramic artifacts of the sedentary peoples in the eastern part of the area, though hunting was paramount and horticulture absent. Bison were most important, though other game animal bones are relatively more frequent than in earlier horizons at this site.

Present are small and some large side notched, concave based projectile points; plano-convex, snub nosed scrapers; ovoid to piriform knives, some hafted obliquely with bone or wood handles; retouched flakes; drills; large rough choppers; grooved mauls; pestles; mano-like stones; longitudinally grooved shaft straighteners; bison rib knapping tools and shaft straighteners; unilaterally multi-barbed harpoon(?) points; a large fluted, barbed, bone point; serrated metapodial fleshers; bone, bison hoof and shell game counters(?); bone whistles; bison scapula side scrapers; wide and narrow antler bracelets; wooden and foreshafted cane arrows with points affixed with pitch(?) and sinew; hearths, simple and foreshafted fire drills; gaming sticks of split halves of small branches; skewers; hard soled moccasin fragments; coiled basketry fragments; and other minor items.

Reflected here is a certain rather well-developed, probably more or less nomadic hunting and gathering culture. Like peoples of the Middle Period, they probably trapped bison, for at the nearby Billings Bison Trap[102] their characteristic projectile points are found in the upper level. Similar projectile points are also predominant at the bison trap near Livingston, Montana.[103] Though most of the artifacts suggest early historic northern Plains cultures, others may represent mountain influence.

The Mill Creek culture of northwestern Iowa and southeastern South Dakota[104] has been mentioned before as a possible Mandan ancestor. The protohistoric or prehistoric Mitchell site[105] near Mitchell, South Dakota, has material which suggests Mill Creek relationships. It is a village of forty to forty-five earth lodges partly surrounded by a double ditch on the edge of a river terrace. Excavated lodges were rectangular in shallow pits with walls of closely spaced vertical posts, and frequent external and internal cache pits. When more is known of Mill Creek-like manifestations in South Dakota, the problem of Mandan antecedents may become much less perplexing.

Will and Hecker have found widely distributed along the Missouri, in the Souris Basin, and many places back from the river, an unidentified type of pottery and other artifacts which appear to be distinctive. Sites mentioned are near Williston, Mannhaven, and Bismarck, North Dakota. The sherds are crude, grit-tempered, well fired, with predominant incised

91. Brinton, 1901, p. 121.
92. Kroeber, 1907, p. 165.
93. Lowie, 1909a, p. 173.
94. Kroeber, 1939, pp. 49–53.
95. Teit, 1930, pp. 304–305.
96. Mooney, 1907b, p. 570.
97. Ewers, 1944.
98. Ewers, 1945.
99. See p. 137.
100. See p. 127.
101. See p. 133.

102. See p. 127.
103. Brown, B., 1932, pp. 80–81.
104. Strong, 1935, p. 286.
105. Meleen, 1938.

or punctate decoration about rim tops. The entire surfaces of pots show brush roughening either horizontal or vertical. Crude projectile points have wide bases and lateral notches. Knives are larger and cruder than those of the historic cultures of the area.[106]

Earth mounds are found throughout the central lowland of North and South Dakota and well into Canada. Some are impressive mounds from one to twelve feet in height and extensive and complex alignments, fortifications, and earthworks exist. Many contain single or group burials in shallow pits. Pottery is relatively rare in the mounds and is characterized by spiral incisions from mid-base to rim, unusual incised decorations and perforated lugs or low castellations. Also present are well-chipped flint blades; small, delicate arrowheads; tubular stone pipes; catlinite tablets with incised animal designs; shaft polishers; sewed birchbark containers; antler tip harpoons and handles; incised antler bracelets; excellent shell work; effigy pipes; and some native copper.

Strong feels that this complex will probably eventually be related to Minnesota mound cultures, though at present this is inconclusive. He also mentions speculations to the effect that the mounds may be peripheral to Ohio mound culture and might reflect the migration of some of the Siouan speakers of the northern Plains out of Ohio, but is careful to point out that these are only speculations for which there is little foundation at present.[107]

Manifestations of Unknown Relationships

"Tipi rings" or circles of stones varying from five to forty feet in diameter and occasionally larger are found all over the area either isolated or in groups of several hundred in which frequently they intersect each other so intricately that it is difficult to separate one from the other. Usually they are simple circles, but eccentric forms also occur. Sometimes they occur near camp sites, but rarely are artifacts found in them. In the Dakotas, some are merely circular depressions in the sod.[108] They are repeatedly referred to as stones for holding down the edges of tipis, but this does not seem plausible in view of the variations in size and the lack of evidence of habitation in their vicinity. Only exceedingly rarely in the writer's experience are remains of fires found in them and they lack packed floors. Most frequently, they are situated on high river terrace fingers and less frequently in sheltered lowland areas. They may be related to the so-called "medicine wheels" of which a stone circle high on a mountain peak in the Big Horns east of Powell, Wyoming, is an example. This circle is over

fifty feet in diameter and includes spoke like lines of stones and small irregular dry masonry walled structures in the center and incorporated in the periphery.

Also frequent are isolated piles of rocks, lines of piles of rocks, and lines of individual stones. Occasionally rock piles cover graves in Montana but most do not. Some of the lines of piles of rocks are parts of bison traps. Offerings were made at some, such as those described in the Crow section and others,[109] while still others are obscure.

Petroglyphs and pictographs are common especially in the western part of the area. In most cases, they cannot be related to specific cultures. A detailed distribution study of them would be significant, but at present this has not been made.

Summary

This brief and incomplete survey has suggested considerable antiquity for northern Plains culture. Though available information provides an inadequate and spotty abstract, an historical picture is beginning to emerge. First, an early postglacial population of nomadic hunters who probably were contemporaneous with animals now extinct and who lived in the western High Plains and surrounding areas. On the eastern borders of the area, the finds of Brown's Valley and Minnesota Man indicate that men were here too in early times.

Subsequently, principally at Signal Butte and Pictograph Cave, the presence of two other successive groups of hunters is indicated. These were probably broadly similar in general culture to their predecessors, though their projectile points particularly were stylistically different and less well made. Bison traps indicate something of their manner of hunting and suggest that at times they were able to take this animal in large numbers.

In the Yellowstone at least, as reflected in Pictograph Cave III and elsewhere, they were succeeded by still another hunting group of distinctive culture who used bison traps. These people apparently remained in the region until very near historic times. It is interesting that, relative to other game animals, bison was less important to these people than to their predecessors.

In the eastern part of the area, sedentary peoples who lived in earth lodges, practiced agriculture, and made pottery, begin to be found in the late prehistoric period. Some of these can be related to surviving peoples and in general their relationships seem to look toward the east and south, rather than the west. Very late in prehistoric and protohistoric times, pottery of the Mandan-Hidatsa tradition was brought westward across Montana to the Continental Divide by a people, probably the Crow, who were in a proc-

---

106. Will and Hecker, 1944, pp. 35–37.
107. Strong, 1940, pp. 385–386; Montgomery, 1906; Will, 1933.
108. Will, 1924, pp. 293–295.

109. *Ibid.*, pp. 295–298.

ess of change from sedentary agriculturalists to nomadic bison hunters. Similar westward movements possibly were taking place further south as suggested by finds of Upper Republican pottery near Cheyenne and in the Laramie Basin as well as in northeastern Colorado beyond the probable range of Indian horticulture. It is significant that this movement with its attendant economic reorientation began before horses were obtained. Later, apparently under the influence of horse economy and other pressures, other peripheral groups began to move into the northern High Plains from both east and west to take over bison-hunting as a primary means of subsistence and to produce the historic Plains culture as it is known ethnologically.

Of at least preliminary usefulness in building an historical framework is the concept of four or possibly five successive technological horizon styles. That is; successive broad technological trends widespread in the area and elsewhere, which place a generalized stamp of similarity in each successive period upon cultures which differ from locality to locality. The writer feels that eventually it will be possible to trace a sequence of technological stylistic changes correlated with successive time periods in many artifacts through cultures which differ rather widely in such aspects as economic orientation.

At present, the best examples of these stylistic changes are to be seen in projectile points. This example will illustrate. In historic times, metal projectile points of a single general type, obtained from the whites are to be found in cultures as widely different as those of the sedentary agriculturalists of the east, through the hunters of the western Plains, to the gatherers of the mountains.

In the late prehistoric period, a small stone, side notched, concave or basilar notched point was pre-dominant, and also found from the agriculturalists to the western hunters and gatherers, as well as more widely.

In the Middle Period, a larger corner notched point with a convex or concave base was predominant in later times and earlier, a somewhat similar point with large notches and much less prominant barbs. These two variants may belong together or at least may be closely related.

In the early period, and probably extending into the middle period, the Folsoms and the "Yuma" variants differ from each other, but still fall into a group in terms of size, excellence of workmanship, and lack of notches.

Stratigraphic superimpositions which confirm all or part of this projectile point sequence are accumulating, e.g., Signal Butte, Pictograph Cave, Billings Bison Trap, Birdshead Cave[110] in the Owl Creek Mountains of Wyoming, Ash Hollow Cave[111] near Ogalalla, Nebraska, Promontory Cave,[112] Blackrock Cave,[113] and Dead Man's Cave[114] around the Great Salt Lake.

Eventually it should be possible to set up sequences of stylistic changes in many other artifacts in such a manner as to add much more content to an historical picture of broadly diffused technological styles superimposed on many peoples of diverse origins living different kinds of lives in different localities. This is not to say that this framework is the only one in which northern Plains prehistory is to be understood, but much of the information likely to be acquired will be of this order.

110. Bliss, 1950, pp. 187–196.
111. Champe, 1946, pp. 37–39.
112. Steward, 1937b, p. 94.
113. Ibid., p. 115.
114. Smith, E. R., 1941, pp. 17–24.

CULTURE SEQUENCE IN THE LOWER MISSOURI VALLEY.

By Carl H. Chapman[*]

THE location of the Lower Missouri Valley in the Midwestern region may be a prime factor contributing to the complexity of the culture problem in the area. According to Wissler, the terrain is located at the approximate junction of three broad cultural areas in post-Columbian times, the Plains, the Northeastern Woodland, and the Southeastern areas.[1] Furthermore, it is evident that this same situation was present in pre-Columbian times in a more aggravated condition. Martin, Quimby, and Collier have four cultural areas meeting in the same region, the Plains, the Illinois, the Middle Southern, and the Ozark Plateau.[2] It is obvious that some of the greatest difficulties in establishing sequence and chronology revolve upon the meeting of cultural areas and the consequent contact of different peoples and their exchange of ideas. The Lower Missouri Valley is a border area, one of overlapping cultures and probably was not often homogeneous culturally.

The limits arbitrarily set for the Lower Missouri Valley are on the west the boundary of the State of Missouri at Kansas City, on the east the mouth of the Missouri River near St. Louis and on the north and south the drainages of the tributaries of the Missouri River within the state. Although the area is comparatively small, a great deal of variation exists in the terrain. In the north, rolling prairies are dissected by sluggish streams whose valleys have cut through a comparatively flat glaciated plain. In the southwest, prairies are again encountered in the upper drainages of the Osage and Blackwater rivers. The western prairie is a gently rolling plain characterized by streams with slight grades and wide flood plains. Valleys have moderate slopes and the divides between the valleys are broad and rounded. Differing considerably from the prairies is the Ozark highland through which flow the two main southern tributaries of the Missouri River, the Osage and Gasconade.

In general, the highland region was much more rugged and isolated than the prairies and had a wider variety of vegetation. The native fauna of the Ozark Highland was also more varied with a greater diversity of fish, small game mammals and birds. The most important game animals, deer, bison, wapiti, bear and beaver were found in all three physiographic divisions. The Missouri River itself, though passing through all three areas, might be considered still another variety of environment with its extremely broad flood plains and loess covered bluffs.[3] The differences in terrain and corresponding varieties of plant and animal life may have had some effect on the life of the peoples in the areas and no doubt were in part responsible for the localization or comparative isolation of some cultures and the widespread and quick change of others.

The probable sequence of the cultures in the Lower Missouri Valley and a suggested time of occupation for each represents the essence of the cultural problem until further research is conducted. Still unsolved is the definite interrelationship of the cultures and their relationships with similar cultures in the Mississippi Valley. These unsolved problems stem in part from the almost complete lack of a chronology such as the one made possible by the tree-ring dating method.

Two methods of approach toward solving the sequence of the area have met with some success. First and most successful is the historical approach, which consists of starting with the most recent Indian cultures, the historic tribes, and working toward the most ancient. The second consists of starting with the ancient cultures associated with extinct mammals and working toward the latest. These establish the beginning and end of the sequence. Direct evidence of stratification has helped fill in the gaps, but confusing the picture are the lacunae of archeological research in much of the lower reaches of the Missouri Valley and the scarcity of direct evidences of sequence in places where considerable investigation has taken place. Therefore it is necessary to depend upon two other approaches for a fuller understanding of the cultural development and sequence. One of these is the comparison with the sequence of similar cultures

* University of Missouri, A.B., 1939, University of Chicago Archeological Field School, 1936; University of New Mexico, M.A., 1946; Assistant Professor in Anthropology, University of Missouri; Director of American Archeology, University of Missouri, 1946——. Chapter received March, 1948.

1. Wissler, 1938, p. 221, Fig. 56; p. 225, Fig. 59.
2. Martin, Quimby, and Collier, 1947, pp. 289–296, 319–368, and map in back of book.
3. Chapman, 1946, pp. 8–14.

in adjacent areas and the other is the apparent similarity of cultural traits that suggest development of one culture into another.

The various cultures in the lower Missouri Valley are placed in rather general time periods. They are discussed in their approximate order of sequence beginning with the early hunting cultures and ending with the historic tribes.

ARCHAIC PERIOD

Preceding the introduction of pottery and perhaps the bow and arrow and agriculture into the Lower Missouri Valley was a long period characterized by slow development of cultural traits and few direct influences from other regions. Theoretically, the period began when the first men discovered and entered the region. The exact time of that discovery and the identity of the people making the discovery may never be known. However, there is some evidence that man was in the Lower Missouri basin contemporaneously with the mastodon, an elephant-like mammal believed to have become extinct in the Pleistocene geologic period.[4] Therefore, it is tentatively assumed that the Archaic period in the Lower Missouri Valley started thousands of years ago at a time when many species of animals that are now extinct roamed the region.

No complex of cultural traits is obtainable from the accounts of the finding of artifacts associated with the extinct mastodon remains. However, one projectile point attributed to the discovery by Koch on the Pomme de Terre River is pictured in an article by Rau and is reproduced in Fig. 59, C.[5] Variant Folsom points are found throughout the region and may indicate an early hunting culture similar to the Folsom complex in the southwest (Fig. 59, D).[6]

One lithic complex, Nebo Hill, has been noted in the western edge of the lower Missouri basin by J. M. Shippee.[7] The complex has been derived from surface finds on small sites situated on the upland bordering the Missouri River. The most characteristic objects of the complex seem to be lanceolate blades and flat celts. Shippee also includes three-quarter grooved axes, flat oval manos, quartzite mortars and hammers and sandstone and pumice abraders in the Nebo Hill complex. The same culture or one similar has been noted in the central part of the area by J. J. McKinny. Artifacts that appear to be typical of the complex in both areas are lanceolate blades (Fig. 59, A) and flat celts (Fig. 59, B).[8]

In all probability more nonceramic complexes will be discovered in the Missouri Valley region in the future.

THE BOONE FOCUS—EARLY WOODLAND PERIOD

The cultural interval following the Archaic is marked by the introduction of pottery and possibly the bow and arrow and an incipient agriculture. It seems to have been a long interval of time judging from the numerous remains left by the people of the period. There is considerable evidence that the known culture of the period, tentatively called the Boone Focus of the Woodland Pattern,[9] in some instances lasted unchanged through perhaps all of the period of Hopewellian influx and possibly was still in existence in somewhat changed form at the time of invasions by Mississippi people. In the Ozark Highland part of the area, there is evidence that the Woodland peoples were more isolated and received far fewer ideas and development was slower. The mortuary complex, for example, was never as highly developed in the southern part of the Missouri basin as in the center. It is probable that other early Woodland cultures preceded the Boone Focus and that it represents the latest phase of development of still earlier cultures of the period. The earlier cultures are insufficiently known to do more than mention their existence at present.

The Boone Focus had the greatest distribution during this Early Woodland Period and held sway along the main stem of the Missouri River. The mortuary complex of the Boone Focus, which was its outstanding feature, may have served as the prototype for the later Hopewellian complex in the Lower Missouri Valley. Trade was maintained in some manner with the Gulf of Mexico by the Boone Focus people as is indicated by seashells, and it is likely that a few ideas as well as materials were obtained along the trade routes. However, the addition of trade materials may have occurred contemporaneously with one of the later periods. The Boone Focus, though probably extending in time through two or possibly three of the general periods (Early and Middle Woodland and possibly into Early Mississippi) is used as the representative of the Early Woodland Period. It is likely, therefore, that some of the traits listed for the Boone Focus should be assigned to later periods, since there is not enough information on the culture to divide it into early and late stages, and the complete range of the Boone Focus as a whole has been included in the description of the culture.

The Boone Focus people were apparently semi-sedentary and depended greatly upon hunting for their subsistence. Deer was the most important food

4. Koch, 1841, pp. 22–24.
5. Rau, 1873, Fig. 1, p. 396.
6. Specimens of variant Folsom form from the Whelply Collection, Academy of Science, St. Louis, Missouri.
7. Shippee, 1948.
8. Artifacts in the collection of Mr. J. J. McKinny, DeWitt, Missouri.

9. Chapman, n.d., pp. 94–103.

animal. Evidence for agriculture by these people is almost lacking. Large flint blades which have been considered agricultural implements because of the polish on one end of the blade could just as well be adzes (Fig. 60, *F*).

Villages were small and were probably made up of flimsy structures.[10]

Although crude pottery vessels were the chief household utensils, the manufacture of earthen vessels was a secondary industry. Pottery vessels were generally brown or reddish-brown in color and were tempered with crushed stone or sand. The characteristic vessel shapes were vessels with globular body and insloping rim (Fig. 60, *D*) and those with pointed base and insloping rim (Fig. 60, *E*). Surfaces were roughly smoothed, brush-marked or cord-marked. Mussel shells were utilized as spoons or scrapers (Fig. 60, *J*).

Sandstone mortars were not of frequent use. Their purpose may have been for the grinding of paint or for preparing food.

The industry of prime importance was the manufacture of stone implements. Large numbers of hammerstones, many of which were pitted, were possibly used in part of the manufacturing process. Roughly oval flint scrapers (Fig. 60, *K*) were probably made to assist in the working of skins for clothing. Cylindrical antler rubbing tools (Fig. 60, *O*) and split bone awls (Fig. 60, *N*) may also have been helpful in the preparation and manufacture of skin clothing. Some of the cylindrical antler tools contained a cavity at one end indicating that the implements may have been handles.

Weapons for the chase were by far the most common of tools manufactured. There was a great variety of stemmed and notched projectile points (Fig. 60, *L*) and knives (Fig. 60, *M*). One type with expanding convex base may be diagnostic or of focal significance (Fig. 60, *Q*). Small stemmed projectile points in replica of larger forms (Fig. 60, *R*) may have been added to the culture in its more advanced stages. Notched, chipped flint axes (Fig. 60, *H*), three-quarter grooved axes (Fig. 60, *I*) and diabase celts (Fig. 60, *G*) were other types of weapons. Perforated deer leg bones (Fig. 60, *P*) were probably employed as arrowshaft straighteners.

Both expanding base (Fig. 60, *S*) and stemmed flint drills (Fig. 60, *T*) were possibly utilized in wood and bone working.

The Boone Focus people apparently did not ornament themselves profusely. Ornamentation consisted of bone beads (Fig. 60, *U*), seashell beads (Fig. 60, *V*), columella of conch shell beads (Fig. 60, *W*) and oval stone pendants (Fig. 60, *X*). The only artifacts of the people suggesting ceremonialism were miniature celts

(Fig. 60, *Y*) and clay and stone pipes of the elbow variety (Fig. 60, *Z*).

The mortuary customs of the Boone Focus people are the best known and the most distinctive features of the culture. Burial was made in mounds constructed especially for that purpose. The mounds varied from round to oval in shape and from small rounded eminences to fifteen feet in height. Some of the oval structures approached seventy-five feet in length.

Inner construction of the mounds varied considerably but there was much overlapping in the same mound or mound groups suggesting a common cultural origin for all. The features of greatest recurrence were (1) earth mounds containing no stone structures, often with graves excavated into the subsoil beneath the mounds (Fig. 60, *A*), (2) stone box graves or a pavement of stones forming the floor, the top, or both, of the graves (Fig. 60, *B*) and (3) large dry masonry burial chambers, round or rectangular in shape and with or without openings (Fig. 60, *C*). The latter have often been termed stone vaults.

The placement of burials in the mounds was more diverse than the structures within the mounds. Burial types were (1) fragmentary burned human remains often mixed with burned earth, ashes and charcoal; (2) fully extended, primary supine burials; (3) secondary bundle burials or bunched masses of disarticulated bones; (4) skulls not associated with other bones; and (5) burial in a fully flexed or semi-flexed position. Mortuary offerings were usually scarce or absent and when present consisted of pottery vessels, pipes, shell beads or a few utilitarian objects.[11] It seems probable that the building of a burial mound was not of frequent occurrence and was practiced perhaps at intervals of several years, the bones of the dead being saved in the interim. Such a practice would account in part for the great variety of burial types. The greatest emphasis of the Boone Focus culture seemed to center about the dead, and perhaps of most importance to the people was the ceremony associated with the construction of a burial tumuli.

HOPEWELLIAN PHASE—MIDDLE WOODLAND PERIOD

The period following the early development of the Boone Focus saw a large scale migration of people and ideas into the area. Extensive travel and trade marked the times. One of the far western outposts of the Hopewellian sphere of influence seemed to lie in the center of the lower Missouri Valley. The Hopewell mode of life appears to have been carried through to this place from the center of Hopewell culture in Illinois. However, it could be that in some instances Woodland peoples already established in the region,

10. *Ibid.*, p. 102.

11. Sources for Boone Focus include: Fowke, 1910, pp. 12–73; Wedel, 1943, pp. 105–191; Berry *et al.*, 1938; Harrington, J. C., 1938; Chapman, 1941; Brownlee, 1936; Fairbanks, 1938.

added to their culture new ideas and customs derived from the eastern Hopewellian. If such was the case, the period saw the overriding of some of the less complicated Woodland cultures until they possessed a striking similarity to the Illinois Hopewell.

The Hopewellian culture centered in Saline County and greatest influence from this outpost or secondary center was felt westward along the main stem of the Missouri River and reached into the Plains Area.[12] The Upper Osage River valley was a region receiving some influence and may have been one route by which the Hopewellian spread to Oklahoma.[13] At the eastern edge of the Lower Missouri Valley is evidence of a small Hopewellian settlement which, however, did not extend its influence up the valley.[14] There seems to be a general lack of evidence of Hopewellian peoples between the Lamine River and the settlement at the mouth of the Missouri River.

The Hopewellian people in the Lower Missouri Valley depended to a large extent on hunting for subsistence. Deer was the main source of meat supply and bison and wapiti were next in importance. Raccoon and beaver may also have been a source of meat but were probably hunted primarily for their fur. Agriculture was practiced to some extent and corn and beans were the principal crops. Large flint objects with polished blades were probably agricultural tools (Fig. 61, G). Gathering and fishing played a small role in the Hopewellian economy.

Villages were generally small, about four to ten acres in area. No evidences of houses have been discovered. Numerous straight-sided, circular pits filled with refuse occurred on the village locations.

Household utensils in greatest quantity were pottery vessels. Pottery was grit-tempered, usually crushed granite, and varied in texture from coarse to fine. The outer surface was smoothed and vessels were small to large in size. Characteristic vessels usually had an inward sloping lip, a slightly bulging rim with a shallow groove or channel on the inside, a body oval in vertical cross-section and a somewhat conoidal base. The lip was flat. Decoration consisted of cross-hatched or rocker marking on the rim bordered on the lower margin by punch-marks. The neck was plain and a single incised line was often present at the bottom margin. The body was frequently covered with closely set bands of vertical edentate rocker impressions (Fig. 61, A). Less common was a wide-mouth jar, ovoid in cross-section with conoidal base. The rim was generally decorated with vertical incised or stamped units below which were punched bosses. The neck area below the bosses was sometimes decorated with dentate stamp impressions and incised lines (Fig.

61, B). The finest type of pottery was thin-walled and harder than the other wares. These vessels varied in shape. Some had globular bodies, others were lobed giving a square appearance to the vessel (Fig. 61, C) and still others were bowl forms (Fig. 61, D). Decorations consisted of the addition of curvilinear designs to the more common motifs. A small percentage of vessels of cruder workmanship had rims flaring outward, a body oval in vertical cross-section and a conoidal base. Decoration consisted of punched bosses on the rim and cord-marking on the body (Fig. 61, E). The latter seems to be a carry-over from the earlier Woodland wares. Miniature vessels were manufactured but were more crudely made than the larger forms.

Pottery manufacture probably ranked first in Hopewellian home industry, but the making of chipped stone implements perhaps surpassed it in importance. Since hunting was so necessary to the existence of the Hopewellian people in this area, most artifacts manufactured were those associated with the chase. Projectile points of the expanding stem variety, shouldered and with either a convex or straight base were most characteristic (Fig. 61, F). Deer antler tips converted into socketed conical projectile points were less (Fig. 61, H) frequently manufactured than the chipped stone varieties. The typical form of ax was three-quarter grooved (Fig. 61, I). Hematite and diabase celts were also common (Fig. 61, L). Grooved sandstone objects may have been atlatl weights (Fig. 61, J).

Clothing was probably made in part from skins and a variety of scrapers were used in the preparation of the skins. Scrapers made of flint were ovoid, snub-nosed and reworked projectile points (Fig. 61, K). Cylindrical antler rubbing tools (Fig. 61, M), and bone beamers for dehairing were other implements probably used in dressing skins (Fig. 61, N). Awls made of bird bones and deer ulnae punches may have assisted in the manufacture of clothing (Fig. 61, O).

A long flat, eyed bone needle may have been utilized for weaving mats (Fig. 61, P). Fine weaving was probably practiced as it was by the Classic Hopewell, but tools associated with such activities have not yet been determined.

Common drills were manufactured of flint and were straight-shafted specimens rounded at the base (Fig. 61, Q). Sandstone abraders were other tools that were probably essential in wood and bone working.

Ornamentation was fairly complex and consisted of imitation canine teeth of bear carved in bone (Fig. 61, R), shell pendants, copper earspools[15] and hematite and limonite paint.

Things suggesting ceremonial life and games were flint disk cones (Fig. 61, S), stone mammiform objects

12. Wedel, 1943, pp. 221–222; notes on field work of the University of Missouri in Saline, Cooper, and Carroll counties, Missouri.
13. Mack, 1942, p. 19.   14. Blake, 1942.

15. Copper earspools from a Hopewellian site in the collection of Fred Winfrey, De Witt, Missouri.

⟨Fig. 61, *T*⟩, stone balls (Fig. 61, *U*), a copper adz or ax (Fig. 61, *V*), clay platform pipes (Fig. 61, *W*), stone effigy platform pipes and clay figurines (Fig. 61, *X*).[16] One large ceremonial earthwork following the contour of a hilltop and enclosing several mounds was probably built by the Hopewellian people (Fig. 61, *Z*).

Mortuary customs have not been definitely established, but at least for the western part of the area it is suggested by Wedel that complicated structures were built for the deposition of the dead.[17] These burial structures consisted of well-built stone chambers, square or rectangular in ground-plan and with walled entranceways (Fig. 61, *Y*). Burial was made within the chamber; the entranceway was closed, and the whole structure was covered with earth to form a rounded mound. Bodies were placed in the chamber in a supine extended position or deposited as bundle burials or masses of bones. Cremated or partially cremated burials were common. Pottery vessels sometimes accompanied the dead.[18]

EARLY MISSISSIPPI AND LATE WOODLAND

After the influx of Hopewellian people was an interval of the cultural history of the Lower Missouri Valley during which there were movements of new people and ideas into the area but on a smaller scale. Mississippi people were well entrenched at the mouth of the Missouri River in late prehistoric times and some had succeeded in making establishments quite far up the Missouri River. It seems that these people were on the march, spreading new ideas and new ways of living wherever they penetrated. The Lower Missouri Valley appears to have been a frontier of the Mississippi people and was never thoroughly converted to the new trend of living. A culture closely related to the Cahokia Area was located on the western edge of the Lower Missouri Valley which indicates that migrations had penetrated that far west. Cultures of the same general period on the southern tributaries of the Missouri River were Woodland peoples with a smattering of Mississippi traits suggesting a spread of ideas rather than people.

THE STEED-KISKER FOCUS

A people of Mississippi affiliation were located in a small area at the western edge of the Lower Missouri Valley. The knowledge of this culture has been derived principally from the investigations of Dr. Waldo R. Wedel at the Steed-Kisker Site[19] and the work of J. M. Shippee.[20] The people living at the Steed-Kisker Site were to all appearances sedentary and dependent to a large extent on agriculture. Corn, pumpkins, sunflowers, and possibly beans were the most important plants cultivated. The people engaged in hunting, and deer was the main source of meat. The diet was further supplemented by the gathering of black walnuts, hickory nuts, hazelnuts, and pecans.

The village was made up of semi-subterranean houses of subrectangular ground plan. Each had an entrance passageway. The roof was supported by four large center posts and smaller posts set around the edges of the excavation. In the center was a fireplace scooped out of the floor to a depth approximating six inches (Fig. 62, *A*). Storage or refuse pits with straight walls were present in the village but were not associated directly with the houses.

Pottery vessels were the most abundant domestic utensils. These vessels were predominantly shell-tempered, but a small percentage of grit-tempered ware was manufactured. The color of the shell-tempered ware was predominantly gray. Outer surfaces were smoothed and rarely polished. Vessels varied considerably in shape. A characteristic vessel was a jar with hemispherical underbody and rounded to angular shoulder. Rims were low and either vertical or flaring. Incised designs decorated the flattish upper body of the jars between the lip and the shoulder (Fig. 62, *H*). Similar to these were jars with no decoration (Fig. 62, *G*). Both often had handles. Another typical shape was a straight-sided bowl with flattened base (Fig. 62, *B*). Bowls of this same general type, perhaps deeper, were sometimes decorated with effigy-head flanges (Fig. 62, *C*). A different bowl-type had a slightly convex bottom and the sides converged toward the top (Fig. 62, *D*). Also present were fragments decorated with incised lines and which were suggestive of "kiva jars" (Fig. 62, *E*). High-necked water bottles found in the vicinity provide still another characteristic vessel shape (Fig. 62, *F*). Miniatures of the larger vessels were also manufactured.

Although the manufacture of pottery vessels was one of the most important home industries, the tools of pottery-making are unknown.

Perforated mussel shells were hafted and used in the cultivation of food plants (Fig. 62, *K*). Mealing stones and mullers were utilized in the preparation of food.

Clothing may have been made of skins, and such things as end scrapers (Fig. 62, *L*) and cylindrical antler rubbing tools (Fig. 62, *J*) probably assisted in the preparation of skins. Deer ulna awls (Fig. 62, *I*) and flake knives were probably used in the manufacture of clothing.

---

16. Clay figurines from a Cooper County Hopewellian site in the collection of Walter M. Davis, Springfield, Missouri.

17. Wedel, 1943, p. 188.

18. Sources for the compilation of Hopewellian traits are: Wedel, 1943, pp. 15–61; 1938, pp. 99–106; 1940, pp. 307–309; Shippee, 1941, pp. 31–32; Chapman, 1947, pp. 78–86, 93–94.

19. Wedel, 1943, pp. 62–98.

20. Shippee, 1941, pp. 28–30.

Simple and expanding-base flint drill-points (Fig. 62, *M*) and sandstone abraders with two or more grooves (Fig. 62, *V*) were other tools utilized in home industries.

The bow and arrow was of greatest importance in hunting and warfare. Small triangular side-notched (Fig. 62, *T*) and unnotched flint points (Fig. 62, *U*) tipped the arrowshafts. Knives were of three types, beveled (Fig. 62, *Q*), oblong with rounded ends (Fig. 62, *R*) and almond shaped (Fig. 62, *S*). Antler tips hollowed at the larger end may have served as handles for knives. Axes of ground stone were fully grooved (Fig. 62, *W*).

Ornaments consisted of subcircular stone pendants (Fig. 62, *N*) and beads made of seashell (*Busycon perversum* Lea) from the Gulf of Mexico. An effigy pipe made of stone (Fig. 62, *P*) would denote some ceremonial life and a phalangeal deer bone drilled lengthwise might be a gaming object (Fig. 62, *O*).

Burial was in an orderly fashion in large cemeteries on the sloping part of hilltops. Graves were shallow and the remains were usually in an extended, supine position. However, a small percentage of flexed and bundle burials did occur. Grave goods were not abundant and were primarily pottery vessels or fragments which were in replica of utility jars found on the village. Sometimes knives or arrowheads accompanied the burials.[21]

THE HIGHLAND ASPECT

It is probable that a Woodland people occupied the southern tributaries of the Missouri River at approximately the same time that the Steed-Kisker Site was inhabited in the western portion of the Lower Missouri Valley. The rough country of the Ozark Highland perhaps isolated the Woodland peoples to a large extent or at least discouraged invasions by the Mississippi groups. Ideas and some trade items did infiltrate the area and exerted greatest force on those living close to the larger streams. The Indians living in the southern and central part of the area during this period appear to have had a fairly homogeneous culture, tentatively named the Highland Aspect.[22]

Hoebel indicates that the top level Woodland culture in Bone Cave (the Bone Cave Focus) may be equated with Late Woodland in Illinois.[23] The Bone Cave Focus can be included under the Highland Aspect. Hoebel also noted an earlier Woodland culture underlying the top level. Unfortunately, earlier investigations did not report stratification and as the Highland Aspect was derived primarily from early reports, it is possible that some of the traits included in the Highland Aspect are of earlier provenience.

The Highland Aspect peoples in the southern part of the Lower Missouri Valley were dependent largely upon game for food, and deer was the common food animal. Gathering also played an important role in the subsistence economy. There is little evidence of fishing and the only suggestion that the people were horticulturists is surmised from perforated shell hoes (Fig. 63, *C*), the use of mortars and pestles and reports of charred corn found by local amateurs. They lived in small groups and were apparently semi-sedentary. It is probable that their houses were flimsy structures for at every opportunity advantage was taken of natural shelter such as caves or rock shelters.

Pottery vessels were the most common household utensils. The type of pottery manufactured was predominantly grit-tempered (frequently crushed limestone) gray to brown in color and with cord marking on the outer surface (Fig. 63, *B*). Vessels were usually large and in shape were wide mouth jars with conoidal base. Other vessels were of globular body shape (Fig. 63, *A*). Rims were generally straight or slightly flaring. Sometimes a decoration of notching was present or adjacent to the lip surface (Fig 63, *A*). A type of less frequent occurrence varied only in the lack of cord marking, the exterior being smoothed. A small percentage of shell-tempered pottery was present in most instances and a number of these vessels were deep bowl forms.[24] Spoons were manufactured from mussel shells, the edges of which were ground smooth (Fig. 63, *D*). In the northern part of the Ozark highland area (Howard County) some of the shell spoons were notched.

The most time consuming home industries of the Highland Aspect peoples were the manufacture of weapons of the chase and of household utensils. Since hunting was a major activity, a large percentage of artifacts were weapons. Stemmed projectile points, knives (Fig. 63, *F*), small stemmed projectile points (Fig. 63, *H*) and full-grooved axes (Fig. 63, *K*) were commonly employed in hunting and perhaps warfare. There was a wide range of projectile point types in general use (Fig. 63, *E*). Small triangular projectile points with convex base made from thin flint flakes seem to indicate Mississippi influence (Fig. 63, *I*). Large, crude, roughly triangular flint blades of undetermined use occur in abundance in Highland Aspect sites (Fig. 63, *G*). Antler flaking tools (Fig. 63, *X*) were used in manufacturing the chipped stone artifacts. Perforated antlers (Fig. 63, *W*) may have assisted in the straightening of arrowshafts. Stone drills (Fig. 63, *L*) may have helped in shaping wooden and bone artifacts.

Clothing was possibly made of skins, and flint scrapers (Fig. 63, *J*) both oval and snub-nosed types as well as antler rubbing tools (Fig. 63, *V*) could have been used in its manufacture. Deer leg bone beamers

21. Wedel, 1943, pp. 62–98.   23. Hoebel, 1946, p. 154.
22. Chapman, n.d., pp. 79–86.

24. Fowke, 1922, p. 77; Ruwwe, 1936, p. 9; Fenenga, 1938.

were other tools useful in the preparation of skins, especially for dehairing (Fig. 63, *T*). Sewing was accomplished with the aid of split-bone awls and deer ulnae punches (Fig. 63, *Y*). If the perforated disks made of pottery sherds are considered spindle whorls (Fig. 63, *O*), there may have been some weaving by the Highland Aspect people. Long bone pins may also have been used in weaving (Fig. 63, *U*).

Ornaments worn by the Highland Aspect people were perforated disk shell beads, unperforated round or oval shell buttons, (Fig. 63, *N*) and small seashell beads (Fig. 63, *M*). Hematite was used extensively for red paint.

The only indication of ceremonial life was the use of clay elbow pipes and pipes carved of limestone (Fig. 63, *P*).

The dead were interred at random on the village sites or buried in the floor of caves. The usual mode of burial was in a fully flexed position (Fig. 63, *Z*), and no grave goods accompanied the body. Bundle burials and fully extended burials were sometimes practiced and in a number of instances the bones of the dead showed evidence of having been burned.[25]

People of this same general culture living nearer the center of the Lower Missouri Valley differed slightly in culture from those in the southern section. A higher percentage of the pottery vessels were shell-tempered and some of these were partially polished. Cord-marked, limestone-tempered pottery vessels were in greatest abundance but a goodly number of these showed evidences of smoothing over the cord marking. Amulets or gaming objects made of phalangeal deer bones drilled lengthwise (Fig. 63, *Q*) and disks of bone (Fig. 63, *R*) were other differences or additions to the culture. Also of note were typical Mississippi projectile points (Fig. 63, *S*) occurring commonly in the central part of the region, some of which may be Mississippi trade articles. One explanation of the differences in this area would be a closer relationship with Mississippi cultures and the absorption of Mississippi traits by Highland Aspect peoples.[26]

EUROPEAN CONTACT PERIOD—LATE MISSISSIPPI

The period of European contact with the Indians in the lower Missouri basin began perhaps as early as 1673 and ended with the removal of all Indians from Missouri in 1830. The two tribes native to the area, the Osage and Missouri, were probably in existence as separate entities as early as 1600 and so that date is used as a marker of the beginning of the period.

The early part of the period, 1600–1720, saw little contact with the Europeans. Marquette and Joliet

mentioned the area in 1673 but did not visit it.[27] It was not until 1719 that there were authenticated accounts of direct contact taking place, but there is little doubt that a few traders and trappers had some relations with the tribes before that time.[28] The only discernible effect on the Indians was the addition of European ornaments to their costume.

The middle part of the period, 1720–1800, brought about great change in the everyday life of the native tribes. Acculturation took place slowly at first and gradually increased in pace until at the turn of the century the material culture of the Indians was primarily European in character.

The last thirty years, 1800–1830, was a time of confusion and sorrow. Most of the Indians frequenting the area were on the march from the east. Such tribes as the Miami, Kickapoo, Shawnee, Delaware, Peoria, Pottawatomie, and Sauk and Fox were hardly more than transients who either settled for a short time or invaded the area on hunting and raiding parties. The Missouri were already gone and the Osage had been divided by the avarice of traders. At the close of the period all Indians were pushed farther west by the Americans crowding from the east.[29]

THE OSAGE

Perhaps the most important of the native historic Indians were the Osage who lived both in the Ozark Highland and in the western prairie. It is probable that their permanent villages in early times were in the rough country bordering the Osage and Gasconade rivers. Unfortunately, the heart of the Osage territory was sealed from archeological investigation by the building of Bagnell Dam in 1932. None of the sites were studied before coverage by waters of the Lake of the Ozarks. Therefore, it is from the non-European cultural objects found on the permanent Osage villages of late time, 1780–1830, located on the upper reaches of the Osage River that the knowledge of the earlier complexes is derived.[30]

According to legend, the Osage migrated to central Missouri from the lower Ohio valley.[31] If this legend is assumed to be true, the resemblance of Osage cultural traits to the Mississippi Pattern is easily explained because at the probable time of the Osage migration, the lower Ohio valley was occupied principally by Middle Mississippi peoples. However, characteristic features of the Middle Mississippi Phase among the Osage, as would be expected, are lacking. The Osage culture is dominantly Upper Mississippi Phase in character and is closely related to the Oneota Aspect. Comparative isolation from the old home

25. Fowke, 1922, pp. 22–100.
26. Field notes on excavation of Bushwhacker Cave (Hd:1), Howard County, 1939–1940, by H. C. Collier, C. H. Chapman, J. E. Wrench, and others.

27. Steck, 1928, p. 159 and Fig. 30.
28. Winsor, 1895, p. 112.
29. Chapman, 1946, pp. 15–40.
30. *Ibid.*, pp. 16–27.
31. Hodge, 1910, Pt. II, p. 156.

land, influence from late Woodland Pattern cultures in the Ozark Highland and close relations with the Upper Phase peoples to the north could be responsible for the resemblance of Osage cultural materials to the Oneota Aspect.

The archeological evidences of the Osage during the early part of their stay in the area come from southwest Missouri where M. R. Harrington found what he called the "Top Layer Culture."[32] Judging from Harrington's report this was a hunting, agricultural, gathering complex found in the top layers of caves or rock shelters. Pottery vessels were shell-tempered, of globular form and vessel rims were straight or recurved. The vessels had handles and were decorated with incised lines and punctations arranged alternately in areas filled with hatching and punctations. Other utensils and tools were sandstone arrowshaft smoothers, sandstone mortars and cupstones, flat circular hammer-grinders, the projecting-stem variety of the elbow pipe, small triangular projectile points, small flint end scrapers and beveled flint knives. Harrington[33] and later Griffin[34] pointed out that the "Top Layer Culture" was probably Osage in origin. Recent investigations on known Osage village sites seem to bear out their conclusions.[35]

The Osage, 1720–1800, appear to have been semi-sedentary, and hunting was the predominant way of obtaining a living. Four hunting expeditions for bison, deer, bear and beaver took place at set times throughout the year. Horses, and earlier, dogs were used in hunting. Agriculture was next in importance in Osage subsistence economy and small patches of maize, beans and pumpkins were cultivated. There was some gathering of wild plant foods but no fishing. The water chinkapin and the persimmon were the most important wild food plants gathered.

The villages of the Osage were usually located near some stream where there was an abundance of water and timber. The lodges were scattered about indiscriminately, but a circular, clear space near the center of the village was used for councils and dances. The permanent village was made up of long rectangular houses constructed of a framework of vertically arched poles interlaced horizontally with saplings. The house frame had a lattice-work appearance until it was covered with woven mats or skins. The houses were thirty to one-hundred feet long and fifteen to twenty feet wide (Fig. 64, Y). In the hunting camps the skin-covered tipi was used. Storage pits within the houses were bell-shaped and sometimes were converted into receptacles for refuse. Other small straight-sided pits were used for storing corn. Firepits were

placed near the center of the dwelling and consisted of circular areas scooped out of the ground. At a distance from the houses were straight-sided, rectangular trenches used for the disposal of refuse.

Domestic utensils and implements before the advent of European trade objects were made of bone, stone and clay. Clay was used most extensively. Pottery ware was shell-tempered, had a smooth finish, and varied in color from buff to gray. Perhaps the most common shape was a wide or medium-mouthed vessel with hemispherical or flattened globular body, but this is conjectural. Rims were either straight or recurved (Fig. 64, K and L). Strap handles were frequently applied to the jar, attaching from the rim to the body (Fig. 64, L). Occasionally, projecting lugs were also applied to vessel rims (Fig. 64, M). Decoration was moderately profuse on the body of vessels but was less frequent on the lip surface. Lip decoration consisted of notching (Fig. 64, L), finger impressions (Fig. 64, N) and punctations (Fig. 64, O). Incised or trailed lines adorned the body of the vessels (Fig. 64, K and L), and sometimes alternated with areas filled with punctations (Fig. 64, P). The motif of design was primarily straight-line hatching. A design element approximating a festoon was often applied (Fig. 64, Q). In early times the decorations were probably made with stone or bone tools, but metal implements were used extensively after 1780.

One of the important home industries of the Osage appears to have been the manufacture of weapons for warfare and hunting. Arrowpoints were made of flint with antler tip flaking tools (Fig. 64, D), and pitted sandstone hammerstones may have played a part in this process. Sandstone arrowshaft smoothers (Fig. 64, G) and rib arrowshaft straighteners (Fig. 64, C) may have been the most important tools associated with shaping arrowshafts.

Sandstone mortars were used in the preparation of food. These were often cupped depressions pecked in the bedrock outcropping on village sites. Pestles associated with the mortars were either round or oval. Smaller cups, perhaps used for a variety of purposes, were frequently cut in sandstone boulders and in the bedrock.

Clothing was made of skins, and small flint end scrapers may have been employed in its manufacture (Fig. 64, T). Large round or oval flint scrapers (Fig. 64, S) were no doubt used in the preparation of skins; sharpened animal leg bones (Fig. 64, A) may also have been utilized for this purpose especially during the latter part of the period. Bone awls, flat in cross-section, were probably employed in sewing.

Some weaving was practiced and perforated pottery disks may have served as spindle whorls (Fig. 64, R). Long bone needles (Fig. 64, B) were probably important in the weaving of flag mats, which were used

32. Harrington, M. R., 1924a, pp. 17–20.
33. Ibid., p. 20.
34. Griffin, J. B., 1937b, pp. 296–297.
35. Berry, Chapman, and Mack, 1944.

as items of household furniture and as coverings of the houses.

The bow and arrow were characteristic weapons of the chase and of war. Arrowpoints were small triangular pieces of chipped flint with concave or straight base (Fig. 64, W), and fairly large stemmed projectile points (Fig. 64, V). Beveled flint knives (Fig. 64, U) were also utilized in warfare and hunting.

Ornamentation of the body and of clothing was generally practiced. Hematite was employed in manufacturing red paint and bone paint-brushes (Fig. 64, H) were devised to apply the paint. Polished tubular bone beads (Fig. 64, J), and disks made of a variety of materials were some of the ornaments in common use. Pieces of bone or antler were sometimes artistically carved.

The pipe was one of the outstanding objects associated with the ceremonial life of the Osage. The pipe was used in councils of war, of peace and in ceremonies of adoption. Pipes were shaped from a variety of stones of which catlinite was the most prized. The projecting-stem variety of the elbow pipe was a common shape. An effigy was sometimes carved on pipe bowls (Fig. 64, I).

The dead were often interred in the ground in a supine, extended position. However, a more typical burial was that under rock cairns. In such instances, the body or bodies were placed on the surface of the ground and stones were heaped above them to form the cairn (Fig. 64, X).

With the steady influx of European trade materials, 1780–1830, the Osage culture appears to have been changed most in the home industries. Beginning sometime prior to 1800, the preparation of skins for purposes of trade became of greatest importance. The art of manufacturing pottery gradually disappeared due to the introduction of copper and iron trade kettles. Weapons for hunting and warfare were no longer manufactured at home on a large scale. Arrowheads were seldom made of flint for copper and iron were used in its stead. More gunflints than arrowpoints were made of native stone. Whetstones of sandstone became very numerous and cones of the same material (Fig. 64, E) were probably used in reworking and sharpening metal tools. Molds (Fig. 64, F) for casting lead and silver ornaments were carved from stone. Handles for knives and other hand tools were some of the most important objects made of bone during this time.

European trade articles were the style. A list of these will serve to indicate some of the changes brought about in the Osage after 1800. Iron and copper kettles, flintlock rifles, iron axes, iron knives, iron hoes, iron awls, copper hawk bells, coils of copper wire, copper buttons, copper and silver crucifixes, porcelain and glass beads, and clay pipes and pipe

stems were some of the more important objects. Artifacts manufactured from broken trade articles included iron and copper arrowpoints, chisels made from flattened rifle barrels, copper disks, cylindrical copper beads, and conical copper spangles.

Many of the Osage were converted to the Christian religion which, among other things, may have affected their mode of burial. The horse became an integral part of the culture and the buffalo a main source of food and clothing. The last thirty years of the period marked an almost complete acculturation of the Osage in the material and some non-material aspects of their culture.[36]

THE MISSOURI

The linguistic stock under which the Missouri Indians have been classed is the Chiwere Sioux.[37] It has been suggested that the Chiwere Sioux (Iowa, Oto, and Missouri along with the Winnebago) had a material culture which can be classed as the Oneota Aspect of the Upper Phase of the Mississippi Pattern.[38] Such a tie-up of historic tribes and an archeological culture would make possible many interesting studies of the people including early migrations. Migration legends are another clue to the past movements of the Indians of history. According to legend the Missouri tribe broke away from the main body of Chiwere Sioux and migrated downstream or from the north via the Grand River.[39] At any rate, early in the period, the tribe had established villages along the Missouri River near the mouth of Grand River in the central part of the Lower Missouri Valley. An Oneota Aspect village, the Utz Site in Saline County, Missouri, was apparently a Missouri Indian village site established prior to A. D. 1720 and perhaps lasting several years beyond that date. It is from this site that most of the knowledge of the Missouri is derived.[40]

The Missouri were hunters and agriculturists, with hunting playing a larger role in their lives than agriculture. The people gathered wild seeds, nuts, roots and berries and caught fish to supplement their diet. Bison, deer, wapiti, beaver and bear were the main game animals hunted, and the whole tribe periodically deserted their villages to go on these hunts. Maize, beans and squash were the important cultivated plants.

Missouri villages were large and though no definite evidences of their houses have been found, it is probable that they were similar in construction to those built by the Osage.

Many bell-shaped pits were excavated three to ten

36. Chapman, 1946, pp. 16–27, 45–52.
37. Hodge, 1907, Pt. I, p. 911.
38. Griffin, J. B., 1937a, pp. 180–181; 1943a, pp. 299–300.
39. Hodge, 1907, Pt. I, p. 911.
40. Berry and Chapman, 1942.

feet in depth for the purpose of food storage and for caching valuables when on hunting trips (Fig. 65, *H*). These pits were often converted into receptacles for refuse suggesting that the Missouri were tidy housekeepers.

The most common household utensils were receptacles for cooking and storage. These were made of clay tempered with crushed river mussel shells. The surface of the pottery vessels was smoothed but not polished or slipped. Vessels were medium to wide-mouthed with hemispherical or flattened-globular body and were generally of greater width than height. Some were round, others elliptical in vertical cross-section (Fig. 65, *A*). Rims were flared, recurved or were straight. Two to four opposed strap or loop handles frequently adorned the rim of the vessel. Sometimes projecting lugs were applied to the rim. Decoration was the rule and consisted of finger impressions, notching and punching on the lip surface and trailing, incising, punctations and finger impressions on the rim and body of the vessels. The motif of design consisted primarily of hatching and combinations of other decorative elements such as chevrons, scrolls, festoons, rows of finger impressions, vertical grooves and lines of punctations or areas filled with punctations. A deep bowl with no decoration was another type of vessel occasionally made. Damaged vessels were sometimes salvaged for further use by cutting away the ragged edges.

The industrial life of the community centered around the manufacture of utensils and implements associated with subsistence economy and warfare. Pottery-making was the largest home industry. Pottery-making tools such as trowels have not been noted on any Missouri Indian sites, but it is probable that smooth river pebbles were used as anvils. Gravers of flint and small sections of bone may be some of the tools used in decorating the vessels. Other household utensils were spoons or scrapers manufactured from mussel shells. Many of these artifacts were notched on the edges (Fig. 65, *L*).

The manufacture of implements associated with hunting and warfare was probably next in importance to making household utensils. Tools for arrowshaft manufacture included arrowshaft straighteners (Fig. 65, *S*) and paired boat-shaped sandstone arrowshaft smoothers (Fig. 65, *D*). Flint hammerstones and antler flaking tools (Fig. 65, *K*) were probably employed in flaking flint arrowpoints, spearpoints, knives, axes and scrapers. Sandstone abrading stones were used in shaping conical antler projectile points and other bone implements.

Flat mealing stones or metates and manos with one flat grinding surface (Fig. 65, *F*) were the means of grinding maize and perhaps other seeds. Notched rib-bones were probably musical rasps (Fig. 65, *M*).

Clothing was made of skins, and side scrapers, end scrapers (Fig. 65, *P*), polished celts and cylindrical antler rubbing tools (Fig. 65, *J*) were probably skin dressing tools. Split bone awls, deer ulnae punches (Fig. 65, *N*) and flat, eyed-needles (Fig. 65, *T*) may have assisted in the manufacture of clothing. That such items as garters and belts may possibly have been woven is indicated by such likely weaving tools as the pottery disk spindle whorl (Fig. 65, *W*) and long bone pins (Fig. 65, *I*).

Much time was spent by the Missouri in digging storage pits with bison scapulae tools (Fig. 65, *B*). Many of the digging tools were notched for hafting and may have served as agricultural implements as well.

Weapons used in hunting and warfare included small triangular flint projectile points with straight base (Fig. 65, *V*), notched crudely worked flint axes (Fig. 65, *C*), conical socketed antler projectile points (Fig. 65, *U*) and large beveled flint knives (Fig. 65, *O*).

Ornamentation was not profuse and consisted of polished tubular bone beads (Fig. 65, *R*) and small triangular stone pendants (Fig. 65, *Q*). Paint was perhaps the most important body decoration and was produced from hematite and limonite. Mortars made of limestone and oval or round pestles were used in the preparation of paint (Fig. 65, *E*).

Pipes were commonly employed in the ceremonial life of the Missouri. The disk-bowl or diminutive-Siouan pipe and a variety of the equal-armed elbow pipe were the types of common usage (Fig. 65, *Y*). Catlinite and siltstone were favorite stones for pipe manufacture. Double-pointed flint drills (Fig. 65, *X*) were probably used to drill the holes in pipes. Tablets of catlinite with engravings on them must also have been important in the ceremonial life of these Indians (Fig. 65, *Z*). Games were no doubt played but the only gaming objects were well-made bun-shaped stones somewhat similar to chunkey stones and possible counters for the cup-and-pin game made of phalangeal deer bones drilled lengthwise.

The dead were buried singly in shallow graves and were fully extended in a supine position (Fig. 65, *G*). A special plot of ground or cemetery was set aside on an abandoned part of the village. However, it appears that bodies were often interred at random within the village. Some grave offerings were included with burials, such as ornaments, utilitarian objects or pipes. Pottery was seldom placed with the dead and there is no evidence that a special mortuary ware was manufactured.

Perhaps after A.D. 1700, objects of European manufacture began to filter into the tribe. Copper kettles were of rare occurrence, but copper spangles, cylindrical copper beads, rings, bracelets, ear coils and blue glass beads became fairly common articles of ornamentation. The establishment of Bourgmont's Fort Orleans near the Missouri village in 1723 was the beginning of closer relations with the Europeans and of corresponding acculturation of the Missouri. Native arts declined and were no longer of great importance by the time the Missouri moved to Nebraska to join the Oto late in the eighteenth century.[41]

SEQUENCE OF CULTURES

The evidence for the sequence of cultures from history, stratification, intrusion, trade and association with extinct species of animals is not abundant. It has been necessary to compare the cultural complexes of the Lower Missouri Valley with those in areas where the sequence is more definitely established in order to suggest a relative chronology. The cultural detail of many of the complexes recognized in the Lower Missouri Valley is insufficient to make well rounded comparisons with cultures in other areas. Therefore, the sequence as it is set forth is a generalization and is subject to change.

The end of the sequence was established by using historical sources. According to history the Osage and Missouri tribes had control of the Lower Missouri Valley as early as A.D. 1673.[42] They were well established on the Osage and Missouri rivers at that time. A conservative estimate would place their arrival in the area at about A.D. 1600.

Both the Osage and the Missouri Indian cultural materials are classed tentatively as Oneota Aspect.[43] Griffin suggests that the Oneota Aspect derived a Mississippian complexion from the Middle Mississippi Phase. He also adds that the distinctiveness of the Oneota Aspect is probably as much a result of its geographical position in an area marginal to later Middle Mississippi as it is of its chronological position.[44] In a later article he indicates that the Oneota developed from a pre-existing Mississippi culture, the most likely predecessor being the Old Village-Aztalan complex.[45] If Griffin's hypothesis is true, it is logical to suppose that a culture of Middle Mississippi provenience would precede the Oneota Aspect if such a culture were in the area. The Steed-Kisker Focus, which is a marginal representation of Middle Mississippi, is therefore, the logical predecessor of the Oneota Aspect in the Lower Missouri basin. On the west still other evidence is at hand indicating that Steed-Kisker should be placed in the sequence before the Oneota Aspect. Wedel notes that the Steed-Kisker is contemporaneous with the Nebraska culture of the Plains area. Trade material of Middle Mississippi provenience found in Nebraska sites and exchange

of ideas between the Nebraska culture and Steed-Kisker determine the contemporaneity of the two. The Nebraska culture antedates the Oneota Aspect which seems to be pre-European contact in the Plains.[46]

From all evidence the Steed-Kisker Focus appears to be a late and dilute representation of Middle Mississippi culture. The migration westward possibly antedated the forming of the Oneota Aspect or the migration of Oneota people to the area. There is no evidence that the Steed-Kisker was the Middle Mississippi group that influenced the Oneota. However, the possibility remains that the focus because of its geographical position in relation to the spread of the Oneota Aspect and its probable nearness in chronology, may have been in part responsible for the Mississippi cast of the Oneota in the area.

Probably contemporaneous with the Steed-Kisker was a late Woodland culture, the Highland Aspect. The contemporaneity of these cultures is suggested by trade objects of Middle Mississippi character associated with the Highland Aspect and by the influence of the Mississippi on the Woodland culture artifacts. Only one instance has been noted of Mississippi trade material associated with the Highland Aspect in the Lower Missouri Valley. Projectile points and fragments of one or two pottery vessels of Mississippi type were found mixed with the Highland Aspect materials in Bushwhacker Cave, near the central part of the area.[47] Another instance of trade objects of Middle Mississippi manufacture was found associated with Highland Aspect artifacts southeast of the area in the Mississippi River drainage. Effigy flange pottery vessel fragments, notched triangular projectile points and biconcave discoidals were exotic trade objects noted in Boulder Cave.[48] Throughout the Highland Aspect the influence of Mississippi is suggested by roughly triangular projectile points with convex base and made of thin flat flint flakes; the use of shell for tempering pottery vessels; flaring rims and bowl-shaped vessels; and incised line decorations.

Hoebel in his Bone Cave report indicates that the latest Woodland culture living in the cave could be equated with Late Woodland in Illinois.[49] Adjacent to the area on the east, Adams found a Late Woodland culture the latest in the sequence and overlying a Middle Mississippi culture.[50] Bennett and Maxwell indicate that the Late Middle Mississippi and Late Woodland are contemporaneous in Illinois,[51] and

41. Chapman, 1946, pp. 27–40, 53–56.
42. Steck, 1928, p. 159.
43. Chapman, 1946, pp. 26, 39.
44. Griffin, J. B., 1943a, p. 302.
45. Griffin, J. B., 1946, p. 90.

46. Wedel, 1943, pp. 213–217.
47. Field notes on the excavation of Bushwhacker Cave (Hd:1), Howard County by H. C. Collier, C. H. Chapman, J. E. Wrench, and others, 1939–1940.
48. Notes on the excavation of Boulder Cave, Crawford County, by C. H. Chapman and Landis Parker, 1934–1935.
49. Hoebel, 1946, p. 154.
50. Adams, 1941.
51. Bennett and Maxwell, 1942, p. 50.

Cole and Deuel described a similar situation.[52] However, MacNeish notes that Maples Mills was earlier than Middle Mississippi in Fulton County, Illinois.[53] Judging from the above reports it seems that there was a Late Woodland Complex in much of Missouri and Illinois which was contemporaneous with Middle Mississippi cultures in some places and later or earlier in others. It is probable that the Highland Aspect in the Lower Missouri Valley was contemporaneous with the Steed-Kisker, a marginal Middle Mississippi culture.

The next earlier period, Middle Woodland (Hopewellian), was established in part by stratification. One instance of stratification was noted in test excavations on the "Old Fort" in Saline County. Oneota Aspect pottery fragments were in the top levels of the tests and Hopewellian type pottery sherds appeared in the lower levels of the tests.[54] Another evidence of stratification was noted on the Givens Site in Saline County, where it was found that a Hopewellian village seemingly overlapped an early Woodland site.[55] The tests were small and further investigation is needed before the stratification is fully verified. Stratification seems to indicate that the Hopewellian appeared in the area after the Early Woodland, Boone Focus, and before the Oneota Aspect. The Hopewellian is placed earlier than Steed-Kisker because Wedel notes a case of intrusive Middle Mississippi burials in a probable Hopewellian burial mound. Wedel also cites no evidence that Steed-Kisker and Hopewellian were contemporaneous and in fact indicates that the Hopewellian was the earlier of the two. He points out that such a sequence is in line with previous findings and interpretations in the Mississippi Valley.[56]

It is suggested that Hopewellian peoples migrated from the east and perhaps mixed to some extent with the Woodland peoples already established in the central and western part of Missouri. Wedel indicates that the more dilute form of Hopewell-like culture in Missouri may represent a secondary dispersion from the Illinois center. He also points out that the most likely migration route was via the Salt River in northern Missouri.[57] Negative evidence supporting Wedel's view is that the Missouri River Valley has yielded no evidence of the Hopewellian Phase in the area from the junction of the Lamine River to Creve Coeur Lake near the mouth of the Missouri. Griffin, on the basis of pottery similarities, also suggests that

the closest cultural connections of the Hopewellian cultures in this area are with the Illinois Valley center.[58] Indications are that many of the Woodland people in the portion of the area between the Lamine River and the eastern edge of the region were not affected by the migration of Hopewellian people or ideas and continued to develop along already established lines. Those not affected may later have developed into a Late Woodland culture similar to the Highland Aspect. Early Woodland, Boone Focus, probably preceded and was contemporaneous with the Hopewell during most of the Middle Woodland period. It is likely that in many instances the Early Woodland was changed considerably by Hopewellian influence.

Not enough is known to attempt to follow the fortunes of the Hopewellian peoples, but it does seem that these people were no longer in the Lower Missouri Valley at the time of the Middle Mississippi (Steed-Kisker) migrations. Stewart in the Platte and Clay County report says in effect that the Steed-Kisker and Hopewellian both from cultural and physical evidence are somewhat peripheral representations of widespread Mississippi Valley population movements.[59] Migration of Hopewellian and Middle Mississippi cultures to the Lower Missouri Valley is probably the best explanation of the peripheral representations of those cultures in the area.

An Early Woodland period represented by the Boone Focus, preceding Hopewellian seems to be indicated by one instance of stratification.[60] There is also evidence that the Boone Focus continued through the Middle Woodland period and was in some instances influenced by the Hopewellian peoples. Griffin indicates a somewhat similar situation in Illinois by suggesting that a number of the small hilltop mounds along the Illinois and Mississippi valleys above the mouth of the Ohio fall in the Early Woodland period. He adds that the Hopewellian intrudes and merges with a continuation of the burial complex producing one of the manifestations of Illinois Hopewell.[61] The exact time relations of specific manifestations of the Boone Focus have yet to be determined. Further investigation is necessary before full definition of the Early Woodland period and the early and late traits and complexes of the Boone Focus can be separated.

The mode of burial of great importance to the Boone Focus was very similar to that of the Hopewellian. Burial in mounds containing dry masonry chambers or vaults and the treatment of the bodies or bones of the dead were common to both people. The Hopewellian mortuary customs differed primarily in the greater elaboration of the burial chamber. Other

52. Cole and Deuel, 1937, p. 206.
53. MacNeish, 1944, p. 42.
54. Tests conducted on the "Old Fort" in Saline County, by Carl Chapman and John Mack for the University of Missouri, 1939.
55. Field notes on the excavation of the Givens Site (Sa:1), by Chapman and Mack, 1939.
56. Wedel, 1943, p. 216.
57. *Ibid.*, p. 220.

58. Griffin, J. B., 1946, p. 67.
59. Stewart, 1943, p. 264.
60. See fn. 55.
61. Griffin, J. B., 1946, p. 54.

traits held in common by the Hopewellian people and the Boone Focus were three-quarter grooved axes; punch and boss, stamping with a cord-wrapped stick and cord marking decorations on pottery vessels; the shape of pottery vessels and perhaps projectile types.

There are indications of other Early Woodland cultures in the Missouri Valley which are probably earlier than Boone Focus, but no such complexes have been defined fully enough to deserve mention. One exception is the Ralls Focus[62] which is closely related to the Boone and perhaps contemporaneous with it, but is centered outside the limits of the Lower Missouri Valley.

Assumed to have preceded the Early Woodland are nonceramic complexes of an Archaic period. The only nonceramic complex in the Lower Missouri Valley for which there is much evidence is Nebo Hill.[63] Another complex is perhaps indicated by variant Folsom points found intermittently throughout the area. Finally there are fairly well authenticated evidences of the association of stone projectile points with extinct species of mammals. The people contemporaneous with the extinct animals were probably the first men to discover the region and are assumed to be the most ancient cultural evidences in the Lower Missouri Valley.

In summation the suggested cultural sequence for the Lower Missouri Valley is as follows. The Archaic

62. Chapman, n.d., pp. 104–109.
63. Shippee, 1948.

was a long period beginning with early hunting peoples contemporaneous with the Mastodon and followed by a number of nonceramic cultures. Among the nonceramic peoples may have been a variant Folsom complex. Nebo Hill is the best known complex of the period.

Pottery was introduced and Woodland Pattern cultures were formed beginning the Early Woodland Period. The Boone Focus, a burial mound Woodland culture is assumed to be a late development of the Early Woodland and is the best known and most widespread in the area for the period. Following and contemporaneous with the Boone Focus was a Hopewellian invasion from the east. The invasion of the Hopewellian people marked the beginning of a Middle Woodland Period. During this period, the Boone Focus apparently changed and perhaps finally graded into a Late Woodland complex similar to the Highland Aspect of the Woodland Pattern. The Highland Aspect was influenced by the Mississippi Pattern and was probably contemporaneous with the Steed-Kisker Focus. The penetration of the area by the Steed-Kisker peoples after the disappearance of the Hopewellian people marked the beginning of the late prehistoric period. The last Indians to hold control of the Lower Missouri Valley for a fairly long period were the historic tribes, the Osage and Missouri Indians, both probably of the Oneota Aspect. Finally in 1830 all Indians were removed from the area, bringing to a close a long, colorful era in the history of the Lower Missouri Valley.

ARCHEOLOGY OF THE ILLINOIS VALLEY: 1950.
*By Donald E. Wray**

THE basin of the Illinois River system is a natural geographical unit which to a great extent determines the distribution of prehistoric culture patterns. Features which are significant for the various cultural adjustments are the flat bottom land, the bluffs and terraces of the main streams, the narrow sheltered valleys of the tributaries, and the expanses of prairie paralleling both sides of the basin.

Current archeological knowledge is confined principally to certain areas along the Illinois River, itself. This is unfortunate, because the marginal valleys and headwaters may contain subcultures and routes of overland contact with other regions. However, the prehistoric populations were concentrated in the Illinois Valley, and the significant cultural periods can undoubtedly be most clearly distinguished in these sites.

Data currently available are concentrated in three sections of the river basin: the Cahokia area and the lower part of the Illinois; the central region in Fulton and Peoria counties; and the northern area between La Salle and Joliet. The Cahokia area is reported in numerous books and articles, of which the more significant are those of Moorehead,[1] Kelly,[2] Titterington,[3] and Griffin and Morgan.[4] The central area is the location of the work by Cole and Deuel,[5] and is also covered, in part, by Griffin and Morgan[6] and McGregor,[7] as well as in many special papers by various authors. The northern area is discussed in the works of Langford,[8] Kelly and Cole,[9] J. B. Griffin,[10] J. W. Griffin,[11] and in current work under Orr and McGregor.

These three areas provide a basis for analysis and comparison between areas and local cultural units. The known differences make such a treatment culturally meaningful as well as pragmatic. Sufficient comparability in the horizons recognized throughout the valley permits the setting up of broad time periods to which localized cultures may be assigned. This temporal-cultural framework serves to correlate those foci which are related and also indicates gaps in our knowledge. It should be noted, however, that ignorance of the intervening territory may exaggerate the apparent distinctions which are described below. In this paper the central area has been used as the base point for the temporal sequence because of the relatively greater amount of data and closer refinement of cultural distinctions.

THE CENTRAL AREA

ARCHAIC PERIOD

The presence of a very early complex in the Illinois basin is possible, but there is still no definite evidence of such an occupation. The most suggestive discovery is reported from Tazewell County.[12] A shell heap with fire hearths was found on a river terrace far above the present valley floor. It had been covered by slides from a higher terrace and may be of considerable age. Unfortunately, no distinguishable artifacts were recovered.

At least one presumed pre-pottery cultural tradition appears in a series of campsites which are typically located in the small tributary valleys. These sites are limited in area and shallow, suggesting brief occupation or a mode of living which did not leave quantities of refuse. This complex is known only through surface collecting, and can be only tentatively defined, but the consistency among the sites lends validity to this complex.

The artifacts include certain types of large stemmed projectile points which do not appear in later horizons, and fully grooved axes which often retain an irregular pebble shape. Very large celts may occur in this or a related complex (Fig. 66). The occurrence of two Folsomoid points at one of these camps may or may not be significant. It should be noted that most of the projectiles have been ground smooth on the base, a trait which appears rather consistently in the Eastern Archaic.

This group of pre-pottery sites is designated as the

* University of Chicago, A.B. 1940; A.M. 1942; Ph.D. 1949; Department of Sociology and Institute of Labor and Industrial Relations, University of Illinois, 1947——. Chapter received December, 1947; revised January, 1951.

1. Moorehead, 1928.
2. Kelly, 1933.
3. Titterington, 1933; 1935; 1938; 1950.
4. Griffin and Morgan (eds.), 1941.
5. Cole and Deuel, 1937.
6. Griffin and Morgan (eds.), 1941; Griffin, J.B., 1941a.
7. McGregor, n.d.
8. Langford, 1927; 1928.   10. Griffin, J. B., 1943a; pp. 268–284.
9. Kelly and Cole, 1931.   11. Griffin, J. W., n.d.
12. Schoenbeck, 1939.

Speight Focus in Fulton and Peoria counties. Other related complexes are suggested by the occurrence of types of projectile which are similar to Speight points yet have distinctive features. These include notched and stemmed blades with serrated edges and possibly an association with the fully dressed three-quarter grooved axe.[13]

EARLY WOODLAND

Three foci can be placed in this period: the Red Ocher sites of Cole and Deuel, here referred to as the Roskamp Focus; the Black Sand Focus of Cole and Deuel; and the Morton Focus as it is redefined below. Each of these is known from a very few sites. All have pottery, although Roskamp and Black Sand ceramics are difficult to describe because of limited data.

Little can be added to the definition of Red Ocher given in Cole and Deuel.[14] It is known only as a burial complex characterized by flexed burials in low mounds and the use of ocher over the burial. The latter trait is too widespread to be meaningful and the purely local term Roskamp is suggested.

Only one projectile type is diagnostic. This is the thin laurel-leaf blade with small side notches, the "turkey tail" form. Sherds of crude pottery with heavy grit temper appear in the mounds. The surface areas have rough cord, fabric or net impression; lips have flat horizontal surfaces which may also be fabric impressed. Other traits are a variety of notched and plain blades, galena, rolled copper beads, copper awls, barrel shell beads, gorgets, small celts, and copper breastplates (Fig. 68).

The temporal position of Roskamp relative to other Early Woodland foci is still uncertain. It may be earlier, since the blade forms are closer to those of the Archaic, and the pottery seems unrelated to Black Sand and Morton or to any succeeding culture.

The Black Sand Focus is known from a very few village sites and a group of burials at Liverpool.[15] Sherds of so-called Black Sand type have been reported in early Hopewell, so their presence on a site does not necessarily mean a Black Sand occupation.[16] The Liverpool burials were beneath a Hopewell mound and consisted of semiflexed burials in pits with associated notched and stemmed projectile points, pitted hammerstones, and possibly the grooved axe. The pottery is grit tempered, usually cord-marked or smoothed-over cord-marked. Decoration is by incising over cord-marking (Black Sand Incised) and embossing. These techniques, in simple geometric patterns, seem to anticipate the later decorations of Morton and Hopewell (Fig. 69).

The term "Morton Focus," as used in this paper, refers to only part of the complex to which Cole and Deuel applied the term.[17] The Morton farm is the type site for this focus, for here the distinctive elements occur without being overlaid by later and related types. Burials were flexed interments in low mounds with few or no grave goods. Village deposits of Morton are more abundant than those of either Roskamp or Black Sand and occur on more sites. Morton sherds appear on many Hopewell sites and suggest cultural evolution or contact.

The artifact assemblage is uncertain, for no distinctive projectile types are known, nor is it certain whether celts or grooved axes are typical. Morton pottery has a greater variety of decorative techniques and motifs than does Black Sand. The typical Morton Incised design is a "herringbone" motif, formed by narrow incised lines (Fig. 70). This design occurs in a band along the rim, probably with cord marking of body areas. Less common motifs are lines or areas of solid or hollow punctates (Sisters Creek Punctated); broad trailed lines over cord marking; and rare use of plaint crescent stamps. Probable vessel form is a large pot with a constricting shoulder and vertical or slightly everted rim.

The Morton Focus represents an Early Woodland culture which is ceramically advanced and probably more numerous than the earlier foci. However, village sites are still quite small and provide no evidence of agriculture. It is likely that a number of similar hunting cultures can be assigned to this period in the future.

MIDDLE WOODLAND

EARLY HOPEWELL[18]

A technological and/or social revolution seems to mark the transition from Early Woodland to Middle Woodland; in the central area this revolution is expressed by the development of Early Hopewell. The number and size of villages increases markedly; the burial and mound complex is greatly elaborated; and the artifact assemblage is greatly enriched. These changes are of such magnitude that certain apparent continuities in local cultural traditions are apt to be forgotten.

Some of the more typical design motifs of Early Hopewell pottery are shown in Figure 71. This includes some of the variants which Cole and Deuel designated as "Type 2A."[19] The influence of Morton tradition is apparent in the use of the crescent stamp (Neteler Stamped), and the modified "herringbone" design. Other techniques include thumbnail impressions, usually arranged in vertical lines on the rim;

13. Speight Focus material is in the collections of W.D. Speight, E. Schoenbeck, and R. A. Wray of Peoria, Illinois. [The Schoenbeck collection is now in the Illinois State Museum, Ed.]

14. Cole and Deuel, 1937, p. 66.

15. *Ibid.*, pp. 136–145.

16. McNeish, 1946, personal communication.

17. Cole and Deuel, 1937, p. 223.

18. [This attempt to recognize significant divisions within Hopewell in Illinois is provocative rather than definitive.—Ed.]

19. Cole and Deuel, 1937, pp. 43–46.

straight dentate stamps applied diagonally to rim zone or combined with trailed lines to form decorative zones on body areas; embossing, usually in combination with dentate stamping; lip notching with a smooth or cord-wrapped stick; and a combination of hollow punctates and trailed lines on body areas.

An important and typical feature of rim decoration in Early Hopewell is the use of a plain band near the lip, separated from a decorated zone by a broad trailed line. This arrangement of plain and decorated bands is rare or absent in Middle and Late Hopewell. Vessels have constricting shoulders, a sharp division of rim from shoulder, and vertical or slightly everted rim sections. Two types of base are known: One is a flattened conoidal form; the second is a flat base with a sharp angle of juncture with the sides. The latter is similar to that of Adena pottery of the Ohio-Kentucky area.[20] Temper is almost always grit, although variations in paste, firing, and decoration indicate further temporal subdivisions. An effort at further refinement is being made in this area by McGregor.[21] This complex is dominant at Havana except in the latest period of the site when it is replaced by new varieties of stamped ware and by limestone tempered "classic Hopewell" pottery. This sequence is also found at the Weaver site.[22]

The Early Hopewell burial complex has been commonly referred to as the "log crypt" type of mound. It is characterized by a rather large tumulus in which extended flesh burials are placed at the floor level and enclosed in a timber structure or crypt. Mounds of this type are well known because of the elaborate grave furniture which they usually contain. While pottery is not commonly present in such mounds, the relationship between the log crypt and the Early Hopewell ceramic complex is indicated in Mound 6 of the Havana group where whole vessels of the early type are among the grave goods.

The "log crypt" mounds include the largest structures in the area; many are from eight to twelve feet high with base diameters of 100 feet or more. Certain structural features are diagnostic. The floor has a cover of clay, sand, or loess; and on this floor is placed a rectangular crypt of logs in which one or more flesh burials are placed. The crypt was often chinked with clay and rock, and sometimes was apparently held together by vertical posts set into the floor parallel to the walls. Stone walls and stone covers or pavements are frequently associated with the crypt. Clay crematory basins also occur in this type of mound, usually outside the crypt.

Associated structural features include: post holes parallel to the crypt walls; fiber mats on the crypt floor; and long bone skewers, or pins, stuck upright in the floor, presumably to hold the matting in place (Fig. 77, A).

The artifacts from Early Hopewell mounds include nearly all of those which can be found in this culture in any area. Copper seems to have been more commonly used in this period than at any other and occurs in the form of axes, breastplates, head plates, earspools, conjoined tubes or pan pipe and beads. Mica is found in round sheets and in flakes sprinkled over burials. Caches of flint disks occur at Havana and Baehr. Obsidian is found at Naples, Whitnah, and F455; it occurs as simple notched blades rather than the elaborate forms of Ohio and in very small quantities. The platform pipe, in both plain and effigy form, is common and many appear to be made of stone imported from Ohio. Cut human and animal jaws are common, as are cut, drilled, and inlaid bear teeth. Pearl beads are used profusely in necklaces, collars, and decorative bands on clothing. Shell is used in spherical and barrel beads and also as large containers made out of ocean species. Human figurines occur at the Baehr Site and in the southern area. Traits of sporadic occurrence are silver beads, copper flakes, stone ear spools, and reel gorgets of stone and copper.

This complex in mound assemblage occurs in the Havana Site,[23] the Liverpool mounds,[24] the Ogden-Fettie group,[25] certain mounds at Naples,[26] and at Baehr.[27]

Early Hopewell in central Illinois suggests a fusion of indigenous culture with a more advanced social group which had close ties with the Ohio Valley. Certainly, close trade relations and cultural bonds with Ohio are indicated along with broadened contacts with other regions. It must be emphasized that the assembly of traits which has here been called "Early Hopewell" probably can be broken down into two or more temporal subdivisions. Suggestions in this direction are the proportions in which effigy and plain platform pipes occur; the possibility that limestone tempered "classic" pottery may be present in the later phases of the early period; and the occurrence of transitional mound types such as the Dickison group near Peoria in which a sand floor and elaborate grave goods are combined with a central subfloor pit.[28]

Changes of this nature, as well as shifts in the ceramic complex, can undoubtedly be used to further define the cultural shifts which took place in Early Hopewell. It is probable that the distinction between "Early" and "Middle" Hopewell is purely arbitrary

20. Griffin, J. B., 1945d, p. 223.   22. Wray, n.d.a.
21. McGregor, n.d.

23. Griffin and Morgan (eds.), 1941, pp. 17–18.
24. Cole and Deuel, 1937, pp. 133–136.
25. Ibid., pp. 171–177.
26. Griffin and Morgan (eds.), 1941, pp. 29–35.
27. Griffin, J. B., 1941a.
28. Deuel, 1940.

and is a matter of convenience rather than an indication of sharp social and cultural differences.

MIDDLE HOPEWELL

Mounds of this period are smaller than those of Early Hopewell, although there is some overlapping. Typical mound construction is a tumulus over a central subfloor pit, which sometimes has a log cover and raised earth rim. Crypts, crematory basins, and matting, are not used; stone walls and pavements are very rare. Mound floors are frequently covered with sand or clay and the central pit is sometimes surrounded by four or five small fire pits. (Fig. 77, B).

Burials in the pit are extended flesh interments, singly or in groups. A new feature is the inclusion of bundle burials in the corners or sides of the pit, or on the mound floor around the pit. Offerings with the pit burials are less elaborate than those of Early Hopewell. Typical inclusions are: plain platform pipes, bear teeth, small numbers of pearl and shell beads, red ocher, cut animal jaws, and rectangular gorgets of stone and copper.

The pottery complex differs from that of Early Hopewell in several ways. Herring bone incising and diagonal dentate stamping disappear; their place is taken by several varieties of straight dentate stamp applied vertically to the rim, by Naples Ovoid stamping, and by combinations of cord-wrapped cylinder and paddle markings (Fig. 75). All of these types are grit tempered.

In this period the "classic Hopewell" pottery types occur in greatest abundance. These have limestone or clay tempering and are generally more finely executed and more ornate than the grit-tempered wares. These wares occur in very small proportions, and are probably imported from the lower Illinois Valley where limestone tempering is much more common.

Among the classic wares the following types can be distinguished: Hopewell Zone Incised, a lobed vessel with a bird design in incised lines; Hopewell Zone Stamped, with geometric or curvilinear areas with stamp roughened contrast; Montezuma Punctated, body and rim covered with semilunar finger punctates; Calhoun Red Filmed, a small bowl, sometimes with wide flattened red painted lip and plain body, also in limestone temper.

A great deal of attention has been given to the classic Hopewell pottery because of its artistic excellence and its esoteric appearance. While these wares are of great significance because of their widespread appearance, it must be emphasized that in central Illinois they rarely amount to as much as one per cent of the total ceramic complex. The high percentage of grit temper in the central area, in contrast to the much larger percentage of limestone tempering in the lower Illinois Valley, emphasizes the regional differences which exist and suggests that indigenous cultural traditions persisted in both areas to a greater extent than would be realized by an examination of the mound complex alone.

Middle Hopewell components appear on most sites of the early period, which implies that population was fairly constant. The increased quantities of classic pottery suggest continued trade relations over a wide area; on the other hand, the disappearance of esoteric materials from remote regions indicates a degree of cultural and social disruption and withdrawal.

Type sites for Middle Hopewell are Hummel,[29] the mounds at Clear Lake,[30] Whitnah,[31] and the Swords village.[32] Components are also present in the Clear Lake, Weaver, and Ogden-Fettie villages.

LATE HOPEWELL–WEAVER FOCUS

There is so little of classic Hopewell in this period that use of the term Hopewell can be challenged; however, important elements of continuity do exist, and the sporadic occurrence of Hopewellian traits seems to justify the classification of the Weaver Focus as representative of the closing period for Hopewell.[33]

The pottery complex is noticably different from that of Middle Hopewell, although some continuities can be seen. Use of the dentate stamp is abandoned, and the cord-wrapped cylinder impression and embossing become more frequent. Vessels are conoidal with constricting shoulders and vertical or inward sloping rims; one series is "cocoanut" shaped; plain shallow bowls are rare. Types which have been suggested for this period are: Clear Lake Stamped, with cord-wrapped stick impressions applied to the lip and rim; Weaver Plain, a smooth thin rim with lip notches or grooves and smooth body; Weaver Cord Marked, a body covered with widely spaced fine cord marks or a coarse cord-marked surface with lip notching or cylinder impression (Fig. 76).

Classic Hopewell pottery occurs rarely in the beginning of this period and then disappears entirely. The localization of ceramic types and the absence of foreign material indicate a sharp reduction of contact with other groups which correlates with a simplification of the burial complex. Mounds of the Weaver Focus are of two or three types. They are very small, often being only a foot high. The most common type has a central subfloor pit containing one or more semiflexed or bundle burials (Fig. 77, D);

---

29. Cole and Deuel, 1937, pp. 166–167.
30. *Ibid.*, pp. 183–185.
31. *Ibid.*, pp. 152–160.
32. Wray, n.d.*b*.
33. The editor is one of those who regarded Weaver as the beginning of Late Woodland. The evidence produced by Wray from burials indicates a transitional period from Classic Hopewell to Late Woodland.

similar burials are placed around the pit on the mound floor. Grave goods include sherds of the type wares, small notched projectile points, shell spoons and disk beads, rectangular and oval two hole gorgets of stone and copper, small celts, and occasional "Maples Mills" points.

A second mound construction consists of a large shallow rectangular pit containing flexed and bundle burials; stone slabs are set around the pit to enclose it and the earth in the pit indicates heavy firing. Another mound type contains a small central fire pit with no other features. These types may indicate temporal change within Weaver.

In this period there is increasing use of small stemmed and notched points and a reduced number of large blades. Broken stone gorgets appear more frequently in village refuse than at any other time. Globular vessels with vertical or flared rims and single cord impressions anticipate the types common in Maples Mills.

The type site for this focus is the Weaver Site (F229). Components occur at Clear Lake, Hummel, and Whitnah. As interpreted by McNeish[34] and Wray,[35] the Weaver Focus represents a period of cultural change which disrupts, although it does not completely sever, the tradition of Middle Hopewell. The decline of Hopewell is reflected in the pottery changes and the simplification of the mound complex. Although contact with other regions seems to decline, and cultural change is very evident, there is no indication of any great population decline.

MAPLE MILLS FOCUS

Maples Mills has no recognizable connection with Hopewell, although there is continuity from Weaver. Some refinements and additions can be made to the analysis of this culture as it is defined by Cole and Deuel.[36]

The ceramic types are very distinctive in the central Illinois area and probably indicate a new cultural impact or migration. Typical vessels are globular, with fairly sharp shoulder angles, fine cord marking on body areas, and sharply separated rims. Rims are vertical or slightly flared, and frequently castellated. Rim and lip decoration consist of single cord impressions in geometric designs, occasionally combined with hollow punctates. Two rim types can be described: Gooden Cord Impressed, a vertical rim with geometric cord design on the rim and cord lines on the inner side of the lip; Maples Mills Cord Impressed, a vertical rim, frequently plain, but with flattened lip with cord impressions.[37] Ceramic types which continue from the Weaver Focus include Weaver Plain with lip notching, Weaver Cord Marked, and

Clear Lake Stamped. The presence of these types in Maples Mills and transitional forms in Weaver indicate a relationship which is confirmed by the artifacts. Projectile forms are quite similar to those of Weaver, although the unnotched triangular point is more frequent. Single- and double-hole gorgets occur in Maples Mills, although less frequently than in Weaver.

The burial complex consists of cemeteries and low mounds containing flexed, bundle, and cremated burials. Grave goods include whole vessels of the type wares, shell beads, projectile points, bone awls, and gorgets. Some burials are placed in shallow pits surrounded by post holes. This may be a final simplified version of the pit and cover idea of earlier periods (Fig. 77, D).

The Maples Mills Focus seems to represent an intrusion of a Late Woodland group from the Northern part of the state. The ceramics indicate a close relationship to Lake Michigan culture. In this period the clear entrance of an alien group, plus the relatively small amount of village material, suggest a population decline and widespread migration. On the other hand, the relationships to Weaver indicate a local continuity and a degree of acculturation which serves to heighten local variations in tradition.

EARLY MISSISSIPPI—GARREN FOCUS

The presence in Maples Mills of triangular points and globular vessels suggests a possible Mississippian influence upon a Woodland tradition. It has been suggested that the Spoon River Focus might be derived from such a cultural blend. At the same time, the presence of Old Village forms in Spoon River raises the problem of the relationship of the latter to the Cahokia region and to early Middle Mississippian tradition. The Garren Site in Fulton County sheds light upon both of these problems.

A group of house sites and refuse pits at Garren indicate a contemporaneous occupation by Maples Mills and Old Village and a blending of the two groups. The resulting pottery types resemble those of Spoon River, although many diagnostic Spoon River elements are absent.[38] Houses are rectangular with wall trenches and possibly corner posts. The Old Village pottery includes Powell Plain, Ramey Incised, and Monks Mound Red. These wares are less well fired and more porous than those from Cahokia, although they are within the range present at that site. Artifacts include unnotched triangular points, split bone awls, deer ulna awls, and "thumbnail" scrapers.

With the Old Village material in these house sites are Maples Mills sherds, principally variants of Gooden Cord Impressed. Simplification of design and

34. McNeish, n.d.d.   36. Cole and Deuel, 1937, pp. 191–198.
35. Wray, n.d.a.   37. Schoenbeck, 1946.
                                    38. Wray, n.d.a.

changes in rim form indicate a partial acceptance of Mississippian pottery standards. Some vessels have Maples Mills cord decoration on shell-tempered paste; others use grit-tempered paste in globular forms with smooth everted rims which duplicate Old Village types. A small shallow bowl with a crude bird head rim effigy in grit-tempered paste is another example of ceramic acculturation. The only artifacts which are definitely Maples Mills are the typical heavy triangular points.

It is significant that the grit-tempered sherds which reflect Mississippian influence tend toward the rim shape and body treatment which are typical of Spoon River. The combination of globular body, round shoulder, and cord-marked surface from Maples Mills with the shell temper and everted rim of Old Village yields the characteristic Spoon River vessel form. The Garren Site suggests that Old Village became a distinctive culture type in the Cahokia region while Maples Mills and, perhaps, the Weaver Focus still existed in the central area. Old Village was then spread up the Illinois valley by actual settlement, at least as far as the central area and possibly farther north. As a result of this penetration the Spoon River and Fisher Foci grew up as local variations in late Mississippian times.

LATE MIDDLE MISSISSIPPI

EARLY SPOON RIVER

Early Spoon River is a distinctive culture complex based partly upon Old Village and Maples Mills, but with additions and elaborations. Villages appear in new locations, indicating some change in cultural tradition or economic adjustment. Sites are small and usually located on bluffs, in contrast to Hopewell and Late Woodland Village sites, most of which are in bottom lands. At the same time, the recurrent presence of Maples Mills sherds suggests either that the spread of Spoon River was rapid and based upon expansion from other regions, or that small groups retained the older culture and lived in larger Spoon River settlements for a time.

The ceramic complex is more variable in form and decorative technique than that of any preceding culture. Forms include the globular pot, Old Village angular shouldered pot, short-necked water bottle, shallow bowl, effigy head bowl, plate, and the beaker (Fig. 79). All have coarse shell tempering, with finer paste in some of the Old Village type pots and the finer bowls and beakers. Decorative techniques include cord marking of body areas, incised line motifs on plate rims, pot shoulders, and rims of bowls and beakers, effigy modeling on bowl rims and beaker handles, and red paint and slip on beakers.

Artifact types include: straight and convex sided celts; plain and side notched triangular points; ex-

panded base drills; diamond and leaf shaped knives; and thumbnail scrapers. Shell is used as hoes, scrapers, disk beads, rectangular strips, fish lures, spoons, *Busycon* pendants and bowls, and hollow disk gorgets. Bone and antler are used in awls, beamers, fish hooks, flakers, jinglers, bracelets, and hair rings. Copper appears rarely in the form of tubular beads and copper-covered wooden ear pendants in the form of bear teeth.

House construction is typically a square or rectangular building set in a shallow pit, with wall trenches and internal and external fire and trash pits. Double wall trenches are common and may indicate either rebuilding or reinforcing walls. Walls are constructed of poles set vertically in the trenches and covered with clay and thatch.

Burial mounds or cemeteries include extended single and multiple flesh burials, with occasional cremation and bundle burial. Grave goods are infrequent and consist of whole pottery, beads, pendants, projectile points, and knives.

MIDDLE SPOON RIVER

This period marks the introduction into the central area of the temple mound complex; these structures are small compared to those around the Cahokia region, since they rarely exceed ten feet in height and seventy feet in length. They are rectangular, and in three instances showed successive building stages and buildings destroyed by fire. Sites of this period are larger than those of Early Spoon River and cemetery mounds are larger with more profuse grave goods. The Kingston Lake Village and the Dickson Mound belong in this stage.

Ceramic types include those of the early period with certain noticable changes. The amount of cord marking decreases from 30 per cent to 15 per cent, with a corresponding increase in smooth body surface. Handles on pots are broader and are more frequently combined with lip nodes and effigy forms. Effigy heads on bowls are more frequent and more conventionalized, and effigy head water bottles occur sporadically. Two new vessel forms are: Dickson Lobed, a globular smooth-surfaced jar with deep lobing of the body; Williams Bottle, a long-necked globular water bottle with smooth or polished surface. The latter is often painted in black and brown on buff. Another new technique is incising through a red slip on beakers and bowls.

New stone artifact types include: the flaring bit celt, polished stone spud, large thin laurel leaf blades, crystal and calcite beads, and full figure human effigy pipes. Some of these traits may be linked with the ceremony of the temple mound complex.

Most utilitarian traits continue from the early period with the following shifts in emphasis. The multiple notched point, bell shaped hoe, and large shell bead are more common; heavy scrapers, shell scrapers, and shell fish lures disappear; unnotched points, oval hoes, elbow pipes, and straight celts become less frequent; bone hairpins, beaver tooth chisels, arrow shaft smoothers, cannelcoal discs, and shell gorgets become more common. The pottery trowel, lip scallops, and grooved pot handles also appear at this time.

LATE SPOON RIVER

In this period the temple mound complex and the Spoon River tradition continue with minor changes, but two new complexes enter the central area. One is a fully developed Oneota complex; the second, a combination of traits from the Cahokia region and, perhaps, more southern regions which includes elements of the Southern Cult. The number of sites in this period is much smaller than in Middle Spoon River. This, plus the introduction of foreign cultural traits, indicates a drastic population disturbance with a decline in the number of villages and a widespread movement of new tribal groups into the area.

Spoon River tradition is modified by the disappearance of polished plain ware and the angular shouldered vessel, and by increased use of cord marking. The burial complex is unchanged except for an increase in the amount of grave goods. New southern traits which appear at this time include: tripod water bottles in fine shell-tempered ware; effigy jars of the frog and *Busycon* shell; carved and painted vessels with the cross and circle motif; shell gorgets with engraved spider figures; polished stone maces and large long thin ceremonial blades. Oneota traits include: globular pots with line and punctate designs on shoulder areas and notching and punctates on the lip (Fig. 80); the paired arrowshaft smoother; the antler "wrench"; and large thumbnail scraper. The Oneota line and punctate technique is applied to non-Oneota vessel forms, such as the deep plate, sometimes in combination with motifs which seem part of the Southern Cult.[39]

Three distinct cultural traditions seem to mingle in this period. Spoon River continues from earlier times but with a very considerable decline in population. The entrance of new elements from the north and from the south (Fig. 81), suggests that Crable and other sites of this period represent a time of migration and tribal disruption such as occurred after 1650.[40]

HISTORIC PERIOD

The only reported village of the early historic period is that of the Peoria tribe of the Illinois Confederacy. This village was visited by Marquette in 1673 and was the locale of a mission, trading post, and a fort. After 1700 the Illinois occupation was sporadic and the region was dominated successively by the Fox, Kickapoo, and Pottawattomi. After 1750 a French village existed within the present city of Peoria and the American Fort Clark maintained Peoria as a trading center. A number of burials near the French settlement and around the site of Fort Clark contained iron tools and weapons, silver ornaments, and glass beads. These represent the late historic period. The only discovery which may be in the early contact span is a copper plate with an engraved "eagle-warrior" which was associated with blue glass beads.[41] Although scattered finds of European objects have been made, no historic site has yet been identified with any degree of certainty.

SOUTHERN ILLINOIS VALLEY AND CAHOKIA AREA

ARCHAIC

Caves and rock shelters may contain evidence of pre-pottery horizons; this is suggested by deep deposits in the lower levels of which occur large heavy projectile points and no sherds.[42] However, no focus in this period can, as yet, be defined.

Titterington has defined a complex which, to date, is nonpottery. The relative elaborateness of this focus and the presence of copper suggest that it may belong in Early Woodland rather than in Archaic. This focus is known from cemeteries and low mounds which contain extended burials covered with red ocher. Limestone slabs are placed over most of the interments. Burial goods include: stemmed and notched projectile points; round or square copper awls; copper celts; full and three-quartered grooved axes; bannerstones; hematite plummets; diorite balls; small shell gorgets; perforated pebbles; and tubular beads of rhyolite (Fig. 67).[43]

The Titterington Focus resembles the Speight Focus in some of the projectile types, although others are distinctive. Bannerstones do not occur in the central area; this may indicate an early regional differentiation.

EARLY WOODLAND

Sites which appear to be related to the Central Area Roskamp Focus are reported in St. Charles County, Missouri and St. Clair County, Illinois.[44] Traits include the "turkey tail" point, laurel leaf blade, copper and hematite plummets, shell spoons, shell gorgets, galena, and stone tube or pipe. These traits suggest affinities with the Roskamp Focus, but are included by Titterington in his nonpottery horizon. Definite placement of this complex can not be made at the present time.

39. Smith, H. G., 1951.   40. Wray and Smith, 1944.

41. Powell, J. W., 1894, p. xxxix.   43. Titterington, 1950.
42. Grimm, 1947.   44. Grindell, 1945.

MIDDLE WOODLAND

HOPEWELL

At the present time the developmental sequence of Hopewell can not be as clearly defined in the southern Illinois Valley as it is in the central area. Some indications of stratification appear at the Knight Site, where extended burials with poorly executed Hopewell objects and pottery are superimposed upon central subfloor pit burials which contain single and multiple extended burials with fairly elaborate grave goods. Associated with the pit burials are copper celts and earspools, drilled bear teeth, conch shell containers, plain and effigy pipes, and grit-tempered pottery. The superimposed burials include similar objects of poor design and grit and limestone-tempered pottery which is a degenerate and poorly executed variant of classic Hopewell.[45] Mounds from the Knight group contain the following grave goods: whole vessels of the Baehr type; flaked knives; galena; a diorite cone; mica; bear teeth; pearl beads; conch shell containers; copper axes; and bone skewers.[46] A group of painted pottery figurines from this group is comparable in style and execution to those from the Turner Site in Ohio. Similar figurines occur at the Baehr Site with a similar artifact assemblage.[47]

The southern Illinois Valley area undoubtedly will show a temporal sequence comparable to that of the central area. However, there appears to be a difference in the ceramic complex which is clearly seen in the higher percentage of limestone-tempered "classic" ware in the lower valley and in the apparent differences in mound construction traits.

LATE WOODLAND

JERSEY BLUFF FOCUS

The mounds which have been assigned to this focus may represent a temporal sequence which can be assigned to a number of local cultural stages.[48] The focus is known from mounds and villages along the bluffs of the lower Illinois River. Burials are single and multiple, predominantly flexed, with occasional extended bundle and cremation types. The use of stone slabs in covers, walls, and vaults along with fire pits and burned areas suggest affiliation with Hopewell and the Weaver Focus.

Ceramic types include grit-tempered smooth and cord-marked "cocoanut" vessels, with smooth or notched lips. Artifact types are: pottery elbow pipes, plummets, cut and perforated animal jaws, drilled animal teeth, disk, cylindrical, and marginella shell beads, spoons and hoes, sheet copper plaques, limestone discoidals, projecting stem pipes of stone or pottery, small celts and spuds.

The Jersey Bluff Focus appears to be a blend of Late Woodland and Mississippian traits. It is probably contemporaneous with both the Weaver and Maples Mills foci and will probably be divided into corresponding periods. It is likely that Mississippian influence appears earlier in this area than in the central part of the valley.

EARLY MISSISSIPPI

OLD VILLAGE FOCUS

The Cahokia area is the presumed origin point of the various foci which make up the Monks Mound Aspect; the latter unit includes all of the Middle Mississippian groups in the Illinois valley as well as those in Jo Daviess County and Aztalan, Wisconsin. The concentration of village, cemetery, and temple mound sites around Cahokia demonstrates the importance of this locality in prehistoric times. Unfortunately, there has been little systematic excavation in the crucial parts of this region.

Cahokia was apparently a cultural center before Old Village with a temple mound complex of southern origin which is pre-Middle Mississippian. This is combined with a utilitarian complex of Jersey Bluff type.[49] The first recognized horizon which can be called Middle Mississippi is a fairly elaborate and distinctive culture which appears to combine traits drawn from a number of different areas. The first suggestion of stratification is Kelly's division of an early "pure village site" and a late "Bean pot-duck effigy" culture.[50] Moorehead had recognized a similar division in the Ramey Mound.[51] Griffin defined these components as the Old Village Focus and the Trappist Focus.[52]

The Old Village Focus is defined primarily in terms of three pottery types: Powell Plain, a fine shell-tempered paste with smooth or polished surface, black, gray or brown, in Old Village angular shoulder jar form with rolled or everted rim; Ramey Incised, the same paste as Powell Plain and the same form but with a shoulder design of trailed chevrons or scrolls with occasional punctates; Monks Mound Red, fine limestone tempering, smooth or polished surface with a slip or wash of red, a bowl form with round constricting shoulder and plain lip, with lines of punctates paralleling the lip (Fig. 78). Sporadic pottery traits are loop handles, effigy heads on bowl rims, pottery trowel, vertical rim on bowl, and the beaker. Other traits of Old Village include split bone awls, stone spades, base and side notched points, and extended burials with few grave goods.

---

45. Titterington, personal communication.
46. McKern, Titterington, and Griffin, 1945.
47. Griffin, J. B., 1941a.   48. Titterington, 1942.

49. Griffin, J. B., personal communication.
50. Kelly, 1933, p. 103.
51. Moorehead, 1928, pp. 39, 48.
52. Griffin, J. B., 1941c; 1946, pp. 86–88; 1949.

Sites of this period occur in northern Illinois[53] and in southern Wisconsin.[54] Trade sherds appear in the early levels at the Kincaid Site in southern Illinois. This indicates a wide distribution of Old Village settlements, in the earliest horizon of Mississippian development in Illinois and adjacent states. It is probable that Old Village incorporated Woodland traits in each locality and was the base out of which later Mississippian variants were evolved.

LATE MISSISSIPPI—TRAPPIST FOCUS

This focus is the later period of occupation at the Cahokia Site, and accounts for most of the remains. The large temple mounds were built or enlarged at this time and the great cemeteries and extensive village deposits suggest an increased population which remained on the spot for a considerable period of time.

Vessel forms and decorative techniques are more varied, with jars, shallow and deep bowls, water bottles, beakers, and plates being typical. Decoration consists of cord marking, trailing, incising, slipping and painting, and effigy modeling. Artifact types include multiple notched triangular points, the flaring bit stone celt, flared and notched hoes, and profuse shell beads and pendants.[55]

The Trappist Focus develops out of Old Village and the distinction between the two is an arbitrary one. The heavy occupation at this time was apparently disrupted before the Southern Cult entered the region. Engraved eagle and spider gorgets found near Collinsville indicate sporadic occupation in very late Mississippian times.[56] This suggests a depopulation of large sites at the end of the Trappist period parallel to that which took place in the central area.

ONEOTA

A small Oneota site is reported from Pere Marquette State Park.[57] It is close to the area of the Orr Focus, and probably belongs to it. Indications of trade contact with an Oneota group are also reported near the Cahokia Site.[58] Nothing comparable to the mixture found at Crable is known from the Cahokia region.

HISTORIC PERIOD

The Tamaroa and Cahokia tribes of the Illinois Confederacy were in the Cahokia area in early historic times. After 1700, most Illinois tribes moved to Fort Chartres and were apparently heavily accul-

turated by this time. The only suggestion of early trade contact is a site near Lebanon, Illinois where a few white materials occur with late Trappist and an excellent example of the Crable High Rim plate.[59] An intrusive pit in the Powell Mound contained silver crosses, buckles, spangles, and sheet silver bracelets, one of which bears the letters, "—treal"; this is probably British material of 1765–1812.[60]

NORTHERN ILLINOIS VALLEY

ARCHAIC AND EARLY WOODLAND

Recent excavations on Starved Rock indicate the presence of a Late Archaic focus which is succeeded by an Early Woodland component.[61] The presence of large notched blades, grooved axes, and heavy grit-tempered pottery on a number of sites suggests a fairly extensive occupation in these periods although no complex can be, as yet, defined. The flexed pit burials at the Fisher Site may belong in this horizon.

MIDDLE WOODLAND

Hopewell villages and mounds are present, although apparently not so numerous as in the central and southern areas. The only defined local variant is the Goodall Focus, reported by Quimby.[62] The pottery types of Goodall seem to cover the span of Hopewell described in the central Illinois area and evolve into a Late Woodland culture which is equivalent to the Weaver Focus. Goodall is probably a result of culture diffusion up the Illinois valley and is, therefore, in a marginal position. It is also possible that Goodall may have incorporated traits which derived from overland trade routes and localized cultures.[63]

A large Hopewell site on the Fox River contains pottery types which seem identical with those of Early and Late Hopewell in the central area.[64] The Utica and Adler mound groups in the Illinois valley contain central sub-floor pits with extended flexed and bundle burials. Ceramic types include Hopewell Zoned, Hopewell Incised, and Montezuma Punctated, with local equivalents of plain dentate stamped and Woodland Plain. Grave goods include whole pottery vessels, ovoid side notched projectiles, tang base drills, bunts, celts, cut and perforated bear teeth, single-hole oval gorgets, square copper awls, and plain platform pipes. The small size and internal features of these mounds suggest that they are Middle Hopewell. The presence of classic Hopewell wares substantiates this placement.[65]

53. Bennett, 1945, pp. 127–155.
54. Barrett, 1933.
55. Titterington, 1938.
56. Huth, Ray, personal communication.
57. Rinaldo, n.d.
58. Perino, 1947, and personal communication.

59. Grimm, Robert, personal communication to editor.
60. University of Illinois Collections.
61. Orr, Kenneth, personal communication.
62. Quimby, 1941b.
63. Quimby, 1943.   64. Steward, J. F., 1903.
65. Griffin and Morgan (eds.), 1941, pp. 44–47.

The "Muskegon Stage" of the Goodall Focus parallels the Weaver Focus in the decline of dentate stamp and classic wares, and the increased use of plain and cord impressed types.

LATE WOODLAND

The Corbin Site near LaSalle has grit-tempered pottery, fine cord-marked bodies, and rims with single cord impressed motifs.[66] This suggests the Maples Mills Focus of the central area and Lake Michigan affiliation. It is probable that Late Woodland groups in this area were relatively unaffected by Mississippian culture and existed into historic times. Late Woodland sherds with European trade goods occur at the Fisher Site, Starved Rock, and Forest Park. These may represent an unbroken occupation or temporary migration in late times. These sherds are so few in number and uncertain in type that classification has, so far, been impossible.

EARLY MISSISSIPPI

This period is not represented by any known site, but its presence, or influence, can be hypothecated because of the Mississippian elements which occur in the Fisher Focus.

LATE MISSISSIPPI—FISHER FOCUS

The Fisher Focus diverges considerably from contemporaneous foci in the central and lower Illinois Valley. Taxonomically, it is Upper Mississippi, although it is different from the Oneota or Fort Ancient aspects. The Fisher Site has been reported by Langford,[67] J. B. Griffin,[68] Deuel,[69] and J. W. Griffin.[70] The stratigraphy indicates successive occupation by Early Woodland, Hopewell, three periods of the Fisher Focus, and one or two historic groups. The three stages of the Fisher Focus probably equate with the three periods of Spoon River.

Early Fisher has rectangular houses in shallow pits, with wall trenches, central fire pits, and four internal roof supports. Pottery is shell-tempered, light brown or gray, and elaborately decorated in a technique which Langford called "antler point." Decoration consists of cord marking, broad trailed lines and punctates, lip notching and crimping, with festoons and chevrons the common motifs. This type of decoration gives a vessel a heavy ornate appearance which makes the ware quite distinctive. J. W. Griffin names two ceramic types: Fisher Trailed, with globular body and trailed and punctate decorations; Fisher Noded, globular vessels with lobing or nodes along the shoulder, often with plain surface. Both of these

types are shell-tempered (Figs. 82 and 83). Stone artifacts are large and small triangular projectiles, small celts and hammerstones. Antler and bone are used in projectile points, bored tines, gouges, fish hooks, cut animal jaws, bone pins and awls, and harpoons. Shell is used for spoons, pendants, scrapers, hoes and beads. Copper is used in sheet covered wooden earspools, celts and rolled beads. These may be a survival from Hopewell or a result of Mississippian influence.

The harpoons occur in Early and Middle Fisher and represent two or three types. This trait sets Fisher apart from any other known culture in Illinois and suggests an, as yet, unknown influence on Early Fisher.

Middle Fisher seems to be the time of heaviest occupation of the site. House types are unchanged and burials tend to be concentrated in low cemetery mounds instead of being scattered through the village area. The pottery complex is changed by the increasing use of grit temper and simplification of decoration which produces a ware closer to Woodland pottery than to Mississippian. Stone artifacts include unnotched triangular points, flaring bit celts, muller, abrading stone, discoidal, equal arm pipe, and rectangular tablets associated with antler cylinders. Other artifacts include: antler and bone projectile points, cylinders, gouges, hoes or rakes, jinglers, beamers, fishhooks, bone tubes, button labrets, and polished racoon penis bones. Shell artifacts are spoons, pendants, scrapers, fish hooks, beads, hoes, and drilled rectangles. Copper is used in celts, pins, tubes, earspools, and beads.

Late Fisher is not as completely known as the other periods, but can be defined in terms of an almost complete use of grit temper and simple decoration with trailed chevrons or festoons (Fig. 83). This type (Langford Plain) is dominant and the only form which can be defined with certainty. Langford Plain is the dominant ware at Plum Island and is very important at Kaskaskia. A number of sites are known which can be assigned to some stage of the Fisher Focus. These include the Kankakee Refuse Heap,[71] Gentleman's Farm Site,[72] Forest Park,[73] Plum Island,[74] and Kaskaskia.[75]

The Fisher Focus is limited to the northern Illinois Valley and represents a cultural development which is quite divergent from that of the central and lower areas. There is some evidence of Fisher materials in the western sites of the Fort Ancient Aspect and in late sites of Indiana and Michigan.[76] Sherds of beakers and polished black ware, as well as the presence of

66. Ceramic Repository, University of Michigan.
67. Langford, 1919; 1927; 1928; 1930.
68. Griffin, J. B., 1943a.
69. Deuel, 1940.
70. Griffin, J. W., n.d.

71. Langford, 1919.
72. Austin, L., personal communication.
73. Morgan, 1933.
74. Kelly, and Cole, 1931.
75. McGregor, J. C., personal communication.
76. Griffin, J. B., 1943a, p. 282.

the discoidal, beamer, and antler cylinder indicate contact with the Spoon River Focus. Taxonomically the Fisher Focus is Upper Mississippian, probably a separate unit, although it is contemporaneous with Middle Mississippi in the central and lower areas of Illinois.[77]

ONEOTA

The Huber, or Blue Island Site near Chicago is Oneota, probably of the Orr or Winnebago foci. Pottery is shell-tempered, smooth surfaced, with decoration on shoulder areas of straight trailed lines, vertical or slanted; punctates in areas or with trailed lines; lip crimping, grooving, or notching. Handles are wide with incised line and punctate decoration. Artifacts include beamers, celts, needles, shell spoons, bone musical rasp, and grooved biconical club head. This site indicates at least a temporary occupation of the northern area by a group with true Oneota culture.[78]

HISTORIC PERIOD

The northern area seems to have been the population center in the historic period since most recorded settlements are in this region and sites with contact materials are more numerous than in the central and southern sections. The Forest Park Site contained Fisher Focus burials with iron axes and knives, copper and silver buckles, copper rings and bracelets, crosses, and kettles.[79] Fisher Site burials contained similar trade objects including a brass sun dial, or compass, and wooden objects.[80] Contact sites are reported in the Fox River Valley,[81] the Arrowsmith Battlefield,[82] and on the Vermilion River.[83]

The Kaskaskia village of the Illinois tribe is the best documented site in the Illinois Valley. After its destruction by the Iroquois in 1680, the French established a mission, trading post, and Fort Saint Louis on Starved Rock. For a decade or more, Kaskaskia was a rallying point for many tribal groups, and the site was occupied for short periods by a number of tribes after 1700.

The village of Kaskaskia contains a major component termed Heally, which is Late Fisher Focus.[84] The extent to which this component contains trade objects is uncertain, although small quantities of such material may be present. A second component, the Danner Focus is a culture foreign to the Illinois Valley. Pottery is shell-tempered, with smooth or cord marked globular body, with rare grooved paddle stamping. Rims are flaring with notched, crimped, or overlapped lip. Strap handles decorated with short

trailed lines and notched edges, sometimes in a tapering hourglass form are common, and conical applique nodes below the lip also occur. This component is similar to the Madisonville Focus in Ohio, and probably represents the Shawnee who came to the site after 1682. There seems to be more trade material with this component than with the Fisher material which may indicate either more trade contact or a temporal difference. Trade objects with the Danner Component include blue glass seed beads, spherical beads and tubes; copper and brass tube beads and jinglers; coiled brass wire ear or hair ornaments; glass bottles; and iron knife and ax blades.

There are possibly other historic components related to Oneota and Late Woodland. With the exception of the Madisonville-Shawnee material, tribal identification of these components is not possible. The only evidence of groups from the central area consists of two sherds of Crable Incised plates; this is puzzling, since numbers of people from the central and lower Illinois valley are known to have been at Kaskaskia.

Artifact types at Kaskaskia which belong to non-Fisher components are serrated triangular points, fingernail scrapers, perforated flat bone awls, polished bone tubes, scapula gouge, and buffalo scapula hoe. Refuse pits containing these artifacts and Danner pottery are bell shaped and resemble the pits of Oneota rather than those of Spoon River.

Buffalo bones are common at Kaskaskia and distinguish it from prehistoric sites in all three geographic areas. This change in faunal remains suggests either a change in hunting techniques or a climatic shift accompanied by large scale migration of buffalo to the eastern prairie.[85] It is possible that a migration of the buffalo was the causal factor in the entry of Oneota cultural groups to the northern and central Illinois Valley in protohistoric times.

SUMMARY AND INTERPRETATIONS

The presence of Archaic occupation throughout the Illinois Valley is now well established. Evidence from the central area suggests further subdivisions which may represent a considerable span of time. These early foci seem related to a general pre-pottery horizon which extended over the entire eastern United States. The resemblance of certain projectile types to those of Early Woodland suggests a cultural continuity; this is also indicated by the relatively numerous sites in the Late Archaic. The Titterington Focus may be such a transitional culture. It contains elements such as the bannerstone and copper implements which do not occur in the central area, yet it does not have pottery. It is probably an extension into the Illinois Valley of a southern complex.

77. *Ibid.*, p. 279; Griffin, J. W., n.d.
78. Griffin, J. B., 1943a, pp. 284–286; Morgan, 1933.
79. Morgan, 1933.   82. Faye, 1935.
80. Langford, 1927.   83. Brigham, 1943.
81. Steward, J. F., 1903.   84. Orr and McGregor, n.d.
85. Griffin and Wray, 1946.

There may be in the Cahokia region an Early Woodland Focus equivalent to Roskamp in the central area.

The earliest complexes contain little evidence of trade relationships, although the similarity of projectile types indicates some kind of contact with adjacent groups. The Roskamp Focus and its correlates contain materials gathered from a wide area and the cultural forms are standardized to a greater degree than is the case in Archaic foci.

The transition from Archaic to Early Woodland can be distinguished arbitrarily by the presence or absence of pottery. This definition would place Roskamp and, perhaps, a part of the Titterington Focus in Woodland. It is likely that both foci are transitional and that no cultural revolution divides these horizons. The Black Sand Focus and the Morton Focus have definite pottery assemblages and appear more commonly in villages than do earlier groups. It seems that these and related foci indicate a slowly increasing population with a gradual elaboration of ceramic tradition.

The Middle Woodland period is marked by the introduction to the Illinois Valley of Hopewell tradition. A revolution in culture, a changed economic base, and increased population are indicated. This change may represent the introduction of agriculture accompanied by an elaborate ritual life. Evidence of agriculture is rare in Early Hopewell; however, the digging stick would leave no archeological clue. It is difficult to see how large permanent villages and "public works" could be sustained by a hunting economy.

Early Hopewell appears in its ceremonial form as a previously established complex with many affinities with the Ohio Valley. Illinois Hopewell seems to result from the expansion of a ceremonial complex, which originated in Ohio, into the Illinois and Mississippi valleys where it incorporated localized Woodland traditions. Such an interpretation seems to be validated by the relatively standardized forms of mound construction and grave goods, and the locally varied utilitarian pottery and village patterns. Early Illinois Hopewell resembles in pottery type and mound construction the pre-Hopewellian cultures of the Ohio and lower Mississippi valleys.

In both the central and the lower Illinois Valley the number of mounds and villages suggests a lengthy duration for Hopewell. The subdivisions of this culture in each area have been indicated. In both areas classic Hopewell is succeeded by an attenuated version which may equally well be called Late Woodland. General similarities in mound construction and ceramics remain, but local variations are more noticeable. In the central area the Weaver Focus merges into Maples Mills; in the southern valley the Jersey Bluff Focus is submerged by Mississippian culture; in the northern area the Goodall Focus tends toward Late Woodland.

The ceramic types which are "classic Hopewell" are more common in the lower Illinois Valley than in the central and northern areas and have been used to separate an "early" from a "middle" Hopewell. In the central region they occur rarely at the close of Early Hopewell, are most frequent in Middle Hopewell, and disappear early in the Weaver Focus. This distribution of pottery types is correlated, in part, with the use of exotic materials and objects, and suggests that Hopewell in Illinois can be interpreted as a sudden initial expansion into a new area, which is followed by a classic period, and closes with a gradual but complete breakdown of trade relations and social contacts. The decline of social organization does not seem to be a result of population reduction, for the sites of the Weaver Focus seem to be as common and intensive as those of the classic period.

There may, however, have been a very drastic population change in the closing period of Weaver Focus and during Maples Mills. The introduction of new culture traits and the relatively slight deposits of Maples Mills indicate a population reduction and rapid acculturation.

Early Mississippi, represented by the Old Village Complex, appears at Cahokia and is a blending of southern Mississippi traits with various local traditions. Old Village culture expanded from the Cahokia region and provided the base out of which developed late Middle and Upper Mississippian foci. It may be that Old Village represents a period of relatively uniform culture comparable to that of Early Hopewell. Old Village influences which moved up the Illinois Valley were the origin, when combined with Woodland traits, of the Spoon River and Fisher foci; in the Mississippi and Rock River valleys they resulted in the Jo Daviess and Aztalan foci.

The Spoon River Focus illustrates the development which grew out of a blend of Old Village and Maples Mills. The Garren Site shows the fusion of these traditions into an early prototype of Spoon River. Later stages show the standardization of this blend into classic Spoon River with an increase in population; Middle Spoon River marks the introduction of the temple mound complex and greater conformity with the Cahokia region; Late Spoon River includes the introduction and incorporation of Oneota and Lower Mississippi elements at a time of sharp population decline.

The Fisher Focus is a development which parallels Spoon River, and is derived from a mixture of Old Village, local Woodland, and probably Lake Michigan influences. This focus, because of its marginal position, diverges progressively from the evolution which takes place in the central and lower Illinois Valley and becomes more Woodland than Mississippian.

In Late Mississippian times, in the closing periods of the Spoon River and Fisher foci, there seems to be a radical decline in population which is accompanied by the appearance of alien cultures and a tendency toward villages in which two, or more, different cultures cohabited. These sites are shallow and are apparently of relatively short duration. Occasional trade materials would indicate that the sites of this type are protohistoric even though they are not listed in European documents.

Historic tribal groups were present in all three areas but their remains are unidentified except in the northern area. In this region it is probable that the Kaskaskia tribe can be related to the Late Fisher Focus at the Kaskaskia site; the Danner component of Kaskaskia represents the Shawnee. The absence of trade material in the numerous Mississippian sites of the central and lower valley areas indicates a population decline and abandonment of most of the large villages before the contact period. The occurrence of distinctive pottery such as Crable Incised at Madisonville, Kaskaskia, and Crable demonstrates the protohistoric dating of these sites; at Madisonville and Kaskaskia, and possibly at Crable, this pottery is associated with European material.

Later tribal migrations which are recorded in historic documents were of relatively short duration and involved groups which were not indigenous to the Illinois Valley. Scattered remains of the later period have been reported, but it is not possible at present to describe the cultures of these tribes. Archeological deposits which are of significant depth and quantity end in the Illinois Valley around 1700.

The archeology of the Illinois Valley has been clarified in the past decade; but a number of problems can be stated on the basis of current knowledge. The detailed analysis and temporal sequence of the Archaic period requires considerable attention. The exact position of the various early Woodland foci remains to be determined. The origin of the Hopewellian ceremonial complex is still uncertain, and the developmental sequences are still open to question. The relationship of Old Village to earlier horizons is not clear, and the impact of Old Village in the northern Illinois Valley area awaits further investigation. Special attention should be given to the period in which there is an apparent population decline with immigration, which in Illinois occurs between 1650 and 1700. In this time span a number of tribes entered the region and the problem of archeological identification with recorded political groups becomes more meaningful. The difficulty of such an effort is shown in the attempts to relate the various components at Starved Rock and Kaskaskia to historical social units.

HOPEWELLIAN DRESS IN ILLINOIS. *By Thorne Deuel*[*]

IN THE pages following I shall try to give a picture of how Hopewellian men and women looked, what clothing they wore, and the kind of jewelry with which they adorned themselves. Archeologists are prone to leave the impression that theirs is an objective science and their obligation to patrons or people generally ends when they relate what they actually find in field work. They are liable to call all pointed bone objects, awls, the majority of chipped flakes without stems or notching, scrapers, and to speak of finely polished stone pieces of unknown use as ceremonials. This is a fairly simple procedure but at that they *have interpreted,* often on the basis of general form only without any other evidence. In reality, of course, "awls" signify not only pointed instruments but those employed for "piercing small holes, as in leather or wood"; scrapers are tools for scraping, and ceremonials signify beautifully executed products used in ceremonies of more or less solemn import.

Having been for a number of years connected with a Museum that continually endeavors to present and explain to everyday people rather than specialists various natural happenings in the world including the doings of men, I feel that archeologists have oversimplified their problem and for one reason or another taken the easiest way out, a well-beaten path which leads through unchanging barren flats with no very definite destination in sight. It seems to me they have missed the exciting, dangerous and uncharted routes through ancient villages, hunting camps, and burial grounds where these ancient inhabitants again go about their homely duties of wigwam and maize plot and bury their dead in tombs with appropriate ceremonies. Who is better equipped to make such a study and supervise the reconstruction of such scenes (whether in words or in sculpture) than the archeologist?

Furthermore as Museum workers, we have been impressed by the apparent lack of appreciation by the average visitor of the usual archeological exhibit, even when tastefully displayed with adequate explanatory labels and an illustrative background. To improve this situation the staff of the Illinois State Museum has felt compelled to develop dioramas to show the prehistoric inhabitants of the state as they looked and in their proper settings. To begin, the help of specialists in the anatomy of the American Indian, has been enlisted to reconstruct the life-like heads of several "average" Indians from different cultural horizons in Illinois. Available literature and field notes have been carefully studied together with much of the pertinent original material with a view to determining the fashions of Hopewellian dress.

I should like to express here my appreciation to Professors W. M. Krogman and Georg K. Neumann for their assistance in the reconstruction of Indian heads from skulls, to Bartlett M. Frost for the photographs of his excellent reproductions of Hopewellians, to Frances Ridgely for her drawings of the fashion plates of these ancient men and women, to Dr. P. F. Titterington and Mr. Willie Smith for the loan of original statuettes and to many others who have cheerfully helped the study in various ways.

The originals of the reconstructions on Figure 84 were made in wax by B. M. Frost. Reconstructions on Figure 85 through 91 were made by Frances S. Ridgely as was Figure 93. The making of all reconstructions was carefully supervised by the writer.

In the course of the work it was noted that certain ornaments were found in some mounds, different objects of the same class in others, while still other sites lacked any definite evidence that the class was known at all. For example, the stud-type copper earspool occurs in some Hopewellian sites, in others ear disks only appear and in still others, earspools of all kinds seem to be lacking. Although this and other variations seem to indicate changes in Hopewellian customs over the years, the evidence is scanty and unconvincing. Consequently no attempt is made here to group styles of dress in chronological order.

The results are presented with no thought that the study of Hopewellian dress is complete nor should the conclusions reached in many instances be considered other than tentative and subject to revision as new evidence warrants.

RECONSTRUCTION

THE WELL-DRESSED HOPEWELLIAN MAN AND WHAT HE WORE[1]

If a warrior, the face of the Hopewellian man is painted white as are the shaven parts of his head

[*] United States Military Academy, West Point, B.S., 1912; University of Chicago, Ph.D., 1935. Director, Illinois State Museum, 1938——. Chapter received December, 1947.

1. Sites mentioned in this article are in Illinois and classified as Hopewellian unless expressly stated to the contrary.

above the ears, behind the temples and the narrow transverse strip separating the pompadour-like forelock from the hair on the back of the head. The hair is drawn into a central, flat-topped knot at the back (see Figs. 84, *A*, and 93, *A*).

Above the breechcloth, his body is painted to the base of the neck a lustreless purplish-red color with the shoulders encircled by broad white bands bounded by narrow black lines and crossed ladder-like by lines in black and possibly other colors such as yellow (orange) or red. An epaulet-like broad white band similarly decorated extends from the circular band at the neck to the middle of the upper arm.

His breechcloth is worn in a roll with the part passing between his legs looped over the portion around his waist at the back. Breechcloths are adorned with batik designs in color or decorated with pearls, ground shell beads, shells or bears' teeth (see Figs. 87, 89, and 91).

In his ears are copper earspools from each of which is suspended a black bear's tooth set with a pearl, or a short string of pearls. Around his neck he wears a string of pearls and a bear's tooth necklace, or a three strand string of metallic beads, from one strand of which is suspended a trifle below the waistline a pair of the cut and shaped halves of a wolf or human lower jaw, possibly the sign of his prowess in the hunt or of success in a hand-to-hand engagement with a valiant enemy (see Figs. 85–87).

A CHIEF'S DRESS

He may be a civil chief, chief of a clan, or head of a secret society who wears a head plate of wood or leather on which are mounted the antlers of a deer. About his neck is a glittering necklace of silver beads from which a cut human maxillary smoothly ground on the upper surface, is suspended a little below the waistline. A poncho-like sleeveless deerskin jacket ornamented with several hundred pearls covers him from the throat nearly to the knee (see Fig. 86).

HOPEWELLIAN WOMEN OF FASHION

Women engaged in household duties especially if they have young children, apparently do not wear much of the usual jewelry or arrange their hair as they do on more formal occasions. The hair is usually parted on the crown and drawn back smoothly over the head, leaving the ear ornaments of burnished copper partly exposed to view. In back the hair is sometimes drawn together into a broad flat rope (or braid) enclosed in netting and allowed to fall to the waistline, or more rarely is twisted up into a heavy plait, doubled back on itself and held together in this position to the back of the head by means of tape or a cord (see Figs. 84, 88, and 93).

Copper "spools" or ear ornaments of some kind seem to be worn generally by the women though the remains in graves do not always bear this out. It is possible that ornaments made of perishable materials such as wood, are popular.

Necklaces of cut shell beads are worn by women as are the cut halves of jaws in the same manner as by men.

Armbands, of leather or cloth decorated with pearl or other beads seem to be generally worn on the upper arms near the shoulders, and on the wrists. Women while engaged in their household or horticultural duties may lay these aside.

The beltless wrap-around skirt of red cloth is the customary dress for women. Dresses of black seem to be worn on important ceremonial occasions. On occasion the red skirt is decorated by three equally spaced broad white vertical stripes of white bordered by heavy black lines. Dresses are frequently decorated with shell or pearl beads sewn on near their upper and lower margins in interrupted double lines.

The women wear ankle-length moccasins probably of leather that are notched at the sides. They are ornamented along the upper borders, at the instep and around the margin of the sole with pearl or shell beads. Black is the favorite color.

THE DANCING WOMAN[2]

The face of the dancer is devoid of paint except for a crescent-shaped patch of white beneath the left eye (see Figs. 84, *B*, and 93, *B*).

Her hair lacks the part in the middle of the crown but is arranged with two protruding knots on top of the head, one inclined forward over the middle of the forehead, the other at the back and left. The knots are dome-shaped with the rounded tops painted red, and the bases wrapped with white leather or cloth bands. The hair is drawn together in the back in the customary rope or braid that falls slightly below the waistline.

The hair on the right side of the head is shaven or closely cropped and above this, appears an arched roll of hair, painted red. The customary earspools are worn, the right one black, the other red.[3]

On the upper arms and wrists, she wears the characteristic bands decorated with shell beads. About her throat is a three-strand necklace of massive flattened-globular beads (cut from the columnella of the *Busycon* shell) graduated in size with the largest at the center front.

A dull purplish belt ornamented with a batik-like

---

2. See Fig. 84, *B*. The largest statuette from the Knight Mound has been interpreted by Mr. Bartlett M. Frost, Dioramist, to be a dancing woman, possibly one taking part in a ceremony. The head fragment in the Willie Smith collection may be from a similar figure.

3. The left earspool showed traces of red when examined by the writer and seemed to have been painted in that color originally.

design in orange-yellow encircles the dancer at the waist and supports the usual wrap-around skirt. This garment is of black cloth decorated with interrupted double-lines of pearl or shell beads sewed on near its top and lower margins. On her feet are the usual high-topped woman's footwear decorated with shell beads. The left moccasin is red, the right is black.

In each hand she carries a wing or fan of turkey feathers and on the back of her skirt just below the waistline is the spread tail of the same bird[4] (see Fig. 93, E and F).

THE EVIDENCE

The evidence that supports the foregoing interpretation and reconstructions is presented below. Much of it was previously given in a paper that appeared in the spring of 1948.[5]

The original sources from which the data were derived are as follows:

The stature, facial appearance, head and body form, sex, age, and health status are based on observation and measurement of long bones and reconstruction of the soft parts on skulls.

The articles of jewelry or of personal adornment as they were worn by their owners when living are determined by their placement with skeletons in graves.

The statuettes and the study of reports on them yield fashions of hair dress, body painting, personal ornaments and clothing styles.

Clothing worn by the dead at burial is often indicated by a pattern arrangement of shell, copper and pearl beads, bears' teeth, cut human and animal jaws with which they were adorned.

Fragments of cords and textiles, including feather cloth, are occasionally preserved by the salts of copper or silver that formed on ornaments or tools in contact with them.

Impressions preserved in clay sometimes yield the type of weave.

Designs in color are occasionally retained by being transferred to clay soil when the textile embedded in it decays.

Where definite evidence is lacking information and illustrations of other prehistoric or modern Indians have been used to fill the gaps. An example of this is the interpretation that the objects carried and worn by the Knight dancing woman are fans and feather bustle.

DRESS AND APPEARANCE OF HOPEWELLIAN MAN

The three male statuettes utilized in the reconstructions given above are the Knight figure (Calhoun County) and the two Baehr ones (Brown County), one of which is headless and neither of which are available for study at this time.

None of the statuettes observed is very revealing as to physical appearance of the Hopewellians since the figures are stylized and the parts in disproportion especially the head and lower legs. They *do*, however, give one the idea that the Hopewellians had short and relatively heavy bodies and that "slant" eyes were considered a mark of beauty. Skeletal remains confirm the general indication of body type.[6]

On the Knight statuette[7] is based the description of hair arrangement, and the painting of face, trunk, and arms (see Fig. 84, A). Except for this and the Turner (Ohio) figures, no other Hopewellian statuette reported to date presents details of hair arrangement for men. Remains of the dead, of course, rarely yield evidence of these customs.

Three of the Turner figures from Ohio according to Willoughby's description and reconstruction wore a single knot above the middle of the forehead. These knots end in rounded (not flat) surfaces similar to those on the Knight female dancing figure and on the Honey Creek head from Oklahoma. A fourth Turner male, sitting cross-legged "represents a warrior with sides of the head shaved, leaving a ridge of short hair extending across the crown from front to back, a method of arrangement characteristic of the warriors of the Pawnee, Sauc and Fox, and various other tribes of the northern half of the United States."[8]

Unfortunately the two Baehr statuettes are known today only from drawings published first by Dr. J. F. Snyder several years ago[9] and recently reproduced by Griffin.[10] The first of these figures has lost its head and the second is conventionalized and yields little information. Covering the crown and back of the head of the last is a hood or head plate that in front ends in a projecting point surmounted by a rosette high over the middle of the forehead. This might from the drawing represent a hairknot inclined toward the front. This strongly resembles in simplified form the headdress and knot worn by a standing Ohio male figurine.[11]

HOPEWELLIAN JEWELRY CHIEFLY FROM THE MALE VIEWPOINT

Ear ornaments were worn by men and women alike in Illinois judging by the Knight, Willie Smith and the second Baehr statuettes.[12] That the disk-like

---

4. These feather objects, of course, are pure interpretations based on historic Western Plains Indian customs. One thing, however, seems certain—the close relationship if not identity of the bustle on this female and that on the back of the human figure represented on the tubular pipe from the Adena mound in Ohio (See Fig. 92, D).

5. Deuel, 1948.

6. Neumann, G. K., personal communication.

7. Of the six Knight figurines, one represents a man, four are women, and "the sixth . . . is extremely simple and devoid of detail, and is not painted." Discovered in Calhoun County by W. L. Wadlow of Versailles, all statuettes are now in the collection of Dr. P. F. Titterington of St. Louis. A comprehensive description of them appears in McKern, Titterington, and Griffin, 1945.

8. Willoughby and Hooton, 1922, p. 73. From the drawing, Pl. 21f, the "ridge of short hair" may represent a copper headplate.

9. Snyder, 1898.

10. Griffin, J. B., 1941a, pp. 179, 180, 183–184.

11. Willoughby and Hooton, 1922, Pl. 21g. For a complete description of the Turner statuettes see *ibid.*, pp. 71–74. Of these figures, three men wear ear ornaments, while the other two and the three women wear none.

12. Griffin, J. B., 1941a, pp. 179, 180, 183–184.

projections at the side of the head of the Knight and Smith figures are ornaments and not ears is plainly evident. The ears themselves are incised in the clay just above and in contact with the projecting disks. In the Baehr figurine, the ornament appears at the very base of the lobe and seems to be single and circular in shape. This may be a simple disk, or a pulley-type "earring" as Dr. Snyder interpreted it.[13]

In some "stud" or "sleeve button" earspools, the front disk is larger than the rear one; in others they are of equal size. Disks may be flattened, curved, or corrugated. The average diameter of a disk probably lies in the neighborhood of two inches. The Hopewellian earspool is fashioned from sheet copper and is relatively heavy. In fastening them in place, the hollow connecting tube (already attached to one disk) may have been passed through the hole in the wearer's ear and riveted to the second disk.

In Ohio, copper earspools have been found in large numbers, a few "plated" with silver or iron, and even "small ear ornaments" of meteoric iron alone.[14] Similar jewelry of copper overlaid with native silver and meteoric iron were recovered at the Turner site.[15]

Earspools were worn on occasion as ornaments elsewhere than in ears. Titterington reports finding them in the Gibson mound (Calhoun County) near the wrists of the dead.[16] Moorehead notes similar cases in Ohio[17] (see Fig. 89).

Two pairs of the pulley-type ornaments were described by Snyder[18] that were found in the Baehr mounds (Brown County) near the ear region of two skeletons and interpreted by him to be ear ornaments. If so used it would appear that they had been suspended from a cord rather than inserted in the ear itself. They are circular with a central axial hole and a wide groove on the circumference as if for a belt or cord. Perforations usually eight or nine in number radiate from the axial hole to the outer groove like the spokes of a wheel.

Beads or pearls have been found in positions indicating they were held to the rim of the "pulley" by a cord passing through the radial holes.[19] This same cord could have been employed to hold the ornament to ear, headdress, or clothing. Pulley-type ornaments of stone, bone, pottery and wood have been reported from Illinois.

The ear ornaments indicated on a pottery figure from the Baehr Site (Brown County), as reported by Snyder and as shown in his drawing may represent the pulley type.[20] Similar ornaments have been recovered in Calhoun[21] and Pulaski[22] counties in Illinois, in a tomb and in a crematory basin respectively.

Rings or "pulleys" similar to those from Illinois have been found in Ohio: of terra cotta or pottery by Putnam at the Turner Site; of stone at the Hopewell site by Squier and Davis.[23]

Necklaces and Pendants

Necklaces of bears' teeth, other teeth, and of pearl, shell, bone and metal beads occur frequently in graves. The metal beads are chiefly of native copper but meteoric iron and silver are sometimes used. The shell beads are either marine or fresh water shells slightly modified to permit stringing, or ground and bored beads cut from the columellae of the Busycon or the thick walls of large "Unios." Sometimes necklaces consist of a single type of bead and sometimes of two or more kinds varying in size, material and shape as for example a string of ground shell discoidal beads alternating with globular and olive-shaped meteoric iron ones from Havana, Illinois.

Necklaces seem to have been worn by men and women alike. Possibly there was a difference in materials or bead forms worn by the sexes but it is not apparent from the evidence available (see Figs. 85 and 88).

At the Baehr Site, at Rome in Peoria County, and at Havana strings of beads were deposited alongside bundle and other burials. The string of shell and iron beads with bundle burial 10, Mound 6 (near Havana in Mason County)[24] and the beads and perforated sharks' teeth in a large marine shell beside skeleton No. 1 in Baehr Mound 2 are cases in point.[25]

Bear-Tooth Necklaces

Bears' teeth were favored as necklaces among Illinois Hopewellians, presumably for men only.[26] Three cases occur where bears' teeth were used alone and three where they were associated with beads at the neck. Six other cases of the use of bears' teeth were noted. At times bears' teeth may have been used in combination with shell beads (see Figs. 89–91).

A set of ten (10) replicas of grizzly bear teeth made of sheet copper came from a rock-walled tomb in

13. *Ibid.*, p. 183.
14. Moorehead, 1922, p. 28.
15. Willoughby and Hooton, 1922 p. 49.
16. Titterington, letter and diagram. Excavation by Mr. L. M. Gibson and son of Alton, Illinois.
17. Moorehead, 1922, p. 121.
18. Griffin, J. B., 1941a, pp. 179–180.
19. Titterington, personal communication.

20. Griffin, J. B., 1941a, pp. 179, 180, 183.
21. Titterington, personal communication.
22. Recovered for the Illinois State Museum by J. C. McGregor in 1947 from a Hopewell Mound in process of destruction during road operations near Olmsted, Illinois.
23. Willoughby and Hooton, 1922, pp. 60–61.
24. McGregor, n.d. The numbers designating mounds in Fulton County are those used by the Illinois State Museum and the University of Chicago in their surveys. Sites in other counties are numbered as in the publications cited.
25. Griffin, J. B., 1941a, p. 176.
26. As far as sex and associations were determinable from the reports, only men wore bear-tooth necklaces.

Liverpool Mound 79.[27] A rough average of their dimensions are: length 3¾, maximum width 1⅛, and thickness 1/32 inches. Some of them having holes in the "root end" may have been hung around the neck. Others may have been sewed to garments as noted below.

METALLIC NECKLACES

Seven instances of metallic beads used in strings and presumably for necklaces (definitely "around the neck" in three cases) are reported from Illinois. Of these one necklace is silver ("with a bit of the fabric string still visible"), five are copper (one with two-strand twisted "hempen" twine still in place) and one is a combination of meteoric iron and ground shell.[28] These necklaces are from central Illinois, two each from Fulton, Mason, and Brown counties and one from Peoria County. Copper beads, association unknown, are reported from Jo Daviess County.[29]

PEARL NECKLACES

Necklaces made of pearls and/or slugs from freshwater shellfish were a popular type of jewelry among both men and women. Occasionally the pearl necklaces were associated with necklaces of other material or combined with other elements in the same string. Five instances of pearl necklaces, and two of pearls in association with cut shell beads, and three other cases of pearls perforated for stringing or for sewing to garments are reported from Illinois.

NECKLACES OF SHELL BEADS

Altogether nineteen (19) references to shell necklaces in Illinois Hopewellian graves have been located in the literature. Of these, eleven (11) are definitely of cut shell (three of these strings were in combination with bear teeth or associated with bear-teeth necklaces), one (1) was of *Marginella* shells, another (1) of mixed marine varieties slightly modified for stringing, the remaining six (6) probably of ground shell only. This is by far the commonest type of necklace and is used by men and women alike.

Differences in shape of bead or species used exclusively by either sex were not determinable in this study. Ground shell beads occur in the following shapes: button or disk, discoidal (thick disk), barrel-shaped, cylindrical, olive-shaped (or elongated globular) and massive flattened globular. Shells of marine species, which were slightly modified to make a hole to permit stringing, include the *Marginella, Campeloma, Goniobasis,* and *Helisoma.*

A necklace of bone beads, probably tubular, 80 in

number, was found with an extended skeleton in the Baehr mound.

NECKLACES OF SMALL MAMMAL TEETH

1. Necklace of squirrel incisors over 200 in number, bored through roots, with a second necklace of olive or barrel-shaped shell beads and a third of copper beads, occurred with a skeleton in the Hemphill (Hemplull) mound (Brown County).[30]
2. Canine teeth of the raccoon, 179 in number, perforated at the base lay in the neck region of a skeleton of a middle-aged person in Baehr Mound 2 (Brown County).[31]

PENDANTS

Mandibles, generally human or wolf (dog?), cut in halves, the chin portion missing, partly ground, polished and bored for suspension, were the most popular type of pendant used by the Hopewellians, men and women alike.[32] Occasionally a fragment of a single half is found; sometimes two or more mandibles occur with a skeleton. More rarely the maxillary, cut from the rest of the skull and perforated, is worn by itself or along with the modified but undivided mandible, and in three instances at least, an unmodified mandible was recovered, e.g., one with the remains of a woman in Whitnah Mound 60, Fulton County.[33] Usually the mandible halves seem to have been suspended somewhat below waist level from a necklace. It is possible that some were attached to the breechcloth (where necklaces are lacking), to hang in the same position. The uncut jaws may have been simply laid near or upon the body of the dead. In a photograph of the log tomb burial in Dickison Mound 478 near Rome, the strands of ground shell beads on Burial 3, are seen to extend down to the pelvic region where they are in contact with the cut halves of a wolf mandible (see Figs. 85–88, 91).

In this study, reports of nineteen cases were noted, totalling three (3) uncut and seventeen (17) cut halves of human mandibles, one (1) cut human mandible undivided at symphasis, six (6) cut maxillaries, eight (8) cut halves of wolf or dog mandibles, and four (4) cut halves of bear mandibles accompanying nineteen or more burials. In one instance, the report is indefinite as to whether the four cut human maxillaries and the undivided cut mandible were associated with more than one burial in the tomb. The number of bear jaws found in the Hopewellian conicals of the Portage group[34] was taken here as two although a greater number seems to be indicated.

27. Cole and Deuel, 1937, p. 144.
28. Grogan, 1948. Also letters dated January 22, 1946, from R. M. Grogan and M. M. Leighton, Illinois Geological Survey, and from E. P. Henderson, U. S. National Musuem, dated April 29, 1946.
29. Bennett, 1945, Pl. 9, Fig. *i.*

30. Griffin, J. B., 1941a, p. 201. In the earlier reports the name "Hemphill" is erroneously written "Hemplull."
31. *Ibid.,* p. 176.
32. Walker, W. M., n.d.
33. Schoenbeck, Ethel, personal communication.
34. Bennett, 1945, p. 161.

Of these nineteen, evidence of the suspension from necklaces of the cut jaws, human or animal is definite in two (2) instances, the inference very strong in three cases, constitutes a possibility in three others and is not determinable in the remaining eleven. The possibility that they may have been sewed to a breechcloth in front exists in one case, is highly improbable in five cases, and doubtful or underterminable in thirteen. Strangely enough, although earspools occur on all the Titterington and Willie Smith figurines, no indication of the wearing of mandibles appears on any statuettes from Illinois or elsewhere.

Since bear and wolf jaws were worn, it would seem that the more powerful fighting wild animals were chosen and hence, that the human mandibles and maxillaries were those of brave enemies and worn for a like reason. However, if the jaws had a protective quality or religious significance, they might rather represent friendly relationships and hence the human jaws might be those of dead friends, patrons or relatives.

OTHER PENDANTS

Other types of pendants are rarely found. A limestone (?) ornament "shaped roughly like a stemmed projectile point" was found with Burial No. 8, Mound 6, at Havana and "probably served as a pendant" on a shell, beartooth, or combination necklace of these elements. It was perforated in the stem.[35]

A bone specimen made to imitate a bears' split canine had a hole in the root end and may have been used as a pendant. Bears' teeth set with pearls or colorful stones were used as pendants, for sewing to garments and possibly for toggles (Figs. 89 and 91).

It is possible other perforated teeth of the bear may have been employed similarly. The Baehr, Knight, and Willie Smith statuettes give no indication of pendants worn by man or woman.

COPPER GORGETS OR BREASTPLATES

Professor William H. McAdams refers to these as "a sort of breastplate, or thin piece of copper, generally square (rectangular?), with holes pierced for fastening, like some of these from Ohio, but . . . corrugated very much like a piece of zinc from a modern washboard. We have found a few smooth ones, but the corrugated ones seem to have been fashionable."[36] None of these mentioned by McAdams have been located by the writer nor has any information been found giving the circumstances of their finding. No copper breastplates from Illinois Hopewellian were available for this study.

Cyrus Thomas reports the finding of a skeleton with "three thin, crescent-shaped pieces of roughly-hammered native copper, respectively 6, 8 and 10 inches in length, with some small holes along the convex margin," in a Hopewellian mound near East Dubuque.[37]

Numbers of rectanguloid breastplates or copper gorgets are reported from the Hopewell[38] and Turner groups in Ohio. "A number of these have been taken from mounds and graves of this culture," says Willoughby. A crescent shaped copper object found in the Turner group is "probably a gorget."[39]

GORGETS OF STONE

These were worn singly as a rule, occasionally in greater numbers. Judging by the reports from Ohio concerning copper gorgets or breastplates and the evidence of the method of stringing found, these were hung from the neck on cords or thongs, with the long axes horizontal, and carefully spaced one from another. They may on occasion have been sewn to cloth or skin clothing.[40] The rectangular gorgets of stone and of copper may have indicated social rank or political station.

In shape the stone gorget, usually two-holed, was most often rectangular but was at times, elliptical, ovoid, or lozenge-shaped. Certain one-holed specimens of the same general shape may have been worn as gorgets with the long axis vertical. A "typical" rectangular gorget of stone would be five to six inches long, $1\frac{1}{2}$ to 2 inches wide and a quarter to $\frac{3}{8}$ of an inch thick.

In the Arthur Gale collection are a number of rectanguloid gorgets of shell each about five inches long, shaped like the usual two-holed stone specimens but with the natural curvature of the material apparent. They are reported to have come from a grave in Union County in association with copper earspools, a string of pearls and of disk shell beads. Though I saw the material twice, no opportunity was offered to examine it closely or to measure any of it. Nor could information as to other details of the find be obtained.[41]

REEL-SHAPED GORGETS

See *Insignia of Political Rank or Social Position,* page 172.

GARMENTS

CLOTH

Needles from the rib bones of deer and from other bones indicate the sewing together of skins and fabrics to make garments.[42]

However, we do not have to depend on such evi-

---

35. Griffin and Morgan (eds.), p. 10, and Pl. 4, No. 8.
36. McAdams, 1895, pp. 263–264.
37. Thomas, C., 1887, p. 35.
38. Moorehead, 1922, pp. 119–120 and Pl. LV.
39. Willoughby and Hooton, 1922, p. 48 and Pl. 10a and 11b.
40. Moorehead, 1922, p. 119.
41. Smith, Willie, personal communication.
42. Griffin and Morgan (eds.), 1941, p. 11 and Pl. 6, Figs. 6 and 7; Cole and Deuel, 1937, pp. 163, 190; Moorehead 1928, p. 164.

dence alone to indicate the knowledge of weaving by Hopewellians. Remains of textiles have been found several times in Hopewellian sites but on account of their fragility, relatively few specimens have been preserved or accurately recorded so they could be studied or reconstructed.[43]

The chief agents by which textile remains are preserved are carbonate of copper salts, impressions on clay or pottery, and by charring. Henderson reports finding cloth preserved on a copper axe in a mound near Naples in Scott County. "On one side the salts of copper have preserved the cloth. . . . The warp and woof . . . are distinctly marked. On the other side of the axe are preserved in the same manner, feathers over the whole surface." These remains he judges, and probably rightly so, to be those of feather-cloth. Henderson thinks the "fabric" to be of wool, though it is possibly of bark.[44]

Cloth with the "distinct impression of a feather" from Mound 2 of the Baehr group should probably be similarly interpreted.[45]

A woven fabric of vegetable fiber left its impression on a copper axe from Mound 1 of the Baehr group.[46]

Henderson refers to another case from Madison County, of feather-cloth made with bark fibers, wool and feathers, that was reported on page 420 of Steven's *Flint Chips,* of which I have been unable to get a copy. Henderson says, "The body, no doubt, was wrapped in a bark mantle, one side of which was covered with feathers in the style in which the Indians of the Mississippi Valley manufactured feather cloth."[47]

Tracings of matting have been discovered as a wrapping for copper axes, to cover the body of deceased persons in tombs and to cover the floor of a tomb.[48] The weave seems to be known from the Scott County find only.[49] In the case of a textile found in the Ogden Mound (F°174) the writer saw the imprint while it was distinctly discernible. A design of concentric circles and bands in red, orange, and black was still visible though it disappeared shortly on drying out.

BREECHCLOTH

The Baehr statuette[50] (headless) and the Knight figure,[51] both male, wear the breechcloth. While the method of looping the cloth over the belt or roll at the back of the two figures seems identical, it is not clear whether the arrangement in front is the same. The Baehr belt as seen in the illustration seems to be double in front with a small semicircular apron. In the Knight figurine, a broad triangular piece extends downward from beneath the rolled belt-like part and narrows to pass between the legs. However, these differences may be more apparent than real and due merely to varying conventions of the artists. Breechclouts were probably of cloth and of leather.

Presumably at times they were decorated by colored designs in resist-dyeing[52] or by sewing on beads,[53] bears' teeth,[54] shells and mandible halves.[55] (see Figs. 87, 89, 90).

A breechcloth is shown on the fragmentary torso of the Honey Creek statuette from Oklahoma. Seen from the drawing this shows no rolled portion and presents a moderately wide triangular outline in front.[56]

Breechcloths are of the same general type on the Turner statuettes as far as can be judged from Willoughby's drawings of the reconstructed figures, except possibly the Ohio examples are broader and may not be secured similarly in back. One shows a roll or belt remarkably similar to the Knight warrior figure in front, though the breechcloth itself is so wide as to give the appearance of "shorts" not unlike modern bathing trunks.

SHIRTS

Reference was made to Hopewellian hunting shirts as long ago as 1887. Thomas evidently quoting from his assistants' report, writes: "Lying across the thighs were dozens of small copper beads, evidently formed by rolling slender wirelike strips into small rings. The assistant who opened this mound, and who is personally well acquainted with Indian habits and customs, suggests that these beads once formed the ornamentation of the fringe of a hunting shirt."[57] Or they might have been sewn on the breechcloth or a belt.

43. For general articles on Amerindian textiles with references to Hopewellian fabrics see Holmes, 1884; 1896; Miner, 1936.

44. Henderson, 1884, p. 691.

45. Griffin, J. B., 1941a, p. 176.

46. *Ibid*, p. 183.

47. Henderson, 1884, p. 691. The mound referred to is the Mitchell Mound. Although "copper implements" were found, there is no certainty from Henderson's account that it is Hopewellian.

48. Cole and Deuel, 1937, pp. 135, 173, 175.

49. Henderson, 1884, p. 695.

50. Griffin, J. B., 1941a, p. 180 (Fig. 11).

51. McKern, Titterington, and Griffin, 1945, p. 296, Pl. XX.

52. There is no clear evidence for a design on this type of garment. The Knight dancing woman has a design in color on her belt. Shetrone and Greenman (1931) show on the frontispiece, a reconstruction of an Ohio Hopewellian man in a breechcloth with a batik-like design characteristic of Hopewellian cloth. The effigy tubular pipe from the Adena Mound (Mills, 1902, pp. 29–31) depicts a similar garment, the incised decoration on which may indicate a design in color. Though this is from an earlier culture, it seems to be one related to Hopewellian.

53. Thomas, C., 1887, p. 35.

54. Griffin, J. B., 1941a, p. 179.

55. See "Pendants—Mandible" above.

56. Through the courtesy of Mr. Frank Phillips and Mr. Pat Patterson of Bartlesville, Oklahoma, photographs and drawings were sent me of the fragment of a statuette, showing the body from the knees to above the waist. Presumably this piece does not belong to the head fragment from the same site, or, if so, the lady was masquerading as a man.

57. Thomas, C., 1887, p. 35.

The only Hopewellian statuette from Illinois or elsewhere that presents anything like a shirt is the Knight warrior. "The entire body above the breech-clout and the left arm above the wrist are painted a dull purplish red, suggesting a shirt. . . . Looping from the top of each shoulder to pass under the adjoining arm is painted a broad band of white bordered with red [black?] and sectioned by transverse black lines at wide intervals. Lateral extensions of this garment or painted design extend outward from the neck well over each shoulder."[58] The shirt if such, extended under the belt. On the other hand, as the color at its margins is not outlined in relief like the readily recognizable garments on these figures, this appears to be body painting rather than clothing (see Fig. 84, A).

Snyder indicates the possibility of a sash or garment from the position of certain beads with skeleton H of Baehr Mound 1. "Over the breast were several flat ovoid beads, made of shell . . . perforated through the long diameter for fastening to the sash or garment, and each having on one side two holes drilled an eighth of an inch deep to receive brilliant [sic] stone or jewel settings."[59] The arrangement of beads and pearls on a skeleton in the Dickison mound near Rome suggested to Walker a "collar and bib" or bead breastplate sewn to a garment (see Fig. 85).[60]

Similarly the large number of pearls and pearl slugs found in the tombs near Liverpool may have been attached to garments. In Mound 77 of this group, it is reported that "Scattered over the chest, as if they had been attached to a garment, were four or five hundred pearl beads" (see Fig. 86).[61]

The remains of fabric and feather cloth mentioned above may be interpreted as blankets or robes. Still another reference to a coat or a cape is given by Shetrone for the Ogden (Lewistown, Illinois) site. "This individual when interred wore a coat or cape on which had been sewed hundreds of shell and pearl beads."[62]

FOOTGEAR

Although the man represented in one of the Turner statuettes wore moccasins and leggings, the Knight warrior seems to be bare of foot and leg. Whether or not the other Turner male statuettes were similarly dressed or barefooted seems doubtful as the evidence apparently was destroyed in the altar fire. Beads near the feet of skeletons 2 and 3 in Dickison Mound 478 may have decorated the moccasins of the dead.[63]

INSIGNA OF POLITICAL RANK OR SOCIAL POSITION (MALE)

The richly "dressed" persons buried in the Hopewellian Mounds were undoubtedly the important individuals of their communities. Possibly some of the accompanying bodies were those of retainers, minor officials or relatives who were sacrificed to go with the spirits of the great to the next world in a manner customary among the historic Natchez.[64] Many of the accompanying adornments such as gorgets, copper breastplates, and feather robes mentioned above may have had special social significance to the wearer and the community.

Moreover, there are other objects that seem almost certainly to indicate rank or social position but whether through birth, political prestige, or religious authority is not now determinable.

COPPER PLUME

"Associated with these charred remains was a thin hammered, plume-shaped copper ornament." This was probably part of a headdress and may represent a feather (see Fig. 90).[65]

HEAD PLATE

A head plate of copper similar to those found by Moorehead[66] in the Hopewell group in Ohio but without visible means for attaching antlers is reported by the same archeologist from a grave in Mound 6 at Havana.[67] "The curved plate of copper has two small perforations along the border of one end and a large perforation in the center of the border of the other end. It probably was a part of a ceremonial headdress."[68]

REEL-SHAPED GORGETS

Two instances of reel-shaped stone gorgets were noted for Illinois. In both cases there was a pair of them associated with a skeleton. One pair came from Mound 6 at Havana,[69] the other from Whitnah Mound 60 across the Illinois River and a few miles away. At Havana they were "at the neck of skeleton 5," and at Lewistown they seemed to lie near the waist of the dead (see Fig. 91).[70]

IMITATION GRIZZLY BEAR TEETH OF COPPER

Of the ten copper replicas of grizzly bear teeth previously described, several had two holes near the center probably made for sewing them to a garment.[71]

58. McKern, Titterington, and Griffin, 1945, p. 296.
59. Griffin, J. B., 1941a, p. 179.
60. Walker, W. M., n.d.
61. Cole and Deuel, 1937, pp. 135, 143–144.
62. Shetrone, and Greenman, 1931, p. 332 under Fig. 207.
63. Walker, W. M., n.d.
64. Swanton, 1911, p. 145.
65. Griffin, J. B., 1941a, p. 174.
66. Moorehead, 1922, pp. 99, 107–108, 109, 112.
67. Moorehead, 1928, p. 161.
68. Griffin, and Morgan (eds.), 1941, p. 10.
69. Ibid., p. 10.
70. Schoenbeck, Ethel, personal communication. These gorgets, before their recovery in 1947, had been disturbed by road-grading operations.
71. Cole and Deuel, 1937, p. 144.

ANTLER HEADDRESS

One of the most interesting finds from the Liverpool group (Mound 77?) consisted of two antlers of a young Virginia buck found near the head of a skeleton and doubtless part of a headdress.[72] No definite record of the grave goods accompanying each burial was made and consequently the skeleton with which the antlers occurred is unknown. If these were associated with the skeleton of the so-called mat burial and its rich trappings, the situation is strikingly similar to one in a Hopewell tomb in Ohio with its wealth of clothing and jewelry, and the imposing headdress with copper antlers. Presumably a wooden plate or leather head covering was used at Liverpool to hold the antlers firm and erect as they were obviously worn from the evidence of engraving,[73] mask,[74] and the relation of the Ohio replica to its owner's body.[75] With the Illinois skeleton (of the "mat burial") were found a necklace of one hundred and twenty "silver beads, of native manufacture . . . [and] scattered over the chest, as if they had been attached to a garment, were four or five hundred pearl beads. Below the feet lay a copper adz, a blade [ax] of the same material, and a human upper jaw cut in the manner frequently found in Hopewellian sites" (see Fig. 86).[76]

For the purpose of comparison, a description of Burial 248 from Mound 25, Hopewell group (Ohio) is given. "The skeleton . . . [had] associated with it . . . some very remarkable objects. At the right shoulder lay a large platform pipe and a beautiful agate spearhead. A copper plate lay on the breast, and another on the abdomen, while a third lay under the hips. These plates, when lifted, were found to have preserved . . . cloth and sinews. . . . Cut, sawed and split bears' teeth covered the chest and abdomen, and several spool-shaped ornaments and buttons of copper were found among the ribs. The body had apparently been dressed in a cloth garment extending from the neck to the knees, upon which had been sewn several thousand beads, some of pearl and others of shell. Upon the skirt of the garment had been sewn some of the largest and most beautiful pearl beads found in any of the mounds, together with bears' teeth, etc. The head had been decorated with a remarkable headdress of wood and copper. . . . The antler-shaped ornaments were made of wood encased in sheets of copper, one-sixteenth of an inch thick. They originally had four prongs of nearly equal length. . . . 'The headplate . . . covered the head from the forehead to the base of the skull, and the branching antlers probably rose perpendicularly.' "[77]

This presents a remarkable parallel to the Illinois find although the Ohio community must have been a much richer one for wealth placed with the dead was greater in amount and more varied than in the Illinois case.

Mound City Group in Ohio yielded a number of horn-like representations usually associated with the head or a headdress. With graves numbered 3 and 4 in Mound 13 were three pairs of antlers fashioned in copper—"one set with a single tine, a second set with 3 tines and a third with 4 tines each. . . . These doubtless were used in conjunction with and attached to bonnet-like coverings of skins and fabrics, as indicated by the provision left at the base of each for attachment. . . . The method of attachment is [in the 3-tined set] . . . by means of tabs at the base, to be passed through skin or cloth and clinched, while that of the 4-tined set is by means of a cord passing through the perforations at the base and through the fabric."[78]

Professor Moorehead mentions finding "number of copper headdresses" in the Hopewell group but space is lacking to describe them here.[79]

A four-tined antler-like headdress in copper was recently reported from the Fisher mound in Kentucky in a phase related to Hopewellian.[80]

It will be noted the antler set from the Liverpool site was two-tined with a point of one broken off and the place worn smooth. Whether or not higher rank was signified by adding a tine is an intriguing thought. The finding of two sets with different numbers of points in the same Ohio grave may point to a promotion achieved shortly before death.[81]

RED OCHER PAINTING OF HEAD

This custom may have been one of sprinkling the body after death with red ocher but since the Knight statuette of the living warrior was painted white on face and possibly red on body, it seems probable that the dead in certain instances were also painted. Red pigment was observed on skulls in Hopewellian graves in three instances at Rome,[82] once near Oak-

72. *Ibid.*, Pl. XXXI, *B.* No mention of the antlers is made in the text. They were designated on the list when transferred from the Ohio State Museum to the Illinois State Museum as follows: "Small pair of deer antlers; part of a headdress with a burial, Liverpool."

73. Moorehead, 1922, pp. 126–127 and Figs. 20–21, p. 128.

74. Burnett, 1945, p. 40 and Pl. LXXVII. This specimen, though not Hopewellian, belongs to a cultural group that seems to have inherited many of the Hopewellian customs.

75. Moorehead, 1922, pp. 107–108.

76. Cole and Deuel, 1937, p. 135 and Pl. XXXI. *B.*

77. Moorehead, 1922, pp. 107–108.

78. Mills, 1922*b*, pp. 366–367.

79. Moorehead, 1922, pp. 126–128; cf. also pp. 109–110 (and **Fig.** 12*a* and Pl. LXXI).

80. Webb and Haag, 1947*a*, pp. 77–79. The authors classify the series of cultural traits, of which the headdress is a part, as Adena.

81. Mills, 1922*b*, pp. 366–367.

82. Walker, W. M., n.d.

ford in Menard County[83] and in the Montezuma Mound near Pearl, Illinois.[84]

MISCELLANEOUS TRAITS

"Conjoined copper tubes" similar to others from Wisconsin, Michigan, Tennessee, and Ohio are mentioned by Snyder as having been "unconnected with any other object" and was considered by him an ornament.[85] Others have thought them musical instruments as the remains of reeds or hollow bone have been recovered in them.[86]

PLUMMETS

A plummet of limestone was found near the left humerus of a skeleton buried in Mound 6 at Havana.[87] It had a groove near the top and may have been suspended from a string about the neck of the owner, although such a heavy object would seem rather awkward to wear as an ornament. It is seldom that these artifacts are found in direct association with Hopewell burials.

WOMEN'S DRESS

As noted for men, the women buried in Hopewellian tombs or represented in sculpture are doubtless from the socially important class.

HAIR ARRANGEMENT, HEADDRESS, FACE AND BODY PAINTING

The three methods of wearing the hair in Illinois mentioned above can be seen on the Knight female figures (see Fig. 93).[88]

The Willie Smith head appears to be identical with that of the Knight dancing woman except the knobs are lacking, (probably having been ground down) and there is no paint on the figure. The body and neck are missing so the complete hair arrangement is not now determinable (see Fig. 92, A and B).

Hopewellian women in Illinois and Ohio seem to have used paint on their faces and bodies very rarely.

On a female statuette from the Hopewell group in Ohio the hair seems to be enclosed in "the meshes of a net . . . represented by incised lines."[89] If the incising consists of two oblique series of lines, that produce lozenge-like areas, it may represent braiding rather than a net.

On the standing Turner woman, the hair is parted in the middle, lies smooth over the head and is secured in a loop at the back very like one of the Knight statuettes.[90]

JEWELRY AND OTHER ADORNMENT

EAR ORNAMENTS

The four Knight women, the Willie Smith head, and the female head from Honey Creek, Oklahoma appear to have ear ornaments of the "sleeve-button" or spool type. The three Turner women (Ohio) lack ear ornaments as do half the six male figures.

NECKPIECES AND NECKLACES

Around the neck of three Knight figures may be seen faintly a background of paint, black in two instances and white in the case of the dancing woman. On each of these are two or three rows of small dots of the opposite colored paint, white on black in two instances, and black on white in the other. These have been interpreted as being neckpieces of cloth or leather to which beads, either pearl or ground shell, are sewed.[91] Or the "neckpieces" may be a stylistic way of representing several strands of beads. *A contrario,* the beads on female skeletons found in tombs may in some instances be from neckpieces rather than necklaces.

In most reports, the sex of the skeletons is omitted when describing finds, so that it is difficult to distinguish differences (if they exist) between grave offerings accompanying men and those with women. From the Liverpool Mounds, the skeleton of a woman is reported to have had a necklace, presumably of ground shell beads.[92] Cole and Deuel report a woman from an intrusive pit in Whitnah mound 54, presumably a Hopewellian burial, that had a necklace of over a thousand cut shell disk beads.[93]

ARM AND WRISTBANDS

On three of the female Knight statuettes, decorative arm and wristbands were painted on both arms. The lower arm of one figure is missing but doubtless it was originally adorned in the same manner. The interpretation given here is that these were bands of black cloth (or leather) ornamented by sewing or tying on pearls or shell beads (see Fig. 88).

In the Knight mound that yielded the pottery statuettes, Dr. Titterington noted bead arrangements on skeletons definitely indicating that the deceased had worn similarly decorated armbands when buried.[94]

83. Personal observation of skull from Noten Wiseman farm kindly loaned by the present owner, Mr. John Harris of Athens, Illinois.
84. Fowke, Bushnell, *et al.,* 1905.
85. Griffin, J. B., 1941a, p. 182.
86. Willoughby and Hooton, 1922, pp. 50–51; Moorehead, 1922, p. 128.
87. Griffin and Morgan (eds.), 1941, p. 10.
88. See also McKern, Titterington, and Griffin, 1945, p. 297.
89. Moorehead, 1922, p. 163.
90. Willoughby and Hooton, 1922, Pl. 21b.

91. The black dots on the white background on the neckpiece of the "dancing woman" seem small in proportion when compared with the white dots on the neckpieces of the other figures. All may represent the same type of adornment, the first featuring very large beads of cut shell. On the other hand, the white background with black spots may be a convention to indicate beads of copper or some other material.
92. Cole and Deuel, 1937, p. 134.
93. *Ibid.,* p. 156.
94. Titterington, personal communication.

GARMENTS

Except for the neckpieces and armbands noted above, the torsos of three Knight female statuettes are devoid of covering. The fourth woman (with nursing child) wears neither garment nor ornament above the waist except the usual earspools. The Turner (Ohio) standing woman lacks the earspools as well.[95]

BELTS

One of the Knight female figures, that of the "dancing woman," is clad with a belt in addition to skirt, apparently decorated in color by resist-dyeing.

RESIST-DYEING

Not only does the design on the belt of this Knight figure give the impression of batik work but actual designs in color on clay in the Ogden Mound[96] and on textile fragments recovered in Ohio[97] seem to demonstrate the common use of this technique by Hopewellians (see Fig. 94).

SKIRTS

All four skirts represented on the Knight statuettes are the blanket type, that was wrapped about the body and secured by folding in at the waist. The lower margin of the dress extends a little below the knees. Considerable variety in the color of the skirts is exhibited: two are a solid, dull red (one without belt or ornamentation), the third is chiefly red decorated with three broad white stripes bordered by heavy black lines; and the fourth or "dancing figure" wears a black skirt.

Two of the skirts are decorated by horizontal interrupted double lines of white at top and bottom, here interpreted to mean pearls or beads sewed on or otherwise attached in strings. Beads are occasionally reported "at the waist and at the knees" of skeletons and may indicate skirts ornamented in a similar way.

95. Willoughby and Hooton, 1922, Pl. 21b.
96. Personal observation of writer.
97. Shetrone, and Greenman, 1931, p. 107, Fig. 53.

The dresses as determined from fragments of the three female figures from the Turner site all seem to be a dull red in color.[98]

MOCCASINS

All the Knight statuettes representing women show moccasins high over the ankle, front and back, but scalloped and lower at the sides. These are decorated by what appear to be white beads around the edges of top and sole, and at the instep. All wear black moccasins except the dancing figure that has the left one red and right one black (see Figs. 84 and 88).

The Turner statuettes of women differ from the Illinois ones in having "low foot coverings of the general form of the woven shoes from the Kentucky caves.[99]

The study given in this paper is the beginning of an undertaking to depict in miniature three-dimensional scenes the manner of life of the Indian groups living in Illinois up to the time of their withdrawal westward. In such a project, the co-operation of anthropologists and artists is essential, the former to interpret the archeological and skeletal evidence, the latter to create the living appearance of these vanished peoples engaged in their customary activities. Much of the information needed for this is sadly lacking from the field notes, written or pictorial, and from the published reports. In some cases it may not have been evident in the material found but in others it is simply omitted or perhaps was beyond the capabilities of those doing the field work. Undoubtedly new techniques are needed to discover the nature of the perishable remains placed in graves or left on campsites. More complete observations and fuller notes would in many cases clarify the picture immensely and enable us to represent more fully the appearance, dress, and cultural habits of people of the past. This and the interpretation of the observations and finds seems to be largely the responsibility of the archeologist.

98. Willoughby and Hooton, 1922, pp. 73–74.
99. Ibid., p. 73. See also Holmes, 1896, pp. 34–35 and Fig. 9.

THE ARCHEOLOGY OF THE LOWER OHIO VALLEY.
By *Moreau S. Maxwell**

INTRODUCTION

IT IS becoming more and more apparent that within the general archeological area of the lower Ohio drainage the primary diffusion of culture was with the current of the watershed. Thus cultural affiliations can be traced from centers into marginal areas —west along the Ohio River from Ohio and Kentucky; west and north along the Green River of Kentucky; west and north along the Cumberland River of Kentucky and Tennessee; north along the Tennessee River of Tennessee and Alabama; south along the Wabash, White and East Fork rivers of Indiana, and south along the Illinois and Mississippi rivers. The river currents, as apparently do the currents of culture diffusion, all converge on the area of southern Illinois, an archeological region about which surprisingly little has been published. Throughout the majority of its prehistoric past the region seems to have been peripheral in character, approaching the status of a minor cultural center only later in Middle Mississippi times. However, the marginal influences manifested in the sites of southern Illinois do bring significant information to bear on the solution of archeological problems closer to the cultural centers. For this reason this article has been focused on the excavations in southern Illinois, conducted by the University of Chicago and by the Works Projects Administration, Museum Extension Project.[1]

THE ARCHAIC

There has long been a suspicion on the part of archeologists in the lower Ohio Valley that nomadic hunters, similar to the Paleo-Indian of the western plains may have penetrated through to the Ohio Valley at a relatively early post-Mankato date. Unfortunately no geological or extinct faunal associations have been found to support this suspicion, but typological evidence continues to mount for the existence in the valley of a Folsom-Yuma type of hunter.

Throughout the area, carefully chipped, fluted points and blades with long diagonal flake scars have been found in sufficient numbers that they cannot be disregarded. Many such points have been found as isolated surface artifacts by collectors in southern Illinois. Particularly in the collection of Irvin S. Peithman of Carbondale there are sixteen of these fluted, concave-based points, found in Jackson, Williamson, and Union counties. These points are uniformly thin, more often fluted on one face only, and range from three to five centimeters in length. The basal edge of the majority of these has been ground smooth, and the secondary chipping is usually more skillfully done than that on projectile points from the Early Woodland cultures of southern Illinois.

A small cache of flint blades were found in a site overlooking the Little Grassy Creek in Williamson County. Typologically, these blades also appear to be early. The blades, now in the collection of Mr. Peithman, were found in a shallow, irregular pit in a site on which there were a number of unmodified flint flakes, broken scrapers and choppers, but no pottery, nor was there any midden accumulation. Six of the seven blades were between fourteen and fifteen centimeters in length, the seventh being twenty-five centimeters in length. The edges were parallel, curving in just at the point, and the bases were incurvate and ground smooth. A carefully controlled pressure flaking had been used producing parallel, oblique scars from the edge to the center of the face of each artifact. This flaking is finer than that on any of the artifacts excavated from Woodland sites in the Carbondale region, and resembles most closely the chipping on artifacts from the Perry Site (Lu°25) of the Lauderdale Focus.[2]

Across the Mississippi River in Jefferson County, Missouri, material found by Adams[3] in the Hidden Valley rock shelter has been considered tentatively as

* University of Chicago, B.A., 1939; M.A., 1946; Ph.D., 1949; Assistant Professor of Anthropology, Beloit College, 1946—. Chapter received December, 1947, reduced one-third in January, 1951.

1. I am especially indebted to Dr. Fay-Cooper Cole and to Roger Willis, Richard MacNeish, Kenneth Orr, and Robert Bell for information concerning the excavations in Pope and Massac counties; to Irvin S. Peithman of Carbondale, Illinois, whose information concerning sites, private collection, and assistance were invaluable; to Dr. Thorne Deuel for advice during excavation in Williamson and Jackson counties; to the Southern Illinois University and the State Museum at Springfield, which were sponsors of the Works Projects Administration excavations; and to Dr. James B. Griffin for a constant flow of information and leads. My indebtedness extends to the numerous authors whose sources I have cited in making this interpretation.

2. Webb and DeJarnette, 1942, Pl. 101, Fig. 2.
3. Adams, 1941, p. 190.

belonging to an early complex. On the floor of this shelter, and underlying a ceramic-bearing layer, was a habitation zone in which no pottery was found. The flint artifacts found in this nonceramic zone were of three types—a large, thin, straight-based knife, large disk scrapers and projectile points of an unusual type. The points were long and carefully flaked. The base was straight and narrow with a stem expanding towards the shoulder, straight shoulders and recurved edges on the blade. In shape they are unlike any projectile points reported from southern Illinois. However, the quality of the chipping indicates a possible relationship with the Little Grassy artifacts.

To date the only cultural complex which might be ascribed to this Paleo-Indian period comes from the Parrish Site in Hopkins County, Northwestern Kentucky.[4] Here, the presence of over one hundred and thirty-five burials indicates a habitation of some duration. Of the projectile points found on the site, six are Folsom-like, fluted points,[5] and three can be compared typologically with blades of the Yuma type—exhibiting "what appear to be identical chipping and shape."[6] Associated with these points were large, plano-convex, hafted scrapers and a number of small gravers, neither of which appear in the assemblages of the Pickwick Aspect. Also in the artifact complex were side scrapers, atlatl weights, large antler chisels, cut antler sections, deer ulna flakers, and one deer metatarsal awl. Pottery was conspicuously absent from the site.

In summary, negative evidence may be invoked, as well as positive, in the attempt to ascribe these artifacts to their temporal position. Extensive excavations carried out in the southeast and the Ohio Valley from 1937 to 1942 served to provide a fairly complete picture of the cultural assemblages from the immediate pre-ceramic period to the time of European contact. With but one exception,[7] points of the Folsom type do not appear in these assemblages, and therefore may be presumed to be earlier. The skill in pressure flaking, not characteristic of later Woodland cultures, and the close typological similarity between certain artifacts and those of the High Plains, gives further weight to the assumption of antiquity for the Ohio Valley artifacts. It is significant that there are no reported associations of grinding tools with these artifacts. Apparently, like the Folsom of the west, these people were primarily hunters, living in small nomadic bands and seldom camping long enough on one site to leave a refuse midden of any size.

Much less tenuous than the evidence for Paleo-Indian occupation of the valley is the information available on the cultural assemblages of the pre-ceramic sites usually associated with shell middens.

Such an assemblage was first reported by Moore, from the Green River Valley of Kentucky.[8] Later the list of traits in the complex was expanded by Webb and Haag[9] and the assemblage established as the Indian Knoll Focus of the Archaic Pattern. Components of this focus have been excavated in McLean and Ohio counties of Kentucky and in Clark County, Indiana.[10] Excavation in the Pickwick Basin of the Tennessee River in Alabama produced evidence of another pre-ceramic complex, known as the Lauderdale Focus.[11] The relationship between these two foci was sufficiently close to warrant the inclusion of the two into a Pickwick Aspect of the Archaic Pattern.

Somewhat later a third focus, the Eva Focus, was included in this aspect as the results of excavations along the Tennessee River in West Tennessee.[12] To some extent the Eva Focus appears to be an intermediate cultural link between the Lauderdale and Indian Knoll foci. Although there is a greater trait identity between Eva and Indian Knoll, there are some significant detail similarities between Eva and Lauderdale, as, for example, the double-basal notched projectile points, and the long narrow points with recurved edges.[13] Significant differences do appear in the complex of the Eva Focus. However, since the authors entertain the possibility that the Eva people "may have survived into the historic period as the ephemeral Mosopelea"[14] such differences may be due to the introduction of traits from later assemblages. (The "beaver tail" stem projectile point, for example, listed as rare in Eva and absent in the other two foci is most common in assemblages of the Adena culture.)

The available information on the Pickwick Aspect points to a homogeneous, conservative culture with rare trading contacts to the Gulf Coast, and in the case of the Eva people perhaps to the Lake Superior region. Physically the people were inbred and relatively homogeneous. They were short in stature (males five feet, four inches and females five feet) and of rather slight build with long, high-vaulted heads, often with a sagittal crest, and short broad-nosed faces.[15] They were a hunting, gathering and probably war-like people, often establishing semipermanent habitation sites along the small rivers where shell fish, which were the staple of diet, could be gathered in abundance. Mounds built of the discarded shells were both dwelling sites and depositories for the

4. Haag, 1942a, pp. 217-218.
5. Roberts, 1939, p. 531 (cf. point in upper right of Pl. 15).
6. Haag, 1942a, p. 218.
7. Lewis and Kneberg, 1941 (fluted points are considered a focal trait in the Candy Creek Focus).

8. Moore, 1916a.
9. Webb and Haag, 1939; 1940; 1947a; 1947b; and Webb, 1946.
10. Guernsey, 1939.
11. Webb and DeJarnette, 1942.
12. Lewis and Kneberg, 1947.
13. Webb and DeJarnette, 1942, Pl. 158, Fig. 2, No. 17.
14. Lewis and Kneberg, 1947, p. 15.
15. Skarland, 1939.

dead. These were buried in small round pits in a flexed position, or occasionally in a sitting position, and the skeletons of children particularly, were often accompanied by the skeletons of dogs or the shells of turtles. Hunting was done primarily with the atlatl, or dart thrower, made of wood with an antler hook and a polished stone weight at the balance. The darts were tipped with long slender flint or socketed antler points. They fished with bone fishhooks and probably nets and weirs. Wild grain and nuts were ground to meal with the cylindrical, bell-shaped pestle, and the shallow, multiple-pitted mortar. In the manufacture of skin garments a bone awl and perforated needle were used. Decoration consisted of long, cylindrical stone and bone beads, shell disk and anculosa beads and perforated animal canine teeth worn around the neck. Children were often buried dressed in short shirts made of strands of shell beads. Adults wore large shell gorgets on the chest, and long bone pins, occasionally engraved, were worn in the hair or in pierced ears. All cooking and storing vessels must have been made of wood or bark since these people were either not yet aware of the techniques of pottery making, or had not begun to utilize the technique. The techniques of agricultural cultivation were also apparently unknown to them.

Apparently there were no centers of this shell mound archaic in Illinois, but cultural traits diffused northward. For a number of years amateur collectors in southern Illinois have found artifacts on the surface which resembled, typologically, many of the focal traits of the pre-ceramic Indian Knoll Focus. In plowed areas and shallow blow-outs, stone atlatl weights, primarily of the bi-winged type; bell-shaped pestles, full grooved axes and long narrow side-notched projectile points were found, but no pottery or midden deposit. Typologically the artifacts were supposed to be earlier than the Early Woodland ceramic horizon. This supposition was proved to be correct by the excavation of the stratified Faulkner Site in Massac County, Illinois, by the Anthropology Department of the University of Chicago.[16]

The Faulkner Site is composed of two middens, a non-ceramic layer overlaid by a Baumer component. Only artifacts of stone were recovered from the non-ceramic layer (Fig. 95). The soil of Massac and Pope counties has proved to be so acid that bone and shell quickly disintegrate. The trait complex for the Faulkner Focus is thus, unfortunately, incomplete. It is possible that many of the bone and shell traits, diagnostic for the Indian Knoll Focus and other foci of the Archaic Pattern, were originally present in the artifact assemblage of the Faulkner Focus.

The projectile points have been grouped into six subcategories of the Type I established by Cole and

Deuel.[17] The most common of the six is a straight-stemmed, square-shouldered point with a flat or slightly excurvate base and straight tapered edges. A distinctive sub-category of projectile point has a small well-defined notch near the base which is usually the widest part of the point. The edges are often parallel, terminating in a short, blunt tip. This subtype is particularly close to some of the Black Sand projectile points,[18] and may possibly be related to the large well-chipped points of the Osceola Site in Wisconsin.[19] Five points were found with basal notches, the shoulders extending nearly to the base. Projectile points of this type have not been reported from the Indian Knoll Focus, but they do occur in the Black Sand Focus[20] and in the Lauderdale Focus at the Perry, Bluff Creek, Mulberry Creek and Georgetown Cave sites.[21] They are especially characteristic of the Eva Focus where they are considered to be early.[22]

Other flint artifacts—expanded base drills, "needle" drills, gravers, large plano-convex scrapers—and a multiple pitted "nutting stone," and a fragmentary atlatl weight, demonstrate further the affiliation of this focus with the Pickwick Aspect and the Black Sand Focus.

In a comparison of traits between the sites of the Indian Knoll Focus and the Faulkner Focus, excluding the traits of bone and shell, MacNeish finds the relationship to be very close, with over 60 per cent of the traits being identical. The relationship between the Faulkner and Lauderdale Focus sites is less close and diminishes further between Faulkner and both the Lamoka Focus and the McCain Site of Dubois County, Indiana.[23]

In spite of the number of traits in common between Faulkner and Indian Knoll, there are a number of specific traits which do not seem to conform. In particular, the grooved ax, the subrectangular bar atlatl weight, the long cylindrical pestle, bell pestle and long stone beads which are characteristic of Indian Knoll are missing at Faulkner. The long, narrow, straight-stemmed projectile point, present at Faulkner, differs in detail from comparable points in the Indian Knoll Focus. In respect to the absence or scarcity of these traits and the presence of such detailed traits as the basal-notched projectile point and the parallel-sided, side-notched point, there seems to be an even closer similarity between the Faulkner and the Eva foci. The fact that the diagnostic Indian Knoll traits, missing in the Faulkner assemblage, have been found in large numbers on the

16. MacNeish, 1948.

17. Cole and Deuel, 1937, p. 53.
18. *Ibid.*, p. 140, Fig. 28—a69, a36, a71.
19. Ritzenthaler, 1946, Pl. 6.
20. Cole and Deuel, 1937, Fig. 28—a82.
21. Webb and DeJarnette, 1942, Pl. 93, 1–3; Pl. 152; Pl. 294, 1–7; Pl. 305.
22. Lewis and Kneberg, 1947, p. 18.
23. Miller, 1941.

surface of sites near Carbondale, suggests that there may have been two lines of diffusion by which Archaic traits entered southern Illinois. One of these lines would be north along the Tennessee River and the other west along the Green and Ohio rivers.

The complex of traits at Faulkner does not, according to MacNeish, bear a genetic relationship with the Early Woodland Baumer Focus found in the same Massac County, Illinois. Only 30 per cent of the traits of these foci are similar. On the other hand, a comparison with the Black Sand Focus (F 77) in Fulton County, Illinois, shows a very close relationship, with 80 per cent of the traits shared by both foci. The notable exception to this relationship is the presence of pottery in the Black Sand Focus (possibly derived from the northeast).[24] From this evidence it is indicated that the Faulkner people continued to migrate northward, influenced at some point by a pottery-bearing culture and should be considered as ancestral to the group responsible for the Black Sand Focus.

In summary, it now appears to be well established that there were population, and cultural centers of Shell Mound Archaic people in the lower Ohio River drainage. From these centers, traits diffused northward to such marginal sites as the McCain site, Dubois County, Indiana,[25] the Faulkner Site in Massac County and various camp sites around Carbondale, Illinois. It is impossible to determine at this time whether such marginal sites represent the diffusion of distinctive Archaic traits to indigenous people, or whether they are habitations of migrant Shell Mound people. The physical resemblance between the Black Sand and Indian Knoll skeletal material seems to suggest the latter. If this is true, however, the subsistence pattern of the people changes as they move outward to marginal areas. In addition some of the distinctive traits of the cultural centers diminish in importance in the marginal assemblages.

EARLY WOODLAND

One of the major problems in interpretation of the archeology of the lower Ohio Valley and the Mississippi is the clarification of the relationship between cultures of the Archaic period and those of later pottery-using people. To many interpretors the grafting of ceramic techniques to a pre-ceramic cultural complex does not produce a radical change in culture.[26] Lewis and Kneberg see a conservative Archaic culture in the Eva Focus persisting unchanged through several pottery horizons.[27]

The relationship between the Lauderdale Focus and the introduction of pottery is not as well defined as could be desired. Pottery appears in the upper

levels of all the sites classified as Archaic.[28] Fiber-tempered, sand-tempered and possibly the limestone-tempered, fabric-impressed pottery all seem to enter the area with no appreciable difference in the cultural complex, suggesting a pottery development on a local base.

Fairbanks[29] suggests that the development of pottery in the Savannah River Focus represents the diffusion of techniques to an indigenous Archaic rather than the introduction of actual objects of a new people. The transition from Copell to Tchefuncte seems to have been of much the same order.[30] The presence of grit-tempered plain and fabric-impressed pottery on six of the seven Kentucky Indian Knoll sites leads Webb and Haag[31] to consider the possibility that late Indian Knoll people made pottery of a Woodland type. In the northeast, pottery seems to have been infused into the later levels of the Brewerton Focus with little change in the culture complex.[32]

The inference from these data is that there is a continuity of culture from the Archaic period to the next (presumably Early Woodland) with a transition marked only by the introduction of pottery and the gradual diminishing of some of the more distinctive Archaic traits. Since, in the Ohio Valley, the greatest elaboration of culture in this immediate post-Archaic period is the Adena complex, the further question is raised of whether Adena represents a development out of the Pickwick Aspect, or whether it represents the intrusion of an alien people. The discontinuity of physical types, dolichocephalic Sylvids in the Pickwick Aspect and the brachycephalic Centralids[33] in Adena, and certain discontinuities in the cultural complexes of the two horizons have led Webb and Snow, Martin, Quimby, and Collier,[34] and others to favor the latter view.

Much of the interpretation of these two problems hinges around the relationship between Adena and the Woodland Pattern. As defined in The First Woodland Conference,[35] this pattern does not include the majority of traits considered characteristic for Adena. However, Griffin[36] sees Adena as merely the elaboration of a burial complex on a basic Woodland background. Webb and Snow[37] accept the interpretation first made by Cole and Deuel[38] of a Woodland culture continuity running from the earliest pottery horizons in central Illinois through Hope-

24. Maxwell, 1947, pp. 22–23.
25. Miller, 1941.
26. Griffin, J. B., 1946, p. 44.
27. Lewis and Kneberg, 1947.
28. Webb and DeJarnette, 1942.
29. Fairbanks, 1942, p. 231.
30. Ford and Quimby, 1945.
31. Webb and Haag, 1947a, pp. 44–45.
32. Ritchie, 1944, pp. 31 ff.
33. Webb and Snow, 1945, p. 251.
34. Martin, Quimby, and Collier, 1947, p. 262.
35. Byers (ed.), 1943, p. 393.
36. Griffin, J. B., 1943a, pp. 306–307.
37. Webb and Snow, 1945, p. 326.
38. Cole and Deuel, 1937.

well. The former authors then extend this continuity backward in time to include the Indian Knoll people, but not Adena. Thus they interpret Hopewell culture as a combination of indigenous Woodland and intrusive Adena peoples and cultures.

In this controversy, two facts significant in interpreting the archeology of the subject area stand out as having been established. The first of these is that a fabric-impressed pottery is one of the early types in the lower Ohio Valley, throughout the Southeast and the Northeast, and that this surface treatment may appear on a sand-tempered, limestone-tempered, grit and clay-grit-tempered ware. The second point is that this characteristic pottery surface treatment has a range in time which bridges the Archaic and Adena horizons, and persists in some areas through the development of Hopewell.

Sand-tempered, fabric-impressed sherds are the predominant ware of the Eva Focus in West Tennessee, appearing during the Archaic and possibly contemporaneous with the fiber-tempered wares of the Pickwick Basin. In East Tennessee the quartzite-tempered, fabric-impressed pottery of the Watts Bar Focus appears to be contemporaneous with at least part of the fiber-tempered horizon of Georgia.[39] In Kentucky there is a possible association between late Indian Knoll culture and grit-tempered, fabric-impressed pottery,[40] and in the Northeast, grit-tempered fabric-impressed pottery appears as a minor form in the Brewerton Focus of the Archaic.[41] In the Adena horizon, fabric impressions appear on the surface of some of the Fayette Thick sherds from the Mt. Horeb Site,[42] a site which Griffin[43] considers to have begun in early Adena. In Georgia, the grit-tempered Dunlap Fabric Marked is considered to be earlier than the general Swift Creek period,[44] and the limestone-tempered, fabric-impressed pottery characteristic of the Candy Creek Focus of east Tennessee.[45] In the Pickwick Basin, the limestone-tempered Long Branch Fabric Marked[46] is a minor part of the pottery complex of the Copena component at Wright Village.[47] In the Crab Orchard Focus, southern Illinois, grit-tempered Crab Orchard Fabric Marked pottery continues through the Hopewell period. Sherds with this surface treatment are in the Turner mound of Ohio Hopewell[48] and the New York Focus of the Hopewellian Phase in the Northeast.[49] It is apparent

that this technique of pottery manufacture, or of decoration, continues through the entire period of cultural development from the late Archaic to late Hopewell. If, therefore, a cultural complex of the area can be determined to have neither characteristic Adena or Hopewell traits, but a predominance of fabric-marked pottery, it would seem to indicate that an indigenous Woodland culture exists before Adena and after the Archaic.

Such a culture, apparently, is the Baumer Focus[50] of Pope and Massac counties, Illinois, in which the dominant ceramic ware is a fabric-marked, limestone-tempered jar.[51] MacNeish[52] has demonstrated the cultural nonconformity which apparently exists between this ceramic focus and the pre-pottery culture in the Faulkner Focus. After the Faulkner people had moved north to the Illinois River Valley, the Baumer people, apparently descendants of a more southern Archaic, moved into southern Illinois.

The two major sites which have been excavated are the Baumer Site and the Avery Lake component. Both are small village sites, with a thin layer of midden refuse, on ridges overlooking two of the many sloughs which border the Ohio River. At the Baumer Site (Fig. 96), five miles south of the Kincaid Site, were large square houses built of logs set in individual holes rather than in wall trenches. Circular pits from three to six feet deep, had been dug in the midden presumably for storage or refuse. One clay-lined pit had been used as a fire basin, but in general, the fire pits were irregular in shape and unlined. The refuse pits were circular with flat bottoms and were either straight sided or bell-shaped with apertures smaller than the base.

Burials, flexed on either the side or the back, were made in both the midden refuse and in irregular oval pits, with no associated grave goods. Unfortunately, the highly acid soil had so decomposed the bone that it was impossible to make significant observations on the skeletons. The acid soil also accounts, no doubt, for the lack of animal bones in the refuse.

The importance of hunting in this culture is inferred from the number of projectile points. That a gathering economy was also important is apparent from the bell-shaped and conical pestles, the pebble mullers and the multiple-pitted lap mortars. Small ovoid hoes of chipped rhyolite, with a high polish on the excurvate blade were unquestionably used for digging in the earth, but more probably for the excavation of pits rather than the cultivation of fields.

39. Lewis and Kneberg, 1946, p. 8.
40. Webb and Haag, 1947a, p. 44.
41. Ritchie, 1944, p. 242, Pl. 114, No. 25.
42. Griffin, J. B., 1943a, p. 668.
43. Griffin, J. B., 1945d, p. 244.
44. Fairbanks, 1942, p. 227.
45. Lewis and Kneberg, 1941, p. 53.
46. Haag, 1939a.
47. Haag, 1942b, p. 517.
48. Willoughby and Hooton, 1922, Pl. 24, Fig. g.
49. Ritchie, 1944, Pl. 92, Fig. 22.

50. Willis, 1941.
51. Roger Willis is preparing the site reports of this focus for publication. I am indebted to him for information regarding the excavated material. Some of the interpretations are my own, and are subject to correction after the publication of the Baumer Focus.
52. MacNeish, 1948.

The projectile points in general fall within the classifications set up by the First Woodland Conference. Secondary chipping is rare and the primary technique is a controlled percussion flaking. Stemmed points predominate, the most common being straight based with a wide-contracting stem and a straight shoulder.

Drills were rare, and conformed to three types—the expanded-based, the winged and the slender, thick, excurvate-based which was the most common. End, side and large disk scrapers were common. A number of roughly worked core tools have been classified as choppers or hand axes.

The pecked and ground tools included, in addition to the bell-shaped pestle, small, thick, fully grooved axes; thick, polished celts with pointed polls, sandstone abraders, pitted hammerstones and one hematite plummet. The polished slate and limestone gorgets were particularly significant. One resembles the "reel-shaped" gorgets of Adena, with angular concave sides. Another gorget is rectangular and one is spade-shaped with a single perforation at the small end.

Seventy per cent of the pottery from the two components is Baumer Fabric Marked on which small pads of fabric were apparently used in modelling the vessels. The tempering material is either a combination of natural clay pellets and angular fragments of limestone, both of which have leached out of the ware; or more infrequently, coarse sand. The surface hardness is between 2 and 3 in both types. Methods of firing seem to be poorly controlled and probably consisted of piling burning brush around the jar since both oxidized and reduced areas appear in the same jar. Wall thickness ranges from four to ten millimeters. No restorable vessels were found with the exception of one miniature jar but the rim and basal sections indicate a deep jar with a wide mouth, slightly curving shoulder and small flat base. Some forms with slightly larger bases may have approached a flower pot shape.

Two other types have been tentatively established on the basis of surface treatment—a plain surface and a cord-marked surface—both occurring on the same ware as the fabric marked. The plain surface is often a fabric surface which has been deliberately smoothed over, indicating the fact that fabric marking was primarily functional in the molding of the jar. Decoration appears most often on this plain surface and consists of single cords impressed in chevrons, straight line incising and punctation. The cord-marked sherds are roughened with a cord-wrapped paddle. Occasionally small groups of cords are intercrossed to produce an intentional design. This technique differs from the common intercrossing of lines when applying the cord-wrapped paddle over the entire surface.

Griffin[53] sees a close relationship between the Baumer pottery and the limestone or grit-tempered Fayette Thick which he considers to be early in Kentucky Adena and part of a widespread Woodland ceramic tradition.

Few of the nonceramic artifacts are characteristic enough to allow comparison with the Adena assemblage. However, this fact in itself testifies to the Woodland nature of the Baumer Focus. Many artifacts can be traced to the Archaic of Kentucky and west Tennessee. The multiple-pitted lap mortar, the fully grooved ax, and the bell-shaped pestle are significant in the Archaic, but do not appear in the Adena of Kentucky or later horizons. One fully grooved ax has recently been found in the Adena Fisher Site (Fal-C) in Kentucky[54] but this isolated occurrence can hardly be considered as characteristic of Adena culture. The straight-stemmed projectile points in Baumer resemble those in the West Tennessee Archaic more closely than they do the rather specialized straight-stemmed point of Kentucky Adena.[55] The contracting-stemmed projectile point, characteristic of Baumer, is found in the Archaic, but is absent or a very minor type in Kentucky Adena. A close relationship has been seen between the "reel-shaped" gorget of Baumer and comparable forms in Adena. However, this begins as an early trait in Adena[56] and also appears in the early ceramic levels of Western Alabama in a complex typologically between "shell mound" and Copena which Griffin refers to as the Colbert Focus.[57]

The Baumer Focus has also been compared with the Candy Creek Focus in East Tennessee. As Lewis and Kneberg have suggested,[58] the affiliations of Baumer are stronger in West Tennessee but there is still a striking similarity between Baumer and Candy Creek. Comparing the traits of Baumer with a partial trait list for Candy Creek,[59] a cultural identity of over 80 per cent is seen for the two foci in spite of Swift Creek influences in the Candy Creek Focus. The similarity, however, need not imply close genetic relationship between the two peoples. Both may simply be manifestations of a widespread, homogeneous, pre-Adena Woodland.

In conclusion, the Baumer Focus is early. In my opinion, the people are the direct descendants of the "shell mound" people of the Pickwick Aspect, probably stemming from some Archaic or early ceramic group along the lower valley of the Tennessee River. Three possible interpretations can explain the pres-

53. Griffin, J. B., 1945d, p. 226.

54. Webb and Haag, 1947b; additional Adena grooved axes are described in Griffin, J. B., 1943a, p. 58.

55. Cf. Webb, W. S., 1942, Fig. 15 1–A.

56. Webb, W. S., 1941, p. 210.

57. Griffin, J. B., 1946, p. 52.

58. Lewis and Kneberg, 1946, p. 5.

59. Anonymous, 1941.

ence of traits in the Baumer Focus which are also found in the Adena sites of Kentucky: (1) Baumer and Adena are contemporaneous, with Baumer marginal to and influenced by the Adena culture center (the absence of characteristic Adena traits argues against this); (2) Adena culture is later than Baumer and is developed from this and other similar early Woodland cultures; (3) the manifestations of Adena culture found in Ohio, Kentucky, Indiana, and Illinois are the work of an intrusive Centralid people who entered an area already sparsely populated by a widespread Woodland group with a relatively homogeneous culture.[60] The meeting of these two groups was a peaceful one[61] and the Adena people borrowed heavily from the Woodland culture complex. Such borrowed traits were, especially, the cord- and fabric-marked pottery and the polished stone work. Adena culture, a blend of early Woodland and traits associated with the burial complex of the *Adena people,* then became the dominant elaboration for the period and influenced to varying degrees the marginal Woodland people who surrounded it.

Excavations in the Crab Orchard Basin near Carbondale from 1939 to 1941[62] supply more of the missing pieces to the puzzle. At a number of sites in Williamson and Jackson counties fabric-impressed pottery, associated with a relatively distinctive stone and bone complex, was found to lie beneath later Woodland and Middle Mississippi components. The largest village in this area, occupying roughly fourteen thousand square feet, was named the Crab Orchard Site and is the type station for the Crab Orchard Focus (Fig. 97 and 98).

The Crab Orchard Site located on a low bluff near the Crab Orchard Creek was apparently occupied from the arrival of the first Indians in the area until nearly protohistoric time. All of the known cultures of southern Illinois are present in superposition from the earliest ceramic horizon to Middle Mississippi. However, in spite of constant occupation over a period of not less than nine hundred years, the midden deposit is not more than two feet thick. This midden, a rich black humus, is organically and physically homogeneous. No sterile lines indicate an abandonment by one group and a subsequent occupation by another. Stratigraphy, therefore, is based on statistical analysis checked against control blocks in the few areas where aboriginal storage pits had not been dug.

Three zones were established by this method. Zone I, from the surface to a depth of approximately six inches, contained Raymond Focus, Dillinger Focus and Middle Mississippi material. Zone II, approxi-

mately thirteen inches thick, and Zone III approximately five inches thick, contained Crab Orchard Focus material. The trait complex of Zone III cannot be adequately determined until an unmixed site can be located. However, in general, this zone contains material very much like the trait complex in the Baumer Focus and is apparently uninfluenced by either Adena or Hopewell.

Zone III is characterized primarily by the pottery. Although fabric-impressed pottery is predominant, Sugar Hill Cord Marked pottery is common in this zone. The tempering material of the cord-marked ware is predominantly hornblende, but granite and limestone may appear in the same sherd. This material is either in the form of pebbles up to seven millimeters in diameter, or large angular fragments. The depth of the cord impressions and the fact that one cord can be followed from lip to base indicates that the cord impression was probably rolled on rather than applied with a paddle. Horizontal cord impressions often appear on the interior of the lip. The color is predominantly a brick red, and the vessel walls unusually thick, from 12 to 20 millimeters. The typical jar shape is exemplified in the complete vessel in Figure 98, a deep conoidal jar with a small flat base. The closest relation to this ware seems to be the Fayette Thick of the early Adena sites.

Crab Orchard Fabric Marked is the predominant ware of this period. The tempering material is grit-quartzite, feldspar, or hornblende in angular chunks. The surface is covered with plain-plaited fabric or cord-wrapped dowel impressions which are applied horizontally. For a short distance below the lip on the interior, fabric or cord-wrapped dowel impressions are applied vertically. The wall thickness ranges from five to nine millimeters. The jar form is subconoidal with a slightly constricted neck and a flat base approximately nine centimeters in diameter. The jar illustrated by Griffin[63] from Jackson County is an example of this type.

The nonceramic traits which can be related definitely to Zone III are closely related both to Baumer and to the Archaic. Long, tanged antler projectile points, and the tines from which they were cut, are common. Circular flat based pits and multiple-pitted lap mortars may be associated with a gathering economy, but the prevalence of animal bones testifies to the major importance of hunting. Bone artifacts consisted of one projectile point, a cut deer mandible and numerous splinter awls. The predominant projectile type, as at Baumer, was long with a contracting stem and a straight or excurvate base. The second most common point also resembles the Baumer form, with a wide straight stem and a straight shoulder.

60. Big Sandy, Ledbetter, Colbert, Watts Bar, Candy Creek, and Baumer sites.

61. Webb and Snow, 1945, p. 315.   62. Maxwell, n.d.*b.*

63. Griffin, J. B., 1941*a,* pl. 16.

Short-bodied points with long, narrow, straight stems are like a point found at Faulkner and long, narrow points with shallow side notches resemble those in the Eva Focus.

Drills were narrow with expanded, triangular or straight-stemmed bases. End and side scrapers, straight-based flake knives, ovoid choppers and small hoes can all be attributed to this zone. One fragment of a grooved ax, pitted hammers or anvils, unworked lumps of galena and a clay figurine complete the trait complex.

In summary there is a very close relationship between the cultural material of Zone III or early Crab Orchard and the Baumer Focus, and both components might be considered as belonging to the same focus. One of the significant differences is in the tempering material, clay and limestone in Baumer and igneous or metamorphosed grit in Crab Orchard. Since there is no other evidence for a temporal difference between Baumer and early Crab Orchard we may assume the temper difference to be on the basis of available material. The most southern extension of glaciation in this area has been determined as a line passing twelve miles south of Carbondale. To the north are the igneous rocks of the glacial till, whereas to the south there are only sedimentary rocks. This explanation has also been used by Haag[64] in interpreting differences between Adena wares.

Whereas the Baumer people appear to have left Massac County at the close of this period, in the Crab Orchard sites there is an unbroken continuity of culture into Zone II, or late Crab Orchard Focus. This later stage of development is marked by the introduction of new traits, or traits that can be identified as emanating from other culture centers. Zone II is the longest period of unbroken occupation of the Crab Orchard Site. Probably semipermanent houses were erected but since holes dug for support posts did not extend to the yellow clay, it was impossible to find any trace of them. The majority of the circular, flat based, straight-walled pits dug throughout the village contained material from this zone.

In twenty-seven different areas throughout the midden human bones were found. However, only nine of these can be definitely recognized as burials. Fragments of maxilla, mandibles, skull vaults, and long bones scattered in the midden refuse were probably deposited when aboriginal storage pits were dug through previous burials. Of the definite burials, all in a poor state of preservation, four were tightly flexed on the side, four were secondary bundle burials, all in shallow, irregularly oval pits, and one was an infant cremation in one of the circular un-lined pits. There

were no artifacts found in unquestioned association with any of the burials, but their depth in the village midden indicates that they were probably made during the occupation of Zone II.

Only one of the skulls could be restored, but the physical type of this individual is highly significant. Ruth Marzano, Department of Anthropology, University of Chicago, who made the reconstruction and measurements, states that this individual is a dolichocranic Sylvid of the Shell Mound type. Interpretations made on the basis of one individual may be invalid, but the suggestion is strong that the Woodland people of the Crab Orchard Focus were relatively little changed physically from their Archaic ancestors.

The trait complex of Zone II shows relatively little change from Zone III. The Crab Orchard Fabric Marked pottery is the predominant ware of this zone, Sugar Hill Cord Marked ware having become less popular. Vessel walls are thinner and there is a refinement in technique of manufacture. The flat bases are larger and some conoidal bases appear. Of the non-ceramic traits, the grooved ax, multiple-pitted lap stone, and mortars disappear. In their place, many traits occur for the first time in the lower levels of this zone. There are antler awls and punches, hammers or "drifts," and drilled handles. In bone, deer metatarsal and bird ulna awls are present but rare, and one notched and polished ring was found. Mussel shells were cut and perforated for pendants. Most of the earlier chipped flint traits persist, but significant new forms appear such as broad projectile points with very small, round bases; small corner notched points, straight-stemmed points with diagonal shoulders, and an excurvate-based point with a weak shoulder, which appears often on one side only. Thin ovate knives were introduced, and chipped and polished chisels and plano-convex adzes or scrapers. Celts were thick and crude with pointed polls. Thin chalky limestone celt-shaped artifacts were probably used in preparing hides. A pecked quartzite ball, a small conical limestone cup and sandstone and hematite tablets were found in the lowest levels of this zone and in the upper level of Zone III.

Some of the new traits which are introduced into the Crab Orchard Focus at this time show a typological similarity to traits in the Adena center in Kentucky. Antler "drifts" and handles, thin ovate knives, and stone tablets are common in Adena.[65]

There are also detailed similarities in the projectile points. In the preparation of this article I made a classification of 1,361 projectile points illustrated or described in detail from twelve Kentucky Adena

64. Haag, 1942c, p. 342.

65. Webb and Snow, 1945.

sites.[66] These points were grouped into twenty "types", a number purposely large to include as many variations as possible. Of these points, 706, or 52 per cent, are the long, excurvate-based weak-shouldered point[67] common in Zone II of Crab Orchard, but absent in Zone III and in the Baumer complex. The expanding-stemmed point and the narrow, straight-stemmed point with diagonal shoulder are present in both Zone II and Adena, but the straight-based, contracting-stemmed point which is the predominant form in Baumer and Zone III of Crab Orchard represents only two tenths of one per cent of the group of Adena points inspected. Another typological clue to the chronological position of this stage in the Crab Orchard Focus is provided by the long, narrow, double-tapered point which also occurs in the Red Ocher Phase,[68] interpreted by Deuel[69] as Adena.

There is further evidence in Zone II of a strong Hopewellian influence from the Illinois River Valley. Possibly this influence followed that of Adena, but unfortunately the stratigraphic evidence is not conclusive. However, the available information points to the fact that Adena-like traits in the Crab Orchard Site are earlier than ceramic and nonceramic traits that are characteristic of Illinois Hopewell. Hopewell pottery, the Type 3 of Cole and Deuel,[70] cut and perforated animal jaws, characteristic deep corner and side-notched projectile points, and a specialized "reel-shaped" gorget, when found in portions of the midden undisturbed by pits, were in the upper levels of Zone II. Artifacts which have been compared typologically with Adena, on the other hand, appear first in the lower levels of this zone. The answer to this problem can be answered conclusively only by further excavation.

In summary, then, it appears that there was in the lower Ohio Valley a cultural complex of the Woodland Pattern which may have emerged from the Archaic, but which was, in southern Illinois at least, earlier than the distinctive Adena complex. In my opinion this lends weight to the hypothesis that the Adena cultural complex is the product of an intrusive people, rather than merely the grafting of a burial mound complex to an existing Woodland base.

The transition between the Archaic Pattern and the Woodland Pattern is marked by the introduction of ceramic techniques, by a reduction in the shell-fish diet, and by a gradual stylistic change in nonceramic artifacts. Possibly the bow and arrow supplanted the atlatl in hunting. Wild plant foods were gathered and milled, but there is no evidence to indicate that the people were agriculturalists. Probably this period, manifested in the Baumer and early Crab Orchard foci, was not of long duration and was either earlier than, or coeval with, the first appearance of the Adena people in the lower Ohio Valley. By the time that Adena cultural influences moved westward to southern Illinois, the Baumer Site had been abandoned. The Crab Orchard people, on the other hand, demonstrate an unbroken cultural continuity through the stage of Adena influence, accepting many of the material traits of Adena but not the elaborate burial complex. In the late Crab Orchard Focus a much stronger influence is felt from the Illinois Hopewell centers and the burial-mound complex is taken over by at least some of the Crab Orchard people. The majority of older Crab Orchard traits, however, persist in association with the new stylistic importations.

MIDDLE WOODLAND

The period of "classic" Hopewell development has been suggested by some as the period during which agriculture spread through the Ohio and Mississippi valleys. Whether or not there was a radical change in subsistence, there certainly was, at least in southern Illinois, a radical change in religious life and an introduction of the burial mound complex. This in itself is sufficient to mark a new or "middle" period of development in Woodland culture. There was no break in cultural continuity, simply the acceptance of a number of new stylistic elements which were added to the older, more generalized cultural traits. In the Crab Orchard Focus, no trait which is present in the pre-Hopewell, or "Adena," levels is conspicuously absent during the period of Hopewell intrusion. This can be explained in part by conservatism, possibly also in part by the continued influx of Adena influence if Griffin[71] is correct in thinking that Adena in Kentucky lasted through some part of the Hopewell development in Ohio.

There is no evidence in southern Illinois for the entrance at this time of a people physically different from those of the Crab Orchard Focus. The basic cultural complex is that of the Woodland Crab Orchard, and although traits stylistically characteristic of Illinois Valley Hopewell appear to have had a utilitarian function in the village, they comprise a minor percentage of the total trait complex.

Surprisingly enough, Hopewell mounds along the Mississippi River in southern Illinois have been generally ignored by pot-hunter and professional alike and yet this area may well be found to be as extensive and highly developed a center as that in the Illinois Valley. The Vogel Mound group in Jackson County, reported by Thomas[72] is undoubtedly

66. University of Kentucky Reports in Anthropology and Archeology."

67. Cf. Webb, W. S., 1940, Fig. 38–*M* and *P*.

68. Cole and Deuel, 1937, Fig. 19–9.

69. Deuel, 1935, p. 430.   70. Cole and Deuel, 1937, p. 42.

71. Griffin, J. B., 1946, p. 57.   72. Thomas, Cyrus, 1894, p. 143.

Hopewell. Here an extended burial was found with a copper earspool, an ovate gorget and pottery which Griffin states is a mixture of Hopewellian decorative techniques and fabric-impressed (Crab Orchard Fabric Marked) and cord-marked (Crab Orchard Cord Marked) sherds. The same mixture of pottery types was found, apparently with other Hopewell traits, at the Hiser Mound group two miles away.[73] Two complete vessels of Hopewell Zoned Stamped from this area are in the Irvin S. Peithman collection. There are also three-quarter grooved axes, platform pipes, copper knives and celts, and sheets of mica in this and various other local collections.

In the Crab Orchard Site, and in five other components in Jackson and Williamson counties, Hopewell traits begin to appear in the upper three-quarters of Zone II. There is a radical change in the Crab Orchard Fabric Marked pottery. Whereas previously the rims of these vessels had been undecorated, suddenly over 80 per cent of the rims are decorated with a row of nodes produced by punching from the interior with a solid or hollow stick. More rarely the punching is done from the exterior, or is a series of two or more rows of nodes. That this is a trait associated with Hopewell is apparent from its appearance in the Ohio, Illinois, and Wisconsin centers.

A new type of pottery, Crab Orchard Cord Marked, is introduced and becomes popular. This is a thin-walled grit or clay-grit ware, cord-marked with fine, tightly-twisted cords. Like the fabric-marked vessels of this period, there is a row of punched nodes below the rim. The vessel form appears to be a narrow conoidal jar with slightly constricted neck and straight rim. This may very possibly be a local variant of a wide-spread type which occurs in association with Hopewell and which has previously been assigned to local Woodland groups. Vessels of similar aspect are found in northeastern Missouri,[74] southern Michigan and northeastern Indiana[75] in Porter County, Indiana,[76] central Illinois,[77] and in the Turner Mound in Ohio,[78] suggesting that this is a utilitarian ware in the Hopewell ceramic complex.

In addition to these ceramic types there was a small percentage of Hopewell Zoned Stamped and Zoned Incised identical with Type 3 of central Illinois.[79] and probably imported as vessels from that center. There were also a number of sherds of the same paste and temper as Crab Orchard Fabric Marked which showed an attempt on the part of the local people to copy the elaborate Hopewellian de-

signs. There is nothing about these sherds that suggests an incipient Hopewell. They are all imitations of developed Hopewell designs and concepts.

Nonceramic Hopewellian traits which occurred in Zone II were cut and perforated racoon, lynx and wolf mandibles; a perforated fox canine, and a cut bear canine; a small polished limestone disk; "reel-shaped" gorgets; ovate projectile points with deep, round side notches; long triangular drills; large disks of hornstone flint, and a very crude clay female figurine. A platform pipe was plowed up in a site in the Crab Orchard Basin which the surface survey had previously assessed as belonging to the Crab Orchard Focus.

Recently a large group of mounds, and what is apparently a Hopewell village site, has been located on the Twenhofel Farm near the Vogel and Hiser mound groups. Here amateurs found an extended burial covered with a coarsely woven fabric and a quantity of pearl and cylindrical shell beads. At the left side of the skull was a small cache of shell beads and four copper earspools, and around both ankles were strings of large, rectangular shell beads. Near the mound two flaring copper celts and some unworked sheets of mica were found. A surface survey of the village site, made two months later, disclosed the fact that Crab Orchard Fabric Marked was the dominant pottery type, but that Hopewell and Hopewell-influenced sherds occurred in a much higher percentage than they had in the Crab Orchard Site.

It appears probable then that Hopewell in southern Illinois is only the acceptance by a local people of a burial complex and an associated elaboration of manufacturing techniques.

The association of Hopewell designs and fabric-marked pottery are of significance in the interpretation of Illinois Hopewell. Somewhere in the chain of Hopewell sites along the Mississippi River from the mouth of the Illinois River to Fountain Bluff there is a break between northern and southern influences.[80] This may be marked by nonceramic traits but it is certainly marked by the Naples Stamped ware in the north and Crab Orchard Fabric Marked in the south. The only site in Illinois where these two types are found in association, in any significant percentage, is the Boulder Site in Clinton County.[81] Naples Stamped has not been found on any of the sites of southern Illinois. Crab Orchard Fabric Marked, on the other hand, has been found rarely along the Illinois River. A large flat-based sherd of this type was found in a Hopewell grave in the Havana Mound.[82] Two fabric-marked body sherds, 137 disks, apparently made of flint from the horn-

73. Griffin and Morgan (eds.), 1941, p. 48.
74. Eichenberger, 1944, p. 220.
75. Quimby, 1941b, Pl. 9, No. 2.
76. McAllister, 1932, Pl. 32 S–1.
77. Cole and Deuel, 1937, Fig. 6, No. 3.
78. Willoughby and Hooton, 1922, Pl. 22, d.
79. Cole and Deuel, 1937, p. 42.

80. McKern, Titterington, and Griffin, 1945, p. 302.
81. Chamberlain, J., n.d.
82. Griffin and Morgan (eds.), 1941, Pl. 12, No. 3.

stone quarry near Carbondale, two specialized "reel-shaped" gorgets like the one from Crab Orchard, and cut and perforated dog mandibles were also found in this same mound group. It has been assumed that the Type 3 pottery vessels in the Crab Orchard Focus were traded down the river from the Illinois Valley. It now seems apparent that pottery, at least, was occasionally traded up the Mississippi Valley as well.

Much of the difference between northern and southern Hopewell in Illinois may be attributed to the differences between the Woodland bases of the two areas. From the time that the Faulkner people went north to establish the Black Sand Focus until the advent of Middle Mississippi cultures, none but the most generalized relationships existed between the Woodland foci of Fulton and the southern counties. This is especially marked in the period immediately preceding Hopewell development. The difference that exists between the Morton Focus and the Crab Orchard Focus is striking when one recognizes the short geographic distance between the two.

Even more striking is the difference that exists between the Early and Middle Woodland of Jefferson County, Missouri, and early and late Crab Orchard separated by sixty-five air miles.[83] The cultural affiliations of the Missouri sites seem to be with the Illinois Valley to the northeast.[84] Strangely enough, north of Hannibal, Missouri, north of the mouth of the Illinois River, Crab Orchard Fabric Marked sherds constitute nine per cent of a Central Basin-Hopewell ceramic complex at Site MA3.[85]

Other instances of Hopewellian manifestations are being reported from the lower Ohio Valley. Black[86] mentions a collection allegedly coming from a large mound in Posey County, Indiana, which includes elaborate copper work of the Ohio Hopewell type. A surface collection made on the site produced Mississippi sherds, "many sherds of the Marksville-Hopewellian type and also sand-tempered sherds bearing upon their surfaces complicated stamp designs identical to the Swift Creek patterns of the Southeast." Recently a Hopewell site has been excavated by Neumann in the lower Wabash Valley near Carmi, Illinois.[87] It seems apparent that further excavation will produce a center for Hopewell culture in the lower Ohio Valley, and that the complex of traits for this center will be significantly different from that of either the Ohio or central Illinois centers.

Late Woodland

The cultural development which follows the Hopewell climax in southern Illinois is not clearly seen.

83. Adams, 1941.
84. Blake, 1942.
85. Eichenberger, 1944.
86. Black, 1941.
87. Griffin, J. B., personal communication.

In the Carbondale area, the Crab Orchard Focus seems to end abruptly. In many Jackson and Williamson county sites a distinctive cord-marked pottery, Raymond Cord Marked, was found on or near the surface, mixed with material of the Crab Orchard Focus. From the evidence derived from stratified sites we can say only that the Raymond Focus is later than Hopewell and earlier than the Mississippi Pattern in Williamson and Jackson counties.

Only one unmixed component of this focus has been excavated. This was on the Raymond farm, on the south bank of the Big Muddy River north of Carbondale (Fig. 100). The midden deposit was thin, approximately eighteen inches, but it was possible to recognize two zones on the basis of typology. The lower zone, six inches thick, contained only material of the early Crab Orchard Focus, comparable to Zone III at the Crab Orchard Site. Except for a few shell-tempered and Dillinger sherds near the surface, the top foot of midden contained Raymond Cord Marked pottery only. This ware is grit-tempered and cord-wrapped paddle impressed. Approximately 50 per cent of the rim sherds had small notches in the exterior or interior lip. Aside from this there was no attempt at decoration, and the nine thousand sherds from Raymond components show an amazing and boring homogeneity. Only two vessel forms were present, both conoidal-based, one with straight sides and the other with a slightly constricted neck.

Remarkably few nonceramic artifacts were associated with these sherds. Unmodified antler tine punches and sharpened bone splinters were rare. Projectile points were crudely made in general and included small, narrow triangular points similar to the ones in the Mississippi Pattern, and straight-based side and corner-notched and straight-stemmed points. Flake knives and scrapers were more common than shaped tools. The latter included only a few crude, straight-based knives and one straight-stemmed hafted scraper. Two gravers were found, their points rubbed smooth by use. Only two types of ground stone artifacts were found—thick ovate celts which are little more than polished pebbles and half of a long plano-convex rectangular bar, possibly an atlatl weight.

There is very little of a positive nature that can be said about the Raymond Focus. We know only that it was a very generalized Woodland group, relatively poor in material culture traits of a non-perishable nature. The Raymond Focus is later than Hopewell in southern Illinois and earlier than classic Middle Mississippi, but there is no indication of a continuity between Raymond and either Crab Orchard or Mississippi. Certainly none of the specialized traits that give late Crab Orchard its Hopewellian flavor have been carried over into the Raymond Focus. Nor have those traits which are characteristic of the indigenous Crab Orchard persisted into the Raymond Focus. Either the Raymond Focus is the manifestation of an indigenous culture in a period of decadence, or it is the trait complex of an alien group, uninfluenced by the widespread Hopewell development, who enter the area for the first time. Sufficient evidence does not exist at the present time to support either hypothesis.

There is a close similarity between the complex of the Raymond Focus and the Lewis Focus (Fig. 99) of Pope and Massac counties[88] and they have been combined in the Bluff Aspect. The pottery is nearly identical with decorative techniques somewhat more common in the Lewis Focus. Like the Raymond Focus, nonceramic traits are meagerly represented, and in the main are nondistinctive. In stratified sites the Lewis Focus lies between the Baumer and the Kincaid (Middle Mississippi) foci. There is, however, no cultural continuity indicated between Baumer and Lewis, as is to be expected from the hiatus indicated in the Carbondale area. In its later stages the Lewis Focus appears to have been influenced by Middle Mississippi traits. This influence is manifested by rectangular small-log houses, extended burials, a red slip on the surface of a few sherds and olla and plate vessel forms. In view of this influence MacNeish has suggested that the Lewis Focus may have continued for a short time after the entrance in the area of the people of the Kincaid Focus.

With the information available the Raymond and Lewis foci present an enigma, both apparently are meager generalized Woodland cultures following in time the elaborate complex of the Hopewell period. In the later stages of development the focus can be compared temporally and in part culturally with the Late Woodland sites of Parker Heights in Adams County, Illinois and the Jersey Bluff Focus of Jersey County, Illinois.[89] The Lewis and Raymond foci not only indicate the fact that Woodland tribes were living in southern Illinois during the beginning of the period when Mississippi influences were entering the area, but also that in this region at least some time elapsed between the end of Hopewell development and the entrance of Middle Mississippi people.

In the Carbondale area, the Raymond Focus is followed by the Dillinger Focus (Fig. 101),[90] a Woodland complex strongly influenced by Mississippi culture. The fact that the Raymond Focus demonstrates no definite signs of encroaching Mississippi influences whereas the Dillinger Focus, in its earliest development, is highly acculturated by a contemporaneous, neighboring, Mississippi group, suggest a cultural hiatus between the Raymond and Dillinger foci.

Components of the Dillinger Focus have been found in the top level of the Raymond Site at a number of sites in the Crab Orchard Basin and in cave sites at Cove Hollow, Chalk Bluff[91] and along Indian Creek.[92] These sites are the remains of a semisedentary culture in which agriculture, as indicated by the chert and shell hoes, is beginning to play an important role, but in which hunting is the dominant economy. There is a marked difference between the variety of foods eaten in the Dillinger Focus and that of the earlier foci. The Dillinger people seem to have eaten everything that moved, from digger wasp larvae to other humans. The pottery is well made, predominantly grit-tempered, cord-marked, and appears in a variety of shapes. The predominant form is a large globular jar with a constricted neck, but deep conoidal vessels, small bowls, shallow plates and large shallow evaporating pans are common. The majority of rim sherds are decorated with applied fillets, lip notches, vertical and horizontal lugs and groups of nodes. Raised points on the lip often give a collared effect to the jars. Associated with this complex is an unusual vessel form, often either sun-dried or poorly fired, which may have been ceremonial in use. This is a small, narrow vase, with very thick walls. The base is small, flat and usually divided into four elements or "feet." Vessels of this type have also been found on the surface of the Cahokia village,[93] in the Pere Marquette Site,[94] in the Korando Site and the Ullin Site in Pulaski County, Illinois.[95]

Two per cent of the sherds from the type site are shell-tempered—from angular shouldered jars and small loop-handled bowls—indicating contact with a Middle Mississippi complex. Further evidence of outside contacts is seen in the rare incised sherds, and sherds with notched applied fillets, most like those of the Yankeetown Site in Warwick County, Indiana.[96]

The distribution of the Dillinger Focus is not well known. A surface survey of the Mississippi bottom lands indicated a probable concentration in the western part of Jackson County with a penetration along the Big Muddy and Crab Orchard waterways into the western part of Williamson County. A Dillinger Component was indicated at both the Guy Smith Site and the Korando Site excavated by the University of Illinois. Dillinger Cord Marked pottery is present in the top levels of the Boulder Site in Clinton County, and from the surface of the Ullin Site on the bank of the Cache River in Pulaski County. Farther west along the Cache River in Alexander County a

88. MacNeish, n.d.c, p. 34.

89. MacNeish, 1944. [In this paper attributed to "Middle Woodland." ED.]

90. Maxwell, n.d.a.

91. Peithman, 1939.

92. Thomas, C. J., 1938.

93. Titterington, 1938.

94. Rinaldo, n.d.

95. Material sent to the University of Chicago by Dr. Bruce Merwin.

96. Black, Glenn A., personal communication.

surface collection was made by Mr. Bus Miller of Makanda from a site known locally as the Fatty Morris Site.

There is a close resemblance of traits between this focus and the Maples Mills,[97] Jersey Bluff, Pere Marquette, Dick, Spencer and Parker Heights foci which some students have grouped together in the Tampico Phase. This resemblance seems to be due partly to the common presence of Middle Mississippi traits on a Woodland base, and not to any genetic relationship. One of the important criteria for this grouping, the burial complex, is not known for the Dillinger Focus. However, unconfirmed reports suggest that some of the stone slab graves along the Mississippi River bluffs in Jackson County contained Dillinger pottery. Ascribing the Dillinger Focus to the Woodland Pattern may be objected to by some. Certainly the trait complex does not fit into the framework established by the First Woodland Conference. The trait complex most nearly resembling that of the Dillinger Focus is found in the Plattin Focus of the Middle Mississippi Pattern in Jefferson County, Missouri.[98] The Plattin Clay Tempered pottery type of this focus resembles very closely the Dillinger Cord Marked pottery of the Korando Site. However, in the Plattin sites this constitutes only 22 per cent of the ceramic complex, with the shell-tempered Imperial Plain constituting 78 per cent. A cross influence or trading relationship seems to have existed between the two foci. In substance, the argument for the Woodland heritage of the Dillinger people is a shaky one. However, the culture complex differs, in subsistence emphasis, in ceramic traits and in some of the projectile point types, from that of contemporary Middle Mississippi people occupying the same area. Since these points of difference are diagnostic of the Woodland-Mississippi culture separation it seems logical to assume that the Dillinger people were an indigenous group living in harmony with and acculturated by the entering Middle Mississippi people. In the main their settlements were up the Kaskaskia, Big Muddy and Cache tributaries, leaving the flat bottom lands for the Mississippi farmers.

Without question the Mississippi influence in the Dillinger Focus stemmed from the Cahokia center rather than from sites of the Tennessee-Cumberland Aspect of southern Illinois and Indiana. Probably these influences continued through both the Old Village and the Trappist foci, although such determinant traits as Powell Plain pottery for the Old Village Focus and the distinctive bean pot shape of Trappist have not been found in Dillinger components. The presence of loop handles and the absence of strap handles and effigy forms indicate that Dillinger was coeval with at least the earlier focus of the Monks Mound Aspect. There is no evidence upon which to postulate a survival of the Dillinger Focus after the Middle Mississippi occupation.

MIDDLE MISSISSIPPI

The late prehistoric Indians of southern Illinois seem to have been affected by the complexes of two culture centers—the Cahokia and the general Tennessee Cumberland centers. The Cahokia (Monks Mound Aspect) spread southward along the Mississippi from the region around St. Louis, establishing large village sites along the flood plain, influencing such indigenous people as the Woodland Dillinger, and penetrating to the interior only in rare hunting forays (as apparent from material in rock shelters and sites along the Crab Orchard Basin). The Linn Site and the Hale Site, both in Union County, may belong to this aspect. In general, however, these sites are no better known now than they were after Thomas' preliminary excavations.[99] Incidentally the Catholic medal found by Thomas in one of the stone slab graves in the Hale Site, if genuinely associated with the culture, is the only indication of European contact with Middle Mississippi in southern Illinois.

The Tennessee-Cumberland Aspect in southern Illinois is best represented at the Kincaid Site in Pope and Massac counties. Since this material is being prepared for publication, a brief summary of the results of excavation and analysis will be sufficient here.

The Kincaid Site consists of sixteen mounds and several areas of village habitation.[100] The mounds are large truncated conicals and pyramids, and low domed circulars with the village areas between the mounds. Agriculture is the dominant economy, supplemented by hunting and fishing. The wattle and daub rectangular houses were arranged close together in the village areas with the walls of adjoining houses parallel. On top of the truncated conical and pyramidal mounds were temples with clay banquettes which probably served as ceremonial centers not only for the people of the Kincaid village, but for isolated farming groups as well. Two burial complexes are present, extended burials in log cists and in stone slab cists. Occasionally infants and adults were buried in a partially flexed position in the village refuse. Grave goods were rare with all types of burials.

Six wood specimens from the Kincaid Site have been dated within the span of 1513 to 1588.[101] This evidence and the indications of internal stylistic change have led the investigators to recognize three time periods within the Kincaid Focus—Early from

97. Cole and Deuel, 1937.   98. Adams, 1941.

99. Thomas, Cyrus, 1894, p. 154. [Examination of ceramic collections from these sites does not support this suggestion of a close connection to the Cahokia area.—ED.]

100. Bennett, n.d.

101. Cole, Bell, Orr, and MacNeish, 1946; see also the chapter by Bell in this volume.

1450 to 1520; Middle from 1520 to 1580 and Late from 1580 to 1613.

In the Early period a few of the domiciliary mounds were built. The houses were small, rectangular wattle and daub structures with open corners. But there was little planning to the arrangement of houses in the village. Burials were made in log cists, in the extended position, with the inclusion of few grave goods. Effigy bowls, rarer than in later times, consist of blank-faced bottles with horned owl-shaped heads, bird heads on bowls and rare fish effigy bowls. Alien potsherds demonstrate a limited trading sphere with Cahokia and western Tennessee and Mississippi.

The Middle period was a transition period between the small village and the later town. Large domiciliary mounds were built and the houses were arranged around a central plaza. These houses were of both open and closed-corner types. Both salt pans and effigy bowls increase in numbers and incised angular guilloche appears for the first time. Bird heads and lugs modeled in the shape of human hands are most common and are executed with more skill. Trade sherds indicate a widening circle of contacts, adding Kentucky, Alabama and the Upper Mississippi Phase to the trading sphere.

The Late period sees the greatest ceremonial activity. The large truncated pyramid with a conical offset was built then. Mounds were arranged in a semicircle around a central plaza and the houses were laid out in parallel rows. The dead were enclosed in slab stone boxes, still with rare grave goods. In the ceramic complex, bird effigies decrease in importance, incising becomes more prevalent and strap handles take the place of loop handles. Some change in the nonceramic complex is also indicated. Stone effigies and long lanceolate blades appear only in the Late period. Equal-armed pipes, the use of fluorspar for disks, earplugs, labrets and beads, and the thin serrated triangular projectile points are more common in the later stages.

There is reason to believe that there was an extensive occupation of Kincaid, and of her sister cities (the King Site at Wycliffe, Kentucky, and the Angel Site at Evansville, Indiana), after the last dendrochronological date of 1588. However, European influences must have been manifested in the late years of the 17th century, and they are completely missing in the three sites. Evidence that there may have been an archeological horizon following Kincaid and preceeding European settlement comes from artifacts of the Southern Cult[102] found in Union County in the late eighteen hundreds. Although cult traits are frequent in the Angel Site and the King Site, they are very rare in the Kincaid Focus. If this cult enters southern Illinois in its final elaboration only after the abandonment of Kincaid it would help to explain the fluorspar human effigy, tripod water bottles and obstetrical jars found in stone box graves near Anna[103] by Perrine and the incised copper plates depicting dancing eagle warriors reported by Thomas from similar graves nearby.[104]

In recapitulation we have a picture of one indigenous culture in the lower Ohio Valley from the earliest inhabitants to a period shortly before the entrance of European influence and of three intrusive waves of people who modify the lives of the original occupants. Through internal culture change plus the borrowing of ceramic techniques there is an emergence of Woodland culture out of the Archaic. In turn Woodland is modified in the areas peripheral to Ohio and Kentucky by Adena people who intrude on the valley. There is some suggestion that the culture centers were more conservative than the peripheral tribes—that Indian Knoll and Adena last longer in Kentucky than they do in either Illinois or Ohio. Again by a process of internal change in the Woodland Pattern plus such influences as Adena and possibly others, the ceremonial Hopewellian culture is developed. In the lower Ohio Valley this seems to enter as a complex from the center in central Illinois rather than from the Scioto Valley of Ohio. Perhaps in the later stages of this development ceremonial centers were established in the lower valley and the area no longer was marginal to central Illinois. There is no fading of Hopewellian culture into a later development. Either a sudden catharsis leaves the Woodland an impoverished people broken into small tribes with little vestige of former techniques, or the bearers of Hopewell culture leave the Ohio Valley and their place is taken by intruding Raymond and Lewis people. The latter persist in the eastern tip of southern Illinois until they are finally forced out by the increasing population of the Middle Mississippi invaders from the southeast. In the western part of this area a Woodland group, the Dillinger people, continued to live in close contact with a Middle Mississippi group which entered from the southwest. It is probable that these Woodland people occupied the forest lands of the interior through the entire period of Mississippi development. But the time from 1600 when Kincaid was in its climax to 1700 when Europeans first entered the valley and found only scattered bands of starving hunters remains a blank for the present.

102. Waring and Holder, 1945.

103. Perrine, 1874.   104. Thomas, Cyrus, 1894, p. 161.

THE TENNESSEE AREA. *By Madeline Kneberg**

THE political, economic, and academic imperialism of states' rights is responsible for this utterly incongruous title, as if culture could be discussed in terms of state areas rather than natural provinces. Like the dachshund that is a dog and a half long and half a dog high, the state of Tennessee has peculiar proportions. Straddling the east-central part of the United States, it extends for over four hundred miles east and west, from the banks of the Mississippi to the crests of the Appalachian Mountains, and is scarcely more than a hundred miles wide from north to south.

In culture, as well as, or because of, geography, the state of Tennessee straddled the prehistoric life of the eastern United States. The ebb and flow of cultures and the march of peoples left their impress. Perhaps, no culture ever reached its apogee in Tennessee, but some version of every cultural horizon in the eastern United States is represented.

Generally speaking, the area can be divided into three natural divisions: East Tennessee, Middle Tennessee, and West Tennessee. The threefold cultural, physical, and political divisions that exist today have their counterparts in the prehistory of the state. But this general tripartite classification is inadequate to explain the sequences and trends of culture.

Actually, there are six distinct physiographic regions that influenced the events that took place. On the eastern border there are two thousand square miles of mountain wilderness broken by narrow valleys and coves. Lofty forests and dense underbrush still exist today, and in a primeval state it must have been almost impassable except by the greatest effort. West of the mountains is the great valley of the eastern channel of the Tennessee River. In this area of about nine thousand square miles are bottom lands, not only along the Tennessee River itself, but also along its many tributaries. Here are to be found hundreds of prehistoric village sites, many of them successively used by different peoples during the centuries of aboriginal occupation. Still part of East Tennessee is the Cumberland Plateau, rising abruptly a thousand feet above the valley. The five thousand square miles of the plateau, extending north and south to the borders of the state, is char-

acterized by a combination of forests and scrub undergrowth masking sharp declivities cut by ancient streams. This region formed a discouraging barrier even to the white man. Thus, nature had an important hand in shaping the entire human story of East Tennessee. Movement was necessarily north and south along the valley, with a few exceptions, to which we shall refer later.

Middle Tennessee begins where the plateau grades into the Highland Rim, and extends to the western valley of the Tennessee River. The Highland Rim includes nearly ten thousand square miles of the poorest land in the state. Thin soil barely supports the cedar glades growing precariously and tenaciously on the limestone. Within this region, however, lies the Central Basin where the Harpeth and Cumberland rivers drain over six thousand square miles of fertile land.

The western valley is scarcely more than twelve miles in width and comprises only twelve hundred square miles. Yet its fertile soil and rich assortment of animal and plant life was a particularly desirable location for hunters and food gatherers in aboriginal times. Only one important river joins the Tennessee from the west. This is the Big Sandy whose flow is parallel to that of the Tennessee for about fifty miles before its confluence near the northern border of the state. The prehistoric occupation of the Big Sandy Valley was significantly influenced by its comparative isolation from the main waterway.

Beyond the western valley is the plateau of West Tennessee which drops gradually to the west, ending in a series of bluffs above the Mississippi bottom lands. Cultures of the prehistoric sites in this region are more directly affiliated with those of the Mississippi Valley, even those on the headwaters of the Obion River, which is less than twenty miles from the banks of the Tennessee.

The very first human beings that came to Tennessee were probably Folsom hunters stalking the mastodon and other game animals of nine or ten millenia ago. Folsom points have been found in nearly every part of the state, but so far none has been associated with extinct animals. Most have been surface finds. Perhaps the earliest recognition of the distinctive Folsom point was by Thruston,[1] who stated they were "a specialty of Maury County," Tennessee. In the

* University of Chicago, B.A., 1932; M.A., 1947; Professor of Anthropology, University of Tennessee. Chapter received in December, 1947.

1. Thruston, 1890, pp. 231–232.

western valley, nine feet below an occupation of the Archaic peoples, was found evidence of hearths and flint chips. But there seems to have been no continuity of occupation between the early Folsom hunters and their successors.

With the Archaic peoples began the continuous story of human life in Tennessee (Fig. 102). Perhaps two thousand years ago the Eva people,[2] an Archaic group, began to settle along the Tennessee River and its tributary, the Big Sandy, in the western valley. Their culture differed little from that of their northern neighbors at Indian Knoll in Kentucky, or from that of the Lauderdale people in northern Alabama. This was an early Neolithic type of culture that lacked pottery and agriculture. We need not postulate that the Eva people were ignorant of these two great Neolithic inventions. They had wide contacts, trading with the Lake Superior Indians for copper and the Gulf Coast Indians for marine shells. They obtained pottery from the Baumer people, and we may suspect that corn may also have been a trade commodity.

In the western valley where the Eva people lived, animals of many species, wild fruits, nuts and roots, and streams full of fish and clams furnished an ample food supply without recourse to agriculture. The thousands upon thousands of clams consumed by Eva mouths are evident in the great refuse heaps of shells that can be found in Eva villages. Agriculture has little advantage when nature supplies food ready for the taking. We are not always justified in calling the Archaic peoples "pre-pottery" and "pre-agricultural." The prefix should be "non-," since many of them, like the Eva people, preferred to buy their pottery and perhaps disdained the menial labor of tilling the soil. The hunter does not take enthusiastically to the hoe and the humdrum existence of the farmer. Nor does the hunter's wife joyfully add the extra burden of agricultural work to her already staggering responsibilities.

The Eva shell heaps were cemeteries as well as garbage piles. The dead were interred in pits dug into the refuse. Occasionally, they even had clambakes on their refuse piles, for here and there are hearths containing calcined shells. Into the general heaps went the broken tools and the bones of the animals eaten. The actual living quarters were almost too close to the village dump. Around its odorous mass clustered the huts with their storage pits.

Not all of the Eva people lived on clams. Some villages are wholly devoid of shells. Instead of garbage heaps, the ordinary refuse accumulated under foot until it sometimes actually became an elevation of two or more feet above the surrounding land. This was a black, greasy soil into which, as in the shell mounds, the graves for the dead were dug.

If we judge by the imperishable remains of the Eva people we should consider their culture to be far simpler than it was. It was very likely just as rich and colorful as that of the historic Plains Indians. Eliminate the wooden, painted, feathered, and woven things, the soft tanned hides, the cradles, baskets, boats and bows, and what remains is a small sample of the arts and crafts preserved in bone, stone, shell, copper, and red ocher. From these and the skeletons we must infer what the Eva people looked like, what they made, how they lived, and why they died, whom they knew, and with whom they fought.

Their craftsmanship in stone grinding was exceptional. The finish and symmetry of their atlatl weights, their flat gorgets and beads is as good as any ground stone made by the North American Indian excepting perhaps, the sculptured images of later peoples. The Eva flint knapper produced an abundance of spearheads, arrowheads, drills, scrapers, gravers, and knives. The larger spearheads or points for atlatl darts far outnumbered the smaller arrowpoints, suggesting that the bow and arrow was known and used, but that the atlatl was preferred. Plano-convex adzes with bits often highly polished from use were the Eva wood-working tools. Large, flat, hoe-like objects may have been merely digging tools and acquired polish on their bits from the sandy soil, or they may actually have been hoes. Such implements seem to have been more common at late settlements, and may indicate that corn or tobacco was being raised. The group, at least, may have known about tobacco, because tubular pipes were used, that is, if the tubes were pipes, and if they didn't smoke sumac or other plants. Or perhaps, these were merely gadgets confined strictly to the medicine man's bag of tricks. The Eva people were sedentary, and exhaustion of natural resources of game and plant food plus an increasing population may have induced them to clear fields and plant corn to supplement their fare. There is no doubt that this group remained in the western valley long after other peoples began to settle there.

From the bones of the thousands of Virginia deer, wild turkeys and other game which they hunted, the Eva artisans made a great variety of implements. Arrowpoints, atlatl hooks, arrow wrenches, adzes, handles, and other things were made from deer and elk antlers. Awls, fishhooks, needles, scrapers, beads, and ornaments of various kinds were made from bone, sometimes finely engraved.

Small *Anculosa* shells were strung for beads. Large marine conchs were made into vessels, ear ornaments, pendants, gorgets and beads. Sometimes thick sheet copper was combined with shell, but usually it was

2. Lewis and Kneberg, 1947.

used alone to make spherical beads, tubes, awls, fish-hooks and pendants. The use of copper for utilitarian objects relates the culture to the "Old Copper Complex"[3] of Wisconsin, and, thus, is an important indicator of the time period.

The Eva people secured pottery vessels from the Early Woodland Baumer[4] group who made flat-based pots and finished the surfaces with impressions of simple plaited basketry or a cord-wrapped stick. Later, pottery was obtained from other Woodland people who used a clay-grit paste, marked the surfaces with a cord-wrapped paddle and notched the lips of the vessels. Sometimes, but rarely, the pottery came from the region of Alabama where the paste was tempered with sand and the decorations either pinched or incised into the surface, the so-called Alexander ware. Still more rare were shell-tempered pots that the late Eva people must have acquired from early Mississippi peoples invading the region.[5]

Eva burials were usually in a tightly flexed position; in fact, they were forced into pits so small that the body was distorted, occasionally the head being bent back until the neck was broken. In late times, the custom of burying cremated remains appeared sporadically. This is strange because the custom was early in the Alabama area, and was not present in the Kentucky Archaic culture.[6]

In physical appearance the Eva people were usually of moderate stature although some individuals were rather tall and robust. The women were quite small and delicately built. The skull shapes varied from long to medium, but many were actually short and broad. The longer-headed individuals usually had narrower and longer faces, the faces being narrow both at the jaws and cheekbones. However, a very broad face is also typical of the Eva physiognomy. One characteristic feature is seen in the excessive wear of the teeth, almost to the gums, which caused absorption of the jaw margins and tends to make the faces appear shorter than normal. An interesting anomaly was the relatively high occurrence of open metopic sutures; it suggests inbreeding.

The Eva culture finally disappeared, but individuals were most likely absorbed by incoming groups. It is even possible that Archaic groups remained in the area, changing culturally through the years. The Southeast, in historic times, contained a number of groups belonging to various linguistic stocks, none of which the linguists consider as indigenous. The Siouans are supposed to have come down from the Ohio region, the Algonquians from the northeast, the Cherokee from the northeast, the Yuchi from the Middle West, and the Muskhogeans

from somewhere west of the Mississippi. It is not beyond the realm of possibility that some one or more of the linguistic stocks actually had representatives in the Southeast in distant times. The historic linguistic diversity was no greater than the prehistoric cultural diversity which existed in chronological sequences in a single area, or contemporaneously in adjacent geographical locations. It has already been suggested that the eastern Siouan groups, such as the Ofo,[7] Biloxi, Catawba and others were survivals of the Archaic peoples.[8] The identification of Mosopelea[9] as the early name of Ofo may furnish a name for the late Archaic people in the western Tennessee region.

Our story now shifts to the eastern valley where little or no trace of the Archaic culture has been found. The shell mounds are not found above Chattanooga, although, shoals where clams might be secured are present, and the entire lower portion of the river shows shell mounds. The earliest settlements in the eastern valley were those of the Upper Valley people, a group of southeastern Woodland Indians.

The earliest of the Upper Valley people who settled along the French Broad River as well as the Tennessee are known as the Watts Bar people. They lived in compact villages in circular houses, dug kettle-shaped storage and cooking pits and buried their fully flexed dead in circular graves. A curious situation confronts us when we try to imagine how they subsisted. Few animal bones, no shells and no evidence of corn have been found. Perhaps, like the eastern Siouan peoples, they destroyed the bones of their game animals. They made rather indifferent arrowheads, some medium-sized with stems and some without, and a few small triangular points with incurved sides. Most of their celts were poorly made; only the bit was ground, while the rest was left roughly pecked. Flat stone gorgets very much like those of the Archaic peoples were practically the only ornaments. A few steatite boatstones and tubular pipes were fairly well made.

Their pottery was usually crudely made and its surface was finished with impressions of plain plaited fabric or a cord-wrapped dowel. It was tempered with crushed quartzite or coarse sand and, except for the bottoms of the pots which were conoidal, it resembled the Baumer pottery used by the Eva people.

As the Upper Valley people became adjusted to their environment they substituted crushed limestone for quartzite in their pottery. In addition to the finish used on the early pottery they wrapped paddles with cord and impressed the vessel surfaces. Along the Hiwassee River, they were not far from

3. Ritzenthaler, 1946.
4. Willis, 1941.
5. Lewis and Kneberg, 1947.
6. Webb and De Jarnette, 1942, pp. 113 and 316.

7. Voegelin, C. F., 1941, p. 247.
8. Lewis, T. M. N., 1943, p. 311.
9. Swanton, 1946, pp. 165–166. [For a different interpretation see Griffin, J. B., 1943a, pp. 11–35,—Ed.]

Georgia where the Swift Creek people had devised a means of decorating their pots by carving wooden paddles which they pressed onto the soft clay. Some paddles were merely grooved, others double-grooved at right angles, and still others carved into remarkably fine and intricate designs. The end results when impressed on pottery, are respectively known as the simple, check, and complicated stamped wares.

The Upper Valley people carried on communications with their Georgia neighbors and learned to make stamped pottery of their own. The group of this period are called the Candy Creek people (Fig. 103).[10] Their settlements extended all along the Tennessee River, and their type of pottery has been found as far downstream as Benton and Henry counties in the western valley. Limestone-tempered, fabric-marked, cord-marked, and check-stamped all appear there, the fabric and cord-marked types as early as late Archaic.

But the western valley shows little evidence of occupation by Early Woodland peoples. Instead, the Archaic population seems to have dominated the area, possibly permitting the establishment of only a few villages by outsiders. At a small number of scattered sites, there appears to have been occupations by people similar in culture to the Upper Valley group.

Somewhere, probably in the region of the middle portion of the valley, where the Copena culture flourished, Woodland Indians related to the Upper Valley people acquired the custom of burying their dead in conical mounds. These Middle Valley mound builders moved down the river into the western valley, and up the river to eastern Tennessee. In the western valley, their village debris lies above that of some of the Eva people. Their mounds are away from the river banks on the second bottoms or uplands. In eastern Tennessee their settlements followed those of the Candy Creek and Watts Bar peoples, the mounds usually being on the upland, but occasionally on the bottom lands near the shore.

The Hamilton people,[11] a group having a Middle Valley culture, lived throughout most of East Tennessee; even along remote streams their mounds can be found (Fig. 104). Villages were composed of households strung out along the river banks, each with its own refuse pile of mussel shells. Like the Archaic peoples, the Hamiltonians esteemed the ubiquitous clam as a dietary staple.

Although the Middle Valley people made pottery almost indistinguishable from that of the Upper Valley group, and their tools and weapons were similar; they differed in burial customs and community plan. The Hamilton group valued marine shells highly, and used them for various kinds of ornaments. They used entire conch columellae as beads, perforating them from end to end with a bore not over one-eighth inch. These ponderous beads were up to nine inches in length and weighed about half a pound.

Among their projectile points, which were usually mediocre, they had a most delicate incurvate-sided, triangular type, especially well-adapted to killing human beings. Many of the skeletons in the mounds revealed that a number of such points had penetrated into more or less vital organs. Sometimes males were buried with quivers full of arrows, tipped with this type of point, lying beside them. These were not enemy arrows—they were homemade, and were used in local squabbles. The contentious Hamiltonians were too much concerned about fighting among themselves, and too complacent regarding any threat from outside. And so they were driven out of the fertile valley by a more united and powerful people, the early Mississippi invaders. For a while they continued to reside in secluded places, but finally they disappeared from eastern Tennessee.

The counterpart of the Hamilton culture in western Tennessee was less homogeneous. There were people who built conical burial mounds, made similar pottery and triangular arrow points, but only in Decatur County, near the southern border of the state did they have individual refuse heaps of mussel shells with the households separated from each other. These Decatur[12] people usually lived in more compact villages, most likely for protection (Fig. 105). They were better able to resist the Mississippi invasion and apparently did so for considerable time.

The Decatur culture is closely related to Copena. In fact, the Decatur sites probably are the villages of the Copena people. The Fisher Mound in Hardin County, Tennessee, reported by Webb[13] showed a log tomb of the type described by Rowe[14] for the Smith Farm in Rhea County in eastern Tennessee. The Hamilton, Copena and Decatur cultures seem to be geographical variations in the culture of the Middle Valley Woodland peoples. And, as a group, they represent a southern variant of a widespread manifestation, to which the Adena culture of the Ohio River Basin also belongs. The changes which transformed Early Woodland culture into Middle Woodland culture represent diffusion of ideas from various sources, the strongest influences probably coming from the Marksville people in the Lower Mississippi Valley.

The continued existence of the Eva people in the western valley discouraged for a time extensive settlement by the Decatur group. But, eventually the resistance slackened and Decatur villages and mounds appeared farther down the Tennessee River.

10. Lewis and Kneberg, 1941, pp. 29–34.
11. Lewis and Kneberg, 1946.

12. Lewis and Kneberg, 1947.   14. Rowe, this volume, p. 203.
13. Webb and De Jarnette, 1942.

In fact, the Decatur people became numerous and progressive. In spite of being strongly influenced by Mississippi peoples, they were not displaced. They seem to have gradually modified their culture until it became a hybrid, part Middle Valley Woodland and part Middle Mississippi. Because in late times they can scarcely be considered as the same Decatur group, they are differentiated as the Harmon's Creek people (Fig. 105).[15] Discussion of their culture is better postponed until the Middle Mississippi culture is introduced into this story.

Beyond the watershed between the Tennessee and Mississippi rivers a powerful, aggressive and culturally advanced people were penetrating the heart of the Mississippi Valley, and settling along tributary streams. On the headwaters of the Obion River, an affluent of the Mississippi in western Tennessee, they built a great town (Fig. 106). Along the South Fork of the Forked Deer River at Pinson, they built the greatest mound group in the state, one of the mounds being over seventy feet high. Beyond the eastern bluffs of the Tennessee River, a group of the same people had penetrated to the Cumberland and Harpeth rivers in the Central Basin. They may have reached these rivers by ascending the Mississippi to the mouth of the Ohio and then travelling along the Ohio to the mouth of the Cumberland.

Their former towns are always identifiable by the great pyramidal substructure mounds upon which their council houses were built. Perhaps one of the earliest colonies of this people in Tennessee was established on the bluffs above the Mississippi at Memphis.[16] The people whom we designate as Middle Mississippi were, in Tennessee, a branch of the Muskhogeans. The various tribal divisions of this group dominated the late prehistoric aboriginal life in the Southeast. In fact, the Creek Confederacy, the Choctaws, and Chickasaws were factors to be reckoned with by the white man in the seventeenth and eighteenth centuries.

The early Mississippians were numerous and spread rapidly over a large territory, carrying with them a culture that was basically homogeneous. They had planned communities with a public square for ceremonies, dances, and games. Bordering the squares were erected large community buildings which gradually became elevated on earthen foundations as the structures were rebuilt upon the same location. Dwellings clustered about the community centers, and often the towns were entirely surrounded by stockades.

Some archeologists object to the hypothesis that the Middle Mississippi culture spread by migration,

but, as seen from Tennessee, there is no question about Middle Mississippi peoples having migrated into this region. It is clear in many other places in the Southeast that this culture superseded earlier ones on the same sites. That the people who brought it were Muskhogeans is scarcely debatable. Muskhogean tradition contains detailed migration legends that fulfil some of the surmises of the southeastern archeologists.

There is an obvious continuity of town-dwelling, pyramidal mound building, agricultural life from the time of its first appearance to the days of De Soto, and there is little doubt that many of the descendants of the early Mississippi peoples became the historic southeastern tribes. It is far more difficult to deduce the origin and earlier home of the Mississippi-Muskhogeans. The generalized resemblances to the cultures of Middle America have been frequently remarked with various explanations offered, most of which suggest diffusion through trade. What seems most probable is that the Muskhogeans once lived on the peripheries of the Middle American cultures. The unsettled conditions which prevailed in the Valley of Mexico about A.D. 1000 as a result of the disintegration of the Toltec Empire caused considerable movements of dissatisfied groups. This was reflected on the eastern coast in the Huastec area for a long time until the Aztecs achieved political domination and stabilized conditions.

If the Huastec area was affected, the chances are good that the movements of peoples caused population pressures over a much larger area. The proto-Mississippi peoples were probably peripheral to the higher cultures of Middle America, but were in more or less constant communication with them. While the Mississippians did not participate in all of the complex developments, they followed a way of life that could scarcely have arisen as a result of trade or desultory diffusion in a relatively short time. The complex of agriculture, town life, central plazas and temple mounds shared by both areas must surely represent numerous contacts over a period of considerable duration. Very likely the extensive immigration of tribal groups out of the Valley of Mexico, due to the internal political conflicts and pressure from migratory tribes, had distant repercussions, causing the marginal peoples to move and seek new homes. The earliest temple mounds of the Mississippi Valley probably date around the first part of the twelfth century.[17] They could represent the movements into the south and southeast of peoples who had formerly lived on the outskirts of Middle American civilization. If so, then the Caddo and Muskhogean peoples must have been immigrants into their later territories. This seems more likely than that the culture

15. Lewis and Kneberg, 1947.
16. [This site identified as Shelby (12–P–2) is regarded as a Late Mississippi site in Phillips, Ford, and Griffin, 1951.—Ed.]

17. Krieger, 1946, p. 257.

bearers were Huasteca traders[18] purveying social, ceremonial and religious concepts along with their trade pots.

A century or slightly later the early Mississippi peoples had immigrated into Tennessee by way of the Mississippi Valley. Their culture was already a well-integrated body of technical, social, and ritual activities that differed widely from the culture of the aborigines then inhabiting the Tennessee Valley. The Obion people, a local branch of the early Mississippians constructed a large town near the Tennessee-Mississippi divide on the headwaters of the Obion River (Fig. 106). Covering more than twenty-five acres, this settlement became an important source of cultural ideas for the nearby region. The great plaza was bordered by five mounds, one of which with its ramp was nearly five hundred feet long. The pottery made by the Obion Indians was a fine, white or light gray ware tempered with clay-grit and exclusively plain-surfaced except for the textile marked salt pans and a few black on white painted vessels. Decorating was modelled or painted and handles were of the cylindrical loop type. Later, incised and engraved decoration and strap handles appeared, and finally shell-tempered pottery came into use shortly before the site was abandoned.

The Obion people were related to the Hiwassee Island[19] people in eastern Tennessee who also had large substructure mounds, plazas and compactly organized towns (Fig. 107). The Hiwassee Island group had already acquired the use of shell to temper their pottery which was quite similar to that of the Obion people except for the temper. The painted pottery of the eastern early Mississippi people was red on buff in contrast to the black on white of the western group. Both groups constructed their buildings, homes and council houses in the same manner. The walls were composed of small saplings closely set in trenches, and all structures were rectangular. Neither group left any evidence of its burial customs and as a result we are deprived of the knowledge concerning costume and ornament. We may conjecture that they were no less adorned than other groups and that their ideas of ornament and costume were somewhat similar to those of later Mississippi peoples with whom they merged in many places. The early Mississippi peoples penetrated to remote valleys in the foothills of the mountains in eastern Tennessee, reaching this region long after the towns on the Obion and Forked Deer rivers had been established. They came to eastern Tennessee as invaders who almost entirely replaced the former inhabitants.

In western Tennessee the early Mississippi peoples were content (or forced) to remain in the Mississippi drainage while the Woodland Indians, and perhaps

some Archaic groups, continued to reside along the Tennessee and tributary streams. An economic and social accommodation took place between these peoples of diverse traditions and produced some unusual local cultural complexes along the Tennessee River. The situation was further colored by the influences from the east, possibly caused by displacements of the Middle Valley, Swift Creek, and Copena peoples due to the incoming Mississippians.

Woodland villages in the southern part of the valley show some pottery with limestone temper and stamped decoration of the check and complicated types, but such sites nearly always have larger quantities of clay-grit-tempered pottery with similar decorative treatments. Both kinds of pottery are distinguished by a high proportion of cord-marked ware. More northern villages have less of the limestone-tempered pottery and the abundant clay-grit pottery has less cordmarking. There is a gradual transition from sites of the Decatur group to those of the Harmon's Creek Indians. While the Harmon's Creek culture is clearly the ceramic heir of the Decatur, still, it is just as obviously the architectural offspring of the Obion culture.

Typical wall trench, open corner, rectangular houses, identical to those of the Obion Mississippians, were built by the Harmon's Creek people. Small disks of stone and pottery, pottery trowels, and pottery pipes with small bore stems differentiate this culture from earlier Woodland and point to Mississippi contacts. Small triangular arrowpoints and cord-marked pottery are traits shared with the earlier Woodland. Neither Woodland nor Early Mississippi people buried their dead within the village area, consequently there is a depressing lack of information on their burial customs. It is possible that a single example of a stone walled crematory hints at the mortuary customs of the hybrid Early Mississippi-Middle Woodland culture. There must have been a complex interaction between the two peoples, because throughout the valley there can be found scarcely two components that could be considered sufficiently alike to belong to the same focus.

Some sites showed a continuity of occupation from the days of the Archaic Eva peoples up to Late Mississippi times. At least, almost every variety of pottery ever known in the region was present in appreciable amounts. One cannot escape the idea that the western valley was an aboriginal melting pot. The only people who failed to settle along the Tennessee were the early Mississippians. Only one substructure mound and a few examples of large community buildings are known and even these are relatively late, being associated with shell-tempered pottery and burials in the village area.

Some sites were inhabited only by the Harmon's

18. MacNeish, 1947, pp. 13–14.   19. Lewis and Kneberg, 1946.

Creek people and only during the Middle Woodland period. Others showed that an early occupation by these people was superseded by a Late Mississippi settlement. Still other sites seemed to have been mixed settlements. This situation was well illustrated by a group of three sites just north of the mouth of the Big Sandy River. The Centerville Landing Site was a single component Woodland settlement, while a quarter of a mile south at the Williams Site was a somewhat earlier Woodland overlain by a Late Mississippi occupation. Just across the river was the large Gray Site where the earliest occupation was Woodland, similar to that of the Centerville Landing Site, followed by an extensive Mississippi occupation which included some amalgamation with the Woodland.

The failure of the early Mississippians to conquer the western valley could be explained in more ways than one. The presence of both Archaic and Woodland people would have been a deterrent, assuming that their accommodation extended to combining forces against Mississippi colonizers. If such were the case, an enclave would have resulted, giving rise to variable cultural entities within its borders. The same situation may have resulted from the disinclination of the Mississippians to settle in the frequently inundated bottom lands. This seems more plausible, since nowhere else in the Southeast did the presence of other inhabitants prevent the Mississippians from moving in. Even here this occurred in later times.

The Late Mississippi culture is represented in the western valley and the Central Basin. Along the Cumberland and Harpeth rivers the Gordon people built great communities with groups of substructure mounds upon which their public buildings stood. The Duck River inhabitants were a western valley group who shared much of their culture with the Gordon group (Fig. 108). The communities were similarly organized and the burial customs were identical. The salient feature of Late Mississippi burials in Middle Tennessee was the use of stone coffins, usually occurring in restricted cemetery areas and superimposed. The coffins were long, narrow boxes made of limestone slabs, and in them the bodies were placed at full length on their backs. Gordon and Duck River funerals often included unceremonious jostling of previous occupants of the coffins, the loose bones being piled at one end, or even dumped out.

The Middle Tennessee people seem to have had almost a monopoly of the Dover flint quarries. As a result, they became expert flint chippers producing such spectacular items as the famous Duck River cache[20] consisting of blades over two feet in length and a variety of symbolic and effigy forms. Middle Tennessee flint exports have turned up far and wide in the Southeast, furnishing a chronological link be-

tween cultures of different peoples. Another widely distributed object of this period is the sculptured stone image. These often are found in pairs, one representing a female, the other a characteristically posed and often excellently sculptured, elderly male. The Gordon and Duck River people both possessed such images but may not have made them. The Muskhogean tribes all recognized a special deity connected with the sacred fire and the sun, the Muskogee tribe calling him "grandfather."[21] There is certainly a "grandpa-like" quality in the elderly male with drooping wattles under his chin shown in Figure 108, D.

Before describing the Late Mississippi period in eastern Tennessee, we should note that a variant of the Gordon and Duck River cultures existed along the Tennessee River in Henry, Benton, and Stewart counties. The Gray Site, mentioned earlier, had originally been a Harmon's Creek town (Fig. 108). This group, already influenced by Early Mississippi culture, was living in circular dwellings constructed by the wall trench method. On the nearby ridge they had established a necropolis whose Hopewellian flavour is immediately recognizable. A large stone walled enclosure covered by a mound of earth had been built around the funeral bier after the cremation of some twenty persons. Adjacent to this was a rectangular pavement also covered by the mound. Other small mounds near the large earthwork afforded comparable burial evidence. In the large crematory were only copper stains, but in one small mound, copper fragments and several large conch shells accompanied the remains.

The Harmon's Creek village gradually acquired a new population element from its Mississippi neighbors, and finally the town became almost indistinguishable from any other Late Mississippi settlement. Amalgamation between the two peoples resulted in the modification of the house floor pattern of the Harmon's Creek people who began to square up their circular houses. The most distinctive products of the Late Mississippi peoples in the local area were engraved pottery and fine, polished flint celts. This Gray culture may have acquired engraved pottery from people along the Mississippi River. The Shelby Negro Park Site near Memphis had not only engraved plate rims, but occasionally Moundville and Arkansas designs on black polished ware.

Designs identical to those on Sanders Engraved[22] from Central Texas embellished Gray plate rims. Aboriginal trade had attained immense proportions by the fifteenth and sixteenth centuries. It is practically impossible to ascertain the direction of influence in many cases. Individual products travelled in all directions. Mississippi groups established themselves at strategic points along the great inland water-

---

20. Lewis, T. M. N. (ed.), 1947.

21. Williams, 1930, p. 111.   22. Kreiger, 1946, p. 335, Pl. 27.

ways and trails. Gossip and ideas flowed along the transportation system, by-products of the trade in tangible items. The stone coffin may have been a Gordon or Duck River invention. The idea travelled far beyond the culture where it originated, and other peoples, in the habit of burying their dead in flexed positions, took it over, changed its shape, but used it for the same purpose.

Some Gray sites failed to use the stone coffins, probably because suitable slabs were hard to find and transport. The burial position and the custom of segregating burials in cemetery areas were the same as in the neighboring Gordon and Duck River regions. The Gray culture seems to have been that of a later group than the Gordon and Duck River people. One might even suspect that it dates around the fifteenth century. Perhaps it represents the penetration of Duck River colonies into the lower portion of the Tennessee River.

While the western valley reveals a curious set of local accommodations between the Eva, Harmon's Creek, and Gray peoples, the valley of eastern Tennessee was more of a Mississippi stronghold. Towns of the Hiwassee Island early Mississippians were to be found far into the wilderness of the Clinch and Powell rivers. Scarcely any of the Woodland groups remained except, perhaps, along the Hiwassee River for a time.

Not later than the middle of the fifteenth century, and maybe somewhat earlier, Muskogee groups began to join the Hiwassee Islanders. The Cherokee, who were then living in the mountains, called them the Ani-Kusa. If these Muskogee were "people from Coosa" as the Cherokee claimed, it is easily understood why so much of their culture resembled that of peoples who inhabited the upper Coosa River and one of its headwaters, the Etowah.

In eastern Tennessee the remains of the ancient Ani-Kusa are called the Dallas culture (Fig. 109). Great Dallas towns were built at many desirable locations not already preempted by the Hiwassee Islanders. Gradually, the two groups merged, intermarriage as well as political bonds serving to cement the communities.

The Dallas council house was a *tcokofa,* or "hot house," similar to that described by Taitt[23] at Tukabachee. It was rectangular in shape and was entered through an outer passage or vestibule which had a turn to keep out drafts. This hot house was the winter counterpart of the summer square ground. Within the Dallas *tcokofa* was a broad bench extending around all four walls and divided into sections or "beds" by clay and wattle partitions. In the center on the floor was the fireplace, whose flames furnished heat, light and supernatural sanction for the deliberations of the council.

Ani-Kusa ceremonies can be inferred from Dallas archeological objects. The old consecrated conch shells from which "the black drink" was imbibed were of religious and military significance. They were frequently buried with men.

The most important Ani-Kusa ceremony was the busk, celebrated annually for four to eight days. Many symbols are associated with busk ceremonies and such symbols can be traced on Dallas objects. The cross symbol is associated with the sacred fire, newly kindled at each busk. Variations of the cross motif appear on fine painted pottery and on shell gorgets. Also engraved on shell gorgets are turkey cocks, the totem cf the turkey clan whose women danced the turkey dance on the first day of the busk. Copper plates, exhibited at Tukabachee during the busk, have counterparts in archeological materials. Space does not permit extended discussion of this subject which is receiving detailed study by Waring.[24] The Tennessee area furnishes considerable information concerning the correlation of Dallas archeological remains with ancient Muskogee ceremonies. The local Dallas culture was evidently derived from the Coosa-Etowah cultural center and was approximately contemporaneous with the great late cultural development at Etowah. The earlier Etowah manifestation equates with the Hiwassee Island horizon in eastern Tennessee.

The busk was the central ceremony which linked the Muskogee groups of the Southeast. The annual performance with its attendant paraphernalia insured peace and harmony between the towns. But, while the busk promoted social unification within the individual town and between the other Muskogee towns, it was extended also to all members of the Creek Confederacy. All of the tribes who united with the Creeks either adopted the busk or altered their own ceremonials to agree with it. Because it was a peace ceremony, we may explain the far-flung occurrence of individual items commonly associated with the busk. The so-called Southern Cult seems to be the extension of essentially Muskhogean symbols over a wide geographical area. The initial spread of these ideas must have preceded the period in which they are best known. The Late Mississippi groups such as the Gordon, Duck River and Dallas people possessed too much else in common with the early Mississippians for us to assume that their ceremonialism was an isolated phenomenon. The absence of early Mississippi burials deprives us of a whole cultural complex derived from the graves, a complex which in every area has furnished the "cult" elements. Late Mississippi culture is a blend of esthetic, ceremonial and technical ideas derived from a multiplicity of sources. The old conch shell dippers and copper objects came down from the Archaic period, cut mica

---

23. Taitt in Mereness (ed.), 1916, p. 503.

24. Waring, Antonio J., personal communication.

and copper-plated wood from Hopewell, frog and fish effigy bowls possibly from as far away as Middle America. Everything was grist for the late Mississippi mill which ground out a cultural *olla-podrida* of great expansive vitality. Southern ceremonialism almost possessed the acculturating power of the modern movie. It was deeply religious in spirit among the groups where it was rooted in their past; it was, perhaps, essentially secular among those to whom its various items diffused through trade, political affiliation, or other means.

The favorite gambling game and athletic sport of the Indians of the eastern United States was the ball play or lacrosse which was borrowed from the Algonquians by the southern Indians. On the outcome of games played between neighboring towns, the people would stake everything, including the shirts off their backs. The winning town gathered up the loot which in many cases must have included "cult" items. From town to town, by the fickle whims of chance passed the "Southern Cult" in payment of gambling debts. At least a part of this much debated phenomenon was spread by rash speculation.

In the very heart of the Ani-Kusa territory of eastern Tennessee was the cultural enclave of the Yuchi or Mouse Creek people (Fig. 110). Along the lower Hiwassee River, an eastern tributary of the Tennessee, and at a few other spots were large towns fortified not only with stockades, but also with deep ditches. The people lived in shallow pit houses, entrance to which was through narrow, covered vestibules. The towns possessed large council houses of the general type of dwellings. An open area in the midst of the houses was reserved for communal activities.

In contrast to the Dallas custom of burial here, there and anywhere in the town, the Mouse Creekers reserved cemetery sections. Also in contrast to the Dallas flexed burial position, Mouse Creek corpses were stretched to the utmost length on their backs, with even their feet extended as far as possible. Hence, long, narrow graves were the rule. The cemetery idea and the full-length position strongly resemble the Gordon and Duck River burial customs of Middle Tennessee. The exclusively plain surfaced Mouse Creek pottery also is reminiscent of Middle Tennessee and contrasts with the characteristic cord-marked Dallas pottery.

Did the Yuchi migrate into eastern Tennessee from the Cumberland area? If so, what became of their substructure mounds? Perhaps, their settlements were too short lived to have built up earthen foundations. They must have been permitted to settle along the Hiwassee by the Dallas people. Perhaps, they had become naturalized Creeks acting as a buffer state between the Dallas and Cherokee towns. They probably did not arrive until the late fifteenth century,

and may have been deliberately encouraged to settle where they did by the Creeks seeking to offset the encroachments by the Cherokee. For the Cherokee mountaineers were pressing into the Tennessee Valley by this time. Cherokee towns of the seventeenth century stood where Hiwassee Island and Dallas towns did earlier on the Little Tennessee River and the upper Hiwassee.

Pushed into the mountains centuries earlier by the Muskhogeans, the Cherokee had not only survived but prospered. With an increasing population they threatened the Dallas hegemony. In former times, when eastern Tennessee was inhabited by the Upper Valley Indians, the Cherokee had been a powerful southeastern people related, at least by tradition[25] to the Yamassee of the Carolina and Georgia coast (Fig. 111). Makers of complicated- and check-stamped pottery in the eighteenth century, they were the heirs apparent of the ancient stamped pottery makers of Georgia who fled to the mountains before the Muskhogean march to the sea. Their coastal cousins, the Yamasee, remained on the coast, but the Cherokee became adapted to the high valleys of the Great Smoky Mountains.

No love was lost between the Yuchi and Cherokee, and through the conniving of a disgruntled trader, the latter finally "cut off" the last Yuchi town of Chestoee in 1715.

Gradually, the Creeks withdrew to the south and the valley of eastern Tennessee was free for Cherokee expansion. Then came the white men to snatch the region from the Cherokee just as they had succeeded in acquiring it. It is true that the Chickamauga band terrorized the settlers along the Tennessee River, but only for a brief time did Cherokee possession of the land justify their claims of ownership. Except for the Little Tennessee and Upper Hiwassee valleys they merely had brief squatter's rights to the abandoned Creek lands of the eastern Tennessee Valley.

By the early eighteenth century, few Indians remained in the Tennessee area except in the eastern portion. The great towns were abandoned and the wilderness closed in. Aboriginal life still flowed along the trails that crossed from east to west, and north to south. Along the same trails traveled Carolina traders west to the Mississippi, French *coureurs de bois* east to the coast, and Indians in all directions. Rum and trinkets had followed the same route as aboriginal trade wares, and with the new things had come disaster in the form of smallpox, diphtheria, measles, and syphilis.

So ends the story of the Tennessee area in aboriginal times, a story only half-told because we know so little about parts of the state rapidly undergoing destruction by the building of many dams.

25. Cheves (ed.), 1894.

WOODLAND CULTURES OF EASTERN TENNESSEE.

By Chandler W. Rowe[*]

THIS paper is primarily concerned with the materials which are affiliated with the Woodland culture pattern and does not consider to any degree the vast amounts of data which are categorically placed with the Middle Mississippi culture or historic occupations. During the years of 1934 to 1942 the University of Tennessee, under the direction of T. M. N. Lewis and Madeline Kneberg (1938–1942), and in conjunction with the TVA and WPA, excavated numerous archeological sites in the Tennessee River Valley. The cultural material which was unearthed in the eastern part of the state (Chickamauga, Norris, Fort Louden, Watts Bar, and Douglas Basins) ran the gamut from relatively early pottery-making complexes through the period of occupation by historic groups.

Sufficient data have been recovered to permit classification of the Woodland cultural material into two aspects, namely, Upper Valley and Middle Valley aspects. These in turn have been broken down into foci: Watts Bar Focus and Candy Creek Focus (Upper Valley Aspect) and the Hamilton Focus (Middle Valley Aspect). In geographical extent, these foci occupy approximately the same area, all being rather widespread throughout East Tennessee. In addition to the cultural and geographical relationships of these foci, a temporal relationship has also been established among them. A relative chronological sequence has been built up through stratigraphic evidence which indicates that the Watts Bar Focus is the first period of the Early Woodland. Apparently it is not the initial cultural level in this region since it is preceded by a shell mound culture in certain areas. That there is a relationship between the latter and the following Woodland horizons has not been determined. Following the Watts Bar Focus in time is the slightly later Candy Creek Focus which has previously been designated by M. R. Harrington[1] as the "Round Grave" culture. Because of the presence of such pottery types as Swift Creek and Napier Complicated Stamp, Long Branch Fabric Marked and simple and checked stamp

wares, the Candy Creek Focus is felt to be contemporaneous with the Early Swift Creek material.

The Hamilton Focus is the fourth cultural period represented in East Tennessee and immediately follows the Candy Creek Focus in time. This is the final period of Woodland occupation in the region as it directly precedes the Hiwassee Island Focus, a Middle Mississippi manifestation.

In the Upper Valley Aspect, the Candy Creek Focus is felt by Lewis and Kneberg to be a slightly later manifestation of the Watts Bar Focus,[2] the distinction being due to new ideas, particularly with regard to the surface treatment of pottery vessels, which tended to modify the original cultural manifestations. The same ethnic group, then, was apparently responsible for the cultural remains which appear in both the Watts Bar and Candy Creek foci.

Both the Upper Valley and the Middle Valley aspects share a number of traits which place them within the broad limits of the Woodland culture pattern and in addition have in common traits which are widespread in the Southeastern Woodland sites. There are, however, traits which make it possible to distinguish between the Upper Valley and Middle Valley aspects. Inspection of various phases of their culture will make this apparent.

CANDY CREEK FOCUS

DWELLING AREA

The areas in which the people lived who left behind the remains assigned to the Upper Valley Aspect provides some evidence as to the type of houses which were used. Although examples are not numerous, it appears that the typical house was circular, with large support posts set in a pattern about twenty-five feet in diameter.[3] The paucity of animal bone and shell indicates that hunting and gathering of river mussels played a small part in the food economy of the people. Because of this fact and also because there is no adequate evidence for agriculture it must be postulated that the Upper Valley peoples subsisted primarily upon food obtained from wild plants. The areas of habitation indicate that the houses or shel-

[*] Beloit College, A.B., 1939; University of Chicago, M.A., 1947; M.A., 1947; Ph.D., 1951. Assistant Professor, Department of Anthropology and Sociology, Lawrence College. Chapter received December, 1947.

1. Harrington, M. R., 1922.

2. Lewis and Kneberg, 1946, p. 4.   3. *Ibid.*, p. 4.

ters were fairly close together since the refuse heaps are situated near each other rather than being strung out along the river banks.

Characteristically the Candy Creek peoples dug a large number of pits in their village areas.[4] Generally speaking, they are circular in form and somewhat more constricted near the top than at the bottom, giving them a "kettle-shaped" appearance. The function of these pits can be inferred from the evidence acquired with them. They do not appear to have had merely a single function. This is evidenced from the fact that many of the pits contained stones blackened by fire which may mean that they were used for cooking. Other pits of the same general appearance contained no stones and may represent storage pits. Still others were used for disposal of the dead, but this would seem to be a secondary rather than a primary function.

POTTERY[5]

The pottery of the Candy Creek Focus is predominantly limestone-tempered, but crushed quartzite was used for tempering material in the early period. It apparently lost its popularity and was rarely used in the later period. Lewis and Kneberg[6] point out this shift in tempering material as one of the changes in the culture pattern of the Candy Creek people during later times. This particular change, they feel, is an environmental one—limestone being more plentiful and easily crushed.

In the limestone-tempered pottery, five different surface treatments are recognizable: fabric-marked (Long Branch Fabric Marked), fine cord-marked (Candy Creek Cord Marked), coarse cord-marked (Hamilton Cord Marked), plain (Hamilton Plain), and stamped. The fabric-marked or cord-wrapped-dowel marked pottery is the early Candy Creek material, but declines to a position of minor importance in later times. The plain ware, on the other hand, is seldom found in the early period but is more common in the late period. The simple stamped pottery is of no particular numerical importance at any time but occurs with greater frequency in the later Candy Creek period than in the earlier one.

The most frequent vessel forms of Candy Creek material are jar and kettle-shaped vessels. The fabric-impressed vessels occur in these two forms, the kettle-shaped primarily which usually exhibits a vertical rim although present with an incurved rim to some extent; and the jar-shaped vessel which is less frequent and has a vertical rim exclusively. Projecting lug handles appear on a few of these jars, but are rare as are appendages in general on Hamilton and Candy Creek pottery. Examples of footed and conoidal bases have been found on both vessel forms of the fabric-impressed type but they are by no means common.

Vessels exhibiting the fine cord-marked surface treatment most frequently take the jar shape, having usually a vertical rim with an exterior fold. Occasionally, however, the slightly excurved rim appears. Kettle-shaped vessels of this type are rare and when present may have either a vertical or incurved rim form.

The coarse cord-marked vessels constitute a minor portion of the Candy Creek Focus pottery. Both the kettle-shaped, incurved rim form and the jar-shaped, vertical or slightly excurved rim, vessel forms are found.

The most frequent vessel form of the plain surface pottery is the kettle-shape with the vertical rim. Jar-shaped, excurved rim vessels appear but are not as common. Also noted, but infrequently, are conoidal and footed bases, notched lip and crude incising.

Simple stamped pottery occurs in one form only, the kettle-shaped vessel with a vertical rim, notched lip, and footed base.

In addition to the type of surface treatment mentioned above, occasional examples of complicated and check stamped pottery are found. The vessel forms are not adequately known but the rim and basal sherds indicate that the kettle-shaped vessel was the principal if not the exclusive form.

The quartzite-tempered pottery is predominantly fabric-impressed and made exclusively in the kettle-shape with an incurved rim. Quartzite-tempered, cord-impressed sherds have been noted but are only infrequently found.

Various foreign or intrusive types occur at Candy Creek sites to some extent although they are not common. Such sherds are all sand-tempered and six surface treatments are present: Complicated stamped in the Swift Creek and Napier traditions, fabric-impressed with a footed base (Dunlap style?), check stamped with a footed base (Deptford style?), simple stamped, (Mossy Oak Simple Stamped?), cord-marked and plain with incised decoration, notched lip and footed base.

BONE

Little evidence of a bone industry among the Candy Creek groups has been obtained. This may be due to the destructive nature of the acid condition of the soil.

PIPES

Pipes are rare in the Candy Creek material. All of the examples found are tubular and made of steatite.

---

4. The Candy Creek cultural traits are illustrated in Fig. 103 of this volume.

5. The pottery type names used are those designated by Lewis and Kneberg, 1946, pp. 80–88.

6. *Ibid.*, p. 33.

SHELL

No shell objects have been found in Candy Creek Focus material.

CHIPPED STONE

The predominant projectile point of the Candy Creek is straight stemmed with a straight shoulder and either a short or elongate blade. These points are quite thick and do not exhibit much secondary chipping.

Stemless points are also fairly common. In general they are shield shaped or are broad, have excurved sides and either a straight or incurved base. Many of these points exhibit longitudinal channeling on one or both sides in the tradition of the Folsom point. This leads Lewis and Kneberg to the conclusion that "at least a great many of the so-called 'Folsom-like' points found in the Southeast should be identified as products of the early Woodland peoples."[7]

Small triangular projectile points with incurved sides and bases have been found on Candy Creek sites but are not a common form.

Both stemmed and stemless knives frequently occur. The asymmetrical type of blade is more common than the symmetrical. Double tapered knives are rare. Chipped stone perforators, crude, thick, double tapered specimens were used. Stemmed end scrapers are common and occasionally biconvex scrapers are found.

GROUND STONE

The ground stone implements of the Candy Creek Focus are similar in kind and manufacture to those of the Hamilton Focus. The thick, conical, pecked celt with a tapered poll is the principal type. Flat celts which do occur in Hamilton material, however, are very rare. Grooved axes occur, all exhibiting a full groove. Double grooved axes have been noted but occur infrequently.

Hammer stones, abrading stones and conical pestles are all similar in form and frequency of occurrence to those of the Hamilton Focus. Steatite vessels had a limited use and steatite was used in the manufacture of engraved bar gorgets. The latter were also made of ground slate.

Pitted stones of the type known as "nut-stones" or "cup-stones" are not uncommon. Their use, however, is problematical.

BURIAL CUSTOMS

As we mentioned earlier, the Candy Creek groups buried their dead in pits located in the village area. The pits are small, round or oval, and apparently were first utilized for storage and only secondarily as graves, since they are not arranged according to any apparent plan nor are they confined to any particular portion of the village area. In almost every case the Candy Creek burials are articulated and the body fully flexed, usually lying on the back. Burials which are partly flexed and lying on the side have been found, but the nature of the pits in which the burials are made generally made the fully flexed position necessary in order to receive the body. Mortuary furniture occurs infrequently.

HAMILTON FOCUS[8]

DWELLING AREA

The households of the Middle Valley peoples (exemplified by Hamilton Focus material) appear to have been scattered up and down the river banks for some distance. Archeology has brought forth no evidence of dwellings of a permanent nature. The only remains of occupation are the accumulations of refuse, primarily mussel shells, fragments of pottery and stone implements, which occur in scattered piles quite widely separated. That some type of community organization existed is postulated by Lewis and Kneberg,[9] due to the presence of groups of burial mounds associated with the general locations of the settlements (Fig. 104).

POTTERY

The pottery of the Hamilton Focus is exclusively limestone-tempered. The surface treatment falls into four categories: fine cord-marked (Candy Creek Cord Marked), coarse cord-marked (Hamilton Cord Marked), plain (Hamilton Plain), and brushed surface treatment; the brushed surface may be a variant of Hamilton Plain. The first three types were made in about the same quantity and comprise the primary types which are present. The fourth type is relatively rare. The vessel shapes vary and should be considered within the categories of surface treatment. Pottery vessels which have a fine cord-marked surface treatment occur in two forms, the so-called kettle-shaped vessel with a vertical rim form are most common, but occasionally found with a slightly excurved rim. The subconoidal type of base occurs in these two forms but is rare.

Coarse cord-marked pottery vessels are also found in both the kettle and jar-shaped forms. But here the kettle-shaped vessels have the incurved rim only and in the jar-shaped forms the vertical rim is predominant, but a slightly incurved rim does occur.

The coarse cord-marked vessels have been noted in a bowl shape with an incurved rim. These are not common but should be mentioned. Here, also, the subconoidal base is of minor importance.

---

7. *Ibid.*, p. 31. [This is not mentioned in the chapter by Kneberg in this volume.]

8. The Hamilton Focus cultural traits are illustrated in Fig. 114.
9. For a detailed discussion of the Hamilton Community plan see Lewis and Kneberg, 1946, pp. 36–37.

The plain ware also is found in these two forms, the kettle shape with a vertical rim generally but with an incurved rim form occasionally, and jar-shaped vessel in which the predominant rim form is vertical, but may also appear as an excurved form. Punctates occur occasionally on the rim or lip. Crude incising has also been noted on both forms to some extent, but is exceptional. Subconoidal and footed bases occur infrequently.

The brushed type of surface treatment has been found only on the kettle-shaped vessel with an incurved rim.

BONE

There is little evidence of the use of bone implements by the Hamilton Focus peoples. Only a very few specimens of bone and antler have been recovered. This is not surprising in view of the scarcity of animal bone on the sites. This fact has led to the assumption that hunting was of little importance as a means of obtaining food. It may be that the acid condition of the soil has destroyed the bone. Reliance upon mussels as a staple in the diet has already been mentioned. A few bone awls have been found both of the splinter type and those in which one articulatory end has been retained.

PIPES

The typical Hamilton Focus pipe is of the elbow variety. The stem is long in relation to the bowl and apparently was complete in itself and did not necessitate the use of a separate stem. The majority of pipes were made of limestone-tempered pottery, although pipes of steatite, in the same form, are occasionally found.

SHELL

All of the Hamilton Focus shell artifacts have been found in association with burials. Beads occur most frequently. They are principally made by grinding off one end of *Olivella* shells to facilitate stringing. Also, although not as commonly, *Marginella* and *Campeloma* shells, river pearls and cylindrical and discoidal beads are found. Pendants are not numerous but some small *Busycon* shells (unworked) or large *Busycon* shells (pear or triangular-shaped and engraved) were used for making ornaments of this type.

One of the most distinctive and frequently used shell ornaments was made from the large marine conch columella. These ornaments are from six to eight inches in length, and, although many are drilled longitudinally, some are found solid or unperforated. The presence of these columellae together with the *Busycon* shell pendants seems to indicate a trade relation, directly or indirectly, with some Gulf coast peoples.

CHIPPED STONE

Projectile points, knives, scrapers and perforators comprise the chipped stone artifacts of the Hamilton Focus.

The stemmed projectile points were made with either a straight or flared stem and usually a short blade, although elongate blades are also found to a considerable extent. The shoulder is straight in most instances but may be barbed.

Stemless projectile points are also common; they usually occur as burial accompaniments. These are small, triangular points with straight or incurved sides and incurved bases.

Knives are stemless and commonly have an asymmetrical blade. Symmetrical blades are rare and have been found only in association with burials.

Both side and end scrapers were made by the Hamilton people but not to any great extent.

Perforators are rarely found and it is interesting to note that none of the specimens is small and thin enough to have drilled the perforations which occur in some of the conch columellae.

GROUND STONE

The typical Hamilton Focus celt is a single bitted, thick, conical shaped implement with a sharply tapered poll and a pecked surface. The only grinding occurred on the bit.[10] One other type was used to some extent, a flat celt with a thin cross-section, a pecked surface and a ground bit.

Grooved axes are seldom found and the only examples found are of the full grooved type. Conical pestles have been noted, but are also uncommon.[11] Hammer stones are rare and do not show any distinctive features.

The presence of a number of sherds indicates that some use was made of steatite vessels. No complete vessels have been found, however. Steatite was also used in making bar gorgets of various shapes.

BURIAL CUSTOMS

One of the outstanding differences between the Hamilton and Candy Creek peoples is the method of disposal of the dead. The Hamilton people buried their dead exclusively in mounds erected for this purpose. Usually, although not always, the topsoil was first removed from the area on which the mound was to be built and the burials made by covering the dead with earth. As additional burials were added the mound grew higher as a result. This was not a hit-or-miss process, however, as several constructional phases are often discernible in the mounds. Frequently these constructional phases are separated by a sort of veneer or capping material such as a layer of soil, mussel shell or stone slabs. In general, the

10. *Ibid.,* p. 116.   11. *Ibid.,* p. 117.

bones of the deceased are articulated, although instances of burial of the skull alone or cremation have been found. The body is usually placed on the surface and covered with soil or, as frequently occurs, a layer of mussel shell or logs.[12] Pit inhumation seldom occurs and often burials of this type represent the intrusion of another (later) cultural group. The position of the inclusive mound burials are partly flexed. Completely extended burials are rare. For the most part the burials do not have grave goods included with them.

A brief description of a Hamilton burial mound will provide a clearer understanding of mound construction and mode of burial. During the early part of the summer of 1941 the writer excavated a mound located about nine miles south of Spring City, Rhea County, Tennessee on the farm of W. D. Smith. This unit was designated as 122 Rh 42 and is a component of the Hamilton Focus, Middle Valley Aspect. The mound was one of several situated on a small rise above the bottom lands of the Tennessee River. The mound itself was eleven feet high, sixty feet long and fifty feet wide. Seventeen burials were removed from the mound. Undoubtedly there were more in the structure, but lack of time permitted only partial excavation. The technique used was a system of coordinate trenches which was adequate in determining the details of mound construction and method of disposal of the dead (Fig. 112).

The profiles obtained by these coordinate trenches showed four distinct building phases (Fig. 113 and 114). All phases were constructed of red clay and could be differentiated due to the discoloration of the surfaces which had been exposed to the elements for a period of time.

The earliest building phase (phase D) was a mounding on the old humus line which had a basal diameter of about twenty feet and a maximum summit elevation of about three feet. The old land surface had not been scraped away except for a small area under the east side of the mound.

Two burials were encountered in this phase. One lay directly on the old humus line at the bottom of phase D and the other occurred in a pit which had its origin in this phase but which extended below the old land surface into the subsoil. Neither burial was accompanied by artifacts.

Directly superimposed upon the early one, the second building phase (phase C) had a basal diameter of about twenty five feet and a maximum elevation of three and one-half feet above phase D. Two burials were also found in phase C and proved to be of particular interest (Figs. 117–119). These individuals were lying side by side, fully extended and covered with six charred logs (Fig. 115). Attempts to locate

post molds around these burials were unsuccessful. The logs were evidently burned in place as the surrounding ground was fire blackened. The burials themselves, however, did not appear to be burned to any great degree. Accompanying each burial were several artifacts lying together near the skull. With one individual (Burial 16, adult male) were three chisel-like stone celts, pecked and ground with tapered polls, measuring about five and one-half inches long, one inch wide and three-fourths of an inch thick, one chipped stone celt of coarse chert with poor conchoidal fracture planes, a projectile point four inches long, one and three-fourths inches wide at the maximum breadth and pentagonal in shape, several pieces of worked bone which are unidentifiable due to decay, and three long and narrow mussel shells of the Tennessee River type. With the other individual (Burial 17) was a cache which contained one mussel shell of the above type, a turkey leg bone (unworked), a projectile point of the Middle Valley incurvate type, a crude chipped stone celt similar to the one described for Burial 16, and plain surface limestone-tempered sherds which appear to be the remains of three pottery vessels. The size and shape of these pots has not been determined. Burials 16 and 17 were located at the bottom of phase C in almost the exact center of the mound. Approximately halfway between the bottom and the top of phase C was a mussel shell layer which was one to one and one-half feet thick at the deepest point and which extended over most of the area covered by phase C.[13]

The summit of phase B was distinguishable due to the presence of a clearly visible old land surface. The maximum summit elevation was eight feet from the old humus line under the mound or two and one-half feet from the top of phase C. The basal diameter was approximately thirty-seven feet. This phase was constructed of the same type of reddish clay which was used in building the other mound phases and also contained a layer of mussel shell. The thickness of the shell stratum in phase B was on the average a little less than one foot and had neither the areal extent nor the vertical depth to compare with C. The shell did not cover the entire phase but occurred only on the east side of the mound.

Seven burials were recovered from phase B. Six of them were included in the mound fill while the other lay in an oval, ash-lined pit which had its origin in phase B but intruded into the fill of phase C. No burials were found in the shell layer. Only three of the burials were associated with grave goods, and in these cases they were meagre. Burial 4 had three longitudinally perforated, long conch columella

12. *Ibid.*, Pl. 89.

13. It may be noted that the mussel shell used in the construction of the mound was somewhat ovoid in shape and is not of the same variety as the specimens which were with Burials 16 and 17, the latter being long, narrow, and "razor-like" in shape.

beads lying on the chest in such a manner as to suggest that they had been strung around the neck. Lying on the pelvis of Burial 8 was a triangular, incurvate projectile point with serrated edges indicating that the point was inflicted rather than included as a mortuary offering. Associated with the burial was a long, narrow celt thirteen and three-fourths inches long, two and one-half inches wide and one inch thick. It has a tapered poll and a pecked and partly ground surface. Also included was an unidentifiable fragmentary projectile point.

Phase A, the last building phase to be applied to the mound, has a basal diameter of about fifty-five feet and a maximum summit elevation of eleven feet, or three feet higher than the top of phase B. As in the case of the others, this phase was built of reddish clay but contained no mussel shell layer as were found in phase C and B. Six burials were removed from phase A, all of which were in a poor state of preservation. One of these (Burial 5) was associated with a large mortar or grinding stone circular in shape with a small circular depression at the center. The other burials in this place had no artifacts with them.

Cultural material was scarce throughout the mound fill. Much of it, particularly the pottery fragments, is in the Candy Creek Focus tradition. This is due to the fact that some of the dirt used in building the mound was scraped up from an earlier Candy Creek village site nearby. The stone work of both the Candy Creek and Hamilton peoples is quite similar and it is therefore difficult to assign projectile points and other stone objects to one focus or another with any degree of accuracy. Scattered throughout the mound fill and occurring in all phases were seventy-four pieces of ground iron ore. These are roughly square or rectangular in shape. None were associated with burials. A few pieces of unworked iron ore were found but these raw pieces were rare.

Only thirty pottery sherds were recovered from the fill of the portion of the mound excavated. All were limestone-tempered. In surface treatment, three were plain, twenty-five fabric-impressed or cord-wrapped dowel and two were check stamped. Twelve fabric-impressed sherds were removed from a pit lying below the mound which had its origin in the old humus lime extending under the mound structure. This pit apparently represents a feature at the periphery of the Candy Creek village site mentioned above. The only pottery definitely associated with the mound are those sherds which were found with Burial 17, limestone-tempered with a plain, smooth surface.

RELATIONSHIPS

The question of the origin and ethnic identification of the bearers of the Candy Creek and Hamilton Focus culture types must remain, at this time, a matter of speculation at best. Inferences can be drawn indicating that the Candy Creek people were not indigenous to the area in which their remains are found archeologically, as was pointed out earlier. Identification with known historic groups cannot be conclusively shown at present, however. Similarity of physical type and culture seems to point to a genetic relationship between the Candy Creek and Hamilton peoples.[14] Since stratigraphy shows that the Hamilton material is later we may, therefore, assume sequential development from one to the other. Such differences as exist between these two groups can probably be explained primarily on the basis of internal change or increased cultural intensity along with isolation to some degree[15] and influence from outside groups.

In its most distinctive cultural aspect, the burial mound, the Hamilton Focus groups appear to be closest to the Copena and Adena complexes. The principal Copena traits[16] which also occur in the Hamilton Focus material are: site in the vicinity of the large river, conical earth mounds, mounds occurring in groups, flexed burials, extended burials, burials inclusive in mounds, disk shell beads, elbow pipes, flat bar gorgets, and limestone-tempered pot sherds. The latter are exclusive in the Hamilton material and although Webb and DeJarnette[17] do not feel that limestone-tempered sherds can be definitely assigned to the Copena material, Griffin[18] presents evidence which indicates that Copena pottery is limestone-tempered predominantly. None of the above traits, however, are particularly diagnostic of Copena and seem insufficient evidence on which to base a cultural relationship.

On the basis of cultural similarity alone, we might test several possibilities in regard to relationship. Copena and Hamilton are either genetically related or they are not. If we assume a genetic relationship between them, it must be determined whether (1) Hamilton is ancestral to Copena; (2) Hamilton developed out of Copena; or (3) Hamilton and Copena are contemporaneous variants of one culture.

There may be other possibilities, but these will suffice. Obviously the chronological sequence is important and the temporal aspect of the problem must first be determined. The Candy Creek material apparently is Early Woodland and in view of the intrusive sherds mentioned earlier seems to correspond

14. Miss Kneberg feels that there is a significant variation in physical type (personal communication).
15. Lewis and Kneberg, 1946, p. 6, state that, although the Upper and Middle Valley groups were contemporaneous for a period of time, there is sufficient evidence to indicate that they were isolated from each other.
16. Webb and DeJarnette, 1942, p. 305, Table 42.
17. *Ibid.*, p. 303.
18. Griffin, J. B., 1945d, pp. 228–234.

in time with the early Swift Creek material and, particularly with regard to projectile points, also with Adena. The Hamilton material has been shown to be later than the Candy Creek Focus material. The presence of vessels with flaring rims and rounded bottoms, the triangular projectile point of the so-called Middle Mississippi type and the emphasis on shell work, especially the small and cut *Busycon* pendants, indicates the late position of the Hamilton Focus. In addition, it is suggested that the Hamilton groups existed at the time of the Middle Mississippi occupation of the Hiwassee Island groups in that area.[19] The Copena material, Webb and Snow[20] feel, is earlier than the Middle Mississippi peoples of the southeast, and the fact that there are no Late Hopewell artifacts in Copena causes them to place the Copena people in a Middle Hopewell period. Griffin[21] points out that wide-mouth, rounded bottom vessels, strap handles and Middle Mississippi-like triangular projectile points have been found on Copena sites. The nature of such evidence would seem to point to contemporaneity of Hamilton and Copena. Such Swift Creek elements as occur with Copena are probably later Swift Creek rather than the early Swift Creek which is identified with the Candy Creek peoples. In view of these facts it is apparent that the hypotheses that Hamilton is ancestral to Copena and that Hamilton developed out of Copena are ruled out. This would leave, for further testing, the proposition that Hamilton and Copena are contemporaneous variants of one culture. The traits which the two have in common are of such a general nature (although the occurrence in both groups as a complex of traits provides additional weight) that it would seem weak evidence upon which to establish a genetic relationship. What is needed are traits held in common which would set the two groups apart from other cultures. For example, conceivably the large number of pieces of squared off iron ore, mentioned above as occurring in the Hamilton burial mound, might be an environmental adaption of the use of galena crystals common to Copena. If these pieces could be demonstrated to be a substitute for galena used by a group in an area where galena was scarce, the common origin position would be more plausible. Such evidence is not forthcoming. Finally, the physical type of the Hamilton people does not appear to be similar to that of the Copena people, particularly with regard to cranial deformation. It must be concluded therefore, that although Hamilton and Copena are probably contemporaneous variants of one culture, such a genetic relationship between them cannot be adequately demonstrated at present.

We may test the same hypothesis in connection with the Hamilton and Adena cultures: (1) Hamilton is ancestral to Adena; (2) Hamilton developed out of Adena; or (3) Hamilton and Adena are contemporaneous variants of one culture.

The relative chronological position of Adena and Hamilton is apparent from the previous discussion. Webb and Snow[22] have derived a chronological bar chart which effectively divides Adena into an early and late period, and places Adena earlier than, but running into Hopewell. The Hamilton material is later than Adena if it is contemporaneous with Copena and Webb's placement of Copena as Middle Hopewell is correct. The possibilities that Hamilton is ancestral to Adena and that Adena and Hamilton are contemporaneous variants of a single culture do not hold. In order to establish a genetic relationship between the two only the hypothesis that Hamilton developed out of Adena remains. Both groups have in common such traits as:[23] conical mounds which occur in groups, the mounds show stratigraphy, borrow pits occur near mounds, the primary purposes of the mound is to cover the burials, mounds built up as burials were added, constructional use of stone, important central graves, skeletons extended, skeletons flexed, body extended in log tomb, steatite vessel fragments, large tubular columella beads, disk and *Marginella* beads.

The mound traits held in common here are more in number than those exhibited by both the Copena and Hamilton peoples. In addition, the Copena traits which are found in the Hamilton Focus trait list are also included in the Adena material. While it is true that the correspondence of mound traits of Hamilton and Adena is impressive, it is also true that here the similarity ends. The copper and mica traits, many of the pottery traits as well as others involving stone and other burial customs are not found in the Hamilton material. Physical types, again, are not similar. In all probability, any attempt to demonstrate a genetic relationship between Hamilton and Adena would meet with no success.

That such a relationship apparently exists between Candy Creek and Hamilton has already been stated. It has further been pointed out that the Hamilton Focus material is later than that of Candy Creek. The burial mound complex which characterizes the Hamilton material does not appear in Candy Creek. The Hamilton material can then be seen as a stage of development of a general southeastern Woodland culture which has been subject to some outside influence, one which was rather specialized with regard to burial customs. This influence was apparently the same one which produced the Copena culture type.

19. Lewis and Kneberg, 1946, p. 9.
20. Webb and Snow, 1945, p. 336.
21. Griffin, J. B., 1945d, p. 245.

22. Webb and Snow, 1945, p. 213.
23. Adena traits as listed *ibid.*, p. 16.

Questions have not been answered and cannot be at this time. Who the Candy Creek and Hamilton people were and who were their closest relatives cannot now be determined. With regard to chronology, it can be said that the Candy Creek Focus is Early Woodland equating in time with early Swift Creek and Adena. The Hamilton Focus material is a somewhat later manifestation, probably Middle Wood-

land (early to late Hopewell), contemporaneous with Copena, and is said to have existed at the time of the Middle Mississippi occupation in that area.

If the problems outlined above seem oversimplified it is due to the fact that the material is only incompletely known at present. Additional information may alter the picture radically.

A FRAME OF REFERENCE FOR THE ARCHEOLOGY OF EASTERN TENNESSEE. *By Andrew H. Whiteford**

SINCE the middle of the nineteenth century the valley of the Tennessee River has been subjected to frequent visitations by persons interested in "Indian relics." Sites were numerous and easy to find, the country was beautiful, specimens were interesting and plentiful, and such items as shell gorgets and effigy pipes were greatly in demand by the museums of the time. An enormous number of the sites of this region were torn apart by interested amateurs who were building up collections and by local gentry searching for "buried treasure."

In spite of the rather large amount of digging which took place through the years, the importance of the region as an archeological area was not apparent and the investigations of the Indian sites did not really begin until 1885 when J. W. Emmert conducted a series of excavations for the Bureau of American Ethnology. These excavations were part of a widespread program under the direction of Cyrus Thomas to prove that the mounds and other earthworks were attributable to the American Indians or their immediate and direct ancestors.

The most important part of Emmert's work was conducted in the valley of the Little Tennessee River in eastern Tennessee, the region in which Timberlake[1] had stayed during his year's sojourn among the Cherokee. The famous map which he drew of the country[2] locates the tribal towns and indicates that the area was definitely inhabited by the Cherokee at that time. A comparison of this map with the location of the sites which were excavated by Emmert shows that some of the investigations coincide directly with the locations of the towns shown by Timberlake. Inasmuch as Thomas fully realized that his material came from sites which were documented Cherokee villages, it can be understood why, when he discussed this material[3] he attributed it wholly to this tribe. In designating the cultural manifestations which were found on the Little Tennessee as Cherokee, Thomas made an interpretation which very strongly affected the interpretations of all the subsequent archeological investigations in eastern Tennessee and the adjacent area. Excavators working in the region naturally had some reason to expect to find Cherokee remains and, when they actually did find material which resembled that described and illustrated by Thomas, they quickly assigned it to that tribal group. The fact that all the material which Thomas described was not necessarily Cherokee and actually represented several distinct prehistoric complexes was not recognized until rather recently.

The next important archeological investigation in this region was conducted by C. B. Moore[4] for the Academy of Natural Sciences of Philadelphia in 1915 when he traveled the Tennessee River from Paducah to Knoxville, excavating en route. The result of this work was presented by Moore in the journal of the academy in a report which is almost entirely of a descriptive nature. He made no attempt to segregate the material into cultural complexes and showed no similarities or relationships beyond a few very broad statements.

One of the most serious attempts to analyze the various archeological phenomena from this area was that of M. R. Harrington,[5] who excavated a number of sites on the Tennessee River in the area between the mouths of the Little Tennessee and the Hiwassee Rivers. Partly because of Thomas' interpretation and partly because the Cherokee were known to have been in the area historically he made a definite attempt to define the archeological complex which might be associated with this group. Harrington's results have been used by all subsequent investigators in the Southeast as the basis of comparison with any other material which might possibly be Cherokee.[6] Because of this it is particularly important that the material which Harrington uncovered be reexamined and related to the results of more extensive investigations in the same area and even on some of the same sites.

With limited excavations such as Moore and Harrington were able to make, the archeology of eastern Tennessee and the adjacent area would have unfolded slowly and normally had it not been for the

* Beloit College, B.A., 1937; University of Chicago, M.A., 1943; Ph.D., 1951; Associate Professor of Anthropology, Beloit College, and Director of Logan Museum of Anthropology, 1946——. Chapter received December, 1947.

1. Timberlake, 1765.
2. Reproduced as Pl. XXVI in Thomas, C., 1894.
3. *Ibid.*

4. Moore, C. B., 1915.
5. Harrington, M. R., 1922.
6. Webb, W. S., 1938.

207

creation of the Tennessee Valley Authority and the government funds which were made available through Federal Emergency Relief, especially W.P.A.

The endeavors of the various states, with federal aid, to recover the prehistoric remains of the region before inundation of the TVA reservoir areas made the Southeast the most archeologically active area in the country. The continuous and extensive excavations which were permissible under this program resulted in the accumulation of so much data and the formulation of so many developmental and relational theories for the cultures of the Southeast that it became nearly impossible to keep pace with the latest.

When W. S. Webb reported on the excavations in the Norris Basin[7] in eastern Tennessee he made an attempt to associate the cultural traits into complexes. The two complexes which he recognized were particularly distinct in their architectural traits and he designated them as the "large log town house complex" and the "small log town house complex". He compared his material with reputed Cherokee traits obtained from Harrington, Thomas, and Heye, Hodge and Pepper,[8] in order to determine whether that group had occupied the Norris Basin area. Comparing these lists[9] with each other and with his sites 19 and 10 he found trait correlations which he did not feel were high enough to suggest that the Cherokee had occupied the Norris Basin. It is interesting, however, that the correlations between the "Cherokee" lists with the Norris Basin sites and the "Cherokee" lists with each other were about the same (63–74 per cent).

A more recent attempt to use the published material on the archeology of eastern Tennessee is that of Setzler and Jennings[10] who again used Harrington's Cherokee list, this time to compare with their data from the Peachtree site in Georgia. Proceeding on the basis that the Cherokee are reputed to have occupied that site in historic times they also compiled a list of traits which they associated with that tribe. By comparison with the data of Webb and Harrington they concluded that manifestations of the same focus to which Peachtree belongs are present in the Norris and Chickamauga Basins.[11]

Since the excavations of the University of Tennessee in the Chickamauga Basin and elsewhere have investigated more extensively some of the exact areas examined by Harrington, Moore, and Thomas, I propose in this paper to review their data and interpretations in the light of more recent and detailed anal-

yses. Such "cultures" as Thomas' "Cherokee," Harrington's "Cherokee," Setzler and Jenning's "Cherokee," and Webb's "large log town house" and "small log town house" will also be examined in order to determine their relationships and resemblances to the archeology of the Chickamauga Basin and to each other. Moore's material and the data which Harrington assigns to manifestations other than the Cherokee also will be related to this recent information. An attempt will be made to weld all the various data, obtained by different people in different times from different sites (but in the same general area), into one unified and correlated body of knowledge, which it is hoped, will simplify the task of other persons making comparisons with data from this section of the Southeast.[12]

THE INVESTIGATIONS IN THE NORRIS BASIN

The comparison of the cultural complexes from the Chickamauga and Norris basins is better than the others which are made here because the original field data from the Norris Basin, as well as the artifacts, were available at the University of Tennessee. This made it possible to deal with fairly complete complexes of traits—a procedure not possible with other materials.

The Woodland horizon was represented in the Norris Basin in the same manner as in the Chickamauga Basin although, in the former, the succession can be determined only by analogy. The earliest of the Woodland aspects in the Chickamauga Basin, the Upper Valley, is widely distributed in the Norris Basin. All sites except the Taylor Farm Mound, Crawford Farm, Freel Farm Mound, Richardson Farm Mound, Hill Farm Mounds, and the Heatherly and Stiner Stone Mounds, showed some occupation or visitation by these people. Although there were no pure Woodland sites, the cave sites of the basin were less mixed than others and at the Hawkins, Doane, Wallace, Saltpeter, and Bullock caves the pottery is almost exclusively the limestone-tempered Woodland type. Upper Valley Aspect affiliations are suggested by the surface finishes: plain plaited fabric-impressed, cord-marked, check and simple stamp. These same surface treatments were also found in grit and sand-tempered wares, and additional Upper Valley traits were found in the conoidal and footed bases at these sites.

The artifact complexes from the cave sites are more difficult to classify. The stone gorgets, sherds and lugs of steatite vessels, and "crude pestles, hammer stones and mortars" can all be associated with Woodland manifestations, but the bone industry is

7. Ibid.
8. Heye, Hodge, Pepper, 1918.
9. Webb also included a list of traits from the Fain's Island Site near Dandridge, Tennessee, which was excavated by the University of Tennessee and which he considered might possibly represent Cherokee culture (Webb, W. S., 1938).
10. Setzler and Jennings, 1941.
11. Ibid., p. 57.
12. This paper is a much abbreviated version of a detailed study done while at the Laboratory of Anthropology, University of Tennessee. A copy is in Harper Library, University of Chicago.

different from anything in the Chickamauga Basin. Practically all the bone and antler found in the Chickamauga Basin were from Mississippi sites, but the artifacts of this material from the Norris Basin caves are distinctly different except for splinter awls, fishhooks, and objects of turtle carapace and bear canine beads.[13] This Norris Basin bone work more closely resembles the bone industry from the Archaic shell mounds of the lower Tennessee River and includes awls of split deer metapodials, cut and hollowed bear femora, engraved bear mandibles, deer ulnae scrapers, carved and socketted deer antler handles, a large propeller-shaped specimen possibly made from a human femur,[14] and an antler celt or scraper.[15] Webb pointed out the similarities between these cave sites and some of the cave sites from Lea, Wolfe, and Powell counties in Kentucky.[16] It may be that the bone industry of these caves represents a culture related to the Archaic which preceded the Upper Valley people who were responsible for the ceramic and worked stone remains. It is significant that these people lived in caves and subsisted on products of hunting and gathering to the exclusion of fishing and clam digging. Some sites of the Archaic culture which are situated back from the rivers and which lack the clam shell middens have been excavated in west Tennessee.

Practically the same group of Upper Valley Aspect Woodland traits found in the cave sites occurred at the Irvin Village[17] and Lea[18] and Bowman[19] farms. At the first two of these, these traits were common enough to suggest the presence of a Woodland component, while at the Bowman Farm the evidence suggests a camp site or temporary occupation. At the Ausmus Farm,[20] Johnson Farm Cemetery,[21] Cox Mound,[22] and Walters Farm Village,[23] the evidence suggests similar short occupations preceding components of the Dallas Focus.

The occurrence in the Norris Basin of sites of the Middle Valley Aspect appears to be limited to two, or possibly three, mounds in Anderson County on the Clinch River considerably below the dam and outside of the Norris Basin proper. The Crawford Farm,[24] and Freel Farm[25] sites are particularly characteristic of the burial mounds belonging to this aspect. No pottery is reported, but the following traits

are typical of the Middle Valley mounds of the Chickamauga and other basins: small mounds built by addition of burials; first burial on surface or in pit covered with small mound, stone slab veneer or capping on mound phases; varied deposition including flexed, extended, reburial, and possibly cremation; large cut columellae, both perforated and unperforated, *Olivella* beads, and small, thin, triangular points with incurvate sides and bases.[26] The long stemmed pipes from the Freel Farm are also found in Middle Valley mounds.

The Taylor Mound[27] is less typical for, although the large monitor pipe is similar to a broken specimen found in a Middle Valley mound on Hiwassee Island, and the slab paving may represent a stone veneer, the pottery is not of Middle Valley type and the poorly formed stone coffin found here is also not characteristic of this culture. The pottery and coffin may belong to a later and intrusive culture. If the Crawford, Freel, and Taylor sites are the only components of the Middle Valley Aspect, it is evident that typical occurrences of this culture did not extend into the Norris Basin but were concentrated to the south on the lower Clinch River.

The Heatherly and Stiner Stone Mounds[28] have been grouped with the Middle Valley mounds in Ford and Willey's Burial Mound I as "attenuated Copena-like sites."[29] The information from these two sites is limited but, aside from their use as burial repositories, they have little in common with the mounds of the Middle Valley Aspect further south. The cut bear canines and bear jaws are unlike anything in east Tennessee and, as is indicated by Webb,[30] resemble specimens which have been found to the north by Black in Indiana[31] and by Smith,[32] and Funkhouser and Webb[33] in Kentucky. Some of these sites were similar low stone mounds, and the indication seems to be that Heatherly and Stiner are related to cultural manifestations to the north rather than to the south.

Mississippi Pattern manifestations in the Norris Basin.—The work in the Norris Basin led to the recognition of two house types and eventually to two cultural manifestations. Webb's observation that "separation of these large and small log houses into two groups on the basis of construction of buildings leads to the correct separation and grouping of these sites as manifested by the presence or absence of other traits,"[34] implies that the congeries of traits as-

13. Webb, W. S., 1938, Pl. 14.
14. *Ibid*, Pl. 14b.
15. *Ibid.*, Pl. 85a.
16. *Ibid.*, p. 364.
17. *Ibid.*, p. 38.
18. *Ibid.*, p. 140.
19. *Ibid.*, p. 10.
20. *Ibid.*, p. 83; Griffin, J. B., 1938, p. 277.
21. Webb, W. S., 1938, p. 130.
22. *Ibid.*, p. 161; Griffin, J. B., 1938, p. 280.
23. Webb, W. S., 1938, p. 115; Griffin, J. B., 1938, p. 266; see p. 288 for data on the Irvin Village.
24. Webb, W. S., 1938, p. 180.
25. *Ibid.*, p. 186.

26. *Ibid.*, Pl. 122b.
27. *Ibid.*, p. 133.
28. *Ibid.*, pp. 9 and 159.
29. Ford and Willey, 1941, p. 337.
30. Webb, W. S., 1938, p. 160.
31. Black, 1934.
32. Smith, H. I., 1910.
33. Funkhouser and Webb, 1928, p. 201.
34. Webb, W. S., 1938, p. 367.

sociated with the construction types had been separated. The only series of traits in the report is the chart on page 327 and as this is a summary of traits by sites, and as practically all the sites had more than one component, the chart does not actually show culture complexes. Unless each site is accepted as homogeneous (a single component) the list of site traits cannot be used in determination of focal affiliations.

Such cases, as at the Lea Farm,[35] where small log houses were found below houses of large log construction, occurred a number of times in the Chickamauga Basin and led to the recognition of a time difference between them. The time precedence of the small log house type does not agree completely with Webb's belief in their contemporaneity,[36] although the two overlapped in time at the extremes of their existence.[37] The earlier complex has been designated in the Chickamauga Basin as the Hiwassee Island Focus of an unknown aspect of the Middle Mississippi Phase and is homologous to the "small log town house complex" of the Norris Basin.[38] Examples of the typical pole construction of these Hiwassee Island Focus houses were at the Richardson Farm Mound[39] and the Hill Farm.[40] These were rectangular, with clay seats and horizontal log braces. The shell-tempered pottery with its plain surface and frequent loop handles is also characteristic of this focus. This assignment is substantiated by the absence of Dallas Focus traits such as strap handles and cord marking.

The Norris Basin sites for which a component of the Hiwassee Island Focus has been recognized and the diagnostic traits of this culture which occur at them are shown in Table 1.

TABLE 1

Hiwassee Island Focus Traits on Sites in the Norris Basin

	Lea Farm	Richardson	Hill	McCarty	Bowman	Irvin	Harris
Pole house construction	x	x	x	x	x	x	x
Wall trenches	x	x		x	x	x	x
Rectangular pattern	x	x	x	x	x	x	x
Horizontal wall braces	?	x			x		
Clay seats		x	x		x	x	x
Red-filmed pottery	x				x	x	x
Loop handles (exclusively)		x		x	x	x	
Plain surface (exclusively)				x	x		
Salt pans	x				x		x
Red-on-buff painted	x						

35. *Ibid.*, p. 140.
36. *Ibid.*, p. 370.
37. Lewis and Kneberg, 1941, p. 22.
38. Lewis and Kneberg, 1946, p. 48.
39. Webb, W. S., 1938, p. 64.
40. *Ibid.*, p. 60.

At the Irvin, Harris, and Lea sites, a component of the "large log town house" or Dallas Focus was also present. No Dallas type houses were found at the Harris site, but much of the pottery and some other traits were typical of this culture. Dallas Focus components were also found at the Ausmus, Cox Mound, Walters, and Johnson sites. Each of these was marked by extensive occurrences of Dallas traits and, with the exception of the Johnson Site, typical log construction Dallas houses. The traits which occurred at these sites and were considered indicative of Dallas occupation are shown in Table 2. All the traits which occured at these are not included in the table, for many of them were not particularly diagnostic—being found in two or more of the Middle Mississippi foci in this area— while others were unique. In most cases, the complexes at the various sites were the basis of classification rather than the isolated traits. Generalized Middle Mississippi pottery features are not in themselves definitive, but when they occur with large log houses or with semiflexed burials, they are indicative of Dallas associations.

In summary it may be said that most of the archeological cultures of the Norris Basin appear to be very similar to other manifestations in eastern Tennessee. This is to be expected in view of its geographical position and its relationship to the river valley system. Certain distinctive features from this basin are discussed in the final summary.

The Investigations of M. R. Harrington

At the time Harrington conducted his excavations on the upper Tennessee River it was believed by American anthropologists that the archeological manifestations in this region could unquestionably be attributed to the Cherokee and to them alone (Table 2). Harrington was to a considerable degree influenced by this concept but found himself forced by his archeological perception to recognize three cultural divisions: the "round grave" culture which he attributed to an Algonkin people;[41] a "second culture" which he considered as possibly ancestral to the Cherokee;[42] and the "Cherokee culture".[43] In addition to these divisions he also suggested the possibility of a Creek occupation on Hiwassee Island directly precedent to the arrival of the Cherokee.[44]

The "Round Grave Culture"[45] was characterized by a particular burial complex consisting of very tightly flexed burials deposited in small circular pits, and by steatite vessels, grooved axes, "rude bone awls, arrow points of many forms, and majority of them stemmed, fine two-holed gorgets, bracers made of bone, and pendants of perforated animal teeth." The

41. Harrington, M. R., 1922, p. 276.
42. *Ibid.*, p. 278.
43. *Ibid.*, p. 281.
44. *Ibid.*, p. 281.
45. *Ibid.*, p. 147.

TABLE 2

DALLAS FOCUS TRAITS FOUND IN SITES IN THE NORRIS BASIN

	Irvin	Harris	Lea	Ausmus	Cox Mound	Walters	Johnson
Sub-structure mounds	x			x	x	x	
Log construction houses	x			x	x	x	x
Logs individually set	x			x	x	x	x
Wide interstices				x	x	x	x
Rectangular house plan	x			x	x	x	
Burials in sub-structure mounds	x			x	x	x	
Flexed or seated burials	x			x	x	x	x
Pit inhumation	x			x	x	x	x
Grave goods	x			x	x		x
Stone slabs on graves	x				x		x
Much cord-marked pottery	x	x	x	x	x	x	
Strap handles		x	x	x	x	x	x
Lugs	x	x	x	x	x	x	x
Appliqué fillets	x	x	x	x	x	x	x
Pointed rims					x	x	
Incised decoration		x	x	x	x	x	
Modeled decoration (effigy)	x	x	x	x	x	x	
Punctate decoration	x			x	x	x	x
Negative painting	x						
Small, thin triangular points				x		x	x
Thin square sided celts				x	x	x	
Spatulate ax					x		
Steatite rings							x
Double tapered knives					x		
Bone pins with carved heads				x	x	x	
Bone flesher or end scrapers	x	x		x		x	
Bone hooks	x			x			
Turtle shell rattles					x	x	
Socketted antler points	x	x		x		x	
Oliva beads				x			x
Massive shell beads	?			x	x		
Marginella beads				x		x	
Shell gorgets—engraved					x		
Shell mask gorgets					x		
Knob-headed shell pins				x	x	x	
Shell earplugs (pulley shape)				x			
Conch shell vessels (Cassis)				x			
Copper beads				x			
Copper covered wooden earspools				x			

pottery was "egg shaped"[46] with pointed bottoms and characterized by "impressions of a very unusual sort of fabric made of reeds and fiber cord."[47] This complex is readily recognizable as that which has been designated at the Upper Valley Aspect of the Woodland Pattern in the Chickamauga Basin.[48]

Harrington believed that the people of the "second culture" possessed the peculiar fabric impressed pottery which he found associated with the "Round Grave" complex, and also a number of traits which he believed to be more closely related to the "Cherokee Culture."[49] The complex which he believed typical of this group included such traits as triangular projectile points "like those of the Cherokee", celts, copper, beads and ornaments of marine shell, burials flexed or extended in burial mounds, partial cremation of bodies after interment, occasional stone graves, and pottery which was simpler and plainer than the "Cherokee" pottery and distinguished by a red-on-buff painted ware.[50]

This complex, for which Harrington was hard put to find an explanation, represents an interesting mixture of Upper Valley and Middle Valley Woodland traits with an additional series of factors which are related to the Hiwassee Island and Dallas foci of the Middle Mississippi Phase.[51] The burial mounds of the Middle Valley Aspect (Woodland Pattern), with their frequent occurrence of intrusive burials of the Dallas Focus, probably formed the basis upon which Harrington postulated this complex.

Harrington recognized that the complex which he assigned to the Cherokee contained a large number of traits, which were widely distributed in the central Mississippi Valley, and that it showed evidences of having been strongly affected by influences from the south and east.[52] Most of the traits which he calls Cherokee may unhesitatingly be equated with either the Dallas or the Mouse Creek Focus.[53]

Harrington first differentiated the Upper Valley Aspect of the Woodland Pattern when he recognized the "Round Grave Culture" on the Mainland Village Site at the junction of the Little Tennessee and Tennessee Rivers.[54] It was not strongly represented at this unit, however, and its occurrence is probably an extension of the strong component of this culture on Lenoir (or Bussell's) Island, which lies directly across one arm of the river. It was at this latter site that the complete complex was distinguished.[55]

In the absence of ceramic information,[56] the only

46. Ibid., p. 154.
47. Ibid., p. 277.
48. Lewis and Kneberg, 1941, pp. 30 ff.
49. Harrington, M. R., 1922, pp. 278 ff.
50. Ibid., p. 279.
51. Lewis and Kneberg, 1941.
52. Harrington, M. R., 1922, pp. 282 ff.
53. Lewis and Kneberg, 1941, pp. 6 ff.
54. Harrington, M. R., 1922, p. 50.
55. Ibid., p. 69.
56. The pottery associated with this culture is not treated by Harrington in his discussion of these sites, but the Candy Creek Fabric Marked is referred to in the general discussion (Harrington, M. R., 1922, Pl. XLVII) and in the description of Mound No. 2 on Hiwassee Island (ibid., p. 112) as having been found at the Lenoir City Mounds. The mounds on the Bussell Place are usually referred to as the Lenoir City Mounds, but since no mention is made of the particular Woodland complex with which this pottery is associated it is probable that the title in the illustration mentioned above refers generally to the three sites at the mouth of the Little Tennessee River, two of which possessed distinct occurrences of the "Round Grave Complex."

traits which offer any key to the identity of the "Round Grave" people are: the presence of steatite sherds,[57] ground stone gorgets,[58] the tightly flexed burial position with deposition in circular pits,[59] and the low point of origin in the great midden. The first of these traits has been found to some extent with components of both aspects of the Woodland Pattern in the Chickamauga Basin, but stone gorgets occur almost exclusively with Upper Valley components.[60] The stemmed projectile points[61] and heavy splinter bone awls[62] which Harrington found with this complex have absolutely no significance in themselves as indicators of cultural affiliations, inasmuch as artifacts of this type have been found with practically every cultural manifestation in this region.

The significant feature which enables us to identify the "Round Grave Culture" with the Upper Valley Aspect is the association of this combination of traits with a non-mound building complex.

Harrington also believed that an occupation of the "Round Grave Culture" existed on Hiwassee Island and indicated it as the village layer underlying Mound 2.[63] It is interesting that the extensive excavations conducted by the University of Tennessee on Hiwassee Island revealed no evidence of such an occupation.[64] Harrington does not describe the sherds which he felt might "be assigned to the 'Round Grave' people,"[65] but the "fragments of vessels with legs," vessels with pointed bottoms, and fragments of steatite vessels may be equated, in this case, not with the Upper Valley, but with the Middle Valley Aspect of the Woodland Pattern, a culture which Harrington did not distinguish but which was responsible for the building of this mound[66] and which shared many artifact traits with the Upper Valley Aspect.

This Middle Valley Aspect of the Woodland Pattern is one of the most interesting cultures found on the upper reaches of the Tennessee River. Its components occur in considerable numbers in the area between Knoxville and Chattanooga and as they are marked by numerous conical burial mounds which are easily seen from the river, they were pitted or excavated by both the numerous pot-hunters of the region and the early archeologists. The mound on Hiwassee Island which Harrington designated as Mound 1 was partially excavated by him and completely excavated during the investigations in the

Chickamauga Basin. It was found to be a typical burial mound of the Middle Valley Aspect into which burials of the Dallas Focus were intruded.[67] Mounds No. 2 and 5, also on Hiwassee Island and excavated by Harrington, can definitely be identified as burial mounds of the Middle Valley Aspect. No ceramics are described which can be associated, but the rest of the complex is typical and includes such traits as large conch columellae, perforated and unperforated; small *Busycon* shells perforated for pendants; masses of *Olivella* beads possibly sewn on garments; and heavy pendants cut from the wall of a large conch.[68] The burial complex of the Middle Valley Aspect is characterized by small conical mounds erected over flexed or extended burials which are deposited either directly upon the surface or interred in pits. Subsequent burials were laid down upon the summit of the mound and then covered with another layer of earth, a series of burials resulting in a fairly large mound with a number of phases. In some cases, as in Mound 5 on Hiwassee Island, each phase is covered with a layer of mussel shells.

A skull burial was also found in this mound. This form of interment, with secondary cremation, is found in the burial complex of the Middle Valley culture and tends to further indicate the affiliation of the two mounds on Hiwassee Island with that aspect.[69]

Another trait which has been demonstrated to be associated with the Middle Valley Aspect by the analysis of the Chickamauga Basin material is the small thin projectile point with incurvate sides and base.[70] Harrington illustrates a number of excellent examples and calls them "Flint Implements of the Cherokee."[71] A cache of these points was found with an extended burial on the Upper Hampton Place in a burial mound which certainly appears to belong to the Middle Valley Aspect.[72] (Another mound on the same site, excavated by Moore,[73] contained a skull burial accompanied by one of the most distinctive traits of this culture, a cut conch columella.) This small thin projectile type which Harrington believed to be Cherokee appeared again on the Bussell Place, and once again, was associated with typical Middle Valley burial mounds.

At this site (Bussell Place or Lenoir City Mounds),[74] although the pottery is described by Harrington in terms too general to be of any comparative value, the Middle Valley association is recognizable by the occurrence of such characteristics as burials laid on subsoil or deposited in shallow pits and covered with a

57. Harrington, M. R., 1922, p. 149.
58. *Ibid.*, p. 160.
59. *Ibid.*, p. 164.
60. This paper, Appendix.
61. Harrington, M. R., 1922, p. 158.
62. *Ibid.*, p. 161.
63. *Ibid.*, p. 112.
64. Lewis and Kneberg, 1941, Map #3; cf. also Lewis and Kneberg, 1946, p. 5.
65. Harrington, 1922, p. 111.
66. Lewis and Kneberg, 1941, p. 27.

67. Lewis and Kneberg, 1946, Unit 73, p. 24.
68. Harrington, M. R., 1922, pp. 108 and 129.
69. Lewis and Kneberg, 1941, p. 27.
70. *Ibid.*, p. 27 and Pl. IV, Figs. 18 and 19.
71. Harrington, M. R., 1922, Pl. LXX.
72. *Ibid.*, p. 89, Pl. XXIX.
73. Moore, C. B., 1915, p. 407.
74. Harrington, M. R., 1922, p. 34.

mound,[75] skull burials[76] and cremations,[77] an unforated stone gorget,[78] and the points referred to above.[79]

A rectangular copper ornament[80] was also found in Mound No. 3 at this site, but no copper has been associated with this complex in the Chickamauga Basin and no interpretation can be made of this single occurrence on the basis of data now available.

On the basis of comparison with data from the Chickamauga Basin it appears certain that components of the Middle Valley Aspect of the Woodland Pattern were excavated by Harrington at the Bussell Place, Upper Hampton Place, and Hiwassee Island sites.

The foci of the Middle Mississippi Phase in east Tennessee are rather difficult to distinguish from each other on the basis of the meager and incomplete data in Harrington's report. It was impossible under conditions of limited time and resources for the excavator to do more than test any of the sites in which he was interested, and the result is necessarily an incomplete picture. Pieces of evidence were recovered which suggest all of the cultural divisions which have been recognized in the Chickamauga Basin, but the complete complex for any single one is not present. Architectural data are completely lacking in Harrington's report, yet this factor is one of the most important in distinguishing the Hiwassee Island Focus from the succeeding Dallas and Mouse Creek foci. The occurrence, however, of sherds of red-filmed and red-on-buff painted pottery definitely suggests Hiwassee Island.[81] It was not possible for the excavator to associate these items with any of the other material from those sites, but Harrington felt that they represented something which was not to be assigned to the Cherokee.[82] This red-on-buff ware has been found in minor quantities from Cox Island, in northeastern Alabama, up the river to the Mainland site at the mouth of the Little Tennessee. Moore found it at Citico (near Chattanooga), the White Place, and the Bennett Place,[83] but the greatest single concentration was found during the excavations of the University of Tennessee on Hiwassee Island[84] for which it has been named. No other material from the Lenoir Island or Mainland sites can be related to this focus, and inasmuch as it was undoubtedly coeval with the succeeding Dallas Focus for a time, a few sherds may be expected to occur on sites which never possessed a component of the Hiwassee Island Focus. Situations of this type were found at the Ledford Island and Dallas Sites in the Chickamauga Basin.[85]

Most of the material which Harrington recovered from his excavations in this area he believed represented Cherokee culture. On the basis of data now available, that material can be assigned to at least three different foci. As has been indicated already, the cut conch columellae, small projectiles with incurvate sides and base, and the burial mound complex, are definitely associated with the Middle Valley Aspect of the Woodland Pattern. Many of the other traits, such as conch vessels, engraved shell gorgets, fishhooks, copper beads, bone fleshers, thick polished celts, and flexed burials in substructure mounds or intrusive into Middle Valley burial mounds, may be recognized as belonging to the Dallas Focus.[86]

The bulk of the pottery which Harrington calls Cherokee[87] is typical of the late Middle Mississippi manifestations in eastern Tennessee and may belong to either the Dallas or the Mouse Creek Focus, (Fig. 109-110) or in some instances, to the Hiwassee Island Focus. Such occurrences as effigy modeling on frog or sun-fish bowls,[88] lugs,[89] incised decoration,[90] appliqué fillet decoration on the rim,[91] strap handles,[92] long and short necked bottles,[93] and a great variety of other shapes, might be found in either of the two later foci. These particular items could be used to determine the specific focus to which they belong, if their quantity or the data pertaining to them were ample for proportionate comparisons, but such an approach is obviously impossible in this study.

Other "Cherokee" traits which are found in both the Dallas and Mouse Creek foci are: flat celts with squared edges,[94] double bitted chisels,[95] stone knives,[96] double tapered bone awls,[97] pestles,[98] nutting stones,[99] *Oliva* beads,[100] perforated bulbous shell earplugs,[101] knobheaded shell pins,[102] large and small spheroid, discoid, and cylindrical shell beads,[103] axe effigy pottery pipes,[104] and stone discs.[105] One of the few dis-

75. *Ibid.*, p. 41.
76. *Ibid.*, p. 43.
77. *Ibid.*, p. 38.
78. *Ibid.*, p. 40.
79. *Ibid.*
80. *Ibid.*, p. 45.
81. Harrington, M. R., 1922, p. 190.
82. *Ibid.*, p. 192.
83. Moore, C. B., 1915.
84. Lewis and Kneberg, 1946, p. 172.

85. Lewis and Kneberg, 1941, p. 175. [Further comment on this type is in Phillips, Ford and Griffin, 1951, p. 133]
86. Lewis and Kneberg, 1946, p. 175.
87. Harrington, M. R., 1922, pp. 173 ff.
88. *Ibid.*, Pl. LIX.
89. *Ibid.*, Pl. LX.
90. *Ibid.*, Pl. LII.
91. *Ibid.*, Pl. LV.
92. *Ibid.*, Pl. LII.
93. *Ibid.*, Pl. LVIII.
94. *Ibid.*, Pl. LXXIII, Figs. *b* and *c*.
95. *Ibid.*, Pl. LXXIII, Fig. *a*.
96. *Ibid.*, Pl. LXXII.
97. *Ibid.*, Pl. LXXV, Figs. *a* and *d*.
98. *Ibid.*, Pl. LXXVI.
99. *Ibid.*, Pl. LXXVII.
100. *Ibid.*, Fig. 48.
101 *Ibid.*, Pl. LXXXII, Figs. *c* and *d*.
102. *Ibid.*, Pl. LXXXII, Figs. *e,f,h,* and *i*.
103. *Ibid.*, Figs. 49 and 50.
104. *Ibid.*, Fig. 61.   105. *Ibid.*, Pl. LXXXVI and Fig. 63a.

tinguishing factors between these two foci which is available in the Harrington material is the difference in burial deposition. An extended burial complex which is accompanied by this series of traits can be assigned to the Mouse Creek Focus with little question, while this same series in occurrence with a flexed burial complex can be assigned to the Dallas Focus.

Components of the Dallas Focus were found by Harrington in Mound 1 and 2 on Hiwassee Island where they were intrusive in typical Middle Valley burial mounds. The burials of these components contained shell-tempered pottery and knob-headed shell pins and also additional traits which were not only typical of the late Mississippi cultures, but also indicative of the Dallas Focus alone. These additional and distinguishing factors were: conch shell vessels,[106] a shell gorget engraved with the triskele design,[107] and the semi-flexed position of the intrusive burials.

On Lenoir Island Harrington made a clear distinction between his "Round Grave Culture" and the people who buried in rectangular graves. The materials found in the graves of this latter group indicate clearly that the burials are to be associated with either the Dallas or the Mouse Creek Focus. All doubt, however, that the proper association is with the Dallas Focus is resolved by the fact that 32 out of 34 burials were deposited in a flexed position, the position of the other two being indeterminable because of decay or previous disturbance.[108]

This typical late Middle Mississippi complex is found also at the Mainland site which produced both flexed and extended burials. The presence of cord-marked pottery with the flexed burials further suggests their affiliation with the Dallas Focus, a suggestion which becomes a certainty with the occurrence of lugs, strap handles, lobed bodies, and zoomorphic effigy modeling on *cord-marked* jars. Such combinations are associated with no other culture in this area but the Dallas Focus.

The artifacts which were found with the extended burials[109] were not of a particularly distinctive nature, but this type of deposition can, in almost every case, be associated with the Mouse Creek Focus, and it is worth noticing that none of the artifact types which are determinants for the Dallas Focus were found with these burials.

It is suggested, then, that components of both the Dallas and Mouse Creek foci are present at this site, and the data presented by Harrington also suggests the possibility of an occupation by the people of the Hiwassee Island Focus. The evidence for an occurrence of each of the three Middle Mississippi foci recognized in eastern Tennessee at this single site is not conclusive, but must be considered in the light of a number of other factors.

One such factor is the possibility of a single, extended occupation by people of the Dallas Focus. In the Chickamauga Basin, as has been pointed out,[110] the time periods for the three Mississippi foci may overlap considerably, thereby accounting for a fairly large number of traits which are held in common by the successive and partially coeval cultural groups. The traits here which seem to be characteristic of the Hiwassee Island or Mouse Creek foci may merely represent the initial and final stages respectively of a single occupation of a long continued Dallas component. Another factor, is that, inasmuch as this site is large and deep and the excavations were necessarily on a small scale, it is rather remarkable that the limited amount of material recovered should so strongly suggest occupations of each of the three foci recognized in the Chickamauga Basin. In view of these facts it seems exceedingly likely that further excavations will reveal the presence of complete components of each of the three foci.

In summary it may be said that components of the Upper Valley Aspect of the Woodland Pattern are suggested by Harrington's material from the Mainland and Lenoir Island sites and conform closely to his "Round Grave Culture"; that components of the Middle Valley Aspect of the Woodland Pattern, which Harrington incorporated with his "Cherokee," are indicated at Mounds 1, 2, and 5 on Hiwassee Island, the Upper Hampton Place, and the Bussell Place; that the Hiwassee Island Focus is known to have occurred also on the Mainland Site and Lenoir Island; and that components of the Dallas Focus are shown to have been present on Hiwassee Island, the Mainland Site, and Lenoir Island, while the Mouse Creek Focus was possibly represented at the two latter sites.

THE INVESTIGATIONS OF C. B. MOORE

The work of C. B. Moore on the Tennessee River in 1915[111] was largely in the nature of an extensive site survey with numerous tests but practically no intensive excavation (Table 3). He was limited by both time and available labor but his investigations resulted in the location of a great number of the sites along the river and at least a brief description of most of those which he located.

As he was traveling by river, most of the sites which contained mounds were observed and checked but he failed to find or record the village sites which could not be seen from a boat. The data for eastern Tennessee which are presented in his report describe only one site which might belong to the earliest culture in this area—the Upper Valley Aspect. This was located at Lowes Ferry between Knoxville and Lenoir City.[112] His excavation at this site was very limited, and it is impossible to assess the artifacts which he described

106. *Ibid.*, p. 125.   108. *Ibid.*, p. 73.   110. Lewis and Kneberg, 1946.   112. *Ibid.*, p. 421.
107. *Ibid.*, p. 124.   109. *Ibid.*, p. 59, Pl. XVI.   111. Moore, C. B., 1915.

as "a shell bead," "flint arrowheads," and "A small discoidal stone." However, he also found flexed burials, a grooved ax, a broken slate gorget, and a kettle-shaped pit. These traits suggest a component of the lowing chart. It will be seen that, although the determining traits are few, they are distinctive of the Middle Valley Aspect as defined in the Chickamauga Basin.

TABLE 3

TRAITS OF THE MIDDLE VALLEY ASPECT DISCOVERED BY C. B. MOORE

	Carter Farm	Montgomery	Lovelady Ldg.	Mattie Igou	Davis Pl.	Hoyal Ferry	Viniard Ldg.	Upper Hampton	Ewing Pl.	Tedder Pl.	DeArmond Pl.	Evans Pl.	Biss Pl.	F. A. Berry	Carmichael	Arthur
Small burial mounds	x	x	x	x	x	x	x	x	x	x	x	x	x	x	x	x
Primary interment	x	x	x	x	x	x	x	x	x	x	x	x	x	x	x	x
Mussel shell layer	x	x	x	x										x		
Rock slab layers		x	x	x												
Semiflexed position		x	x		x		x						x	x	x	x
Partial burials							x							x	x	
Subsoil pits	x	x				x	x	x	x		x				x	
Small, thin projectile points, incurvate						?		?					?			?
Conch collumelae	x	x		x		x	x						x	x		x
Olivella beads	x			x												x
Marginella beads				x												
Large, discoid shell beads					x											

Upper Valley Aspect, an identification which was corroborated by a survey of the site by this author and the finding here of limestone-tempered sherds with plain plaited fabric-impressed surfaces.[113]

Probably the most significant single contribution which Moore's research made to the archeological picture of eastern Tennessee was his discovery of the many small burial mounds along the river between Knoxville and Chattanooga. Even the limited excavation which he did at these sites was sufficient to give an indication of their nature and to allow their recognition as mounds of the Middle Valley Aspect of the Woodland Pattern. A number of the characteristics of this culture are so very distinctive that even a small amount of information makes identification possible.

Moore's tests of these sites indicated definitely that many of them were burial mounds and belonged to the Middle Valley Aspect in spite of the paucity of artifacts and the complete absence of pottery. The sites which may be assigned to this culture with considerable certainty are: Carter Farm, Montgomery Place, mound near Lovelady Landing, Mattie Igou Site, Davis Place, Hoyal Ferry Mound, Viniard Landing Mounds, Upper Hampton Place, Ewing Place, Tedder Place, De Armond Place, Evans Place, Biss Place, F. S. Berry Place, Carmichael Place, and the Arthur Place. These sites, and the group of diagnostic traits described for each, are summarized on the fol-

Moore described other details and finds from these sites, but those in the chart are the only ones which are culturally meaningful.

A number of other mounds were excavated which also seem to have belonged to the Middle Valley Aspect but for those in this group the data are too scanty to make more than a "possible" identification. These mounds are: Shellmound, Jones Place, Mounds near Cook Landing, Lower Hampton Place, Campbell Place, Mounds near Hood's Ferry, mounds near Huffine Ferry, W. W. Blair Place, and the Edward Prater Place.

Moore attempted to excavate at only two of the large sub-structure mounds which are found along the river in eastern Tennessee. These were the Citico Mound[114] and the mound on the Bennett Place,[115] both near Chattanooga. This Citico Mound, which is at the mouth of Citico Creek, should not be confused with the Citico Mound on the Little Tennessee River, which Emmert excavated in 1885 and which was supposed to stand on the site of the Cherokee town of Settacoo.[116]

There is little question but that components of the Dallas Focus were present at the Citico Mound and the mound on the Bennett Place, for at both of these localities were found large mounds of the Dallas substructure type. Table 4 shows some of the typical Dallas traits which were described by Moore from these sites and, although they represent only a frag-

113. Site survey of the Fort Loudon Basin with C. W. Rowe for the Laboratory of Anthropology, University of Tennessee, 1942.

114. Moore, C. B., 1915, p. 370.
115. *Ibid.*, p. 338.   116. Thomas, C., 1894, p. 374.

ment of the total complex, they are diagnostic of this culture.

Nothing is known about the structures within these mounds except that clay floor or "burned areas" are described, and Read described post holes which were encountered when he tunneled into the Citico Mound in 1860.[117] Moore described the burial complexes in considerable detail so that it is possible to recognize a number of different burial positions (semi-flexed seems to be predominant) and associate with them such typical Dallas traits as covers of stone or wood, accompanying shell gorgets in variety of designs, large stone knives, shell face masks, shell ear-plugs, sheet copper ornaments, and modeled effigy pottery.

One of the most interesting aspects of Moore's report on the Citico Mounds is the finding of two small iron chisels and four blue glass trade beads in association with the Dallas complex. The fact that white trade goods occurred in such a small number of the burials from this site would indicate that the contact between these people and the traders had been limited. Their presence here is another indication that the Dallas culture persisted into the historic period. One of the burials (No. 23) which contained trade goods also included such typical Dallas artifacts as a rattlesnake shell gorget and a stemmed ax or spud, while another (No. 79) had a sheet copper ornament and a grooved shell ear plug.

Moore's description of the pottery from this site tells practically nothing, but the pictures or references to modeled and incised specimens, as well as strap handles and lugs, are indicative of the Dallas component. Paradoxically he also mentions one stamped sherd and two pieces of painted red-on-buff. These cannot be interpreted but may indicate accidents or possibly an occupation by people of the Hiwassee Island Focus in the unexcavated section of the mound.

The large Bennett Mound is an outstanding example of the large Dallas type mound although the traits described by Moore do little more than suggest the nature of the occupation here. The burial complex, effigy modeled pottery, double tapered knives, shell gorgets, and copper ornaments, are sufficient to identify at least one component. This same thing may be said for the other Dallas components which Moore discovered—their presence is indicated, but on the basis of minimum evidence. At the Wilson, Mattie Igou, and Hampton Place sites, it is the burial complex which suggests Dallas.

At the Wilson Site, a large mound was present which was possibly of the sub-structure type, but the burials were excavated from the surrounding village area. Some of the traits are not diagnostic, but the excavation of a semi-flexed burial in a partial stone slab grave and accompanied by large tubular copper beads strongly suggests the Dallas Focus. This type of stone slab grave was also found at the Mattie Igou site where it was intruded into the top of a Middle Valley mound. That it belonged to the Dallas culture is indicated by its contents—large marine shell beads, and a small pointed rim pot.

The Hampton Place in Hamilton County was important because of the large number of trade specimens found here in association with seated and semi-flexed burials. Webb suggested that the seated burials found in the Norris Basin might have been Creek,[118] and these, like the seated burials discovered on the DeArmond Site in the Watts Bar Basin,[119] were definitely associated with the Dallas Focus. Unfortunately, the extensive occurrence of aboriginal grave goods which was typical of the situations mentioned above was not found at the Hampton Place. In this case the native products were almost completely displaced by such trade items as iron knives and bracelets, glass beads, and various items made of sheet brass. In the absence of diagnostic artifacts the association with the Dallas Focus is based upon the burial complex—its similarity to other seated pit burials where the associations are definitely Dallas.

Moore also discovered some items which are impossible to interpret. On William's Island in Hamilton County,[120] he found a group of ten burials which he described as fully extended. The traits associated with them are definitely Middle Mississippi and the burial position suggests (if he is correct) relationship to the Mouse Creek Focus. At the Kimbrough Place[121] he uncovered something unique in this area—circular stone slab floors about six feet in diameter, surrounded by a low stone wall. Only one of these possessed the wall, but both held burials lying near their center. These are unlike anything from the Chickamauga Basin but may be similar to the walled features on the McGee Farm and in the Callaway Mound (No. 2) in Monroe County on the Little Tennessee River.[122] The partial stone slab graves in the mound at the Kimbrough Site are also unlike other occurrences. The stone slabbing in the mound suggests Middle Valley association, but these burials appear to have been incomplete stone coffins and more nearly similar to some Dallas materials. The only artifacts which can be related to a known culture are the long slender copper celts which are similar to examples found at the Hixon Site,[123] an outstanding Dallas mound.

Burial characteristics at the Eldridge Place and the

117. Read, 1868.

118. Webb, W. S., 1938, pp. 112 and 242.
119. Excavated by John Alden for the University of Tennessee.
120. Moore, C. B., p. 354.
121. Ibid., p. 403.
122. Thomas, C., 1894, pp. 378 and 385.
123. Lewis and Kneberg, 1941, p. 17.

R. A. Sharp Place are also difficult to interpret. At each, the chief suggestion of Dallas affinity comes from the semi-flexed burial position. At the Sharp Place, there were also a great number of discoidal shell beads which strengthen the identification, but the stone box graves from the Eldridge Place are not so helpful. These graves were occasionally found in the Chickamauga Basin but never in the concentration represented at this site. In the light of the incomplete information the suggestion that Dallas components were present here should be recognized as tentative, to say the least.

In much of Moore's material from this area information is sparse, and it may appear that the cultural affiliations suggested here are based upon less than significant evidence. This is not always the case, for some of the traits described by him are clearly diagnostic of certain recognized complexes. His mention of a small burial mound immediately suggests a Middle Valley component, and if he further notes a subsurface burial pit containing two conch columellae, there can be little doubt concerning identification, for these traits do not occur with any other culture in this area. In similar manner the occurrence of such "key traits" as shell masks and rattlesnake gorgets in a substructure mound can suggest nothing more or less than a component of the Dallas Focus. It is recognized that cultural comparisons and identifications would be more valid if there were based upon an item for item examination of a complex of traits, but, when this is not possible, the best must be made of available data.

THE INVESTIGATIONS UNDER THE DIRECTION OF CYRUS THOMAS

It is impossible to use the data presented by Thomas in the Twelfth Annual Report of the Bureau of American Ethnology[124] with any conviction that they present a complete or even, in some cases, an accurate picture of the material which Emmert excavated in the Tennessee Area. The majority of descriptions are so general as to be worthless for comparative purposes, and those excavations which produced only unspectacular materials were treated summarily.

Quite a number of the sites described appear to resemble the burial mounds of the Middle Valley Aspect of the Woodland Pattern (Table 3). As the artifacts recovered here were usually few in number and not particularly colorful, they are given very little mention in the report. On Long Island in Roane County[125] (identified erroneously by Thomas as the site of the Brakebill Mound which is at the junction of the French Broad and Holston rivers) three of the mounds (Nos. 11, 12, and 14) appear to belong to

124. Thomas, C., 1894.   125. Ibid., p. 358.

TABLE 4

DALLAS FOCUS TRAITS FROM C. B. MOORE'S EXCAVATIONS

	Citico	Wilson	Mattie Igou	Hampton Pl.	Bennett Pl.
Burials in sub-structure mounds	x				x
Pit inhumation				x	x
Wood or stone grave covers	x	x	x		
Burials flexed or seated	x	x		x	x
Burials intrusive into Middle Valley mounds			x		
Grave goods	x				x
Strap handles	x				
Lugs	x				
Pointed rims			x		
Incised decoration	x				
Modeled effigy decoration	x				x
Negative painting					?
Small, thin triangular points					x
Spatulate ax	x				
Double tapered knives					x
Ax-shaped pipes	x				
Flanged rim pipes	x				
Shell gorgets—engraved	x				x
Shell mask gorgets	x				
Knob-headed shell pins	x				
Shell ear plugs (pulley shape)	x				
Conch shell vessels				x	
Copper beads		x			
Copper ornaments	x				x
Trade goods	x		x		

this aspect. Each was a small burial mound; number 11 was built over burials deposited on the original surface, and number 12 and 14 possessed in addition a veneer of mussel shell over each phase. No artifacts are described, but the character of the mounds suggest the Middle Valley burial complex. The mounds on the Hagler[126] and Lee[127] farms, also in Roane County, were probably Middle Valley. Mound No. 2 at the Lee site possessed a stone slab veneer, but certain other features are unique. The circular burial mound (No. 2) on the McMurray Farm[128] resembles those above except for the occurrence of two stone coffins which might have been intrusive. Mound No. 8 in the Citico group (McSpaddin),[129] also in the valley of the Little Tennessee, also resembles, in its general features, the mounds of the Middle Valley Aspect. The same may be said for the burial mounds on the Pate Farm[130] nearly opposite old Fort Loudon, the Tipton[131] and Lane[132] farms in Loudon County,

126. Ibid., p. 363.   130. Ibid., p. 388.
127. Ibid., p. 364.   131. Ibid., p. 391.
128. Ibid., p. 367.   132. Ibid.
129. Ibid., p. 377.

at Park's or Jackson's Ferry,[133] and on the Jackson Farm.[134] Mound No. 3 at Bat Creek[135] is also rather similar but apparently possessed non-typical traits such as copper ornaments and enigmatic engraved stone.

On Lenoir Island at the junction of the Little Tennessee and Tennessee rivers, Emmert found other burial mounds which apparently belong to this same complex. His mound No. 1,[136] although intruded into by historic burials, possessed a clay veneer and other traits of the Middle Valley complex. In the neck of land called Hall's Bend,[137] mounds 15 and 16 (they cannot be distinguished in the report) was a burial mound with stone veneer built over a pit into the original surface. The fact that two burials found in the pit were "seated" would cause more doubt concerning its Middle Valley affiliation if we were able to depend on Emmert's designation of burial position.

It is possible that some of the sites which are here assigned to the Middle Valley Aspect may be misinterpreted because of the inadequate data; however, in view of the fact that all the burial mounds in the areas directly adjacent to this were associated with this culture and usually characterized by submound pits and/or veneered phases, the identifications are probably valid.

In spite of the many shortcomings in Thomas' report, he presents one of the best early pictures of Middle Mississippi culture from this area. This was derived chiefly from Emmert's excavations in the valley of the Little Tennessee and in mound No. 2 on Lenoir Island. The size of the mounds, the tradition that they were built by the Cherokee, and the occurrence of such traits as engraved shell gorgets, effigy pottery, negative painting, and superimposed fireplaces, led to their being extensively described and illustrated. There can be little doubt that these are substructure mounds of the Dallas type, for, in practically each case, were found clay floors, fireplaces, and even post molds, which Thomas describes for the Lenoir Island mound as eighteen inches in diameter.[138]

The outstanding Dallas components described by Thomas are those excavated by Emmert at the following sites: the McMurray Mound (No. 3—Chilhowee),[139] the McSpaddin Mound (No. 4—Citico)[140] the mounds on the Callaway Farm (No. 1, the Toco or Toqua Mound,[141] and No. 2, the Callaway mound),[142] and Mound No. 2 on Lenoir Island.[143] In addition to these the Bat Creek No. 1[144] was apparently another sub-structure type mound, although

133. Ibid., p. 394.   139. Ibid., p. 367.
134. Ibid., p. 396.   140. Ibid., p. 374.
135. Ibid., p. 391.   141. Ibid., p. 280.
136. Ibid., p. 397.   142. Ibid., p. 269.
137. Ibid., p. 404.   143. Ibid., p. 369.
138. Ibid., p. 399.   144. Ibid., p. 392.

very little more information is available. Table 5 shows the occurrence of Dallas Focus traits at these sites.

TABLE 5

DALLAS FOCUS TRAITS FROM EMMERT'S EXCAVATIONS

	McMurray No. 3	McSpaddin	Callaway Farm	Callaway Mound	Bat Creek No. 1	Lenoir Ld. No. 2
Sub-structure mounds	x	x	x	x	x	x
Burials in sub-structure mounds*	x	x	x	x		x
Pit inhumation	x	x	?			
Wood or stone grave covers	x					
Burials intrusive into Middle Valley mounds	x					
Grave goods		x	x	x		
Cord-marked pottery		x				x
Strap handles		x	x			x
Lugs			x			x
Appliqué fillets		x	x			x
Incised decoration		x	x			x
Modeled effigy decoration		x	x	x		
Negative painting				x		
Small thin triangular points						x
Flat, square sided celts						x
Spatulate ax			x			
Large stone disks						x
Bone pins with carved heads		x	x			
Bone flesher or end scraper			x			x
Massive shell beads	x		?			x
Marginella beads						x
Shell gorgets—engraved	x		x			x
Shell mask gorgets	x	x	x			x
Knob-headed shell pins		x	x			
Conch shell vessels				x		
Copper ornaments				?		
Trade goods	x	x				x

*It should be noted that Emmert described practically all the burials from this area as extended unless they were bundled or seated. The occurrence of his "extended" burials at many of the sites appears doubtful in view of further excavations at these same sites. At that Fain's Island site in Jefferson County where he described the burials as "in most cases, lying at full length" (Thomas, C., 1894, p. 358) the University of Tennessee found the majority of burials in flexed or semiflexed positions. Emmert's excavations around Lenoir City also produced results which, in regard to burial position, were directly contradictory to Harrington's later observations. This is particularly significant when it is remembered that burial position is an important distinction between the Dallas and Mouse Creek foci.

The relationships and cultural significance of much of the material excavated by the earlier archeologists in this area can be explained in the light of recent and intensive investigations, but some of the phenomena uncovered by Emmert has never been duplicated. Nothing resembling the mass bundle burials which he found on Long Island in Roane County[145] and on the McGhee Farm in Monroe County[146] has

145. Ibid., p. 362.   146. Ibid., p. 378.

been recovered in more recent work. The clay canoe-shaped coffin containing an extended burial and surrounded by four seated burials, which also came from Long Island,[147] remains a unique occurrence. The same is true of the circular burial areas paved with rock and enclosed within stone slab walls which he found in the McGhee Mound,[148] in the Callaway Mound No. 2,[149] in the Bat Creek Mound,[150] and on the Blankenship Place.[151]

Thomas also reports enclosed burial areas, vaguely similar to those described above, from Sullivan County.[152] To our knowledge no recent investigation has uncovered anything resembling the stone domed vaults, or "stone hives" which he describes. Piles of limestone slabs covering graves are reported from near Kingsport in northeastern Tennessee and, although nothing similar was recovered in the Chickamauga Basin, they may have resembled the Heatherly and Stiner stone mounds from the Norris Basin.[153]

OTHER INVESTIGATIONS IN EASTERN TENNESSEE

Even before 1885, when Emmert conducted his excavations for the Bureau of American Ethnology, considerable archeological investigation had been going on in this area. Although this work was done by the Reverend E. O. Dunning for the Peabody Museum of Yale University and the Peabody Museum of Harvard and by Dr. E. Palmer for the National Museum, the excavators published no comprehensive reports, and it is only through the use which other authors made of this material that we are able to learn any details.

Palmer's excavations at the McMahan Mound near Sevierville produced a large amount of material and, although he listed it in catalogue fashion,[154] it was Holmes's work on shell artifacts which really described them.[155] It is obvious from the large number of fine shell gorgets and face masks that a strong component of the Dallas Focus must have been present here. Most of them are identical with specimens from this culture in the Chickamauga Basin and surrounding area.

The references in the report to burned clay areas, layers of charcoal, and upright posts are almost positive indications that this 16 foot mound was one of the Dallas type sub-structure mounds. The pottery described confirms this identification with the mention of shell-tempering, cord marking, appliqué fillets, nodes and modeling. Some trade goods were also found, and, although Palmer felt that they came from deep in the mound, they can probably be accepted

as additional evidence that the Dallas culture continued into the historic period.

A small number of other finds at this site do not belong with the Dallas material and possibly indicate a component of the Woodland Pattern in the immediate vicinity. These specimens are the bannerstone and boatstone found in the nearby fields and the fragment of "a rudely made vase, in which we have the impression of a fabric, the warp of which, whether wood or cord, has consisted of fillets more than one-fourth of an inch in width, the woof being of fine cord."[156] The description sounds very much like Woodland plain plaited fabric-impressed pottery, an identification which is almost assured by the further description that the pot had an incurved rim and a slightly flattened base.

The chief source of information for the discoveries of the Reverend Dunning at the Brakebill, McBee, and Lisle mounds, is the paper written by George Grant MacCurdy who described and illustrated the artifacts but made no analysis and drew no conclusions from them.[157] The Brakebill Mound was most certainly of the Dallas substructure type and MacCurdy quotes Dunning as referring to "layers of charcoal and burnt clay several yards square.[158] He also quotes Dunning's observation that some of the gorgets "were deposited under the head of a human skeleton, which was doubled up in the usual manner."[159] This reference seem to indicate Dallas gorgets associated with typical Dallas semi-flexed burials.

The numerous artifacts described and illustrated from this site substantiate the recognition of a Dallas component. These are indicated in Table 6.

The materials from the McBee Mound[160] in Jefferson County, which are also suggestive of Dallas affiliations, are also shown in Table 6, and it will be seen that the shell gorgets are not found here, nor are there references by the excavator which give positive indications of house floors in the mound. In spite of this, the burial complex, the projectile points, and the shell vessels and pins suggest a Dallas component. Dunning made a brief reference to a rectangular enclosure surrounding one of the burials and, while this cannot be equated with anything from more recent excavations, it should be recognized that he may have misinterpreted some of the house post holes which were undoubtedly in the mound.

We have practically no information about the details of the Lisle Mound in Greene County on the Nolichucky River but, if shell masks, small thin triangular projectile points, and massive conch shell beads, are diagnostic of the Dallas Focus then a component of this culture is represented here. The only

147. Ibid., p. 359.
148. Ibid., p. 291.
149. Ibid., p. 385.
150. Ibid., p. 392.
151. Ibid., p. 393.

152. Ibid., p. 353.
153. Webb, W. S., 1938, pp. 9 and 159.
154. Holmes, 1884b.
155. Holmes, 1883.

156. Holmes, 1884b, p. 445.
157. MacCurdy, 1917a.
158. Ibid., p. 60.

159. Ibid.
160. Ibid., p. 68.

other candidate in this area might be the other Late Mississippi culture represented by the Mouse Creek Focus, but this would be eliminated by the presence of the large mound which is exclusively Dallas in this area.

TABLE 6

DALLAS FOCUS TRAITS FROM MISCELLANEOUS EXCAVATIONS

	McMahan	Brakebill	McBee	Lisle	Lick Creek	Williams Island
Sub-structure mounds	x	x			x	
Burials in sub-structure mounds	x	x	x		x	
Wood or stone grave covers			x		x	
Burials flexed or seated			x	x	x	
Grave goods	x	x	x		x	
Cord-marked pottery	x				x	
Strap handles						x
Appliqué fillets						x
Pointed rims						x
Incised decoration						x
Modeled effigy decoration					x	
Punctate decoration						x
Small, thin, triangular points			x	x	x	x
Flat, square sided celts			?		x	x
Spatulate ax						x
Double tapered knives				x		
Bone flesher or end scraper			x	x	x	x
Oliva beads		x				
Massive shell beads		x	x			x
Shell gorgets—engraved	x	x			x	x
Shell mask gorgets	x	x		x	x	x
Knob-headed shell pins				x	x	x
Conch shell vessels				?		
Copper celts					x	
Trade goods	x					x

One site which Dunning described himself was the Lick Creek Mound at the junction of the Nolichucky River and Lick Creek.[161] Definitive Dallas features are described in the author's reference to a layer of sand covered with burned clay, ashes, charcoal, and animal bone. In this thirty foot mound, this sounds very much like a house floor. Below the "floor" were found typical Dallas burials in flexed positions and covered with wood and bark. The burial complex is somewhat confused by Dunning's description of a rectangular wooden vault containing a burial at the center of the mound. It is impossible to tell whether this was simply a well preserved Dallas log covered burial or something unique. The only artifact found

with the "vault" was a copper celt—a trait associated with the Dallas Focus.

The extensive group of artifacts, which further identify this mound as a component of the Dallas Focus, is listed in Table 6, but the shell gorget complex from this site is particularly worthy of mention. It is described by Dunning, but most of the gorget types are illustrated by Holmes. Examples of the rattlesnake gorget were apparently found in some numbers,[162] and others included the triskele, cross,[163] and conventionalized human figure.[164] Interestingly enough, some of the information given about the pottery allows the use of quantitative criteria. Dunning states that the pottery was distinguished by a large proportion of cord marking, a feature distinctive of the Dallas Focus. He also describes additional diagnostics as *effigy modeling and textile impressed* fragments.

There are some artifacts from this site which cannot be absolutely assigned to a Dallas component. these include: the wooden "vault," axes with ridges bordering the groove, the long steatite tubes, and a scalloped stone disk. The axes are the only things which appear distinctly out of place, but it is probable that more than one component was present at this site.

The excavation by C. B. Moore at William's Island has been described in this paper, but additional digging at this site was done by George D. Barnes, a local "professional" collector, who sold the material to a Mr. A. R. Crittenden who presented it to the museum of Wesleyan University. This material was finally described in an article by G. G. MacCurdy.[165] No records were kept during the excavation and, although the author tried to get information from the parties concerned, he was able to do nothing more than describe and illustrate the specimens.

Although nothing is known of the burial complex, nor of the mound, the shell complex is distinctly Dallas. The total list of artifacts which can be associated with this component is included in Table 6. In addition, the polished stone pipe is similar to Dallas materials from Fain's Island, and the shell "buttons" resemble others associated with this culture in the Norris Basin. Some of the small thin projectile points appear to be authentic, but much of the chipped stone must be viewed with suspicion. This was a region in which many fine small points were manufactured by certain parties and sold to dealers throughout the country. The two rows at the top of Figure 24 in the MacCurdy article are suspect.

Two other items are significant at this site. The stone gorgets which are illustrated[166] are undoubt-

161. Dunning, 1872.

162. Holmes, 1884, Pl. LXV, 2 and 6.
163. *Ibid.*, Pl. LII.
164. *Ibid.*, Pl. LXXV.
165. MacCurdy, 1917b.
166. *Ibid.*, Figs. 33 and 34.

edly Woodland and (if they actually come from this site) would suggest a component of this culture. The other items of importance are the trade goods illustrated in the report. Some glass beads are reported, and an examination of the pictures indicates that the "copper" artifacts are very similar to those made from brass trade kettles in this same area. The same thing is true of the rolled beads,[167] and it may be noted that one of the large perforated metal discs was found on a string with some glass beads.[168] The "copper" complex described is very probably trade sheet brass and indicative of historic contact at this site.

SUMMARY AND CONCLUSIONS

This paper has been written primarily to examine the early published data on the archeology of eastern Tennessee and to ascertain the possibilities of reinterpretation in terms of the recent archeological analysis of the cultures of the Chickamauga Basin in the same region.

It must be understood of course, that each interpretation which is presented is of a tentative nature. This must be the case when so much evidence is taken from early published materials, but every effort has been made to check all data carefully and to

167. *Ibid.,* Fig. 55.   168. *Ibid.,* Fig. 53.

weigh them against the numerous factors which influence interpretation of similarities and relationships.

That at least some of the site analyses are correct was demonstrated when the Division of Anthropology of the University of Tennessee reexcavated or completed the excavations of some of the sites tested or partially excavated by the early workers. In these cases, it was gratifying to discover that the various components which had been suggested in this paper from the data in the early literature were substantially correct. In some cases, all the components had not been recognized, largely because of limited excavation or lack of published detail by the early writer. However, the components which were suggested did appear during the course of more extensive excavation in every case.

Table 7 is arranged by sources; placing the reports which were used in this study in chronological order of publication with the sites arranged culturally. This, of course, is for the use of those who are consulting the original sources and desire further information on the interpretation of the data there presented.

Information is combined for such sites as the Hiwassee Island Site for which the interpretation on the

TABLE 7

SUGGESTED CULTURAL AFFILIATIONS
(Arranged by Publications)

SITES	WOODLAND PATTERN		MISSISSIPPI PATTERN			HISTORIC AND UNKNOWN	
	Upper Valley Aspect	Middle Valley Aspect	Hiwassee Island Focus	Dallas Focus	Mouse Creek Focus	Historic	Unknown
Norris Basin:							
Hawkins Cave (14)	UV*						
Doan Cave (23)	UV						
Wallace Cave (12)	UV						
Saltpeter Cave (3)	UV						Un
Bullock Cave (13)	UV						Un
Irvin Village (5)	UV		HI	D			
Lea Farm Village & Mounds (17)	UV		HI	D			
Bowman Farm (2)	UVm		HI				
Ausmus Farm Mounds (10)	UVm			D			
Johnson Farm Cemetery (15)	UVm			D			
Cox Mound (19)	UVm			D			
Walters Farm Village (11)	UVm			D			
Crawford Farm Mounds (21)		MV					
Freel Farm Mound (22)		MV					
Taylor Farm Mound (16)		MV?				Ov	
Heatherly Stone Mound (1)							Un
Stiner Farm Stone Mounds (18)							Un
McCarty Farm Mounds (4)			HI				
Hill Farm Stone Mounds (6)			HI				
Richardson Farm Mound (8)			HI				
Harrison Farm Mounds (9)			HI	D			

TABLE 7—Continued

Sites	Woodland Pattern		Mississippi Pattern			Historic and Unknown	
	Upper Valley Aspect	Middle Valley Aspect	Hiwassee Island Focus	Dallas Focus	Mouse Creek Focus	Historic	Unknown
Harrington's Work:							
Mainland Site	UV		HI	D	MC		
Lenoir Island Site	UV		HI	D	MC		
Hiwassee Island		MV	HI	D		Hi	
Mound 1		MV		D			
Mound 2		MV		D			
Mound 5		MV					
Upper Hampton Place (Rhea Co)		MV					
Bussell Place		MV					
C. B. Moore's Work:							
Prater Island	UV						
Carter Farm		MV					
Montgomery Place		MV					
Mound near Lovelady Landing		MV					
Mattie Igou Site		MV		D			
Davis Place		MV					
Hoyal Ferry Mound		MV					
Mounds near Vineyard Landing		MV					
Upper Hampton Place (Rhea Co)		MV				Hs	
Ewing Place		MV					
Tedder Place		MV					
DeArmond Place		MV					
Evans Place		MV					
Biss Place		MV					
F. A. Berry Place		MV					
Carmichael Place		MV					
Arthur Place		MV					
William's Island				D?	MC?		
Jones Place		MV?					
Mounds near Cook Ldg.		MV?					
Lower Hampton Place		MV?					
Campbell Place		MV?					
Hood's Ferry		MV?					
Huffine Ferry		MV?					
W. W. Blair Place		MV?					
Edward Prater Place		MV?					
Bennett Place				D			
Citico Mound (Hamilton Co.)				D		Hs	
W. S. Wilson Site	UV?			D			
Hampton Place (Hamilton Co.)				D?		Hs	Un
Kimbrough Place				D?			Un
R. A. Sharp Place				D?			
Eldridge Place				D?			Un
Cyrus Thomas' Work:							
Long Island							Un
Mound 11		MV					
Mound 12		MV					
Mound 14		MV					
Hagler Farm		MV					
Lee Farm		MV					
Pate Mound		MV					
McSpaddin Farm Mound No. 8		MV					
Tipton Farm		MV					
Lane Farm		MV					
Park's Ferry		MV					

TABLE 7—*Concluded*

SITES	WOODLAND PATTERN		MISSISSIPPI PATTERN			HISTORIC AND UNKNOWN	
	Upper Valley Aspect	Middle Valley Aspect	Hiwassee Island Focus	Dallas Focus	Mouse Creek Focus	Historic	Unknown
Jackson Farm		MV					
Hall's Bend		MV					
Tellico Plains		MV					
Bat Creek Mound No. 3		MV?					
Bat Creek Mound No. 1				D?			
McMurray—Mound No. 2		MV?					
Lenoir Island							
Mound No. 1		MV?				Hs	
Mound No. 2				D		Hs	
McMurray Mound No. 3 (Chilhowey)				D			
McSpaddin Farm (Citico) No. 4				D			
Callaway Farm (Toco Mound) No. 1				D			
Callaway Farm—Mound No. 2				D			Un
McGhee Farm (Chote)							Un
Blankenship Place							Un
Latimore Farm							Un
The Chickamauga Basin (University of Tennessee):							
Candy Creek Site	UV			Dm		Hs	
Hiwassee Island		MV	HI	D		Hs	
Spivey Site	UV	MV					
McGill Site		MV					
Sale Creek Site	UV	MV	HI	D			
Hixon Site	UV	MV	HI	D			
Dallas Site	UV	MV		D			
Davis Site	UV	MV	HI	D			
Rymer Site		MV			MC		
Mouse Creek Site		MV	HI		MC		
Ledford Island	UV				MC		
Ocoee	UV				MC	Ov	
Varnell		MV					
Minor Excavations:							
McMahan Mound	UV?			D		Hs	
Brakebill Mound				D			
McBee Mound				D			
Lisle Mound				D			
Lick Creek Mound				D			
Williams Island	UV?			D		Hs	

*Symbols: UV —Upper Valley Aspect.   Hs —Historic.
MV—Middle Valley Aspect.   Ov —Overhill Focus (Cherokee).
HI —Hiwassee Island Focus.   Un —Unknown or unidentifiable manifestation.
D —Dallas Focus.   m —Minor occurrence.
MC—Mouse Creek Focus.

basis of extensive excavations by the University of Tennessee is given. This will automatically be the complete information unless some of the early workers discovered manifestations which they removed or destroyed and which were not available to later investigations. Other instances, sites at which the University of Tennessee has not conducted excavations, are even better for this table. An example is Lenoir Island where Emmert excavated material which can be construed as representing Middle Valley Aspect burial mounds (Woodland Pattern), a Dallas Focus substructure mound (Middle Mississippi Phase), and historic material (relationships unknown). Harrington, at a later date, investigated Lenoir Island and published data which indicate that components of the Upper Valley Aspect (Woodland Pattern), are also present as well as indications of the Hiwassee Island and probably Mouse Creek foci (Middle Mississippi Phase.) This paper may be conceived of by some as a distribution study. In some respects it is.

It must be remembered, however, that the differentiating factors between the Hiwassee Island, Dallas, and Mouse Creek foci are largely architectural and ceramic, and many of the distinctions are made upon quantitative occurrence of types. It is impossible in about 90 per cent of the published data consulted to determine these highly significant factors. The fact that the Hiwassee Island Focus is found almost exclusively in the Norris and Chickamauga basins means nothing more than that these two areas are the only ones in which complete and careful excavations have been conducted which would allow the discernment of the particular features of the Hiwassee Island Focus.

One absence which is possibly significant is that of the Mouse Creek Focus from the Norris Basin area. In view of the fact mentioned above that this region was extensively and systematically excavated (and also that the material and original field notes as well as the published interpretation were completely restudied by this writer), it can be stated with considerable assurance that this particular culture did not extend into that area. The few other instances of its occurrence outside of the Hiwassee River Valley, where it was first defined, may be viewed with caution, but its identification at a number of sites on the Tennessee River in the Watts Bar Basin (upriver from the Chickamauga Basin) seem to substantiate these judgements.

The widespread occurrence of the Upper Valley Aspect of the Woodland Pattern is very much as might be expected, but the paucity of its manifestations, as compared with the great number of Middle Valley Aspect sites (Woodland Pattern), again means very little. The chief factor which accounts for this difference is the type of excavations which were carried on by early investigators. The Upper Valley sites are usually extremely unimpressive in appearance, being distinguishable only by the darkening of the soil because of organic deposits, and the occurrence of pot sherds and pieces of stone. Even when excavated these village sites gave poor returns to the worker in terms of beautiful artifacts or museum display pieces, and as a result, they were usually not identified as sites, and if identified, were passed by for richer hunting.

The Middle Valley Aspect burial mounds (Woodland Pattern) are of exactly the reverse nature. They are seen from the river as small conical mounds large enough to be fairly well explored by a small party in a comparatively short period. This met the requirements of such explorers as Moore, and, as a result, about twenty-four of these small mounds were excavated by his group between Chattanooga and Knoxville.

The most significant feature of Middle Valley distribution is its absence from the Norris Basin on the upper Clinch River. Four sites associated with this culture have been identified on the lower Clinch, (Freel, Crawford, Lee, and possibly Taylor) but the only other burial mounds (Stiner and Heatherly) are distinctly different and probably are related to similar types of stone mounds to the north in Kentucky and Indiana.

This absence of components of the widespread Middle Valley Aspect from the upper Clinch and Powell rivers, the presence of the northerly related stone mound culture, and the materials from the cave sites, which suggest the possibility of components of the Archaic, indicate that a slightly different archeological picture obtains here from that in the adjoining river valleys to the south. The earliest occupation of the area was by a non-pottery-making group which lived in inland caves and made extensive use of bone and antler implements. (Saltpeter and Bullock caves) Their remains are similar to materials from Kentucky and suggest other more distant manifestations of the Archaic horizon. With the exception of one non-pottery site in the Watt's Bar Basin these are the only remains which might relate to the numerous Archaic sites in the Tennessee valley in Alabama and western Tennessee, and the related sites to the north in Kentucky.

The earliest Woodland people (Upper Valley Aspect) probably followed the cave-dwellers down to the area from the north and east[169] and absorbed or dispossessed them. This would seem to be more probable than a genetic relationship which would require proof that the early peoples were directly ancestral to the later Woodland groups. Although the remains of both groups are found in some of the same caves and stratigraphic separation is lacking, it is possible to distinguish between the cultural congeries, because the Upper Valley Woodland remains have been found in so many instances without any sign of the distinctive bone and antler implements of the earlier culture. Any suggestion that the mixed cave sites represent the earlier section of a developmental sequence would require the acceptance of a culture change during which a large number of distinctive traits were lost while practically no additional ones were being added to the inventory. Inasmuch as the Upper Valley Aspect sites are widespread and common, it would be expected that some indication of change would be found suggestive of this transition.

The relationship between the Upper Valley Woodland peoples and those who built the stone burial mounds is impossible to define. It is also impossible to do more than guess about the relationships of these stone mounds to the widespread burial mound complexes, but they would seem to be very closely related

169. Lewis and Kneberg, 1946, p. 8.

to such mounds to the north as the Precht, Pierson, Martin, and Burkham stone mounds of Indiana,[170] and, on the basis of a few traits, to the Adena complex, rather than to any other. In general the burial mound building Woodland peoples seem to have arrived in this area at a later time than those related to the Upper Valley Aspect. If this should be true in this case, it would indicate that the stone mound builders might be coeval with the Middle Valley Woodland peoples in the southern part of the valley. However, it hardly matters whether the relationship between the Upper Valley peoples and the builders of the stone mounds is one of succession or contemporaneity; the significant point seems to be that the area of the Upper Clinch and Powell rivers was inhabited by one or both in sufficient numbers to discourage the invasion of the area from the south by the Middle Valley peoples who were spreading up the Tennessee River and its tributaries.[171] The Woodland people of the Upper Valley Aspect remained in possession of this area until the later invasions by Early Middle Mississippi peoples of the Hiwassee Island Focus.

In spite of the necessary cautions in the use of these data it is hoped that they will prove of some help to students who are interested in the archeological cultures of the Southeast. If it is possible to reinterpret the older writing in archeology, the usable information in every area will be substantially increased. Such attempts should result, if nothing more, in modern archeological publications which future archeologists may easily and profitably interpret in the light of their further and more enlightened analyses.

170. Setzler, 1930, and Black, 1934. The only other mention of such mounds in this area is by Thomas (1894), whose mention of stone mounds with such items as slab floors, circular walls, mass burials, etc., suggests the mounds in Indiana and with additional traits as copper beads are suggestive of Adena. These sites are Bat Creek No. 3, McGhee, Kimbrough, Callaway No. 2, Blankenship, and McMurray No. 2.

171. It is conceivable that this movement up the Tennessee River of the burial mound building Middle Valley people may have displaced the Upper Valley groups, which are known to have occupied the upper Tennessee Valley at an earlier time, and pushed them upriver into the cul de sac of the Clinch River Valley, eventually causing such a concentration of Upper Valley peoples in this area that they were able to defend themselves successfully and turn the encroachers east up the Tennessee River.

PREHISTORIC CULTURES OF THE CENTRAL MISSISSIPPI VALLEY. *By James B. Griffin**

THE archeological richness of the Central Mississippi Valley has been known for years, but the available material all pertained to the cultural group known as Middle Mississippi. It was almost all obtained from the large fortified towns, large open village and cemetery areas, often in association with pyramidal mounds which belong to the last major period of prehistoric occupation in the area. Nothing was known of the earlier periods. In fact, very little thought was given to the idea that there might be earlier material there.

It was this large blank area which tempted those connected with the Central Mississippi Valley Archeological Survey.[1] It was unreasonable to believe that the earlier ceramic cultures at least, were unrepresented in this area. Another attraction was the general belief that somewhere in this region lay the spawning ground, so to speak, of the Mississippi cultures which had spread throughout the Mississippi Valley and Southeast in the last few hundred years before the historic period.

The information in the literature on the archeology of this area was based on the brief reports of early travellers and of a few archeologists. Squier and Davis, whose *Ancient Monuments of the Mississippi Valley* was largely concentrated on Ohio and Wisconsin, give but brief mention to the wealth of sites in this area.[2] The "Report on the Mound Explorations of the Bureau of American Ethnology" by Cyrus Thomas provides descriptions of the excavations made by his field men.[3] These reports tell of mounds with successive structures, or burials, or ruined houses with hard clay floors, and baked clay from the walls, of pottery vessels from within the house ruins and with burials, and other features. Most of the area discussed in this chapter Thomas called the "Arkansas district," with the "Central or Tennessee district" to the east. There was, however, little attempt to portray the artifacts recovered and to interpret the relationship of the various sites one to another or to the cultural groups in contiguous areas. Thomas clearly recognized the close connection to other Middle Mississippi material in southern Illinois and in Kentucky and Tennessee. Thruston, however, recognized the fundamental similarity of the material from southeastern Missouri, western Kentucky, southern Illinois and the area around Nashville and suggested that the regional differences probably reflected local tribal units.[4] Putnam, basing his interpretation on the collections in the Peabody Museum of Harvard University, reached the same conclusion.[5] A number of Missourians excavated in southeast Missouri and published their results.[6] These publications provide the best early information on this area. At the beginning of this century W. H. Holmes produced his study of the aboriginal pottery of the eastern United States, which placed heavy emphasis on what he called the Middle Mississippi Province.[7] This portion of the paper was based on the collections in the Davenport Academy of Science made by a Captain Hall (unfortunately this was very poorly documented) and upon the collections made under the direction of Cyrus Thomas. Clarence B. Moore conducted excavations along the major streams and his reports form the largest single source of information on the area.[8] Somewhat later, valuable information has been provided by Calvin S. Brown on western Mississippi,[9] Webb and Funkhouser in western Kentucky,[10] by Lemley, Dickinson, and Dellinger on eastern Arkansas,[11] and by Winslow M. Walker and Robert McCormick Adams on southeastern Missouri.[12]

Unfortunately there are no documented historic sites in this area. By this, I mean there are no definite locations recorded by early explorers, traders, or missionaries as the site of an Indian town or a definite tribal group. There are sites and culture complexes such as the Walls and Wallace foci, to be described later, where European artifacts have been found in

* University of Chicago, Ph.B., 1927; M.A., 1930; University of Michigan, Ph.D., 1936; Director, Museum of Anthropology and Professor of Anthropology, University of Michigan. Chapter received June, 1948.

1. Phillips, Ford, and Griffin, 1951.
2. Squier and Davis, 1848.
3. Thomas, C., 1894.
4. Thruston, 1890, p. 61.
5. Putnam, 1878a, p. 204; 1878b, p. 310.
6. Beckwith, 1911; Conant, 1878; Croswell, 1878; Evers, 1880; Potter, 1880; Swallow, 1875.
7. Holmes, 1886; 1903.
8. Moore, 1908; 1910; 1911; 1916b.
9. Brown, C. S., 1926; particularly the Walls site.
10. Webb and Funkhouser, 1933.
11. Dickinson and Dellinger, 1940; Dellinger and Dickinson, 1940.
12. Walker and Adams, 1946.

association with the last aboriginal complexes of the area. The Wallace Focus can probably be assigned to the Quapaw, but Walls is as yet not connected with a specific tribal group.

A number of tribes and towns were mentioned by the chroniclers of the De Soto expedition. Somewhere in the neighborhood of Friars Point, Mississippi, was the habitat of the Quizquiz, who have not been connected with any later group. The Spaniards crossed the Mississippi and were first in Aquixo close to the river and then moved north to the territory of the Casqui which is identified as the lower end of Crowley's Ridge. A short distance to the north and at war with the Casqui were the Pacaha. Swanton has equated the Casqui of De Soto with the later Kaskinampo. By 1650 he locates the Kaskinampo on the Cumberland, a short distance above its mouth and in 1700 they join the Koasati on the Tennessee River in northeastern Alabama. The Pacaha were for some time regarded as the Quapaw, but this identification was based on the name Capaha given by one of the De Soto chroniclers. Swanton is "rather inclined to regard them as a branch of the Tunica, as also the Aquixo and Quizquiz, since Tunica Oldfields near Friars Point marks a former location of the Tunica tribe. However, this is highly speculative."[13] The last group mentioned in the area covered by this paper were centered in the large village of Quiguate which Swanton is inclined to equate with the Menard mound a few miles east of Arkansas Post. Unfortunately there are no known authentic De Soto relics from any of the sites in this area and it must be admitted that the tribal identifications are not too successful. Pacaha was a fortified village and there are not many such recorded sites in northeastern Arkansas.[14] The description of Pacaha is sufficient evidence that the inhabitants were in the cultural stage which for reasons to be more fully detailed below we can recognize as the mature or classic Mississippi period.

The next Europeans to venture into this section were Jolliet and Marquette in 1672, and here too the historical evidence is not too satisfactory. The available accounts of the voyage were written by neither explorer. One record is the story of the voyage recorded by Father Dablon from Jolliet, but Dablon's original manuscript has not been preserved.[15] Another record is the autograph map of Marquette which represents his knowledge of the course of the river and the Indian tribes located in the vicinity.[16] On this map there are Indian tribes identified in the area described in this chapter. The location of a Metchigamea village in the area reached by the explorers is questioned by Delanglez. He points out that the site of the supposed Illinois village was actually the first

Quapaw village. Here the explorers talked with an old man in the Illinois tongue about other villages to the south. The account of the voyage which has been credited to Marquette was instead written by Dablon based on Marquette's map, Jolliet's verbal story to Dablon and a copy of Jolliet's letter to Frontenac. "Hence what we read in the *Recit* about this part of the journey is not what was in Marquette's journal, but is Dablon's interpretation of the information derived from the above sources."[17] Dablon also says that explorers were told of an Illinois village four days journey to the west which had European artifacts. This statement is apparently based on a statement of Jolliet in which the name of the tribe trading with "those of California" does not appear. the evidence is not good for the location of an Illinois Confederacy tribe in this area.

There were four Arkansas villages in the neighborhood of the mouth of the Arkansas River which were consistently visited by the French from this date up to about 1700.[18] They are, moreover, the only Indians consistently mentioned in this area as permanent inhabitants for this period. In the early eighteenth century certain Quapaw Indians denied any knowledge of the builders of the mounds near the mouth of the St. Francis.[19] Unfortunately there are no sites in this area which we can confidently date at this period on the basis of the European material found in association with a homogeneous archeological culture. Such an identification may not be too far in the future.

Another Indian tribe is identified as the Monsopelea on Marquette's map about in the neighborhood of Memphis. The name of this group does not appear in the *Recit* of Dablon. This is presumed to be the group to whom Marquette gave a letter which eventually turned up in Virginia. Various attempts have been made to identify these Indians, but our factual knowledge is negligible.[20] Another tribe placed on early maps is the Aganahali on the east bank of the Mississippi, but almost nothing can be done about identifying them.

The Mississippi Valley from Cairo south might be regarded as the heart of the area occupied by the Indians north of the Rio Grande. Certainly as a mighty waterway which could and did carry Indians from the north to the south, and back again, its banks also offered excellent spots for the locations of towns and villages. It received its waters from the Rockies to the Appalachians and reached north almost to Canada and not so long ago had drained part of the Great Lakes. The water in the river then went south and so in the main did the earliest ancestors of the Indians as they entered the Central Mississippi Val-

13. Swanton, 1946, pp. 54–55.
14. Lewis, T. H., 1894.
15. Delanglez, 1944b, p. 301.
16. Delanglez, 1945a.
17. *Ibid.*, p. 45; 1946d.
18. Delanglez, 1945a, pp. 43–44.
19. Delanglez, 1946b, p. 37.
20. Griffin, J. B., 1943a; Delanglez, 1946a; 1946c; 1946d.

ley, drifting down from the north to enter a completely new land as far as occupation by man was concerned. How long ago this was is not known, but it must have been some thousands of years. Just what cultural equipment was brought by these first migrants we are still unable to describe except in the most general terms. The remains of the early Indians have been plentifully found in the Plains to the west associated with earth features indicative of a time when the great glaciers were still retreating to the north to finally melt away. On the northern shores of Lake Huron evidence of early man from one of the late glacial lake beaches is clear and unmistakable.[21] As yet, to the east such uncontrovertible evidence has not been presented but early Indian fishweirs in Boston's Back Bay area are thought by conservative New England students to be at least four thousand years old.[22] There are claims of high antiquity from Florida but while suggestive it would be best to wait for additional finds. Certainly the great fresh water shell heaps along the St. John's without a bit of pottery are evidence in themselves of the length of time of the Indian occupation. Elsewhere in the Southeast were other tremendous shell heaps accumulated through the years by generation upon generation of people. On these pottery is rarely found below the top few feet. To the south, in the Lower Mississippi Valley near the Gulf, one site has been found which is comparable to a part of the Archaic Indian cultures of the Southeast. Somewhat farther up the river another site, quaintly called Poverty Point, is also of the pre-ceramic period. On all sides then we know that early man, or at least fairly early man, occupied the eastern United States area.

Unfortunately, there is very little evidence for the presence of man in the Central Mississippi Valley during the Archaic Period. This is true not only in the records of the early archeologists but also in the most recent work of various archeologists. Part of the reason for this is that the earlier men concentrated on the larger more spectacular sites with burials, pottery, and pyramidal mounds. These sites were easy to find. The Central Mississippi Valley Archeological Survey obtained projectile points on a few sites which typologically might be ascribed to an early Archaic period. Some of these sites were almost devoid of pottery. The recognition, excavation, and description of material of this Archaic period awaits intelligently directed effort toward finding early sites which will take into account the physiographic factors which have helped to obscure the earliest period. Since this earliest material has an age of some two thousand years or more it is reasonable to believe that the considerable shifting of the Mississippi river

bed and of the beds of many of its tributaries has washed or eroded away or covered many of the older sites. There must, however, be sites which have been left on islands above the floods, or on land which was not swept away, or in places along long abandoned ancient river channels.

A possible reference to an early occupation is given by Beckwith in his discussion of baked pottery balls similar to the Poverty Point specimens which he found in the Charleston area. These were in the lower levels of the sites he dug and in the last foot of a red clay deposit.[23] Unfortunately no other artifacts are described from this level.

EARLY AND MIDDLE WOODLAND PERIOD

The next major periods were also not well known in this area before the work of the Central Mississippi Valley Archeological Survey. There were references in various publications to burial mounds but it would have been hazardous to allocate any of the sites mentioned to a particular period for so little data was available. On the basis of a conical mound shape and mound location on bluffs bordering the Mississippi Valley, plus a ceramic complex from a nearby village site, a highly tentative Helena Focus was recognized which more or less arbitrarily named a regional representative of the Early Woodland period.[24]

The same vacuum existed with regard to the succeeding Hopewellian period. The recognition of a southern variety of Hopewellian in the Lower Mississippi Valley strongly implied that similar material would be located in the area between Louisiana and the central Ohio and Illinois valleys. Published references are scanty however.[25] Moore recovered a platform pipe in western Tennessee from a small mound with a subfloor rectangular grave.

"Centrally in the smaller excavation, beginning at the base and extending 2 feet into the underlying clay, was a grave 3 feet 4 inches wide by 8 feet long, containing the remains of a skeleton at full length, having at the right hand a coarse, undecorated pot in fragments, and at the outer side of the left shoulder a pipe of claystone, of the monitor type, also greatly broken, which, put together and slightly restored, is shown in Fig. 26."[26]

The angularity of shape of this pipe, the horizontally expanded rim with an incised decoration suggestive of a Weeden Island–Troyville ceramic style all serve to make this a decidedly unusual specimen.

21. This volume, pp. 99–100.   22. Johnson *et al.*, 1942.

23. Beckwith, 1911, pp. 24–25 and Pl. 1. Survey and excavation in southeast Missouri in 1950 by the University of Michigan has confirmed the association of a Late Archaic occupation and the clay ball horizon as pre-ceramic.

24. Ford and Willey, 1941, Fig. 2; Griffin, J. B., 1946, Fig. 4.

25. Indianapolis Archeological Conference, 1935, p. 64.

26. Moore, C. B., 1916*b*, p. 501.

West presents a photograph of the pipe[27] and in his text states that it is made of Ohio pipestone.[28] He also thought he detected knife marks on it and so believed it had "no great age."

Near the mouth of the Ohio near Wickliffe, Kentucky, a recent mound excavation, still incompletely reported, obtained short, thick copper beads, copper axes, a green stone celt, four celts of flint, projectile points and scraps of flint. The finds are said to have been with a burial in a rectangular subfloor pit.[29]

These two sites at least are within the Middle Woodland or Hopewell period. Farther south the surface collections of the Central Mississippi Valley Archeological Survey indicate an occupation with small conical or dome-shaped mounds and a ceramic complex with fabric-impressed, cord-marked, and plain surfaces on the undecorated ware, and zone stamped and rocker stamped treatment on the decorated pieces. The decorated pottery forms less than 10 per cent of the sherds as is common throughout the Mississippi Valley in Hopewellian sites.

Any reasonably complete presentation of the Early and Middle Woodland periods in this area will require excavation of a number of key mounds and village sites to recover the maximum amount of information on the material culture.

The pre-Mississippian ceramic complexes in this area were provisionally called Baytown, after a site in Monroe County, Arkansas.[30] This was divided chronologically into an Early and Late Baytown to accommodate Adena-Hopewellian sites at the beginning of the sequence and those with pyramidal mounds and clay-tempered pottery at the end of the period. Only one published report has appeared which gives any idea of the cultural attributes of the Late Baytown period. This is the Oliver Site in Coahoma County, Mississippi. At this site, however, there is also a late occupation with a full Middle Mississippi complex resembling that of the Lower Arkansas area which is associated with European trade goods.[31] These two complexes should not be confused.

Moore's field work in the White and Black river valleys discovered only one site which can be reasonably assigned to the early Mississippi Period. In the mounds near Chandler Landing, Prairie County, Arkansas,[32] Moore excavated pipes of clay and stone which belong to the styles in use at Spiro and probably belong to the asserted early occupation of that Oklahoma site. Two of these are modified platform pipes of stone with a projecting base, while the third is an elbow clay pipe with a long stem. Two slender chisel-like forms of slate and green quartzite, six boat stones—only one of which has a hollowed-out base—a copper coated wood object, leaf-shaped blade, and the absence of pyramidal mounds are other traits indicating a chronological placement for the site in the early or developmental Mississippi period (Fig. 123, A–E).

The surface survey in the New Madrid area by Adams and Walker produced good evidence of at least the Middle Woodland period in the area. Some sites, with small mounds in association, had clay and grit-tempered plain, cord-marked, and fabric-impressed sherds. One vessel illustrated by Adams and Walker is a good Woodland conoidal base jar with slightly insloping shoulders.[33] Other illustrations in this same publication are of cord-marked vessels with added outer rimstrips and fabric-impressed sherds with a cord-wrapped stick impression on the outer lip edge. Various stemmed, side-notched and corner-notched Woodland points were also found by this survey.

NEW MADRID FOCUS

The larger sites in southeast Missouri are often located on land which would be above normal river floods and are along the banks of former streams which probably still contained water at the time of the occupancy of the site. When these sites were first surveyed in the latter part of the last century, circular depressions about 30 feet in diameter with slightly raised ridges were called house circles and prompted the supposition that the aboriginal houses were circular in shape. Actually the floor plan is rectangular and was located slightly below the ground surface (Fig. 120, A and B). The walls were supported by posts with interwoven cane and plastered with mud containing vegetal material. This was left rough on the outside but was smoothed on the inside and was painted with red ocher. In some of the houses the posts were set in a previously excavated wall trench which was then filled in. The larger interior posts supporting the roof were placed about the central fireplace. The main habitation area was enclosed by a three-sided rectangular earthwork open on the side bordering the stream bank. The central area within the enclosure was not filled with houses and is relatively devoid of occupation debris. In connection with this central area there are one or more large pyramidal mounds placed on the periphery. On some of the sites there are four of these mounds one of which is likely to be distinctly higher and larger than the others.

The earthwork which supported the palisade sur-

27. West, 1934, Part 2, Pl. 55, Fig. 5.
28. *Ibid.*, p. 161.
29. King, 1939.
30. Griffin, J. B., 1941*b*; Ford and Willey, 1941, have a hypothetical account of this complex.
31. Peabody, 1904.
32. Moore, C. B., 1910, pp. 341–348.
33. Adams and Walker, 1942.

rounding the town was found by excavation to be about 7 feet wide with a double row of post-molds in the top (Fig. 120, C). On the outer side of the embankment there was a ditch. The earth from this had probably been used to help raise the earthen wall in which the upright posts were placed and at the time of excavation formed a ridge of some 3½ feet. There were no indications of bastions either in the early surveys or from the later excavations such as have been identified at sites in Tennessee, Indiana, and Wisconsin.

Burials were either placed in small cemeteries adjacent to the house sites or in burial mounds, formed by successive layers of interments. The burials are primarily extended and accompanied by pottery vessels and other artifacts. Additional burial forms are bundle, flexed, and mass burials.

The projectile points are usually small, well-shaped, triangular examples (Fig. 120, D). The elaborate modifications common in the Cahokia area are not part of the New Madrid Focus, while the willow leaf point of eastern Arkansas, and the antler tip point were not commonly manufactured by this group. There are some stemmed and side-notched knives or larger projectile points and a few side-notched scrapers. Flint chisels, celts, drills, and large flint hoes (Fig. 120, H) are fairly common. Small polished stone celts (Fig. 120, J) and an occasional spud (Fig. 120, E), biconcave discoidals (Fig. 120, G), hammers, tool sharpeners, and polishers (Fig. 120, F) are also identified with the New Madrid Focus. Stone and flint artifacts are relatively rare.

Bone implements are not particularly common being limited to deer ulna awls, small needles with a central eye, antler tip flakers, worked deer astragulus and blunt bone cylinders. Probably with additional village site and refuse deposit excavation the artifact inventory of bone, stone and shell may be enlarged. Shell dippers of *Busycon*, small *Busycon* pendants, columella beads, and engraved shell ornaments have been taken from sites assignable to this division (Fig. 120, K–M). One of the famous, but relatively rare spider gorgets is from the Matthews Site. Others, very similar to this have come from Cahokia. Two other engraved gorgets from this area which certainly belong to the New Madrid complex have representations of human figures. One of these is the famous "long-nosed god" throwing a discoidal stone.

Copper artifacts are very rare to absent in the New Madrid Focus. This is somewhat unusual since these sites are certainly in the time period and culture complex when the use of sheet copper was widespread in the Mississippi Valley and Southeast. North and west of this focus in Dunklin County, the famous copper plates, described and illustrated by Fowke,[34]

34. Fowke, 1910, p. 98.

were recovered from a field by a farmer, but there was no other associated material.

If there is little nonpottery material data with which to connect the New Madrid Focus with other areas or to set up a cultural complex, the ceramic material presents a striking contrast. This has been one of the rich fields for pot hunters and the common aboriginal practice of this group of placing vessels with the burials enabled many individuals to acquire large collections. Adams and Walker interpreted the cord-marked clay-tempered pottery found on the Middle Mississippi sites as the cooking ware while the fine clay or shell-tempered vessels are the mortuary pottery. This may or may not be true. Our interest, however, can be centered on the Middle Mississippi pottery.

The wide-mouth, shell-tempered jar with globular body and short rim with two loop or strap handles is present here (Fig. 122, A–E). Most of the specimens in Museums or in private collections are of relatively small jars placed with burials. The handles are usually circular to oval in cross-section and true strap or ribbon handles are rare. Bifurcated lug handles are not common and are found on vessels with loop handles. A shape modification is made by lobing the shoulder area. The incised decoration is placed on the shoulder area. The motifs are curvilinear and rectilinear meanders, the rectilinear guilloche, and the use of a punctate band placed between incised arches, or punctates bordering on an incised arch, or punctates filling spaces between incised arches. This jar complex has interesting suggestions of late decorative techniques found also in Oneota and Fort Ancient, but has even closer ties to the Cumberland. This interpretation of close Cumberland affinities of the New Madrid area has been emphasized earlier by Putnam, Thomas, Thruston, and Phillips. The shoe-form pot is also found in this area.

Most of the mortuary and better made vessels are either tempered with fine shell, fine granular particles or a mixture of both. They were polished to burnished on the outer or upper surface. In color they range from brown to greyish black with many vessels having a bluish tinge. By far the most common bottle form has been called a "carafe" by Phillips (Fig. 121, M). This has a tall, narrow neck which is usually slightly flared at the rim and at the area of attachment to the body. The body is subglobular with a somewhat flattened base. There are many modifications of this basic form. Lobing, vertical grooving from the outside, a small fillet at the neck-shoulder juncture, or medallion heads are placed on this shape. A combination of the jar body with typical decoration and the bottle neck makes a compound form. Annular or ring bases are fairly common (Fig. 121, P) and bulbous tripods are also sometimes found

(Fig. 121, Q). There are "head vessels" reminiscent of northeast Arkansas but in this area they form the body of a carafe and also have an annular base (Fig. 122, P). Another effigy form is a dog vessel with carafe neck (Fig. 122, G–H). Negative painting also was used for decoration on this vessel shape (Fig. 122, N–O).

There are also a minor proportion of bottles with a short, medium-wide neck (Fig. 122, F) and others with a gradual curve between rim and shoulder that might be described as pear-shaped. A modification of this low necked bottle has been called the "hooded" bottle which may either have an animal or human face or a plain surface (Fig. 121, S–T).

Another major group of fine ware is included within the considerable variety of bowls. The simple hemispherical bowl with an almost vertical to incurving rim (Fig. 121, A) is not as common as the outsloping wall bowl which usually has a flattened base (Fig. 121, B). The rims are often scalloped with four or more raised sections (Fig. 121, D). Some of these are similar to the "prayer bowl" also found at Moundville, in Alabama (Fig. 121, D). Incised decoration is placed on some of these scalloped bowl rims. Rectangular bowls are fairly common. There are also straight rimmed plates with incised or engraved decoration on the upper rim surface usually with a line filled triangle pattern. The bean pot is so rare as to suggest a definite importation from Cahokia when it occurs in the area. Another bowl feature, besides the considerable variety of shapes, is the rim effigy which usually is of a conventionalized bird head which is flattened and looks as though it were produced by a cookie cutter rather than modelled (Fig. 121, H). The head usually faces the bowl interior. The lug tails are usually small. There are a small number of human effigy heads on bowls some of which have a hair form and dunce cap headdress very similar to Cumberland forms (Fig. 121, F–G). Other effigies associated with the bowl are shell, both bivalve and univalve (Fig. 121, J), and gourd forms (Fig. 121, L).

Other effigies of gourds are found on hooded bottle types (Fig. 121, O), while fish, frog, beaver, and other animals were formed on either bowl or jar shapes (Fig. 121, I; Fig. 122, I–K). The most famous effigy, however, is the human effigy bottle which is usually portrayed as a seated woman (Fig. 122, M). There are many variations in portrayal but a humped back with small nodes indicating vertebra are quite common. On some figures the ribs, scapula, and clavicles are indicated. There are other treatments of the human form adapted to vessels which are more unique to this particular area.

Painted and slipped wares are an important part of the complex and are of particular significance. Vessels with all-over red slip are rare and the only effigy form is the owl. In contrast to the scarcity of red-slipped pottery is the relative abundance of negative painted vessels. This is one of the two major areas of negative painting in the eastern United States (the other being the Cumberland) and probably has the most varied and complex designs. In addition, this technique was used at times on the same vessels with direct painting, to the confusion of the modern classifier. Almost all of these painted vessels are on the carafe bottle shape (Fig. 122, N–O). In the painted ware group Phillips proposed the following divisions: red on buff; red and white (Fig. 122, L); polychrome (red, white, and black), negative painting, and combination (negative painting and direct painting). The most prominent design motif is the cross or four world quarter placed within a circle. At times the cross arms are straight while in others they are curved suggesting a whirling swastika. The circle surrounding the cross sometimes has rays or a zigzag star design. There are also scrolls, nested triangles, and concentric circles.

Other ceramic objects include perforated disks, labrets or lip plugs, trowels (Fig. 120, O–P), miniature vessels, ladles, and pot supports. There is also the short-stemmed elbow pipe with the stem hole equal in size to that of the bowl.

There are sites on the western border of Kentucky which are very close to this complex.[35] Its western and northern extent are not known although it probably reaches close to Cape Girardeau. There is an indefinite and perhaps merging zone into the Lower St. Francis basin although there are few evidences of trade vessels in either subarea. This is also true to the south along the Mississippi where from Pecan Point to northwest Mississippi there are a series of related sites which form a definite complex distinct from New Madrid, St. Francis, or the Lower Arkansas.[36] The cultural connection of the New Madrid Focus to the Cumberland is unusually clear indicating a relationship of close ethnic ties.

LOWER ST. FRANCIS AREA—PARKIN FOCUS

This Middle Mississippi division is concentrated along the St. Francis River in northeastern Arkansas. To the north it merges with the New Madrid Focus north of Marked Tree and is blended with the Walls-Pecan Point complex to the east and south. Two of the most noticeable features of this focus are the large rectangular dwelling areas which have themselves been built up into a mound by accumulation of refuse, and the relatively poor quality of most of the pottery.

The Parkin site is a typical one in this regard and for its description I quote from Moore.

35. Webb and Funkhouser, 1933.
36. Holmes, 1886, p. 369.

On the river bank, immediately at the town of Parkin, is a famous aboriginal cemetery. . . .

. . . The Parkin Mound, similar in type to the Rose Mound, has a great upper surface, as a rule flat, on which are many humps and rises. According to a rough measurement the sides of the mound are of the following lengths: north, 617 feet; south, 525 feet; east, 938 feet; west, 863 feet. It is surrounded on three sides by depressions whence unquestionably material to make the lower part of it was taken. Subsequently the height of the mound increased by the accumulations due to long occupancy. This made-ground we found to have a depth no greater than 4.5 feet in the various holes sunk by us. The height of the mound above the general level probably is from 3 to 6 feet, though of course it appears considerably greater when viewed from the depressions which partly surround it, or from the river.

There is a pond in the level ground on the northern side of the mound, no doubt caused by the removal of material for its making.

On the western edge of this great mound, on the river bank, is a mound 20 feet in height, on which doubtless, dwelt the chief who ruled over the great settlement. The diameter of this domiciliary mound was not taken by us, as the base had been greatly impaired in places by the cutting through of a road, and in other parts by the wash of the river.[37]

Pyramidal mounds are often on the west side of these large platforms. Smaller mounds are, on some sites, placed opposite the major structures. There are no evidences of fortifications either with or without bastions. While house circles or house rings have been reported it is likely that excavation would uncover a rectangular floor pattern as suggested by Thomas' excavators' results where they found not only such structures but suggested several of these had been attached to form a series of connecting rooms. The houses are of wattle and daub construction.

In the lower St. Francis area such sites as the Rose Mound exhibit a mixture of the St. Francis and Walls complexes. At such sites I believe the Walls complex to last longer and come up into the early historic period. Farther north in the St. Francis sites there are evidences of trade vessels from the sites along the Mississippi or at least the joint possession of common concepts. The most typical St. Francis sites are like Parkin, Neely's Ferry, Castile, and Fortune.

The burials are almost all extended on the back. There are some cremations, flexed burials and bundle burials. Burials were made in the domiciliary mounds, in natural ridges near the village site, and in the occupied zone which itself becomes sort of a habitation mound. By far the most common artifact with the burials is pottery. The vessels were usually placed near the head and then alongside the body depending on the number of vessels. In many cases vessels with burials were accompanied by musselshell spoons.

37. Moore, C. B., 1910, p. 303.

Artifacts besides pottery were not commonly placed with the burials. The common projectile point is a small thin laurel leaf with either an almost pointed, convex, or straight base (Fig. 123, J). The small triangular point is not common. Flint pebble chisels were a part of the stone implement complex (Fig. 123, F). Flint spades are rare (Fig. 123, G). Small stone celts were made from sandstone, quartz, or limestone (Fig. 123, H). Rude discoidals, sandstone hones, and hammerstones are occasionally collected.

There were quite a number of antler arrowpoints (Fig. 123, P), some bone awls (Fig. 123, O, Q), a few bone beads, a bone comb at the Rose Mound (Fig. 123, S), and antler flaking tools.

Besides the shell spoons (Fig. 123, M), there were various kinds of shell beads, *Oliva* shells pierced for stringing; disk, square, and tubular beads, ear plugs of shell of the blunt pin variety, ear plugs with mushroom head, large marine coast shell drinking cups are rare, shell gorgets with a weeping-eye design are from the Rose Mound (Fig. 123, T) and Turkey Island (Fig. 123, N); a shell gorget carved to represent a turtle with perforating holes for attachment which enter and leave on the same side is from Neely's Ferry. One engraved marine univalve was taken by Moore from a site in Independence County, which does not seem to be of the St. Francis complex. Blunt pin shell ear plugs have been found placed close to the skull near each ear cavity (Fig. 123, L).

Copper artifacts are not particularly common. Copper beads were found at Big Eddy, Rose, Neely's Ferry, and Miller Place. An unusual copper bead was taken from a grave at the Rose Mound. A copper head band covered with fabric and bark and with two central holes was found on the frontal bone of one burial at the Rose Mound. This same burial also had a copper breast plate. Both copper specimens were undecorated. Only one possible copper repoussé copper plate has been found in this area.[38] There is a single copper cross in the Peabody Museum collection at Harvard from the Rose Mound. This probably is with the other late Rose Mound objects for a similar cross was at Madisonville.

Clay artifacts other than pottery include labrets or ear plugs, pottery supports (Fig. 123, I), perforated and unperforated disks, elbow pipes with stem and bowl about the same length. Some of these have small feet to aid the pipe to maintain an upright position (Fig. 124, N). Other pipes have a short projection in front of the bowl (Fig. 124, O) while others have incised decorations or attempts at effigy figures.

If there is little that is diagnostic or outstanding in the nonpottery complex, the situation is changed

38. Phillips, 1940, Fig. 31j. This specimen is from Shugtown, not Spiro, Arkansas.

somewhat when the pottery is studied. In general, the St. Francis area is not notable for the quality of its shell-tempered paste characteristics, shapes, modeling, or other decorative features. Moore remarked on this feature:

Quantity rather than quality seems to have been the aim of its makers, for the ware is insufficiently fired, and the vessels are frequently thick and out of shape—"lop-sided," to use an expression exactly describing them.

The high polish of the surface often found on vessels from Mississippi, Alabama, and Louisiana, is almost absent on the St. Francis.

A very large proportion of the vessels are undecorated or have some trivial form of decoration such as beaded, notched, or scalloped margins, or else loop-handles below the rim or ears projecting from it (if handles and ears, which were used to aid suspension, may be classed as decoration). Superior trailed or incised decoration is almost never seen on the St. Francis pottery, the inferior surface of most of the ware being unsuited to incised decoration of excellent quality, even had it been attempted. When incised decoration is met with on the St. Francis ware, it is as a rule rude and scanty, being confined to parts just below the rim, and usually is restricted to vessels intended for culinary purposes. On the few vessels found by us having incised decoration, it is almost invariably of a kind so elementary in design and execution that the vessels are entirely outclassed in this respect by those found in some other regions. But one really superior piece of incised work was found by us on the whole St. Francis river, and but two or three of even medium quality. This comparative absence of incised decoration on St. Francis pottery is conducive to great monotony in the appearance of its vessels, since very many of them, which would have decoration in other regions, are wholly without it on the St. Francis.[39]

He then mentions that his party found some 1,400 vessels in the St. Francis sites of which about eight per cent were worthy of much comment.

A most common vessel shape and one which is very representative of the St. Francis is a deep, vertical walled bowl which often has notches on the outer lip and lug handles (Fig. 124, A). There are other shallower bowls (Fig. 124, D). All have a tendency toward a flattened bottom. Lugs are either two or four to a vessel. The deep bowls are frequently decorated to represent fish effigies (Fig. 125, E).

The jars either have an over-all plain surface or have a punctate body or rim decoration (Fig. 124, G), or an incised decoration on the rim. This latter is sometimes placed alone on the rim, is sometimes associated with punctates, and is also found on jars with punctate bodies. The jars have a wide mouth, rounded shoulders and a short vertical to slightly flaring rim. They are thick-walled and have a rather coarse texture. There are both loop and strap handles with the latter somewhat more common. There are usually two to a vessel. Lug handles are either two or four to a vessel and sometimes are alternated with loop or strap handles.

39. Moore, C. B., 1910, p. 260.

The most common bottle form is a short neck, wide-mouth type (Fig. 124, L). The upper part of the neck slants outward slightly and the lip is rounded. Small medallion heads are sometimes placed on the shoulder area (Fig. 124, B). The body is globular and seldom flattened. The annular or ring base is a marked feature of the bottles, particularly of a shape with a tall neck flaring outward toward the lip (Fig. 124, M). There are some disk bases with indented edge. Tripod vessels with both bulbous and slab legs are part of the bottle complex (Fig. 124, J).

One interesting vessel shape which is absent is the salt pan which does not appear in either the plain or fabric-impressed form.

The effigy forms on the St. Francis as a whole are not impressive. Some deep bowls have fish attributes or serpent, bird and animal. Human effigy heads on bowls are very rare in the St. Francis. Bird heads are usually modeled (Fig. 125, A–B). The serpent-cat monster is neither abundantly nor adequately represented. Some curious vessels have an odd effigy figure on the lug tail. The human effigy bottle and head effigy are not common in the St. Francis nor are they well executed (Fig. 125, K–L). The tea pot shape at the Rose Mound is a part of the late complex at that site and is not a common St. Francis feature.

In the St. Francis the double-necked bottle or connected double bottle, and the stirrup-handle bottle are both exciters of curiosity as to their possible Middle American connections (Fig. 125, C).

Vessels with a red filmed surface, particularly bottles, are fairly common in the St. Francis. The vessel shapes are the same as in the plain ware. Red on buff is also common in this cultural subdivision. Somewhat less common is red on white (Fig. 125, G–J), while polychrome and negative painting are very rare. These more complicated painting techniques are almost always on the bottle form.

WALLS—PECAN POINT

Another significant archeological unit can be recognized in the area along both sides of the Mississippi for a relatively short distance above and below Memphis. The sites range from Kent, Arkansas, and Walls, Mississippi, on the south, to Mississippi County, Arkansas, and the adjoining Tennessee section on the north. Some of the sites which can be included in this group are Gosnell, Chickasawba, Nodena, Bell, and Pecan Point, all in Mississippi County, Arkansas; Hales' Point and Richardson's Landing in Tennessee; Golightly, Bradley, and Rhodes in Crittenden County, Arkansas; Kent in Lee County, Arkansas; Shelby in Tennessee; Walls, De Soto County, Commerce, Hollywood, and some others in Tunica County, Mississippi.

It should perhaps be pointed out at the beginning

that this Walls Focus (originally called Alpika)[40] comes into the historic period. This is based on the presence of a small amount of European goods at Bradley,[41] Rhodes,[42] and Kent in indubitable association with the Walls complex.[43] Some importance can be attached to this point for it serves to connect this culture group to the period of early European map making and tribal identifications. Secondly, it demonstrates that in this area also, an Indian culture which participated in the ideology of the Southern Cult came into the early historic period.

Burial No. 22, adult, was the one to which reference has been made as having been found in the summit-plateau of the mound. This skeleton, which was partly flexed on the right side, lay 4 feet down, a depth greater than that of any other burial found by us at the Kent Place. At the left of the skull was a rude ornament of sheet-copper, 7.75 inches in length and 3.5 inches in maximum width, and having three perforations at one end for suspension or attachment. Small bits of copper had been pieced on with rivets to complete the ornament. At the neck were shell beads and glass beads mingled. At the left of the pelvis was a bowl, and a few badly decayed shell beads lay at the left knee.[44]

At the Rhodes site which furnished Moore with some excellent pottery pieces one burial was associated with a blue glass bead.

Burial No. 42, a child of seven or eight years of age, had at the neck two shell beads and one tubular bead of blue glass. On the left side of the thorax was a small, face-shaped gorget of shell, without decoration, having two perforations at the upper, or broader, end. On the right side of the thorax was a rude, discoidal stone of ferruginous clay with a secondary ferruginous coating. The six vessels which lay with this burial, most of which were small, had the following arrangement: a pot at the right of the skull; a bowl over the right shoulder; a pot at the right elbow; a bottle at the left elbow; a large bowl at the left side of the pelvis; a bottle at the middle of the left femur. A shell bead lay near one of these vessels.[45]

At the Bradley site Moore's crew excavated ten and one-half days and discovered one hundred eighty-one burials. Moore stated "at the Bradley Place was abundant evidence of aboriginal intercourse with the whites."[46] This is only supported by the description of one burial..

Burial No. 75, a child two or three years of age, had at the left of the skull a mass of red oxide of iron, ground for use as pigment. Dr. H. F. Keller speaks of this pigment as highly ferruginous. At the neck were: thirty-six shell beads one-third to one-half inch in length; one small, tubular bead of sheet-copper or of sheet-brass, corroded through and through; two beads of glass. With the beads were the spire of a marine shell, greatly decayed, having two perforations for suspension, and what seem to be two diminutive, copper bracelets, one placed above the other and joined together through corrosion when found. These bracelets, if such they are, are made of rods of copper with overlapping ends, but are bent to have an inside diameter of .75 inch, and hence, with such proportions, could hardly have encircled the wrists of even a young infant. Perhaps placed together, they served as a pendant ornament, in connection with the beads. Attached to these by corrosion was a metal bead similar to the one already described. On the chest of the skeleton was an undecorated gorget of shell, irregularly oblong, 3 by 3.5 inches, having at the broader end four perforations, two in line immediately above two others also in line. To the right of the pelvis stood a bottle.[47]

While we can admit that the Walls Focus comes in to the historic period we are by no means certain as to its initial or terminal date. Only a few burials had European goods and even these had only a token accompaniment of the rare and valuable new trinkets. We have little on which to go but our final date here is surely between 1540 and about 1682. The Walls Focus has the distinctive teapot form which is also in the historic Lower Arkansas Valley and is also associated with European objects farther south in Mississippi. This leads to the conclusion that Walls has an end date closer to 1700 than to 1540.

As a rule these sites do not have either large groups of mounds or very large pyramidal mounds. Neither do they have evidence of ramparts or fortifications. The mound at Pecan Point was 150 feet in its north to south dimension and 180 feet east and west. In the 1880's the height is given as 15 feet but at the time of Moore's visit in 1910 the mound height is given as 12 feet. When the timber was first cleared from the field, many small hillocks or elevations were observed scattered irregularly over the surface. Both Thomas and Moore stressed the considerable evidence of Indian occupation and the size of the burial area. One of the excavators for Thomas suggested the small mounds or hillocks had been used as a dwelling site and that when a death occurred the dwelling was burned over the body. Moore uncovered three hundred and forty-nine burials. Of this number, two hundred and fifty-three were extended, five of them face down, the rest were placed on the back. Some burials were flexed or semiflexed. These are the normal burial positions for this focus with the exception that in some of the southern components such as Commerce, the bunched or bundle burial is the most common type. It is in this focus also that a few "urn burials" have been excavated.[48] The made ground or occupied zone at these sites is from three to five feet deep.

The most common projectile point is the small, thin, triangular form with a straight or concave base

40. Griffin, J. B., 1946, p. 81, Figs. 2 and 7.
41. Moore, C. B., 1911, pp. 427–446.
42. Ibid., pp. 413–426.
43. Ibid., pp. 406–411. [This association is not accepted by Ford in Phillips, Ford and Griffin, 1951, p. 230.]
44. Ibid., p. 409.
45. Ibid., p. 415.
46. Ibid., p. 435.
47. Ibid., p. 431.
48. Hampson collection at Wilson, Arkansas, from the Turnage, Shawnee Village, and Nodena sites. These are primarily fetal bones in bowls or on large jar fragments. There is also the famous "casket" from Hales' Point, Tennessee, reported in Holmes, 1903, p. 38.

(Fig. 126, G). A minority are the small leaf-shaped points which are much more common in the St. Francis. Knife forms are narrow with convex sides and a straight base or with a broad, short stem. The ground stone celts are short with a rectangular outline and flattened rather than ovoid in cross-section. There are a few rectangular celts of shale with a central perforation near the poll end (Fig. 126, D). Another celt or ax is the well-known "hoe-shaped variety" (Fig. 126, C). Much more common than any of the other celts or axes are the chipped pebble chisels of jasper or yellowish jasper slate which are usually from two to five inches long, one to two inches wide and one-half inch thick (Fig. 126, B). Many have very well polished bits.

Shallow stone mortars (Fig. 126, M) and grinding stones have been obtained by private collectors from these sites as well as hammerstones, whetstones of pumice, discoidals with two plane surfaces (Fig. 126, R) and biconcave surfaces. Flint hoes, some with "Cahokia type" notches are known from these sites (Fig. 126, F, I).

Flint was not the only material used for projectile points for there are antler tip points and also the scales of the gar pike which were hafted. There are large antler flaking tools, awls of deer ulna and other "bone perforators"; tortoise carapace, presumably for either a cup or rattle; bone beads, perforated or grooved dog or panther canines for suspension; and bone beads. Two distinctive utilizations of bone by these people have been observed. Fairly common as grave goods are the metacarpal bones of large size birds such as the wild swan, wild goose and wild turkey. There are also the astraguli of elk and deer which were cut and smoothed to be employed presumably as dice or game counters (Fig. 126, E). Mention should also be made of bison bones which are not commonly found on sites in this area, particularly east of the Mississippi.

Face masks cut from the side walls of large marine gastropods are occasionally found but there is no record of other shell ornaments such as the rattlesnake gorget, cross, spider or human figures which sometimes accompany the masks. Shell earplugs are of both the expanded head (Fig. 126, K) and blunt pin (Fig. 126, J) type. Shell beads are found but are not described further in the literature. Some mussel shell pendants with a perforation at the hinge end were recovered at the Kent Site. Mussel shell spoons are reported from some sites.

Copper artifacts are of rare occurrence and are limited to small tubular beads and pendants. Most of the pipes are of clay of the Middle Mississippi equal armed type (Fig. 126, N). Some of these have incised designs. One from Pecan Point has an incised swastika with the spiral arms on the side walls while on

the bowl there is a crude human face with horns or plumes. At the Kent Site a pipe was modeled after the shape of the human effigy bottles. Clay trowels, sometimes called bottle stoppers, clay earplugs, labrets (Fig. 126, L), perforated and unperforated clay discoidals (Fig. 126, O–P), and clay balls (Fig. 126, Q) are parts of this culture complex. Mention has already been made of the few blue glass beads found with burials. Turquoise beads and a pendant are reported from the Oliver Site in Coahoma County, Mississippi and is the only recorded instance east of the Mississippi.[49] They were with a child burial with associated glass beads and belong to the last occupancy of the site presumably associated with a Natchezan and Lower Arkansas Complex.

Pottery vessels were very common with burials. "Usually in the graves of horizontal skeletons there was found with each a pot, bowl, or jug near the head, at the feet, or by the hips; often two and sometimes all three with one skeleton, but it was seldom that two vessels of the same kind or intended for the same use were with one skeleton."[50] Moore excavated five hundred thirty-five vessels at Pecan Point; two hundred fifty-eight at Bradley Place, one hundred twenty-three at Rhodes Place and sixty-nine at Kent. In addition to this, known collections have many hundreds of vessels from these Walls Focus sites so that it is safe to say that thousands of vessels were buried with the dead by these people. From these vessels we have our best evidence of the cultural connections of their makers.

There are quite a number of indicators that the Walls-Pecan Point complex is late in the area. Not only do a few of the sites have actual European trade material but many of the traits of the complex are held in common with culture complexes such as Natchezan, Wallace, and Glendora which not only have quite an assortment of European objects but which can be rather definitely ascribed to historic tribes such as the Natchez, Arkansa and Caddo. The teapot vessel is common in at least the southern Walls-Pecan Point sites. This vessel shape has aroused considerable interest among archeologists. Holmes thought it might have evolved in the Lower Arkansas Valley from an animal effigy form, while Vaillant compared it to Middle American spouted vessels as a part of the ill-fated "Q" complex which was supposed to have moved in from Mexico and stimulated the growth of the high cultures in the Southeast. One of the most recent interpretations is that the teapot is an imitation of French teapots.[51] This is rather far removed from Vaillant's interpretation and is much closer to the truth since the distribution of this shape along both sides of the river from the Lower Arkansas

49. Peabody, 1904, pp. 50–51.
50. Thomas, C., 1894, p. 221.   51. Quimby, 1942.

area south into Natchez territory, and its appearance at many sites with European goods is adequate testimony to its time period if not to its origin.

There are three human effigy head bowls from the Walls Site which suggest three different physical types, Indian, Caucasian, and Negroid. Whether these are "portraits" it is impossible to say. At the Kent Site two animal effigy bottles are suggestive of European animals. One of these looks like a pig, while the other looks like a horse head. The Kent Site had a small number of European articles and it is not unlikely that the native potter accustomed to producing in clay effigies of the indigenous flora and fauna would take naturally to the production of an effigy of these new animal forms.

The two major "wares" in this Walls complex are Bell Plain, and its associated decorated types, which often have a polished surface and a fine texture with little or no shell-temper. The other is called Neely's Ferry Plain and is the shell-tempered Mississippi jar and other forms. The Neely Ferry Plain and the decorated forms such as Kent Incised (Fig. 127, C) or Fortune Noded (Fig. 127, A) from Walls Focus sites almost always have a noticeably thinner wall than do comparable types from the St. Francis. Another fairly common feature is the beveled inner lip which was given to both jars[52] and bottles.[53] This distinctive treatment is not found on typical St. Francis, Lower Arkansas, or New Madrid area sites nor farther south in Mississippi or Arkansas. Another significant ceramic development is the variety of treatment based on the strap handle. The loop handle is almost, if not entirely, absent and the strap handle is the normal form. When there are two or four to a vessel, they are regarded as functional. Multiple handles form an arcaded rim with an opening between the outer vessel wall and the inner handle surface.[54] A further specialization transforms the handle from any association with the suspension of the vessel to a decorative embellishment and was applied as an added clay strip (Fig. 127, B–C). Holmes presented an interpretation of this handle change from functional to decorative in two reports.[55] While multiple handles (more than four) are known from central Alabama at both Moundville and the Montgomery area, the closest parallel is from eastern Nebraska in the Lower Loup Focus commonly thought to be protohistoric Pawnee. These resemblances can be regarded as parallel developments without specific connection from one area to the other.

It has been indicated that the closest connections of the New Madrid Focus seem to be the Cumberland Aspect sites in the Nashville area. The Walls–Pecan Point Complex is also rather closely connected to the Cumberland Aspect but evidences an even closer blend into the Moundville Complex. This relationship should not, I think, be interpreted as a movement of a group of people from one area to the other but is a reflection of their close geographical location and an approximately contemporary existence. There are too many features of the Walls–Pecan Point culture which indicate its intimate association with the lower St. Francis, New Madrid, and even Lower Arkansas to believe that it is anything but a development of the area where it is most common. Some of the highly specific Moundville resemblances are a strong use of engraving; an engraved bird design on a wide-mouth bottle; bottles with ogee symbol on the upper shoulder area; skull, long bones, hand and eye designs on bottles; engraved rattlesnake "god"; and the wide mouth bottle with short neck, globular body and disk base. More general connections can be seen in such items as the common possession of frog effigy jars with broad strap handles, multiple strap handles on jars, compound vessel of a half bottle placed on a jar, the hooded water bottle, and the hoe-shaped ceremonial ax. This more general list might be expanded considerably. Moundville connections have been emphasized in the past to the northern Alabama-Tennessee Valley sites,[56] to the Cumberland Aspect,[57] and to Etowah.[58] While these connections are certainly valid and not to be minimized, the ties of Moundville to the Montgomery, Alabama area and to the Walls–Pecan Point are equally important.

The engraved technique of decoration in the Walls Focus is one of its most distinctive ceramic traits. This was almost certainly derived from the Caddoan area to the west and south into Texas where its early appearance in the ceramic history of east Texas has been interpreted as influence from northeast Mexico.[59] This technique apparently moved eastward as a diffused trait rather than as a part of the cultural baggage of a migrating group of people, for vessel shapes and other cultural features do not suggest a movement of people from eastern Texas, eastern Oklahoma, or southern Louisiana, into this Central Mississippi Valley area. From this Walls area engraving moved eastward to the Moundville center and was further diffused from that center to Etowah and the Chattahootchie Valley. Engraving is found to the north in the New Madrid Focus and in the Trappist and Spoon River foci of the St. Louis–Peoria area.

52. Brown, C. S., 1926, Fig. 268; Moore, C. B., 1911, Figs. 37, 38.
53. Moore, C. B., 1911, Figs. 29, 40, 49–51, 78.
54. Ibid., Fig. 36.
55. Holmes, 1886, pp. 393–398; 1903, Pl. VI.

56. Webb and DeJarnette, 1942, pp. 319–322; DeJarnette and Wimberley, 1941, pp. 99–110.
57. Ford and Willey, 1941, p. 356.
58. Willoughby, 1932.
59. Du Solier, Krieger, and Griffin, 1947.

THE MENARD FOCUS

A cultural division can be recognized in the lower Arkansas Valley in the Late Mississippi period. One of the first to call attention to this complex was Moore. He pointed out that the "aboriginal pottery of the Arkansas river possesses the distinctive features belonging to the ware of both the region above and the region below that stream."[60] This was actually a statement indicating that the Caddoan pottery penetrated as far north as the Arkansas while the other part of the Menard complex resembles the St. Francis–Walls material. Somewhat later Harrington called attention to the similarity of a portion of the Carden Bottoms complex west of Little Rock, to material from the eastern Arkansas Valley.[61] Dickinson and Dellinger discussed some late features from the lower Arkansas and called attention to their time position and association with the Quapaw.[62]

As with the other cultural complexes recognized in this chapter there is not sufficient data to provide anywhere near a well-rounded presentation. At a site such as Menard there is apparently a fair time depth represented. When Moore and others have dug there they have labeled as "Menard" objects from nearby sites so that recognition of a specific or homogeneous association of objects is difficult to present. For this paper we will call the "Menard Focus" artifacts of a late time horizon that are found from the mouth of the Arkansas to the Little Rock area. Of particular importance is the association of European manufactured objects at site after site with native Indian artifacts as grave associations. Glass beads, brass beads or other objects of brass and a few objects of iron are the nonnative items mentioned in the literature. The relative scarcity of these indicate a date around 1700. While there are some records of trade contact with the Spanish in the Southwest and the Southeast by 1673 it is not likely that any considerable amount of European objects were a part of the native culture until the early part of the eighteenth century. This dating is somewhat substantiated by comparable dates for the related Glendora and Natchezan material.

Moore was not particularly impressed with the Lower Arkansas area with its lack of large mound groups or extensive cemeteries with attractive burial offerings. Burial positions were extremely varied with the bundle burial being perhaps the most common form in the area below Pine Bluff, while to the west extended and flexed burials were the prevalent forms. On the basis of a few measurable skulls from the Menard area and the Greer Site, Hrdlička recognized this late population as a part of his Gulf type and emphasized that Greer and Menard represented "one well defined type."[63] Burial offerings were usually placed near the skull. Most of these grave goods were pottery vessels.

The eastern part of the area has little available stone for artifacts so that in general such material was not abundant on the sites. The projectile points are small and triangular in shape with a small number of leafshaped points of the type more common in the St. Francis. Small snub-nosed end scrapers were quite common on some of the sites in the Menard area such as Wallace. The small chert pebble chisel and celt, small disks of fine-grained sandstone about 3 inches in diameter, hammerstones and rubbing stones complete the utilitarian materials of stone. The famous carved stone disk did not come from the Menard Site proper but from the Almond Site two miles to the north along the north bank of Lake Dumond.[64] A quartz crystal came from the mound at the Wallace Site.

Many bison bones were identified at the Menard Site but the majority of the bone implements were made of deer. Bone artifacts include awls of various kinds, projectile points from antler tines, beaver incisors, bone beads and long pins with a beaded head. Shell spoons were placed inside pottery vessels, shell beads were not common, and other objects of shell are rare.

The most common pottery is plain shell-tempered Mississippi ware (Fig. 128, A–C). The incised decoration was made with a broad flattened instrument producing a distinctive type of incising (Fig. 128, D–F). It is found on jars and flaring walled bowls. The designs on the bowls are usually volutes while line filled triangular areas are found on the jars. On the bowls and jars this decoration is usually fairly deep and on the jars particularly a cameo effect is produced on the interior surface. Decoration on the bottles is almost always a scroll design. Some small jars with globular body and short vertical rim have a design formed by a combination of a punctate band placed within incised lines. This has been called Owens Punctated. Another style of incising is a combination of curvilinear trailed lines and incised circles placed on a vessel shape usually thought of as Natchezan (Fig. 128, I).

One of the most distinctive features of the Menard Focus is the shape of the bottle neck which is placed on most of the plain or decorated bottles. It is a low truncated cone with a short outsloping rim (Fig. 128, C, K, N–Q). The teapot bottle has aroused considerable controversy. It is found in this area with a number of minor variations (Fig. 128, N, Q). It is concentrated in the lower Arkansas and the adjacent Mississippi Valley where its late chronological position should have made its association with an early

60. Moore, C. B., 1911, p. 370.
61. Harrington, M. R., 1924b, p. 90.
62. Dickinson and Dellinger, 1940.
63. Hrdlička, 1908, p. 563.   64. Moore, C. B., 1908, p. 492.

Middle American complex seem unreasonable. Besides this explanation, Holmes has suggested the teapot developed from an effigy form[65] and Quimby has proposed that it is a copy of the French teapot.[66] The bottles are often painted with a completely covered red exterior or red and white on buff in a scroll design. The neck area is painted red.

Effigy bowls and other forms are much less common than in the St. Francis and Pecan Point–Walls complexes. Effigy bowls have a low side wall and a horizontal band of red paint on the outer rim (Fig. 128, J–M). Similar low bowls have both an outer and an inner red rim band, while on the interior designs of broad red pigment lines form a cross, scroll, or swastika.

A strong percentage of the Menard complex is a Caddoan intrusion from the south and west. One element of this may be recognized in the Owens Punctated type. Another is the scroll trailed decoration which is very close to the type called Keno Trailed in the Glendora Focus, while still others are close to Taylor Engraved or Natchitoches Engraved (Fig. 128, K). This influence grows increasingly stronger as one ascends the Arkansas. It is probable that in the Greer area and to the west a significant increase in the proportion of Caddoan traits will cause the recognition of a complex distinct from that of the Menard area. This, however, cannot be done at the present writing.

65. Holmes, 1886, p. 403.
66. Quimby, 1942, p. 263.

SURVEY OF CADDOAN AREA ARCHEOLOGY. *By Kenneth G. Orr**

THE Caddoan area is recognized as the territory embraced within the corners of the present states of Oklahoma, Texas, Arkansas, and Louisiana (Fig. 129). The name is derived from tribes of the Southern Caddoan linguistic division which occupied the area in historic times. It includes the Ouachita Mountains, a fringe of the eastern Plains, and the Gulf Coastal Plain. It might be referred to as the Arkansas-Red River region. Some prefer the geographical term; an apt designation might be the *Habiúkut* area occupied by the "co-tradition" represented by the Fulton and Gibson aspects. The physiographic provinces of the Caddoan area shared in common a moderate climate, adequate rainfall and soil for agricultural purposes, and imposed no serious barriers to movements of peoples. The Ozark Plateau on the northern fringe of the area was an effective buffer against the penetration of northern influences such as northern Woodland, Hopewellian, and Middle Mississippian. The most important physiographic factor in the growth of culture was the network of south-flowing streams which embrace the area. Of these, the Arkansas, Red, Sabine, and Neches rivers were the largest and most thoroughly occupied. Their many tributaries allowed free access into the most remote sections. No geographic barriers existed to the Plains area on the west, yet only in Fulton Aspect times have we evidence of contact of Caddoan area groups with Plains groups. At this time an exchange with Puebloan groups in the southwest also presumably took place.

Archeological investigations on the Red and Ouachita rivers conducted by Clarence B. Moore at the beginning of the century opened up the rich Caddoan area. Somewhat later, Harrington, Moorehead, and Thoburn followed with intensive field surveys. More recently the contributions of individuals such as Webb and Dodd, Lemley, Dickinson, Hodges, and Walker have greatly added to our knowledge of the eastern and southern part of the area. During the 1930's large-scale excavations supported by the Works Progress Administration and directed by the universities of Oklahoma and Texas

initiated large extensive excavations. The first area conference held at the University of Oklahoma brought together individuals interested in the archeology of the area who pooled their information to form the first comprehensive picture of Caddoan area history. This paper rests heavily on the concord reached at this conference, and particularly the pioneer synthesis work of Alex Krieger of the University of Texas. Krieger's results agree closely with my own arrived at independently.

The "Stage" concept used in this paper is primarily for convenience in relating Caddoan area cultures to those of the southeastern United States. The concept of an Archaic, Early, and Middle Woodland stages as commonly used in the Southeast apply rather successfully to the Caddoan area. But "Early and Late Mississippi stages" have little more than chronological meaning in this area. For example, the increasing complexity of culture from Early to Late Mississippi stages in the Southeast (as seen in Middle Mississippi) certainly is not reflected in the Caddoan area. Actually, Gibson Aspect culture ("Early Mississippi stage") is more complex than the succeeding Fulton Aspect ("Late Mississippi stage") and, if anything, a simplifying process took place. Both aspects are clearly distinguishable from Middle Mississippi in all periods of development. A broad concept of Mississippi Pattern might embrace Gibson and Fulton aspects but there are as sharp differences between these aspects and Mississippi units as between the Mississippi Pattern and the Marksville–Troyville–Coles Creek cultures of the Lower Mississippi Valley. The differences between Middle Mississippi and Gibson–Fulton (Habiúkut) now impress me as the result of two distinct traditions. Middle Mississippi, including the St. Francis–Alpika materials have suggestive similarities with cultures of the Antilles and the north coast of South America. Weeden Island, Swift Creek, and Lamar ceramics might be included in this group. Gibson's ties are with Hopewell and Middle America. The taxonomic devices focus and aspect are sufficient for the purposes of this mainly intra-area study; more inclusive problems including phase and pattern must follow our concern with the classificatory units.

Data are scarce for the earlier stages, and the few representative sites are described in some detail. But

* Columbia College, B.A., 1937; University of Chicago, M.A., 1942, Ph.D., 1944; Assistant Professor of Anthropology, University of Oklahoma, 1945–1946; Assistant Professor of Anthropology, University of Chicago, 1946–1950. Chapter received June, 1948; reduced one-third by the editor in January, 1951.

sites are plentiful in the Gibson and Fulton Aspect horizons and comparably extensive descriptions are not possible in this paper. Throughout the study I have allowed myself the benefit of following promising leads and hypotheses with the hope that they will prove a stimulus in pointing the way for future work. It is earnestly desired that the preliminary nature of the work in the Caddoan area be recognized, and that the conclusions of this paper be regarded as tentative postulates.

ARCHAIC STAGE

Information on the earlier stages of culture in the Caddoan area is both rare and piecemeal. However fragmentary, the evidence is sufficient to indicate an apparently long occupation of relatively simple Archaic cultures in the Caddoan area.

Basing his conclusions on surface explorations and the study of private artifact collections, Clarence H. Webb presents evidence for what may be a series of prepottery cultures in northwestern Louisiana.[1] Typologically earliest are the 12 fluted points, 6 Clovis-like points, and 59 Yuma-like points (Fig. 130, I–P) reported to have been collected in the area. While these finds do not, of course, establish a Folsom culture they give an interesting suggestion of the presence of part of a Folsomoid complex. Whatever the time level represented, the absence of points of this type in pottery cultures of the Caddoan area makes it clear that they are of the prepottery horizon.

While the Folsomoid points have not been found in occupational sites prepottery sites are present in the area: "scattered sites are present along the lateral escarpments bordering the Red River Valley, also in the hill sections between major streams, at which large, crude projectile points and scrapers, grooved axes, hammerstones, pitted stones, mortars and occasional tubular stone beads are found, and where sherds of pottery are absent or scarce. These sites are usually small and without evidence of dense habitation."[2] Other evidence of the Archaic horizon in northwestern Louisiana includes: two-holed gorgets, pierced tablets, boatstones, bannerstones (bipennate, prism, expanded center, biconcave form), grooved axes, large drills, and tubular stone beads, as well as an "Albany type beveled scraper" and "San Patrice type projectile point" (Fig. 130, N).[3] The San Patrice point suggests a late survival of traits of concave base, smoothed basal margin and thinning of basal segment by removal of longitudinal flakes. Webb admits that certain of the types occur in pottery-bearing units, and may be shared with early pottery cultures.

The Folsomoid-Yuma and San Patrice points do not occur with pottery-bearing cultures. This data along with the occurrence of typologically early materials make the case for prepottery units in northwestern Louisiana highly probable. The variety of projectile points means two or more cultural divisions. Folsomoid connections, however far removed in time from early Folsom of the Plains, are a distinct possibility. Much less conjectural is the finding of prepottery materials as a complex in situ at Gulpha, southwestern Arkansas.

GULPHA

The Gulpha unit occupied a long, flat-topped knoll (265 by 90 feet) some 30 feet above the Ouachita River at the junction of Gulpha Creek, 6 miles southeast of Hot Springs, Arkansas.[4] The knoll, extending to a depth of over 9 feet, had been built up by successive layers of occupation on alluvial soil presumably deposited by periodic floods. The soil contained quantities of flint chips, "broken rejects," blades, and projectile points with occasional evidence of fire and burnt animal bones. Potsherds were confined to the top one-foot level. The top culture appeared to be connected with that of a group of mounds located some 600 yards up Gulpha Creek which supposedly belonged to an early Gibson Aspect or pre-Gibson Aspect horizon.

Mortars, hammerstones, and celts found in the earlier levels appeared similar to those of the top-layer pottery unit. Notched stone net sinkers were confined to the top levels, while only grooved net sinkers were found in the earlier levels. Projectile points from the two levels were also different. Tiny and delicately chipped points were found only in the top level, whereas the non-pottery levels contained an abundance of larger, stemmed or (rarely) notched points of less precise manufacture. Projectile points of several types came from the lower levels (Fig. 130, A–H). We are unable to determine whether this range of forms represents a single unit or a series of cultural units, since levels are not given for the artifacts. A large, relatively crude point comes from the lowest depth (9 feet 9 inches), and augmented by the projectile point variations suggest that several nonpottery cultures may have been represented. Roughly triangular scrapers or knives are also listed for the lower levels (Fig. 130, D).

Harrington interprets the site as a flint workshop area used repeatedly by successive groups of Indians who quarried flint farther up the Gulpha Creek, and returned to form their artifacts. This theory might account for some of the nonpottery levels as representing short occupations by miners of late pottery-bearing cultures. The evidence, favors a "pre-pottery" interpretation of the lower levels: (1) the top

1. Webb, C. H., 1948.
2. *Ibid.* 3. Webb, C. H., 1946, pp. 15–17.

4. Harrington, M. R., 1920, pp. 103–110; recognized as Archaic by Griffin, J. B., 1946, Fig. 3.

layer pottery represents one of the earlier pottery-bearing cultures in the Caddoan area, still earlier pottery cultures are improbable; (2) the quantities of projectile points, mortars, hammerstones and celts found in the debris would imply a more sedentary occupation than the mining expeditions which Harrington suggests; (3) in view of the copious presence of lithic artifacts, sherds would almost certainly be present if the earlier units had pottery; (4) the profusion of flint chips is not unusual in a culture making extensive use of stone artifacts. It seems logical to conclude then that one or more prepottery units occupied the knoll. As Harrington points out, the height of the site above the river would prevent frequent flooding, and an alluvial deposit of 8 to 9 feet in depth could represent some degree of age.

EARLY OZARK BLUFF DWELLERS

The University of Arkansas investigators[5] and Harrington[6] agree on an extensive prepottery stage underlying the pottery cultures of the Ozark Plateau bluff sites. They also agree that a "Bluff Dweller' unit underlies a "Top Layer" culture. The late Bluff Dweller pottery resembles Marksville, Coles Creek, and Gibson Aspect types, whereas the succeeding Top Layer pottery resembles types from Oneota and Fulton Aspects. All investigators conclude that the non-pottery culture grades into the pottery horizons of the Bluff Dwellers,[7] but that the "Top Layer" represents a clearly identifiable horizon. It is regrettable that the prepottery artifacts are not clearly distinguished from the pottery unit artifacts in the reports. But the noted connection between the two and occasional specific references enable us to suggest the probable cultural complex of the earlier levels.

Large flint projectile points commonly occurred in the form of "diamond-shaped points with more or less pointed bases," as well as side-notched and stemmed forms. The presence of the atlatl and cane-shafted darts indicate extensive use of the throwing stick in the earliest period. "True arrows are only found on the surface," and the larger points are considered more fitting for spears and darts rather than arrows. The few points illustrated have square stems. Double bitted, flint axes were the only ax form. Fishhooks and notched pebbles ("net-sinkers") were absent. Various types of fabric bags, baskets, bark vessels, and a series of fabric articles of clothing were used throughout the Bluff Dweller period. Pitch smeared on the interior of baskets and bags provided liquid containers in lieu of pottery vessels. Because of non-availability of data, corn, sunflowers, pumpkins, beans, and squash commonly found in bluff shelters[8] cannot be proven to extend into the earlier prepottery levels, but this possibility allows for lively speculation on the problem of the origin or origins of agriculture in the southeastern United States.[9] Quantities of animal and some fish bones indicate the main food supply. Cache pits lined with grass baskets, leaves, or stone slabs were used for food storage. Individual flexed burials, a few or no grave goods were found in grass-lined pits.

The hills of northeastern Oklahoma are on the fringe of the Ozark Plateau and are connected with the heart of the Bluff Dweller country in northwestern Arkansas by the Cowskin and other rivers. It is logical to look for close cultural connections between the two areas. Unfortunately the Oklahoma bluff sites have yielded little by way of organic artifacts, and the rich fabric complex of the Bluff Dwellers is lacking here. This is almost certainly due to the more humid condition of the Oklahoma shelters which has prevented preservation of such perishable materials. A general correspondence is seen in the lack of pottery, large stemmed flint points, and relatively crude knives and scrapers, as well as individual flexed burials in pits. As in the case of the Arkansas units the material is found in thick deposits, some exceeding 15 feet in depth. Again, pottery levels overlie the prepottery levels; in the Oklahoma units a Hopewellian culture is succeeded by the Neosho Focus,[10] which resembles the Oneota Aspect, as does Harrington's top-layer culture.

The possibility of a distinct prepottery group in the Ozarks is seen in Harrington's brief mention of finding grooved axes in association with a variety of projectile points "lacking in character" and in appearance cruder than the main run of Bluff Dweller point types. He suggests that this as yet unnamed unit is typologically and possibly chronologically earlier than other Bluff Dwellers in the area.

The Bluff dwelling peoples of the Ozarks are readily distinguishable in the pottery horizons which closely parallel developments in the Caddoan area and the east-central Plains area. Our data, however, are insufficient to distinguish the various groups of prepottery cultures which undoubtedly roamed the 300 miles area of the Ozarks. Some of these groups acquired pottery and agriculture in later times, though not necessarily both traits at the same time. Since the earliest pottery types identified to date are Marksvillian-Hopewellian, the suggestion is that pottery was acquired sometime after the earliest Woodland cultures had come into being in the surrounding areas.

5. Dellinger and Dickinson, 1942.
6. Harrington, M. R., 1924a.
7. This has been called Proto-Bluff Dweller also in a theoretical reconstruction by Martin, Quimby, and Collier, 1947, pp. 338–339.

8. Gilmore, 1931; 1932.
9. Quimby, 1946.
10. Baerreis, 1939; 1951.

COMPARISON OF ARCHAIC UNITS

The wealth of data on organic artifacts found in the dry shelters of the Ozark Bluff Dwellers may well have originally been present in Gulpha and other Archaic units. Cross comparisons are restricted by our meager data. We may note the common sharing of a general hunting-gathering mode of life, relatively crude flint artifacts, and large projectile points which were probably used on spears and atlatl darts. Differences are seen in projectile point styles—and it is this artifact which promises to be of greatest aid in eventually separating the cultural units and periods. Net sinkers, present at Gulpha are notably absent, or of different form, in the Ozark sites. The Ozark double-bitted ax, grooved ax, and Gulpha "celt" further indicate separate cultural units. Gorgets, pierced tablets, boatstones, bannerstones, plummets, and tubular stone beads are suggested, though not proven, archaic artifacts from northwestern Louisiana.

Gulpha and Ozark straight stemmed points correspond with similar types from the Tchefuncte site, an Early Woodland period in southern Louisiana.[11] The trianguloid knife or scraper of Gulpha (Fig. 130, D) has counterparts in Tchefuncte[12] and Copell, the Archaic site preceding Tchefuncte. Other Gulpha points do not appear to be closely related. These few resemblances as well as the similarity to early eastern United States sites in general, place early Caddoan area units in the Archaic stage, but there is little to be said at this time regarding degrees of relationships. Harrington[13] and Griffin[14] suggest a connection between the early Basket Maker culture of the Southwest and the Bluff Dwellers of the Ozarks, and comparable Kentucky units. Data, however, are lacking on the necessary cultural and stratigraphic details to allow a detailed comparison of the early eastern and western makers-of-baskets. "Basket-maker finds" in western Oklahoma near Kenton, as well as prepottery units of the Edwards Plateau, central Texas, narrows the gap between the two areas, and the hypothesis appears promising.

We may visualize a long period of prepottery occupations, during which time a series of not greatly differentiated hunting-gathering groups occupied the bluffs and stream terraces of the Caddoan area. These groups were culturally related to others of the Archaic stage in the southeastern United States, and perhaps to initial stages of the Anasazi sequence in the Southwest, as well as to some Folsomoid manifestation. The problem of their ultimate origin is bound to that of the Archaic problem as a whole. As in the case of several eastern units (Lauderdale, etc.), certain of the prepottery cultures acquired pottery probably from advanced outside sources and proceeded into the pottery horizons.

EARLY WOODLAND STAGE

At widely scattered points throughout the southeastern United States, Early Woodland cultures gradually emerged from those of the Archaic period. The best example of Early Woodland level is that called Fourche-Maline, which not only resembles Tchefuncte, but has been found superimposed on prepottery levels with which it shares most of the nonceramic traits.[15] It is furthermore dissimilar to the latest pottery cultures in the area but has direct relations to the pre-Gibson, Evans Component at the Spiro Site. There can be little doubt that the mounds of the Fourche-Maline area contain artifacts from several time periods and it would be well to apply the term Fourche-Maline to earlier manifestations, especially as seen in the Williams mound. This was a circular area 150 feet by 130 feet and 5 feet high which occupied the flat bottom land flanking the Fourche-Maline Creek 2½ miles west of its junction with the Poteau River. The lack of a village site or other features, despite extensive testing in the surrounding area, makes it highly probable that the Fourche-Maline people lived on the mound, building it up with debris and dark brown soil. The evidence of small basin-shaped cache pits (3) (containing animal bones, ash, and mussel shell) at the base of the mound, and a house feature in the body of the mound substantiates this idea. The mound also functioned as a burial container, witnessed by the 122 human burials and 3 dog skeltons (presumably burials) found apparently inclusive, interspersed with mixed mound soil.

Most burials were single, full-flexed, primary interments without common orientation of the head. One burial consisted of 5 individuals. Fifteen burials contained 2 to 4 individuals all tightly flexed. The nearby and closely related Adams mound contained one grave having 11 individuals in it. A deposit of hard white ash was found in many of the burials, but no burnt earth to give indisputable evidence of fire. Three burials were partially cremated, and a few skeletons were disarticulated, suggesting either secondary burial or posthumous disturbance by rodents. Neumann identified the physical type as Iswanid, a longheaded, delicate boned group similar to types found in the Indian Knoll shell heap of Kentucky.[16] Grave goods were rare or absent, and when present consisted of a few flint or bone implements.

Owing to the dark midden soil underlying the

---

11. Ford and Quimby, 1945, Fig. 8, *a, b, f, h.*
12. *Ibid.,* Fig. 9, *F.*
13. Harrington, M. R., 1924*a.*
14. Griffin, J. B., 1946, p. 43.

15. Newkumet, 1940*a;* 1940*b;* Griffin, J. B., 1946, Fig. 2, was the first to indicate an early level for Fourche-Maline. See also Krieger, 1947*b,* p. 202.
16. See pp. 17–20, this volume.

house, it was impossible to identify a post pattern. The house area was roughly rectangular in form, 15 feet wide, and showed evidence of having been burned. Wattle-and-daub construction was indicated by the presence of chunks of fire-hardened mud daub over the house area.

A collection of approximately 6,000 pottery sherds was excavated. The dominant pottery type was a plain, thick (average ½ inch), sherd-tempered paste, with smooth brown and red-brown surface, in the form of large, deep, utilitarian bowls one foot or more in depth and diameter (Fig. 131, I). The vessel forms include: collared and collarless, large vertical rimmed bowls; flaring rimmed bowls; recurved rim; oval, constricted neck, collarless bowls; and one shallow, flaring rim bowl. Fully 68 per cent of the sherds were tempered with ground sherd (or hardened clay?) 22 per cent were of grit, 5 per cent shell, and the rest bone, organic, and combinations. The bases were almost uniformly circular, flat discs (Fig 131, U), some having a slight concavity. Some bases (45) showed impressions of twined basketry or matting, suggesting a basket container used in the moulding process. Decorated sherds were rare (90). Of these, a few (14) had fine to deep fingernail impressions and pinched-up rough nodes (Fig. 131, U). The one square flat base found was covered with deep fingernail impressions. Applique features were absent with the exception of a few (6) vertical, handle-like lugs located 1 inch down from the lip. Most of the decorated sherds were incised in straight-line designs which ranged from narrow (most) to broad trailed. Designs consisting of chevron, diamond, parallel groups of line and ladder were made by long, deeply cut lines (Fig. 131).

A large series of projectile points (4720) were found, most being a large, shouldered or slighted barbed type with tapering haft (Fig. 131, L). The predominance of large, heavy points, along with bone atlatl hooks, found in other Fourche-Maline sites, establishes the use of the throwing stick and dart. A few small points were found (level not stated), but these were crude and thick. Corner tang knives (4), "bunt" scrapers (3), a few drill points, including the T-shaped form, chipped "hoes" (19), and an abundance of laurel-leaf shaped knives (Fig. 131, M–N) and double bitted axes (120) (Fig. 131, K) complete the list of chipped flint artifacts. With few exceptions, the flint work was roughly executed; delicately chipped specimens were extremely rare.

The ground stone industry included: gorgets (2 complete, 21 fragments), pendants (10 fragments), boatstones (5 fragments, 9 complete), grooved pebbles, oval pitted manos (96), and heavy metates with a wide, shallow depression. The boatstones, made of dark, polished hematite, were usually solid, only a few being hollowed out (Fig. 131, S, T). Gorgets included the winged or "reel-shaped" type (Fig. 131, E), and an elongated oval form (Fig. 131, O). A problematical object was a cylindrical bar with expanded center and notches at both ends. Gorgets and pendants were made of ground and polished slate. Hammerstones were found in abundance. A few paint stones of limonite, hematite, and soft clay as well as fragments of a soapstone-like material were listed. Several pendants were notched, or finely scratched with parallel zigzag lines. Though abundant in later horizons, only two polished stone celts were found here. The double bitted ax was apparently the main hafted cutting tool, and the suggestion is that the celt is late in Fourche-Maline (Fig. 131, G). Two flattened, tubular stems, one of pottery and the other of fine sandstone, were thought to represent pipes—the only evidence of smoking.

Bone awls (154) were mainly of split animal bones, but also of deer cannon and ulna bones, antler tips, and bird bones. A few long rounded pins (7) came from this mound and resembled those from the related Adams mound (Fig. 131, B). At the Adams mound, long, curved bone pins with expanded heads, having rows of small drilled holes, were found associated with the skulls as hair ornaments (Fig. 131, A). Bone whistles and tubes have been found in other Fourche-Maline mounds. One pendant made of thin conch shell is also reported.

In attempting to place the Fourche-Maline Focus culturally and chronologically, we may first note that many traits such as boatstones, atlatl hooks, "reel-shaped" gorgets, bar gorgets, bone pins, and contracting stemmed darts are found in southeastern Archaic and Early Woodland units. Flexed primary burials with little or no burial goods and burial mounds combined with refuse mounds are also early traits. Large, stemmed points along with double bitted axes are found in prepottery Ozark levels. The following traits appear to be shared with Tchefuncte: burial mound[17] and burial type, tubular pipes, large, contracting stemmed points, boatstones, atlatl hooks, large shallow metates, oval and pitted manos, bone awls, and possibly simple shell gorgets. The Tchefuncte boatstones are much more amorphous than those of Fourche-Maline. Tchefuncte-Fourche-Maline resemblances are further seen in the pottery. Fourche-Maline plain pottery shares tempering, general paste appearance, thickness and bowl forms with Tchefuncte Plain. Notably absent, however, are the Tchefuncte tetrapodal base supports. Certain forms of Tchefuncte Incised show marked similarities with Fourche-Maline incised types in technique and in the use of parallel line designs on the rim.[18] Tche-

17. Ford and Quimby, 1945, Pl. 3, a–g.
18. Newkumet, 1940b, p. 8.

functe Tammany Pinched is also similar to Fourche-Maline fingernail pinched types. Apparently absent in the eastern Oklahoma unit are stamped and red-filmed pottery types as well as the jar form.

A comparison of the two units show close relationships and marked differences. In evaluating such a comparison it is significant that Fourche-Maline resembles Tchefuncte more closely than any other known pottery culture of the Caddoan area—as discussed later, however, similarities are seen between the Evans component at the Spiro Site and Fourche-Maline. While Fourche-Maline is obviously not a Tchefuncte Focus site, the similarities are sufficient to indicate a general contemporaneity, and to justify placing this unit (as represented by the Williams mound) as the earliest pottery culture yet found in the Caddoan area. The extension of the Fourche-Maline pottery complex is suggested by the finding of similar pottery types in an adjacent area to the east at Strickland Island Site, Scott County, Arkansas.[19]

"EARLY WOODLAND" IN NORTHEASTERN OKLAHOMA

In a preliminary field report Baerreis suggests the possibility of a Woodland unit underlying Hopewellian material at the bottom layers of a bluff shelter, located on a small tributary of Honey Creek, Delaware County, Oklahoma.[20] This important site contained four cultures in the following sequence from bottom to top: (1) Woodland, (2) Hopewellian, (3) Neosho Focus, and (4) materials relating to either the Gibson or Fulton Aspect—probably the latter. The Woodland level was marked by the presence of grit-tempered, cord-marked pottery with the roughening slightly smoothed over in some cases. With the exception of this site, and another nearby unit, cord-marked pottery appears to be absent in the Caddoan area. This Woodland level apparently has affiliations to the north with early Plains manifestations.

SUMMARY

The Early Woodland stage in the Caddoan area appears as a development from archaic roots in much the same manner as in the rest of the Southeast. Pottery is present along with well-developed Archaic traits. As in the case of Tchefuncte, the pottery in its first manifestations is well developed. More rudimentary stages may be discovered, but at present the genesis of the potter's art is not to be discovered in this area. The resemblances of Tchefuncte and Fourche-Maline pottery, as well as the differences, suggest a common source for both rather than a development from one to the other. The presence of

cord-marked pottery in the northwest part of the area suggests a southerly thrust of possibly contemporaneous Early Woodland units in the Central Plains. The presence of pottery, large burial repositories, as well as heavy manos and metates in Fourche-Maline suggests a more sedentary culture subsisting on an assured food supply—although no evidence of agriculture has been found. With the accumulation of these material benefits the stage is set for further complexity of culture in the succeeding period.

MIDDLE WOODLAND STAGE

In most of the Caddoan area there is little evidence for this stage. There has not been sufficient material excavated or analyzed to give a clear picture of the position and the content of this Middle Woodland period as a functioning cultural group in the area. The most complete published evidence comes from the Kirkham Place, located on the Little Missouri River, a tributary of the Ouachita, in Clark County, southwestern Arkansas.[21] This is a refuse mound indicating a time range from late Marksville to Coles Creek for its major occupation. Subsequently a "Caddoan" culture used it for a wattle-and-daub house platform and for a few burials. Vertical stratigraphy within the area was not noted, but Coles Creek sherds predominated on the extremity and decreased toward the center. The pottery was similar, if not identical with the lower Mississippi Valley types, Churupa Punctated, Yokena Incised, Troyville Stamped, and Coles Creek Incised (Fig. 132, A–F). Most of the sherds were plain and smooth surfaced, with volcanic tuff as aplastic. While jar and bowl forms were common, bottles were completely absent. A few fragments of pottery pipe stems probably represented "platform" pipes. Chipped stone traits included: triangular or oval, leafshaped knives (Fig. 132, I, L), flake scrapers, T-shaped drills, and large stemmed projectile points (Fig. 132, G, H, J), most of which were "lozenge-shaped having tapering hafts with shoulders or barbs." Small points were significantly absent. A few fragments of chipped stone, double-bitted and notched axes (Fig. 132, M) came from the midden and site surface. The ground stone assemblage included: a few celts, fragments of unpolished limestone vessels suggesting semi-spherical bowls, a broken "gorget" (pendant?) (Fig. 132, O), and a few fragments of hollowed boatstones (Fig. 132, T). One perforated shell disk made of the whorl of a large marine shell was found. Both the ceramic and nonceramic artifacts had close affiliations with Middle Woodland units of the Lower Valley.

To the north, Marksville and Coles Creek pottery has been reported widely distributed in bluff shelters from the southern periphery of the Ozark Plateau

---

19. Dellinger and Dickinson, 1942, Pls. XVIII and XXIII.
20. Baerreis, n.d., p. 2.

21. Dickinson and Lemley, 1939.

to the Missouri state line.[22] Yokena Incised, Marksville, and Troyville Stamped, and Coles Creek Incised are among the types recognized. Accepting the ceramic similarities to Marksville–Coles Creek, although some types (especially basket impressed disk bases) were equally similar to Fourche-Maline and Early Spiro types—we are unable to call these units Marksvillian or Coles Creek. With the exception of lozenge-shaped projectile points, the rest of the Bluff Dweller complex has little in common with lower Mississippi Valley units. The investigators doubt that "Marksville–Coles Creek pottery is intrusive or trade ware because it is widespread." In fact, "most potsherds in our collections from the final stage of the Bluff Dweller culture are Marksville."[23] A plausible interpretation is that pottery-making Bluff Dwellers had come under Marksville–Coles Creek ceramic influences which seem to have emanated from the lower Mississippi Valley centers.

In view of the supposed Marksville affiliation of cultures in the Arkansas Ozarks, it is interesting to note the occurrence of a series of Hopewellian sites in the neighboring area of northeastern Oklahoma.[24] The sites, excavated by the WPA–University of Oklahoma project from 1938 to 1941, were found as large village refuse areas and in bluff shelters. Griffin applied the term "Cooper" to this complex.[25] The main village sites were located near the mouth of Honey Creek, Delaware County. Here Hopewellian pottery had been found in stratigraphic sequences at two sites: (1) superimposed over nonpottery material at the Evans Site, and (2) over a "Woodland" unit and underneath Neosho Focus and Fulton Aspect (?) material. Sufficient variation was seen in pottery decoration to postulate an earlier and a later period. The material is interpreted as bearing a close association to northern Hopewell units, particularly as seen in the Kansas City area and in central Illinois.[26]

The extension of the Fourche-Maline culture into the Middle Woodland is highly probable. This position appears inescapable, especially since certain Fourche-Maline traditions appear to carry through to Evans which is associated with early Coles Creek influences. Indeed it may be that most of Fourche-Maline belongs chronologically with the Middle Woodland period, although the pottery seems to have earlier Tchefuncte-Adena connections. In this case, Fourche-Maline might be regarded as a "cultural-lag" situation. Marksville and Hopewellian apparently exerted remarkably little direct influence on the western Caddoan area. To date only one Marksville sherd has been recognized in Fourche-Maline.

Krieger reports Tchefuncte-like Marksville and/or Troyville sherds along with examples of sand-tempered wares at the Davis mound in east-central Texas. He believes that highly polished sherds with engraved lines, typical of the Alto Focus, also belong with this horizon, and that the Alto Focus belongs chronologically with Marksville or Troyville, although typologically it is classed with the Gibson Aspect, a later horizon elsewhere (see p. 246). It may be that the Marksville sherds of the Davis Site are related to the Orange Focus of eastern Texas, a cultural relative of Marksville regarded by Griffin as earlier than the main Alto Focus occupation.[27]

Considering the area as a whole, the interpretation most probable in terms of present evidence visualizes two Middle Woodland thrusts. The northern Hopewellian thrust appeared to have skirted the western fringe of the Ozarks, penetrating a short distance into this area. The Marksvillian thrust spread westward along the course of the Red River and its tributaries from centers in the lower Mississippi Valley. It was of sufficient force to establish representative units in the eastern and southeastern parts of the Caddoan area and to influence pottery developments in the Ozarks(?), but failed to penetrate into the western area.

EARLY MISSISSIPPI STAGE

In the lower Mississippi Valley the Early Mississippi stage is considered to begin with the appearance of a new complex of traits including: rectangular temple mounds, rectangular houses, clay elbow pipes, thin, small projectile points, pottery clay trowels, solid clay figurines and so forth. A number of traits, such as celts, boatstones, quartz crystals, bone atlatl hooks, survived from the earlier period.[28] Ford and Willey would begin this period with Troyville, but Griffin and Quimby tend to equate Troyville with Marksville and consider Coles Creek a better marker of this new development.[29] In the Caddoan area cultures containing Coles Creek influence are the next chronological group to be discussed. It would be well to keep in mind, however, that the complexes of "Early Coles Creek" and "Late Coles Creek" have not been clearly delimited. Though a "blunt tool" for fine chronological distinctions, the idea of a "Coles Creek horizon" is sufficient to demarcate cultures of the Early Mississippi stage.[30] Additional aid in placing Caddoan area units in this stage comes in the recogni-

22. Dellinger and Dickinson, 1942.
23. *Ibid.*, p. 278.
24. Baerreis, 1939, n.d.
25. Griffin, J. B., 1946, p. 67 and Fig. 5.
26. Baerreis, David, personal communication.

27. Griffin, J. B., 1946, p. 84; 1950.
28. Ford and Willey, 1941, p. 345.
29. Griffin, J. B., 1946, pp. 62 and 66–67.
30. *Ibid.*, p. 81. Speaking of the divisions between lower valley time periods, Ford says: "There is no clear-cut line at which any of these time periods suddenly stop and the succeeding one starts—the transition between them is a gradual replacement of pottery types" (personal correspondence, December, 1947).

tion of "early Middle Mississippi" traits occurring either as part of the complex or as intrusions.

GIBSON ASPECT

Krieger was first to apply the term "Gibson Aspect" to five related foci of the Early Mississippi stage in the Caddoan area. He has defined the main traits and outlined the basic information on the aspect as well as presented a detailed report on the Sanders[31] and Alto foci.[32] The first symposium on the Caddoan area recognized the reality of this unit, and although it hasn't been established in print most workers in the area utilize the concept. The Sanders Focus is located on the western edge of the Caddoan area in northeastern Texas and south-central Oklahoma. Brown, Norman, and possibly Hughes of eastern Oklahoma are related units. Gahagan Focus is represented by a single component, the Gahagan Site on the Red River in northwestern Louisiana.[33] Craig, Brackett, Eufaula, and several Delware County sites in northeastern Oklahoma and two small units in northeastern Texas form the Spiro Focus.[34] The Haley Focus is composed of Haley, Crenshaw II, Mineral Springs, Washington, and Ozan I sites in southwestern Arkansas.[35] The Davis Site and other components ranging from east-central Texas eastward to the Red River, Louisiana, from the Alto Focus.[36]

At present controversy has arisen regarding relationships of the Gibson Aspect units to each other and to outside cultures, and the chronological position. The problems involve possible Middle American influences in the southeastern United States and the whole concept of the "Southern Cult." A symposium on the Caddoan area held at the University of Oklahoma in 1946[37] did much to clarify the problems of the Gibson and succeeding Fulton Aspect. A round table on the "Southern Cult" held at the University of Michigan, 1947,[38] provided more clues to the solution of this difficult problem. Krieger's recent summaries[39] are a major contribution toward ordering the data of the Caddoan area both for the Early and Late Mississippi stages.

EVANS COMPONENT[40]

Thirty-five burials at the base of the Craig mound and the nearby house foundation afford the main information concerning the initial period of occupation at the Spiro Site in Le Flore County, eastern Oklahoma. Three of these burials were multiple, containing over 10 individuals each, superimposed in a small burial mound 25 feet in diameter and 6 feet high. Loosely bound bark matting was found under and above the mound burials (Fig. 133, P, T, U). Burial goods included pottery vessels, quartz crystals, boatstones, stone beads, a few river-shell and land-snail beads, red and green pigment and small caches of pebbles suggesting rattles. Other burials usually containing two individuals in "spooned" flexed position, had little or no burial goods. Several showed evidence of burning and one was a complete cremation contained in a bi-sected, gourd-shaped pottery vessel (Fig. 133, Q). A large crematory basin (19′ in diameter, Fig. 133, O), found at the base of the Craig mound was associated with this period. The wattle and daub houses were roughly square and ranged from 18 to 25 feet to a side, having four center posts (not strictly aligned), and short parallel trench entrances (Fig. 133, A).

The main type of pottery (Evans Plain) was a relatively thick, dark brown ware with clay or sherd tempering and (rarely grit), in the form of hemispherical globular bowls and squat, amorphous jars (Fig. 133, M, N, S, W, X). The jars which flared slightly had flat disk bases, or in rare instances, square bases. Most Evans Plain vessels had a dull, occasionally rough surface, but a few specimens were polished, with narrow, incised line(s) around the orifice (Fig. 133, R, V). A very thick sherd-tempered ware (Spiro Plain) with plain surface, light brown to orange in color, formed unusually large vertical-rimmed jars with inverted pear-shaped bodies, and hemispherical bowls. Spiro Plain was the main utilitarian ware in the succeeding Craig component. Several vessels with Coles Creek influences were associated with Early Spiro burials. Other Coles Creek types (French Fork Incised, Coles Creek Incised) came from disturbed areas and may be associated with Evans or Craig (Fig. 133).

The chipped stone industry consisted of small, delicately chipped, stemmed points often with serrated edges (Fig. 133, F, H, I); large points with contracting hafts (Fig. 133, G); thick ovate knives or scrapers (Fig. 133, J). Large triangular blades with recurved edges, a concave base, and knobs at the basal extremities (Fig. 133, K) were found associated with stone beads in stratigraphically low burials, but lacked pottery associations. This type occurred in Craig also and may be entirely associated with this period (Fig.

---

31. Krieger, 1946, p. 175.
32. Newell and Krieger, 1949.
33. Moore, C. B., 1912; Webb and Dodd, 1939.
34. Orr, K. G., 1939; 1941; 1946; Howard, L. E., 1940; Finklestein, 1940. The Spiro Focus formerly was considered to include Brown, Norman, and Hughes. These are excluded in the revised concept (see pp. 247–251).
35. Moore, C. B., 1912; Lemley, 1936; Harrington, M. R., 1920.
36. Krieger, 1946; 1947b.
37. Krieger, 1947b.
38. Orr, K. G., n.d.c.
39. Krieger, 1946.
40. Because of possible ambiguity in terminology the four com-

ponents at the Spiro Site have been given distinguishing names as follows: Evans, formerly Early Spiro; Craig, formerly Early Middle Spiro; Brown, formerly Late Middle Spiro; and Clayton, formerly Late Spiro.

136, O). An unusually fine specimen of an effigy boat-stone made of quartz in the shape of a locust came from a burial (Fig. 133, L). Celts with wide, flat polls were typical. One of the best markers of the Evans component was the abundance of black stone beads of spheroidal or cylindrical form (Fig. 133, C–E). It was clear that Evans lacked the elaborate ground stone industry (pipes, earspools, batons, spatulate celts, etc.), marine shells, copper objects, and engraved, polished pottery as well as the bottle form of the succeeding period. No trace was seen of the "Southern Cult."

Evans is both stratigraphically and typologically earlier than the succeeding Gibson Aspect unit, the Craig component. We may also note the near identity of Spiro Plain and the main undecorated pottery type of Fourche-Maline. The amorphous Evans Plain jars have a form similar to Adena Aspect jars[41] and a genetic connection might be suspected here. Boatstones, stone beads, cremations and crematory basins, small accretion mounds with extensive use of bark matting, as well as flexed individual and varied skeletons are generally regarded as Middle Woodland traits. The presence of Coles Creek pottery traits as well as small projectile points, however, tends to bring Evans, the first unit, into the Early Mississippi stage. The only units discovered thus far with a complex at all comparable to Evans is the Fourche-Maline culture and (remotely) Crenshaw I.

CRENSHAW I

The Crenshaw Site, located on the west bank of the Red River, 14 miles east of the Texas line in southwestern Arkansas, consisted of an earlier Coles Creek unit (Crenshaw I) and later "Caddoan" units. Krieger recognizes two later units: Crenshaw II which represents the Haley Focus (Gibson Aspect), and Crenshaw III representing the Texarkana Focus (Fulton Aspect).[42] The Coles Creek people had built up part of the mound (measuring 50 by 30 by 6 feet in height) by accretion of layers containing burials. The Haley and finally Texarkana people had cut burials into the mound. A nearby flat burial ground was used by Coles Creek people as well as the later "Caddoans." Group burials in which the skeletons were laid in rows were reported for both Coles Creek and Haley. Burial furniture included pottery, caches of projectile points, and a few beads and rattles.

The Coles Creek pottery included a thin polished, brown ware as well as a heavy, thick ware; both were grit-tempered. Bowls, jars, "vases," and a platter (Fig. 134) comprised the pottery forms with bottles being significantly absent (excepting Fig. 134, I). A major design element was the large spur or curl terminating in a circular punctate, and arranged in scroll-like bands with area-filling punctates. The types corre-

sponded closely with Coles Creek and French Fork types of the "Early" Coles Creek period. Long stemmed pottery pipes are also recorded.

Other artifacts were boatstones, oval pebbles, triangular celts, and a chisel. The projectile points were mainly small, delicately chipped stemmed forms with long, slightly flaring blades and flaring barbs (Fig. 134, Q–S). Bone needles, awls (deer leg bone), and tortoise shell rattles containing pebbles, a shell bead, perforated mussel shells used as a girdle, and several quartz crystals complete the list of artifacts.

The identification of Crenshaw I as Coles Creek has been substantiated by Ford who considered the main difference between this unit and the Coles Creek of the lower Mississippi Valley the greater use of curvilinear design at Crenshaw.[43] Webb and Dodd note connections with the Weeden Island culture of Florida, which in turn is also related to Coles Creek.

Crenshaw I and Evans have several traits in common: mounds built by accretion of burials, cremations, double flexed burials in cemeteries, flaring bladed points(?), rattles, thick utilitarian ware, similar hemispherical bowls, Coles Creek influence, and absence of major Gibson Aspect traits. Crenshaw I, however, had in addition close resemblance to Craig and Gahagan, including: parallel rows of skeletons in burials, long stemmed pottery pipes, flaring edge points, and specific pottery vessels. The Crenshaw polished jar with square base and outflaring rim, small bowls with triangular orifice, and spheroidal bowls are close to Evans-Early Craig. The data point to near contemporaneity of Crenshaw and Early Gibson as seen at Gahagan and Craig but Crenshaw may have preceded these units by a short time period. At any rate, it seems clear that Evans connections are with indigenous cultures such as Fourche-Maline or unknown units, and Crenshaw is an intruder from the Lower Valley. Both traditions were submerged by the advent of the distinctive and elaborate features of the Gibson Aspect.

CRAIG COMPONENT

The cultural sequence at the Spiro Site confirms the idea of varying time periods for the different Gibson foci. The Brown component at Spiro was superimposed on the Craig component. Craig is much like Alto, Gahagan, Eufaula, Brackett and the Delaware County Spiro Focus sites, while Brown closely resembles Sanders, Haley, Norman, and the earlier period of occupation at the Hughes Site. With the Spiro data in mind we are able to place the full florescence of the Southern Cult at a point in time between Gahagan and Alto representing the initial cult period, and the Brown, Sanders, and Haley groups representing the decline of the cult.

The Craig component at Spiro is early within the

41. Webb and Snow, 1945, Fig. 2.
42. Krieger, 1946, p. 213.

43. Ford, 1937, p. 195.

Gibson Aspect. It has the same four center post house with trench entrance as does Evans but is more rectangular, lacked interior fireplaces, has an additional row of wall posts, and was oriented to the cardinal directions (Fig. 135, G). Engraved conch shells are rare and the art form is rudimentary. This contrasts with the elaborate shell carving found in Brown. Other sites presumed to be contemporaneous with Craig also lack conch shells. This is important since most of the realistic concepts associated with the "Southern Cult" are found as shell engravings at Spiro.

A few Evans burial traits such as stone beads, "Copena" point blades, use of red and green pigment, group burials, cremations, tiny stemmed projectile points survived. Earlier Craig burials were circular, usually with bark or cane matting over and under the bones. The skeletal material was too poorly preserved to indicate more than a probably primary interment and some partial cremations. As Craig developed, stretchers of cedar logs with cane mat bases used to contain bodies and gifts (Fig. 135, C) appeared and this procedure was also followed during the life of the Brown component. While earlier Craig burials had few or no conch shells, they contained many pottery vessels. Later Craig and Brown burials contained dozens of shell dippers and thousands of shell beads but rarely a pottery vessel. Earlier Craig stone beads and "Copena" points gave way to shell beads in great abundance and form, and long elliptical blades in later Craig and Brown times. Earlier recurved edge points became less popular as a variety of new small stemmed types made their appearance (Fig. 136, A–G).

Spiro Plain continues as the main utilitarian ware (Fig. 136, E'). The polished dark brown ware of Evans may be related to the polished black ware of Early Craig. Hemispherical bowls and jar shapes were generally similar, but bottles were a striking innovation. The paucity of pottery vessels in later burials of the Craig component presented a serious problem of tracing the development of many of the pottery types. All forms found, however, can be considered as intermediate between Early and Late Gibson types. Necks of bottles which were long and conical, with narrow mouths, in the early Craig period became shorter though still tapering in the intermediate period (Fig. 136, X), and cylindrical in the Brown component. Early carinated bowls had deep rims (Fig. 136, J'), later, the rims became shorter and the vessel wider (Fig. 136, F'). The spheroidal bowl disappeared after Early Craig. Early Craig designs are carefully engraved with excellent symmetry, but those of the intermediate period show increasing carelessness, and design elements undergo changes. The earlier interlocking scroll with circle nucleus (Fig. 136, Y) were found in a variety of modified forms as the culture proceeded through time. Earlier polished pottery was black, but later becomes dark to light brown prior to the crystallization of the Brown component.

One is left with the strong impression that much of the earlier culture, perhaps the bulk of it, at Spiro survived the arrival of Early Gibson and that Early Gibson was essentially a ceremonial complex imposed on a firm indigenous base at Spiro to create the Craig Focus at that latter site. The almost complete lack of polished engraved pottery, stone spatulate celts, earspools, and other key traits of Gibson in the Craig and Brown houses of the village shows a sharp dichotomy between the utilitarian complex regarded as largely indigenous, and the ceremonial complex which is regarded as intrusion from Early Gibson sites to the south. If Early Gibson polished pottery is a feature of the common culture at the Davis Site of the Alto Focus, and is apparently a superimposed ceremonial complex at Craig of the Spiro Focus, it would be logical to think of this complex as being earlier in Alto. The origin of the bulk of the Early Gibson ceramic complex is not to be found in the lower Mississippi Valley, since specific resemblances either to Marksville-Troyville or Coles Creek are lacking. The finding of the Marksville and Troyville sherds with Alto Focus material at the Davis Site in east-central Texas strongly suggests a pre–Coles Creek inception for Gibson pottery in this part of the Caddoan area.[44]

Various explanations have been given for the complex which seems to be gathered together in the Early Gibson sites. The proximity of Alto to Middle America and its probable early date gives us the best present clue to the origin of Caddoan pottery. MacNeish believes that many ceramic traits, as well as nonceramic traits, of the Southern Cult came directly in from the Huastec area.[45] Webb and Dodd found Gahagan nonpottery traits so similar to types from the St. Johns and Crystal rivers, Florida, that they postulated a direct migration from that area to northwestern Louisiana.[46] They also pointed out a connection between the Florida materials and Ohio Hopewell. Krieger stressed the Hopewell similarities to much of the Southern Cult complex and indicated that many of the concepts and techniques were already known from Middle Woodland times, as seen especially in northern Hopewell material.[47] Griffin, while noting certain connections between Hopewell and Mississippi, feels that the connections into the Alto Focus and Middle Mississippi levels are fairly vague.[48] I have been impressed with the greater correspondence of Gibson material to northern Hopewell than to Marksville, and also feel that a hiatus existed between

44. Krieger, 1947b, p. 201.
45. MacNeish, 1947.
46. Webb and Dodd, 1939, p. 121.
47. Krieger, 1945, p. 510.
48. Griffin, J. B., 1946, pp. 75–77, 83.

known Hopewell and Early Gibson. The extent to which the culture change as seen in the Craig-Brown continuum reflects a general development from Early to Late Gibson cannot be estimated accurately due to lack of comparable sequences. However, artifacts representing the intermediate stage between Early and Late Gibson are also found in southwestern Arkansas at such sites as Washington and Ozan. The problem of this transition is still to be worked out in detail but the reality of development cannot be doubted. Probably the final interpretation will recognize a continuous exchange of cultural ideas across most of the Caddoan area during this period along with additional impulses from Middle America. While Alto-Gahagan seems culturally far removed from Sanders the fact that Alto-Gahagan culture is ancestral to Sanders culture is borne out at the Spiro excavation where the one grades into the other.

THE LATE PERIOD OF THE GIBSON ASPECT

The late period of the Gibson Aspect is represented by Brown, Sanders, Haley, Norman, and probably the early phase at the Hughes Site (Fig. 129). The earliest part of the period and the last of the preceding Early Gibson period represented the high point of cultural development at Spiro. This was especially expressed in the elaborate working of shell dippers, shell gorgets, wooden masks and effigies on sticks, repoussé copper effigies (eagles, woodpeckers) stone double bowl T-pipes with shell inlays, a great variety of shell and wooden beads, ground stone implements such as the baton, monolithic ax and intricately incised stone earspools covered with copper (Fig. 136). The small-stemmed pottery pipe with basal spurs made its appearance. In the later part of the period the entire ceremonial complex underwent a decline and before Clayton times had nearly disappeared. Engraved shells became increasingly rare and there was a definite decadence in the art style as the Brown period progressed.

Correlated with the continuous impoverishment of the burial complex was the increased use of pottery as burial goods. The pottery was still mainly sherd-tempered, but shell was used increasingly for tempering. Red filmed types similar to Sanders Plain were common and occurred in the form of large and small bottles and wide carinated bowls with short rims (Fig. 136, F'). Bottle bodies, oblate spheroidal in the earlier period were now spherical, oblate spheroidal, and sometimes had shoulders. Strap handles occurred on red carinated bowls. A distinctive, large shell-tempered jar with short outslanting rim and clusters of nodes on the body occurred frequently in the burials. In one case human hand and feet bones were found in a jar of this type. Most of the pottery may be interpreted as developments from Craig, but some

forms—particularly those with shell tempering and handles appeared inspired by an outside source which might be termed "Mississippian." The thick Spiro Plain ware so common in the earlier Spiro periods was replaced by thinner, though related types, in which bone tempering was used exclusively.

The rectangular four center post house with trench entrance and double wall posts of earlier times now became a rectangular, two center post form with post entrance and single wall posts (Fig. 135, J). But it was still oriented strictly in the cardinal directions. In the following Ft. Coffee period (Fulton Aspect) the two center post rectangular house was the dominant form, but orientation was casual (Fig. 137, A). This same house type was retained by Caddoan groups in Anadarko until the later part of the nineteenth century.[49] Stretcher burials were replaced with group interments in circular pits. The skeletons were extended with heads at one end and clusters of pottery vessels at the other end. The Brown component burial was identical with the Sanders burial type (Fig. 135, I).

Norman traits closely parallel those of Brown and Sanders but had as a dominant vessel shell-tempered jars with handles. Norman may have been close to the source of the shell-tempered wares which became increasingly common in Late Middle Spiro and Late Spiro.

THE CHRONOLOGICAL POSITION
OF THE GIBSON ASPECT

The chronological position of the Gibson Aspect has still to be firmly established. Certain leads are indicated, however, in the cultural similarities between Gibson and cultural units in the eastern United States and Plains, as well as in the affiliations of succeeding Fulton Aspect units with later horizons in the southwestern United States and with historic European trade materials. Little doubt remains that all of the Gibson Aspect was "prehistoric" in the sense of lacking any trace of European trade materials. European goods were rare except in the latest Fulton Aspect units, and were found here only in those units geographically nearest French and Spanish trade sources.

It now appears probable that the eastern "cult" material is later than the "cult" in the Caddoan area. Important data on this problem came from recent work on the Kincaid Site, a Middle and late Middle Mississippi unit in southern Illinois. Pottery studies showed the presence of Moundville sherds in Middle and Late period levels at Kincaid. Bell dated these horizons between approximately A.D. 1500 and 1600.[50]

49. Swanton, 1942, Pl. 14. Old Caddos in Anadarko, Oklahoma, were raised in similar wattle-and-daub houses, according to information which I gathered in an ethnological survey of the Social Science Research Council during the summer of 1946.
50. Bell, n.d.; also this volume, pp. 345–51; Orr, K. G., n.d.b.

Moundville contained "cult" materials closely similar to those of the Gibson Aspect; its motifs tying closely with shell motifs of Middle and Late Gibson. In addition to Moundville, Cahokia trade sherds were also found at Kincaid. "Old Village" trade sherds from Cahokia underlaid Middle Kincaid and consequently Moundville.[51] And there were connections between "Old Village" and the Gibson Aspect.

Krieger found connections between Sanders and "Old Village" in the presence of Cahokia type, notched triangular points; vessels like Cahokia "bean pots" (present in Old Village but more common in Trappist, at Cahokia). "Bean pot" forms similar to Sanders types occurred at Spiro in a burial regarded as transitional between Craig and Brown. This same burial (Burial No. 51) contained a globular shell-tempered jar with loop handles resembling early Middle Mississippi forms. Notched triangular projectile points of the same form and material as the common Cahokia type occurred in a Late Craig or Brown burial. The flaring-bitted celts of Late Craig-Brown are essentially identical in form and material to those found at Cahokia.[52] Other possible ties between Gibson and Old Village includes the following traits found at Cahokia:[53] spatulate celts, human and frog effigy pipes,[54] by-cymbal earspools (a small type of bone or wood with copper veneer), small projectile points with expanding stems and flaring blades, cross and circle motif, falconidae eye motif, interlocking scroll motif, black polished pottery, one sherd of Spiro Fine Incised, polished flint baton,[55] conch shell dippers and beads. The lack of engraved shell at Cahokia and realistic "cult" figures may be significant. An increasingly strong web of evidence is being recognized to relate Middle or Late Gibson to earlier Cahokia, which in turn is tied to Early Kincaid at *ca.* 1450 or earlier.[56] A study of cross influences between the two dominant centers, Spiro and Cahokia, promises fruitful research since both appear to represent largely distinct traditions.

Besides Coles Creek connections Brown had increasing contact with an unknown culture which had shell-tempered pottery. The Craig-Brown burial containing the globular shell-tempered jar with loop handles has been mentioned. Loop handles are considered good indicators of early Middle Mississippi. A small shell-tempered jar with short out-slanting rim, and brush-marked surface also came from a house site underneath a Craig-Brown mound (Brown mound) at Spiro. In Brown, shell-tempered ware becomes increasingly common. The fact that the Norman ceramic complex is largely shell-tempered with an abundance of handled jars suggests that it had proximity to a source of this Mississippian tradition. Possible sources of the shell tempering are the St. Francis Focus in eastern Arkansas, or an unclassified "Mississippi" Plains unit to the north and possibly west. The Henrietta Focus of north-central Texas,[57] although of the succeeding Fulton Aspect period, had shell-tempered pottery; the possibility of earlier shell-tempered horizons on the western and/or southern Plains must be borne in mind. A blank-faced effigy bottle with shell tempering was the only clear-cut connection between Craig-Brown and Classical "Middle Mississippi" of the southeast.[58] This specimen came from a burial regarded as somewhat earlier than the Brown component (Burial No. 99). A few red-on-buff sherds, common in the St. Francis Focus appeared at Spiro in disturbed soil, but are sufficient to indicate a possible connection with this area. Large shell-tempered jars identical with the Brown component type were found in top layer cultures of the Ozarks.[59]

For purposes of interpreting chronology of the "Southern Cult" it is important to note that it did not reach its full development until middle and later portions of the Gibson period. The apex of engraved shell art came after earliest Gibson but prior to latest Gibson. This would fall into the Middle portion of the Middle Mississippi period as seen in early Kincaid, and leaves no hiatus to the succeeding Moundville "cult" manifestation which was tied by trade sherds to Middle and Late Kincaid. From this standpoint some of the "cult" elements, probably a majority of them, first appeared in the Caddoan area then spread to the Southeast where they occurred frequently in later horizons. The florescence of the "cult" at Spiro must have been of short duration since most of the more elaborate objects, particularly carved shell, occurred in only a few burials, apparently of a single time period. During this short period of florescence many Huastecan similarities are seen: in the cut-out and engraved gorgets, the

---

51. Richard S. MacNeish identified the Kincaid trade sherds with the aid of the Ceramic Repository for the Eastern United States of the University of Michigan.

52. Robert Bell identified the Spiro flaring celts as being made of flint from the Kaolin Quarry, Union County, Illinois.

53. These notations are from personal observations of the P. F. Titterington collection unless specified. See Titterington, 1938. [The justification for regarding many of these traits as "Old Village" at Cahokia is not clear. It should also be remembered that in the definitive publication defining the Spiro Site trait associations do not appear.—Ed.]

54. Moorehead, 1928, Pl. XXXIII.

55. Whelpley Collection, St. Louis Academy of Science. Information courtesy of Dr. P. F. Titterington.

56. MacNeish, 1947, pp. 10–11, proposed this train of reasoning.

57. Krieger, 1946, pp. 87–150.

58. Earlier Gibson lacks handles, effigies, painted ware, negative painted ware and shell tempering—when found in later Gibson these traits appear intrusive from "Middle Mississippi." "Middle Mississippi," in turn, lacks the polished engraved wares which are dominant in Gibson. These differences argue strongly for separate origin of the two ceramic traditions.

59. Dellinger and Dickinson, 1942, Pl. XXVI, *L*; Griffin, J. B., 1937*b*.

figure with a conical cap in Huastecan manner, spurred base, right-angled pottery pipes, and so forth. We may postulate additional Middle American impetus or, at least, close contact to account for the highest period of development at Spiro.

After a short period of decline of ceremonialism—marked by the disappearance of stretcher burials, conch shells, and elaborate stone artifacts— the "cult" disappeared at Spiro, and the Clayton component continued with mere fragments of the earlier burial complex. The great change between Gibson and Fulton is especially due to the disappearance of the Gibson burial complex and associated ceremonialism. At the same time new elements begin to come in mainly from the Plains area: triangular projectile points, scapula hoes, L-shaped pipes, perhaps derived from some unit like the Great Bend Aspect of central Kansas.[60] However sharp the changes from Gibson to Fulton, they can be explained as a rapid change of ceremonialism and the introduction of a relatively few new items rather than by wholesale cultural replacement. The evidence suggests that the shift from Gibson to Fulton did not represent a true cultural disconformity. The short transition period between the two aspects is seen in early Texarkana and McCurtain, and in Belcher. With the passing of the Gibson Aspect we enter the final phase of cultural history, termed the Late Mississippi stage.

LATE MISSISSIPPI STAGE

FULTON ASPECT

The concept of the Fulton Aspect as developed by Krieger[61] closely agrees with my own deductions arrived at independently.[62] He has set up seven foci as follows: (1) a Texarkana Focus located on the Red River in northeastern Texas and southwestern Louisiana;[63] (2) a closely related McCurtain Focus located north of Texarkana in southeastern Oklahoma;[64] (3) a Belcher Focus on the Red River in northwestern Louisiana and southwestern Arkansas;[65] (4) Titus Focus on a tributary of the Red River in northeastern Texas;[66] (5) Bossier Focus occupying the hills above tributaries of the Sabine and Neches rivers in east-central Texas;[67] (6) Frankston Focus occupying the upper reaches of the Sabine and Neches rivers in the southwestern part of the Caddoan area;[68] (7) Glendora Focus, a series of widely scattered sites in southeastern Arkansas, northeastern and

central western Louisiana, and one site in northeastern Texas (Fig. 129).[69] an additional unit, the "Mid-Ouachita" Focus defined by Hodges[70] for the Ouachita River in southwestern Arkansas, should be added.

Glendora and Frankston are associated with European trade materials and definitely represent the latest period in the area. Frankston is thought to be the culture of the Hasinai Caddo; the Glendora culture was found at Natchitoches village in west-central Louisiana and in the vicinity of the Kadohadacho in southwestern Arkansas; and Mid-Ouachita is thought to represent the Cahinnio Caddo encountered by De Soto on the upper Ouachita. Glendora is always a top-layer unit, and presumably latest in the area, while Frankston is considered to have depth of development, perhaps into the prehistoric (pre-1540) period.

Lack of European trade goods may not in itself, be accepted as meaning pre–De Soto (1541) or even pre–La Salle (1682). It will be noted that sites with trade materials are on the eastern, southern, and southwestern extensions of the Caddoan area where they would have easiest access to French trading posts in the lower Mississippi Valley or Spanish trading centers in the Southwest. Even in these cases trade materials are relatively scarce in Glendora and Frankston sites. It is entirely possible that Fulton Aspect units in remote areas of the Caddoan region, as the Fort Coffee Focus on the northwestern fringe, and the Texarkana and McCurtain foci in the west-central area, may have received only driblets of white goods or none at all until a late period. They could have existed well past La Salle's time without evidence of trade materials at the sites.[71]

Krieger is correct in pointing out an early, and perhaps extensive trade between the Frankston Focus and the Spanish southwestern centers via the "Jumanos."[72] The account attributed to Father Douay in 1686 reported the presence of many Spanish trade articles among the Hasinai Caddo.[73] How much exaggeration went into this report, perhaps to impress the French Court with the trade encroachments of the Spanish, or how many of the reported objects

60. Wedel, 1942, 1947.

61. Krieger, 1946.

62. Orr, K. G., n.d.a.

63. Dickinson, 1941; Harrington, M. R., 1920 (Ozan 11 and 15); Krieger, 1946.

64. Baerreis, n.d.

65. Moore, C. B., 1912 (Foster, Friday, McClure sites); Webb and Dodd, 1941; Krieger, 1946.

66. Krieger, 1946.

67. Ibid.   68. Jackson, 1936 (Saunders); Krieger, 1946.

69. Moore, C. B., 1908 (Greer, Douglas); 1909 (Glendora, Keno), 1912 (Battle); Walker, W. M., 1935; Webb, C. H., 1945; Dickinson, 1941; Orr, K. G., 1941; Krieger, 1946.

70. Hodges in Krieger, 1947b, p. 200; Hodges, 1945.

71. A comparable situation was encountered at the Zimmerman site in north-central Illinois during excavations of the University of Chicago and the Illinois State Museum in 1947. Here were found units of what is considered the Kaskaskia Illinois group surrounding LaSalle's Fort St. Louis about 1683 with only slight traces of European goods in a few features. The situation will vary from area to area. I believe a considerable time period elapsed after first extensive European contact, and the appearance of white goods in site features.

72. Krieger, 1946, p. 40.

73. [For the questionable veracity of the "Douay" account see Delanglez, 1938.—ED.]

would turn up in Hasinai trash pits are other problems. We would certainly not expect to find Spanish clothing or the papal "Bull." Even if we grant extensive European acculturation to the Hasinai in the late 1600's, we have no reason to suspect that other Caddoan units to the north would fare equally well. Indeed there is only slight evidence of cross-contacts between the Frankston and other Fulton Aspect units and these groups may well have been in a state of war, or, at least, culturally isolated. Fort Coffee has ceramic similarities with Glendora including swollen neck bottles and negative elements surrounded by hatchuring. Several Fort Coffee vessels were identical to McCurtain and Texarkana types (Fig. 137). Consequently, we would regard Late Fort Coffee as well as Late McCurtain and Texarkana units as extending well into the 1600's and perhaps 1700's. Fort Coffee, however, had probably gone by 1739 for the Mallet expedition following the Arkansas River through this area made no mention of the extensive settlements.[74]

Traits differentiating Fulton from Gibson were as follows: lack of mounds and most of the Gibson ceremonial complex, individual burials in flat cemeteries with pottery around head or feet, a great variety of engraved polished pottery including some effigy forms; shell tempering in all but the southwestern part of the area; pottery elbow or stone L-shaped pipes and absence of T-pipes or effigy pipes, very little or no marine shells or beads; and few or no earspools. The split-backed type earspool found in Clayton was apparently a last survivor of this artifact. The presence of Plains traits in units on the western perimeter especially was distinctive. These included: sandstone hones, thumb nail scrapers, diamond-shaped knives, L-shaped stone pipes, scapula hoes, and small triangular projectile points (Fig. 137, E, F).

The strongest evidence for the close relationship of Fulton to the preceding Gibson traditions is seen in the ceramics. The basic vessel forms of carinated and shouldered bowl, hemispherical and conical bowl, bottle, and small jar with outflaring rim had prototypes in late Gibson. The pottery designs, especially those based on the spiral and the scroll, were retained in much modified and frequently elaborated form. A common geometric design on Craig-Brown shell dippers, a concentric semicircular "sun burst" motif, appeared in identical form on Texarkana, McCurtain, and Fort Coffee bowls (Fig. 137, B'). The Clayton component had a majority of types which were intermediate in form between Brown and the later Fort Coffee types. The Fulton Aspect house in the Spiro area was the Late Gibson rectangular two center post type without alignment in the cardinal directions (Fig. 137, A).

74. Folmer, 1939, p. 4.

If our theory of the emergence of Fulton foci from Late Gibson is correct evidence of time differences between the Fulton units would reflect this emerging process. Glendora was furthest removed typologically from Gibson and had European trade materials. The Frankston Focus had perhaps least claim to Gibson connections; there is a real problem in locating the cultural ancestor for this group. The Clayton component, Belcher Focus, Titus Focus, and earlier McCurtain Focus have the closest similarities to the Gibson Aspect. These units continued to utilize mounds for burials and perhaps for temples, had group burials in shafts in the mounds, and some traces of Late Gibson ceremonialism, including: earspools, marine shells, some with rough engravings (Belcher), and gorgets (McCurtain Focus). Fronto-occipital head deformation practiced by Gibson people is also found in Fulton skeletal materials.[75]

There is stratigraphic evidence supporting the contention that time differences existed within Fulton. Clayton burials intrude into a Gibson mound and latest Fort Coffee materials overlie the surface at the Spiro Site. At the Hatchel mound, Belcher and Texarkana materials underlie Glendora materials found along with Texarkana in the top layer. An extensive period of Texarkana occupation is indicated in the presence of a 14-foot layer of refuse on the mound.[76] Krieger indicates that Belcher and Titus clearly provide convenient prototypes for Glendora pottery.[77]

It then appears plausible to postulate an earlier Fulton Aspect period representing an intermediate cultural zone between Late Gibson and Late Fulton. The earlier unit would consist of Early Fort Coffee (Clayton component), Early Texarkana, and McCurtain, Belcher, Titus and perhaps Bossier. The Late Fulton period would be represented by Glendora (developing out of Belcher and Titus), Late Fort Coffee developing out of Clayton and Late Texarkana and McCurtain. Frankston apparently occupied both periods with the late period marked by European trade goods and the presence of a new pottery type (Patton Incised).

The problem of providing dates for the Fulton Aspect thus has as its major problem the starting point of Early Fulton. Glendora dates in the late 1600's and 1700's at which time French trading goods were becoming plentiful in the lower Mississippi Valley. Krieger believes that Frankston was encountered by Moscoso, De Soto's lieutenant, in 1541

75. At the Moore Site, Fort Coffee Focus, see also Hrdlička, 1909, p. 173. Neumann is studying relationships of Gibson and Fulton skeletal material.

76. [C. H. Webb and others believe that this is not an accumulated refuse deposit, as Krieger indicates, but is a mound zone constructed from village site material.—ED.]

77. Krieger, 1946, p. 211.

and this seems highly plausible. At this time the Caddo of the Frankston area were engaged in trade with the Puebloan groups from whom they received cotton blankets and turquoise.[78] Evidence of this trade is also seen in the Moore component of the Fort Coffee Focus where a turquoise necklace was found in a burial. Puebloan contributions to the Fulton Aspect consist of the turquoise, cotton blankets, neck banding (Fig. 137, Z) (found also in Fort Coffee), olla forms in Titus, and a few Puebloan trade sherds also in Titus. Pecos Pueblo presumably received in return carinated and shouldered bowls found from Glaze III to Glaze VI periods. The Late Fulton Aspect shouldered bowl, particularly one with a recurved rim called "cazuela" bowl bears closest resemblance to Middle American forms.[79] Consequently, it may not be impossible that both the Caddoan area and Southwest received these forms from a common source in Middle America. Whatever the nature of the exchange between the Southwest and Caddoan area, the fact of contact in Early Fulton times appears undeniable. The Puebloan pottery types found to date have not been in archeological context and are not particularly sensitive types for dating, but they do indicate a date of *ca.* 1400 to 1600 which would agree with the general time period now accorded for the Fulton Aspect. The possibility of further Puebloan finds in Fulton gives promise of accurate dates for the later history of the Caddoan area.

During the Fulton Aspect, close contacts were maintained with the Plains group but slight evidence is seen of contacts with late Middle Mississippi groups to the east. This contrasts with the Gibson period where contacts to the east must have been extensive. Also suggestive is the greater homogeneity of Gibson material as contrasted with the heterogeneity of Fulton material. These data suggest a politically well-organized Gibson culture in which the common ceremonialism, the "Southern Cult," represented a powerful influence with wide radiations. With the collapse of the "cult" and its inferred political structure, Caddoan area units returned to local autonomy which was reflected in the local development of various cultural differences. Plains units, possibly held in check during the Gibson period, were free to impress their culture on the high centers of the Caddoan area, and as a result a number of Plains traits became part of the Fulton complex.

With the establishment of the Europeans the Caddoan cultures became acculturated and began to disintegrate. The various Caddo tribes were placed on a reservation on the Brazos River, Texas, for a while and about the time of the Civil War were removed to the Anadarko reservation in western Oklahoma, where they remain today.[80] Reflecting the innumerable cultural influences which have played on them from Early Fulton times to the present day, Caddos now numbering nearly 2000 individuals, have a highly polyglot culture. Much of the original ideology still remains, though apparently well integrated with many other traditions. When I visited them in 1946 the older members, a number of them over 70, still remembered important details of the culture of the last century, including house building. Pottery making, for which they had been justly famous was forgotten in the memory of even the oldest. The recent peyote cult and commonly held social and semi-religious dances including the "Ghost Dance" had replaced the earlier ceremonialism. The dead were buried in small wooden houses, a practice picked up from the Creeks. Myths and tales, as well as occult lore known to a few individuals may provide a fruitful harvest for the ethnologist who arrives before too late.

CONCLUSIONS

The results of this survey of Caddoan area archeology gives only the broadest outlines of culture history. The gaps in our data are especially obvious in the earlier stages. Even within the relatively well-represented later stages the process of intensive cross comparisons and synthesis has only begun. Inevitably the conclusions presented here will be altered by future work.

The Archaic stage was definitely present in the Caddoan area as well as in most surrounding areas. A variety of artifact types, particularly in projectile points, ranging from Folsomoid-Yuman to Early Woodland types, represented a series of small hunting-gathering groups who ranged over the area probably for thousands of years. The correspondence of cultural traits with those of the Southeastern Archaic stage indicates that the process of development must have been largely parallel in both areas. As in the Southeast, the prepottery artifact complex was found also in early pottery-bearing cultures. The transition from Archaic to Early Woodland was a gradual process in which pottery, burial mounds, and a few other traits were added. The importance of the Archaic here lies in its key geographical position. Future work will undoutedly aid greatly in clearing up problems of early cultural relationships between the east and the west.

Only Fourche-Maline (Williams mound) of eastern Oklahoma represented the Early Woodland and may well be of considerably greater distribution than found to date. It is similar in many respects to Tchefuncte of the lower Mississippi Valley. Indications

78. Krieger, 1947b, p. 207.
79. Noguera and Du Solier in Krieger, 1947b, pp. 205–206.
80. Swanton, 1942.

are that the same influences produced the two cultures. On the northwestern fringe of the Caddoan area cord-marked Woodland sherds were found underlying Hopewellian material. Except for this occurrence northern Woodland cultures utilizing cord-marking made no discernible impression on the area.

Although Fourche-Maline traditions must have existed through the Middle Woodland period, the distinguishing characteristics of this phase of the culture have not been determined. Marksville expanded up the Red River and its tributaries, establishing relatively pure sites at the Kirkham Place in southwestern Arkansas, and perhaps in the Orange Focus of eastern Texas. Strong Marksville-Troyville influence extended as far as the Davis Site in east-central Texas, and well into the Arkansas Ozarks. But the northwestern part of the Caddoan area remained largely unaffected. A northern Hopewell thrust intruded a short distance into northeastern Oklahoma but exerted no apparent influence beyond this point. During the later part of this period the Gibson Aspect presumably in part from Middle America, made its initial appearance at the Davis Site.

In the transition period between Middle Woodland and Early Mississippi, Evans appeared as a recipient of Fourche-Maline traditions plus Early Coles Creek influences(?). Burial mounds were used in conjunction with a dominantly Middle Woodland complex, suggesting a cultural lag in this peripheral area. A pure, early Coles Creek site, Crenshaw I, in southwestern Arkansas represented the last stronghold of lower Mississippi Valley traditions. Both Middle Woodland and Coles Creek influences were seen submerged by the rapidly expanding Gibson Aspect.

Early Gibson, seen in Alto, Gahagan, and Craig, dominated the area with a radically new series of cultural traits, including: polished, engraved pottery, delicately chipped projectile points and blades, an elaborate groundstone industry (earspools, T-shaped and effigy pipes, spatulate celts) marine shells, and deep shaft burials in temple mounds. In Alto the ceramic complex appeared as everyday utilitarian materials, but at Spiro, Eufaula, and Brackett it was a ceremonial (burial) complex fused with the Early Spiro utilitarian complex of Fourche-Maline tradition. While the bulk of the ceramic complex is of Middle American inspiration the nonceramic artifacts have Hopewellian relationships. The socio-religious ceremonialism as seen in the shell carvings and burial complex might best be interpreted as a blend of Hopewellian and Middle American practices.

Early Gibson developed into Late Gibson through seriations noted in the Craig-Brown sequence at Spiro, in which additional Middle American and "Middle Mississippian" influences also contributed. The transition was marked by the high development of the "Southern Cult" seen especially in the florescence of shell carving. During the high point of "Cult" activity many ceremonial concepts were diffused eastward to large Middle Mississippi sites such as Etowah, Georgia, and Moundville, Alabama. The similarities of southeastern ceremonialism of this time period, along with the homogeneity of Caddoan area Gibson culture indicates strong political and religious control as well as widespread trading activities. In Late Gibson, seen in Brown, Sanders, Haley, and Norman, the intensity of the ceremonialism began to decline. By Early Fulton times overt manifestations of the "Cult" have virtually disappeared and the final, or Late Mississippi stage emerged.

With the decline of the "Cult," strong Plains influences appeared on the western edge of the area. Scapula hoes, shell-tempered pottery, triangular points, L-shaped pipes and other Plains traits composed an increasingly important part of the complex. Continued Middle American influences introduced some new pottery vessels and pipe types, but the bulk of the ceramics was a much modified and elaborated continuation of Gibson ceramics. For the early part of this period there is evidence of trade with Puebloan groups, and strong suggestions of cultural exchange of pottery ideas between the Southwestern and Caddoan areas. The Early Fulton units, including Clayton, Early Texarkana and McCurtain, Belcher and Titus, retained a dying grasp on Gibson ceremonialism, but this quickly disappeared in Late Fulton. Glendora, Frankston, Late Fort Coffee, Late Texarkana and McCurtain reached historic levels and probably extended into the 1700's in the final stage. Fulton had given up mound-building as well as most of the Gibson nonceramic industries, but ceramics continued to be a major achievement.

The Natchez and Taensas of western Mississippi had acquired some of Gibson-Fulton culture via the earlier Plaquemine. Along with the Creeks these tribes may have been the final recipients of the "Southern Cult." The exotic caste society of the Natchez with its Suns, Nobles, and Commoners might well reflect the elaborate social structure which accompanied the Gibson Aspect. The final heirs of the long Gibson and Fulton Aspect development included the Hasinai, Kadohadacho, Natchitoches, and Cahinnio(?) Caddo. The remnants of the Caddos, now living in Anadarko, southwestern Oklahoma, have been much acculturated by Spanish and French, Southeastern and Plains Indian contacts; but still retain memories of their earlier culture.

From an early period in the Archaic stage up to the advent of the Gibson Aspect, the Caddoan area was peripheral to dominant cultures of the lower Mississippi Valley. With the appearance of the Gibson Aspect, partially at least from Meso-America, a highly unique and elaborate culture became established and sent out strong ceremonial influences into the Southeast. During the height of this period, few outside influences, with the exception of Meso-America, affected the cultural autonomy of the Gibson Aspect. But with the breakdown of Gibson ceremonialism, and presumably political organization as well, strong influences swept in from the Plains, with even the distant Puebloans making cultural contributions. To the end, however, Fulton maintained distinctive characteristics especially seen in its elaborate pottery.

Because of its key position at the cross-roads of the Southwest, Plains, and Meso-America, all stages of Caddoan area history can shed light on widespread cultural interactions. The Early and Late Mississippi stages in the eastern United States were especially affected by happenings in the area. The intricate details of intra- and inter-area cultural relationships have still to be worked out. When this is achieved, with the help of tree-ring dating, a tapestry rich in detail and significance will replace the present vague outlines of Caddoan area history.

PREHISTORY OF THE LOWER MISSISSIPPI VALLEY.

By Jesse D. Jennings*

THE present chapter has for its objective the description of the Indian cultures of Mississippi as a center and their arrangement into proper chronological order. A summary of present knowledge, rather than a development of new theses, is proposed. The traits, material and non-material, which characterize these different periods will be synoptically presented. Although great detail is not attempted, the cultural effect one period had upon another will be shown where this is possible.

Although many students gathered and reported data in the South, the first systematic attempt to learn and define the sequence of cultures in the Lower Valley can be credited to Henry B. Collins and his student James A. Ford. Beginning with speculations of Collins as a guide, Ford studied the sherds from scores of sites. The results of the analysis of surface collections were then supplemented by stratigraphic tests at selected sites. In this way Ford and his associates built up a knowledge of a sequence of prehistoric Indian occupations. There is no doubt as to the validity of the sequence of material objects, but the full content of some of the complexes—e.g., Deasonville and Caddoan—is being and will continue to be drastically questioned and revised.

Although, as indicated, the succession of Lower Valley cultures has come to be regarded as reasonably accurate in its present form, it must not be forgotten that the sequence was first set up and has subsequently been modified, largely on the basis of pottery. Pottery from the surface was used as a guide for test excavation.[1] The results of tests in turn dictated the few complete site excavations undertaken by the Louisiana survey group in the late 1930's. Therefore, the reader is warned that the continuing emphasis, at all times during the continuing study, has been on ceramics, and as a result no thorough analysis, with equal emphasis upon all phases of Indian life, is at hand for any period.

Aside from the strong ceramic bias mentioned above, any unevenness of data can, to some degree, be further explained in terms of spotty excavation. In some cases, sites are dug but not yet reported. Data from Texas and Arkansas are scanty. Particularly valuable, but not yet available will be the results of the Central Mississippi Valley Survey, conducted over several seasons since 1940. Preliminary conclusions resulting from this survey are very important. In that critical region of the river from Memphis to Vicksburg, the careful work of the survey has discovered ceramic evidence of the strong occurrence of every major cultural horizon defined elsewhere in the South, except for the Archaic, which is very scantily represented.[2] Moreover, these cultures are repeatedly found in stratigraphic sequences confirming those of the Lower Valley and in the rest of the East generally. Many sites yield material showing a transitional position from one stage to another. The facts and speculations resultant from this survey, when published, will have a powerful effect upon the detailed prehistory of the Lower Valley.

The first broad cultural grouping to be presented here is the Archaic. Universal over the east, it was a simple level of life which contained within it the prototypes of many later specialized artifacts and customs. The river valley or river drainage pattern of subsistence and community development was here initiated. Included in the Archaic period are, of course, the cultures called Archaic, Copell, Poverty Point, Lauderdale Focus of Alabama, and certain sites near Natchez, Port Gibson, and Jackson, Mississippi.

Early Woodland comes next. It includes Tchefuncte proper, early Adena, Miller I, Early Baytown,[3] and the Alexander sites of Alabama. Pottery came into use during this period. Copper used as tools and ornaments is found. Agriculture may have been introduced or developed. Burial of the dead in mounds appeared. Tobacco may have been used.

---

* Montezuma College, Montezuma, New Mexico, A.B., 1929; University of Chicago, Ph.D., 1943; Professor of Anthropology, University of Utah, 1948——. Chapter received December, 1947; reduced by one-third, January, 1951.

1. Ford, 1936.

2. Phillips, personal communication.

3. Phillips, Ford, and Griffin, 1951. Baytown is an ill-defined term first used by the Central Mississippi Valley Survey to designate the culture characterized by cord-marked pottery, clusters of low domed mounds, etc. found in the alluvial valley of the Mississippi River. No detailed account of the total complex of traits which distinguish the culture yet exists, although it includes and absorbs the Deasonville of Ford, and should possibly absorb the Miller series I have described from northeast Mississippi, Jennings, 1941. Ford and Willey use the term, but only touch upon its general significance.

The third group is the Middle Woodland. This period may be regarded in the South as a shift from a generalized to a specialized pattern of living. The direction of cultural expansion was established. Larger mounds of more elaborate construction still served as burial places. Special pottery forms and surface finishing techniques appeared. Tobacco became much more popular and pipe form began its development to the currently popular elbow type. Here I have lumped Marksville, Early Baytown, Miller II, Copena, the Hopewellian of Alabama and north Mississippi, the Santa Rosa of Florida, and many small, unstudied sites of the Tombigbee, Mobile, Chickasawhay, and Pearl rivers.

The next stage in the chronology is the Mississippi period, which is marked by flamboyance in pottery, copper work, shell, and flint. Mounds became specialized foundation structure rather than tombs. A strong religious caste heavily encumbered by ritual is thought to have existed. Within this stage I have lumped Troyville, Coles Creek, Plaquemine, Middle and Late Baytown, Gahagan, Moundville, Spiro, Koger Island, Tennessee Cumberland, and the many other remains categorized as Early and Late Middle Mississippi.

After A.D. 1600, the Lower Valley was characterized by what I have called the Historical Decline. In this stage of decadence of technology, an apparent corresponding loss of ritual and ritually used objects, and a decline in tribal strength, can be inferred. This period includes the Natchezan[4] and the Chickasaw.[5]

ARCHAIC AND EARLY WOODLAND

Since data on the nomadic hunters are too scanty to permit more than the heaping of speculation upon earlier speculation, it behooves us to consider the somewhat better known cultural stages. Here we consider the manifestations found in sites on the Yazoo River in the broad alluvial valley of the Mississippi which extends from Vicksburg to Memphis, on the Big Black and Bayou Pierre rivers of Mississippi, and along the Gulf Coast. Two divisions are readily recognized. The earlier of these, the Archaic, is ubiquitous in the Southeast (Fig. 138). The other, Early Woodland, called Tchefuncte[6] and/or Burial Mound I,[7] is at present less well known than the Archaic. The early Archaic of Louisiana and the Gulf Coast is the cultural and near-chronological counterpart of the Tennessee and Kentucky rivers inland shell-heap dwellers, and those of the East Coast such as the Stallings Island settlement or the Lamoka Focus in New York. Early Woodland (Tchefuncte) is related to Adena and Red Ocher, Miller I, Deptford to the east, Middlesex in New York, many sites

lying between Natchez and Jackson, Mississippi, and many unnamed sites in south Mississippi. It is true that between the Archaic (this term is here meant to include the general level of *prepottery* development found all over the Southeast) and the Early Woodland cultures (we here allow Tchefuncte to typify) the differences are not great. The early blends with, or gives way to, the later without a clear line of demarcation. At present our knowledge is too scanty to differentiate between the stone, shell, and bone artifacts of the prepottery and pottery levels. A new site in Louisiana would presumably be categorized as Archaic or Tchefuncte on the basis of the presence or absence of pottery, mound burial, copper artifacts, and upon site location. In any discussion of the prepottery horizons of the Southeast it must first be realized that from Nova Scotia to Corpus Christi along the Atlantic Coast, as well as in the Caribbean and on all the important interior water courses, the Archaic peoples once lived. From place to place their material and non-material traits were variable, but as Haag[8] says: "An examination of the material culture content of the non-pottery horizons shows a significant percentage of correlation." He further says that the trait assemblages from site to site are not identical "but the cultural level of aboriginal economy . . . clearly indicates a marked accordancy of advancement along common lines of development." Fairbanks[9] makes this point even clearer by demonstrating through a comparison of traits that Stallings Island in Georgia has from 51.8 to 32.7 per cent of traits in common with four Kentucky and two New York sites.

Archaic remains, at least in the area under discussion, are usually shell middens ranging greatly in size (Fig. 138, A). An idea of their magnitude and artifactual richness, which implies either a very heavy or very long occupational history, can be quickly given. At Indian Knoll, Webb[10] reports 880 burials; from the entire excavation he reports 55,280 artifacts. These were divided thus: flint, 13,806; ground stone, 3,270; copper, 3; bone, 8,466; antler, 4,342; shell, 25,125; and all other 267. Or from Ct°27 Webb and DeJarnette[11] show 1,346 specimens of worked flint from one 5-foot thick slice across the shell bank. Other sites have been equally prolific.

The Archaic peoples lived, as far as we know, a simple, unfettered life, uncomplicated by stringent religious and civic duties. Although their remains are sometimes found in caves, the people usually favored high spots along the rivers or coasts where mussel shoals or oyster flats were easily and constantly available. A stable food supply thus permitted the development of semipermanent "villages" prior to the knowl-

4. Quimby, 1942.
5. Jennings, 1941.
6. Ford and Quimby, 1945.
7. Ford and Willey, 1941.
8. Haag, 1942a.
9. Fairbanks, 1942.
10. Webb, W. S., 1946.
11. Webb and DeJarnette, 1942.

edge of agriculture. Tremendous quantities of shell fish were eaten. (Cook[12] has some interesting speculations on population based on the re-analysis of California shell heaps.) Augmenting the evidently basic shellfish food were deer, bear, raccoon, rabbit, turkey, and various waterfowl. Fish were also eaten—these were caught with hook and line, and presumably with nets or weirs. Seeds, tubers, berries, and nuts were probably eaten in season. The people lived upon the shell heaps, in flimsy little shelters made of small poles and boughs presumed to have been no more than windbreaks or shade from the sun. Food was cooked on rude hearths scattered about the midden. The dead were buried at random in the site, usually in a tightly flexed position and crammed into small round pits. (Fig. 138, B). Even dogs were sometimes accorded pit burial. The chief weapon or hunting tool appears to have been the lance or dart, used with spear thrower. The latter was evidently of great importance to them. The hook or notch, against which the lance butt rested, was carefully carved of antler to resemble an outsize crochet needle (Fig. 138, E). The hook was affixed to a shaft which may have been weighted with a carefully shaped object of stone (called bannerstone) or pieces of cut shell. Usually the shaft slipped through a drilled hole in the weight. With these slender throwing sticks, evidently made with the greatest care, the Archaic hunters were probably expert. Most of their flint objects (tens of thousands have been recovered) are heavy, rudely chipped points thought to have been spear or lance points (Fig. 138, J). In later Archaic levels, at most sites there are stronger percentages of smaller flint tools.

How long did these people dominate the east? Webb and DeJarnette[13] imply that they lived unmolested on the Tennessee River for many centuries, even while in other sections much more advanced ideas were being practiced. They base their belief on a continuity of certain types of bone and stone artifacts found from early to late, found in the upper levels in undisturbed association with pottery known to have been used by later groups. However, if the collections from the Tennessee River sites were closely restudied for typological variation from bottom to top, it is possible that significant cultural change could be shown within the time spanned by the material. This is not intended to refute any statement that the shell heaps possibly remained in intermittent use over a long period, and possibly until fairly recently. Obviously, pottery of very recent type or burials intrusive into the shell deposits or accumulating upon the shell bear only an accidental physical relation to the Archaic remains.

Excellent summaries of these Archaic potteryless cultures by Fairbanks,[14] Haag,[15] and Webb and DeJarnette[16] are startlingly similar in their conclusions regarding the uniformity of the basic characteristics which can be considered diagnostic of this widespread, once numerous group.

Whether the Archaic groups possessed clay pottery is a simple matter of definition. Here we assume that they did not. Moreover, in the Lower Valley the Archaic as now known did not possess such a variety of implements or tools as the general run of Archaic sites in other sections, although this may be no more than a reflection of the inadequate sample of the Louisiana data as compared to other areas. The significant thing now appears to be that the Lower Valley Archaic differs little from the prepottery shell mound remains found elsewhere. Specific differences include pottery pipes, tubular in form, and the amorphous "Poverty Point" objects of clay which are two items not found elsewhere. Notable absentees in southern sites are such artifacts as grooved axes, pestles of any kind, firecracked stones in fireplaces, burials in round pits, dog burials, shell beads, bone bodkins, or pins, incisor teeth as tools, and copper in any form. The consistent absence of these items can be, and has been, interpreted in two ways. One explanation is that in the Lower Valley there exists an early level which lacks certain sophisticated elements and is therefore earlier than, and ancestral to, other more northerly centers, where the basic cultural form originating in the Lower Valley base was enriched by new ideas—either borrowed or invented. The alternate explanation is that the Lower Valley Archaic and Tchefuncte (Early Woodland) represent local peripheral forms of an Archaic level which arose to the east in Florida and Georgia or to the north in Tennessee, Alabama, and Kentucky, or possibly both.

In order to determine the content of the "average" Archaic site in Louisiana, I have compared all the traits except pottery which are found in the five midden sites reported by Ford and Quimby.[17] The objects or practices listed below are found at one or more of five sites: Little Woods, Big Oak, Tchefuncte A and B, and Copell. This list inventories the Archaic data fairly well.

Community	Burial
Shell middens	Burials in midden
Burned areas in midden	Primary burial flexed
Burned pits in midden	Human bones scattered
Middens along beach lines	Grave goods absent
Bundle burials	Burial in pits
Grave goods in burials	Poverty Point clay objects

12. Cook, 1946.   13. Webb and DeJarnette, 1942.

14. Fairbanks, 1942.
15. Haag, 1942a.
16. Webb and DeJarnette, 1942.
17. Ford and Quimby, 1945.

Flint
  Ovate triangular stemmed
    projectile points, 1–A
  Ovate triangular stemmed
    projectile points, 1–B
  Ovate triangular stemmed
    projectile points, barbed,
    1–A
  Narrow lanceolate
  Drills
  Flake scrapers
  Plano-convex scraper

Ground Stone
  Boatstone
  Plummets, grooved
  Sandstone saws
  Rubbing stones
  Hammerstones
  Bar weight
  Quartz
  Pitted stones(?)
  Metates
  Stone beads

Shell
  Shell gouges
  Conch container
  Circular gorgets

Rectangular gorget
Chisel
Inner whorls

Bone
  Socketed antler projectile
    points
  Antler harpoons
  Socketed deer bones
  Socketed metatarsals
  Socketed bones of small
    birds and animals
  Bone splinter points
  Ulna flakers
  Antler drifts
  Antler bones, unmarked
  2 Canine teeth, perforated
  Pelvis bones, otter
  Pelvis bones, coon
  Cut jaw
  Ulna awl
  Antler flaker
  Fishhook
  Splinter awl
  Antler handles
  Chisel
  Awls-cannon
  Turtle shell
  Asphaltum

At each site except Copell, however, pottery was found. Copell may therefore be considered for the sake of argument to be pre-pottery, i.e., true Archaic, and yet its chief significant difference from the others seems to lie only in its lack of pottery. The crude "Poverty Point" objects of clay appear to be earlier than pottery vessels.[18] At Poverty Point in Louisiana, C. H. Webb[19] reports quantities of stone vessel sherds (Fig. 138, I). Stone vessels characterize the Archaic of the Tennessee River and probably should, on the basis of his work, be considered as a trait of the Lower Mississippi Valley Archaic as well. They have been regarded here as typical Archaic artifacts.

Although the Archaic remains have been defined as lacking pottery, many sites continued to be occupied after pottery came into use. The history of the earliest pottery of the Southeast is briefly reviewed here before we leave the Archaic for a consideration of the Early Woodland groups. Throughout the Southeast the earliest pottery appears to have been fiber-tempered. The fibrous materials were vegetable shreds which disappeared during the firing of the clay, leaving channels or vesicles in the paste. At Stallings Island and the Bilbo Site, Georgia, and from the many Tennessee River sites in North Alabama, fiber-tempered sherds without decoration are the earliest forms. But there are in the Southeast at least three centers for the fiber-tempered pottery.[20] These

employed differing decorative techniques. The restricted St. Johns area emphasized incising to the exclusion of other techniques; whereas in Georgia punctating in various forms was the first decoration employed. In northern Alabama the fiber-tempered pottery was plain. Very early, however, a sand-tempered ware appeared on which the technique of rim embossing with nodes punched from the inside was coexistent with zoning and the punctating of Stallings Island. At the Tchefuncte site the pottery employed techniques observed in both St. Johns and north Alabama wares. The chronological significance of these variations in early pottery treatment is obscure. For the purposes of this paper, the Archaic is considered to be pre-pottery. Within limits a pre-pottery site would be considered older than an adjacent one which contained pottery.

Now, in order to describe the Early Woodland horizon, what must be done? To the Archaic complex just described one needs only to add several pottery types and mound burial, suspect that horticulture was practiced, and a new period exists! Note that the Lafayette Site differs from the sites just described in having a different location and in mound burial, in the possession of a celt, a stone effigy head, but, however, it lacks a rich industry in bone. What Ford and Quimby have called Tchefuncte can best be understood as a late Archaic or, better, a transition from the generalized Archaic base to the more specialized patterns of life which ensued.[21]

No attempt is made to minimize or belittle the few but significant additions to the aboriginal way of life which marked the beginning of Early Woodland (Tchefuncte) times. The very existence of pottery, its form, and the techniques of decoration proved to be of lasting importance. Numerous pottery types have been recognized and described (Fig. 139, D–T).[22] These types can be thus described in general. Tempered with angular pellets of clay and fine sand, it was predominantly plain surfaced, having been smoothed after coiled construction. The finished ware was soft and chalky, and therefore fragile. The form could be called a cylindrical pot, with nearly vertical sides. A slight enlargement in the middle was often combined with a slight taper to the flat base which might also have four legs. The legs varied in form but can be described as slab-like lumps or small cones firmly fastened to the base. Rims tended to be simple vertical ones. Occasional thickening of the rim by means of an exteriorly added coil is common. Lips were sometimes notched. When any surface decoration was applied, it generally extended from lip to base. Incising, stamping, pinching between thumb and forefinger, incising or trailing with deeper indentations of the incising tool in the bottom

18. Based on excavation by Phillips at Jaketown, Mississippi, Griffin, personal communication. This is also borne out by C. H. Webb and his work at Poverty Point.
19. Webb, C. H., 1944.
20. Griffin, J. B., 1945a.
21. Ford and Quimby, 1945.   22. Ibid.

of the grooved line, and dimple-like punctations inside zones (which made geometric figures) set off by incised lines are the characteristic techniques. One type of finish, found only on wide mouthed bowls, was a red film or wash applied over the entire vessel. Another very characteristic decorative treatment, found all over the Southeast wherever early sites have been worked, is a row of tiny nodes encircling the rim just below the lip. These nodes are made by pushing a small round-pointed tool or segment of reed into the still plastic clay from the interior of the vessel until the soft clay bulges outward to form the small but sharply defined conical knob. The pottery types set up to distinguish various combinations of characteristics in Louisiana are not unique. Similar, even identical, types are reported from Georgia (Stallings Island), Alabama (Pickwick Basin), Florida, and north Mississippi (Lee County).

While the Tchefuncte people were experimenting with a new way of life, there was a comparable culture, Miller I, in the northeast quarter of Mississippi, whose outlines can be faintly recognized. This local group was subject to influence from the inhabitants of the Tennessee River of north Alabama.

Miller I communities were small affairs located on the low terraces of the valleys of lesser creeks or on low bluffs along the myriad streams in the Tombigbee headwaters and on down the river toward Mobile. There is some evidence that there were houses built of small singly-set vertical posts, but this remains conjectural. Pottery vessels differed from that of the Lower Valley in being conoidal, small mouthed utensils with simple rim. Gritty and abrasive to the touch, made of sand and clay-tempered paste, the pottery is dull brown to fiery red in color and is characterized by fabric-marked (or cord-wrapped stick) impressions. In conjunction with this characteristic pottery, plain fiber-tempered pieces indistinguishable from the fiber-tempered specimens of the Tennessee River, occur in significant percentages. The one known burial lay flexed, face and chest downward in a small pit. Over the burial had been placed a cover or "paving" of large fabric-marked sherds (Fig. 139, C). The physical type to which this individual belonged has not been determined.

Mound burial in Louisiana on the basis of data at the Lafayette site[23] was not yet such a complex series of events as was typical in other areas where, at the same time, other groups were practicing mound burial (Fig. 139, B). The Lafayette Mound was one of a group of three located on the banks of the Vermillion River. It was essentially and only a burial mound. In a very shallow irregular pit, cleared of surface soil, a number of bodies were laid down. Then a low dome of earth about 2½ feet high was built over, and larger

23. Ibid.

than, the pit. This first eminence built of black earth, filled with debris, was covered by another 2½ foot mantle of similar earth. The final accretion contained no burials. There was an arc of post molds under the mound. This arc probably is referable to the village site, and its inclusion within the circumference of the mound a coincidence. At least no evidence of structural relationship between the vertical pole construction and the earthen mound was brought out. These facts can be generalized thus: mounds were built in one or more increments, but contained no burials in the secondary mantle. In other areas where the burial mound was in use, a much more complex series of events evidently transpired during the period of construction. In Kentucky, Indiana, and Illinois the Adena culture and its variants were coexistent with the Tchefuncte of Louisiana. Their burial complex was more elaborate. Cremation, both partial and complete, was practiced. Clay lined basins or pits beneath the mound served as crematories. Log tombs, ranging from simple pens one log high, to roofed log cribs several logs in height, were frequently built as the nuclei of burial mounds; the conical mounds were often in groups sometimes within earthen well-like enclosures.

Physically, there are differences between the people of the Archaic and Early Woodland stages. In Archaic times we note a longheaded, slender individual of medium height who did not deform their heads. In the Tchefuncte population, however, there was a broadheaded element. These latter also practiced skull deformation. The presence of a new physical type is interpreted as evidence that new peoples had arrived; with them they brought the idea of mound burial, and possibly the news of pottery. In any event the new folk and the complex of new ideas seem to have appeared simultaneously.

Summaries are often simplified to a point past strict accuracy, but to conclude this section, a brief recapitulation of the known Early Woodland cultural practices is offered. The stage is characterized by burial mounds. Uusally the mounds are small, conical ones, located on elevated sites where there are elevations available (Fig. 139, A). Mounds are frequently not near a village or dwelling site. Bodies were placed on prepared floors (Louisiana) or in pits beneath the original surface. Burial in small open pits was also in vogue. Dwellings were built of posts set vertically in the ground. House shape was circular or rectangular. Tobacco probably came into use during this period; in any event tubular clay and stone pipes are a diagnostic artifact (Fig. 139, U). Copper apparently enjoyed a precious metal status and was employed for various ornaments. There is a faint suspicion that agriculture characterized the life of the people. Pottery making was adopted and a distinct complex of associated types developed. Plain vessels predominated. Flat bases and an unusual four footed basal treatment were predominant (Fig. 139, *H*) and a globular jar with slightly constricted neck and outflaring rim were the common vessel forms. The characteristic basal forms were used for both types of vessel.[24] Decoration of pottery was still done by incising, stamping, and pinching. Then, in some cases, the area inside the zoning lines was further emphasized by rocker stamping or punctation. Another significant item is that by the end of the period fiber tempering of pottery had been abandoned. Sand, crushed clay pellets, or crushed grit were now used exclusively. Generally this cluster of new ideas is grafted almost imperceptibly onto the widespread Archaic habits of living.

The distribution of these first burial mounds and the thousands of villages is extensive. They are found on the valley floors as was true of the Louisiana Tchefuncte sites; along the Mississippi River from New Orleans to Illinois, up the major tributaries of this river and in the hills of Mississippi, Alabama, Tennessee, and Georgia, as well as Arkansas and Missouri. These conical mounds also occur on ridges and on low terraces beside streams of all magnitude. Not enough of them are excavated to permit an accurate synthesis of the general culture of the day, or its extreme limits of occurrence.

MIDDLE WOODLAND

Continuing the basic trends of the earlier stages, the Middle Woodland depends for its characteristic flavor upon relatively few new trait complexes (Fig. 140). Its most noticeable differences from the Archaic and Early Woodland lie in the elaboration of earlier concepts in new forms. Included within this Middle Woodland stage are the Louisiana phenomena called Marksville, the Early Baytown of Arkansas and Mississippi, Miller II, the Copena of Alabama, the Santa Rosa of west Florida,[25] the Hopewellian of south Alabama,[26] and possibly the small conical mounds which lie between Natchez and Jackson, Mississippi. Most or all of these are local variants of a culture manifestly related to the Hopewellian of Ohio. The term "Delta Aspect" has been proposed for Marksville and Troyville.[27] According to Ford,[28] Marksville period pottery is found in collections in a continuous zone along the bluffs and alluvial valley of the Mississippi River from Baton Rouge almost to Memphis. The recent survey of the Central Mississippi Valley confirms Ford's distribution map, however, by discovery of a number of sites where Marksville pottery types

occur as a minor type. Relatively full data about the Marksville remains of Louisiana have been recovered from the Crooks Site[29] and from Marksville proper.[30]

Before becoming too greatly preoccupied with related cultures, it behooves us to review the traits which characterize the Marksville of Louisiana. Details of mound construction are available from three sites. These are Marksville Mounds 4 and 8,[31] Crooks,[32] and McQuorquodale.[33] The mound sites are found in a flood plain away from the associated village. Mounds are domed or conical in shape, as much as 100 feet in diameter and as much as 20 feet in height. In each known case the construction of a mound began with the removal of top soil over the area to be used for mound base. Then a low, flat-topped platform of earth roughly 30 feet or 40 feet square, and no more than three or four feet high was fashioned. In the case of Crooks the earth for the platform was evidently borrowed immediately beside the platform site. After a mass or group burial (6 individuals at McQuorquodale; over 250 at Crooks) was made on the platform, a conical heap of earth was placed upon the platform. This earth, of course, covered the dead. At Marksville this procedure varied in that there were log tombs for the dead let down into the prepared platform. At Crooks 168 bodies had been included within the primary mound itself. In all cases, however, the ceremony was apparently incomplete until the final conical mound was built. The fill over the platform was always followed by a second mantle of earth which enveloped the entire original structure or structures. In the secondary accretion burials were sometimes included, as in the case of Crooks. These burials were placed at random and singly throughout the layer, usually in shallow basins or depressions made to receive the body or bodies (Fig. 140, *A*).

The facts of mound construction outlined above can be reduced to this: Mounds are primarily built as burial monuments or tombs. First, was made the low rectangular platform. Bodies were placed on the platform. Then a second stage—an enveloping mantle—was added. A third stage was the further enlargement and increase in height by addition of another mantle of earth. There were various uses for the initial platform. It might surround one or more log structures; it might have many bodies included within it at the time of construction; and it was apparently always used for a mass funeral. As for the treatment of individual dead, the predominant position is still full flexion, although many cases of isolated skull burial occur. The partially flexed or

24. *Ibid.*, Figs. 17, 18.
25. Willey and Woodbury, 1942.
26. Wimberly and Tourtelot, 1941.
27. Griffin, J. B., 1946.
28. Ford, 1935.

29. Ford and Willey, 1941.
30. Setzler, 1933, 1940.
31. Fowke, 1928; Setzler, 1940.
32. Ford and Willey, 1940.
33. Wimberly and Tourtelot, 1941.

the bundle burial was common; the extended position is very rare. The practice of blanketing the body in mussel shell occurs often enough to be considered a diagnostic trait. The practice of placing some object with the dead was still far from common, but it was becoming more popular. Eighty-four per cent of all burials at Crooks had no artifacts with them. Grave goods, although present in 16 per cent of the cases, were scanty in amount.

At both Crooks and Marksville grave pits were sometimes lined with bark or matting. Many of the artifacts of the Marksville period inventory are objects familiar from the earlier cultures. Chipped stone implements exist in greater variety. The predominant projectile point type is the stemmed; both barbed and simple forms occur (Fig. 140, G–K). According to a very worthwhile analysis[34] there appears to be a chronological significance in the frequency of occurrence of various types of these crudely executed tools. Briefly, this significance is that there appears to be a trend in the more recent cultures toward greater precentage of the barbed haft types, with a resultant decrease in simple hafting. This does not mean that one lone projectile point will carry a chronological tale. All these types occur from Archaic to historic times, but on a percentage basis the trend may exist.

Marksville pottery is distinctive and again provides the most clearcut cultural clue (Fig. 140, R–V; Fig. 141, A–L). Many types have been isolated and described. A generalized description will here be adequate to demonstrate the specialized direction of development. The pottery was made by coiling, the aplastic was burned clay, with both sand and grit also present. In plain vessels the texture was coarse, the paste contorted. Decorated vessels tended to have a fine paste with less contortion. Vessel shapes were varied. Bowls, shallow bowls, beakers, pots or jars with constricted neck and outflaring rims were common in plain ware. In the decorated ware, the most common form was the globular pot. These vessels had high rounded shoulders with the lower two-thirds of the vessel sloping inward toward a small flat base. A special four-lobed vessel was very characteristic. The rim, which is a special diagnostic feature, was either vertical or slightly outflaring, and might be either simple, thickened on the exterior by addition of an extra coil, or cambered (camber is here used to mean a slight horizontal interior concavity matching the exterior bulge of the rim or collar). The fine hatching or cross-hatching of the cambered rim was a prime decorative characteristic of all types of the period. Whether plain or decorated the pottery possesses the flat bottom. It was sometimes square (as in the case of lobed pots) but usually was round.

Decoration, if present on a vessel without a specialized rim, covered the vessel from lip to base. A separate zone of neck decoration appeared on those vessels with specialized rim. Two basic decorative techniques exist—the deep U-trough made by incising or trailing with a round tipped tool and a toothed rocker stamp. Designs consisted of smooth zones, set off by trailed or incised lines. The zones make figures, the background was almost always roughened by the rocker stamp. Smooth and rough bands alternate. The raptorial or spoon bill bird is the most commonly used figure. Although each figure is unique, the conventional bird motif dominates. Other vessels were covered by parallel trailed lines, which are looped and arced over the entire vessel to make graceful imaginative designs. Nested circles and squares were also used. All decorative techniques can be found on the rare, but diagnostic, "boot" shaped vessel. A variation on the rocker stamping was found at the Crooks Site where one type is characterized by roughening produced by the crinkled edge of some species of scallop. The fabric (or cord-wrapped stick) marked pottery of Miller I is represented at the Crooks Site.[35]

A new technique of pottery decoration first appeared in the Southeast at this time. This was the use of a film of red pigment to set off the negative zone in place of the rocker stamping. Relatively rare, it may stem from the red filming of the Early Woodland stage and it presages a time when color was to be widely used (Fig. 140, V). It should be remembered in the welter of distinctive decorated types and new techniques that plain undecorated ware was the overwhelming style. For example, at Crooks the plain types comprised 33 of 84 whole vessels and in total sherds 11,620 of 14,402—approximately three out of four.

The other material objects possessed by the people of Crooks and Marksville are not as spectacular as the pottery, but are, within certain limits, of diagnostic value. Several new items have appeared. In stone the ground celt had been acquired (Fig. 140, M). Sandstone human effigies and the monitor or platform pipe are new in the region (Fig. 140, B, C). Platform pipes of pottery were new; tubular clay pipes continued to be used. Copper was used more commonly; solid copper earspools, rolled tubes (small and large), and copper bracelets were now made (Fig. 140). Galena in the form of beads was known, but was evidently rare (Fig. 140, L). Quartz crystals were still highly prized. Bone, at Crooks, was almost nonexistent. Five fishhooks and two awls were the only bone tools found (Fig. 140, D–F). This, of course, may be explained on the basis that the mounds contain fewer items of all kinds than do the shell

---

34. Ford and Willey, 1940.

35. *Ibid.*, Fig. 20k and *j*, Fig. 28c; Fig. 34.

middens. Pearls were used for the first time.

Below is a condensed listing of artifacts, minus pottery, lifted bodily from Ford and Willey:[36]

MARKSVILLE ARTIFACTS

Chipped Stone
  Barbed haft projectile
    points
  Simple haft projectile
    points
  Chipped celt
  Drills
  Polished chipped stone
  Hammerstones
  Knives
  Rough chipped stone, various rejects
  Scrapers

Ground Stone
  Boatstones
  Plummets
  Stone beads
  Monitor pipe
  Gorgets
  Celts
  Effigies, human
  Effigies, grasshopper
  Hammerstones
  Miscellaneous stone and pebbles

Shell
  Pearl beads
  Shell, small, beads
  Deposits of shell
  Conch columnella pendant

Bone
  Fishhooks
  Awls

Ceramic
  Pipe, curved base
  Pipe, curved base effigy
  Pipes, tubular
  Clay effigy
  Balls, biconical

Mineral
  Copper earspools
  Copper tubular bead
  Copper bracelet
  Galena bead
  Quartz crystals
  Red ocher masses

While Marksville dominated the Lower Valley, there existed at the same time a very closely related series of cultures in other areas. The Copena of Tennessee and Alabama built conical burial mounds, possessed the log tomb, indulged in the practice of cremation, used a limestone-tempered pottery, made and treasured a wide variety of copper objects, used bone for many tools, utilized many galena crystals for some purpose, and made massive zoomorphic pipes of stone.

There exists along the Florida and Alabama coasts a culture called Santa Rosa[37] which is the cultural equivalent of Marksville. It shares more traits with Marksville than does Copena.

As for the distribution of material, it can be said to blanket the Lower Valley.[38] Since the work of the Central Mississippi Survey, Marksville is known to occur in Middle Woodland levels as far up the river as Memphis[39] and to follow each major tributary of the Mississippi as it ascends the river. I suspect that gaps in its occurrence as plotted by Setzler[40] mean nothing except that the blank spaces are unexplored. The main river does not seem to have been the path of Hopewell spread. The early pottery seems to have come into the valley from the east down the west flowing streams.

In the delta of Mississippi and Arkansas as well as the hinterlands of Mississippi, the Baytown–Miller II cultures coexisted with the more spectacular Marksville–Santa Rosa–Hopewellian–Copena groups. These former folk built groups of two to six domed conical mounds, employed copper for artifacts, used Gulf shell for ornaments and pretty generally followed the habits of the times. But they are characterized by a radically different pottery technology. Their sand-tempered or burned clay-tempered wares nearly universally had cord-marked paddle surface treatment (although fabric-impressed pieces were still made). Vessel shapes also differ from the Marksville specimens. This pottery tradition stemmed from eastern sources, and did not become popular in the Lower Valley, although cord-marked pottery is reported 18 inches deep in a 24 inch deposit from the Marksville village site.[41] One vessel at Crooks was textile-impressed or marked with a cord-wrapped stick. This same distinctive style of finish was coexistent with cord marking in northeast Mississippi in heavy percentages in Miller I, but less frequent in Miller II. Another diagnostic trait of these interior peoples is the small crude projectile point. This is found, in significant percentage, wherever cord marking is predominant. The projectile point is poorly chipped by percussion from a rough piece of flint. In section it is lozenge like. A rudimentary stem or haft and a slim, carelessly executed body characterize the form, which is about an inch long.[42] This form, of course, is in addition to the larger points reported from other Middle Woodland cultures.

To exemplify the cultural practices of this less publicized interior group, the Miller II complex is reviewed.[43] Twin burial mounds, conical or domed, are common. At the type site in Lee County, Mississippi, the mounds were 13 feet by 85 feet in size. Built exclusively for burial purposes, the mounds were constructed of clean sterile clay containing no cultural material. Either construction was continuous or the surface of one stage was carefully cleaned before additional earth was put in place, because there was no hint of more than one construction phase. The yellow soil used in construction was quite uniform in color throughout. Before the mound was built, humus was first cleared away for a base. Then a quick-burning fire was lighted over much of the cleared area, two or three dignitaries were either placed in shallow pits in the burned area or (in one case) placed between two thin layers of contrasting yellow clay, and the placing of mound fill began.

36. *Ibid.*
37. Willey and Woodbury, 1942.
38. Ford, 1935, Fig. 1; Setzler, 1940, Fig. 16, show its known distribution on these dates.
39. Phillips, personal communication.
40. Setzler, 1940, Fig. 16.
41. Ford and Willey, 1940.
42. Collins, 1932, Pl. 9.
43. Subsequent paragraphs based on Jennings, 1941; 1944.

Burials were also included at random within the mound as it was raised. Normally burials were made in extended positions; graves rarely contained grave goods. If grave furniture was included it was usually pottery, although a double burial which was blanketed in clay had copper earspools of undetermined type, a conch shell vessel, and a limestone platform pipe as grave objects (Fig. 141, *M*). Oval (15 × 20 feet) or subrectangular (20 × 20 feet) houses were built of vertical posts set singly in individual post holes in shallow irregular depressions two to three feet in diameter by three or four inches deep near the center of the house. Houses were heated by fires. No attempt was made to model a rim or otherwise shape the fire basins. The celt and plano-convex discoidals both were made of ground stone. One cube of galena was found on a village site. Irregular pitted stones, roughly shaped milling stones, and rough pebble hammerstones were found. Flint objects, most of which were stemmed points and knives, were usually large and of relatively rough workmanship. The small, poorly executed projectile point, elsewhere mentioned as diagnostic of the era, occurred quite frequently (Fig. 141, *O*). About 96 per cent of the pottery was plain or cord-marked (Fig. 141, *P*). Two types were discernible. One is made of a homogeneous paste heavily tempered with fine sand. Sherds are gritty and friable in the hands. A second, slightly later type, contains less sand but includes clay pellets as tempering material. Both occur in plain form or have cord-wrapped paddle marks irregularly over the surface. Both types are varying shades of grey-brown and red in color. Associated with this dominant cord-marked complex were numerous minority pottery types known from contemporary cultures in other portions of the Southeast (Fig. 141, *Q*). This important group of sherds comprises only 4 per cent of the entire assemblage from the type site.

The Middle Woodland levels of the Lower Valley can be briefly recapitulated as follows: Mounds, in groups, are located on flood plains near rivers away from the villages. Mounds are still built in two or more stages, but the various stages are specialized. The nucleus of the mound is the primary platform. The log tomb continued in use as was cremation. Bone was now used only for awls, projectile points, and fishhooks. Atlatl hooks and handles have disappeared. In ground stone the grooved ax is supplemented by the celt. Platform pipes, plain and effigy, and the elbow pipe are new stone objects. Shell cups, beads, and gorgets occur as well as pearls. Flint is still generally heavy, but some small, delicately chipped points appear. Pottery displays a very characteristic complex of associated traits, the cambered rim, flat bottom, four-lobed pot, and shouldered jar, the raptorial bird design, and zoned decorative techniques, are all developments of earlier styles. In fact the raptorial bird is a constant decorative element. It appears on hundreds of vessels. Its appearance is modified to fit the medium, but this bird, its talons, and a series of conventionalized symbols seemed to dominate the thinking of the craftsmen of the age. This device was common in the north as well. In the interior, the Baytown-Miller cultures flourished; their differing traits have been indicated.

EARLY MISSISSIPPI

Considering how generally widespread the evidences of the Mississippi cultures are over the south, there is surprisingly little systematic published work upon which to base a synthesis.

In the Lower Valley, Early Mississippi includes two important cultures which have been called Troyville and Coles Creek. Coles Creek is a form which is evidently widespread, but at present only the pottery complex has been adequately defined. Whether the rest of the culture is uniform and widespread is unknown. Typical Coles Creek pottery is found all over most of the area with which this study is concerned. Troyville, considered by Ford and Willey[44] to possess the dignity of a full cultural phase, will finally be considered, I think, nothing more than a transition site where new traits moving west from Florida and east from Texas in a leisurely fashion were in part adopted by what was probably a late Marksville group. It must again be pointed out that, as a period, Troyville exists only as a pottery complex; moreover, it is a pottery complex which is often difficult to distinguish from the closely related Marksville complex. The one site, at Troyville, Louisiana, was never thoroughly explored. Walker[45] has published a short report of certain salvage data, but by no means did he completely analyze the culture. For practical purposes Troyville is a transition site, equal in age to Coles Creek and Middle Baytown of the same region, since in all but pottery it possesses the new traits of the Mississippi period. There are no well reported Mississippi sites from the Lower Valley, although Ford[46] has, as mentioned above, segregated a well defined pottery complex labeled Coles Creek, which typifies the Lower Valley Mississippi material (Fig. 142, *D–M*).

The Mississippi cultures represent the impact of a new series of ideas upon the widespread Middle Woodland peoples. What these new ideas were can be fairly well sorted out.

Opening phases of the new stage can first be detected in a new mound form, built in a new way, for a different purpose. Mounds became squared truncated pyramids, built, rebuilt, and many times en-

44. Ford and Willey, 1940.   46. Ford, 1935; 1936.
45. Walker, W. M., 1936.

larged. Each rebuilding or addition served as a foundation for one of a series of successive temples or other structures of religious function. The mound was thus no longer a grave marker or monument to the dead—it was a foundation for a temple or town house. It is true that burials of presumably important personages may be found in these mounds in grave pits let down from the hard packed floors of the current summit but the primary reason for mound construction had changed from burial crypt to temple site. And the arrangement of mounds had altered. Previously the tumuli were loosely grouped, or occurred singly. Now the square, flat-topped eminences were usually grouped so as to outline a hollow square or plaza. The plaza and mounds were the heart of a religious center where it is assumed a sacred governing cast of priest-rulers dwelt. Some of the mounds were huge. Thirty to sixty feet height is ordinary for the dominant mound of a group. On the plaza side of some mounds lay a ramp with a lesser gradient than that of the steep mounds. Sometimes logs were embedded in these ramps, or log stairs very like modern stairs were built to provide easy access to the surrounding buildings.

Continuous emphasis in the descriptive literature upon the pyramidal nature of the new type of mounds has implied the entire disappearance of the domed burial mound. However, this did not happen. In the Mississippi flood plain (at such early sites as Lake George,[47] Fig. 142, C) there was often a huge mound, pyramidal in shape; compactly satellite to it were 10 to 40 lower mounds—some domed and some flattened. Around the entire site will usually be found a deep ditch, and inside the ditch or moat an earthen rampart. These large sites are located in wide river valleys or alluvial lands where fertile soils were, and still are, found.

Burial customs also shifted somewhat. Fleshing of burials, as well as cremation, was practiced, although cemeteries are presumed to have been in use by Coles Creek times. The practice of burying the personal possessions of the dead with them began to be popular. All these significant new trends imply, we assume, the existence of a social and religious system of considerable complexity, with its attendant castes and privileges.

The number of mound groups indicates a denser population than at any previous time. There are hundreds of villages and mound groups. The mounds represent literally millions of man-days of labor. Time thus lost from food-getting argues for a stable food supply which only an advanced agricultural practice could have supplied. Archeological evidence supports the view that these people were good farmers, tilling the best lands of the wide rich river terraces, and possessed therefore of certain leisure seasons. Evidently various craft guilds or individual artisan specialists developed. In flint and copper and shell, the work grew finer. But in pottery, with its new techniques of construction, its variety of form and diversity of specialized appendages and the use of shell as tempering material, lies the greatest departure from the relatively narrow limits of tradition.

Some of the innovations in pottery treatment are the loop handle, polishing of plain vessels, thinner, stronger wares, and nodes or ears around the rim; beakers, bowls, and plates are new shapes replacing the commoner simple jars of the previous cultures. Decoration is normally confined to the upper part of the vessel. Incising, punctating, and trailing were still the common decorative techniques, but the designs and the manner of execution would not be confused with the Marksville ceramic tradition. Red painting in zones defined by incised lines continued to be popular. Sometimes the whole vessel received a thin wash of red clay. Pottery elbow pipes were very common but the platform style had disappeared. Heavy effigy pipes, human and animal, were realistically carved (Fig. 143, O–Q). These massive effigy pipes are virtually a new form, different both from the earlier effigies which in one form (Copena) were rude and heavy and from the platform pipes of Marksville which were realistically carved but small in size. In architecture vertical poles were set in trenches, rather than in individual holes as had been previously done. The round community house still was popular in some areas, although square houses and temples were also being built with the trench-pole type of construction.

On some sites, such as Troyville, the older pottery tradition seems to have continued dominant while the ceremonial mound, the plaza, and the temple pattern were being fixed. On the other hand, at sites in the hill lands back from the Mississippi River, the domed mounds and the cord-marked pottery style were still popular well after the Mississippi influence had been felt. Early Mississippi period sites in the Mississippi flood plain show the temple mound and plaza as an idea strongly fixed, while the Baytown pottery remains in use.

The Mississippi culture has been long regarded as having arisen, and developed, somewhere on the Mississippi River, probably south of Memphis. Although this may be true, recent developments have led some scholars to think the original impetus for the culture may have entered the Mississippi Valley from the Southwest or from Mexico, and that the earliest Mississippi culture remains are those in eastern Texas and Oklahoma on the sites of the Gibson Aspect.[48]

47. [There is reasonable doubt that Lake George is entirely an early site. It begins in Coles Creek but continues up to Late Mississippi times.—Ed.]

48. Krieger, 1947a.

Too little data are at hand for a settlement of this question as to where the Mississippi culture developed its basic identifying characteristics. There is no doubt that the Mississippi culture is essentially Mexican in inspiration. From precisely what area or how or at what point in time this thrust occurred is still conjectural.

After the initial period of impact and dominance just described and called Early Mississippi, came a period of climax. Upon the complicated social and religious system which undoubtedly existed and into an already full technology, an incredible elaboration appeared. This cultural zenith, while widespread, did not penetrate into all the remote areas. It is the best known of any of the prehistoric levels of the Southeast. It is characterized briefly thus: the huge mound sites were now composed of square and linear mounds arranged about a plaza. The mounds were still built in stages; upon each stage a temple—square in outline—had been built; each building was destroyed by fire before additional construction began. There is evidence that each construction stage was initiated by the death of a priest or other sacred person because so often there was a burial inside the temple in a pit let down from the floor before the temple was burned and new construction started. The extended burials had numerous artifacts with them. Burial of commoners was made in cemeteries, whereas religious and civil leaders were interred in the temple mounds. The bundle burial of fleshed bodies was common in the Lower Valley. Certain stone objects were well chipped but in the Lower Valley small, rather crude projectile points, greatly resembling the forms of the Woodland cultures but smaller in size, predominated. Polished celts were common. Beautiful shell gorgets, shell beads, hairpins, and earpins were generally used. Pottery, shell-tempered, was exuberantly varied in form. Painting, including polychrome painting, in the Lower Valley was highly developed. In the states of Mississippi and Tennessee the cord marking of pottery may have persisted. Houses and temples continued in the square or rectangular shape which predominated in the earlier stages. Specialization in burial system occurred in the Tennessee-Cumberland region where stone slab graves in vast cemeteries was the common burial technique.

In all its phases and wherever found, the Mississippi was a rich culture. Tools and utensils were numerous and varied. Farming tools included stone or shell hoes as well as the digging stick. Myriads of triangular well chipped points imply the heavy use of the bow and arrow, although heavier flint specimens (drills, knives, and scrapers) are common. No grooved axes were used, but the hafted polished celt in all sizes was abundant, and used for woodworking. Bone and stone fishhooks were common.

To most people, students and layman alike, this climax typifies the prehistoric southern Indian. And the objects best known are those referable to what has been called the Southern Cult. Numerous students have recently offered analyses of these artifacts.[49] Whatever its origin or significance, the Southern Cult sat supreme upon the land.

The entire aggregation of artifacts which make up the very late prehistoric culture of the Mississippi Valley seems to be no more than the climax of the chain of aesthetic and social development begun on the thousand miserable shell heaps of the seashores and river banks. Its abrupt disappearance has been credited to the simultaneous appearance of Europeans and smallpox, syphillis, or the common cold. In any event, it waned to be finally observed in a decadent form by the French among the Taensa and Natchez tribes. That its star declined rapidly is undenied. But its beginning was slower and can almost be charted. At Spiro, Orr's[50] preliminary analysis is presented in such a way as to show that the Southern Cult was not exotic but developed from earlier levels most closely allied in form and content to the Coles Creek remains. At Emerald[51] near Natchez (Fig. 142, A), one recovers Coles Creek sherds, Southern Cult material (massive kneeling effigy pipes), and historic Natchez pottery. I anticipate that exploration of this gigantic site may produce another "cult center"; at nearby Anna (an even more spectacular site), a comparable sequence of artifacts has been recovered (Fig. 142, B).

The general account of the Middle and Lower Valley climax remains just finished is oversimplified. Actually for the southern part of our area it is misleading. What happened apparently was that the complex of traits of the Middle River did not achieve universal popularity in the Lower Valley. Numerous characteristic climax sites now known lie north of a line running east-west through Alexandria, Louisiana, and McComb, Mississippi, even though the typical pottery is to be found on the shores of Ponchartrain and on the fan of the delta at the mouth of the Mississippi River. The traits (painted pottery, the exotic stone, copper, and shell) of this late climax phase are not generally found south of Natchez, although they are spectacularly numerous near Natchez and farther north along the bluffs to Vicksburg and along the streams of the alluvial plains of Arkansas and Mississippi. At Gahagan[52] most of the artifacts recovered appear to be in the late style, although

49. Waring and Holder, 1945; Phillips, 1940; Krieger, 1945; Webb and Snow, 1945; Griffin, 1944a; Waring, 1945a; and others.
50. Orr, K. G., 1946.
51. This site was first called Emerald, after the plantation name, by B. L. C. Wailes in the 1850's. Later it took the name Selsertown from a small town, now extinct, which grew up around a tavern operating alongside the Natchez Trace.
52. Webb and Dodd, 1939.

Gahagan has been considered as belonging to the Gibson Aspect.

The Late Mississippi of the Lower Valley differs in several ways from the remains higher up the river. What these differences are, are fairly well known to those working with the material but no published data are at hand. A local culture called Plaquemine has been isolated.[53] This has not yet been fully described, but in a general way this short period can be defined more in terms of what it lacks than in what it possesses. The late era here, as elsewhere, often poses a delicate choice of selection. The period is so recent that it is hard to separate from the historic decline of the seventeenth century. As best I can determine, the Plaquemine of Louisiana still possessed and used the burial mound in conjunction with the temple mound. The pottery was often plain, did not possess the same flamboyance of form, nor was the use of paint so common. Large sites where many mounds represented the large religious center for an adjacent village were lacking.

The traits which generally characterize the latest prehistoric period in the Lower Valley were cited by Ford.[54] Here he indicates the significant elements of a complex he calls the Big Black series of his Tunica complex (Fig. 143, A–D, F–H, M). The Big Black series comprises sites in the vicinity of Jackson, Mississippi. To these sites the Anna, Ferguson, and many other sites near Natchez can be added. From Anna, as a result of the construction of a trench silo through one of the mounds, typical Coles Creek Incised and Natchez Incised pottery were recently recovered— but from different places in the mound. Ford[55] also tabulates Natchez material from Anna. Nearby, the fabulous Emerald (Selsertown) site yields Coles Creek and Natchez sherds plus many effigy pipes.[56] The percentages of Coles Creek sherds from these sites, however, is low. The site also has many late elements in its detail of construction, being very similar to the sites on the St. Francis River in Arkansas. I fancy that extensive research will demonstrate that the Big Black and Natchez area sites will prove to have existed from early Mississippi times to the last decades of the seventeenth century.

Ford's list of characteristic Big Black elements follows:

Small, steep conical burial mounds	Biconcave discoidal stones
Large rectangular truncate mounds	Quartz crystals
Liberal burial furniture	Elbow pipes
Skeletons extended	Stone earspools, plated with copper
Skeletons flexed	Fossil shark's teeth
Isolated skull burials	Unshaped lumps of galena
Bundle burials	Plummets of iron ore
Skulls capped with bowls	Lens-shaped masses of green clay

Masses of red ocher	Chipped celts of flint
Ear pins of *Busycon columnella*	Grooved sandstone abraders
Disk-shaped beads of shell	Chert knives or side scrapers
Tubular beads of shell	Leaf-shaped flints
Beads of Marginella	Triangular-shaped projectile points
Tubular beads of stone	Stemmed projectile points
Smooth ground celts, usually greenstone	Flint awls or hand drills
	Terrapin carapaces

The traits which typify Plaquemine in Louisiana will probably not be greatly different from the list above.

Since the above was written, an ambitious attempt to assess the Indian cultures of the south, and their relationship to each other, has been put forward by Griffin.[57] He has therein mentioned the many points of similarity, and disparity, between the widespread cultures of the eastern half of the continent. Some of his statements of relationship are categorical, but in many cases examples are adduced. In his general treatment of the late Lower Valley cultures[58] he, I think quite correctly, points out the culturally mixed and uncertain content of Deasonville, as well as the elusive nature of Coles Creek, and further says of the Big Black Focus that it "has relationship to the earlier Coles Creek on the one hand and, on the other, to such late Middle Mississippi foci as Alpika . . . and to Moundville." Throughout this paper Griffin also emphasizes the centuries of continuity of many cultural objects and customs in the south; he also takes cognizance of changed emphases and an acceleration of cultural development.

HISTORICAL DECLINE

Despite the relatively elusive nature of the more recent Lower Valley cultures, we observe in the Historical Decline period an even greater inconclusiveness. Ford[59] recognized how uncertain his evidence for his latest periods was. He was compelled to lump together ceramic material now recognized as belonging to separate eras. He delineated a series of related pottery complexes which were the most recent in the Lower Valley. These he called Natchez, Caddo, Tunica, and Choctaw, tentatively identifying them as the prehistoric debris left by the tribes historically bearing these names. Since that time Quimby[60] has shown that this first roughing out can and will be refined into clear subdivisions, some of which will be allocated to the Late Middle Mississippi period, and others to the Historical Decline. Ford showed that in the latest of his three periods the conical burial mound remained in use until historic times, and the pottery of his four complexes is remarkably similar, the differences being temporal (Tunica) or local development (Natchez or Choctaw). Ford's difficulty with the recent data emphasizes how uncertain is the

---

53. Quimby, 1942.
54. Ford, 1936, p. 128.
55. *Ibid.*
56. Brown, C. B., 1926.
57. Griffin, J. B., 1946. The paper was written, however, in 1939–1942.
58. *Ibid.*, pp. 80 ff.
59. Ford, 1936.
60. Quimby, 1942.

point where climax becomes historic decadence. I hasten to point out that no one thinks that material outlined by Quimby as being typical of the Natchez or Choctaw was used *only* by these two groups. Although I regard the Choctaw and Natchez materials as more effectively tied to an historic ethnic group than is that which is labeled Caddo, it would be folly to assert that wherever a sherd of Chickachae Combed was found, there too had been a Choctaw. But the pottery types listed by Quimby can be regarded as reliable indicators of time. The distribution of both these types extends as far as the extreme northeast county of Mississippi.

The sketch of the content of Historical Decline cultures now provided has been abridged from Quimby's Natchezan.[61]

In layout and location the Natchezan sites follow the precedent of earlier time by being on sizeable streams near arable lands (Fig. 144, *A*). Flat topped mounds are arranged about a plaza but the low domed burial mound appears alongside the truncated pyramids. Probably most of the villages, and possibly the temple and plaza areas as well, were palisaded, but archeological evidence is lacking. Early accounts do not mention palisades except for the Bayogoula. Upon the flat topped mounds, temples of priest-chieftain houses were constructed. These houses were rectangular as were the dwellings. The dwellings were made of posts set in trenches. The temples were characterized by bird effigies upon the roof-tree.

In burial customs the historic groups were following two traditions. Priest-rulers were buried inside the temples, which of course meant that they were interred, with rich and bloody ceremony, in the upper level of the pyramidal mounds upon which the temple stood. But, at the same time, bodies of less important tribesmen were placed in burial mounds. Others probably went into cemeteries. Many burials were bundle type which means that the historically observed practice of placing the dead on platforms until decomposition had separated flesh from bones was common. The bundle burials, of course, had occurred to the north since the Early Woodland period. Presumably, the historic practice of platform burial also began in that era. Both the extended and flexed positions for flesh burials were still in use.

Again we are forced to discuss a culture largely in terms of its pottery. Coil made, thin, and generally well baked, the pottery is tempered with fine grit, fine sand, fine ground shell, tiny clay pellets, or combinations of these substances. Vessel form varies rather widely. There were wide shallow bowls with rounded bottoms, water bottles, both long and short necked, with flat bottoms, the small mouthed, short necked pot, deep wide mouthed vessels, both with

and without outflaring rims, a few jars, a few shallow plate-like forms, and some compound shapes. The rounded bottom was usual, although the flattened base is quite common. Plain wares are commonest. Decoration tends to be confined to the rim and shoulder area, but may cover the entire vessel. Incising and combing, some zoning with zones set off by hatching, or by occasionally punctating, are the usual decorative treatments. Curvilinear designs such as whorls, and scrolls are commonest. Pottery of the types Chickachae Combed and Choctaw Incised are regarded as Choctaw marker types. Natchez Incised and Fatherland Plain are the marker types for historic Natchez (Fig. 144, *B, G*). Projectile points tend to be small and generally triangular, but they are sometimes stemmed, and even barbed (Fig. 144, *O*).

The archeologically derived diagnostic traits of the Natchezan which Quimby[62] felt were valid are thus summarized:

Pyramidal mound	European trade objects
Burial mound	present
Intrusive burial pits in	Pottery (see earlier para-
mound	graphs)
Cemetery burial pits	Clay elbow pipes
Abundant refuse pits	Gar fish scale projectile
Mound summit structures	points
Rectangular houses, trench	Large oval stemmed points
construction	Fish shaped flint points
House partitions	Triangular stemmed points
Palisade trenches	Triangular "fir tree" points
Plazas	Discarded stones—perforated
Secondary bundle burial	Quartz crystals
Extended burials	Grooved quartz crystals
Flexed burials	Effigies of stone or fired clay
Burials in wooden chest	Thick shell beads
Burial furniture abundant	Small shell gorgets

From the early journals the fragmentary archeological record can be enlarged, but as Quimby says,[63] the ethnologic data is not of a type readily comparable to the material recorded archeologically. In fact his paragraph so well analyzes some of the problems inherent in discovering the material content of the historic cultures that I quote it in full.

The correlation between the ethnological evidence and the archeological evidence leaves much to be desired. The reason for this lack of correlation is threefold. In the first place, many of the traits described by contemporary French observers are not suited for comparison with archeological data. Secondly, the archeological data are incomplete; they do not represent complete complexes by site. In the third place, there was considerable shifting about by the early historic tribes in the lower Mississippi Valley. There was widespread trade and communication among the Muskhogean and Caddoan tribes as well as intertribal and intervillage wars. With the Bayogoula, Mugulasha, Houma, and Taensa all occupying the same village in the course of seven years it would seem useless to hope for archeological data sufficient to differentiate such closely related peoples. Further, it seems that all tribes had captives or refugees from other tribes dwelling among them,

61. *Ibid.*

62. *Ibid.*   63. *Ibid.*, p. 273.

and it would not seem improbable to find Caddo potters at work in a Tunica or Houma village.

The presumed Caddoan ceramic and other traits of the historic period are sufficiently summarized by Ford and Willey.[64] The southern Caddo, in northwest Louisiana, and adjacent portions of Arkansas and Texas possessed:

Elaborate pottery decorated with negative designs, red slip ware, polished ware, incising, punctating, rocker stamping, and many other features are characteristic. A few burial mounds were used in Arkansas and Texas and numerous temple mounds are also found. However, the trait of mound building appears to have been on the decline. Other traits were derived from Middle Mississippi or were the result of parallel development from common influence. Some of these were primary burial extended in graves, very copious deposits of grave goods in which pottery figured prominently, shell ear pins knobbed at one end, copper plated ear spools, discoidal stones, and small sharp celts.

Ford and Willey here repeat their conviction that Caddoan as they define it was largely the end product of the developmental chain which began with Marksville, continued through Troyville and Coles Creek until historic times. Most of their evidence, as the cited paragraph shows, is found in the ceramic complex. It must be said however, that there is no certainty that the complex they have summarized is necessarily Caddoan.

The foregoing sections have tended to demonstrate that the fabric of associated traits which characterize each of the cultures of the Lower Valley from early to late contain basic concepts first observed in the earliest levels, even though the development may not be uniform throughout the area. In developing this emphasis I may have failed to show my realization that, even though traits may persist, their significance may shift, or that a complex of associated traits may characterize one culture, whereas the lack of this same complex may characterize its temporal and spatial neighbor. As an example of this latter phenomenon, we see at the Archaic level that the presence or absence of bell pestles helps distinguish an assemblage of Archaic artifacts in Louisiana from one found in the valley of the Tennessee. More important, however, in the proper handling of Southeastern artifacts is the knowledge that technological variation in the fabrication, or a difference in design, may set off the artifact of one period from its subsequent outgrowth. The copper earspool, for example, is a recognizable trait of both the Marksville and Spiro sites: thus both cultures share a general trait which itself can be broken down into several lesser traits. But the earspools are of different construction and may bear upon them different designs, with the result that the objects can be assigned to their proper cultural bracket on the basis of their intrinsic qualities. Thus,

although earspools are common to both periods, the specific earspool, with its technique of fabrication, constitutes a trait of one or the other, but not both cultures. The differences in the object are regarded as being the result of, and being evidence of, numerous cultural developmental processes. The differences may also be culturally significant. And again, even within one cultural level, a general trait may characterize the level, but its nature will differ from one local center to another. As an example, note the effigy vessel of Late Mississippi cultures. In the headwaters of the Tennessee River the raccoon or bear effigy and the owl are reasonably frequent effigy types. In the Middle Mississippi Valley and in the southeast corner of Arkansas, the fish, the frog, and the human form are commonest. All are effigy vessels, coeval, having developed under similar cultural conditions, but they, with other locally associated traits make up a distinctive local deviant of the dominant culture of the time.

It seems hardly necessary to mention that intraterritorial contact began early and was continuous from Archaic times on. As an example, note the number of marine shells recovered at Indian Knoll in Kentucky.[65] Copper and galena objects in Tchefuncte sites are equally good evidence. Then in each succeeding level, evidence of exchange of either finished manufactures or basic raw material is ample. Bell[66] has shown from Spiro that numerous basic raw materials used for tools or ornaments (flint, copper, galena, hematite, mica, shell, quartzite, turquoise) were imports from distances up to 1,000 miles. Whether there was a tribe or class of professional traders or peddlers, or whether parties from one town went directly to the nearest source of the items they coveted, is not important. What is important is that there was throughout the Southeast a constant movement of peoples and a consequent exchange of objects (and ideas?) which resulted in a surprising uniformity of culture objects over wide areas of the south. A uniformity of custom and ritual also seems to have existed. If we may judge by the large scale tribal shifts of the eastern seaboard in historic times, in response to various dislocating factors, equally extensive migrations in prehistoric times for similar reasons can be invoked to explain, for example, the distribution of Hopewell cultures, without too great a strain on the credulity. I think it not too much to assume that there was never a time when Indian population was geographically stable. Migration by units of all sizes, from the family to the tribe, was probably routine. Add to this the constant, if not heavy, traffic in materials, and there is little wonder that all over the east, a generally similar succession of occupations is observed. It behooves students of prehistory to con-

64. Ford and Willey, 1941, p. 353.

65. Webb, W. S., 1946. 66. Bell, 1947.

tinue to recognize that this movement existed and attempt in their restorations to take account of it, without forgetting the facts of local idiosyncrasy, which may in early research obscure a basic trend or relationship.

A short statement specifically clarifying the relation of the southern half of the area under consideration (the states of Mississippi and Louisiana) to the northern half of the same area is desirable to pull together the scattered references throughout this chapter.

Briefly the situation appears to have been this: in early times the Lower Valley seemed to dominate. Tchefuncte and Marksville appear to have been scantily distributed over the entire region, but Early Baytown, coexistent with Tchefuncte and Marksville, is the stronger in the Mississippi River alluvial plain region and on eastward in the hills of central and south Mississippi. Subsequently, while Troyville, Coles Creek, and other Mississippi cultures worked out their destinies within the main valley, the backwoods tribes tended to freeze and perpetuate the Baytown tradition. Here the complex of small domed mounds, cord-marked pottery, and rough flint work was never generally replaced by the exuberant technology and ritual complexes of the Middle Mississippi period. All through the hinterlands of the area south and east from Durant, Mississippi, we find sites where the Early and Late Baytown ideas appear to have persisted until nearly historic times. An occasional fragment of Marksville or Mississippi pottery is found often enough to confirm the suspicion that these sites were occupied during the greater elaboration of the cultures of the main river. Natchezan pottery is also found on sites where the bulk of the material is of earlier origin.

It is of interest to note that the Big Black River sites, the Bayou Pierre sites, sites around Natchez, and those on the Yazoo, and other rivers tributary to the Mississippi represent in varying degree, without lacunae, the entire sequence of cultural development from early to late, excepting the Archaic. This lack, I think can be explained by the fact that these sluggish rivers, flowing through earthen channels, did not possess the long rock-bottomed shoals where mussels and related forms are most often found in great abundance. Conditions merely were not right for the ecological adjustments the Archaic peoples had made. However, on such rivers as the Pearl, Tombigbee, Mobile, Chickasawhay, and others which led to the Gulf of Mexico rather than into the Mississippi river, the catalogue of cultural succession is incomplete. Cordmarked sand-tempered pottery, small domed mounds, and many, but small, village sites predominate, thus giving evidence that there was no great enthusiasm here for the Mississippi way of life. However, on

these smaller sites which perpetuate an early tradition, very recent pottery, identified as Natchezan can be found; it is assumed, but not proved, that the small sites were continuously occupied.

To me these distribution facts argue that the cultures lumped under the term Mississippi were spread by actual movement of segments of the population. What probably happened was that the complex resulted from an actual movement of peoples from Mexico. Originally few in number they amalgamated with, and soon dominated, those already in the Valley in Late Woodland times. Each Mississippi site found outside the Mississippi Valley proper may be considered as a colony where local populations had joined the settlement. And where the colonies did not go, there we find a long continued adherence to the earlier manner of living. The Woodland pattern yielded only at the very end to a decadent version of the climax cultures which in their earlier strength had passed around them. We can consider the extreme Lower Valley and the interior provinces as laggardly in their adoption of new ideas, but by 1680 the tribes of the entire area had a diluted Mississippi culture which we have presented in terms of Natchezan, although the Chickasaw of northeast Mississippi would have demonstrated the same trend.

In this region there are many problems beckoning the student. Of prime importance is the closer definition of the material culture of the historic tribes; the relation, if any, of the persisting Baytown-Miller materials to the historic tribes is mysterious at present. Beginning steps have already been made toward the identification of historic tribes with archeological material. Examples are the Yuchi, Creek, and Cherokee identifications made by Lewis and Kneberg.[67] Ford[68] and Quimby[69] seem to have pinned the Natchez down; they and Collins[70] have begun on Choctaw, while I have in part defined Chickasaw material cultures of the 1700's.[71]

We know virtually nothing about the content of either Early or Late Baytown mounds or villages. At such sites as Anna and Emerald we know nothing of the early history, which is effectively sealed by the last construction stages, although Cotter has pretty well demonstrated these sites to be recent.

Until some such sites are dug, and we can perchance perceive an unbroken line of ceramic, architectural, and religious development, the present chronological structure will perforce, remain as much conjecture as fact. Of course, the individual problems are legion. How far down the Mississippi River will the Southern Cult material be found? And how common is it in the vast areas between the present "key

67. Lewis and Kneberg, 1946.
68. Ford, 1936.
69. Quimby, 1942.
70. Collins, 1927.
71. Jennings, 1941.

sites"? Where were the Chickasaw towns in De Soto's day? What archeologically is historic Caddo? Do, as I suspect, the Choctaw and Chickasaw material objects of the eighteenth century perpetuate Baytown forms of an earlier day?

Conclusions

In the pages of this chapter scores of important unanswered questions challenge the reader as well as the author. Partially accepted, this challenge resulted in many pages of speculation, but space limits have made it necessary to strike out this section. Suffice it to say that the narrative account was presented in a way intended to bring into relief two basic facts which the prehistory of the south seems to teach (1) that there is a coherent, cohesive core of cultural ele-

ments which color and influence all cultures of the south, and (2) that the true story of the region is a story of accretion and enrichment of this basic core. In other words, I can see continuity (ideas if not population), which was richly modified by accretion at periodic intervals.

The welter of conflicting ideas regarding the dating of aboriginal cultures have in part been precipitated by Carbon 14 analyses. There is little point in speculating further on the matter. Suffice it to say that I have consistently been guilty of extreme conservatism in my assignment of guess dates. The full span of time, from earliest Archaic to the decline of the 1700's, now appears to have been at least 5,000 years.

ALABAMA ARCHEOLOGY: A SUMMARY.

By David L. DeJarnette[*]

THE GEOGRAPHIC BACKGROUND

PHYSIOGRAPHY

THAT portion of the Southeastern United States encompassing Alabama includes five physical areas[1] varying from the highlands of the Appalachian Plateau to the lowlands of the Gulf Coastal Plain, with relief tapering from 2,407 feet above sea level in North Alabama to sea level in South Alabama.

The Appalachian Plateau reaches into the northeastern part of the state and makes up Alabama's boldest topography. This plateau represents the southernmost prongs of the Appalachian Mountains. Falling away northwestward from the Appalachian Plateau is the less bold Interior Low Plateau. On the other (southeastward) side of the Appalachian Plateau is the small Valley and Ridge Province. Paralleling the Valley and Ridge Province southward is the Piedmont Province, another finger of upland area, which juts into the east-central portion of the state. These four physical areas include all of the high relief of Alabama and make up, roughly, the northeastern diagonal half of the state. Terrain in the other half gives way to the Gulf Province where rolling foothills gradually drop to the delta, dune and beach country of the extreme southern portion of the state.

There are eight major rivers in Alabama, all of which served as routes of migration and commerce in aboriginal times (Fig. 145). The Tennessee River, making its way from the Cumberland Plateau to the Ohio, dips through the northern part of Alabama, and along its banks are innumerable shell heaps and other remains of aboriginal occupancy. On the Warrior River, which flows southward in the western section of the state, is the large prehistoric site of Moundville. The Warrior River empties into the Tombigbee, which in turn joins the Alabama River to form the Mobile River. *Mabila,* the sixteenth-century Indian town where the Spaniard De Soto

and his followers fought their disastrous battle with the Mobile Indians, is believed to have been located in the area where the Tombigbee and Alabama join.[2] On the banks of the Coosa River in eastern Alabama was the Creek town of *Coca,* one of the best-established points along De Soto's route.[3] The Coosa flows southward as does the neighboring Tallapoosa River, and these two meet to form the Alabama River, which cuts across south-central Alabama. Where the Coosa and Tallapoosa rivers meet there is a heavy concentration of burial urn sites, and all along the Coosa, Tallapoosa, and Alabama, as well as along the Chattahoochee, which forms the southeastern boundary of the state, are numerous aboriginal sites showing Caucasian contact. The Mobile River mentioned above empties into the Gulf of Mexico. It was into the mouth of this river that the Spaniard Pineda sailed in the year 1519.[4]

Along ridges paralleling the rivers which flow through the upland sections of Alabama, and especially along the Tennessee River, are numerous caves, some of which show evidence of aboriginal occupation.

GEOLOGY

Geologic ages from the Archean to the Cenozoic are represented in Alabama. The northeastern part of the State, that which includes the Appalachian spurs, is the oldest. Here igneous and metamorphic formations offer mica, which seems to have been highly prized by the Indians; slate, from which they frequently made pendants, whetstones and other objects; steatite (soapstone) from which they carved bowls and tobacco pipes; greenstone, a favorite material for celts; sandstone, which they used for abraders and other objects; and quartzite, used for knives and projectile points.[5] Throughout the state limestone, chert, flint and chalcedony are widespread and were availed of extensively in aboriginal manufacture. Excellent pottery clay is also widespread. In the southwestern part of Alabama are salt springs used by Indians as a source of salt.

* University of Alabama, B.S., 1929, Member of University of Chicago Field Party, Summer, 1932; Curator of Alabama Museum of Natural History, University, Alabama, 1933-49. Curator and Chairman, American Museum of Atomic Energy, 1949——. Chapter received November, 1947.

1. Fenneman, 1938.

2. Swanton (ed.), 1939, p. 216.
3. *Ibid.*, p. 206.
4. Swanton, 1946, p. 35.
5. Jones, W. B., 1939, pp. 9 ff.; 1942, pp. 327 ff.

CLIMATE AND SOIL FERTILITY

Aborigines found the Alabama climate temperate and comparatively pleasant, averaging 60° Fahrenheit in the extreme northern part of the state and 67° Fahrenheit in the southern part. They found here abundant rainfall plus a long growing season (averaging nine months out of the year). They found the elements friendly—snow is rare and there is little wind, as a general rule, though brief windstorms are frequent in the northern and central portions of the state during the spring months. Hurricanes from the West Indies area sometimes reach the Gulf shores of Alabama, but this is infrequent.

Agricultural groups found Alabama soil productive and easily cultivated. A "Black Belt" crossing the central portion of the state is a strip of rolling terrain having a black, sticky, calcareous clay soil which is highly fertile. The extensive site of Moundville is located at the northern edge of this very fertile area. Sandy loam and reddish clay cover the other regions of the state. While these other areas are not so fertile as the "Black Belt" they are highly productive because of favorable climatic conditions.

FLORA AND FAUNA

Plant life in Alabama is abundant and shelters an abundant animal life. Even today Alabama is well supplied with the bounty of forest and stream, and the aborigines found here plenteous provision for the comforts and necessities of their existence.

Theirs for the gathering were blackberries, dewberries, and many other wild berries; wild grapes and muscadines; pawpaws, wild cherries, wild plums, crabapples, haws, persimmons; smilax roots and other edible roots; hickory nuts and many other nuts including the pecan.[6]

There was good hunting here. Deer is still plentiful in many areas of the State; and mink, muskrat, fox, raccoon, opossum, squirrel, rabbit, bat, and shrew are numerous throughout Alabama. Bears, cougars (panthers), wolves, and lynx were common until after Caucasian settlement. Bison reportedly wandered into Alabama only rarely. Wild turkeys were abundant up until a few years ago; wild ducks, wild geese, quail, mourning doves, woodpeckers, buzzards, owls, and numerous other birds are still plentiful, as is a wide variety of aquatic life including fish, mussel, eel, frog, turtle, and, in the southern portion of the state, alligator.

Pine, oak, gum, hackberry, cypress, and red cedar are some of the more common trees of Alabama and they were used by the Indians in numerous ways. Cypress was a favorite material for dugouts,[7] pine was used for house frames, gum was used for drums,

etc. Among other Alabama plants useful to the Indians were mulberry and yucca, both of which furnished fiber; yaupon, from which the "black drink" was brewed; sassafras and numerous other shrubs which yielded dyes and medicines; cane, used for blowguns, matting, pipestems; and, in the southern section of Alabama, spanish moss, which was worn by the Indians as clothing and used in many other ways.

There are four kinds of poisonous snakes in Alabama, the rattlesnake, copperhead, cotton-mouth, and coral, as well as many nonpoisonous snakes.

THE GENERAL ARCHEOLOGICAL PICTURE

AREAS EXCAVATED

The federal government, sponsoring intensive archeological investigations along the Tennessee River during the TVA dam construction program, made possible a more thorough archeological examination of the Tennessee Valley Region of Alabama than has yet been attained in any other portion of the state. Most of our knowledge of Alabama archeology is therefore derived from that region. All of the other principal river areas of the state have had a measure of investigation by a number of agencies.

FOLSOM-YUMA

In Alabama there has been found no cultural assemblage which can be equated with Folsom-Yuma, though Folsomoid points are reported as random finds in several areas of the State. Yuma-type flaking has been recognised on several projectile points found in the lower levels of a shell heap on an island in the Tennessee River,[8] and in this same region two broken Folsomoid points were found in the mound fill of two burial mounds, one in each mound,[9] while another broken Folsomoid point was found, with no particular context, in a village area.[10]

IDENTIFIED CULTURAL HORIZONS

The details of the stratigraphic picture in Alabama have not as yet been interpreted. The present stage of the study indicates certain *trends* only. The most perceptible trend is a generalized chronology in which the following sequence is indicated: Archaic (pre-pottery), Transitional Archaic and Early Woodland (introduction of pottery), Hopewellian and Middle Woodland, and, finally, Transitional Woodland and Middle Mississippian. These horizons as they are indicated in Alabama are described on the following pages.

---

6. Harper, 1928.   7. Swanton, 1946, pp. 244 ff.

8. Webb and DeJarnette, 1942, Pls. 101–102.
9. *Ibid.*, p. 304 and Pls. 132–No. 2; broken Folsomoid point is in lower row of plate artifacts, fourth from left.
10. *Ibid.*, p. 304.

ARCHAIC IN ALABAMA

GENERAL FEATURES

The Archaic horizon is represented in North Alabama in shell heaps along the Tennessee River (Fig. 146). Other than distinguishing this period as *pre-pottery,* we have not clearly differentiated it from succeeding horizons; neither are the developmental and acculturative changes within Shell Mound Archaic itself clear. Further interpretation of Shell Mound Archaic awaits a restudy of shell mound material—a restudy based on detailed analytical breakdowns and comparisons with unstratified sites.

Pending this analysis it is possible to present the following generalizations based on traits associated with burials inclusive in apparent pre-pottery levels.

ARCHAIC DWELLINGS

The Shell Mound Archaic people apparently erected only crude temporary shelters. There are in their occupational levels only scattered post holes and a few clay floors. They had numerous fired areas and many fire basins floored with stones.

SUBSISTENCE

Shellfish played a major role in the diet of the Shell Mound Archaic people, the shell middens themselves being formed by the shell which was discarded meal by meal.

Fresh-water fish, wild turkey and venison were also on the Shell Mound menu from time to time. The Shell Mound Archaic people caught fish with bone fishhooks (Fig. 147, *E*) and killed game with stone-tipped or bone-tipped spears (Fig. 147, *F–H*) thrown with the aid of atlatls (Fig. 147, upper left inset figure). Tools used in manufacturing their spears and other implements were antler shaft-straighteners (Fig. 147, *A*), antler drifts (Fig. 147, *B*) and tines, grooved stone axes (Fig. 147, *V*), circular pebble hammerstones (Fig. 147, *Y*), and flint drills (Fig. 147, *U*). They probably gathered roots which they ground with stone bell pestles (Fig. 147, *X*); they must have gathered nuts which they cracked on "nutting stones" (Fig. 147, *W*).

They cooked in vessels carved of sandstone or steatite (Fig. 147, *Z*), apparently using preheated pebbles to bring their mixtures to the desired warmth.

APPAREL AND ORNAMENT

The art of weaving was evidently known to the Shell Mound Archaic people; remains of a fabric breechclout have been found with a Shell Mound Archaic burial.[11] Leather garments, also, were probably fashioned with bone awls and needles (Fig. 147, *M–Q*) which had been sharpened with grooved shale

11. *Ibid.,* p. 189 and Pl. 217–2.

abraders. Shell and bone pins were used (Fig. 147, *J'*).

The Shell Mound Archaic Indian adorned himself with necklaces and bracelets. He had beads of both marine and fresh-water shell (Fig. 147, *E', H'–I', P'*), beads of stone and bone (Fig. 147, *G'*); he had charms made of animal and human teeth (Fig. 147, *D'*); he had pendants of shell (Fig. 147, *O'*), and bar gorgets of stone.

CEREMONIAL CUSTOMS

Tubular tobacco pipes (Fig. 147, *C'*), which the Shell Mound Archaic people carved from stone, may have served in ceremonial rites. A bowl which they made from a human skull may have had a ceremonial use (Fig. 147, *N'*). They also had carved bone "spatulas" which suggest ceremonial significance (Fig. 147, *L'*).

BURIAL CUSTOMS

Although all of the foregoing comments on the Shell Mound Archaic people are based on artifacts associated with Archaic burials, most Archaic burials in Alabama do not have any artifacts associated with them, other than personal ornaments. When they buried children, however, these people were more inclined to lay down some accompanying object—more often than when they buried adults.

They buried their dead in the shell midden, placing the body in a tightly flexed (Fig. 147, *B'*) or a sitting position (Fig. 147, *A'*; Fig. 148). It may be that the body was sometimes bound by wrappings into this flexed position. Occasionally, but not often, they gave only slight flexure to the knees and elbows. In a few instances they buried the body in an extended position, sometimes with the face downward. Very often, regardless of whether they flexed the body or laid it down extended, they removed the head before burial.

Cremation was also popular in Shell Mound Archaic times. Sometimes the body was cremated away from the spot where the calcined bones were finally buried; at other times the bones were left lying in the spot where cremation had taken place.

The Shell Mound Archaic people showed either ceremonial or personal regard for the dog; dogs seem to have been buried with the same care accorded people, and sometimes dog burials accompanied human burials.

TRANSITIONAL ARCHAIC AND EARLY WOODLAND IN ALABAMA

GENERAL FEATURES

Transitional Archaic and Early Woodland marks (1) the introduction of pottery into the region of Alabama; (2) the first widespread occupation of the state, so far as present investigation has indicated;[12] and (3) later stages of this period mark the first construction of burial mounds here.

Comments on the people of this period will be followed by descriptions of their pottery, after which there will be noted an early burial mound of Alabama.

THE TRANSITIONAL ARCHAIC AND EARLY WOODLAND PEOPLE

People of this period in North Alabama continued to use as habitation sites shell heaps along the Tennessee River. They also settled in villages along the smaller streams of northern Alabama[13] and west central Alabama.[14] There is a suggestion of their occupation of south-central Alabama.[15] And in southeast Alabama there were at this time people with affiliations toward the Atlantic coastal area.[16] The influence of these people soon spread westward to southwest Alabama.[17]

The very first introduction of pottery into Alabama was apparently unaccompanied by any other important changes. The people of this "new era" continued to use atlatls; vessels of sandstone and steatite did not go out of style; "nutting stones," bell pestles, grooved axes, shale abraders and circular pebble hammerstones were still common. Ornaments worn during Shell Mound Archaic times seemed to remain popular; tubular tobacco pipes continued to be used; and sitting burials and tightly flexed burials continued to be made.[18]

While medium sized, simple stemmed, barbless flint projectile points were still used extensively, larger points—especially the large, straight based, ovate triangular, stemless forms—seemed to lose favor.

TRANSITIONAL ARCHAIC AND EARLY WOODLAND POTTERY

Transitional Archaic and Early Woodland pottery in Alabama is of three general series: Wheeler, Alexander, and Deptford. The Wheeler and Alexander series are most prominent in northern Alabama,[19] and occur also in west-central Alabama[20] and in southwest Alabama.[21] Wheeler has been found also in southeast Alabama,[22] while Alexander has been found in south-central Alabama.[23] The Deptford series occurs in southeast Alabama[24] and Deptford influence extends to southwest Alabama, where a Deptford-like ware has been called McLeod Deptford.[25]

WHEELER POTTERY

The Wheeler pottery series in Alabama is fiber-tempered and consists of simple open bowls with flat to flat-rounded bottoms. Crudely shaped annular bases are common. Wheeler ware from northern Alabama is often decorated, the decoration being either a carelessly applied dentate stamping, or a simple stamping or punctation. Punctations are sometimes arranged in neat rows, but often are only haphazard markings made with a hollow reed, or some bluntly pointed object, or the fingernail. These decorations are vaguely similar to those found on the Alexander series. Wheeler ware found outside the Tennessee Valley in Alabama usually has no surface decoration and is crudely smoothed. The Wheeler pottery series is apparently a western extension of the fiber-tempered pottery of the Carolina, Georgia, Florida region.

ALEXANDER POTTERY

The Alexander pottery series in Alabama is sand-tempered and is represented in forms varying from medium-sized globular jars to small, flat-based cups or beakers. Tetrapodal supports on a subsquare base have been noted. The series has a characteristic rim treatment in which the rim is embellished exteriorly, just below the lip, with a row of small, rounded bosses or nodes, while immediately below this row of nodes are several parallel incised lines. Lips are usually lightly notched. With this characteristic rim treatment the exterior surface may be plain or it may be covered wholly or partially by reed punctations, by pinched ridges or fingernail punctations, by geometric patterns, or by zoned decorations[26] in which parallel lines form zones filled with rectangular punctations or stampings. Rocker stamping occurs on a few sherds.

Pottery of the Alexander series has been found in Tchefuncte sites in Louisiana.[27] Chronological equa-

12. Folsomoid finds in various sections of the state have been inconclusive, and no evidence of Shell Mound Archaic (pre-pottery) in Alabama has yet been found outside the Tennessee Valley Region.

13. Mgv64, the Robinson Site; unpublished data in files of Alabama Museum of Natural History, University, Alabama.

14. The Huster Component near Tuscaloosa, Alabama; unpublished data, loc. cit.

15. Griffin, J. B., 1946, p. 51.

16. As suggested by Deptford pottery described on following pages.

17. As suggested by McLeod Deptford pottery described on following pages.

18. Sitting burials and tightly flexed burials were found at Mgv64, the Robinson Site, a Transitional Archaic site having stone vessels and Alexander pottery. Unpublished data in files of Alabama Museum of Natural History, University, Alabama.

19. First described in Griffin, J. B., 1939. See also Haag, 1939a; 1942, also described in Dunlevy, n.d.

20. Griffin, J. B., 1946, p. 51.

21. Wimberly and Tourtelot, 1941, pp. 20, 33; Wimberly, n.d.b.

22. Hurt, n.d.

23. Griffin, J. B., 1946, pp. 50, 51.

24. Hurt, n.d.

25. Wimberly, n.d.b.

26. Griffin, J. B., 1939, Pl. 11b; Haag, 1942b, pp. 514–516, Pls. 100, 156; Haag, 1939a; Dunlevy, n.d.

27. Ford and Quimby, 1945, pp. 64, 65.

tion of the Alexander series with Tchefuncte is further strengthened by the evidence, based on typology, that the Alexander pottery series could well have lain the background out of which certain Hopewell pottery characteristics developed. This is especially evident in the rim treatment whereby small exterior nodes are made by punching a cylindrical tool through the vessel rim from the interior. Decorative patterns made up of zoned areas, appearing in the Alexander series, indicate a cross-over with similar Hopewell designs, as does also the rocker stamping which occurs on a few Alexander sherds. Some typological similarities between the Alexander series and Adena pottery have also been noted.[28]

DEPTFORD POTTERY

Pottery of the Deptford series has been found in surface collections in southeast Alabama.[29] This Alabama ware, found in limited quantities, is typologically similar to the "classic" Deptford of Georgia.[30]

McLEOD DEPTFORD POTTERY

McLeod Deptford occurs as a concentration in southwest Alabama. Here it appears as an assemblage of decorative types, each of which is somewhat variant to the decorative types diagnostic of the Georgia Deptford assemblage.

McLeod Deptford is sand-tempered. Vessels are medium sized. Forms are: bowls with straight sides; globular bowls with slightly to moderately constricted mouth; jars with sloping shoulders and inslanting to slightly flaring rims. Exterior rim folds are a constant characteristic. Bases are flattened-rounded. Decoration consists of simple stamping, linear check stamping, and check stamping, the latter two being applied with a carved paddle or roulette bearing five or more check-rows. A plain ware similar in form to the decorated ware accompanies the assemblage.

Summarily, McLeod Deptford is better made than Deptford and expresses a refined version of Deptford.[31] The Deptford pottery along the Chattahoochee River in southeastern Alabama may represent the western-most extension, in its basic style, of the Georgia pottery assemblage. The southwest Alabama variant (McLeod Deptford) is hinged to Deptford of Georgia on the basis of its appearance as an assemblage containing the three decorative styles of early Georgia Deptford, simple stamping, check stamping, and linear check stamping, and not on close typological resemblances of individual pottery types. The most noticeable difference between Georgia Deptford and McLeod Deptford is the refinement in deco-

ration and modeling of the latter. In McLeod Deptford ware, decorative units (checks and stamped lines) are appreciably smaller and applied with more care. McLeod Deptford check stamped ware expresses refinements that appear in the check stamped ware so liberally sprinkled throughout the Southeast.

AN EARLY BURIAL MOUND

During the later stages of the Transitional Archaic and Early Woodland period there was built one of the earliest burial mounds yet identified in Alabama. This is the McQuorquodale Mound near the Tombigbee River in southwest Alabama. It enclosed ten burials, and there were indications that others had been included in the mound, but had deteriorated beyond positive recognition when the mound was excavated.

A whole pottery vessel was an apparent burial association. It was a small, deep, sand-tempered bowl or jar having features suggestive of the time period of Late Tchefuncte–Early Hopewellian.[32] In the mound fill were a few steatite vessel fragments, five Wheeler sherds (plain), several Alexander sherds, a few Deptford sherds,[33] and a few clay-tempered sherds. These clay-tempered sherds express relationship to Marksville. Some are incised with Marksville-like technique and bear designs vaguely similar to Marksville pottery; one sherd indicates a beaker form which is common in Marksville pottery.

The people who built the McQuorquodale Mound used "nutting stones," pebble hammers, medium to small side-notched and stemmed projectile points. Some of them wore beads of rolled sheet copper, and cymbal-shaped copper earspools. They had greenstone celts, flat bar gorgets with two perforations, a conical stone cup. They used as burial offerings sheet mica, faceted galena, and perhaps tar.[34]

MIDDLE WOODLAND AND HOPEWELLIAN IN ALABAMA

GENERAL FEATURES

The Middle Woodland and Hopewellian period in Alabama marks (1) the introduction of new pottery types into different areas of Alabama, and (2) the appearance of a specialized burial-ceremonial system known as Copena (Fig. 149).[35]

28. Griffin, J. B., 1945d, p. 228.

29. Hurt, n.d.

30. For description of Deptford pottery of Georgia see Caldwell and Waring, 1939.

31. Wimberly, n.d.b.

32. See illustration in Wimberly and Tourtelot, 1941, *Fig. 12*. The four vestigial podal supports resemble late Tchefuncte to Early Marksville. See also Marksville-like form of sherd shown in *Fig. 15*, lower right corner.

33. These Deptford sherds were not recognized as such during initial study of the McQuorquodale Mound material; later study of pottery in this area (Wimberly, n.d.b.) has brought out the Deptford relationship.

34. Because of the decayed condition of the burials it could not be determined whether or not the tar, "nutting stones," greenstone celts and flat bar gorgets were definitely burial associations.

35. Webb, W. S., 1939, p. 201; Webb and DeJarnette, 1942, p. 301.

The new pottery types introduced during this period will be noted, together with the people who used them, after which the Copena burial-ceremonial system will be discussed.

THE POTTERY AND THE PEOPLE IN NORTH ALABAMA

In northern Alabama, potters during the Middle Woodland and Hopewellian period favored a limestone-tempered ware which they made in great quantities. They effected onto this ware few suggestions of the features which we call Hopewellian,[36] even though they were manufacturing it while strong Hopewellian adumbrations were being cast on burial-ceremonial activities of the area.

NORTHERN ALABAMA LIMESTONE-TEMPERED POTTERY[37]

Vessels are medium to medium large jars with wide mouths and moderately flaring rims. Bases may be conoidal, subconoidal, or they may be flattened, bearing four podal supports. Smoothed (plain) ware and fabric-marked, check stamped, simple stamped and complicated stamped ware are the most common types; cord-marked ware and brushed ware is less usual; incised ware is a minority type and is represented by simple geometrical patterns (chevrons and diagonal parallel lines) on the rim area.

Limestone-tempered pottery is most abundant in the eastern section of northern Alabama. It has apparent affiliations to the north and to the east and probably entered Alabama from a general northeast direction.

The northern Alabama villagers who used limestone-tempered pottery buried some few of their dead in the village middens, scooping out pits large enough to contain the body either in a partly flexed or a fully flexed position, (and it has been speculated that the *Copena* burials—which were contemporaneous, and for which, as yet, no definite village connections are known—may have been theirs).

There is as yet little insight into their daily lives. They used stone implements that are either spades or hoes, possibly indicating an acquaintance with agriculture. (The spades or hoes are made of limestone; some are notched, others are unnotched.) Other implements which they used were grooved stone axes (chipped); mediumly large, simple stemmed stone projectile points; antler drifts and flakers; and splinter bone awls.

THE POTTERY AND THE PEOPLE IN
SOUTHWEST ALABAMA

Southwest Alabama potters of this period gave their ware the "Hopewellian look" so conspicuously

absent in northern Alabama. Hopewellian zone stamping, incising and punctating appear on a ware that has been found in abundance in southwest Alabama and has been called the Porter Hopewellian series.[38]

PORTER HOPEWELLIAN POTTERY

Porter Hopewellian pottery is characteristically tempered with sand, although sometimes clay tempering occurs, and even less frequently there is a combination of sand and clay tempering. Vessels are small to medium sized. Forms are: beakers or cups with outslanting sides; jars with high shoulders; open bowls; and bowls with incurving rim (constricted mouth). Bases are typically flattened and are circular or square. Exterior surfaces may be plain or they may have a single incised line around the rim area, or they may be decorated, except for the rim and basal areas, with zone stamping or with incising. Zone stamping is characterized by flowing patterns outlined by incised lines. The conventionalized bird motif seems to be represented. Stamping within the patterns was effected by rocking an implement—sometimes notched, sometimes unnotched—back and forth between the incised lines. There are also rectilinear patterns of nested triangles and squares as well as circular punctations. Plain, incised curvilinear patterns, both flowing and confined, occur, as do plain, incised rectilinear patterns. These plain, incised patterns are similar to the zone stamped patterns except that the incised lines are closer together.

In most respects the Porter Hopewellian series resembles the Florida Northwest Coast variety of Hopewellian pottery[39] more than it does the Marksville or the Troyville series.[40] The Marksville rim (cambered and crosshatched), for example, is lacking in the Porter Hopewellian series.

The people who used the Porter-Hopewellian ware in southwest Alabama had crudely chipped, double-bladed chalcedony axes; small lapstones; medium sized, simple stemmed flint and quartzite projectile points, usually barbless; a fewer number of medium sized notched quartzite and flint projectile points; siltstone "boatstones" (imperforate, not hollowed out) which may have been atlatl weights; bone projectile points or awls cut to provide for insertion of shaft; bone fishhooks; antler tines; splinter bone awls and deer ulna awls. A fragment was found of one of their stone (sandstone) bar gorgets having a biconical perforation; this fragment is probably a part of a two-hole bar gorget similar to those used in the Transitional Archaic and Early Woodland periods. There are three pottery elbow pipes which

---

36. The vessel illustrated in Webb and DeJarnette, 1942, Pl. 206–2, has a zoned decoration on the rim and shoulder suggestive of Hopewellian zoned designs, but this vessel is unusual in Alabama.
37. Griffin, J. B., 1939; Haag, 1939a; 1942; Dunlevy, n.d.

38. Wimberly, n.d.b.
39. Willey and Woodbury, 1942.
40. Ford and Willey, 1939; 1940.

they used—two sand-tempered and one clay-tempered; these elbow forms modeled in clay appear to have replaced the earlier tubular forms carved from stone.

They were probably acquainted with the custom of building burial mounds.[41] Other burials were made, in partly flexed positions, in village middens.

THE POTTERY AND THE PEOPLE IN SOUTHEAST ALABAMA

People along the Chattahoochee River in the southeastern section of Alabama used Hopewellian pottery[42] similar to the Porter-Hopewellian series. They also used another type, Swift Creek Complicated Stamped,[43] which has a decorative similarity to some of the limestone-tempered pottery used during Woodland-Hopewellian times in northern Alabama.[44]

THE COPENA BURIAL-CEREMONIAL SYSTEM

A specialized burial-ceremonial system appeared in northern Alabama during the Middle Woodland and Hopewellian period. The people of this "sect" built burial mounds to enclose elaborate graves and skillfully wrought burial offerings. Because they frequently included copper and galena among their offerings, this burial-ceremonial assemblage has been called Copena, using combined elements of the words "copper" and "galena." Where these followers of the Copena burial system lived, where they obtained their burial offerings, and what characterized their daily existence has not been fully determined.

Copena mounds are typically conoidal in form and are constructed of sand and clay. They are found most often along small streams, and sometimes occur in pairs.

Before beginning the actual mound construction, Copena adherents usually buried separately several individuals (precedent burials) in long, oval pits. They would shape each pit with care and make the bottom level; then they would floor the bottom with a layer of clay, spreading the clay by puddling it. Sometimes they would shape a low, clay "pillow" and foot rest. They would then lower the body (in an extended position, face upward) into the grave, and after placing with the body carefully arranged burial offerings, they would often completely seal both body and offerings with another layer of clay (Fig. 150, B). Sometimes they would place small logs on either side of the body; at other times they might cover the body with bark.

Leaving piled beside the grave the earth they had thrown up in digging it, they would bring sand and clay from elsewhere to refill the grave.

After they had made in this manner a number of closely grouped burials the Copena people began the actual mound construction, bringing sand and clay to cover all the graves in the group, and covering also the heaps of earth that had been piled up in digging the precedent graves. As they deposited the sand and clay, and before any definite mound had been formed, they would add other burials (inclusive burials). In making these inclusive burials they sometimes flexed the body fully (Fig. 150, E), sometimes extended it, sometimes laid down lone heads or skulls (Fig. 150, D), or disarticulated body members or bones. Sometimes they laid down the burned fragments of bodies that had been cremated (Fig. 150, A).

When their deposits of sand and clay had accumulated to a moderate size, mound construction was completed with a final capping of sand and clay, after which no further burials (no intrusive burials) were added.

They buried with their dead, objects which were expertly made and obviously valuable. Bodies were sometimes buried wearing copper earspools (Fig. 150, J), copper bracelets (Fig. 150, M), beads of drilled copper or rolled copper (Fig. 150, I, R), copper breast plates (rectangular); *Olivella* or marine columella shell beads (Fig. 150, G–H). Fabric was used, sometimes, at least, in shrouding the body; we have found fragments of cloth adhering to copper ornaments. Other articles found with Copena dead are: fragments of mica; lumps of galena which are often faceted (Fig. 150, N); a distinctive type of long, stemless, leaf-shaped projectile point (Fig. 150, L), copper reel-shaped objects (Fig. 150, F); small to medium sized copper axes; massive spades or hoes of chipped and polished greenstone (Fig. 150, P); large, polished greenstone celts which are thick, ovate in cross section, and have long, tapering, round-pointed polls (Fig. 150, Q); marine shell cups (Fig. 150, O); a pottery discoidal (limestone-tempered); tobacco pipes of stone (Fig. 150, T), and one tobacco pipe of pottery (Fig. 150, S).

The Copena stone tobacco pipes are usually carved from steatite and are usually elbow-shaped, though one zoomorphic steatite pipe has been found—an elongate form representing most likely a dog (Fig. 150, U). A siltstone elbow pipe is decorated with an incised curvilinear design; one portion of the design forms a human figure having facial features represented by an incised cross.

41. As has been noted, the McQuorquodale Mound, built in this area during the "late" Early Woodland period, contained in the mound fill a few clay-tempered sherds. These sherds occur as a minority variation in the Porter Hopewellian series. The clay-tempered Porter Hopewellian sherds together with other Hopewellian features of the mound—the conical cup, mica, copper earspools and other copper artifacts—makes the building of the mound compatible with both the "late" Early Woodland period and the "early" Middle Woodland and Hopewellian period.

42. Hurt, n.d.   43. *Ibid.*   44. Haag, 1939b.

The one pottery tobacco pipe which has been found in a Copena mound is slightly smaller than the typical stone elbow pipes, but it is identical with them in form. It is limestone-tempered and was made by a skilled potter.

Village economy of the people who practised Copena customs has not yet been recognized in any North Alabama occupational level. No by-products that would have been left where Copena articles were manufactured—rejected Copena points, broken Copena celts, culled raw materials—have been found. There are limestone-tempered pottery sherds[45] scattered through Copena mound fills, however, and this, together with the limestone-tempered pottery pipe and the limestone-tempered pottery discoidal, points to some relationship between Copena and the northern Alabama villagers who used limestone-tempered pottery.[46]

But there is a suggestion of Copena in only one of these villages.[47] Here there were found several projectile points similar to the stemless, leaf-shaped points distinctive of Copena, a large greenstone spade similar to those found in Copena mounds, and a small fragment of copper. Also found here were polished greenstone celts, but they are not of the long, pointed poll variety characteristic of Copena.

OTHER TRAITS OF THIS POSSIBLE COPENA VILLAGE

This village site (Lu^{v}65)[48] contained thousands of limestone-tempered sherds, a few sand-tempered sherds, and a few clay-grit-tempered sherds. Decorative types represented in the limestone-tempered ware are: plain, fabric-marked, check stamped, simple stamped, complicated stamped, and incised. (Sherds from this village cover a wider variety of decorative types than those found in Copena mounds.) Decorative types represented in the sand-tempered ware are: plain, incised, pinched, and cord-impressed. The clay-grit-tempered sherds are all of plain ware. Also present at this village site were: circular structure pattern and wattle; circular puddled clay fire basin; a number of storage or refuse pits; lapstones; circular hammerstones; flint knives, scrapers and drills; a broken Folsomoid point; stemmed projectile points, small triangular projectile points; bone and antler projectile points; antler drift or flaker; two-holed bar gorget; and splinter bone awls.

Interpretation of the Copena burial-ceremonial

system and its relationship to prehistoric Alabama awaits further investigation.[49]

TRANSITIONAL WOODLAND IN ALABAMA

GENERAL FEATURES

Transitional Woodland marks the introduction of more new pottery types into Alabama. The term "Transitional" has been used in describing this period because the new pottery appears to represent a continuation of older characteristics plus a minority of new characteristics which appear to indicate contact with Middle Mississippian.

TRANSITIONAL WOODLAND IN NORTH ALABAMA

In northwestern Alabama the use of limestone-tempered pottery was gradually replaced by a ware that has been called the McKelvey Series.[50]

MCKELVEY POTTERY

Pottery of this series is clay-grit-tempered, the clay particles being either crushed sherds or lumps of dried clay. The grit is often grains of chert, sandstone, quartzite, jasper, and rarely grains of quartz-sand. Vessel forms are medium sized globular pots with spherical bottoms and slightly flared rims. Bowl forms, both shallow and deep, occur. Some have ears projecting outward from the rim. Decorative treatments occurring most commonly are smoothed (plain), cord-marked and check stamped. Fabric-marking occurs as a minor decorative style and sherds bearing this treatment are indistinguishable, except for tempering material used, from fabric-marked limestone-tempered ware. Incising, forming chevrons and diagonal parallel lines on the lower rim area, occurs infrequently. Sherds bearing zoned punctated areas occur sporadically in small numbers.

McKelvey pottery carried on such Woodland decorative traits as cord marking and check stamping. Although basically Woodland, McKelvey pottery includes some traits not derived from a Woodland background. The use of clay tempering was probably derived from the West where clay tempering was characteristic during this period at Coles Creek sites in the Delta Region of the Mississippi River. Certain characteristics of vessel form (flattened bases and eared rims) were probably derived from this same region. Supporting this theory of certain western derivations is the fact that McKelvey pottery occurs most abundantly in the western portion of North Alabama. Other non-Woodland pottery characteristics such as noded handles appear to have been copies

45. Types occurring with most frequency are plain and fabric-marked. Check stamped is usually minority type and is often represented by only one sherd. At one Copena mound, however (Lu63, Haag, 1942b, p. 525), check stamped ware was predominant.

46. See Griffin, J. B., 1945d, pp. 229–234, 243; also Lewis and Kneberg, 1946, p. 87.

47. Lu^{v}65, described in Webb and DeJarnette, 1942, p. 173, Pls. 198–207.

48. Webb and DeJarnette, 1942, loc. cit.

49. Relationship of Copena to some of the other Hopewellian divisions is shown in a comparative trait list in Webb and Snow, 1945; see also Ford and Willey, 1940, p. 140; and Griffin, J. B., 1946, p. 72.

50. First described by Griffin, J. B., 1939. See also Haag, 1939a; 1942; also described in Dunlevey, n.d.

from shell-tempered pottery of the Middle Mississippian period.

The McKelvey pottery series has been equated with the period marking the introduction of Middle Mississippian into Alabama not only because of its apparent Coles Creek affiliations but also because of its frequent occurrence at the temple mound sites in various parts of the state. It occurs in the fills of temple mounds of the Tennessee River Valley Region of Alabama, at Moundville and at the Bessemer Site. At the Bessemer Site there were a few definite typological similarities between the McKelvey pottery and the shell-tempered ware.[51]

The real relationship between the clay-grit-tempered ware and the Middle Mississippian shell-tempered pottery is not clear. Certainly the McKelvey pottery did not lay the background out of which the latter pottery might have developed. On typological grounds the McKelvey pottery series is definitely more Woodland than it is Middle Mississippian. Summarily, McKelvey appears to represent a combination of Woodland pottery characteristics and characteristics of clay-tempered pottery of the Delta Region of the Mississippi River, into which Middle Mississippian pottery characteristics were sometimes blended.

TRANSITIONAL WOODLAND OF SOUTH ALABAMA

Surface survey of the Chattahoochee River Valley Region in southeast Alabama has revealed a pottery sequence analagous, perhaps, with the transitional period between Woodland and Middle Mississippian in northern Alabama. In the Chattahoochee Valley a common site assemblage includes a dilute Weeden Island[52] ware accompanied by later Fort Walton and Lamar types.[53] Weeden Island pottery, unaccompanied by later wares, is also found here in limited quantities.[54] Clarence B. Moore excavated a Weeden Island burial mound in this same region.[55]

Studies now being made of the Mobile Bay Region of southwest Alabama show Weeden Island and Coles Creek pottery occurring there.[56] In Clarke County, just north of the Mobile Bay Region, Moore excavated Weeden Island burial mounds along the Tombigbee River.[57]

MIDDLE MISSISSIPPIAN IN ALABAMA

GENERAL FEATURES

The Middle Mississippian period in Alabama marks (1) the most extensive aboriginal occupation of the state; (2) the highest aboriginal cultural stage attained in Alabama, characterized by agriculture, temple mounds, highly developed arts and industries; and (3) a decline (taking place just before and in the wake of Caucasian penetration and settlement of the state) during which the custom of burying in pottery urns came into use in south-central Alabama.

Middle Mississippian in Alabama and its relation to preceding periods will be outlined; the highlights of Middle Mississippian activities will be drawn, along with comments on the most extensive Middle Mississippian site in Alabama, Moundville; and, finally, burial urns and certain pottery changes marking the declining stages of Middle Mississippian in Alabama will be noted.

RELATION OF MIDDLE MISSISSIPPIAN TO PRECEDING PERIODS

The older cultural stages of Alabama do not lay a background out of which Middle Mississippian in its entirety might have developed. Copena offers the only typological link between the Woodland and Middle Mississippian periods in Alabama. If Middle Mississippian is in part a continuation of Copena traits, the following traits could have been derived from Copena: earthen burial mounds; the practice of burying the dead in extended position; the use of copper, especially for axes and earspools, the use of galena; the manufacture and use of polished greenstone celts; elbow tobacco pipes of stone and pottery, and elongate zoomorphic stone tobacco pipes.

Triangular, stemless projectile points as well as the puddled clay fire basin and wattle-work house construction so characteristic of the Middle Mississippian period might conceivably have their prototypes in Copena, if the fire basin, the structure and the triangular points[58] from Lu^v65 (described on preceding pages) are Copena.

Archaic and Woodland horizons of Alabama might have furnished to the Middle Mississippian period utilitarian objects such as bone awls, antler tines, bone fishhooks, whetrocks, grooved sharpening stones, lapstones, pebble hammers; the non-utilitarian use of marine shell for beads, pins and gorgets; and canine teeth beads. These traits, however, are widespread through various cultural horizons of the entire Southeast, so their occurrence in the Archaic and Woodland levels of Alabama has no special meaning so far as the problem of intrusion or indigenous development of the Middle Mississippian traits are concerned.

Middle Mississippian traits of Alabama having no apparent relationship whatever with the older complexes in Alabama are: temple mounds; planned

51. DeJarnette and Wimberly, 1941, p. 108 and Fig. 73.
52. Early Weeden Island apparently equates with the Transitional Woodland period.
53. Hurt, n.d.
54. For an analysis of the Weeden Island culture see Willey, 1949.
55. Moore, C. B., 1907c, pp. 442–445.
56. Wimberly, n.d.
57. Moore, C. B., 1905b, pp. 253–262.

58. Webb and DeJarnette, 1942, Pl. 207–1; lower row of plate artifacts.

orderly arrangement of village features; entrenched post construction for houses; shell-tempered pottery with its varied form and its varied decorative and surface treatments; pottery trowels; spatulate ceremonial axes; large stone discs; the numerous and varied "cult" manifestations including such designs as hand-eye, the forked (weeping) eye, the open eye, the barred oval, skull-and-bones, feathered serpent, spider, woodpecker, crouching or dancing figure, the cross and its variants, the sun symbol, the bilobed arrow and other cryptic symbols, some or all of which appear on various materials—pottery, copper, marine shell and stone.

THE MIDDLE MISSISSIPPIAN PEOPLE OF ALABAMA

Agriculture was the principal means of support for the Middle Mississippian people. We find widespread evidence of agriculture in their villages—portions of charred corn and beans, replicas of the gourd and squash in their pottery shapes. This concrete evidence, together with testimony of first Caucasian contacts, is supplanted by a consideration of the large size and permanent aspect of many of the Middle Mississippian villages, a situation possible only in the light of an abundant food supply, more than dependence on fishing, hunting and gathering would afford.

MOUNDS

At many of their villages in Alabama, Middle Mississippian people erected one or more large flat-topped mounds (Fig.151, upper left). Excavations of these mounds have revealed that they served as foundations for structures. It is speculated that these elevated structures served as temples or as chief's houses while the villagers occupied houses of similar construction on the unelevated surfaces surrounding the mound or mounds.

All such mounds excavated, so far, in Alabama have consisted of layers of earth successively laid down after the top surface of each layer had been used for a time as a structure floor. Ramps of earth gave an easier approach to the tops of steep-sided mounds.

At some Middle Mississippian villages, burial mounds were built in addition to temple mounds. These burial mounds, built of sand and clay were usually gradual accumulations of bodies and earth. At the Bessemer Site in central Alabama there was an unusual mound consisting of earth heaped over a "pavement" of limestone rocks which in turn overlay structure patterns. The mound was topped at one end by a conical "tower." A single burial was found in this mound.

DWELLINGS

Houses which the people of this period built (Fig. 151, upper right), both on the mounds and the surrounding village surfaces, had a typically rectangular floor plan and varied in size from small (10 X 15 feet) to larger ones (25 X 40 feet). Most commonly they made the walls of the structures by placing rows of upright posts in long narrow trenches outlining the floor. Earth was heaped into the trenches and tamped about the bases of the poles. Then the posts were interwoven with split cane after which this completed wall framework was plastered over with a clay and sand mixture (wattle-and-daub construction). Little is known of the roof detail, but it is probable that roof members were attached to the wall and met above the center of the structure to form a support for the thatch which probably topped the structure.

Variations of this type of structure are those which were laid out by digging holes for individual posts rather than by digging trenches. These structures were usually rectangular, but a few circular and semicircular structure patterns have been found.[59]

Interiors of all the structures were simple so far as archeological investigations reveal. Usually a circular puddled clay fire basin occupied a central position on the floor of the structure, while a few structures have revealed a single clay "seat" along one of the walls.

IMPLEMENTS

The Middle Mississippian people of Alabama utilized many of the raw materials directly available in the vicinity of their villages, but very often obtained foreign raw materials from distant places. Copper and galena were imported from outside the state, and marine shells were brought in either from the Gulf region or from the Atlantic coastal region.

From flint, chert, and jasper they made small, triangular projectile points (Fig. 151, *T*), scrapers, drills, (Fig. 151, *U*) and knives.

From greenstone they made polished celts, usually smaller than the Copena celts of similar style and flatter in cross-section (Fig. 151, *R*).

For needles and awls they utilized mainly the leg bones of the deer, although leg bones of birds, especially the turkey, were used (Fig. 151, *M–P*).

Sections of deer and bird bones were cut and shaped into fishhooks (Fig. 151, *K*).

Antler tines were used as implements (Fig. 151, *L*), and antler tips were perhaps used during this period for projectile points, but such use was not widespread.

Utilitarian objects of copper are rare and even such objects as copper axes and fishhooks, neither

59. At Moundville no complete circular patterns have been found.

of which are widespread through the Middle Mississippian material from Alabama, may have had a use more ceremonial than utilitarian.

ORNAMENTS AND CEREMONIAL OBJECTS

Ornaments which the Middle Mississippian Indians in Alabama wore were usually shell, rarely copper, occasionally stone and bone.

Both fresh-water and marine shells were used in making beads and pendants (Fig. 151, Y–B', E', F'). Tubular shell beads, disc shell beads, globular shell beads, and beads made of small univalves were often worn about the arms and legs, less often around the neck. These beads have a long history, having been worn in nearly identical styles by the Shell Mound Archaic peoples of Alabama. Long shell pins were perhaps hairpins, while shorter, knobbed pins were worn through perforations in the ear. Shell gorgets and pendants, often elaborately engraved, were worn over the breast.

Ornaments made of copper were pendants and earspools, and a very few beads. Pendants were often embossed with symbolic designs and earspools were made more elaborate by embossing them with single or concentric circles and rows of nodes (Fig. 151, C', D'). Compared with the use of shell for ornaments, copper was used but rarely.

Animal teeth, usually the canine tooth, were worn as necklaces after being drilled. Among the Middle Mississippian peoples of Alabama, however, this use of animal teeth for ornaments was restricted.

Stone was sometimes used for pendants and beads, but only occasionally.

Ceremonial objects other than those worn as ornaments were discoidals of stone and pottery (Fig. 151, X), stone spatulate axes, stone "batons," large stone disks which were occasionally engraved with "cult" symbols, copper axes with straight or curved (expanded) blades.

At Moundville appear two specialized items of ceremonial nature, counterparts for which have not been found in other Middle Mississippian units of Alabama. These are the monolithic axe (blade and handle carved from a single piece of stone), and the carved-stone bird effigy bowl.

TOBACCO PIPES

Although most Middle Mississippian pipes from Alabama are made of pottery and are of the elbow (equal armed) variety (Fig. 151, H'), there are occasionally human and animal effigy forms (Fig. 151, W). There are stone pipes, both in the equal-armed form and effigy form. The larger of these stone effigy pipes find their nearest relative in the Copena "dog pipe" mentioned earlier.

POTTERY

Middle Mississippian people in Alabama used most extensively a shell-tempered pottery. Use of this characteristic ware was spread throughout the state. A specialized variety of this ware, called salt-pan, occurs in some localities.

MIDDLE MISSISSIPPIAN POTTERY IN ALABAMA

Middle Mississippian pottery is typically shell-tempered. It has various forms: bottles (both large and small-mouthed) cups, bowls, plates, pots, and jars; a variety of effigy forms, with the bird (duck or turkey) being most common, but human, animal, fish, and vegetable (gourd) forms also occurring (Fig. 151, A–I).

Although much of this pottery is plain, it is often decorated, sometimes with elaborate designs.

Decorative treatment varies from painting in colors of red, tan and white to engraving executed after vessels had received their final firing. The simpler decorations were usually incised (while the clay was still soft), and consisted of single line decorations often accompanied by a row of punctations or short oblique incised lines. Another simple decorative style was the pasting of nodes and strips on the vessel rim (appliqué ware). Painting of pottery was relatively rare and consisted of geometric patterns directly applied or "Cult" patterns applied by negative painting (drawing the design on the vessel with grease or some other combustible agent and covering the entire vessel with paint, after which the vessel was fired, burning away the paint covering the design and leaving the painted surfaces outside of the design area only).

Engraving was the favorite means of applying "Cult" designs on pottery, although incising was common also. The engraved designs appear characteristically on vessels that had first received a black wash or film. The engraving, cut through this black film into the lighter color of the paste core, stood out boldly and for this reason was probably the favorite style of decorating with symbolic figures. The "Cult" figures and symbols occurring on Moundville pottery were usually reproduced in this manner (Fig. 152). Some few of these vessels have been found in the Tennessee River Valley Region of Alabama and have been found in fewer numbers at Middle Mississippian sites throughout the state. Other decorative styles occurring more or less infrequently throughout most of the state on shell-tempered ware are cord marking, check stamping, and, especially on those occurring with Caucasian trade material, brushed and complicated stamped. Appliqué of strips and nodes, sometimes accompanied by punctations, occurs on late ware of this period.

SALT-PAN WARE

A specialized form of Middle Mississippian shell-tempered ware is the thick, large basin known as "salt-pan ware," so-called because it is believed to have been used for evaporating saline solutions for obtaining salt. This ware is usually strikingly marked with an over-all pattern showing it had been impressed with a woven fabric. Perhaps a woven fabric form was used to support the clay as the vessel was formed. A few of the salt-pans lacked this feature and were plain, crudely smoothed.

At one place in Clarke County, Alabama, a great amount of this ware was found in the immediate vicinity of a large salt spring where even in late times salt was abundantly available. (During the War between the States, a Confederate saltworks was located here.)

MIDDLE MISSISSIPPIAN POTTERY IN SOUTH ALABAMA

Shell tempering is characteristic of the South Alabama Middle Mississippian ware, but here we find more sand-tempered ware in the Middle Mississippian horizon than in any other Middle Mississippian component of the state. The sand-tempered vessels, except for the tempering materials, are no different from the shell-tempered vessels.

The vessels are mainly open bowls and "casuela" bowls, with shallow plates, interiorly decorated, being common. Jars and bottles are infrequently found. The open bowls, casuela bowls and plates are often decorated with incised designs usually forming some variation of the scroll. Punctated dots often make up parts of the designs; "Cult" figures sometimes decorate the exterior of bowls (both the open and casuela types). The hand-eye design is the most common of these, and the skull-and-bones and the "weeping" eye occur sporadically. The bowls are occasionally black-filmed with a true wash-slip. Engraving as well as incising occurs on the slipped ware.[60]

Bird effigy vessels resemble those of North Alabama and Moundville. Human head effigies occur in abundance and are as a whole better executed than the modeled heads farther north in Alabama. The effigy bowls are usually steep-sided, shallow bowls with the head (either human or bird) facing inward above the lip of the bowl. Appendages other than the head are lacking except for a flange segment along the portion of the vessel lip opposite the head.

Influence exerted on the wares of the Middle Mississippian period of the Mobile Bay region seems to have been derived from Weeden Island, Coles Creek, and Moundville, and therefore shows a close relationship to Fort Walton ware.

Fort Walton ware is represented in Alabama mainly in the Chattahoochee River Valley Region where it occurs with Lamar ware, the two being apparently contemporaneous.

BURIALS

Burials were made in pits either directly in the village or in small burial mounds. Bodies were most often extended (fully) or with the trunk extended and the legs and arms only slightly flexed. Bundle burials (reburials) were not uncommon, and partly flexed to fully flexed burial was occasionally practiced. Personal ornaments, and evidently clothing, were left on the dead buried in the flesh; and very often pottery vessels, stone and bone implements, pipes and other objects were placed with the dead.

THE MIDDLE MISSISSIPPIAN SITE AT MOUNDVILLE, ALABAMA

Moundville represents the most extensive Middle Mississippian center in Alabama. A complete trait list for Moundville has not been drawn up, but the present stages of study indicate that Moundville is properly classed as Middle Mississippian.[61]

A superficial glance at Moundville material is greeted immediately with objects of ceremonial and "Cult" import. As yet there is no evidence that Moundville was occupied prior to the time that the "Cult" influence appeared in Alabama, but there is abundant evidence that Moundvillians had a day to day existence not occupied altogether with the manufacture and admiration of ceremonial objects. If all objects of ceremonial or "Cult" nature were removed from the Moundville material, there would still remain a mass of material that includes nearly all items found at the many Middle Mississippian sites of Alabama. In other words, Moundville is "basic" Middle Mississippian.

The illustrated trait list for Moundville presented in this paper shows a number of these "basic" traits (Fig. 151). These have been emphasized to show that Moundville may be equated not only with the specialized ceremonial sites of Etowah and Spiro but also with less ornate Middle Mississippian components.[62]

THE DECLINE OF THE MIDDLE MISSISSIPPIAN PERIOD

Marking the decline of the Middle Mississippian period in Alabama is the disappearance of the custom of building temple mounds and the discontinuance of the use of many "Cult" symbols. There seems to have been adopted just prior to or during this stage the custom of burying in pottery urns.

Concentrated in the south-central area of Alabama,

---

60. See illustrations in Moore, C. B., 1905 c, p. 291, Fig. 7; p. 294, Fig. 9; p. 296, Fig. 10.

61. See DeJarnette and Wimberly, 1941, for preliminary trait list of Moundville.

62. The ceremonial nature of Alabama is emphasized in Moore, 1905a; 1907a; A, and in Waring and Holder, 1945.

and extending both eastward and northwestward from there, are burial grounds containing burial urns.[63] The urns often contain the remains of more than one individual and may contain as many as five small children. Usually the flesh has been removed from the body when it was placed in the urn, although flesh burials of children had been common.

Little is known of the village life of the peoples practicing urn burial, but the urns themselves link them with the Middle Mississippian period. The urns are tempered with ground shell as is the typical Middle Mississippian ware of Alabama, and the decorations on the urns are very similar to the incised decoration of Mississippian ware. Objects of European manufacture often accompany the skeletons in the urns.

BURIAL URNS

The burial urns found in Alabama are typically very large jars, many measuring more than 50 cms. in maximum diameter, having high shoulders, straight to slightly flaring rims, and bodies either globular of flattened globular and spherical to sub-conoidal bases. Some have angular shoulders. Decorations are usually confined to the rim and upper shoulder areas.

63. Arrowpoints, 1922; see also Moore, 1899; 1904.

Some of the variations of decoration which the burial urn ware shares with other late wares of Alabama are: single and multiple incised scroll; diagonal parallel incised lines followed by rows of punctations; incised designs on the upper surfaces of out-turned bowl rims. Nearly always the urns are provided with some sort of cover. Most often this covering is a shallow or deep bowl and sometimes is a smaller urn. Many of the covers are large casuela bowls (incurved rims and angular shoulders). Less often a large fragment of an urn or a slab of stone is used as a cover. Sometimes the covering vessel, especially if another urn, fits inside the rim of the urn and rests on the flaring rim. The bowl type of cover usually fits over the urn and rests on the urn shoulder. Decorations on the cover are usually incised decorations similar to those on the urns except that the designs are characteristically drawn with more care, and appliquéd multiple strips placed either vertically or horizontally on the rim area.

The burial urn ware as well as most of the later-than-Moundville Middle Mississippian ware appears to be a dilute Moundville ceremonial ware, with degeneration in care of execution, and a loss of "Cult" designs except for an occasional occurrence of the hand-eye and the cross designs.

CREEK AND PRE-CREEK. *By Charles H. Fairbanks**

GEORGIA is rich in archeological sites but the systematic excavation has only been accomplished in recent years. C. C. Jones in 1873 noted most of the prominent sites and described many artifacts and some whole pottery vessels, but his work was not especially systematic and serves as little more than a survey. Holmes covered Georgia in his South Appalachian Group and does not further subdivide the material. In the light of recent work it is possible to divide his South Appalachian Group into several cultural complexes. Some of his illustrations remain the best available for the area. C. C. Moore touched the Georgia coastal areas briefly and got into southwest Georgia to some extent from the northwest Florida coast. In all these cases he missed the big sites and adds little to our knowledge of Georgia archeology. With the work of Heye at Nacoochee and Moorehead at Etowah the large-scale excavation of important sites was begun. This culminated with the extensive WPA excavations at Macon and Savannah. These tremendously increased the specific knowledge of the area and have resulted in a number of detailed papers which will be referred to later. Under Dr. Robert Wauchope the University of Georgia conducted a statewide survey to supplement the work done at Ocmulgee National Monument. The results of this survey are now being prepared for publication. The Georgia area has been surveyed by the Society for Georgia Archeology over a period of years and most of the material has been deposited at Ocmulgee National Monument. More recently the building of large multi-purpose dams on the Etowah (Alatoona Dam) and Savannah rivers (Clark Hill Dam) has resulted in surveys by Joseph Caldwell for the Smithsonian Institution. All of this work has resulted in an increasingly detailed knowledge of the early inhabitants of Georgia. It is now possible to identify the historic and prehistoric remains of the Creeks who were the largest Indian group in colonial times. Suggestions will be made as to the origins and developments of the various culture groups but obviously much work, both in the field and laboratory, must yet be done.

The earliest remains in the central Georgia area are probably the patinated flints of the early Macon period described by Kelly (Fig. 154, *A–DD*).[1] These flints are mainly chips but flake tools and fully chipped tools do occur. Side and end scrapers as well as a variety of gravers and one generalized Folsom point make up the collections together with a tremendous amount of flint scrap. The tool series is believed by Kelly to resemble the Folsom complex. All are heavily patinated in comparison with the patination shown on tools from the oldest pottery levels occurring in essentially the same soils. The flints occur in weathered clays underlying the oldest pottery levels and the mean depth of patination is at least twice that for the flint in the lowest pottery levels. I am not sure how much weight can be given to the evidence of patination as soil leaching and soil activities are much more rapid in the humid southeast than in areas where leaching studies have largely been made. There is as yet no evidence of association with fossil animal forms. Kelly discusses the possibility of "migration" from higher levels but the great bulk of the material would seem to rule out this possibility which challenges the very basis of systematic archeology as never again could we believe things belong where we find them. I would regard the patinated flints as belonging to the widespread Archaic group but not directly related to the nonceramic levels at the bases of the shell mounds. The flint types in detail do not closely resemble the types from the shell mounds and seem to be related to some Swift Creek types. Kelly found the flints scattered and did not locate a true occupation level. Thus they may be redeposited from some other location. At other points in Georgia generalized Folsom points have been found. A private collection at Ways, Georgia, had a large number, many with full channels. Thus there is some evidence of an old nonceramic occupation of Georgia. If a more satisfactory site could be found perhaps some of the ambiguities of the Macon patinated flints could be cleared up.

With the next group there begins a fairly continuous series of occupations in central Georgia. It is not intended that this series should be considered the work of one people or even that a steady process of development from one base is indicated. In fact, at least one major cultural break is present. But the occupation seems to have been fairly continuous and

* University of Chicago, B.A., 1939; University of Michigan, M.A., 1950; Teaching Fellow, University of Michigan, 1948–1950. Chapter received November, 1947.

1. Kelly, 1938.

there are few blank spots of major length. The oldest levels are again nonceramic but are not well known. At Tuft Springs, Adkins Mound, and Shell Rock Cave in the Macon area a flint industry was found below the pottery levels. It consists of large, heavy, generally triangular points with straight stems and a few plano-convex end scrapers. In general it seems to be related to the nonceramic levels at the bases of the shell mounds on the Tennessee and Savannah rivers. The fiber-tempered or Stalling's Island Focus does not seem to be developed to the extent it is in the Savannah Valley and so it is not surprising to find less evidence of the early and nonceramic stages. Most of the sites so far excavated in central Georgia are mounds or villages of later groups, chiefly Lamar, with midden and flint tools underlying the ceramic levels. The material has not yet been analyzed but it does not seem to develop directly into the ceramic levels as in Tennessee. It is distinct from the patinated flints of the Macon Plateau in shape of the points and the fact that it shows very little patination.

In central Georgia besides these sites there is also evidence of a buried flint industry that has shown up repeatedly in clay pits operated by the brick companies. These flints occur without any evidence of pottery and are in general like the Tuft Springs types. Colored (red, tan, white, and mottled) flints were extensively used. Long, wide, stemmed points, with several kinds of stems and shoulders, together with both ovate and triangular blades make the complex (Fig. 155). The flint work looks a lot like the flint from Stalling's Island and I believe is rather closely related. The sites have not been excavated except incidentally to clay mining because they are found from six to twenty feet below the present surface of the river swamps. The locations seem to follow the banks of sloughs through the swamp. The deep overburden is probably of fairly recent age but still quite respectable antiquity is indicated. A Lamar site in the area shows about 2 feet of overburden. It is probably that the rate of deposition of silt has increased rapidly in historic times. In northern Georgia local collections show highly similar points in fairly large numbers. All the points are large and most of them are long in proportion to width. Many are asymmetric. The sites from which these were collected are in general without pottery. Due to the fact that local collections are the only source of information and that, so far as I know, no sites have been excavated not much can be said about the nonflint traits.

Most of the river bottoms in central Georgia are overlain with a heavy mantle of recent alluvium and more early sites may be present. The sites so far found do not show the gradual development of pottery as on the Savannah River or the Georgia coast or even the Tennessee River Valley. Fiber-tempered

pottery is present as a minority ware in the next period and it is altogether possible that these early nonceramic people did not remain in central Georgia long enough to develop pottery and that the main center of development was on the Savannah with only a later penetration of the characteristic pottery during Swift Creek times. But a river bottom nonceramic level is clearly present. The people must have been simple hunters and collectors as were their relatives along the Savannah and the Georgia coast. Little can be said about their way of life until more has been learned of their material traits.

A form of simple stamping on fiber-tempered ware has been reported from the Stalling's Island site and from northern Alabama. This may be ancestral to the later simple stamping on sand-tempered ware. The impressions on this fiber-tempered simple stamped are more separate and look like individual impressions rather than the later type which seems to be a thong wrapped stick or possibly a simple grooved paddle. However there is definitely a suggestion that they are related techniques. It is unfortunate that the Mossy Oak period is not well known as it seems to be widespread. These people were hunters and collectors who seem to have moved rather frequently in small groups. The sites are small and generally thin. At the Mossy Oak Site in central Georgia the complex is found pure, below Lamar and separated from it by a sterile sand alluvium. The Mossy Oak trait list is quite similar to Swift Creek except that less is known about it and the list is probably not complete (Fig. 156, A–N). The general pattern of life of the two groups must have been very similar. Projectile points are often of white quartz and consequently heavy and rather shapeless. Pottery is sand-tempered with conoidal bases and rarely tetrapodal feet. The jars are quite deep and of small to medium size. The rim is usually straight and slightly flaring with sometimes an incised line at the neck. The simple stamping usually covers the entire vessel. In some cases it is rather carefully arranged so that adjacent impressions connect and the lines run roughly parallel. In most cases the stamping was rather carelessly done and does not present a neat appearance. Boatstones and two-hole, oval, flat gorgets are fairly common. They, presumably, in connection with the heavy projectile points, indicate the use of the atlatl or throwing stick. In central Georgia the only form of pipe is a short, conical tube of steatite.

In northern Georgia there is evidence that simple stamped pottery is associated with elements of the Adena complex such as copper celts, mica plates,[2] galena and magnetite lumps, plummets, etc.[3] The sites near Cartersville were not carefully excavated and much of the detail is lost but enough is known

2. Waring, 1945b, p. 120.   3. Fairbanks, 1946a, p. 127.

to show that Adena traits do occur and that they were associated with simple stamped and checked stamped pottery. Thus there is ample evidence of a more elaborate aspect to Mossy Oak life than the central Georgia remains at first indicated. Many of the elaborate carved stone pipes in the shape of animals from northern Georgia can be provisionally assigned to a slightly later Copena level which is contemporary with Middle Swift Creek. In central Georgia simple stamped pottery occurs on the same sites as the rock effigy mounds and is probably associated with their builders. There are two large rock effigy mounds in the shape of eagles(?) near Eatonton. One has a rock enclosure around it. In the same area are a number of small, conical rock mounds with depressed centers. They are located on hills in the same area and in very similar spots to the rock effigies. Only one effigy mound and none of the conical mounds has been excavated. At that one excavation Dr. A. R. Kelly found only simple stamped pottery which he called Vining Simple Stamped. The Vining site appears to have been a multiple occupation so the type name was changed to Mossy Oak Simple Stamped. Simple stamped pottery has been found on all these sites where surface collections have been made. There is no large amount or consistent occurrence of other pottery types. I feel certain that the effigy mounds and conical mounds belong to the Mossy Oak complex. Thus the bird symbolism found in Adena and Hopewell is present in Georgia along with other traits associated with these early manifestations. Perhaps it is premature to call this material Adena but the comparative term "Adenoid" has very little to recommend it. The term "Early Woodland" has been used in this volume as a period term for this level. At any rate there is in central and northern Georgia, associated with Mossy Oak Simple Stamped pottery, a group of traits that suggests a variety of the early ceremonial also found in Adena. So far the burial complex has not been excavated. The actual cultural picture may be that there was a widespread religious and economic pattern of which these elements are the only remains. This may well enough be the substratum from which so much later material developed. On the basis that Mossy Oak is earlier than Swift Creek or equivalent with Early Swift Creek and that Copena is contemporary with Middle Swift Creek the dating of the Mossy Oak period would agree well with the situation as it has been determined in the Tennessee Valley.

The best preserved of the early levels in central Georgia is the Swift Creek period named from a site a few miles south of Macon excavated by A. R. Kelly. Sites of this period are fairly numerous and widespread in north, central and south Georgia. Most of them are simple village sites in or near river swamps.

At Swift Creek itself an accretional mound of sand and humus was present. Some sites may contain burial mounds such as the large Kolomoki Site in southwest Georgia. These sites seem, however, to be Late Swift Creek.[4] The Evelyn Mound on the central Georgia coast was probably pyramidal but the occupation seems to be an aberrant or very late form of Swift Creek. Kolomoki also has a very large pyramidal mound but that site again shows Weeden Island pottery types and may be very late in the Swift Creek period. All this indicates a long time span for the Swift Creek occupation. Georgia seems to be definitely the center of distribution of the complex. The accretional mound seems to be definitely an experiment but whether it is an attempt to copy Middle Mississippi pyramidal mounds or the early shell mounds is far from clear. Or it may have been purely a practical expedient dictated by the rise of river water in the swamp location of the site. The presence of domed accretional mounds, some pyramidal mounds and some burial mounds would indicate some ceremonial practices but show that Swift Creek was removed from the main stream of mound building. I do not think Swift Creek can be regarded as the source of mound building in this area. Evidence of burials is so far lacking in excavated sites. The trait list so far determined is quite varied (Fig. 157). Agriculture may have been present but was certainly not important and the presence of shallow stone mortars and bun-shaped mullers might as well indicate the use of wild seeds and nuts. Chipped stone is abundant and usually of brightly colored pebble flints. Points are usually medium to large with heavy chipping, in general quite different from the Stalling's Island types. Stems are usually straight, with narrow shoulders, some side or diagonal notches, some opposite beveled or "spinner" points that are probably knives. There are many side and end scrapers and quite a variety of drills. These drills may be simple, with an expanded base, or with a cruciform base. Many points are asymmetric. Most of the chopping tools are fairly large and none seem to be true hoes. Some large chipped or battered notched choppers could have been used for almost anything. Large flat celts, smaller elliptical cross-section celts and the three-quarter grooved axes are well made but not common. Small flat whetstones suggest the sharpening of bone tools though none have been found. Small stone disks were found in a few cases but are probably intrusive from higher levels. Winged and prismatic bannerstones as well as boatstones indicate the use of the atlatl. Some types are very similar to those from Stalling's Island. The use of the atlatl was, of course, suggested by the large projectile points. Perforated steatite net sinkers are identical with those from

4. Fairbanks, 1946a.

Stalling's Island. Steatite vessels found on Swift Creek sites along with the abundant pottery are another hold-over from the Stalling's Island period. Rough hammerstones and small pebbles battered on the ends are common. The smaller pebbles may be flint working hammers. Steatite tubes are very scarce and indicate a rather tentative use of tobacco unless some form of cigar was used. A small seated human effigy of pottery suggests a religious life of some complexity. Stone pipes from northern Georgia seem to belong to this level on the basis of contemporaneity of Middle Swift Creek and Copena. One at Ocmulgee National Monument is an extremely well done and lifelike mountain lion, another a rather stiffly executed bear, others are long tubes. Thus there are suggestions of a rather elaborate side to Swift Creek life that is not yet well documented. On the whole the complex is archaic in its use of the atlatl and the suggestions of a collecting economy rather than a full fledged agriculture. The bulk of the complex seems to be the old hunting and collecting pattern with a few elements of the later agricultural periods. The pottery shows an unusual sophistication.

Swift Creek Complicated Stamped pottery is the most elaborate and neatest of all the Southeastern stamped wares (Fig. 157, Q–Y). It is grit-tempered, thin, well made, and completely stamped over the entire surface of the vessel. It can be divided on the basis of style and stratigraphy into Early, Middle, and Late periods. In the Early period it is comparatively weakly impressed, with narrow lands, more rectilinear elements, smaller folded rims and somewhat simpler designs. In the Middle period the designs become more curvilinear, bolder with broader lands, and the folded rims more prominent. In the Late period, not well represented at the type site, the designs tend to become large and more carelessly applied, rim folds large, and perhaps a tendency to decorate only the upper third of the vessel. On the basis of these types the more southern sites toward Florida fall into the Late period, though Florida also has Middle and Early material. The stamping is on deep jars with a conoidal base, slightly flaring rim and sometimes tetrapodal feet. These feet seem to occur at all levels. Towards Florida there is a tendency to decorate only the upper third of the jar. Plain shallow bowls may be more abundant in southern Georgia than in the central area. Towards northern Georgia the Swift Creek Complicated Stamped horizon breaks up into a number of subtypes on the basis of segregation of curvilinear and rectilinear motifs. In the central area this segregation does not seem to exist except as indicated from Early to Late. In northern Georgia also there is a tendency to fill rectangular areas with parallel lines. As the use of parallel lines seems to be an element of Early Swift Creek the northern material would seem to be early. However, the late Etowah Complicated Stamped uses this device and seems at the same time to be an outgrowth of Napier Complicated Stamped. At the present time the question as to whether the use of parallel lines in northern Georgia is simply a late development or a matter of spatial specialization is far from clear. Some of the north Georgia sites are certainly as early as central Swift Creek.

At the large Kolomoki Mound Group in southwest Georgia there are pyramidal mounds as well as some conical mounds with protruding boulders that suggest burial mounds. Here there is a large amount of rather Late Swift Creek Complicated Stamped, some zoned punctate and red filmed sherds that definitely tie in with Weeden Island. Rims on Swift Creek sherds are greatly thickened and have a very deep fold. Some of the stamped and punctate sherds seem to have exactly the same characteristics of paste and temper. This is apparently a mixed group such as the Santa Rosa–Swift Creek of northwest Florida. It is probably quite late in Swift Creek times and, as one of the few Swift Creek sites having a pyramidal mound, probably falls at the very end of the period. Smaller sites in the same region seem to be earlier on the basis of surface collections of Middle and Late Swift Creek Complicated Stamped sherds.

Swift Creek is usually associated in central Georgia with minority wares of fiber-tempered (Stalling's Island types), simple stamped (Mossy Oak), fabric-impressed and Napier Complicated Stamped. If the presence of Stalling's Island types in Swift Creek should prove to be the rule as more sites are excavated it would show that Swift Creek occupied the central Georgia piedmont during at least the later parts of the Stalling's Island period. However, Swift Creek does not appear on the coast until late Deptford times, a full period later than Stalling's Island. When it does appear it is Middle Swift Creek. We would have then a Savannah River area for Stalling's Island distribution and a central Georgia center for Swift Creek. At present that explanation agrees well with the known occurrence and distribution of trade sherds in central Georgia. These minority types are present in different proportions in the various Swift Creek sites. They will probably have considerable significance for the detailed chronological position of the whole range of sites. In the Tennessee Valley Webb found Pickwick Complicated Stamped[5] in the shell mounds above fiber-tempered and also associated with Copena sites. This type is extremely similar in decoration, form and lip treatment to Middle Swift Creek Complicated Stamped, except that it is tempered with crushed limestone. In the upper Tennessee Valley Lewis found Swift Creek Complicated

5. Webb, W. S., 1939, p. 52, Pl. 60a.

Stamped in the Candy Creek Focus, Upper Valley Aspect.[6] Here again the type is highly similar to Georgia specimens and they feel that some sherds are actual imports from the Swift Creek area. The sherds illustrated could certainly all be Middle Swift Creek. Some are limestone-tempered like Pickwick Complicated Stamped and others are grit-tempered and indistinguishable from Swift Creek Complicated Stamped. This would indicate that Swift Creek, Copena and Candy Creek are all contemporary, during the Middle period of Swift Creek. The Copena trait list as now known shows a number of variations from either Swift Creek or Candy Creek. This is due to the fact that the sites excavated in the Copena area are burial sites whereas burial traits are largely unknown from Swift Creek and Candy Creek. The Candy Creek trait list is very similar to Swift Creek except for the higher percentages of simple stamped and fabric-marked and the small triangular projectile points with incurvate sides. The fabric-marked sherds might almost be expected to be more abundant in the northern variant as the bulk of that type of decoration lies to the north. Again we get the impression that Swift Creek in central Georgia was a long period and probably outlasted both Copena and Candy Creek. In the Savannah area Brewton Hill Complicated Stamped[7] is again similar to Middle and Late Swift Creek and is found in the late Deptford period which comes between fiber-tempered and the Wilmington (cord-marked) periods. Brewton Hill Complicated Stamped seems to be stylistically almost transitional between Swift Creek Complicated Stamped and Lamar Complicated Stamped and thus is a very late type within the period. On the coast it seems to be later than in central Georgia and to reflect the late position of areas peripheral to the piedmont of central Georgia. The fact that it is not found as a majority type in the coastal region suggests that it was grafted onto an already existing ceramic complex. In southern Georgia and northern Florida, Swift Creek becomes merged with check stamped types to form the Santa Rosa–Swift Creek period.[8] The material seems to be Swift Creek of the Early, Middle and Late types. While the Kolomoki Mound Group is a large group and probably had a longer existence than the majority of sites it seems to indicate that Swift Creek and the allied Santa Rosa–Swift Creek continued up into Weeden Island times. Thus in the southern area as on the eastern coast there is a merging of Swift Creek with groups both earlier and later and it is not the dominant type it is in central Georgia. In both peripheral areas the check stamped type seems to be much

stronger and to have formed the dominant occupation. The tradition of zoning areas with punctations, which was first seen in fiber-tempered, is especially strong in Florida and is reminiscent of the Alexander series. Only late in Swift Creek, as a Weeden Island type, does it occur with Swift Creek. Swift Creek probably developed into Lamar although the precise steps cannot yet be demonstrated. In central Georgia it is found stratigraphically below Lamar at the Lamar and Cowerts Landing sites. It is also below Macon Plateau. Thus the evidence as I see it shows Swift Creek beginning while the last of the Stalling's Island people were still around, at about middle Deptford times. It also runs up into the beginning of Weeden Island times. The presence of minority amounts of Mossy Oak Simple Stamped and checked stamped fits in well with this dating. The minority sherds of fiber-tempered are less easy to account for on the basis of present information. If we assume that fiber-tempered lingered in central Georgia as a sort of refuge area during Deptford times we can account for the sherds. This might also account for the variations within the fiber-tempered types.

Swift Creek presents a number of problems the first of which is why the earliest of the complicated stamped wares should be so much the best in design and execution. That it was preceded by a long and rich art in wood carving seems certain. That it developed out of checked stamping or Mossy Oak Simple Stamped is hard to believe until indeterminate types forming a full complex are found. Types combining check stamped backgrounds with curvilinear designs superimposed are known but do not seem to form a clear-cut, complete complex. Holmes' idea,[9] that stamping came from the Antilles and developed on the Georgia coast, seems to have a number of objections. To begin with the Swift Creek sort of complicated stamping is not especially strong in precisely those areas along the coast where influences from the Antilles would be expected to be strongest. Rouse has shown that there is nothing in the Caribbean that is like Southeastern stamping.[10] The most that can be said now is that complicated wood carving may have spread from the Caribbean into the southeast. If Swift Creek subsequently grew out of this carving tradition it would seem to be begging the question to claim that stamping itself had it origins in Antillean cultures. The presence of even very similar sherds in Mexico or even China is outside the scope of the present problem unless we can demonstrate routes and stages of the diffusion. It seems to me that complicated stamping in the Southeast is a development in that area and an elaboration essentially within the area. The ultimate origins may be in the Caribbean, Mexico, or Asia, and these leads should be eagerly

6. Lewis and Kneberg, 1946, Pls. 46 and 47.
7. Caldwell and McCann, 1941.
8. Willey and Woodbury, 1942, pp. 241–242.

9. Holmes, 1894.   10. Rouse, 1940.

followed; but as a problem of Southeastern archeology it is uniquely our own and offers rich material for further research.

With Swift Creek the art of stamping in the Southeast begins a long and tortured existence. Lewis and Kneberg[11] suggest that Swift Creek may have been early Cherokee. As will be brought out in the discussion of the Lamar period, the northern sites of Lamar are late Cherokee. There is definitely a development from Swift Creek to Lamar, although it is not well documented at present. But present evidence seems to indicate that the Cherokee arrived in the Southeast in comparatively recent times. That they could have been in central Georgia as early as Swift Creek times I find hard to believe. The Swift Creek–like sherds from the Ohio region are of infrequent occurrence and peripheral to the Swift Creek area so they probably do not represent the location of the Cherokee with complicated stamping before their removal to the Southeastern mountains. I would like to suggest that complicated stamping (Swift Creek in its early form) became so firmly established in central Georgia that all later migrants to the area, including Cherokee and Creek, became infected with it and that no one ethnic group can be tied to the technique during its entire existance. The late arrival of Creek and Cherokee who used it does not agree with the long time span of stamping in Georgia. The arrival of Creek and Cherokee in the Southeast in comparatively recent times displaced numbers of earlier groups (perhaps Yuchi and Timucua?) and it is probably among some of these that the inventors (or adaptors) of complicated stamped pottery are to be found.

During the Swift Creek period people making Mossy Oak Simple Stamped pottery continued to live in central Georgia. Others making checked stamped, and another type of complicated stamped (Napier) lived here or nearby. In midden pits at Macon sherds of Swift Creek Complicated Stamped, Mossy Oak Simple Stamped, check stamped and Napier Complicated Stamped were present in varying percentages. Simple stamped and check stamped are generally below Swift Creek on the Georgia coast and in northern Florida. However in central Georgia they are contemporary on some sites at least. Napier Complicated Stamped (Kelly's Delta ware) is known from only one pure site in central Georgia but is apparently more abundant in northern Georgia from surface collections. It is characterized by thin, sand-tempered pottery decorated with a fine line, predominantly rectilinear complicated stamping. Usually the designs are chiefly rectangular areas filled with parallel lines. Lip folds are much taller than in Swift Creek Complicated Stamped (Fig. 156, O, W). On the whole the

11. Lewis and Kneberg, 1946, p. 99.

material is very easily distinguished from Swift Creek Complicated Stamped on the basis of temper, color and style. In northern Georgia this type seems to persist in time at the expense of curvilinear elements and to culminate in Etowah Complicated Stamped at a much later period. Another north Georgia variant has lozenge-shaped areas filled with parallel lines. It might be suggested that the Napier preoccupation with parallel lines reflected a hold-over from simple stamping types. This is also borne out by the fact that both Napier and Mossy Oak have a definitely gritty feel and appearance. But until complete stylistic studies are made of the Southeastern stamping types it is impossible to document such a development. At any rate Napier Complicated Stamped is much easier to derive from Mossy Oak Simple Stamped on stylistic and technical grounds than is Swift Creek. Check stamped is not at present known from pure sites in central Georgia and the presence of sherds in the Swift Creek sites must be ascribed to trade from the Georgia coast and Florida.

By far the most thoroughly excavated area in central Georgia is the Macon Plateau, now Ocmulgee National Monument. The Macon Plateau Focus ushers in the Middle Mississippian elements for the Southeast and temporarily interrupts the complicated stamping tradition. It is above Swift Creek, Mossy Oak and Napier, and below Lamar and Ocmulgee Fields. Macon Plateau makes a definite break with the old hunting-collecting economy and has a full-fledged agriculture. There is evidence of a field inside the town but the bulk of the gardens must have been outside and the mound group probably served as an assembly point for scattered family groups. The large mounds, fortifications, and ceremonial buildings indicate an economy with sufficient leisure for non-subsistence pursuits. They probably had a priesthood who ran things in the ceremonial center and may have had an elaborate political and military organization. The whole system was much more complicated than anything that had preceded it in central Georgia.

Macon Plateau traits include: sites (2) on hills above river plain and towns protected by large open ditches. The locations of the sites and the fortifications suggest that times were not very peaceful and that these Macon Plateau people had to defend their positions. Other traits are: Platform mounds, clay and log steps to mound top, plating of mound slopes with varied colored clays, water sorted sand on top of mounds, burials in and under platform mounds, extended, re-articulated burials of cleaned bones, partial cremations, bundle burials, extended burials in the flesh, log cribs around burials, agriculture important, row agriculture, at least one small field inside village fortifications, circular earthlodges paired with rectangular "Small Log Town House" type buildings, rectangular town houses on pyramidal mounds, earthlodges on village level, preferential seating in earthlodges, special platforms in earthlodges, pottery grit-tempered (early), shell or mixed shell and grit-tempered (later), plain surface large jars, either flaring or surged rims, expanded lips, loop handles (two per pot), erect effigies on lip of shallow bowls, blank face effigy water bottles, plain water bottles, simple twined impressions on salt pans, some fugitive red paint, pottery trowels, medium sized projectile points, stemmed and triangular projectile points, oval celts, discoidals, spud, cut disk shell beads, olivella shell beads, tubular shell beads, conch shell cup, plain oval circular shell gorgets, grooved bone pins, copper-covered cut puma jaws, copper embossed plaque, modified monitor type pipe of pottery or stone, caches of ovate flint blanks. The various activities of the communities will be discussed in detail but the list as a whole shows a remarkable similarity to those of the Hiwassee Island Focus of Lewis and Kneberg, and to the Small Log Town House of Webb in the Norris Basin. An added series of traits so far not recorded for either group in Tennessee and probably not present there is the burial complex suggestive of Adena or Hopewell (tombs under mounds, log tombs or cribs, partial cremations, re-articulated burials, caches of flint blanks, oval celts, etc.).

The two Macon Plateau communities known are large and the type site is very large. Both are on flat ridges some height above the flood plain. At the Macon Plateau Site there is a large series of two ditches around the village. Kelly believes these were combined defenses and semi-subterranean dwellings. The ditches seem to be primarily defensive and if they were ever used as dwellings it must have been as a refuge only. At Brown's Mount there was formerly a stone wall encircling the village area. At Macon Plateau there are seven flat topped mounds which had the usual rectangular structures on them. At the present there are few details of these buildings but they were basically of the small log type as described by Webb for the Bowman, Irvin, Richardson and Harris sites.[12] Mound C besides being a pyramidal mound had sub-mound pits and a large number of inclusive burials. It seems to have been the burial center of the community. This reflects a much different attitude toward burials than is found in the Small Log Town House and Hiwassee Island Foci in Tennessee. Two smaller mounds also may have been building platforms but the evidence was not clear. The most spectacular feature of the town was the pairing of rectangular buildings on mounds with circular earthlodges at village level. Basically, the earthlodges are the most universal American type but many details

12. Webb, W. S., 1938.

seem to fit rather well with southeastern historic, and especially, Creek social organization and religious practices. Such items would be: pairing of circular earthlodges and rectangular buildings, the dais opposite the door, the seats around the side, the suggestion of preferential seating, the tunnel-like entrance and the basins in front of the seats which I have suggested may have been vomative basins for use with the black drink so widely used in the Southeast. Webb has described a circular Adena structure that in features of the special clay dais opposite the door and the circular arrangement of seats suggests that Adena may have had a proto-type of the Macon earthlodge. In connection with the Adena traits in the burial complex this definitively suggests a connection between Macon Plateau and Adena or Hopewell. I do not mean to imply that Macon Plateau is a direct and lineal descendent of Adena, or its southern cousin Copena, but that it does share some ceremonial traits typical of the Adena-Hopewell groups. As Macon Plateau, on the basis of cross dating, is later than Copena it would seem that the Macon Plateau people came in contact with Copena or Hopewell before their arrival in Georgia. It is probable that they did not have a fully developed Middle Mississippi culture at that time. This would indicate the persistence of an Early Woodland religious cult, in a modified form, into the period of Middle Mississippi and the beginnings of the Southern Cult.

Chipped stone is not common and the conditions of the soil had destroyed most of the bone implements so we do not know much about the common tools of the Macon Plateau people. However, slender, split, and completely ground bone pins with encircling grooves at the top were found. Projectile points of flint are fairly large, stemmed, and rather crudely chipped. Tapered poll, oval cross-section, polished celts, bi-concave discoidals, and a bi-lobed spud comprise the polished stone traits. The spud is notable as it is an element of the Southern Cult. The celt is fairly large and suggestive of Copena celts. Two sets of copper covered cut puma jaws and an embossed sheet copper plaque were found with burials. I am not sure whether we should regard these as early traits or as elements of the Southern Cult. The copper plaque is not of the Eagle-man type but does seem more suggestive of the Cult than of the earlier type of plaque. *Olivella*, cut disk, cut tubular shell beads, plain shell gorget, and plain conch shell dipper indicate a simple shell industry and fair trade contacts. The plain shell work and the copper make Macon Plateau look like one of the earliest forms of Middle Mississippi. Pipes, usually of clay but sometimes of stone, have a projection ahead of the bowl suggesting a modified monitor type. There are types that seem to have been used without a stem as well as ones that were fitted with separate stems. All are much more massive than pipes of the Lamar period (Fig. 158).

The dominant characteristic of Macon Plateau pottery is that it is drab. There is none of the ornamentation of later Middle Mississippi and in general the types are hard to define in relation to other plain types. Nevertheless they are distinct from other central Georgia types. The predominant type is Bibb Plain, which in the earlier levels is grit-tempered but later becomes shell-tempered. Probably the bulk of it is mixed shell and grit-tempered. The common shape is a large, round bottomed jar with quite definite shoulder, flaring or surged rim, lip rounded or flattened and extruded. Only loop handles occur and often have a longitudinal groove or paired raised knobs at the top. These handles are the most common feature suggesting decoration on the jars. There are occasional paired nodes on the shoulder but they are quite rare. Shallow bowls of Bibb Plain are scarcer than the jars and are the only type generally decorated. They have small modeled heads projecting above the rim, one to a bowl and never any other part of the animal shown. The most common form seems to be a very generalized owl or perhaps eagle. A somewhat refined type of Bibb Plain confined to water bottles is called Halstead Plain. It is much finer in workmanship and finish, usually a polished black. Blank face as well as simple water bottles were found. Some bottles and perhaps some bowls were red filmed, but this treatment was rare. Fabric-impressed and plain salt pans have been called Hawkins Fabric Impressed and McDougal Plain, respectively. The most aberrant type is Macon Thick which was found in cylindrical jars of small diameter and thick walls. The thickness of the walls was often up to 20 mm. on jars only 100 mm. in diameter. The surface decoration was either deep incising, cord impressions, concentric circle stamped, occasionally punctated or often plain. The various decorative styles occurred singly on the jars and never seemed to have been combined. The only comparable types are some jars with roughly similar shapes from the northwest Florida area, probably Weeden Island period.[13] And these do not seem to be strictly comparable. Minority types at the Macon Plateau included Dunlap Fabric Impressed and some cord impressions on Bibb Plain type jars. One or two sherds of a thin, brown, zoned punctate type suggestive of Weeden Island were found but there is too little of the material to be sure of the exact period. Aside from the Macon Thick the pottery complex is highly similar to the pottery from the Small Log Town House sites as described by Griffin and the pottery of the Hiwassee Island Focus as described by Lewis and Kneberg. However Hiwassee Island has much more red filmed and a unique red-on-buff. The Hiwassee Island Complicated Stamped which seems to be very similar to Etowah Complicated Stamped is also absent from the Macon Plateau Focus. In the Macon period cord-marked sherds were present in small numbers but are universally grit-tempered and do not seem to have been as important in the complex as cord-marked at Hiwassee Island. The whole pottery complex seems to me to represent an early Middle Mississippi affair with very little of the emphasis on decoration that developed in later Middle Mississippi times. In the dominant pottery type, Bibb Plain, the Macon Plateau period is close to the Small Log Town House of Webb and the Hiwassee Island of Lewis and Kneberg. It seems to be closer to the Small Log Town House than to Hiwassee Island as a whole. Only in a few details of architecture and burial customs is there any great variation. The evidence from the pottery would seem to indicate that Macon Plateau was slightly earlier than Hiwassee Island and Etowah. But it must fall into the same general period.

Burials were more diverse than is usually found in one period and suggest that several elements were mixed in the Macon Plateau period. They were buried in the flesh; as typical bundle burials; partly cremated; or as re-articulated burials of cleaned bones. Some were in log cribs under one of the platform mounds, others inclusive in the mound or the adjacent village site. This mound had the additional Adena trait of inclusive burials during stages of mound construction. While the mound was definitely a platform and not the Adena type of burial mound it does have a vaguely Adena flavor.[14] It was probably the site of temples where burial rituals took place and the bodies were prepared for burial. The whole thing looks more like historic descriptions of bone picking among the Natchez and Choctaw than anything else described for the Southeast. The Southeast seems to have developed bone picking more and is the center of distribution of this trait. As one goes out from the Southeast the pattern becomes modified as on the North Carolina coast where White's drawings show keeping of bodies in special houses but there is no mention of a separate class of bone pickers. In addition to the Adena or Hopewell traits of burial forms, caches of flint blanks and the oval celt there were a number of traits such as the spud, conch shell cup, plain shell gorget, discoidals, copper placque, and the cult bird with weeping eye that suggest a formative stage of the Southern Cult. On the basis of cross dating Macon Plateau is slightly earlier than the large centers of the Southern Cult at Etowah and Moundville. Macon Plateau does not have the elaborate incising on pottery or shell shown at Etowah and can be presumed to be earlier on that basis. Other

13. Holmes, 1903, Pls. 91b and 106a.

14. Webb and Snow, 1945.

similar stylistic arguments could be shown, and I am definitely convinced that Macon Plateau is earlier than the maximum spread of the Cult. The elements of the Cult are present at Macon but are simple and do not yet seem to have permeated the entire life of the community as at Etowah, Moundville, or Spiro. It may be that the population pressures which developed in full Middle Mississippi gave an impetus to the spread and elaboration of the Cult that was lacking in the first invasion from the west. I am assuming that there is little argument that Middle Mississippi came into central Georgia from the west as it certainly did not develop out of Swift Creek. The only trouble is that as yet there is no group described for the western area that seems to have been the base for Macon Plateau.

All evidence points toward the Cult being mainly prehistoric in its maximum spread and having only remnants left in historic times. On the basis of an elaborate sherd cross dating Kreiger proposed the dates 1300–1400 for the cult.[15] This would seem to check well with my own conclusions from the central Georgia material. It has been suggested that the Southern Cult arose out of the old-time southern religion when it was faced with wild rumors of what Cortez did to the Aztecs.[16] Kreigers dates would seem to effectively quash that explanation. The cult may or may not be related to the Adena-Hopewell religion. The birds do not look closely related and the other presumed cult objects in Adena are in general not like those of the Southern Cult. But there is such a large time gap that the Adena bird could have grown to almost anything. Whatever the origins of the Southern Cult it does seem to have a formative period at the Macon Plateau level. Only later did it elaborate and thoroughly permeate the societies involved. I doubt that the Southern Cult was a "death" cult except in that the burial of the dead had a rather important place in the rituals of southern Indians of most periods. In view of the suggestion that the Macon Plateau people were invaders I think we have a clue to the pressures back of the spread of the Cult. With the spread of full agriculture populations evidently increased considerably. Populations had been slowly increasing since Archaic times but they reached a critical stage in Middle Mississippi times. The resulting pressures could well have been behind the Macon Plateau migration. Could these pressures also have generated the Cult? It seems certain Macon Plateau was agricultural as the cultivated field excavated by Kelly indicates. Probably the agricultural deities increased in importance during this period. I believe the Cult persons represent an agricultural deity identified with the sun and that the Cult spread

with Middle Mississippi agriculturists prior to any white contacts. I would doubt that either renegade Mexicans from the DeLuna expedition[17] or wild rumors of Cortez were responsible for the origin or spread of the Southern Cult. It is noteworthy that only the weeping-eyed bird is well developed at Macon Plateau. The more elaborate representations of cult deities are absent. At the level of Etowah and Lamar the more elaborate Cult items become common and seem to represent the full flower of the Cult.[18]

The Etowah Site near Cartersville in northwest Georgia is one of the most interesting sites in the south. The material is in general Lamar with mounds arranged around a court, complicated stamped pottery on deep jars, incised cazuela bowls, strap handles, shell-temper, grit-temper, red-painted pottery in a minority, etc. The Cult items are numerous and varied reflecting the metropolitan character of large sites. Such Tennessee traits as seated images and stone-box graves also show wide trade contacts. The pottery seems to be largely Etowah Complicated Stamped—a large deep jar with conoidal base, moderate shoulder and flaring rim. It generally lacks the notched, pinched or punctated rim fold of Lamar. The design elements are usually rectilinear; i.e., nested diamonds or triangles. This is a style highly reminiscent of Napier where there was an emphasis on parallel lines. If one must look for the origins of Etowah Complicated Stamped it would be in Napier rather than in Swift Creek. There is also some curvilinear complicated stamped material from Etowah but it seems to be in the minority. It more closely resembles Lamar than Swift Creek in execution, style, paste, temper, interior surface finish, etc. (Fig. 159).

Etowah has more elements of the later phase of Middle Mississippi than does Macon Plateau and seems to be slightly later but in the same general period. The lateness is borne out by the much more elaborate Cult objects. It seems that Etowah and Lamar are roughly contemporary and that, in Georgia as a whole, Macon Plateau falls into the early part of this period. Of course, at Macon the Lamar period succeeds Macon Plateau, but as a whole Lamar must have had a long time span. And the Cult seems to have developed during the Lamar-Etowah period. (To the north Lamar extends up into the eighteenth century but apparently does not last that long in central Georgia.) There is some suggestion that Etowah is earlier than Lamar but this results largely from a selection of earlier sites from the Etowah group in contrast to a series of later sites within the Lamar group. The complexes are roughly contemporary and I should imagine also closely enough related to form one aspect. What is notable about Lamar and Etowah

15. Krieger, 1947a.
16. Martin, Quimby, and Collier, 1947, p. 361.

17. Griffin, J. B., 1944a.   18. Waring and Holder, 1945.

in this context is the "mixed" pottery. Cazuela bowls often have stamped lower portions and "late" Middle Mississippi incised rims. This is a mixing on one object of two styles, the old stamping of the Southeast and the new incising of Middle Mississippi. Even without the hybrid forms the two styles are as separate jars throughout the complex. Thus there is clear evidence of mixing of two pottery styles. It seems to me that it also reflects the mixing of two societies. I do not know whether the skeletal material will show whether there is evidence of physical hybridization. But the material culture certainly does show a mixture. I would like to suggest that this cultural mixture may also have sparked the spread of the Southern Cult. The mixture is most apparent in Georgia but exists to some extent in all Middle Mississippi groups who were usually the possessors of the Cult.

We have seen that the Middle Mississippi invaders (Macon Plateau) possessed the simplest elements of the Cult. Then in the later period when mixing had taken place the Cult becomes exuberant and evidently becomes the dominant element of the various cultures involved. Did this exuberance of the Cult result from the mixture or from the conflict involved in the movement of Middle Mississippian peoples into the Southeast? I do not know and would certainly hesitate to suggest that the concept of hybrid vigor can be transferred to cultural affairs. Perhaps studies of other complexes which possess the Southern Cult with a view toward detecting evidence of this mixture would help solve some of the present problems of this widespread Cult.

Both the Small Log Town House and the Hiwassee Island Foci are just about contemporary with Macon Plateau, although Hiwassee Island at least may have lasted longer. They do not seem to be enough older or simpler to be ancestral to Macon Plateau. Hiwassee Island has a highly specialized ceremonial building complex different from Macon Plateau, a number of pottery types that are different and a completely different burial complex apparently. The Macon Plateau burial complex seems to be much more complex than anything suggested for Hiwassee Island and the elaborate ceremonial building complex of paired circular and rectangular structures is completely different. This then leaves us with little information on the origin of Macon Plateau. I do not know of any group in the general area of western Tennessee that could serve as the parent and yet that is the area that would most logically seem to be the location of their former home. It may be that Macon Plateau picked up the burial complex to the northwest where either the Adena-like complex of north Georgia or Copena could have loaned them to Macon Plateau. The whole appearance of the period suggests that it is the remains of a migrant people just arrived in central Georgia. It is hard not to compare the suggested origins of Macon Plateau with the origins of the Creeks as recounted in their migration legend, and assume that it represents the first wave of the Muskogeans to enter the area. There are plenty of small Muskogean-speaking groups lying at the fringes of the Muskogee proper who could fill these requirements. Perhaps the Hitchiti would be my best guess. In the next period the picture becomes much more complicated. If we do not assume that Macon Plateau is at least early Creek or Hitchiti we must postulate two separate pushes from the west and so far there is no ethnographic basis for such an assumption.

Macon Plateau is followed by the Lamar period (Fig. 160). There is at present among students of the Southeast and of adjacent areas a good deal of confusion about just what is meant by Lamar in central Georgia. This is due in part to the fact that excavations at the Lamar Site are not complete and that the dominant pottery type, Lamar Complicated Stamped, is widespread from the Carolinas and eastern Tennessee south to Florida. The same complex without stamping spreads westward into central Alabama. Some features of Lamar are present in the Fort Walton period of northwest Florida. In central Georgia, as possibly nowhere else, it is evident that a linguistic group cannot be tied irretrievably to a given pottery type and that the totality of the complex must be used in making ethnic comparisons. It is highly probable that further detailed analysis of the complex will have considerable bearing on the identification of the people using it and the cultural mechanisms at work. In central Georgia the Lamar period is to be identified with the protohistoric Creek, specifically the lower Creek and the various Hitchiti-speaking towns that were in the area during the time De Soto made his march through the Southeast. In the Carolinas it is Cherokee. In some sites in the Carolinas it seems to be Siouan. In eastern Tennessee it is Overhill Cherokee. At most sites where Lamar Complicated Stamped pottery is present there are also elements assigned to the late period Middle Mississippi. I would like to emphasize that Lamar Complicated Stamped is not associated with any one ethnic group but represents a strongly established local pottery making style, developed out of Swift Creek, and the later part of the Muskogeans moving into the southeast took over the technique and perhaps even the potters themselves. It is also recognized that, to some extent, early people with the technique already established were gradually modified by late Middle Mississippi diffusions such as incising, cazuela bowls, strap handles, etc. It is well established that the Creek had this culture and that they had recently come into the Southeast. If, as suggested in the Macon Plateau section, that group represents these Muskogean migrants, then Lamar must represent a later stage of Muskogean life. It may represent the same group after they had absorbed certain Southeastern elements or it may be an additional wave of migrants. It is certainly a period of hybridization of cultures and perhaps physical types as well. It seems simplest to assume only one migration, but that in waves and not as a single movement.

There are a large number of Lamar sites in Georgia. Some of the larger ones are: the Lamar Site at Macon, Nacoochee, Hollywood near Augusta (at least in the upper levels), Neisler on the Flint River, Shoulderbone and Shinholster's near Milledgeville, Maxey's near Athens, Singer in southwest Georgia and Bull Creek near Columbus, Turnbull in northeast Georgia and Irene near Savannah. Sites outside Georgia are Peachtree in North Carolina and the Fort Loudon Stockade in Tennessee. In addition there are numerous small sites covering a considerable range of time, many without mounds and most represented only by notes and surface collections at Ocmulgee National Monument. It seems to be the most widespread unit in the southeast and is about the equivalent of the South Appalachian of Holmes, although he does include some material now called Swift Creek. In central Georgia the typical sites have two mounds facing each other across an open court. At the Lamar Site the smaller mound is circular and has a counterclockwise spiral ramp, the only one known. At Lamar there is also an encircling palisade of individually set posts. The palisade showed a number of extra lines probably representing repair jobs and indicating a fairly long occupation. The site is located on a low natural rise in the river swamp. Other Lamar sites, especially around Eatonton, are located on bluffs or hills. In general, however, they seem to have preferred swamp hammocks for defensive or agricultural purposes. Villages were generally small or at least compact. At Lamar there were wattle-and-daub rectangular houses, often set on low dirt platforms. At Carroll Village Site near Eatonton house posts were set in wall trenches. Burials were in the village area, usually flexed and often without grave goods. But when they were accompanied by goods there was usually quite a collection; vessels, pipes, celts, shell gorgets, conch columella knobbed pins, copper plates, etc. Urn burials are found sporadically throughout Lamar and I am not sure what significance can be attached to their distribution. They may be early traits. Some projectile points were large and stemmed, some small triangular, probably the bow and arrow was the chief weapon. Agriculture is indicated by the presence of burned corn cobs and burned beans. Celts were small and triangular in shape, usually flat in cross-section. Shell work is more abundant than in the earlier levels and consists mainly of rather large shell beads, knobbed shell pins and large circular shell gorgets with the carved designs of the Southern Cult. There are probably time differences indicated by these shell gorgets but the details have not yet been worked out. Pipes were more abundant and one of the most spectactular items of the Lamar culture. It is evident that tobacco smoking became much more prevalent in Lamar than in previous periods. This may indicate an increased ceremonial use of tobacco or that smoking was released from ceremonial contexts and became habitual as in present American society. The known use of the Black Drink by the historic Creek suggests that the latter alternative was the reason for the increase in pipes. These pipes were almost always of clay and were fitted with detachable and perishable stems. Grotesque men's faces which suggest some of the cult deities were most common. Other types were the hafted celt, "boat shaped", bird heads, animal heads, phallic, and some with handles. Bone tools are slightly more prevalent than in earlier levels and consist of turkey leg bone awls, split and polished bone awls and probably antler points. Lamar Complicated Stamped and Lamar Bold Incised were the principle pottery types. It is as yet impossible to prepare detailed trait lists for the various subdivisions as we begin to distinguish them. But an attempt will be made to discuss some of the differences and indicate their significance. At present these differences show up as regional variations but I am not certain that some of the apparent regional specializations are not actually time differences.

The pottery of Lamar shows as much variation as the nonceramic traits and is much easier to handle on the basis of surface collections. Here I will only attempt to describe the central Georgia ceramic complex and note a few regional variations. As yet no systematic study of the pottery has been made. In central Georgia Lamar Complicated Stamped forms the bulk of the collections. It is grit-tempered with shell temper rare in the Macon area. Colors are gray, brown or black, interiors smooth and black or bluish-black. Most common are curvilinear designs such as the filfot cross, concentric circles, concentric figure eights, etc. Jars are deep with slightly flaring rim, lips either folded and pinched or reed marked on the folded rim strip. Reed marked rim bosses are rare in the central area, commoner toward the northeast, especially along the Savannah River. The filfot cross also seems to be commoner, and often exclusively used, on the coast and at points in North Carolina. Jars are generally large over most of the area. Shallow bowls, usually carinated, are almost always stamped with the exception of the rim area. Bases are generally flat. Rims were straight or sloping inward slightly. These rims are incised with broad line designs. Lips are simple, rounded or flattened. Handles are almost unknown on stamped jars and on bowls. Cord marking and simple stamping occur rarely. There is also some plain ware on jars and bowls. Red and white paint is sometimes found on the interior of plates and shallow bowls. At the Lamar site there were several examples of a plain surfaced, deep jar with conoidal base and four raised, noded points on the rim. This is similar to a type of the Dallas Focus of Tennessee.[19] There was also a vessel suggestive of the Southeastern basket shape with a square base. While the bodies of most incised bowls were stamped a fair proportion of them have plain lower parts (for Lamar pottery types see Fig. 160, S–DD).

Toward the west the pottery complex gradually changes. In view of the known movements of the Creek during the seventeenth century back towards central Alabama it is tempting to consider this a temporal change. Swanton has indicated that there was a gradual concentration of the Creek in the western part of their area during the time that must be the later part of the Lamar period. However, it does in part seem to be a function of space as stamping lingered longer on the coast. At the Neisler Site on the Flint River there was less grit and more shell temper, less stamping and more plain and incised surfaces. Simple water bottles, negative painted effigy water bottles ("dog pots"), gourd effigy dipper and incised and punctate sherds of a type reminiscent of Fort Walton of Florida were also present. Some sherds suggestive of the Gulf coast were also present in the Macon area, especially in the upper levels at Mossy Oak, but they were far from common. At Bull Creek near Columbus on the Chattachoochee there was even less stamping and more plain and incised sherds, with stamping still fairly strong. Again "dog pots" were found with burials. Across the Chattahoochee at such sites as the Abercrombie Mound in Alabama the stamping is even less common but the same incising is present in the cover jars of urn burials. South along the Chattahoochee from Columbus the Lamar horizon seems to gradually fade out and its place is to be taken by incised and punctate types from the Gulf coast (Fort Walton and the earlier Weeden Island). North of Macon the Lamar sites run pretty much like the central sites to the region of Atlanta and Athens. From that line north there are a number of changes. At the Turnbull Site on the Tugaloo River there is more plain ware, temper is crushed limestone, there is a late check stamped. Nonceramic traits, based on local collections, are: rattlesnake and turkey shell gorgets, knobbed shell pins, semicircular shell bracelets, bi-concave, bi-convex, or single-tapered stone discoidals plus a quantity of historic materials. This mound is probably the historic location of the Chero-

19. Lewis and Kneberg, 1946, Pl. 60g.

kee town of Tugaloo. At the Hollywood Mound near Augusta there was what appears to be fairly typical Lamar in the upper portions of the mound mixed with historic materials. The lower part of the mound was a mixture of Southern Cult (repoussé copper plates, copper ax, conch cup, sun disk water bottles, etc.) with Moundville incised, pipes of Lamar type except for one elaborate one of soapstone showing a seated person. Thus at Hollywood Lamar is historic (probably Cherokee) and stratigraphically above the Southern Cult. In general Lamar seems to be slightly later than the greatest spread of the Cult but the Cult is present in many Lamar sites. In other words Lamar was a fairly long period and the Southern Cult flourished in the earlier parts of the Lamar time zone. The profusion of historic material from the Hollywood mound is confusing as Thomas seems to say it occured with Cult materials. If so this would be a very late Cult site. Most of the Cult materials from historic sites seem to be a rather modified form and the objects often show a rather sloppy execution.

The Nacoochee Mound in northern Georgia yielded a great amount of material of the northern variant of Lamar. The large platform had rectangular structures on it but there is little information on their structural details. Some burials were precedent to the mound but there were also large numbers in the general village area. Burials were flexed and many were accompanied with grave goods. The pottery was of the Lamar type with some late elements. Temper was grit, sand and shell or shell alone. There was some red filmed material and one "dog pot" or effigy water bottle with negative painted design. The stamping was generally rectangular but seems to resemble Lamar rather than Etowah. Pinched rims of the Lamar type were common. There was at least some simple stamped and a good deal of plain ware. Bowls were common and usually incised in the Lamar style. Late pottery elements not common in central Lamar were: frog effigy bowls, lugs on bowls, human effigy heads on bowls, and occasional strap handles on globular jars. Pottery stamps, flamboyant Lamar type pipes, pottery disks, knobbed ear pins and conical pottery objects complete the ceramic complex. The stamps may be textile stamps rather than for working pottery as they do not seem adapted to the impression of clay. Shell work was abundant and included large gorgets, conch shell beads, knobbed ear pins, marginella beads, cups, pearls and shell hoes. Celts were flattened, slightly elliptical and often placed with burials. Small triangular projectile points were found as well as larger notched forms. Bone awls, pins, and antler tips, punches and chisels were common. Metal was used for ornaments and celts. Some of the copper was probably historic but much seems to have been prehistoric. Copper plates show a human torso and an eagle claw. The whole Nacoochee complex shows much more Southern Cult material than does central Lamar but it is not too aberrant to be assigned to the Lamar group. The chief changes were the presence of painted pottery and such traits as effigy bowls. As these were found in Lamar sites west of Macon (Neisler and Bull Creek) they are certainly part of the complex. I have suggested that these traits found on the western Georgia sites may be a function of the late position of the western sites and the picture at Nacoochee would seem to bear this out. However, there is no indication as to whether the Nacoochee materials are all one period. In fact the site probably represents a fairly long occupation, mostly in the Lamar period. The historic materials suggest that Nacoochee was occupied into the historic period and thus probably Cherokee. The notes as published are not sufficiently clear to rule out the possibility of an intrusion. In general the material seems to be slightly earlier than the European materials would indicate. Perhaps the best explanation would be that Nacoochee was occupied for a long period by one group who late in the life of the site got European trade goods. The alternative, that the Cult persisted until historic times in northern Georgia, is indicated by Hollywood but we need more data. Nacoochee is most closely related to Tugaloo, Neisler, and the upper levels of Hollywood. Of this group of sites Nacoochee, Tugaloo, and Hollywood seem to fall in the Cherokee orbit, and Neisler is in the Creek group. This obviously demands more analysis to determine what differences there are between the two groups. Of course all may some time be proved to belong to the same group, Cherokee or Creek, as there was a good deal of wandering around in the Southeast during this and the succeeding periods.

From the above discussion I hope that I have indicated that Lamar is fairly homogeneous but that regional and probably temporal differences do occur. At one time studies were under way to set up a Lamar Aspect on the basis of trait comparisons for the various sites. It was realized that this would be largely a study in virtuosity as the temporal position of Lamar was pretty generally established and the addition of aspectual and focal terminology would simply becloud the issue. However, it is apparent that we are dealing with areal as well as temporal units and some smaller breakdown of the material is needed. This should be done on the basis of trait comparison of a number of sites. It is apparent that different linguistic groups are involved, the Cherokee and Creek. Lamar is definitely later than Macon Plateau in central Georgia and probably, as a period, continued later than the Etowah Site occupation. I believe, however, that the Etowah and Lamar periods are roughly synchronous. In central Georgia material, ascribed to the Creek of the period just before Europeanization, complicated stamping was abandoned earlier than in the Tennessee material which can be ascribed to the Cherokee. I would regard this not alone as evidence of a more conservative attitude of the Cherokee but as a function of position as well. Some changes are undoubtably due to time but many must arise from geographical position. The Cherokee, in their mountains, were less in the movement of ideas and things than the Creek on the relatively open piedmont. The Southeastern stamping tradition was interrupted by the arrival of Macon Plateau people (perhaps the Muskogee). Then in Lamar times there followed a period when the return of stamping, and its incorporation into a pottery complex with other elements, indicates the return or resurgence of the people submerged by the Macon Plateau invasion. This is, of course, precisely what could be expected to happen. It is not usual for any group to disappear completely. During the Lamar period there seems to have been a continual pressure of late Middle Mississippian elements on the area. This was probably a period of diffusion of ideas through trade and tribal contact rather than a period of actual replacements. Actually some large movements of groups took place during this period but they seem to have been mainly within the area. The pressure of diffusion was felt most sharply by the towns to the west and it is precisely there that the most plain pottery, the most incising, painting, strap handles, effigy forms, and the least stamping, conoidal bases, etc., is found. Large metropolitan centers like Nacoochee and Etowah also attracted trade and show a greater variety of traits. As the process continued the late elements spread farther toward the coast. But it seems that stamping persisted into the historic period on the Georgia and Florida coasts (historic Timucuan sherds from the Castillo de San Marcos National Monument at St. Augustine, Florida, show a Lamar-like stamping). Just why the Cherokee resisted these late elements until the 1760 period when the Lower Creeks had given them up by 1700 is hard to explain. The Lower Creeks had close relatives in central Alabama and there was certainly a good deal of movement by whole towns back and forth between Alabama and Georgia. There must also have been much movement of individuals between Creek towns and these could carry word of the latest styles. The Southern Cult, in spite of its great homogeneity, does not seem to have been a unifying element as it is found in markedly different complexes. But it does indicate basic ceremonial beliefs in common over the entire area. The beginnings of the Lamar period were probably not sharply drawn except where actual intrusions took place as at Macon. In other places there was a gradual absorption of late elements. The end of the period is everywhere hard to define and in most cases is complicated by the appearance of European traits.

The Ocmulgee Fields period grew out of Lamar and is the remains of Lower Creek towns of the period from 1690 to about the American Revolution (Fig. 161). These towns so far investigated were Kasita, Coweta, Ocmulgee, and Oconee of the colonial period. The documentation is sufficiently exact so that we can be sure we are dealing with the Lower Creek towns in the period just before they lost the bulk of their ancestral methods of manufacture and took on an European technology. The chief characteristics of Ocmulgee Fields are the modification or loss of Lamar elements and they are best presented in tabular form (Fig. 161):

Lamar	Ocmulgee Fields
1. Pottery complicated stamped	1. Pottery brushed or stippled
2. Folded, pinched or punctated band below lip	2. Lip notched or applique fillet below lip
3. Large jars and bowls	3. Small to medium jars and bowls
4. Jar bases conoidal	4. Jar bases rounded
5. Bowl bases flat	5. Bowl bases rounded
6. Grit or later shell temper	6. Shell temper or temperless (Carbon flecks)
7. Simple bowl lips	7. Complex, shelf-like bowl lips
8. Cazuela bowl	8. Cazuela bowl
9. Some Woodland forms	9. Some forms derived from European
10. Handles on jars rare	10. Handles on jars common, strap type
11. Incising bold and rhythmic	11. Incising weak and sloppy
12. Incised scroll, guilloche, nested tables, nested triangles	12. Same elements but incomplete and unfinished
13. Mounds on most large sites	13. Mounds very rare
14. Anthropomorphic shell gorgets	14. Few shell gorgets
15. Knobbed conch shell pins	15. Knobbed conch shell pins.
16. Large conch shell beads	16. Large conch shell beads
17. Medium stemmed and small triangular projectile points	17. Small triangular projectile points only
18. Pipes flamboyant, complex elbow type, effigy, etc.	18. Pipes English clay or native copy of trade pipes
19. Burials flexed	19. Burials flexed or extended
20. Urn burials sporadically	20. Rarely inverted pot over infant bones
21. Grave goods not common	21. Grave goods common (trade goods)
22. European materials very rare	22. European materials common 1650–1730
23. Southern Cult usually	23. Only remnants of Southern Cult

From this comparative listing it will be seen that there are few added traits over the previous Lamar except those added through European influence. There is a steady modification of Lamar traits on the pattern already suggested in Lamar from eastern to western sites. The added Indian traits are definitely late Middle Mississippi such as the increased use of strap handles, rounded bases on jars, small triangular projectile points, etc. Two trends from Lamar seem to be present. One is the progressive loss of traits like mounds, flamboyant shell gorgets, effigy pipes, breakup of courtyard and mound arrangement of the villages, and in general the more complex Lamar traits. This tendency may reflect the gradual loss of aboriginal religious life as it is reflected in the material remains. We know the Creek by no means lost their old religious beliefs but they seem to be having a less pervasive effect on the entire economy. The other tendency is the progressive modification along lines already present in Lamar. As an instance of the first trend we have the fact that the elaborate material of the Southern Cult is pretty definitely religious in nature. Its loss in Ocmulgee Fields suggests the effect of the missionary showing up in the material remains. Many elements of historic Creek ceremonial practices are parallel or complimentary to the Cult and there can be little doubt that they are to be regarded as phases of the same basic religious belief. But the loss of much of the Cult objects reflects the changing way of life. The Creek in historic times must have moved rapidly into a cash and barter economy if the vast amount of deer skins shipped by the English is any indication. This also is reflected in the presence of vast amounts of European materials in the graves. These trade goods date from the closing years of the seventeenth century and the beginning of the eighteenth century. In other words, the Creek stopped making their own tools, ornaments and weapons and began to trade deer skins for European counterparts. This change to a barter economy must have profoundly effected the crafts, religion, economics and even diet. The lack of mounds and village plan may reflect the loss of community religious life. The added emphasis on grave goods may show an increased interest in the after life produced by Christianization. It should be possible to demonstrate the parallelisms between what is preserved of Creek religious ceremonial and the Southern Cult. I believe further studies will also show how the changing basis of Creek economy is reflected in the changing material culture.

The derivation of Ocmulgee Fields pottery styles from Lamar is undoubted and clinches the identification of the two complexes as historic and protohistoric Creek. Admittedly the pottery types alone are not enough to identify ethnic groups but the documentation and the comparisons of the total complexes leaves little doubt. In Lamar designs are bold and rhythmic and have a definite flare. The design is usually on the rim of cazuela bowls and almost always balances alternate rectangular and curvilinear; rectangular and diagonal, or diagonal and curvilinear elements. The designs "connect" or run smoothly from one element to another. The crossing of lines in the guilloche is exact, for instance. There is a certain amount of variation and especially toward the southwestern part of Georgia there is a good deal of more naturalistic designs, often accompanied by punctates. This is evidently a borrowing from Weeden Island and Fort Walton of the northwest Florida coast. But in general Lamar incising is very well drawn. In Ocmulgee Fields, on the other hand, the incising tends to be sloppy. Individual lines are weak and almost hesitant in execution. In the guilloche the lines do not meet at the crossing. The regular alternation of balanced elements breaks down. Many earlier elements such as the spiral, nested triangles, and nested tables are still present but they would be almost unrecognizable without the fine examples of Lamar. Often key lines that complete the element are omitted and the result is a more or less random incising. It is tempting to say that in Lamar the designs had meaning and that the potter knew what she was drawing while in Ocmulgee Fields she had forgotten the meaning or significance of the elements. Thus she was rather vaguely copying an effect rather than creating something with cultural meaning. The brushing and stippling of deep jars in the same way reflects the loss of Lamar techniques. In Lamar the stamping is pretty sloppy in comparison with Swift Creek but at least they were cutting recognizable dies and had in mind such elements as the filfot cross and concentric loops. In many ways the brushing and stippling of Ocmulgee Fields looks like an attempt to produce the rough surface of Lamar Complicated Stamped by someone who was too lazy to cut a stamp. This is assuming that stamping is a decorative technique and not a technical process. If it is technical (to compact the surface) the historic Creek had decided to do it an easier way. If the excellence of Lamar incising can be taken as an indication of the function of the designs in the culture, then the lack of coherence in Ocmulgee Fields shows a society in process of change where the old elements had lost their meaning. Thus Ocmulgee Fields would show both the loss of social and religious organization and the loss of tools, skills, and techniques of aboriginal life. This is further demonstrated by the use of European materials for old tools such as bottle glass for thumb-nail scrapers.

At least three excavated sites can be called full Ocmulgee Fields: Ocmulgee Fields at Macon, Lawson Field at Columbus (Kasita), and Big Sandy at Indian Springs. Another series such as the Arthur Tarver Site near Macon and the Ennis Site near Milledgeville seem to be transitional but predominately in the historic period. A large number of small sites show the presence of both Lamar and Ocmulgee Fields pottery types and only excavation could show whether there was a continuous occupation with cultural change or an intermittant occupation during both Lamar and Ocmulgee Fields periods. All of these sites fall in the area occupied by the Creek during the later part of the seventeenth and the first half of the eighteenth centuries. From about the middle of the eighteenth century the Creek seem to have been living more or less as farmers in log cabins, owning slaves and further acting like white colonials. They kept many social and religious traits but have left very little in the way of aboriginal artifacts. The early acceptance of European materials by the Creek with the consequent breakdown of old styles is a recurrent facet of the old problem of Creek and Cherokee. This process is much slower among the neighboring Cherokee and even the coastal Muskogean groups who kept stamping (as one item of many) until the beginning of the eighteenth century. The Cherokee seem to have been more conservative in many ways. They fiercely resisted the white inroads on their lands. But the Creek, following the example of Emperor Brim after his unsuccessful Yamassee War in 1715, seem to have adopted a policy of diplomatic maneuver. Spanish, French and English were played off one against another and trade advantages eagerly sought. This policy continued until the time of McGillivray after the American Revolution. Of course, once begun it could not be abandoned as the Creek could not relearn the forgotten crafts. It did succeed in maintaining Creek territory slightly later than did neighboring tribes. But from the early times on the presence of traders, largely Scotch and French, among the Creek was significant. These men probably did more to mix both blood lines and culture items than all the Spanish conquistidores and priests. The Creek had a well-developed pattern of adoption of conquered individuals and even fragmentary tribes such as the Yuchi. Probably this is reflected in their mixed culture of such varied parentage. It may also account for their ready acceptance of European traits. But even granting that the Creek had socially recognizable methods of accepting new ideas the breakdown of the old ways was rapid. The force of English traders was undoubtedly one element, Spanish Jesuit and Franciscan missionaries another. Perhaps the relative ease of travel over the rolling hills of central Georgia and Alabama was another factor in their readiness to change the ancestral way of life. These problems of why change took place at varying rates among different groups are ones that cannot be solved on archeological data alone. But the archeologist has the opportunity and duty to provide at least some of the data for their final solution.

To summarize very briefly the archeological periods of Georgia I would say that the earliest levels were the Early Macon Flint industry and possibly the deeply buried flints. These were followed by the very scattered evidences of the fiber-tempered or Stallings Island group. They were not well represented in central Georgia. Next comes the general period of Swift Creek. During early Swift Creek times the Mossy Oak people also inhabited central Georgia and may have preceded Swift Creek. But in general they are partly contemporary with early Swift Creek, which lasted much longer and is terminated by the Macon Plateau invasion. Macon Plateau is relatively isolated and falls into the beginning of the more widespread Lamar-Etowah period. This period is again fairly long and shows considerable development. It was during this period that the Southern Cult developed. Lamar is chiefly noteworthy because it exhibits a hybrid character evidencing mixture of old and new elements. If the Macon Plateau invasion is to be ascribed to some such group as the Hitchiti, then the Lamar period with its clear indications of cultural affiliation with the Lower Creek of the sixteenth century, is almost what could be expected of the mixture of old and new people in Georgia. The last or Ocmulgee Fields period is a logical outgrowth of Lamar and represents the material remains of the Lower Creek towns of Kasita, Ocmulgee and Oconee during the closing years of the seventeenth and early eighteenth centuries.

THE CULTURAL SEQUENCE OF THE CAROLINA PIEDMONT.

By Joffre Lanning Coe*

THE territory of North Carolina undulates like a multi-colored ribbon from the forested heights of the Great Smoky Mountains to the sandy waste of Cape Hatteras. Encompassed in this area of 57,000 square miles may be found segments of the entire range of southeastern habitat, varying from the birch and hemlock forests on the rugged Alleghenian highlands to the palm trees on the sandy islands in the estuary of the Cape Fear. The political boundaries of North Carolina cut arbitrarily across the natural regions of the Atlantic slope, isolating a portion of each from the whole. What is true of these environmental zones is also true of the people who inhabit them and of the culture that is theirs. Yet, for many years archeologists have thought of North Carolina as a homogeneous area—a kind of no-man's land between the great stamped pottery cultures of the South and the fabric-marked pottery cultures of the North Atlantic Coast. This interpretation, emphasized by the sharp contrast between two apparent culture areas, has tended to obscure the true nature of the problem. It has implied that North Carolina and the adjoining portions of Virginia and South Carolina are marginal areas partaking only of the crumbs from the higher tables of culture. It has denied for the Central Piedmont a cultural development paralleling and integrating with those to the south, to the west, and to the north. No progress was possible in this area until its uniqueness was realized. Now it is beginning to be demonstrated that there was a long and widespread cultural sequence and that it terminated in historic times with the decimation of the eastern Siouan tribes. To understand this sequence, it is necessary to see it in context as one of many interrelated facies of the whole prehistory of the region.

The early colonists soon discovered that "the Indian" was in reality many autonomous peoples who differed physically, culturally, and linguistically. Those with whom they first came in contact lived along the shores of the landlocked sounds of the tide-water region and spoke dialects of a language that is now known as Algonquian. Further inland the Tuscarora Indians lived along the Neuse River, and like the Cherokee in the mountains to the west, spoke a dialect of the Iroquoian language. Between the Tuscarora and the Cherokee, between the mountains and the coast, there lies a broad span of broken and rolling country called the Piedmont Plateau. In this area south of the Potomac and north of the Santee, there lived twenty-four other tribes who are believed to have spoken Siouan languages. Thus, by the beginning of the eighteenth century the traders and explorers were acquainted with over thirty different tribal dialects spoken in the Carolina area. Although these dialects have been classified as belonging to only three major linguistic families, the Algonquian, the Iroquoian, and the Siouan, many of those in the same family were not mutually intelligible. The Tuscarora could not understand his linguistic cousin, the Cherokee, and the Tutelo language showed a greater similarity to the western Dakota than to its neighbor, the Catawba.

This variety of languages observed at one point can serve only as an index to the complex nature of the aboriginal occupation; it does not identify cultures! There is no necessary relationship between the language a people spoke and the other elements of their culture. Some of these tribes with different speech participated in the same basic culture while some of those sharing a common language varied considerably in their cultural expression.

The identification and description of the cultures of these thirty historic tribes is a problem which can never be completely solved. With the possible exception of the Cherokee nearly all of the needed information will have to be obtained by archeological techniques. It was unfortunate, at least for the solution of this problem, that "the tribes between the mountains and the sea were of but small importance politically; no sustained mission work was ever attempted among them and there were but few literary men to take an interest in them. War, pestilence, whiskey and systematic slave hunts had nearly exterminated the aboriginal occupants of the Carolinas before anybody had thought them of sufficient im-

* University of North Carolina, B.A., 1944; University of Michigan, M.A., 1948. University of Chicago Archeological School, 1935; Director, Laboratory of Anthropology, University of North Carolina, 1948——. Chapter received March, 1950.

portance to ask who they were, how they lived, or what were their beliefs and opinions."[1]

Of even greater importance is the problem of reconstructing the cultural antecedents of these historic tribes. How much of their way of life in the seventeenth century was the result of influences from other parts of the country and how much was the result of a long period of development in this local area? Or did they migrate *in toto* into the area? There is every reason to believe that the Middle Atlantic States have been inhabited for several thousand years, and it is the task of archeology to isolate and describe the cultural change or continuity that has taken place.

The romanticist's picture of the "barbarian, headed by hunters and warriors and grouped in shifting tribes led by the chase"[2] is more rhetoric than fact. These primitive people seldom left their local territory unless forced to do so by circumstances beyond their control. The cultural complexes in North Carolina cannot be explained in terms of frequent and varied migrations. Nor can they be explained solely as the result of cultural stimuli from "higher" groups. This area was not just a convenient Basin Street where the north and south folks met. It has a long history of cultural development in its own right. There were no Etowahs or Spiros along the way, and the comparatively small, drab village sites scattered throughout the area have offered little incentive for extensive research. Furthermore, the quality of some of the early work that was attempted by the Bureau of American Ethnology in 1887 is reflected in the investigator's apparent free use of imagination in giving his finds the necessary local color. Nevertheless, the key to much of the cultural history of the Central Atlantic states is to be found in an understanding of the Siouan occupation of the Piedmont. This observation was originally made by William Henry Holmes nearly fifty years ago. His opinion was:

> Two tribes of Siouan stock, the Tutelo and Catawba, and perhaps others not so well known, inhabited parts of . . . Carolina . . . and it is probable that much of the confusion observed in the ceramics of these sections is due to this occupation. The stock was a vigorous one, and must have developed decided characteristics of art. . . . Whether the work of the various tribes was sufficiently individualized to permit of the separation of the remains at the present day is a question yet to be decided, but there is no doubt that the task may be at least partially accomplished by systematic collection and study.[3]

Such studies have been in progress since 1936 and there is now some evidence available to indicate the path along which this historic Siouan culture developed. Much further work will have to be done before all of the landmarks or waystations can be identified, but now that the general direction has been established the details will follow more rapidly. Unfortunately, the same cannot be said for the other areas of North Carolina. With the exception of a few localities along the coast, very little is known of the archeology of the region east of Raleigh. The cultures of the mountains section of the state are also poorly known. One site has been competently excavated in the classic Cherokee territory,[4] but the area north of Asheville has yet to be explored. The reader must keep in mind that the material presented here is a theoretical reconstruction. Much of the information for the early periods is based upon typological seriation of surface collections, and this evidence will have to be verified by controlled excavations. In general, however, this sequence for the Central Piedmont is believed to be sound and future work should serve to round out this image and complete the background.

To facilitate comparison between various culture complexes throughout the eastern United States six terms are in current usage to identify the major known horizons. These terms, Archaic, Early Woodland, Middle Woodland, Early Mississippi, Late Mississippi, and Late Woodland, were not intended to be regarded as classificatory units of culture or as strict time markers. They merely indicate a general cultural trend within a rather flexible period of time. The chronology for these periods is essentially that established for the Mississippi Valley, and it was hoped that cultural units in other areas could be tied on to this stem for the elucidation of the problems for the area as a whole. The Archaic generally refers to that period prior to the introduction or participation in pottery making. Early Woodland is the period characterized by the first extensive use of pottery, and Middle Woodland identifies the period of the Hopewellian expansion. Early and Late Mississippi are the great periods of pyramidal mound building in the Mississippi Valley, while the Late Woodland refers to a continuation of the Middle Woodland tradition in other areas. Unfortunately, these quasi-time-cultural periods cannot be satisfactorily used in all of the areas treated in this volume. The inadequacy of information or the very nature of the problem has made the correlation uncertain. This has frequently been the result of greater specialization along certain lines and the lack of adequate typological markers along others. For the North Carolina area these terms have been used wherever possible for comparison, but they cannot at present be adequately used to identify either stages or particular cultures. In this paper, the "Formative Phase" includes all cultural activity up to the introduction and

1. Mooney, 1894, p. 6.
2. McGee, 1897, p. 157.
3. Holmes, 1903, p. 142.

4. Setzler and Jennings, 1941.

general use of fired clay vessels. There is no reason to believe that this innovation took place at the same time or developed at the same rate in all parts of the state. Therefore, it does not mark a definite time period, but rather a certain cultural level. The "Developmental Phase" identifies the succeeding cultural level which is characterized by the extensive use of pottery and the development of agriculture; by the concentration of populations and the development of widespread cultural intercourse. The "Climactic Phase" began about 1550, near the time of European contact, and lasted through two centuries. This was the period of maximum expansion of the local groups and was marked by conflict, movement, and rapid cultural change, ending with the near extermination of all autochthonous cultures in the area.

THE FORMATIVE PHASE

The further back into time one tries to go in reconstructing man's history, the more difficult the task becomes. Ancient man lived in smaller social groups, populated less of the earth's surface, and produced fewer and cruder implements to mark his existence. Furthermore, the normal processes of nature, erosion and deposition, combine with man's own activities to destroy or hide the frugal remains that were left. It is not surprising, therefore, to find that so little is known about the early stages of man's life.

There has not been found in North Carolina, or in the region east of the Appalachians, any evidence that can reasonably demonstrate man's life there much before the beginning of the Christian era. This does not mean, however, that such evidence will not be found in the future. There are already some suggestions that the Piedmont Plateau may have been inhabited as early as 10,000 years ago by small bands of people who lived by hunting, fishing, and gathering of wild plants.

Most of the evidence so far advanced in support of a very early culture in the Piedmont has been the occasional finding of a fluted projectile point. These points are similar in form to the Folsom points found in Colorado, and it has frequently been assumed that the common use of such an unusual technique also indicated approximate contemporaneity. Unfortunately, no specimen of the eastern variety has been found in an early geological context. So far, these points have not been found clustered in an area small enough to suggest the presence of an actual habitation site. They are usually found singularly and on the surface. Soon after the Folsom point had become fashionable, considerable attention was centered on the Chase City–Oxford area of Virginia and North Carolina. This section was thought to be unusually rich in fluted points and attempts are still being made to find the precise location of the "Folsom" camps.

Actually this apparent concentration of fluted points was an illusion created by two enthusiastic collectors[5] in an area otherwise poorly known. Fluted points have now been found throughout the Piedmont and it appears that the makers of these points never showed a preference to the Chase City–Oxford area.

It is generally accepted that similarity in form alone does not prove contemporaneity, but in the case of the Folsom point any similarity of form has implied great age and perhaps in some cases rightly so. Yet, the desire to prove great antiquity for these points has hindered rather than helped the search for early cultures. Attention has been focused on this one particular form while an abundance of other typologically early material has gone unnoticed or has been obscured when miscast in an eastern version of the Folsom complex.

In 1938 the occurrence of an early stone tool culture was reported in Central Georgia. This complex consisted of a series of heavily patinated flakes, scrapers, knives, perforators, and points, and was found to underlie all other cultural material on the Macon Plateau. Some of these finds were unquestionably old, but their unique character was not realized apparently when the finding of one fluted point fragment influenced the conclusion that the whole complex "both the cutting tools and the projectiles have a 'Folsomoid' aspect."[6] Actually the specimens illustrated, in spite of their heavy patination, are closely related to the Badin Focus of the Central Piedmont. This focus has many traits that are reminiscent of Folsom, but like the Parrish Site in Western Kentucky[7] it also has polished stone atlatl weights. Furthermore, the Badin Focus people made pottery and clearly lived during the Early Woodland Period. It is fantastic to assume that they represented a Folsom continum separated from the parent stock by half a continent and 10,000 years.

There is no reason to believe that Folsom man was alone in this New World. His contemporaries were in many parts of the country, and signs of their existence are constantly being found. The early stone industries of the southeast are part of a general widespread chopper-scrapping-grinding tool complex that represents their legacy from the Old World. While they shared much of their basic culture with their contemporaries in other parts of the country, they also developed traits that distinguished them from their neighbors. In the High Plains the greatest specialization is to be found in the Folsom and Yuma points. In Southern California the Lake Mohave and Pinto Basin points are unique and in the Central

5. Mr. Arthur Robertson, Chase City, Virginia, and Mr. A. D. Capehart, Oxford, North Carolina.
6. Kelly, 1938, p. 7.
7. Haag, 1942a, pp. 217–218.

Piedmont the trademark is the Guilford point (Fig. 162,C).

THE GUILFORD FOCUS

The assemblage of traits known as the Guilford Focus is the most widespread and commonplace of all the early stone industries in the Piedmont and is well represented in every known collection of archeological material from this area. This abundance of specimens and their regional-wide distribution, however, cannot be counted among the archeologists' blessings because it is for this very reason that it has not been recognized before. This thin, widespread distribution has resulted in their being mixed with the remains of nearly every other succeeding culture and rarely have they been found in sufficient quantity at any one site to suggest their former independent existence. As more work was accomplished in the area, it gradually became apparent that there was an early, recurring complex that could be separated from the other known cultures. Once this complex was consciously looked for, it was found easy to recognize, and it has been established both typologically and stratigraphically as the earliest recognized culture on the Piedmont Plateau.

All known Guilford sites are small. They are usually found situated on top of a knoll or on the end of a long ridge nearest a stream. Water, however, appears to have been used primarily for drinking or cooking and there is no evidence that these people gathered shell fish or other aquatic life to any great extent. They were hunters of large game, for the most part, and preferred to make their camps in the hills rather than along the larger streams. The remains found at one place are usually scant, but their widespread distribution throughout the Piedmont and adjoining areas seems to indicate a long period of occupation for these small family groups. It also indicates that the Guilford culture changed very little during a period that may have lasted for a thousand or more years. The tools and weapons of these people were chipped from stone except for an occasional shallow mortar ground into the flattened surface of a small boulder (Fig. 162). Most of the flaking was done by means of direct percussion and retouching or pressure flaking was rarely practiced. Stone grinding was used only to smooth the edge and base of projectile points and occasionally the cutting edge of a celt-like tool. Ground and polished tools such as axes and atlatl weights were unknown. The most characteristic projectile point was a long, slender, but thick blade. Its base was usually concave, although less frequently it was made straight or slightly convex. In cross-section it was more rounded than eliptical and in some cases it appeared almost diamond shaped. On the most typical point (Fig. 162, C) the base and both edges of the blade for about one-third of the length were usually smoothed by grinding. Frequently the flaking runs diagonally across the body of the blade and, in general, suggests the Yuma type in a degenerate form.

The companion tool to the Guilford point is a crudely chipped stone ax. These axes are relatively small, seldom exceeding six inches in length, and invariably notched on either side for hafting. The poll of the axe is frequently as heavy as the blade, but usually thick, while the blade has a reasonably thin and often resharpened cutting edge. Some of the axes show signs of wear or polishing where they were hafted, but no instances of intentional grinding or polishing has been found.

Although the typological relationship of the Guilford point to the Yuma type is tenuous, there are occasionally found associated with this complex two other points that are remarkable because of the apparent close relationship to early Western types. These points appear to be identical in every respect to the Lake Mohave and Gypsum Cave types and, while this similarity in form may have little meaning in itself, the fact that they occur and reoccur consistently as part of the Guilford culture is significant and suggests that the Guilford culture is typologically, at least, one of the oldest in the Piedmont. This has recently been substantiated with the discovery of Guilford type materials buried to the depth of 12 feet in the flood plains of the Upper Pee Dee River and overlaid stratigraphically by the Savannah River and other known later cultures.

Just what connection these people may have had with Southern California and the Southwest is unknown, but the present information would seem to indicate that they probably shared a common cultural heritage in the not too far distant past. Except for the implements described above, the rest of the materials composing the Guilford complex is not distinctive. Large flakes were retouched and used as scrapers and simple, roughly executed, oval blades are common. Occasionally a flake or broken blade has been reshaped to form a long slender point which could serve for drilling and perforating. No burials have been found and there is no evidence of these people ever erecting houses or structures of any type. They lived as isolated families and moved frequently leaving behind scattered stone chips of their manufacture and an occasional lost or broken tool. What became of these people and their culture is unknown, although the presence of rudimentary stemmed blades (Fig. 162, F, G), especially in what are thought to represent the later Guilford sites, suggests that it could be one of the ancestors of the later Savannah River culture.

The second nearly universally distributed culture in the Piedmont may be identified with the Savannah River Focus of Georgia. However, this culture did not persist into pottery-making times in the Piedmont and the comparison must be made with the early prepottery levels of this culture where found along the Savannah River in Georgia and South Carolina. It is a true representative of the Archaic Period in the sense that it was prepottery yet the progenitors of polished stone tools. In its basic form, it appears to have been distributed east of the Appalachians from southern Delaware to central Alabama and no marked areal specialization can be noted until the introduction of the technique of firing clay vessels. The more southern groups appear to have oriented themselves with the technique of tempering the clay with vegetable fibers while the groups in the Upper Piedmont shared in the widespread northeastern technique of tempering pottery vessels with crushed rock. In general, these people were prolific users and manufacturers of soapstone vessels, having as one of the earliest forms a large, elongated tub-like vessel with crude lug handles at each end.

One of the clearest pictures of the transition from the soapstone vessels to pottery is to be found in the northern Piedmont where clay mixed with broken fragments of soapstone vessels were molded and fired in the form of the original stone prototype. This was pointed out nearly fifty years ago by William Henry Holmes, who stated with remarkable insight:

> It may be mentioned as a curious fact that as we approach the head of tide water on the Potomac and enter the district furnishing soapstone we observe the influence of this material on both the paste and the form of the earthenware. The sites about West Washington contain many sherds tempered with pulverized steatite, and the vessels to which they belonged were, in cases, supplied with rude nodes set a little beneath the rim, closely resembling the handles characterizing the steatite pots of the same section. From this circumstance it is clear that the making of pottery and the working of the soapstone quarries were contemporaneous events, a fact shown also by the intermingling of articles of both classes in the debris of many village sites.[8]

If Holmes had had at his disposal the present knowledge of cultural sequences in the East, he would have undoubtedly carried this hypothesis one step further and suggested that most of the early Woodland pottery of the northeast, such as Vinette I and Fayette Thick or the fabric-marked, grit-tempered sherds of the late Indian Knoll sites, may have shared their origin with the steatite tempered vessels made on the Potomac.

For some reason the people living in the Carolina Piedmont who participated in this Savannah River culture were not particularly fond of shell fish, al-

8. Holmes, 1903, p. 157.

though this seemed to be a favorite food of their more southern cousins. Numerous sites have been found along streams and rivers where mussels and various types of aquatic gastropods grew in abundance yet few are ever found in their camp refuse. Like their predecessors, the Guilford people, they appeared to have been much more interested in the hunting of large game and the gathering of forest products than in fishing. This, however, seems to be the main distinction. They ground and polished stone in the form of full grooved ax heads and prismatic atlatl weights. They chipped large but relatively thin knife blades and spear points that would be hard to distinguish from the materials found along the Savannah River. The spear points were broad but relatively short, averaging not more than four inches in length. The stem is straight with the base and shoulders being squared off precisely. The juncture of the stem with the shoulder was frequently evened up by grinding, so as to make this juncture a truer right angle. The knife blades were frequently made as large as 10 inches in length and four inches in width and were seldom stemmed. When stems were made they were rudimentary in form, being quite wide, but projecting beyond the blade very little. These blades were formed by strong, well-controlled blows, leaving large but relatively thin flake scars. While the overall appearance of these specimens is crude, their makers were undoubtedly the masters of the percussion technique. Their finished product was large, but thin and symmetrical without resorting to retouching by pressure flaking. They used most any handy flake as a scraping tool without much alteration, although flakes are occasionally found that have had their edges retouched to a nearly circular form. Drills were frequently made by rechipping a long slender point on a broken or discarded spearhead which often resulted in a cruciform appearance.

So far, this archaic culture is known only through its nonperishable remains and no objects manufactured from bone or shell are known. This is undoubtedly due to poor preservation in the sites rather than their absence in the original culture. Burials are unknown and there is no evidence for the use of any type of shelters or the existence of any organized communities. Like the earlier Guilford people, they were still wandering family groups, though somewhat larger in size, and made their homes wherever the hunting was good within the local area. Scattered fireplaces with an abundance of burned and fire-cracked stones in otherwise sandy soil would seem to indicate stone boiling as one means of cooking. The Savannah River period in the Carolina Piedmont was terminated with the displacement of the Savannah River–like cultures by a new culture and a new people. While it is reasonable to expect that the transition from the Guilford to the Savannah River culture may be more thoroughly demonstrated, it seems unlikely that their successors have any continuity with these early cultures in the Piedmont.

THE DEVELOPMENTAL PHASE

This new way of life, enforced by the invaders of the Piedmont, is by no means clear to us now. It was an event of considerable magnitude, however, equaling in many respects a similar invasion by the European colonist over a thousand years later. An understanding of what happened during this period will do much toward explaining many of the subsequent changes that have been observed but not interpreted.

Into the central Piedmont there came a new culture and, apparently, a new people. They penetrated the area like a wedge splitting the older communities into two parts isolating each from the other. From this time on the cultures of the Piedmont developed in three separate spheres. To the south, the Savannah River culture continued its logical development until the manufacture of a fiber-tempered pottery was commonplace. To the north, their cousins were soon to manufacture a soapstone-tempered clay vessel essentially as the result of their own ingenuity and the trend of the time. But in the central area the intruders introduced a new cultural tradition. They brought with them very definite ideas about the manufacture of clay pottery. They also brought with them the techniques and skill for the production of an unsurpassed stone industry. This culture is called the Badin Focus.

BADIN FOCUS

These people had a passion for engraving stone (Fig. 163, *K, O, S, W*). They used any stone available, although fragments of slate about the size of their hand was generally preferred. These engraved designs were both naturalistic and geometric. Some, however, were covered with such a maze of crisscrossed lines that they could hardly be called a design at all. It would be interesting to know for what purpose all of this engraving was done. Some of the slate pieces were obviously used only as a medium for the execution of the design, while others show considerable use, perhaps the result of grinding minerals for paint. Others that have only random lines on their surface may have served as a cutting block. Many of the waterworn river pebbles that were engraved were also perforated and worn as ornaments (Fig. 163, *K*). The graving tool used for this work was made from a large thin stone flake. Two notches were made side by side in the sharpest edge, leaving a fine point in between. This was a very effective tool, easily made and profusely used.

The Badin projectile point (Fig. 163, *A, G*) is the single trait most diagnostic of the culture. It is a side-notched point with a broad, rounded blade. The base is rounded at the edges, but concave at the center and usually finished by grinding smooth. When held with the base up, the tangs produced by the side notching resemble the horns of a ram. This point is the most unique, but not the most common type made by the Badin People. They were very fond of serrated edges and straight, square stems (Fig. 163, *M*) and made them in great quantities. Less frequently they used corner notches (Fig. 163, *N*) and simple tapering stems. Serrated edges and ground bases are two outstanding characteristics of the Badin chipped stone points.

These people were also fond of exotic forms of atlatl weights. They made the conventional forms of prismatic and butterfly weights (Fig. 163, *V*), but they preferred a double-pointed pick type (Fig. 163, *X)* or a semilunar variant with blunted ends (Fig. 163, *T*).

In considering the Badin culture one thing stands out above everything else, that is its great similarity to the Indian Knoll culture of Kentucky. The correlation of traits is so great that some direct connection must be postulated. This connection is further strengthened by the fact that the Badin culture appeared in the Piedmont about the same time the shell mound culture was being displaced by that of the Adena people in Kentucky. They appear to be the same physical type and they buried their dead in the same type of round pit. They were both beginning to make pottery: a crude clay-grit tempered ware usually smooth on the exterior, but sometimes paddled with a heavy wicker-type fabric.[9] Their stone industry was nearly identical. They both made essentially the same types of projectile points, drills, scrappers, stone balls, choppers, axes, and atlatl weights. No bone or shell objects have been recovered from a Badin site, but many of the engraved stones are reminiscent of the engraved bone objects found in Kentucky. They both did make heavy barrel-shaped stone beads.

On the basis of trait comparison, it would seem that the Badin–Indian Knoll relationship is closer than any other yet reported. The two are not identical, however, and, if these cultures are the product of the same people, considerable time must have elapsed between their exodus from Kentucky and their arrival in the Carolina Piedmont, since, among other things, they lost their taste for shell fish along the way and became more dependent upon large game. They also became more efficient and prolific potters and learned new styles for projectile points and atlatl weights.

The early stages of pottery making are absent in

9. Webb and Haag, 1947a, p. 27.

the central Piedmont, and the Badin culture represents the beginning of the ceramic era when it introduced well-developed pottery techniques. Although this culture is essentially "archaic" in form, it is roughly contemporaneous with the fiber-tempered pottery cultures further south and lies well within the Early Woodland Period. It represents the only major outside influence upon the local people until the beginning of European colonization. It is believed that these people were the direct lineal ancestors of the historic Siouan tribes and that this culture, modified through time and space, was the foundation for their later way of life. The remarkable thing about these people is their apparent conservatism and their resistance to change. Physically, the historic Siouan tribes have their closest counterpart among the skeletons of the Kentucky shell heaps,[10] and, culturally they changed very slowly until the Climactic Period. They were the rugged individuals of the early American way.

YADKIN FOCUS

The Yadkin culture is distinguished from its predecessor primarily by an advance in ceramic technology. Clay was abandoned as a tempering medium and was replaced entirely by sand or crushed rock. They continued to roughen the exterior surfaces of their vessels with a wicker-type fabric. It resembled that used by the Badin people, but was of a much finer weave. In addition another small group of vessels were either smoothed or roughened with a cord-wrapped paddle. The vessels were still just a cheap substitute for baskets or stone bowls and showed little of the imagination that characterizes true ceramic art. The simple bowl and the conoidal jar was the usual form, although a few pieces had a slight shoulder with a flaring rim.

Cigar-shaped clay pipes as well as carefully carved stone ones were smoked. The stone pipes were either of the simple platform type or of the large zoomorphic type, and they were made from local cholorite-schists or soapstone.

In the rest of the stone industry a number of changes were taking place. The three-quarter-grooved ax had replaced the full-grooved type, and it, in turn, was being discarded in favor of the large, roughly ground celts. The atlatl weights were still being made as well as some of the stemmed projectile points. A large broad base, triangular point, however, was gaining much favor, and perhaps this indicates the first appearance of the bow and arrow.

The Yadkin Focus belongs to the Middle Woodland Period. It represents the logical growth and change in the area without the benefit of much outside influence. For some reason the Hopewell cere-

10. Neumann, n.d.

monialism, so readily accepted elsewhere, made little impression upon the peoples of the Piedmont. The platform pipes suggest some contact, but its extent is unknown. The large celts, the more frequent zoomorphic pipes, and certain pottery characteristics suggest a closer relationship to the Copena culture to the west than to the classic Hopewell to the north. This seems a little strange since one of their principle sources of mica was the Western Carolina Mountains. A fairly close connection can be established, however, between the Yadkin Focus and the Deptford culture on the coast of Georgia. Linear checked stamped and dentate stamped pottery have been found in considerable quantity on several Yadkin sites. Some pieces resemble the Deptford series so closely that they may have actually been received in trade.

UWHARRIE FOCUS

The practice of agriculture was well established in the Piedmont by A.D. 1200. The small hunting groups of the preceding periods were beginning to settle down into village communities. Fields were cleared and permanent houses were being constructed. The sedentary aspects of agriculture were beginning to effect every phase of their daily life. Hunting was still their main occupation, but agriculture, as it was then practiced, gave the Uwharrie people greater security and stability. This security was soon reflected in a rapid growth of their population, and their villages increased in number throughout the length of the Yadkin River. Other Uwharrie villages spread northward into Virginia and southward along the Catawba and Broad Rivers into South Carolina. The Uwharrie was the most homogeneous and widespread of all of the pottery making cultures in the Piedmont. It was the parent culture out of which the later ones emerged, specialized, and diverged.

The Uwharrie village was composed of a cluster of small circular houses usually situated along the banks of the larger rivers. The frame of the houses were constructed of small interwoven saplings, and the roof and sides were covered with bark and skins. The fire pits were lined with stone and located near the center of the house, but nothing else is known about their interior furnishing. Burials were made in a cemetery area and not in the floor of the house as was the later custom. The usual practice was to bundle the body into as tight a flexed position as possible then place it in a round or oval pit three to four feet deep. Individuals were frequently buried with shell bead necklaces or bracelets and other objects such as gorgets and smoking pipes of polished stone. The Uwharrie individual had a long head and a high vault and is unquestionably the ancestor of the historic eastern Siouan Indians.

Pottery of the Uwharrie Focus represents a culmination of the Badin-Yadkin traits. The slight areal variations that were distinctive in the early periods were absorbed in the Uwharrie style. The pottery was simple in form, crude in execution, but functionally adequate. The vessels were invariably either a hemispherical bowl or a conoidal base jar with a slightly constricted neck and a short vertical rim. These forms were still conventional and showed little change from the styles originally introduced by the Badin culture (Fig. 163, Q, U). The temper became almost entirely crushed quartz. Some of the particles used were so large that they protruded through both sides of the vessel wall. The interior surfaces were invariably scraped with a serrated edged tool. The exterior surfaces, however, were finished in several ways. Cord-marking was continued from the preceding period, but the wicker fabric was no longer used for this purpose. A heavy net woven from two loosely twisted cords and wrapped around a paddle was one of the new innovations of this period for surfacing the exterior of vessels. Scraping the exterior surface was another new style that was soon to become commonplace. The Uwharrie potters were also the first in the area to use incising for decoration, but they went little beyond a series of parallel lines placed below the rim. These lines were crudely executed and continued completely around the vessel in groups of four or six. Frequently, on the cord-marked or net-impressed surfaces the rim area was scraped prior to the incision of these parallel lines. So far, in the ceramic history of the Piedmont, neither lugs, feet, or any other kind of appendages have been used.

Smoking pipes were made both from clay and stone. The former were still the large, tubular, and rather crudely executed type. The latter, however, were skillfully carved and invariably works of art. The stone used in almost every instant was a dark green chlorite-schist. In form, they represented the transition between the Hopewell platform type and the winged-stemmed type of the historic Piedmont tribes. The platform was still well defined, but the bowl had migrated toward the front end and had tipped from a vertical position to one of about thirty or forty degrees. The platform in some cases still projected a short distance beyond the base of the bowl. These pipes were carefully carved and polished to a high luster. After completion they were frequently engraved with various combinations of geometric designs. These designs varied from a ladder of cross-hatched triangles (similar to Fig. 163, O) to a series of concentric squares or rectangles. The designs were apparently engraved long after the completion of the pipe and by persons who were obviously less skillful than the original manufacturer.

Work in stone appears to have less importance now than during the previous period. Crudely ground celts replaced the three-quarter grooved axes and the bow and arrow had long replaced the atlatl. The typical projectile point was now in the form of a small, narrow triangle which seldom exceeded one and one-half inches in length and three-quarters of an inch in width. These points were usually well made with slightly concave sides and bases. Hoes were made from roughly chipped blades and were frequently resharpened as the cutting edge became dull with use.

The Uwharrie culture disappeared as the local tribal groups which once shared it gradually developed their own specialized arts and crafts. Its dissipation marked the close of the Developmental Phase which began nearly a thousand years ago with the invasion of the Piedmont by the Badin people. It was a period that saw the development of the ceramic arts and a basic change in the way of life of a people. It saw a migratory hunting and gathering existence change into a sedentary hunting and agricultural economy. It saw the change from temporary camps and open windbreaks to permanent villages and comfortable houses. It was a period of basic development for the peoples of the Piedmont.

THE CLIMACTIC PHASE

By the year A.D. 1550 a great many changes had taken place (Fig. 164). A new virile culture in central Georgia called Lamar was extending its influence northward through the Piedmont. The Iroquois Nation and the Powhatan Confederacy were pushing their political domination southward. At the same time, the coastal relatives of Lamar were moving their towns up the rivers away from the coast, possibly to escape Spanish interference. The old inhabitants of the Piedmont were being pressed upon from all sides and were soon faced with a grim struggle for their very existence. It was indeed a fight for life, and it lasted less than two hundred years.

PEE DEE FOCUS

One of the best archeological records of the movement of a people in the southeast is that of the Pee Dee Culture. It moved into the upper Pee Dee River Valley with household and baggage about the middle of the Sixteenth Century, forcing the Uwharrie descendants into the hills of the Piedmont. They established large villages and cultivated large fields. They were mature agriculturists. Yet, they never crossed the narrows of the Yadkin and after less than five generations of constant warfare, they left the region to return to the coast. They contributed nothing to the indigenous cultures except strife and received the same in return. Their period of success is stratigraphically sealed between the deposits of the dispossessed Uwharrie people and those of the historic Siouan tribes who finally forced their withdrawal.

The Pee Dee Focus gives contrast and life to the study of Piedmont cultures. It appeared so suddenly and was gone so quickly that it resembles a beam of light flashing across a dark sky. It tells us little about the slow plodding growth of the Piedmont hill tribes, but it does give us a better means of establishing relative age as well as a better understanding of the events that happened during the Climactic Phase.

The Pee Dee people lived in large compact villages protected by stockades and situated close to the banks of the river. Their domestic houses were the usual oval type, but their public buildings were square or rectangular in plan with plastered walls and a peaked roof of thatch. Some of their religious buildings were covered with earth and others were placed upon the top of pyramidal mounds. They buried their dead in pits dug into the floor of houses dedicated for that purpose.

The burial customs varied somewhat depending, apparently, upon the individual. Some were extended while others were completely flexed. All individuals, however, were carefully prepared for burial. The body was wrapped in cloth and skins and the pit was lined with bark. Roof timbers were placed over the burial so that the earth would not come into contact with it. Most of the infants that died were buried in large clay urns (Fig. 165, *W*). These urns were ritually killed by knocking out their bottoms, and then they were placed into pits along side the other burials in the houses of the dead.

These people were skillful potters as the large burial urns would indicate, yet they had very little imagination or creative drive. The vessel form, the surface finish, and the applied decoration were all stereotyped. All of the burial urns were made in the same shape, varying only in size from five to twenty gallons, and their usual surface finish was the complicated stamp. No decoration was ever applied to these urns. The smaller domestic ware was equally prosaic. There were only three types of surface finish: smooth, complicated stamped, and textile wrapped. Decoration consisted of small nodes or punctates around the shoulder of the cazuela type bowls (Fig. 165, *I, P*). Furthermore, the nodes, punctates, and rosettes were used almost exclusively on plain surfaced vessels. The textile-wrapped pottery (Fig. 165, *D*) is unique and, apparently, the private innovation of the Pee Dee potters. In surfacing a vessel in this fashion, it was first wrapped with strips of textile and then beaten all over with a plain paddle. This is the reverse of the usual procedure of wrapping a paddle with textile and then applying the paddle to the vessel.

Among the lesser crafts, work in shell was quite extensive and ranged from large conch masks and dippers to gorgets (Fig. 165, *A*) and a variety of beads.

Copper was used frequently for axes (Fig. 165, *C*) and in the manufacture of ornaments such as copper-coated wooden ear disks (Fig. 165, *X*). Bone splinters were sharpened into awls and, in some cases, they were made into ceremonial scratchers (Fig. 165, *F*). Clay pipes were carefully made, but, like the pottery, conformed strictly to the stereotype. The usual form had a short stem with a right angle bowl (Fig. 165, *S, T*). Their work in stone was nondistinctive except for a small pentagonal arrowpoint. Some of them were symmetrical and well-made, but the greatest number were asymmetrical (Fig. 165, *K*). It was deliberately done and not just poor workmanship. They used a thin flake to begin with and retouched it only as much as was necessary to make it conform to the desired shape.

The Pee Dee individual, like his culture, was unique for the Piedmont. He was rather short of stature and round-headed with severe head deformation or flattening. It is not possible at present to identify the tribal name of the people who possessed the Pee Dee culture, but it is fairly certain that they were a Muskogean-speaking people.

DAN RIVER FOCUS

When the Pee Dee communities began expanding northward, the small tribes of Uwharrie descent moved out of the lower valley and took refuge among their kinspeople in the hill country above the great narrows of the Yadkin. At about the same time their relatives in Virginia were moving south to a more secure position on the islands in the Roanoke River near Clarksville. The isolation once enjoyed by the Uwharrie people was no longer possible. External pressure herded them into a restricted area and forced them to co-operate in order to survive. The earlier trend of cultural isolation and specialization was reversed, and their constant contact with foreign cultures resulted in the assimilation of many new traits. The Climactic Phase was a period of rapid and radical change in many aspects of the culture of these people.

The Dan River Focus is the archeological reconstruction of the culture of the Sara Indians who were living along the Dan River in 1650. It represents the transition from the basic Uwharrie pattern to the climax of the Siouan cultures of the Piedmont in 1700. It shows the influences that effected this change and illustrates the generic relationship of one to the other.

The Sara Indians of this period were living in small palisaded villages that differed very little from those of their Uwharrie ancestors. Hunting and fishing supplied them with most of their food and that was supplemented with a variety of agricultural products. Their fields were cultivated with hoes made from roughly chipped stone blades, and a thick oval celt was their principle tool for cutting and clearing timber. Drills and knives were made by retouching small thin flakes of stone, and their arrowpoints were made in the traditional Uwharrie style. Although they retained the shape of a narrow triangle, with straight or slightly concave sides and base, they were somewhat smaller and seldom exceeded an inch in length. Bone tools were very common and consisted of a variety of awls, fish hooks, and flakers. The awls were made from both whole and split bones, but the most common type was made from the ulna of a deer. Fish hooks were cut from a flattened piece of bone and were grooved around the shank for attaching the line. Turtle shells were cut and scraped to serve as cups and were occasionally made into rattles as well.

Ornaments were made from both bone and shell. Bird bones were cut into short cylinders and used for beads, and certain phalanges from the wing were drilled and used as pendants. The large barrel-shaped shell beads of the Uwharrie period were made smaller, and a variety of small oval and disk-shaped beads were popular. More frequently, however, small marginella shells were perforated for stringing and used in their original shape.

Pipes were made from clay with considerable skill and imagination. Although a few large heavy tubular pipes were still made, the majority were carefully constructed and artistically designed. Some were made in the form of a straight tube, while the bowl of others were bent up to an angle of as much as thirty degrees. A few of the pipes were decorated with punctated designs, and one had the engraved figure of a man covering most of the stem and bowl. Their stone pipes were equally as well made as were those of the Uwharrie, and they were essentially the same type. These later pipes, however, had a less pronounced platform and the bowl was tipped farther toward the front of the stem.

The typical Uwharrie jar was still made. Coarse sand, however, had partially replaced the crushed quartz as tempering material, and combinations of straight and curved lines together with punctates supplemented the simple parallel lines of the earlier style. The traditional jar with restricted neck, short vertical rim, and conoidal base was seldom made. Instead, they preferred a wide-mouthed vessel with a flaring rim, but retained the conoidal base. Strap handles, in use for the first time, were added to the rim, and the outer edge of the lip was consistently notched or scored. The interior of the vessels was scraped with a serrated tool which left a rough striated surface, but the treatment of the exterior differed considerably from its ancestral form. Although the majority of the Dan River pottery was net-impressed, the heavy net-impressed and cord-marked surfaces most typical of the Uwharrie were completely absent. These later nets were woven from a fine thread and tied with small tight knots. Several kinds of weaves were used, but there seems to have been no preference. Cord-marked vessels were rare but when they were made, a thin, tightly twisted cord was used for wrapping the paddle. Some of the surfaces were only roughly scraped, but a few were carefully smoothed. The only radically new technique to appear at this time was the use of a corncob as a tool for finishing the exterior surfaces.

The Dan River Focus was a contemporary of the Pee Dee as attested by the numerous Pee Dee trade sherds yet no attempt was made by them to copy or use a stamp of any kind. They did, however, borrow the strap handle idea together with its peculiar punctate decoration from the Fort Ancient Culture of the Ohio Valley and casually experimented with the use of shell for temper in their own pottery. They traded with their northern relatives on the Roanoke and adopted lip notching as a decoration, but not the folded rim which was so characteristic of the Clarksville pottery. The presence of Catawba trade sherds on Dan River sites and their attempt to incorporate this more sophisticated incised decorations on their own pottery gives an early indication of the developing Lamar influence which was to spread throughout the Piedmont in another two generations.

HILLSBORO FOCUS

The Hillsboro Focus is a representative of the climax of the aboriginal Siouan culture in the Carolina Piedmont. It is the archeological remains of the Occaneechi Indians of 1700. A generation later they, together with the other Piedmont tribes, had lost their homes, their country, and their tribal integrity. They were reduced to the status of displaced families and attached themselves to any group who offered them shelter. Yet, as late as 1700 they were more concerned with intertribal warfare than with the ominous expansion of the English farmers, rogues, and gentlemen. European traders were well known to them, and a few of their products were finding favor in everyday use. The gun, however, had not replaced the bow and the copper kettle had not replaced the earthenware pot. Their crops were good and game was plentiful. "Their Cabins were hung with a good sort of Tapestry, as fat Bear, and barbacued or dried Venison; no Indians having greater Plenty of Provisions than these. The Savages do indeed, still possess the Flower of Carolina, the English enjoying only the Fag-end of that fine Country."[11] This oversight, however, was soon to be corrected.

It is known from historical records that the Hills-

11. Lawson, 1709, p. 54.

boro Focus and the Clarksville Focus are the remains of the same people separated by less than two generations. Their community plan, a small palisaded village of circular huts, remained unchanged and, in all probability, their other basic patterns of life as well. It was in the more fickle art of the potters, like the female fashions of today, that the change was most rapid. There is little doubt but that many of the Hillsboro potters also made pottery in the Clarksville style during their youth, yet a superficial study of the pottery alone would not indicate this close a relationship. The traditional net-wrapped paddle was entirely abandoned in favor of a carved paddle with either a simple or check stamp design (Fig. 166, A, S). Other vessels were rolled with corncobs and a great many more were finished smooth. The earlier characteristic rough interiors were now carefully smoothed, and the only temper used was fine sand. They were still conservative in decorating their pots and continued to use the folded rim or notches on the lip or a combination of the two. The notches or punctates on the lower edge of the rim-fold, however, were no longer made. Incised and punctate decorations were becoming more acceptable, and the standard conoidal jar (Fig. 166, S) was being supplemented with a bowl having a flat base and an incurving rim (Fig. 166, G). This cazuela type bowl, together with its crude bold incised decoration, clearly shows the effect of the Lamar cultural influence spreading from the southwestern part of the Piedmont, and it is further illustrated in an interesting attempt to combine the incurved rim of the new "Lamar type" bowl with the traditional outflaring rim (Fig. 166, R).

Compared with the pottery, the other crafts changed slowly. The arrowpoint remained a small equilateral triangle which seldom exceeded one-half an inch in length. Some were still made from quartz, although the majority were made from a silicified slate of local origin. Stone knives and scrapers were less frequently made and were soon to be replaced altogether by metal trade knives. In the same fashion the rather rough oval stone celt was being discarded in favor of the new metal ax. Bone tools, however, continued to be made in quantity. Awls made from bone splinters or the whole bone were in everyday use (Fig. 166, B, F, M). Needles were made from cut fragments of bone and a hide scraper formed out of the cannon bone of a deer was commonplace (Fig. 166, O, P). Antler fragments were carved into flaking tools (Fig. 166, D, N). Turtle shells were cut and scraped to form small drinking cups or drilled and mounted as rattles. Mussel shells were notched and used as scrapers in the manufacture of pottery. Marine shells were imported, cut, and ground into beads

of several sizes and shapes. A large oval variety was invariably worn in a string around the neck while those in the shape of a small disk were worn both in a string and embroidered on wrist and ankle bands. Whole marginella shells were ground for stringing and embroidered on a vest-like garment, and large sections of conch shells were fashioned into gorgets and engraved.

Smoking pipes were still made from both clay and stone, usually in the form of a simple tube (Fig. 166, K). Some pipes, however, had a swollen bowl set at a slight angle on a stem which had been flattened on top and decorated with small notches down the side (Fig. 166, J). The stone "platform pipe" of the Uwharrie and subsequent groups had become, basically, a tube. The nearly horizontal bowl was attached to the end of the winged stem which was frequently decorated with engraved designs composed of concentric rectangles and hatched triangles. Unlike certain pottery styles the short stemmed elbow pipe of the Lamar culture was not acceptable in their conservative smoking ritual, and the traditional tube form remained essentially unchanged as it has throughout the known history of these people.

Of all the changes that have occurred in the Piedmont cultures since the introduction of pottery the most dramatic was the appearance of a new mode of burial in the Hillsboro Focus. It was a shaft and chamber type of burial previously unknown in the Piedmont, but well known in certain areas of South and Central America.[12] The connection, if any, is unknown, but its uniqueness in this area and similarity of construction are not questioned. The Hillsboro burials were fully flexed and wrapped in skins or textiles and placed in a bark lined chamber cut into the side of a narrow vertical shaft at a depth of four to six feet. A pottery vessel was placed with the burial then the chamber was sealed with stone slabs or timbers and the entrance shaft filled with earth.

After 1700 nothing is really known about the Occaneechi Indians or the later changes in the Hillsboro Focus. It is thought that they may have joined the Tutelo and Saponi in their move toward the mouth of the Roanoke River. Again in 1722 they were mentioned as living with the Saponi and Tutelo at Fort Christanna in Virginia. Twenty years later, however, they had all left Virginia to seek protection among the Iroquois, and in 1753 they were formally adopted by the Cayuga and became a part of the Six Nations. In 1871, Waskiteng, the last of the full-blooded Tutelos died. There is no record of the last Saponian or of the last Occaneechian.

12. Ford, 1944.

THE ARCHEOLOGY OF EASTERN GEORGIA AND SOUTH CAROLINA. *By Joseph R. Caldwell*[*]

UNTIL quite recently little has been known of the archeology of eastern Georgia and South Carolina. This chapter will present briefly the prehistory of these regions, so far as it is now understood, by describing the successive archeological manifestations in the order of their appearance on the prehistoric scene, beginning with the oldest. The geographical area under consideration is an arbitrary one and more detailed surveys will need to be made before prehistoric cultural boundaries can be determined.

"EASTERN FOLSOM"

The distinctive flint and chert projectile points shown in Figure 167 may be the most ancient evidence of human activity in this region. Somewhat similar stone points have been found in New Mexico and Colorado associated with extinct fauna geologically datable to the close of the last glacial age.[1] The artifacts from Georgia and South Carolina have been random surface occurrences, without Pleistocene associations, and their relation, if any, to the western types is not clear.[2]

All the points shown in Figure 167 are in the United States National Museum. *A, B,* and *C* are from Kiokee Creek, Columbia County, Georgia; *D* is from Milledgeville, Baldwin County; *E* is from Forsythe County; and *F, G,* and *H* are from Buckhead Creek, Burke County.

THE SAVANNAH RIVER FOCUS

Aside from the Folsom-like points, concerning which little can yet be said, the earliest archeological remains in this area have been found in certain shell heaps on the Savannah River and adjacent portions of the Georgia and South Carolina coasts. The materials occurring at these sites are indicative of a simple hunting and gathering economy and the artifacts are sufficiently similar from one site to another to suggest their having been left by a single people or by a group of peoples of closely related culture. The two major shell heaps which have been excavated, Stalling's Island and Bilbo, were occupied more than once and in both cases the materials characteristic of the Savannah River Focus were stratigraphically below, and hence antedated, the other remains.

Stalling's Island on the Savannah River eight miles above Augusta is largely covered by an imposing heap of freshwater mussel and other shells. C. C. Jones described the pile in 1873 as roughly three hundred by one hundred twenty feet in extent and fifteen feet high. He trenched the shell heap, finding human burials, fragments of pottery, and implements and ornaments of animal bone, stone, and shell.[3]

In 1931 Claflin, working for Peabody Museum, made extensive excavations at Stalling's Island.[4] It soon became apparent that the materials he was finding were unusual and unlike the specimens of pottery and other artifacts which had hitherto been considered characteristic of the region. He named this archeological assemblage the "Stalling's Island Culture." Claflin also noted later refuse, storage, and burial pits cutting into the shell heap from higher levels. The pits contained fragments of most of the more common varieties of aboriginal pottery in the district, indicating that the distinctive Stalling's Island pottery and other material must have been older. A survey of the surrounding country showed the presence of several other Stalling's Island Culture sites.

Additional work at Stalling's Island was conducted by Fairbanks in 1940, and the Stallings Island Culture is now recognized as a component of the Savannah River Focus.[5] Fairbanks' excavations resulted from his interest in Claflin's statement that pottery was absent from the lower levels of the shell heap. Excavating three stratigraphic blocks, Fairbanks found that potsherds occurred mainly in the uppermost twelve inches of the heap and did not appear deeper than two feet. Other artifacts of stone and

* University of Chicago, M.A., 1943; now Archeologist, River Basin Surveys, Smithsonian Institution. Chapter received December, 1947.

Article published with permission of the Smithsonian Institution. Certain of the illustrations are reproduced through the courtesy of the above-named Institution, the Robert S. Peabody Foundation, the University of Georgia Press, *American Antiquity,* and Messrs. Charles C. Fairbanks and Antonio J. Waring, Jr.

1. Bryan and Ray, 1940, pp. 69–72.

2. Kelly, 1938, pp. 2–8, Fig. 5, and Wauchope, 1939, pp. 344–346, Fig. 30.

3. Jones, C. C., 1873, p. 197.   5. Fairbanks, 1942.

4. Claflin, 1931.

animal bone, however, continued downward for more than six feet. It was evident that the inhabitants of Stalling's Island had not begun to use pottery until relatively late in their history. A similar situation has been found at early and apparently related sites in northern Alabama,[6] where a variety of pottery comparable to the ware at Stalling's Island was preceded by vessels of steatite and sandstone.

The Bilbo shell heap, excavated by Waring near the mouth of the Savannah River yielded materials similar to those found at Stalling's. Bilbo was a much smaller site and contained no burials, but while Stalling's has some cultural traits which Bilbo does not have, Bilbo possesses hardly any which are not also found at Stalling's.[7] At the base of the Bilbo deposit was a shell layer which contained no artifacts at all, possibly a pre-pottery level. Examination of the strata above suggested that the culture had undergone changes with the passage of time: decorated pottery gradually increased at the expense of the plain pottery and there were apparent modifications in the types of bone pins and stone projectile points. The topmost layer, which included the humus zone and several intrusive pits, contained paddle stamped pottery of a subsequent period (Deptford).

From the excavations at Stalling's Island and Bilbo and from observations on other sites, we can deduce a number of the characteristics of the culture and economy of the Savannah River Focus people. Their favorite dwelling places were close to the Savannah River and the Ocean, on islands or knolls in tidal swamps, the better to collect the shellfish which formed a principal portion of their diet. Mussels were eaten near Stalling's Island and on the upper river, but oysters were the usual fare on the coast and in tidewater areas. Gar, sturgeon, and other fish were taken on lines with bone hooks (Fig. 168, G). The hooks were fashioned in an ingenious way, one step of the process being shown in Figure 168, D. Nets may also have been used. Pierced flat fragments of steatite, particularly abundant at Stalling's (Y) have been called net sinkers, although it is by no means certain that they were so employed. Another variety of stone objects also called net sinkers are pebbles, usually quartzite, with an encircling groove (W).

The atlatl-propelled spear is believed to have been the chief weapon of the chase because the stone projectile points, which occur abundantly, seem too large to have been arrowheads and because objects which might have been parts of atlatls have been found.[8] No complete specimen of the atlatl, which

was probably of wood, has survived, but antler hooks (E) and "bannerstones" (U) are currently identified as atlatl hooks and weights. Animal and bird bones found in the shell heaps testify which species were hunted and eaten. These included deer, bear, racoon, rabbit, turkey, waterfowl, and others. The dog may have been used for hunting; Claflin found four human burials accompanied by small animals with canine teeth, perhaps dogs although they were not identified as such in the original report.

For some reason, serviceable bone and stone tools have been found in greater abundance and in more variety at these early sites than in areas which were occupied in later times. Even the later shell heaps, where one might expect such specimens to be best preserved, have yielded relatively fewer artifacts of bone. Bone implements comprised awls and perforators made of various animal bones (Fig. 168, H, I, J), tubes, chisels (N), and flakers (N, O, P). Stone tools included hammerstones and mullers (V), mortars (AA), chipped stone knives and scrapers (Q, R), drills (T), and grooved axes (Z). Most stone tools were chipped by percussion but some objects were polished.

As we have already indicated, earthenware began to be used late in the history of Stalling's Island. There is no evidence so far that the adoption of pottery was accompanied by simultaneous changes or additions in the other material culture, although changes were doubtless being made as Waring has shown in the case of Bilbo. The pottery was crude compared to later southeastern wares and differs from them in being tempered with vegetable fiber, modeled rather than made by the more usual coiling process. Many vessels were merely smoothed before firing but others were decorated by varieties of punctation and occasionally by incising. A curious combination of an incised and punctated line (Fig. 169, C) is the hallmark of this ware. The simple bowl was the predominate vessel form.

Nothing of the apparel of these people is known, but ornaments were made of bone, stone and shell. They wore shell pendants and beads of several forms, bone pins sometimes incised with geometric designs (Fig. 168, A) or occasionally painted (B), and "gorgets" with two drilled holes which may have been for suspension.

When an individual died it was customary to bury him in a small round grave scooped out of the shell heap, sometimes abandoned storage pits were so used. In most cases the body was laid on the side with the knees drawn up, sometimes very tightly. There were occasional secondary or bundle burials, in which the bones only were interred after the flesh had been removed or allowed to disintegrate. Ornaments and implements were found with about one-fourth of the

6. Webb and DeJarnette, 1942, p. 308.

7. Waring, A. J., Jr., n.d.

8. The atlatl, or spear thrower, widespread in the Americas, served as an extension of the arm enabling the spear to be thrown with considerable force and range. See Webb, W. S., 1946, pp. 319–333, for a discussion of the atlatl and the arrangement of its parts.

burials at Stalling's, and we have already mentioned the occurrence of a small animal with some human burials.

The skeletal material obtained by Claflin was unsatisfactory for study purposes. The Stalling's Island people are said by Hooton to have been round-headed[9] which is interesting, if correct, for at other comparably early sites in the Southeast longheaded skulls were the rule.

There were many features of later aboriginal culture in the Southeast which were never known to the people of the Savannah River Focus. They did not build artificial mounds, they probably did not have the bow and arrow, and there is no evidence that they possessed permanent dwellings, agriculture, or tobacco.

Eight other sites located by Claflin in the vicinity of Stalling's Island on the Savannah River and Big Stevens Creek should be tentatively considered as belonging to the Savannah River Focus on the basis of Claflin's statement that "there is sufficient material from all the sites . . . to establish them as having been at one time occupied by the Stalling's Island people." Other Savannah River Focus sites are found at the mouth of the Savannah River near the Bilbo shell heap. The pottery is similar to that found at Stalling's Island and Bilbo. Excavations have been limited and few non-ceramic artifacts are known although there is a high correspondence in type among those which do occur. The Meldrim Site consisted of a fringe of low shell heaps on the shore of Wilmington Island near Savannah, Georgia. Two test pits yielded nothing but pottery, and the Stalling's Island–like sherds were mixed with later types (Deptford and Wilmington). The Oemler Marsh middens were two horseshoe-shaped deposits of considerable size in tidal swamp a few hundred feet from the shore of Wilmington Island. A small excavation in one of them revealed no materials other than pottery which was all similar to the Stalling's Island and Bilbo types. It has been suggested that these horseshoe-shaped sherd deposits may once have surrounded pile dwellings. A site at the upper end of Ossabaw Island, which was not visited by the writer, is represented in the National Museum by a collection of sherds, some of which are shown in Figure 169, A–D.

Across the river in Beaufort District, South Carolina, several sites of these people were investigated by Moorehead in 1933.[10] At Chester Field he found a large horseshoe-shaped ridge of piled oystershell containing pockets of periwinkles—the remains of dinners—some graceful bone pins, a bone scraper, a projectile point made from an antler tip, and fragments of worked antler and flint. Jones Island nearby

yielded identical pottery, a bone pin, a bone comb, and two pitted stones probably used to pound food. At Cat Island and Lake Plantation similar sherds were found but with pottery of later occupations as well.

Southward along the Georgia coast at Valona in McIntosh County many large Stalling's–like sherds have been found washing out on the beach. In Glynn County south of the Altamaha River, Holder found several sites which had such pottery along with later varieties but his work has not been published. These and more distant sites are not included in the Savannah River Focus, but the similarity of their pottery indicates, at least, a certain degree of contemporaneity. In the St. Johns area of northeast Florida a somewhat similar pottery again seems earliest.[11]

The material culture at Stalling's Island and at the other sites of the Savannah River Focus has many similarities with early assemblages which are widely distributed from Florida to Kentucky and which Ford and Willey classified into an "Archaic Stage" of eastern prehistory.[12] The term Archaic is still useful and is used in this volume. Fairbanks has suggested that the Savannah River Focus be included with the Lauderdale Focus of northern Alabama and the Indian Knoll Focus of Kentucky in a "Shell Mound Aspect,"[13] but Webb has placed Lauderdale and Indian Knoll together in a "Pickwick Aspect,"[14] and that is how matters stand at present. Ford and Quimby's discussion of the Tchefuncte "Period" in Louisiana was more concerned with establishing its relative time position than in placing it in any classificatory scheme,[15] but it is interesting to note that comparison of the Tchefuncte sites with the Savannah River, Lauderdale, and Indian Knoll Foci shows Tchefuncte to be by far the most divergent.

With the partial exception of Tchefuncte, the consimilarity of Archaic southeastern sites reflects a certain degree of contemporaneity, emphasized as Ford and Willey have pointed out, by the absence of traits which later sites possess.[16] Their common nonagricultural economy is the basis for other resemblances. Yet the artifacts from widely separated sites correspond to such a degree that genetic and diffusionistic relationships are certain, though as yet not delineated. To do this we shall need many more sites excavated, detailed comparisons among separated areas, more human skeletal material, and within each area comparisons of the pre-pottery with the pottery bearing levels.

---

9. Claflin, 1931, p. 45.
10. Flannery, 1943; Griffin, 1943b.

11. Griffin, 1945a, pp. 218–223.
12. Ford and Willey, 1941, pp. 332–334.
13. Fairbanks, 1942, pp. 230–231.
14. Webb and DeJarnette, 1942, p. 317.
15. Ford and Quimby, 1945, pp. 90–92.
16. Ford and Willey, 1941.

THE THOM'S CREEK AND HORSE ISLAND
MANIFESTATIONS

There is yet little evidence that the Savannah River Focus extended far into South Carolina but other sites occur which are somehow closely related. At Thom's Creek and at another site below Columbia is found pottery resembling that of the Savannah River but distinguished by sand tempering and by minor differences in form and decoration.[17] One hundred miles away at Horse Island in Charleston District on the Coast a similar though not identical ware (Fig. 169) is in the majority,[18] and some such sherds have been noticed at Stalling's Island. The question arises whether Thom's Creek is the South Carolina equivalent of the horizon represented by the Savannah River Focus or whether it is somewhat later.

THE DEPTFORD PERIOD

The Deptford Site occupied a high bluff on the Georgia side of the Savannah River about two miles below Savannah. Shell deposits extended for several hundred feet along the bluff and sparser occupational evidence continued for a considerable distance back. There was a small burial mound about a quarter mile to the southwest.

In 1937, stratigraphic work by Waring and Holder showed that several varieties of pottery at Deptford occurred in a definite sequence,[19] interpreted as follows. The first occupation was during Savannah River Focus times when relatively small amounts of Stalling's-like pottery were left by a people who evidently belonged to that cultural grouping. Then, after an interval of unknown duration the site was reoccupied during a period which we call Deptford. The abundant, well-made, and often elaborately stamped Deptford pottery indicates that this occupation must have been heavy, or long in duration. The next period, called Wilmington, saw another heavy habitation of the site, this time characterized by abundant pottery decorated by cord-wrapped paddle. An even later period, named Savannah I, was indicated as a result of excavations in the burial mound by H. Thomas Cain.[20]

Thus we see that the Deptford Site was occupied during four periods of the coastal sequence. The second occupation at Deptford, the Deptford Period proper, is the one with which we are concerned here. Unfortunately little is known of the Deptford Period aside from its pottery. In 1940 Catherine McCann excavated a considerable portion of the bluff at Deptford in order to obtain a sampling of the material culture assemblages of the Deptford and Wilmington

period.[21] Although her work brought to light about forty burials and many artifacts, it was difficult to segregate the materials of the two occupations. Most of the burials apparently belonged to Wilmington times, but many of the artifacts, shown in Figure 170, can pertain to either period or to both.

Figure 170, *A, B, C,* are representative potsherds of the Deptford Period, and *D* shows the most common shapes of vessels. The decoration of *A* is called linear check stamping,[22] in this case probably impressed with a carved wooden paddle although specimens occur suggesting use of a roulette. The decoration of *B* is termed simple stamping[23] and might have been made with the edge of a stick. The decoration of *C* is referred to as complicated stamping,[24] and was probably executed by use of a large elaborately carved wooden paddle. The distribution of complicated stamped sherds in the stratigraphic pits suggested that this variety of decoration was a late addition to the pottery of the Deptford Period. There are other Deptford pottery types which occurred less frequently.[25] Deptford Period pottery was made by the coiling method, and is very sandy, suggesting that sand was intentionally added as temper.

Figure 170, *K* and *O,* are respectively a platform pipe and a small cup representing a number of such objects found at Deptford. The pottery of which they are made has paste similarities to Deptford vessels, and we suppose that it is to the Deptford Period that these artifacts belong. The pipes provide the first evidence of the smoking custom on the Georgia coast. The other objects in Figure 170 may pertain either to Deptford or Wilmington times: *E, F, G,* and *H* are respectively shell gorgets, a shell bead, and a chisel, all made from conch; *I* comprises awls or perforators of various mammalian bones, except the third from the left which is of a fish spine; *V* is probably a bone projectile point; and *J* are pins, which we distinguish from awls on the basis of delicacy or presence of decoration. Objects *L, M, N,* are respectively flint projectile points or knives, a drill and a long curved flake, possibly also a knife; *P* is a polished stone plummet, *Q* a fragment of a bannerstone or atlatl weight, *R* a polished hemispherical stone, *S* possibly a whetstone, *T* a stone gorget, and *U* a celt.

Deptford Period sites are not too common at the mouth of the Savannah River, or anywhere for that matter, although stray sherds often are found. A site occurs on upper Pipemaker's Creek and another is reported on the road between Savannah and Coffee

17. Griffin, 1945*b*.
18. United States National Museum Collections.
19. Waring, A. J., Jr., personal communication.
20. Caldwell, McCann, and Hulse, n.d.

21. *Ibid.*
22. Type name is Deptford Linear Check Stamped. The names of other pottery types are footnoted in passing.
23. Deptford Simple Stamped.
24. Deptford Complicated Stamped.
25. Deptford Plain, Deptford Zone Punctated and Deptford Cord Marked. The last type might be transitional to the next period.

Bluff. Much farther south, Deptford pottery appeared in some of Holder's Glynn County excavations.

Deptford pottery is present in collections from Beaufort District South Carolina, a site is reported at Union Landing, Jasper District,[26] and sherds have been identified in southeastern North Carolina.[27]

A pottery with some Deptford characteristics, but more like the early stamped wares of northern Georgia and eastern Tennessee is found in central South Carolina. It also appears in the upper Savannah basin and is stratigraphically above the Savannah River Focus at Stalling's Island. In the western part of the state it has been noted near Greenville, and at Colonoy and Reedy River.[28]

From the foregoing it will be seen that we know practically nothing about the people who lived on the Georgia coast during the Deptford Period, and some definite knowledge must await excavation of one or more "pure" Deptford Period sites. The distinctive Deptford pottery types however do provide some interesting chronological and distribution data concerning the Deptford Period, although we cannot yet guess their significance in terms of peoples or cultures.

We have already seen that Deptford sherds were restricted to the upper level of Bilbo. In a stratigraphic pit at Deptford some Stalling's-like sherds were found at the bottom. The length of time between these two horizons is not known but the gross differences between the fiber-tempered, non-coiled, non-paddle stamped simple bowls of the Savannah River Focus, and the sand-tempered, coiled jars and elaborate stamped decoration of Deptford, are far greater than between any two successive complexes in the area. There are hints of transition in certain of the pottery from Stalling's Island, in the Thom's Creek series of South Carolina and in the fiber and the sand-tempered potteries of northern Alabama. Recent work by Waring near the mouth of the Savannah is expected to clarify this.

Potteries resembling the major Deptford types occur at sites on the Georgia and South Carolina coasts and on the northwest coast of Florida.[29] In interior Georgia, northern Alabama, and eastern Tennessee there are other early stamped potteries which resemble the Deptford types to a lesser degree. The complicated stamped type at Deptford appears to be the coastal equivalent of the well known Swift Creek type of central Georgia.[30] Another Deptford type is similar to one of the north Georgia simple stamped types which is in turn associated with Swift Creek

sherds at sites in the interior.[31] The Deptford Check Stamped types are probably the analogues of the check stamped types associated with these others in the interior, although the linear check stamping variant is most frequent and most flamboyant on the coast.

There is an interesting parallelism in the succession of pottery styles between the Georgia coast and the northwest coast of Florida. The stratigraphic pits at Deptford indicated that the complicated stamped pottery type was probably a late addition to the other Deptford varieties. On the northwest Florida coast the end of the Deptford Period is marked by the introduction of complicated stamped pottery of Swift Creek Type.[32]

THE WILMINGTON PERIOD

The stratigraphic pits at Deptford showed that the Deptford pottery styles were in time followed by those which we call Wilmington (Fig. 171, A, F), representing the next period on the Coast. We do not know if a new population came into the area or whether the new pottery was adopted by the people already there, perhaps as a result of diffusion from the north or northwest.

The typical Wilmington vessel[33] is decorated by cord wrapped paddle with the individual cord impressions large, usually vertical and parallel. The shape is a cylindrical jar with slightly incurving rim and a sub-conoidal or rounded base. Vessel walls and bases are rather thick and the interiors are carelessly finished, showing scraping and brushing impressions, and often large lumps of partially extruded tempering material consisting of clay or fragmented potsherds. There are other new styles of decoration as well.[34] In spite of the differences between Deptford and Wilmington pottery, they do have fundamental similarities which Deptford did not share with the earlier Savannah River Focus: coiled construction, paddle stamping, and the presence of jar as well as bowl shapes. There are also less frequent Wilmington sherds which show the persistence of Deptford decoration styles.[35]

Artifacts other than pottery were not abundant at the "pure" Wilmington Period sites which have been investigated. Figure 171 shows bone awls (D), pins (E), the blade of a hafted scraper (G) and a two-hole bar gorget (H). The purpose of the perforated conical pottery object (C) is unknown. The pipe (B) was found with a fragment of another in a Wilmington burial mound, but we do not know if it is a typical

26. Floyd, Marmaduke H., personal communication.
27. Waring, A. J., Jr., personal communication.
28. In collections made by John R. Swanton, which are now in the U. S. National Museum.
29. Willey and Woodbury, 1942, pp. 240–241.
30. Kelly, 1938, pp. 25 ff.

31. Ibid., pp. 31, 39; see also Fairbanks, 1946b, p. 103.
32. Willey and Woodbury, 1942, p. 241.
33. Wilmington Heavy Cord Marked.
34. Wilmington Brushed, Wilmington Net Marked.
35. Wilmington Check Stamped, Wilmington Simple Stamped, Wilmington Complicated Stamped.

form. The absence of "atlatl weights" and, at some sites, the occurrence of small stone projectile points suggest that the bow and arrow was present by Wilmington times, if not earlier.

The major Wilmington habitation areas at the mouth of the Savannah are the Walthour Site on Wilmington Island,[36] and on the mainland, Cedar Grove[37] and Deptford[38] (later occupation). Excavations at these sites showed numerous midden pits and patches of stained soil, but no house patterns, though it is probable that these people had permanent habitations.

The earliest small burial mounds on the coast were built during the Wilmington Period.[39] They are fairly frequent from Beaufort, South Carolina, to Brunswick in Glynn County, Georgia, and many of them were excavated by Moore.[40] It will be interesting to determine, in connection with the problem of the nature of the Wilmington occupation, whether the introduction of the mounds to the coast is attributable to the same source as the Wilmington pottery.

Wilmington mounds are fairly similar in structure, circular, seventy-five to one hundred and fifty feet in diameter, and from one to four feet high (Fig. 171, I). In a few cases they contain nothing which is now apparent, but usually there is a central deposit of several cremated individuals or a central burial pit below the original ground surface. Other interments may or may not be found beyond the center: pockets of calcined bones, skull burials, flexed, sitting, extended, or bundle burials. Infrequent grave offerings comprise deposits of hematite or mica, a bone awl, a few shells, or a pottery vessel. Greenseed Field and King's New Ground Field, both in Liberty County, Georgia, are notable in having a high proportion of extended burials.[41]

Moore stated that he had received no report of mounds farther north than Beaufort,[42] but Wilmington ceramics may be allied to the abundant cord-marked pottery of the Middle Atlantic states and surveys should be made in the intervening area of both Carolina coasts. In Georgia and South Carolina the Wilmington manifestation seems to be restricted to the Coast.

THE SAVANNAH I PERIOD

It was earlier stated that the Deptford burial mound was built in Savannah I times. This period follows Wilmington, apparently without a sharp break and might easily have been named "late Wilmington." In this case the evidence is not stratigraphic, but is provided by the typologies of Savannah I pottery and burial traits which are almost exactly intermediate between the types of Wilmington and Savannah II. Presumably the people who lived on the Coast during the Savannah I Period were descended from the Wilmington population.

Figure 172 shows representative Savannah I sherds and vessel forms, the cord-marked type (A)[43] is like its earlier Wilmington analogue in having a straight rim, but resembles the later Savannah II type[44] in the crisscross application of the stamp, in relative thinness of the vessel wall, and in careful finishing of the interior surfaces. The undecorated sherds (C, D)[45] are quite similar to the plain type of the Savannah II Period.[46] At some sites Savannah I pottery is tempered with sherd or clay after the manner of Wilmington but at others the material is quartz grit as in the Savannah II Period. This seems to indicate that the shift in temper type took place later than the shift in form and decoration and also confirms the intermediate position of Savannah I.

Several of the burial mounds dug by Moore[47] appear to belong to Savannah I times, but have not been visited by this writer and will not be further mentioned here.

The principal sites at the mouth of the Savannah River include: the Oemler village, the Deptford burial mound,[48] one of the Cedar Grove burial mounds, the Dotson mounds,[49] and the Haven Home burial mound and village.[50] The Oemler village, which had an earlier Wilmington occupation, was distinguished by a considerable number of midden pits, some pertaining to the Savannah I period. As at Wilmington habitation areas there was no architectural evidence. The Deptford Mound contained only a few burials, none distinguished by accompaniments. The Dotson burial mounds were an adjacent pair, situated in pine barren land on upper Pipemaker's Creek. A number of burials were found, all individual cremations, and the pottery, which was abundantly scattered through the mounds, was almost altogether undecorated suggesting a preferred mortuary type. A string of conch columella beads, a few of which are shown in Figure 172, F, were the only nonceramic artifacts with a burial.

The Haven Home Site, about eight miles south of Savannah, is designated on a 1736 map of Savannah as "Indian King's Tomb." It formerly comprised a

36. Caldwell and McCann, n.d.
37. *Ibid.*
38. Caldwell, McCann, and Hulse, n.d.
39. With the possible exception of the Evelyn Mound excavated by Preston Holder, which may be slightly older.
40. Moore, C. B., 1897; 1898a; 1898b, various sites. This writer has not personally visited all of them. See also Flannery, 1943, Kempfer Place.
41. Moore, C. B., 1897, pp. 81–89.
42. Moore, C. B., 1898a, pp. 147–148.

43. Savannah Fine Cord Marked.
44. Also called Savannah Fine Cord Marked (Caldwell and McCann, 1941, pp. 43–44).
45. Savannah Plain.
46. Savannah Burnished Plain (*ibid.,* pp. 45–46).
47. Moore, C. B., 1897.
48. Caldwell, n.d.
49. *Ibid.*
50. Waring, n.d.

mound about forty feet in diameter and five and one-half feet high with a surrounding village area. The mound, excavated by Waring, contained flexed, bundled, and cremated burials, some accompanied by conch columella beads, olivella beads, and pierced carnivore teeth. A conch shell bowl was present, also an effigy pottery vessel resembling a dog or raccoon, and small triangular flint projectile points. The presence of a late check stamped pottery along with Savannah I types suggests that this may be the latest of the Savannah I sites, verging upon the Savannah II Period.

Altogether, the Savannah I burial mounds were similar to Wilmington burial mounds with a few new traits: cremated burials in a central shell deposit, pottery intentionally broken and scattered through the mound, cremated urn burials (lacking cover vessels), and shell vessels occasionally with burials. Pottery vessels are more frequent with burials than in Wilmington times.

We know of no Savannah I sites in South Carolina, but in Georgia they may have the same geographical range as Wilmington. Southward in Liberty County, Georgia, the Eulonia mound[51] can probably be assigned to this period and here as at Dotson there seems to have been a preference for plain pottery with burials. The interesting Cox burial mounds near Darien, McIntosh County, have some similarities with the Savannah I Period but the connection has not been established.[52] The Sea Island burial mound in Glynn County is reported by Waring to be a Savannah I mound.

THE SAVANNAH II PERIOD

Most of our data concerning the Savannah II Period come from the Irene Site where its chronological position was fixed as underlying the Irene Period, the last prehistoric one on the Coast.[53] Mound D of the Middle Settlement on Ossabaw Island,[54] several other burial mounds dug by Moore, and the Glendenning Site on Wilmington Island may belong to Savannah II but this is not certain. Two Savannah II vessels were found at Hollywood near Augusta,[55] and several sherds at the McCollum Site, Chester District, South Carolina, but the Savannah II manifestation is most apparent, perhaps essentially localized, at the mouth of the Savannah River.

The lower panel of Figure 173 shows typical potsherds and vessel shapes of the Savannah II Period at Irene. The cord-marked variety (I)[56] is like its Savannah I predecessor except that vessel rims show a marked flare. The plain sherds (N, O)[57] are similar to the Savannah I plain, although some vessels are more highly burnished. The incidental fluting on the rim (O) was also present on the earlier pottery (Fig. 172, C). The occurrence of two new pottery types also distinguishes this period: a check stamped variety (K)[58] and a complicated stamped (J, M).[59] Some examples of the latter have the bar designs (J) found at Etowah, in northern Georgia.[60]

The primary deposit at the base of the Irene burial mound belonged to Savannah II times and showed an interesting continuity of the burial customs which were first used as early as the Wilmington Period. About half the traits noted had been present in both the Wilmington and Savannah I periods, and about half in Savannah I alone. Burial offerings were relatively more abundant than before.

During the Savannah II period, for the first time on the coast, we find platform mounds, a discernible village plan, extensive inclosure walls, and wattle and daub houses. At Irene seven successive platform mounds (Fig. 173, H, L), some and probably all containing rectangular buildings on their summits, were built just east of the burial mound. Each was pentagonal in plan with an ascending ramp, and the last five were palisaded. These were doubtless public structures and the infrequency of permanent houses in the village area suggests that the site was primarily a ceremonial center.[61]

Representative specimens of nonceramic artifacts from Irene are shown in the right-hand panel of Figure 173. Most of the types depicted were made both during this period and the one following, except those lettered Q, R, and S, the specific features of which belong to the latter period. T and U are respectively a shell gorget and pin, made from conch; V are awls or perforators, W a needle, and X a fishhook, all from animal bone; Y and AA are respectively a polished stone disc and a celt, and Z are the most common forms of flint projectile points.

In contrast to earlier times on the Coast the Savannah II period at Irene has a definitely Middle Mississippian cast, even though Middle Mississippi-like pottery is absent. Evidently Mississippian cultural characteristics were being transmitted from the interior, and provide evidence of approximate contemporaneity between Savannah II and some Middle Mississippi cultures in the west.

The Savannah II Period may be regarded as a fusion of the old coastal culture with Middle Mississippian influences from the interior. The pottery and

51. Waring, n.d.
52. Visited by the writer.
53. Caldwell and McCann, 1941.
54. Moore, C. B., 1897, pp. 113–128.
55. Thomas, C., 1894, pp. 317–326. The vessels are not illustrated in Thomas.
56. Savannah Fine Cord Marked (Caldwell and McCann, 1941, pp. 43–44).

57. Savannah Burnished Plain (ibid., pp. 45–46).
58. Savannah Check Stamped (ibid., pp. 44–45).
59. Savannah Complicated Stamped (ibid., p. 45).
60. Ashley, 1932, Figs. 84, 85a, b, c.
61. Caldwell and McCann, 1941, p. 69.

burial complexes were essentially a coastal development, but the stimulus for the platform mounds and village layout must have been derived from the west. That this cultural mixture resulted from the actual mingling of diverse peoples was remarkably shown by the skeletons of the people themselves. Hulse found that outsiders had appeared at Irene at this time,[62] and there was also evidence (a rare tooth anomaly) that an old coastal family line, and thus presumably others, had survived in this area from Savannah I times to the much later Irene Period.[63]

Many years ago at the Hollywood burial mound near Augusta, Georgia, Reynolds found evidence of cultural stratification.[64] A burial group associated with Middle Mississippian pottery and "Southern Cult" objects[65] (Fig. 174, lower) underlay a very similar group associated with some Savannah II pottery and Irene Period pottery (Fig. 174, upper). The Savannah II period precedes the Irene Period on the Coast so the Savannah–like types probably were retained somewhat longer in the Augusta area to have been placed in the same burial deposit with Irene types. The lower burial deposit and its Mississippian and cult materials was contemporary with Savannah II or slightly earlier, and the people were a group perhaps involved in the movement which impinged upon the Coast.

THE IRENE (LAMAR) PERIOD

The mixture of old coastal and intrusive interior culture elements which formed the Savannah II Period eventually became modified, and we recognize a new period, Irene, named after the large site where it was so well represented.[66] At Irene the last of the Savannah II platform mounds was capped by a large round topped mound (Fig. 173, G). Additional layers were placed on the burial mound, and a wattle and daub mortuary building was constructed (E, F). A circular council house or rotunda was built opposite the large mound and the space between was inclosed by walls or palisades. There is every indication that the site was occupied during the transition between Savannah II and Irene. The pottery types were radically changed but some sherds and vessels showed combinations of the distinctive features of both periods, and the nonceramic artifact types remained fairly constant (Fig. 173). The coastal burial complex which had had a remarkable stable development since Wilmington times continued with none of the earlier traits lost, but a few more added: the use of a mortuary structure, shell earpins with burials, burials with

charcoal or ash; at other sites with wood or bark, with nests of pebbles (presumably the remains of rattles).

There are many Irene Period sites on the Coast, a number of which were excavated by Moore,[67] and the limits of the coastal variant have not been distinguished. Four major coastal sites which have many common traits and which may later be set up as a focus are: Irene, St. Catherine's Island (south end) in Liberty County, and Creighton and Sapelo Islands in McIntosh County.[68] Traits shared by these sites include urn burial of infants and adults, perforated urns, discoidals or stone discs with burials, fragments of steatite vessels with burials, and the rattlesnake design on shell gorgets, often with burials.

Three mounds A, B, C, at Lawton's field, McIntosh County, can be set apart on the absence of the traits just mentioned and frequency of burials inclosed in wood or bark.[69]

The small mound at Little Island in Beaufort District, South Carolina, was distinguished by having only cremated burials.[70]

The sites of the Irene Period on the Coast may be classed as "Lamar–like" on the resemblance of their pottery to that of the Lamar Site excavated by Kelly in central Georgia.[71] Scores of sites throughout Georgia, South Carolina, and perhaps Tennessee and eastern Alabama share a remarkably close ceramic similarity, and the term Lamar "culture" or "aspect" has frequently been used to group them, although no careful comparison has been made. It is certain that they were more or less contemporary, but we have little understanding of the nature or degree of their other relationships.

Similarities in the pottery of the Irene Period and central Georgia Lamar are many and detailed. In both areas the complex consists of three types: a complicated stamped, an incised, and a plain; all are grit-tempered and the particular decoration types are commonly restricted to particular vessel forms. The stamped types of the two areas[72] are each on an elongated globular vessel with a slight shoulder, flaring rim and rounded base, although straighter rims occur. In central Georgia the body is less elongated than on the Coast. Stamped decoration in central Georgia comprises curvilinear and rectilinear motifs including the filfot cross, but the latter is most usual on the Coast (Fig. 173, B). The incised and plain types[73] are usually on bowls. A special rim decoration characteristic of stamped vessels and some of the incised or plain consists of a row of reed punctations, less

62. Hulse, 1941, pp. 67–68.
63. Hulse, n.d.
64. Thomas, C., 1894, pp. 317–326.
65. See Waring and Holder, 1945, for a discussion of the Southern Cult.
66. Caldwell and McCann, 1941.
67. Moore, C. B., 1897; 1898a.
68. Moore, C. B., 1897, pp. 28–43, 55–66, 75–81.
69. Ibid., pp. 15–20.
70. Moore, C. B., 1898a, pp. 162–163.
71. Kelly, 1938.
72. Lamar Complicated Stamped and Irene Filfot Stamped.
73. Irene Incised and Lamar Bold Incised, Irene Plain and Lamar Plain.

frequently of pinching or incising, on or without an added rim strip.

The Lamar Site at Macon and the Irene Site on the Coast are among the latest prehistoric sites in their respective areas. No historic materials have been found at either, but Waring has reported Spanish wheel-made pottery from other coastal Irene sites[74] and historic chinaware and iron nails were found in the upper levels at Hollywood.[75] A number of historic Cherokee sites in eastern Tennessee and western North Carolina have a Lamar–like pottery which is considerably later than in Georgia.[76] It is likely that many and perhaps all Lamar-like sites are post–De Soto.

In central Georgia a Lamar "focus" is identified "on documentary grounds with the lower Creek towns of the period from 1540 to about 1650."[77]

In South Carolina sites having Lamaroid or Irene pottery are fairly common. There are several mounds on the Wateree-Broad drainage, among which are one twelve miles below Columbia, the Greenhill mound and McCollum mounds in Richland District, and the McDowell mounds in Kershaw District (Fig. 175).[78] The Wateree-Broad area in north central South Carolina seems to have had a concentrated population in aboriginal times. According to Morton: "All the mounds that I have observed in this State . . . do not amount to as many as are found on the Wateree within the distance of twenty-four miles up and down the river, between Lancaster and Sumpter Districts."[79] Other sites noted by Blanding were quoted in Squier and Davis.[80] It will be interesting to determine which of these too are Lamar or Irene.

In 1924 George Pepper illustrated a typical Irene vessel from Fairfield District as an example of Wateree (Siouan) pottery since this group had formerly resided in the district where it was found.[81] His identification may be correct and if not specifically Wateree the vessel should be Siouan. Since most if not all Irene and Lamar pottery postdates De Soto, and since the Siouans had already obtained their greatest expansion in South Carolina before that time, it follows that they must have made the Lamar pottery found in their area. This widespread ceramic was no respecter of linguistic boundaries for it was made by Muskogeans in Georgia, and a variant has been claimed for the Cherokee in eastern Tennessee. An important problem for the future and one which should be productive of many concrete results will be the precise correlation of the various sub-areas of Lamar-like pottery with historic ethnic and tribal groups.

In earliest historic times the Georgia Coast was inhabited by Muskogean speaking peoples, and a contiguous fringe of the Coast north of the Savannah River in South Carolina was occupied by the Cusabo, Edisto, and Stono, probably also Muskogeans. The coast north of the Savannah River was called by the Spaniards the province of Santa Elena; the coast south as far as St. Andrews Sound was known as the province of Guale. Since the Guale Indians and the other Muskogeans just northward were in their historic positions at least as early as 1562,[82] it is probably these who were responsible for the Irene Period archeological sites of the immediate region.

Swanton, using ethnological data exclusively, suggested that the Georgia Coast was marginal to the interior in historic times.[83] This trend is noticeable in the Middle Mississippi influences in the Savannah II Period, and is continued in the ceramic and other similarities between the interior Lamar-like sites and the Irene sites of the Coast. The increasing cultural rapprochement was culminated in historic times by establishment of Creek hegemony on the Georgia Coast.

THE FULL HISTORIC PERIOD

The researches of Swanton, Milling, and many others have provided a large body of information concerning the historic period in South Carolina and the Georgia Coast, but correlation of archeology and history has only begun. While historic potteries are clearly related to those of prehistoric times, known sites are rather small, late, with few aboriginal artifacts, and not strictly comparable to the prehistoric sites.

For a considerable time before De Soto (1539–1542) most of South Carolina had been inhabited by peoples speaking a Siouan dialect, related to some of the languages of North Carolina, and to the speech of many of the tribes later found on the western Plains. The first description of a Siouan tribe, ca. 1521, indeed of any tribe in the present United States, was Francisco of Chicora's testimony regarding the country of Duhare, near Winyaw Bay, South Carolina, which has been critically presented by Swanton.[84]

When the Georgia Coast was first explored it appears to have had "a kind of confederacy with a head chief, more closely centralized in this particular than the Creek Confederacy."[85] At that time there was no mention of alliance or allegiance to tribes of the interior. The Muskogeans of Guale finally merged with the Yamassee, reputedly a group belonging to the hinterland of the province. These are said to have

74. Waring, n.d.
75. Thomas, C., 1894, pp. 320–321.
76. Lewis and Kneberg, 1946, p. 98.
77. Fairbanks, 1946b, p. 103.
78. Collections from these sites are in the U.S. National Museum.
79. Morton, 1846.
80. Squier and Davis, 1848.
81. Pepper, 1924.

82. Swanton, 1946, pp. 128, 135.
83. Swanton, 1928c.

84. Swanton, 1940.
85. Swanton, 1922, p. 94.

been subject to the Hitchiti (lower Creeks) which later became important in the Creek Confederacy, if indeed they not already were. The major seat of the Yamassee was probably on the Altamaha,[86] and the Hitchiti themselves were at the headwaters of that stream. In 1733, at a conference between the Indians and the Georgia Colony, the Confederacy assumed the right to dispose of the lands.[87]

The historic site of Fort King George at the mouth of the Altamaha River was occupied by the Yamassee Huspaw in 1715 who were said to have formerly lived there.[88] The Indian village area contained numerous sherds of Spanish wheel-turned pottery (Fig. 176, I) in direct association with late types of aboriginal pottery. The latter have a number of general similarities with coastal Irene pottery, which itself has been found with Spanish sherds at other sites, but more specific resemblances of the Fort King George pottery are with the historic Hitchiti pottery of the interior.[89]

The historic situation is far more complex than we have made it appear and was especially so on the lower Savannah River where numerous alien groups were settling in late times. These included such diverse peoples as Yuchi, Shawnee, Creeks, and even a few Natchez. At Parachukla, Hampton District, South Carolina, Marmaduke H. Floyd found burials with abundant historic glass beads washing out of the river bank (Fig. 176, G). Fragments of European clay pipes (H, lower right), a bullet (H, lower left), iron nails (A), china (C), and crockery were mingled with Indian shell beads (G, upper) and pottery.[90] The aboriginal pottery (B, D, E, F) was again similar to the historic Hitchiti complex of central Georgia. The Parachuckla Site had been occupied by the Appalachicola, a Hitchiti group, and their town was abandoned during the Yamasee War of 1715.

86. *Ibid.,* p. 101.
87. *Ibid.*
88. Lewis, B., 1939.

89. Caldwell, n.d.
90. Materials presented to the United States National Museum.

PREHISTORIC FLORIDA: A REVIEW. *By John W. Griffin**

WHILE broad areal differences were noted in the archeology of Florida many years ago, the development of time perspective and the definition of specific cultural configurations in time and space are relatively recent phenomena. The recency of much of the work on which sequences and complexes rest, and the fact that some of the major works are still unpublished, renders the task of summary and synthesis difficult. Without the full cooperation of workers in the field, the writing of this paper would have been impossible.[1]

Before the pottery sequence for the northwest Florida coast was established by Willey and Woodbury,[2] most of the available information had been derived from burial mounds. On the other hand, the majority of the more recent work has been concentrated in middens and village sites. This has led to a somewhat unbalanced situation which can only be corrected by future work and excavation. However, sequences, based largely on ceramics, have been erected for various portions of the state within the past few years, and these provide a framework for Florida archeology.

Our approach in this summary of Florida archeology will be through the periods and areas now recognized. The earlier periods, Paleo-Indian and "Archaic", are treated in state-wide terms. Periods following the "Archaic" are then discussed by geographical areas; the areas used being those proposed by Goggin.[3] The final phase of Florida Indian archeology, that of the Seminole, is not dealt with in the present paper.

The geographical areas shown in Figure 177, although they possess certain cultural validity in one or more periods, are utilized for the sake of convenience rather than through any conviction that they represent cultural reality in the sense that any concept of "archeological areas" or "culture areas" would imply. Certain of the areas, such as the Glades Area, possess greater validity through time than do others, but at present it is more satisfactory to regard them as a convenient framework within which to present the data than as an interpretation of cultural conditions.

PALEO-INDIAN

The problem of early man in Florida is one on which a voluminous literature exists. The two finds of human skeletal material which have caused the most controversy were made by Sellards at Vero in 1915[4] and Gidley at Melbourne in 1925.[5] Except for the recent papers of Sellards,[6] Hrdlička,[7] Stewart,[8] and Rouse,[9] the majority of the literature has been listed by Sellards,[10] and is not noted in this paper.

At both Vero and Melbourne human skeletal material was found under conditions which led geologists, although not all geologists, to regard it as contemporary with the fossil-laden beds in which it was said to have been found. Anthropologists, under the leadership of Hrdlička, were practically unanimous in rejecting these claims for antiquity. In view of the amount of controversy concerning these two finds it is strange that careful cranial reconstructions were not made, and measurements were not published, until 1946.[11]

Stewart's analysis of the physical anthropology of the Vero and Melbourne remains is enlightening. He found the reconstruction of the Melbourne specimen unbelievably poor. Careful reconstruction changed its cranial index from hyperbrachycranic (89.0) to dolichocranic (73.1). The Vero skull was found to have a cranial index of 72.4. Stewart points out that the two skulls were found under similar circumstances less than forty miles apart, and that only about 4 per cent of the Florida crania on record exhibit an index of less than 75. This, in and of itself, is not a proof of antiquity, but it is suggestive.

Rouse, in two recent papers,[12] has carefully examined the available evidence on the Vero and Melbourne specimens from the geological and archeological point of view. He comes to the conclusion

* University of Chicago, M.A., 1946; now Archeologist, Florida Park Service, Gainesville, Florida.

1. This paper was originally written in 1947 but was substantially revised in December, 1951. By this latter date many manuscripts initially used had been published. Nevertheless, the writer wishes to express his appreciation to Ripley P. Bullen, John M. Goggin, Irving Rouse, Hale G. Smith, and Gordon R. Willey for permitting him to use their unpublished material. The illustration which accompany this paper were prepared in 1947 by Andrew R. Janson; had they been done in 1951, many more artifacts could have been related to the ceramic complexes.
2. Willey and Woodbury, 1942.
3. Goggin, 1947b; see also Goggin, 1949a.

4. Sellards, 1916.
5. Gidley, 1926.
6. Sellards, 1937.
7. Hrdlička, 1937.
8. Stewart, 1946.
9. Rouse, 1950, 1951.
10. Sellards, 1940, pp. 380–385.
11. Stewart, 1946.
12. Rouse, 1950, 1951.

that the skulls date from either preceramic or Orange (fiber-tempered) times, which he dates as occurring during the Melbourne–Van Valkenburg interval (2000 B.C. to 0). The Vero skull lay on the unconformity representing this interval, while the Melbourne skull had seemingly been intruded into the underlying Melbourne formation. If Rouse's conclusions are correct, and they seem to be, Vero and Melbourne represent an early Indian population, older then Hrdlička would have granted, but more recent than the Pleistocene dating of some of the geologists. Strictly speaking, the Vero and Melbourne remains are not those of Paleo-Indians, but relate instead to the "Archaic" horizons discussed below.

There are, however, a few artifacts which point to the presence of early man in Florida. Some of these have been found in river bottoms in association with extinct animals. This in itself may mean nothing, for all sorts of fortuitous associations can occur under such conditions. However, some of these artifacts may be early. Jenks, for example, has described two beveled bones artifacts from the Itchtucknee River that are of a type similar to those found at early sites near Clovis, New Mexico.[13]

Folsom-like stone points have been found at various places in Florida. Many of these points have all of the attributes of the Folsom and similar points except for the grooving, and even this is rudimentarily represented in one or two specimens.[14] Goggin has in several places called these Suwannee Points, but has not formally defined the range which he includes under this term.[15] William Edwards, who is now pursuing the study of Paleo-Indian sites in Florida, has announced the finding of Folsom-like points under fiber-tempered pottery horizons.[16] As his studies progress we may expect more interesting information.

Goggin has published a paper in which he outlines a Santa Fe Complex, consisting of several types of chipped stone artifacts which he believes to be early.[17] He considers his Suwannee Points to be a part of this complex, although they have not yet been found in association with the other tools. Some pottery is found in sites of the Santa Fe Complex which have so far been excavated. More work in the field is needed before the various problems connected with the complex are clarified.

While the problem of early man in Florida is far from solved, the anthropological evaluation of the antiquity of man in the state has shifted from an emphatic negative to a cautious positive in recent years.

13. Jenks, 1941.
14. Simpson, 1948.
15. Goggin, 1949a; 1950c.
16. Edwards, William, personal communication.
17. Goggin, 1950c.

ARCHAIC PERIOD

PRE-POTTERY HORIZON

There is considerable evidence for a pre-ceramic "Archaic" period in northeast Florida and in the Indian River area, but only suggestive hints from elsewhere in the state. Wyman was the first to call attention to certain of the large shell heaps along the St. Johns River which contained no pottery, and were presumably built at a time when pottery was unknown.[18] To this observation Moore added the significant information that pottery was found only superficially in some shell heaps, with the lower levels devoid of ceramics although containing other evidences of human origin.[19] Nelson suggested that a nonpottery horizon underlay pottery at the Oak Hill shell heap.[20]

The pre-pottery shell heaps of the St. Johns have not been exhaustively examined in recent years. A report on the Palmer-Taylor Site has appeared,[21] and quite recently some stratigraphic work was conducted at the large Bluffton shell heap.[22] Stemmed projectile points and incised expanded-head bone pins were found at Palmer-Taylor, while the Bluffton site has definitely yielded plain bone pins, *Strombus* celts, *Busycon* gouges, and a fragment of a steatite bannerstone. The artifact inventory as it is now known is duplicated, with the exception of the bannerstone, by that of the succeeding fiber-tempered horizon, although the latter is better known and represented by a larger variety of types. The addition of pottery would seem to be the only major addition differentiating the two horizons. This of course argues for continuity and culture change rather than for change due to migration.

A slightly different complex, presumably relating to pre-ceramic times, comes from a site south of St. Augustine. Large, stemmed, finely flaked blades, polished bannerstones, a stone celt and stone beads, some of them corner perforated, were found here.[23] The relationship of this group of materials to those discussed earlier remains obscure.

FIBER-TEMPERED HORIZON

The fiber-tempered pottery horizon of the St. Johns River was recognized almost as early as the pre-pottery horizon. Wyman[24] noted the presence of the ware but drew no chronological implications from it, while

18. Wyman, 1875.
19. Moore, 1892, p. 916.
20. Nelson, 1918.
21. Dyson and Tooker, 1949.
22. This was a joint project of the Florida Geological Survey and the Florida Park Service, conducted by William Edwards, Ripley P. Bullen, and the writer.
23. Material in a private collection in St. Augustine; notes from John M. Goggin.
24. Wyman, 1875.

Moore definitely recognized its early nature, lying as it did above the pre-pottery levels and below later pottery. Holmes termed the fiber-tempered and early St. Johns Incised pottery "midden ware" and placed it in a middle period, after pre-pottery and before the late wares of the region.[25] In more recent years James B. Griffin has published a description of the pottery and a discussion of its relationships.[26] Even more recently, Rouse[27] and Ferguson[28] have given us more detailed information from the upper St. Johns. Reports on at least two other sites are in progress.[29]

One of the last mentioned sites, Bluffton, has provided us with the first stratigraphic demonstration of a plain fiber-tempered pottery period preceding the better known Orange Period. Here a considerable depth and quantity of plain fiber-tempered material overlies the pre-ceramic. In turn it is capped by some decorated fiber-tempered pottery. The plain pottery not infrequently possesses lip modifications resembling pouring spouts on pitchers. Triangular lip lugs are also found. Neither of these features seem to appear in later levels producing incised fiber-tempered pottery.

The most common decorated fiber-tempered type along the St. Johns River and the adjacent Atlantic coast has been called Orange Incised.[30] It is the marker for the Orange Period.[31] It is decorated with straight line incising (Fig. 178, A–I); vessel form is most commonly straight-sided with a flat bottom. The ware is thick and porous for the most part, although some specimens are remarkably thin when the crudeness of the ware is considered.

Artifacts of the Orange Period include steatite vessel sherds (which may be confined to late portions of the period),[32] stemmed projectile points, plain and incised bone pins (Fig. 178, M), splinter bone awls, incised turtle bone (Fig. 178, N), *Strombus* celts and adzes, shell disc, and *Busycon* gouges. The evidence seems to indicate that dogs were used as food. The Orange Period is well represented along the St. Johns River and parts of the adjacent Atlantic coast. It occurs as far north as the Georgia state line on the east coast. Inland, and on the west coast, finds of fiber-tempered pottery are less frequent, but future work may alter present appearances.

A less common decorated pottery type, with a more limited distribution, is Tick Island Incised.[33] Most

of the sherds of this type, which possess curvilinear incising and punctate filled areas (Fig. 178, J–L) come from the Tick Island site itself, or nearby sites along the St. Johns River. The precise relationship of this type to Orange Incised remains to be worked out, but the writer suspects that it is a late regional variant.

An incised chalky type marks the transition between fiber-tempering and the later periods in northeast Florida. Many of the motifs of Orange Incised are found on this type, which is called St. Johns Incised. Whether this pottery is included in the last stages of the Orange Period, the first part of St. Johns times, or assigned a period of its own, seems of little consequence to this writer.

THE NORTHWEST COAST

The sequence for the Florida Northwest coast was defined by Willey and Woodbury in 1942,[34] and with the exception of the addition of a new period, Leon-Jefferson, has not undergone change of any consequence since that time. This sequence is based on a series of excavations in shell heaps and village sites, supplemented by surface collections, and related to the earlier published data of C. B. Moore,[35] which was primarily from burial mounds.[36]

The Northwest Coast sequence is not one of superimposed discrete cultures, but rather a cultural continuum which can conveniently be broken into a series of periods on the basis of the appearance and disappearance of certain pottery types.[37] Thus, the periods discussed below are abstracted blocks from a continuum, and should be understood as such.

DEPTFORD PERIOD[38]

This is the earliest known period in the area, with the possible exception of a fiber-tempered period which has not been isolated, although sherds are occasionally found. As the name suggests this period is basically related to Deptford in Georgia. Knowledge concerning Deptford in Florida is somewhat scanty. Pottery is sand-tempered and decorated with simple stamped and check stamped designs; three major pottery types occur, Deptford Simple Stamped, Deptford Bold Check Stamped (Fig. 179, C), and Deptford Linear Check Stamped (Fig. 179, A–B). Tetrapodal supports are found on vessels. Artifacts include a few large triangular bladed projectile points, with and without barbs, pebble hammerstones, and small flat whetstones. The evidence for burial mounds is

25. Holmes, 1903, pp. 120-122.
26. Griffin, J. B., 1945a.
27. Rouse, 1951.
28. Ferguson, 1951.
29. By Griffin and Smith for the Cotten Site, and Edwards, Griffin, and Bullen for the Bluffton Site.
30. Griffin, J. B., 1945.
31. Period name by Goggin, 1947.
32. This statement is based on unpublished data from the Cotten Site, and that implicit in Ferguson, 1951.
33. Griffin, J. B., 1945a.

34. Willey and Woodbury, 1942.
35. Moore, 1901; 1902; 1918.
36. Willey, 1949b, has analyzed Moore's material in the light of the pottery sequence.
37. Willey, 1949b, p. 4, has expressed this concept for the area.
38. Summary largely drawn from Willey and Woodbury, 1942; see also Willey, 1949b.

very weak, and the only seemingly reliable evidence of midden burial indicates cremation, but this is based on only two burials.

SANTA ROSA-SWIFT CREEK PERIOD[39]

The succeeding Santa Rosa-Swift Creek Period once again is related to Georgia complexes, this time to the early Swift Creek horizon of central Georgia. In addition to this influence, however, there are marked connections with the Mississippi and Ohio valleys in the form of pottery types and other artifacts of a general Hopewell time level. This latter influence is particularly marked in the western part of the area. The distinctive pottery type for the period is Swift Creek Complicated Stamped (Fig. 179, G–H), although it continues into the next period as well. Other pottery types are shown in Figure 179. Burial mounds are definitely present in the Santa Rosa-Swift Creek of Florida, but they are not too well known. Seemingly these mounds are less elaborate and contain less spectacular materials than do Weeden Island mounds.

WEEDEN ISLAND PERIOD[40]

The materials grouped under the name Weeden Island are perhaps the best known of any from the state of Florida. Weeden Island is a full burial mound complex, and extensive excavations have been made in the mounds, which contain much cultural material. The fact that Weeden Island ceramics and artifacts are aesthetically pleasing has also given impetus to excavations of mounds of this period.

On the Northwest Coast, Weeden Island has been divided into two periods on the basis of ceramic changes. According to Willey and Woodbury, Swift Creek Complicated Stamped, common in the preceeding Santa Rosa-Swift Creek Period, continues into Weeden Island I and is replaced by Wakulla Check Stamped (Fig. 180, I) in Weeden Island II.[41] A great variety of both form and decoration, as suggested by Figure 180, is to be noted in Weeden Island ceramics. Weeden Island Incised (Fig. 180, A, J) is more abundant than Weeden Island Punctated (Fig. 180, F) in this area.

Burial is in low sand mounds, and is predominately secondary in form, although primary burials occur in many mounds. Single burials on or below the mound base are noted. Bundle burials, single skull burials, and flexed burials seem to be the commonest types, in that order. Pottery and artifacts, sometimes in considerable numbers, are found in the mounds. Pottery tends to be found in a mass pottery deposit, usually on the east side of the mound, while artifacts are generally scattered throughout, although there are many instances of artifacts associated with specific burials.

Artifacts include polished stone celts, stone pendants or plummets (Fig. 181, B, D), projectile points, "lances" (Fig. 181, A), hammerstones, shell cups or dippers (Fig. 181, E), shell pendants or plummets, shell beads, clay pipes (Fig. 181, C), and fragments of sheet mica and sheet copper. Hematite is found in many of these mounds.[42]

FORT WALTON PERIOD[43]

The Fort Walton Period is dated as extending from approximately A.D. 1450 to 1650. Culturally, it seems to represent a blending of Floridian (Weeden Island) elements with Middle Mississippian elements. Burial mounds are abandoned for the most part, and burials are placed in cemeteries. Some Fort Walton burials are found intruded into Weeden Island mounds.[44] A type of urn burial, consisting of a large bowl inverted over a skull, is fairly common.

It now appears likely that we can view Fort Walton as a development out of Weeden Island. The postulated earlier end of the range discloses many more similarities to Weeden Island ceramics than does the later end.[45] Nevertheless, the Mississippian influence is very strong, and some movement of peoples may be involved as well. Much of the variation within the period remains to be worked out in the field.

Viewing the period as a whole we find that large coarse grit has replaced the fine sand temper of Weeden Island times. Shell tempering appears, particularly in the western part of the area. Vessel form is commonly a large shallow bowl, sometimes of cazuela form, and the design, when present, is usually confined to a band on the upper portion of the vessel. Rim and lip modifications are common; lugs and handles are used and animal head adornos are reminiscent of the Mississippi Valley. The use of the stamping technique, so common in preceeding periods, is virtually abandoned. Selected pieces of Fort Walton pottery are illustrated in Figure 182.

The culture complex is incompletely known, but a pooling of C. B. Moore's burial site excavations[46] and village excavations at the Lake Jackson Site[47] gives us some information. House form remains unknown, but pyramidal mounds with successive building stages and occupation levels are known. Projectile

39. Summary largely drawn from Willey and Woodbury, 1942, with nomenclatural changes from Willey, 1949b.

40. Summary from Willey and Woodbury, 1942; Willey, 1945; Willey, 1949b.

41. This shift may not be mutually exclusive.

42. Only the more common types are listed here; for more extensive listings see Willey, 1945; 1949b.

43. Summary of this period is based on Willey and Woodbury, 1942; Willey, 1949b; and J. W. Griffin, 1950.

44. Moore, 1903b, pp. 445–466, describes a mound near Chipola Cut-off which obviously represents this kind of mixture.

45. Griffin, J. W., 1950, pp. 108–109.

46. Moore, 1901; 1902; 1918.

47. Griffin, J. W., 1950.

points are customarily large (Fig. 181, *I*), although small triangular points found in the area should also belong to the complex.[48] The "bunt," or scraper, is known (Fig. 181, *H*). Stone celts are fairly common, as are fragments of clay pipes of an equal-arm type (Fig. 181, *G*). Moore found bi-concave discoidal stones infrequently and rough sandstones discs more commonly; the latter occur in numbers at the Lake Jackson site, and some have incised lines on the surface (Fig. 181, *F*). Discs cut from potsherds are frequent. Sandstone slabs with sharpening grooves complete the inventory.

In the earlier part of its time range Fort Walton is prehistoric (in the sense that it does not have trade goods), but other sites are known which contain European materials. Willey and Woodbury have quite reasonably postulated that the Fort Walton sites represent the Apalachee and their neighbors. Since this is almost certainly the culture which De Soto found in the region in 1539–1540, we may be certain that it was based on a rather intensive maize agriculture, as indicated in the narratives of that expedition.

LEON-JEFFERSON PERIOD[49]

In the years immediately following 1633 Spanish mission activity was extended to the Apalachee region. By 1675 this mission field had reached a peak, and in 1702 it was wiped out. Several of the mission sites have been located and two of them—one a mission, the other a fort—have been excavated. Both of these sites presumably date from the years near 1700, and we do not know at just what point in time the shift from Fort Walton to Leon-Jefferson took place.

Leon-Jefferson differs markedly from Fort Walton, not only in the possession of quantities of European materials, but in the aboriginal ceramic complex as well. Some of the motifs on incised pottery are obviously related to Fort Walton, although the execution is slovenly. Quite interesting is the reappearance, in quantity of complicated stamped and check stamped types after their virtual absence in Fort Walton. Red painting, much of it in zones, occurs most frequently on plate forms with annular ring bases, which resemble the forms of Spanish pottery very closely. Trade sherds of Ocmulgee Fields Incised, an historic central Georgia type, are not infrequent. The two sites excavated to date disclose slightly different complexes, which may be the result of the different tribal groups to be found in the mission area.

Only a few aboriginal artifacts are known. Pro-

jectile points are large for the most part, and some are notched. The small triangular point also occurs. Discoidal stones, similar to those mentioned for Fort Walton, are found, as are smoothers and sharpeners. To these few items may be added a broken stone maul. Interinfluence of Spanish and Indian culture is noticeable. The missions are of wattle-and-daub construction, but with spike fastened roof beams. Spanish forms in Indian pottery have been noted, and a scraper from glass should be added. European artifacts are in such variety that it is best not to summarize them at this point.

THE CENTRAL GULF COAST

Despite a considerable bibliography,[50] stratigraphic information for the Central Gulf Coast is limited. Particularly in pre–Weeden Island times the picture is little short of confusing. No single period, or group of periods, can be made to apply to the region as a whole, and sites within a few miles of one another display disturbing dissimilarities.

PRE-WEEDEN ISLAND HORIZONS

Although a few sherds of fiber-tempered pottery have been found, a period containing only this ware has not been isolated. Perhaps the earliest manifestation which we know from the area is represented in the lower portions of the Johns Island Site, where St. Johns Incised and the related limestone-tempered Pasco Incised suggest a temporal position equivalent to the transition from fiber-tempering in the St. Johns Area.[51] At Johns Island, Deptford influence is noted above this level, and Goggin has found even stronger representations of Deptford elsewhere in the area.[52]

In the northern portions of the area, and perhaps toward the south as well, limestone-tempered pottery, usually plain, dominates the scene at least through Weeden Island times. What the relationship of this ware may be to the Perico Period of the Manatee Region is not too clear, but that there is some relationship is evident.

Swift Creek relationships are also noted at a number of sites, and particularly at the famous Crystal River site.[53] It is now evident, however, that this latter site does not date from a single period. Stratigraphic tests, while they contain very little decorated pottery, clearly indicate several periods of occupation. Both Santa Rosa–Swift Creek and Weeden Island are indicated, and Safety Harbor types have

---

48. The scarcity of small triangular points is interesting. They may be a very late introduction into the area, paralleling the situation at Kincaid (Cole *et al.*, 1951, pp. 356–357).

49. Summary based on Boyd, Smith, and Griffin, 1951; see also Smith, 1948*a*; 1948*b*.

50. The more important references for the area are Walker, 1880; Moore, 1899; 1903*a*; 1907; Fewkes, 1924; Rainey, 1935; Simpson, 1936; Willey, 1945; 1949*b*; Willey and Phillips, 1944; Goggin, 1947*b*; Bullen and Bullen, 1950; Griffin and Bullen, 1950.

51. Bullen and Bullen, 1950.

52. Goggin, John M., personal communication.

53. Crystal River has an extensive bibliography, including the following: Moore, 1903*a*; 1907; Greenman, 1938; Willey and Phillips, 1944; Willey, 1948*b*; Smith, 1951*b*; Bullen, n.d.

been found on the surface.[54] While this recent work casts no light on the associations of the Hopewellian objects and negatively painted vessels from the site which have been the source of so much of the literature, it does indicate that the site as a whole was occupied over a long time, and does expand the possibilities for interpretation.

WEEDEN ISLAND PERIOD[55]

The type site of the Weeden Island Period is on Weeden Island, near St. Petersburg, and is actually near the southern boundary of Weeden Island distribution. In the Central Gulf Coast area it is usually difficult to draw a distinction between Weeden Island I and II, as was done on the Northwest Coast. Both complicated stamped and check stamped sherds occur at many of the sites, some of them of Northwest Coast types and others of types peculiar to the area. There are certainly sites which equate with Weeden Island II times, and some are probably equivalent to Weeden Island I. Whether a late introduction of Weeden Island into the area can be postulated is at present uncertain.

There are regional differences in the ceramics of Weeden Island times which may be noted. In contrast to the Northwest Coast, Weeden Island Punctated is more abundant than Weeden Island Incised. The fine sand-tempered paste of the Northwest Coast is often replaced by a chalky paste (Papys Bayou and St. Johns series), and check stamping appears more closely related to St. Johns Check Stamped of the east coast than to Wakulla Check Stamped.

SAFETY HARBOR PERIOD[56]

Safety Harbor is the name given to the protohistoric and historic horizon in this area. In time, it is partially equivalent with both Fort Walton and Leon-Jefferson of the Northwest Coast. Safety Harbor ceramics, exclusive of the Pinellas types, are clearly a development out of Weeden Island, and are repeatedly described as a degenerate Weeden Island in motif and execution. The Pinellas types are often identical with those at the postulated late end of the Fort Walton range.

Sites lacking trade goods are found, but ones with trade goods seem to be more frequent. There is some suggestion that temporal change occurred in Safety Harbor similar to that suggested for Fort Walton. While ceramic shifts, other than the addition of Leon-Jefferson types, could not be demonstrated for the Safety Harbor Site itself, a change from stemmed projectile points to small triangular ones does seem to

be indicated.[57] For the period in general we may indicate that Mississippian influence was not as strong as in Fort Walton; pyramidal mounds appear, but mound burial persists.

In addition to the projectile points, previously mentioned, artifacts of the Safety Harbor Period include hammerstones, grindstones, plummets of stone and shell, *Busycon* picks, *Busycon* dippers, columella chisels, neatly made bone pins, and splinter bone awls.

While Safety Harbor and Fort Walton exhibit many differences when viewed in their totality, some confusion is apt to result from their definition as cultural blocks. Actually, both cultures stem from Weeden Island under the influence of extraneous, i.e., Mississippian, cultures. As we have seen, there are regional differences in the parent Weeden Island culture, and stronger Mississippian influences are found as one nears the Southeastern area proper. In other words, Fort Walton and Safety Harbor occupy a continuous range, and will probably show gradations in time and space as (1) the parent Weeden Island was different, (2) as the Mississippian influences penetrate through time, and (3) as the source of Mississippian influence is left farther behind in traveling southward. The period abstractions are very useful for many purposes, but the dynamic picture is also of importance.

THE MANATEE REGION

The Manatee Region extends along the west coast of Florida from the lower end of Tampa Bay to Charlotte Harbor, and runs inland for a yet undetermined distance. The area occupies a peripheral position between the Gulf Coast areas and the Glades Area, a position which is reflected in the archeological picture.[58]

PERICO ISLAND PERIOD

The Perico Island Site, near Bradenton, may be considered the type site for this period. Perico Plain, the characteristic pottery type of the period, is tempered with large particles of crushed limestone or coquina, much of which has leached out.[59] A few sherds of this ware have been found with incision or linear punctation. Almost as common in many of the sites is Glades Plain, the dominant type of the Glades Area. Belle Glade Plain, from the same area, is also present. A few fiber-tempered sherds found at Perico Island point to an early ceramic occupation of the area, and a few sherds of Deptford Bold Check Stamped would

---

54. Bullen, n.d.
55. Willey, 1945; 1949*b*, gives detailed information for the period.
56. Summary based on Willey, 1949*b*, and Griffin and Bullen, 1950.

57. Griffin and Bullen, 1950. Once again, this suggests a trend similar to that at Kincaid (Cole *et al.*, 1951, pp. 356–357).
58. Summary based primarily on Willey, 1948*a*; 1949*b*, supplemented by Bullen, 1951, and several shorter papers.
59. Relationship of this type to the limestone-tempered Pasco Plain is not completely understood.

seem to indicate at least partial contemporaneity with Deptford and perhaps Santa Rosa-Swift Creek levels of the Northwest Coast.

Artifacts include shell hammers or picks, shell celts, plummets and beads, bi-pointed bone projectile points, bone daggers, and bone awls. Burial for the most part is primary flexed in shell-lined burial pits. At the Perico Island site there is a burial mound built of village site refuse.

The pre-Weeden Island position of this period seems to be established by its presence under the Weeden Island mound, the absence of Weeden Island and later pottery types in the middens, and the few cross ties to early periods of the Northwest Coast. At Terra Ceia, Bullen recognizes a similar manifestation which, however, has more sand-tempered pottery than Perico Plain. This latter limestone-tempered ware when it does appear is still pre–Weeden Island, but a later introduction than the sand-tempered.[60] Willey's opinion would coincide with this data.[61] While some eventual divisions may be made within what is now called the Perico Period, it is apparent that in pre-Weeden Island times the relations of the Manatee Region were closer with the Glades Area than with the Gulf coast farther north.

WEEDEN ISLAND PERIOD

Weeden Island material is not particularly abundant in the Manatee Region, and there is no basis for dividing it into two stages as on the Northwest Coast. Characteristic Weeden Island pottery types occur in several burial mounds, together with varieties of complicated stamped pottery not known from the Northwest Coast. Essentially, Weeden Island in this region is similar to that from the Tampa Bay portion of the Central Gulf Coast Area.

ENGLEWOOD POTTERY SERIES

At the present time this series is best represented at a single sand burial mound, Englewood, near Sarasota. Burials were both bundle and single skull interments, with a few primary flexed skeletons. The bulk of the pottery was in a mortuary deposit at the mound base. The characteristic pottery is incised and punctated in a manner similar to, but different from, Safety Harbor pottery. Englewood Plain and Incised are sand-tempered, and similar in ware quality to Weeden Island pottery. Sarasota Incised is chalky. St. Johns Check Stamped is common. Glades Plain and a few sherds of Fort Drum Punctated show relations with the Glades Area. There are a few Safety Harbor sherds. It would appear that Englewood had a span overlapping both Weeden Island and Safety Harbor.

SAFETY HARBOR PERIOD

The Safety Harbor Period is well represented in both proto-historic and historic sites of the region. It is essentially the same as described for the Central Gulf Coast.

THE GLADES AREA

As Kroeber has pointed out, South Florida is a distinct natural area, marked off from the remainder of the Southeast by its sub-tropical, and even tropical, features.[62] Archeologically, too, this area may be separated from the remainder of Florida. Stirling[63] was the first to call this the Glades Area, a term which has been taken over by Goggin, who has done most of the definitive work in the area.[64] The northern boundary of the Glades Area begins on the west coast slightly north of the Caloosahatchee River, passes north of Lake Okeechobee, and goes out into the Atlantic near Fort Pierce. Within the Glades Area, Goggin has defined three sub-areas, Tekesta, Calusa, and Okeechobee, with boundaries roughly as shown on the map (Fig. 177). He has formulated an overall sequence for the area, and has erected periods for each sub-area.

The chronological framework rests, for the most part, on ceramics, but wherever possible other traits have been related to the ceramic sequence. Actual stratigraphic excavations in the area are still at a minimum, although several have been made in the last few years. The stratigraphic data has been supplemented by controlled surface collecting and by the analysis of previously excavated sites.

Pottery of the Glades Area has been divided into three wares, Glades, Biscayne, and Belle Glade. The Glades ware is characteristically heavily tempered with sand and feels very gritty to the touch. The Biscayne ware, on the other hand, is soft and chalky to the touch; it is closely related to, if not identical with, St. Johns ware. The Belle Glade ware is somewhat intermediate between the other two. The Glades ware has a number of decorated types, executed in incision and/or punctation. Check stamping appears on the Biscayne ware but not on the others. Belle Glade ware is apparently not decorated. Recently, Goggin has established the type Goodland Plain as a recognizable variant of Glades Plain.

EARLY HORIZONS

Although present evidence would not indicate an intensive occupation of the Glades Area in "Archaic" times, there are a few hints that the region was not

60. Bullen, 1951, pp. 14–15.
61. Willey, 1949b, p. 181.

62. Kroeber, 1939, p. 69.
63. Stirling, 1936, pp. 354–355.
64. Goggin, 1939; 1940; 1944a; 1944b; 1947a; 1949a; 1949b; 1950a; 1950b; Goggin and Sommer, 1949. Unless otherwise noted summaries are from these sources.

totally uninhabited. A single fiber-tempered sherd is known from a midden at Palm Beach,[65] and a sherd from a steatite vessel was recovered from another site in the same city.[66] Fiber-tempered pottery occurs on Useppa Island, at about the same latitude on the Florida Gulf Coast.[67] A single sherd of the type St. Johns Incised, together with several gritty sherds containing a fair amount of fiber-tempering, suggests a transitional occupation at Old Fort Center near the west shore of Lake Okeechobee.[68] Doubtless, more information will be forthcoming from the area.

GLADES I PERIOD

Glades I has been divided into two portions. The first of these, called Glades I early, is retained for a plain pottery period dominated by Glades Plain, but also including Goodland Plain. The subperiod is not too well known, but sufficient evidence is available to justify its definition. Glades I, late, sees the addition of decorated pottery in the form of the types Fort Drum Punctated (Fig. 183, A) and Fort Drum Incised (Fig. 183, B). The artifact assemblage for Glades I, late, includes Strombus celts, stone celts, socketed bone points, bone pins, and probably Busycon picks of Type A.

GLADES II PERIOD

The Glades II Period has been divided into three sub-periods in the Tekesta subarea. Ceramically, Glades IIa is marked by the presence of Key Largo Incised (Fig. 183, G), Miami Incised (Fig. 183, F), and Opa Locka Incised. Glades IIb sees the continuation of Key Largo Incised and the addition of Matecumbe Incised (Fig. 183, I). Toward the end of this subperiod incised arcs appear on vessel lips, providing a basis for differentiating Glades IIb early and Glades IIb late. Glades IIc is apparently a period of predominately plain pottery, but may have the type Plantation Pinched as a marker. This subperiod is less firmly established than the others, and, in the writer's opinion, requires further confirmation.

In the Calusa subarea Glades II has not been as finely divided as in the Tekesta subarea. Glades IIa and IIb have not been segregated in the ground, and Glades IIc is questionably present, according to Goggin's analysis of Goodland Point.[69] In this subarea, Gordons Pass Incised (Fig. 183, H) and Sanibel Incised (Fig. 183, C) are the markers for Glades II. In the Okeechobee subarea Glades II is represented by Belle Glade I, and is dominated by Belle Glade Plain pottery. Decorated trade sherds found at Belle Glade enabled cross dating with neighboring areas.

Many of the characteristic artifacts of the Glades Area make their appearance at the Glades II level. With the exception of ornaments, most of the important types found later are now present. Among the artifacts are shell celts (Fig. 183, Q), Strombus hand hammers (Fig. 183, L), columella chisels, bone points, flint points, perforated Arca shells, notched shell weights, groved stone weights, bone pins (Fig. 183, D–E), shell pendants, and Busycon dippers (Fig. 183, R). Burial mounds cannot definitely be assigned to this period; burial type in the middens is predominately extended primary.

GLADES III PERIOD

Glades III is also divided into three sub-periods. In Glades IIIa the decorated types of Glades II are no longer being made, and the type Surfside Incised (Fig. 183, N–O) is introduced. This type may overlap somewhat into Glades IIIb, which is marked by the introduction of Glades Tooled (Fig. 183, P). The final sub-period, IIIc, is delineated by the addition of European trade goods.

Pottery types for the period as a whole include Glades Plain, Surfside Incised, Glades Tooled, Belle Glade Plain, Biscayne Check Stamped (Fig. 183, K), Glades Red, and Biscayne Red. With the disappearance of incision as the dominant decorative device, embossing, grooving, and lip notching are found to occur. Rim lugs are found on some vessels, and asymmetrical vessels appear for the first time.

Many of the artifact types are those found in Glades II, but various new types appear. Chipped stone projectile points seem to be on the decline, but Busycon cups, perforated stone weights, Cassis lip implements, and more varieties of ornaments are added to the complex. Most of the woodworking known from the area dates from Glades III, although there is no reason to believe that it was not important previously. Ceremonial mounds and works of earth and shell, some of considerable magnitude, are known for the period. Burial mounds are numerous, and many contain European trade goods. Trade sherds from Weeden Island, Safety Harbor, and Englewood aid in correlating this period with other areas.

THE KISSIMMEE REGION

This area, comprising the drainage of the Kissimmee River, has received very little attention. The cultural affinities of the region seem to lie largely with the Okeechobee subarea of the Glades Area, which is not surprising inasmuch as the drainage comprising the area empties into Lake Okeechobee. Belle Glade Plain and some Glades Plain pottery is found on sites in the region.[70] One small excavated midden,

---

65. Goggin, John M., personal communication.
66. Collections, Florida State Museum, Gainesville.
67. Griffin, J. W., 1949.
68. Collections, Florida Park Service.
69. Goggin, 1949b.

70. Goggin, John M., personal communication; Griffin and Smith, 1947.

the Skipper Site, contained only Belle Glade Plain pottery. Near the midden was a small sand mound, without burials, postholes, or any other evidence of possible use.[71]

Historic material in considerable quantity is known from the burial mounds in this region. "Ceremonial tablets" of gold and silver have come from at least two sites.[72] This type of artifact is more common in the Glades Area.[73] The Goodnow Mound contained both primary extended and secondary burials accompanied by numerous glass beads, iron scissors, celtiform iron axes, copper and silver pendants, brass and silver hawk's bells, a knife, most of a Spanish olive jar, and other European items.[74]

The sequence in the area is little known. Goggin uses the term Alligator Lake to cover some early material from the area.[75] He also places the Skipper Site in Glades II times,[76] whereas the writer considers it as possibly Glades III. Obviously there was a considerable population in historic times, with mound burial still being practiced. Possibly this region will eventually be classified as a part of the Glades Area; at least the present evidence all points toward relationships in that direction.

THE INDIAN RIVER REGION

This region includes the Atlantic coast and the St. Johns River drainage from Cape Canaveral south to the Glades Area. The region is peripheral, both geographically and culturally, to the northern St. Johns and Glades areas. In the earliest periods the strongest ties are to the northern St. Johns, while in later times influence was strong from both directions. A recent monograph by Rouse is based on all available evidence for the region, and the present summary is based primarily on this source.[77]

EARLY PERIODS

Both the Vero and Melbourne remains, discussed in the section on the Paleo-Indian, were from this region. Preceramic and fiber-tempered periods have been dealt with in the general section on the "Archaic."

MALABAR I PERIOD

Although Rouse indicates the possibility that the markers of this period may really be part of the preceding Orange Period, he has segregated it out because of the possibility that it may represent a distinct period.[78] Malabar I is characterized by St. Johns In-

cised pottery, which is the chalky type bearing motifs derived from the fiber-tempered Orange Incised. Most of the artifacts are carry overs from the Orange Period, although some new types, such as the stone celt, do appear. The one burial which may be assigned to the period was extended and lacked grave goods.

MALABAR I' PERIOD

The Malabar I' Period corresponds to the St. Johns I Period farther north. It is poorly defined as yet, and the vast majority of the data comes from surface collections.[79] In the absence of clear stratigraphic excavations the period is difficult to recognize because it is characterized by plain pottery types occurring in other periods as well.

Two shifts seem to occur at this time. Rouse postulates a shift of the center of population from the St. Johns River to the coastal lagoons, and also notes that burials are now of a roundheaded type. Pointing up the geographical intermediacy of the region is the fact that St. Johns Plain predominates in the northern part of the area, is about equal in frequency with Glades Plain in the center, and is sharply subordinated to Glades Plain in the south. Burial mounds are definitely present in this period, and "Hopewellian" materials are found, for example, a platform pipe.

MALABAR II PERIOD

This is the best known period of the area, both in number of sites investigated and size of collections.[80] The site locations indicate continued concentration of population on the Indian River, and the number of them indicates an increase of population. The period extends up into historic times, when it may be identified with the Ais Indians.

St. Johns Check Stamped pottery appears, and serves as a marker for the period. St. Johns Plain, Glades Plain, and Belle Glade Plain continue. A number of trade sherds of the general Weeden Island time level appear. Projectile points are more varied than formerly, and include notched, stemmed, and triangular forms. Bone implements remain about the same, but there is a greater variety of shell implements. Toward the end of the period European items find their way into sites.

The chalky St. Johns pottery continues to be most common in the north of the area, while the Glades pottery remains dominant in the south. There is no marked cultural change from the previous period; it is set aside by pottery differences and an increase in types of artifacts. In general, the sites are larger than before and are more commonly accompanied by burial mounds.

71. Griffin and Smith, 1947.
72. Douglass, 1890; Griffin and Smith, 1947.
73. See Goggin, 1947a, for a discussion of these tablets in Florida.
74. Griffin and Smith, 1947.
75. Goggin, 1949a, Fig. 3.
76. Ibid.
77. Rouse, 1951.
78. Ibid., pp. 88–89. Period summary ibid., pp. 244–247.

79. Summary for ibid., esp. pp. 247–251.   80. Ibid.

ST. AUGUSTINE PERIOD

This period is represented in the area only at the Higgs Site.[81] This intrusion of a more northerly pottery complex is presumed by Rouse to be the result of Yamassee invasion. The site itself, however, may be more than just an Indian village, and much of the historic material found there may result from the Plate Fleet wreck of 1715, rather than from normal acculturation of the Indians. Since, aside from the St. Augustine Period pottery, the site is primarily of interest for its European materials it will not be discussed in any detail.

THE NORTHERN ST. JOHNS AREA

This area has attracted archeological attention over a long period of time, but the perspective provided by stratigraphic work is only now beginning to emerge. Outstanding work in the area includes that of Wyman, Moore, Douglass, Butler, Nelson, and Stirling.[82] At the time of this writing a comprehensive survey of the area by Goggin is in press.[83]

EARLY PERIODS

The pre-ceramic and fiber-tempered periods of this area have been discussed in a previous section of this paper. The period marked by St. Johns Incised pottery, which is transitional in nature, has also been mentioned.

ST. JOHNS I PERIOD

The existence of a period characterized by plain chalky pottery was first demonstrated by Nelson at the Oak Hill shell heap.[84] While at first glance the existence of such a period contemporaneous with such nearby complexes as Deptford in which stamped pottery is so important seems inconceivable, there is sufficient evidence to indicate that it really exists. Some small amount of decoration does occur at some sites, but the check stamp, which dominates St. Johns II times, is lacking except as noted below.

James B. Griffin has placed the Racey Point and Murphy Island sites of Moore[85] in this period.[86] He tentatively places the Racey Point Site as slightly earlier than Murphy Island. Taken together, these sites contain plain pots with tetrapodal supports, pottery pipes, pottery pendants, sheet copper ornaments, shell dippers, stone celts, chipped stone projectile points, and fragments of mica. Some complicated stamped pottery is present, but no check stamping is noted or figured. Items from these sites are shown in Figure 184, *A–I*, together with some from the low mounds south of the Grant Mound and the Alicia Mounds, both near Jacksonville.[87]

Goggin suggests that these latter two sites represent another, and slightly later, unit within this period.[88] These mounds contain sherds of a late Swift Creek Complicated Stamped type, and the low mounds south of the Grant Mound also contain a ridge-pinched type reminiscent of Tucker Ridge-Pinched of Weeden Island times on the Northwest Coast. Again, it cannot be demonstrated that check stamping occurs.

Goggin defines three subperiods within St. Johns I on the basis of actual trade sherds and indigenous sherds displaying outside influence.[89] St. Johns Ia early is defined on the basis of trade sherds of the Deptford complex and the presence of tetrapod vessels. He notes some influence of the Deptford types on the local chalky ware, but feels this was of short duration. St. Johns Ia late sees some introduction of Swift Creek Complicated Stamped pottery and Hopewellian traits, including copper objects and monitor pipes. St. Johns Ib is marked off by the presence of some examples of Weeden Island I pottery. The period as a whole possesses burial mounds, and a considerable quantity of red-painted chalky pottery is found.

ST. JOHNS II PERIOD

The marker for this period is the appearance of check stamping on the chalky pottery of the area. Once again, Goggin has established sub-periods.[90] Various artifacts are illustrated in Figure 184, *J–W*.

St. Johns IIa includes sites containing both Weeden Island influences and check stamped pottery. Presumably this period is contemporaneous with Weeden Island II on the Gulf coast. St. Johns IIb exhibits Mississippian and Southern Cult influences. Influence from the Southern Cult is present at several sites, but Mt. Royal is perhaps the best known of these.[91] The similarity between the "weeping eye" copper tablet from Mt. Royal[92] and the one from Spiro[93] is very striking, and the dating of either of these sites should closely date the other. Finally, Goggin recognizes a St. Johns IIc horizon which is defined by the presence of historic trade goods.

Work in coastal middens dating from St. Johns II times has provided data which cannot readily be placed in Goggin's subdivisions because of the rela-

81. *Ibid.*, p. 256; see Smith, 1949, for a site report.
82. Wyman, 1875; Moore, 1892–1894; 1894*a*; 1894*b*; 1896; 1922; Douglass, 1885*a*; 1885*b*; 1882; Butler, 1917; Nelson, 1918; Stirling, 1935.
83. To appear in the "Yale University Publications in Anthropology."
84. Nelson, 1918.
85. Moore, 1894*b*, pp. 181–185; 1896, pp. 502–516.
86. J. B. Griffin, 1946, pp. 49–50 and Fig. 2.

87. Moore, 1896, pp. 488–494 and 498–500
88. Goggin, 1947*b*.
89. Goggin, 1949*a*.
90. *Ibid.*
91. Moore, 1894*a*, pp. 16–35; 1894*b*, pp. 130–146.
92. Moore, 1894*a*, frontispiece. *See* also Fig. 184, *U*, present paper.
93. Burnett, 1945, Pl. LXXVI.

tive lack of sherds with extra-areal features. On the other hand, divisions within St. Johns II at one of these sites, Green Mound, has been proposed on the basis of change in the size of checks on the pottery.[94] The apparent shift is from large checks to small, and then back to large, but this needs confirmation from another site. Near the end of the check stamped range some chalky simple stamped and scored pottery is found.

The Timucua village of Nocoroco, known to have been occupied in 1605, yielded both chalky and gritty pottery in approximately equal amounts throughout its shallow depth. The chalky pottery is similar to the upper levels of Green Mound and the gritty sherds, while mostly plain, are also check stamped, simple stamped, and scored. This complex belongs neither in St. Johns II nor the St. Augustine Period, but it may be taken as the pottery complex of the Timucua of that part of the Florida coast in the early seventeenth century.[95]

ST. AUGUSTINE PERIOD

The St. Augustine Period was originally defined by Smith from pottery recovered in excavations in the city of St. Augustine.[96] One of the collections came from the moat of the Castillo de San Marcos, where construction dates of 1672 to 1687 set a lower limit on the dating of the material. The most distinctive type, San Marcos Stamped, is limestone-tempered or coarse grit-tempered and is decorated with simple, check, or complicated stamping, or combinations thereof. There is also an incised type similar to Lamar Bold Incised of Georgia, and a red-filmed type related to Mission Red Filmed of the Leon-Jefferson Period.

Since the initial definition of the complex, specimens have been found over a broad area in Florida. Basically the complex is related to material along the Georgia coast, and it is probable that it represents the ceramic complex of Georgia Indians who came into Florida. Goggin is working on a refinement of this material in relation to both time and tribal affiliation.

THE CENTRAL FLORIDA AREA

Central Florida was one of the last areas in the state to receive systematic treatment. There are still too few published reports, but others, particularly by Goggin, are in preparation.

EARLY HORIZONS

Folsom-like, or Suwannee, points are more common in this area than elsewhere in the state. The Santa Fe Complex, mentioned earlier, is from this area. Fiber-tempered sherds have been found, includ-ing an example of Stallings Island Linear Punctated, a Georgia type.[97]

PRE-CADES POND PERIOD

This period includes Deptford material found in the area.[98]

CADES POND OR ST. JOHNS IB

The Cades Pond Period is characterized by St. Johns Plain and Dunns Creek Red pottery and burial in mounds. It may be considered a westward extension of St. Johns Ib.[99] Until more information is available there would seem to be little reason for not calling the period St. Johns Ib, thereby reducing somewhat the growing nomenclatural complexity in the state.

HICKORY POND

Although St. Johns influence is still present in this period, a basic shift seems to have taken place. Both this and the following period are grouped into what Goggin calls the Alachua tradition. Grit-tempered pottery enters the area, villages are extensive and located in regions of good soil, and burial mounds, while constructed, are not common. The pottery is both cord-marked and cob-marked, with the former predominating.[100] Goggin regards the Alachua tradition as a fusion of St. Johns and Gulf traditions with influence from southern Georgia.[101]

ALACHUA PERIOD

This period is a developmental continuation of Hickory Pond. In ceramics, cob-marking becomes more common than cord-marking. Although it corresponds in time with Fort Walton, no temple mounds are noted. The period almost certainly represents the culture of the western Timucua Indians in early historic times.[102]

POTANO PERIOD

This period has been named by Goggin to cover the Spanish-Indian mission period in the area.[103] Reports have not yet been published, but apparently there are differences between it and both the contemporary Leon-Jefferson and St. Augustine periods.

SUMMARY AND CONCLUSIONS

We have briefly surveyed the known culture sequences in the various areas of Florida. It is to be noted immediately that these sequences are for the

94. J. W. Griffin, 1948. 96. Smith, 1948a.
95. Griffin and Smith, 1949.

97. Goggin, John M., personal communication.
98. Goggin, 1950c, p. 49.
99. Goggin, 1949a, p. 25.
100. The Alachua Tradition is discussed by Goggin, 1949a. The pottery shift is noted in Goggin, 1948b, p. 60.
101. Goggin, 1949a, p. 40.
102. Ibid. 103. Ibid., Fig. 3.

most part based on ceramics, and that in many instances very few artifacts can definitely be assigned to the complexes. Even the Weeden Island periods, perhaps the best known of Florida horizons, are known primarily from burial mounds; some work in middens and village sites has enabled the archeologist to place Weeden Island in its proper time relation to other horizons, but the details of the village life are not known to any extent. These inadequacies in the data render it immediately apparent that the sequences outlined are tentative and rough. This is not to disparage the work already done, but merely to point out how much more remains to be done before the cultural picture is rounded out to a satisfactory level.

We have seen that the hints of early man in Florida continue to multiply, even though the first candidates, Vero and Melbourne, are now assigned to the "Archaic". We have also seen that, particularly along the St. Johns River, there is evidence of a long "Archaic" occupation, beginning in pre-pottery times and continuing through both a plain and decorated fiber-tempered phase. Although the decorated fiber-tempered pottery is distinctly local, there is little doubt that it is related to, and probably contemporaneous with, other fiber-tempered levels in the Southeast. We look forward to radiocarbon dating of these early periods.

Following fiber-tempered pottery times we discussed the archeology of Florida in terms of eight geographical areas, but a broader view discloses three, or perhaps four, major ceramic traditions. Along the Gulf coast a sand or grit-tempered ware begins in Deptford times and continues into historic times. The sequence in the region gives evidence of a cultural continuum with periods rather arbitrarily divided on the basis of the appearance and disappearance of certain pottery types. In South Florida a distinctive ware, Glades, dominates the ceramic picture throughout the sequence. Again, the data suggests continuity, coupled with interesting "Archaic" survivals. In the northern St. Johns area a soft chalky ware dominates the scene until it is replaced in historic times by a complex which seemingly originates outside the state. A possible fourth division is the Alachua Tradition of central Florida. Temporally, this tradition does not cover the span of the others, and information on it is still meagre.

Some of the areas used for description are marginal to others. The Indian River Region derives its distinctiveness from its marginal position in relation to both the St. Johns and Glades areas. The Manatee Region is marginal to the Gulf Coast and Glades areas. The Kissimmee Region is geographically marginal to the Central Gulf Coast, Manatee, Glades, and Indian River areas, but present evidence seems to indicate its strongest connections were with the Glades Area. Central Florida is marginal to the Gulf Coast and St. Johns areas; in earlier periods its affiliations seem to be with the St. Johns, but later it is the locus of a distinct tradition, the Alachua, which, however, exhibits ties with areas both east and west of it.

In addition to the obvious continuity in at least three areas of the state, with each of these areas differing markedly from the others, there is evidence of influences which made themselves felt throughout the state. The introduction of burial mounds is one such influence. Burial mounds are first known with certainty on the Northwest Coast in Santa Rosa–Swift Creek times, and probably reached the Central Gulf Coast somewhat later. It may be as late as Glades III before the trait penetrates the Glades Area, but this is not certain. Burial mounds appear in St. Johns I, and the introduction may be contemporaneous, or nearly so, with that on the Northwest Coast.

Mississippian culture, too, affected all parts of the state, and once again intrudes into the various areas without obliterating the continuity within each. On the Northwest Coast pyramidal mounds appear in the Fort Walton Period, together with other traits, ceramic and non-ceramic, indicating heavy Middle Mississippi influence. The Safety Harbor Period on the Central Gulf Coast discloses the same influence, but in a much more attenuated manner. Pyramid mounds, some of considerable size, appear in Glades III, but the native ceramic tradition remains relatively unaffected. A few pyramid mounds occur in the St. Johns area, but their exact temporal position is unknown. An historical hint of earlier introduction of the trait on the west coast than on the east is provided by the mention of such mounds in the De Soto narratives of 1539–1540, and the absence of any such mention in the French accounts in 1565. There is, of course, the possibility that the construction of such mounds had ceased on the northeast coast by 1565, rather than that they had not yet been introduced, but this seems unlikely to the writer. Their scarcity may be due to the early truncation of aboriginal culture in the area.

The influence of the Southern Cult is statewide, although no sites of the magnitude of Etowah, Moundville, or Spiro are known. In the Fort Walton Period "weeping eyes" are found on pottery vessels, and specimens of Moundville pottery occur.[104] Mount Royal on the St. Johns contains the most distinctive Southern Cult material in the state, and the famous Key Marco site of Cushing[105] also contains material which can be attributed to Southern Cult influence.

104. It is of interest to note that the Moundville sherds at Kincaid come from the Middle and Late periods of that site (Cole and others, 1951, p. 152). This would date these specimens as post-1500, which coincides nicely with the accepted datings of Fort Walton.

105. Cushing, 1897.

The specific form of the influences differs from area to area, as does the intensity of influence, and, again, the local traditions carry through.

The coming of the Europeans set the stage for another group of influences on the Indian. Some of the influences was through trade, but in the Leon-Jefferson, Potano, and St. Augustine periods we find mixed Spanish-Indian settlements and evidence of acculturation. At this same general time level, strong influences from late Georgia aboriginal periods are noted.

From the point of view of anthropology, the archeology of Florida is of extreme interest. Three, or perhaps four, ceramic traditions, areally separated, persist through a relatively long period of time. During this time they undergo internal development, some of which is doubtless independent, while some is due to major influences from the adjacent Southeast. In addition they influence one another. The final stage sees the introduction of the disrupting European influence. In the late periods these factors enable us to examine native cultures, insofar as they are represented by material remains, in the process of change due to the simultaneous action of two diverse traditions, aboriginal and European.

HISTORIC SITE ARCHEOLOGY IN THE UNITED STATES.

By Jean C. Harrington*

AS THE bulk of the contributions to this volume attest, archeological field work in this country is largely concerned with American Indian cultures. However, within the past two decades a number of sites of white occupation have been investigated by archeologists. These have been of considerable variety, from the earliest English settlement at Fort Raleigh to the site of the discovery of gold in California at Sutter's Sawmill; from towns inhabited for over a century to sites occupied only during one short military engagement.

Excavating historic sites is, of course, not a new thing, but it is a new thing in the study of American history, and its effects on both historical and archeological research are becoming evident. In this paper I would like to review a few examples of historic site archeology, indicating its special problems and characteristics, and pointing out its possible contributions to American history.

Probably the immediate impetus to this research has been the relatively recent interest in restoring old houses, villages, forts, and other historic remains. The explanation, however, is really more fundamental, and reflects, among other things, a growing interest in what we often refer to as the "American scene." Concomitant with this new interest, or possibly a result of it, has been the realization that historic sites themselves, as well as the physical remains at these sites, are rapidly being destroyed and that organized action must be taken if our historic landmarks are to be preserved. Such organized action began slowly with the formation of state and local societies and associations. The American Scenic and Historic Preservation Society, one of the first and most effective organizations, was founded in 1895. It was early recognized that active participation by the federal government was necessary, both to preserve and interpret the remaining physical evidences of our historic background, and to encourage and stimulate the efforts of private and public groups in this field. The first step in this direction was the passing of the Antiquities Act in 1906 which gave the President of the

United States authority "to declare by public proclamation historic landmarks, historic and prehistoric structures, and other objects of historic and scientific interest that are situated upon the lands owned or controlled by the Government of the United States to be national monuments."

Public interest grew steadily and a number of organizations were formed for the express purpose of protecting historic sites. Typical of these is the Society for the Preservation of New England Antiquities, founded in 1910. Like the National Park Service, the programs of most of these organizations went beyond the basic purpose of preservation and included the development of the sites for enjoyment by the public. During this same period many established societies, such as the American Institute of Architects, the American Association of Museums, and the Colonial Dames of America, became more aggressively interested in historic site preservation and actively sponsored programs in this field. The restoration of Williamsburg, Virginia, which John D. Rockefeller, Jr., has been carrying on over the past twenty years, is one of the best known and most ambitious examples of restoration and interpretation. It has been a definite incentive for other restoration projects and has been responsible for a wider interest in historic site preservation.

Another evidence of this growing interest was the participation by the federal government during the years immediately preceding World War II. Through its several public works programs, including the Civil Works Administration, the Works Progress Administration, and the Civilian Conservation Corps, a great many buildings and other historic remains were measured, restored, or stabilized and historic sites throughout the country otherwise developed. Most important, these programs provided funds for detailed historical and archeological research in connection with the interpretive development and preservation of the sites.

Preservation of historic remains was further implemented by the enactment of the Historic Sites Act in 1935. The Act states that "it is hereby declared that it is a national policy to preserve for public use historic sites, buildings, and objects of national signifi-

* University of Michigan, B.S., 1924; Graduate Study, University of Chicago, Department of Anthropology, 1932–1936; Regional Archeologist, Region One, National Park Service, Richmond, Virginia. Chapter received September, 1947.

cance for the preservation and benefit of the people of the United States." Among other authorizations, it makes it possible for the Secretary of the Interior, through the National Park Service, to enter into cooperative agreements with states and with local or private agencies in the development and administration of historic areas of national interest, regardless of whether titles to the properties are vested in the United States. The act empowers the National Park Service to make surveys, measured drawings, and investigations relating to historic and archeologic sites, and preserve and develop such sites. It also authorized the creation of the Advisory Board on National Parks, Historic Sites, Buildings and Monuments, which is composed of outstanding scholars and leaders in the fields of American history, architecture, archeology, and conservation generally.

One of the latest evidences of this rapidly growing interest in the preservation of historic remains is the newly formed National Council for Historic Sites and Buildings. The object of the Council, as stated in its by-laws, is "to further the preservation and interpretation, for the public benefit, of sites and buildings situated in the United States and its possessions and significant for American history and culture."

The history of archeological collaboration in the study of historic sites in this country roughly parallels the history of site preservation as outlined above. Due both to the rapid growth of public interest in historic remains and active participation by the federal government through its public works programs, archeological exploration of historic sites has accelerated rapidly since about 1933, and there is every indication that this particular field of research will become even more active in the years to come.[1]

Ever since archeologists have been excavating sites, on this continent, of people of European origin, there has been no satisfactory or generally accepted term for this type of work. *Historic archeology*, a name sometimes applied to it, is unsatisfactory because it implies a historic *kind* of archeology, as for example, the discovery of fossil man at Tepexpan by geophysical methods. *Historical archeology* is better, but in addition to involving the questionable distinction between history and prehistory, it covers too wide a field and would include Indian sites within the historic period. *Historic site archeology*, on the other hand, avoids these difficulties, and seems to be the most satisfactory term yet suggested. It is precise and, I believe, self-explanatory, since a *historic site* is generally accepted to mean a place which is a specific and notable part of the historical record, either of itself, or by virtue of associated events or personalities.

1. For a more detailed review of historic site preservation and development in the United States see Stauffer and Porter, 1943.

COLONIAL ARCHEOLOGY

A major subdivision of historic site archeology is *colonial archeology*.[2] I shall apply the term to those situations in which a segment of an established culture is transplanted to a "foreign" territory, but at the same time retains certain ties with the "mother country." The term, used in this sense, would cover sites of both the Colonial period and the Frontier, and might include a sixteenth-century Spanish colony in Peru, a seventeenth-century English settlement in Virginia, or a nineteenth century-frontier settlement in Kentucky or Oregon. Each involves a group, or community, having a common European culture, implanted in a new and unfamiliar environment, and with influence of the parent culture continuing in effect by political ties, trade, visits to the homeland, and immigration. In each instance, the colonists leave a relatively stable society and established way of life, to be faced with new and different situations, unfamiliar problems with which they must cope, and all the difficulties and dangers of colonial life. Artisans become farmers, and farmers become soldiers and builders. Many lives are lost, much property is destroyed, and many changes are likely to be made, before the community achieves a permanent and well organized form.

There are other conditions which are usually characteristic of colonies, and which relate directly to the application of archeological research in the study of colonial sites. The exigencies of the situation would not always be conducive to the making and keeping of many records, documentary or otherwise. A shopkeeper set down in the woods with a house to build, food to raise, and Indians to fight, is not so likely to record the birth of his children, or make a detailed will and inventory before he dies. And if he does, the record is more apt to be lost than it would in a more stable, established community. Although the colonists probably sent back to the homeland numerous and detailed official reports, there is today a comparative scarcity of such material. A great deal of it has undoubtedly been lost through the ravages of time, while other documents, though extant in private collections and uncatalogued depositories, are inaccessible to the scholar. Consequently, a student of the period will find many gaps in the account of its history and culture. Almost certainly, the inhabitants of Jamestown in 1625 did not live in the same way, follow the same occupations, or have the same kind of household goods as their compatriots in England at the same time. But it is not easy to ascertain from written records just what these differences were. Ar-

2. I believe F. M. Setzler was the first to suggest the term "colonial archeology" for the broad field of historic site archeology, in place of the term "historical archeology." He objected to "colonial," however, on the grounds that it would exclude sites falling outside the Colonial period (Setzler, 1943).

cheology can fill some of the gaps, and provide valuable historical data. Depending both on the quantity and condition of the physical remains encountered, and on the amount of documentary evidence available, excavation of a colonial site can greatly assist in reconstructing the story of the colony's establishment and growth. Dealing as it does with the objects used by colonists and the tangible results of their handiwork and labors, archeology can aid in interpreting the adaptation of these people to their new environment, and can help explain changes that are made and become characteristic in the post-Colonial period.

It must be realized, of course, that archeology can provide only a small part of the source material for study of a historic site, and it is not to be expected that the archeologist's findings will revolutionize the story. The excavation of a site might be compared to the study of a new collection of documentary material. It is possible that nothing new will be learned, but there is always the chance that something will be found that will bring about a new interpretation, or a complete revision of the historical account. It is more likely, however, that the excavating will result simply in throwing more light on the picture and in filling in some of the details missing from the study of written records. The colonial archeologist must therefore know something of the methods and problems of the other fields of study involved. He should certainly know something about historical research and the documentary source material relating to his site. It is also highly desirable that he have some acquaintance with the special fields of knowledge that will be required for proper use of the artifacts and the interpretation of the physical remains encountered. For the complete understanding of these remains, however, and more exact dating and identification, the services of specialists in many fields, such as architecture, ceramics, weapons, numismatics, Indian trade goods, and glassware, will of course be needed.

Because of the extensive and scattered background material for most colonial sites, it has been found to be extremely helpful to the archeologist to have prepared a preliminary orientation report for use before and during the excavating. Such a report compiles and interprets all material relating to the site or portion of the site involved in the immediate excavating program, drawing on the documentary sources, comparative architectural studies, studies of other contemporary sites and of objects from the period concerned, and on the results of any previous excavating at the same site. Such a report need not be a narrative treatise, but rather an orderly accumulation and synthesis of data which will best serve to direct the course of the excavating and assist the archeologist and other specialists in interpreting the data recovered from the ground.

It can easily be seen that a general review of this phase of American archeology cannot be a summary of accomplishments, nor can it be a series of new hypotheses and interpretations. Perhaps eventually, when great numbers of colonial sites have been excavated and the results studied, it will be possible to make certain general statements dealing with the contribution of archeology to American history, or to other fields of study. But at present, the sites that have been excavated have been so widely scattered in location and period, that results can only be considered individually.

I shall not attempt to review each of the projects falling within this field, nor even to list them here. Typical of such projects, in addition to those subsequently discussed, are the following: The work at Plymouth, Massachussetts, by Henry Hornblower, II; the excavations at Whitman Mission, Washington, by the National Park Service under the supervision of Thomas R. Garth; J. O. Brew's work at Awatovi, which included the excavation of the Mission San Bernardo de Aguatubi; excavations now under way at Fort Frederica National Monument in Georgia, under Charles Fairbanks' direction; John W. Griffin's recent excavation of a Spanish Mission near Waukenah, Florida; and the work at Sutter's Sawmill in California by the University of California in collaboration with the California State Park Commission and the National Park Service.

Two outstanding projects lying outside the boundaries of continental United States should be mentioned. Both are excellent illustrations of the contribution that can be made through the combined use of historical and archeological methods and data. One is the work of Adolfo de Hostos at the site of Capara in Puerto Rico.[3] The other is the excavation of the site of Fort Ste. Marie 1, Ontario, Canada, by Kenneth E. Kidd.

I have selected four typical projects to describe in some detail. These particular ones were chosen only because I am more familiar with them, either from participation or because detailed reports are at hand.

FORT RALEIGH[4]

At Fort Raleigh, scene of Sir Walter Raleigh's abortive colonizing effort in the late sixteenth century, the problem is more nearly like that of some

3. Hostos, 1938.
4. A tract of approximately 16 acres, located on Roanoke Island, North Carolina, which presumably embraces part of the settlement sites of 1585 and 1587. This land, including the fort, was transferred to the federal government by the state of North Carolina in 1940, and in 1941 it was designated the Fort Raleigh National Historic Site, under provisions of the Historic Sites Act of 1935. It is administered by the National Park Service, United States Department of the Interior. Archeological explorations were conducted there in the spring of 1947 by the National Park Service under the direction of the author. For a review of pre-excavating knowledge of the site see Porter, 1943.

Indian sites. Although several narrative accounts give the history of this colony, which existed for a short time and then disappeared without a trace, relatively few records concerning it are available. The exact location of the settlement cannot be determined from available sources, though the evidence is fairly definite that it was on the north end of Roanoke Island and adjacent to the traditional site of "The new Fort in Virginia," built in 1585. However, there was no positive evidence that the low rise of ground, known for many years as Fort Raleigh, was actually the fort in question. Archeology, it is hoped, can (1) establish the location of the settlement; (2) secure detailed information concerning it—the number, size, and appearance of the houses, and the layout of the town; (3) determine the original size and appearance of the fort; (4) learn something about the lives of the colonists—their trades, their tools, implements and utensils, and other details of their life; (5) throw some light on the cause of the abandonment of the town, whether from conflict with the Indians or Spanish, or for other reasons; and (6) establish the cultural position of the Indians with whom the colonists came in contact.

Excavations carried on during the spring of 1947 completed only a part of the preliminary exploratory project. The fort was identified and excavated sufficiently to determine the general nature of its construction and its orientation. An area adjacent to the fort, and on the side of the fort's entrance, was partially explored by a series of five-foot trenches. No positive evidence of the village was found, such as wall footings, fireplace remains, or the accumulation of ashes and other typical habitation refuse. However, a number of early European artifacts were found, which, together with the information on the fort, is sufficient evidence to state that the area is unquestionably the site of the Raleigh settlements.

Assuming that further excavation will locate the houses of these early settlers, much should be learned that can make a really major contribution to American history.

JAMESTOWN [5]

At Jamestown, Virginia, the problem is somewhat different from that at Fort Raleigh, and much more complex. Jamestown, founded in 1607, was the site

5. All of Jamestown Island, with the exception of approximately 21 acres, is now part of Colonial National Historical Park, administered by the National Park Service, United States Department of the Interior. The 21-acre tract, which was designated a National Historic Site in 1940, belongs to the Association for the Preservation of Virginia Antiquities and has been preserved and exhibited by that organization since 1893.

The research program at Jamestown after 1936 was under the supervision of the author. There is no single report on the results of the excavating, but individual unit reports are available in manuscript at the office of the Director, National Park Service, U.S. Department of the Interior.

of the first permanent English settlement in America, and capital of the colony of Virginia until 1699. Its location, in a general way, was known, for the remains of the old church are still standing and reports of travellers within the past century have mentioned ruined brick walls in the vicinity. In spite of the great body of source material, the exact location of the first settlement could not be determined. No maps of the town existed, and no adequate descriptions of the town or of its buildings were available, for most of this source material deals only with political, social, or economic history of the period. A few land records have come down to us, but so far not a single inventory of a house or a room has been found, and there is very little documentary information which would tell us what the town looked like and what the inhabitants used and wore.

A broad program of research was carried on from 1934 through 1941, including, in addition to archeological excavating at Jamestown, documentary research at several libraries and other repositories in this country. It has not yet been possible to pursue these studies in England, although valuable material is undoubtedly available there. It is important to emphasize that at such a site documentary, architectural, and other research must be carried on concurrently with the excavating. For maximum results and efficiency in the conduct of each line of research, new source material and interpretations must be constantly compared and the research directed accordingly. Only about ten per cent of the town site proper has been excavated, but a great deal of material and information has been secured, many of the gaps have been filled, and many questions posed which may be answered by further study of the accumulated source material or from additional excavation.

Of primary interest, especially since Jamestown is a National Park Service area, is the information relating to the location and physical appearance of the town at various stages in its development. The area in which the original palisaded settlement is believed to have been located has not been excavated, but information secured from the excavation of other parts of the site, studied in relation to documentary evidence, indicates its probable location. In other parts of the town, house foundations, streets, paths, wells, kilns, ditches (Figs. 185–188), fence lines, and other remains have been found, and many of them have been dated and identified with specific persons and their land holdings. This information, in conjunction with the few available land records, permits partial reconstruction of the plan of the town at several different periods. An enormous mass of cultural material has been recovered, some of which has contributed directly to the interpretation of the house remains, and gives a good picture of the useful and ornamental articles possessed by the Jamestown colonists.

A good example of the interrelationship of the documentary and archeological research is found in the excavations of the season of 1939.[6] The land records pertaining to the area selected for investigation that year, as well as identifiable features previously uncovered in adjacent areas, made possible the tentative location of a one-acre tract of land owned successively by at least five people between 1661 and the close of the century. Documentary evidence showed that the first owner, William May, built a house on this lot shortly after he acquired it in 1661. Whether the second owner lived there is not known, but the third owner apparently occupied a house on the property. The fourth owner, Henry Hartwell, disposed of the property in 1695. There was no evidence from the records to show whether the original May house had stood throughout this period, or had been destroyed, possibly during Bacon's Rebellion in 1676, as had most of the houses in the town. In other words, the pre-excavating knowledge concerning this part of Jamestown consisted mainly in the chain of title for a one-acre tract of land and its approximate location.

In excavating the area, additional physical remains, including several property line ditches, were located which could be identified as those mentioned in the land records. The remains of only one house were found. Over thirty bottle seals bearing the initials "H-H" were recovered from the refuse in and near the house foundations, showing that Henry Hartwell had lived there (Fig. 194). From the total evidence—archeological and documentary—it is now known that only one house ever occupied this site; that it was built soon after 1661, and was still standing in 1695. We know that Henry Hartwell, an important figure in Jamestown history during the latter part of the century, actually lived in that house. Architectural details of the house as well as a number of other interesting facts concerning this particular area are known. Location and identification of the property line ditches and certain fence lines permitted more exact location of adjacent tracts, which in turn provided the location of several earlier features, including certain streets and the shore line of the river. This is just one small example, although many others might be cited, illustrating how the combined use of archeological and documentary evidence provides a more complete or more sharply defined picture.[7]

The artifacts found at Jamestown not only assist in interpreting the remains with which they were associated, as well as reveal the material culture of the Jamestown people, but also contribute information on the cultural history of the seventeenth century.[8] Much more should be learned as specialists are able to make detailed studies of the tools, ceramics, and the extensive collections of other materials excavated at Jamestown. For this period in the history of the Virginia colony, relatively little is known concerning the technology and decorative arts, and the only source of information in many fields has been the study of contemporary practices in England. In architecture, for instance, a great deal is known about the later Georgian period, but almost nothing concerning the seventeenth century. Building materials found at Jamestown, ranging from heavy floor tiles to fine decorative plaster, in addition to the foundations themselves, provide a reasonably accurate picture of the typical Virginia house of that period.

Development of the arts and crafts is of interest, and studies have already thrown some light on this subject. Brickmaking is one example. It was generally believed, although unsupported by documentary evidence, that the bricks used in the buildings at Jamestown were imported from England as ballast in ships. Discovery of brick and tile kilns, however, disposes of this theory (Fig. 186). But more important, it provides material for comparative studies which may show to what extent the Jamestown artisans were getting away from the controls of the powerful craft guilds of England. In this connection, it will be interesting to see if Jamestown bricks varied more from the statute size than those made in England during the same period.

The ceramic collection is revealing as to the extent of trade and commerce of the period. No pottery kiln has yet been found, but the large amount of crude earthenware material certainly suggests that some was made locally. However, a great deal of finer ware was imported, and not only from England, but also from Spain, Holland, Italy, Mexico, and even China (Fig. 189).

One of the most valuable historical contributions made by the Jamestown studies is in providing an over-all picture of the material wealth and social status of the colonists. Here was no impoverished frontier settlement, once the first hard years were past, but a well-built town, lived in by people of culture and, in many cases, of relative wealth. This is well illustrated by their houses (Figs. 187–188). Following the style of the time, the houses were small, particularly in comparison with those of the later Georgian period. But they were by no means crude cottages, as is shown by finds of brick-floored cellars, hearths of Dutch brick, fireplaces faced with im-

6. Harrington, J. C., n.d.

7. For a more detailed example of correlated research at Jamestown see Harrington, J. C., 1940.

8. Of the numerous publications describing the physical remains and cultural objects uncovered in the Jamestown excavations, the most exhaustive study is by H. C. Forman (1938); see also Atwood, 1942. Detailed unpublished manuscript reports are available in the National Park Service files.

ported Delft tiles, plastered walls, wine cellars, casement windows with glass panes, fine wrought iron hinges and locks, ornamental plaster work, tile and slate roofs, and well-laid brickwork.[9]

Excavations at Jamestown have contributed valuable information for the study of historic and protohistoric Indian sites in Virginia. The dating of European trade pipes, as well as other objects of European manufacture found in Indian sites, has been facilitated by the Jamestown research (Fig. 191). It is anticipated that excavation of the site of the Jamestown glass house, recently acquired by the Federal Government, will provide data on the first glass articles manufactured on this continent. There is no reliable documentary evidence as to what objects were actually made there, although it has always been assumed that beads for Indian trade were the principal output. If this point can be established, it will not only be of interest for the history of glass making in America, but will be extremely useful in dating Indian sites in eastern Virginia. The glass works operated for two short, distinct periods—1608–1609 and 1621–1624—and determination of the exact type of beads made there will be of value to the student of Indian archeology. Beads were traded to the Indians in this region from 1607 until probably well toward the close of the century, but it has not been possible to assign precise dates to the sites or strata in which trade beads occur. Beads of known date and origin should prove very useful, and even though the Jamestown beads may resemble those of European manufacture, there should be some unique characteristics which will permit their identification when found in Indian sites.

From a methodological point of view, the research at Jamestown has clearly demonstrated the fruitful results of the close collaboration of historical and archeological approaches to the study and interpretation of colonial sites. Here the most meticulous study of land records and contemporary accounts could yield only a vague and incomplete picture of the town of Jamestown. Exhaustive study of records and museum collections were exceedingly inconclusive in the matter of architecture and material culture. On the other hand, archeological excavation by itself would have revealed only a rather meaningless welter of house foundations, pottery, glassware, and other artifacts. For though Jamestown's near-century period of occupancy seems long, it was not long enough to produce many marked typological variations or much stratigraphy. But with each field of research being carried on in close cooperation, the activities of the archeologist were directed to the best advantage, and the finds in the ground in turn guided historical research and interpretation. As a result, a detailed

and dated picture of Jamestown has emerged, which, aside from being of great interest to the average American, provides valuable material for the study of American history.

FORT RIDGELY[10]

One of the best examples of the application of archeological research to the study of an historic site is the excavation of Fort Ridgely in Minnesota. This frontier post, well known for its part in the Sioux Outbreak of 1862 and one of the focal points of the struggle between the Sioux and the whites in the Minnesota Valley, was established by the War Department in 1853. Rapid advance of the Northwest frontier soon caused the post to be abandoned, and it was not long before most of the buildings had been torn down and the site, for the most part, forgotten. In 1911, however, it was set aside as a state park by act of the Minnesota legislature. Identity of the site had not been lost, since portions of some of the original buildings were still being used as farm buildings. Moreover, there existed fairly good records of the post.

The aim of the excavating was much the same as that of the Jamestown project, namely to secure data which would permit the best possible interpretation of the site to the visitor. One of the buildings was restored for use as a museum and public assembly hall, while other stone foundations were stabilized and left exposed as nearly as possible as they appeared when excavated. In addition to the information secured on the physical appearance of the fort, the excavations produced a large quantity of cultural objects. "Included are military articles, building hardware, household utensils, personal articles, tools and implements, and examples of the farrier's art and harness. Not only do these objects vividly illustrate 'the conditions imposed upon every day existence' during the period involved, but they recall social and economic trends of the period in manufactures, the arts, and inventions."[11]

A secondary result of the excavating at Fort Ridgely was the discovery of previous occupation of the site by Indians. Associated with the Indian material, and stratigraphically separated from the Fort Ridgely horizon, were four gunflints. Indian burial mounds located in the area were shown to be of the same period as the other material which preceded the white occupation. Smith points out that although the ethnic position of this Indian culture is not clear, it is

---

9. Forman, 1938, pp. 81–101.

10. Excavation of Fort Ridgely was begun in 1936 by the National Park Service, under the supervision of G. Hubert Smith, in cooperation with the Minnesota Historical Society and the Minnesota Division of State Parks, as a part of the development planned for Fort Ridgely State Park. The project was carried out under the program of the Civilian Conservation Corps. See Smith, G. H., 1939.

11. *Ibid.*, p. 154.

significant that in the protohistoric period, at least at this site, pottery making and flint working by the natives were contemporary with the use of flintlock guns, and probably both with the custom of mound burial.

Although the excavations at Fort Ridgely were carried on principally for the purpose of developing the site for visitor use, valuable information was secured through closely integrated archeological and historical research. By making full use of available documentary evidence and modern archeological methods, a maximum of information concerning the history of the site was obtained, as well as certain historical knowledge of broader interest.

THE MACON TRADING POST[12]

The Macon Trading Post illustrates another class of sites quite distinct from those reviewed above. Examples have been mentioned ranging from Fort Raleigh, where the written record is extremely meagre, to Fort Ridgely, where the records are much more complete and where physical evidences of the original structures were still visible when the excavating began. But no matter how incomplete the documentary sources may have been, the archeologist set out with at least some historical facts concerning the site. In the case of the Macon Trading Post, however, specific information relating to the Post, or even to the fact that one had existed there, was lacking. The site was discovered by merest accident in the course of excavating what was presumably only an Indian site.

First evidence of the Trading Post was the discovery of a small ditch enclosing a five-sided area. This ditch, upon complete excavation, was interpreted to indicate the line of a stockade wall, probably of horizontal logs. Two openings in the wall were evidently entrances, since remains of an old trail were found leading from these openings. The trail was followed by means of vertical cross sections at intervals of fifty to one hundred feet for a distance of nearly a mile. In addition to the wall ditch and the trail, evidence of log cabins was found inside the enclosure, and remains of Indian lodges appeared in the excavations, both within and without the stockade. Numerous European objects were found, many associated with Indian burials. Evidence from the excavation of nearby Indian village occupations, as well as from the Post itself, showed quite clearly that the

same people had lived on the site before, during, and after the operation of the Trading Post.

Study of the European trade objects indicates a date for the Post within a narrow span of years in the neighborhood of 1700. As A. R. Kelly points out, this is a period in which very little is known of central Georgia history. He suggests that "the Macon Trading Post was established by traders from Carolina late in the 17th century and that it was probably destroyed incident to or following the Yamasee Wars of 1715. The historical significance of the site is enhanced by the probability that Colonel James Moore came to this spot on the Ocmulgee in 1704 in company with fifty Carolinians, that he concentrated 1,000 Creek Indian warriors on the meadow behind the Trading Post, armed them, and proceeded to Florida where he defeated a large force of Spanish and Appalachi Indians in the Appalachi country."[13]

The historical importance of this find is apparent, and the archeological evidence should take on more meaning as historians re-study available sources in the light of that evidence, and as they find new documentary materials relating to this site or to the incidents associated with it. Interesting as this find is to early American history, its importance to Southeastern archeology is of even greater significance. As stated by Kelly, the work at Macon "has given fresh demonstration of [the] increasingly closer relationship between history and archeology in presenting a series of explored sites which fit demonstrably into a chronological series culminating in the more recent documented period of early European contact with the American Indian."[14]

RESTORATION ARCHEOLOGY

It is obvious that colonial archeology does not include all historic site archeology. Another subdivision of this field might be called "restoration archeology," and would include the many projects in which building sites, military sites, and other remains are excavated for the purpose of locating structures exactly and obtaining information for their restoration. It differs from colonial archeology in its aims, and includes sites that do not come under the broad definition of colonial, as I am using it here. But the subject should have some discussion, however, because it is closely associated in most of our minds with projects which I have grouped under colonial archeology, and because many of the projects in these two fields have dealt with sites closely related, both chronologically and culturally. I would like to describe briefly two projects which are representative of restoration archeology.

A good example of military restoration archeology was the excavation and restoration of the earthworks

---

12. The site is located near Macon, Georgia, in Ocmulgee National Monument. Beginning in 1933, excavations were carried on under the sponsorship of the Smithsonian Institution and the National Park Service, and under the auspices of various Federal relief agencies. In addition to the Trading Post and related historic and protohistoric Indian sites described here, several important prehistoric sites in the area have been explored. See Kelly, 1939.

13. *Ibid.*, p. 332.   14. *Ibid.*, p. 329.

on the battlefield of the siege of Yorktown, which concluded the American Revolution.[15] A considerable mass of documentary material and maps was available on the site, and the location of the trenches and batteries was known approximately before the excavations were started. Minute details of the earthworks were known from contemporary accounts, and military standards and manuals of that day made possible the drawing of conclusions regarding height and contour of the fortifications. In fact, the restoration project was originally conceived without regard to any excavation because of the completeness of information from documentary sources. As a result of the excavating, the earthworks were restored exactly in their original location. In fact, they were actually rebuilt in the manner in which they were originally constructed, by first locating the trenches and then throwing out the fill to form the embankments. Excavation and restoration were combined, essentially, in one operation. Remains of the wooden gun platforms were found, which permitted the correct types of guns to be accurately placed in the restored fortifications.

In this instance the work was directed by experts in military history and Revolutionary War fortifications, rather than by archeologists, but the resulting restorations undoubtedly approach the appearance of the original structures as nearly as the archeological and documentary evidence would permit.

Excavation of the site of the McLean House at Appomattox Court House, Virginia, where Lee surrendered to Grant in 1865, is an excellent example of digging to secure information for the restoration of a house.[16]

To my knowledge, this is one of the most thoroughly executed projects yet conducted in the field of house restoration archeology. The house had stood until 1893, and at the time of its demolition detailed plans were made, with the idea of rebuilding it in another location. Those plans, in addition to several photographs of the building, are available. Consequently, the problem was entirely one of obtaining location and construction details, to corroborate the existing plans, and to fill in the record on the area adjacent to the house. As a result of the excavating, remains of the fences, walks, a well, a terrace, as well as many details of the house construction, were found, and minor variations from the plans were recorded for use in the restoration.

15. The Yorktown battlefield is part of Colonial National Historical Park, which also includes Jamestown Island. The excavation and restoration work described here was carried on by the National Park Service between 1933 and 1938 under the program of the Civilian Conservation Corps.

16. The site is located in Appomattox Court House National Historical Monument. Excavation of the McLean House was carried on in 1941 by the National Park Service, under the supervision of Preston Holder. See Holder, n.d.

I would hesitate to go so far as to say that the work described here, and many similar projects throughout the country, is not archeology, although that has not infrequently been suggested. There is possibly some basis for such a suggestion, however. In the first place the information sought is limited and directed specifically to the restoration of the structures involved. The digging is usually localized, and once the structure is found, no effort is made to go outside the immediate area concerned. Interpretations of soil conditions and position of artifacts, provided such observations are made, are in relation to the appearance and construction of the structure. In this respect, Holder says of the McLean House excavation: "It was obvious from the analysis presented in [the historical study] that the major problems would be tectonic in nature. The surface details bore out this conclusion and indicated that little or no exploratory trenching would be necessary. It seemed probable that stratification, artifact analysis, and problems generally so significant in prehistoric archeology would play little part at the McLean Site."[17]

Another way in which restoration archeology differs from colonial archeology is that the problems of construction and restoration are so specialized that the archeologist is not much more than a digging technician, and in most cases the conclusions and interpretations must be left to military specialists and architects. The collaboration required here is quite different, if only in degree, from the cooperative relationship of the historian, archeologist, and antiquarian in colonial archeology.

Whether we refer to these two activities under the single term of historic site archeology, or separate them as suggested here, the fact remains that restoration archeology has specific but limited objectives, whereas the various projects I would group under colonial archeology seek to establish chronology, determine cultural sequences, reconstruct the material culture of a community, and in other ways contribute to the history of the site and of the people who lived there. In some cases the two sorts of digging are both involved on the same site, and the two cannot be separated easily. At such times it is important that the objectives and possibilities of colonial archeology be recognized so that all possible historical information can be recovered through the employment of recognized archeological methods.

OTHER HISTORIC SITE ARCHEOLOGY

Although most excavations of historic sites in this country would fall under one, or both the fields for which the terms colonial archeology and restoration archeology are suggested, there are examples which cannot be classified under either. One such project is

17. *Ibid.*, pp. 1–2.

the work at Hopewell Village National Historic Site in Pennsylvania. Excavation of this eighteenth and early nineteenth century iron-making village was carried on by the National Park Service, not only for restoration data, but for the purpose of securing historical information on the iron-making industry of that period. For the present, it would seem sufficient to refer to such projects under the broader designation of historic site archeology.

I have spoken rather loosely of colonial archeology and restoration archeology as being two "subdivisions" of historic site archeology, but I am aware that they are not of the same order. Certainly they are not two mutually-exclusive categories within the broader field. They are, however, fairly comprehensible names for the two convenient groupings, in one or the other of which most of the excavating at historic sites in this country can be placed.

CONCLUSIONS

The sites considered thus far have been of considerable variety both in problems and in material. But they have more in common than a cultural background of European origin. I think it proper to say that excavation in this field constitutes a new kind of archeology, on a par with Classical archeology, American prehistoric archeology, or paleolithic archeology. Historic site archeology involves a distinctive kind of site, develops a distinctive approach, both in field techniques and manner of interpretation, and produces characteristic conclusions and results.

First, in most cases the sites were occupied for relatively short periods. This means that stratigraphy and seriation, two of the archeologist's most reliable standbys, are not applicable. Actually, chronology is seldom a concern at such sites, for in most cases exact date of the settlement's founding and occupation is known. If not, an approximate date can usually be established from datable artifacts found in the excavation and from superficial historical study. In other words, the problem of chronology is usually not one that taxes the acumen of the excavator.

But, though this problem is usually a minor consideration, a different problem, and one of great influence on the way the excavating is conducted, arises from the fact that the culture represented at these sites is relatively modern and highly complex. It is obvious that no one person can be an authority on every aspect of present day, or even seventeenth century, civilization. Consequently, the investigations of historic sites call for collaboration between, or at the very least, the consultation of, specialists in a number of fields. An effect of this situation, in addition to discouraging archeologists from embarking on research in this field, is to hold up publication of the results of the excavations pending authoritative analysis of the various classes of cultural material.

The archeologists who have worked on the excavation of historic sites have in most cases been trained in departments of anthropology, which means that their experience has usually been in the field of American prehistory. They are almost completely lacking in knowledge of the material objects associated with the period of the sites. In a somewhat comparable field, that of Classical archeology, the worker has specific training in the history and culture of the field with which he is dealing. He has studied art and architecture, language and folklore. To offset this disadvantage, American Indian archeology has equipped the worker at historic sites in this country with careful and meticulous field techniques. Because of all these factors, field work in historic site archeology has been carried on possibly more slowly and precisely than necessary. Other considerations also tend to bring this about. The archeologist knows that other specialists will be checking his work, and that they will perhaps want types of information that he might overlook or might not consider important. So he tries to prepare for every eventuality. Dealing as he often does with sites of outstanding historical importance, there is the feeling that every fragment of information is, or may be, a sacred "historical document." As a result of all these factors, historic site archeology has begun to acquire a reputation for slow, meticulous procedure. I see no immediate remedy, if, indeed, the situation needs correction. However, as workers become experienced in this specialized field, they will be able to proceed more expeditiously and be able to appraise each situation more accurately and with more assurance. Maturity of judgment will come eventually, but in the meantime the workers in this field will have to feel their way.

As mentioned earlier, the results of the work in colonial archeology cannot as yet be stated in terms of new hypotheses and contributions to American history or any other field. But certain results of a more general nature may be cited. First, this work has provided detailed information concerning the physical appearance of the sites at the time of their occupancy, and has made available actual physical remains associated with the settlements. Both the structural remains and the artifacts have a definite and highly effective use in making the areas of interest to the people who visit them.[18] Authentic materials, recovered from the original site, and displayed there, in conjunction with the original setting, have a great educational value. These things give life and substance to the interpretation of the history of the site, and help people to understand better the historical event or period connected with it. This, of course,

18. Harrington, J. C., 1946.

is eminently worthwhile. It is the primary reason for excavating these sites, and would alone justify the work.

Another effect the excavation of historic sites should have is to foster studies of physical objects. Historians are recognizing that more use might well be made of cultural remains, but this interest has not been particularly conspicuous, partly because of academic inertia and partly because adequate materials were not available. The most pressing need at present is the training of specialists in the study of objects associated with colonial sites. Historic site archeology will not only provide the materials to work with, but it should also provide the incentive for students to specialize in the field of identification and interpretation of historic objects.

In a different direction, these studies often make definite contributions to history. Such contributions so far have been minor, and arrived at incidentally to the physical study of the site and artifacts, but they are real and should not be overlooked. It is obvious, even to the layman, that there has been in recent years a growing tendency among historians to broaden their approach to the study of American history. More attention is being paid to the so-called cultural aspects. I do not mean that there has been a shifting of emphasis from political and economic interests, but rather a recognition that there is more to human history than official documents and biographies of public figures. Although the few archeological-historical investigations of colonial sites have probably had no effect on this trend, it is possible that they will have as time goes on. In this regard, the anthropological background of the colonial archeologist has made an important contribution. Rather than approaching the project with a restricted interest, such as architecture or ceramic arts, he has had an ethno-historical interest, which definitely conforms to this new trend in historical research. The published results of this type of archeological work should appeal more to the historian than a more limited, specialized approach, and in the course of time may have some influence on the study of American history generally.

The requirements of historic site archeology are also having an influence on historical research, for an archeologist needs information on his site perhaps never required before. Land records and other documentary materials are subjected to scrutiny from quite a different point of view. Although the number of such studies has been limited, and relatively few students have actually pursued this line of research, historians are beginning to recognize that it has a definite place in historiography.[19]

Outside its own immediate field colonial archeology has furnished data of distinct value in the study of aboriginal history, as has been indicated in the discussion of the various sites. American archeologists have talked a great deal about working from the known to the unknown, but they have been tardy in actually doing it. Study of historic and protohistoric Indian sites will be benefited materially once the work on colonial sites progresses to the point that European trade objects can be accurately dated. We still have a long way to go in this respect, and progress will continue to be slow because of the complexity of the culture involved and the dearth of authorities in the field.

In summary, the work in historic site archeology in this country has established itself as a new field, with characteristic materials, problems, and results. Primarily, it has produced information and physical remains of great value in interpreting places and happenings of significance in American history. It has, in a small way, helped to broaden the approach to American history, and has encouraged the use of physical objects in historical studies. By providing the medium, and possibly an incentive, it should encourage the training of specialists in this field. Historic site archeology is still a foundling, and its course will not be easy, for historians will always depend largely upon the written record, and most archeologists will prefer the romance and excitement of greater antiquity, where much of the broad frame of the historical record still needs filling in. Fortunately the few workers in this field have had the unstinting support and encouragement of such men as Frank Setzler, Alfred Kidder, J. O. Brew, and Clark Wissler. The National Park Service, because of its trusteeship over many of our nationally important historic sites, has had a conspicuous part in the progress of historic site archeology, and will necessarily continue to have. But other individuals and organizations outside the Federal Government have taken an active interest in this new discipline, and I am sure that its full recognition by scholars in every field is not far off.

19. For a good example of historical research directed along these lines see Hatch, 1942.

DENDROCHRONOLOGY IN THE MISSISSIPPI VALLEY.
By Robert E. Bell[*]

DENDROCHRONOLOGY, or tree-ring analysis, is a relatively new technique used in establishing archeological chronologies. Through the work of Dr. A. E. Douglass[1] and his students, dendrochronology has supplied the archeologist with specific calendrical dates which can be used in establishing an exact chronology for prehistoric cultures. By the assignment of true annual dates to wood specimens removed from prehistoric structures, it has been possible to apply specific dates to certain archeological sites and, consequently, to extend them in a more general manner to a single or related cultural complex or cultural horizon. Within the archeological area generally referred to as the Southwest, many sites have been dated by the use of tree-ring analysis.[2] This information has enabled archeologists working in that area to reconstruct the prehistory of the region with much greater reliability than could have been possible without accurate dating. Tree-ring evidence frequently gives us information which shatters the structural framework of reconstructions based upon less precise data. In giving the answer to one problem, however, tree-ring data usually create many new problems. The progress made, nevertheless, is cumulative, and our present knowledge and understanding of Southwestern archeology has a firm foundation which is not equalled by any other area of the United States. This position and understanding of Southwestern prehistory is a result, primarily, of the application of dendrochronology to the archeological problems encountered.

The success in using dendrochronological methods in assigning absolute dates to archeological horizons within the Southwest has been viewed with envy by archeologists in other localities. Tree-ring dating and its use in assigning dates to archeological sites offers a new and better method for establishing an accurate chronology. It is only natural that archeologists should wish to apply this new technique in areas outside of the Southwest in an attempt to solve some of the problems with which they are concerned.

Until recently, however, the development of dendrochronological methods had been limited to the Southwest, and there was some question as to whether or not this technique could be satisfactorily applied in other areas. The Southwest was especially suited to tree-ring analysis by virtue of the environment and the availability of a plentiful supply of archeological specimens. Research work carried on in the past few years has indicated that dendrochronological methods can be applied to other regions, and that the usefulness of this technique is not restricted to the Southwest. Tree-ring research has been carried out with varying degrees of success in Alaska,[3] Mexico,[4] Scandinavia,[5] the Near East,[6] and the Mississippi Valley.[7]

Dr. Fay-Cooper Cole of the University of Chicago has been the prime instigator in getting dendrochronological research started in the Mississippi Valley. In 1934 a dendrochronology laboratory was established at the University of Chicago, the primary objective being the application of tree-ring methods of analysis to the dating of archeological remains of the Mississippi drainage. The research and direction of the activities of the laboratory were initially under the guidance of Dr. Florence Hawley. A report of the accomplishments and activities of the laboratory was published in 1941.[8] Since that time, the dendrochronological research under the direction of the present writer has been directed primarily toward a single problem, namely, the dating of a specific site which represents an example of the Middle Mississippi cultural phase.

The dating of the Kincaid site,[9] located in southern Illinois, was selected as the primary objective for all dendrochronological research. Of the three archeological horizons represented at the site, Baumer, Lewis, and Kincaid, we are here concerned only with

---

[*] University of New Mexico, B.A., 1940; University of Chicago, M.A., 1943; Ph.D., 1947; Chairman, Department of Anthropology and Curator of Anthropology, University Museum, University of Oklahoma, 1947———. Chapter received April, 1947.

1. Douglass, 1935.
2. McGregor, 1941; *Tree-Ring Bulletin*.
3. Giddings, 1941; 1942.
4. Schulman, 1944a.
5. Schulman, 1944b; Zeuner, 1946.
6. Gindel, 1944.
7. Hawley, 1941; Bell, 1943. n.d.
8. Hawley, 1941.
9. A report upon the Kincaid site is in preparation and should be published within the present year (1947). See Cole and others, 1951.

the latest manifestation, which is Kincaid. The most recent horizon at this site, and the one considered here, represents the Kincaid component, Kincaid Focus, Tennessee-Cumberland Aspect of the Middle Mississippi Phase.[10] The Kincaid site was selected for several reasons: (1) it was centrally located with reference to other sites of the central Mississippi Valley; (2) extensive excavations had been made so that a fairly complete picture of the Kincaid component was available; (3) wood specimens which appeared to be dateable by tree-ring methods had been found; (4) the presence of foreign pottery trade sherds at the Kincaid site made it especially useful for the extension of resulting dates to other sites or localities.

There had been a total of about five hundred wood specimens salvaged from excavations at the Kincaid site. This included specimens of all sizes, condition, and species; all wood samples which were sufficiently preserved to be removed were collected and submitted to the laboratory. Naturally, this collection, without a critical selection of specimens in the field, contained much material which was unsuitable for tree-ring analysis. Of this group, approximately forty-five specimens represented red cedar, the species which was to be used in this study. From these specimens, twenty pieces showed possibilities for analysis, the remainder of this series having so few rings that the records were obviously undateable. This small group of twenty specimens, then, supplied the basic material which was studied for possible dating of the Kincaid site. Of these twenty pieces, eight specimens were dated; the remaining specimens had records that were either too complacent, too short, or were too erratic in one way or another. Considerable time has been spent in trying to date these latter twelve specimens, but it has been without success, and it is doubtful if dates for these pieces will ever be forthcoming.

Eight wood specimens, then, from the Kincaid site have been assigned true annual ring dates.[11] The outside ring dates for these specimens range from 1513 to 1588. This range of dates, unfortunately, does not cover the entire span of the Kincaid occupation; both earlier and later occupational levels are not included within this dated period.

There are dates from two of the Kincaid sites, Mx^{v}1C, a village site, and Mx^{0}4, a domiciliary mound. Figure 196 illustrates a diagrammatic cross-section of these two sites and shows the levels with which these dated wood specimens were associated.

On the basis of stratigraphy and developmental changes in ceramics and cultural content, the Kincaid component has been divided into three periods: Early, Middle, and Late.[12] By the use of estimated

bark-ring dates and from the association of wood specimens with specific archeological levels, dates have been assigned to these three divisions of the Kincaid sequence.[13] All of Early Kincaid is considered as having been before 1523; Middle Kincaid ranged from 1523 to 1598, and Late Kincaid lasted from 1598 until sometime after 1613. Since all levels are not represented by specimens which have been dated, both limits of the Early and Late periods cannot be accurately established.

With dates assigned to the various Kincaid periods, it is possible to correlate other sites with Kincaid on the basis of similarities in the total cultural complex,[14] similarities in the ceramic development,[15] and by the use of pottery trade wares which are sufficiently distinctive so that they may be identified as to the original source.[16] Assuming contemporaneity for the cultures which can thus be correlated with Kincaid, such cultures can be indirectly dated by use of the Kincaid chronology. Although actual contemporaneity between two such sites remains to be tested, a suggested correlation should be given and offered as an hypothesis. Certainly minor errors such as might be introduced by cultural lag are not, in this case, of sufficient magnitude to forbid such an extended correlation.

Figure 197 presents a diagrammatic chart of the dated Kincaid periods with the suggested correlations for other foci of the Mississippi Valley. One example should suffice to illustrate the type of evidence upon which this chart is based. In the Early period at Kincaid, foreign trade sherds of four pottery wares were found: Powell Plain, Ramey Incised, Monk's Mound Red, and Cahokia Red Filmed. These wares were associated with the Old Village horizon at Cahokia. In the levels of the Upper or Late period at Kincaid, trade sherds representing three Cahokia Trappist pottery types were found: Tippett Bean Pot, Cahokia Cord Marked, and Cahokia effigy ware. The Kincaid Middle period contained a mixture of Old Village and Trappist trade sherds: Ramey Incised, Powell Plain, Tippett Bean Pot, and Cahokia Cord Marked. From such evidence Cahokia Old Village is correlated with Early Kincaid, and Cahokia Trappist is correlated with Late Kincaid. From such data one cannot, of course, place limits to the correlated horizons. For example, the duration of Old Village horizons may be considerably longer than that for Early Kincaid. What may be suggested, however, is that some portion of the time period represented by Old Village levels and the Early Kincaid levels were contemporaneous.

It is necessary to point out at this time that the

10. Bennett, n.d.   11. Bell, n.d.
12. MacNeish, n.d.a; Orr, K. G., 1944b.

13. Bell, n.d. [Also the Chapter by Bell in Cole and others, 1951.]
14. Bennett, n.d.   15. Orr, K. G., 1944b.
16. MacNeish, n.d.b.

dates assigned to the Kincaid periods, Early, Middle, and Late, are not to be considered as time markers in a rigid sense. Although these dates are based upon true annual tree-ring dates which can be accepted chronologically, the transference of the date from a wood specimen to an archeological level or cultural horizon involves the loss of a certain amount of accuracy. The interpretation of what a tree-ring date may mean with reference to the archeological manifestation involved can become quite complicated, and it is necessary to exercise considerable caution before applying such dates to archeological levels or periods. Although these difficulties in interpretation have been presented by archeologists working in the Southwest,[17] it may be beneficial to discuss a few cautions here. In general, the archeologist working within the Mississippi Valley has not felt the need to consider an interpretation of tree-ring dates, but since such information is becoming available and will be used as evidence for archeological reconstructions, it is advisable that these limitations be considered.

There are no bark dates for the Kincaid site; each specimen has an unknown number of rings missing from the outside of the original ring sequence. These rings have been lost from the outside through weathering, fire, or damage loss of some other kind. The number of rings which are missing can be estimated roughly, and it is suggested that most of the Kincaid specimens would have a bark ring falling from ten to twenty-five years after the outside ring date.[18] For example, specimen Mx⁰4, 1050, has an outside ring date of 1514 with from ten to twenty-five rings estimated to be missing from the outside. This means that the bark date of specimen 1050 is estimated as falling somewhere between 1524 and 1539. There are various lines of evidence which may be used in estimating the bark date: (1) the presence of sap-wood rings on the specimen, (2) the general contour and curvature of the outside rings, (3) the width of the outside rings and a consideration of the general growth curve, (4) the archeological setting from which the specimen was removed. Regardless of how well the evidence may support an estimated bark date, the chance for error is still present, and it must be remembered that the accuracy of these dates is less precise than for the actual outside ring dates.

Assuming that the estimated bark dates can be accepted or that actual bark dates are present, there are several additional cautions to consider. Most archeological wood specimens represent samples taken from a prehistoric structure. If there is a bark date for a single house post representing a structure, can it be assumed that the bark date represents the construction date for that building? Such an assumption allows for a considerable amount of error. The timber in question may have been cut and allowed to dry out or season for some time before it was utilized; a dead tree may have been used which could have a bark date much older than the actual construction date, or the beam or post in question may represent a repair timber placed in the structure at a date much later than the actual construction date. When there are several dated specimens representing the same structure, some of these difficulties in interpretation can be smoothed out, especially if several bark dates fall within the same year. The availability of many dates for a given structure, however, will not always simplify the interpretation. Brew cites an example where 143 dated specimens from a single large room produced dates ranging from 1202 to 1701, with a maximum number of fifty specimens from any single century.[19] A complete and accurate archeological record of the specimen's association and relationships can always help in untangling such difficulties, but interpretation of the significance of the tree-ring dates must still be very carefully considered.

It is important for the archeologist to note whether a specimen is a part of a structure or whether it is merely associated with the structure. Wood specimens taken from refuse, fireplaces, or some such associated feature may date considerably later or earlier than the building containing them. In a case where a burned house has collapsed and been covered over, the field archeologist must be careful not to confuse a specimen from the roof timbers with one from an enclosed fireplace.

Some of these difficulties which apply to the Southwest in regards to the interpretation of tree-ring dates may not be so relevant in the Mississippi Valley. Mound excavations of the cultures representing the Middle Mississippi Phase indicate that most of the wooden structures were destroyed by fire. These ruins were then either buried and covered over or cleared away, and a new structure was put up on the same surface. Moreover, the Kincaid dates indicate that no single structure was used over a long period of time such as often occurs in the Southwest. The number of occupational levels represented by the dated Kincaid sequence suggests that twenty years would be a maximum time period for the length of a single occupation.[20] If we are correct in thinking that most buildings were used for but a few years and that many of them were destroyed by fire, the chance for a re-use or replacement of timbers is greatly reduced. Also, with an urgent need created, the chances are against the use of seasoned timber, for it is doubtful that such a need would have been anticipated far

17. Haury, 1935; Brew, 1946, pp. 89–91.
18. Bell, n.d. The bark ring refers to the last growth ring deposited by the cambium of the growing tree. The outside ring refers to the last ring present on the wood specimen when prepared for analysis.

19. Brew, 1946, p. 89.   20. Bell, n.d.

enough in advance for much seasoning to have taken place. With reference to the possible use of dead trees, the evidence from the Southwest indicates that this was very unlikely in that area. In cases where sufficient data are available, it appears that it was the custom to collect timbers from growing trees for construction rather than from dead ones. This may also be assumed to have been the case in the Mississippi Valley.

Difficulties can sometimes arise from an assumption that the associated artifacts are of the same age as the archeological level in which they are found. In such a case, it is the archeologist's responsibility to recognize that certain objects are foreign intrusions and not to be considered as a part of the horizon involved.

There are undoubtedly other ways in which error may creep into the assignment of tree-ring dates to archeological horizons, but enough has been presented to indicate that one cannot be too dogmatic when applying dendrochronological results to archeological interpretations. This is especially true when the interpretation is based upon a small number of available dates. Errors in interpretation can usually be reduced to a minimum through the accuracy of detailed records kept by the excavator who recovers the wood specimens.[21] Admitting the difficulty in interpretation, however, the results of tree-ring dating still afford the archeologist with the best and most precise method available for establishing a chronology.

With the advent of results achieved by dendrochronological methods which are to be utilized by archeologists, it becomes imperative that these results be accurate. Only too often workers in one field readily accept the results of work done in another field without questioning the validity of such results. This is done, moreover, even though the results frequently remain questionable within the discipline involved. Such has been the case with the archeologist and the dendrochronologist. The archeologist has accepted the dates offered by the tree-ring analyst without reservation; he has not demanded nor expected any proof for the conclusion.

Recognizing the need for accuracy before presenting tree-ring dates to the public, the Southwestern dendrochronologists, through the Tree-Ring Society, have required that all tree-ring dates be checked upon the original material by more than one individual prior to public release. In this way, no single worker could release tree-ring dates without their accuracy being tested and checked by another competent dendrochronologist.

This procedure has been quite satisfactory until recently, but the developments in dendrochronology are such that a more suitable method for checking now appears necessary. This necessity is indicated by the following facts: (1) McGregor and Gladwin have arrived at different sets of dates for certain of the Medicine Valley sites;[22] (2) tree-ring dates which were apparently not checked by other dendrochronologists have been presented to archeologists.[23]

The varying conclusions arrived at by McGregor and Gladwin in dating the Medicine Valley sites are a result of the application of two different methods of tree-ring dating. McGregor utilized the standard Douglass method while Gladwin used a new method which he has developed independently. Gladwin presented his *Methods of Correlation* in 1940.[24] Encountering some difficulties in the application of the Douglass method, he devised a new method whereby certain troublesome factors could be eliminated. He experimented with various procedures which resulted in a method of correlation (crossdating), based upon actual ring width measurements, in which the result of agreements and disagreements in the compared ring patterns could be expressed in terms of a percentage index. By use of this index or percentage of agreement as indicated by correlations on specimens of known date, he should have a device whereby he could judge the accuracy of the correlation when dating a specimen of unknown date.

Although Gladwin is to be complimented upon his attempt to eliminate some of the subjective factors in dendrochronological techniques and to place tree-ring methods upon a more objective footing, his method does not appear to be as reliable as the Douglass method. While Gladwin has eliminated some of the objections which he saw in the Douglass system, he has at the same time introduced more serious objections in his new method. His technique is not only more complex, but spurious correlations can result.

Experiments have been made with Gladwin's method of dating at the Dendrochronology Laboratory of the University of Chicago. The specimens used were from a restricted locality, of known cutting date, and easily crossdated by the Douglass system. It was found that in some cases, according to the Gladwin method, a higher percentage of agreement was present for specimens correlated at a known false cross-match than resulted from a correlation at the correct crossdate. Gladwin's method, then, supported dates which were known to be incorrect much better than it supported the true dates. Obviously, when this is the case, the reliability of such a method for dating wood specimens cannot be accepted. The

21. We have specimens in the dendrochronology laboratory which have no available data except that they came from a specific mound or site. Obviously the meaning of an assigned date to such a specimen has little real significance.

22. McGregor, 1938; Gladwin, 1944.
23. Hill and Metcalf, 1941; Will, 1946; Champe, 1946. .
24. Gladwin, 1940.

Douglass method, when applied to these same true and false cross-matches, definitely did not support the false dating. Using this latter method, comparisons on both the actual wood and with skeleton plots made from the specimens betrayed the false identification.

These data suggest that Gladwin's method, as it has been presented, is not entirely suitable for tree-ring dating. The desirability for more objective methods in dendrochronology is certainly commendable, and Gladwin has made a step in the right direction, but his goal has not been achieved. Some objective criteria by which certainty or the quality of crossdating could be expressed would undoubtedly be a worthwhile adjunct to dendrochronological method. Douglass has expressed the opinion that no mathematical manipulation of tree-ring data can replace a sound judgment based upon experience and familiarity with tree-ring materials.[25] This appears somewhat pessimistic in view of the fact that dendrochronological methods are so new and relatively uninvestigated. If experience in the crossdating of tree-ring specimens can result in the ability of the worker to distinguish between a true date and one which is false, and this is certainly admitted, then it must be possible to devise some method whereby such a distinction can be determined mathematically.

There are several occasions in which tree-ring dates for the Mississippi Valley area have been presented to archeologists. In some cases, tree-ring dates have been presented without evidence to support the conclusion or without the necessary verification of the dates by another competent dendrochronologist.[26] This material, on one occasion, at least, has been offered as a preliminary announcement with a complete report concerning the dendrochronological evidence to be presented at a later date.[27] Without verification of the suggested dates, however, they cannot be considered as anything but tentative until the supporting evidence is presented for judgment.

With the development of dendrochronological methods and the application of these methods in new localities, it is not always convenient to have the conclusions of one individual checked by another. Dendrochronologists have their own work to consider, and they do not always have the time to spare for checking a co-worker's materials. The task of checking, if there is a large number of specimens or if some of them are especially difficult, may be quite time consuming. With tree-ring research expanding over wider areas, the problem of accessibility enters into the picture; dendrochronologists who can check the material are not relatively handy or available.

This presents the difficulty of transporting fragile specimens from one place to another, or special trips must be made by individuals to examine specific materials. In addition, the environment and the type of specimens with which one worker is concerned may be quite different from that encountered by the individual checking the material. This is a factor which necessitates a much greater amount of time than usual for an accurate and critical checking of the results. Furthermore, the archeologist is impatient to utilize the results, and he does not like to wait for what appears to him to be an unnecessary bit of technicality. However, if this important step is eliminated, it becomes imperative that evidence supporting the dates be presented along with their original release.

When tree-ring dates are presented without verification by other dendrochronologists, or when two sets of dates are available for the same series of specimens, the archeologist is faced with a choice between two conclusions. In many cases, the supporting evidence presented for either conclusion is not sufficiently adequate for a valid judgment as to which may be correct. In view of these difficulties, the time has certainly arrived when published tree-ring dates should be supported with all evidence necessary to permit other individuals an opportunity to evaluate the conclusion presented. This would afford a basis for judgment in any case which appears to have a questionable conclusion. Certainly some procedure of this sort would be more satisfactory and beneficial to the development of dendrochronology than that which exists at present. Without strict controls to insure accuracy of tree-ring dating, various factions are likely to develop which would result in a mistrust and ridicule of all dendrochronological methods.

In view of this situation and the need for presenting a sufficient amount of data so that tree-ring results may be properly evaluated, the author has not only had the results of his work[28] carefully rechecked upon the actual wood by other dendrochronologists,[29] but measurements and graphs of the specimens concerned have been presented so that anyone can examine this material and arrive at some conclusion concerning its accuracy.

In the past, crossdating of tree-ring specimens has been demonstrated by skeleton plots, line graphs based upon actual measurements, and photographs.[30] The writer has presented crossdating by the use of histograms or bar-graphs in which measurements for each year are plotted along a base line on a strip of graph paper.[31] Histograms of specimens to be compared can be placed one above the other, or the bases may be opposed with the compared histograms drawn

25. Douglass, 1943, p. 7.
26. Hill and Metcalf, 1941; Will, 1946; Champe, 1946.
27. Champe, 1946.
28. Bell, n.d.
29. John C. McGregor, Virginia Bell.
30. Glock, 1937.
31. Bell, n.d.

above and below a mid-line. This means of comparison appears to offer certain advantages over these other methods.

The skeleton plot is not entirely satisfactory because of its subjective nature. No two dendrochronologists will produce identical plots when "reading" a wood specimen; in fact, two plots made at different times by the same individual may vary somewhat due to the accentuation of certain rings and reducing the significance in the consideration of others. Moreover, skeleton plots are used as a tool to suggest crossdating which must be confirmed by testing this match on the actual wood specimens. Since crossdating in the laboratory is not established by skeleton plots but with additional ring by ring comparisons, these plots can hardly be expected to serve as satisfactory evidence for crossdating in publication. Histograms offer a much better presentation of evidence for crossdating in that they are based upon objective criteria and that a ring by ring comparison is represented. If a skeleton plot is desired, it may be drawn from histogram data.

Line graphs and histograms are based upon identical data; the difference lies in the type of graph used to present the growth measurements. In line graphs each year is represented by a single point upon a line connecting the various year measurements; in histograms each year is represented by a column, the height of which represents the ring width. Histograms offer an advantage in that diagnostic rings, agreements, or disagreements in the ring patterns may be marked by coloring the columns for the years concerned. Also, by having columns to represent the ring width, the division between spring and summer growth may be demonstrated, and rings which appear as variable or unstable can be designated. Through the advantages of including more information about the record or marking features which are important, a more graphic picture of the crossdating can be obtained by the use of histograms than by line graphs, even though both methods do utilize the same basic data.

Photographs of specimens to demonstrate crossdating can be quite satisfactory. Tree-ring records, however, especially on charcoal or rotted wood, are difficult to photograph, and successful pictures require a considerable amount of patience, preparation, and equipment. Furthermore, the expense and space necessary for reproduction is greater than that required by histograms. Certainly the time required for producing suitable histograms to demonstrate crossdating is much less than that necessary for adequate photographs. Either histograms or photographs can present sufficient evidence to successfully demonstrate crossdating; histograms are probably more expedient and less expensive. Obviously, a combination of both methods would represent an ideal procedure. Certainly if tree-ring dates are to be presented for archeological sites, they should be supported by sufficient objective evidence so that other individuals can either confirm or question the results.

Figure 198 illustrates the crossdating by the use of skeleton plots, line graphs, and histograms, of two Mississippi Valley cedar specimens.

The application of dendrochronological techniques to the solution of chronological problems within the Mississippi Valley has produced results; the method has been tested and has proven to be of value in this area. The Kincaid Site, an example of the Middle Mississippi cultural phase, has been dated, and an accurate cedar master chart which extends from 1942 back to 1430 has been prepared. A tentative chart, based upon two specimens only, extends back to the early part of the twelfth century. This cedar chart is known to be useful for an area including the eastern part of Missouri south of St. Louis and the southern part of Illinois. The final limits of this specific tree-ring area have not been determined, but the dating of archeological specimens coming from within the present area, and provided they fall within the range of this master series, is a probable accomplishment as material becomes available. There are some charcoal specimens on hand at present from sites in eastern Missouri[32] which should date with this master chart. Analysis of these specimens is expected to produce additional dates with a minimum of effort.

The present cedar master chart must be lengthened if at all possible. The finding of two specimens which extend back into the early 1100's suggest that other equally old cedars may be found in the same general locality. Field collections should be made to lengthen and support this early portion of the present record. In addition to expanding the length of this chart, research should be undertaken to determine the size of the tree-ring area to which it will apply. An expansion of the tree-ring area will eliminate the need for more local master charts in those areas which may be included in the present one. Such an expansion will certainly reduce the amount of preliminary work necessary for additional archeological dating.

With the knowledge that cedar can be used for successful dating, it would be expedient to extend the development of cedar studies to other localities where the present master chart does not apply. There are excellent archeological specimens of cedar from Tennessee which should be dateable,[33] and much of the preliminary work necessary for this dating has already been done.

Good archeological specimens of oak, ash, and pine

32. Submitted by the Academy of Science of St. Louis.
33. Submitted by W. S. Webb and T. M. N. Lewis.

are available. The dating of these specimens has been handicapped by the lack of a master chart which is long enough to include the period of years which they represent. Our present oak and pine charts are too short for archeological dating. If these master charts cannot be lengthened, then research is necessary to learn more about the possibility of crossdating specimens of these species with a cedar chart. Considerable investigation is necessary to determine the accuracy and reliability of crossdating between different species, but the knowledge that certain species are crossdateable would be of infinite value. Obviously a single master chart for several species would be much easier to prepare than a separate chart for each kind of wood.

Schulman has presented evidence that crossdating with pines in the Mississippi Valley can be improved by a consideration of the spring and summer growth.[34] If this modification in technique can increase the area over which specimens may be crossdated or if it would permit the use of less sensitive specimens, such a consideration would be quite valuable. Certainly this addition to crossdating technique should be tested and applied for areas not studied by Schulman.

Although sufficient material is now available for such research, little work has been done to ascertain from the tree-ring records information concerning past climate in the Mississippi Valley area. Investigations along this line, especially information concerning droughts, may give us ideas as to reasons for the movements of, or the effects of climate upon, prehistoric populations. This approach to the solution of certain archeological problems, which has been so successful in the Southwest, awaits development in this area.

One of the most serious handicaps to the development of tree-ring dating in the Mississippi Valley is the scarcity of modern specimens which exhibit a long ring record. Throughout most areas of the midwest, virgin timber was cleared away years ago, and the occasional survivor is very difficult to locate. Wood specimens having four hundred year's growth represented are very rare, and yet it is this kind of material which is needed to build a master chart by which our archeological remains may be dated. Individuals familiar with any such material should record its occurrence or, preferably, collect samples in order to augment our present meager collections. Certainly, without an accurate and adequate master chart archeological specimens cannot be dated.

The role played by tree-ring analysis within the Mississippi Valley will become more and more important as research work proceeds. The progress made will depend upon the general interest shown in the method and upon the amount of time and the number of individuals engaged in dendrochronological research. In the past, research has been limited to the activities of one or two individuals, working on it continuously for only short periods of time or intermittently in conjunction with other pursuits. There is a need for trained individuals to conduct tree-ring research directed toward the solution of specific problems and toward the dating of archeological horizons in all sections of the Mississippi Valley area. This would greatly speed up the achievements of dendrochronology generally as well as produce a maximum of results with respect to archeology. Because of the scarcity of available materials, the method will probably not be developed to the extent that it will be as useful in this area as in the Southwest. Nevertheless, a brilliant future lies ahead for its development within the Mississippi drainage.

One of the first objectives of future research should be the dating of other sites which appear to be contemporaneous with horizons already dated. This would give us some indication as to how far afield one may go in extending the dates from one site to another on purely archeological evidence. In addition to items mentioned earlier, every effort should be made to extend the dating farther and farther into the past. Once the later horizons are dated, there is no reason to believe that older cultures cannot be dated. As the work progresses to older cultural horizons and is expanded over wide areas, chronological problems will become less and less a matter of primary concern to the archeologist, and he will be able to devote more effort toward a dynamic reconstruction of the prehistoric peoples with which he is working.

34. Schulman, 1942.

CULTURE PERIODS IN EASTERN UNITED STATES ARCHEOLOGY. *By James B. Griffin*

FROM the eastern slopes of the Rocky Mountains to the western shores of the North Atlantic Ocean the American Indians and their ancestors had explored, peopled, and possessed a vast territory. Present estimates of the time at which the initial explorations began would range back well beyond ten thousand years ago. The period of human occupancy has been long. Our present understanding of this occupation has been produced by some eighty years of organized archeological investigations and the invaluable aid of studies in many branches of scientific endeavor. The main outline of the development of Indian culture in this area is now reasonably clear.

We can present this outline as a series of prehistoric periods which will be called the (1) Paleo-Indian, (2) Archaic, (3) Early Woodland, (4) Middle Woodland, and (5) Mississippi and Late Woodland. The areal distribution of many of the cultural units discussed in this is presented in Figures 199–204, and their temporal relationship on Figure 205.

The description of these periods will emphasize a generalized cultural picture of the major features which characterize each of these stages by and large throughout the entire area. There are important areal subdivisions which will receive only summary treatment. Some of these are identifiable, others are but dimly perceived, and still others are probably not recognized due to insufficient data.

The general trend of cultural growth in the eastern United States is a familiar one to all who possess a knowledge of human history. It begins with a simple hunting-gathering period with very few individuals living in small bands with temporary, easily built shelters, regularly on the move following game and taking advantage of the food supply available in localized areas. Evidence of this occupation is scattered and limited to a few objects of material culture which were most resistant to destruction. As time passed and as man became increasingly familiar with the natural resources available to him on this primitive technological level, somewhat larger populations could be supported. The most favorable areas in terms of food production would sustain the largest number of people and evidence of more intensive occupation is revealed in various areas, particularly along streams, near springs, and lakes. While cultural growth and change were progressing at a slow pace it is quite evident that there were continuing additions to both culture and physical type from groups of peoples moving into the western hemisphere from northeast Siberia. In the meantime bands of people had moved into and through Middle America to occupy most of the South American continent. Their cultural descendants with many ancient traits and observances may still be found in relatively inaccessible areas of the eastern tropical forests or in the southern tip of South America. The latest estimate is that man had reached this far south some eight thousand years ago.

While the eastern United States was still in the late Archaic period events of considerable importance were transpiring in the region called Nuclear America, which ranges from southern Peru and Bolivia to the Mexican Plateau. In this area is found not only the earliest evidence of agriculture but its most intensive development and the most complex and elaborate Indian cultures. The origin of agriculture is still obscure as to both place and manner. It is less certain now than ten years ago that it was built entirely from independent domestications. In any event this major addition to man's culture in Nuclear America is now called the Formative Stage and may be said to have begun about 1000 B.C. and lasted for approximately a thousand years.

In the eastern United States due primarily to cultural increment in the area plus certain important additions to the cultural complex such as the extensive utilization of polished stone implements and ornaments, the manufacture of pottery vessels, and the construction of earthen mounds as monuments to the enclosed burials, a new stage begins which marks the early part of the Woodland culture. It is probable but not yet satisfactorily demonstrated that agriculture was introduced during this period and provided the economic base for population increase and the cultural elaboration evident in Early Woodland. It is not, however, until Middle Woodland times that a cultural climax is reached in the Hopewellian Phase. This is primarily a culmination of long resident artistic, ceremonial, and social habits which were stimulated and benefitted by additions from Meso-America.

The Hopewellian culture as a distinctive entity

passes out of existence but there is a continuation of some of its cultural practices in the northern and eastern Late Woodland cultures in the Mississippi period. By and large, however, the Mississippi culture which eventually embraced most of the area east of the Rocky Mountains with its center in the central south is so markedly different from the preceding Hopewell that it is quite clear that the major new cultural impetus which gave this period its dominant social and religious pattern is from Meso-America. The exact method of transmissal is not clear, but approximately a thousand years ago the peoples in the area of the lower Mississippi Valley and eastern Texas began to construct earthen mounds upon which the important building of the community was erected and in a plaza or town square before this mound the social and religious ceremonies of the group were performed. At the time of the first European explorations of the southeast this pattern of life had developed to a level which commanded the respect of the invaders. These population centers with attendant developed structures were not common in the Middle Atlantic, New England, or Great Lakes areas. Here the tribal groups preserved the way of life of Middle Woodland times while sharing some of the cultural changes which are markers for the Mississippi peoples.

PALEO-INDIAN PERIOD

In the western Plains some eight to twelve thousand years ago there were present Indian groups which subsisted largely on the products of the chase with evidence of their association with extinct animal forms such as the elephant and the bison (Fig. 199). The most widely known culture group is called Folsom after a distinctive type of projectile point which was found near the town of Folsom, New Mexico, and is known to be associated in many sites with evidences of considerable geological activity. Our best information on this culture is from the Lindenmeier Site in northeastern Colorado. In the eastern United States area, as reported by most of the individual chapters of this volume, projectile points very closely resembling the distinctive Clovis and Lindenmeier Folsom forms have been found for many years. Unfortunately, most of these important finds have been made by local collectors from surface deposits, many times without any accurate record as to the association of the projectile point with other evidences of human occupation so that our evidence is none too good for a specific complex of other materials associated with these fluted points in the eastern United States. We are becoming increasingly aware, however, that these projectile points do represent an early period in the east in which the Paleo-Indian groups were utilizing this type of fluted projectile point

along with other implement forms not now definitely known to be associated. Some of our best evidence for an actual occupation within a reasonable time of that of the Folsom culture in the west is the identification of these fluted forms at the bottom levels of some of the shell mounds in Kentucky, or in association with early Archaic forms in the shell heaps of the same state. Most recently there has been a report on the Shoop site in eastern Pennsylvania where a considerable number of fluted points have been associated with a distinctive stone complex. It is only a question of time until the associations of the fluted blade in the east will become apparent.

In a number of areas these fluted blades have been found in sites attributable to much later cultural units, and some archeologists have suggested that in the east the fluted blade tradition lingered on until the late horizons, representing perhaps a movement of people from the west into the eastern United States as the high plains became temporarily a difficult region in which to hunt. This might have accounted for the presence of these projectile points in certain mounds. It would not account for the great majority of the fluted points which have no association with any such structures, nor would it explain the very small number as a part of these late cultures.

Another recent archeological discovery has been that of the Guilford Focus in North Carolina which is described in the chapter by Joffre Coe. This is one of the late Paleo-Indian groups and has distinctive connections, as has been indicated, to some of the early peoples in the Southwestern and West Coast areas known as Gypsum Cave and Pinto Basin. Another archeological unit which perhaps belongs in this early period is that of the George Lake culture in northern Lake Huron which is a very crude and limited quartzite industry which has indications of considerable geological antiquity. The early projectile point forms of some of the early shell mounds of the Tennessee River and adjacent areas have resemblances to the projectile forms which have been called Yuma. There seems to be little doubt that in the eastern United States there is a cultural horizon which is reasonably close to what has been called Yuma in the western Plains area.

There can be no question that in this early period the people were organized into small groups, probably of closely associated family units whose activities were limited to rather restricted hunting areas and who utilized the various native floral products for food. It is doubtful if many of the large extinct beasts of the western Plains were equally widespread at this time in the east. We also do not know whether they lasted as long in the eastern United States as they apparently did in the more favorable ecological areas in the western Plains. Thus, there is no reason to expect an intimate association of the earliest Paleo-Indian in the east with the same faunal complex with which they are found in the western area.

THE EARLY ARCHAIC PERIOD

While there is no available skeletal material which we can assign with confidence to the Paleo-Indian in the eastern United States, such is not the case with the Archaic stage which follows. Here at least two longheaded populations have been recognized, one concentrated in the area of the Ohio drainage and in the southeast, and the other seeming to dominate in the region from Minnesota to the Atlantic Ocean. The southern population, which Neumann has called Iswanid, appears in the early Archaic populations of the Indian Knoll Focus of the lower Ohio River down into the Gulf Coast area of Louisiana where it is found in Copell and into Florida as Melbourne man. This population, he has pointed out, has relationships to the Southwest-Plateau group who are first known to us as the Basket-Makers. Within this general Iswanid group in the southeast, physical anthropologists have been able to recognize minor population variants and are able to distinguish the peoples who lived in northern Alabama along the Tennessee River from those who occupied the north flowing tributaries of the Ohio in central and western Kentucky. It may well be in the future with additional skeletal material studied and analyzed that other population variants will be recognized in this area. The same should be true of the populations in the northern section of the east in this early level where inbreeding populations within relatively restricted geographical ranges might tend to perpetuate certain minor characteristics which would serve to identify or characterize family lines. It is to be hoped that such more meaningful groups within the northern early Otamid group will be recognized.

From our knowledge of the general cultural stage of these early Archaic people we may assume that they lived as groups or bands of closely related people who probably reckoned descent through the father and were probably patrilocal. Males were the dominant members of the group because of their importance in hunting and fishing activities. The local bands were usually exogamous. They probably lived in bands of twenty or thirty or perhaps a few more, ranging over a fairly specific hunting territory. These movements would be adjusted to the seasonal variation in the available food supplies through the natural yearly cycle such as we have in the eastern United States. Individuals in this society among the men would be outstanding or important according to their ability as individual hunters or according to their talent as shamans or medicine men. We have little or no indication of any degree of specialization in particular crafts, or of the development of specific roles in the community. The men as hunters would spend a considerable amount of time in obtaining game both by means of the spear-thrower and perhaps some use of the bow and arrow. Some employment would also be made of traps and snares, fish-weirs were probably known and even at this early period fishhooks and gorgets were employed, in certain areas where fish were important. Fish poisoning with local plants may have been used in the southeast. Mussels were extensively utilized on the interior streams and oysters and related bivalves and gastropods on the coastal areas from New England around to the Texas Coast. Women would provide food supplies from seeds, roots, and berries, and perhaps knowledge of the value of various tuberous roots had developed. Some foods were prepared in shallow stone mortars with hand stones for mullers, in some cases with cylindrical pestles and in others with a bell-shaped pestle. There are evidences which suggest large roasting pits and also evidences indicating that stone boiling or "hot rock" cooking was practiced with heated stones being placed in the containers of bark, skin, or basketry, since pottery was unknown in this early period. Shelters were almost certainly of a very transient character with little evidence now remaining of their exact type. In all likelihood they were merely a lean-to structure, in others dome-shaped wigwams, or perhaps even a teepee-like shelter. Some floor areas have been recognized in Lamoka shell heaps, in middens in New York, and clay covered areas suggesting house floors in the shell heaps of Alabama. Clothing of dressed skins was probably utilized if we may judge from the number of awls and needles, scrapers and other implements that are found on sites of this period. There was probably very little production of basketry or fiber clothing, although the distribution of basketry throughout the New World and its identification in the late Archaic in the eastern United States suggests strongly that it was known in the early Archaic.

In the early Archaic there does not seem to have been much, if any, production of polished stone artifacts and instead there are flaked choppers, axes, or hoes, which are the forerunners of the polished or ground forms. Projectile point and other implements were produced by both percussion and pressure chipping. Bone implements were fractured, cut, and ground. In certain areas, such as the Florida Coast where suitable stone material was not common, the extensive employment of shell gouges and celts took the place of cognate stone forms. The burials in this early period are primarily flexed, often in round graves some of which had been previously used as storage pits. There are also secondary and bundle burials, and an occasional cremation. Even at this early period there was not strict uniformity throughout the whole area, or even within a limited zone. Burials were usually made in the habitation areas such as the shell heaps and in some cases later burials would be dug through previous interments. There is no indication of a complex ceremonialism associated with death.

During this early Archaic period these local groups as they lived in particular areas became increasingly familiar with the natural resources that could be utilized with their particular stage of cultural development. Thus, they would become familiar with the best materials for the production of large stone implements and projectiles and other smaller tools where a chipped stone implement was necessary, with the best natural sources for food, such as different types of berries, seeds and roots, the best locations for obtaining game of various kinds, and develop an extensive utilization of the flora for food, medicinal, and magical purposes. Cultural exchange of ideas would be fostered by marriages outside of the local group, bringing in not only new individuals but also new ideas in regard to the surrounding territory. In addition these groups almost certainly would have had certain times during the year to which some ceremonial importance was attached connected with the marked periodicity of different types of food supply. Probably a number of bands would congregate at food-rich locations and thus provide some degree of cultural interchange which would have enabled larger and larger aggregates of people to become familiar with larger territories. There were probably a variety of games known at this time and perhaps boys' and girls' puberty rites. During the early Archaic the dog arrived in the New World, descended from an Old World ancestor, and is found associated with the early Archaic horizons, both in the Southeast and in the Northeast. In a number of places the dog was afforded intentional burial and placed with humans, a practice which had almost ceased by the time of the development of the Woodland pattern of life throughout the eastern United States.

Our best samples of this early Archaic period are at present localized in the northern Alabama area where immense shell heaps were excavated in the middle and late thirties and in the New York area where Ritchie's intensive study of the pre-Iroquoian remains has provided considerable data on early human occupations there. As has been emphasized by a number of the contributors, however, there are sufficient indications from small scattered sites throughout the entire area under consideration that the people of this period occupied many different sites from time to time. But these were not places where the ecological conditions were satisfactory for providing the resources for long continued recurrent occupation of restricted localities, which provided sufficient refuse material to build up deep complex middens. These large shell heaps are the result then of long-continued recurrent occupation by small bands of people and are thus more a reflection of time than they are of occupation by groups of people continuously over a relatively short period of time.

THE LATE ARCHAIC PERIOD

This substage may be characterized by the appearance of various implements which were produced in polished stone (Fig. 200). Among these are the celts which probably preceded the appearance of the full-grooved ax, numerous forms which have been called bannerstones and boatstones, some of which were almost certainly used along with the atlatl as has been evidenced by numerous instances, particularly in the southeast, and the tubular or subconical form called a pipe. There is also more evidence of the use of shell for beads and other ornaments, for the appearance of geometric and incised designs on bone pins and on shell ornaments, for the use of paint on bone implements to provide decoration. We find a considerable development of stone bowls made out of steatite, and of sandstone in the northern Alabama area. Steatite containers were most common in the east along the Appalachians from New England down to Georgia and northern Alabama. These steatite containers provided an artifact which was traded into northern Florida and the lower Mississippi Valley where such raw material was not available. The center for the development of the polished stone complex was in the northern Great Lakes area and in the middle South; it only feebly penetrated into the lower Mississippi Valley and into the far Southeast. At least part of the introduction of this stone polishing or grinding seems to have appeared with the Laurentian culture in the Northeastern area and this culture is also said to be marked by the introduction of a short, stocky, brachycephalic people who practiced extended burial and cremation, along with extensive utilization of red ocher with burials. Cremation was an emphasized form of the burial complex. In the northern area barbed bone harpoons are fairly common. This type of fishing implement did not spread into the middle or far South. Stone plummets were extensively utilized in fishing in the Northeast and this type of artifact found its way through much of the South. Another important development in the late Archaic horizon is the introduction of copper tools in the Lake Superior area. The finds of these are largely concentrated in the adjacent areas of Minnesota, Michigan, and Wisconsin, but were extensively traded probably north of the Great Lakes to the Canadian, New York–New England area. They also were traded into the shell heaps of the middle South.

In the far Southeast an extensive use of marine shells for implements and some ornaments is noticeable during the early Archaic period. In the Northeast and the middle South the marine shells were made into ornaments. This reflects the growing interchange of ideas, probably produced by the somewhat larger populations which have resulted from a fairly complete mastery of the available materials in the particular local environments. Favored raw materials were sometimes carried several hundred miles and then made into finished implements. Plummets throughout much of the eastern United States were made out of stone, but in the general St. Louis area were made out of hematite. This particular type of plummet was traded into the lower Mississippi Valley where it appears in some of the late Archaic sites. Another distinguishing feature of the late Archaic is the production of tubular pipes or of tubular forms which are called pipes. These appear in the middle southern area as a generally short conical form and while they perhaps were not pipes in the late Archaic they almost certainly were in the succeeding Early Woodland period.

The recognition of quite a number of distinctive subdivisions of the late Archaic period, as has been evidenced in the chapters in this volume, almost certainly is a reflection of band or even tribal differences on a relatively uniform time level throughout the entire area. It is certainly far too early to attempt to interpret this accurately in terms of linguistic or even tribal units. Some attempts have been made based on the evidence of the early Iswanid people persisting as a definite physical type to the historic horizon as Siouan speaking peoples of the Piedmont area. Here there is also a direct cultural continuity which has been suggested in the chapter by Joffre Coe. There are also indications that the physical type called Otamid by Neumann has reached the historic horizon in the Northeast as part of the Algonkin–speaking groups. It has also been recognized by a number of students of ethnology that the general cultural pattern of some of the marginal Northeastern Algonkian groups is on at least the same cultural base as that of the late Archaic people in the eastern United States.

Among some of the intriguing practices of the late Archaic people are the production of artifacts made of human skeletal material, such as the shaping of the skull cap into a cup and cutting out portions of the crania for bone gorgets. Antler headdresses formed part of the ceremonial costume of the shamans as they performed magical and religious rites. In the late Laurentian engraved combs of antler and spoons and cups of antler formed part of the utilitarian complex.

One of the results of increased attention paid to burials and burial ceremonies is found in the Glacial Kame culture of lower Ontario and the Great Lakes area where both cremated and flexed burials were accompanied by ceremonial deposits of red ocher, copper beads, and shell materials largely made from large marine conch shells. This burial complex has connections into the late Archaic Titterington Focus of the St. Louis area and also connections are indicated into the somewhat later red ocher complex of central Illinois.

EARLY WOODLAND PERIOD

In the Early Woodland (Fig. 201) in the eastern United States there is no new cultural group which came in as a large body from the outside bringing significantly new cultural features, or producing a sudden violent change in the general way of life of the people of the area. The basic economy throughout most of the eastern United States remains about the same as the late Archaic period. Some of the significant traits which are used as markers for this period, such as the building of mounds over the dead and the accumulation of the dead in these structures, thus increasing their size, the presence of specialized tubular pipes which in this period are likely to have been used for smoking, since tobacco has been found in one of the Kentucky shelters which has been asserted to be associated with Adena artifacts by the Kentucky authorities. There are also changes and specializations in projectile point forms, particularly in the central Ohio area. There is an elaboration of the polished stone forms which perhaps reach their height in Early Woodland. There is a tendency for the full grooved ax to become three-quarter grooved in this period. Finely woven cloth makes its first appearance along with short tooth bone "combs" which may have been used for weaving rather than hair ornaments. They bear a striking morphological relationship to the "combs" used for weaving in the Southwest. Copper becomes primarily an ornamental type of material rather than utilitarian as it was in the late Archaic. Other minerals such as mica were extensively used for ornaments.

The introduction of pottery was probably first made in the north-central and northeastern area where it is a heavy, thick, coarse, granular-tempered ware with plain surfaces, or, more often cord-marked on both the interior and exterior surfaces. In the south-central area the surfaces of the pottery are plain or cord-marked, but much more commonly are fabric impressed. In this latter region is the most frequent occurrence of the Woodland-flowerpot shape sometimes with a pronounced heel at the base, or the vessels are conoidal and round bottomed. This pottery is built up by coiling, subsequently shaped by paddles with different kinds of surfaces thus leaving the impression upon the plastic clay. The vessels were then fired at a low temperature. Along the coastal Piedmont area from New York into the Carolinas the earliest pottery has steatite particles incorporated as tempering, suggesting a gradual shift from stone bowls to ceramic forms. In the far southeast the earliest pottery is tempered with fiber and the shapes are those of the earliest stone containers. The surfaces are predominantly plain in the initial period of pottery construction, or have been treated to resemble the scraped surfaces of the stone vessels which preceded them in the area. This southeastern fiber-tempered ware was probably the result of stimulus diffusion from the north-central area and comes gradually into the Southeast where it is associated with materials of the late Archaic cultural type. Another divergent area is in the lower Mississippi Valley where there is a predominantly plain surfaced pottery and where solid tetrapodal feet were first placed on the flowerpot shaped vessels of the central northern Woodland basic form. The north-central area also seems to be the region in which mounds make their first appearance in eastern United States with outliers found in the lower Mississippi Valley and the far Southeast. They are relatively rare in those areas in Early Woodland as they are east of the Appalachians and in New England. They do not appear in New York in any number until the Middle Woodland. South of the Arkansas and west of the Mississippi in the area which retains predominantly plain surfaced pottery from the period of its first introduction, there are relatively few burial mounds at any period.

The outstanding culture center for this stage is the central Ohio Valley where the Adena culture reached a high development. Ohio archeologists believe that the majority of the burial mounds in the state belonged to the Adena culture and this is certainly true of northern Kentucky. Since burial mounds are not built one on top of the other it is difficult to provide a sequential ordering within Adena. What evidence we have indicates that there was a gradual growth in mound size and the complexity of the inclusive mound features. These culminate in tumuli of great size such as those of the Grave Creek mound of West Virginia, the Wright mound in Kentucky, the Adena mound in Ohio, and the Nowlin mound in southeastern Indiana.

Throughout much of the Southeast the ceramic material of the fiber-tempered period has been attributed to the Archaic which then by inference means that pottery arrived there earlier than it did in the north-central area, because obviously the Archaic is earlier than Early Woodland. On the other hand, the fiber-tempered pottery can also be interpreted, as has been done in this paper, as a marginal borrowing in the Southeast. The additional cultural changes which took place in the north-central area about the time of the appearance of the first ceramic material

did not occur in the far south. This Early Woodland pottery, it is now rather commonly believed, has come into the area from northeast Asia. In northern Asia this ware is associated with the same general type of burials and mound constructions that are found in the eastern United States.

In the Early Woodland stage, particularly in Adena, there is evidence for significant shifts in the socio-economic patterns. There were small house clusters located near streams with an arable flood plain or second terrace, as if the people were now more restricted in their movement, possibly because of the growing importance of farm land. The best village site collection in Kentucky indicates a fairly long occupation because of the variety of projectile points and ceramic types. The continuing importance of the family and the family house structure may be reflected in the predilection for ceremonial interment within the house as practiced in the smaller Adena mounds. On the other hand, the larger Adena mounds with elaborate burials suggest the growing importance of group solidarity expressed in ceremonial terms with recognition of the importance of preserving the relationship in death as in life. These large earthen tombs cannot be regarded as single family burial plots but as primitive mausoleums where the more significant members of various families within a recognized social division must be buried. Presumably smaller village or band units within a relatively small distance would have contributed over the years to the erection of these imposing structures which represent in a sense a group symbol.

Incontrovertible evidence of agriculture in Early Woodland is simply not available. True it is that many of the Kentucky and Ohio rock shelters have produced corn, squash, tobacco, gourd, goosefoot (*Chenopodium*), sunflower, marsh elder, and other local nuts, seeds, and edible plant material. The projectile points and other stone artifacts of Newt Kash Hollow are similar to the Early Woodland Adena culture. The pottery might belong to Early Woodland if not to more specific Adena types. This pottery was "taken from the surface debris or from the miscellaneous material in the storage pits." In other words, we cannot separate the agricultural complex at this site from the ceramic material, or indeed indicate its priority over the flint complex. In other shelters in Kentucky there are Archaic occupations sometimes overlaid with later materials up to and including the Late Mississippi period. It is unfortunate that the excavation of these was made before field techniques had progressed to their present development. The reasonable assumption is then made that agriculture did come into the eastern United States and helped produce Early Woodland, yet it probably did not penetrate into the far Southeast or north until the

Middle Woodland period. It is not believed that this introduction was by a movement of people bringing agriculture and a distinctive culture complex. There is the possibility that agriculture was introduced into the Ozark Plateau area from the Southwest rather than through the Texas area from Mexico. It must be admitted that this argument is partly based on propinquity, partly on the preservation possible in the Ozark shelters as well as the appearance of Basket Maker corn in the Ozark and central eastern area.

This is also the period of additional evidence of a feeling of group solidarity expressed in ceremonial practices. The construction of large earth circles associated with the post mold pattern of a former walled enclosure is likely to represent the ceremonial area in which a considerable number of socially and biologically related families gathered to participate in ceremonies under the direction of individuals who took the responsibility for the performance of such observances.

The Adena people are remarkably similar in physical type and as such they seem to have persisted for a considerable period of time. This suggests that they probably represent a single linguistic division with subunits occupying river drainages and with some marked areal groupings such as in eastern Kentucky, north central Kentucky, the Scioto drainage, and the Miami valleys. Cultural interchange was predominantly within the Adena culture as it was localized in the central Ohio Valley. Another feature of the Early Woodland period is the recognition of a considerable number of regional variants sufficiently homogeneous to indicate occupation by a closely related people who attained some degree of tribal integration. By and large, there can then be seen from this Early Woodland period the gradual development of these local units through time with continuing exchange of ideas and materials representing cultural contact, the growing importance of trade and in some cases, probably representing definite traders moving about through the area picking up specific types of raw materials to bring back for manufacture. This is a development which reaches a high point in the next period. The recognition of and the study and interpretation of these regional sequential developments will afford one of the most stimulating phases of archeological research in the eastern area in the next few years. This has been done notably in the pre-Iroquoian horizons in the New York area within the last few years. The same type of sequential development in the lower Mississippi Valley has been amply demonstrated by the interpretations of the archeologists in that area. The same thing is certainly true in such areas as lower Illinois and in the central Illinois Valley. In North Carolina, as Coe has pointed out in his chapter, there is a clear developmental sequence from the Early Woodland period of the Badin Focus type through into the historic period with not only continuity in the cultural development, but also a continuation apparently of the same physical type throughout this rather long period.

THE MIDDLE WOODLAND PERIOD

The arrival of Middle Woodland (Fig. 202) is recognized by the appearance of cultural materials which are associated with the Hopewell culture of Ohio and in its broader manifestations often referred to as the Hopewellian phase. This cultural development has two major centers in the north. One of these is in the central Ohio Valley in southern Ohio, and the other is in the Illinois Valley and the immediately adjacent Mississippi Valley to the west. There is also a center in the Kansas City area and adjacent Kansas, and northeastern Oklahoma. In the lower Mississippi Valley comparable units are recognized to which the local names Marksville and Troyville have been given, and along the Florida Gulf Coast another Hopewellian manifestation has been called Santa Rosa–Swift Creek. Throughout the entire eastern United States area there can be recognized cultural units which participate in some of the specific items which are attributable to the Hopewell culture. There can be no question, however, as far as the variety and proliferation of cultural elements or of outstanding artifact manufacture is concerned, that the Hopewell center in southern Ohio is preeminent. We recognize that the Hopewell culture has obtained many of its basic ideas from the preceding Adena complex in this same area. There is the same emphasis on burial mounds with the utilization of the same kinds of raw materials for implements and ornaments, and evidence of continuity in quite a number of the cultural traits.

If one views the eastern United States as a whole it is evident that the major cultural progress is still taking place in the north-central portion of the area and that by and large, the western and southern fringes of the area were still marginal to this cultural development. This is the cultural climax of the Middle Woodland tradition and in many ways artistic levels were reached in this period which were not excelled even in the succeeding Mississippi stage. The excellence of these artistic products in stone, bone, copper, shell, mica, and other materials and the close similarity of many of the outstanding products made of such raw materials indicates a high development of craftsmanship with almost certain specialization by individuals who achieved prominence along these particular lines. The large size of many of the Hopewell sites in the Ohio area indicates that there was a considerable increase in population in this period, and also that these major site centers were occupied for a fairly long period of time. The ceramic materials from the famous Turner Site near Cincinnati indicates a long period of occupation at that particular site, for the material represents a spread of time from late Early Woodland well up through the Middle Woodland period. The areal extent of some of these major Hopewell sites, such as Turner, the large number of earthworks and mounds in what is now the heart of Cincinnati, of Portsmouth, of Circleville, Newark, and other large Ohio sites, indicates that these people had a definite plan in mind as to the type of earthworks which were to be constructed and that this major plan was recognized and carried out over a considerable period. The majority of them are certainly not defensive structures, but are part of a ceremonial and sacred precinct.

We know that at least some of the ceremonial earthworks in Ohio cover village site materials and that some of them are associated with post hole patterns, almost certainly marking the presence of former house units. Perhaps the circular form of these earthworks is associated with the village plan present in the Middle Atlantic area at the historic period where the houses were arranged around the inside of a circle. The important announcements to the village were made by the headman from a slightly raised area in the center of the circle. Extensive village site material was discovered during the excavation of the major Turner Site and the Hopewell Site. Excavations at Fort Ancient have produced occupation debris from the interior of the "fort." There was also a village site area outside of the eastern wall.

New studies on the physical type of Ohio Hopewell have indicated that approximately three-fourths of the population belonged to the large northeastern dolichocephalic people which Neumann has called Otamid in this publication, the remainder of the individuals are very closely connected with the Adena physical type. The above mentioned study of the physical type would seem to indicate that there was an intermarriage of Hopewell and Adena people or an actual merging of groups of individuals of the Adena physical type with the dominant Hopewell physical type in Ohio and also in Illinois. If we were to theorize we might suggest that the development of the Adena culture in the central Ohio Valley in southern Ohio and northern Kentucky produced a type of culture which was attractive to the peoples to the north and that there was some actual movement from the New York area and perhaps even from the west and north into southern Ohio where these people gradually took on quite a bit of the developed ceremonialism of the Adena culture and elaborated on this with their own particular art styles and cultural background to produce the Ohio Hopewell. This interchange and contact between these groups plus the widening horizons of the general Middle Woodland period produced the cultural efflorescence which we recognize as Ohio Hopewell.

Even though there are indications of population increase during the Middle Woodland the general social organization would seem to be somewhat similar to that found in Early Woodland. Certainly the ceremonial aspects of the Hopewell culture are a continuation of those of the Adena group. Such house structures as have been found do not indicate any large multiple family structures such as those of the Iroquoian and eastern Atlantic states in the latest prehistoric period. It can certainly be said that the development of the earthwork pattern is along ceremonial lines devoted to the religious concepts and beliefs of the group and that this was probably dominated by male shamans who were promulgating the interpretation of the relationship of man to the universe for the population as a whole. This suggests the development of a specialized priesthood.

It has been said by competent authorities that the hairdress and clothing of the Ohio Hopewell figurines is a style utilized by northern Algonkian groups and also indicates materials and types of clothing found in Kentucky shelters. This is coupled with the conventionalized art style which is bilaterally symmetrical and which continues on in the northeast to the historic horizon, associated particularly with the northern Algonkian groups. This same art style is also found very strongly in the northeast Asia area. Some of the art developments, such as the engraved tablets, the engravings on human bone, were found in the Adena culture, and these would have continued from that source into the Hopewell period. The bear was of considerable importance in their life as indicated in their art. This is suggestive of northeastern groups. Another important feature of the art is the representations of the horned serpent. Representations of Michabo, the Great Hare, an Algonquian culture hero, are known from the Hopewell group in Ross County, Ohio. Antler headdresses were worn in the historic period by Algonkian priests. They are represented by copper antler effigies in place with the burial of individuals who were probably priests. The ceramic material of Ohio Hopewell is certainly primarily 90 per cent, at least, northern, and has some interesting connections with the Point Peninsula pottery of the lower Great Lakes. Projectile points associated with Ohio Hopewell also fit into the northern sequence pattern much better than to any other area, and the same situation is markedly true of the Illinois Valley projectile point types. In the far Southeast along the Gulf Coast and in the lower Mississippi Valley there was a noticeable lag in the development of projectile points and associated stone complexes which reflects the position marginal to the more rapidly changing projectile point styles and forms of the north and south-central areas.

Ohio Hopewell was a very closely knit area culturally, with marked interchange of specific types made out of identical native or imported raw materials and many of these were found in the majority of the major sites. This indicates contemporaneity and that there was a strong cultural connection and feeling of uniformity between these groups. The physical type at the Ohio sites seems to be also homogeneous. If one considers these factors and the differences between the Ohio area as a unit, compared with other regions to the east and west, it is possible to suggest that Ohio Hopewell people spoke a common language and probably constituted a tribal unit. To the west, it is likely on the basis of our present information that there were closely related groups of the Hopewellian culture occupying quite a number of sites from the area of St. Louis north into the upper Illinois Valley and along the adjacent Mississippi Valley to the west. These groups, again, are so closely connected on the basis of their total cultural complex and have such marked distinctions in many of their materials from Ohio Hopewell that here too one might postulate that there was a significant linguistic and tribal grouping. Although the evidence is not too clear we can also point to a recognizable different unit in the Mississippi Valley south of St. Louis down to Cairo where people on a Hopewell level had a close homogeneity, which by and large although closely connected to the Illinois Valley, still was sufficiently different so that a separate "tribal" grouping is indicated. Somewhat the same thing is true of the lower Wabash Valley, but here the association is complicated by the few known sites. Certainly the lower Mississippi Valley in its Marksville-Troyville grouping on the Hopewell level indicates a marked cultural difference from the northern centers and certainly represents a different tribal group and probably linguistic stock as well. This lower valley unit was more closely associated with the Santa Rosa-Swift Creek sites on the Northwest Coast of Florida.

Wide-flung trade or cultural connections of the Hopewellian people, particularly in the Ohio area indicates a considerable knowledge of the entire area east of the Rocky Mountains. There was fairly extensive contact with the far southeast and probably the Florida area, for it was from this general region that most of the large, marine *Busycon* and *Cassis* shells have come. The *Cassis* shell is almost a time marker in the Hopewellian horizon. Its live range is from Cape Hatteras down the east coast of the United States and on into the West Indies. It is not found on the Gulf Coast of Florida. It is reasonable to suppose that the barracuda jaws, the shell of the sea tortoise, spade fish, and live shark's teeth were derived from

the cultural connection into the northern and northwestern Florida area. Santa Rosa–Swift Creek probably received the copper earspools, copper breastplates, the copper so-called pan pipes, the idea of utilization of platform pipes, stone imitation carnivore teeth from the Ohio center. Also in this same general direction of course were the mica mines of Virginia and North Carolina which were so extensively worked by peoples on a primitive level with probably most of the utilization of this mineral being made in the Hopewellian culture. Another time marker for this period was the extensive utilization of obsidian, particularly in Ohio Hopewell, and this is a very distinctive time marker. Obsidian also appears in some ten or twelve Illinois Valley Hopewell sites, although mostly in the form of flakes. It is not known where the source was for this material, whether in the northern Rockies, the southern Rockies in eastern Arizona and New Mexico, or in Middle America. Obsidian has not been found in the southeast, the lower Mississippi Valley, or the Caddoan area. The grizzly bear teeth were also extensively utilized by the Hopewell peoples and even ivory is reported. Additional examples of the connection between Ohio Hopewell and the southeast are the presence of simple stamp, check stamp, and complicated stamp impressions on a small percent of the pottery. There are also such vessel shapes as that called the T-shaped lip and the vertical compound vessels which connect Ohio Hopewell into the Florida area.

These extensive trade relations are sometimes spoken of as though they were conducted on a rather drab economic level, whereas it would appear that the primary purpose for the acquisition of these materials was for their ceremonial utilization by the living people, and then placement with the honored dead in their large and complicated burial tumuli. There would seem to have been a religious motivation for their acquisition, for certainly the majority of the specimens had practically no utilitarian importance or significance. It was not acquisition of materials for exchange in order to build wealth for handing down to one's descendants, but rather the accumulation of such items perhaps for prestige value which would be accorded to those who were dead and to those close relatives who were still living. It has been suggested many times that these trade connections seem to indicate trips of individuals into the far southeast, or into the Plains, or into the northern Mississippi Valley and Lake Superior area, and that they were on regular, definite missions to obtain these raw materials. It may have been because of the common cultural foundation which existed through the Hopewellian period that such individuals were welcomed in foreign tribal groups while on such a mission to obtain these raw materials and it is likely that these travelers would take along with them some of the finished products from the Ohio area associated with the ceremonial complexes which were dominant at the time.

Ohio Hopewell marked a high peak in ceremonial and artistic forms based on a long tradition of cultural development in the area. In achieving this cultural peak they may have reached a level beyond which they found it impossible to go. Certainly the large ceremonial earthworks and associated features in the Ohio area would have taken a considerable amount of the energy of the people and perhaps produced what has been called "cultural fatigue." We can also, I think, see in the art forms that in many cases they represent a very unified style made by relatively few craftsmen. These art forms are recovered primarily from the ceremonial deposits which were placed with the dead. If there was an inclination because of the sacred nature of these materials for these craftsmen to restrict the skills which they had developed to a small, closely integrated group, then it would have been relatively easy with the ceremonial destruction and burial of so many of these fine products, if anything such as a catastrophe or ennui had developed for this art style to go into a marked period of decline.

Another possible explanation for the disappearance of the fine products of this general tradition would be that during the closing phase of its existence there were already pushing in from the south and west into the central Mississippi Valley those cultural influences which later became the Mississippi pattern. At first on a small scale, but with a significantly different village organization and ceremonial associations this new cultural development may have cut in between the northern and southern Hopewell centers so that contact was lost between them. The new society and its values may have been influential in producing a dissatisfaction in the Hopewell orientation and hastened its decline. Perhaps these two explanations given above coincided to some degree. In any event there is a marked cultural decline in the north-central area following the Hopewell period before the first indications of the Middle Mississippi tradition arrived on the scene.

Cultural connections at this time level with Middle America do not seem to have been particularly strong. Certainly it may be acknowledged that agriculture has come in from the south, but its direction as indicated in the Early Woodland discussion is still far from clear. The presence of figurines on this time level, flake knives, the use of obsidian, the development of earspools, are some of these indications which may point to a connection with Middle America.

Another distinctive enclave in Middle Woodland is represented by the Copena culture of northern Alabama and adjacent Tennessee. This is a culture unit of sufficient distinctiveness, along with a specific physical type, which strongly indicates that Copena was a separate tribal and perhaps linguistic group of the Hopewellian complex. Similar significant culture units may be recognized in the far southeast for the developing complicated stamp groups now considered under the general head of the Swift Creek culture. In the northeast we may yet recognize in Point Peninsula one or more cultural, physical, and linguistic groups with a background of some historic depth which continued on without much evidence of marked cultural intrusion well into the Late Woodland cultures of the area.

THE MISSISSIPPI PERIOD

This new cultural expansion may be said to begin with the appearance of the pyramidal earthen mound in the southeast (Fig. 203). This was utilized as a substructure for the important buildings of the community, such as the dwelling of the outstanding political chief, or as the center of operations of the outstanding religious leader. This pyramidal mound and associated plaza complex reflects both a new form of social organization and more extensive utilization of agricultural crops than anything which had gone on before, so that they have become the primary symbol of the Mississippi period and we can say that this general culture development begins with its introduction. Almost certainly this is derived from the Mexican area and presumably through east Texas. We still do not have specific information as to the initial area in which this introduction took place. It does not look as though this was the result of the movement of any large body of individuals into the southwestern part of the eastern United States, but rather a dissemination of some of the outstanding cultural features which were then taken over by the populations in that area. Gradually a new cultural orientation unfolded which was augmented by additional increments from the Meso-American area. In the lower Mississippi Valley this introduction of pyramidal mounds is associated with the Coles Creek culture which was also receiving influences from the Weeden Island culture of the northwest coast of Florida. Soon there was introduced the concept of engraving pottery vessels along with some distinctive new vessel forms, some of which were added to the Mississippi ceramic complex. The initial Mississippi period in this area is marked, by and large, by relatively small sites with a few mounds, none of which on sites occupied for a short period attained any impressive size.

In the area north of the Ohio which has heretofore been the heart area of cultural development from the late Archaic into Hopewell there is a cultural complex marking the beginning of the Late Woodland which indicates a period of rest and quiescence, so to speak, from the preceding Hopewell period. Many basic Woodland characteristics continue with some change but the definitive Hopewellian features fade away. In some local areas these definitely intercede between Hopewell and the appearance of Mississippi, although in others, such as the great Cahokia center, they seem to have existed along with and to have participated to some degree in the development of Early Mississippi. The Cahokia center marks one of the early developments of various complexes which participated in the Early Mississippi period. It had a marked individuality which enables one immediately to recognize specimens of this complex. It seems to have primarily influenced the areas to the north and west of St. Louis. Early Mississippi developments in the southeast, such as those in eastern Tennessee and central Georgia, indicate some relation to the Cahokia center, but this is in generalities rather than specific types. Early Mississippi is not marked archeologically by a strong artistic development or association with elaborate ceremonial performances or rites in any area where it has been recognized. It took some time for the new cultural orientation to achieve sufficient stability for the subsequent florescence which took place in the middle part, or what we might call the Classic Mississippi. This is a development which has a marked parallel to that of the Hopewell culmination in southern Ohio in that some time elapsed during which the new culture type reached its peak. This time, however, the culture center is north and west of the fall line of the Atlantic and Gulf Coast areas, running roughly from north-central Georgia in an east-west belt through northern Alabama, northern Mississippi, western Kentucky, southern Illinois, and into southeast Missouri. There we find the great centers of the Mississippi period, and the products of the Classic Mississippi ceremonial developments in village site alignments, in fortified villages, in tremendous pyramidal mounds, sometimes a score or more on a single site, and in the elaborate art forms which were representative of the height of the southeastern Mississippi culture.

There is abundant evidence of marked population increase represented by considerably larger village or ceremonial center groupings, by the depth of refuse deposits, by the abundant burials, and by the large amount of ceramic and other materials associated with these sites. Sites of this prehistoric division were such a prominent feature of the archeological landscape that for many years the attention of archeologists was concentrated on this group as well as the Hopewell sites. The long period of development which was in back of these groups was hardly realized. These tribal centers were large and impressive, but they were not cities or city states. This level of cultural development was not reached in aboriginal eastern United States.

The Mississippi period was in full bloom at the time of the De Soto entrada into the southeast and at the time of the other early intermittent Spanish and French contacts with this area. We can therefore utilize with considerable confidence the information obtained from these chroniclers and from the late seventeenth and eighteenth century European explorers, colonists, missionaries, and soldiers for a reconstruction of the social structure as it existed in the Mississippi period in the southeast. There can also be recognized definite connections between many of the local Mississippi pattern variants in the southeast and definite tribal and linguistic alignments. As we are able to carry these backward in time from this Mississippi stage into the earlier periods we will be able perhaps eventually to arrive at a reasonable reconstruction of the population and linguistic distributions for some thousands of years into the prehistoric past. That, however, is certainly a matter to be worked out in the future.

One of the significant linguistic groups in the western part of the southeast was the Caddo stock of Louisiana, Arkansas, Oklahoma, and Texas. Here very promising beginnings have been made in the recognition of distinctive areal culture units and it is only a question of time until these will be understood in terms of significant tribal divisions within the Caddo group. By and large, though the late Caddoan area culture is chronologically part of the Mississippi period it is in many respects somewhat marginal and throughout time retains an individuality of its own on the western outskirts of the major Mississippi pattern development.

The dominant linguistic group in the southeast were the Muskoghean-speaking peoples, the Creeks and associated Choctaw, Chickasaw, and related tribes. Their social organization may be utilized as a model in which we can find the reflections of the Mississippi ceremonial developments expressed in the archeological remains.

The social organization of the dominant southeastern tribes is characterized by matrilineal, matrilocal, exogamous totemic clans. The majority of the tribes were further grouped into two major divisions or moieties which were themselves exogamous. These social structures helped to regulate marriage relationships, partnerships in ball games, and functioned at ceremonial observances, such as funerals and seasonal rites. Among the Creek each clan had its special area around the square while each clan of the Cherokee had a designated space in the council house. In some tribes one moiety was concerned primarily with war observances and the other with peace. One moiety would serve to assume the responsibilities of the funeral rites for members of the other moiety. The Chitimacha are said to have had a real caste system, while the Natchez closely approached the solidification of class groupings, which were widespread in the area. Marriage was usually within a specific town or sub-tribal unit and this helped to promote group solidarity at that level. The clan structure within the tribe enables an individual visiting a town not his own to find "blood" relatives and give him a feeling of belonging to these other communities within his own particular tribal group. This certainly acted to unify the tribal group and helped also to spread ideas developing in the various local town communities within the tribe. The family organization was built around the matrilineal lineage.

Political authority had passed from the small local group of the Archaic and Early Woodland to a larger body, the tribe. Tribal power was concentrated in the person of the head chief or in an upper class council. The major political offices were inherited by outstanding individuals through the female line. Tribute was exacted from the weaker groups by dominant village centers and these dominant centers were also obligated to pay tribute to the chief and his associated higher class tribal members. In some groups the tribal chief not only possessed civil and military authority, but also was the highest individual in the priestly class. In these groups the civil authority was strengthened by priestly sanctions, in others there was a division between the civil authorities and the war leaders and the class of priests. In historic times this general configuration seems to have reached its height in the Natchez; or perhaps, on the other hand, the Natchez are a remnant survival of a societal organization which had been more common some few hundred years before the French observed the Natchez. The chief had personal bodyguards and servants. Organized warfare was under the direction of experienced war leaders. Raiding or war parties were formed after council deliberation which decided whether the tribe had received an injury calling for group action. Participation in these war parties was usually voluntary. There was considerable attention to the ceremonial aspect of warfare with group fasting, abstinence from sexual intercourse during this preparation period, group dancing during which propitiation was made to sacred powers for success in the group enterprise. The Creeks took along with them on war parties a chest with sacred paraphernalia to secure religious authority for the success of the war party. The priests of the community were forbidden to shed blood and purification ceremonies were required for those who had been polluted by contact with the dead. Warfare was not for territorial aggrandizement, but was still primarily for blood revenge. Probably some part of the elaborate art forms depict-

ing ceremonially attired individuals in warlike attitudes and regalia represent the performances associated with the pre-war observances and the post-conflict ceremonies.

We, unfortunately, know little about the ceremonies and the ceremonial beliefs of this period in the southeast. A number of accounts are available describing the green corn ceremony (or busk of the Creeks) and its related rites in the eastern United States. This four day ceremony took place at the ripening of the new corn. No one was permitted to eat of the new crop until after the ceremony. Many features of this ceremony, such as the use of the central plaza of the village, the alignment of the principal dwellings (or mounds), the major house (or mound) on the west of the plaza facing east, the keeping of the central plaza cleared of occupational debris, drinking the "black drink" from large Gulf Coast shell containers, the description of the costumes of the dancers, some of whom carried fans, fireplaces with four logs pushed in toward the center from the corners, ceremonial destruction of household material and even temple structures, carrying staffs with feathers attached, all find parallels in the archeological record of the period. It would, however, probably be a mistake to attribute all of the southeastern art forms to the single major ceremony of which we have an at all adequate record. We can, however, be quite sure that the general social organization and religious beliefs and practices of the southeastern Indians were sufficient to account for all of the paraphernalia and expressions which are found in Mississippi stage archeology. Most of the elaborate art forms so often figured in southeastern archeology have come from a relatively few major centers, the big towns of tribal groups, with lesser amounts from outlying villages. This is an indication of the ceremonial importance of these objects to tribal units. Their production and interpretation and display rested in particular clan groups for ceremonial names and observances as well, were the property of specific clans. Such materials while perhaps found most commonly with male burials are also found associated with female and child burials.

Some ten years ago (1940) when eastern archeologists were following a foreshortened chronology and were misled by inaccurate association of a lower valley culture with the De Soto tour most of these ceremonial art forms were thought to be post–De Soto. As a result the total time span was compressed considerably, and this style and art form were thought "to have swept through the late prehistoric southeast very much as the Ghost Dance swept from tribe to tribe across the Plains in the late nineteenth century." Certain archeologists thought they saw in these art forms an expression of a nativistic revival cult which developed in the southeast as a reaction to death, destruction, and social disintegration brought about by De Soto's ruthless campaign and the European diseases introduced by him and other explorers in the sixteenth and early seventeenth centuries. Additional analysis, excavation, reflection and publication have considerably lengthened the time period in which the Mississippi culture existed. It now seems that there was a definite peak period of ceremonial activity which had a fairly long history and that there is then a period of gradual decline in the post–De Soto period, but many of the ceremonial artifacts were produced of native made objects at the Indian sites one hundred to one hundred and sixty years later.

Students of social organization (see p. 38) are now emphasizing study of the changes which take place in the social structure of a group as a result of shifts in subsistence patterns or as a result of strong outside influences which affect group solidarity and values. Thus many of the alterations in the implied social organization of the Mississippi culture from that of the preceding period, coupled with the greater length of time which archeological research attributes to the growth of the Mississippi culture pattern, plus the presence of the Walcolid physical stock in the area long antedating the Mississippi period, rather effectively removes the need for interpreting this cultural development as the result of a major migration of people from outside the southeast. Recognition that a similar subsistence basis can produce similar social structures, as Eggan has suggested, may be the case with the Iroquois, coupled with the increasing archeological evidence of a long local lower Great Lakes Iroquoian development, plus the physical connection of the Iroquois with early northeastern skeletal material rather completely eliminates the earlier arguments of a relatively late movement of the Iroquois into the northeast from either a southern Appalachian or central Mississippi Valley homeland.

The Atlantic seaboard, the Gulf Coast area, and the Plains were certainly "marginal" to this major development in the southeast. Yet their cultural problems still to be understood are of considerable complexity. In each of these areas there is strong local continuity, modified both by diffusion from the central area, and in the case of the eastern Plains, by movements of people during the late Middle Mississippi stage from the Mississippi Valley. The prime example of this is the Iowa, Oto, and Missouri who moved on a late prehistoric level from the northern Mississippi Valley into the Missouri Valley to the west. These people are associated with the Oneota Aspect of the Upper Mississippi. Somewhat earlier is the movement of the Omaha, Ponca, Kansa, and Osage. On somewhat tenuous archeological grounds I would agree with Eggan's hypothesis of a location of these tribes along the Mississippi, presumably south of the Missouri and north of the Arkansas where in the latter area the related Quapaw were still in existence in 1672. During the Mississippi stage the central Ohio Valley was the home of a tribe divided into a number of distinctive subgroups or by a number of closely related tribes with a recognizable culture which was predominantly of the Middle Mississippi phase with interesting and unmistakable Woodland undertones. It now seems reasonably clear on ethnohistorical, linguistic, and archeological grounds that at least part of the Fort Ancient archeological culture was Shawnee. This has received confirmation in an ethnological study of mortuary customs in which it became clear that the Shawnee were primarily a north-central group strongly influenced by burial practices of the south-central area. It is also increasingly likely that the southern members of the Illinois Confederacy were late Middle Mississippi culture bearers while the northern Illinois were more closely allied archeologically to the Siouan Oneota to the north. Other central Algonkian groups such as the Pottawattamie and Miami left remains indicating their marginal position to the Mississippi development and their gradual loss of the older Woodland pattern characteristics. The Menominee and Ojibwa-Chippewa took on few of the Mississippi pattern features due to their northern habitat. The Minnesota Siouan tribes also maintained their old Woodland attributes with but minor modifications.

The eastern Algonquian groups, particularly in southern New England and in the northern Middle Atlantic area, participated in the series of cultural changes which have been identified with the Iroquois. At some sites it is a wise archeologist who can certainly say he is dealing with the remains of an Iroquois or an Algonkian village. In Virginia and the Carolinas both the Algonquian and the Siouan peoples preserved their Woodland heritage and had not made the shift to the Mississippi pattern of behavior and material products.

RADIOCARBON DATES FOR THE EASTERN UNITED STATES.

By James B. Griffin

ONE of the major tasks of the archeologist is to understand the chronology or time sequence of the cultural events with which he deals. This can be done by a number of methods. The development of radiocarbon dating by W. F. Libby and his associates at the Institute for Nuclear Studies at the University of Chicago has provided an excellent technique for the sequential ordering of the prehistory of the Eastern United States.[1] In order that the latest information might be made available to the readers of this volume this appendix has been prepared to present the dates for the Eastern United States which have been issued by the University of Chicago and by two other radiocarbon laboratories.[2,3] In the tabular presentation which follows, abbrevations are used for the dates issued by these three research units. By the time this book is published other counters will be in operation at Yale University and at the University Museum of the University of Pennsylvania.

The initial series of dates issued by W. F. Libby was of considerable importance for the Eastern United States because of the absence in the area of an adequate time scale. Dendrochronology had only been applied to southern Illinois. Other dates depended on European trade goods and the association of archeological material with geological phenomena. In the Plains some correlations had been made with the Southwest. On the whole, however, time scales had been erected without any sound foundation. By the time most of the chapters in this book were written there was a definite trend among archeologists to lengthen the estimates of the durations of the various major archeological periods. The radiocarbon dates should, then, be compared with the relative chronologies presented in the individual chapters in the text and with Figures 197 to 205.

1. Willard F. Libby, *Radiocarbon Dating* (University of Chicago Press, 1952).

2. J. Laurence Kulp, Herbert W. Feely, and Lansing E. Tryon, "Lamont Natural Radiocarbon Measurements, I," *Science*, November 30, 1951, Vol. 114, No. 2970, pages 565–568: a report on the results of the Lamont Geological Observatory (Columbia University), New York.

3. University of Michigan Memorial–Phoenix Project Radiocarbon Laboratory under the direction of Professor H. R. Crane, Department of Physics, University of Michigan. These dates are announced through the courtesy of Dr. Crane and the archeologists concerned.

Sample Number	Description	Age in Years
	PALEO-INDIAN PERIOD	
	FOLSOM SITES	
University of Chicago—Institute for Nuclear Studies Number		
451	Lindenmeier, Colorado; Sample of charcoal from Lindenmeier Folsom Site, submitted by F. H. H. Roberts, Jr. This specimen came from deposits near the top of the occupied zone. It does not date the Folsom fluted occupation in the lower zone of the site.	5020 ± 300
377	Folsom, New Mexico. Sample of charcoal collected by H. J. Cook from a secondary channel which had cut down into the levels at which the original Folsom find was made. This date also is not the age of the original Folsom level.	4283 ± 250
558	Lubbock, Texas. Burned bone from diatomaceous earth zone containing extinct bison as the dominant fossil. This level is associated with the Folsom fluted points. Specimen excavated by Glen Evans and Grayson Meade. Submitted by E. H. Sellards.	9883 ± 350
	"YUMA" SITES	
302	Partially burned bison bone with high organic content, from Sage Creek, Wyoming. This is a Yuma site. The material was submitted by G. L. Jepsen.	6619 ± 350 / 7132 ± 350
454	Charcoal from a site in the Angostura Reservoir area, South Dakota. Sample submitted by F. H. H. Roberts, Jr. Some of the projectiles from this level are like a Yuma form from eastern Wyoming. An example of the Plainview point also came from this level.	7715 ± 740
604	Charcoal from the Long Site, South Dakota. From the Angostura Reservoir in southwestern South Dakota. Collected by Richard P. Wheeler and submitted by Paul L. Cooper.	7073 ± 300
470	Medicine Creek, Nebraska. Charcoal from soil B at Ft–50. Lower occupation zone of feature 18, N155/E45. Collected later and more carefully, otherwise duplicate of 108a. Submitted by C. B. Schultz.	10493 ± 1500

108a Medicine Creek, Nebraska. Charcoal from soil B at Ft–50 in Nebraska. Submitted by C. B. Schultz.   8274 ± 500

65 Medicine Creek, Nebraska. Charcoal from Site Ft–50 in Nebraska. It is a mixture of soil bands A and B which are two feet apart. Submitted by C. B. Schultz.   5256 ± 350

471 Lime Creek, Nebraska, Charcoal from Site Ft–41, Frontier County, Nebraska. Submitted by C. B. Schultz. Points of Scottsbluff type found *in situ* at this site.   9880 ± 670
9167 ± 600
av.
9524 ± 450

EASTERN ARCHAIC PERIOD

116 Annis Mound, Butler County, Kentucky. Indian Knoll Archaic. Local mussel shell from the 6.5 foot level. Submitted by W. S. Webb, University of Kentucky.   5149 ± 300

251 Annis Mound, Butler County, Kentucky. Deer antler from 6.5 foot level. Indian Knoll Archaic. Submitted by W. S. Webb, University of Kentucky.   4900 ± 250

180 Annis Mound, Butler County, Kentucky. Local mussel shell from the 3.0 foot level. Submitted by W. S. Webb, University of Kentucky.   7374 ± 500

254 Indian Knoll, Ohio County, Kentucky. Antler from Indian Knoll, site Oh2, at 1.0 foot level. Submitted by W. S. Webb, University of Kentucky.   5709 ± 350
4894 ± 560
av.
5302 ± 300

191 Frontenac Island, Cayuga County, New York. Lamoka Focus of the Archaic. Charcoal from hearth in deepest refuse levels (trench 4, section 4). Collected in 1939 and now attributed to Lamoka by the collector, W. A. Ritchie, who also submitted the specimen.   4930 ± 260

288 Lamoka Lake Site, Schuyler County, New York. Charcoal from hearth in subsoil under 5 feet of undisturbed refuse. Some rootlets were present in this sample. They were segregated under a low power magnifying glass. This sample was less carefully collected then 367. Collected by A. Frank Barrott. Submitted by W. A. Ritchie.   4395 ± 350
4344 ± 300
av.
4369 ± 200

367 Lamoka Lake Site, Schuyler County, New York. Charcoal from earliest occupation level 5 feet below midden surface. Probably this sample is more suitable than No. 288. Submitted by W. A. Ritchie.   5383 ± 250

417 Boylston Street Fishweir, Boston, Massachusetts. Lower peat underlying the fishweir. Presumably the fishweir should be younger. Submitted by E. S. Barghoorn, Biological Laboratories, Harvard University.   5717 ± 500

418 Boylston Street Fishweir. Fragment of coniferous wood from marine silt overlying the lower peat and the fishweir. Submitted by E. S. Barghoorn.   3851 ± 390

LATE ARCHAIC TO EARLY WOODLAND PERIOD

Lamont Geological Observatory Number

104A Signal Butte, Scotts Bluff County, Nebraska. Signal Butte I horizon (levels II and III not represented). Charcoal collected by W. D. Strong and John Champe, November, 1950 from lowest level (A) in I; below sterile split (B), and upper I occupation zone (C).

Lot I—S. B. IA   one sample,   3420 ± 300
Lot II—S. B. IA   two counts   3450 ± 150
av.   3445 ± 120

104B Signal Butte I horizon, three lots combined, Lot III S. B. 1C (above split B) and Lots IV and V S. B. I in an area where there was no split in strata 1. Charcoal from C insufficient for test, hence the combination.
Lot III—S.B. IC
Lot IV—S.B. I (no split)   2950 ± 200
Lot V—S.B. I (no split)

114 Carbonized plant material collected by James A. Ford from Jaketown Site (20–0–1), 3 miles north of Belzoni, Humphries County, Mississippi. This material is from the prepottery Poverty Point culture.   2400 ± 150
2300 ± 100
av.   2350 ± 80

University of Michigan Memorial–Phoenix Project Radiocarbon Laboratory Number

39 Midden shell from Sapelo Island, McIntosh County, Georgia. This material should date the plain fiber-tempered period on the Georgia Coast. Submitted by Dr. A. J. Waring, Jr.   3800 ± 350
3600 ± ?

EARLY WOODLAND PERIOD

U.C.–I.N.S.

192 Charcoal from cremation (burial 6) on the Oberlander component No. 2 at Brewerton, Oswego County, New York. Collected in 1938 by W. A. Ritchie and submitted by him to the University of Chicago. Dr. Ritchie interprets this as dating the Early Woodland II period in New York.   2817 ± 270
3080 ± 200
av.   2948 ± 170

126 Drake Mound, site No. 11, Fayette County, Kentucky. Fragments of bark preserved by contact with copper reel-shaped breast plate in association with burial No. 7, lying on bottom of pit, the central feature of this site. Submitted by W. S. Webb, University of Kentucky. Mound regarded by Webb as Late Adena.   1168 ± 150

214 Charred wood from sub-floor fireplaces just outside house structure under Cowan Creek Mound, Clinton County, Ohio. Submitted by Raymond S. Baby, Ohio State Museum, who regards the mound as Adena.   1509 ± 250

150 Charcoal from top six inches of Tchefuncte Site ST2, upper level of Midden A, St. Tammany Parish, Louisiana. Submitted by G. I. Quimby, Jr., Chicago Museum of National History. This specimen is regarded as not definitely attributable to the Tchefuncte occupation. — 633 ± 150

151 Shell from top six inches of Tchefuncte Site ST2, surface of Midden A, St. Tammany Parish, Louisiana. Submitted by G. I. Quimby, Jr., Chicago National History Museum. This specimen is also not certainly Tchefuncte in age. — 1233 ± 250

U.M.M.–P.P.R.L.

31 Grass and other plants from Newt Kash Hollow, Menifee County, Kentucky. Collected by W. S. Webb and submitted by V. H. Jones. Much of the cultural material from this cave is Early Woodland. Webb has equated it with Adena and bases part of his argument for Adena agriculture on the material from this site. — 2650 ± 300 / 2600 ± 300

MIDDLE WOODLAND—HOPEWELL PERIOD

U.C.–I.N.S.

136 Charcoal from altar 1, section 3, Mound 25, Hopewell Mound Group, Ross County, Ohio. Collected by W. K. Moorehead, 1891. Specimen no. 56424, Chicago Natural History Museum. Submitted by G. I. Quimby, Jr. — 1951 ± 200

137 Conch shells associated with skeltons 260 and 261, section 1 (?), almost certainly from Mound 25, Hopewell Mound Group, Ross County, Ohio. Collected by W. K. Moorehead, 1891. Specimen nos. 56358, 56606, Chicago Natural History Museum. Submitted by G. I. Quimby, Jr. — 2285 ± 210

139 Bark associated with skeleton 248, section 2, Mound 25, Hopewell Mound Group, Ross County, Ohio. Collected by W. K. Moorehead, 1891. Specimen no. 56094, Chicago Natural History Museum. Submitted by G. I. Quimby, Jr. — 2044 ± 250

152 Wood from wood and bark capping, lower edge of primary mound in Mound 9, Havana Group, Mason County, Illinois. Collected by R. S. MacNeish. Submitted by Thorne Deuel, Illinois State Museum. — 2336 ± 250

Sample number not known

Charcoal from northwest corner of subfloor log tomb in the Wilson Hopewell mound, Wh°6, White County, Illinois. — 710 ± 310 / 736 ± 200 / av. 723 ± 180

143 Charcoal from secondary mantle near junction with primary mantle of east slope of Mound A, Crooks Site, La–3, — 1158 ± 250

La Salle Parish, Louisiana. Submitted by G. I. Quimby, Jr.

154 Vegetal material from base of Mound B from pit in mound, Bynum Site (Mc 1–16), Mississippi. Submitted by John L. Cotter, National Park Service. — 1276 ± 150

U.M.M.–P.P.R.L.

15 Assorted local mussel shells from the Poole Site, Pike County, Illinois. Collected in 1949 by John C. McGregor of the University of Illinois and submitted by him. This is regarded as a middle to late Illinois Hopewell site on cultural grounds. — 2500 ± 300

40 Charcoal from a conical mound in Effigy Mounds National Monument, McGregor, Iowa. The cultural material from this mound is strongly suggestive of Illinois Hopewell. Excavated by Paul Beaubien. Submitted by M. J. Mattes, National Park Service, Omaha, Nebraska. — 900 ± 300

41 Charcoal from a bear effigy mound in Effigy Mounds National Monument. Excavated by Paul Beaubien. Submitted by M. J. Mattes, National Park Service, Omaha, Nebraska. — 930 ± 300

MISSISSIPPI PERIOD
MISSISSIPPI PERIOD

U.C.–I.N.S.

153 Corncobs from the Davis Site, Cherokee County, Texas. These specimens were taken from the occupational debris under the Davis Mound. — 1553 ± 175

U.M.M.–P.P.R.L.

30 Charred miscellaneous plant material from the Gordon Site (the original Coles Creek site), in the Yazoo basin, Mississippi. This site is predominantly Placquemine in time. Submitted by John L. Cotter, National Park Service, 1950. — Barely Pre-Modern

33 Charred miscellaneous plant material from a pit underneath the slope of Mound 34, Cahokia Mound Group, Madison County, Illinois. — 700 ± 300 / 900

THE PALEO-INDIAN PERIOD

The radiocarbon dates for the Folsom culture are in substantial agreement with the dates obtained for geological strata with which the Folsom culture was believed to be associated. The Lindenmeier Site was attributed to a late stage of the Mankato ice age and the maximum of the Mankato in Wisconsin is roughly 11,000 years ago. Dr. Frank H. H. Roberts, Jr., has informed the editor in regard to University of Chicago Institute for Nuclear Studies Number 451 from the Lindenmeier Site, "The charcoal from which it was obtained came from a hearth in the fill of a secondary channel and geologically the level from which it came should be somewhat less than half as old as the culture bearing layer at the site. As a matter-of-fact the date we have probably is approximately that for the slowing down of an extensive period of erosion which followed the human occupation of the area during Folsom times."[4]

A similar explanation is also valid for the initial run of charcoal from the Folsom, New Mexico Site. The only satisfactory date, geologically speaking, for the Folsom culture is that from Lubbock, Texas. In this connection I can do no better than to quote again from the above mentioned letter from Dr. Roberts.

"The points found at Lubbock belong in the Classic Folsom category. Geologically the horizon from which they came should be the same as that at Clovis from which the Classic type points and bison were taken. The Clovis fluted and mammoth bones came from a lower level. In general I think it is a fair assumption that the Lubbock date is approximately correct for the classic horizon at Clovis and probably even for the original Folsom Site itself. On the basis of the geology and its location, I think it possible that the Lindenmeier Site may be somewhat older. However, the general date of 10,000 probably will not be very far out of line even for Lindenmeier."

It is now reasonably well established that the smaller Folsom fluted point is correlated with the giant bison forms and, by and large, follows the earlier, larger Clovis fluted point associated with the mammoth. No radiocarbon dates have been obtained from this level in the west.

The dates obtained for the "Yuma" culture or period are also confirmatory of the archeological and geological evidence with the exception of attempts to place some sites in Nebraska in a pre-Mankato geological position. There is now current a tendency to abandon the term "Yuma" as one which has lost any specific cultural significance. It might be better to retain it as a term similar to Folsom which would acquire cultural meaning from the complexes at the Finley Site, and at Sage Creek, Wyoming and other excavated and reported sites in the same general area and with a similar archeological inventory. The Yuma dates, then, seem to cluster around 6,000 to 8,000 years ago and are substantially later than Folsom. They are consistently earlier than any of the dates attributed to the eastern Archaic.

It has been stated repeatedly in this volume that eastern evidence of Folsom fluted points are not a part of the Archaic cultures except for one or two possible exceptions where they may have been utilized in the early levels of some Archaic sites. The data gathered by John Witthoft on the Shoop Site and that by W. A. Ritchie on a fluted blade site in northern Vermont are rather clear indicators that the

4. Letter to J. B. Griffin, May 28, 1952.

eastern Folsom is significantly earlier than the Archaic. The considerable distribution of fluted blades from New England to Florida should also be considered in this regard.

EASTERN ARCHAIC

As with all of the other periods, the amount of information available is not sufficient to allow anyone to be dogmatic about the actual time position of eastern Archaic units or their relative priority. The remains of this period both in New York and Kentucky are consistent in their range of approximately 4,000 to 5,000 years ago. It should not be assumed that these are the earliest or latest dates attributable to Archaic materials. The date of approximately 7,400 years obtained for the 3-foot level of the Annis Mound (U.C.–I.N.S. No. 180) does not seem in accord with the two other dates for the site. W. S. Webb has suggested that perhaps samples 180 and 251 were inadvertently exchanged in the radiocarbon laboratory so that the age as given for sample 180 might be the age for the lowest level of the Annis Mound. The University of Chicago laboratory will run additional Archaic samples, and a number of additional samples are being processed at the University of Michigan. The increased antiquity of the eastern Archaic will stimulate both interregional research and comparisons throughout the Americas. The considerable body of data available on this period will afford excellent sources for these comparisons.

TRANSITIONAL TO EARLY WOODLAND

The radiocarbon dates for this "period" may be regarded as somewhat contradictory. Archeologists familar with southeastern pre-history regard the Poverty Point horizon of the Lower Mississippi Valley as slightly later than Archaic and earlier than the first ceramic levels. The radiocarbon dates, however, for the Sapelo Island fiber-tempered level are roughly 1,200 to 1,400 years earlier than the early Jaketown occupation. Additional samples from comparable ceramic levels in Georgia and Florida are now awaiting analysis at the University of Michigan.

Some archeologists regard the date for the Oberlander No. 2 Site in New York as somewhat early for the transition between the earliest Woodland to Point Peninsula. Dr. Ritchie is, however, satisfied with this figure and regards this level on cultural grounds as close to the Adena of the Ohio Valley. The most surprising result of radiocarbon dating in the east is the indication that the Adena culture does not primarily preceed Hopewell as most archeologists have indicated, but instead post-dates it by a considerable time period. If the Oberlander date is correct and Ritchie's correlation with Adena is valid, then it is difficult to accept the Ohio Valley dates from mound sites. Some light is shed on this by the date obtained at the University of Michigan on vegetal material from Newt Kash Hollow in Kentucky. The cultural materials from this site have been attributed to the Early Woodland–Adena level by a number of archeologists, and Professor W. S. Webb has based his belief in Adena agriculture on the Adena affiliations of the site. If this date of 2600 is valid and the cultural attribution is also valid how are the mound dates to be evaluated?

The dates now available from the Tchefuncte Site are not satisfactory because the samples were not obtained at a sufficient depth to insure their association with a pure early ceramic group in the Lower Mississippi Valley. Mr. William McIntire of Louisiana State University has collected shell specimens from the lower levels of the Big Oak Island Site in Orleans Parish on the shores of Lake Ponchartrain. This sample which is now at the University of Michigan should give a reliable date. The Tchefuncte ceramic period and the Poverty Point period are probably not separated by more than a few hundred years.

MIDDLE WOODLAND–HOPEWELL PERIOD

One of the major surprises in eastern radiocarbon dating has been the antiquity indicated for the Hopewellian period. In 1940 most of the eastern archeologists estimated Hopewell to be around A.D. 1200 to A.D. 1400. By 1949 some of them were willing to consider a beginning date of A.D. 500 and a longer time span for Hopewell up to around A.D. 800 to A.D. 900. The initial runs on Ohio and Illinois Hopewell at the University of Chicago gave the former a date of roughly 2,100 years ago and the latter some 2,300 years ago. Furthermore, the Ohio runs were obtained from charcoal, marine conch shells and from bark. These were internally consistent and conformed with the wood specimen from Illinois. Since that time the Poole Site has been dated from local Pike County, Illinois mussel shells in the village refuse with an age of 2,500 years ago. The University of Chicago laboratory has run charcoal from the Wilson Mound, Wh°6, in White County, southeastern Illinois with an age of 723 years ago. The other possible exception to this trend is the date obtained from the conical mound in Effigy Mounds National Monument in northeastern Iowa. Through the courtesy of the National Park Service photographs of the materials from this mound were made available. The projectile points and other features are clearly indicative of Hopewell, but the date of 900 years ago is at variance with the previously obtained dates.

Only two runs have been made on southern Hopewellian sites. They are consistent with each other at around 1,200 years ago, but they are, of course, considerably later than the northern Hopewellian dates.

With rare exceptions eastern archeologists believe that northern and southern Hopewellian are of relatively the same age. There is some evidence which suggests a possible priority for the northern area, but certainly the Hopewellian culture at its climax was widely spread throughout the entire eastern United States area. Highly specific artifact types such as the copper earspools, copper conjoined tubes, effigy platform pipes, and the Hopewell zoned stamped pottery should be as good time markers as comparable cultural materials are in other archeological areas.

MISSISSIPPI PERIOD

Very few samples have been dated for this period. The radiocarbon laboratories have been somewhat reluctant to accept carbonaceous material because of the difficulty of distinguishing specimens from the relatively recent past from contemporary carbon. The date for the Davis Site is certainly attributable to the appearance there of eastern type corn and is also to be attributed to the Alto Focus people who built the mound. Mr. A. D. Krieger of the University of Texas is inclined to believe that the Alto Focus is significantly earlier than other Mississippi Pattern sites in the Caddo area. He also is willing to accept a pre-Marksville period for the introduction of the Alto Focus at the Davis Site. This view is not shared by many of his colleagues who believe that the Alto Focus equates with the Coles Creek–Plaquemine cultures of the Lower Mississippi Valley. It is well known that Coles Creek stratigraphically overlies Marksville.

The Gordon Site date is not regarded as satisfactory because of the difficulty of distinguishing it from contemporary specimens. The date of 700 to 900 years ago obtained from Cahokia is, I think, the most valid one at present available on a Mississippi period site. The associated ceramic material indicates that the charred fragments belong to the major development at Cahokia when the culture had reached a peak of ceramic development. These dates are somewhat earlier than the dendrochronology dates for Kincaid. I would not think that the major development at Cahokia was significantly earlier than the dated levels at Kincaid. It should be said that none of the dated specimens from Kincaid were from an Early Mississippi context since Orr's analysis, as reported in the Kincaid volume, was done on pottery which is not Early Mississippi typologically and stratigraphically anywhere in the Southeast. If the Cahokia date is valid then present archeological estimates of a beginning time for the Mississippi cultures of about 1,000 years ago is substantiated.

SUMMARY

Radiocarbon dates have been of great value to an understanding of eastern United States archeology, for they have demonstrated a considerably greater antiquity than the prehistorians had been willing to recognize. The agricultural horizons also have been pushed backward in time so that there is not as great a differential between the Southeast and the Southwest as was formerly thought. The present apparent discrepancies between archeologists' interpretations and the available dates will gradually be resolved by improvements in the technique of radiocarbon measurement, by more carefully controlled selection of specimens, and by time which heals all wounds.

BIBLIOGRAPHY

ABBOTT, C. C.
1876. "The Stone Age of New Jersey." *Annual Report of the Board of Regents of the Smithsonian Institution for 1875*, pp. 246–380, Washington.

ADAMS, ROBERT MCCORMICK
1941. "Archaeological Investigations in Jefferson County, Missouri, 1939–40." *Transactions of the Academy of Science of St. Louis*, Vol. 30, No. 5, pp. 151–221.

ADAMS, ROBERT MCCORMICK, and WINSLOW M. WALKER
1942. "Archaeological Surface Survey of New Madrid County, Missouri." *The Missouri Archaeologist*, Vol. 8, No. 2, pp. 3–23, Columbia.

ANNUAL REPORTS FOR ONTARIO
1886–1928. 36 volumes, irregularly numbered and titled, Toronto.

ANONYMOUS
1941. "Trait Complexes of Cultural Manifestations in East Tennessee." Laboratory of Anthropology, University of Tennessee, Knoxville.

ANTEVS, ERNST
1935. "The Spread of Aboriginal Man to North America." *Geographical Review*, Vol. 25, No. 2, pp. 302–309, New York.
1937. "The Age of the 'Minnesota Man.'" *Carnegie Institution of Washington Year Book*, No. 36, pp. 335–338, Washington.
1938. "Was Minnesota Girl Buried in a Gulley?" *The Journal of Geology*, Vol. 46, No. 3, Pt. 1, pp. 293–295, Chicago.

ARROWPOINTS
1922. Monthly Bulletin, Alabama Anthropological Society (Peter A. Brannon, ed.), Vol. 4, Nos. 1–6, Montgomery.

ASHLEY, MARGARET E.
1932. "A Study of the Ceramic Art of the Etowans." *Etowah Papers* (Warren K. Moorehead, ed.), No. 3, pp. 107–132, New Haven.

ATWOOD, ALBERT W.
1942. "Tidewater Virginia, Where History Lives." *National Geographic Magazine*, Vol. 81, No. 5, pp. 617–656, Washington.

AUGUSTINE, EDGAR E.
1938a. "Recent Discoveries in Somerset County." *The Pennsylvania Archaeologist*, Vol. 8, No. 1, pp. 6–12, Milton.
1938b. "Indian Fortifications in Somerset County." *The Pennsylvania Archaeologist*, Vol. 8, No. 2, pp. 41–45, Milton.
1938c. "Somerset County Excavations: The Powell Sites." *The Pennsylvania Archaeologist*, Vol. 8, No. 3, pp. 60–63, Milton.
1938d. "Important Research on Peck and Martz Rock Shelter Sites in Somerset County." *The Pennsylvania Archaeologist*, Vol. 8, No. 4, pp. 83–88, Milton.

BABBIT, FRANC E.
1884. "Vestiges of Glacial Man in Minnesota." *American Naturalist*, Vol. 18, Nos. 6 and 7, pp. 594–605; pp. 697–708, Philadelphia.

BARREIS, DAVID A.
1939. "Two New Cultures in Delaware County, Oklahoma." *Oklahoma Prehistorian*, Vol. 2, No. 1, pp. 2–5, Tulsa.
1951. *Preceramic Horizons of Northeastern Oklahoma.* Anthropological Paper No. 6, Museum of Anthropology, University of Michigan, Ann Arbor.
n.d. "Summary of the Results of the Archaeological Excavations Conducted in Delaware County by the Department of Anthropology, University of Oklahoma, in conjunction with the Works Project Administration, August, 1938, to March, 1940." Manuscript, University of Oklahoma.

BAILEY, JOHN H.
1940. "A Stratified Rock Shelter in Vermont." *Proceedings of the Vermont Historical Society*, Vol. 8, No. 1, pp. 3–30, Brattleboro.

BARRETT, SAMUEL A.
1933. *Ancient Aztalan.* Bulletin of the Public Museum of the City of Milwaukee, Vol. 13.

BARRETT, SAMUEL A., and ALANSON B. SKINNER
1932. *Certain Mounds and Village Sites of Shawano and Oconto Counties, Wisconsin.* Bulletin of the Public Museum of the City of Milwaukee, Vol. 10, No. 5.

BASTO, ARTHUR
1939. "The Second Summer's Field Work at the Village Site at South Woodstock, Connecticut." *Bulletin of the Archaeological Society of Connecticut*, No. 8, pp. 27–44, New Haven.

BEAUCHAMP, WILLIAM M.
1900. *Aboriginal Occupation of New York.* Bulletin of the New York State Museum, Vol. 7, No. 32, Albany.

BECKWITH, THOMAS
1911. *The Indian or Mound Builder.* Cape Girardeau.

BELL, ROBERT E.
1943. "Tree Ring Chronology." *Chicago Naturalist*, Vol. 6, No. 1, pp. 2–8, Chicago.
1947. "Trade Materials at Spiro Mound as Indicated by Artifacts." *American Antiquity*, Vol. 12, No. 3, pp. 181–184, Menasha.
n.d. "Chronology in the Middle Mississippi Valley." Unpublished Ph.D. thesis, Department of Anthropology, University of Chicago.

BENNETT, JOHN W.
1943. "Recent Developments in the Functional Interpretation of Archaeological Data." *American Antiquity*, Vol. 9, No. 2, pp. 208–219, Menasha.
1944a. "Hopewellian in Minnesota." *American Antiquity*, Vol. 9, No. 3, p. 336, Menasha.
1944b. "Archaeological Horizons in the Southern Illinois Region." *American Antiquity*, Vol. 10, No. 1, pp. 12–22, Menasha.
1945. *Archaeological Explorations in Jo Daviess County, Illinois.* Chicago.
n.d. "A Preliminary Study of the Kincaid Component and Its Affiliations." Unpublished M.A. thesis, Department of Anthropology, University of Chicago.

BENNETT, JOHN W., and MOREAU MAXWELL
1942. "Archaeological Horizons in Southern Illinois." (Abstract) *Transactions of the Illinois State Academy of Science*, Vol. 35, No. 2, p. 50, Springfield.

BERRY, BREWTON, and CARL CHAPMAN
1942. "An Oneota Site in Missouri." *American Antiquity*, Vol. 7, No. 3, pp. 290–305, Menasha.

BERRY, BREWTON, CARL CHAPMAN, and JOHN MACK
1944. "Archaeological Remains of the Osage." *American Antiquity*, Vol. 10, No. 1, pp. 1–11, Menasha.

BERRY, BREWTON, J. E. WRENCH, CARL CHAPMAN, and WILBER SEITZ
1938. "Archaeological Investigations in Boone County, Missouri." *The Missouri Archaeologist*, Vol. 4, No. 3, pp. 2–36, Columbia.

BIRD, JUNIUS
1939. "Artifacts in Canadian River Terraces." *Science*, Vol. 89, No. 2311, pp. 340–341, Lancaster, Garrison.

BLACK, GLENN A.
1934. *Archaeological Survey of Dearborn and Ohio Counties.* Indiana History Bulletin, Vol. 11, No. 7, Indianapolis.
1935. *Excavation of a Blackford County Site.* Indiana History Bulletin, Vol. 12, No. 5, Indianapolis.
1936. *Excavation of the Nowlin Mound.* Indiana History Bulletin, Vol. 13, No. 7, Indianapolis.
1941. "Cultural Complexities of Southwestern Indiana." *Proceedings of the Indiana Academy of Science*, Vol. 50, pp. 33–35, Indianapolis.

BLACK, GLENN A., and PAUL WEER
1936. "A Proposed Terminology for Shape Classification of Artifacts." *American Antiquity*, Vol. 1, No. 4, pp. 280–294, Menasha.

BLAKE, LEONARD W.
1942. "A Hopewell-like Site Near St. Louis." *The Missouri Archaeologist*, Vol. 8, No. 1, pp. 2–7, Columbia.

BLISS, WESLEY
1942. "Archaeological Field Activity of the Pennsylvania Historical Commission in 1941. IV: The Sugar Run Mound Cluster." *The Pennsylvania Archaeologist*, Vol. 12, No. 2, pp. 35–38, Milton.
1950. "Birdshead Cave, A Stratified Site in Wind River Basin, Wyoming." *American Antiquity*, Vol. 15, No. 3, pp. 187–196, Menasha.

BOAS, FRANZ
1892. "Physical Characteristics of the Tribes of the North Pacific Coast." *Report of the Sixty-first Meeting of the British Association for the Advancement of Science, Held at Cardiff in August, 1891*, pp. 424–447.
1905. "The Jessup North Pacific Expedition." *Proceedings of the Thirteenth International Congress of Americanists*, pp. 99–101, New York.

BOAS, FRANZ, and LIVINGSTON FARRAND
1899. "Physical Characteristics of the Tribes of British Columbia." *Report of the Sixty-eighth Meeting of the British Association for the Advancement of Science, held at Bristol in September, 1898*, pp. 628–644.

BOYD, MARK F., HALE G. SMITH, and JOHN W. GRIFFIN
1951. *Here They Once Stood.* University of Florida Press. Gainesville.

BREW, JOHN OTIS
1946. *Archaeology of Alkali Ridge, Southeastern Utah.* Papers of the Peabody Museum of American Archaeology and Ethnology, Harvard University, Vol. 21, Cambridge.

BRIGHAM, WILLIAM B.
1943. "The Arrowsmith Battlefield." *Transactions of the Illinois State Academy of Science*, Vol. 36, No. 2, pp. 71–72, Springfield.

BRINTON, DANIEL G.
1901. *The American Race.* Philadelphia.

BROWER, JACOB V.
1898–1903. *Memoirs of Explorations in the Basin of the Mississippi.* 8 volumes, St. Paul.

BROWN, BARNUM
1932. "The Buffalo Drive." *Natural History*, Vol. 32, No. 1, pp. 75–82, New York.

BROWN, CALVIN S.
1926. *Archeology of Mississippi.* Mississippi Geological Survey, University, Mississippi.

BROWN, CHARLES E.
1907. "The Implement Caches of the Wisconsin Indians." *The Wisconsin Archeologist*, old series, Vol. 6, No. 2, pp. 47–70, Milwaukee.

BROWNLEE, RICHARD
1936. "Mounds on Chariton River in Macon County." *The Missouri Archaeologist*, Vol. 2, No. 2, pp. 7–8, Columbia.

BRYAN, KIRK
1935. "Minnesota Man: A Discussion of the Site." *Science*, Vol. 82, No. 2121, pp. 170–171, Lancaster, Garrison.

BRYAN, KIRK, and PAUL McCLINTOCK
1938. "What Is Implied by 'Disturbance' at the Site of Minnesota Man." *Journal of Geology*, Vol. 46, No. 3, Pt. 1, pp. 279–292, Chicago.

BRYAN, KIRK, and LOUIS L. RAY
1940. *Geologic Antiquity of the Lindenmeier Site in Colorado.* Smithsonian Miscellaneous Collections, Vol. 99, No. 2, Washington.

BRYAN, KIRK, HENRY RETZEK, and FRANKLIN T. McCANN
1938. "Discovery of Sauk Valley Man of Minnesota, with an Account of the Geology." *Bulletin of the Texas Archaeological and Paleontological Society*, Vol. 10, pp. 114–135, Abilene.

BULLEN, ADELAIDE K., and RIPLEY P. BULLEN
1950. "The John's Island Site, Hernando County, Florida." *American Antiquity*, Vol. 16, No. 1, pp. 23–45, Menasha.

BULLEN, RIPLEY P.
1948. "Culture Dynamics in Eastern Massachusetts." *American Antiquity*, Vol. 14, No. 1, pp. 36–48, Menasha.
1949. *Excavations in Northeastern Massachusetts.* Papers of the Robert S. Peabody Foundation for Archaeology, Vol. 1, No. 3, Andover.
1951. "The Terra Ceia Site, Manatee County, Florida." *Florida Anthropological Society Publications*, No. 3, Gainesville.
n.d. "The Famous Crystal River Site." Manuscript on file, Florida Park Service, Gainesville.

BULLEN, RIPLEY P., and EDWARD BROOKS
1947. "The Squam Pond Indian Site, Nantucket, Massachusetts." *Bulletin of the Massachusetts Archaeological Society*, Vol. 8, No. 4, pp. 56–59, Boston.

BURNETT, E. K.
1945. *The Spiro Mound Collection in the Museum.* Contributions from the Museum of the American Indian, Heye Foundation, Vol. 14, New York.

BUSHNELL, DAVID I., JR.
1922. *Villages of the Algonquian, Siouan, and Caddoan Tribes West of the Mississippi.* Bureau of American Ethnology, Bulletin 77, Washington.
1927. *Burials of the Algonquian, Siouan, and Caddoan Tribes West of the Mississippi.* Bureau of American Ethnology, Bulletin 83, Washington.
1935. *The Manahoac Tribes in Virginia, 1608.* Smith-

sonian Miscellaneous Collections, Vol. 94, No. 8, Washington.

1937. *Indian Sites Below the Falls of the Rappahannock, Virginia.* Smithsonian Miscellaneous Collections, Vol. 96, No. 4, Washington.

BUTLER, AMOS W.

1917. "Observations on Some Shell-Mounds of the Eastern Coast of Florida." *Proceedings of the Nineteenth International Congress of Americanists,* pp. 104–107, Washington.

BUTLER, MARY

1939. *Three Archaeological Sites in Somerset County, Pennsylvania.* Bulletin of the Pennsylvania Historical Commission, No. 753, Harrisburg.

1947. "Two Lenape Rock Shelters near Philadelphia." *American Antiquity,* Vol. 12, No. 4, pp. 246–255, Menasha.

BYERS, DOUGLAS S.

1942. "Fluted Points from Wisconsin." *American Antiquity,* Vol. 7, No. 4, p. 400, Menasha.

BYERS, DOUGLAS S., editor

1943. "The First Archaeological Conference on the Woodland Pattern." *American Antiquity,* Vol. 8, No. 4, pp. 392–400, Menasha.

BYERS, DOUGLAS S., and FREDERICK JOHNSON

1940. *Two Sites on Martha's Vineyard.* Papers of the Robert S. Peabody Foundation for Archaeology, Vol. 1, No. 1, Andover.

CADZOW, DONALD A.

1933. "Mr. George Fisher's Discoveries in Western Pennsylvania." *The Pennsylvania Archaeologist,* Vol. 3, No. 3, pp. 3–5, Harrisburg.

1936. *Archaeological Studies of the Susquehannock Indians of Pennsylvania.* Publications of Pennsylvania Historical Commission, Vol. 3, Safe Harbor Report No. 2, Harrisburg.

CALDWELL, JOSEPH R.

n.d. "Cultural Relations of Four Indian Sites of the Georgia Coast." Unpublished Ph.D. thesis, Department of Anthropology, University of Chicago.

CALDWELL, JOSEPH R., and CATHERINE McCANN

1941. *Irene Mound Site, Chatham County, Georgia.* Athens.

n.d. Unpublished manuscript.

CALDWELL, JOSEPH R., CATHERINE McCANN, and FREDERICK HULSE

n.d. Unpublished manuscript.

CALDWELL, JOSEPH R., and ANTONIO J. WARING, JR.

1939. *News Letter.* Southeastern Archaeological Conference, Vol. 1, Nos. 5 and 6, pp. 5–9; pp. 1–12. Mimeographed.

CARPENTER, E. S.

1950. "Five Sites of the Intermediate Period." *American Antiquity,* Vol. 15, No. 4, pp. 298–314, Menasha.

n.d. Unpublished manuscript. University of Pennsylvania.

CHAMBERLAIN, JOSEPH

n.d. "The Boulder Site." Unpublished manuscript, Department of Anthropology, University of Chicago.

CHAMBERLAIN, T. C.

1902. "Review of Kakabikansing." *Journal of Geology,* Vol. 10, No. 6, pp. 794–798, Chicago.

CHAMPE, JOHN L.

1946. *Ash Hollow Cave.* University of Nebraska Studies, New Series, No. 1, Lincoln.

CHAPMAN, CARL

1941. "Horse Bones in an Indian Mound." *The Missouri Archaeologist,* Vol. 7, No. 1, pp. 2–8, Columbia.

1946. "A Preliminary Survey of Missouri Archaeology: Part 1, Historic Indian Tribes." *The Missouri Archaeologist,* Vol. 10, Pt. 1, Bulletin No. 20, pp. 1–55, Columbia.

1947. "A Preliminary Survey of Missouri Archaeology: Part II, Middle Mississippi and Hopewellian Cultures." *The Missouri Archaeologist,* Vol. 10, Pt. 2, Bulletin No. 21, pp. 60–94, Columbia.

1948a. "A Preliminary Survey of Missouri Archaeology: Part III, Woodland Cultures and the Ozark Bluff Dwellers." *The Missouri Archaeologist,* Vol. 10, Pt. 3, Bulletin No. 22, pp. 98–132, Columbia.

1948b. "A Preliminary Survey of Missouri Archaeology: Part IV, Ancient Cultures and Sequence." *The Missouri Archaeologist,* Vol. 10, Pt. 4, Bulletin No. 23, pp. 136–164, Columbia.

n.d. "A Study in the Classification, Distribution and Sequence of the Archaeological Cultures of Missouri." M.A. thesis, University of New Mexico.

CHAPPLE, ELIOT D. and CARLETON S. COON

1942. *Principles of Anthropology.* New York.

CHATELAIN, VERNE E.

1941. *The Defenses of Spanish Florida, 1565 to 1763.* Carnegie Institution of Washington, Publication 511, Washington.

CHEVES, LANGDON, editor

1894. "Journal of the March of Carolinians into the Cherokee Mountains, in the Yemassee Indian War, 1715–1716." In *Year Book of the City of Charleston, S. C., 1894,* Charleston.

CLAFLIN, WILLIAM H., JR.

1931. *The Stalling's Island Mound, Columbia County, Georgia.* Papers of the Peabody Museum of American Archaeology and Ethnology, Harvard University, Vol. 14, No. 1, Cambridge.

CLAUSEN, CARL

1932. "The Wolves' Den Shelter." *The Pennsylvania Archaeologist,* Vol. 3, No. 2, pp. 7–9, 19, Harrisburg.

CLAUSER, CHARLES E.

1948. "The Relationship Between a Coastal Angonkin and a Karankawa Cranial Series." *Proceedings of the Indiana Academy of Science,* Vol. 57, pp. 18–23, Indianapolis.

COLE, FAY-COOPER, and others

1951. *Kincaid, A Prehistoric Illinois Metropolis.* University of Chicago Press, Chicago.

COLE, FAY-COOPER, and THORNE DEUEL

1937. *Rediscovering Illinois: Archaeological Explorations In and Around Fulton County.* Chicago.

COLLIER, DONALD

n.d. Field Notes on Local Groupings in the Northern Plains.

COLLINS, HENRY B., JR.

1927. "Potsherds from Choctaw Village Sites in Mississippi." *Journal of the Washington Academy of Science,* Vol. 17, No. 10, pp. 259-263, Menasha.

1932. "Excavations at a Prehistoric Indian Village Site in Mississippi." *Proceedings of the U. S. National Museum,* Vol. 79, Art. 32, Washington.

1940. "Outline of Eskimo Prehistory." In *Essays in Historical Anthropology of North America,* Smithsonian Miscellaneous Collections, Vol. 100, pp. 533–592, Washington.

1941. "Relationships of an Early Indian Cranial Series from Louisiana." *Journal of the Washington Academy of Science,* Vol. 31, No. 4, pp. 145–155, Menasha.

1943. "Eskimo Archaeology and Its Bearing on the Problem of Man's Antiquity in America." In *Recent Advances in American Archaeology,* Proceedings of the American

Philosophical Society, Vol. 86, No. 2, pp. 220–235, Philadelphia.

CONANT, A. J.
1878. "Archaeology of Missouri." *Transactions of the Academy of Science of St. Louis*, Vol. 3, pp. 353-366.

CONKLIN, A. W.
1875. "Ancient Mounds of Interior Florida." *Field and Stream*, Vol. 6, pp. 329–331, New York.

COOK, S. F.
1946. "A Reconsideration of Shellmounds with Respect to Population and Nutrition." *American Antiquity*, Vol. 12, No. 1, pp. 50–53, Menasha.

COON, CARLTEON, S.
1939. *The Races of Europe*. New York.

COOPER, JOHN M.
1941. *Temporal Sequence and the Marginal Cultures*. The Catholic University of America, Anthropological Series, No. 10, Washington.

COOPER, L. R.
1933. *Red Cedar Variant of the Wisconsin Hopewell Culture*. Bulletin of the Public Museum of the City of Milwaukee, Vol. 16, No. 2.

COTTER, JOHN L.
1937. "The Significance of Folsom and Yuma Artifact Occurrences in the Light of Typology and Distribution." In *Twenty-fifth Anniversary Studies*, Publications of the Philadelphia Anthropological Society, Vol. 1, pp. 27–35.

COUES, ELLIOTT, editor
1893. *The History of the Expedition under the Command of Lewis and Clark*. 4 volumes, New York.

CROSS, DOROTHY
1941. *Archaeology of New Jersey*, Vol. 1, Trenton.

CROSWELL, C.
1878. "Mound Explorations in Southeastern Missouri." *Transactions of the Academy of Science of St. Louis*, Vol. 3, pp. 531–538.

CUNNINGHAM, WILBUR M.
1948. *A Study of the Glacial Kame Culture in Michigan, Ohio, and Indiana*. Occasional Contributions from the Museum of Anthropology of the University of Michigan, No. 12, Ann Arbor.

CUSHING, F. H.
1897. "'Exploration of Ancient Key Dwellers' Remains on the Gulf Coast of Florida." *Proceedings of the American Philosophical Society*, Vol. 35, No. 153, pp. 329–432, Philadelphia.

DEJARNETTE, DAVID L., and STEVE B. WIMBERLY
1941. *The Bessemer Site: Excavation of Three Mounds and Surrounding Village Areas Near Bessemer, Alabama*. Geological Survey of Alabama, Museum Paper 17, University, Alabama.

DELANGLEZ, JEAN
1938. *The Journal of Jean Cavelier*. Institute of Jesuit History, Chicago.
1944a. "The Voyages of Tonti in North America, 1678–1704." *Mid-America*, Vol. 26, No. 4, pp. 255–300, Chicago.
1944b. "The 1674 Account of the Discovery of the Mississippi." *Mid-America*, Vol. 26, No. 4, pp. 301–324, Chicago.
1945a. "Marquette's Autograph Map of the Mississippi River." *Mid-America*, Vol. 27, No. 1, pp. 30–53, Chicago.
1945b. "The Discovery of the Mississippi. Primary Sources." *Mid-America*, Vol. 27, No. 4, pp. 219–231, Chicago.
1946a. "The Discovery of the Mississippi. Secondary Sources." *Mid-America*, Vol. 28, No. 1, pp. 3–22, Chicago.
1946b. "The Journal of Pierre Vitry, S. J." *Mid-America*, Vol. 28, No. 1, pp. 23–59, Chicago.

1946c. "The Jolliet Lost Map of the Mississippi." *Mid-America*, Vol. 28, No. 2, pp. 67–144, Chicago.
1946d. "The 'Recit des voyages et des decouvertes du Pere Jacques Marquette,' Part 1." *Mid-America*, Vol. 28, No. 3, pp. 173–194, Chicago.
1946e. "The 'Recit des voyages et des decouvertes du Pere Jacques Marquette' Part 2." *Mid-America*, Vol. 28, No. 4, pp. 211-258, Chicago.

DELLINGER, S. C., and S. D. DICKINSON
1940. "Possible Antecedents of the Middle Mississippian Ceramic Complex in Northeastern Arkansas." *American Antiquity*, Vol. 6. No. 2, pp. 133–147, Menasha.
1942. "Pottery from the Ozark Bluff Shelters." *American Antiquity*, Vol. 7, No. 3, pp. 276–289, Menasha.

DEUEL, THORNE
1935. "Basic Cultures of the Mississippi Valley." *American Anthropologist*, Vol. 37, No. 3, pp. 429-445, Menasha.
1940. "Archaeological Fieldwork of the Illinois State Museum." *Bulletin of the Illinois State Archeological Society*, Vol. 3, No. 1, pp. 3–7.
1948. "Illinois Records of 1000 A.D." *Journal of the Illinois State Historical Society*, Vol. 41, No. 3, pp. 219–230, Springfield.

DICKINSON, S. D.
1941. "Certain Vessels from the Clements Place: An Historic Caddo Site." *Bulletin of the Texas Archaeological and Paleontological Society*, Vol. 13, pp. 117–132, Abilene.

DICKINSON, S. D., and S. C. DELLINGER
1940. "A Survey of the Historic Earthenware of the Lower Arkansas Valley." *Bulletin of the Texas Archaeological and Paleontological Society*, Vol. 12, pp. 76–97, Abilene.

DICKINSON, S. D., and H. J. LEMLEY
1939. "Evidences of the Marksville and Coles Creek Complexes at the Kirkham Place, Clark County, Arkansas." *Bulletin of the Texas Archaeological and Paleontological Society*, Vol. 11, pp. 139–189, Abilene.

DIXON, ROLAND B.
1923. *The Racial History of Man*. New York.
1928. *The Building of Cultures*. New York.

DOUGLASS, A. E.
1882. "A Find of Ceremonial Axes in a Florida Mound." *The American Antiquarian and Oriental Journal*, Vol. 4, No. 2, pp. 100–109, Chicago.
1885a. "Some Characteristics of the Indian Earth and Shell Mounds of the Atlantic Coast of Florida." *The American Antiquarian and Oriental Journal*, Vol. 7, No. 2, pp. 74–82, Chicago.
1885b. "Earth and Shell Mounds on the Atlantic Coast of Florida." *The American Antiquarian and Oriental Journal*, Vol. 7, No. 3, pp. 140–147, Chicago.
1890. "A Gold Ornament from Florida." *The American Antiquarian and Oriental Journal*, Vol. 12, No. 1, pp. 14–25, Chicago.

DOUGLASS, A. E.
1935. *Dating Pueblo Bonito and Other Ruins of the Southwest*. National Geographic Society, Contributed Technical Papers, Pueblo Bonito Series, No. 1, Washington.
1943. "Notes on the Technique of Tree-Ring Analysis. IV: Practical Instruments." *Tree-Ring Bulletin*, Vol. 10, No. 1, pp. 2–8, Tuscon.

DUNLEVY, MARION L.
n.d. "Guntersville Basin Pottery." In *An Archaeological Survey of Guntersville Basin in Northeastern Alabama*. In manuscript.

DUNNING, E. O.
1872. "Explorations in Tennessee." *Fifth Annual Report*

of the Trustees of the Peabody Museum of American Archaeology and Ethnology, Harvard College, pp. 11–22, Boston.

DU SOLIER, WILFRIDO, ALEX D. KRIEGER, and JAMES B. GRIFFIN
1947. "The Archaeological Zone of Buena Vista, Huaxcama, San Luis Potosí, Mexico." *American Antiquity*, Vol. 13, No. 1, pp. 15–32, Menasha.

DYSON, ROBERT H., JR., and ELIZABETH TOOKER
1949. The Palmer-Taylor Mound, Geneva, Florida. Anthropology Society, Peabody Museum (Hectographed). Cambridge, Massachusetts.

EGGAN, FRED
1937a. "Historical Changes in the Choctaw Kinship System." *American Anthropologist*, Vol. 39, No. 1, pp. 34–52, Menasha.
1937b. "The Cheyenne and Arapaho Kinship System." In *Social Anthropology of North American Tribes* (Fred Eggan, ed.), pp. 35–95, Chicago.
1939. "The Plains Area." Typescript of paper presented at the annual meeting of the American Anthropological Association, Chicago.

EICHENBERGER, J. ALLEN
1944. "Investigations of the Marion-Ralls Archaeological Society in Northeast Missouri." *The Missouri Archaeologist*, No. 19, pp. 3–69, Columbia.

ENGBERG, ROBERT M.
1930. "Archaeological Report," in "Archaeological Work in Westmoreland and Fayette Counties, 1929." *Western Pennsylvania Historical Magazine*, Vol. 13, No. 2, pp. 71–103, Pittsburgh.
1931. "Algonkian Sites of Westmoreland and Fayette Counties, Pennsylvania." *Western Pennsylvania Historical Magazine*, Vol. 14, No. 3, pp. 143–184, Pittsburgh.

EVERS, EDWARD
1880. "Ancient Pottery of Southeastern Missouri." *Contributions to the Archaeology of Missouri*, Archaeological Section of the St. Louis Academy of Science, Part 1, pp. 21–30.

EWERS, JOHN C.
1944. "The Blackfoot War Lodge: Its Construction and Use." *American Anthropologist*, Vol. 46, No. 2, pp. 182–192, Menasha.
1945. "The Case for Blackfoot Pottery." *American Anthropologist*, Vol. 47, No. 2, pp. 289–299, Menasha.

FAIRBANKS, CHARLES H.
1938. "The Kirksville Site." *The Missouri Archaeologist*, Vol. 4, No. 2, pp. 2–4, Columbia.
1942. "The Taxonomic Position of Stalling's Island, Georgia." *American Antiquity*, Vol. 7, No. 3, pp. 223–231, Menasha.
1946a. "The Kolomoki Mound Group, Early County, Georgia." *American Antiquity*, Vol. 11, No. 4, pp. 258–260, Menasha.
1946b. "The Macon Earth Lodge." *American Antiquity*, Vol. 12, No. 2, pp. 94–108, Menasha.

FAIRBANKS, CHARLES H., ARTHUR R. KELLY, GORDON R. WILLEY, and PAT WOFFORD, JR.
1946. "The Leake Mounds, Bartow County, Georgia." *American Antiquity*, Vol. 12, No. 2, pp. 126–127, Menasha.

FAYE, S.
1935. "The Foxes' Fort—1730." *Journal of the Illinois State Historical Society*, Vol. 28, No. 3, pp. 123–163, Springfield.

FENENGA, FRANKLIN
1938. "Pottery Types from Pulaski County." *The Missouri Archaeologist*, Vol. 4, No. 2, pp. 5–7, Columbia.

FENNEMAN, NEVIN M.
1938. *Physiography of the Eastern United States*. New York.

FENTON, WILLIAM N.
1940. "Problems Arising from the Historic Northeastern Position of the Iroquois." In *Essays in Historical Anthropology of North America*, Smithsonian Miscellaneous Collections, Vol. 100, pp. 159–251, Washington.

FERGUSON, ALICE L. L.
1937a. "Burial Area in Moyaone." *Journal of the Washington Academy of Sciences*, Vol. 27, No. 6, pp. 261–267, Menasha.
1937b. *Moyaone and the Piscataway Indians*. Washington.
1940. "An Ossuary near Piscataway Creek." *American Antiquity*, Vol. 6, No. 1, pp. 4–13, Menasha.

FERGUSON, VERA MASIUS
1951. "Chronology at South Indian Field, Florida." *Yale University Publications in Anthropology*, No. 45, New Haven.

FEWKES, JESSE WALTER
1924. "Preliminary Archeological Explorations at Weeden Island, Florida." *Smithsonian Miscellaneous Collections*, Vol. 76, No. 13, Washington.

FINKELSTEIN, J. JOE
1940. "The Norman Site Excavations Near Wagoner, Oklahoma." *Oklahoma Prehistorian*, Vol. 3, No. 3, pp. 2–15, Tulsa.

FISCHEL, HANS E.
1939. "Folsom and Yuma Culture Finds." *American Antiquity*, Vol. 4, No. 3, pp. 232–264, Menasha.

FISCHER-MØLLER, K.
1937. *Skeletal Remains of the Central Eskimos*. Report of the Fifth Thule Expedition, 1921–24, Vol. 3, No. 1, Copenhagen.

FLANNERY, REGINA
1939. *An Analysis of Coastal Algonquian Culture*. The Catholic University of America, Anthropological Series, No. 7, Washington.
1943. "Some Notes on a Few Sites in Beaufort County, South Carolina." *Anthropological Papers*, No. 21, *Bureau of American Ethnology Bulletin* 133, pp. 143–153, Washington.

FLASKERD, GEORGE A.
1945. "Some Folsom and Yuma Type Points from Minnesota." *Minnesota Archeologist*, Vol. 11, No. 2, pp. 32–33, Minneapolis.

FOLMER, H.
1939. "The Mallet Expedition." *Colorado Magazine*, Vol. 16, No. 5.

FORD, JAMES A.
1935. *Ceramic Decoration Sequence at an Old Indian Village Site Near Sicily Island Louisiana*. Anthropological Study No. 1, Department of Conservation, Louisiana Geological Survey, New Orleans.
1936. *Analysis of Indian Village Site Collections from Louisiana and Mississippi*. Anthropological Study No. 2, Department of Conservation, Louisiana Geological Survey, New Orleans.
1937. Review of "Ceramic Relationships of the Pre-Caddo Pottery from the Crenshaw Site" by S. D. Dickinson. *American Antiquity*, Vol. 3, No. 2, pp. 195–196, Menasha.
1944. *Excavations in the Vicinity of Cali, Columbia*. Yale University Publications in Anthropology, No. 31, New Haven.

FORD, JAMES A., and GEORGE I. QUIMBY, JR.
1945. *The Tchefuncte Culture, An Early Occupation of*

the Lower Mississippi Valley. Society for American Archaeology, Memoir No. 2, Menasha.

FORD, JAMES A., and GORDON R. WILLEY
1939. *News Letter.* Southeastern Archaeological Conference, Vol. 1, No. 3, pp. 1–12. Mimeographed.
1940. *Crooks Site: A Marksville Period Burial Mound in La Salle Parish, Louisiana.* Anthropological Study No. 3, Department of Conservation, Louisiana Geological Survey, New Orleans.
1941. "An Interpretation of the Prehistory of the Eastern United States." *American Anthropologist,* Vol. 43, No. 3, pp. 325–363, Menasha.

FORMAN, HENRY CHANDLEE
1938. *Jamestown and St. Mary's—Buried Cities of Romance.* Baltimore.

FORTUNE, REO
1932. *Omaha Secret Societies.* Columbia University Contributions of Anthropology, Vol. 14, New York.

FOWKE, GERARD
1894. *Archeologic Investigations in James and Potomac Valleys.* Bureau of American Ethnology, Bulletin 23, Washington.
1902. *Archaeological History of Ohio.* Columbus.
1910. *Antiquities of Central and Southeastern Missouri.* Bureau of American Ethnology, Bulletin 37, Washington.
1922. *Archeological Investigations.* Bureau of American Ethnology, Bulletin 76, Washington.
1928. "Archeological Investigations—II: Explorations in the Red River Valley in Louisiana." *Forty-fourth Annual Report, Bureau of American Ethnology, 1926–1927,* pp. 405–540, Washington.

FOWKE, GERARD, N. D. McEVERS, JOHN WULFING, and DAVID I. BUSHNELL, JR.
1905. "The Montezuma Mounds." *Missouri Historical Society Collections,* Vol. 2, No. 5, St. Louis.

FROST, NEDWARD M.
1941. "The Sheep Eaters." *Wyoming Wild Life,* Vol. 1, No. 8, pp. 17–19.

FUNKHOUSER, W. D., and W. S. WEBB
1928. *Ancient Life in Kentucky.* Kentucky Geological Survey, Vol. 6, No. 4, Frankfort.
1937. *The Chilton Site in Henry County, Kentucky.* University of Kentucky Reports in Archaeology and Anthropology, Vol. 3, No. 5, Lexington.

GEREND, ALPHONSE
1904. "Potsherds from Lake Michigan Shore Sites in Wisconsin." *The Wisconsin Archeologist,* old series, Vol. 4, No. 1, pp. 3–19, Milwaukee.

GIDDINGS, J. L., JR.
1941. *Dendrochronology in Northern Alaska.* University of Arizona Bulletin, Vol. 12, No. 4, Tuscon.
1942. "Dated Sites on the Kobuk River, Alaska." *Tree-Ring Bulletin,* Vol. 9, No. 1, pp. 2–8, Tuscon.

GIDLEY, J. W.
1926. "Fossil Man in Florida." (Abstract) *Bulletin of the Geological Society of America,* Vol. 37, p. 240, New York.

GILBERT, WILLIAM H., JR.
1937. "Eastern Cherokee Social Organization." In *Social Anthropology of North American Tribes* (Fred Eggan, ed.), pp. 285–338, Chicago.
1943. "The Eastern Cherokees." *Anthropological Papers,* No. 23, *Bureau of American Ethnology,* Bulletin 133, pp. 169–413, Washington.

GILMORE, MELVIN R.
1931. "Vegetal Remains of the Ozark Bluff-Dweller Culture." *Papers of the Michigan Academy of Science, Arts, and Letters,* Vol. 14, pp. 83–102, Ann Arbor.
1932. *The Ethnobotanical Laboratory at the University of Michigan.* Occasional Contributions from the Museum of Anthropology of the University of Michigan, No. 1, Ann Arbor.

GINDEL, J.
1944. "Aleppo Pine as a Medium for Tree-Ring Analysis." *Tree-Ring Bulletin,* Vol. 11, No. 1, pp. 6–8, Tucson.

GLADWIN, HAROLD S.
1937. *Excavations at Snaketown. II. Comparisons and Theories.* Medallion Papers, No. 26, Globe.
1940. *Tree-Ring Analysis.* Methods of Correlation. Medallion Papers, No. 28, Globe.
1944. *Tree-Ring Analysis. Problems of Dating, I. The Medicine Valley Sites.* Medallion Papers, No. 32, Globe.
1947. *Men Out of Asia.* New York and London.

GLOCK, WALDO S.
1937. *Principles and Methods of Tree-Ring Analysis.* Carnegie Institution of Washington, Publication No. 486, Washington.

GODCHARLES, FREDERIC A.
1934. "Rich Variety of Andaste Indian Material Yielded by Excavating Long House Sites in Clinton County, Pennsylvania." *Pennsylvania Archaeologist,* Vol. 4, No. 3, pp. 13–15, Milton.

GOGGIN, JOHN M.
1939. "A Ceramic Sequence in South Florida." *New Mexico Anthropologist,* Vol. 3, pp. 36–40, Albuquerque.
1940. "The Distribution of Pottery Wares in the Glades Archaeological Area of South Florida." *New Mexico Anthropologist,* Vol. 4, pp. 22–33, Albuquerque.
1944a. "Archaeological Investigations on the Upper Florida Keys." *Tequesta,* Vol. 4, No. 4, pp. 13–35, Coral Gables.
1944b. "A Tentative Formulation of Pottery Types for the Glades Area, Florida." Mimeographed.
1947. "A Preliminary Definition of Archaeological Areas and Periods in Florida." *American Antiquity,* Vol. 13, No. 2, pp. 114-127, Menasha.
1948a. "Some Pottery Types from Central Florida." *Bulletin No. 1,* Gainesville Anthropological Association. Mimeographed.
1948b. "A Revised Temporal Chart of Florida Archaeology." *The Florida Anthropologist,* Vol. 1, Nos. 3–4, pp. 57–60, Gainesville.
1949a. "Cultural Traditions in Florida Prehistory." *The Florida Indian and His Neighbors,* pp. 13–44, Winter Park.
1949b. "Cultural Occupation at Goodland Point, Florida." *The Florida Anthropologist,* Vol. 2, Nos. 3–4, pp. 65–91, Gainesville.
1950a. "Stratigraphic Tests in the Everglades National Park." *American Antiquity,* Vol. 15, No. 3, pp. 228–246, Menasha.
1950b. "The Snapper Creek Site." *The Florida Anthropologist,* Vol. 3, Nos. 3–4, pp. 50–64, Gainesville.
1950c. "An Early Lithic Complex from Central Florida." *American Antiquity,* Vol. 16, No. 1, pp. 46–49, Menasha.
n.d. *The Archaeology of the Glades Area, Southern Florida.* Manuscript, to be published by Yale University.

GOGGIN, JOHN M., and FRANK H. SOMMER III
1949. *Excavations on Upper Matecumbe Key, Florida.* Yale University Publications in Anthropology, No. 41, New Haven.

GOODE, JOHN PAUL
1937. *Goode's School Atlas.* New York.

GOSLIN, ROBERT
1944. "A Bone Atlatl Hook from Ohio." *American Antiquity,* Vol. 10, No. 2, pp. 204–205, Menasha.

GRAHAM, WILLIAM J.
1935. *The Indians of Port Tobacco River, Maryland, and Their Burial Places*. Washington.

GREENMAN, EMERSON F.
1927. "Michigan Mounds, with Special Reference to Two in Missaukee County." *Papers of the Michigan Academy of Science, Arts, and Letters*, Vol. 7, pp. 1–9, Ann Arbor.
1931. "Department of Archaeology." *Museum Echoes*, Vol. 4, No. 8, p. 55, Columbus.
1932. "Excavation of the Coon Mound and an Analysis of the Adena Culture." *Ohio Archeological and Historical Quarterly*, Vol. 41, No. 3, pp. 369–410, Columbus.
1935a. "Excavation of the Reeve Village Site, Lake County, Ohio." *The Ohio State Archaeological and Historical Quarterly*, Vol. 44, No. 1, pp. 2–64, Columbus.
1935b. "Seven Prehistoric Sites in Northern Ohio." *The Ohio State Archaeological and Historical Quarterly*, Vol. 44, No. 2, pp. 220–237, Columbus.
1937a. *The Younge Site; An Archaeological Record from Michigan*. Occasional Contributions from the Museum of Anthropology of the University of Michigan, No. 6, Ann Arbor.
1937b. "Two Prehistoric Villages near Cleveland, Ohio." *The Ohio State Archaeological and Historical Quarterly*, Vol. 46, No. 4, pp. 305–366, Columbus.
1938. "Hopewellian Traits in Florida." *American Antiquity*, Vol. 3, No. 4, pp. 327–332, Menasha.
1939a. "Cultural Relationships of Archaeological Sites in the Upper Great Lakes Region." *Papers of the Michigan Academy of Science, Arts, and Letters*, Vol. 24, Pt. 4, pp. 1–10, Ann Arbor.
1939b. *The Wolf and Furton Sites, Macomb County, Michigan*. Occasional Contributions from the Museum of Anthropology of the University of Michigan, No. 8, Ann Arbor.
1943. "An Early Industry on a Raised Beach near Killarney, Ontario." *American Antiquity*, Vol. 8, No. 3, pp. 260–265, Menasha.
1945. "The Hopewellian in the Detroit-Windsor Area." *Papers of the Michigan Academy of Science, Arts, and Letters*, Vol. 30, pp. 457–464, Ann Arbor.

GREENMAN, EMERSON F., and GEORGE M. STANLEY
1940. "A Geologically Dated Camp Site, Georgian Bay, Ontario." *American Antiquity*, Vol. 5, No. 3, pp. 194–199, Menasha.
1941. "Two Post-Nipissing Sites Near Killarney, Ontario." *American Antiquity*, Vol. 6, No. 4, pp. 305–313, Menasha.
1943. "The Archaeology and Geology of Two Early Sites Near Killarney, Ontario." *Papers of the Michigan Academy of Science, Arts, and Letters*, Vol. 28, pp. 505–530, Ann Arbor.

GRIFFIN, JAMES B.
1937a. "The Archaeological Remains of the Chiwere Sioux." *American Antiquity*, Vol. 2, No. 3, pp. 180–181, Menasha.
1937b. "Culture Identity of the Ozark 'Top Layer'." *American Antiquity*, Vol. 2, No. 4, pp. 296–297, Menasha.
1938. "The Ceramic Remains from Norris Basin, Tennessee." In *An Archaeological Survey of the Norris Basin in Eastern Tennessee* by William S. Webb, Bureau of American Ethnology, Bulletin 118, pp. 253–358, Washington.
1939. "Report on the Ceramics of Wheeler Basin." In *An Archeological Survey of Wheeler Basin on the Tennessee River in Northern Alabama* by William S. Webb,

Bureau of American Ethnology, Bulletin 122, pp. 127–165, Washington.
1941a. "Additional Hopewell Material from Illinois." *Indiana Historical Society, Prehistory Research Series* Vol. 2, No. 3, pp. 165–223, Indianapolis.
1941b. "The Central Mississippi Valley Archaeological Survey." *News Letter*, Southeastern Archaeological Conference, Vol. 2, No. 4, pp. 17–19. Mimeographed.
1941c. "Report on Pottery from the St. Louis Area." *The Missouri Archaeologist*, Vol. 7, No. 2, pp. 1–17, Columbia.
1942. "Adena Pottery." *American Antiquity*, Vol. 7, No. 4, pp. 344–358, Menasha.
1943a. *The Fort Ancient Aspect, Its Cultural and Chronological Position in Mississippi Valley Archaeology*. Ann Arbor.
1943b. "An Analysis and Interpretation of the Ceramic Remains from Two Sites Near Beaufort, South Carolina." *Anthropological Papers*, No. 22, *Bureau of American Ethnology*, Bulletin 133, pp. 155–168, Washington.
1944a. "The De Luna Expedition and the 'Buzzard Cult' in the Southeast." *Journal of the Washington Academy of Science*, Vol. 34, No. 9, pp. 299–303, Menasha.
1944b. "The Iroquois in American Prehistory." *Papers of the Michigan Academy of Science, Arts, and Letters*, Vol. 29, pp. 357–374, Ann Arbor.
1945a. "The Significance of the Fiber-tempered Pottery of the St. Johns Area in Florida." *Journal of the Washington Academy of Science*, Vol. 35, No. 7, pp. 218–223, Menasha.
1945b. "Ceramic Collections from Two South Carolina Sites." *Papers of the Michigan Academy of Science, Arts, and Letters*, Vol. 30, pp. 465–478, Ann Arbor.
1945c. "An Interpretation of Siouan Archaeology in the Piedmont of North Carolina and Virginia." *American Antiquity*, Vol. 10, No. 4, pp. 321–330, Menasha.
1945d. "The Ceramic Affiliations of the Ohio Valley Adena Culture." In *The Adena People* by William S. Webb and Charles E. Snow, University of Kentucky Reports in Anthropology and Archaeology, Vol. 6, pp. 220–246, Lexington.
1945e. "An Unusual Oneota Vessel from Minnesota." *American Antiquity*, Vol. 11, No. 2, pp. 120–121, Menasha.
1946. Cultural Change and Continuity in Eastern United States Archaeology." In *Man in Northeastern North America* (Frederick Johnson, ed.), Papers of the Robert S. Peabody Foundation for Archeology, Vol. 3, pp. 37–95, Andover.
1949. "The Cahokia Ceramic Complex." *Proceedings of the Fifth Plains Conference for Archeology*, Notebook No. 1, pp. 44–57, Laboratory of Anthropology, University of Nebraska, Lincoln.
1950. Review of *The George C. Davis Site, Cherokee County, Texas* by H. Perry Newell and Alex D. Krieger. *American Anthropologist*, Vol. 52, No. 3, pp. 413–415, Menasha.

GRIFFIN, JAMES B., and RICHARD G. MORGAN, editors
1941. "Contributions to the Archaeology of the Illinois River Valley." *Transactions of the American Philosophical Society*, Vol. 32, Pt. 1, Philadelphia.

GRIFFIN, JOHN W.
1948. "Toward Chronology in Coastal Volusia County." *The Florida Anthropologist*, Vol. 1, Nos. 3–4, pp. 49–56, Gainesville.
1949. "Notes on the Archaeology of Useppa Island." *The Florida Anthropologist*, Vol. 2, Nos. 3–4, pp. 92–93, Gainesville.
1950. "Test Excavations at the Lake Jackson Site."

American Antiquity, Vol. 16, No. 2, pp. 99–112, Menasha.
n.d. "The Upper Mississippian Occupation at the Fisher Site." Unpublished M.A. thesis, Department of Anthropology, University of Chicago.

GRIFFIN, JOHN W., and RIPLEY P. BULLEN
1950. "The Safety Harbor Site, Pinellas County, Florida." *Florida Anthropological Society Publications*, No. 2, Gainesville.

GRIFFIN, JOHN W., and HALE G. SMITH
1948. *The Goodnow Mound, Highlands County, Florida.* Contributions to the Archaeology of Florida, No. 1, Florida Park Service, Tallahassee.
1949. "Nocoroco: A Timucua Village of 1605 Now in Tomoka State Park." *Florida Historical Quarterly*, Vol. 27, No. 4, pp. 340–361, St. Augustine.

GRIFFIN, JOHN W., and DONALD E. WRAY
1946. "Bison in Illinois Archaeology." *Transactions of the Illinois State Academy of Science*, Vol. 38, pp. 21–26, Springfield.

GRIMM, R. E.
1947. "Excavation of a Rock Shelter near Prairie du Rocker, Illinois." *Amateur Archeology Club*, Bulletin 1, pp. 16–23, St. Louis.

GRINNELL, GEORGE B.
1918. "Early Cheyenne Villages." *American Anthropologist*, Vol. 20, No. 4, pp. 359–380, Lancaster.
1923. *The Cheyenne Indians.* 2 volumes, New Haven.

GROGAN, ROBERT M.
1948. "Beads of Meteoric Iron from an Indian Mound near Havana, Illinois." *American Antiquity*, Vol. 13, No. 4, pp. 302–305, Menasha.

GUERNSEY, ELAM Y.
1939. "Relationships among Various Clark County Sites." *Proceedings of the Indiana Academy of Science*, Vol. 48, pp. 27–32, Indianapolis.

GUTHE, CARL E.
1930. "The Committee on State Archaeological Surveys of the Division of Anthropology and Psychology, National Research Council." *Proceedings of the Twenty-third International Congress of Americanists*, pp. 52–59, New York.
1939. "The Basic Needs of American Archeology." *Science*, Vol. 90, No. 2345, pp. 528–530, Lancaster, Garrison.

HAAG, WILLIAM G.
1939a. *News Letter.* Southeastern Archaeological Conference, Vol. 1, No. 1. Mimeographed.
1939b. *News Letter.* Southeastern Archaeological Conference, Vol. 1, No. 2. Mimeographed.
1939c. *News Letter.* Southeastern Archaeological Conference, Vol. 1, No. 5, Mimeographed.
1942a. "Early Horizons in the Southeast." *American Antiquity*, Vol. 7, No. 3, pp. 209–222, Menasha.
1942b. "A Description and Analysis of the Pickwick Pottery." In *An Archeological Survey of Pickwick Basin in the Adjacent Portions of the States of Alabama, Mississippi and Tennessee* by William S. Webb and David L. DeJarnette, Bureau of American Ethnology, Bulletin 129, pp. 509–526, Washington.
1942c. "The Pottery from the C. and O. Mounds at Paintsville." In *The C. and O. Mounds at Paintsville, Sites JO 2 and JO 9, Johnson County, Kentucky* by William S. Webb, University of Kentucky Reports in Anthropology and Archaeology, Vol. 5, No. 4, pp. 341–349, Lexington.

HAAS, MARY R.
1939. "Natchez and Chitimacha Clans and Kinship Terminology." *American Anthropologist*, Vol. 41, No. 4, pp. 597–610, Menasha.
1940. "Creek Inter-town Relationships." *American Anthropologist*, Vol. 42, No. 3, pp. 479–489, Menasha.
1941. "The Classification of the Muskogean Languages." In *Language, Culture and Personality* (Leslie Spier, A. I. Hallowell, and Stanley S. Newman, eds.), pp. 41–56, Menasha.

HADDON, A. C.
1925. *The Races of Man and Their Distribution.* New York.

HADLOCK, WENDELL S.
1939. *The Taft's Point Shell Mound at West Gouldsboro, Maine.* Bulletin of the Robert Abbe Museum, No. 5, Bar Harbor.

HALDEMAN, S. S.
1881. "On the Contents of a Rock Retreat in Southeastern Pennsylvania." *Transactions of the American Philosophical Society*, Vol. 15, Pt. 3, pp. 351–368, Philadelphia.

HALL, ROBERT L.
1950. "A Style Analysis of Wisconsin Woodland Pottery." *Wisconsin Archeologist*, Vol. 31, No. 1, Milwaukee.

HARPER, ROLAND M.
1928. *Economic Botany of Alabama.* Geological Survey of Alabama, Monograph 9, University, Alabama.

HARRINGTON, J. C.
1938. "Report on the Excavation of Mound B01:1." *The Missouri Archaeologist*, Vol. 4, No. 1, pp. 1–11, Columbia.
1940. "Partnership at Jamestown." *The Regional Review*, Vol. 5, Nos. 2–3, pp. 3–6.
1946. "Interpreting Jamestown to the Visitor." *The Museum News*, Vol. 24, No. 11, pp. 7–8, Washington.
n.d. "Archeological Report, May-Hartwell Site, Jamestown." Manuscript, National Park Service.

HARRINGTON, M. R.
1920. *Certain Caddo Sites in Arkansas.* Indian Notes and Monographs, No. 10, New York.
1922. *Cherokee and Earlier Remains on Upper Tennessee River.* Indian Notes and Monographs, No. 24, New York.
1924a. "The Ozark Bluff-Dwellers." *American Anthropologist*, Vol. 26, No. 1, pp. 1–21, Menasha.
1924b. "A Pot-Hunters' Paradise." *Indian Notes*, Museum of the American Indian, Heye Foundation, Vol. 1, No. 2, pp. 84–90, New York.

HATCH, CHARLES E., JR.
1941. "Glassmaking in Virginia, 1607–1625." *William and Mary College Quarterly Historical Magazine*, 2d series, Vol. 21, Nos. 2–3, pp. 119–138; 227–238, Williamsburg.

HAURY, EMIL W.
1935. "Tree-Rings-The Archaeologist's Time Piece." *American Antiquity*, Vol. 1, No. 2, pp. 98–108, Menasha.

HAWKES, E. W., and RALPH LINTON
1916. *A Pre-Lenape Site in New Jersey.* Anthropological Publications, University of Pennsylvania, Vol. 6, No. 3, Philadelphia.

HAWLEY, FLORENCE
1941. *Tree-Ring Analysis and Dating in the Mississippi Drainage.* University of Chicago Publications in Anthropology, Occasional Paper, No. 2.

HAYDEN, FERDINAND V.
1862. "On the Ethnography and Philology of the Indian Tribes of the Missouri Valley." *Transactions of the American Philosophical Society*, Vol. 12, Pt. 2, Art. 3, pp. 231–458, Philadelphia.

HENDERSON, JOHN G.
1884. "Aboriginal Remains Near Naples, Illinois." *An-*

nual Report of the Board of Regents of the Smithsonian Institution, 1882, pp. 686–721, Washington.

HEYE, GEORGE G., and GEORGE H. PEPPER

1915. *Exploration of a Munsee Cemetery near Montague, New Jersey.* Contributions from the Museum of the American Indian, Heye Foundation, Vol. 4, No. 3, New York.

HEYE, GEORGE G., FREDERICK W. HODGE, and GEORGE H. PEPPER.

1918. *The Nacoochee Mound in Georgia.* Contributions from the Museum of the American Indian, Heye Foundation, Vol. 2, No. 1, New York.

HIGGS, CHARLES D.

1942. "Spanish Contacts with the Ais (Indian River) Country." *The Florida Historical Quarterly,* Vol. 21, No. 1, pp. 25–39, St. Augustine.

HILL, A. T., and GEORGE METCALF

1941. "A Site of the Dismal River Aspect in Chase County, Nebraska." *Nebraska History,* Vol. 22, No. 2, pp. 158–215, Lincoln.

HINSDALE, W. B.

1925. "The Missaukee Preserve and Rifle River Forts." *Papers of the Michigan Academy of Science, Arts, and Letters,* Vol. 4, Pt. 1, pp. 1–11, New York.

1929. "Indian Mounds, West Twin Lake, Montmorency County, Michigan." *Papers of the Michigan Academy of Science, Arts, and Letters,* Vol. 10, pp. 91–101, Ann Arbor.

1930. "Reports of Archaeological Field Work in the Summer of 1928 in Montmorency, Newaygo and Lake Counties, Michigan." *Papers of the Michigan Academy of Science, Arts, and Letters,* Vol. 12, pp. 127–135, Ann Arbor.

1931. *Archaeological Atlas of Michigan.* Michigan Handbook Series, No. 4, University Museums, University of Michigan, Ann Arbor.

HODGE, FREDERICK W., editor

1907–1910. *Handbook of American Indians North of Mexico.* Bureau of American Ethnology, Bulletin 30, Pts. 1 and 2, Washington.

HODGES, MR. and MRS. T. L.

1945. "Suggestion for Identification of Certain Mid-Ouachita Pottery as Cahinnio Caddo." *Bulletin of the Texas Archaeological and Paleontological Society,* Vol. 16, pp. 98–116, Abilene.

HOEBEL, E. ADAMSON

1946. *The Archaeology of Bone Cave, Miller County, Missouri.* Anthropological Papers of the American Museum of Natural History, Vol. 40, Pt. 2, New York.

HOLDER, PRESTON

n.d. "Archeological Excavations at the McLean Site, Appomattox Court House National Historical Monument, Virginia, 1941." Manuscript, National Park Service.

HOLMES, WILLIAM H.

1883. "Art in Shell of the Ancient Americans." *Second Annual Report, Bureau of American Ethnology, 1880–1881,* pp. 179–305, Washington.

1884a. "Prehistoric Textile Fabrics of the United States, Derived from Impressions on Pottery." *Third Annual Report, Bureau of American Ethnology, 1881–1882,* pp. 393–425, Washington.

1884b. "Illustrated Catalogue of a Portion of the Collections Made by the Bureau of American Ethnology during the Field Season of 1881." *Third Annual Report, Bureau of American Ethnology, 1881–1882,* pp. 427–510, Washington.

1886. "Ancient Pottery of the Mississippi Valley." *Fourth Annual Report, Bureau of American Ethnology, 1882–1883,* pp. 361–436, Washington.

1893. "Vestiges of Early Man in Minnesota." *American Geologist,* Vol. 11, No. 4, pp. 219–240, Minneapolis.

1894. "Caribbean Influence in the Prehistoric Art of the Southern States." *American Anthropologist,* old series, Vol. 7, No. 1, pp. 71–79, Washington.

1896. "Prehistoric Textile Art of Eastern United States." *Thirteenth Annual Report, Bureau of American Ethnology, 1891–1892,* pp. 3–46, Washington.

1903. "Aboriginal Pottery of the Eastern United States." *Twentieth Annual Report, Bureau of American Ethnology, 1898–1899,* pp. 1–201, Washington.

1914. "Areas of American Culture Characterization Tentatively Outlined as an Aid in the Study of Antiquities." *American Anthropologist,* Vol. 16, No. 3, pp. 413–446, Lancaster.

1919. *Handbook of Aboriginal American Antiquities.* Part I: *Introductory: The Lithic Industries.* Bureau of American Ethnology, Bulletin 60, Washington.

HOOTON, EARNEST A.

1930. *The Indians of Pecos Pueblo: A Study of Their Skeletal Remains.* New Haven.

1933. "Racial Types in America and Their Relation to Old World Types." In *The American Aborigines, Their Origin and Antiquity* (Diamond Jenness, ed.), pp. 131–163. Toronto.

HOOTON, EARNEST A., and CHARLES C. WILLOUGHBY

1920. *Indian Village Site and Cemetery near Madisonville, Ohio.* Papers of the Peabody Museum of American Archaeology and Ethnology, Vol. 8, No. 1, Cambridge.

HOSTOS, ADOLFO DE

1938. *Investigaciones historicas.* San Juan de Puerto Rico.

HOUGHTON, FREDERICK

1922. "The Archeology of the Genesee County." *Researches and Transactions of the New York State Archeological Association,* Vol. 3, No. 2, pp. 39–66, Rochester.

HOWARD, EDGAR B.

1939. "Folsom and Yuma Points from Saskatchewan." *American Antiquity,* Vol. 4, No. 3, pp. 277-279, Menasha.

1943. "The Finley Site; Discovery of Yuma Points in Situ near Eden, Wyoming." *American Antiquity,* Vol. 8, No. 3, pp. 224–234, Menasha.

HOWARD, LYNN E.

1940. "Preliminary Report on Cherokee County, Oklahoma, Archaeology." *Oklahoma Prehistorian,* Vol. 3, No. 1, pp. 2–11, Tulsa.

HOWELLS, WILLIAM W.

1938. "Crania from Wyoming Resembling 'Minnesota Man'." *American Antiquity,* Vol. 3, No. 4, pp. 318–326, Menasha.

1946. "Physical Types of the Northeast." In *Man in Northeastern North America* (Frederick Johnson, ed.), Papers of the Robert S. Peabody Foundation for Archaeology, Vol. 3, pp. 168–177, Andover.

HRDLIČKA, ALEŠ

1908. "Report on a Collection of Crania from Arkansas." *Journal of the Academy of Natural Sciences of Philadelphia,* second series, Vol. 13, Pt. 4, pp. 558–563.

1909. "Report on an Additional Collection of Skeletal Remains from Arkansas and Louisiana." *Journal of the Academy of Natural Sciences of Philadelphia,* second series, Vol. 14, Pt. 1, pp. 173–249.

1916. *Physical Anthropology of the Lenape or Delawares, and of the Eastern Indians in General.* Bureau of American Ethnology, Bulletin 62, Washington.

1925. "The Origin and Antiquity of the American Indian." *Annual Report of the Smithsonian Institution for 1923,* pp. 481–494. Washington.

1927. "Catalogue of Human Crania in the United States National Museum Collections: The Algonkin and Related Iroquois; Siouan, Caddoan, Salish and Sahaptin, Shoshonean and California Indians." *Proceedings of the U.S. National Museum*, Vol. 69, Art. 5, Washington.

1930. "Anthropological Survey in Alaska." *Forty-sixth Annual Report, Bureau of American Ethnology, 1928–1929*, pp. 19–374, Washington.

1931a. "Anthropology of the Sioux." *American Journal of Physical Anthropology*, Vol. 16, No. 2, pp. 123–166, Philadelphia.

1931b. "Catalogue of Human Crania in the United States National Museum Collections: Pueblos, Southern Utah Basket-Makers, Navaho." *Proceedings of the U. S. National Museum*, Vol. 78, Washington.

1937a. "The Minnesota 'Man'." *American Journal of Physical Anthropology*, Vol. 22, No. 2, pp. 175–199, Philadelphia.

1937b. "Early Man in America: What Have the Bones To Say?" In *Early Man* (George G. MacCurdy, ed.), pp. 93–104, Philadelphia.

1940. "Catalogue of Human Crania in the United States National Museum: Indians of the Gulf States." *Proceedings of the U. S. National Museum*, Vol. 87, pp. 315–464, Washington.

HULSE, FREDERICK S.
1941. "The People Who Lived at Irene: Physical Anthropology." In *Irene Mound Site, Chatham County, Georgia* by Joseph Caldwell and Catherine McCann, pp. 57–68, Athens.
n.d. Unpublished manuscript.

HURT, WESLEY R., JR.
n.d. "Surface Survey of the Chattahoochee River Valley Region of Alabama." Manuscript.

INDIANAPOLIS ARCHAEOLOGICAL CONFERENCE
1935. Indianapolis Archaeological Conference, National Research Council, Division of Anthropology and Psychology, Committee on State Archaeological Surveys. Mimeographed.

JACKSON, A. T.
1936. "A 'Perpetual Fire' Site." *Bulletin of the Texas Archaeological and Paleontological Society*, Vol. 8, pp. 134–173, Abilene.

JEFFERSON, THOMAS
1794. *Notes on the State of Virginia.* Philadelphia.

JENKS, ALBERT E.
1932. "The Problem of the Culture from the Arvilla Gravel Pit." *American Anthropologist*, Vol. 34, No. 3, pp. 455–466, Menasha.

1935. "Recent Discoveries in Minnesota Prehistory." *Minnesota History: A Quarterly Magazine*, Vol. 16, No. 1, pp. 1–21, St. Paul.

1936. *Pleistocene Man in Minnesota.* Minneapolis.

1937. *Minnesota's Browns Valley Man and Associated Burial Objects.* American Anthropological Association, Memoir 49, Menasha.

1938. "Minnesota Man: A Reply to a Review by Dr. Aleš Hrdlička." *American Anthropologist*, Vol. 40, No. 2, pp. 328–336, Menasha.

JENKS, ALBERT E., and MRS. H. H. SIMPSON, SR.
1941. "Beveled Artifacts in Florida of the Same Type as Artifacts Found near Clovis, New Mexico." *American Antiquity*, Vol. 6, No. 4, pp. 314–319, Menasha.

JENKS, ALBERT E., and LLOYD A. WILFORD
1938. "The Sauk Valley Skeleton." *Bulletin of the Texas Archaeological and Paleontological Society*, No. 10, pp. 136–168, Abilene.

JENNESS, DIAMOND
1941. "Prehistoric Culture Waves from Asia to America." *Annual Report of the Smithsonian Institution for 1940*, pp. 383–396. Washington.

JENNINGS, JESSE D.
1939. "Recent Excavations at the Lamar Site, Ocmulgee National Monument, Macon, Georgia." *Proceedings of the Society for Georgia Archaeology*, Vol. 2, No. 2, pp. 45–55.

1941. "Chickasaw and Earlier Indian Cultures of Northeast Mississippi." *The Journal of Mississippi History*, Vol. 3, No. 3, pp. 155–226.

1944. "The Archaeological Survey of the Natchez Trace." *American Antiquity*, Vol. 9, No. 4, pp. 408–414, Menasha.

1946. "Hopewell-Copena Sites Near Nashville." *American Antiquity*, Vol. 12, No. 2, p. 126, Menasha.

1947. Review of *Hiwassee Island* by T. M. N. Lewis and Madeline Kneberg. *American Antiquity*, Vol. 12, No. 3, pp. 191–193, Menasha.

JOHNSON, FREDERICK, and HUGH M. RAUP
1947. *Grassy Island.* Papers of the Robert S. Peabody Foundation for Archaeology, Vol. 1, No. 2, Andover.

JOHNSON, FREDERICK, et al.
1942. *The Boylston Street Fishweir.* Papers of the Robert S. Peabody Foundation for Archaeology, Vol. 2, Andover.

1949. *The Boylston Street Fishweir, II.* Papers of the Robert S. Peabody Foundation for Archaeology, Vol. 4, No. 1, Andover.

JOHNSON, FREDERICK, assembler.
1951. *Radiocarbon Dating: A Report on the Program to Aid in the Development of the Method of Dating.* Society for American Archeology, Memoir No. 8, Salt Lake City.

JOHNSON, FREDERICK, editor.
1946. *Man in Northeastern North America.* Papers of the Robert S. Peabody Foundation for Archaeology, Vol. 3, Andover.

JONES, CHARLES C., JR.
1873. *Antiquities of the Southern Indians.* New York.

JONES, ROBERT W.
1931. "The Clemson Mound." *Annual Report of the Pennsylvania Historical Commission*, No. 5, pp. 89–111, Harrisburg.

JONES, WALTER B.
1939. "Geology of the Tennessee Valley Region of Alabama, with Notes on the Topographic Features of the Area, and the Effect of Geology and Topography Upon Aboriginal Occupation." In *An Archeological Survey of Wheeler Basin on the Tennessee River in Northern Alabama* by William S. Webb, Bureau of American Ethnology, Bulletin 122, pp. 9–20, Washington.

1942. "Geology of the Pickwick Basin in Adjacent Parts of Tennessee, Mississippi and Alabama." In *An Archeological Survey of Pickwick Basin in the Adjacent Portions of the States of Alabama, Mississippi and Tennessee* by William S. Webb and David L. DeJarnette, Bureau of American Ethnology, Bulletin 129, pp. 327–335, Washington.

JUDD, NEIL M.
1929. "The Present Status of Archaeology in the United States." *American Anthropologist*, Vol. 31, No. 3, pp. 401–418, Menasha.

JURY, WILFRID
1937. *The Alway Prehistoric Site in Lobo Township, Middlesex County.* Bulletin of the Museums, University of Western Ontario, No. 1, London.

1941. *Clearville Prehistoric Village Site in Orford Township, Kent County, Ontario.* Bulletin of the Museums, University of Western Ontario, No. 2, London.

KAY, GEORGE F., and MORRIS M. LEIGHTON
1938. "Geological Notes on the Occurrence of 'Minnesota Man'." *Journal of Geology*, Vol. 46, No. 3, Pt. 1, pp. 268–278, Chicago.

KEITH, ARTHUR
1928. "The Evolution of the Human Races." *Journal of the Royal Anthropological Institute*, Vol. 58, pp. 305–321.

KELLY, A. R.
1933. "Some Problems of Recent Cahokia Archaeology." *Transactions of the Illinois State Academy of Science*, Vol. 25, No. 4, pp. 101–103, Springfield.
1938. "A Preliminary Report on Archeological Exploration at Macon, Georgia." *Anthropological Papers*, No. 1, *Bureau of American Ethnology*, Bulletin 119, pp. 1–68, Washington.
1939. "The Macon Trading Post, an Historical Foundling." *American Antiquity*, Vol. 4, No. 4, pp. 328–333, Menasha.

KELLY, A. R., and FAY-COOPER COLE
1931. "Rediscovering Illinois." In *Blue Book of the State of Illinois 1931–1932*, pp. 318–341, Springfield.

KEYES, CHARLES
1942. "An Outline of Iowa Archeology." *Minnesota Archeologist*, Vol. 8, No. 1, pp. 4–7, Minneapolis.

KIDD, KENNETH
1948. "A Prehistoric Camp Site at Rock Lake, Algonquin Park, Ontario." *Southwestern Journal of Anthropology*, Vol. 4, No. 1, pp. 98–106, Albuquerque.

KIDDER, ALFRED V.
1924. *An Introduction to the Study of Southwestern Archaeology*. New Haven.
1932. *The Artifacts of Pecos*. New Haven.

KING, B. B.
1939. *Under Your Feet*. New York.

KINIETZ, W. VERNON
1940. *The Indians of the Western Great Lakes, 1615–1760*. Occasional Contributions from the Museum of Anthropology of the University of Michigan, No. 10, Ann Arbor.

KINNAMAN, J. O.
1912. "Mounds of Florida." *The American Antiquarian and Oriental Journal*, Vol. 34, No. 3, pp. 215–217, Benton Harbor.

KNOBLOCK, BYRON W.
1939. *Bannerstones of the North American Indian*. La Grange.

KOCH, ALBRECHT KARL
1841. *Description of the Missourium or Missouri Leviathan*. St. Louis.

KRIEGER, ALEX D.
1945. "An Inquiry into Supposed Mexican Influences on a Prehistoric 'Cult' in the Southeastern United States." *American Anthropologist*, Vol. 47, No. 4, pp. 483–515, Menasha.
1946. *Culture Complexes and Chronology in Northern Texas*. University of Texas Publication, No. 4640, Austin.
1947a. "The Eastward Extension of Puebloan Datings Toward Cultures of the Mississippi Valley." *American Antiquity*, Vol. 12, No. 3, pp. 141–148, Menasha.
1947b. "The First Symposium on the Caddoan Archaeological Area." *American Antiquity*, Vol. 12, No. 3, pp. 198–207, Menasha.

KROEBER, ALFRED L.
1907. *Shoshonean Dialects of California*. University of California Publications in American Archaeology and Ethnology, Vol. 4, No. 3, Berkeley.
1928. *Native Cultures of the Southwest*. University of California Publications in American Archaeology and Ethnology, Vol. 23, No. 9, Berkeley.
1939. *Cultural and Natural Areas of Native North America*. University of California Publications in American Archaeology and Ethnology, Vol. 38, Berkeley.

DE LAGUNA, FREDERICA
1947. *Prehistory of North America as Seen from the Yukon*. Society for American Archaeology, Memoir 3, Menasha.

LANDES, RUTH
n.d. "The Santee or the Eastern Dakota." Manuscript based on field notes.

LANGFORD, GEORGE
1919. "The Kankakee River Refuse Heap." *American Anthropologist*, Vol. 21, No. 3, pp. 287–291, Lancaster.
1927. "The Fisher Mound Group, Successive Aboriginal Occupations near the Mouth of the Illinois River." *American Anthropologist*, Vol. 29, No. 3, pp. 153x–206x, Menasha.
1928. "Stratified Indian Mounds in Will County." *Transactions of the Illinois State Academy of Science*, Vol. 20, pp. 247–253, Springfield.
1930. "The Fisher Mound and Village Site." *Transactions of the Illinois State Academy of Science*, Vol. 22, pp. 79–92, Springfield.

LAPHAM, INCREASE A.
1855. "The Antiquities of Wisconsin." *Smithsonian Contributions to Knowledge*, Vol. 7, Art. 4, Washington.

LAWSON, JOHN
1709. *A New Voyage to Carolina; Containing the Exact Description and Natural History of that Country, etc.* London. (Reprinted as Lawson's *History of North Carolina*, Richmond, 1937)

LEMLEY, H. J.
1936. "Discoveries Indicating a Pre-Caddo Culture on Red River in Arkansas." *Bulletin of the Texas Archaeological and Paleontological Society*, Vol. 8, pp. 25–55, Abilene.

LEWIS, BESSIE
1939. *The Story of Old Fort King George*. Brunswick.

LEWIS, T. H.
1894. "The 'Old Fort' of Cross County, Arkansas." *The Archaeologist*, Vol. 2, No. 11, pp. 319–325, Waterloo.
1896. "Mounds and Stone Cists at St. Paul, Minnesota." *The American Antiquarian and Oriental Journal*, Vol. 18, No. 6, pp. 314–320, Chicago.

LEWIS, T. M. N.
1943. "Late Horizons in the Southeast." In *Recent Advances in American Archaeology*, Proceedings of the American Philosophical Society, Vol. 86, No. 2, pp. 304–312, Philadelphia.
1947. "The Duck River Cache." *Tennessee Archaeologist*, Vol. 3, No. 4, pp. 54–57.

LEWIS, T. M. N., editor
1947. "Famous Duck River Flint Cache Returns to Tennessee." *Tennessee Archaeologist*, Vol. 3, No. 3, pp. 38–41.

LEWIS, T. M. N., and MADELINE KNEBERG
1941. *The Prehistory of the Chicamauga Basin in Tennessee*. Tennessee Anthropology Papers No. 1, Knoxville.
1946. *Hiwassee Island: An Archaeological Account of Four Tennessee Indian Peoples*. Knoxville.
1947. *The Archaic Horizon in Western Tennessee*. Tennessee Anthropology Papers No. 2, The University of Tennessee Record, Extension Series, Vol. 23, No. 4, Knoxville.

LILLY, ELI
1937. *Prehistoric Antiquities of Indiana*. Indiana Historical Society, Indianapolis.

1942. "A Cedar Point 'Glacial Kame' Burial." *Proceedings of the Indiana Academy of Science,* Vol. 51, pp. 31–33, Indianapolis.

LINTON, RALPH
1936. *The Study of Man.* New York.

LOWIE, ROBERT H.
1909a. *The Northern Shoshone.* Anthropological Papers of the American Museum of Natural History, Vol. 2, Pt. 2, New York.
1909b. *The Assiniboine.* Anthropological Papers of the American Museum of Natural History, Vol. 4, Pt. 1, New York.
1916. *Plains Indian Age-Societies: Historical and Comparative Summary.* Anthropological Papers of the American Museum of Natural History, Vol. 11, Pt. 13, New York.

McADAMS, WILLIAM H.
1895. "Archaeology." *Report of the Board of World's Fair Commissioners at the World's Columbian Exposition,* pp. 225–304, Springfield.

McALLISTER, J. GILBERT
1932. "The Archaeology of Porter County." *Indiana History Bulletin,* Vol. 10, No. 1, pp. 6–66, Indianapolis.

MacCURDY, GEORGE GRANT
1913. "Shell Gorgets from Missouri." *American Anthropologist,* Vol. 15, No. 3, pp. 395–414, Lancaster.
1917a. "Some Mounds of Eastern Tennessee." *Proceedings of the Nineteenth International Congress of Americanists,* pp. 59–74, Washington.
1917b. "The Wesleyan University Collections of Antiquities from Tennessee." *Proceedings of the Nineteenth International Congress of Americanists,* pp. 75–95, Washington.

McGEE, W. J.
1897. "The Siouan Indians: A Preliminary Sketch." *Fifteenth Annual Report, Bureau of American Ethnology, 1893–1894,* pp. 153–204, Washington.

McGREGOR, JOHN C.
1938. "Southwestern Dated Ruins: III." *Tree-Ring Bulletin,* Vol. 4, No. 4, p. 6, Tuscon.
1941. *Southwestern Archaeology.* New York.
n.d. "The Havana Site." Manuscript.

MACK, JOHN
1942. "Archaeological Work at the University of Missouri." *The Missouri Archaeologist,* Vol. 8, No. 1, pp. 19–20. Columbia.

McKERN, W. C.
1931. *A Wisconsin Variant of the Hopewell Culture.* Bulletin of the Public Museum of the City of Milwaukee, Vol. 10, No. 2.
1935. "Editorial." *American Antiquity,* Vol. 1, No. 2, pp. 81–83, Menasha.
1937. "An Hypothesis for the Asiatic Origin of the Woodland Pattern." *American Antiquity,* Vol. 3, No. 2, pp. 138–143, Menasha.
1939a. "The Midwestern Taxonomic Method as an Aid to Archaeological Culture Study." *American Antiquity,* Vol. 4, No. 4, pp. 301–313, Menasha.
1939b. "Wisconsin Archaeology in the Light of Recent Finds in Other Areas." *The Wisconsin Archeologist,* Vol. 20, No. 1, pp. 1–5, Milwaukee.
1942. "The First Settlers of Wisconsin." *Wisconsin Magazine of History,* Vol. 26, No. 2, pp. 153–169, Madison.
1945. *Preliminary Report on the Upper Mississippi Phase in Wisconsin.* Bulletin of the Public Museum of the City of Milwaukee, Vol. 16, No. 3.
1946. "Aztalan." *The Wisconsin Archeologist,* Vol. 27, No. 2, pp. 41–52, Milwaukee.

McKERN, W. C., and ROBERT RITZENTHALER
1945. "Trait List of the Prehistoric Wisconsin Cultures: The Woodland Peoples." *The Wisconsin Archeologist,* Vol. 26, No. 4, pp. 66–79, Milwaukee.
1946. "The Middle Mississippi Peoples." *The Wisconsin Archeologist,* Vol. 27, No. 2, pp. 25–40, Milwaukee.

McKERN, W. C., PAUL F. TITTERINGTON, and JAMES B. GRIFFIN
1945. "Painted Pottery Figurines from Illinois." *American Antiquity,* Vol. 10, No. 3, pp. 295–302, Menasha.

MacNEISH, RICHARD S.
1944. "Middle Woodland Cultures." *Transactions of the Illinois State Academy of Science,* Vol. 37, pp. 41–44, Springfield.
1947. "A Preliminary Report on Coastal Tamualipas, Mexico." *American Antiquity,* Vol. 13, No. 1, pp. 1–15, Menasha.
1948. "The Pre-Pottery Faulkner Site of Southern Illinois." *American Antiquity,* Vol. 13, No. 3, pp. 232–243, Menasha.
n.d.a. "Stratigraphy at Kincaid." Unpublished manuscript, Department of Anthropology, University of Chicago.
n.d.b. "A Ceramic Study of Foreign Sherds Found at the Kincaid Site." Unpublished manuscript, Department of Anthropology, University of Chicago.
n.d.c. "The Establishment of the Lewis Focus." Unpublished M.A. thesis, Department of Anthropology, University of Chicago.
n.d.d. "The Weaver Site." Unpublished manuscript.

MANSON, CARL
1948. "Marcey Creek Site: An Early Manifestation in the Potomac Valley." *American Antiquity,* Vol. 13, No. 3, pp. 223–227, Menasha.

MANSON, CARL, HOWARD A. MacCORD, and JAMES B. GRIFFIN
1944. "The Culture of the Keyser Farm Site." *Papers of the Michigan Academy of Science, Arts, and Letters,* Vol. 29, pp. 375–418, Ann Arbor.

MARTIN, PAUL S., GEORGE I. QUIMBY, JR., and DONALD COLLIER
1947. *Indians before Columbus.* Chicago.

MATTHEW, WILLIAM D.
1915. "Climate and Evolution." *Annals of the New York Academy of Sciences,* Vol. 24, pp. 171–318, New York.

MAXWELL, MOREAU S.
1947. "A Summary of Illinois Archaeology." *The Wisconsin Archeologist,* Vol. 28, No. 2, pp. 19–33, Milwaukee.
1951. *Woodland Cultures of Southern Illinois: Archaeological Excavations in the Carbondale Area.* Logan Museum Publications in Anthropology, Bulletin No. 7, Beloit College, Beloit.

MELEEN, ELMER E.
1938. *A Preliminary Report of the Mitchell Indian Village Site and Burial Mounds.* Archaeological Studies, Circular 2, Pt. 1, University of South Dakota Museum, Vermillion.

MERCER, HENRY C.
1897. *Researches upon the Antiquity of Man in the Delaware Valley and the Eastern United States.* Publications of the University of Pennsylvania, Series of Philology, Literature and Archaeology, Vol. 6, Boston.

MERENESS, NEWTON D., editor
1916. *Travels in the American Colonies.* New York.

MILLER, REX K.
1941. *McCain Site, Dubois County, Indiana. Prehistory Research Series,* Indiana Historical Society, Vol. 2, No. 1, Indianapolis.

MILLS, WILLIAM C.
1902. "Excavations of the Adena Mound." *Ohio Archaeo-*

logical and Historical Quarterly, Vol. 10, No. 4, pp. 452–479, Columbus.

1906. "Baum Prehistoric Village." Ohio Archaeological and Historical Quarterly, Vol. 15, No. 1, pp. 44–136, Columbus.

1907. "The Explorations of the Edwin Harness Mound." Ohio Archaeological and Historical Quarterly, Vol. 16, No. 2, pp. 113–193, Columbus.

1909. "Explorations of the Seip Mound." Ohio Archaeological and Historical Quarterly, Vol. 18, pp. 268–321, Columbus.

1912. "Archaeological Remains of Jackson County." Ohio Archaeological and Historical Quarterly, Vol. 21, pp. 175–214, Columbus.

1916. "Exploration of the Tremper Mound." Ohio Archaeological and Historical Quarterly, Vol. 25, No. 3, pp. 262–398, Columbus.

1922a. "Exploration of the Mound City Group." Ohio Archaeological and Historical Quarterly, Vol. 31, No. 4, pp. 423–584, Columbus.

1922b. "Exploration of the Mound City Group." In Certain Mounds and Village Sites in Ohio, Vol. 3, No. 4, pp. 245–406, Columbus.

MINER, HORACE M.
1936. "The Importance of Textiles in the Archaeology of the Eastern United States," American Antiquity, Vol. I, No. 3, Menasha.

MOFFETT, ROSS
1946. "Some Shell Heaps in Truro, Massachusetts." Bulletin of the Massachusetts Archaeological Society, Vol. 7, No. 2, pp. 17–23, Boston.

1949. "The Raisch-Smith Site: An Early Indian Occupation in Preble County, Ohio." The Ohio State Archaeological and Historical Quarterly, Vol. 58, No. 4, Columbus.

MONTGOMERY, HENRY
1906. "Remains of Prehistoric Man in the Dakotas." American Anthropologist, Vol. 8, No. 4, pp. 640–651, Lancaster.

MOONEY, JAMES
1894. The Siouan Tribes of the East. Bureau of American Ethnology, Bulletin 22, Washington.

1907a. "Hidatsa." Bureau of American Ethnology, Bulletin 30, Pt. I, pp. 547–549, Washington.

1907b. "Siksika." Bureau of American Ethnology, Bulletin, 30, Pt. I, pp. 570–571, Washington.

MOORE, CHARLES
1897. "The Ontonagon Copper Bowlder in the U. S. National Museum." Report of the U. S. National Museum for the Year Ending June 30, 1895, pp. 1021–1030, Washington.

MOORE, CLARENCE B.
1892. "Certain Shell Heaps of the St. John's River, Florida, Hitherto Unexplored." Pt. 1. American Naturalist, Vol. 26, pp. 912–922, Philadelphia.

1894a. "Certain Sand Mounds of the St. John's River, Florida." Journal of the Academy of Natural Sciences of Philadelphia, second series, Vol. 10, Pt. 1, pp. 5–103.

1894b. "Certain Sand Mounds of the St. John's River, Florida." Journal of the Academy of Natural Sciences of Philadelphia, second series, Vol. 10, Pt. 2, pp. 129–246.

1894c. "Certain Shell Heaps of the St. John's River, Florida, Hitherto Unexplored." Pt. 5. American Naturalist, Vol. 28, pp. 15–26, Philadelphia.

1896a. "Certain River Mounds of Duval County, Florida." Journal of the Academy of Natural Sciences of Philadelphia, second series, Vol. 10, Pt. 4, pp. 448–502.

1896b. "Two Mounds on Murphy Island." Journal of the Academy of Natural Sciences of Philadelphia, second series, Vol. 10, Pt. 4, pp. 503–516.

1896c. "Certain Sand Mounds of the Ocklawaha River." Journal of the Academy of Natural Sciences of Philadelphia, second series, Vol. 10, Pt. 4, pp. 517–543.

1897. "Certain Aboriginal Mounds of the Georgia Coast." Journal of the Academy of Natural Sciences of Philadelphia, second series, Vol. 11, Pt. 1, pp. 4–138.

1898a. "Certain Aboriginal Mounds of the Coast of South Carolina." Journal of the Academy of Natural Sciences of Philadelphia, second series, Vol. 11, Pt. 2, pp. 146–166.

1898b. "Certain Aboriginal Mounds of the Savannah River." Journal of the Academy of Natural Sciences of Philadelphia, second series, Vol. 11, Pt. 2, pp. 167–172.

1899. "Certain Aboriginal Remains of the Alabama River." Journal of the Academy of Natural Sciences of Philadelphia, second series, Vol. 11, Pt. 3, pp. 289–347.

1900. "Certain Antiquities of the Florida West-Coast." Journal of the Academy of Natural Sciences of Philadelphia, second series, Vol. 11, Pt. 3, pp. 350–394.

1901. "Certain Aboriginal Remains of the Northwest Florida Coast, Pt. 1." Journal of the Academy of Natural Sciences of Philadelphia, second series, Vol. 11, Pt. 4, pp. 419–497.

1902. "Certain Aboriginal Remains of the Northwest Florida Coast, Pt. 2." Journal of the Academy of Natural Sciences of Philadelphia, second series, Vol. 12, Pt. 2, pp. 125–335.

1903a. "Certain Aboriginal Mounds of the Florida Central West-Coast." Journal of the Academy of Natural Sciences of Philadelphia, second series, Vol. 12, Pt. 3, pp. 361–438.

1903b. "Certain Aboriginal Remains of the Apalachicola River." Journal of the Academy of Natural Sciences of Philadelphia, second series, Vol. 12, Pt. 3, pp. 440–492.

1904. "Aboriginal Urn Burial in the United States." American Anthropologist, Vol. 6, No. 5, pp. 660–669, Lancaster.

1905a. "Certain Aboriginal Remains of the Black Warrior River." Journal of the Academy of Natural Sciences of Philadelphia, second series, Vol. 13, Pt. 2, pp. 125–244.

1905b. "Certain Aboriginal Remains of the Lower Tombigbee River." Journal of the Academy of Natural Sciences of Philadelphia, second series, Vol. 13, Pt. 2, pp. 245–278.

1905c. "Certain Aboriginal Remains of Mobile Bay and Mississippi Sound." Journal of the Academy of Natural Sciences of Philadelphia, second series, Vol. 13, Pt. 2, pp. 279–297.

1905d. "Miscellaneous Investigations in Florida." Journal of the Academy of Natural Sciences of Philadelphia, second series, Vol. 13, Pt. 2, pp. 298–325.

1907a. "Moundville Revisited." Journal of the Academy of Natural Sciences of Philadelphia, second series, Vol. 13, Pt. 3, pp. 337–405.

1907b. "Crystal River Revisited." Journal of the Academy of Natural Sciences of Philadelphia, second series, Vol. 13, Pt. 3, pp. 406–425.

1907c. "Mounds of the Lower Chattahoochee and Lower Flint Rivers." Journal of the Academy of Natural Sciences of Philadelphia, second series, Vol. 13, Pt. 3, pp. 426–456.

1908. "Certain Mounds of Arkansas and Mississippi." Journal of the Academy of Natural Sciences of Philadelphia, second series, Vol. 13, Pt. 4, pp. 481–600.

1909. "Antiquities of the Ouachita Valley." Journal of the Academy of Natural Sciences of Philadelphia, second series, Vol. 14, Pt. 1, pp. 6–170.

1910. "Antiquities of the St. Francis, White, and Black Rivers, Arkansas." Journal of the Academy of Natural

Sciences of Philadelphia, second series, Vol. 14, Pt. 2, pp. 254–362.

1911. "Some Aboriginal Sites on Mississippi River." *Journal of the Academy of Natural Sciences of Philadelphia*, second series, Vol. 14, Pt. 3, pp. 366–476.

1912. "Some Aboriginal Sites on Red River." *Journal of the Academy of Natural Sciences of Philadelphia*, second series, Vol. 14, Pt. 4, pp. 482–640.

1915. "Aboriginal Sites on Tennessee River." *Journal of the Academy of Natural Sciences of Philadelphia*, second series, Vol. 16, Pt. 3, pp. 431–487.

1916a. "Additional Investigation on Green River, Kentucky." *Journal of the Academy of Natural Sciences of Philadelphia*, second series, Vol. 16, Pt. 3, pp. 431–487.

1916b. "Additional Investigation on Mississippi River." *Journal of the Academy of Natural Sciences of Philadelphia*, second series, Vol. 16, Pt. 3, pp. 492–508.

1918. "The Northwestern Florida Coast Revisited." *Journal of the Academy of Natural Sciences of Philadelphia*, second series, Vol. 16, Pt. 4, pp. 514–577.

1922. "Additional Mounds of Duval and Clay Counties, Florida." *Indian Notes and Monographs*, Museum of the American Indian, Heye Foundation, New York.

MOOREHEAD, WARREN K.

1909. "A Study of Primitive Culture in Ohio." In *Putnam Anniversary Volume of Anthropological Essays*, pp. 137–150, New York.

1910. *The Stone Age in North America*. 2 volumes, Boston.

1922. "The Hopewell Mound Group of Ohio." *Field Museum of Natural History, Publication 211, Anthropological Series*, Vol. 6, No. 5, Chicago.

1928. *The Cahokia Mounds*. University of Illinois Bulletin, Vol. 26, No. 4, Urbana.

MORANT, G. M.

1937. "A Contribution to Eskimo Craniology Based on Previously Published Measurements." *Biometrika*, Vol. 29, Pts. 1 and 2, pp. 1–20, London.

MORGAN, RICHARD G.

1933. "Archaeology of the Chicago Area." *Transactions of the Illinois State Academy of Science*, Vol. 25, No. 4, pp. 91–92, Springfield.

1946a. Review of *The Adena People* by William S. Webb and Charles E. Snow. *American Antiquity*, Vol. 12, No. 1, pp. 54–58, Menasha.

1946b. "Fort Ancient." *The Ohio State Archaeological and Historical Quarterly*, Columbus.

MORGAN, RICHARD G., and H. H. ELLIS

1943. "The Fairport Harbor Village Site." *The Ohio State Archaeological and Historical Quarterly*, Vol. 52, No. 1, pp. 3–64, Columbus.

MORTON, SAMUEL G.

1846. "Some Observations on the Ethnography and Archaeology of the American Aborigines." *The American Journal of Science and Arts*, second series, Vol. 2, No. 1, pp. 1–17, New Haven.

MOTT, MILDRED

1938. "The Relation of Historic Indian Tribes to Archaeological Manifestations in Iowa." *Iowa Journal of History and Politics*, Vol. 36, No. 3, pp. 227–314, Iowa City.

MULLOY, WILLIAM

1942a. *The Hagen Site: A Prehistoric Village on the Lower Yellowstone*. University of Montana Publications in the Social Sciences, No. 1, Missoula.

1942b. "A Prehistoric Campsite Near Redlodge, Montana." *American Antiquity*, Vol. 9, No. 2, pp. 170–179, Menasha.

1945. "An Indian Village in the Little Cayuse Mountains of Montana." *Papers of the Michigan Academy of Science, Arts, and Letters*, Vol. 30, pp. 511–521, Ann Arbor.

MULLOY, WILLIAM, and OSCAR LEWIS

1943. "Some Early Types of Points from the Lower Yellowstone Country." *American Antiquity*, Vol. 8, No. 3, pp. 298–299, Menasha.

MURDOCK, GEORGE P.

1941. *Ethnographic Bibliography of North America*. Yale Anthropological Series, Vol. 1, New Haven.

NATIONAL RESEARCH COUNCIL

1921. *Fifth Annual Report of the National Research Council*. Washington.

1929. "Report of the Conference on Midwestern Archaeology, held in St. Louis, Missouri, May 18, 1929." *Bulletin 74*, Washington.

1930. "Guide Leaflet for Amateur Archaeologists." *Reprint and Circular Series*, Number 93, Washington.

1935. *Report of the National Research Council for the Year July 1, 1933–June 30, 1934*. Washington.

1941. *Report of the National Research Council for the Year July 1, 1939–June 30, 1940*. Washington.

1946. *Report of the National Academy of Sciences, National Research Council, Fiscal Year 1944–1945*. Washington.

n.d.a. "Conference on Southern Pre-history Held under the Auspices of the Division of Anthropology and Psychology, Committee on State Archaeological Surveys, National Research Council, Birmingham, Alabama, December 18, 19, and 20, 1932." Washington. Mimeographed.

n.d.b. "The Indianapolis Archaeological Conference Held under the Auspices of the Division of Anthropology and Psychology, Committee on State Archaeological Surveys, National Research Council, Indianapolis, Indiana, December 6, 7, and 8, 1935." Washington. Mimeographed.

n.d.c. "Grants-in-Aid made by the National Research Council within the Fields of Anthropology and Psychology, 1929–1936." Mimeographed.

NELSON, NELS C.

1918. *Chronology in Florida*. Anthropological Papers of the American Museum of Natural History, Vol. 22, Pt. 2, New York.

NEUMANN, GEORG K.

1937. "Preliminary Notes on the Crania from Fulton County, Illinois." In *Rediscovering Illinois* by Fay-Cooper Cole and Thorne Deuel, pp. 227–264, Chicago.

1941a. "Crania from the Porter Mound, Ross County, Ohio." *Papers of the Michigan Academy of Science, Arts, and Letters*, Vol. 26, pp. 479–488, Ann Arbor.

1941b. "The Crania from the Hagan Mound and Their Relationship to Those of Two Late-Prehistoric Populations of Central Illinois." *Transactions of the American Philosophical Society*, Vol. 32, Pt. 1, pp. 79–82, Philadelphia.

1942. "The Origin of the Prairid Physical Type of American Indian." *Papers of the Michigan Academy of Science, Arts, and Letters*, Vol. 27, pp. 539–542, Ann Arbor.

n.d. "The Skeletal Remains from Keyauwee." Unpublished manuscript.

NEWELL, H. PERRY, and ALEX D. KRIEGER

1949. *The George C. Davis Site, Cherokee County, Texas*. Society for American Archaeology Memoir No. 5, Menasha.

NEWKUMET, PHIL J.

1940a. "Preliminary Report on Excavation of the Williams' Mound, Le Flore County, Oklahoma." *Oklahoma Prehistorian*, Vol. 3, No. 2, pp. 2–10, Tulsa.

1940b. "Excavation of 'Black Mound' Reveals Ornate

'Hair Pins.'" *Oklahoma Prehistorian*, Vol. 3, No. 2, pp. 1–8, Tulsa.

NEWMAN, MARSHALL T., and CHARLES E. SNOW
1942. "Preliminary Report on the Skeletal Material from Pickwick Basin, Alabama." In *An Archeological Survey of Pickwick Basin in the Adjacent Portions of the States of Alabama, Mississippi and Tennessee* by William S. Webb and David L. DeJarnette, Bureau of American Ethnology, Bulletin 129, pp. 393–507, Washington.

OEHLER, CHARLES M.
1950. *Turpin Indians.* Cincinnati Museum of Natural History, Popular Publication Series No. 1.

OETTEKING, BRUNO
1930. *Craniology of the North Pacific Coast.* Memoirs of the American Museum of Natural History, Vol. 15, Pt. 1, New York.

ORR, ELLISON
1914. "Indian Pottery of the Oneota or Upper Iowa Valley in Northeastern Iowa." *Proceedings of the Iowa Academy of Science*, Vol. 21, pp. 231–239, Des Moines.

ORR, KENNETH G.
1939. "Field Report on the Excavations of Indian Villages in the Vicinity of the Spiro Mound, Le Flore County." *Oklahoma Prehistorian*, Vol. 2, No. 2, pp. 8–15, Tulsa.
1941. "The Eufaula Mound: Contributions to the Spiro Focus." *Oklahoma Prehistorian*, Vol. 4, No. 1, pp. 2–15, Tulsa.
1946. "The Archaeological Situation at Spiro, Oklahoma; A Preliminary Report." *American Antiquity*, Vol. 11, No. 4, pp. 228–256, Menasha.
n.d.*a*. "A Preliminary Study of Certain Components in the Caddoan Archaeological Area." Unpublished manuscript, Department of Anthropology, University of Chicago.
n.d.*b*. "Culture Change at Kincaid, A Study in Statistical Analysis." Unpublished Ph.D. thesis, Department of Anthropology, University of Chicago.
n.d.*c*. "Report on the Southern Cult Roundtable, University of Michigan." Unpublished manuscript, Department of Anthropology, University of Chicago.

ORR, KENNETH G., and J. C. McGREGOR
n.d. "Excavations in LaSalle County, 1947: A Preliminary Report." Unpublished manuscript.

OVER, W. H.
1936. "The Archaeology of Ludlow Cave and Its Significance." *American Antiquity*, Vol. 2, No. 2, pp. 126–129, Menasha.

OSGOOD, CORNELIUS
1940. "The Organization and Aims of the Eastern States Archaeological Federation." *Archaeological Society of New Jersey News Letter*, Number 2.

PARKER, ARTHUR C.
1907. *Excavations in an Erie Indian Village and Burial Site at Ripley, Chautauqua County, New York.* New York State Museum Bulletin, No. 117, Albany.
1922. *The Archeological History of New York.* Parts 1 and 2. New York State Museum Bulletin, Nos. 235–238, Albany.

PEABODY, CHARLES
1904. *Exploration of Mounds, Coahoma County, Mississippi.* Papers of the Peabody Museum of American Archaeology and Ethnology, Vol. 3, No. 2, Cambridge.

PEITHMAN, IRVIN
1939. "Evidences of Early Woodland Culture at Chalk Bluff Rock Shelter." *American Antiquity*, Vol. 4, No. 3, pp. 268–272, Menasha.

PEPPER, GEORGE H.
1924. "Wateree Artifacts." *Indian Notes*, Museum of the American Indian, Heye Foundation, Vol. 1, No. 2, pp. 74–75, New York.

PERINO, G.
1947. "Cultural Clues from Cahokia." *Amateur Archaeologist Club of St. Louis*, Bulletin 1, pp. 14–16.

PERRINE, THOMAS M.
1874. "Antiquities of Union County, Illinois." *Annual Report of the Board of Regents of the Smithsonian Institution for 1873*, p. 410, Washington.

PHILLIPS, PHILIP
1940. "Middle American Influences on the Archaeology of the Southeastern United States." In *The Maya and Their Neighbors*, pp. 349–367, New York.

PHILLIPS, PHILIP, JAMES A. FORD, and JAMES B. GRIFFIN
1951. *Archaeological Survey in the Lower Mississippi Alluvial Valley, 1940–1947.* Papers of the Peabody Museum of Archaeology and Ethnology, Vol. 25, Cambridge.

PORTER, CHARLES W., III
1943. "Fort Raleigh National Historic Site, North Carolina: Part of the Settlement Sites of Sir Walter Raleigh's Colonies of 1585–1586 and 1587." *The North Carolina Historical Review*, Vol. 20, No. 1, pp. 22–42.

POTTER, W. B.
1880. "Archaeological Remains in Southeastern Missouri." *Contributions to the Archaeology of Missouri*, Archaeological Section of the St. Louis Academy of Science, Pt. 1, pp. 5–19.

POWELL, J. W.
1894. "Report of the Director." *Twelfth Annual Report, Bureau of American Ethnology, 1890–1891*, pp. XXI–XLVIII, Washington.

PUTNAM, FREDERICK W.
1878*a*. "Report of the Curator." *Eleventh Annual Report of the Trustees of the Peabody Museum of American Archaeology and Ethnology*, Vol. 2, No. 2, pp. 191–206, Cambridge.
1878*b*. "Archaeological Explorations in Tennessee." *Eleventh Annual Report of the Trustees of the Peabody Museum of American Archaeology and Ethnology*, Vol. 2, No. 2, pp. 305–360, Cambridge.
1882. "Notes on the Copper Objects from North and South America, Contained in the Collections of the Peabody Museum." *Fifteenth Annual Report of the Peabody Museum of American Archaeology and Ethnology*, Vol. 3, No. 2, pp. 83–148, Cambridge.

QUIMBY, GEORGE I., JR.
1938. "Dated Indian Burials in Michigan." *Papers of the Michigan Academy of Science, Arts, and Letters*, Vol. 23, pp. 63–72, Ann Arbor.
1939*a*. "Aboriginal Camp Sites on Isle Royale, Michigan." *American Antiquity*, Vol. 4, No. 3, pp. 215–223, Menasha.
1939*b*. "European Trade Articles as Chronological Indicators for the Archaeology of the Historic Period in Michigan." *Papers of the Michigan Academy of Science, Arts, and Letters*, Vol. 24, Pt. 4, pp. 25–31, Ann Arbor.
1941*a*. "Hopewellian Pottery Types in Michigan." *Papers of the Michigan Academy of Science, Arts, and Letters*, Vol. 26, pp. 489–494, Ann Arbor.
1941*b*. *The Goodall Focus: An Analysis of Ten Hopewellian Components in Michigan and Indiana.* Prehistory Research Series, Indiana Historical Society, Vol. 2, No. 2, Indianapolis.
1942. "The Natchezan Culture Type." *American Antiquity*, Vol. 7, No. 3, pp. 255–275, Menasha.
1943. "The Ceramic Sequence within the Goodall Focus."

Papers of the Michigan Academy of Science, Arts, and Letters, Vol. 28, pp. 543–548, Ann Arbor.

1944. "Some New Data on the Goodall Focus." *Papers of the Michigan Academy of Science, Arts, and Letters,* Vol. 29, pp. 419–423, Ann Arbor.

1946. "The Possibility of an Independent Agricultural Complex in the Southeastern United States." In *Human Origins, Selected Readings,* Series II, No. 19, pp. 206–210, Chicago.

RADCLIFFE-BROWN, ARTHUR R.

1935. "Patrilineal and Matrilineal Succession." *Iowa Law Review,* Vol. 20, No. 2.

RADIN, PAUL

1923. "The Winnebago Tribe." *Thirty-seventh Annual Report, Bureau of American Ethnology, 1915–1916,* pp. 35–550, Washington.

RAINEY, FROELICH G.

1935. "An Indian Burial Site at Crystal River, Florida." *The Florida Historical Society Quarterly,* Vol. 13, No. 4, pp. 185–192, Tallahassee.

RAU, CHARLES

1873. "North American Stone Implements." *Annual Report of the Board of Regents of the Smithsonian Institution for 1872,* pp. 395–408, Washington.

READ, M. C.

1868. "Ancient Mounds Near Chattanooga, Tennessee." *Annual Report of the Board of Regents of the Smithsonian Institution for 1867,* pp. 401–402, Washington.

READ, M. C., and CHARLES WHITTLESEY

1877. "Antiquities of Ohio, Report of the Committee of the State Archaeological Society to the Centennial Commissioners of Ohio." *Final Report of the Ohio State Board of Centennial Managers to the General Assembly of the State of Ohio,* Pt. 2, pp. 6–131, Columbus.

REYNOLDS, ELMER R.

1880–1881a. "Aboriginal Cemeteries Near Piscataway, Maryland," *Abstract of the Transactions of the Anthropological Society of Washington, D.C.*

1880–1881b. "Ossuary at Accotink, Virginia." *Abstract of the Transactions of the Anthropological Society of Washington, D.C.*

RICHARDS, ELIZABETH A.

n.d. "A Comparative Study of a Series of Crania from Dutch Harbor, Alaska." Unpublished M.A. thesis, Department of Anthropology, University of Chicago.

RINALDO, J. B.

n.d. "The Pere Marquette Park Sites." Unpublished M.A. thesis, Department of Anthropology, University of Chicago.

RITCHIE, WILLIAM A.

1932. *The Lamoka Lake Site: The Type Station of the Archaic Algonkin Period in New York.* Researches and Transactions of the New York State Archaeological Association, Vol. 7, No. 4, Rochester.

1936. *New Evidence Relating to the Archaic Occupation of New York.* Researches and Transactions of the New York State Archaeological Association, Vol. 8, No. 1, Rochester.

1937. "Culture Influences from Ohio in New York Archaeology." *American Antiquity,* Vol. 2, No. 3, pp. 182–194, Menasha.

1938a. *Certain Recently Explored New York Mounds and Their Probable Relation to the Hopewell Culture.* Research Records of the Rochester Museum of Arts and Sciences, No. 4.

1938b. "A Perspective of Northeastern Archaeology." *American Antiquity,* Vol. 4, No. 2, pp. 94–112, Menasha.

1940. *Two Prehistoric Village Sites at Brewerton, New York, Type Components of the Brewerton Focus, Laurentian Aspect.* Research Records of the Rochester Museum of Arts and Sciences, No. 5.

1944. *The Pre-Iroquoian Occupations of New York State.* Rochester Museum of Arts and Sciences, Memoir No. 1.

1945. *An Early Site in Cayuga County, New York; Type Component of the Frontenac Focus, Archaic Pattern.* Researches and Transactions of the New York State Archaeological Association, Vol. 10, No. 1, Rochester.

1946. *A Stratified Prehistoric Site at Brewerton, New York.* Research Records of the Rochester Museum of Arts and Sciences, No. 8.

1949a. *The Bell-Philhower Site, Sussex County, New Jersey.* Prehistory Research Series, Indiana Historical Society, Vol. 3, No. 2, Indianapolis.

1949b. *An Archaeological Survey of the Trent Waterway in Ontario, Canada.* Researches and Transactions of the New York State Archaeological Association, Vol. 12, No. 1, Rochester.

RITCHIE, WILLIAM A., and RICHARD S. MACNEISH

1949. "The Pre-Iroquoian Pottery of New York State." *American Antiquity,* Vol. 15, No. 2, pp. 97–124, Menasha.

RITZENTHALER, ROBERT

1946. "The Osceola Site: An 'Old Copper' Site near Potosi, Wisconsin." *The Wisconsin Archeologist,* Vol. 27, No. 3, pp. 53–70, Milwaukee.

ROBERTS, FRANK H. H., JR.

1935. *A Folsom Complex, Preliminary Report on Investigations at the Lindenmeier Site in Northern Colorado.* Smithsonian Miscellaneous Collections, Vol. 94, No. 4, Washington.

1936. *Additional Information on the Folsom Complex, Report on the Second Season's Investigations at the Lindenmeier Site in Northern Colorado.* Smithsonian Miscellaneous Collections, Vol. 95, No. 10, Washington.

1939. "The Folsom Problem in American Archeology." *Annual Report of the Board of Regents of the Smithsonian Institution for 1938,* pp. 531–546, Washington.

1940. "Developments in the Problem of the North American Paleo-Indian." In *Essays in Historical Anthropology of North America,* Smithsonian Miscellaneous Collections, Vol. 100, pp. 51–116, Washington.

ROBBINS, MAURICE

1944. *The Faulkner Spring Site.* Papers of the Attleboro Museum of Art and History, No. 1.

1946. "The Ford Site, a Prehistoric Station in Norton, Massachusetts." *American Antiquity,* Vol. 12, No. 2, pp. 80–94, Menasha.

ROUSE, IRVING B.

1940. "Some Evidence Concerning the Origins of West Indian Pottery-Making." *American Anthropologist,* Vol. 42, No. 1, pp. 49–80, Menasha.

1945. "Styles of Pottery in Connecticut." *Bulletin of the Massachusetts Archaeological Society,* Vol. 7, No. 1, pp. 1–8, Boston.

1947. "Ceramic Traditions and Sequences in Connecticut." *Connecticut Archaeological Society Bulletin,* No. 21, pp. 10–25, New Haven.

1950. "Vero and Melbourne Man: A Cultural and Chronological Interpretation." *Transactions of the New York Academy of Sciences,* Series 2, Vol. 12, No. 7, pp. 220–224, New York.

1951. "A Survey of Indian River Archaeology, Florida." *Yale University Publications in Anthropology,* No. 44, New Haven.

ROWE, JOHN H.

1940. "Excavations in the Waterside Shell Heap, Frenchman's Bay, Maine." *Papers of the Excavators' Club,* Vol. 1, No. 3, Cambridge.

RUWWE, J. W.
1936. "Primitive Man in Phelps County." *The Missouri Magazine,* Vol. 8, No. 9, pp. 8–9, Jefferson City.

SAGARD, THÉODAT GABRIEL
n.d. *Le Grand voyage au pays des Hurons, situé en Amérique vers la mer douce, aux derniers confins de la Nouvelle France, dite Canada.* In *Trois Voyages au Canada: Jacques Cartier, 1534 et 1536; Samuel de Champlain, 1608 et 1611; et Frere Gabriel Sagard, 1624.* Collection Voyages et Decouvertes, Paris.

SAPIR, EDWARD
1916. *Time Perspective in Aboriginal American Culture.* Canada Department of Mines, Geological Survey, Memoir 90, Anthropological Series, No. 13, Ottawa.
1929. "Central and North American Indian Languages." *Encyclopedia Britannica,* Vol. 5, 14th edition, pp. 138–141, Chicago.

SCHMITT, KARL
n.d. "Patawomeke: An Historic Algonkin Site." Unpublished M.A. thesis, Department of Anthropology, University of Chicago.

SCHMITT, KARL, and RICHARD G. SLATTERY
n.d. "The Shepard Site, Montgomery County, Maryland." Unpublished manuscript.

SCHOENBECK, ETHEL
1939. "Discovery of a Buried Aboriginal Shellheap in the Illinois River Valley." *Transactions of the Illinois State Academy of Science,* Vol. 32, No. 2, pp. 61–62, Springfield.
1946. "Cord-decorated Pottery in the General Peoria Region." *Transactions of the Illinois State Academy of Science,* Vol. 39, pp. 33–42, Springfield.

SCHRABISCH, MAX
1915. *Indian Habitations in Sussex County, New Jersey.* Geological Survey of New Jersey Bulletin 13, Union Hill.
1926. "Aboriginal Rock Shelters and Other Archaeological Notes of Wyoming Valley and Vicinity." *Proceedings and Collections of the Wyoming Historical and Geological Society,* Vol. 19, pp. 47–218, Wilkes-Barre.

SCHULMAN, EDMUND
1942. "Dendrochronology in Pines of Arkansas." *Ecology,* Vol. 23, No. 3, pp. 309–318, Lancaster.
1944a. "Dendrochronology in Mexico, I." *Tree-Ring Bulletin,* Vol. 10, No. 3, pp. 18–24, Tucson.
1944b. "Tree-Ring Work in Scandinavia." *Tree-Ring Bulletin,* Vol. 11, No. 1, pp. 2–6, Tucson.

SELLARDS, E. H.
1916. "Human Remains and Associated Fossils from the Pleistocene of Florida." *Eighth Annual Report of the Florida Geological Survey,* pp. 121–160, Tallahassee.
1937. "The Vero Finds in the Light of Present Knowledge." In *Early Man* (George Grant MacCurdy, ed.), pp. 193–210, Philadelphia.
1940. "Early Man in America: Index to Localities." *Bulletin of the Geological Society of America,* Vol. 51, pp. 373–431, New York.

SELTZER, CARL C.
1944. *Racial Prehistory in the Southwest and the Hawikuh Zunis.* Papers of the Peabody Museum of American Archaeology and Ethnology, Vol. 23, No. 1, Cambridge.

SETZLER, FRANK M.
1930. *The Archaeology of the Whitewater Valley.* Indiana History Bulletin, Vol. 7, No. 12, Indianapolis.
1931. *The Archaeology of Randolph County and the Fudge Mound.* Indiana History Bulletin, Vol. 9, No. 1, Indianapolis.
1933. "Pottery of the Hopewell Type from Louisiana."

Proceedings of the U. S. National Museum, Vol. 82, Art. 22, Washington.
1940. "Archeological Perspectives in the Northern Mississippi Valley." In *Essays in Historical Anthropology of North America,* Smithsonian Miscellaneous Collections, Vol. 100, pp. 253–290, Washington.
1943. "Archaeological Explorations in the United States, 1930–1942." *Acta Americana,* Vol. 1, No. 2, pp. 206–220.

SETZLER, FRANK M., and JESSE D. JENNINGS
1941. *Peachtree Mound and Village Site, Cherokee County, North Carolina.* Bureau of American Ethnology, Bulletin 131, Washington.

SETZLER, FRANK M., and W. DUNCAN STRONG
1936. "Archaeology and Relief." *American Antiquity,* Vol. 1, No. 4, pp. 301–309, Menasha.

SHAPIRO, HARRY L.
1934. "Some Observations on the Origin of the Eskimo." *Proceedings of the Fifth Pacific Congress,* pp. 2723–2732, Toronto.

SHETRONE, HENRY C.
1920. "The Culture Problem in Ohio Archaeology." *American Anthropologist,* Vol. 22, No. 2, pp. 144–172, Lancaster.
1924. "Exploration of the Wright Group of Prehistoric Earthworks." *Ohio Archaeological and Historical Quarterly,* Vol. 33, pp. 341–358, Columbus.
1926. "Explorations of the Hopewell Group of Prehistoric Earthworks." *Ohio Archaeological and Historical Quarterly,* Vol. 35, No. 1, pp. 1–227, Columbus.
1928. "Some Ohio Caves and Rock Shelters Bearing Evidences of Human Occupancy." *Ohio Archaeological and Historical Quarterly,* Vol. 37, No. 1, pp. 1–34, Columbus.
1930. *The Mound Builders.* New York.
1936. "The Folsom Phenomena as Seen from Ohio." *The Ohio State Archaeological and Historical Quarterly,* Vol. 45, No. 3, pp. 240–256, Columbus.

SHETRONE, HENRY C., and EMERSON F. GREENMAN
1931. "Explorations of the Seip Group of Prehistoric Earthworks." *Ohio Archaeological and Historical Quarterly,* Vol. 40, No. 3, pp. 343–509, Columbus.

SHIPPEE, J. M.
1941. "Hopewellian and Middle Mississippi Remains from the Kansas City Area." *The Missouri Archaeologist,* Vol. 7, No. 2, pp. 28–32, Columbia.
1948. "Nebo Hill, a Lithic Complex in Western Missouri." *American Antiquity,* Vol. 14, No. 1, pp. 29–32, Menasha.

SIMPSON, J. CLARENCE
1936. "Report on the Activities in Hillsborough County." *Second Biennial Report to State Board of Conservation, Florida,* pp. 109–116, Tallahassee.
1948. "Folsom-like Points from Florida." *The Florida Anthropologist,* Vol. 1, Nos. 1–2, pp. 11–15, Gainesville.

SKARLAND, IVAR
1939. "The Skeletal Material." In *The Chiggerville Site, Site 1, Ohio County, Kentucky* by William S. Webb and William G. Haag, University of Kentucky Reports in Anthropology and Archaeology, Vol. 4, No. 1, pp. 28–49, Lexington.

SKINNER, ALANSON B.
1913. *Social Life and Ceremonial Bundles of the Menomini Indians.* Anthropological Papers of the American Museum of Natural History, Vol. 13, Pt. 1, New York.
1915. *Associations and Ceremonies of the Menomini Indians.* Anthropological Papers of the American Museum of Natural History, Vol. 13, Pt. 2, New York.
1921a. "Notes on Iroquois Archaeology." *Indian Notes*

and Monographs, Miscellaneous No. 18, Museum of the American Indian, Heye Foundation, New York.

1921*b*. "Material Culture of the Menomini." *Indian Notes and Monographs*, Miscellaneous No. 20, Museum of the American Indian, Heye Foundation, New York.

1925. *Observations on the Ethnology of the Sauk Indians*. Bulletin of the Public Museum of the City of Milwaukee, Vol. 5.

1927. *The Mascoutens or Prairie Potawatomie Indians*. Part III: *Mythology and Folklore*. Bulletin of the Public Museum of the City of Milwaukee, Vol. 6, No. 3.

SLATTERY, RICHARD G.

1946. "A Prehistoric Indian Site on Selden Island, Montgomery County, Maryland." *Journal of the Washington Academy of Sciences*, Vol. 36, No. 8, pp. 262–266, Menasha.

SMITH, CARLYLE S.

1950. *The Archaeology of Coastal New York*. Anthropological Papers of the American Museum of Natural History, Vol. 43, Pt. 2, New York.

SMITH, ELMER R.

1941. *The Archaeology of Deadman Cave, Utah*. Bulletin of the University of Utah, Vol. 32, No. 4, Salt Lake City.

SMITH, G. HUBERT

1939. "Excavating the Site of Old Fort Ridgely." *Minnesota History: A Quarterly Magazine*, Vol. 20, No. 2, pp. 146–155, St. Paul.

SMITH, HALE G.

1948*a*. "Two Historical Archaeological Periods in Florida." *American Antiquity*, Vol. 13, No. 4, pp. 313–319, Menasha.

1948*b*. "Results of an Archaeological Investigation of a Spanish Mission Site in Jefferson County, Florida." *The Florida Anthropologist*, Vol. 1, Nos. 1–2, pp. 1–10, Gainesville.

1949. *Two Archaeological Sites in Brevard County, Florida*. Florida Anthropological Society Publications, No. 1, Gainesville.

1951*a*. *The Crable Site, Fulton County, Illinois*. Anthropological Papers, No. 7, Museum of Anthropology, University of Michigan, Ann Arbor.

1951*b*. "Crystal River, Revisited, Revisited, Revisited." *American Antiquity*, Vol. 17, No. 2, pp. 143–144, Salt Lake City.

SMITH, HARLAN I.

1910. *The Prehistoric Ethnology of a Kentucky Site*. Anthropological Papers of the American Museum of Natural History, Vol. 6, Pt. 2, New York.

SMITHSONIAN INSTITUTION

1928–1932. Annual Reports of the Board of Regents. Washington.

1940. *Essays in Historical Anthropology of North America*. Smithsonian Miscellaneous Collections, Vol. 100, Washington.

SNODGRASS, JESSE

1894. "Carved Shell." *The Archaeologist*, Vol. 2, No. 4, pp. 114–115, Waterloo.

SNOW, CHARLES E.

1948. *Indian Knoll Skeletons of Site Oh2, Ohio County, Kentucky*. The University of Kentucky Reports in Anthropology, Vol. 4, No. 3, Pt. 2, Lexington.

SNYDER, J. F.

1898. "A Group of Illinois Nomads." *The Archaeologist*, Vol. 3, No. 3, pp. 77–81, Waterloo.

SPAULDING, ALBERT C.

1946. "Northeastern Archaeology and General Trends in the Northern Forest Zone." In *Man in Northeastern North America* (Frederick Johnson, ed.), Papers of the Robert S.

Peabody Foundation for Archaeology, Vol. 3, pp. 143–167, Andover.

SPECK, FRANK G.

1907*a*. "Some Outlines of Aboriginal Culture in the Southeastern States." *American Anthropologist*, Vol. 9, No. 2, pp. 287–295, Lancaster.

1907*b*. *The Creek Indians of Taskigi Town*. American Anthropological Association Memoir, Vol. 2, No. 2, Lancaster.

1909. *Ethnology of the Yuchi Indians*. Anthropological Publications, University Museum, University of Pennsylvania, Vol. 1, No. 1, Philadelphia.

1920. *Decorative Art and Basketry of the Cherokee*. Bulletin of the Public Museum of the City of Milwaukee, Vol. 2, No. 2.

1926. "Culture Problems in Northeastern North America." *Proceedings of the American Philosophical Society*, Vol. 65, No. 4, pp. 272–311, Philadelphia.

SPIER, LESLIE

1918. *The Trenton Argillite Culture*. Anthropological Papers of the American Museum of Natural History, Vol. 22, Pt. 4, New York.

1921. *The Sun Dance of the Plains Indians: Its Development and Diffusion*. Anthropological Papers of the American Museum of Natural History, Vol. 16, Pt. 7, New York.

SPOEHR, ALEXANDER

1941. *Camp, Clan, and Kin among the Cow Creek Seminole of Florida*. Field Museum of Natural History, Anthropological Series, Vol. 33, No. 1, Chicago.

1942. *Kinship System of the Seminole*. Field Museum of Natural History, Anthropological Series, Vol. 33, No. 2, Chicago.

1944. *The Florida Seminole Camp*. Field Museum of Natural History, Anthropological Series, Vol. 33, No. 3, Chicago.

1947. *Changing Kinship Systems*. Field Museum of Natural History, Anthropological Series, Vol. 33, No. 4, Chicago.

SQUIER, EPHRAIM G., and EDWIN H. DAVIS

1848. *Ancient Monuments of the Mississippi Valley*. Smithsonian Contributions to Knowledge, Vol. 1, Washington.

STATE HISTORICAL SOCIETY OF IOWA

1923. *Bulletin of Information*, No. 11, Iowa City.

STAUFFER, ALVIN P., and CHARLES W. PORTER

1943. "The National Park Service Program of Conservation for Areas and Structures of National Historical Significance." *Mississippi Valley Historical Review*, Vol. 30, No. 1, pp. 25–48.

STEARNS, RICHARD E.

1940. *The Hughes Site*. Proceedings of the Natural History Society of Maryland, No. 6, Baltimore.

STECK, FRANCIS-BORGIA

1928. *The Jolliet-Marquette Expedition, 1673*. Quincy.

STEVENS, EDWARD T.

1870. *Flint Chips*. London.

STEWARD, JOHN FLETCHER

1903. *Lost Maramech and Earliest Chicago*. Chicago.

STEWARD, JULIAN H.

1936. "The Economic and Social Basis of Primitive Bands." In *Essays in Anthropology Presented to A. L. Kroeber* (Robert H. Lowie, ed.), pp. 331–350, Berkeley.

1937*a*. "Ecological Aspects of Southwestern Society." *Anthropos*, Vol. 32, Nos. 1–2, pp. 87–104, St. Gabriel Mödling bei Wien.

1937*b*. *Ancient Caves of the Great Salt Lake Region*. Bureau of American Ethnology, Bulletin 116, Washington.

1938. *Basin-Plateau Aboriginal Sociopolitical Groups*.

Bureau of American Ethnology, Bulletin 120, Washington.

1942. "The Direct Historical Approach to Archeology." *American Antiquity*, Vol. 7, No. 4, pp. 337–343, Menasha.

STEWARD, JULIAN H., and FRANK M. SETZLER

1938. "Function and Configuration in Archaeology." *American Antiquity*, Vol. 4, No. 1, pp. 4–10, Menasha.

STEWART, T. DALE

1939a. *Anthropometric Observations on the Eskimos and Indians of Laborador.* Field Museum of Natural History, Anthropological Series, Vol. 31, No. 1, Chicago.

1939b. "Excavating the Indian Village of Patawomeke (Potomac)." *Explorations and Field-Work of the Smithsonian Institution in 1938*, pp. 87–90, Washington.

1940. "The Finding of an Indian Ossuary on the York River in Virginia." *Journal of the Washington Academy of Science*, Vol. 30, No. 8, pp. 356–364, Menasha.

1943. "Skeletal Remains from Platte and Clay Counties, Missouri." In *Archeological Investigations of Platte and Clay Counties, Missouri* by Waldo R. Wedel, United States National Museum Bulletin 183, pp. 245–273, Washington.

1946. *A Reexamination of the Fossil Human Skeletal Remains from Melbourne, Florida.* Smithsonian Miscellaneous Collections, Vol. 106, No. 10, Washington.

STEWART, T. DALE, and WALDO R. WEDEL

1937. "The Finding of Two Ossuaries on the Site of the Indian Village of Nacotchtanke (Anacostia)." *Journal of the Washington Academy of Science*, Vol. 27, No. 5, pp. 213–219, Menasha.

STIRLING, MATTHEW W.

1935. "Smithsonian Archeological Projects Conducted under the Federal Emergency Relief Administration, 1933–1934." *Annual Report of the Board of Regents of the Smithsonian Institution for 1934*, pp. 371–400, Washington.

1936. "Florida Cultural Affiliations in Relation to Adjacent Areas." In *Essays in Anthropology Presented to A. L. Kroeber*, (Robert H. Lowie, ed.), pp. 351–357, Berkeley.

1940. "The Historic Method as Applied to Southeastern Archeology." In *Essays in Historical Anthropology of North America*, Smithsonian Miscellaneous Collections, Vol. 100, pp. 117–123, Washington.

STRONG, W. DUNCAN

1930. "A Stone Culture from Northern Laborador and Its Relation to the Eskimo-like Cultures of the Northeast." *American Anthropologist*, Vol. 32, No. 1, pp. 126–144, Menasha.

1933. "Studying the Arikara and Their Neighbors on the Upper Missouri." *Explorations and Field-Work of the Smithsonian Institution in 1932*, pp. 73–76, Washington.

1935. *An Introduction to Nebraska Archeology.* Smithsonian Miscellaneous Collections, Vol. 93, No. 10, Washington.

1936. "Anthropological Theory and Archaeological Fact." In *Essays in Anthropology Presented to A. L. Kroeber* (Robert H. Lowie, ed.), pp. 359–370, Berkeley.

1940. "From History to Prehistory in the Northern Great Plains." In *Essays in Historical Anthropology of North America*, Smithsonian Miscellaneous Collections, Vol. 100, pp. 353–394, Washington.

1943. *Cross Sections of New World Prehistory.* Smithsonian Miscellaneous Collections, Vol. 104, No. 2, Washington.

STUART, JAMES

1876. "The Yellowstone Expedition of 1863. (From the Journal of Captain James Stuart, with Notes by Samuel T. Hauser and Granville Stuart)." *Contributions to the Historical Society of Montana*, Vol. 1, pp. 149–233, Helena.

SULLIVAN, LOUIS R.

1920. *Anthropometry of the Siouan Tribes.* Anthropological Papers of the American Museum of Natural History, Vol. 23, Pt. 3, New York.

SWALLOW, G. C.

1875. "Abstract of Report." *Eighth Annual Report of the Trustees of the Peabody Museum of American Archeology and Ethnology*, Vol. 1, No. 8, pp. 17–18, 28, 45–46, Cambridge.

SWANTON, JOHN R.

1911. *Indian Tribes of the Lower Mississippi Valley and Adjacent Coast of the Gulf of Mexico.* Bureau of American Ethnology, Bulletin 43, Washington.

1922. *Early History of the Creek Indians and Their Neighbors.* Bureau of American Ethnology, Bulletin 73, Washington.

1928a. "Social Organization and Social Usages of the Indians of the Creek Confederacy." *Forty-second Annual Report, Bureau of American Ethnology, 1924–1925*, pp. 23–472, Washington.

1928b. "Religious Beliefs and Medical Practices of the Creek Indians." *Forty-second Annual Report, Bureau of American Ethnology, 1924–1925*, pp. 473–672, Washington.

1928c. "Aboriginal Culture of the Southeast." *Forty-second Annual Report, Bureau of American Ethnology, 1924–1925*, pp. 673–726, Washington.

1928d. "Social and Religious Beliefs and Usages of the Chickasaw Indians." *Forty-fourth Annual Report, Bureau of American Ethnology, 1926–1927*, pp. 169–273, Washington.

1930. "Some Neglected Data Bearing on Cheyenne, Chippewa, and Dakota History." *American Anthropologist*, Vol. 32, No. 1, pp. 156–160, Menasha.

1935. "Notes on the Cultural Provinces of the Southeast." *American Anthropologist*, Vol. 37, No. 3, pp. 373–385, Menasha.

1940. "The First Description of an Indian Tribe in the Territory of the Present United States." In *Studies for William A. Read* (Nathaniel M. Caffee and Thomas A. Kirby, eds.), pp. 326–338, Baton Rouge.

1942. *Source Material on the History and Ethnology of the Caddo Indians.* Bureau of American Ethnology, Bulletin 132, Washington.

1946. *The Indians of the Southeastern United States.* Bureau of American Ethnology, Bulletin 137, Washington.

SWANTON, JOHN R., editor

1939. *Final Report of the United States De Soto Expedition Commission.* House Document 71, 76th Congress, 1st Session, Washington.

SWAUGER, JAMES L.

1940. "A Review of F. H. Gerrodette's Notes on the Excavation of the McKees Rock Mound." *The Pennsylvania Archaeologist*, Vol. 10, No. 1, pp. 8–10, Milton.

TAITT, DAVID

1772. "Journal of David Taitt's Travels from Pensacola, West Florida, to and through the Country of the Upper and Lower Creeks, 1772." *See* Mereness, Newton D. (ed.), *Travels in the American Colonies*, pp. 493–565, New York.

TAYLOR, WALTER W.

1948. *A Study of Archaeology.* American Anthropological Association, Memoir 69, Menasha.

TEIT, JAMES A.

1930. "The Salishan Tribes of the Western Plateaus." *Forty-fifth Annual Report, Bureau of American Ethnology, 1927–1928*, pp. 23–396, Washington.

THOMAS, C. JOE

1938. "Bluff Shelters of Union County." *Transactions of*

the *Illinois State Academy of Science,* Vol. 31, No. 2, pp. 77–78, Springfield.

THOMAS, CYRUS
1887. "Burial Mounds of the Northern Sections of the United States." *Fifth Annual Report, Bureau of American Ethnology, 1883–1884,* pp. 3–119, Washington.
1894. "Report on the Mound Explorations of the Bureau of American Ethnology." *Twelfth Annual Report, Bureau of American Ethnology, 1890–1891,* pp. 3–730, Washington.
1898. *Introduction to the Study of North American Archaeology.* Cincinnati.

THRUSTON, GATES P.
1890. *The Antiquities of Tennessee.* Cincinnati.

THWAITES, REUBEN GOLD, editor
1896–1901. *The Jesuit Relations and Allied Documents.* 73 volumes, Cleveland.
1906. *Travels in the Interior of North America* by Maximilian, Prince of Weid. In *Early Western Travels, 1784–1846,* Vol. 23, Cleveland.

TIMBERLAKE, HENRY
1765. *Memoirs of Lieutenant Timberlake.* London.

TITTERINGTON, PAUL F.
1933. "The Cahokia Mound Group and Its Surface Material." *The Wisconsin Archeologist,* Vol. 13, No. 1, pp. 7–14, Milwaukee.
1935. "Certain Bluff Mounds of Western Jersey County, Illinois." *American Antiquity,* Vol. 1, No. 1, pp. 6–46, Menasha.
1938. *The Cahokia Mound Group and Its Village Site Materials.* St. Louis.
1940. "Outline of Cultural Traits of the Jersey County, Illinois, Bluff Focus." *Bulletin of the Illinois State Archaeological Society,* Vol. 3, No. 1, pp. 15–22.
1942. "The Jersey County, Illinois, Bluff Focus." *American Antiquity,* Vol. 9, No. 2, pp. 240–245, Menasha.
1950. "Some Non-pottery Sites in St. Louis Area." *Illinois State Archaeological Society,* n.s., Vol. 1, No. 1, pp. 19–30.

TREE-RING BULLETIN
1934–1946. Vols. 1–12. The Tree-Ring Society, Tucson.

THE VALENTINE MUSEUM
1898. *The Valentine Museum.* Richmond.

VOEGELIN, CARL F.
1941. "Internal Relationships of Siouan Languages." *American Anthropologist,* Vol. 43, No. 2, pp. 246–249, Menasha.

VOEGELIN, CARL F., and ERMINIE W. VOEGELIN
1946. "Linguistic Considerations of Northeastern North America." In *Man in Northeastern North America* (Frederick Johnson, ed.), Papers of the Robert S. Peabody Foundation for Archaeology, Vol. 3, pp. 179–194, Andover.

VON BONIN, GERHARDT, and G. M. MORANT
1938. "Indian Races in the United States. A Survey of Previously Published Cranial Measurements." *Biometrika,* Vol. 30, Pts. 1 and 2, pp. 94–129, London.

VON EICKSTEDT, EGON
1934. *Rassenkunde und Rassengeschichte der Menschheit.* Stuttgart.

WALKER, S. T.
1880a. "Preliminary Explorations among the Indian Mounds in Southern Florida." *Annual Report of the Board of Regents of the Smithsonian Institution for 1879,* pp. 392–413, Washington.
1880b. "Report on the Shell Heaps of Tampa Bay, Florida." *Annual Report of the Board of Regents of the Smithsonian Institution for 1879,* pp. 413–422, Washington.

WALKER, WINSLOW M.
1935. *A Caddo Burial at Natchitoches, Louisiana.* Smithsonian Miscellaneous Collections, Vol. 94, No. 14, Washington.
1936. *The Troyville Mounds, Catahoula Parish, Louisiana.* Bureau of American Ethnology, Bulletin 113, Washington.
n.d. Field Notes on the Dickinson Mounds Near Rome, Illinois.

WALKER, WINSLOW M., and ROBERT McCORMICK ADAMS
1946. "Excavations in the Matthews Site, New Madrid County, Missouri." *Transactions of the Academy of Science of St. Louis,* Vol. 31, No. 4, pp. 75–120.

WALLIS, WILSON D.
1947. *The Canadian Dakota.* Anthropological Papers of the American Museum of Natural History, Vol. 41, Pt. 1, New York.

WARING, ANTONIO J., JR.
1945a. "The De Luna Expedition and Southeastern Ceremonial." *American Antiquity,* Vol. 11, No. 1, pp. 57–58, Menasha.
1945b. "Hopewellian Elements in Northern Georgia." *American Antiquity,* Vol. 11, No. 2, pp. 119–120, Menasha.
n.d. "The Bilbo Site." Unpublished manuscript.

WARING, ANTONIO J., JR., and PRESTON HOLDER
1945. "A Prehistoric Ceremonial Complex in the Southeastern United States." *American Anthropologist,* Vol. 47, No. 1, pp. 1–34, Menasha.

WAUCHOPE, ROBERT
1939. "Fluted Points from South Carolina." *American Antiquity,* Vol. 4, No. 4, pp. 344–346, Menasha.

WEBB, CLARENCE H.
1944. "Stone Vessels from a Northeast Louisiana Site." *American Antiquity,* Vol. 9, No. 4, pp. 386–394, Menasha.
1945. "A Second Historic Caddo Site at Natchitoches, Louisiana." *Bulletin of the Texas Archaeological and Paleontological Society,* Vol. 16, pp. 52–83, Abilene.
1946. "Two Unusual Types of Chipped Stone Artifacts from Northwest Louisiana." *Bulletin of the Texas Archaeological and Paleontological Society,* Vol. 17, pp. 9–17, Abilene.
1948. "Evidences of Pre-Pottery Cultures in Louisiana." *American Antiquity,* Vol. 13, No. 3, pp. 227–231, Menasha.

WEBB, CLARENCE H., and MONROE DODD, JR.
1939. "Further Excavations of the Gahagan Mound; Connections with a Florida Culture." *Bulletin of the Texas Archaeological and Paleontological Society,* Vol. 11, pp. 92–127, Abilene.
1941. "Pottery Types from the Belcher Mount Site." *Bulletin of the Texas Archaeological and Paleontological Society,* Vol. 13, pp. 89–116, Abilene.

WEBB, WILLIAM S.
1938. *An Archeological Survey of the Norris Basin in Eastern Tennessee.* Bureau of American Ethnology, Bulletin 118, Washington.
1939. *An Archeological Survey of Wheeler Basin on the Tennessee River in Northern Alabama.* Bureau of American Ethnology, Bulletin 122, Washington.
1940. *The Wright Mounds: Sites 6 and 7, Montgomery County, Kentucky.* The University of Kentucky Reports in Anthropology, Vol. 5, No. 1, Lexington.
1941. *Mt. Horeb Earthworks, Site 1, and the Drake Mound, Site 11, Fayette County, Kentucky.* The University of Kentucky Reports in Anthropology and Archaeology, Vol. 5, No. 2, Lexington.
1942. *The C. and O. Mounds at Paintsville, Sites JO 2 and JO 9, Johnson County, Kentucky.* The University of

Kentucky Reports in Anthropology and Archaeology, Vol. 5, No. 4, Lexington.

1946. *Indian Knoll, Site Oh 2, Ohio County, Kentucky.* The University of Kentucky Reports in Anthropology and Archaeology, Vol. 4, No. 3, Pt. 1, Lexington.

1950. *The Carlson Annis Mound, Site 5, Butler County, Kentucky.* University of Kentucky Reports in Anthropology, Vol. 7, No. 4, Lexington.

WEBB, WILLIAM S., and DAVID L. DEJARNETTE
1942. *An Archeological Survey of Pickwick Basin in the Adjacent Portions of the States of Alabama, Mississippi and Tennessee.* Bureau of American Ethnology, Bulletin 129, Washington.

WEBB, WILLIAM S., and W. D. FUNKHOUSER
1933. *The McLeod Bluff Site in Hickman County, Kentucky.* The University of Kentucky Reports in Archaeology and Anthropology, Vol. 3, No. 1, Lexington.

1934. *The Occurrence of the Fossil Remains of Pleistocene Vertebrates in the Caves of Barren County, Kentucky.* The University of Kentucky Reports in Archaeology and Anthropology, Vol. 3, No. 2, Lexington.

WEBB, WILLIAM S., and WILLIAM G. HAAG
1939. *The Chiggerville Site, Site 1, Ohio County, Kentucky.* The University of Kentucky Reports in Anthropology, Vol. 4, No. 1, Lexington.

1940. *Cypress Creek Village Sites 11 and 12, McLean County, Kentucky.* The University of Kentucky Reports in Anthropology, Vol. 4, No. 2, Lexington.

1947a. *Archaic Sites in McLean County, Kentucky.* The University of Kentucky Reports in Anthropology, Vol. 7, No. 1, Lexington.

1947b. *The Fisher Site, Fayette County, Kentucky.* The University of Kentucky Reports in Anthropology, Vol. 7, No. 2, Lexington.

WEBB, WILLIAM S., and CHARLES E. SNOW
1945. *The Adena People.* The University of Kentucky Reports in Anthropology and Archaeology, Vol. 6, Lexington.

WEDEL, WALDO R.
1936. *An Introduction to Pawnee Archeology.* Bureau of American Ethnology, Bulletin 112, Washington.

1938. *The Direct-Historical Approach in Pawnee Archeology.* Smithsonian Miscellaneous Collections, Vol. 97, No. 7, Washington.

1940. "Culture Sequence in the Central Great Plains." In *Essays in Historical Anthropology of North America,* Smithsonian Miscellaneous Collections, Vol. 100, pp. 291–352, Washington.

1942. *Archeological Remains in Central Kansas and Their Possible Bearing on the Location of Quivira.* Smithsonian Miscellaneous Collections, Vol. 101, No. 7, Washington.

1943. *Archeological Investigations in Platte and Clay Counties, Missouri.* U.S. National Museum Bulletin 183, Washington.

1947. "Culture Chronology in the Central Great Plains." *American Antiquity,* Vol. 12, No. 3, pp. 148–156, Menasha.

WEIDENREICH, FRANZ
1939. "On the Earliest Representatives of Modern Mankind Recovered on the Soil of East Asia." *Peking Natural History Bulletin,* Vol. 13, No. 3, pp. 161–180.

WESLAGER, C. A.
1942. "Ossuaries on the Delmarva Peninsula and Exotic Influences in the Coastal Aspect of the Woodland Period." *American Antiquity,* Vol. 8, No. 2, pp. 141–151, Menasha.

WEST, GEORGE A.
1905. "The Aboriginal Pipes of Wisconsin." *The Wis-*

consin Archeologist, old series, Vol. 4, Nos. 3–4, pp. 47–171, Milwaukee.

1934. *Tobacco, Pipes and Smoking Customs of the American Indians.* Bulletin of the Public Museum of the City of Milwaukee, Vol. 17.

WHITEFORD, ANDREW H.
1947. "Description for Artifact Analysis." *American Antiquity,* Vol. 12, No. 4, pp. 226–239, Menasha.

WHITTLESEY, CHARLES
1871. *Ancient Earth Forts of the Cuyahoga Valley, Ohio.* Western Reserve and Northern Ohio Historical Society, Tract 5, Cleveland.

WILFORD, LLOYD A.
1941. "A Tentative Classification of the Prehistoric Cultures of Minnesota." *American Antiquity,* Vol. 6, No. 3, pp. 231–249, Menasha.

1942. "Minnesota Archaeology: Current Explorations and Concepts." *Proceedings of the Minnesota Academy of Science,* Vol. 10, pp. 20–26.

1944. "The Prehistoric Indians of Minnesota: The Mille Lacs Aspect." *Minnesota History: A Quarterly Magazine,* Vol. 25, No. 4, pp. 329–341, St. Paul.

1945a. "The Prehistoric Indians of Minnesota: The Headwaters Lakes Aspect." *Minnesota History: A Quarterly Magazine,* Vol. 26, No. 4, pp. 312–329, St. Paul.

1945b. "Three Villages of the Mississippi Pattern in Minnesota." *American Antiquity,* Vol. 11, No. 1, pp. 32–40. Menasha.

WILL, GEORGE F.
1924. *Archaeology of the Missouri Valley.* Anthropological Papers of the American Museum of Natural History, Vol. 22, Pt. 6, New York.

1933. "A Resumé of North Dakota Archaeology." *North Dakota Historical Quarterly,* Vol. 7, Nos. 2–3, pp. 150–161, Bismarck.

1946. *Tree Ring Studies in North Dakota.* North Dakota Agricultural College, Bulletin 338, Fargo.

WILL, GEORGE F., and THAD C. HECKER
1944. "Upper Missouri River Valley Aboriginal Culture in North Dakota." *North Dakota Historical Quarterly,* Vol. 11, Nos. 1–2, pp. 5–126, Bismarck.

WILL, GEORGE F., and HERBERT J. SPINDEN
1906. *The Mandans.* Papers of the Peabody Museum of American Archaeology and Ethnology, Vol. 3, No. 4, Cambridge.

WILLEY, GORDON R.
1939. "Ceramic Stratigraphy in a Georgia Village Site." *American Antiquity,* Vol. 5, No. 2, pp. 140–147, Menasha.

1945. "The Weeden Island Culture: A Preliminary Definition." *American Antiquity,* Vol. 10, No. 3, pp. 225–254, Menasha.

1948a. "Culture Sequence in the Manatee Region of the Florida West Coast." *American Antiquity,* Vol. 13, No. 3, pp. 209–218, Menasha.

1948b. "The Cultural Context of the Crystal River Negative Painted Style." *American Antiquity,* Vol. 13, No. 4, pp. 325–328, Menasha.

1949a. *Excavations in Southeast Florida.* Yale University Publications in Anthropology, No. 42, New Haven.

1949b. *Archaeology of the Florida Gulf Coast.* Smithsonian Miscellaneous Collections, Vol. 113, Washington.

WILLEY, GORDON R., and PHILIP PHILLIPS
1944. "Negative Painted Pottery from Crystal River, Florida." *American Antiquity,* Vol. 10, No. 2, pp. 173–185, Menasha.

WILLEY, GORDON R., and RICHARD W. WOODBURY
1942. "A Chronological Outline for the Northwest Flor-

ida Coast." *American Antiquity,* Vol. 7, No. 3, pp. 232–254, Menasha

WILLIAMS, SAMUEL C.
1930. *Adair's History of the American Indians.* Johnson City.

WILLIS, ROGER K.
1941. "The Baumer Focus," *Society for American Archaeology* Notebook, Vol. 2, No. 2, p. 28. Mimeographed.

WILLOUGHBY, CHARLES C.
1932. "Notes on the History and Symbolism of the Muskhogeans and the People of Etowah." In *Etowah Papers* (Warren K. Moorehead, ed.), No. 2, pp. 7–66, New Haven.
1935. *Antiquities of the New England Indians.* Cambridge.

WILLOUGHBY, CHARLES C., and EARNEST A. HOOTON
1922. *The Turner Group of Earthworks, Hamilton County, Ohio.* Papers of the Peabody Museum of Archaeology and Ethnology, Vol. 8, No. 3, Cambridge.

WIMBERLY, STEVE B.
n.d.*a.* "Archaeological Investigations in the Mobile Bay Region, Southern Alabama." Unpublished manuscript.
n.d.*b.* "Archaeological Investigations in Clarke County, Southern Alabama." Unpublished manuscript.

WIMBERLY, STEVE B., and HARRY A. TOURTELOT
1941. *The McQuorquodale Mound: A Manifestation of the Hopewellian Phase in South Alabama.* Geological Survey of Alabama, Museum Paper No. 19, University, Alabama.

WINCHELL, N. H.
1878. "Primitive Man at Little Falls." *The Geological and Natural History Survey of Minnesota, Sixth Annual Report,* pp. 53–64, Minneapolis.

WINCHELL, N. H., editor
1911. *The Aborigines of Minnesota.* Minnesota Historical Society, St. Paul.

WINSHIP, GEORGE P.
1896. "The Coronado Expedition, 1540–1542." *Fourteenth Annual Report, Bureau of American Ethnology, 1892–1893,* Pt. 1, pp. 329–613, Washington.

WINSHIP, GEORGE P., editor
1904. *The Journey of Coronado, 1540–1542. . . . As Told by Himself and His Followers.* New York.

WINSOR, JUSTIN
1895. *The Missippi Basin.* Boston and New York.

WINTEMBERG, WILLIAM J.
1928. *Uren Prehistoric Village Site, Oxford County, Ontario.* National Museum of Canada, Bulletin No. 51, Anthropological Series, No. 10, Ottawa.
1936. *Roebuck Prehistoric Village Site, Greenville County, Ontario.* National Museum of Canada, Bulletin No. 83, Anthropological Series, No. 19, Ottawa.
1939. *Lawson Prehistoric Village Site, Middlesex County, Ontario.* National Museum of Canada, Bulletin No. 94, Anthropological Series, No. 25, Ottawa.
1946. "The Sidey-Mackay Village Site." *American Antiquity,* Vol. 11, No. 3, pp. 155–182, Menasha.
1948. *The Middleport Prehistoric Village Site.* National Museum of Canada, Bulletin No. 109, Anthropological Series, No. 27, Ottawa.

WISSLER, CLARK
1907. "Diffusion of Culture in the Plains of North America." *Proceedings of the Fifteenth International Congress of Americanists,* pp. 39–52, Quebec.
1910. *Material Culture of the Blackfoot Indians.* Anthropological Papers of the American Museum of Natural History, Vol. 5, Pt. 1, New York.
1914. "Material Cultures of the North American Indians." *American Anthropologist,* Vol. 16, No. 3, pp. 447–505, Lancaster.
1920. *North American Indians of the Plains.* American Museum of Natural History, Handbook Series No. 1, second edition, New York.
1922. *The American Indian.* Second edition, New York.
1926. *The Relation of Nature to Man in Aboriginal America.* New York.
1927. *North American Indians of the Plains.* American Museum of Natural History, Handbook Series No. 1, third edition, New York.
1938. *The American Indian.* Third edition, New York.

WITTHOFT, JOHN
1947. "Smooth-base Projectile Points from Eastern Pennsylvania." *The Pennsylvania Archaeologist,* Vol. 16, No. 4, pp. 123–130, Milton.

WOOD, E. F.
1936. "A Central Basin Manifestation in Eastern Wisconsin." *American Antiquity,* Vol. 1, No. 3, pp. 215–219, Menasha.

WOODBURY, GEORGE
1937. *Notes on Some Skeletal Remains of Texas.* The University of Texas Bulletin, No. 3734, Austin.

WORMINGTON, HELEN M.
1949. *Ancient Man in North America.* Denver Museum of Natural History, Popular Series, No. 4, third edition. Denver.

WRAY, DONALD E.
n.d.*a.* "The Weaver Site." Unpublished manuscript.
n.d.*b.* "The Swords Site." Unpublished manuscript.

WRAY, DONALD E., and HALE G. SMITH
1944. "An Hypothesis for the Identification of the Illinois Confederacy with the Middle Mississippi Culture in Illinois." *American Antquity,* Vol. 10, No. 1, pp. 23–27, Menasha.

WREN, CHRISTOPHER
1914. "A Study of North Appalachian Indian Pottery." *Proceedings and Collections of the Wyoming Historical and Geological Society,* Vol. 13, pp. 131–221, Wilkes-Barre.

WYMAN, JEFFRIES
1875. *Fresh-Water Shellmounds of the St. Johns River, Florida.* Memoirs of the Peabody Academy of Science, Vol. 1, No. 4, Salem.

ZEUNER, FREDERICK E.
1946. *Dating the Past: An Introduction to Geochronology.* London.

ILLUSTRATIONS

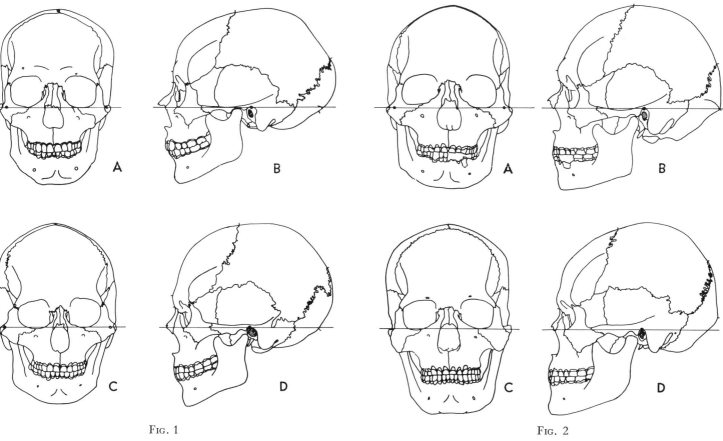

Fig. 1

A–B. Front and side views of an Ashiwid Variety Basket-Maker
C–D. Front and side views of an Iswanid Variety from a Kentucky
Archaic site

Fig. 2

A–B. Front and side view of the Lenapid Variety from the Fort
Ancient Aspect, Ohio
C–D. Front and side view of the Walcolid Variety from the Spoon
River Focus, Illinois

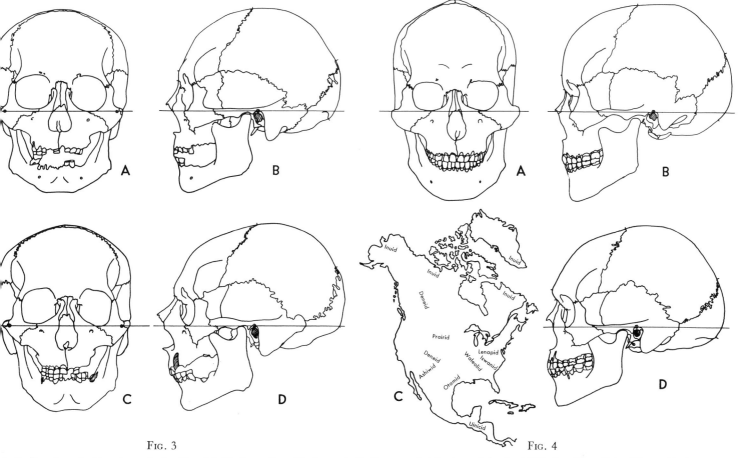

Fig. 3

A–B. Front and side view of the Deneid Variety, San Carlos
Apache
C–D. Front and side view of the Lakotid Variety, Brule Dakota

Fig. 4

A–B. Front and side view of the Inuid Variety from Point Hope, Alaska
C. Map of North America with the distribution of Indian varieties
D. Early Woodland skull with Otamid contours from Fulton County, Illinois

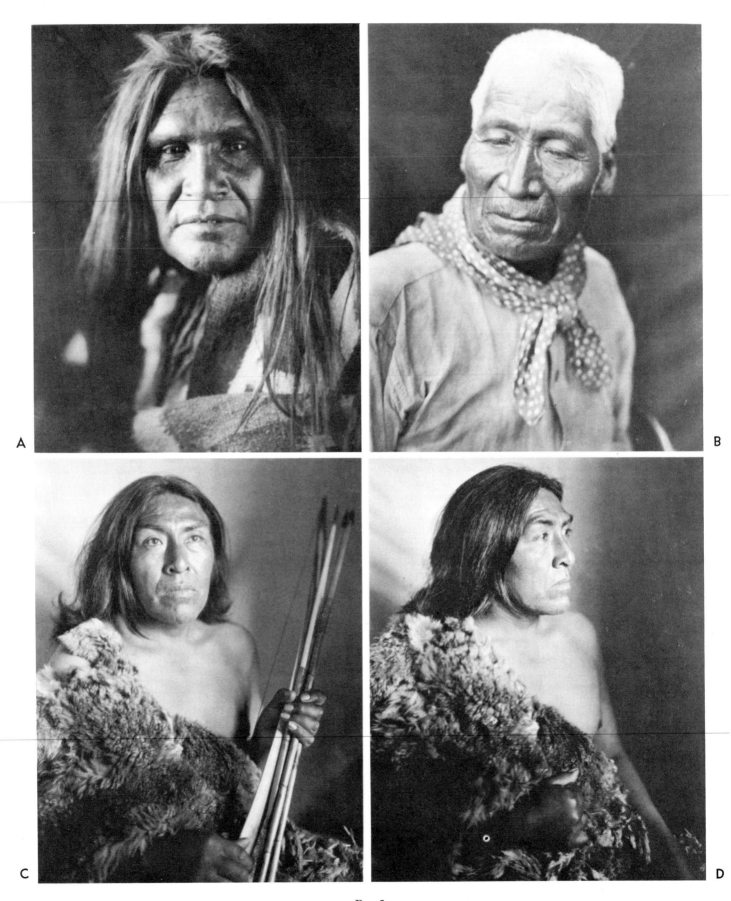

Fig. 5

A. Mohave   *B.* Papago   *C–D.* Southern Yana

Fig. 6

A. Ashiwid Variety from Acoma
B. Ashiwid Variety from Cahuila (California)

C. A Catawba representative of the Iswanid Variety
D. Inuid Variety, Cape Wales Eskimo

FIG. 7

A. An Assiniboine of the Lenapid Variety   C. Wind River Shoshone of the Lakotid Variety
B. A Seneca of the Lenapid Variety   D. Gros Ventre of the Lakotid Variety

FIG. 8

A. Salt River Arizona representative of the Walcolid Variety   C. A Hopi Walcolid

B. A Chickasaw Walcolid   D. A Choctaw of the Uinicid Variety

Fig. 9.—Representatives of the Deneid Variety from different tribal groups

A. White Mountain Apache   *B.* Uncompahgre Ute   *C.* Klamath   *D.* Navajo

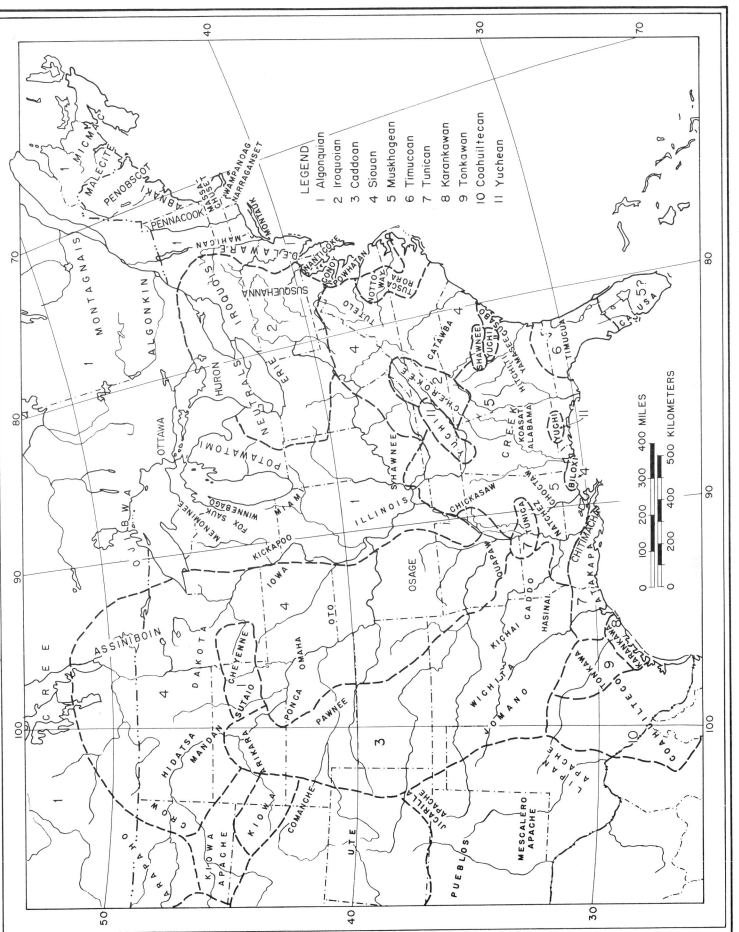

FIG. 10.—Tribes and linguistic stocks in the eastern United States *ca.* A.D. 1700 (after Swanton)

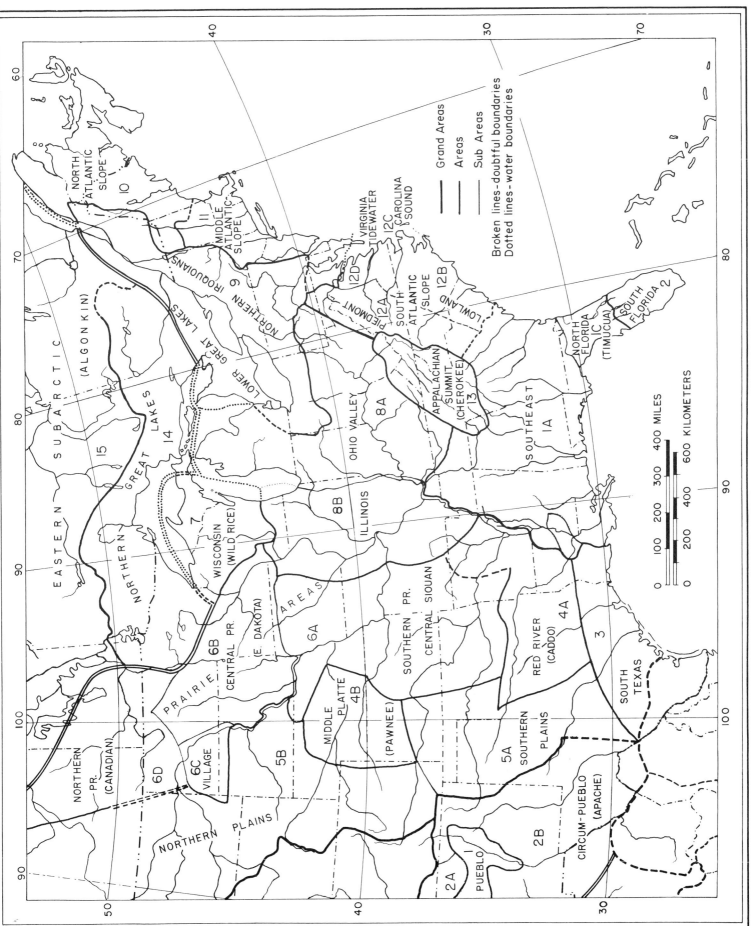

Fig. 11.—Culture areas in the eastern United States (after Kroeber)

Fig. 12.—Lamoka Focus artifacts (drawn from artifacts at the Rochester Museum from the Lamoka Lake site)

A. Narrow, side-notched projectile point
B. Narrow-stemmed projectile point
C. Large narrow-stemmed, expanding based projectile point
D. Expanding based, side-notched drill
E. Side-notched based drill
F. Expanding based drill
G. Straight based drill
H. Ovate knife
I. Lanceolate, convex-based knife
J. Triangular celt ($\frac{1}{2}$ actual size)
K. Rectangular celt ($\frac{1}{2}$ actual size)
L. Rectangular, plano-convex adz ($\frac{1}{2}$ actual size)
M. Beveled adz ($\frac{1}{2}$ actual size)
N. Plano-convex scraper ($\frac{1}{2}$ actual size)
O. Rectangular chopper ($\frac{1}{2}$ actual size)
P. Antler punch
Q. Dagger segment
R. Deer ulna awl
S. Deer radius awl
T. Deer metapodial awl
U. Polished turkey bone awl
V. Polished splinter awl
W. Perforated, polished splinter awl
X. Segment of a polished bone dagger
Y–Z. Double-pointed pins
A'. Perforated deer styliform (plume-holders)
B'. Splinter bone awl or projectile point with a notched base
C'. Splinter bone awl or projectile point with engraved edges
D'. Bone fishhook
E'. Pointed bone whistle
F'. Reworked notched objects with the ends blunt
G'. Pointed, chisel-like objects with notched edges
H'. Flaker from long-bone section with chipped edges
I'. Bone weaving tool
J'. Pronghorn antler objects (trap sticks)
K'. Whistle(?) with single perforation
L'. Tubular bird-bone beads
M'. Deer scapula scraper

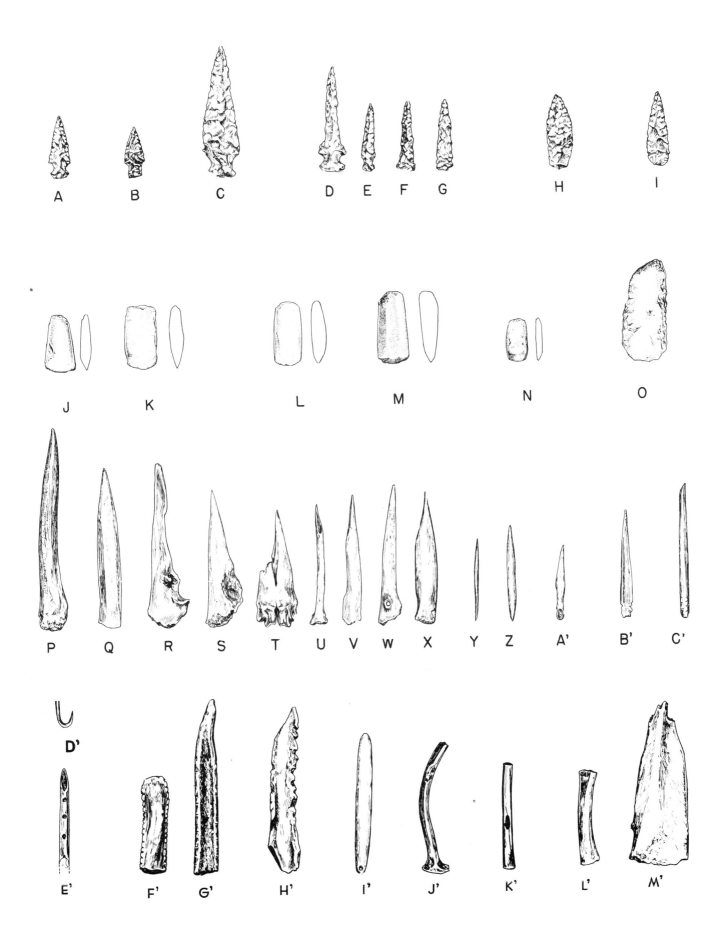

A　B　C　D　E　F　G　H　I

J　K　L　M　N　O

P　Q　R　S　T　U　V　W　X　Y　Z　A'　B'　C'

D'

E'　F'　G'　H'　I'　J'　K'　L'　M'

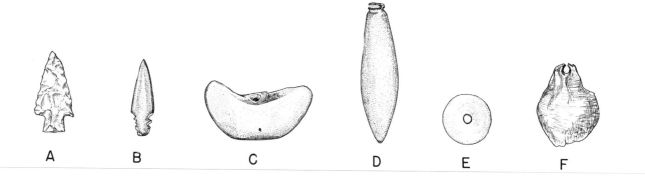

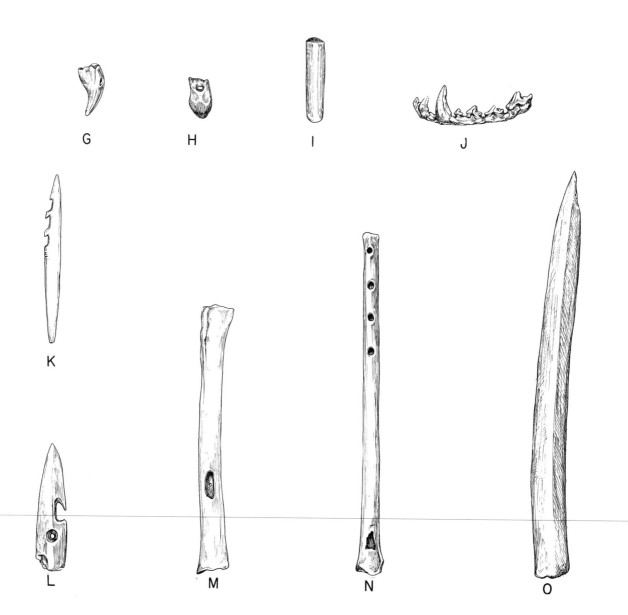

Fig. 13.—Frontenac Focus artifacts (from material in the Rochester Museum from the Frontenac Island site)

A. Narrow-stemmed projectile point
B. Ground slate projectile point
C. Crescentic bannerstone
D. Elongated plummets with grooved base
E. Conch-shell pendant

F. Piriform conch-shell pendant
G. Canine of immature bear, perforated through interior wall
H. Perforated elk canine bead
I. Antler flaker
J. Cut wolf mandible

K. Harpoon with multi-unilateral barbs
L. Harpoon with single barb and single line hole
M. Whistle with single perforation
N. Whistle with multiple perforations
O. Bone dagger

Fig. 14.—Brewerton Focus (from material in the Rochester Museum from the Oberlander and Robinson sites)

A–F. Broad, side-notched projectile points
  G. Corner-notched projectile point
  H. Narrow, side-notched point
  I. Round-based corner-notched point
J–K. T-shaped based drills
  L. Drill or graver based on rough spalls
  M. Triangular point with a straight base
N–O. Flake knives
  P. Crescentic chipped chopper
  Q. Straight-stemmed end or thumbnail scraper
  R. Side-notched end or thumbnail scraper
  S. Oval chopper
  T. Amygdaloid chopper
  U. Rectangular chopper
  V. Copper gouge
  W. Copper celt
  X. Copper pin
  Y. Short, broad gouge
  Z. Rectangular bannerstone
  A'. Bone projectile point
  B'. Short bone needles
  C'. Conical antler projectile points
  D'. Split beaver-tooth cutting tool
  E'. Beaver-tooth gouge or scraper
  F'. Long, narrow gouge

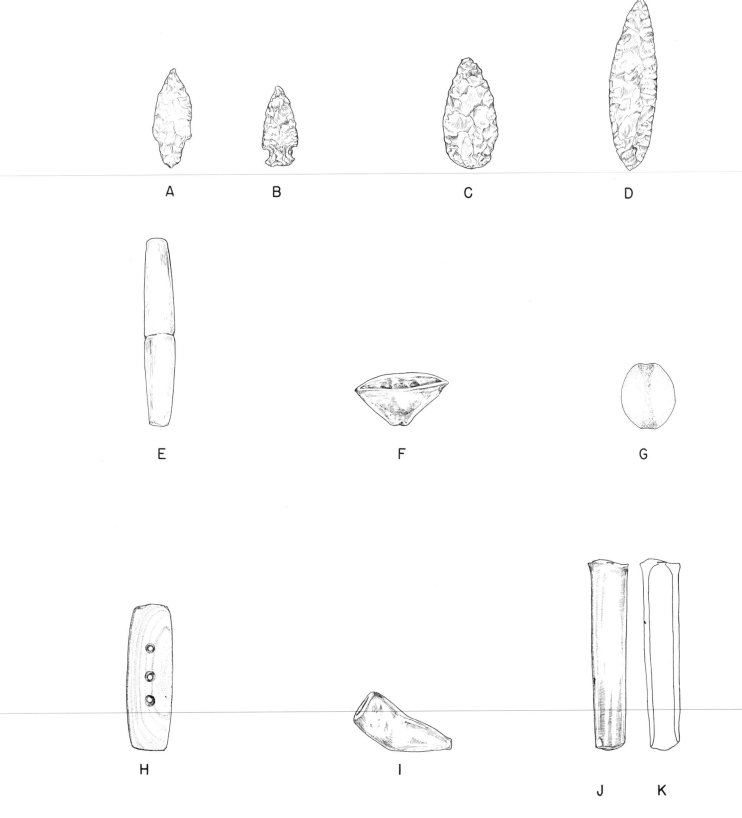

Fig. 15.—Middlesex Focus (artifacts selected from the collections of the Rochester Museum)

A. Contracting stemmed projectile point
B. Corner-notched projectile point
C. Fine cache blade
D. Ovate chipped knife

E. Plano-convex bar amulet (atlatl weight?)
F. Double perforated boatstone (atlatl weight?)

G. Grooved bola stone
H. Rectangular gorget
I. Obtuse-angle elbow clay pipe
J. Blocked-end stone tube pipe
K. Cross-section of blocked-end pipe

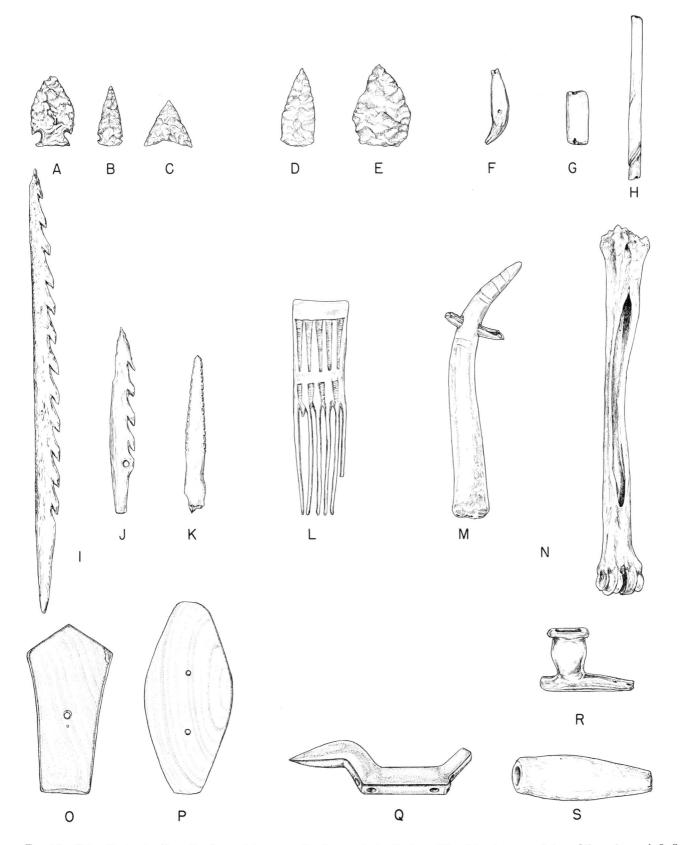

FIG. 16.—Point Peninsula (from Rochester Museum collections, principally from Kipp Island, except *L* from Wray site and *O–S* from various sites in western New York State).

A. Corner-notched projectile point
B. Side-notched projectile point
C. Isosceles, broad-based projectile point (only Late Point Peninsula)
D. Thin cache blade (Early Point Peninsula)
E. Crude, thick cache blade (Late Point Peninsula)
F. Perforated bear-canine pendant

G. Short columella bead
H. Long columella bead
I. Multi-unilateral barbed harpoon (Late Point Peninsula)
J. Multi-unilateral barbed harpoon with line hole (Late Point Peninsula)
K. Multi-bilateral barbed harpoon or dentate stamping tool (Late Point Peninsula)

L. Bone comb (Late Point Peninsula)
M. Antler-hafted beaver incisor for scraping
N. Bone beamer
O. Pentagonal polished-stone pendant
P. Polished-stone gorget
Q. Birdstone (atlatl weight)
R. Stone platform pipe
S. Clay tube pipe

Fig. 17.—Owasco and Point Peninsula pottery types

A. *Bainbridge Linear* (a Late Owasco type from the Bainbridge site; see Ritchie, 1944, Pl. 16, No. 2). Decoration on the collar is linear punctate, at the base of the collar cord-wrapped stick, on the neck incising, while the body is check-stamped.

B. *Bainbridge Incised Neck* (a Late Owasco type from the Castle Creek site, in the Broome County Historical Society Collection at Binghampton, N.Y.). Collar decoration is cord-wrapped stick, neck decoration is incised, shoulder decoration is oblique cord-wrapped-stick impressions, and bodies are check-stamped.

C. *Castle Creek Punctate* (reconstructed from sherds at the Castle Creek site; see Ritchie, 1944, Pl. 21, No. 5). Collar decoration is of tube-impressed punctate, neck is incised, shoulder decoration is cord-wrapped-stick decoration, and the body is finished by cord-wrapped paddling.

D. *Castle Creek Beaded* (Late Owasco type from the Castle Creek site; see Ritchie, 1944, Pl. 12). Oblique cord-wrapped-stick decoration above and below the beaded rim, incised neck decorations, oblique cord-wrapped-stick impressions on the shoulder, and a check-stamped body decoration.

E. *Castle Creek Incised* (from the Castle Creek site, in the Broome County Historical Society Collection at Binghamton, N.Y.). Oblique cord-wrapped-stick impressions on the rim, incised line on the neck, oblique cord-wrapped-stick on the shoulder, and cord-marked body.

F. *Bainbridge Notched Lip* (reconstructed from sherds in the Rochester Museum collections from the Bainbridge site). A Late Owasco type having incised decorations on a flattened, Outflared lip with herringbone linear punctate on the body and a check-stamped body decoration.

G. *Owasco Corded Collar* (in the Rochester Museum collections from the Castle Creek site; see Ritchie, 1944, Pl. 13). A Middle or Late Owasco type having horizontal cord-wrapped stick impressed lines on the collar, cord-wrapped-stick impressions on the neck and shoulder, and a cord-marked body.

H. *Owasco Oblique* (reconstructed from sherds from the Sackett Farm in the collections of the Rochester Museum). A Middle Owasco variant of the type which has oblique and cord-wrapped-stick impressions on the rim, neck, and shoulder, and a cord-marked body.

I. *Owasco Oblique* (reconstructed from sherds from the Castle Creek site in the collections of the Rochester Museum). A type prevalent during old Owasco times which has horizontal rows of oblique cord-wrapped-stick impressions on the rim, neck, and shoulder, with cord-marked body.

J. *Owasco Horizontal* (reconstructed from sherds in the Rochester Museum collections). An Owasco type with oblique cord-wrapped-stick impressions (sometimes) on the rim, horizontal cord-wrapped-stick lines on the neck, oblique cord-wrapped-stick impressions on the shoulder, and with frequently a cord-marked body.

K. *Owasco Platted* (reconstructed from sherds in the Rochester Museum collections). An Owasco type having sometimes oblique cord-wrapped stick on the rim, always cord-wrapped stick plats on the neck, oblique cord impressions on the shoulder, and a cord-marked body.

L. *Owasco Herringbone* (the drawing is copied from one found by the Rochester Museum at the Castle Creek site). Cord-wrapped-stick herringbone designs on the shoulder, neck, and rim, while the body is cord-marked.

M. *Levanna Corded Collar* (based on sherds from the Levanna site which are now in the Rochester Museum collections). The decoration on an appliquéd collar are oblique lines of cord-wrapped-stick impressions. The whole vessel is cord-marked.

N. *Levanna Cord on Cord* (based on sherds from the Levanna site which are now in the Rochester Museum collections). The vessel is cord-marked with cord impression on a flattened lip.

O, P, Q. *Carpenter Brook Cord on Cord* (reconstructed from sherds from the Carpenter Brook site in the Rochester Museum Collections). On this type are found Owasco Oblique, Platted, and Herringbone superimposed on cord-marking.

R. *Wickham Corded Punctate* (reconstructed from sherds from the Wickham and Carpenter Brook sites which are now in the Rochester Museum collections). An Early Owasco type with punctates made by the end of a cord-wrapped stick or corner of a cord-wrapped paddle, as well as cord-wrapped-stick designs on a cord-marked surface.

POINT PENINSULA SERIES

S. *Jack's Reef Corded Collar* (reconstructed from sherds in the Rochester Museum collections from the Jack's Reef site). A Late Point Peninsula type very similar to Levanna Corded Collar.

T. *Jack's Reef Corded* (reconstructed from sherds from the Kipp Island site which are now in the Rochester Museum collections). A Late Point Peninsula type very similar to Levanna Cord on Cord, except that the lip is not flattened.

U. *Jack's Reef Punctate* (reconstructed from sherds from Jack's Reef which are now in the Rochester Museum collections). Similar to the Jack's Reef Corded Collar type except that the decoration is done by dentate stamping.

V. *Point Peninsula Corded* (based on sherds in the Rochester Museum collections). A Point Peninsula type similar to Carpenter Brook Cord on Cord, except that the decoration is on the body and the lips are pointed or rounded.

W. *Kipp Island Crisscross* (in the Rochester Museum collections; see Ritchie, 1944, Pl. 58, No. 11). A Late Point Peninsula type with cord-wrapped-stick impressions over cord-marking.

X. *Jack's Reef Corded Punctate* (based on sherds from the Jack's Reef site which are now in the Rochester Museum collections). A Late Point Peninsula type like Wickham Corded Punctate.

Y. *Vinette Dentate* (reconstructed from sherds from the Vinette site which are now in the Rochester Museum collections). A Point Peninsula type, decorated by bands of oblique and horizontal dentate stamp impressions on the rim, neck, and body; surface finish is smooth.

Z. *Vinette Complex Dentate* (based on sherds in the Rochester Museum collections). A type having bands of closely spaced vertical dentate impressions ornamented in horizontal bands.

A'. *Vinette Pseudo-Scallop Shell* (based on sherds in the Rochester Museum collections from the Wickham site). A Middle Point Peninsula type with vertical scallop shell-like impressions on the neck and body.

B'. *Wickham Punctate* (based on sherds from the Wickham site which are now in the Rochester Museum collections). Dentate stamp impressions on the rim, neck, and body, with circular punctate on the lower rim. This is a Middle Point Peninsula type.

C'. *Point Peninsula Rockered* (based on sherds from the Wickham site which are now in the Rochester Museum collections; see Ritchie, 1946, Pl. 8, No. 21). Decorated with rocker dentate impressions.

D'. *Vinette I* (based on a pot exhibited in the Rochester Museum). An Early Point Peninsula and pre–Point Peninsula type having vertical cord markings on the exterior and horizontal cord or fabric markings on the interior.

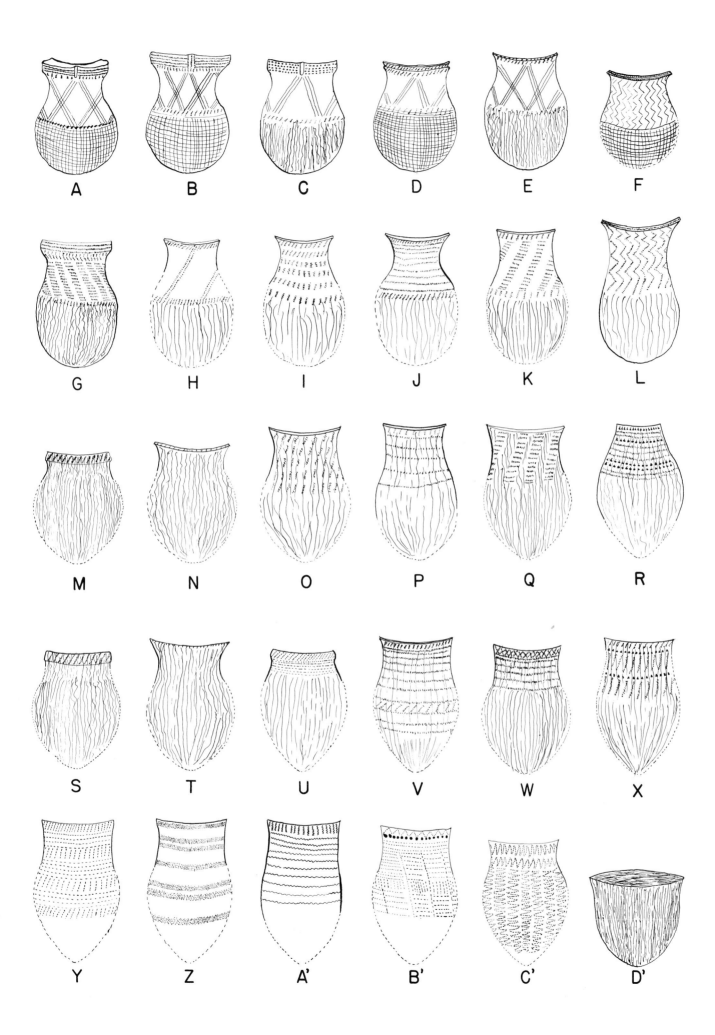

A   B   C   D   E   F

G   H   I   J   K   L

M   N   O   P   Q   R

S   T   U   V   W   X

Y   Z   A'   B'   C'   D'

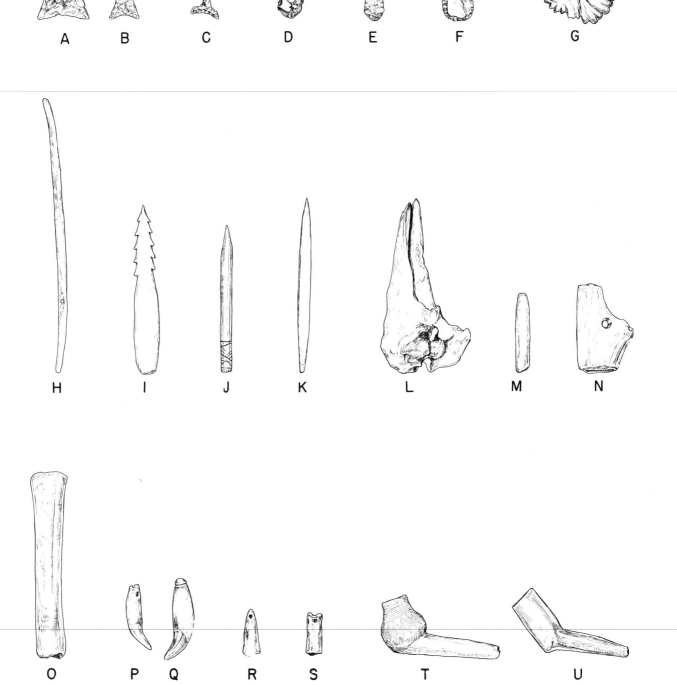

Fig. 18.—Owasco artifacts (based on artifacts in the Rochester Museum collections)

A. Early Owasco projectile point
B. Late Owasco projectile point
C. Drill
D. Drill or perforator
E. Strike-a-light
F. Scraper
G. Sinew stone

H. Bone needle
I. Multi-bilateral barbed harpoon
J. Decorated bone awl or pin
K. Polished bone awl
L. Bone beamer
M. Antler flaker
N. Perforated bone handle

O. Large bone bead
P. Pierced bone canine pendant
Q. Grooved bear-canine pendant
R. Ground and cut phalange bead or tinkler
S. Cut phalange bead or tinkler
T. Clay pipe with *pointillé* decoration
U. Plain clay pipe

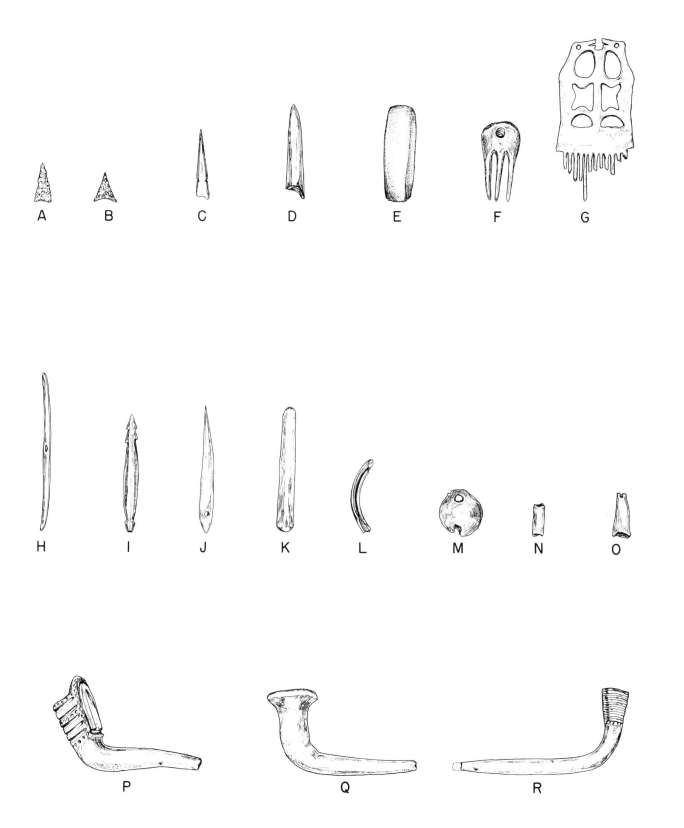

Fig. 19.—Iroquois artifacts (all artifacts except *G* are in the collections of the Rochester Museum; *G* is in the collection of H. Schoff of Honeyoye Falls; artifacts *G*, *Q*, and *R* are Onondaga-Oneida, while the others are Seneca).

A. Projectile point of an early type
B. Projectile point of a late type
C. Notched bone projectile point
D. Conical antler projectile point with a basal tang
E. Small rectangular celt
F. Prehistoric bone comb

G. Historic bone comb
H. Bone needle
I. Multi-bilateral barbed bone harpoon
J. Perforated awl
K. Antler flaker
L. Split beaver incisor gouge
M. Epiphyseal perforated cup pendant

N. Tubular bird-bone bead
O. Cut and polished phalange bone tinkler or bead
P. Effigy pipe
Q. Trumpet pipe
R. Ringed bowl pipe

FIG. 20.—Iroquois pottery types (based upon an analysis of Iroquois pottery by MacNeish)

MOHAWK TYPES

A. A late Mohawk type, Mohawk Notched Lip
B. A late Mohawk-Oneida-Onondaga type, Fonda Incised
C. A late Mohawk-Oneida-Onondaga type, Wagoner Hollow Incised
D. An early Mohawk type with corded decoration, Oak Hill Corded Lip
E. An early Mohawk type with cord-wrapped-stick decoration, Oak Hill Corded
F. An early Mohawk type with incised decoration, Chance Incised

ONONDAGA-ONEIDA TYPES

G. A late Oneida-Onondaga type, Roebuck Punctate
H. A late Oneida (Onondaga?) type, Thurston Figured
I. A prehistoric type, Durfee Incised
J. An early type, Swarthout Dentate
K. An Oneida-Onondaga type, Pompey Triangular
L. An early type, Ivey Corded

CAYUGA TYPES

M. Richmond Mills Incised
N. Genoa Fort Linear Punctate
O. Genoa Fort Notched Collar
P. Hummel Corded, an early type
Q. Hummel Linear, an early type
R. Myer's Station Notched Collar

SENECA TYPES

S. Warren Notched Collar, a late type
T. Dutch Hollow Notched Lip
U. Long Point Notched Collar
V. Dansville Corded, an early type
W. Dansville Linear, an early type
X. Dansville Notched Collar

NEUTRAL (ERIE?) TYPES

Y. Ontario Horizontal, a Neutral-Erie type
Z. Pound Necked, a late Neutral type
A'. Lawson Incised, a Neutral-Erie type
B'. Middleport Oblique, a Neutral type with grooved paddle body decoration
C'. Uren Linear, an early Neutral type
D'. Krieger Corded, an early Neutral type

ERIE POTTERY TYPES

E'. Ripley Plain Collar, a late Erie type
F'. Ripley Cord Marked, a late Erie type
G'. Ripley Plain, an Erie type
H'. Ripley Triangular, a late Erie type

HURON POTTERY TYPES

I'. Warminster Crosshatched, a late Huron type
J'. Warminster Oblique, a Huron type

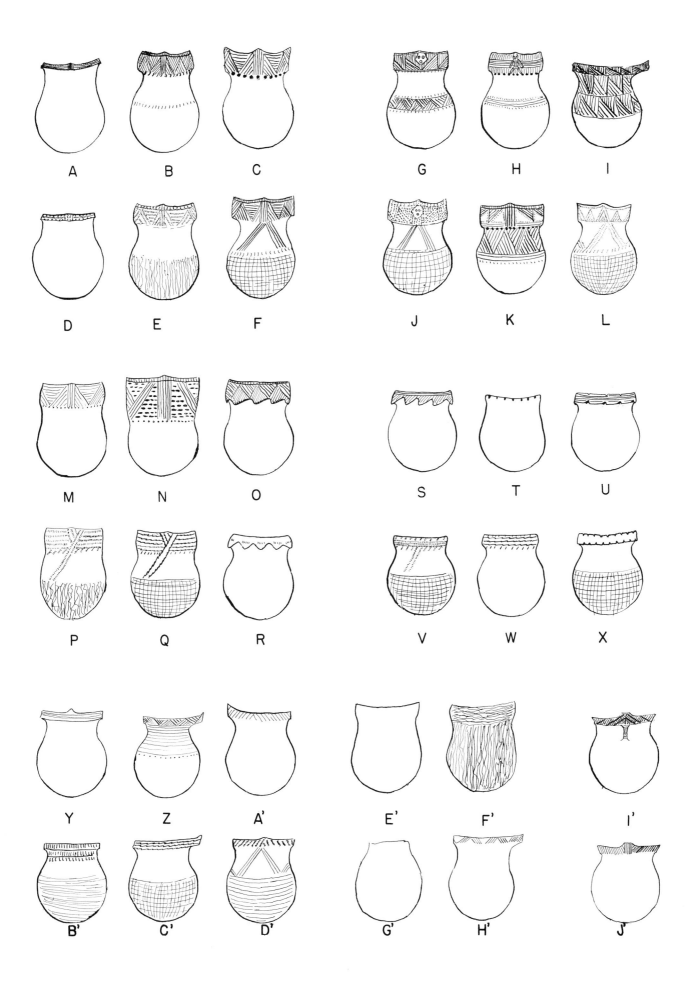

A   B   C   G   H   I

D   E   F   J   K   L

M   N   O   S   T   U

P   Q   R   V   W   X

Y   Z   A'   E'   F'   I'

B'   C'   D'   G'   H'   J'

FIG. 21.—Representative traits of the Archaic and Early Woodland: Middle Atlantic States

A–C. Stemmed projectile points from the Koens-Crispin site, New Jersey (after Hawkes and Linton, 1916, Pls. XVI, *l*, and XVII, *a* and *g*)

D. Stemmed point ("fish spear") from the Red Valley site, New Jersey (after Cross, 1941, Pl. LVIII, *b*)

E. Stemmed point with bifurcated base ("fish-tail") from Zakiah Swamp site, Maryland

F. Notched copper blade from Abbott Farm site, New Jersey (after Putnam, 1887, Fig. 30)

G. Pestle-like implement from Koens-Crispin site, New Jersey (after Hawkes and Linton, 1916, Pl. XIX, *j*)

H. Oval hammerstone from Koens-Crispin site, New Jersey (after Hawkes and Linton, 1916, Pl. XIX, *l*)

I. Chipped and slightly polished celt from Koens-Crispin site, New Jersey (after Hawkes and Linton, 1916, Pl. XVI, *m*)

J. Knobbed celt from the Koens-Crispin site, New Jersey (after Cross, 1941, Pl. XXXVIII, *a*)

K. Stone gouge from Red Valley site, New Jersey (after Cross, 1941, Pl. LVI, *a*)

L. Flaked chopper from New Jersey (after Abbott, 1876, Fig. 6)

M. Steatite-tempered basal sherd exhibiting impression of coarse fabric from Goose Island site, New Jersey (after Cross, 1941, Pl. XXVI, *a*)

N. Semilunar knife from Burlington County, New Jersey (after Abbott, 1876, Fig. 114)

O. Full-grooved ax from Salisbury site, New Jersey (after Cross, 1941, Pl. XX, *a–4*)

P. Steatite-tempered basal sherd exhibiting coarse fabric impressions from Selden Island site, Maryland (after Slattery, 1946, Fig. *1*, *g*)

Q. Steatite-tempered vessel fragment exhibiting flat base and cord-roughened body from Selden Island site, Maryland (after Slattery, 1946, Fig. 1, *a*)

R, T. Winged bannerstones from the Koens-Crispin site, New Jersey (after Hawkes and Linton, 1916, Pl. XXI, 2, and Pl. XXIV, 6)

S. Steatite vessel with lugs from Virginia (after Bushnell, 1931, Pl. XIV)

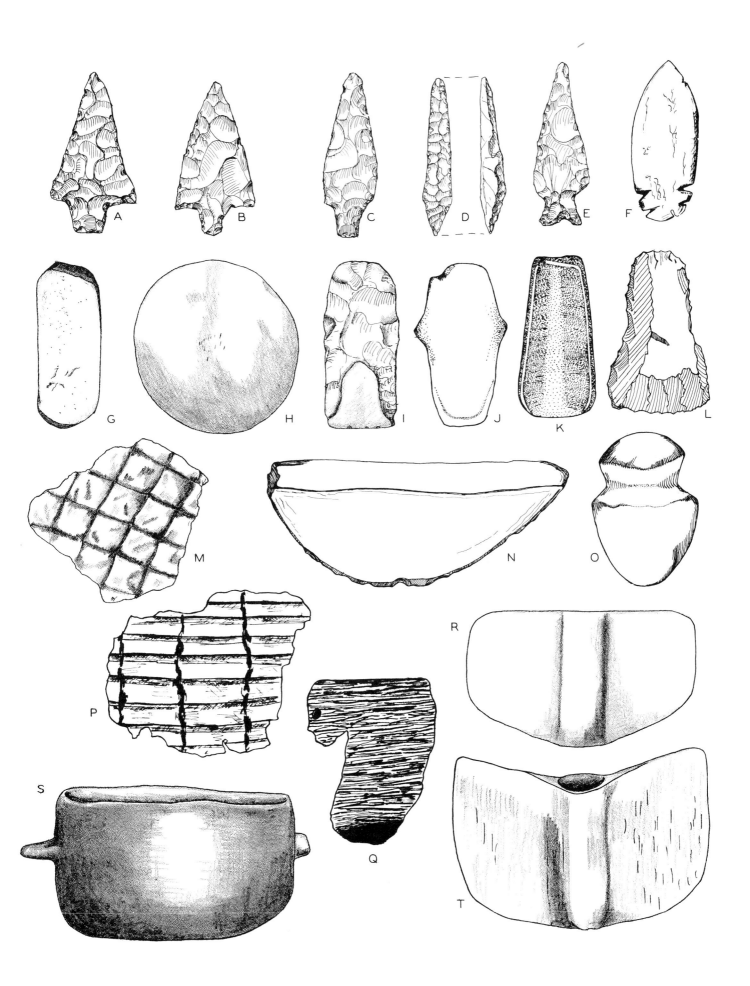

Fig. 22.—Representative traits of the Middle Woodland period: Middle Atlantic States

A. Schematic profile of a Mountain Focus Mound, Virginia, exhibiting subfloor pits, rock pile, inclusive bone lenses, and surrounding ditch

B. Schematic profile of a Thomas Focus Mound, Pennsylvania, exhibiting subfloor pit, stone cist, and rock slabs placed on mound periphery

C. Straight-based stone platform pipe with raised ridge over stem hole from Henry Brumback Mound, Virginia (after Fowke, 1894, Fig. 14)

D. Pottery pipe from Linville Mound, Virginia (United States National Museum Cat. No. 169922)

E. Curved-base stone platform pipe from Williamsburg Mound, Virginia (after Fowke, 1894, Fig. 5)

F. Stone gorget from Dickinson Mound, Virginia (after Fowke, 1894, Fig. 4)

G. Stone gorget from Philip Long Mound, Virginia (after Fowke, 1894, Fig. 10)

H. Copper gorget from the Crall Mound, Pennsylvania (after description of Thomas, 1894)

I. Stone gorget from New Jersey rock shelter (after Cross, 1941, Pl. LXIX, a–5)

J. Cylindrical shell bead made from a conch columella

K. Grooved stone ax of type prevalent in surface collections from Virginia and Maryland

L. Triangular blade or projectile point of type associated with Mountain Focus of Virginia

M. Notched projectile point of type widespread over entire Middle Atlantic area

N. Bone or antler comb from the Linville Mound, Virginia (after Fowke, 1894, Fig. 8)

O. Stone celt (artifacts of this category associated with the Mountain Focus of Virginia)

P. Pottery vessel from the Linville Mound, Virginia, with fabric-impressed surface finish (United States National Museum Cat. No. 169869)

Q. Pottery vessel from the Linville Mound, Virginia, with simple stamped or thong-wrapped paddled surface finish (United States National Museum Cat. No. 167877)

R. Pottery vessel from Luzerne County, Pennsylvania, exhibiting cord-marked surface treatment, punctating and interior nodes, and patterned arrangement of dentate stamping (after Wren, 1914, Pl. II)

S. Artist's conception of pottery vessel from the Clover Creek Focus, Virginia, drawn from sherds in the collections of the United States National Museum

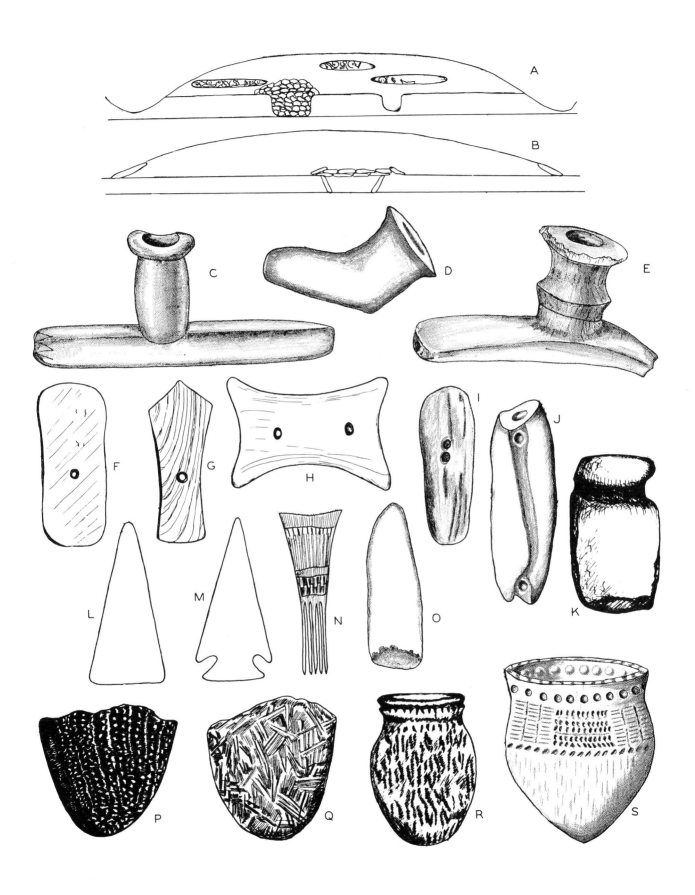

Fig. 23.—Representative traits of the Late Woodland period in Virginia and Maryland

A. Diagram of ossuary burial as found at various historic sites in the Virginia-Maryland tidewater area

B-C. Sherds of Potomac Creek Cord-Impressed (after Stewart, 1939b, Fig. 87, and Schmitt, n.d., Pl. I, Fig. 3)

D. Sherd of Rappahannock Incised (after Stewart, 1939b, Fig. 87)

E. Shell gorget from site of Patawomek, Virginia, exhibiting design produced by drilled-dot technique (after Schmitt, n.d., Pl. II, Fig. a5)

F. Shell mask from Tidewater, Virginia (after Holmes, 1883, Pl. LXVII)

G. Clay bead from the vicinity of Port Tobacco Creek, Maryland (after Graham, 1935, Pl. VI, Figs. 7–8)

H. Pottery pipe from vicinity of Port Tobacco Creek, Maryland, exhibiting dentate stamped decoration (after Graham, 1935, Pl. VI, Fig. 9)

I. Triangular arrowpoint of the type prevalent in the Chesapeake Tidewater area

J. Artist's conception of pottery vessel of the Shepard Cord Marked type exhibiting cord-wrapped-stick decorations, drawn from sherds from the Shepard site, Maryland, in the United States National Museum collections

K. Pottery vessel of the Keyser Cord Marked type from the Keyser site, Virginia (after Manson, MacCord, and Griffin, 1944, Pl. X, Fig. 2)

L. Restored pottery vessel of the Keyser Cord Marked type from the Hughes site, Maryland (after Stearns, 1940, Pl. II, Fig. 1)

M. Diagram of semiflexed burial associated with the Luray and Montgomery foci of Virginia and Maryland

N. Pottery pipe exhibiting incised decoration from the Shepard site, Maryland (after Schmitt and Slattery, n.d.)

O. Bone fishhook from the Hughes site, Maryland (after Stearns, 1940, Pl. IV, Fig. 2j)

P. Pottery pipe from the Hughes site, Maryland (after Stearns, 1940, Pl. III, Fig. 1)

Q-S. Projectile point type from the Shepard site, Maryland (after Schmitt and Slattery, n.d.)

T. Bone beamer from the Hughes site, Maryland (after Stearns, 1940, Pl. IV, Fig. 1)

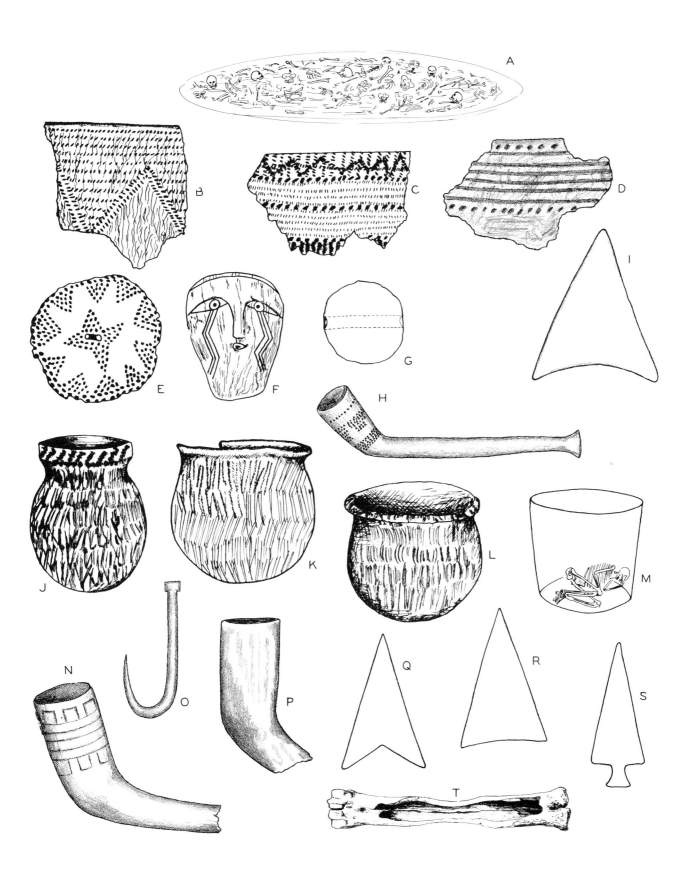

Fig. 24.—Representative traits of the Late Woodland period in southwestern Pennsylvania

A. Diagram of fortification and house types (based on Butler, 1939)

B–E. Pottery vessels exhibiting cord-marked surface finish (after Butler, 1939, Pl. 3c, Table 4c, Pl. 4c, Pl. 16a)

F–H. Sherds exhibiting various appendages (after Butler, 1939, Pl. 5, Figs. a and j, and Pl. 7, Fig. j)

I. Sherd exhibiting punctating and incised decoration ("chevron") (after Butler, 1939, Pl. 9c)

J. Pottery pipe exhibiting dentate stamped decoration and swollen bowl (after Butler, 1939, Table 6a)

K. Pottery pipe exhibiting dentate stamped decoration and rim band (after Butler, 1939, Table 6d)

L. Stone pipe (after Butler, 1939, Table 7a)

M. Stone discoidal (after Engberg, 1930, Pl. II, Fig. 3)

N. Stone celt (after Butler, 1939, Pl. 13)

O–Q. Stone projectile points (after Butler, 1939, Pl. 18)

R. Antler projectile point (after Butler, 1939, Pl. 14c)

S. Bone chisel (after Butler, 1939, Pl. 15u)

T. Bird-bone tube (after Engberg, 1931, Pl. IV, Fig. 10)

U. Perforated phalange (after Butler, 1939, Pl. 14q)

V. Bone fishhook (after Butler, 1939, Pl. 22)

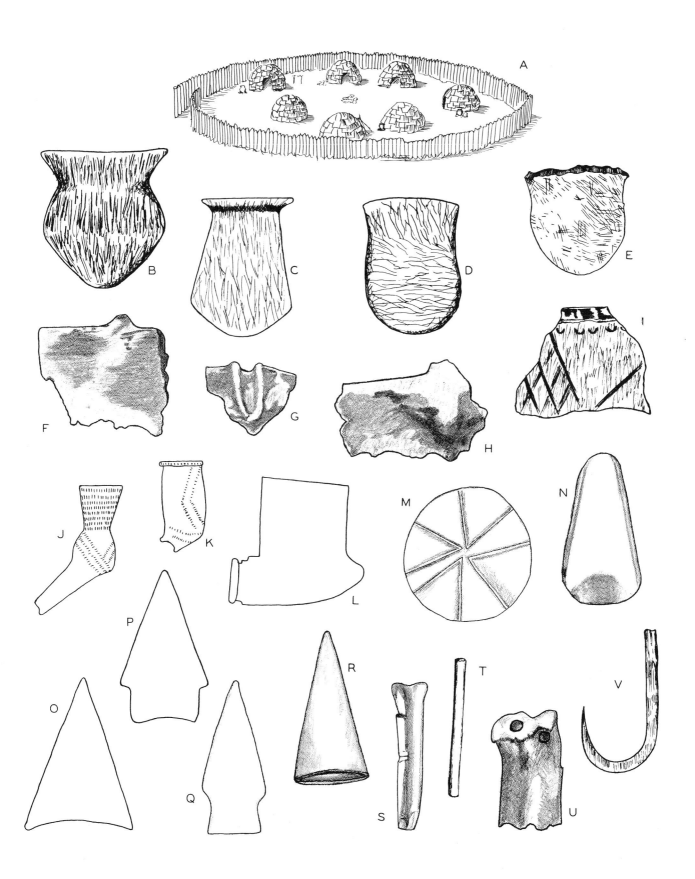

A

B

C

D

E

F

G

H

I

J

K

L

M

N

O

P

Q

R

S

T

U

V

Fig. 25.—Representative traits of the Late Woodland period: Susquehanna Focus

A. Restored pottery vessel from the Washington Borough site, exhibiting high collar and incised decoration (after Cadzow, 1936, Pl. 68)

B. Restored pottery vessel from the Washington Borough site, with double neck, conventionalized human faces, mammiform projections, and incised decoration (after Cadzow, 1936, Pl. 71)

C. Restored pottery vessel from the Washington Borough site, exhibiting conventionalized human face, mammiform projections, and incised decoration (after Cadzow, 1936, Pl. 62)

D. Pottery vessel from the Strickler site, exhibiting roughened surface finish, narrow collar, and gashed lower edge of collar (after Cadzow, 1936, Pl. 27b)

E. Pottery pipe from the Strickler site (after Cadzow, 1936, Pl. 30)

F. Triangular stone projectile point from the Washington Borough site (after Cadzow, 1936, Pl. 95)

G. Antler arrowpoint from the Washington Borough site, with serrated base (after Cadzow, 1936, Pl. 93b)

H. Pottery pipe from the Strickler site, with animal effigy bowl (after Cadzow, 1936, Pl. 31a)

I. Bone fishhook from the Schultz site (after Cadzow, 1936, Pl. 116)

J. Stone celt from the Schultz site (after Cadzow, 1936, Pl. 130)

K. Bone chisel or graver from the Schultz site (after Cadzow, 1936, Pl. 111c)

L. Barbed bone point from the Schultz site (after Cadzow, 1936, Pl. 114d)

M. Knobbed antler object from the Schultz site (after Cadzow, 1936, Pl. 118c)

N. Carved bone comb from the Washington Borough site (after Cadzow, 1936, Pl. 83c)

O. Stone face from the Washington Borough site (after Cadzow, 1936, Pl. 60b)

P. Stone turtle effigy from the Washington Borough site (after Cadzow, 1936, Pl. 60f)

Q–V. European or Colonial trade items from various Susquehanna Focus components:

Q. Brass kettle

R. Rum bottle

S. Iron ax

T. Metal "hawkbell"

U. Jew's-harp

V. Gun part

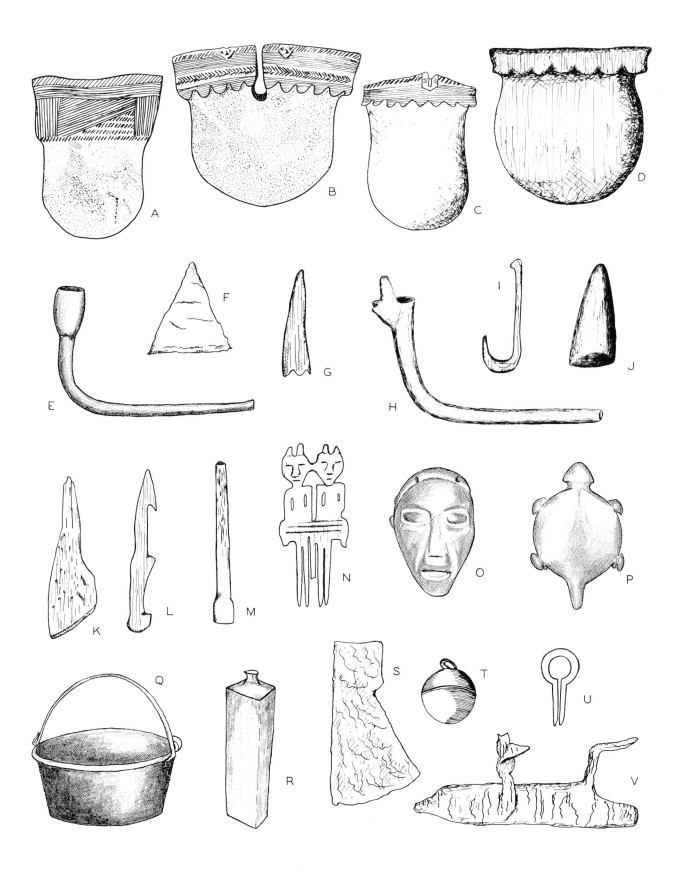

Fig. 26.—Representative traits of the Late Woodland period: eastern Pennsylvania, New Jersey–Delaware.

A. Restored pottery vessel from the Minisink site, New Jersey, exhibiting roughened surface finish, and narrow collar (after Heye and Pepper, 1915, Pl. XXI)

B. Portion of incised "Iroquois" vessel from the Minisink site, New Jersey (after Heye and Pepper, 1915, Pl. XXII*b*)

C. Restored pottery vessel of the "Iroquois" type from the Minisink site, New Jersey (after Heye and Pepper, 1915, Pl. XXIII*a*)

D. Portion of pottery vessel of the Owasco type from the Minisink site, New Jersey (after Heye and Pepper, 1915, Pl. XX*b*).

E. Pottery vessel of the Owasco type from Bradford County, Pennsylvania (after Wren, 1914, Pl. 9, Fig. 3)

F. Pottery vessel from Bradford County, Pennsylvania, with Owasco characteristics and incised designs (after Wren, 1914, Pl. 13, Fig. 5)

G. Restored shell gorget with incised decoration from the Minisink site, New Jersey (after Heye and Pepper, 1915, Fig. 5)

H. Shell gorget with engraved decoration from the Minisink site, New Jersey (after Heye and Pepper, 1915, Fig. 7)

I. Shell bird pendant with incised and drilled-dot designs from the Minisink site, New Jersey (after Heye and Pepper, 1915, Fig. 12)

J. Bone or antler comb with dog effigy from the Minisink site, New Jersey (after Heye and Pepper, 1915, Fig. 2)

K. Restored pottery vessel from the Broomall rock shelters, Pennsylvania, exhibiting cord-marked surface finish and incised decoration (after Butler, 1947, Pl. 12*g*)

L. Restored pottery vessel from the Prime Hook Neck site, Delaware, exhibiting cord-marked surface finish and incised decoration

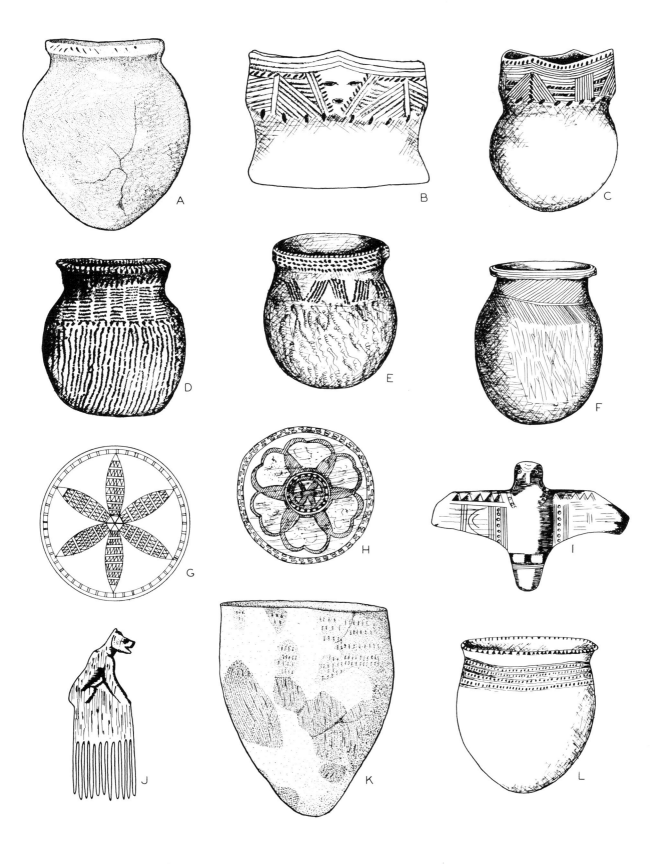

A

B

C

D

E

F

G

H

I

J

K

L

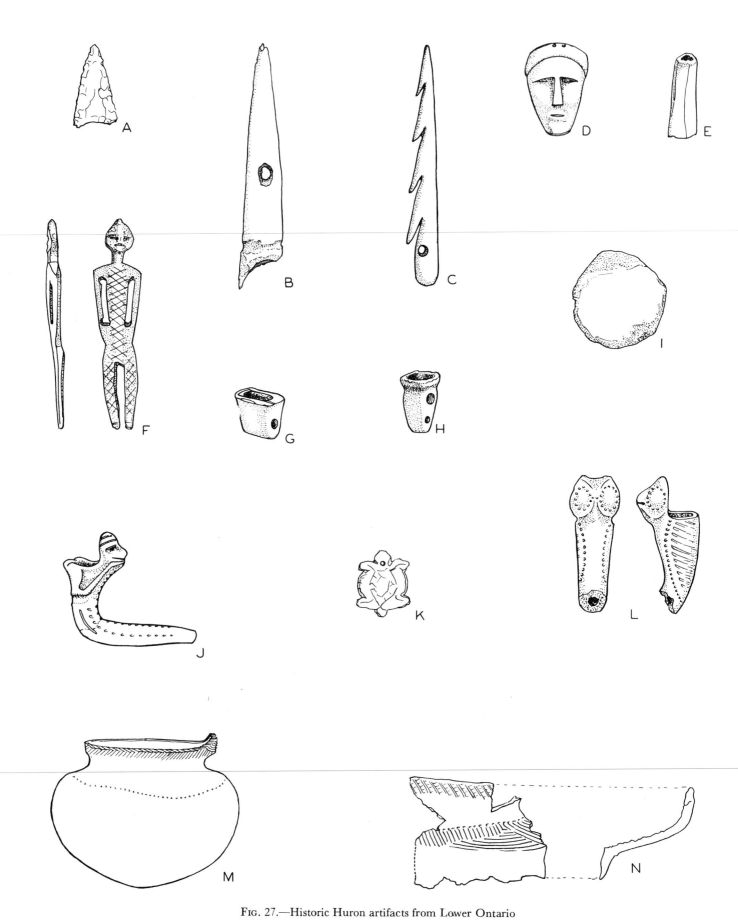

Fig. 27.—Historic Huron artifacts from Lower Ontario

A. Chert projectile point
B. Bone projectile point
C. Bone harpoon point
D. Bone bead, carved

E. Bone tubular bead
F. Bone figurine
G–H. Stone pipe bowls

I. Pottery disk
J. Clay pipe
K. Pipestone bead

L. Clay pipe bowl
M. Clay vessel
N. Part of rim sherd

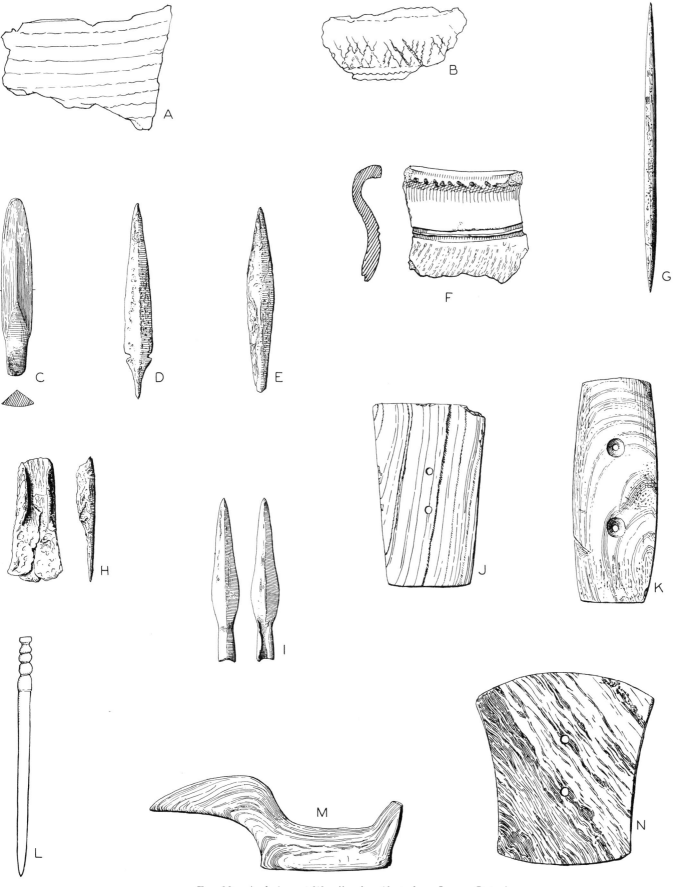

FIG. 28.—Archaic and Woodland artifacts from Lower Ontario

A–B. Sherds
C. Ground slate projectile point
D–E, I. Copper points
F. Rim sherd

G. Copper pike
H. Copper spud
J, N. Ground slate palette

K. Bar amulet
L. Bone pin
M. Slate birdstone

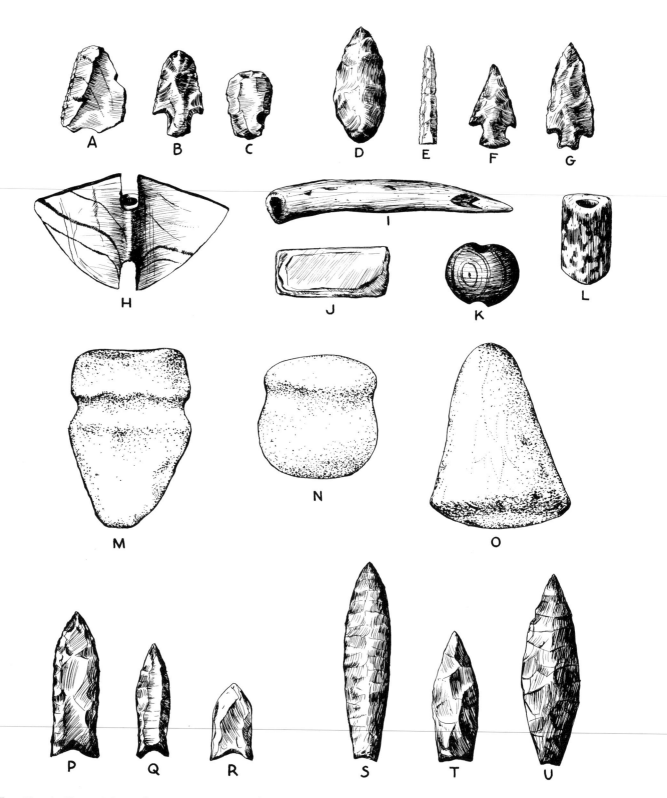

FIG. 29.—Artifacts of the Archaic period. *A–O* are types similar to those of the Indian Knoll or Shell Mound Focus of Kentucky

A. Flake scraper
B. Hafted scraper
C. End scraper
D. Blade or knife
E. Drill
F. Corner-notched point
G. Stemmed point

H. Winged bannerstone (atlatl weight)
I. Antler atlatl hook
J. Subrectangular bar (atlatl weight)
K. Ovoid slate object (atlatl weight)
L. Prismoidal atlatl weight
M. Fully grooved ax

N. Grooved hammer
O. Conical pestle
P–R. Folsom-like points or fluted blades
S. Yuma-like point
T. Nonfluted point
U. Yuma-like point

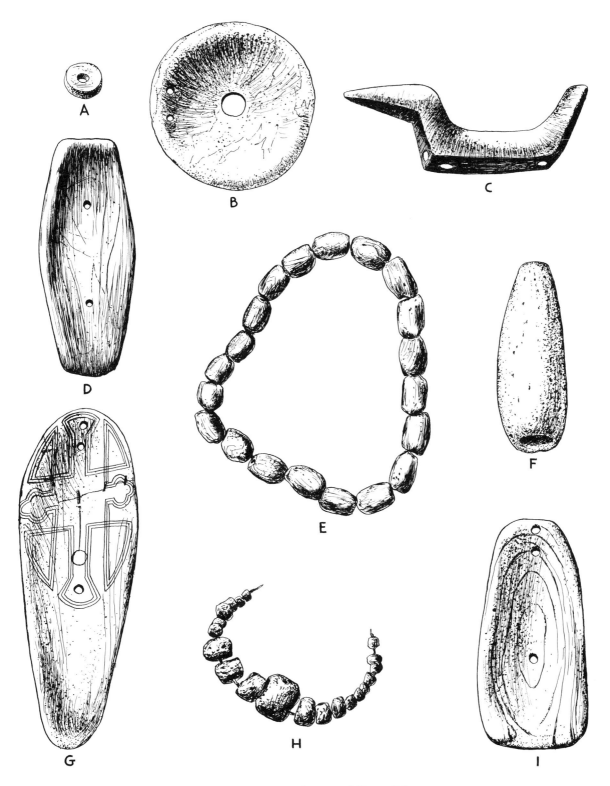

Fig. 30.—Artifacts of the Glacial Kame Culture

A. Disk-shaped marine-shell bead
B. Marine-shell gorget
C. Birdstone of slate

D. Rectanguloid marine-shell gorget
E. Marine-shell (columella) beads
F. Tubular stone pipe

G. Sandal-shaped, marine-shell gorget
H. Spheroidal beads of copper
I. Rectanguloid slate gorget

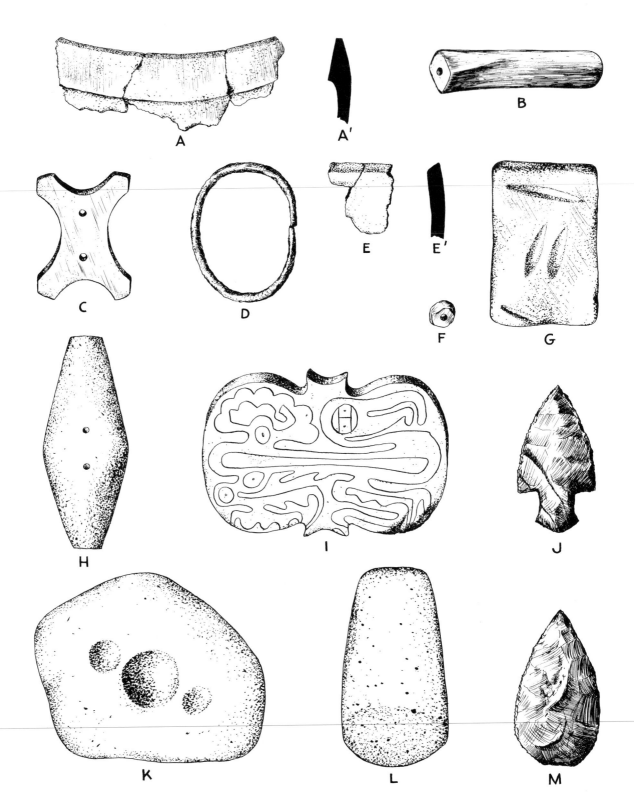

FIG. 31.—Artifacts of the Adena Culture in the Ohio Valley

A–A′. Adena plain pottery, thickened rim
    B. Tubular stone pipe
    C. Reel-shaped stone gorget
    D. Copper bracelet
E–E′. Plain rim sherd

    F. Disk-shaped marine-shell bead
    G. Grooved sandstone tablet
    H. Expanded center stone gorget
    I. Inscribed tablet (Berlin) with rap-
       torial bird design

    J. Stemmed projectile point
    K. Cupstone
    L. Ungrooved stone ax
    M. Leaf-shaped blade

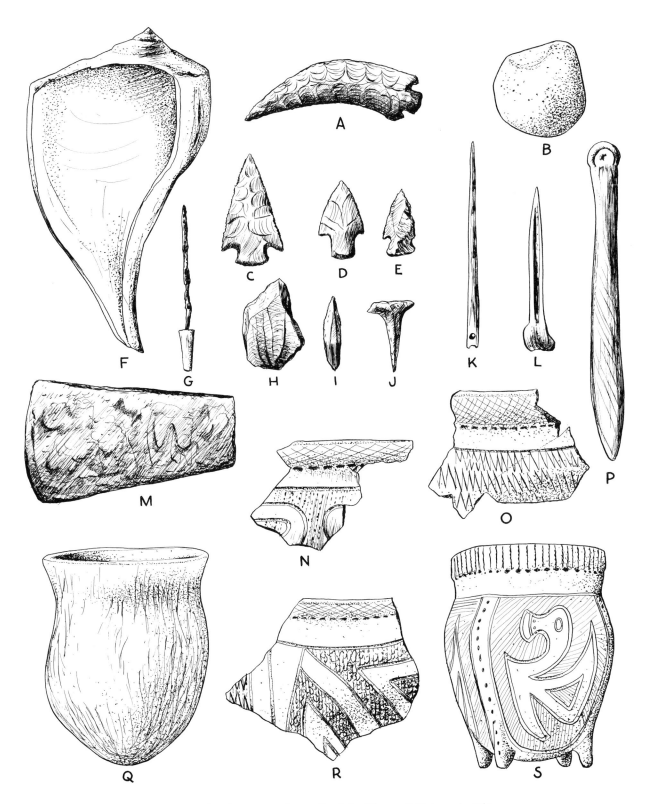

Fig. 32.—Implements and utensils of the Hopewell Culture in Ohio

A. Flint knife
B. Hammerstone
C. Corner-notched projectile point
D. Stemmed projectile point
E. Crude, corner-notched projectile point
F. Marine-shell (*Busycon perversum*) container
G. Copper awl with bone handle

H–I. Flint core and flake knife
J. Drill
K. Bone needle
L. Bone awl
M. Copper ax
N–S. Characteristic ceremonial pottery:
  N. Dentate stamped body areas alternating with smooth bands

O. Plain rocker design on body
P. Skewer, deer metapodial bone
Q. Typical, cord-marked, utilitarian vessel (Woodland)
R. Check-stamped areas alternating with smooth bands
S. Tetrapodal vessel with duck design and cord-impressed background

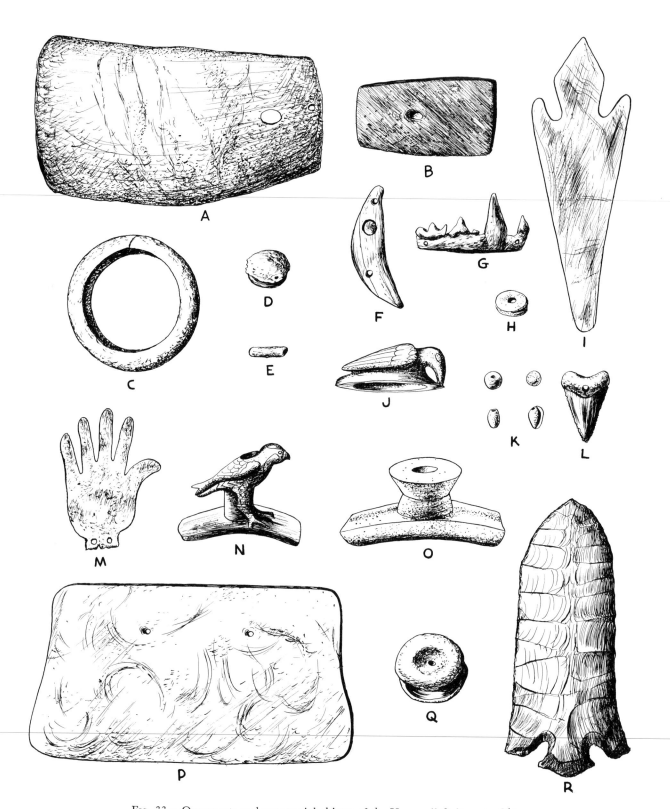

Fig. 33.—Ornaments and ceremonial objects of the Hopewell Culture in Ohio

A. Copper headdress

B. Stone gorget

C. Copper bracelet

D. Copper-covered wooden "button"

E. Copper bead

F. Bear tooth with pearl setting

G. Cut animal jaw (mountain lion)

H. Disk-shaped marine-shell bead

I. Spear-shaped mica ornament

J. Bird effigy boatstone

K. Shell beads, pearl (*upper right*), *Marginella apicina* (*lower right*)

L. Perforated shark tooth

M. Hand of sheet copper

N. Effigy platform pipe (duck hawk)

O. Platform pipe

P. Copper breastplate

Q. Copper earspool

R. Obsidian spearpoint

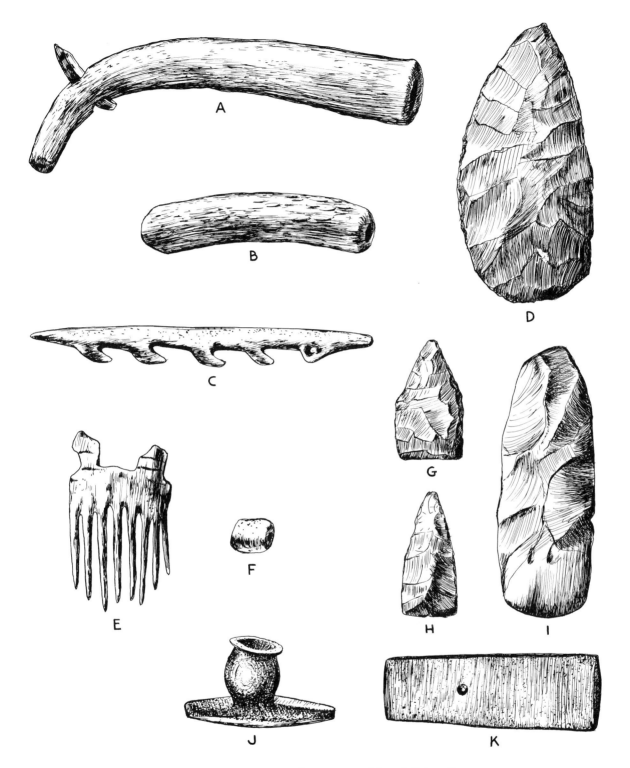

Fig. 34.—Artifacts of the "Intrusive Mound Culture"

A. Beaver tooth hafted in antler handle
B. Antler handle
C. Harpoon (antler)
D. Knife-scraper

E. Comb (antler)
F. Bead (columella of marine shell)
G. Projectile point, angular blade
H. Triangular blade

I. Flint ax, chipped and polished
J. Platform pipe (keeled stem)
K. Stone gorget

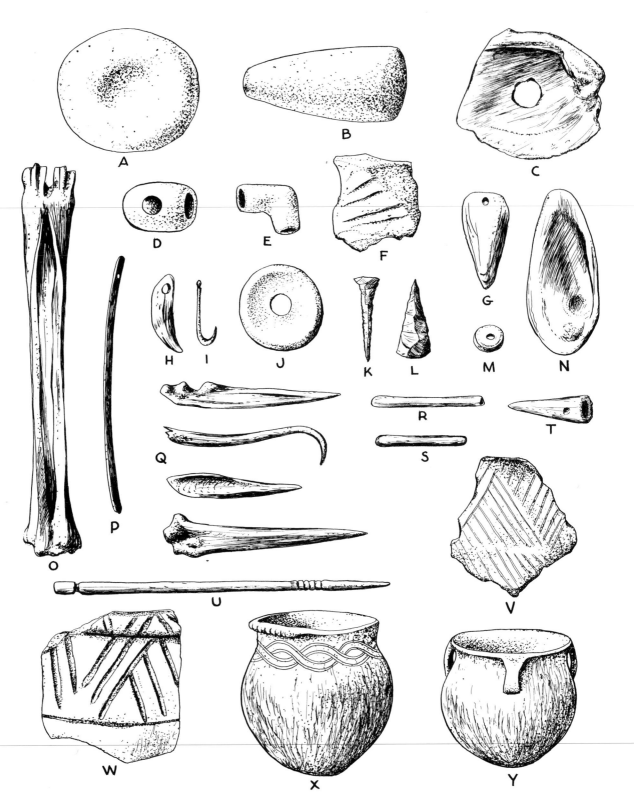

Fig. 35.—Artifacts of the Fort Ancient Aspect

A. Pitted hammerstone
B. Ungrooved ax
C. Mussel-shell hoe
D. Conoidal tobacco pipe
E. Elbow tobacco pipe
F. Grooved abrading stone
G. Shell pendant
H. Perforated wolf tooth
I. Bone fishhook
J. Discoidal stone

K. Drill
L. Triangular projectile point
M. Disk-shaped shell bead
N. Mussel-shell spoon
O. Beamer (deer metapodial bone)
P. Bone needle
Q. Bone awls, ulna (top), raccoon penis, splinter, turkey metatarsal
R. Bone (bird) bead

S. Flaking tool (antler)
T. Projectile point (antler)
U. Hairpin
V. Pottery rim sherd, Feurt Focus
W. Rim sherd, Anderson Focus
X. Pottery vessel (lip diameter 24.2 cm.), Baum Focus
Y. Pottery vessel (height 15.6 cm.), Madisonville Focus

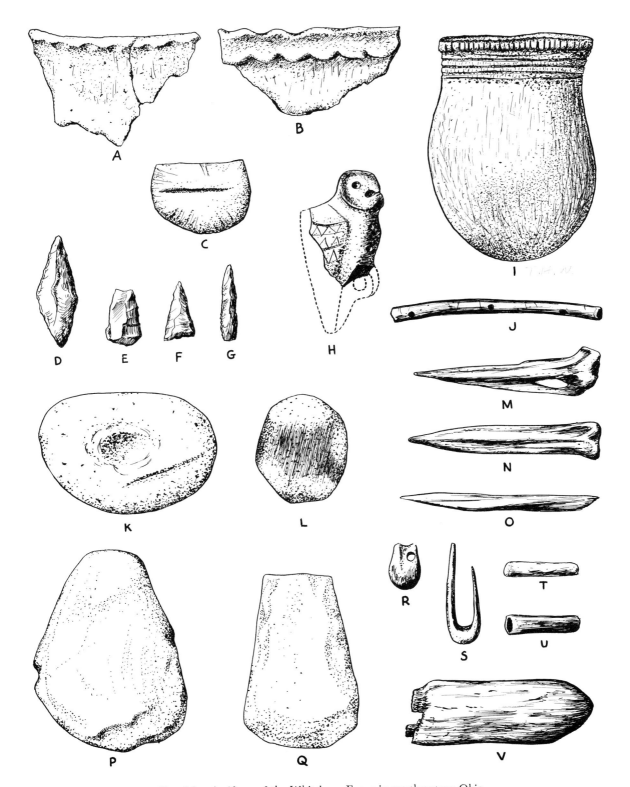

FIG. 36.—Artifacts of the Whittlesey Focus in northeastern Ohio

A–B. Typical rim sherds
  C. Grooved abrading stone
  D. Knife
  E. End scraper
  F. Triangular projectile point
  G. Drill
  H. Keel-shaped tobacco pipe (owl)

  I. Pottery vessel with typical rim
      designs
  J. Bird-bone flute
  K. Pitted hammerstone
  L. Faceted hammerstone
  M. Turkey metatarsal awl
  N. Split bone awl

  O. Bone splinter awl
  P. Notched "net-sinker"
  Q. Stone ax, chipped and ground
  R. Elk-tooth pendant
  S. Bone fishhook
  T. Flint flaking tool (antler)
  U. Bird-bone bead
  V. Gouge or scraper (elk antler)

Fig. 37.—Simplified visual outline of the prehistory of the Upper Great Lakes Region, based on selected characteristics for each period. Periods from bottom to top are earliest to latest.

LATE WOODLAND

A. Reconstructed vessel from Wolf site, Macomb County, Michigan

B. Incised vessel of kind on sites which are presumably Erie

C–D. Cord-marked vessels from northern Ohio post-Hopewell sites

E. Elbow pipes of the Younge Focus with punctate or *pointillé* decoration

F. Wide- and narrow-base triangular points

TRANSITION TO LATE WOODLAND

G–I. Cord-marked vessels of the Gibraltar Focus of southeastern Michigan

J. Side-notched projectile points, West Twin Lakes Focus

K. Clay elbow pipe, West Twin Lakes Focus

L. Antler tines with inserted beaver incisors, West Twin Lakes Focus

M. Bone harpoon, West Twin Lakes Focus

MIDDLE WOODLAND

N. Cord-marked vessel of Hopewell group

O. Summerville Incised vessel from the Goodall Focus

P. Norton Crosshatched vessel from the Goodall Focus

Q. Goodall Dentate Stamp

R. Copper ax and adz, Goodall Focus

S. Corner-notched projectile points, Goodall Focus

T. Platform pipe from the Brooks Component of the Goodall Focus

EARLY WOODLAND (AND OLD COPPER)

U. Cord-marked pottery vessel

V. Stemmed projectile point

W. Scraper

X. Side-notched projectile point

Y. Copper rat-tailed spear

Z. Long, narrow copper celt

A'. Copper point with perforation at base of socket

B'. Copper point with socket handle

C'–E'. Copper points illustrating variations in shape

F'. Short-socketed copper spud

G'. Copper celt

H'. Short-socketed copper spud

I'–J'. Copper crescents with two prongs

K'. Copper awl

LATE ARCHAIC

L'–P'. Flint implements

Q'. Fluted projectile point of type found in western Michigan

EARLY ARCHAIC

R'–X'. Large quartzite implements of the George Lake Complex

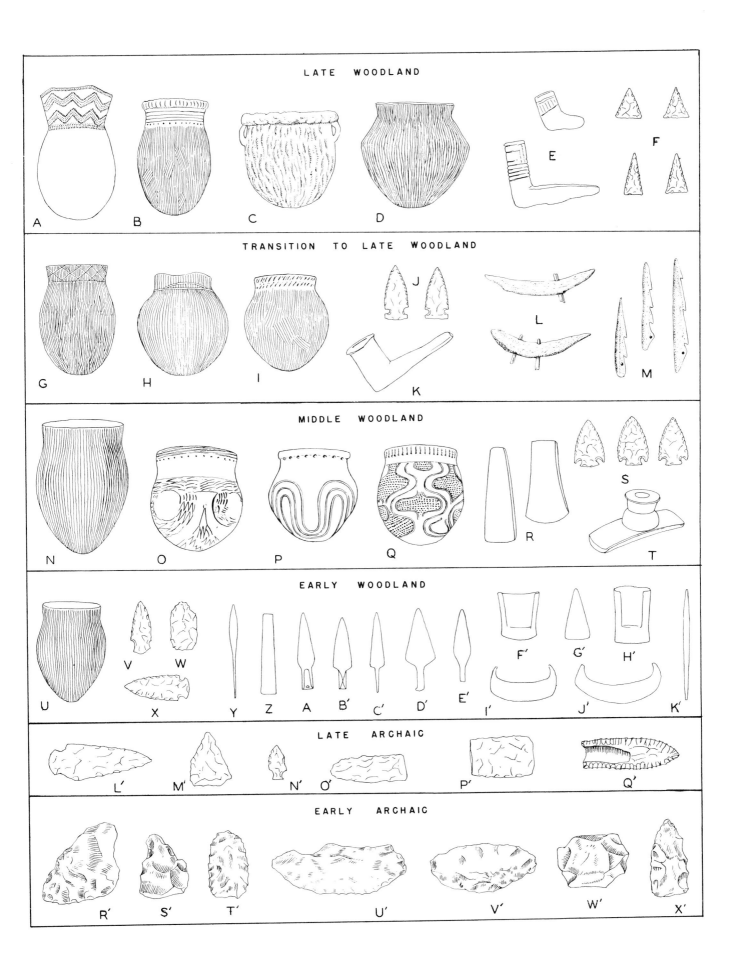

LATE WOODLAND

A B C D E F

TRANSITION TO LATE WOODLAND

G H I J K L M

MIDDLE WOODLAND

N O P Q R S T

EARLY WOODLAND

U V W X Y Z A' B' C' D' E' F' G' H' I' J' K'

LATE ARCHAIC

L' M' N' O' P' Q'

EARLY ARCHAIC

R' S' T' U' V' W' X'

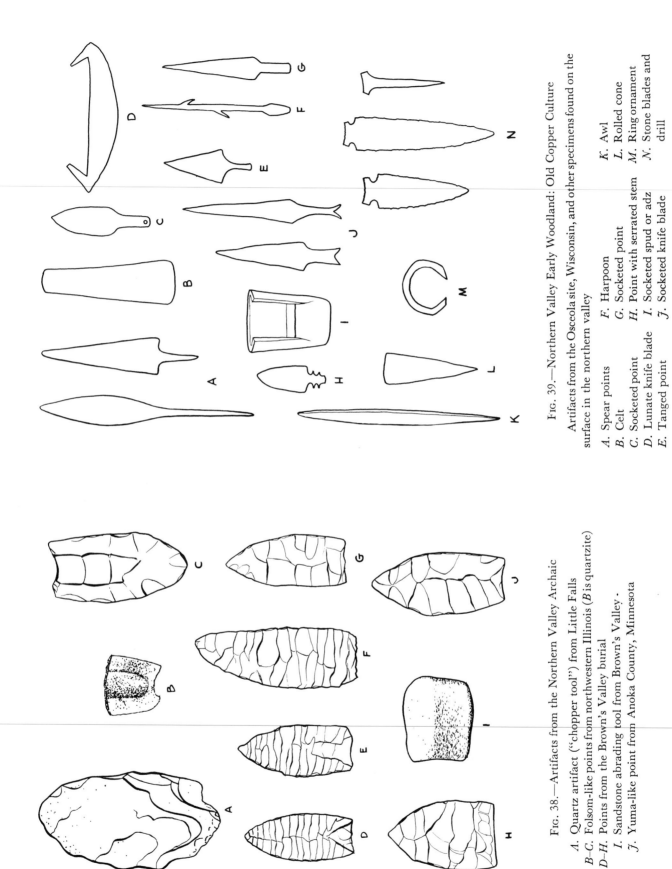

FIG. 39.—Northern Valley Early Woodland: Old Copper Culture

Artifacts from the Osceola site, Wisconsin, and other specimens found on the surface in the northern valley

A. Spear points
B. Celt
C. Socketed point
D. Lunate knife blade
E. Tanged point
F. Harpoon
G. Socketed point
H. Point with serrated stem
I. Socketed spud or adz
J. Socketed knife blade
K. Awl
L. Rolled cone
M. Ring ornament
N. Stone blades and drill

FIG. 38.—Artifacts from the Northern Valley Archaic

A. Quartz artifact ("chopper tool") from Little Falls
B–C. Folsom-like points from northwestern Illinois (B is quartzite)
D–H. Points from the Brown's Valley burial
I. Sandstone abrading tool from Brown's Valley.
J. Yuma-like point from Anoka County, Minnesota

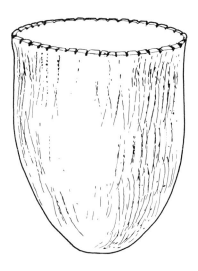

FIG. 40.—Northern Valley Early Woodland. Pottery vessel from the Cooper Rock Shelter site, Wisconsin. Assignment to Early Woodland tentative.

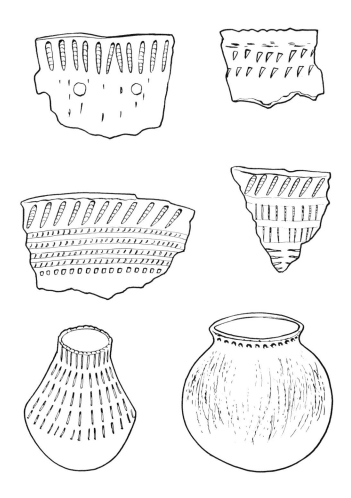

FIG. 41.—Northern Valley Middle Woodland: Laurel Focus. Sherds and vessels typical of Laurel pottery

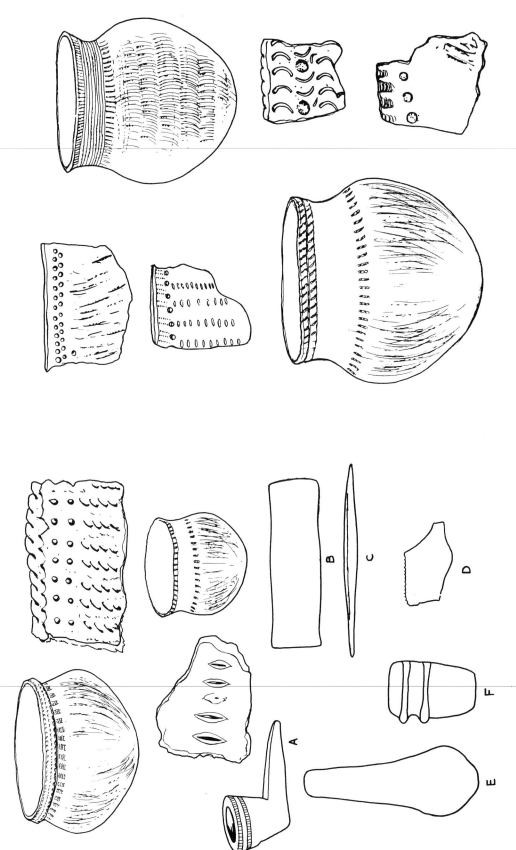

Fig. 43.—Northern Valley Middle Woodland: Iowa pottery. Two vessels from Lane Farm Mound Group. Right top vessel shows combination of single-cord-impressed decorations and rocker-stamped body. Sherds are from village and rock shelter sites in central and northern Iowa and feature various styles of stamping, punching, embossing, and incising and are tentatively assigned to the "Amana Culture."

Fig. 42.—Northern Valley Middle Woodland: Effigy Mound Aspect

Top: Sherds and vessels typical of Effigy Mound pottery. Top, right, has heavy cord-marking in vertical columns, small perforations, crenellated and thickened lip. Lower left sherd had fingernail incisions. Vessels have cord-marked bodies, decorations of single cord impressions, and cord-wrapped stick.

A. Typical pipe
B. Copper celt
C. Copper awl

D. Serrated slate implement
E. Greenstone spud-celt
F. Three-quarter-grooved ax

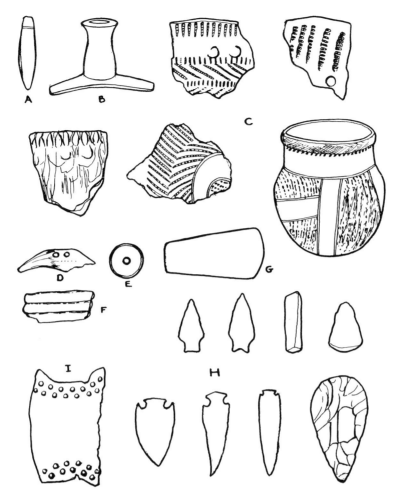

FIG. 44.—Northern Valley Middle Woodland: Trempealeau Focus

A. Grooved bar or "net-sinker"
B. Platform pipe
C. Various sherds found in mound fill and village debris, with stamped, incised, punched, cord-marked designs and single Hopewellian-type funerary vessel
D. Perforated bear canine
E. Copper ear-disk

F. Copper conjoined tubes
G. Copper celt
H. *Top:* Utilitarian points, flake knife, scraper. *Bottom:* Various ceremonial stonework pieces from jasper, chalcedony, flint, and obsidian
I. Top of copper sheet gorget with embossing

FIG. 45.—Northern Valley Middle Woodland: Nickerson Focus. Pottery vessel from Jo Daviess County, Illinois. Body cord-marked, except for zoned design.

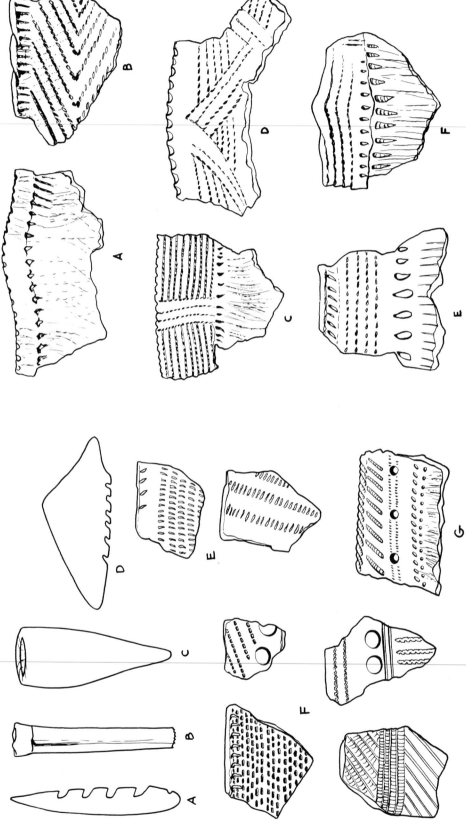

Fig. 47.—Northern Valley Transitional Woodland: Lake Michigan pottery.

A–C. Sherds from Woodland manifestation associated with Middle Mississippi manifestation at Aztalan site, Wisconsin (A and C have raised corners; B has typical paneled single-cord impressed motifs)
D–F. Sherds from a village site at Two Rivers, Wisconsin (D has paneled design; E and F typical combinations of punctated and cord-wrapped-stick impressions with cord-marking).

Fig. 46.—Northern Valley Transitional Woodland: Minnesota manifestations.

A–D. Bone artifacts from Arvilla Focus:
  A. Harpoon point
  B. Skin-dresser with serrated lower edge
  C. Tubular pipe with belled bowl
  D. Serrated scraping implement
E. Typical cord-wrapped-stick-impressed sherds from Kathio Focus
F. Typical stamped and embossed sherds from Howard Lake Focus (lower left sherd has cord-wrapped-stick impressions and horizontal incising)
G. Typical cord-wrapped-stick-impressed and punched rim sherd from Blackduck Focus.

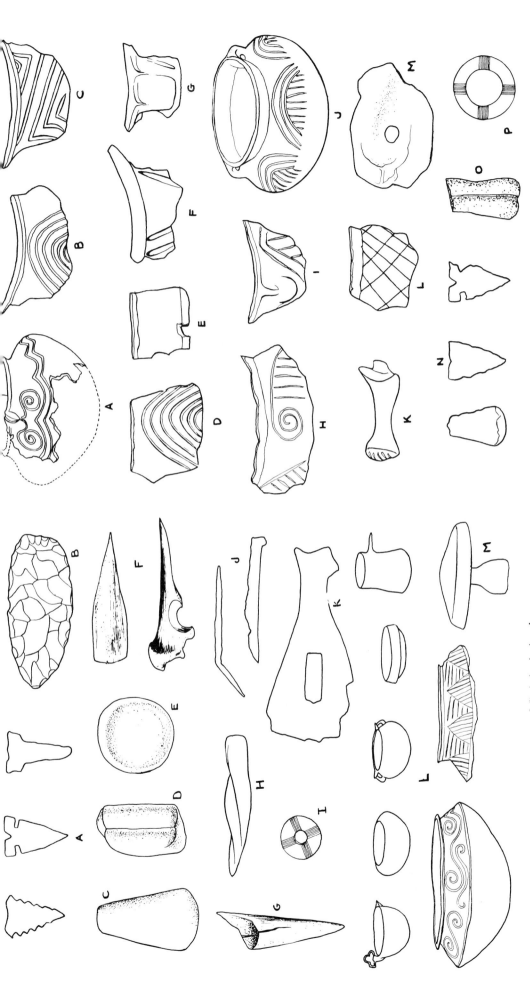

Fig. 48.—Northern Valley Early Mississippi: Aztalan

A. Aztalan notched and serrated triangular points and drill
B. Stone hoe
C. Stone celt
D. Sandstone shaft abrader
E. Sandstone discoidal
F. Bone awls
G. Antler-tip projectile point
H. Pendant from *Busycon* columella
I. Steatite earspool, with incised lines
J. Copper fish gorge and copper knife blade
K. Bison scapula "fiber shredder"
L. *Top*: Outlines of typical Aztalan vessel forms. *Bottom*: Typical designs on rims
M. Pottery trowel

Fig. 49.—Northern Valley Early Mississippi: Cambria and Apple River foci

A. Cambria vessel
B, C. Sherds from John Chapman site, showing Aztalan-type Middle Mississippi characteristics
D–G. Sherds from Mills site, showing mixture of Middle and Upper Mississippi characteristics (*E* has sharply angular shoulder; *F* sharply flaring rim; *D* rounded-angular shoulder; *G* strap handle and short flaring rim)
H–J. Sherds and vessel from Savannah site, showing Upper Mississippi traits as dominant
K, L. Sherds with red slip (*L* is scratched-incised) found in all three Apple River Focus sites, identified with Trappist Focus of Cahokia
M–P. Artifacts from Mills site:
M. Shell hoe
N. Scraper and two triangular projectile points
O. Sandstone shaft abrader
P. Steatite earspool of definite Aztalan type

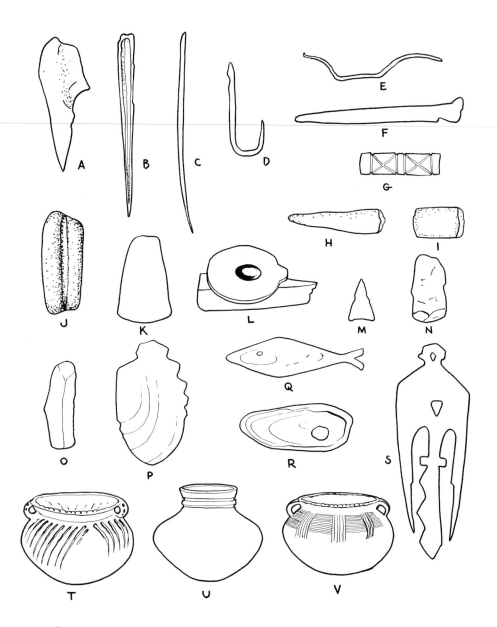

Fig. 50.—Northern Valley Late Mississippi: Oneota Aspect. Artifacts and pottery characteristic of various Oneota foci.

A, B. Bone awls
   C. Bone needle
   D. Copper fishhook
   E. Copper gorge
   F. Copper knife blade
   G. Incised bone tube
   H. Antler-tip projectile point
   I. Antler "counter"

   J. Sandstone abrader
   K. Stone celt
   L. Disk-bowl pipe
   M. Triangular projectile point
   N. Snub-nosed scraper
   O. Flake knife
   P. Shell spoon with sculptured edge
   Q. Shell fish effigy

   R. Shell hoe
   S. Sheet copper pendant (the copper artifacts and shell objects are especially characteristic of Lake Winnebago and Grand River)
   T. Lake Winnebago vessel
   U. Grand River vessel
   V. Orr vessel

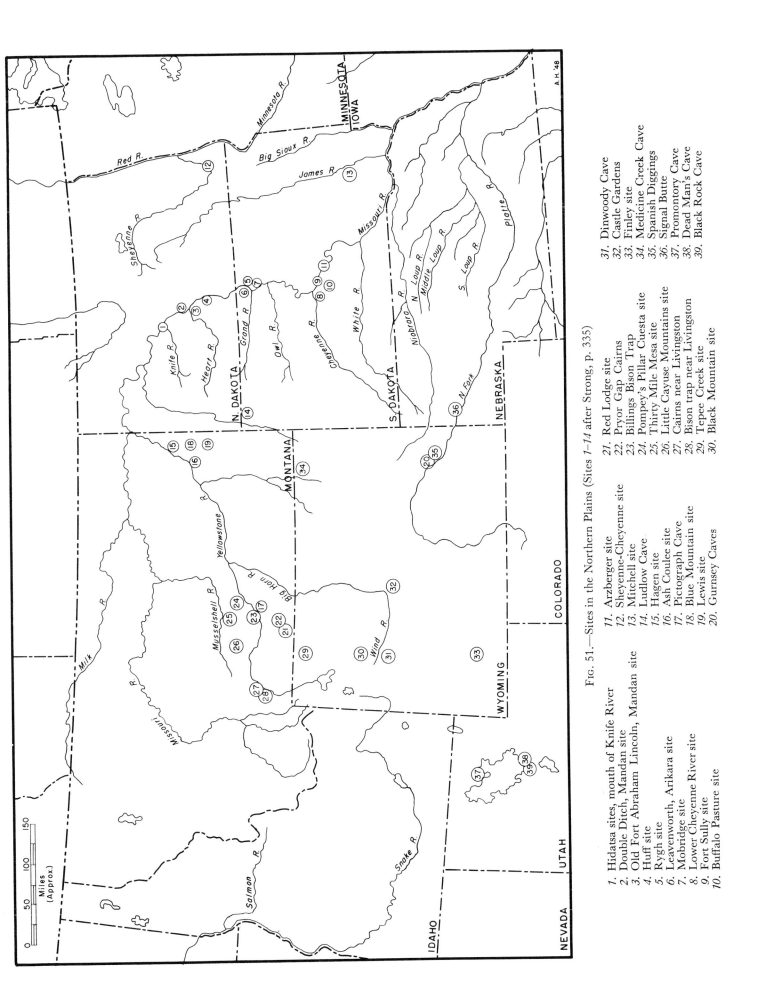

Fig. 51.—Sites in the Northern Plains (Sites *1–14* after Strong, p. 335)

1. Hidatsa sites, mouth of Knife River
2. Double Ditch, Mandan site
3. Old Fort Abraham Lincoln, Mandan site
4. Huff site
5. Rygh site
6. Leavenworth, Arikara site
7. Mobridge site
8. Lower Cheyenne River site
9. Fort Sully site
10. Buffalo Pasture site

11. Arzberger site
12. Sheyenne-Cheyenne site
13. Mitchell site
14. Ludlow Cave
15. Hagen site
16. Ash Coulee site
17. Pictograph Cave
18. Blue Mountain site
19. Lewis site
20. Gurnsey Caves

21. Red Lodge site
22. Pryor Gap Cairns
23. Billings Bison Trap
24. Pompey's Pillar Cuesta site
25. Thirty Mile Mesa site
26. Little Cayuse Mountains site
27. Cairns near Livingston
28. Bison trap near Livingston
29. Tepee Creek site
30. Black Mountain site

31. Dinwoody Cave
32. Castle Gardens
33. Finley site
34. Medicine Creek Cave
35. Spanish Diggings
36. Signal Butte
37. Promontory Cave
38. Dead Man's Cave
39. Black Rock Cave

FIG. 52.—Early Period artifacts from the Lewis site, Montana

A–D. Oblique Yuma points
E–G. Fluted points
H–I. Eden Valley Yumas
J. Scottsbluff Yuma

EARLY MIDDLE PERIOD ARTIFACTS FROM PICTOGRAPH CAVE, MONTANA

K–U. Projectile points
K. Fluted point
P. Eden Valley Yuma
V. Plano-convex end scraper
W, X, A′, D′, H′. Bifacially chipped knives
Y–Z. Spoke shaves
B′–C′. Gravers
E′–G′. Game counters

LATE MIDDLE PERIOD ARTIFACTS FROM PICTOGRAPH CAVE II

I′. Shaft straightener
J′. Game counter
K′. Knife
L′–S′. Projectile points (L′–N′ are characteristic types of this horizon)
O′–S′. Types similar to Pictograph Cave I

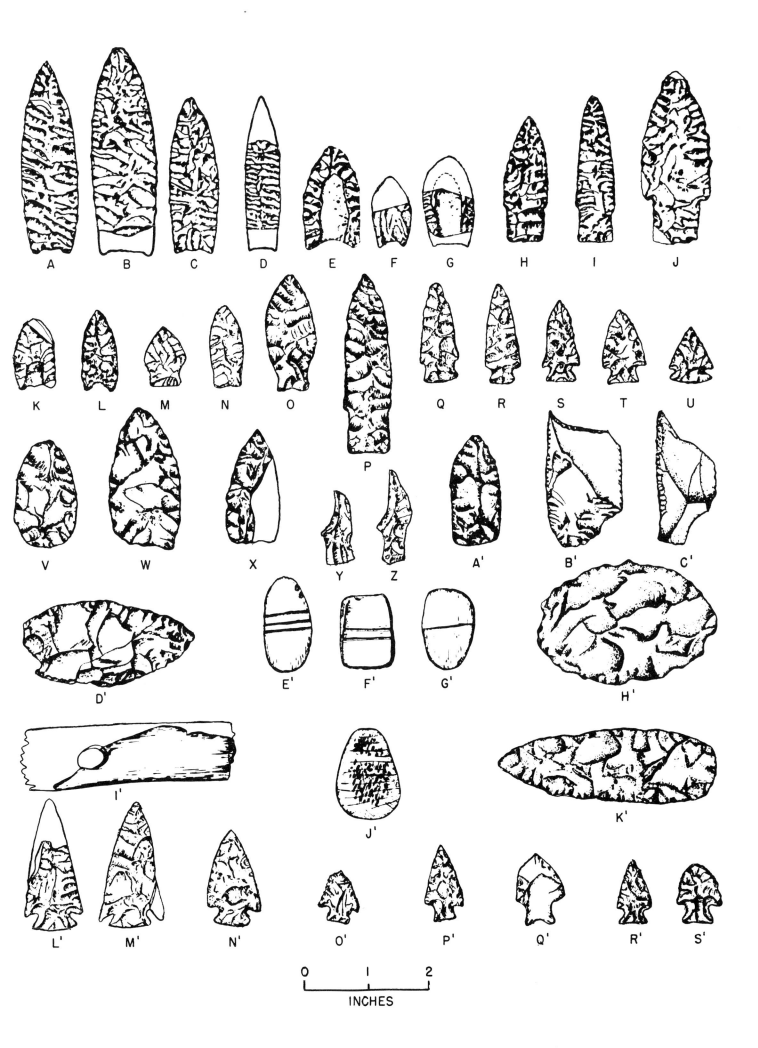

A B C D E F G H I J

K L M N O P Q R S T U

V W X Y Z A' B' C'

D' E' F' G' H'

I' J' K'

L' M' N' O' P' Q' R' S'

0   1   2

INCHES

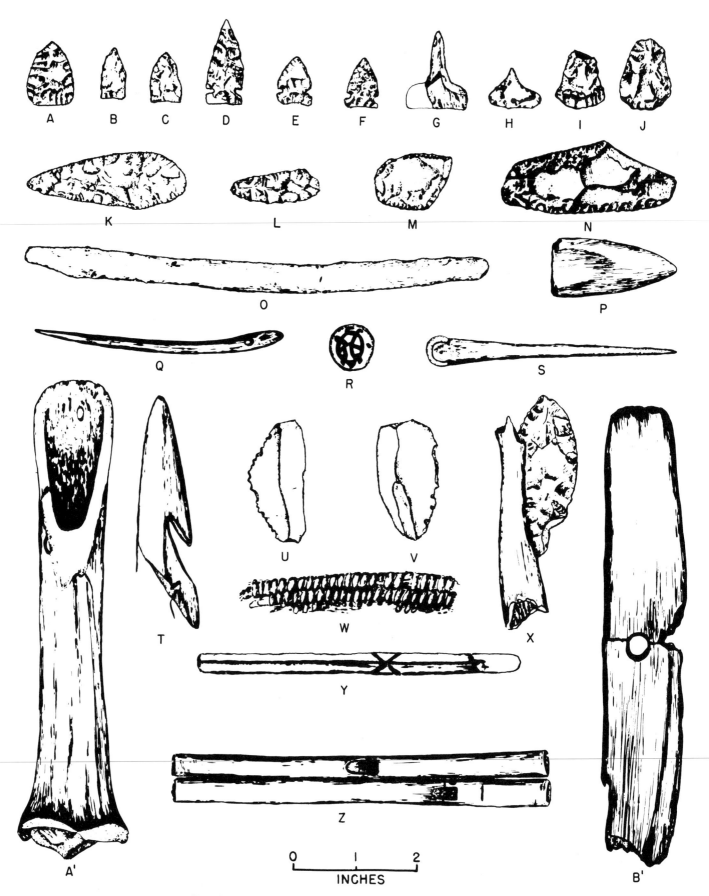

FIG. 53.—Early, Late Period artifacts from Pictograph Cave III

A–C. Unnotched, triangular projectile points
D–F. Notched, triangular projectile points
G–H. Drills
I–J. Plano-convex end scrapers
K–N. Knives
O. Stone chipping tool of bison

P. Fluted bone point
Q. Pierced bison-horn needle
R. Horn game counter
S. Bone awl
T. Fragment of a barbed antler projectile point
U–V. Serrated blades

W. Fragment of coiled basketry
X. Obliquely hafted knife with bone handle
Y. Split-twig game counter
Z. Bone whistle
A'. Serrated fleshing tool
B'. Shaft straightener of bison rib

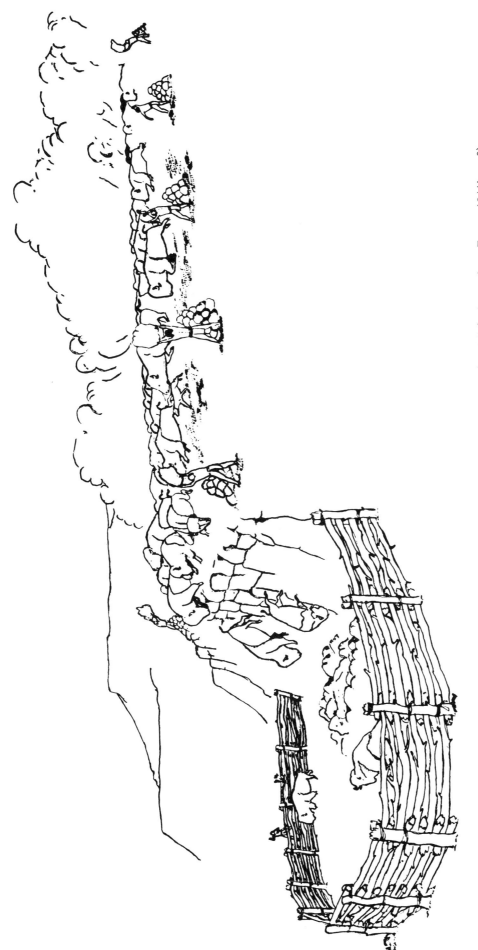

Fɪɢ. 54.—Probable manner of use of a bison trap together with enclosure below the cliff (redrawn from Ewers, 1944b, p. 9)

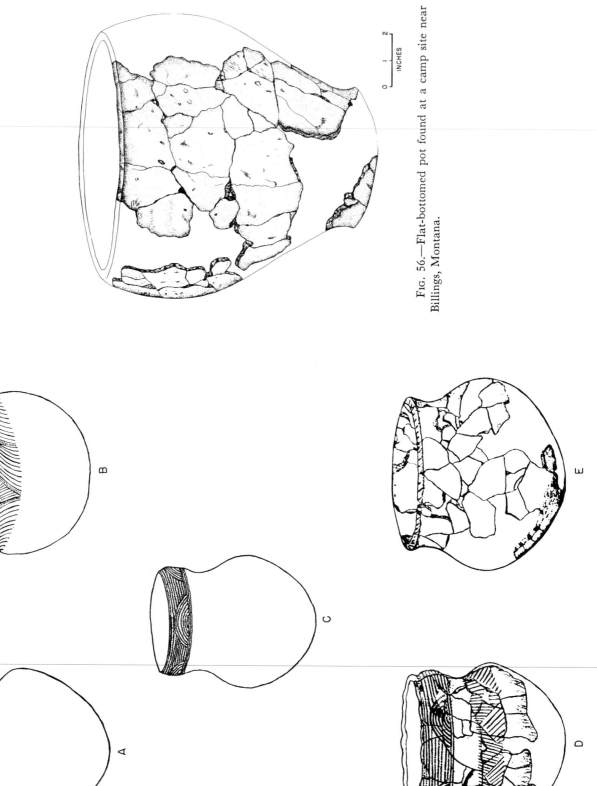

Fig. 56.—Flat-bottomed pot found at a camp site near Billings, Montana.

Fig. 55.—A–C, Early, Middle, and Late Mandan pottery (after Will and Hecker, 1944, Pls. 8 and 10); D–E, Mandan-Hidatsa tradition pottery from the Hagen site.

0   1   2
INCHES

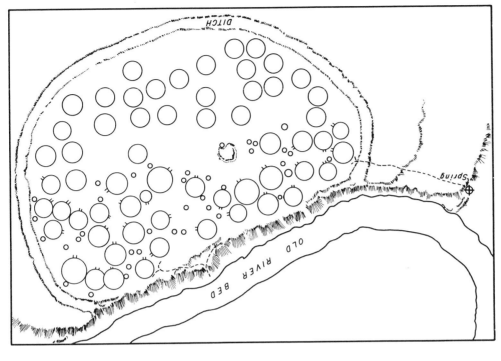

Fig. 58.—Map of the Sheyenne–Cheyenne site near Lisbon, North Dakota.

DITCH

Spring

OLD RIVER BED

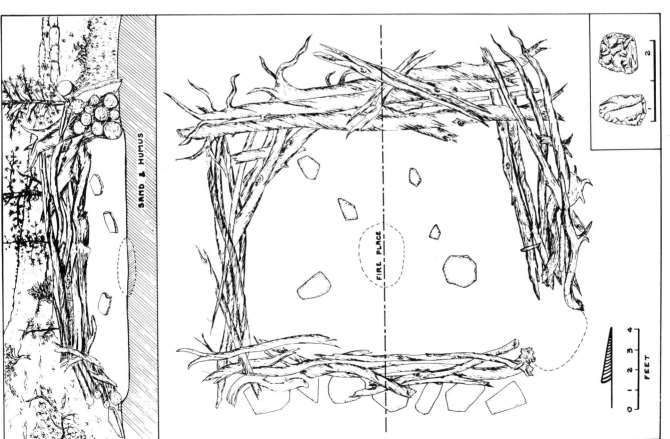

SAND & HUMUS

FIRE PLACE

1

2

0 1 2 3 4
FEET

Fig. 57.—Remains of a cribbed Log Lodge at Thirty Mile Mesa Village. *Inset:* 1, plano-convex end scraper; 2, homemade gun flint (both from lodge fill).

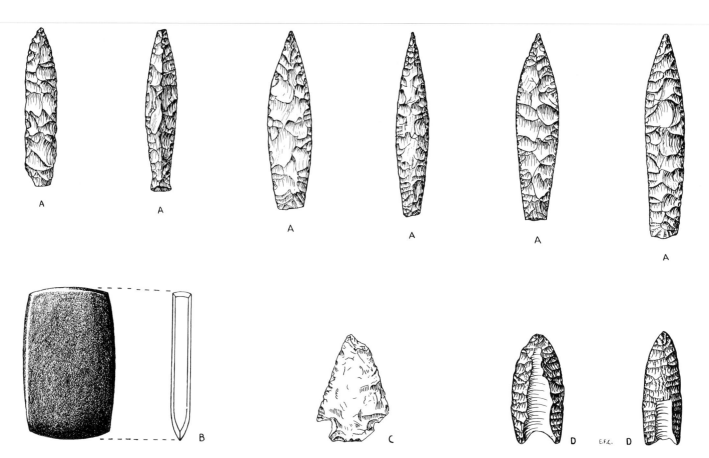

FIG. 59.—Artifacts associated with nonceramic Archaic complex in Missouri

A. Lanceolate blades of the Nebo Hill facies   *C.* Projectile point reported in association with mastodon remains (after Rau, 1873)
B. Flat celt of Nebo Hill   *D.* Variant Folsom projectile points

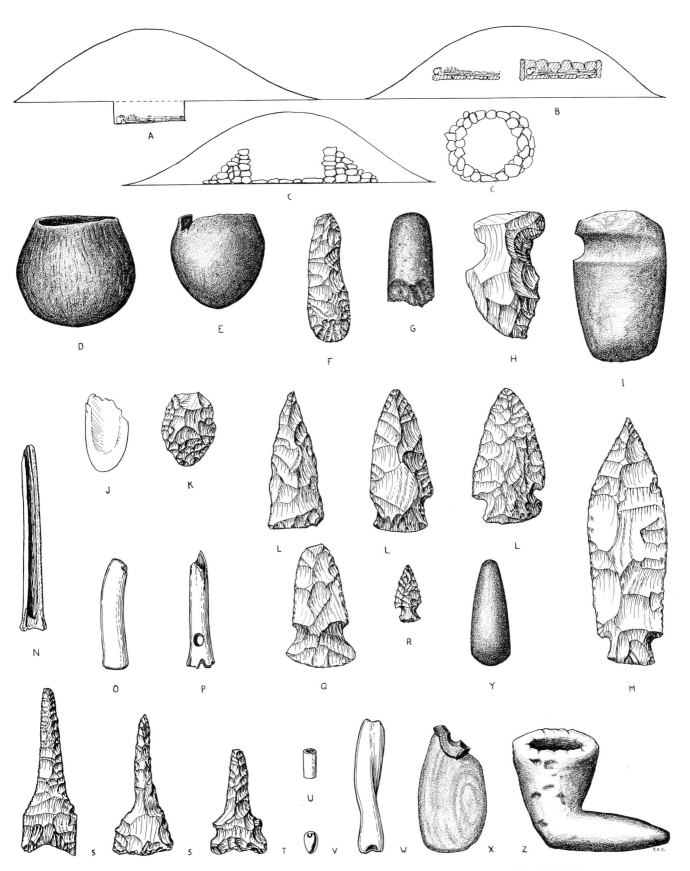

Fig. 60.—Cultural complex of the Boone Focus, central Missouri (*D* and *E* after Wedel, 1943)

A–C. Diagrammatic representation
of burial structures
D. Cord-marked vessel
E. Plain surface vessel
F. Hoe
G, Y. Celt forms

H–I. Chipped and three-quarter-
grooved axes
J. Shell spoon
K. Scraper
L, Q, R. Projectile points
M. Knife
N. Bone awl

O. Antler rubbing tool
P. Bone arrowshaft straightener
S–T. Drills
U. Bone bead
V–W. Seashell beads
X. Stone pendant
Z. Clay elbow pipe

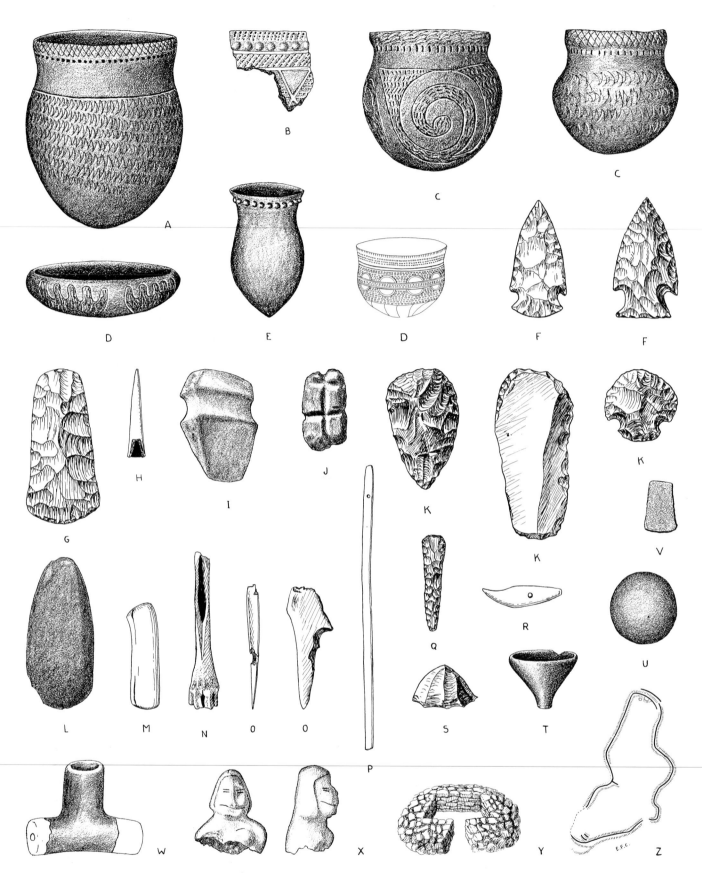

FIG. 61.—Cultural complex of the Hopewellian Phase in the Kansas City area (*C–H, M–R*, and *T–V* after Wedel, 1943)

A–E. Pottery vessels
F, H. Projectile points
   G. Hoe
   I. Three-quarter-grooved ax
   J. Grooved stone, possibly an atlatl
      weight
   K. Thumbnail, keeled and hafted
      scraper

   L. Celt
   M. Antler rubbing tool
   N. Broken section of bone beamer
   O. Split bone and ulna awls
   Q. Drill
   R. Imitation bear tooth
   S. Flint disk core
   T. Stone mammiform object

   U. Stone ball
   V. Small copper ax
   W. Broken clay platform pipe
   X. Clay figurine
   Y. Stone burial chamber of the type
      enclosed within an earth mound
   Z. Ceremonial earthwork

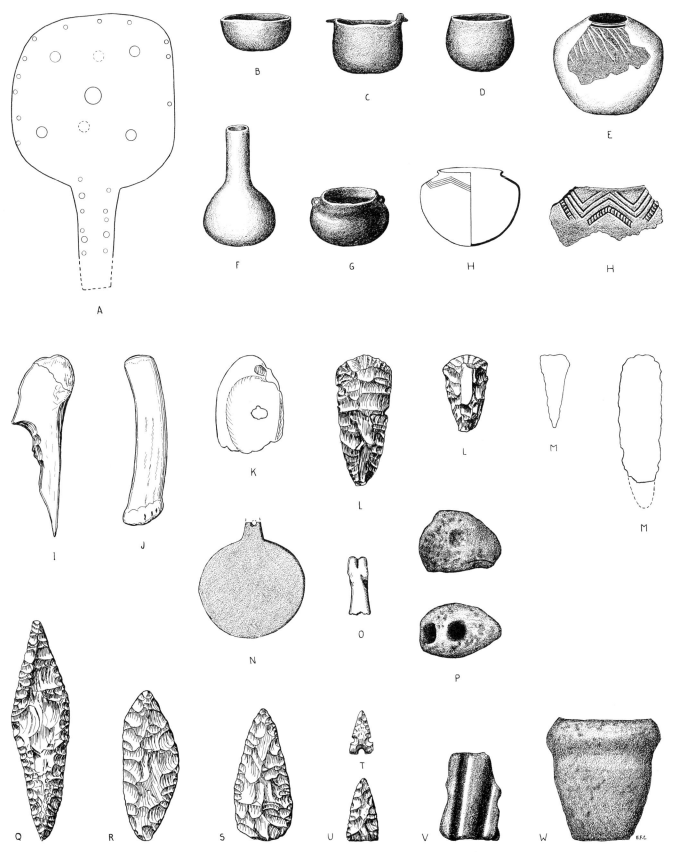

Fig. 62.—Steed-Kisker house floor plan and artifacts (all but *G, L, O, T, U*, and *V* after Wedel, 1943)

A. Ground plan of house
B–H. Pottery vessels
I. Bone ulna awl
J. Antler flaking or rubbing tool
K. Shell hoe

L. End scraper
M. Drills
N. Pendant
O. Bone ornament or gaming object
P. Effigy pipe

Q–S. Knife types
T–U. Projectile points
V. Abrading stone
W. Ax

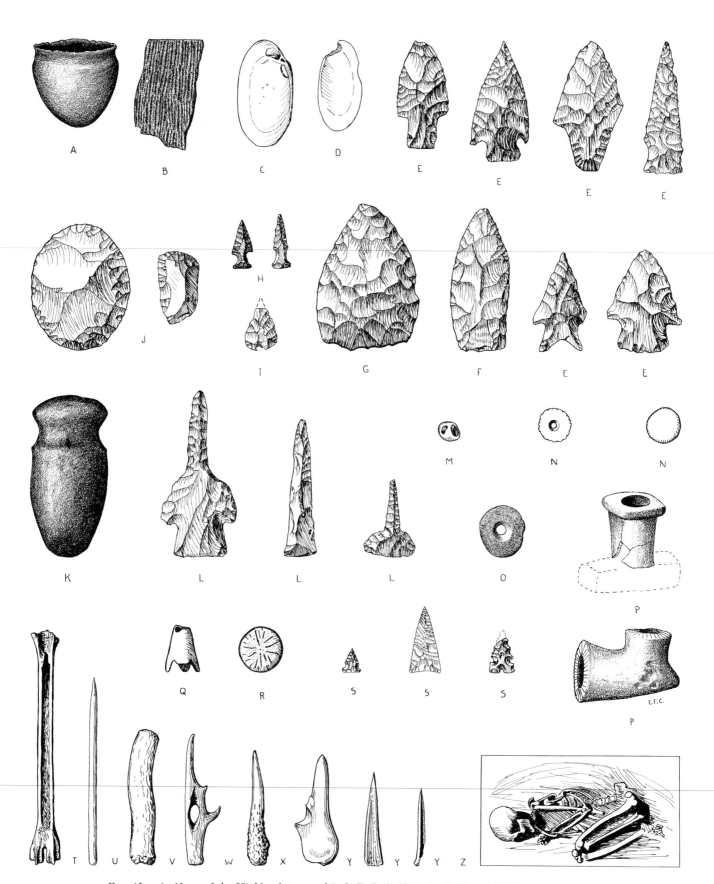

FIG. 63.—Artifacts of the Highland Aspect (*A, C–E, G, J–K, O–P, T–U,* and *W–Y* after Fowke, 1910)

A–B. Plain and cord-marked pottery
  C. Unperforated shell hoe(?)
  D. Shell spoon
E, H, I, S. Various projectile point types
  F. Knife
  G. Rough blade
  J. Scrapers
  K. Full-grooved ax

  L. Drill types
  M. Seashell bead
  N. Shell beads
  O. Pottery disk
  P. Reconstructed platform(?) pipe and
     elbow pipe
  Q. Bone ornament or gaming object
  R. Bone disk

  T. Beamer or fleshing tool
  U. Bone pin
  V. Antler rubbing tool
  W. Antler arrowshaft straightener
  X. Flaking tool
  Y. Bone awls
  Z. Flexed burial

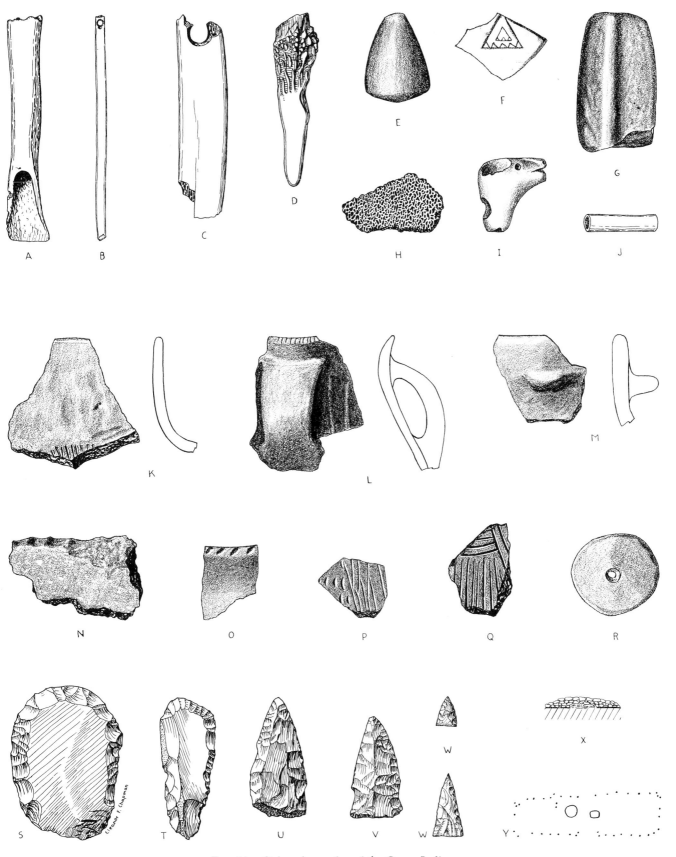

FIG. 64.—Cultural complex of the Osage Indians

A. Bone fleshing tool
B. Bone needle
C. Bone arrowshaft straightener
D. Antler flaking tool
E. Cone-shaped whetstone of sandstone
F. Mold

G. Sandstone arrowshaft smoother
H. Bone paint brush
I. Effigy pipe
J. Bone bead
K–Q. Pottery fragments
R. Pottery disk

S–T. Scrapers
U. Knife
V–W. Projectile points
X. Stone cairn
Y. Floor plan of narrow rectangular house

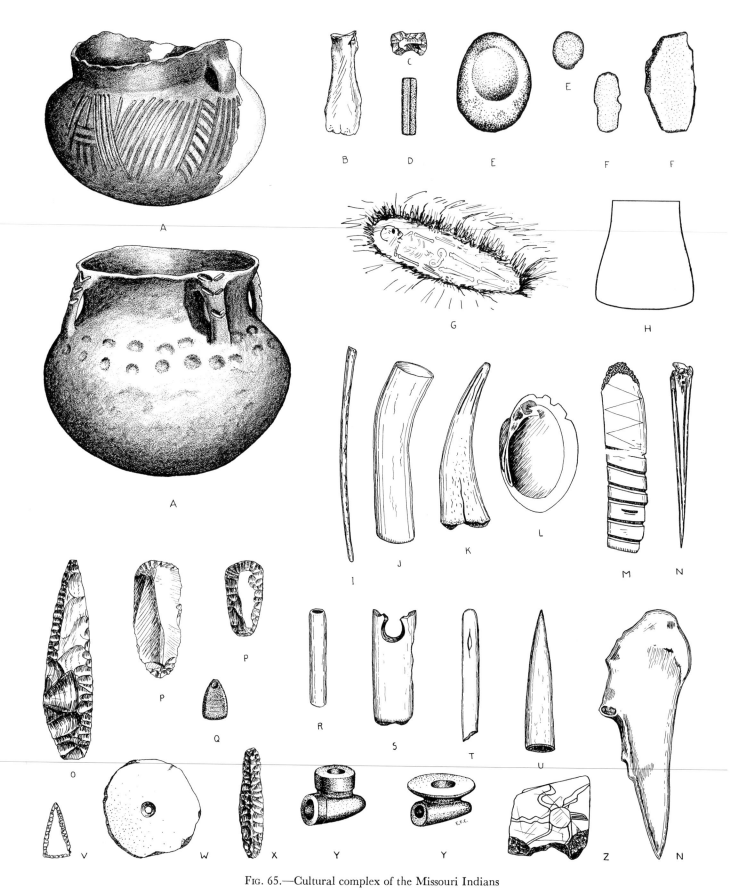

FIG. 65.—Cultural complex of the Missouri Indians

A. Pottery vessels
B. Scapula digging tool
C. Flint ax
D. Sandstone arrowshaft smoother
E. Mortar and muller
F. Metate and mano
G. Extended burial in single grave

H. Storage-pit outline
I. Bone pin
J. Rubbing tool
K. Antler flaking tool
L. Shell spoon
M. Bone musical rasp

N. Bone awl
O. Knife
P. End scraper
Q. Stone pendant
R. Bone bead
S. Bone arrowshaft straightener

T. Eyed bone needle
U–V. Projectile points
W. Pottery disk
X. Drill
Y. Pipes
Z. Engraved catlinite tablet

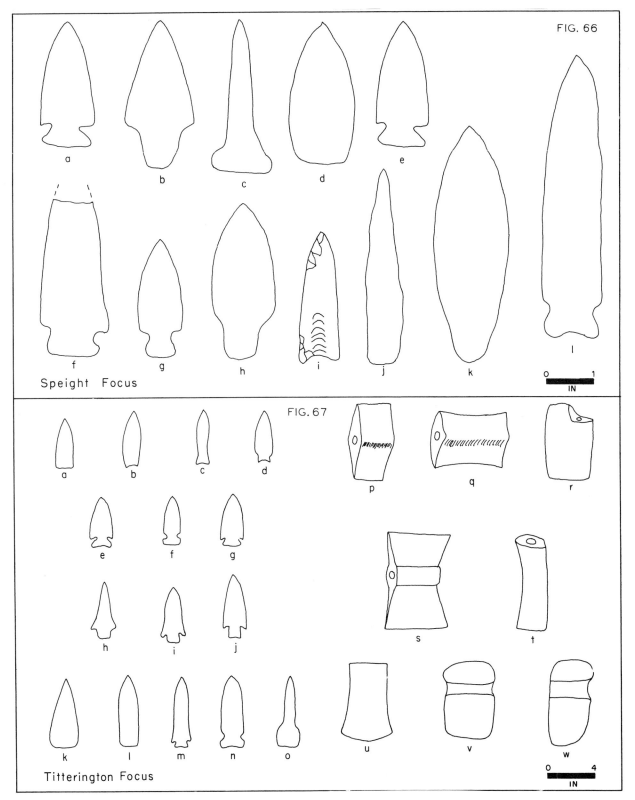

FIG. 66.—Speight Focus points from central Illinois

I. Folsomoid type possibly associated with Speight site

FIG. 67.—The Titterington Focus of the Archaic in the St. Louis area

A–N. Various projectile point types   *P–T.* Various bannerstones   *V.* Full-grooved stone ax
O. Drill   *U.* Copper ax   *W.* Three-quarter-grooved stone ax

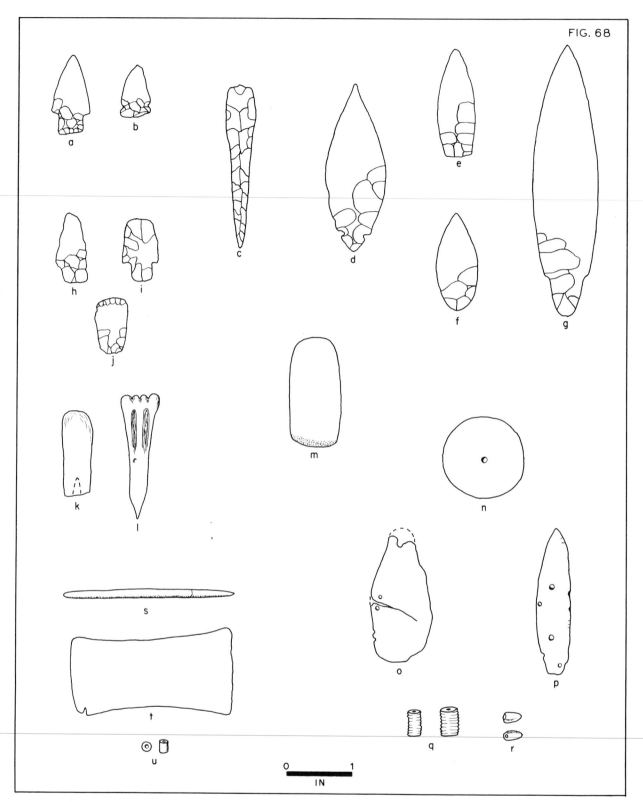

FIG. 68

FIG. 68.—Roskamp Focus of Early Woodland

A. Stemmed projectile point
B. Small notched projectile point
C. Expanded base drill
D. Side-notched, double-pointed blade or "turkey tail"
E–F. Lanceolate or leaf-shaped blades
G. Excellently chipped large thin blade
H. Stemmed, asymmetric knife

I. Stemmed scraper or chisel
J. Scraper
K. Socketed antler handle
L. Awl from bisected deer metapodial
M. Polished celt, rectangular section
N. Circular gorget of marine shell
O. Pear-shaped shell gorget or pendant
P. Crescentic shell object from burial

Q. Crinoid stems probably worn in necklace
R. Marginella shell beads with apical perforation
S. Copper awl, square section
T. Copper plaque from burial
U. Rolled copper beads

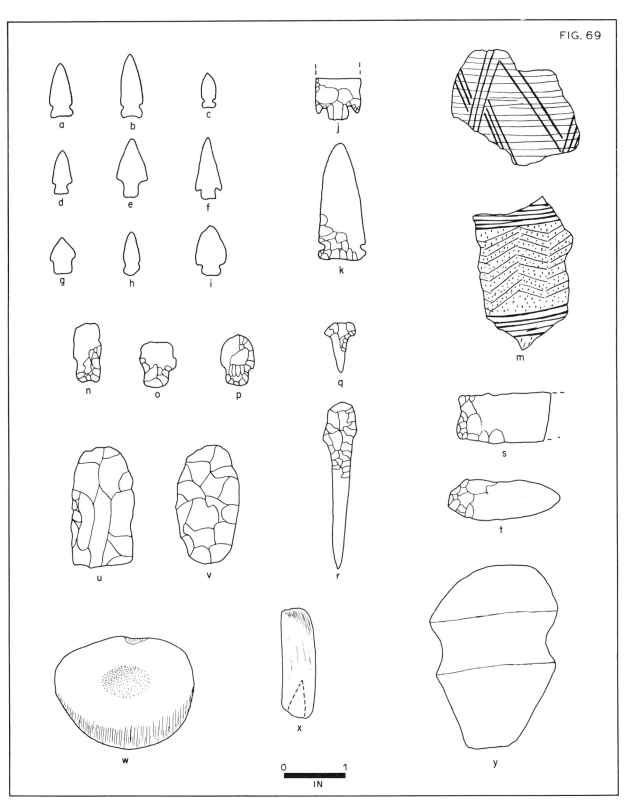

FIG. 69

FIG. 69.—Black Sand Focus of Early Woodland

A–K. Various projectile points
L–M. Black Sand Incised pottery
N–P. Stemmed scrapers or chisels
  Q. Winged drill

R. Expanded base drill
S. Thin, well-made knife (broken)
T. Asymmetric stemless knife, common
   type

U–V. Celt or hoe-like tools of chipped
     flint
  W. Pitted hammerstone
  X. Socketed antler handle
  Y. Full-grooved ax

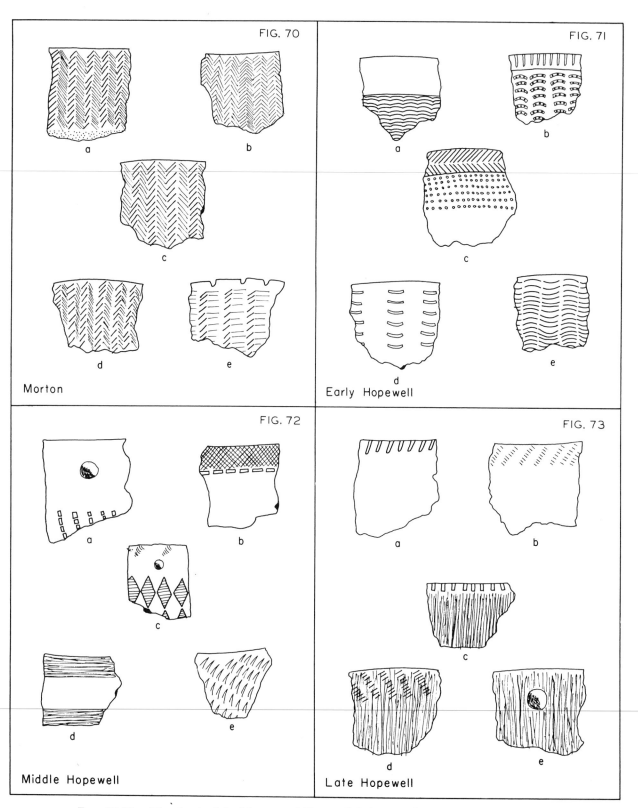

FIGS. 70–73.—Rim sherds of the Morton and Hopewell Culture in the Central Illinois Valley

FIG. 70.—*A–E*, Morton Incised.

FIG. 71.—*A, D, E*, Plain crescent stamp. *B.* Crescent dentate stamp. *C.* Incised and punctated rim.

Fig. 72.—*A, C*, Naples Stamped. *B.* Hopewell Rim Incised. *D*, Baehr Brushed. *E.* Plain rocker stamp.

Fig. 73.—*A.* Weaver Plain. *B.* Clear Lake Stamped. *C–E.* Weaver Cord Marked.

FIG. 74.—Early Hopewell pottery of the Central Illinois Valley

A. Diagonal hemiconical punctates in lower rim zone

B–C. Plain crescent stamp in rim zone

D. Hollow cylinder punctates on upper rim zone

E. Horizontal cord-wrapped-stick impressions on lower rim

F. Crescent dentate stamp on rim area

G. Plain rocker stamp on body

H. Diagonal dentate stamp on lower rim zone

I. Dentate stamp in herringbone pattern on lower rim zone

J. Diagonal dentate stamp on lower rim zone

K. Plain crescent (fingernail) stamp

L. Havana Zoned Incised

FIG. 75.—Middle Hopewell ceramics

A. Havana Zoned Stamped   C. Havana Zoned Stamped   E–I. Variations of dentate stamping on the rim
B. Hopewell Rim Incised   D. Incurving bowl rim of zoned incised type

Fig. 76.—Pottery of the Weaver Focus

A–C. Cord-wrapped-stick impressions on outer rim   *G–I.* Weaver Cord Marked
D–F. Clear Lake Cord-Stamped on Weaver Plain

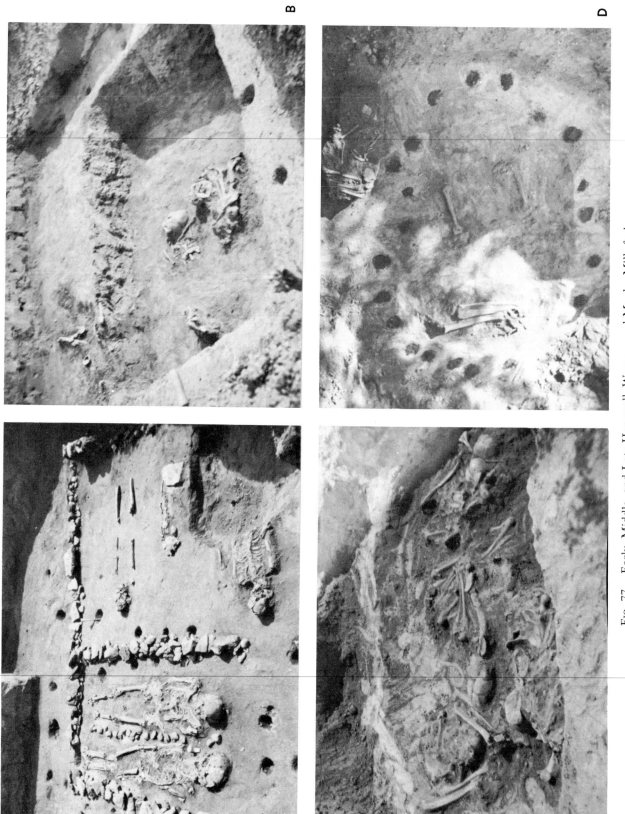

Fig. 77.—Early, Middle, and Late Hopewell, Weaver, and Maples Mills foci

A. Early Hopewell (Fᵛ234) (floor level extended burial within log crypt and rock walls; bone skewers in post molds and effigy pipes)

B. Middle Hopewell (Fᵛ410) (central subfloor pit with log cover; disarticulated burials in pit and around margin)

C. Late Hopewell-Weaver Focus (Fᵛ909) (shallow central pit; semiflexed bundle burials)

D. Maples Mills (Fᵛ911) (semiflexed burial in shallow pit; post molds around pits)

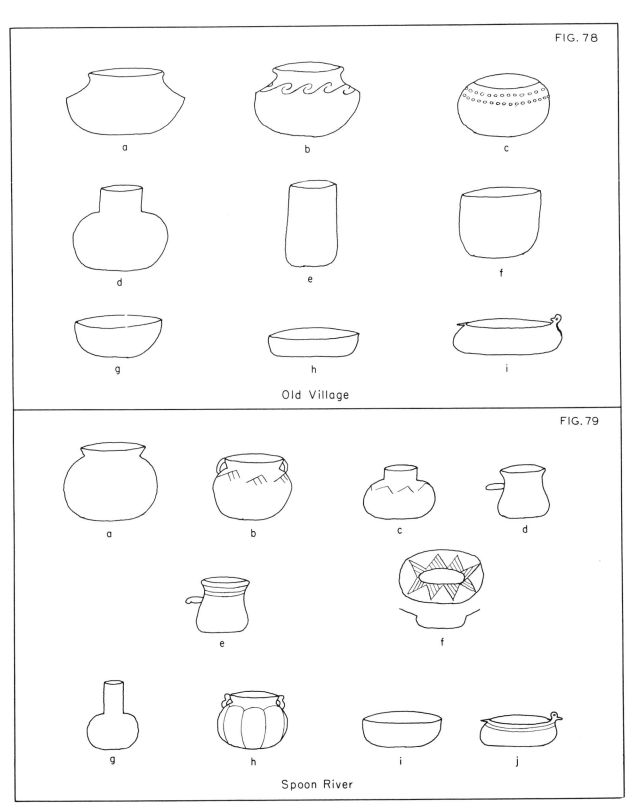

FIG. 78

Old Village

FIG. 79

Spoon River

Fɪɢ. 78.—Old Village Ceramic Complex

A–B. Angular shouldered jars of Powell
    Plain and Ramey Incised
  C. Bowl of Monks Mound Red

D. Short-neck, wide-mouth water bottle
E. Tall, beaker-like form

F. Deep bowl
G–I. Shallow bowls

Fɪɢ. 79. Spoon River and Trappist Ceramic Complex

A–B. Globular bodied jars
  C. Short-neck water bottle
D–E. Beaker or "bean-pots"

F. Plate with incised decoration on rim
G. Long, cylindrical neck bottle

H. Lobed jar
I–J. Shallow bowls

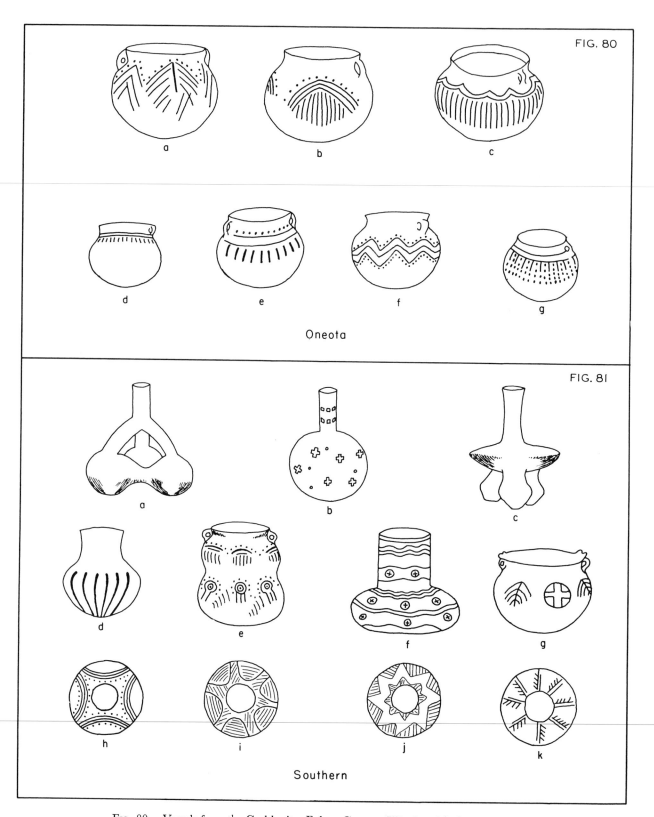

FIG. 80

Oneota

FIG. 81

Southern

Fig. 80.—Vessels from the Crable site, Fulton County, Illinois, with Oneota designs

Fig. 81.—Pottery vessels from southern Illinois of the Mississippi period

A, C. Trilobed bottles   *E, G.* Jars with Oneota and "Southern Cult" designs
B. Negative-painted bottle   *F.* Engraved bottle
D. Deeply lobed bottle   *H–K.* Deep plates with incised and punctate designs on the rim

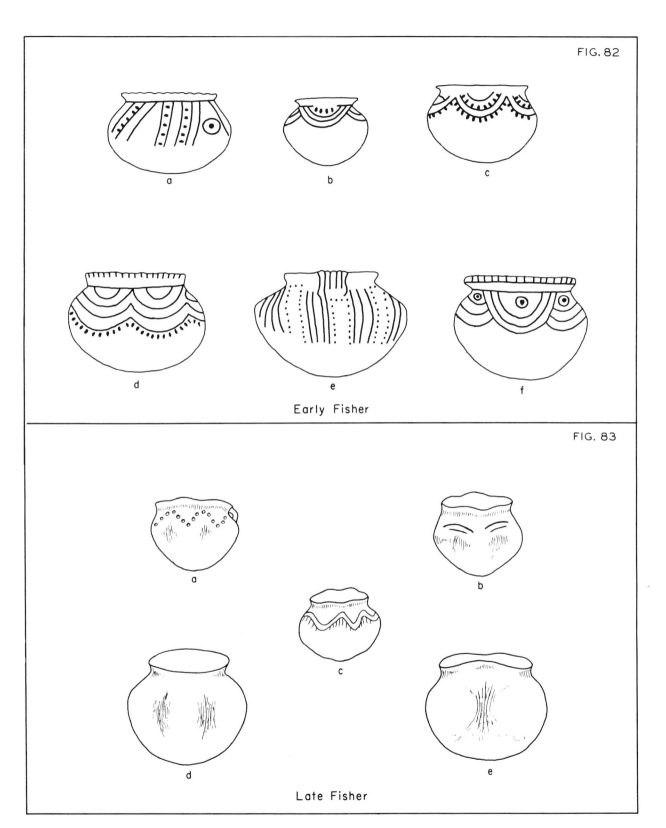

Early Fisher

Late Fisher

FIG. 82.—Early Fisher Focus ceramic specimens

FIG. 83.—Late Fisher Focus pottery

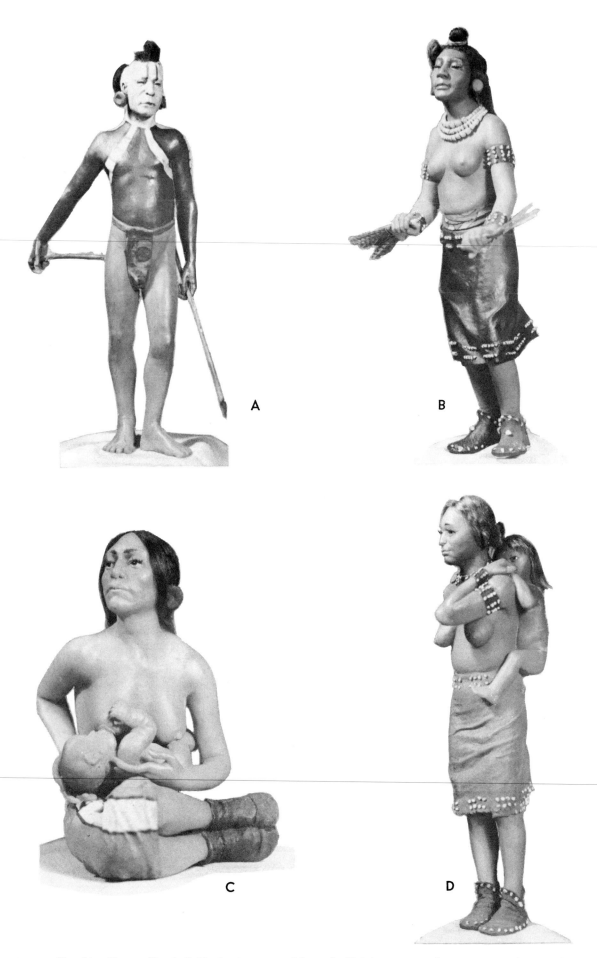

FIG. 84.—Hopewellian individuals reconstructed from the Knight statuettes (sculpture and photographs by B. M. Frost).

A. Warrior with spear   *B.* Dancing woman   *C–D.* Women with children

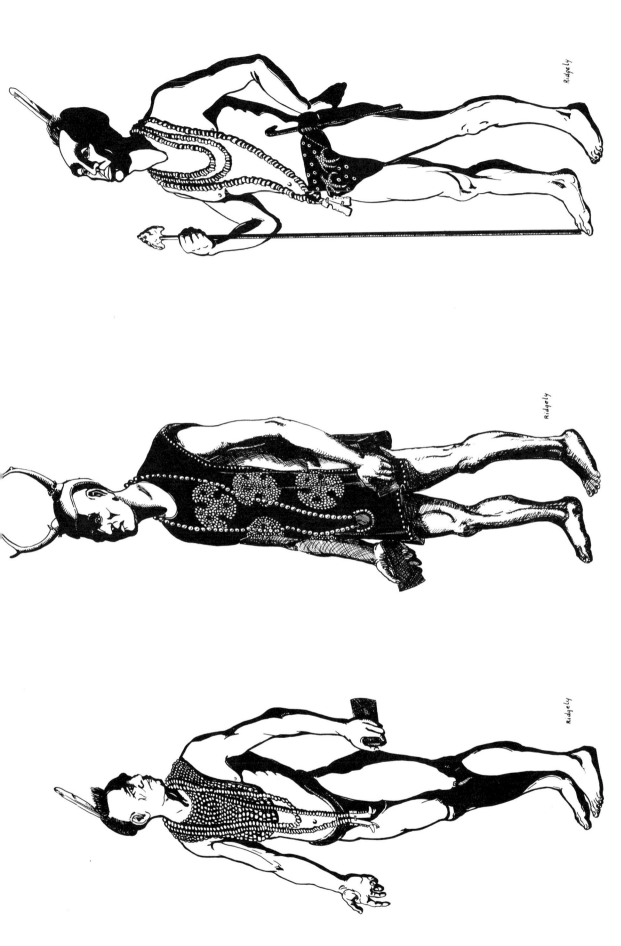

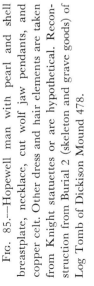

Fig. 85.—Hopewell man with pearl and shell breastplate, necklace, cut wolf jaw pendants, and copper celt. Other dress and hair elements are taken from Knight statuettes or are hypothetical. Reconstruction from Burial 2 (skeleton and grave goods) of Log Tomb of Dickison Mound 478.

Fig. 86.—Hopewell official in ceremonial regalia. Necklace of globular silver beads and a cut human maxillary with teeth as a pendant, numerous pearl beads over body "as if sewed to garment," and copper axes or hatchets were found with skeleton of the "mat burial" in Liverpool Mount 77. The antler portion of the headdress was found with a skeleton at Liverpool but possibly not with the mat burial. The pearl beads are sewn on the cloth in a design found at the Hopewell site in Ohio, where it occurred in sheet copper. Other elements of the dress are hypothetical.

Fig. 87.—Hopewell warrior, with necklace of disk shell beads, with halves of human mandible as pendants, a spearhead and small rings of shell, and hawk claws. The other objects and dress elements are taken from Knight statuettes or are hypothetical, as is the arrangement of hawk's claws and shell rings on the breechcloth. Reconstruction from the principal skeleton (No. 4), Log Tomb 2, Whitnah Mound 54.

FIG. 88.—Hopewell woman from Log Tomb of Dickison Mound 478. Her skeleton lay next to the principal male (Fig. 85) of the group. The necklace of ground shell beads and their general arrangement on the body and relation to the wolf mandible halves, the skull of a hawk, and the beads at the feet occurred with this skeleton. The pot is restored with its design as found on a fragment recovered from the mound earth, though not in the tomb. The remaining articles of dress and hair arrangement are hypothetical or based on the Knight figurines.

FIG. 89.—A Hopewell man as revealed by a burial in the Gibson Mound, from the notes and diagram furnished by Dr. Paul F. Titterington. The copper earspools and bear-tooth pendants at ears and wrists, the bear-tooth pendant near each shoulder, a characteristic platform pipe, bears' teeth at the waist, and a copper ax accompanied this skeleton when found. Other dress elements are based on Knight figurines and traits from other sites.

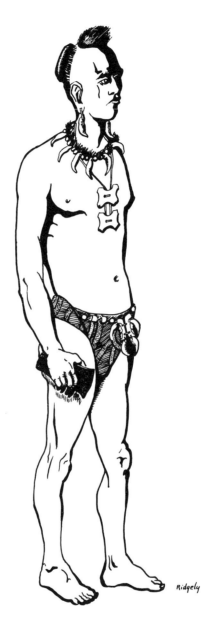

FIG. 90.—A Hopewell male with accoutrements chosen from finds in the Baehr Mounds of Brown County, Illinois. The copper earspools, copper plume, the human portrait clay pipe (bowl), bears' teeth, stone celt, and bone beads were a part of the material found with the charred remains of a small group of skeletons in Baehr Mound 1. The *Helisoma* shell beads, the hint of feather cloth, and shape of headdress (from complete figurine) and the kind of breechcloth (from headless figurine) all came from the Baehr group.

FIG. 91.—Hopewell Male reconstructed from Burial 5, Mound 6, near Havana, Mason County, Illinois. The deceased when buried wore two reel-shaped gorgets on the chest, had a black bear canine near each ear, bear canines about the neck together with ground shell beads (shape unknown), two halves of a wolf jaw, shell beads, and black bear canines in the waist region. The copper ax lay beside the body. Barrel-shaped and flattened globular beads came from this mound. Hair arrangement and type of breech-cloth were derived from the Knight statuettes, design on cloth from an Ohio Hopewell site, and decorated fur collar from Catlin illustrations of Plains Indians.

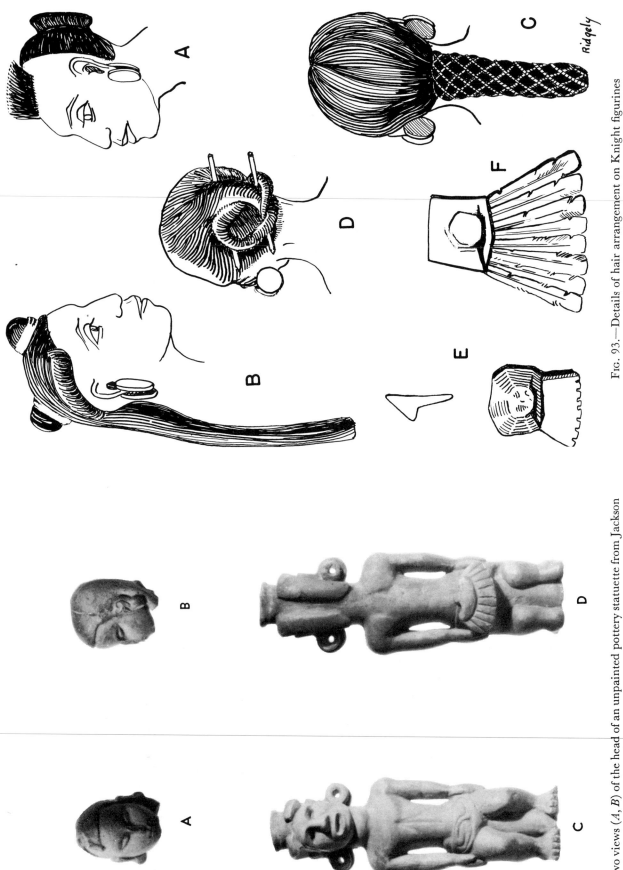

FIG. 93.—Details of hair arrangement on Knight figurines

A. From Hopewell man (see Fig. 84, A)
B. From dancing woman (see Fig. 84, B)
C. From mother with nursing child (see Fig. 84, C)
D. From standing women with child (see Fig. 84, D)
E. Bustle as it appears on Knight dancing woman, from the side and from the back
F. Bustle reconstructed of turkey-tail feathers

FIG. 92.—Two views (A, B) of the head of an unpainted pottery statuette from Jackson County, Illinois, in the collection of Mr. Willie Smith of Murphysboro. There are ear-spools in the ears, and the hair roll and shaved portion of the right side of the head that duplicates a like arrangement on the Knight dancing figure. The front view (C) is of a cast of the Adena human effigy pipe, showing the breechcloth and its decorative design. The back view (D) of the same pipe shows the bustle-like ornament. Mold for pipe loaned by the Illinois State Museum through the courtesy of the Ohio State Museum.

Fig. 94.—Hopewellian cloth fragment with batik-like design preserved on a copper breast-plate from Ohio. Reproduced here through courtesy of the Ohio State Museum.

Fig. 95.—Cultural traits of the Faulkner Focus in southern Illinois

A (1). Irregular oval pit
B (2). Flexed burial
C (3). Stemmed projectile points
D (4). Stemless projectile points
E (5). Gravers
F (6). Various types of drills
G (7). Hafted scrapers
H (8). End scrapers
I (9). Large knife forms
J (10). Plano-convex scraper
K (11). Pebble pestle
L (12). Multiple-pitted "nutting stone"
M (13). Fragment of prismoid atlat weight
N (14). Small single-perforation pendant
O (15). Single-pitted hammerstone or lap anvil

THE FAULKNER FOCUS

1

2

3

4

5

6

7

8

9

10

11

12

13

14

15

FIG. 96.—Outstanding traits of the Baumer Focus

A (1). Round, straight-sided, flat-based pit
B (2). Bell-shaped pit
C (3). Square house plan
D (4). Various types of projectile points
E (5). Hafted and end scraper
F (6). Disk knife or scraper
G (7). Drills
H (8). Chisel
I (9). Knives
J (10). Broken poll and bit portions of celts
K (11). Conoidal pestle
L (12). Disk-shaped knife or scraper
M (13). Ovate hoe with a high dirt polish on bit

N (14). Two-holed "reel-shaped" gorget
O (15). Pendants and plummet stone
P (16). Full-grooved ax
Q (17). Cord-impressed rim from Baumer Fabric Impressed vessel
R (18). Incising on rim of plain ware
S (19). Punctates on rim sherd
T (20). Cord impressions and small punctates on plain ware
U (21). Parallel rows of punctates on plain ware
V (22). Body sherd of Baumer Cord Marked
W (23). Baumer Fabric Impressed vessel with constricted flat base
X (24). Baumer Fabric Impressed vessel with flat base
Y (25). Miniature vessel with plain surface

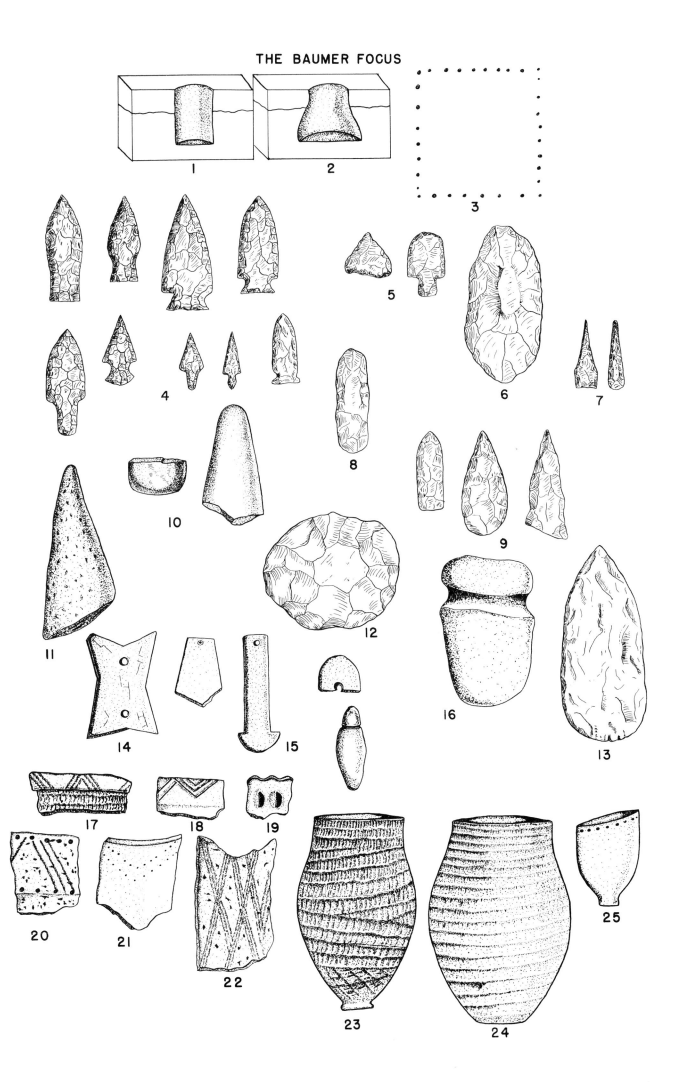

THE BAUMER FOCUS

Fig. 97 —Various culture traits of the Crab Orchard Focus

A. Round, straight-sided, flat-based pits
B. Round conoidal pits
C. Flexed burials
D. Bundle reburials
E (1). Antler projectile points
F (2). Antler tines from which projectile points have been cut
G (3). Antler punch
H (4). Antler ring
I (5). Cut and drilled wolf mandible
J (6). Drilled fox canine
K (7). Clay female effigy
L (8). Antler awl
M (9). Cut antler
N (10). Antler flaking tool or hammer
O (11). Antler handle
P (12). Deer metatarsal awl

Q (13). Bird-bone awl
R (14). Split bird-bone awls
S (15). Bone chisel
T (16). Disk knife or chopper
U (17). Knives
V (18). Projectile points
W (19). Flint eccentric forms
X (20). Flake knife
Y (21). Hafted scrapers
Z (22). End scraper
A' (23). Side scrapers
B' (24). Drills
C' (25). Polished chert chisels
D' (26). Soft claystone tablet
E' (27). Vertically grooved celt
F' (28). Tapering polled celt
G' (29). Fragment of grooved ax

H' (30). Notched flint ax
I' (31). Sandstone abrader
J' (32). Single-pitted anvil
K' (33). Ovoid hoe
L' (34). Chalky limestone celt
M' (35). Limestone disk
N' (36). Quartzite ball
O' (37). Sandstone pitted or cupstone
P' (38). Hematite concretion used as paint mortar
Q' (39). Hematite tablet
R' (40). Limestone conoidal cup
S'–U' (41–43). Limestone "reel-shaped" gorgets
V' (44). Shell pendant
W' (45). Bar atlatl weight
X' (46). Pebble pendant

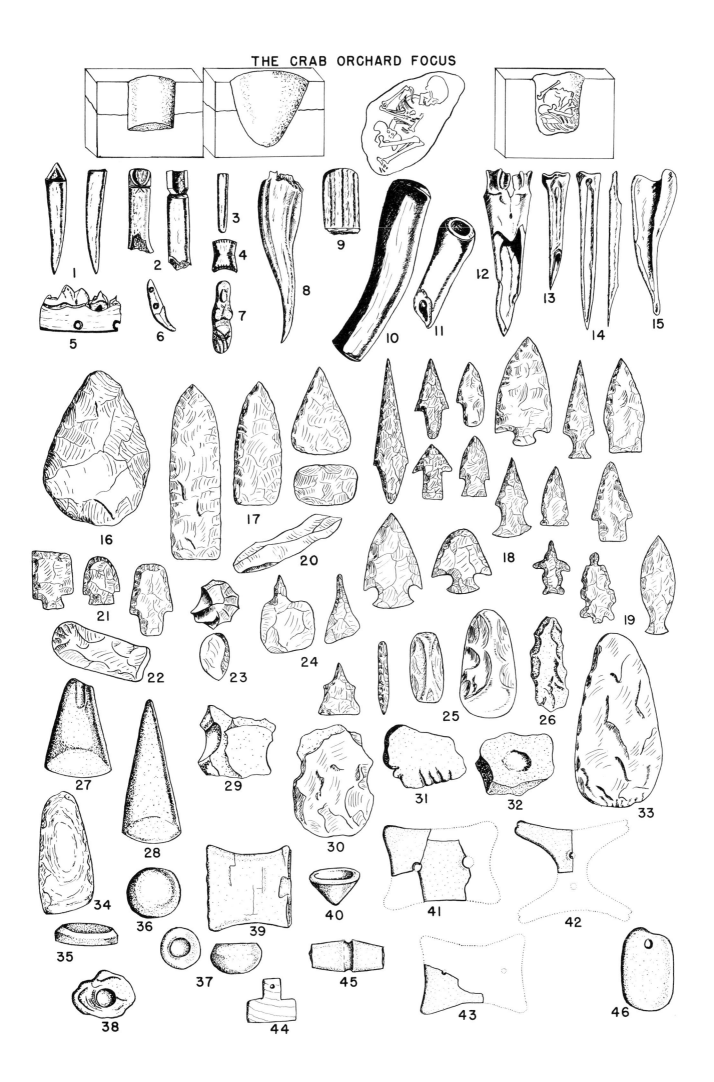

THE CRAB ORCHARD FOCUS

Fig. 98.—Ceramic traits of the Crab Orchard Focus

A (1). Conoidal, flat-based Sugar Hill Cord Marked jar

B (2). Crab Orchard Fabric Marked jar from the Cove Hollow rock shelter (the punctated design is unique)

C (3). Crab Orchard Cord Marked jar with a horizontal row of nodes around the rim punched from the interior

D (4). Reconstruction of atypical shouldered jar of Crab Orchard Fabric Impressed

E (5). Miniature vessels with plain surfaces

F (6). Conoidal-based Crab Orchard Fabric Impressed

G (7). Cord-impressed rim sherd with the individual impressions forming part of the design

H (8). Incised decoration over Sugar Hill Cord Marked surface

I (9). Oblique cord-wrapped-stick impressions on the outer rim

J (10). Typical rim sherd of the late part of the Crab Orchard Focus

K (11). Hopewell crosshatched rim

L (12). Noded and incised body sherd (the ware is similar to Crab Orchard Fabric Impressed, while the decoration is derived from Hopewell)

M (13). Punctate decoration over Crab Orchard Fabric Impressed

N (14). Hemiconical punctates over Crab Orchard Fabric Impressed

O (15). Copy of Hopewell crosshatched rim by Crab Orchard potters

P–Q (16–17). Variants of Hopewell rim treatment on local ware

R (18). Dentate stamped sherd—a type very common in the Illinois Valley at this period

S (19). Zoned plain rocker stamping

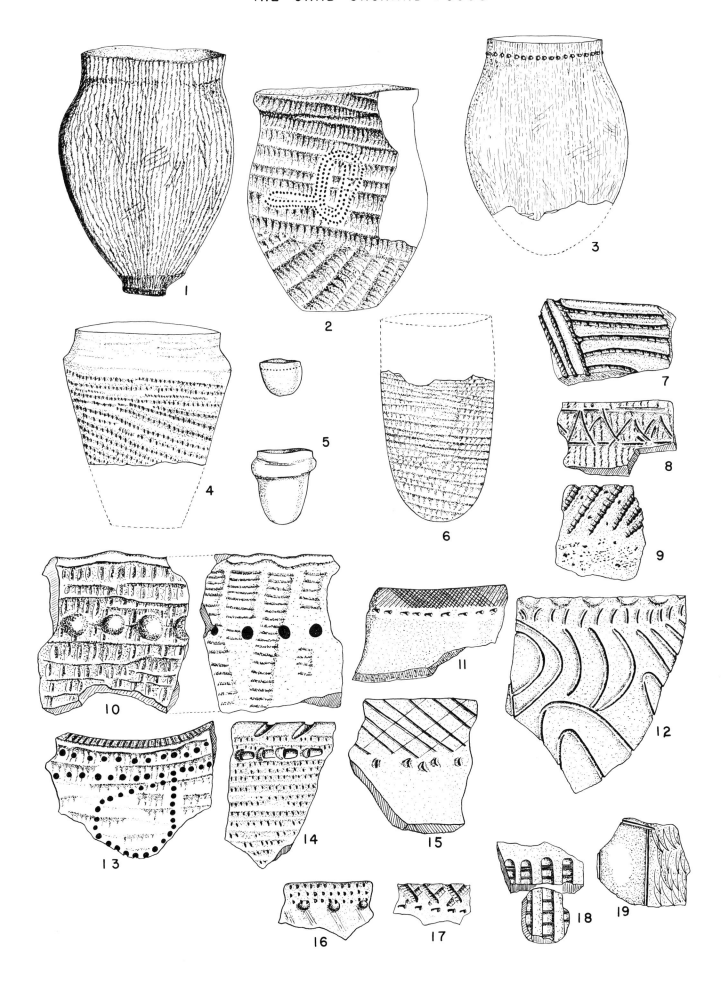

FIG. 99.—Features of the Lewis Focus

A (*1*). Circular, straight-sided pits
B (*2*). Floor plan of rectangular house
C (*3*). Stone cairns
D (*4*). Double extended burial
E (*5*). Projectile point types
F (*6*). Knife
G (*7*). End scraper
H (*8*). Plano-convex scraper or adz
I (*9*). Flaking tool
J (*10*). Clay beads

K (*11*). Incised clay disk
L (*12*). Celt poll
M–Q (*13–17*). Reconstructed vessel forms of Lewis Cord Marked
P (*18*). Scalloped lip on Lewis Cord Marked
R (*19*). Interior view of notched lip
S (*20*). Lewis Incised rim sherd
T (*21*). Notched outer lip edge
U (*22*). Lewis Incised rim sherd

THE LEWIS FOCUS

Fɪɢ. 100.—The Raymond Focus of the Late Woodland period

A (1). Cut antler tips
B (2). Antler awl
C (3). Split bird-bone awl
D (4). Projectile points of various types
E (5). Drill or reamer
F (6). Ovoid knives
G (7). Side scrapers
H (8). Trianguloid knife
I (9). Flake knife
J (10). Hafted scraper
K (11). Thumbnail scraper
L (12). Graver
M (13). Chisel
N (14). Grooved bar—possibly an atlatl weight
O (15). Pebble celt of basalt

P (16). Clay disk ornamented with impressed cords
Q (17). Shapes of Raymond Cord Marked jar
R (18). Miniature bowl of plain ware
S (19). Exterior views of rim and lip treatment of Raymond Cord Marked
T (20). Interior view of notched inner lip edge on Raymond Cord Marked
U (21). Inner rim notching with cord-wrapped-stick impressions
V (22). Exterior lip-edge notching or knicking

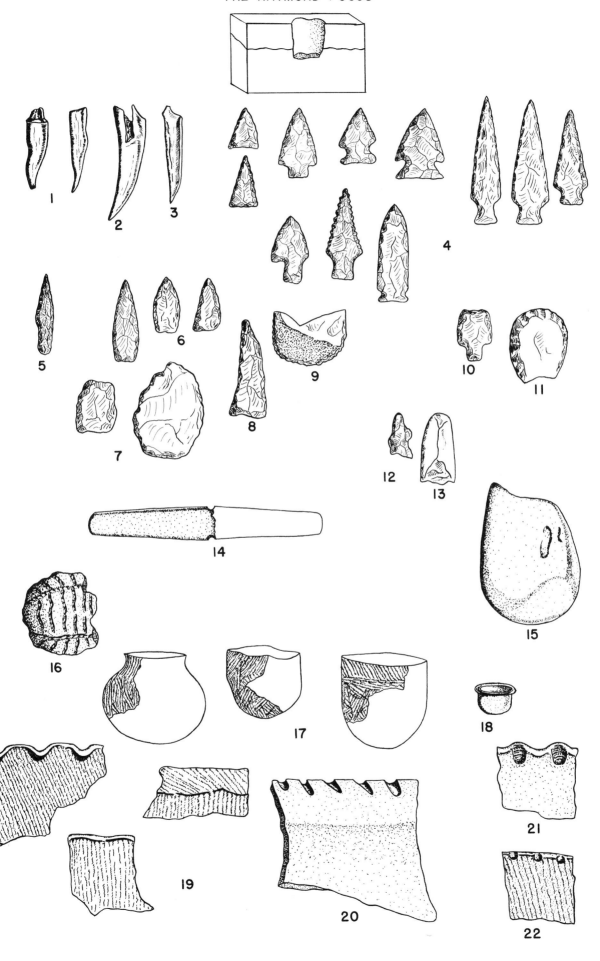

THE RAYMOND FOCUS

Fig. 101.—The Late Woodland Dillinger Focus

A (1). Circular, straight-sided, flat-based pit
B (2). Circular pit with expanded base
C (3). Circular pit lined for short distance above floor with baked clay
D (4). Fishhook blank and completed hooks
E (5). Antler projectile points
F (6). Deer phalanx jingler
G (7). Grooved canine tooth
H (8). Antler awl
I (9). Antler tally
J (10). Antler flaking hammer
K (11). Deer metatarsal awls
L (12). Bird-bone awl
M (13). Bird-bone tallies
N (14). Carved bone pins
O (15). Stem of clay pipe
P (16). Clay anvil
Q (17). Clay dippers

R (18). Clay plummet-like effigy
S (19). Clay discoidals
T (20). Pottery disk
U (21). Shell hoes
V (22). Various projectile point types
W (23). Various types of drills
X (24). Knives
Y (25). Pierced stone pendant
Z (26). Sandstone discoidals
A' (27). Sandstone abraders
B' (28). Hafted and end scrapers
C' (29). Stone celts
D' (30). Hematite concretion rubbing stone
E' (31). Flint hoe
F' (32). Vessel form—angular-shouldered jar and loop-handled vessel on extreme right are shell-tempered plain ware, while the remainder are Dillinger Cord Marked

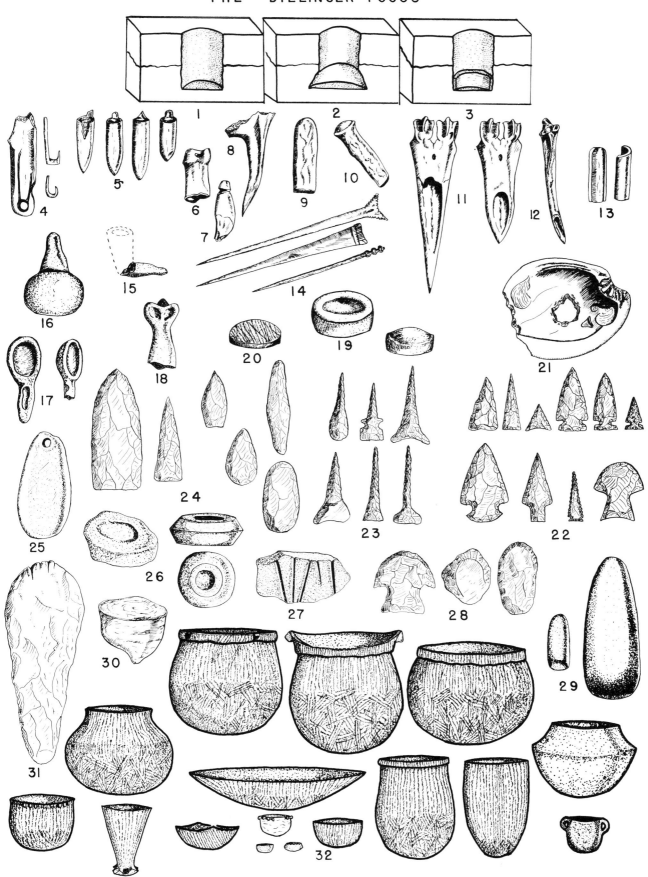

THE DILLINGER FOCUS

Fɪɢ. 102.—Archaic Culture of western Tennessee

A. Community plan: refuse mound cemetery, pits, shelters
B. Fully flexed burial
C. Spearpoints
D. Basal-notched point
DD. Side-notched point
E. Corner-notched points
EE. Triangular point
F. Hoe blade
G. Tubular stone pipe
H. Drills
I. Graver
J. Stemmed scraper
K. Adz
L. Flake scraper
M. Hoe
N. Atlatl weights
O. Bone needles or bodkins
P. Bone pendant
Q. Bone scraper or flaker
R. Antler atlatl hooks
S. Arrow wrench
T. Shell two-hole gorget
U. Shell vessel
V. Shell beads
W. Copper objects
X. Stone bead
Z. Slate two-hole gorget

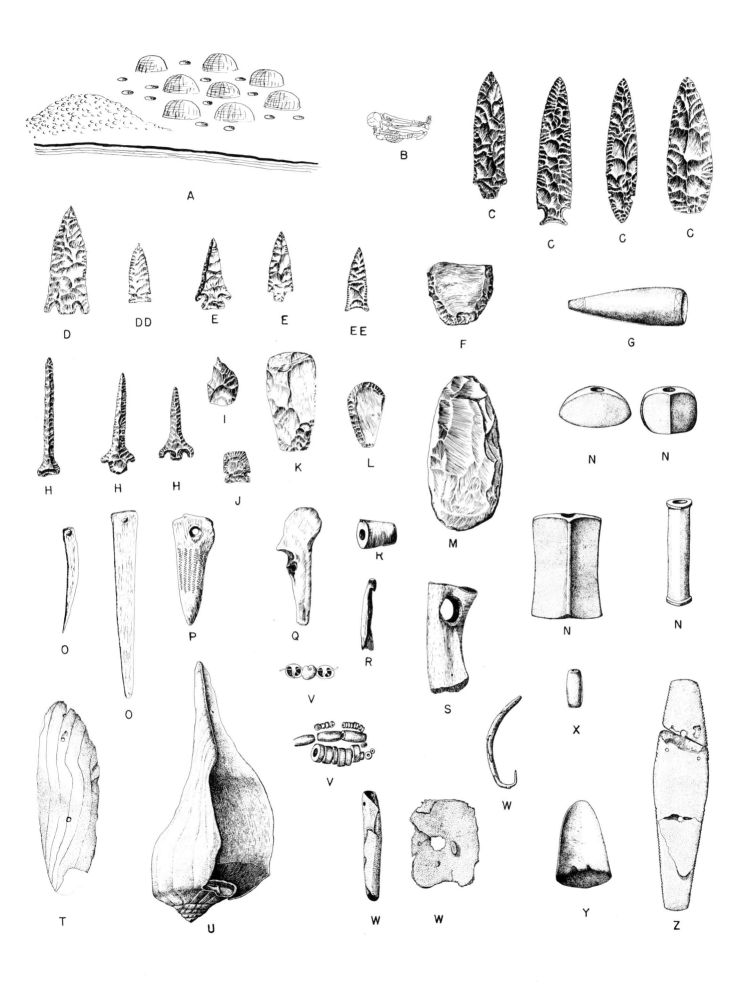

A

B

C   C   C   C

D   DD   E   E   EE   F   G

H   H   H   I   J   K   L   M   N   N

O   O   P   Q   R   R   S   N   N

V   V   X   W   Z

T   U   W   W   Y

Fɪɢ. 103.—Candy Creek Culture of eastern Tennessee

A. Community plan
B. Circular dwelling pattern, tapered post molds
C. Kettle-shaped pit, cross-section
CC. Kettle-shaped pit, from above
D. Fully flexed burials
DD. Partly flexed burial
E. Pecked celts
EE. Grooved axes
F. Heavy, stemmed projectile points
G. Side-notched projectile points
H. Stemless projectile point
I. Drills
J. Stemmed scraper
K. Engraved bone pendant
KK. Engraved bone fragment
L. Bear canine pendant
M. Slate gorgets
MM. Steatite gorgets
N. Steatite tubular pipes

NN. Boatstones
O. Limestone-tempered simple stamped pottery
OO. Sand-tempered check-stamped pottery
P. Limestone-tempered check-stamped pottery
PP. Sand-tempered check-stamped pottery
Q. Limestone-tempered fabric-marked pottery
QQ. Sand-tempered fabric-marked pottery
R. Limestone-tempered cord-marked pottery
S. Limestone-tempered complicated stamped pottery
SS. Sand-tempered complicated stamped pottery, Swift Creek type
T. Same as SS, Napier type

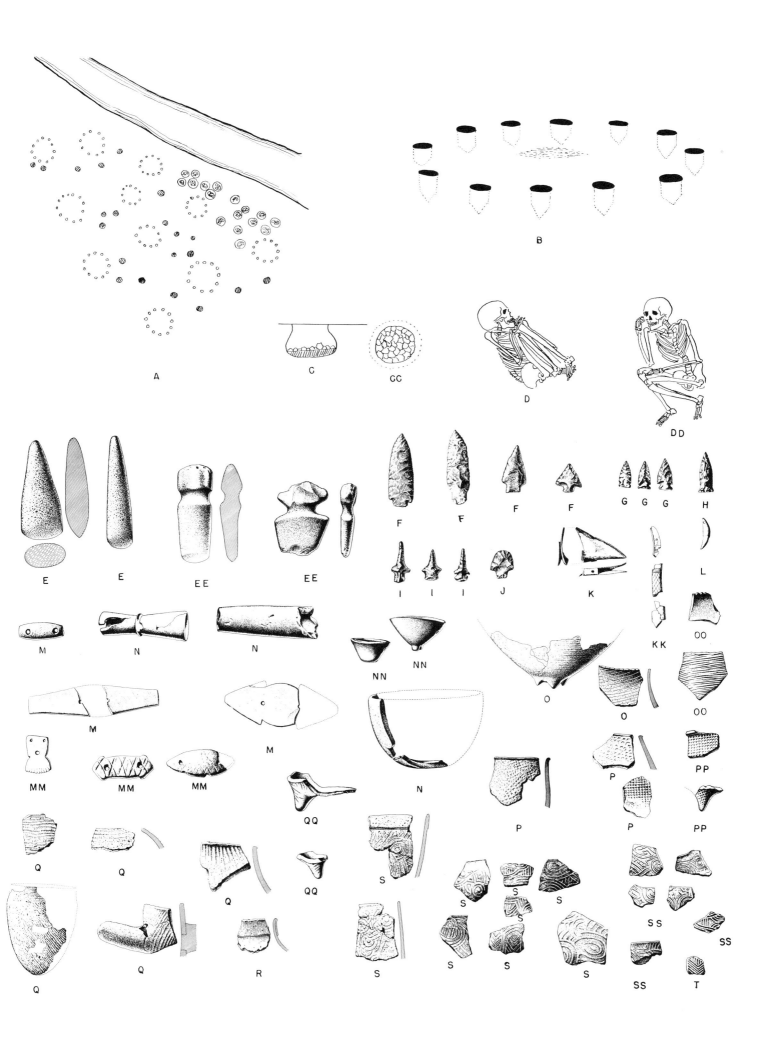

FIG. 104.—Hamilton Culture

A. Community plan
B. Burial mound cross-section
C. Partly flexed burial
D. Rare projectile point type
DD. Common projectile point type
E. Triangular projectile points
F. Stemmed scrapers
G. Pecked celts
H. Carved bone object
I. Shell pendants
II. Large pendant
J. Engraved shell
K. Columella ornaments

L. Steatite bowl rim fragment with lug
LL. Steatite gorget
M. Steatite pipe
MM. Pottery pipes
N. Limestone-tempered, cord-marked pottery
O. Limestone-tempered, plain pottery, decorated with punctates
P. Sand-tempered, complicated stamped pottery, Napier type(?)
Q. Sand-tempered, check-stamped pottery

A

B

C

D   DD   E E E E   F   F

G   G   G   H   L   I   I   J   K

I   I I I I   II

LL   M   MM   MM   MM

N   N   N   N   O   P

N   N   N   O   O   P

O   Q

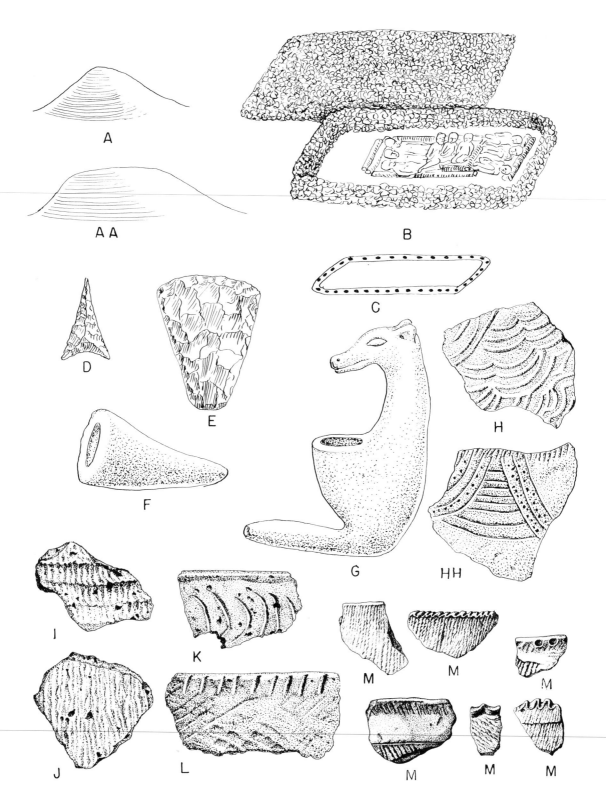

Fig. 105.—Decatur and Harmons Creek cultures of western Tennessee

A. Decatur conoidal burial mound
AA. Harmons Creek conical burial mound
B. Crematory and ceremonial pavement within an elliptical mound
C. Harmons Creek dwelling pattern
D. Incurvate triangular projectile point

E. Harmons Creek flint hoe
F. Harmons Creek pottery pipe
G. Decatur effigy pottery pipe
H. Harmons Creek complicated stamped pottery
HH. Harmons Creek incised and punc-

tate pottery
I. Decatur fabric-marked pottery
J. Decatur cord-marked pottery
K. Decatur incised pottery
L. Decatur check-stamped pottery
M. Harmons Creek cord-marked pottery

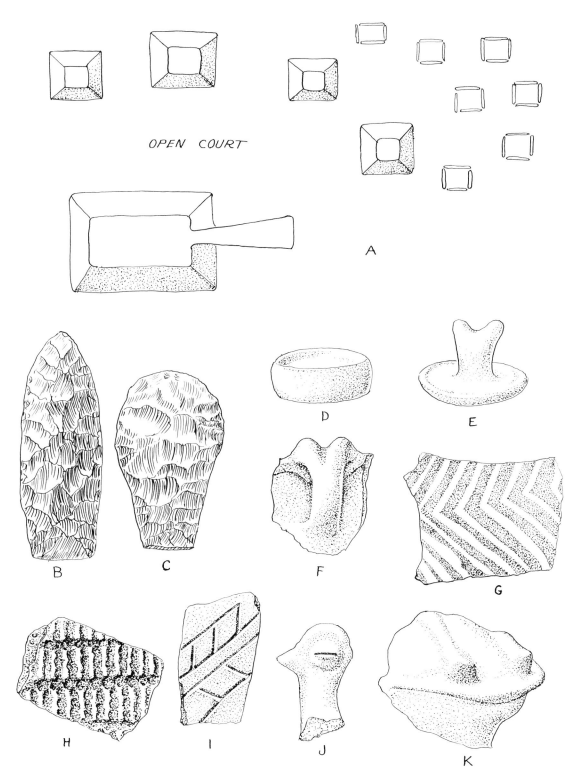

OPEN COURT

FIG. 106.—Obion Culture

A. Community plan   F. Loop handle   I. Incised pottery
B–C. Large hoes   G. Black-on-white painted pottery J. Modeled effigy head
D. Biconcave stone disk   H. Textile-marked pottery   K. Frog effigy bowl fragment
E. Pottery trowel

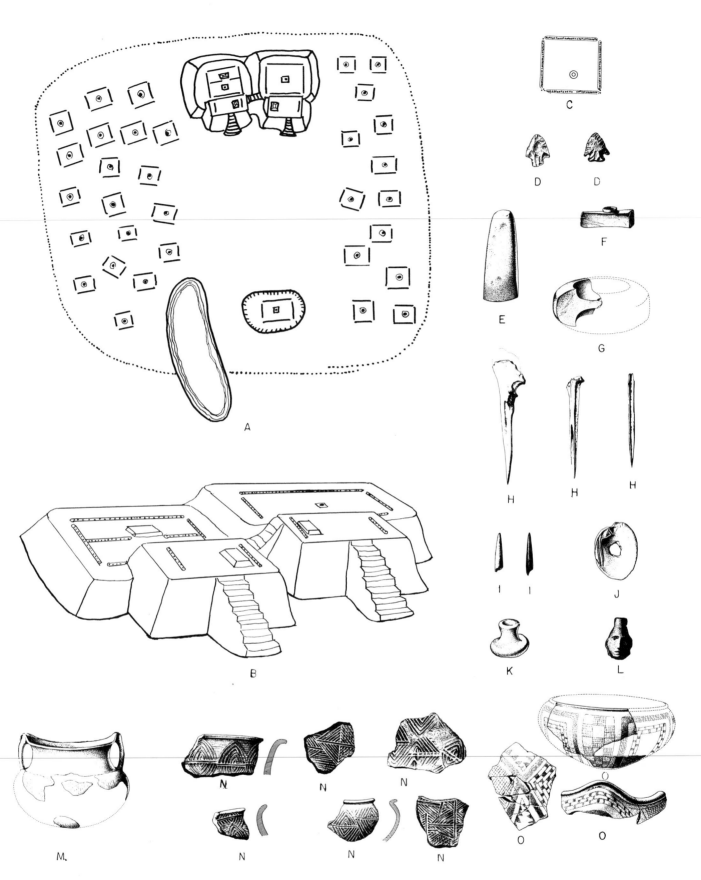

FIG. 107.—Hiwassee Island Culture

A. Community plan
B. Substructure mound plan
C. Dwelling house pattern
D. Projectile points
E. Polished celt
F. Stone pipe

G. Chunkey stone
H. Bone awls
I. Antler projectile points
J. Shell hoe
K. Pottery trowel
L. Pottery effigy head

M. Shell-tempered cord-marked pottery jar
N. Shell-tempered complicated stamped pottery
O. Red-on-buff painted pottery

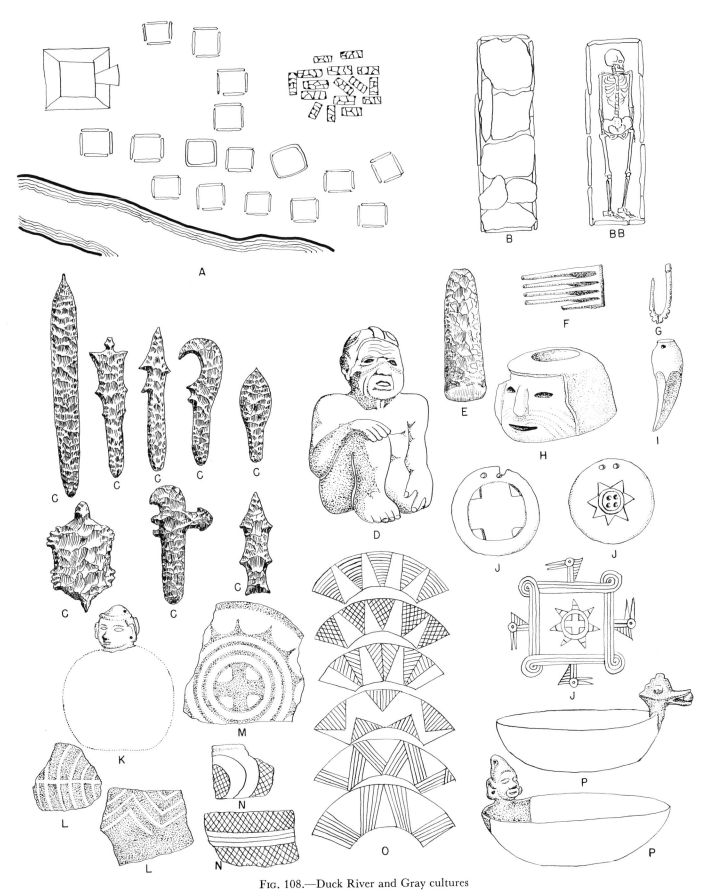

FIG. 108.—Duck River and Gray cultures

A. Community plan: substructure, dwellings, and stone coffin cemetery
B. Stone coffin
BB. Extended burial in stone coffin
C. Duck River ceremonial flints
D. Stone sculpture
E. Gray type flint celt

F. Bone comb
G. Composite bone fishhook
H. Claystone effigy pipe
I. Copper-covered wooden effigy bear canine
J. Shell gorget designs
K. Effigy bottle

L. Black-on-white exterior negative-painted pottery
M. Negative-painted bowl, interior
N. Engraved black ware
O. Engraved plate rims
P. Modeled effigy head bowls

Fɪɢ. 109.—Dallas Culture

A. Community plan
B. Dwelling house pattern
C. Typical partly flexed burial
D. The "tcokofa" ground plan
E. Cut shell beads
EE. Natural shell beads
F. Shell pin earplug
FF. Pully-type shell earplug
G. Shell-disk gorgets
GG. Shell-mask gorget
H. Bone awls
HH. Bone point
I. Scraper
J. Turtle-shell rattle
K. Stemmed projectile point
KK. Triangular projectile point
L. Ceremonial blade
M. Bear canine pendant
N. Raccoon splanchnic bodkin

O. Stone disks
OO. Steatite ring
P. Polished celts
Q. Spatulate ax
QQ. Monolithic ax
R. Shell vessel
S. Copper ornaments and celt
T. Short-stemmed elbow pipes
TT. Ax effigy pipe
U. Bird-head effigy pottery bowl
UU. Human-head effigy pottery bowl
V. Long-neck pottery bottle
W. Conventionalized zoömorphic pottery jars
X. Incised pottery jars
XX. Pottery trowel
Y. Noded pottery vessel
Z. Negative-painted pottery bottle

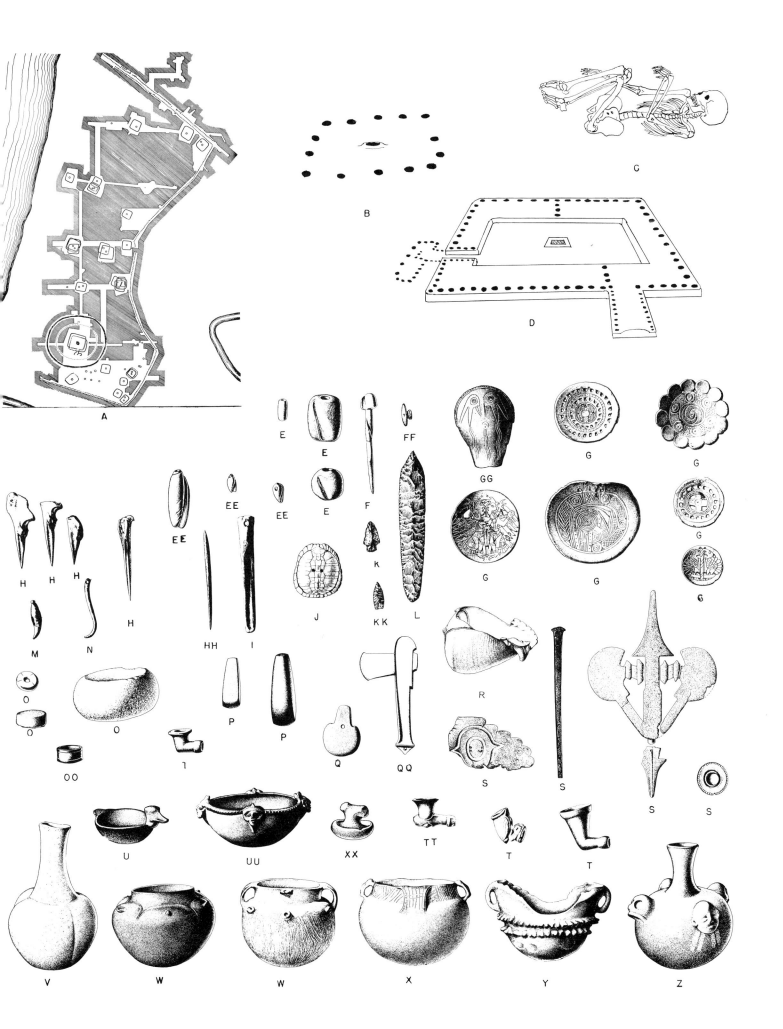

A

B

C

D

E E E EE EE F FF K KK J L GG G G G G G G

H H H H M N HH I O O OO P P 1 Q QQ R S S S S S

U UU XX TT T T

V W W X Y Z

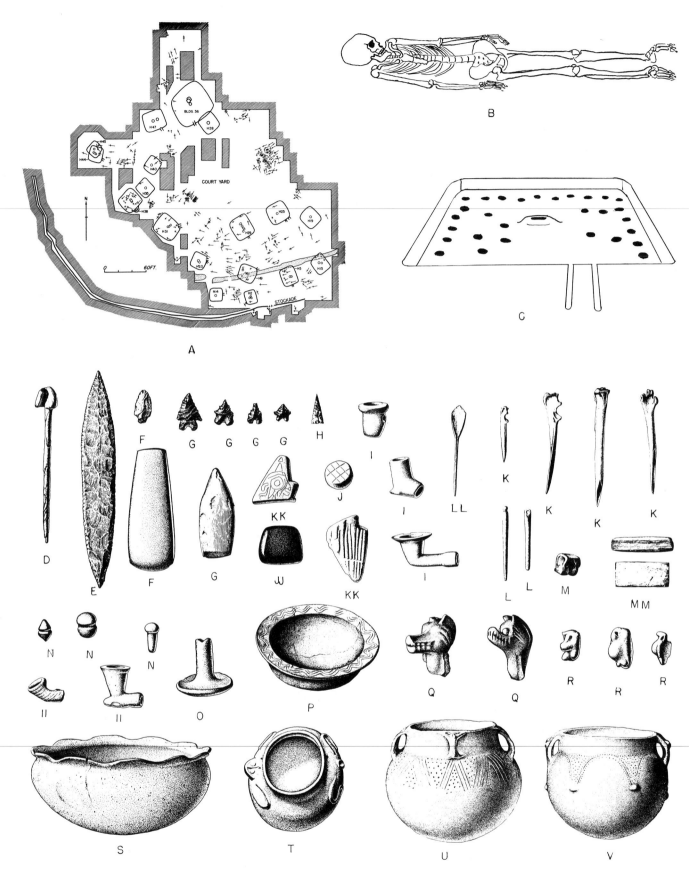

FIG. 110.—Mouse Creek Culture

A. Community plan
B. Fully extended burial
C. Shallow-pit house floor plan
D. Shell earpin
E. Flint blade
F. Stemmed projectile point
G. Notched-base projectile points

H. Triangular projectile point
I. Stone pipes
II. Pottery pipes
J. Stone disk
JJ. Cannel coal polisher
K. Bone awls
KK. Claystone awl sharpener

L. Bone bodkins
LL. Bone pin
M. Polished astragalus die
MM. Bone net-spacers
N. Pottery earplugs
O. Pottery trowel
P. Incised pottery bowl

Q. Pottery effigy heads
R. Pottery figurines
S. Plain pottery bowl
T. Frog effigy bowl
U–V. Decorated pottery jars

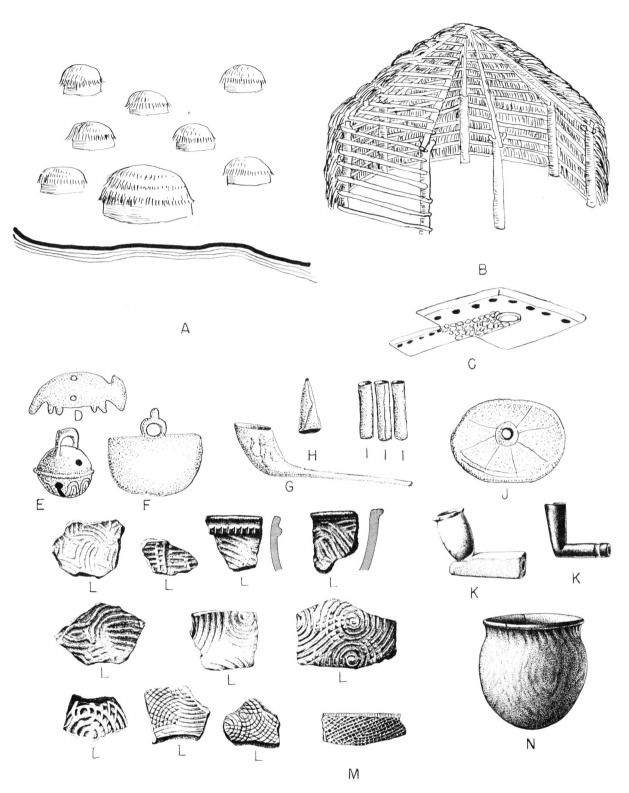

Fig. 111.—Cherokee Culture

A. Community plan
B. Architectural details of council house
C. Sweat-house floor plan
D. Brass effigy
E. Brass hawk bell
F. Iron hoe
G. English trade pipe

H. Conical brass ornament
I. Tubular brass ornaments
J. Shell-disk pendant
K. Stone pipes
L. Complicated stamped pottery
M. Check-stamped pottery
N. Stamped jar

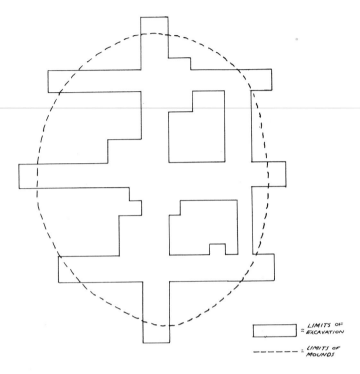

LIMITS OF
EXCAVATION

LIMITS OF
MOUNDS

FIG. 112.—Method of excavation of Hamilton Burial Mound 122RH42

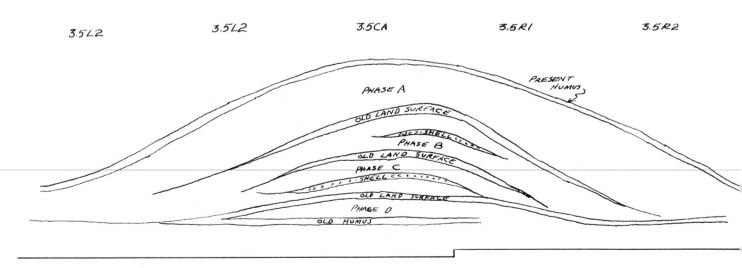

3.5L2   3.5L2   3.5CA   3.5R1   3.5R2

PHASE A

PRESENT HUMUS

OLD LAND SURFACE

SHELL

PHASE B

OLD LAND SURFACE

PHASE C

SHELL

OLD LAND SURFACE

PHASE D

OLD HUMUS

FIG. 113.—East-west profile, Mound 122RH42

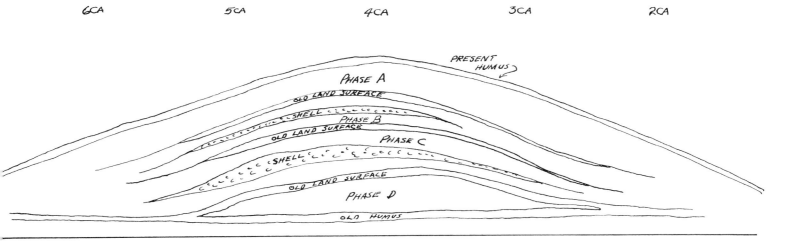

Fig. 114.—North-south profile, Mound 122RH42

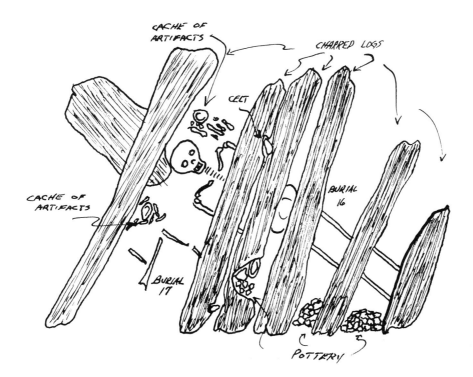

Fig. 115.—Details of log-covered Burials 16 and 17, Mound 122RH42

FIG. 116.—Hamilton Burial Mound (122RH42) viewed from the north

FIG. 117.—Burials 16 and 17 with logs in place

Fig. 118.—Burials 16 and 17 with logs removed

Fig. 119.—Detail of Burials 16 and 17 showing caches of artifacts

FIG. 120.—Material from the Sikeston Ridge area of the New Madrid Focus. (*A–J* are drawn after illustrations in Walker and Adams, 1946, and Adams and Walker, 1942; *K* is after MacCurdy, 1913, Fig. 67; *L* and *M* are after Thruston, 1890, Fig. 245 and Pl. XVII; *O* and *P* are after photographs by Dr. P. F. Titterington of specimens in his collection from southeastern Missouri.)

A. Cross-section through house pit at the Matthews site, New Madrid County, Missouri

B. Floor plan of rectangular house at the Matthews site

C. Ground and section of corner of embankment at the Matthews site

D. Various projectile point shapes from the Matthews site

E. Long-handled spud from the Matthews site

F. Grooved sandstone "shaft polisher" from the Matthews site

G. Discoidal stone from the Matthews site

H. Chipped flint hoe from New Madrid County

J. Small polished celt with narrowed poll from the Matthews site

K. Spider effigy shell gorget from Perry County, Missouri

L. Engraved shell gorget from southeastern Missouri

M. Engraved shell gorget from New Madrid County, Missouri

O–P. Pottery trowels thought to have been used in working the mud house walls

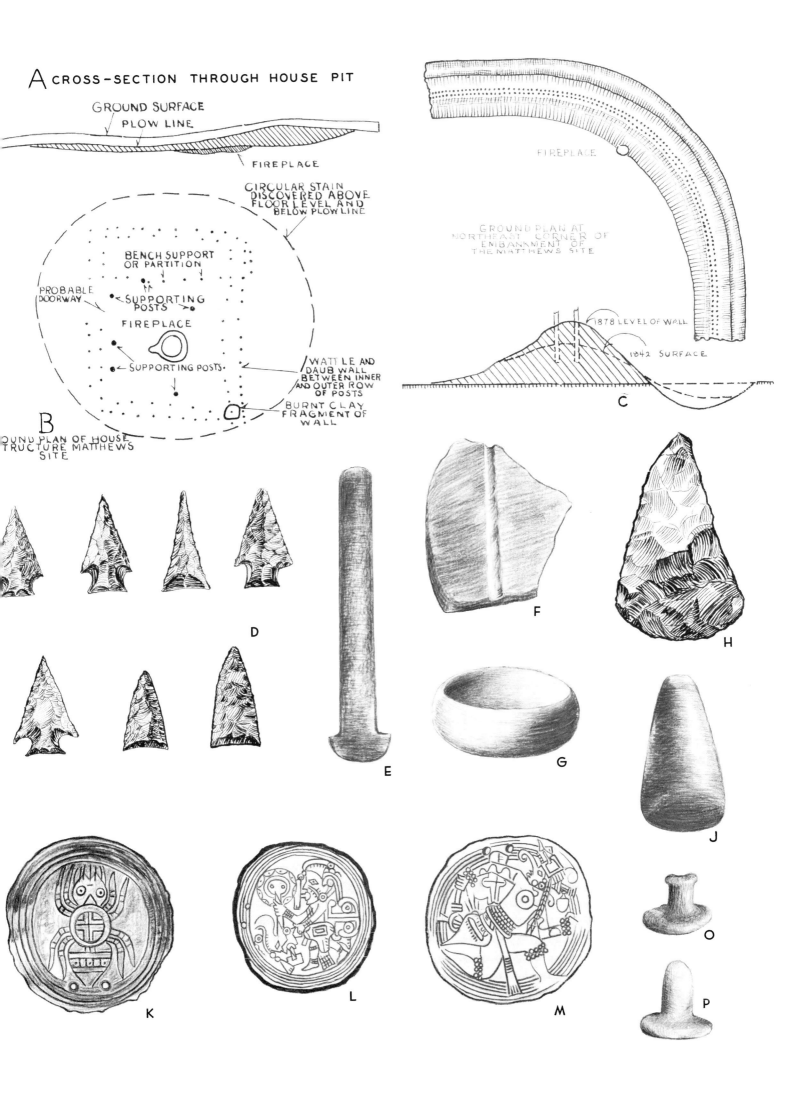

A CROSS-SECTION THROUGH HOUSE PIT

GROUND SURFACE
PLOW LINE

FIREPLACE

CIRCULAR STAIN
DISCOVERED ABOVE
FLOOR LEVEL AND
BELOW PLOW LINE

BENCH SUPPORT
OR PARTITION

PROBABLE
DOORWAY

SUPPORTING
POSTS

FIREPLACE

SUPPORTING POSTS

WATTLE AND
DAUB WALL
BETWEEN INNER
AND OUTER ROW
OF POSTS

BURNT CLAY
FRAGMENT OF
WALL

B GROUND PLAN OF HOUSE
STRUCTURE MATTHEWS
SITE

FIREPLACE

GROUND PLAN AT
NORTHEAST CORNER OF
EMBANKMENT OF
THE MATTHEWS SITE

1878 LEVEL OF WALL

1842 SURFACE

C

D

E

F

G

H

J

K

L

M

O

P

FIG. 121.—Various vessels of Bell Plain from the Sikeston Ridge area. (Drawing after photographs by Dr. Philip Phillips: In the American Museum of Natural History; from mounds near Charleston, Mississippi County, Missouri, *A, B, F, N, O,* and *T;* from New Madrid County, Missouri, *C.* In the Peabody Museum, Harvard University, from New Madrid County, Missouri, *D, E, H, I, L, M, P,* and *Q.* Drawings after photographs by P. F. Titterington in his own collection: from Stoddard County, Missouri, *G* and *J;* from New Madrid County, Missouri, *K* and *S;* from Pemiscott County, *R.*)

A. Bowl with short vertical notches on outer lip margin (diameter 16.5 cm.)

B. Bowl with four notched lugs below rim (diameter 22.3 cm.)

C. Bowl with raised rim sections (diameter 23 cm.)

D. Elaborately scalloped bowl rim (diameter 19 cm.)

E. Effigy bowl with three parallel horizontal lines on the outer rim (diameter 18.5 cm.)

F. Bowl with human effigy head facing the bowl interior (diameter 18 cm.)

G. Bowl with human effigy head rattle (height 7.5 cm.)

H. Effigy bowl with duck head facing the interior of the bowl (diameter 16.7 cm.)

I. Fish effigy bowl (diameter 9.5 cm.)

J. Conventionalized conch-shell bowl

K. Bowl with "basket" handle (diameter 15.3 cm.)

L. Ladle or gourd effigy (length 11.5 cm.)

M. The most common bottle shape (the carafe) in southeast Missouri (height 23 cm.)

N. Carafe bottle with unusually deep and broad incising on body (height 25.3 cm.)

O. Effigy gourd bottle with flattened base (height 22.4 cm.)

P. Carafe bottle with tall annular base and four sets of four perforations

Q. Hollow-leg tripod bottle with legs connecting with vessel interior (height 22.7 cm.)

R. Stirrup-neck bottle (diameter 17.7 cm.)

S. Hooded bottle with owl effigy face (height 16.6 cm.)

T. Hooded bottle (height 12.6 cm.)

Fig. 122.—Various vessels from the Sikeston Ridge area of the New Madrid Focus. (Drawings after photographs by Dr. Philip Phillips: In the American Museum of Natural History from mounds near Charleston, New Madrid County, Missouri, *A*, *D*, *E*, and *P*. In the Peabody Museum, Harvard University, from sites in southeastern Missouri, primarily New Madrid County, *B*, *C*, *F–J*, *N*, and *O*. Drawings after photographs by P. F. Titterington of his own collection: from Scott County, Missouri, *K*; from Dunklin County, Missouri, *M*. Drawing after Holmes, 1903, Pl. XLII, *d*, is vessel *L*.)

A. Matthews Incised two-handled jar (diameter 16.5 cm.)

B. Matthews Incised two-handled jar (diameter 16.5 cm.)

C. Matthews Incised two-handled jar with lobed shoulders; the punctates on this specimen are often accompanied by incised lines (diameter 19.7 cm.)

D. Matthews Incised two-handled jar with design suggestive of Oneota (diameter 17.2 cm.)

E. Matthews Incised two-handled jar (diameter 15.3 cm.)

F. Short-neck, wide-mouth bottle of Bell Plain (height 12.7 cm.)

G–H. Two views of an effigy bottle of Bell Plain with carafe type neck (height 21.6 cm.)

I–J. Two views of effigy fish bottle with wide, short neck of Bell Plain type (height 15.2 cm.)

K. Turtle effigy bottle of Bell Plain with hollow legs and six toes; the turtle has a weeping-eye design on the left eye which is not reproduced in this drawing (length from tail tip to nose tip 25.9 cm.)

L. Long straight-neck bottle of Nodena Red and White

M. Seated woman human effigy bottle of Bell Plain (height 19.7 cm.)

N. Negative-painted bottle with neck fillet (height 15.3 cm.)

O. Negative-painted bottle with neck fillet; upper portion of carafe(?) neck now broken (height 19.7 cm.)

P. Human head effigy bottle of Charleston type; upper section of carafe(?) neck broken away; there is an annular base (height 22.3 cm.)

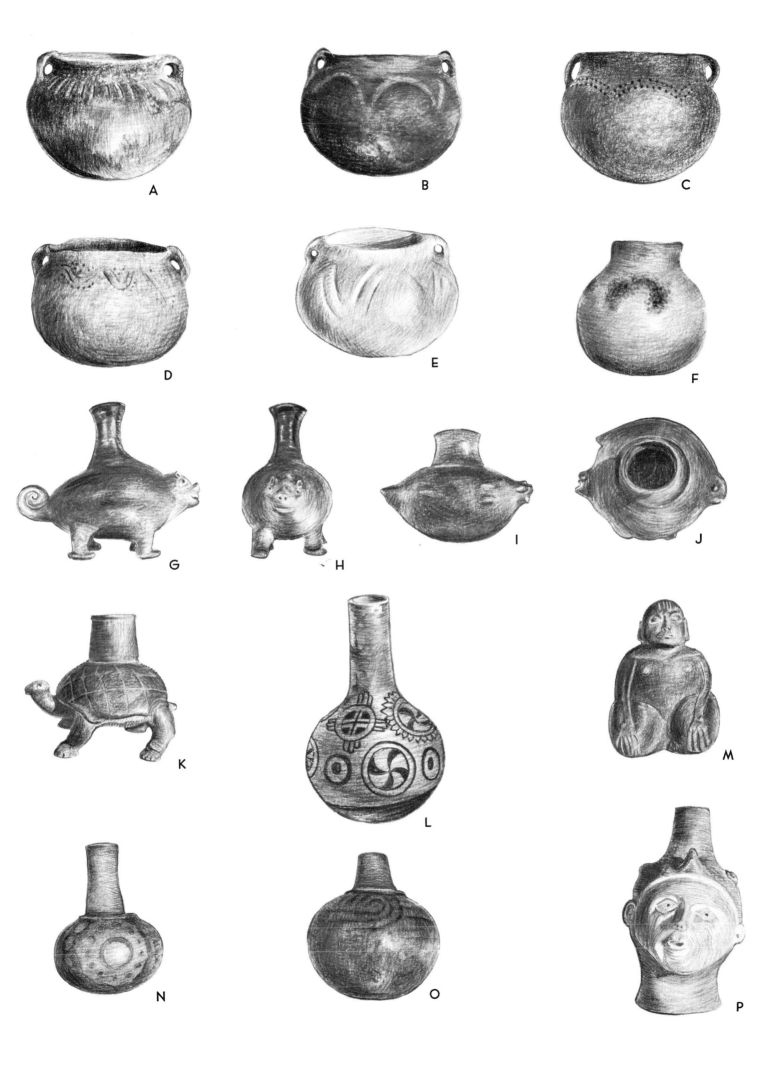

Fig. 123.—Artifacts from Chandler Landing of Early Mississippi period (*A–E*) and from the Lower St. Francis area (*F–T*) of Middle to Late Mississippi. (*A–E, I, L, N, S,* and *T* are after Moore, 1910; *F–H, J, K, M, O–R* are from specimens in the Hampson Collection, Wilson, Arkansas.)

A. Small flat-base jar of Baytown Plain from Chandler Landing, Prairie County, Arkansas (height 8.6 cm.)

B. Two views of a rock-crystal boatstone from Chandler Landing

C. Ceremonial ax of greenstone from Chandler Landing (length 21 cm.)

D. Earthernware pipe from Chandler Landing (length 13.3 cm.)

E. Stone pipe of shale with projecting stem from Chandler Landing (length 18.5 cm.)

F. Flaked pebble chisel from Togo, Cross County, Arkansas

G. Large flint hoe of type found in Upper St. Francis area

H. Stone celt from Togo

I. Clay pot support from the Rose Mound, Cross County, Arkansas (height 9.5 cm.)

J. Flint projectile points from the Vernon Paul Place, Cross County, Arkansas

K. Flint drills from the Vernon Paul Place

L. Earplug of shell from the Rose Mound

M. Shell spoon of a type found in the St. Francis area

N. Shell mask gorget from Turkey Island, Cross County, Arkansas

O. Deer ulna awls from Togo

P. Antler projectile point from Togo

Q. Bone sliver awl from Togo

R. Split deer metatarsal perforator from Togo

S. Bone comb from the Rose Mound

T. Shell mask gorget from the Rose Mound

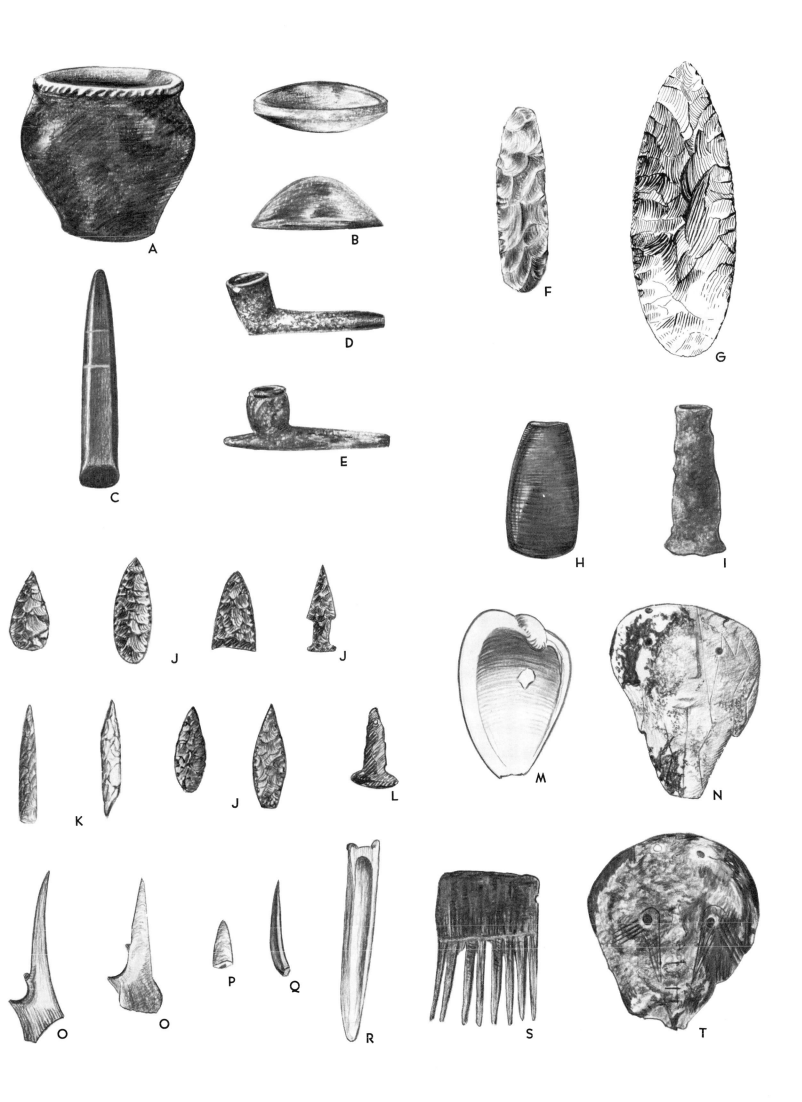

Fig. 124.—Pottery vessels and pipes from the Lower St. Francis area. (Vessels *A*, *D*, *J–L* are in the Peabody Museum, Harvard University; vessels *C*, *G*, and *H* are in the University of Arkansas collections; vessel *M* is in the Museum of the American Indian, Heye Foundation; they are drawn from photographs by Dr. Philip Phillips. Vessels *B*, *E*, *N*, and *O* are drawn after Moore, 1910. Vessel *F* is in the Lemley Collection in Hope, Arkansas, and is drawn after a photograph by Dr. P. F. Titterington. Vessel *I* is in the University of Michigan, Museum of Anthropology.)

A. Deep straight-sided bowl of Neeley's Ferry Plain from the Halcomb Mounds, Cross County, Arkansas

B. Small bottle of Neeley's Ferry Plain with small medallion heads from the Parkin site, Cross County, Arkansas (height 17.5 cm.)

C. Straight-neck bottle of polished Neeley's Ferry Plain from Barton Ranch, Crittenden County, Arkansas

D. Shallow bowl of Neeley's Ferry Plain from the Fortune Mounds, Poinsett County, Arkansas

E. Tazza vessel of Neeley's Ferry Plain from the Rose Mound, Cross County, Arkansas

F. Straight-neck bottle with ovoid body of Neeley's Ferry Plain type from Twist Place, Cross County, Arkansas

G. Strap-handle jar of Parkin Incised from Barton Ranch

H. Jar with four strap handles of Vernon Paul appliqué from the Vernon Paul site, Cross County, Arkansas

I. Small jar of Fortune Noded from the Williamson site, Cross County, Arkansas

J. Bulbous leg tripod bottle of Neeley's Ferry Plain from Neeley's Ferry

K. Bottle of Neeley's Ferry Plain with high perforated ring base from the Neeley's Ferry site (height 20.5 cm.)

L. Short wide-mouth bottle of Old Town Red from the Rose Mound (height 18 cm.)

M. Long straight-neck bottle with disk base of Neeley's Ferry Plain from Turkey Island, Cross County, Arkansas (height 23.5 cm.)

N. Effigy elbow pipe of clay with medallion head and "knees" from Potter Place, Poinsett County, Arkansas (about one-third size)

O. Clay elbow pipe with projecting stem from Turkey Island (about one-third size)

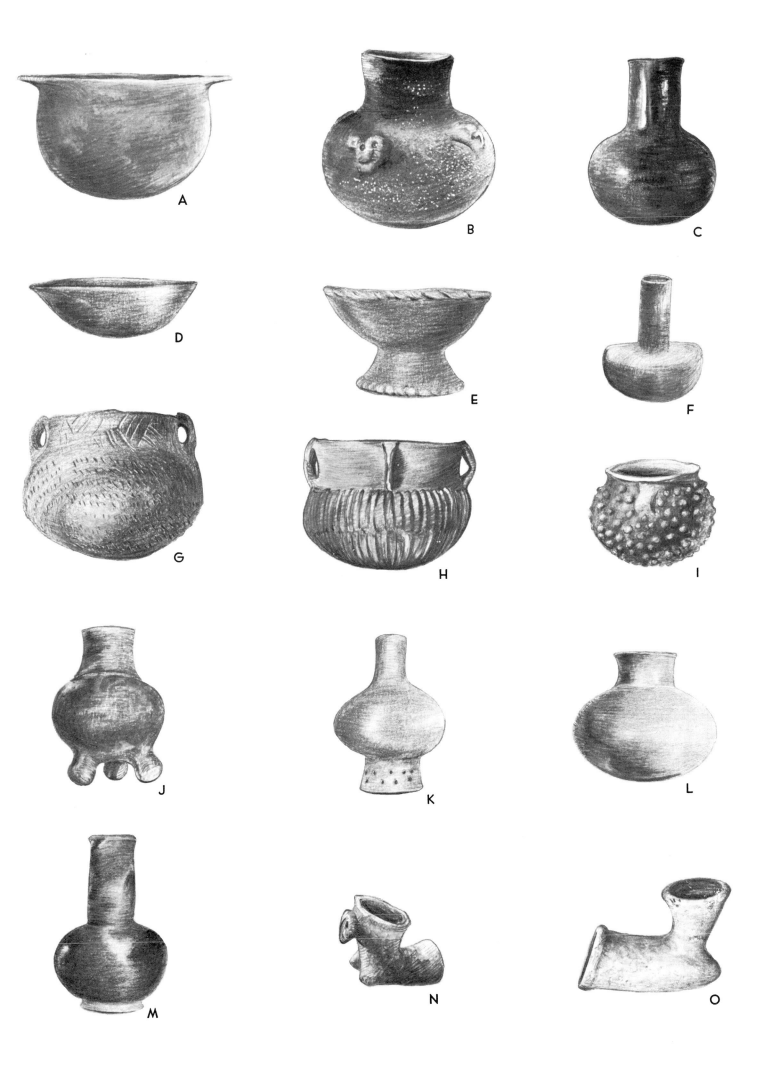

FIG. 125.—Pottery vessels from the Lower St. Francis area. (Vessels *A*, *G*, and *J* are in the Lemley Collection in Hope, Arkansas. They are drawn from photographs by Dr. P. F. Titterington. Vessels *B*, *D–F*, *H*, and *I* are in the Peabody Museum, Harvard University; they are drawn from photographs by Dr. Philip Phillips. Vessels *C* and *K* are after Moore, 1910. Vessel *L* is in the Chicago Natural History Museum; it is drawn after a University of Michigan, Museum of Anthropology, Neg. 6004.)

A. Effigy bowl of Neeley's Ferry Plain from Hazel Place, Poinsett County, Arkansas (height 17 cm.)

B. Effigy bowl of Neeley's Ferry Plain from Neeley's Ferry, Cross County, Arkansas.

C. Stirrup-neck bottle of Neeley's Ferry Plain from Neeley's Ferry (height 16 cm.)

D. Elaborate fish effigy bowl of polished Neeley's Ferry Plain from Fortune Mound, Poinsett County, Arkansas

E. Fish effigy bowl of typical Neeley's Ferry Plain Type from Cross County, Arkansas

F. Compound vessel of Neeley's Ferry Plain from Rose Mound

G. Marine-shell effigy bowl of Nodena Red and White from Vernon Paul Place, Cross County, Arkansas (height 11.5 cm.)

H. Long straight-neck bottle with ring base of Carson Red-on-Buff from Rose Mound, Cross County, Arkansas

I. "Duck" effigy tetrapod vessel (legs broken) of Nodena Red and White from Halcomb Mounds, Cross County, Arkansas

J. Slab leg tripod, long straight-neck bottle of Nodena Red and White from Vernon Paul Place (height 24 cm.)

K. Human male effigy figure of Old Town Red from Vernon Paul Place (height 22.5 cm.)

L. Human male face bottle of Old Town Red from Cross County, Arkansas (height 19 cm.)

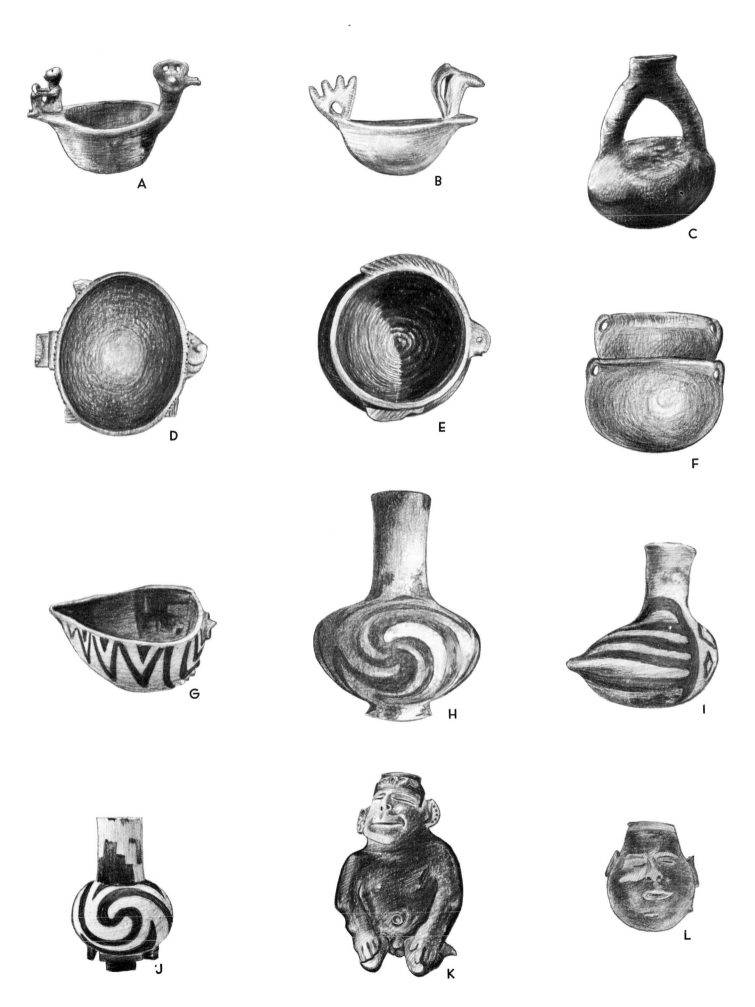

Fig. 126.—Culture traits of the Walls Focus from the Memphis area. (*A* is drawn after a photograph of the Alabama Museum of Natural History. *B, C, F, I, J, K, M–Q*, and *S* are drawn after Brown, C. S , 1926. *D, E, H*, and *L* are drawn after Moore, 1911. *G* is drawn from specimens in the Hampson collection of Wilson, Arkansas. *R* is drawn from a specimen in the University of Michigan, Museum of Anthropology.)

A. Extended burial with a bottle and bowl found at Nodena, Mississippi County, Arkansas

B. Partly polished chipped celts from Walls, De Soto County, Mississippi

C. Unperforated handled "ceremonial" celt from Walls

D. Perforated rectangular "ceremonial" Celt from Pecan Point, Mississippi County, Arkansas

E. Deer, elk, and bison astraguli smoothed for use as dice from Pecan Point

F and *I*. Flint hoes from Walls

G. Projectile points from Nodena

H. Three views of a stone earspool from Bradley Place, Crittenden County, Arkansas

J. Shell earplug from Walls

K. Shell ornament from Walls

L. Clay earplug or labret from Rhodes Place, Crittenden County, Arkansas

M. Stone mortar from Walls

N. Clay pipe from Walls

O. Plain pottery disk from Walls

P. Perforated pottery disk with incised lines from Walls

Q. Biconical clay object from Walls

R. Discoidal stone object of type associated with Walls

S. Stone pipe of frog design from Lake Cormorant, De Soto County, Mississippi

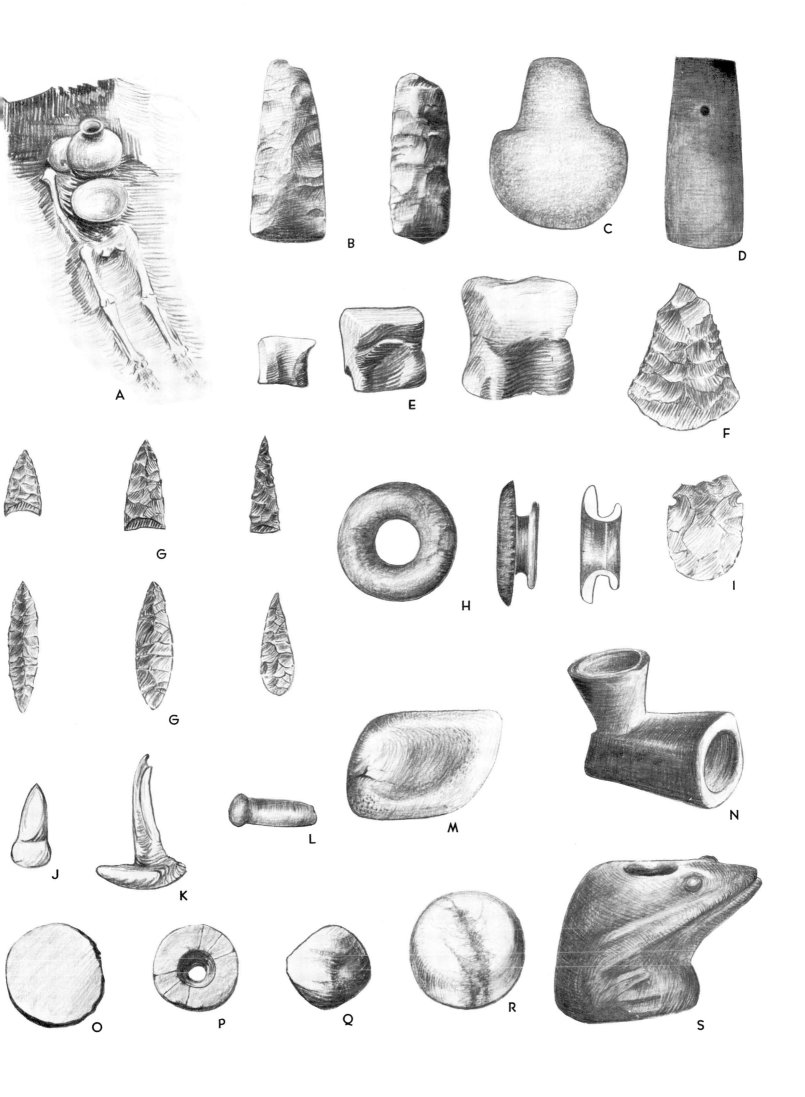

A

B

C

D

E

F

G

G

H

I

J

K

L

M

N

O

P

Q

R

S

FIG. 127.—Pottery representative of the Walls Focus from the Walls site, De Soto County, Mississippi. (These vessels are in the collection of the University of Mississippi except for the design in S, which is in a private collection. All drawings are after Brown, C. S., 1926, except G, H, and L, which are drawn after prints of the University of Michigan, Museum of Anthropology, Negs. 4350 and 4348.)

A. Fortune Noded (diameter 12 cm.)
B. Rhodes Incised (diameter 15.2 cm.)
C. Kent Incised (diameter 19 cm.)
D. Teapot vessel of Bell Plain (diameter 25.5 cm.)
E. Neeley's Ferry Plain frog effigy vessel (height 11 cm.)
F. Bell Plain bowl with "monster" head and curled tail
G. Bell Plain bowl with human effigy head (diameter 23 cm.)
H. Bell Plain bowl with human effigy head of Negroid appearance (diameter 22.6 cm.).
I. Bell Plain bottle with decoration in imitation of cord (height 19 cm.)
J. Bell Plain conjoined bottles (height 9.5 cm.)
K. Bell Plain bottle with jar-shaped neck (height 15.2 cm.)

L. Bell Plain bowl with human effigy head of Caucasoid appearance (height 8.6 cm.)
M. Bell Plain jar with hand decoration (height 13.7 cm.)
N. Bell Plain vessel with narrow orifice (height 14 cm.)
O. Bell Plain bottle with ogee symbol on shoulder area (height 20.3 cm.)
P. Avenue Polychrome tripod bottle (probable height 32 cm.)
Q. Walls Engraved bottle with head, hand, long bones, and scroll design; there is a swastika engraved on the base (height 13.8 cm.)
R. Reproduction of design on neck area of above vessel
S. Stylized bird design from a Walls Engraved vessel

Fig. 128.—Vessels from the Lower Arkansas area. (Vessels drawn from photographs by Dr. Philip Phillips are *A–O* and *Q* in the Museum of the American Indian, Heye Foundation; vessel *P* is drawn after Holmes, 1903.)

A. Deep jar of Neeley's Ferry Plain from Carden Bottom, Yell County, Arkansas (diameter 14 cm.)

B. Narrow-neck olla of Neeley's Ferry Plain from Carden Bottom (height 24.3 cm.)

C. Long narrow-neck bottle with angled rim of late eastern Caddoan connections from Old River Landing, Arkansas County, Arkansas (height 24.3 cm.)

D. Wallace Incised bowl from Greer, Jefferson County, Arkansas (diameter 19 cm.)

E. Wallace Incised high rim bowl from Greer (height 9.7 cm.)

F. Wallace Incised bowl from Greer (height 9.0 cm.)

G. Small shell-tempered jar of a type related to Cowhide Stamped from Old River Landing (height 12 cm.)

H. Small shell-tempered jar with stamped neck band like Cowhide Stamped but with a body design resembling Oneota; from the Greer site (diameter 15.3 cm.)

I. Platform base jar of Fatherland Incised from the Menard Mound, Arkansas County, Arkansas (height 11.5 cm.)

J. Effigy bowl variant of Old Town Red with a red outer border typical of the Lower Arkansas in the protohistoric period from the Old River Landing (diameter 19 cm.)

K. Natchitoches Engraved bottle from Greer (height 23 cm.)

L. Engraved shell-tempered bowl with two vertical lugs from Carden Bottom (diameter 11.4 cm.)

M. Effigy bowl from Old River Landing, very similar to *J* (diameter 19 cm.)

N. Frog effigy bottle of Old Town Red with typical Lower Arkansas bottle neck shape from Old River Landing; the teapot spout tail shown in Moore, 1908, Pl. XVII, is now missing (height 10.7 cm.)

O. Nodena Red and White bottle with Lower Arkansas style neck from Old River Landing (height 23 cm.)

P. Human male effigy figure of Nodena Red and White from a grave near the Menard Mound (height 26.7 cm.)

Q. Old Town Red teapot bottle from near Menard Landing (height 14 cm.)

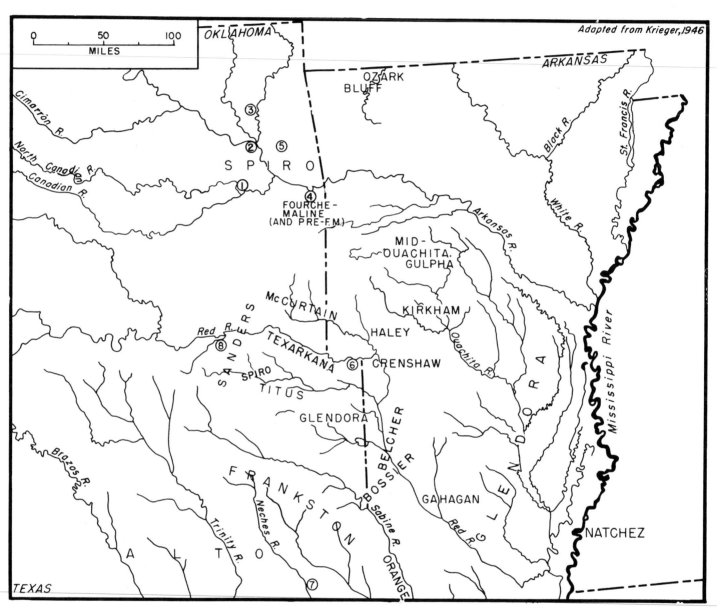

FIG. 129.—Map of Caddoan archeological area showing location of main cultural units. Numerals locate sites as follows: (*1*) Eufaula (Groseclose), (*2*) Hughes, (*3*) Norman, (*4*) Spiro, (*5*) Brackett, (*6*) Hatchel, (*7*) Davis, (*8*) Sanders.

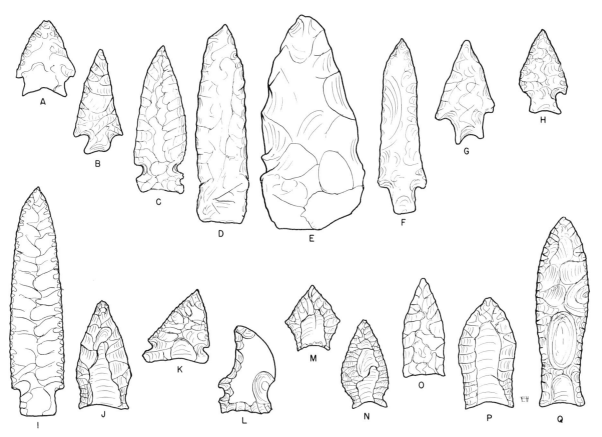

Fig. 130.—Flint artifacts of the Archaic Stage (approximately one-half natural size).

A–H. Gulpha (after Harrington, 1920)   *I–Q.* Northwestern Louisiana sites (after Webb, C. H., 1946, 1948)

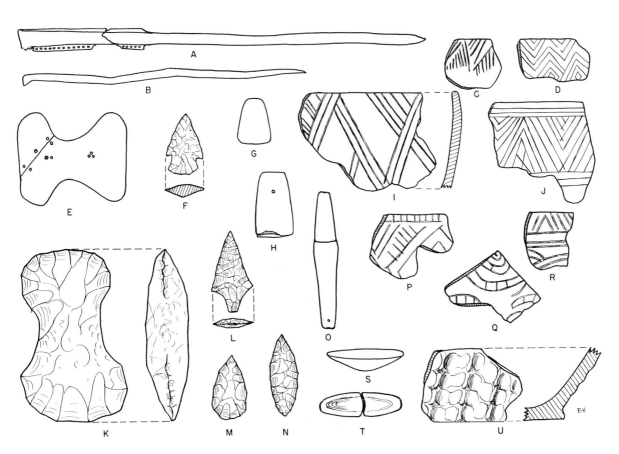

Fig. 131.—Artifacts of the Fourche Maline Focus (after Newkumet, 1940; approximately one-fourth natural size).

A–B. Bone pins	*F, L.* Chipped-stone points	*M.* Scraper
C–D, I–J, P–R, U. Sherds	*G.* Celt	*N.* Blade
E, H, O. Ground-stone gorgets and pendants	*K.* Double-bitted ax	*S–T.* Boatstones

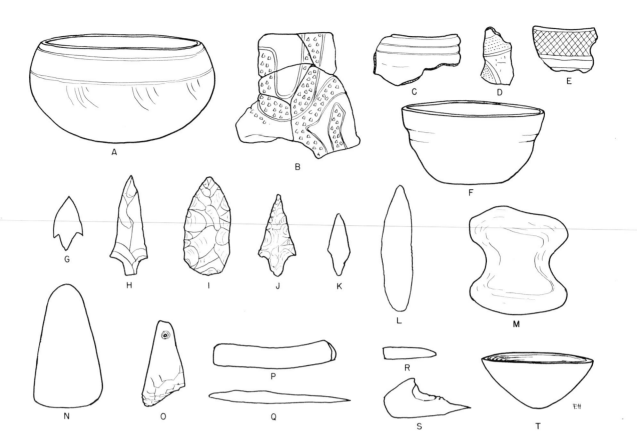

Fɪɢ. 132.—Artifacts of the Kirkham Site (after Dickinson and Lemley, 1939; approximately one-fourth natural size).

A–F. Pottery
G–L. Chipped-stone points and blades

M. Ground-stone notched ax
N. Celt

O. Gorget
P. Bone flaker(?)

Q–S. Bone awls
T. Boatstone

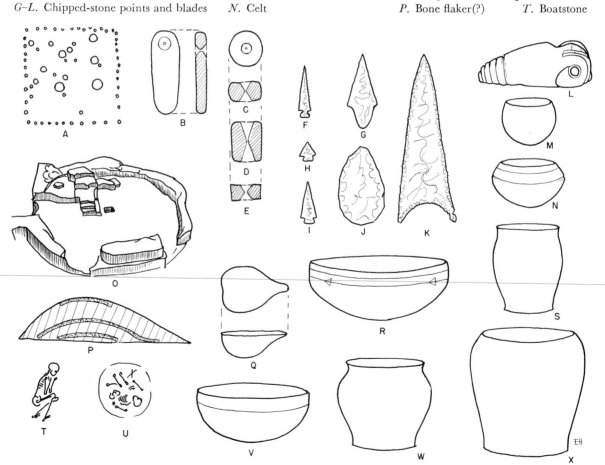

Fɪɢ. 133.—Traits of the Evans Component

A. House plan (approximately 24 feet square)
B. Black stone pendant
C–E. Black stone beads (approximately one-half natural size)
F–K. Chipped-stone artifacts (approxi-

mately one-fourth natural size)
L. Quartz crystal locust effigy boatstone (approximately one-half natural size)
M–N, Q–S, V–X. Pottery vessels (approximately one-sixth natural size)

O. Puddled clay crematory basin (19 feet in diameter)
P. Burial mound with burial layers (6 feet high, 25 feet in diameter)
T–U. Burial positions

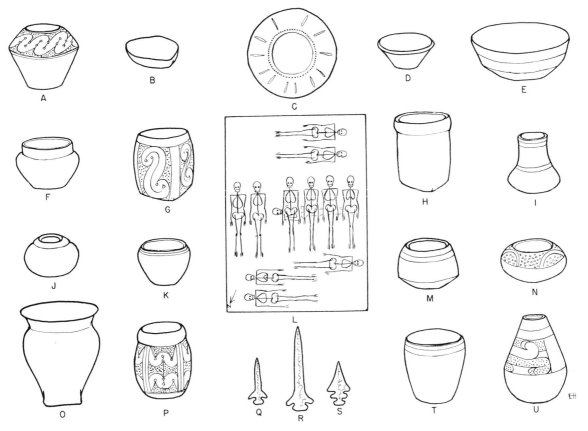

FIG. 134.—Artifacts of Crenshaw 1 (after Lemley, 1936).

A–K, M–P, T–U. Pottery vessels (approximately one-fourth natural size)

L. Burial type

Q–S. Chipped-stone pendants (approximately one-half natural size)

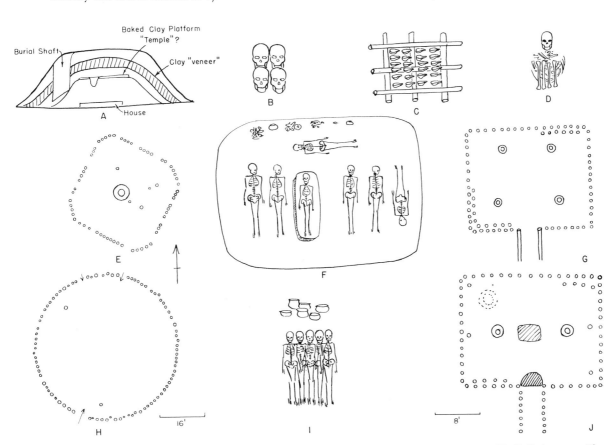

FIG. 135.—Burial, house, and mound types of the Gibson Aspect (house scales: *E, H* shown at *H; G, J* shown at *J*).

A. Idealized cross-section of the Brown
   3 mound (approximately 175 by
   15 feet)
B–D. Craig burials

E. Alto house
F. Gahagan burial (after Webb and
   Dodd, 1939)
G. Craig house

H. Haley and/or Alto house
I. Brown burial
J. Brown house

Fig. 136.—Artifacts of the Gibson Aspect. Unless otherwise mentioned, all artifacts are approximately one-eighth natural size. Artifacts from Craig-Brown with exception of *H* (Gahagan, after Webb and Dodd, 1939); *I′* (Haley); *K′* (Haley); *H′* (Alto); *L′* (Alto, Gahagan); *M′* (Haley); after Krieger, 1946.

A–G. Chipped-stone points (approximately one-half natural size)
H. Copper mask
I–M. Shell beads (approximately one-half natural size)

N–O. Blades (approximately one-fourth natural size)
P. Ground-stone baton fragment
Q. Conch-shell gorget
R–S. Ear spools
T. Copper bird effigy plate

U. Wooden mask
V–W. Stone pipes
X–Y, D′–M′. Pottery vessels
Z. Spatulate celt
A′. Celt
B′. Flaring celt

Fig. 137.—Traits of the Fulton Aspect. All traits from the Fort Coffee Focus with the exception of *F* (Belcher); *P* (Titus and Belcher); *K, S* (Glendora); *R* (Bossier); *V, Z* (Titus); *W* (Frankston); *A'* (Belcher); *B', C', D'* (Texarkana), after Krieger, 1946.

A, C. House types (*C* is 28 feet in diameter)
B. Burial type
D. Scapula hoe (approximately one-eighth natural size)
E–F. Chipped-stone points
G–H. Chipped-stone blades (approximately one-half natural size)

I. Pitted mano (approximately one-fourth natural size)
J. Awl (approximately one-eighth natural size
K, R–D'. Pottery vessels (approximately one-eighth natural size)
L. Plano-convex scraper (one-half natural size)

M. Sandstone shaft polisher (approximately one-half natural size)
N. Pecking pebble (approximately one-half natural size)
O. Stone pipe (approximately one-fourth natural size)
P–Q. Clay pipes (approximately one-fourth natural size)

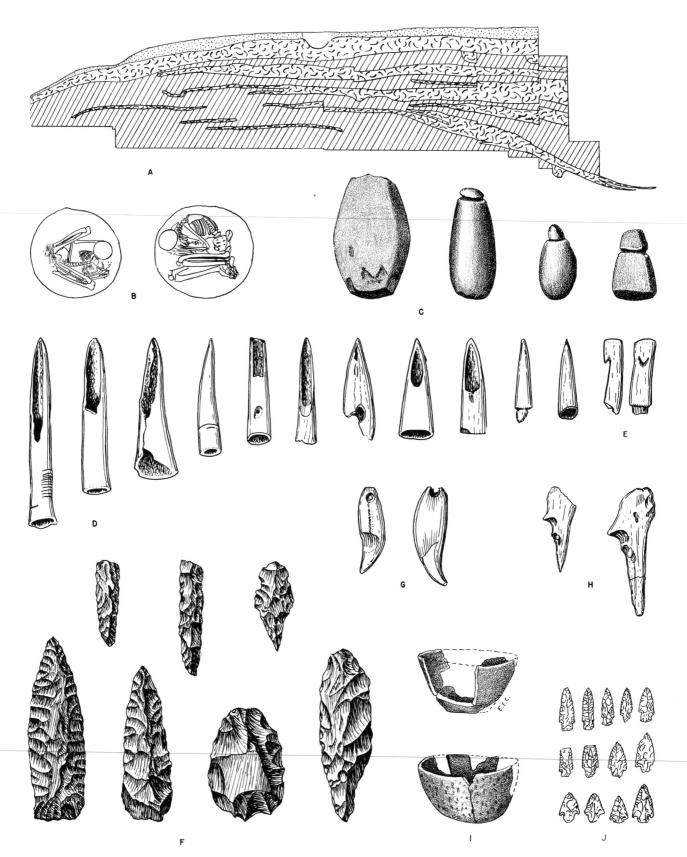

FIG. 138.—Representative traits of the Archaic Cultures in the Lower Mississippi Valley and Southeast. All specimens were taken from Ford and Quimby, 1945, except *A* (Webb and DeJarnette, 1942), *B* (Webb, W. S., 1946), and *I* (Webb, C. H., 1944).

A. Cross-section of shell heap on Tennessee River
B. Round grave burials at Indian Knoll, Kentucky
C. Plummets and other ground-stone objects
D. Projectile points of antler and bone
E. Atlatl hook of antler
F. Knives, drills, and other flint tools
G. Perforated canine teeth of bear
H. Bone awls
I. Steatite vessels from Poverty Point Site, Louisiana
J. Common projectile point forms

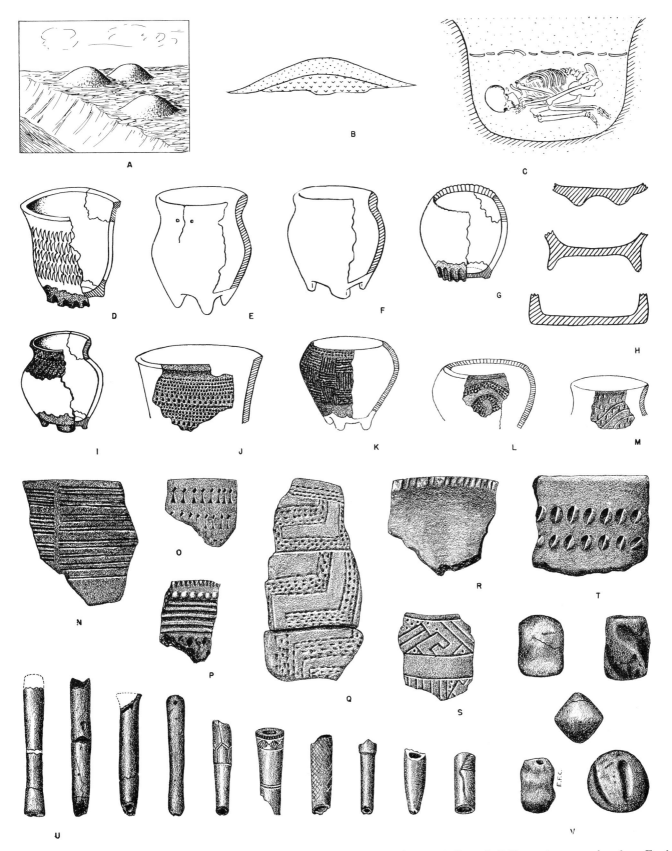

Fig. 139.—The Tchefuncte Culture of the Early Woodland period. Unless otherwise indicated all illustrations are taken from Ford and Quimby, 1945.

A. Hypothetical mound group of Early Woodland period
B. Cross-section of Lafayette mound
C. Generalized Miller I burial from Lee County, Mississippi; body is covered by a layer of Saltillo Fabric (textile) Marked sherds
D–G, I–M. Vessel shapes common to Tchefuncte Plain, Tchefuncte Stamped, Lake Borgne Incised, Orleans Punctated, and Tammany Pinched pottery types
H. Bottoms from Tchefuncte Plain vessels
N. Chinchuba Brushed sherd from Tchefuncte site
O. Mandeville Stamped sherd from Tchefuncte site
P. Alexander Incised sherd from Tchefuncte site
Q. Orleans Punctated sherd from Little Woods site
R. O'Neal Plain sherd
S. Lake Borgne Incised sherd
T. Tammany Pinched sherd from various Louisiana sites
U. Tubular clay pipes from Tchefuncte period sites
V. Clay Poverty Point objects from Little Woods site

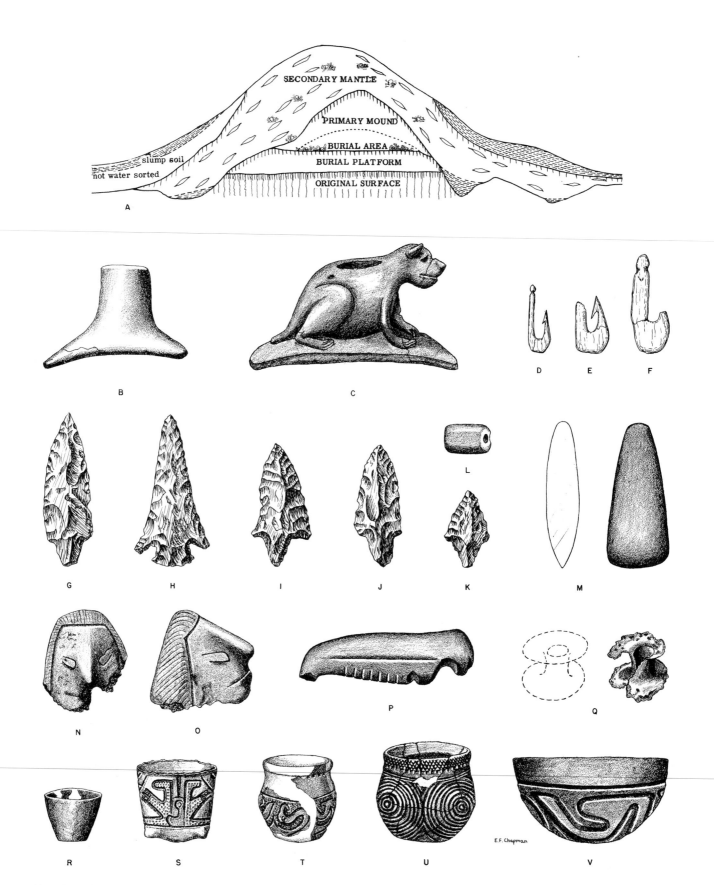

Fig. 140.—Marksville characteristics of the Middle Woodland or Hopewellian period. All illustrations are of objects recovered at the Crooks site and are taken from Ford and Willey, 1940.

A. Cross-section of Crooks Mound
B–C. Clay pipes
D–F. Fishhooks
G–K. Projectile points
L. Galena bead

M. Ground-stone celt
N–O. Clay head
P. Bituminous shale grasshopper
Q. Fragmentary copper earspool
R. Marksville Plain vessel

S. Marksville Stamped vessel
T. Marksville Stamped vessel
U. Marksville Incised vessel
V. Marksville Red Filmed vessel

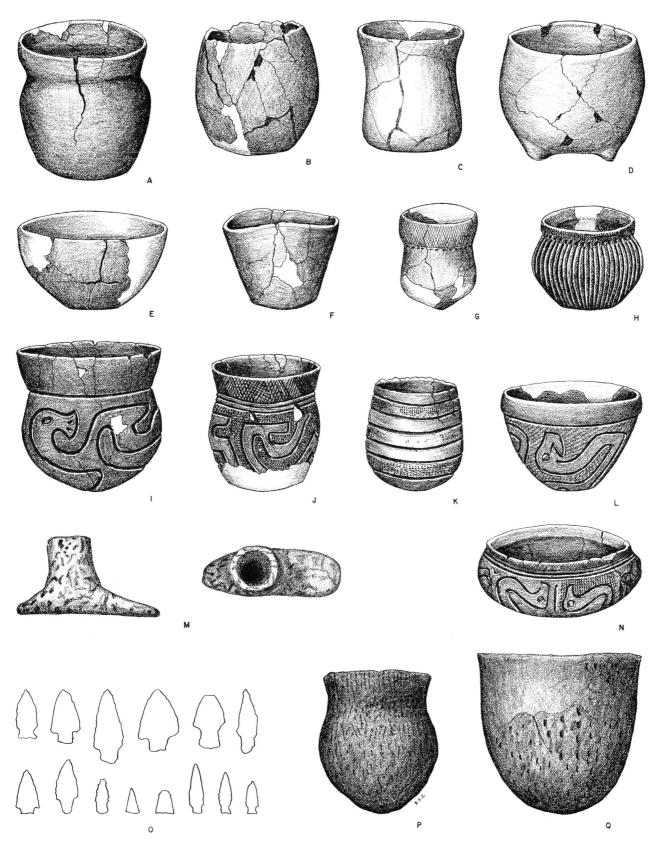

Fɪɢ. 141.—Middle Woodland vessels and projectiles. Specimens on this plate are after the following sources: *A–L, N* (Ford and Willey, 1940, Figs. 22, 23, 24, 25, 29, 32, 35, 36); *M, P, Q* (Jennings, 1941, Pl. 10); and *O* (Collins, 1932).

A–G. Marksville Plain vessels	*M.* Platform pipe from Miller II mound, northeastern Mississippi	*P.* Furrs Cordmarked vessel
H–I. Marksville Incised vessel		*Q.* Variant form of Alexander Pinched vessel
J–K, N. Marksville Stamped vessels	*O.* Typical Miller and Deasonville projectile point	
L. Crooks Stamped vessel		

Fig. 142.—The Early Mississippi period: Coles Creek and related groups. Specimens on this plate are after the following sources: *A–C* (based on topographic data furnished by the Natchez Trace Parkway, National Park Service, Tupelo, Mississippi). *D–M* (Ford and Willey, 1939).

A. Emerald Mound, speculative restoration (present form in inset)

B. Anna Mound group, speculative restoration (present form in inset)

C. Lake George Mound group, present form

D–M. Coles Creek Plain and Coles Creek Incised vessels

FIG. 143.—Representative traits of the Mississippi period. Specimens on this plate are after the following sources: *A–H, K–M* (Ford, 1936, Figs. 23 and 27); *I–J, O* (Brown, C. S., 1926, Figs. 225–227, 327, 342); and *N* (generalized examples).

A–H, K–M. Vessels from burials in mounds in the valley of the Big Black River, Mississippi, and from historic Tunica graves at Angola Farm, Louisiana

I. Incised vessel from Emerald Mound, Mississippi

J. Engraved vessel from Franklin County, Alabama

N. Discoidal gaming stones

O. Human effigy pipe from Ferguson Mound, Mississippi

P–Q. Human effigy pipes from Emerald Mound, Mississippi

FIG. 144.—Late Mississippi: the historic decline in the Lower Valley. Specimens on this plate are after the following sources: *A–B, D–H, K, N* (Ford, 1936, Figs. 9 and 11); *C, J, P–Q* (Jennings, 1941, Pls. 5 and 10); and *I, L–M, O* (Quimby, 1942, Pls. XIV, XVI, XVII).

A. The Fatherland site—Grand Village of the Natchez tribe, A.D. 1650(?)–1730

B. Natchez Incised vessel

C. Shell-tempered vessel from historic Chickasaw site, Lee County, Mississippi

D. Wilkinson Incised vessel

E–F, H. Fatherland Incised vessel

G. Natchez Incised vessel with red slip between incised lines

I. Manchac Incised vessel

J. Shell buttons from historic Chickasaw(?) grave, Lee County, Mississippi

K. Clay head from Fatherland Mound

L–M. Pipes from Bayou Goula site

N. Plate from Fatherland site

O. Predominant projectile point forms—Natchezan sites

P. Oktibbeha Plain vessel

Q. Wilson Plain vessel

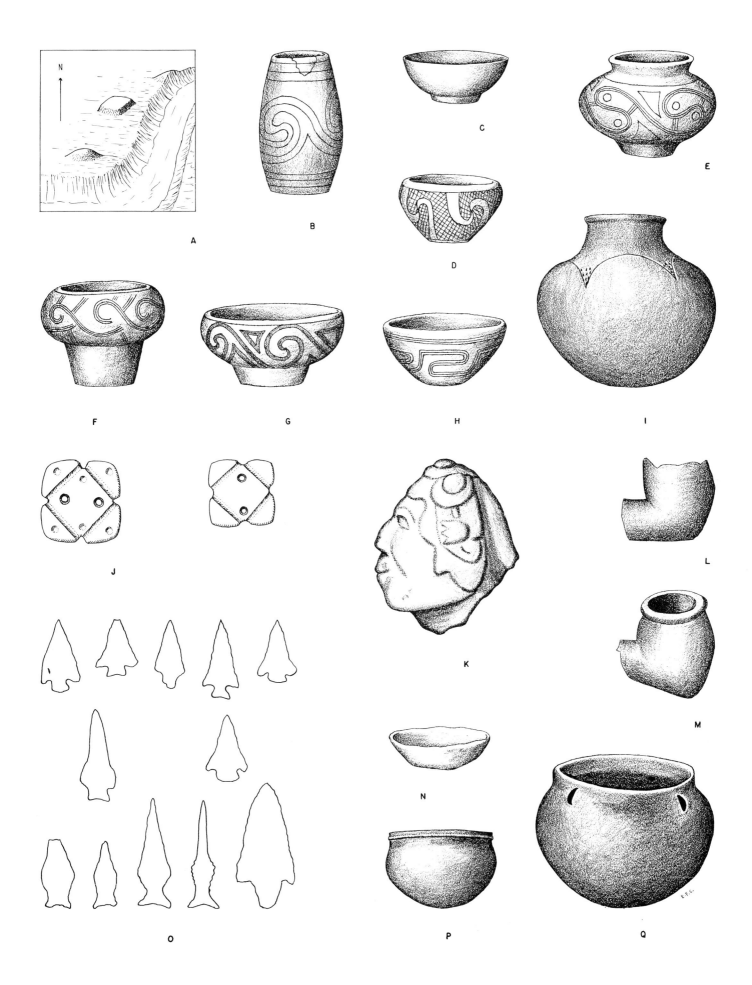

A

B

C

D

E

F

G

H

I

J

K

L

M

N

O

P

Q

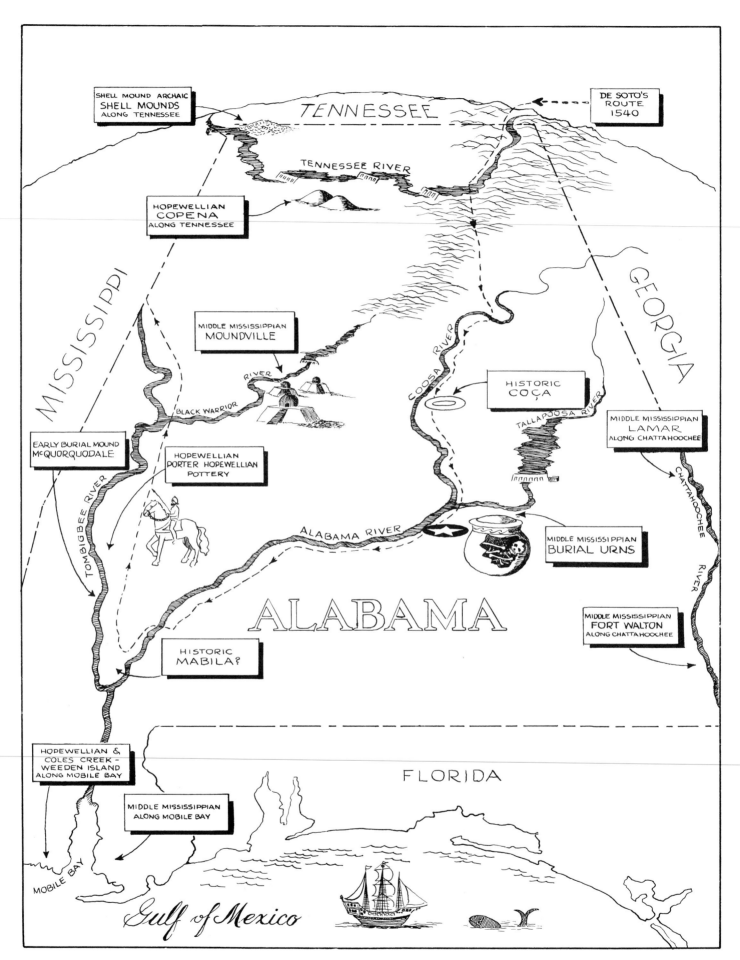

TENNESSEE

SHELL MOUND ARCHAIC
SHELL MOUNDS
ALONG TENNESSEE

DE SOTO'S
ROUTE
1540

TENNESSEE RIVER

HOPEWELLIAN
COPENA
ALONG TENNESSEE

MISSISSIPPI

GEORGIA

MIDDLE MISSISSIPPIAN
MOUNDVILLE

RIVER

BLACK WARRIOR

HISTORIC
COÇA

COOSA RIVER

TALLAPOOSA RIVER

MIDDLE MISSISSIPPIAN
LAMAR
ALONG CHATTAHOOCHEE

EARLY BURIAL MOUND
McQUORQUODALE

HOPEWELLIAN
**PORTER HOPEWELLIAN
POTTERY**

TOMBIGBEE RIVER

CHATTAHOOCHEE RIVER

ALABAMA RIVER

MIDDLE MISSISSIPPIAN
BURIAL URNS

ALABAMA

MIDDLE MISSISSIPPIAN
FORT WALTON
ALONG CHATTAHOOCHEE

HISTORIC
MABILA?

HOPEWELLIAN &
COLES CREEK -
WEEDEN ISLAND
ALONG MOBILE BAY

FLORIDA

MIDDLE MISSISSIPPIAN
ALONG MOBILE BAY

MOBILE BAY

Gulf of Mexico

Fig. 145.—Panorama of Alabama archeology

Fig. 146.—Excavating Mulberry Creek Shell Mound (Ct∘27) on the Tennessee River in Colbert County, Alabama

FIG. 147.—Archaic Complex of northern Alabama (Objects *L′–P′* are not to scale)

A (*1*). Antler arrow shaft straightener
B (*2*). Antler drift
C (*3*). Antler projectile point
D (*4*). Bone projectile point
E (*5*). Bone fishhook
F (*6*). Bone atlatl hook
G–H (*7–8*). Antler atlatl hooks
I (*9*). Shell atlatl weight (composite)
J (*10*). Stone atlatl weights
K (*11*). Boatstone
L (*12*). Bar gorget
M (*13*). Bone awl
N (*14*). Deer ulna awl
O (*15*). Bone awl
P (*16*). Bone needle
Q (*17*). Bone awl
R–T (*18–20*). Stone projectile points
U (*21*). Stone drill
V (*22*). Grooved stone ax
W (*23*). Lapstone or nutting stone
X (*24*). Stone bell pestle

Y (*25*). Circular hammerstone
Z (*26*). Small steatite vessel
A′ (*27*). Sitting burial
B′ (*28*). Fully flexed round grave burial
C′ (*29*). Tubular stone pipe
D′ (*30*). Human tooth bead
E′ (*31*). Shell-disk beads
F′ (*32*). Canine tooth bead or pendant
G′ (*33*). Tubular stone bead
H′–I′ (*34–35*). Tubular shell beads
J′ (*36*). Shell columella pin
K′ (*37*). Crinoid stem bead
L′ (*38*). Engraved bone spatula (28 cm. long)
M′ (*39*). Human fibula awl (36 cm. long)
N′ (*40*). Bowl from human skull (18.5 cm. greatest diameter)
O′ (*41*). Shell pendant (2.5 cm. long)
P′ (*42*). Shell beads (individual beads, 1.3 cm. long)

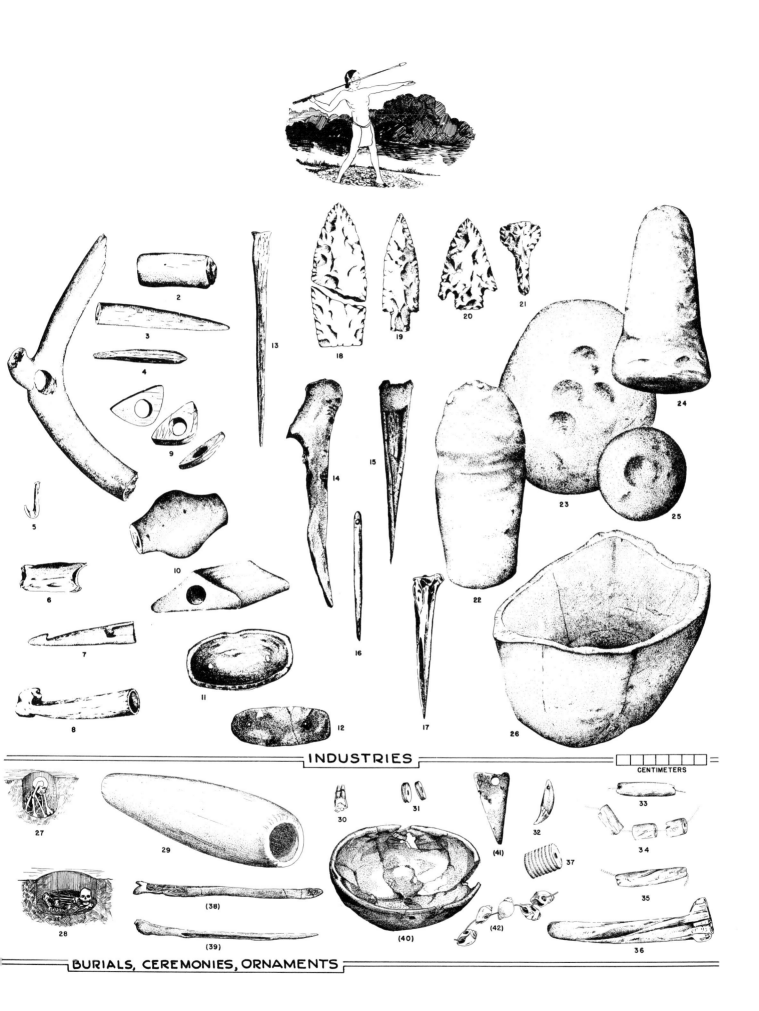

INDUSTRIES

CENTIMETERS

BURIALS, CEREMONIES, ORNAMENTS

FIG. 148.—Sitting burial (No. 11) in Alabama Shell Mound Archaic at Perry site (Lu°25), Lauderdale County, Alabama

Fig. 149.—Profile of a Copena Burial Mound, the Colbert Creek Mound (Lu°54) in Lauderdale County, Alabama. Pedestals mark location of burials.

FIG. 150.—Important features of the Copena Cultural Complex

A (1). Cremated burial remains
B (2). Extended burial with puddled clay covering shown partly removed
C (3). Multiple burial
D (4). Isolated skull burial
E (5). Flexed burial
F (6). Copper reel-shaped gorget
G–H (7–8). Shell beads
I (9). Drilled copper beads
J (10). Copper earspools
K (11). Shell pendant
L (12). Flint projectile point (Copena point)
M (13). Copper bracelet
N (14). Galena (cabochon-abraded)
O (15). Marine-shell cup
P (16). Greenstone spade
Q (17). Greenstone celt
R (18). Copper bead of rolled plate copper
S (19). Limestone-tempered pottery tobacco pipe
T (20). Stone tobacco pipe
U (21). Zoömorphic tobacco pipe of steatite

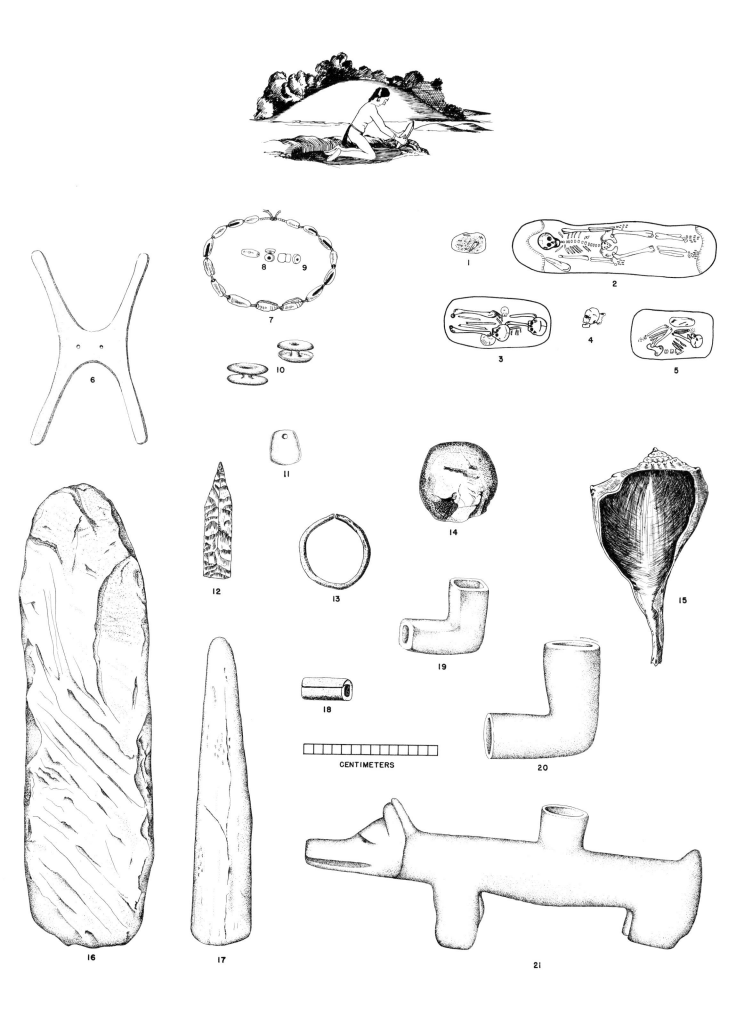

1

2

3

4

5

6

7

8 9

10

11

12

13

14

15

16

17

18

19

20

21

CENTIMETERS

Fig. 151.—Middle Mississippi features at Moundville

A–I (1–9). Shell-tempered pottery vessels
J (10). Pottery trowel
K (11). Bone fishhook
L (12). Antler tine
M (13). Woodpecker bill awls
N (14). Deer ulna awls
O (15). Bone needle
P (16). Bone awl
Q (17). Greenstone chisel
R (18). Greenstone celt
S (19). Lapstone
T (20). Flint projectile point

U (21). Flint drill
V (22). Pebble hammer
W (23). Frog effigy pipe of pottery
X (24). Stone discoidal
Y–B' (25–28). Various types of shell beads
C'–D' (29–30). Earspool disk (copper over
    wood)
E' (31). Earplug of shell
F' (32). Shell pendant
G' (33). Canine tooth pendant
H' (34). Elbow tobacco pipe of pottery

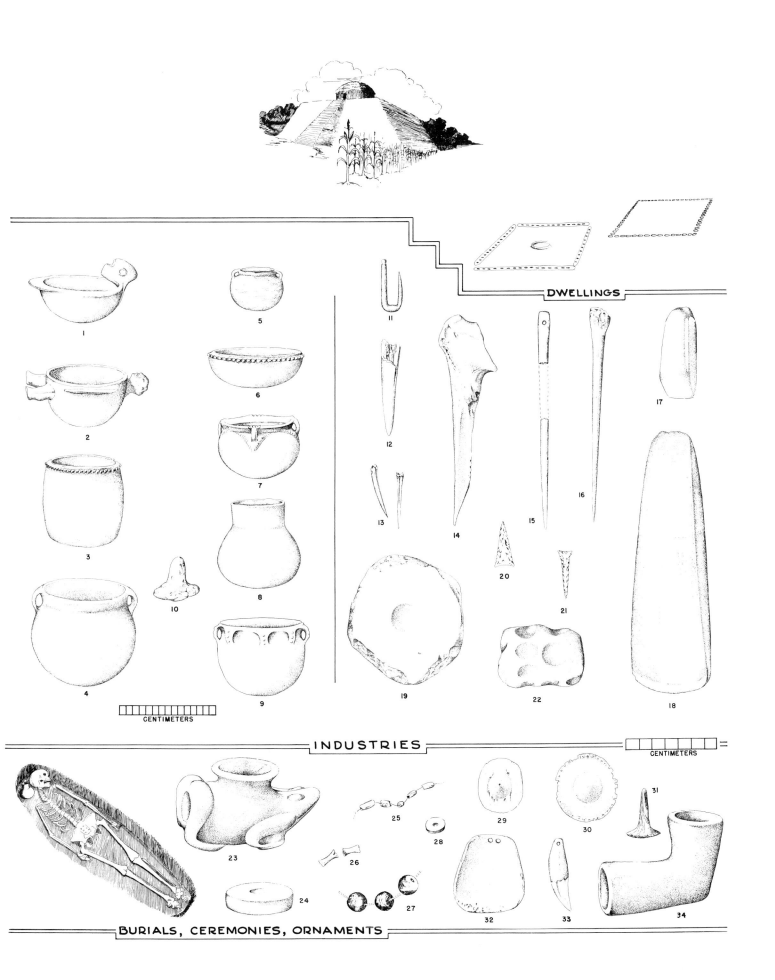

DWELLINGS

INDUSTRIES

CENTIMETERS

CENTIMETERS

BURIALS, CEREMONIES, ORNAMENTS

Fig. 152.—Ceremonial pottery from Moundville: *upper right*, skull and leg bones (height 13 cm.); *left*, engraved bottle (height 20 cm.); *lower*, engraved bottle with head of mythological bird (height 14.5 cm.).

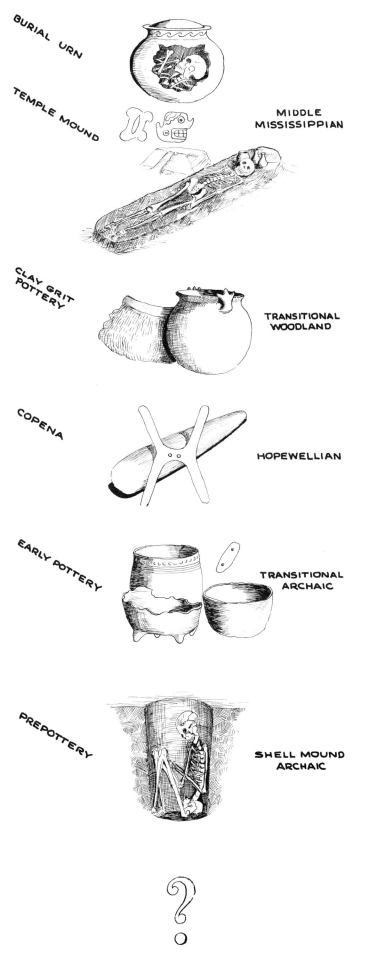

BURIAL URN

TEMPLE MOUND

MIDDLE MISSISSIPPIAN

CLAY GRIT POTTERY

TRANSITIONAL WOODLAND

COPENA

HOPEWELLIAN

EARLY POTTERY

TRANSITIONAL ARCHAIC

PREPOTTERY

SHELL MOUND ARCHAIC

FIG. 153.—Outstanding features of the various Alabama cultures arranged in time sequence from bottom to top.

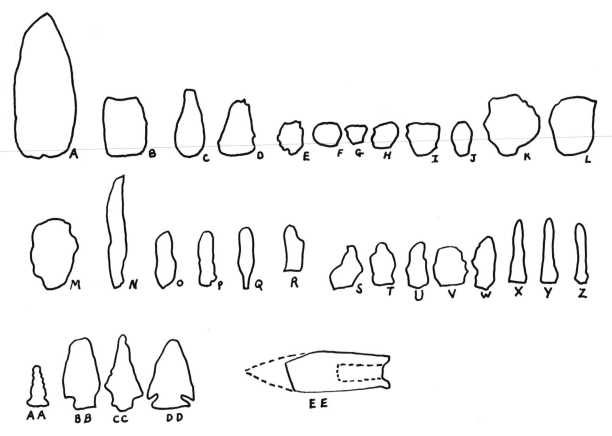

Fig. 154.—Early Macon flint industry (after Kelly, 1938)

A. Large blade
B. Chisel-like knife
C–D. Flake end scrapers
E–W. Small flake forms without secondary chipping

X–Z. Drills
AA. "Spinner Point" or opposite beveled point
BB–DD. Stemmed and notched forms
EE. Folsom point

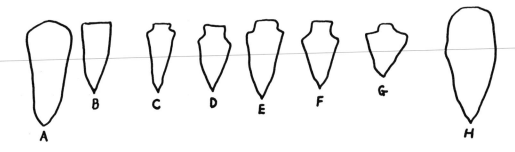

Fig. 155.—Flint forms from deep levels of Ocmulgee River flood plain

A, B, H. Large blades   C–G. Various stemmed points

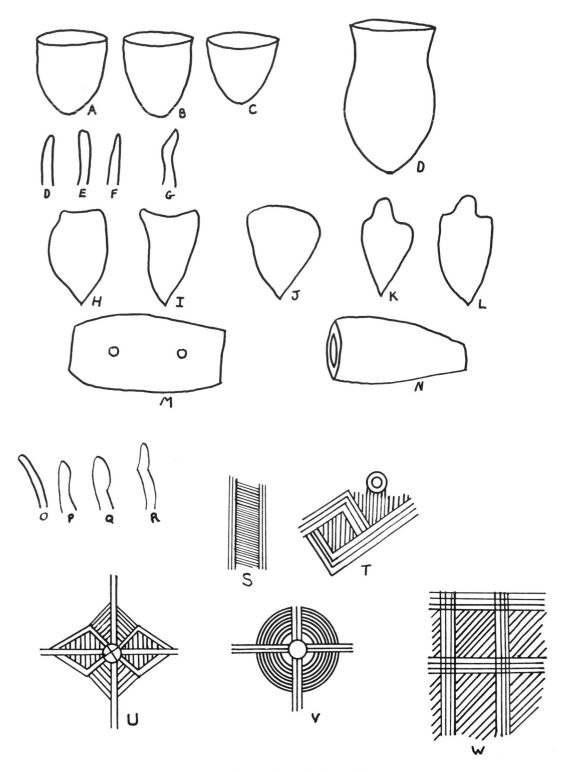

FIG. 156.—Mossy Oak and Napier artifacts

A–D. Vessel shapes of Mossy Oak Simple Stamped
E–G. Rim forms of Mossy Oak Simple Stamped
H–J. Triangular blades
K–L. Stemmed points

M. Two-hole flat gorget
N. Tubular pipe
O–R. Napier Complicated Stamped rim forms
S–W. Napier Complicated Stamped designs

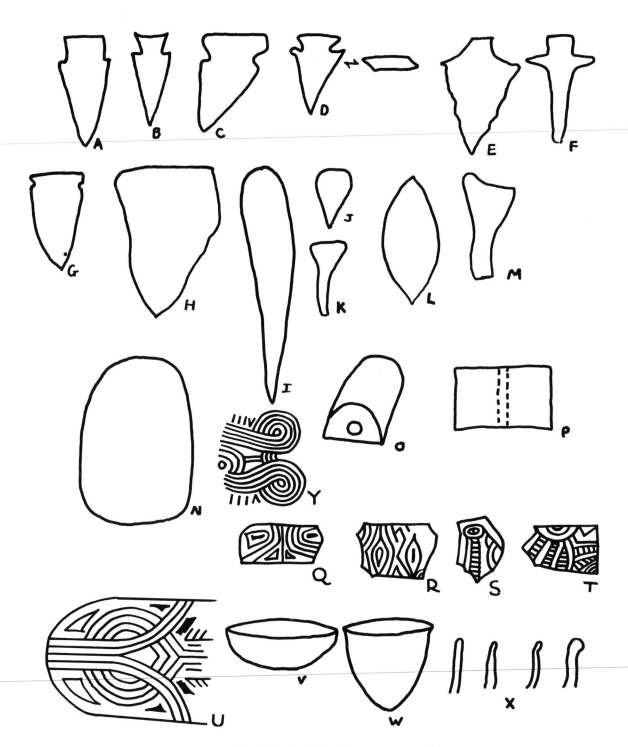

FIG. 157.—Swift Creek period

A–E, G. Stemmed projectile points

H, L. Fully chipped blades

I–K, M. Flake knives or side scrapers

F. Cruciform drill

N. Bun-shaped muller

O. Bun-shaped bannerstone

P. Winged bannerstone

Q–T. Swift Creek Complicated Stamped sherds

U, Y. Designs from Swift Creek Complicated Stamped jars

V–W. Swift Creek vessel shapes

X. Rim forms

FIG. 158.—Macon Plateau Complex of the Early Mississippi period

A. Schematic section of pyramidal mound with submound burial pits
B–C. Earth lodge
D. Spatulate stone spud
E. Plain shell gorget
F. Elliptical shell object
G. Conch-shell dipper or cup
H–I. Cut disk and barrel-shaped shell beads
K–L. Medium-sized triangular projectile points

M. Large ovate blades from cache
N, P. Stemmed and notched projectile points
O. Biconcave stone discoidal
Q. Large triangular blade from cache
R. Large polished stone celt
S. Pottery pipe
T. Small bowl with effigy head
U–V. Salt pans
W–GG. Various vessel shapes; Y is Macon Thick

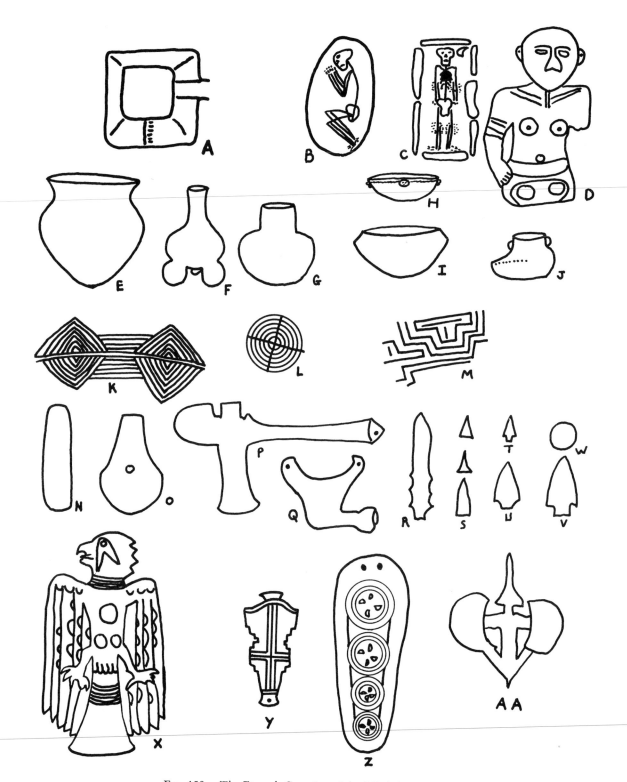

FIG. 159.—The Etowah Complex of the Mississippi period

A. Pyramidal mound with ramp and terraces
B. Flexed burial
C. Extended burial in stone box grave with conch-shell cup, gorget, and beads
D. Seated stone effigy
E. Etowah Complicated Stamped vessel shape
F. Tripod water bottle, usually with negative-painted sun symbol

G. Plain water bottle, occasionally negative painted
H–I. Bowl shapes
J. Moccasin pot
K–M. Etowah Complicated Stamped designs
N. Polished stone celt
O. Perforated spud
P. Monolithic ax
Q. Pottery pipe

R. Flint blade
S. Three types of small projectile points
T–V. Three types of stemmed projectile points
W. Pottery disk
X. Copper eagle placque
Y. Copper badge
Z. Copper badge with sun symbols
AA. Bilobed arrow copper placque

FIG. 160.—The Lamar Complex of Late Mississippi

A. Plan of village with palisade and mounds
B. House pattern on small dirt platform
C. Flexed burial
D. Urn burial
E. Fragment of shell gorget portraying a Southern Cult mythological being

F. Knobbed conch-shell pin
G. Ulna awl
H. Bear-tooth pendant
I. Discoidal
J. Antler point
K. Polished stone celt
L. Polished stone chisel

M–N, R. Pottery pipe forms
O. Small triangular projectile points
P–Q. Large stemmed projectile points
S–T. Designs from Lamar Bold Incised
U–V. Designs of Lamar Complicated Stamped
W–DD. Lamar vessel shapes

Fig. 161.—Ocmulgee Fields Culture of the early seventeenth century

A. House plan with central firebasin
B. Flexed burial
C. Extended burial
D–G. Small triangular projectile points
H–I. Thumbnail scrapers of flint and glass
J. Polished celt

K. Large flint triangular blade
L. Knobbed conch-shell pin
M. Barrel-shaped conch-shell beads
N. Pottery disk
O. Steatite pipe suggesting European influence
P. English white clay pipe

Q. Copper cone
R. Brass hawk bell
S. Iron hoe
T. Sword
U–W. Vessel forms derived from Lamar
X–Y. Vessel forms derived from Europe

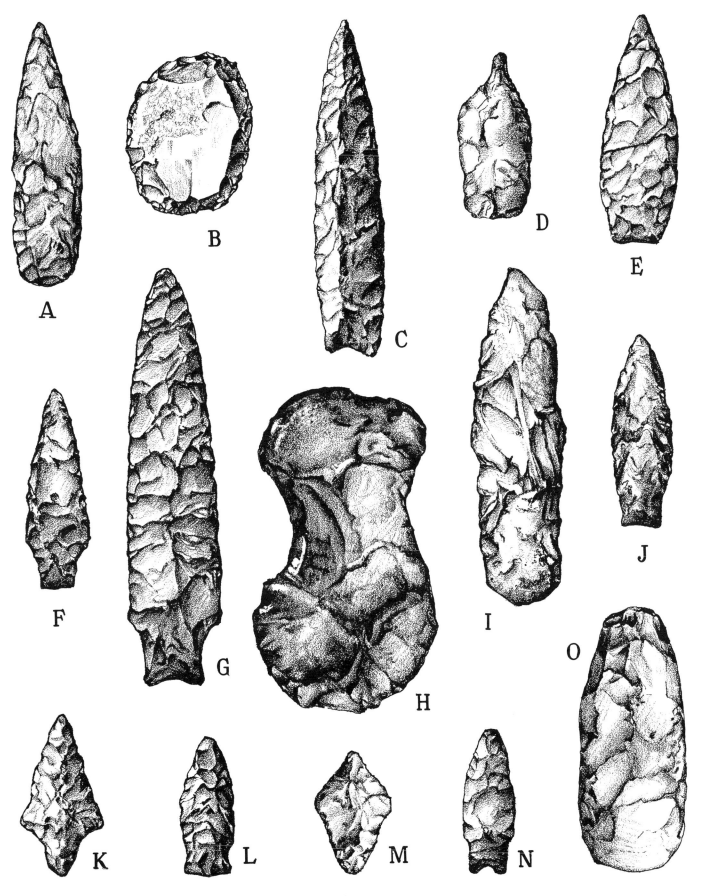

FIG. 162.—The Guilford Focus

A, C, E. Characteristic projectile points
F, G, J, K, L, M, N. Associated but atypical
    forms of projectile points

B. Scraping tool
D. Drill
I. Knife

H. Ax
O. Celt

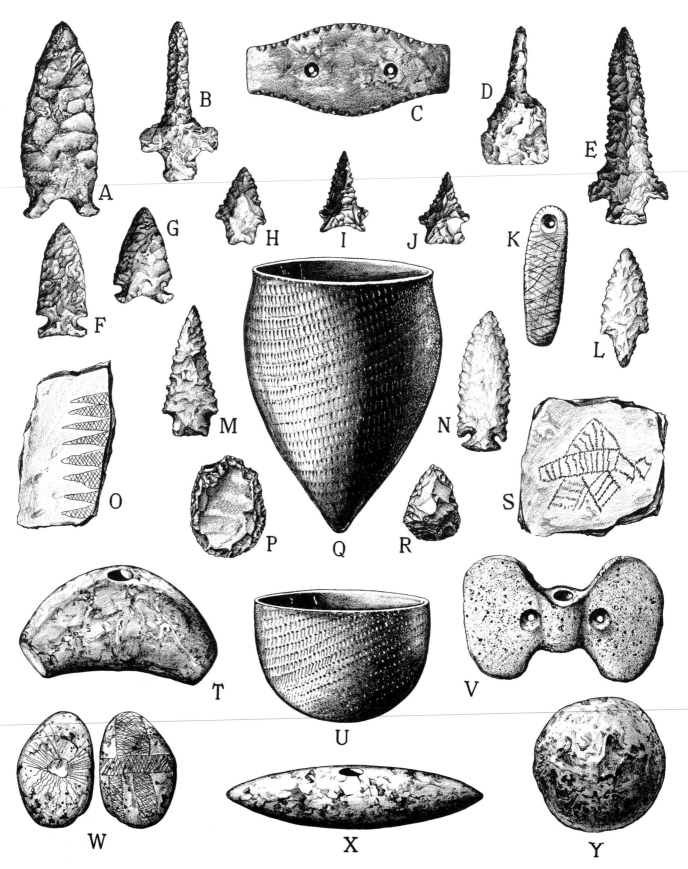

FIG. 163.—The Badin Focus

A, F, G, M, N. Typical projectile point forms
E, H, I, J, L. Minority types of projectile points

B, D. Drills
C. Thin, flat, slate gorget
K, O, S, W. Engraved slate tablets
P, R. Scraping tools

Q, U. Pottery vessels
T, V, X. Atlatl weights
Y. Hammerstone

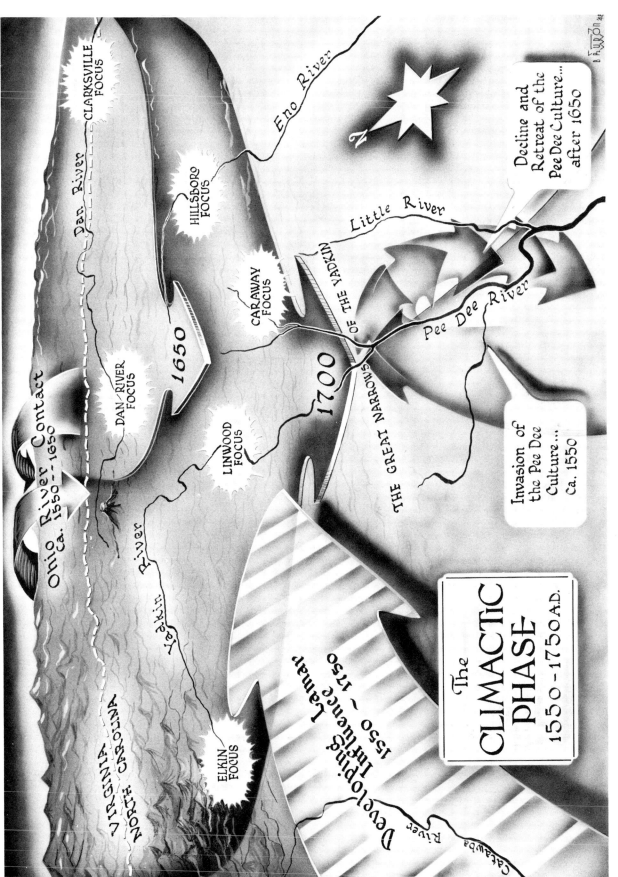

Fig. 164.—The movement and development of the Piedmont cultures during the Climactic Phase

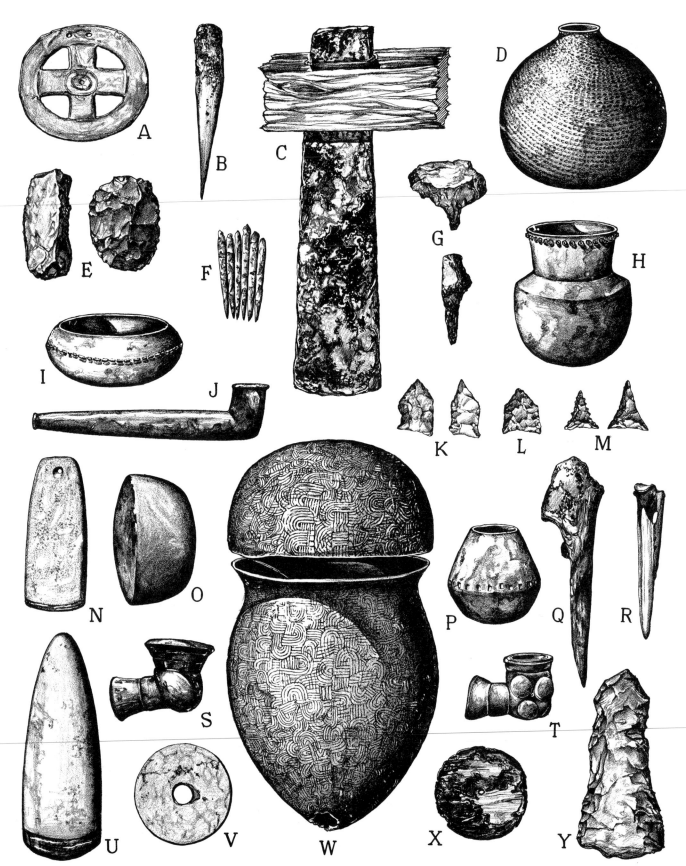

FIG. 165.—The Pee Dee Focus

A. Shell gorget
B, Q, R. Bone awls
C. Copper ax
D. Textile-wrapped pottery jar
E. Scraping tools
F. Bone skin scratcher
G. Stone drills

H, I, P. Typical smooth-surfaced pottery vessels
J, S, T. Clay pipes
K, L, M. Typical projectile points
N, U. Polished stone celts
O. Polished stone discoidal or gaming stone

V. Polished stone ear ornament
W. Complicated stamped pottery burial urn and cover
X. Copper-coated wooden ear ornament
Y. Hoe

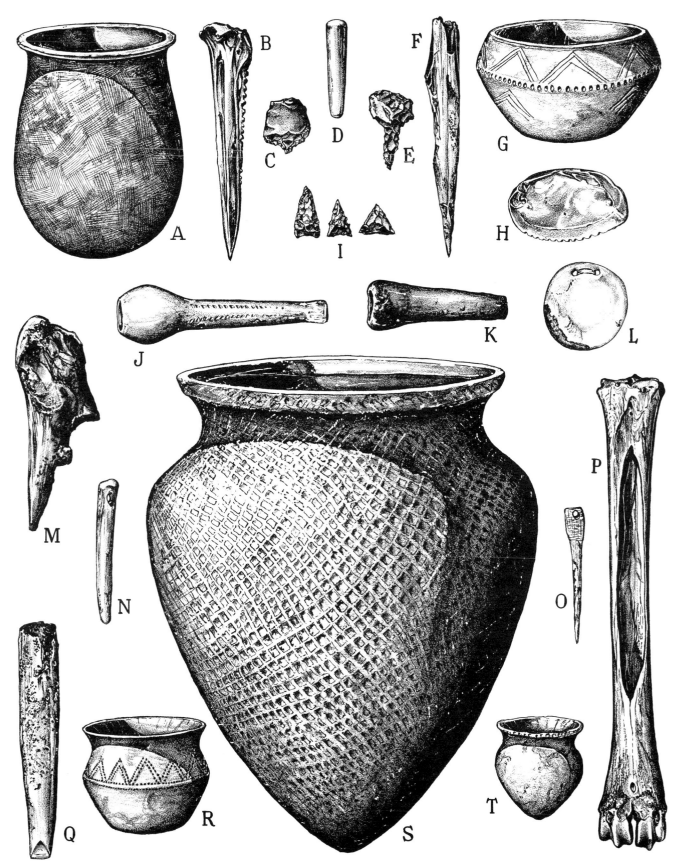

Fig. 166.—The Hillsboro Focus

A. Simple-stamped pottery jar
B, F, M. Bone awls
C, E. Drills
D, N. Antler flakers
G, R. Smooth-surfaced decorated bowls

H. Serrated mussel shell
I. Projectile points
J, K. Clay pipes
L. Shell gorget
O. Bone needle

P. Bone beamer
Q. Antler chisel
S. Check-stamped pottery jar
T. Smoothed-over check-stamped jar

Fig. 167.—Folsomoid projectile points from Georgia

A–C. From Kiokee Creek, Columbia County, Georgia   E. From Forsythe County, Georgia
D. From Milledgeville, Baldwin County, Georgia   F–H. From Buckhead Creek, Burke County, Georgia

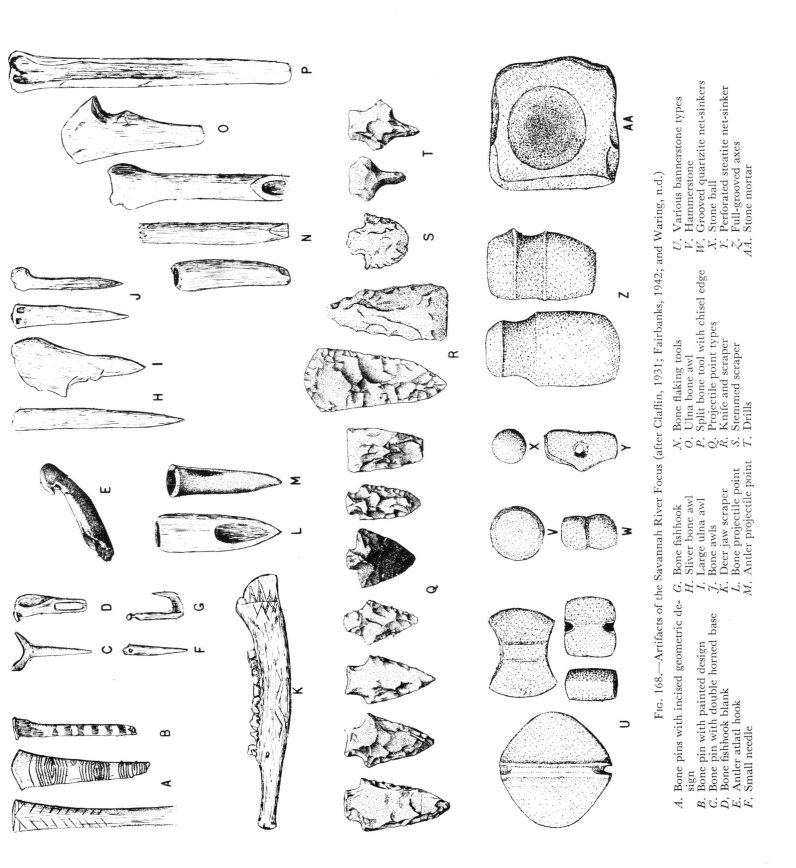

Fig. 168.—Artifacts of the Savannah River Focus (after Claflin, 1931; Fairbanks, 1942; and Waring, n.d.)

A. Bone pins with incised geometric design
B. Bone pin with painted design
C. Bone pin with double horned base
D. Bone fishhook blank
E. Antler atlatl hook
F. Small needle
G. Bone fishhook
H. Sliver bone awl
I. Large ulna awl
J. Bone awls
K. Deer jaw scraper
L. Bone projectile point
M. Antler projectile point
N. Bone flaking tools
O. Ulna bone awl
P. Split bone tool with chisel edge
Q. Projectile point types
R. Knife and scraper
S. Stemmed scraper
T. Drills
U. Various bannerstone types
V. Hammerstone
W. Grooved quartzite net-sinkers
X. Stone ball
Y. Perforated steatite net-sinker
Z. Full-grooved axes
AA. Stone mortar

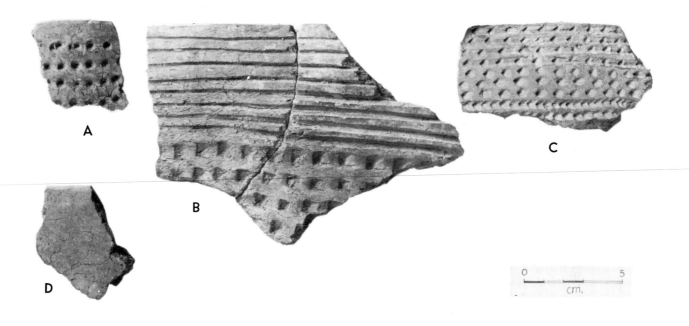

FIG. 169.—Fiber-tempered Pottery of the Late Archaic in the Georgia Coastal area

A–D. Stallings Punctate sherds from the upper end of Ossabaw Island, Chatham County, Georgia   *E–H.* Rim sherds of Stallings Punctate from Horse Island, Charleston District, South Carolina

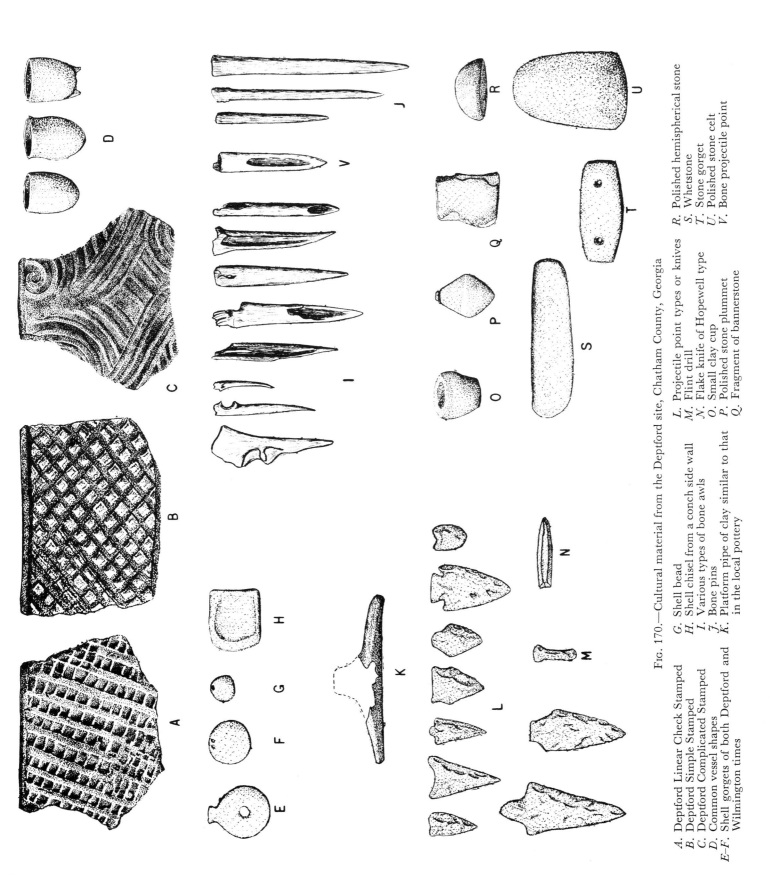

Fig. 170.—Cultural material from the Deptford site, Chatham County, Georgia

A. Deptford Linear Check Stamped
B. Deptford Simple Stamped
C. Deptford Complicated Stamped
D. Common vessel shapes
E–F. Shell gorgets of both Deptford and Wilmington times

G. Shell bead
H. Shell chisel from a conch side wall
I. Various types of bone awls
J. Bone pins
K. Platform pipe of clay similar to that in the local pottery

L. Projectile point types or knives
M. Flint drill
N. Flake knife of Hopewell type
O. Small clay cup
P. Polished stone plummet
Q. Fragment of bannerstone

R. Polished hemispherical stone
S. Whetstone
T. Stone gorget
U. Polished stone celt
V. Bone projectile point

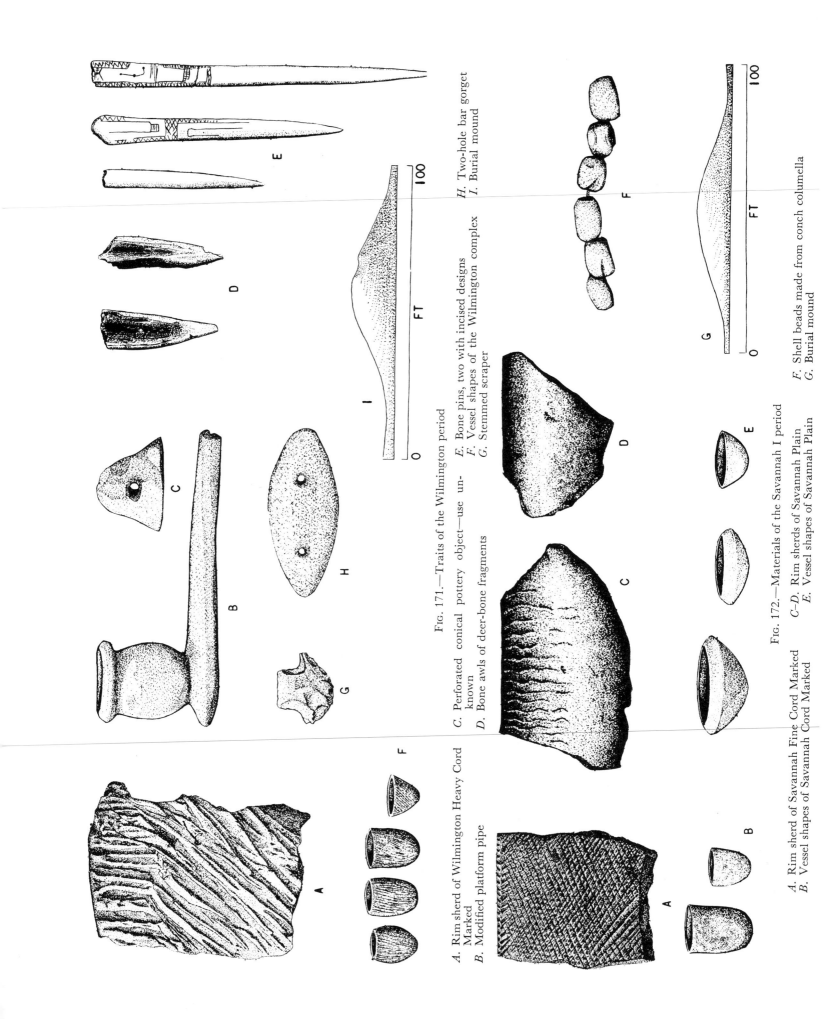

Fig. 171.—Traits of the Wilmington period

A. Rim sherd of Wilmington Heavy Cord Marked
B. Modified platform pipe
C. Perforated conical pottery object—use unknown
D. Bone awls of deer-bone fragments
E. Bone pins, two with incised designs
F. Vessel shapes of the Wilmington complex
G. Stemmed scraper
H. Two-hole bar gorget
I. Burial mound

Fig. 172.—Materials of the Savannah I period

A. Rim sherd of Savannah Fine Cord Marked
B. Vessel shapes of Savannah Cord Marked
C-D. Rim sherds of Savannah Marked
E. Vessel shapes of Savannah Plain
F. Shell beads made from conch columella
G. Burial mound

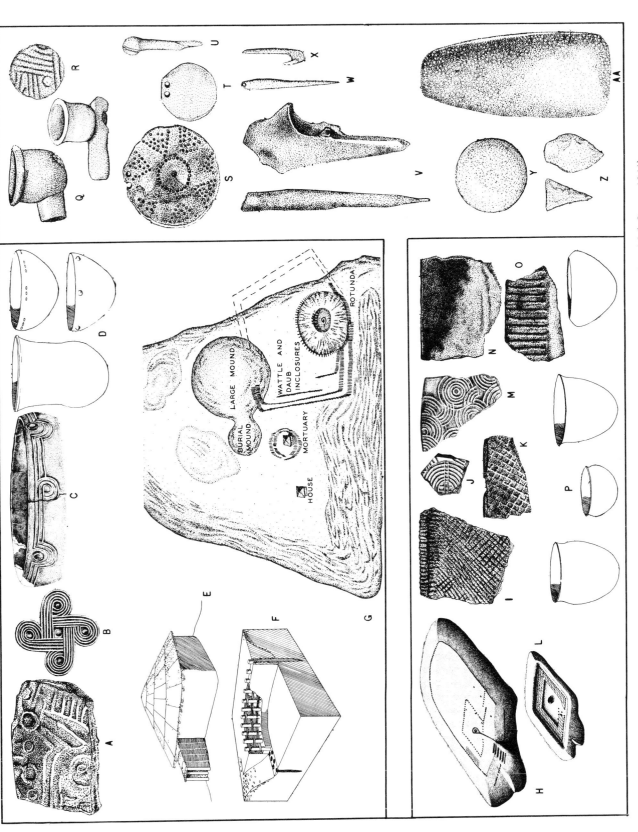

FIG. 173.—Materials from the Irene site, Chatham County, Georgia (after Caldwell and McCann, 1941)

A. Rim sherd of Irene Filfot Stamped
B. Drawing of complete design of Irene Filfot Stamped
C. Upper rim section of Irene Incised
D. Vessel shapes of Irene Period
E–F. Wattle-and-daub mortuary building of the Irene Period
G. Ground plan of Irene Period
H. Floor plan of the fifth structure in the Irene Mound
I. Savannah Fine Cord Marked rim
J. Savannah Complicated Stamped
K. Savannah Check Stamped
L. Floor plan of the second structure in the Irene Mound
M. Savannah Complicated Stamped
N–O. Savannah Burnished Plain rim sherds
P. Vessel shapes of the Savannah Period
Q. Pottery pipes of the Savannah and Irene periods
R. Pottery disk
S. Shell gorget with punctate decoration
T. Shell gorget
U. Shell pin
V. Bone awls of sliver and ulna handle types
W. Bone needle
X. Bone fishhook
Y. Polished stone disk
Y. Most common projectile point forms
AA. Polished stone celt

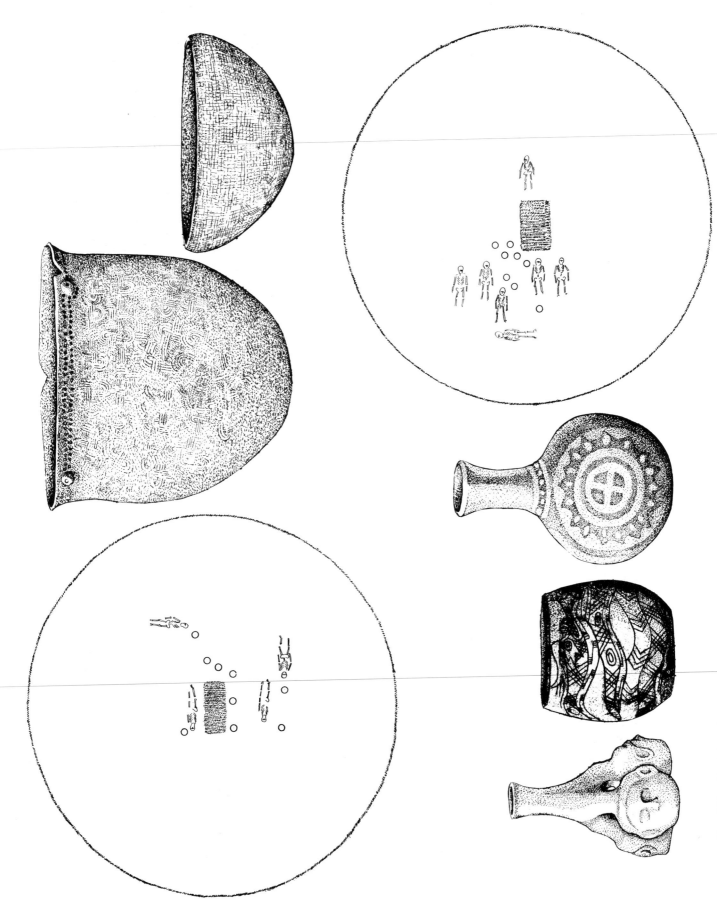

Fɪɢ. 174.—Burials and pottery vessels from the Hollywood Mound, Richmond County, Georgia: *upper*, late burial level; *lower*, early burial level

Fig. 175.—Material from the McDowell Mounds, Kershaw District, South Carolina in the Lamar period

A. Complicated stamped sherd
B. Rim sherd of deep bowl(?) with design like Lamar Incised
C. Discoidal stone with two(?) pitted faces
D. Hammerstone
E. Hand-wrought iron nail(?)
F. Fragment of metal—use unknown
G. Stone elbow pipe with circular dots outlined by engraved line
H. Small discoidal for gaming
I. Pottery disk probably for gaming
J. Bone awls

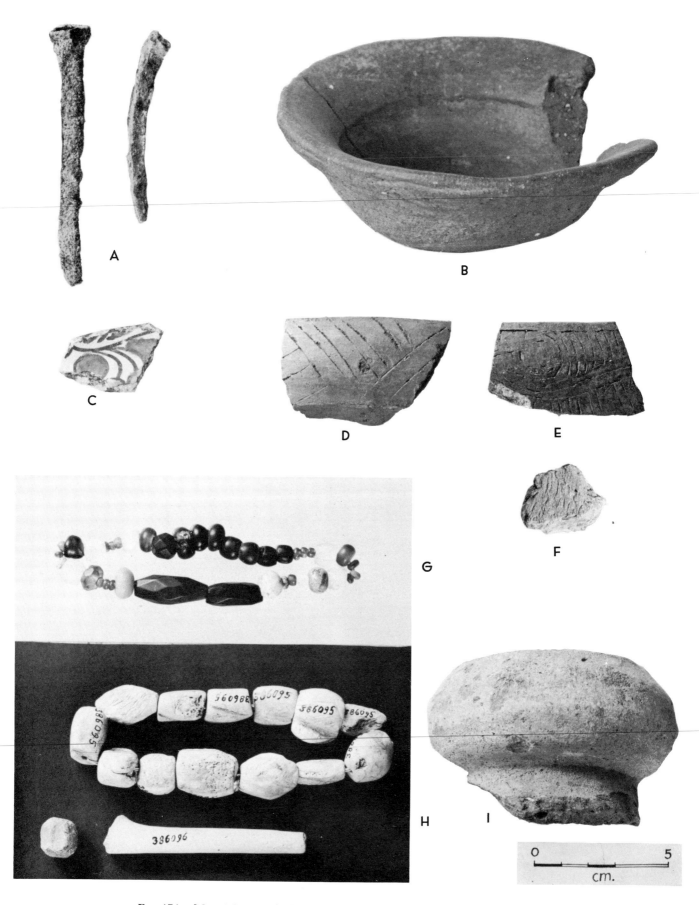

FIG. 176.—Materials from the historic sites of Parachuckla and Fort King George

A. Iron nails
B. Flaring-rim bowl of native ware
C. Imported china

D–E. Rim sherds similar to Ocmulgee
  Fields Incised
F. Body sherd similar ·to Walnut
  Roughened of Macon area

G. European glass beads
H. Native shell beads, a fragment of a
  European clay pipe, and a bullet
I. Spanish wheel-turned pottery

FIG. 177.—Archeological areas of Florida

1. Northwest Gulf Coast
2. Central Gulf Coast
3. Manatee

4. Glades
   4A. Calusa
   4B. Tekesta
   4C. Okeechobee

5. Kissimmee
6. Indian River
7. Northern St. Johns
8. Central Florida

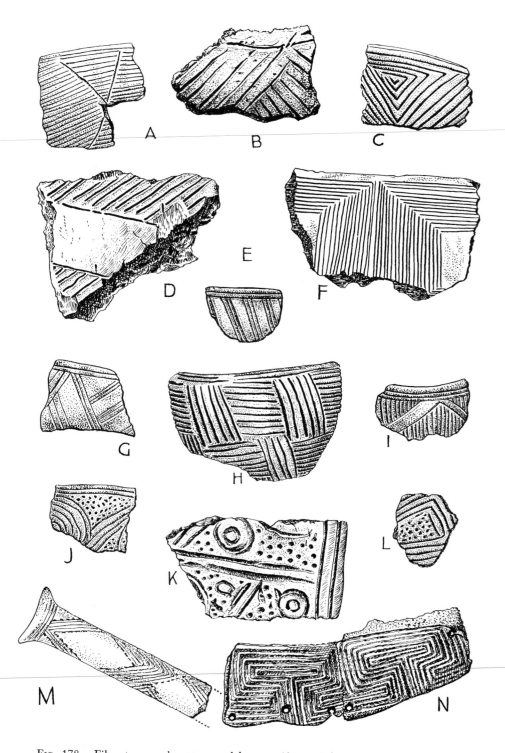

Fɪɢ. 178.—Fiber-tempered pottery and bone artifacts of the Archaic period in the St. Johns area of East Florida.

A–I. Orange Incised
J–L. Tick Island Incised

M. Incised bone pin with design similar to that on the pottery
N. Incised and drilled turtle bone

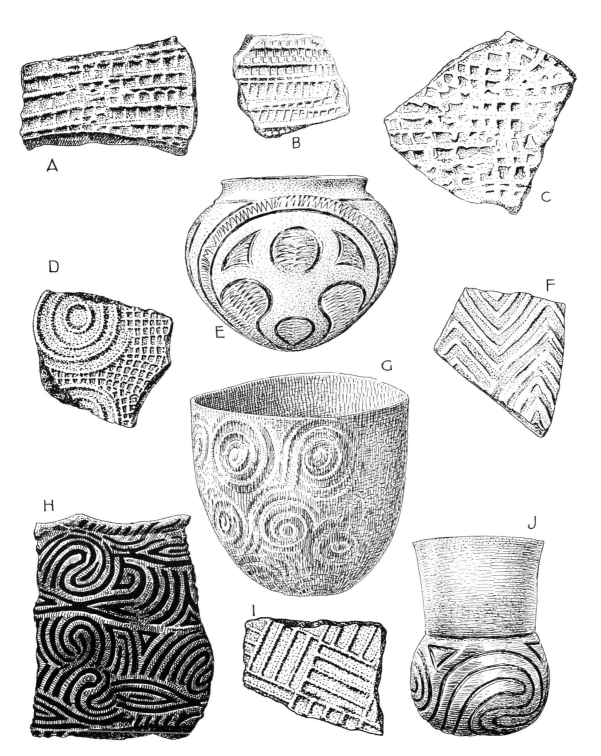

FIG. 179.—Deptford and Santa Rosa–Swift Creek pottery types

A–B. Deptford Linear Check Stamped
   C. Deptford Bold Check Stamped
   D. New River Complicated Stamped
   E. Alligator Bayou Stamped

F. Crooked River Complicated
   Stamped
G–H. Swift Creek Complicated
   Stamped

I. St. Andrews Complicated
   Stamped
J. Basin Bayou Incised

Fig. 180.—Weeden Island pottery types

A, J. Weeden Island Incised
B. Indian Pass Incised
C. Tucker Ridged Pinched
D. Hare Hammock Surface Indented

E. Carrabelle Punctated
F. Weeden Island Punctated
G. Weeden Island Zoned Red
H. Carrabelle Incised

I. Wakulla Check Stamped
K. Keith Incised
L. Weeden Island Plain

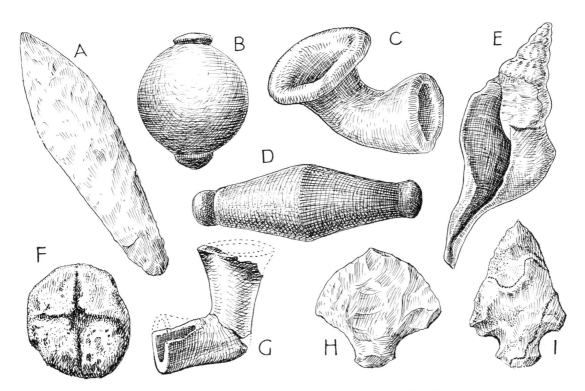

FIG. 181.—Weeden Island (*A–E*) and Fort Walton (*F–I*) artifacts

A. Large projectile point
B, D. Stone plummets
C. Clay elbow pipe with flaring rim
E. Shell cup

F. Incised sandstone disk
G. Clay elbow pipe
H. "Blunt" scraper
I. Projectile point

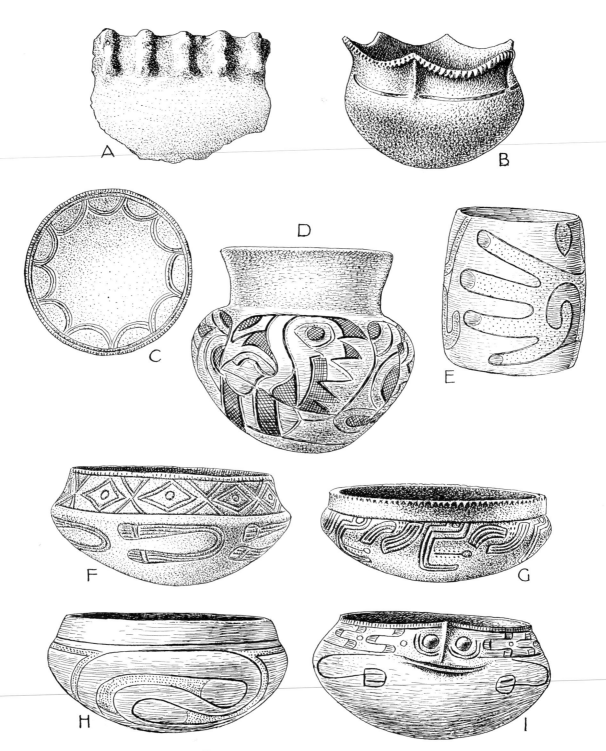

FIG. 182.—Fort Walton pottery vessels

A–B. Lake Jackson Plain
C, F–I. Fort Walton Incised
D–E. Atypical designs found on vessels
in association with Fort Walton

Incised vessels; *E* shows a design motif associated with the Southern or Buzzard Cult

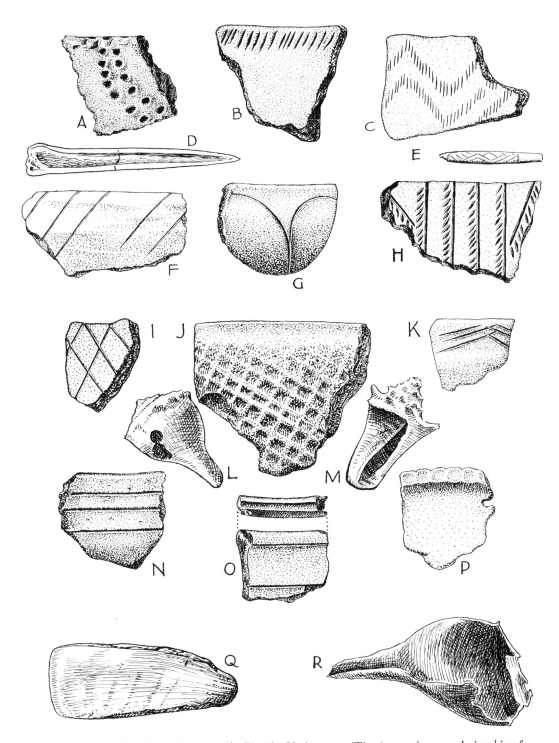

FIG. 183.—Cultural materials from the Florida Glades area. (The time and space relationship of these items is noted in the text.)

A. Fort Drum Punctate
B. Fort Drum Incised
C. Sanibel Incised
D. Split bone awl or pin
E. Engraved bone pin
F. Miami Incised

G. Key Largo Incised
H. Gordon's Pass Incised
I. Matecumbe Incised
J. Biscayne Check Stamped
K. Dade Incised
L. *Busycon* shell pick

M. Strombus hand hammer
N-O. Surfside Incised
P. Glades Tooled
Q. Strombus celt
R. *Busycon* dipper

FIG. 184.—Tentative Complexes of St. Johns I and II

ST. JOHNS I

A, E. St. Johns Plain
B. Projectile point
C. Complicated stamped sherd

D. Stone plummet
F. Pottery ring
G. Pottery elbow pipe

H. Copper conjoined tube
I. Incised and punctated vessel

ST. JOHNS II

J. Effigy pottery vessel
K, T. Two types of pottery vessels
L. Pottery dipper
M. St. Johns Check Stamp
N, P. Pottery effigies

O. Copper-covered limestone earspool
Q. Stone celt
R. Projectile point
S. Pottery tube

U. Copper plate from Mount Royal with cult design motif
V. Stone "spud"
W. Copper ornament

Fig. 185.—Three old ditches at Jamestown are revealed here in the bottom of an exploratory trench and in the profile at the far end of the trench by the darker earth that has gradually filled up these ditches. Most such ditches, several thousand feet of which have been uncovered, were originally dug to mark property lines. They have made it possible to locate exactly a large number of recorded land holdings on Jamestown Island.

Fig. 186.—Remains of a brick kiln excavated at Jamestown, Virginia. In it were still stacked, just as they were left some three hundred years ago, several hundred poorly fired bricks and a large quantity of flat roof tiles. Contrary to popular belief that bricks were brought from England as ship ballast, the bricks used at Jamestown were actually made right on the spot. In the areas thus far explored at Jamestown, remains of two brick kilns and four lime kilns have been uncovered.

FIG. 187.—One of the most interesting of the remains uncovered at Jamestown was this series of three brick foundations. The major foundation, with brick-floored cellar, was the second of the three to be constructed and was probably the house built by Robert Sherwood in the latter part of the seventeenth century. Its construction largely destroyed the earlier foundation walls of the first "country house," or governor's mansion. The last house, represented by the wall built on a layer of dirt on the cellar floor of Sherwood's house, was a wing of a large plantation house built after Jamestown was abandoned.

FIG. 188.—Typical small house foundation, with uneven brick floor. Both the walls and the floor were made of bricks salvaged from another structure, a common practice at Jamestown. Under the loose earth at the left side of the cellar was found a brick-lined, wood-covered pit containing several wine bottles and the upper leg bone of a deer.

FIG. 189.—Two *sgraffito* slip-ware dishes typical of a large number found at Jamestown in a ditch fill back of the foundations of Henry Hartwell's house. This ware, probably made in the Barnstable district of North Devonshire, England about 1650, has not been found extensively at any other American Colonial sites.

FIG. 190.—Four earthenware vessels and a glass bottle; all restored from fragments excavated at Jamestown, Virginia. The three largest dishes of lead-glazed earthenware were probably made at Jamestown.

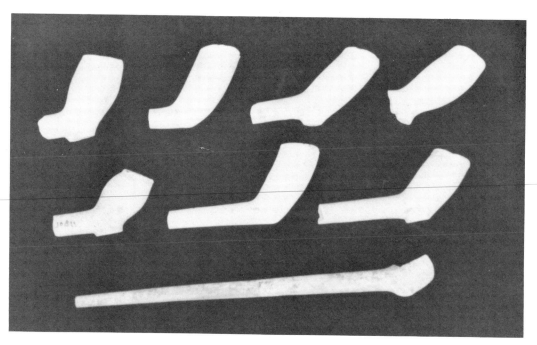

FIG. 191.—Seventeenth-century clay pipe bowls and a clay pipe stem, typical of the several thousand found in the Jamestown excavations. Because the styles changed often, and because of their fragility, pipes are one of the most valuable aids in dating historic sites.

FIG. 192.—In this selection of implements and utensils found during the excavation of the first State House at Jamestown, Virginia, are a latten spoon, clay tobacco pipe, bone-handled knife, brass buckle, brass cock for wine cask, brass ladle, iron hoe, and iron ax. More abundant in the excavations, however, are pottery, glass bottles, and building materials.

FIG. 193.—Typical glass bottles found in the excavations at Jamestown, Virginia. The squat wine bottles are possibly the oldest. The square gin bottle probably came from Holland.

FIG. 194.—Two of the thirty-odd "H–H" bottle seals found near the foundation of a house, which helped to identify it as belonging to Henry Hartwell. Seals, such as these, were impressed on the shoulders of wine bottles and often carried the initials of the owner.

FIG. 195.—Most of the wells at Jamestown were relatively shallow, with a barrel, such as this, placed at the bottom below the level of the normal ground water. Some of the best-preserved objects from the Jamestown excavations came from the bottoms of wells. Material such as bone, wood, and leather was preserved by being continuously under water.

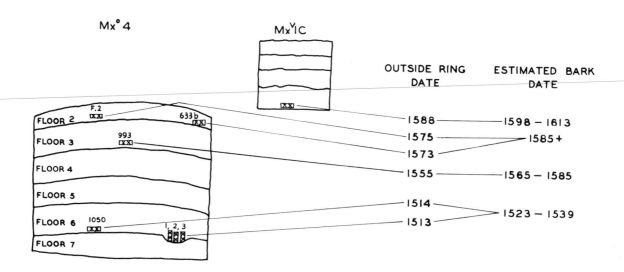

FIG. 196.—Diagrammatic cross-section of sites Mx°4 and Mx^{v}IC illustrating the location of dated wood specimens from the Kincaid site.

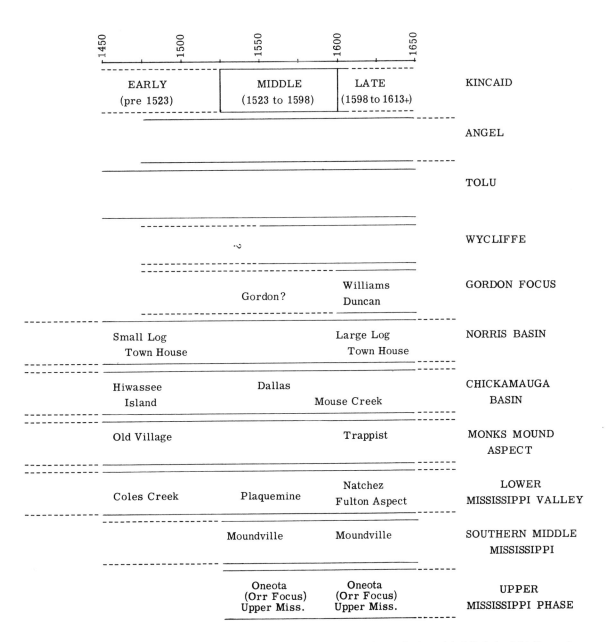

FIG. 197.—Dated Kincaid periods by dendrochronology and suggested correlation with Mississippi Valley units

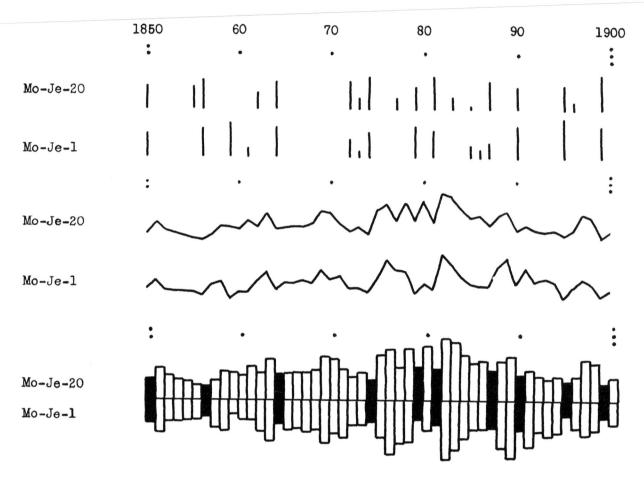

Fig. 198.—Cross-dating of two cedar specimens by skeleton plots, line graphs, and histograms. Rings which are narrow on both specimens have been colored black in the histogram to aid comparison. The base lines have been opposed in the histogram.

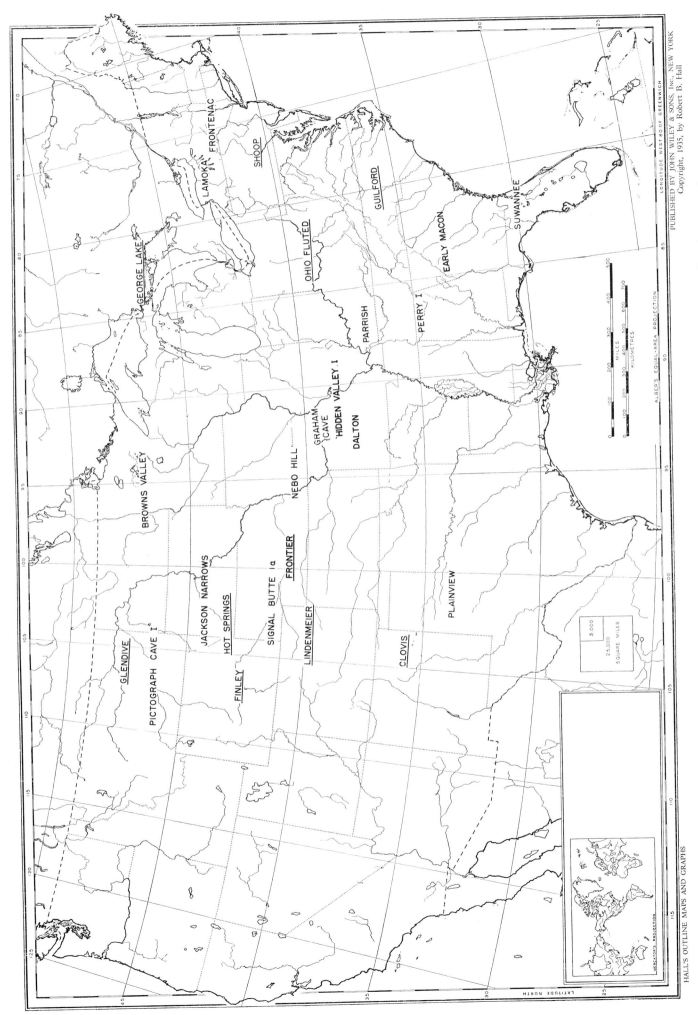

FIG. 199.—Distribution of sites and culture units during the Paleo-Indian and Early Archaic periods. Paleo-Indian sites are under-lined on this map.

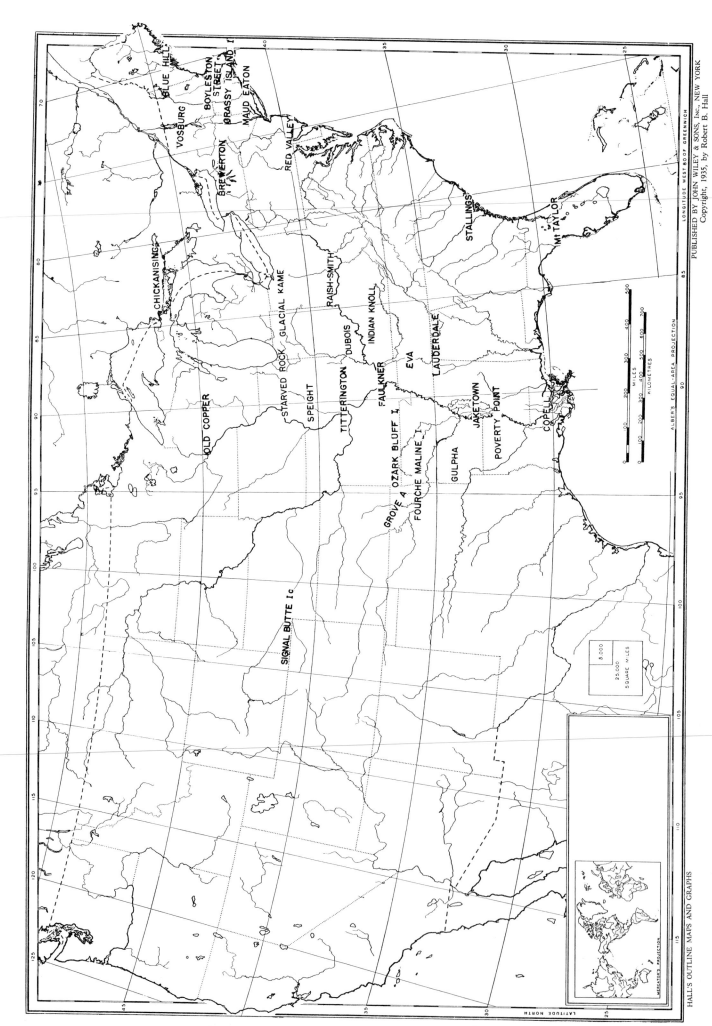

PUBLISHED BY JOHN WILEY & SONS, INC., NEW YORK
LONGITUDE WEST 80° OF GREENWICH
Copyright, 1935, by Robert B. Hall

Fig. 200.—Distribution of sites and culture units during the Late Archaic period

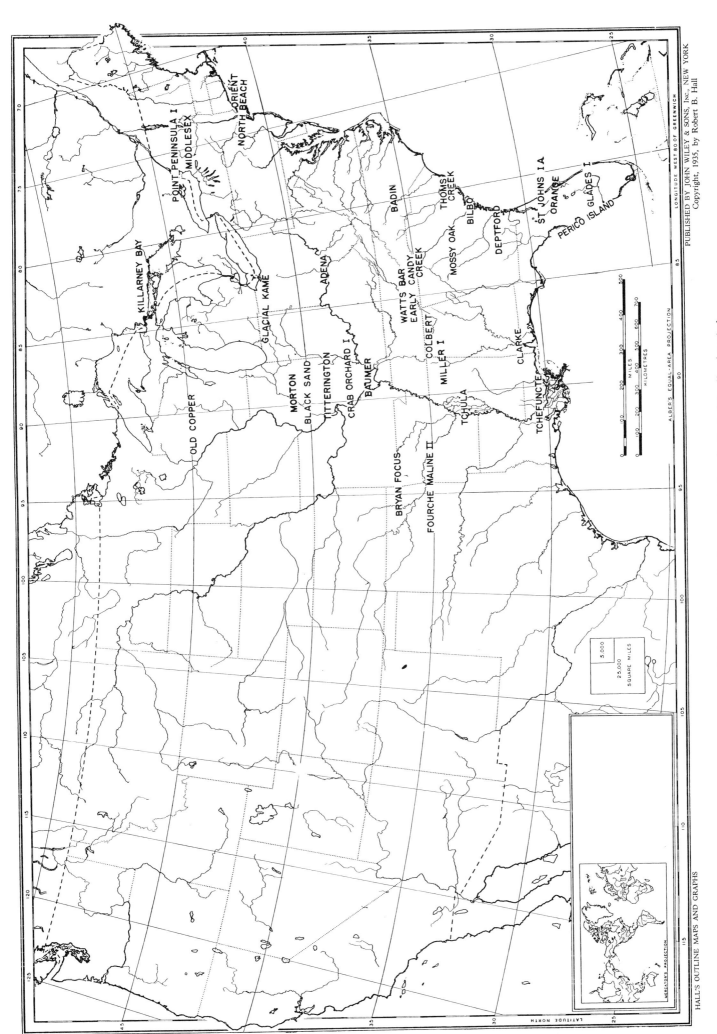

Fig. 201.—Distribution of sites and culture units during the Early Woodland period

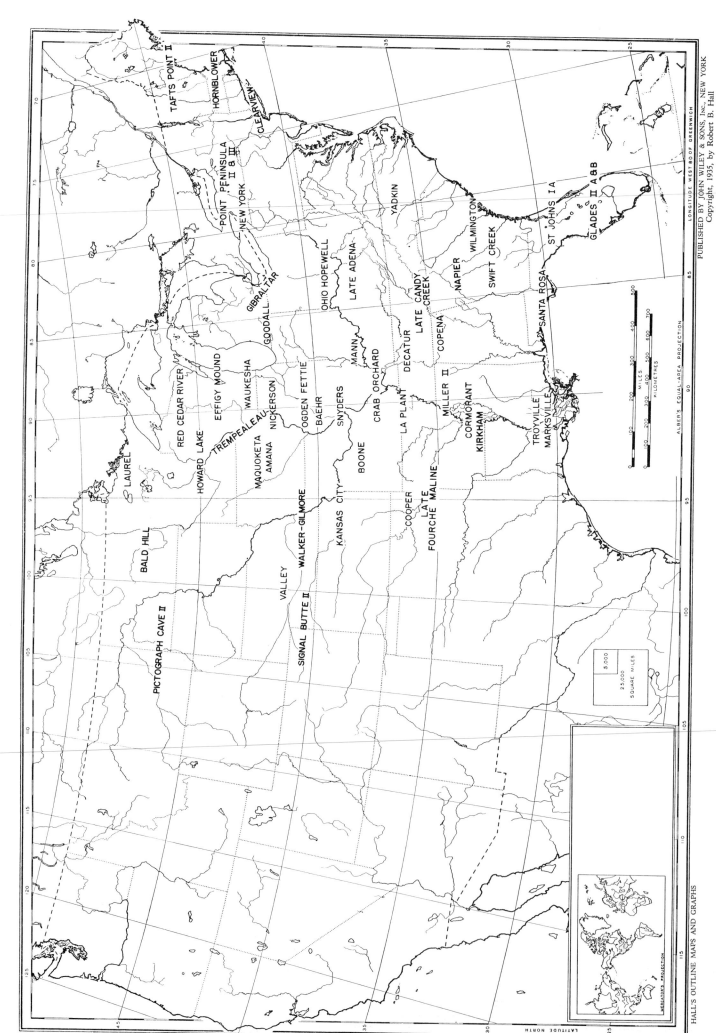

PUBLISHED BY JOHN WILEY & SONS, INC., NEW YORK
Copyright, 1935, by Robert B. Hall

FIG. 202.—Distribution of sites and culture units during the Middle Woodland (Hopewellian) period

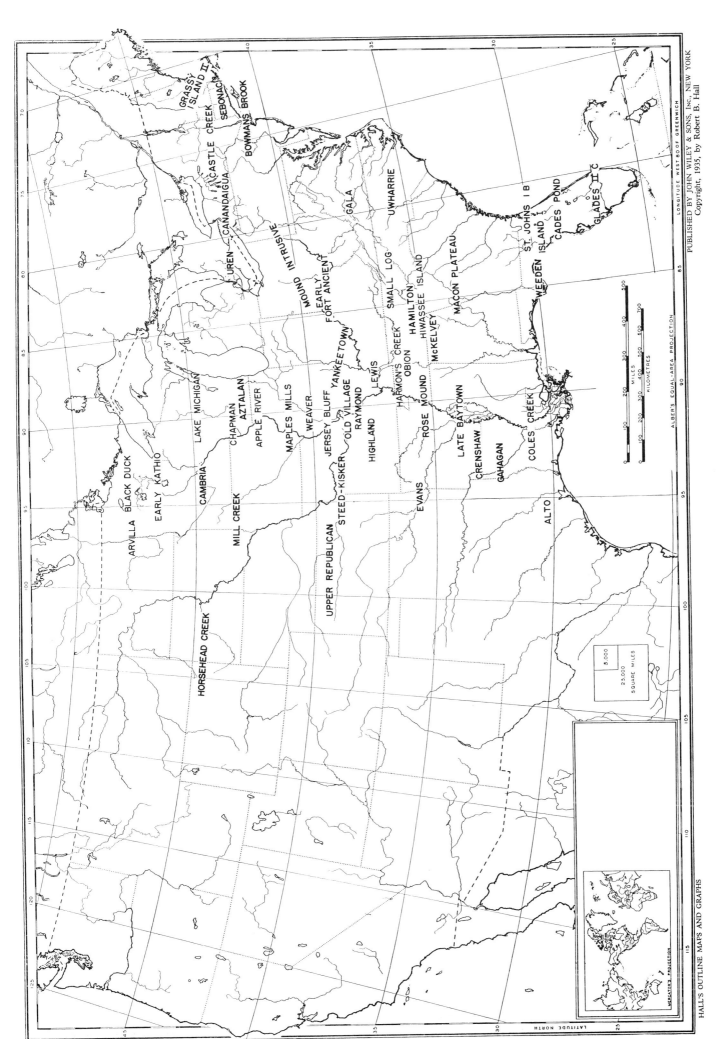

Fig. 203.—Distribution of sites and culture units at the beginning of the Mississippi period

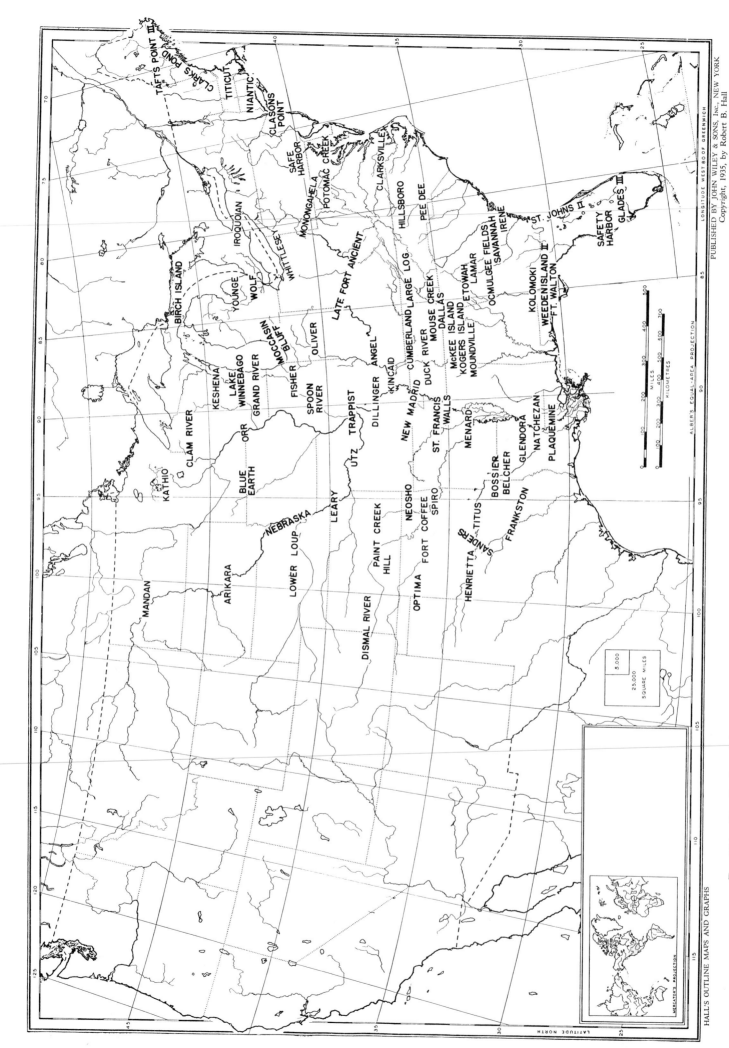

Fig. 204.—Distribution of sites and culture units during the climax and decline of the Mississippi period. Identified groups on the northern and northeastern periphery still maintained their basic Woodland tradition during this period.

HALL'S OUTLINE MAPS AND GRAPHS

Time scale (top and bottom): 1700 A.D. — 1450 A.D. — 1200 A.D. — 950 A.D. — 600 A.D. — 350 A.D. — 100 A.D. — 1000 B.C. — 3000 B.C. — 8000 B.C.

Period headers (top): LATE | MISSISSIPPI | EARLY | MIDDLE WOODLAND | EARLY WOODLAND | LATE ARCHAIC | EARLY ARCHAIC | PALEO-INDIAN
LATE WOODLAND

THE EASTERN AREA

LATE · CLARKS POND · TITICUT · NIANTIC · POTOMAC CREEK · CLARKSVILLE · HILLSBORO · ST. AUGUSTINE · SAFETY HARBOR · LEON-JEFFERSON · IRENE · OCMULGEE FIELD · MOUSE CREEK

MISSISSIPPI · LATE WOODLAND · GRASSY ISLAND II · SEBONAC · CLASONS POINT · CHANCE · IROQUOIAN · MONONGAHELA · UREN · UWHARRIE · PEE DEE · GALA · ST. JOHNS II · GLADES III · CRYSTAL RIVER II · FORT WALTON · WEEDEN ISLAND II · SAVANNAH · KOLOMOKI · MACON PLATEAU · LAMAR · SMALL LOG · ETOWAH · DALLAS · HIWASSEE ISLAND

EARLY · BOWMANS BROOK · OWASCO · ST. JOHNS IB · GLADES II · CADES POND · WEEDEN ISLAND I · WOODSTOCK · WILMINGTON · NAPIER · HAMILTON

MIDDLE WOODLAND · TAFTS POINT II · HORNBLOWER · CLEARVIEW · POINT PENINSULA · NEW YORK · YADKIN · CRYSTAL RIVER I · SANTA ROSA · SWIFT CREEK · CANDY CREEK

EARLY WOODLAND · GRASSY ISLAND I · NORTH BEACH · ORIENT · ROSENKRANS · RED VALLEY · MIDDLESEX · BADIN · ST. JOHNS IA · ORANGE · GLADES I · PERICO ISLAND · BILBO · THOMS CREEK · DEPTFORD · MOSSY OAK · WATTS BAR

LATE ARCHAIC · TAFTS POINT I · BOYLESTON · MAUD EATON · VOSBURG · LAMOKA · BREWERTON · FRONTENAC · MT. TAYLOR · STALLINGS ISLAND I

EARLY ARCHAIC · GUILFORD

PALEO-INDIAN · SHOOP · SUWANNEE · EARLY MACON (?)

THE CENTRAL AREA

WHITTLESEY · OLIVER · OLD BIRCH ISLAND · WOLF · MOCCASIN BLUFF · MCKEE ISLAND · NATCHEZAN · FISHER · SPOON RIVER · GLENDORA · LOWER ARKANSAS · UTZ · KESHENA · CLAM RIVER · KATHIO

DUCK RIVER · HARMONS CREEK · DECATUR · OBION · FORT ANCIENT · MOUND INTRUSIVE · GIBRALTAR · YOUNGE · MOUNDVILLE · COPENA · YANKEETOWN · KOGERS ISLAND · MCKELVEY · WALLS · KINCAID · DILLINGER · MAPLES MILLS · RAYMOND · JERSEY BLUFF · OLD VILLAGE · TRAPPIST · PLAQUEMINE · COLES CREEK · TROYVILLE · NEW MADRID · ST. FRANCIS · ROSE MOUND I · BOONE · STEED-KISKER · HIGHLAND · APPLE RIVER · LAKE MICHIGAN · AZTALAN · BLUE EARTH · CHAPMAN · CAMBRIA · BLACK DUCK · ARVILLA

CLARKE · COLBERT · BLUFF CREEK · OHIO HOPEWELL · GOODALL · MANN · MILLER II · CORMORANT · LEWIS · WEAVER · CRAB ORCHARD · ILLINOIS HOPEWELL · MARKSVILLE · LA PLANT · KIRKHAM · KANSAS CITY HOPEWELL · EFFIGY MOUND · WAUKESHA · TREMPEALEAU · RED CEDAR RIVER · HOWARD LAKE · LAUREL

ADENA · KILLARNEY BAY · MILLER I · BAUMER · MORTON · SPEIGHT · TITTERINGTON · BLACK SAND · TCHEFUNCTE · TCHULA

EVA · GLACIAL KAME · STARVED ROCK · FAULKNER · POVERTY POINT · COPELL · JAKETOWN · HIDDEN VALLEY I · OLD COPPER

CHICKANISING · RAISCH-SMITH · DUBOIS · INDIAN KNOLL · LAUDERDALE · DALTON · NEBO HILL · GRAHAM CAVE

GEORGE LAKE (?) · PERRY I · BROWN'S VALLEY (?)

EARLY PARRISH · LITTLE FALLS (?) · MINNESOTA MAN (?)

THE WESTERN AREA

BELCHER · BOSSIER · FORT COFFEE · BROWN · CRAIG · EVANS · FRANKSTON · NEOSHO · SANDERS · GAHAGAN · CRENSHAW I · TITUS · OPTIMA · ALTO · HENRIETTA · LEARY · HILL · LOWER LOUP · NEBRASKA · DISMAL RIVER · MILL CREEK · PAINT CREEK · ARIKARA · UPPER REPUBLICAN · SIGNAL BUTTE II · BALD HILL · MANDAN · HORSEHEAD CREEK · PICTOGRAPH CAVE II

FOURCHE-MALINE · COOPER · GROVE - C · GROVE - B · GROVE - A · GULPHA · WALKER-GILMORE · VALLEY

SIGNAL BUTTE Ic · PLAINVIEW · HOT SPRINGS

SIGNAL BUTTE Ia · PICTOGRAPH CAVE I · JACKSON NARROWS · FRONTIER · GLENDIVE · FINLEY · LINDENMEIER · CLOVIS

Period headers (bottom): LATE | MISSISSIPPI | EARLY | MIDDLE WOODLAND | EARLY WOODLAND | LATE ARCHAIC | EARLY ARCHAIC | PALEO-INDIAN
LATE WOODLAND

FIG. 205.—This figure, presenting the geographical and temporal position of eastern United States archeological units, is organized more or less along the temporal ideas current when most of the papers in this volume were written during 1947–49. The cultural alignments on this figure and on Figures 199–204 are the product of the editor. This is definitely a pre-radiocarbon figure. Interarea correlations are not to be examined too closely with the idea of determining which local region has received or developed new ideas before adjacent or far distant areas. Such priorities are still in the realm of conjecture rather than established fact. This figure should be compared with the dating so far obtained by the radiocarbon method and by dendrochronology as explained in pages 345–351. Some adjustments in temporal allocations must be left for future work.